Random House

DATE			

Random House

Japanese-English
English-Japanese
Dictionary

Seigo Nakao

Random House
New York

Random House Japanese-English English-Japanese Dictionary

Copyright © 1997 by Random House, Inc.

All rights reserved under International and Pan-American Copyright Conventions. No part of this book may be reproduced in any form or by any means, electronic or mechanical, including photocopying, without the written permission of the publisher. All inquiries should be addressed to Reference & Information Publishing, Random House, Inc., 201 East 50th Street, New York, NY 10022. Published in the United States by Random House, Inc., New York and simultaneously in Canada by Random House of Canada, Limited.

Hardcover edition of this dictionary was published by Random House, Inc. in 1995.

Library of Congress Cataloging-in-Publication Data
Nakao Seigo.
　　Random House Japanese-English English-Japanese Dictionary /
　　compiled by Nakao Seigo.
　　　　p.　　cm.
　　ISBN 0-679-44149-2 (hardcover)
　　ISBN 0-679-78001-7 (paperback)
　　1. Japanese language—Dictionaries—English. 2. English language—
Dictionaries—Japanese. I. Title.
PL679.N294 1995
495.6'321—dc20
　　　　　　　　　　　　　　　　　　　　　　　95-15508
　　　　　　　　　　　　　　　　　　　　　　　CIP

Typeset and printed in the United States of America

9 8 7 6 5 4 3
0-679-78001-7 (PB)

New York　Toronto　London　Sydney　Auckland

This book is available for special purchases in bulk by organizations and institutions, not for resale, at special discounts. Please direct your inquiries to the Random House Special Sales Department, toll-free 888-591-1200 or fax 212-572-4961.

Please address inquiries about electronic licensing of the content, for use on a network or in software or on CD-ROM, to Subsidiary Rights Department, Random House Reference & Information Publishing, fax 212-940-7370.

Acknowledgments

I owe my thanks to many people for the completion of this dictionary. Without their cooperation and patience, it would have been an overwhelming job.

I would like to express my sincerest thanks to Sol Steinmetz, who helped me to launch this project, and Carol Braham, both of Random House. I am grateful to them for their extensive efforts to organize the formulae of this dictionary and solve numerous problems that I confronted owing to the drastic differences between Japanese and English.

I particularly would like to express my deepest gratitude to Erivan Morales for his extensive editing, sound advice, and constant moral support. Without his enthusiastic help, it is doubtful that I could have completed this project at all. This dictionary is dedicated to him.

Guide to the Dictionary

Main Features

The *Random House Japanese-English English-Japanese Dictionary* is primarily intended for two types of English-speaking users: those who have no knowledge of Japanese and those who already have some knowledge of the language but still need a dictionary in which all Japanese words and phrases are explained from the standpoint of English and in English grammatical terms. It should also prove indispensable to anyone who needs a bilingual dictionary that presents the basic vocabulary of both languages in an accessible, easy to use format.

This dictionary includes not only those essential words and idiomatic phrases that are most often used in daily conversation in Japan but also words and expressions that appear frequently in newspapers and magazines. And since the Japanese written forms of Japanese words are given after the romanized form on first mention within an entry, the dictionary will also serve as an aid to those who are learning to read and write the language. However, because the romanized forms always appear first, the user does not have to know the Japanese writing system to look up a word or pinpoint a definition.

Arrangement and Content of Entries

In both sections of the dictionary, Japanese to English and English to Japanese, **main entries** are in strict letter-by-letter alphabetical order, ignoring punctuation and parentheses except when doing so would violate common sense. (A special case is the many Japanese adjectives that are followed by the syllable **na** or **no** in parentheses: alphabetization stops before the parenthesis when listing these as entries.)

In both sections, **main entries** are in boldface type. Many entries in both sections contain **subentries,** which are also in boldface type. These subentries, which consist of idioms, common expressions, compounds, phrases, and example sentences, increase the usefulness of the dictionary, and they were included to the extent permitted by space limitations.

Japanese-English Section

In this section, the boldfaced Japanese **main entry** in **rōmaji** (roman letters) is followed (in most cases) by an italicized **part-of-speech** label and then by the Japanese written form of the entry word or phrase, either in **kana** (the Japanese phonetic script), **kanji** (Chinese characters), or a mixture of kanji and kana, following common Japanese usage. These are followed by English equivalents or definitions and, in some cases, by boldfaced **subentries** (idioms, phrases, etc.).

Although main entries are always followed by the same word or phrase in Japanese writing, in the case of subentries, the Japanese written form is omitted if part of it would repeat Japanese writing that has already appeared elsewhere in the entry. For example, the entry for **fukushi** (welfare) contains a subentry for **shakaifukushi** (social welfare) for which the Japanese written form is not given because it would repeat the kanji for the word **fukushi.** (Users who wish to find any Japanese written forms that have been omitted can often do so by searching elsewhere in the dictionary. In this case, **shakaifukushi** has its own main entry, and the kanji for **shakai** can also be found in the English-Japanese section under **social.**)

When an entry has two or more distinct meanings or can be used, from the point of view of English grammar, as more than one part of speech, its English equivalents are numbered. However, English equivalents that are closely related in meaning are separated by semicolons rather than being numbered, and in any case there is never more than one sequence of numbers: if numbers have been used to separate parts of speech, then any distinctions of meaning within those divisions are merely separated by semicolons.

Examples:

ippuku, *n.* 一服 1. puff (tobacco). 2. one dose; one portion.

ippō 一方 1. *n.* one side; the other party. 2. *adv.* on the other hand.

ireru, *vb.* 入れる 1. put in(to); let in. 2. send someone to. 3. comply with; accept. 4. make (tea, coffee).

In cases like the second example above, where parts of speech are separated by numbers, the part-of-speech labels are given after the numbers rather than immediately following the main-entry word or phrase.

When a Japanese main-entry word is borrowed from a foreign language other than Chinese, the source language is indicated in parentheses before the English equivalent(s). The original word in the source language is also given, in italics, when it would be difficult to guess from its Japanese pronunciation. Examples: **burashi,** *n.* (E.) brush; **buranko,** *n.* (Pg. *balanço*) swing.

English-Japanese Section

In this section, the boldfaced English **main entry** is followed by an italicized **part-of-speech** label, then the entry's Japanese equivalents. All Japanese equivalents for main entries are given in both **rōmaji** and Japanese writing (**kanji** and/or **kana**). However, in the case of boldfaced English **subentries,** the Japanese written form is omitted if part of it would repeat Japanese writing that has already appeared elsewhere in the entry. For example, in the entry for **domestic,** the Japanese written forms for the subentries **domestic flight** (kokunaisen) and **domestic car** (kokusansha) are not shown because the kanji corresponding to the syllables **kokunai** and **kokusan** (which convey the root meanings of two different senses of "domestic") were given earlier in the entry.

When an English entry has two or more distinct meanings, their Japanese equivalents are numbered. When the separate meanings are closely related, they are separated by semicolons rather than being numbered. In either case, the Japanese equivalents of the separate meanings are often followed by English glosses in parentheses to identify the sense that is being translated by the Japanese.

Examples:

bridge, *n.* 1. hashi 橋 2. burijji ブリッジ (game).

hair, *n.* kami(noke) 髪(の毛) (head hair); ke 毛 (body hair, fur).

When the sense that is being translated is considered self-evident, a parenthesized gloss is not given. For example, in the above entry for **bridge,** the second of the two numbered Japanese equivalents is glossed as referring to the game; therefore, the first can be assumed to refer to the most common meaning of "bridge," which is the structural one. In the same way, a parenthesized gloss that has been given in one entry is sometimes not repeated in nearby entries for related English words. In the following example, the entry for **austere,** glosses are given for three different Japanese words, but in the entry for the related word **austerity,** there are no glosses for the Japanese words that are related to those three.

austere, *adj.* 1. kibishii 厳しい (stern). 2. kanso (na) 簡素 (な) (plain). 3. mazushii 貧しい (frugal).

austerity, *n.* 1. kibishisa 厳しさ. 2. kanso 簡素. 3. mazushisa 貧しさ.

When only the last of a group of Japanese equivalents has a parenthesized gloss, the gloss refers to all Japanese equivalents to its left until either another gloss or another definition number is encountered. In the following example, the entry for **accord,** the Japanese words **itchi** and **chōwa** both mean "harmony."

> **accord,** 1. *n.* itchi 一致; chōwa 調和 (harmony); kyōtei 協定 (agreement); **of one's own accord** jihatsu-teki ni 自発的に. 2. *vb.* itchi suru 一致する; chōwa suru 調和する.

Lastly, when an English main entry can be used as more than one part of speech (as in the above example), the Japanese equivalents are numbered, with part-of-speech labels following the numbers rather than the boldfaced entry itself. In entries of this type, distinctions of meaning are separated by semicolons rather than being numbered.

Romanization of Japanese

The system of romanization used in this dictionary is a modified form of the widely used Hepburn system. The only significant modification is the use of an apostrophe to indicate a break between certain double letters.

The apostrophe is widely used in the Hepburn system to indicate a break between "n" and a following vowel or the glide "y." In this dictionary, the use of the apostrophe is extended to certain double letters such as "nn" and "uu," where an apostrophe is inserted between the letters (n'n and u'u) to indicate that there is a break between them and they are not pronounced as a single letter.

For a table of the basic syllables of Japanese as spelled in the Hepburn system and as represented in the two types of kana scripts, hiragana and katakana, see pages xix–xx.

Pronunciation

Vowels

Japanese has five basic vowels, usually referred to as short vowels, which are romanized as **a, i, u, e,** and **o.** These are pronounced approximately like the "a" in "father," the "ee" in "feet," the "oo" in "mood," the "e" in "met," and the "o" in "fort," respectively. They are all pronounced in a relatively short, clipped manner in contrast to the so-called long vowels, which are produced by drawing out the sounds of the short vowels to approximately twice their normal length. In the Hepburn system, the long vowels corresponding to **a, u,** and **o** are written by placing a macron over those letters, producing **ā, ū,** and **ō.** The Hepburn system writes the long vowels for **i** and **e** in two ways: in words borrowed from languages other than Chinese, they are written with a macron as **ī** and **ē;** otherwise they are written as **ii** and **ei,** respectively.

(The actual pronunciation of **ē**, or **ei**, varies considerably: some speakers pronounce it as an elongation of the short vowel **e**, others as a sequence of the short vowels **e** and **i**.)

Other vowel combinations, aside from the long vowels **ii** and **ei**, are pronounced as sequences of the two vowels, though sometimes with a glide between them. Such vowel combinations as **ai, au, oi,** and **ue** often sound like "eye," "ow" (as in "cow"), "oy" (as in "boy"), and "we" (as in "wet") to the ears of English speakers. The contrast between **ai** and **ae** is important. The former ends in a sound like the "ee" of "feet" and the latter in a sound like the "e" of "met."

The vowel **u** in the syllable **su** tends to be pronounced very faintly or not at all (so that the syllable sounds like **s**) before some consonants, as in **sukoshi** ("a little bit"), and at the end of some words, as in the polite copula **desu** and the polite verb suffix **-masu**. These examples are often pronounced "skoshi," "des," and "mas."

The vowel **i** also has a tendency to be pronounced very faintly or even whispered in certain contexts, especially in the syllable **shi**, but also in the syllables **chi, hi, ki,** and **pi**. This muting of the **i** sound most commonly occurs when **shi, chi, hi, ki,** or **pi** precedes any of the following consonants: **ch, f, h, k, p, s, sh, t,** or **ts**. For example, **shikata** (way, method) is often pronounced "shkata," and **hito** (person, human being) is often pronounced in a way that sounds like "hto" or "shto" to most English speakers. However, Japanese speakers hear the **i**, as it is whispered rather than dropped entirely. These pronunciation patterns are widespread, but they are seldom indicated in dictionaries and textbooks. They are best learned by observing the speech of native speakers.

Consonants

Most Japanese consonants are pronounced more or less the way the same letters would be pronounced in English. However, there are some important differences.

1. The combination **ch** is always pronounced as in "chair," never as in "character" or "charade."
2. The letter **g** is always pronounced as in "gift" or "get," never as in "ginger" or "generation."
3. The **ts** of the syllable **tsu** corresponds to nothing in English. It sounds rather like the "ts" of "footsore"; however, it is really a single consonant, and it always begins the syllable in which it occurs.
4. The **f** of the syllable **fu** often sounds more like an "h" than like an English "f." (It is produced more by narrowing the gap between the upper and lower lips rather than by bringing the upper teeth close to the lower lip as in English.) A glance at the table of Japanese syllables on page xix will reveal that **fu** belongs to the **h** row.

5. The Japanese **r** is not at all like the retroflex American "r," in which the tongue is rolled back, then forward. Instead it is produced by flapping the tip of the tongue downward from just behind the upper front teeth. It often sounds very much like an "l" to English speakers. Aside from this, Japanese has no "l" sound, and the **r** is used in pronouncing foreign loanwords that contain the letter "l."

6. The letter **y** that appears after some consonants is a glide between the consonant and the following vowel rather than a vowel as it sometimes is in English. Thus **tōkyō** (the name of the city), which is often pronounced in English as three syllables (to-ky-o), is actually two syllables in Japanese (**tō** and **kyō**).

7. The Japanese **n** has two pronunciations. One is at the beginning of the syllables **na, ni, nu, ne,** and **no,** where it is pronounced like the English "n." The other is the so-called syllabic **n.** This is a nasalized "n," sometimes described as always coming at the end of a syllable. However, the nasalized "n" is counted as a syllable by itself, so that the word **kin** (gold) consists of two syllables (**ki** and **n**). The word **nan** (what) contains both types of **n.** When the syllabic **n** comes before a vowel (or the glide **y**) within a word, it is important to distinguish it from the syllable-beginning type. In speech, there is a break between this **n** and the following vowel. In the Hepburn system, it is often marked with an apostrophe, as in **kan'en** (hepatitis), and this dictionary follows that practice.

Double Consonants

When a word contains double consonants, for example, the two "p's" in **kippu** (ticket), the two are pronounced separately with a break between them rather than as a single consonant. In this case, the two "p's" are pronounced like those in "hip pocket" and not like those in "hippie." In the same way, the two "k's" of **gakkō** (school) are pronounced like the "kc" of "bookcase" and not like the "k" of "bookies." Other such consonant pairs are **ss, tt,** and **nn.** In this dictionary, the two "n's" of **nn** are separated by an apostrophe, as in **kan'nen** (idea, sense), since the first of the pair is the syllabic **n.**

The consonant combination "tch," as in **itchi** (accord), also has a break between the "t" and the "ch," being pronounced like the "tch" in "hatcheck" and not like that in "hatchet."

Accent

The Japanese accent pattern is fundamentally different from the English one, in which accented syllables are stressed more heavily than unaccented ones. The Japanese accent pattern is often described as flat, meaning that every syllable is stressed equally. Japanese does have an accent, which consists of a change in pitch on certain syllables, and this change in pitch can be used to differentiate between two words that are otherwise pronounced the same, as **háshi** (chopsticks) and **hashí** (bridge). However, such distinctions are not as crucial as they would be in English, where a misunderstanding might arise if a particular syllable is not stressed. A general guideline for the Japanese accent is to avoid putting a heavy stress on any syllable. Even without a proper pitch accent, meanings can be understood from context. On the other hand, if a speaker does put a strong stress accent on any syllables, the words will sound foreign to most Japanese ears.

Pronunciation of Foreign Words

As can be seen from the table on pages xix–xx, the typical Japanese syllable consists of either a vowel alone or a consonant (or consonant plus glide) followed by a vowel. Aside from the doubling of certain consonants and the frequent appearance of syllabic **n** before other consonants, Japanese has few consonant clusters, especially compared to English and some other European languages. As a result, when a loanword from English (as pronounced in English) contains a succession of consonants, its pronunciation in Japanese often requires a vowel between the consonants. This pronunciation is of course reflected when such words are romanized. For example, pronunciation of the word "illustration" in Japanese requires insertion of a vowel between "s" and "t" and between "t" and "r," resulting in **irasutorēshon.**

Japanese also has few vowel sounds compared to English, and one Japanese vowel often has to do the work of several English ones. The Japanese **a** is used to represent the English short "u," as in the example above, and the Japanese long **ā** is often used for both the short English "a" of "fast" and the rather different vowel sound of English "first."

Japanese does not have a "v" sound, and English "v" becomes "b" in borrowed words. For example, "vest" and "best" are both pronounced (and romanized) as **besuto.** Although there is no "v" in rōmaji, the constant influx of foreign words into Japanese is so great that many consonant sounds that were previously nonexistent are being gradually added to both spoken Japanese and the rōmaji alphabet. For example, **ti** and **tī** are now commonly used for such borrowed words as **tisshū** (tissue) and **aisu-tī** (iced tea). Since modern Japanese originally lacked the "f" sound of English, some earlier loanwords using this sound were given an approximate pronunciation, as in the case of **kōhī** for "coffee." More recently, however, such syllables as **fa, fi, fe,** and **fo** have gained currency, especially among younger people.

Word Division, Special Marks

Spacing and Hyphens

In the Japanese writing system, the language is written without spacing between words. There are punctuation marks, such as commas, brackets for quotations, and the equivalent of a period at the end of a sentence. Otherwise, however, the characters within a sentence are spaced equally, with divisions between one thought unit and another being recognized in terms of inflectional endings, case markers, and function words, much as they would be in speech. The use of **kanji,** or Chinese characters, which are seen as sense units, also aids in the process of comprehension.

When writing Japanese in romanization, without the visual aid of kanji, it is obvious that the words need to be divided by spaces as they would be in European languages. The tendency of Japanese to build words into longer units by compounding and the addition of prefixes and suffixes sometimes makes it difficult to do the dividing without separating elements that really go together logically. In this dictionary, longer Japanese sense units have been divided into smaller units by spacing except when it was felt that doing so might obscure the overall sense. When spacing was ruled out, hyphens were often used to show the divisions within the compound word.

Aside from such commonsense (and admittedly subjective) decisions, a number of general rules have been followed.

1. When introducing a word of the type that is never used alone but always forms part of another word, e.g., **sū-** (several), a hyphen is used to indicate that it would begin (or end) another word. However, in examples of use, the hyphen is omitted, as in **sūshūkan** (several weeks).
2. Hyphens are used to link doubled words, as in **moshi-moshi** (hello).
3. When a word consists of more than seven syllables, it is divided with hyphens to aid in comprehension and pronunciation, as in **teiki-kankōbutsu** (journal, periodical).
4. The suffix **-teki** (or **-teki na**), which is used to form adjectives from certain nouns, is always hyphenated.
5. Compounds of two or more foreign loanwords are usually hyphenated, as are compounds of a Japanese word and a foreign loanword. Examples: **kurisumasu-pāti** (Christmas party); **ha-burashi** (toothbrush, from Japanese **ha,** or tooth, and English "brush").

Ellipses

Ellipses indicate that some word or phrase (as a subject, object, indirect object, etc.) must be added in order to complete the thought: for example, **... ni hitteki suru** (correspond to), in which a noun needs to be supplied before the **ni** (as after English "to").

Parentheses

Throughout the dictionary, parentheses are used in Japanese words and phrases to indicate parts of the word or phrase that could be omitted without changing the meaning. Examples: **irasshai(mase)** (Welcome!); **kitchiri (to)** (exactly).

A special use of parentheses is for the words **na** and **no** following certain types of adjectives or noun modifiers: for example, **akiraka (na)** (obvious). The **na** or **no** is used only when the adjective appears before a noun as its modifier, not when it appears in the predicate as a complement.

The Slash

Throughout the dictionary, the slash is used to indicate alternate constructions or meanings. In other words, either of the alternatives separated by the slash can be used in the context indicated. When the slash is used to indicate two variants that can be used to form a Japanese word without a difference of meaning, the first variant has a hyphen to avoid confusion. For example, **buryoku-kainyū/-kanshō** is to be interpreted as **buryoku-kainyū** or **buryoku-kanshō**. In such cases, the hyphens are used even though the compound word might otherwise be spelled closed up or as separate words.

The Japanese Writing System

Japanese is written using three different basic scripts: **kanji** (Chinese characters), **hiragana,** and **katakana,** the latter being two distinct types of the Japanese phonetic script known as **kana.** The basic vocabulary of Japanese, of which Chinese loanwords are an integral part, is written in a mixture of kanji and hiragana. In contemporary Japanese, katakana is most commonly used to write loanwords from languages other than Chinese and to write foreign personal and place names; however, it is also sometimes used to write Japanese words for some special reason such as emphasis.

The Use of Kanji

When **kanji** are used to write uninflected words such as nouns, they often represent the whole word. In the case of inflected words such as verbs and adjectives, the kanji, when used, represent the stem of the word, with inflectional endings being written in **hiragana.** Function words, including the particles that are used to indicate case, are always written in hiragana. Certain other very common words are now often written in hiragana even when kanji exist for them. For example, **watashi** (the pronoun "I") can be written either in hiragana as わたし or in kanji as 私. The choice is a matter of usage. This dictionary gives the kanji for a Japanese word (if kanji exist) whenever the word is more frequently written in kanji than in hiragana in such publications as newspapers and magazines.

The merit of using kanji is that it can differentiate homonyms, which abound in Japanese. For instance, **kiru** has two different meanings: 着る (wear) and 切る (cut). The two words are easily distinguishable when they are written in kanji; in speech or when written phonetically, however, they can be confused unless the context makes their meaning clear.

Hiragana and Katakana

The **hiragana** and **katakana** scripts are shown in the table on pages xix–xx, along with their pronunciations, shown in **rōmaji.** Each of the scripts has 46 basic **kana** characters, each of which represents one syllable. These are combined to express more complex syllables such as **bya, gya,** and **kya,** making a total of more than one hundred syllables. In the hiragana script, long vowels are represented by combining two hiragana characters, as in **tanoshii** 楽しい (enjoyable, pleasant), where the kana for **shi** (し) is followed by that for **i** (い) to form the long vowel **ii.** In katakana, on the other hand, long vowels are represented by a dash (ー) placed after a kana containing a short vowel, as in both syllables of **kōhī** (coffee), which is written コーヒー.

Parts of Speech

The parts of speech of English and Japanese do not correspond exactly. While both languages share the basic concepts of noun, pronoun, verb, adjective, and adverb, Japanese lacks the article, the relative pronoun, and the relative adverb. What are called auxiliary verbs in Japanese are quite different from English auxiliary verbs, and where English has prepositions that appear before the noun, Japanese has particles (sometimes called "postpositions") that appear after the noun.

Even within the shared concepts of noun, verb, and adjective, there are significant differences. Japanese nouns and verbs lack the concept of number. On the other hand, some types of Japanese adjectives are inflected for tense, Japanese verbs and verb phrases can be used to modify a noun directly, and a number of grammatical forms that correspond to the category of adjectives in English are considered separate parts of speech in Japanese.

In labeling parts of speech, this dictionary takes an approach that is thought to be in the best interests of the average English-speaking user. Rather than burdening the reader with Japanese grammatical categories, words are labeled according to the way they are used in the sense being defined. This means that Japanese words are in many cases labeled from the point of view of English rather than that of traditional Japanese grammatical categories. In most cases, there is no difference. If a Japanese word is labeled as a noun, it is a noun. If it is labeled a verb, it is a verb. On the other hand, if it is labeled an adjective, it might be one of a number of Japanese parts of speech that can be used to modify a noun. In the same way, the Japanese particle, which always appears after the word it governs, might sometimes be identified as a preposition, sometimes as an adverb, depending on the way it is used or, to put it another way, depending on the way the English word with which it corresponds is used. Some examples of these special cases follow.

Adjectives

Japanese words that are identified as adjectives are of several types. One type is the inflected adjective or **keiyōshi,** for example, **akai** (red). This is the "normal" Japanese adjective, which ends in an **i** preceded by another vowel such as **a, i, u,** or **o.**

Another type is the **keiyōdōshi** (referred to in English by a number of names, such as "copular noun" or "-na adjective"). This grammatical form is essentially a noun (often of Chinese or other foreign origin), which can be used in Japanese as an adjective. When used before a noun as its modifier, this type of word is followed (before the noun) by **na** or **no.** When used in the predicate of a sentence, it is not followed by **na** or **no.** In this dictionary, adjectives of this type are identified by the **na** or **no** (or both) that follows them in parentheses.

Examples:

akiraka (na), *adj.* 明らか (な) obvious; apparent; clear.

abekobe (na, no), *adj.* あべこべ (な、の) opposite; topsy-turvy.

In the first example, the adjective **akiraka** can be either a complement (without **na**) or a modifier (with **na**). In the second example, the adjective **abekobe** can take either **na** or **no** to be a modifying adjective. When a word of this type is shown with **na** or **no** without parentheses, it indicates that this adjective is mainly used as a modifier, and that its use as a complement is nonexistent or highly rare.

A great many nouns, including loanwords, become modifying adjectives when they are followed by **na** or **no.** For example, **gendai** (present day) may be transformed into the modifying adjective **gendai no** (present-day): hence **gendai no mondai** (present-day problems). In this dictionary, some adjectives originating in this manner from nouns are indicated with **no** in parentheses, and accordingly their definitions are adjectival. They may be converted into nouns by eliminating **na** or **no.**

Some words in this dictionary that are verbs in grammatical form are labeled as adjectives because they are mainly used, or are being presented in the dictionary, as modifiers of nouns.

Examples:

aiteiru, *adj.* 開いている open.

aitsugu, *adj.* 相次ぐ continuous; successive.

In form, **aiteiru** is the present progressive tense of the verb **aku** (to open), and **aitsugu** is the "nonpast" (present or future) form of a verb that means "to follow one after another." However, here they are being used as adjectives, equivalent to the English words cited.

The Particle

The functions of the Japanese particle (**jodōshi**) are multiple: subject marker, object marker, direction indicator, and possessive marker, to name a few. In the **Japanese-English** section of this dictionary, they are normally identified as particles, after which their different uses are given grammatical labels that correspond with those of their English counterparts.

Example:

to, *parti.* と 1. *conj.* and; **anata to watashi** you and me. 2. *prep.* with; **haha to** with my mother. 3. *conj.* when; **uchi ni kaeru to** when I came back home. 4. *conj.* if; **ame ga furu to** if it rains.

In the **English-Japanese** section, they are merely labeled according to the English part of speech that they are being used to define.

Table of Japanese Syllables in Rōmaji, Hiragana, and Katakana

1) R = rōmaji; H = hiragana; K = katakana
2) An asterisk (*) marks those syllables that, to a speaker of English, appear to have beginning consonants that do not match those of the other syllables in the same row. They do not appear inconsistent from the standpoint of Japanese, which originally lacked such sounds as "si," "ti," "tu," etc.
3) The syllables shown in parentheses are essentially used in Japanese only in words borrowed from other languages.

	R	H	K	R	H	K	R	H	K	R	H	K	R	H	K
	a	あ	ア	i	い	イ	u	う	ウ	e	え	エ	o	お	オ
k+vowel	ka	か	カ	ki	き	キ	ku	く	ク	ke	け	ケ	ko	こ	コ
s	sa	さ	サ	*shi	し	シ	su	す	ス	se	せ	セ	so	そ	ソ
t	ta	た	タ	*chi	ち	チ	*tsu	つ	ツ	te	て	テ	to	と	ト
n	na	な	ナ	ni	に	ニ	nu	ぬ	ヌ	ne	ね	ネ	no	の	ノ
h	ha	は	ハ	hi	ひ	ヒ	*fu	ふ	フ	he	へ	ヘ	ho	ほ	ホ
m	ma	ま	マ	mi	み	ミ	mu	む	ム	me	め	メ	mo	も	モ
y	ya	や	ヤ				yu	ゆ	ユ				yo	よ	ヨ
r	ra	ら	ラ	ri	り	リ	ru	る	ル	re	れ	レ	ro	ろ	ロ
w	wa	わ	ワ										wo	を	ヲ
n'	n'	ん	ン												
g	ga	が	ガ	gi	ぎ	ギ	gu	ぐ	グ	ge	げ	ゲ	go	ご	ゴ
z	za	ざ	ザ	*ji	じ	ジ	zu	ず	ズ	ze	ぜ	ゼ	zo	ぞ	ゾ
d	da	だ	ダ	*ji	ぢ	ヂ	*zu	づ	ヅ	de	で	デ	do	ど	ド
b	ba	ば	バ	bi	び	ビ	bu	ぶ	ブ	be	べ	ベ	bo	ぼ	ボ
p	pa	ぱ	パ	pi	ぴ	ピ	pu	ぷ	プ	pe	ぺ	ペ	po	ぽ	ポ
ky	kya	きゃ	キャ				kyu	きゅ	キュ				kyo	きょ	キョ
sh	sha	しゃ	シャ	shi	し	シ	shu	しゅ	シュ	(she)	(しぇ)	(シェ)	sho	しょ	ショ
ch	cha	ちゃ	チャ	chi	ち	チ	chu	ちゅ	チュ	(che)	(ちぇ)	(チェ)	cho	ちょ	チョ
ny	nya	にゃ	ニャ				nyu	にゅ	ニュ				nyo	にょ	ニョ
hy	hya	ひゃ	ヒャ				hyu	ひゅ	ヒュ				hyo	ひょ	ヒョ
my	mya	みゃ	ミャ				myu	みゅ	ミュ				myo	みょ	ミョ
ry	rya	りゃ	リャ				ryu	りゅ	リュ				ryo	りょ	リョ

Table of Japanese Syllables in Rōmaji, Hiragana, and Katakana

	R H K	R H K	R H K	R H K	R H K
gy	gya ぎゃギャ		gyu ぎゅギュ		gyo ぎょギョ
j	ja じゃジャ	ji じ ジ	ju じゅジュ	(je)(じぇ)(ジェ)	jo じょジョ
by	bya びゃビャ		byu びゅビュ		byo びょビョ
py	pya ぴゃピャ		pyu ぴゅピュ		pyo ぴょピョ

4) Katakana characters for words borrowed from foreign languages. Owing to their frequent use in words from other languages, the syllables "ti," "tu," "di," and "du" have become common both in writing and in speech. However, "va," "vi," "ve," and "vo" exist only in writing. These sounds are naturally expressed only in katakana, not in hiragana. Not shown in the table but also gaining currency are the combinations テュ and デュ, which are used in writing the "tu" and "du" of such words as "tuner" and "duet," respectively. If transcribed into the Hepburn system, they would have to be represented as "tyu" and "dyu."

t				ti テイ	tu トゥ		
d				di ディ	du ドゥ		
f	fa ファ	fi フィ				fe フェ	fo フォ
v	va ヴァ	vi ヴィ				ve ヴェ	vo ヴォ

5) Long vowels.

ā	ああ	ī	いい	ū	うう	ē	ええ	ō	おお
	アー		イー		ウー		エー		オー
	あー		いー		うー		えー		おう
									おー

Abbreviations

Source Languages of Loanwords

(D.) Dutch; (E.) English; (F.) French; (G.) German; (It.) Italian; (Pg.) Portuguese; (Sp.) Spanish; (Skt.) Sanskrit.

Parts of Speech

adj. adjective
adv. adverb
art. article
aux. vb. auxiliary verb
conj. conjunction
interj. interjection
n. noun
parti. particle
prep. preposition
pron. pronoun
vb. verb

Japanese-English Dictionary

辞典

A

abaku, *vb.* 暴く expose; reveal.

abara(bone), *n.* 肋(骨) rib.

abaraya, *n.* あばら家 hovel.

abareru, *vb.* 暴れる become violent.

abekku, *n.* アベック (F. *avec*) a couple (on a date).

abekobe (na, no), *adj.* あべこべ (な、の) opposite; topsy-turvy.

abekobe ni, *adv.* あべこべに on the contrary; upside down; inside out.

abiru, *vb.* 浴びる take a bath or shower; bask in sunlight; abundantly receive (praise or criticism).

abiseru, *vb.* 浴びせる pour; throw; lay (blame on).

abunai, *adj.* 危ない dangerous; risky; doubtful; life-threatening.

abunakkashii, *adj.* 危なつかしい insecure; unsteady; unreliable.

abunōmaru (na), *adj.* アブノーマル (な) (E.) abnormal.

abura, *n.* 油 oil.

abura, *n.* 脂 fat.

aburage, *n.* あぶらげ fried bean curd.

abureru, *vb.* あぶれる be left unused; **shigoto ni abureru** be unemployed.

aburu, *vb.* あぶる roast; broil.

āchi, *n.* アーチ (E.) arch.

achira あちら 1. *pron.* that; that person, thing, or place. 2. *adv.* over there; abroad.

achi(ra)kochi(ra) ni, *adv.* あち(ら) こち(ら) に here and there; in various places; back and forth.

achira no, *adj.* あちらの 1. that

(object). 2. of a foreign country.

āchisuto, *n.* アーチスト (E.) artist.

ada, *n.* 徒 uselessness; **ada ni naru** turn out to be useless.

adana, *n.* あだ名 nickname.

adeyaka (na), *adj.* あでやか (な) gorgeous.

adobaisu, *n.* アドバイス (E.) advice.

adokenai, *adj.* あどけない innocent; artless.

aegu, *vb.* あえぐ gasp; groan; suffer.

aemono, *n.* 和え物 vegetables or seafood dressed with vinegar, miso, or mashed tofu.

aete, *adv.* 敢えて positively; bravely; purposely.

aete suru, *vb.* 敢えてする dare to do; act bravely.

afureru, *vb.* あふれる overflow.

afurika, *n.* アフリカ (E.) Africa.

agaku, *vb.* あがく struggle.

agameru, *vb.* 崇める worship; adore.

aganau, *vb.* あがなう atone; make up for.

agari 上がり 1. *n.* ascent; increase. 2. *n.* earnings; income. 3. *adj.* completed or ended; prepared; ready; **Sushi itchō agari.** Sushi coming up!

agaru, *vb.* 上がる 1. climb; go up; (price) rise. 2. enter (a house or room). 3. eat; drink. 4. improve. 5. stop (rain or snow). 6. become shy.

ageku, *n.* 挙句 negative outcome; **ageku no hate ni** what is worse.

agemono, *n.* 揚げ物 deep-fried

food.

ageru, *vb.* 上げる 1. raise; lift.
2. give. 3. turn up (volume).
4. hold (a ceremony).

ageru, *vb.* 揚げる deep-fry.

ago, *n.* あご chin; jaw.

agohige, *n.* あごひげ beard.

agura o kaku, *vb.* あぐらをかく sit
cross-legged.

ahen, *n.* 阿片 opium.

ahiru, *n.* あひる duck; **minikui
ahiru no ko** ugly duckling.

ahō, *n.* 阿呆 fool; silly person.

ahorashii, *adj.* あほらしい silly.

ai, *n.* 愛 love.

ai, *n.* 藍 indigo; **ai'iro** deep violet
blue.

aibiki, *n.* 逢引 secret rendezvous.

aibō, *n.* 相棒 associate; partner;
buddy.

aibu, *n.* 愛撫 caress.

aibu suru, *vb.* 愛撫する caress.

aichaku, *n.* 愛着 affection;
attachment.

aida, *n.* 間 interval; time; distance;
relationship; **... no aida ni**
between; during; while.

aidea, aidia, *n.* アイデア、アイデ
ィア (E.) idea.

aidoku suru, *vb.* 愛読する read
with pleasure; subscribe (to a
periodical).

aidoru, *n.* アイドル (E.) idol.

aigan suru, *vb.* 愛願する entreat;
implore.

aigo, *n.* 愛護 protection; **dōbutsu
aigo kyōkai** Society for the
Prevention of Cruelty to Animals.

aihansuru, *adj.* 相反する
conflicting; contradictory.

aiji, *n.* 愛児 one's child.

aijin, *n.* 愛人 love; lover; mistress;
the other woman.

aijō, *n.* 愛情 love; affection.

aikagi, *n.* 合鍵 spare key; master
key; passkey.

aikawarazu, *adv.* 相変らず as
usual; as ... as ever.

aiken, *n.* 愛犬 one's (pet) dog;
aikenka dog lover.

aiko あいこ 1. *n.* tie (in sports).
2. *adj.* even; quits.

aikoku, *n.* 愛国 love of one's
country.

aikokusha, *n.* 愛国者 patriot.

aikurushii, *adj.* 愛苦しい adorable.

aikyō, *n.* 愛敬 charm.

aima, *n.* 合間 interval; spare time.

aimai (na), *adj.* あいまい (な)
ambiguous; vague; unsure.

ainiku, *adj., adv.* あいにく
unfortunate(ly); disappointing(ly);
Oainiku(sama). That's too bad!

ainoko, *n.* 合の子 half-breed.

ainori suru, *vb.* 相乗りする share a
vehicle (esp. a cab) with others;
ride together.

airashii, *adj.* 愛らしい (person or
animal) amiable; captivating.

airon, *n.* アイロン (E.) iron; **airon
o kakeru** press.

aisaika, *n.* 愛妻家 loving husband.

aisatsu, *n.* 挨拶 greeting;
salutation.

aisatsujō, *n.* 挨拶状 greeting card.

aiseki, *n.* 哀惜 lamentation on
someone's death.

aiseki suru, *vb.* 相席する share a
table.

aisha, *n.* 愛車 one's favorite car.

aisha, *n.* 愛社 loyalty to one's
employer.

aishadō, *n.* アイシャドー (E.) eye
shadow.

aishaseishin, *n.* 愛社精神 devotion
to one's employer.

aishō, *n.* 愛称 pet name.

aishō, *n.* 相性 affinity;

compatibility; **...to aishō ga ii** compatible with.

aishū, *n.* 哀愁 loneliness.

aiso, aisō, *n.* 愛想 sociability; friendliness; cheerfulness; **aiso ga ii** friendly; **aiso ga tsukiru** be disgusted or disappointed.

aisu-hokkē, *n.* アイスホッケー (E.) ice hockey.

aisu-kōhī, *n.* アイスコーヒー (E.) iced coffee.

aisu-kurīmu, *n.* アイスクリーム (E.) ice cream.

aisu-kyandē, *n.* アイスキャンデー (E.) ice cream on a stick; popsicle.

ai suru, *vb.* 愛する love.

aisu-sukēto, *n.* アイス スケート (E.) ice skating.

aisu-tī, *n.* アイスティー (E.) iced tea.

aita, *adj.* 開いた open.

aita, *adj.* 空いた unoccupied; vacant.

aite, *n.* 相手 1. partner; associate; **aite o/ni suru** keep company with; deal with a person sincerely; **aite ni shinai** ignore a person. 2. rival; opponent.

aiteiru, *adj.* 開いている open.

aitō, *n.* 哀悼 condolence.

aitsu, *n.* あいつ that damn person.

aitsugu, *adj.* 相次ぐ continuous; successive.

aitsuide, *adv.* 相次いで continuously; one after another.

aitsume, *interj.* あいつめ Damn him (her)!

aiyoku, *n.* 愛欲 lustful love.

aiyō no, *adj.* 愛用の favorite (thing).

aizō, *n.* 愛憎 simultaneous feeling of love and hatred.

aizu, *n.* 合図 sign; signal.

aizuchi, *n.* 相槌 nod of assent;

aizuchi o utsu nod one's agreement.

aji, *n.* あじ horse mackerel.

aji, *n.* 味 1. taste; flavor; **aji ga ii** taste good; **aji ga warui** taste bad. 2. sensation.

ajia, *n.* アジア (E.) Asia.

ajikenai, *adj.* 味気ない uninspiring; insipid; dreary.

ajiru, *vb.* アジる (E.) agitate.

ajisai, *n.* あじさい hydrangea.

ajiwau, *vb.* 味わう 1. taste; savor. 2. experience; go through (hardship).

aka 赤 1. *n.* red; crimson; scarlet. 2. *adj.* total; stark; **aka no tanin** perfect stranger.

aka, *n.* 垢 dirt.

akachan, *n.* 赤ちゃん baby (affectionate usage).

akademikku (na), *adj.* アカデミック (な) (E.) academic.

akadenwa, *n.* 赤電話 public phone.

akago, *n.* 赤子 baby.

akai, *adj.* 赤い red; crimson; scarlet.

akaji, *n.* 赤字 deficit.

akaku naru, *vb.* 赤くなる blush (with embarrassment, shame, or drink).

akarasama (na), *adj.* あからさま (な) frank; open; forthright.

akarasama ni, *adv.* あからさまに frankly; openly; without reserve.

akari, *n.* 明り light; **akari o tsukeru** turn on the light.

akarui, *adj.* 明るい bright; lively.

akarumi, *n.* 明るみ lighted spot; **akarumi ni deru** be brought to light.

akarusa, *n.* 明るさ brightness; liveliness.

akasen, *n.* 赤線 red-light district.

akashingō, *n.* 赤信号 red (traffic)

light.

akasu, *vb.* 明かす 1. disclose; reveal. 2. sit up the whole night.

akatsuki, *n.* 暁 1. daybreak; beginning. 2. ending.

akazatō, *n.* 赤砂糖 brown sugar.

-ake 明け the end of a thing or event; **tsuyuake** the end of the rainy season.

ākēdo, *n.* アーケード (E.) arcade.

akegata, *n.* 明け方 daybreak.

akehanasu, *vb.* 開け放す throw open; leave open.

akeru, *vb.* 明ける 1. start. 2. end; expire.

akeru, *vb.* 開ける 1. open. 2. unwrap. 3. turn over (pages). 4. pierce; make a hole.

akeru, *vb.* 空ける empty; make room for.

akesuke ni, *adv.* あけすけに without reserve; openly.

akewatasu, *vb.* 明け渡す surrender; vacate.

aki, *n.* 秋 autumn; fall.

aki, *n.* 空き vacancy.

aki-heya/-ma, *n.* 空き部屋／〜間 vacant room; room to rent.

akinai, *n.* 商い trade; business.

akinau, *vb.* 商う trade in.

akippoi, *adj.* 飽きっぽい easily bored; capricious.

akiraka (na), *adj.* 明らか（な) obvious.

akirame, *n.* あきらめ resignation; abandonment.

akirameru, *vb.* あきらめる resign oneself to; yield to.

akireru, *vb.* あきれる be astounded; be disgusted.

akiru, *vb.* 飽きる get tired of.

akishitsu, *n.* 空き室 vacant room; room to rent.

akisu(nerai), *n.* 空き巣(狙い)

sneak thief.

akitarinai, *adj.* 飽き足りない insufficient; unsatisfying.

akiya, *n.* 空き家 vacant house; house to rent.

akka suru, *vb.* 悪化する go from bad to worse.

akkenai, *adj.* あっけない (thing or event) over too soon; abrupt.

akke ni torareru, *vb.* あっけにとられる be taken aback; be flabbergasted; be dumbfounded.

akogareru, *vb.* 憧れる long for; yearn after.

aku, *n.* 悪 evil; vice.

aku, *vb.* 空く become vacant; become unused; **te ga aku** become free.

aku, *vb.* 開く open; start.

akubi, *n.* あくび yawn.

akudoi, *adj.* あくどい 1. vicious; nasty. 2. gaudy; garish.

akuheki, *n.* 悪癖 bad habit.

akuhitsu, *n.* 悪筆 poor handwriting.

akuhyō, *n.* 悪評 bad reputation; bad review.

akui, *n.* 悪意 malice; ill will.

akuji, *n.* 悪事 wrongdoing; crime.

akujo, *n.* 悪女 bad woman.

akujōken, *n.* 悪条件 bad condition; handicap.

akujunkan, *n.* 悪循環 vicious circle.

akuma, *n.* 悪魔 devil; demon; Satan; devilish person.

akumade(mo), *adv.* 飽くまで(も) to the utmost; to the end.

akumu, *n.* 悪夢 nightmare.

akunin, *n.* 悪人 wicked person; villain.

akusai, *n.* 悪妻 bad wife.

akusei, *n.* 悪政 poor government.

akusei (no), *adj.* 悪性 (の)

malignant.

akuseku suru, *vb.* あくせくする fuss about; fidget; work in a restless manner; work constantly.

akusento, *n.* アクセント (E.) accent.

akuseru, *n.* アクセル (E.) accelerator.

akusesarī, *n.* アクセサリー (E.) accessory.

akushitsu (na, no), *adj.* 悪質 (な、の) nasty; bad; of poor quality.

akushu, *n.* 握手 handshake.

akushū, *n.* 悪習 bad habit; evil practice.

akushū, *n.* 悪臭 bad smell.

akushumi, *n.* 悪趣味 poor taste.

akutenkō, *n.* 悪天候 bad weather.

akutoku, *n.* 悪徳 vice.

akuyū, *n.* 悪友 bad friend.

ama, *n.* 海女 fisherwoman; female pearl diver.

ama, *n.* 尼 nun.

amachua, *n.* アマチュア (E.) amateur.

amadare, *n.* 雨垂れ raindrop.

amadera, *n.* 尼寺 nunnery.

amado, *n.* 雨戸 rain shutter.

amae, *n.* 甘え dependence.

amaeru, *vb.* 甘える depend on other people's goodwill; behave disrespectfully.

amagasa, *n.* 雨傘 umbrella.

amagumo, *n.* 雨雲 rain cloud.

amai, *adj.* 甘い 1. sweet. 2. indulgent.

amaku miru, *vb.* 甘く見る slight; underestimate.

amami, *n.* 甘味 sweetness.

amamizu, *n.* 雨水 rainwater.

amanattō, *n.* 甘納豆 sugared red bean.

amanogawa, *n.* 天の川 Milky Way.

amanojaku, *n.* あまのじゃく perverse person; stubborn person.

amari, *n.* 余り rest; surplus.

amari, *adv.* 余り 1. very much; excessively; more than. 2. not very. 3. **... no amari** as a result of.

amarimono, *n.* 余り物 leftovers.

amari ni (mo), *adv.* 余りに (も) excessively.

amaru, *vb.* 余る be left (over); remain.

amarugamu, *n.* アマルガム (E.) amalgam.

amayakasu, *vb.* 甘やかす spoil (a person); indulge.

amazake, *n.* 甘酒 sweet sake.

ame, *n.* 雨 rain; rainfall; **Ame ga furu.** It is raining. **Ame ga yanda.** It has stopped raining.

ame, *n.* あめ candy; sweet.

amerika(gasshūkoku), *n.* アメリカ(合衆国) the United States.

amerikajin, *n.* アメリカ人 American (person).

amerika no, *adj.* アメリカの American (thing).

amidana, *n.* 網棚 rack (luggage).

amimono, *n.* 編み物 knitting.

amu, *vb.* 編む knit.

an, *n.* 案 idea; plan; proposal; **an o dasu** make a proposal; **meian** good idea.

an, *n.* あん sweet bean paste.

ana, *n.* 穴 hole; opening; crevice; cavity.

anaba, *n.* 穴場 little-known but pleasing spot (such as a restaurant).

anadoru, *vb.* 侮る look down upon; slight; underestimate.

anagachi, *adv.* あながち not necessarily.

anago, *n.* 穴子 sea eel.

anākisto, *n.* アナーキスト (E.)

anarchist.

anākizumu, *n.* アナーキズム (E.) anarchism.

anarogu, *n.* アナログ (E.) analog.

anata, *pron.* あなた you; darling (used by a woman to her husband or boyfriend).

anaunsā, *n.* アナウンサー (E.) announcer; TV newscaster.

anaunsu, *n.* アナウンス (E.) announcement.

anbaransu, *n.* アンバランス (E.) imbalance.

anchoku (na) *adj.* 安直 (な) easy; cheap.

anchoku ni, *adv.* 安直 (に) in an easy or cheap way.

anchūmosaku suru, *vb.* 暗中模索 する grope in the dark.

andārain, *n.* アンダーライン (E.) underline.

ando suru, *vb.* 安堵する feel relaxed; feel relieved.

ane, *n.* 姉 older sister.

angai, *adv.* 案外 unexpectedly; surprisingly.

angō, *n.* 暗号 code.

ani, *n.* 兄 older brother.

an'i (na), *adj.* 安易 (な) easy.

anime, animēshon, *n.* アニメ, アニメーション (E.) animated cartoon; animation.

an'i ni, *adv.* 安易に easily; lightly.

aniyome, *n.* 兄嫁 older brother's wife.

anji, *n.* 暗示 hint; suggestion; insinuation.

anjiru, *vb.* 暗じる worry about; be concerned with.

anjū, *n.* 安住 peaceful living.

anka (na), *adj.* 安価 (な) inexpensive.

ankēto, *n.* アンケート (F. *enquête*) questionnaire.

anki, *n.* 暗記 memorization.

ankoku, *n.* 暗黒 darkness.

ankokumen, *n.* 暗黒面 dark side.

ankōru, *n.* アンコール (F.) encore.

anma, *n.* あんま masseur; masseuse; massage.

anmari あんまり 1. *adj.* irrational; cruel. 2. *adv.* unusually; extremely; very (much); not very.

anmin, *n.* 安眠 sound sleep.

anmin bōgai, *n.* 安眠妨害 disturbance of someone's sleep.

anmoku (no), *adj.* 暗黙 (の) implicit; tacit.

anmonia, *adj.* アンモニア (E.) ammonia.

an'na, *adj.* あんな (derogatory) that; that sort; such; **An'na yatsu.** That creep!

an'nai, *n.* 案内 information; guidance; invitation; introduction.

an'naigakari, *n.* 案内係 informant; guide.

an'naisho, *n.* 案内所 information booth.

an'naisho, *n.* 案内書 handbook; guidebook.

an'nai suru, *vb.* 案内する guide; show; introduce.

an'na ni, *adv.* あんなに such; so much; that much.

an ni, *adv.* 暗に implicitly; indirectly.

ano, *adj.* あの that; those; **ano hi** on that day; **ano koro** in those days.

ano ne, *interj.* あのね Well! Look!

ano yo, *n.* あの世 afterworld.

ano yō (na), *adj.* あの様な that kind of.

ano yō ni, *adv.* あの様に in that manner.

anpi, *n.* 安否 safety.

anraku (na), *adj.* 安楽 (な) cozy;

comfortable.

anrakushi, *n.* 安楽死 mercy
killing.

ansanburu, *n.* アンサンブル (F.
ensemble) harmony; balance.

ansatsu, *n.* 暗殺 assassination.

ansatsusha, *n.* 暗殺者 assassin.

ansei, *n.* 安静 rest; **zettai ansei**
absolute rest (doctor's orders).

anshin, *n.* 安心 peace of mind;
relief; **anshin dekiru** reliable.

anshō, *n.* 暗誦 recitation.

anshōbangō, *n.* 暗証番号 code
number.

antai, *n.* 安泰 peace.

antei, *n.* 安定 stability.

antena, *n.* アンテナ (E.) antenna.

an'yaku suru, *vb.* 暗躍する
maneuver behind the scenes.

an'yo, *n.* あんよ baby's toddle.

anzan, *n.* 安産 easy delivery (of a
baby).

anzan, *n.* 暗算 mental calculation.

anzen, *n.* 安全 safety; security.

anzen (na), *adj.* 安全 (な) safe;
secure.

anzen-beruto, *n.* 安全ベルト seat
belt.

anzenkamisori, *n.* 安全かみそり
safety razor.

anzen-pin, *n.* 安全ピン safety pin.

anzu, *n.* 杏 apricot.

ao, *n.* 青 blue; green.

aoba, *n.* 青葉 green leaf.

aogu, *vb.* 仰ぐ look up; look up to;
ask for (advice); depend on.

aogu, *vb.* 扇ぐ fan; instigate.

aohige, *n.* 青ひげ bluebeard (bluish
appearance of man's face after
shaving).

aoi, *adj.* 青い blue; green; unripe;
inexperienced.

aoitori, *n.* 青い鳥 bluebird.

aojashin, *n.* 青写真 blueprint.

aojiroi, *adj.* 青白い pale.

aomono, *n.* 青物 vegetable.

aomuke ni, *adv.* 仰向けに on one's
back.

aonisai, *n.* 青二才 greenhorn.

aonori, *n.* 青海苔 (dried) green
seaweed.

aoru, *vb.* 煽る fan; instigate; stir up.

aoshingō, *n.* 青信号 green light.

aozora, *n.* 青空 blue sky.

apāto, *n.* アパート (E.) apartment
(for rent).

apīru, *n.* アピール (E.) appeal.

appaku suru, *vb.* 圧迫する
suppress; oppress.

appare (na), *adj.* あっぱれ (な)
admirable; **Appare.** Splendid!
Good job!

appu, *n.* アップ (E. *up*) upswept
hairdo; closeup.

appu suru, *vb.* アップする (E. *up*)
lift; raise; improve.

ara, *interj.* あら Oh!

ara, *n.* あら shortcoming;
weakness.

ara-arashii, *adj.* 荒々しい rough;
violent; impudent.

arabia, *n.* アラビア (E.) Arabia.

arabiago, *n.* アラビア語 Arabic
language.

arabiajin, *n.* アラビア人 Arabian
(person).

aragoto, *n.* 荒事 (kabuki) stylized
movements (by a samurai or
warrior character).

arai, *adj.* 荒い violent; rough; rude.

araizarai, *adv.* あらいざらい
entirely.

arakajime, *adv.* あらかじめ
beforehand.

aramashi, *n.* あらまし outline;
story line; plot.

arankagiri, *adv.* 有らん限り with
all one's might.

arankagiri no, *adj.* 有らん限りの utmost.

aranu, *adj.* あらぬ groundless; unjust.

arare, *n.* あられ 1. hail. 2. rice cracker.

arashi, *n.* 嵐 storm.

arasou, *vb.* 争う fight; dispute; compete.

arasuji, *n.* 荒筋 story line; plot.

aratamaru, *vb.* 改まる 1. be renewed. 2. (person) become formal.

aratameru, *vb.* 改める change; renovate; correct.

aratamete, *adv.* 改めて again; anew; another time.

arata (na), *adj.* 新らた (な) new; fresh.

arata ni, *adv.* 新らたに newly; anew; over again.

arau, *vb.* 洗う wash; **sara o arau** do the dishes.

arawa (na), *adj.* あらわ (な) open; uncovered.

arawa ni suru, *vb.* あらわにする expose.

arawareru, *vb.* 現われる appear; show up.

arawasu, *vb.* 表わす signify; represent; express.

arawasu, *vb.* 現わす show; show up; demonstrate.

arawasu, *vb.* 著わす write; publish.

arayuru, *adj.* あらゆる all; every possible.

are, *pron.* あれ that.

arekakoreka, *pron.* あれかこれか this or that.

are(k)kiri, *adv.* あれ(つ)きり since then.

arekore, *pron.* あれこれ this and that; every possible thing.

areru, *vb.* 荒れる deteriorate; decline; become uncontrollable.

arerugī, *n.* アレルギー (G. *Allergie*) allergy.

ari, *n.* 蟻 ant.

ariamaru, *vb.* 有り余る be abundant; have more than necessary.

ariari to, *adv.* ありありと vividly; clearly.

ariawase, *n.* 有り合わせ anything on hand; something available.

aribai, *n.* アリバイ (E.) alibi.

arifureta, *adj.* ありふれた ordinary; banal.

arigachi (na, no), *adj.* ありがち (な、の) common; frequent.

arigatai, *adj.* 有難い grateful; welcome; appreciative.

arigata-meiwaku, *n.* 有難迷惑 misplaced or unwanted kindness.

arigatō, *vb.* 有難う be grateful; thank; **Arigatō.** Thank you! **Dōmo arigatō gozaimasu.** Thank you very much.

arika, *n.* 在りか whereabouts.

arikitari (na, no), *adj.* ありきたり (な、の) commonplace; conventional.

arinomama ni, *adv.* ありのままに as it is; frankly; honestly.

arisama, *n.* 有り様 state; circumstance.

arisō (na), *adj.* ありそう (な) likely; probable; believable.

arittake (no), *adj.* ありつたけ (の) all; utmost.

aru, *adj.* 或る a; an; a certain; some; **aru hi** one day; **aru hito** someone; a certain person; **mukashi mukashi aru tokoro ni ...** Once upon a time, there lived ...

aru, *vb.* ある 1. have; there is (are); exist; be located. 2. happen; take

place. 3. experience; **-ta koto ga
aru** have experienced; **mita koto
ga aru** have seen before.

arubaito, *n.* アルバイト (G. *Arbeit*)
part-time job; moonlighting.

arubamu, *n.* アルバム (E.) album.

aruchū, *n.* アル中 alcoholic;
alcoholism.

arufabetto, *n.* アルファベット (E.)
alphabet.

aruite, *adv.* 歩いて on foot.

aruiwa あるいは 1. *conj.* or. 2. *adv.*
perhaps; maybe.

arukōru, *n.* アルコール (E.)
alcohol; liquor.

arukōru-chūdoku, *n.* アルコール
中毒 alcoholic; alcoholism.

aruku, *vb.* 歩く walk.

arumi-hoiru, *n.* アルミホイル (E.)
aluminum foil.

arumi(niumu), *n.* アルミ(ニウム)
(E.) aluminum.

arumi-sasshi, *n.* アルミサッシ (E.)
aluminum window frame.

arupusu, *n.* アルプス (E.) the Alps;
nihon arupusu the Japanese
Alps.

aryū (no), *adj.* 亜流 (の) imitative;
counterfeit.

asa 朝 1. *n.* morning. 2. *adv.* in the
morning.

asa, *n.* 麻 hemp; linen.

asagao, *n.* 朝顔 1. morning glory.
2. urinal.

asagohan, *n.* 朝御飯 breakfast.

asahaka (na), *adj.* 浅はか (な)
superficial; thoughtless; silly.

asahi, *n.* 朝日 morning sun; rising
sun.

asai, *adj.* 浅い shallow; short
(days); inexperienced.

asakusa nori, *n.* 浅草海苔 dried
seaweed.

asamashii, *adj.* 浅ましい

despicable; base; miserable.

asameshi, *n.* 朝飯 breakfast.

asameshimae, *adj.* 朝飯前 easy.

asaru, *vb.* 漁る rummage; forage;
search for.

asatte, *n., adv.* あさって、明後日
the day after tomorrow.

ase, *n.* 汗 sweat; perspiration; **ase
ga deru/ase o kaku** to sweat;
perspire.

asemo, *n.* あせも prickly heat.

aseru, *vb.* 焦る get impatient; be in
a hurry; be anxious and eager.

aseru, *vb.* 褪せる fade; discolor.

ashi, *n.* 足 1. foot; leg; foot of an
animal. 2. transportation. 3. **ashi
o arau** quit; **ashi ga deru**
overspend.

ashi, *n.* 葦 reed.

ashidematoi, *n.* 足手まとい
burden; nuisance.

ashidome, *n.* 足止め delay;
stalemate; **ashidome o kū** be
delayed; be held up.

ashika, *n.* あしか sea lion.

ashikake, *adv.* 足掛け
approximately; **ashikake ninen**
approximately two years.

ashikarazu 悪しからず I don't
mean to be impolite; Don't take it
badly.

ashikubi, *n.* 足首 ankle.

ashimoto, *n.* 足元 step; **Ashimoto
ni ki o tsukete.** Watch your step.

ashioto, *n.* 足音 footstep.

ashirau, *vb.* あしらう deal with
indifferently (lightly, badly).

ashisutanto, *n.* アシスタント (E.)
assistant.

ashita, *n., adv.* 明日 tomorrow.

ashiwaza, *n.* 足技 footwork (in
judo and sumo).

asobaseru, *vb.* 遊ばせる leave idle;
let play.

asobi, *n.* 遊び 1. play; game; diversion; relaxation. 2. playing around; dissipation. 3. having a good time. 4. visit; **Asobi ni kite kudasai.** Please come to see me.

asobihanbun de/ni, *adv.* 遊び半分で／に playfully; insincerely.

asobinin, *n.* 遊び人 philanderer; idler; gambler.

asobu, *vb.* 遊ぶ 1. play; enjoy; philander. 2. be idle; be left unused. 3. be unemployed.

asoko, *n., adv.* あそこ (on) that spot; there; over there.

assari (to), *adv.* あっさり（と） simply; lightly; easily.

assari shita, *adj.* あっさりした simple; light; easy.

assei, *n.* 圧制 tyranny.

assen, *n.* 斡旋 assistance; help; good offices.

asu, *n., adv.* 明日 tomorrow.

asupirin, *n.* アスピリン (E.) aspirin.

asurechikku-kurabu, *n.* アスレチックラブ (E.) athletic club.

ataeru, *vb.* 与える give; award; cause.

atafuta suru, *vb.* あたふたする be in a hurry; be in a fluster.

atai, *n.* 価 value; price.

atakamo, *conj.* あたかも as if.

atakku, *n.* アタック (E.) attack.

atama, *n.* 頭 1. head; face; hair. 2. brain; intelligence. 3. beginning.

atamadekkachi (na, no), *adj.* 頭でっかち（な、の）1. top-heavy. 2. quixotic.

atamakin, *n.* 頭金 down payment.

atarashii, *adj.* 新しい fresh; new; latest.

atarashisa, *n.* 新しさ freshness; novelty.

atari 辺り 1. *n.* neighborhood; area. 2. *adv.* around.

atari, *n.* 当たり hit; success; (lottery) winning.

-atari 当たり per; **hitoriatari** per person; **kokuminhitoriatari** per capita.

atarihazure, *n.* 当たり外れ hit or miss.

atarikuji, *n.* 当たりくじ winning number.

atarimae (no), *adj.* 当たり前（の）right; reasonable; natural.

atarisawari no nai, *adj.* 当たり障りのない innocuous; safe.

ataru, *vb.* 当たる 1. hit. 2. guess correctly.

ataru, *vb.* あたる become sick from food poisoning; **fugu ni ataru** be poisoned by eating fugu (puffer or blowfish).

ataru, *vb.* あたる treat badly; take it out on.

atatakai, *adj.* 暖かい、温かい 1. mild; warm. 2. warmhearted; happy.

atatamaru, *vb.* 暖まる、温まる get warm.

atatameru, *vb.* 暖める、温める heat up; warm up.

ate, *n.* 当て expectation.

ate ga hazureru, *vb.* 当てが外れる be disappointed.

atehamaru, *vb.* 当てはまる fit; apply to.

atena, *n.* 宛名 address; addressee.

ate ni naranai, *adj.* 当てにならない unreliable.

ate ni suru, *vb.* 当てにする count on; depend upon; trust.

ateru, *vb.* 当てる 1. hit. 2. touch (by hand). 3. guess correctly. 4. expose (to the sun). 5. win (lottery or prize).

ateru, *vb.* あてる allocate.

ateru, *vb.* 宛てる address (mail).

ato 後 1. *adj.* another (with a number); **ato san'nin** another three people.　2. *prep.* after; behind.

ato, *n.* 後 1. the rear.　2. the rest.　3. successor; descendant.

ato, *n.* 跡 1. track; trace.　2. ruins.

āto, *n.* アート (E.) art.

atoaji, *n.* 後味 aftertaste.

ato de, *adv.* 後で later.

atogaki, *n.* 後書き afterword; postscript.

atokata, *n.* 跡形 trace.

atokatazuke o suru, *vb.* 後片付けをする clean up a place after using it.

atomawashi ni suru, *vb.* 後回しにする postpone.

atomodori o suru, *vb.* 後戻りをする retreat; regress.

atorie, *n.* アトリエ (F. *atelier*) studio.

atosaki, *n.* 後先 consequence; cause and effect.

atoshimatsu o suru, *vb.* 後始末をする settle (a problem); put in order.

atotsugi, *n.* 跡継ぎ heir; inheritor; successor.

atsui, *adj.* 熱い hot (food or material); passionate.

atsui, *adj.* 暑い hot (weather).

atsui, *adj.* 厚い thick.

atsukamashii, *adj.* 厚かましい impudent; brazen.

atsukau, *vb.* 扱う treat; deal with; deal in; transact.

atsumari, *n.* 集まり meeting; collection.

atsumaru, *vb.* 集まる get together; meet; assemble.

atsumeru, *vb.* 集める collect;

attract; summon.

atsuryoku, *n.* 圧力 pressure.

atsuryoku-dantai, *n.* 圧力団体 pressure group.

atsuryoku-gama/-nabe, *n.* 圧力釜／～鍋 pressure cooker.

atsusa, *n.* 熱さ、暑さ heat.

atsusa, *n.* 厚さ thickness.

atto iu ma ni, *adv.* あっという間に in an instant.

atto iwaseru, *vb.* あっと言わせる take by surprise.

attō suru, *vb.* 圧倒する overwhelm; overpower.

attō-teki (na), *adj.* 圧倒的 (な) overwhelming.

au, *vb.* 会う see (a person); meet; **tomodachi ni au** see a friend.

au, *vb.* 遭う be involved in (an accident); get caught in.

au, *vb.* 合う fit; suit; match; agree with.

auto, *n.* アウト (E.) out (in sports).

awa, *n.* 泡 bubble; foam.

awabi, *n.* あわび abalone.

aware, *n.* 哀れ pity; misery.

awaremu, *vb.* 哀れむ feel pity for; feel sympathetic.

aware (na), *adj.* 哀れ (な) pitiful; miserable.

awaseru, *vb.* 合わせる 1. put together; combine.　2. harmonize; adjust.　3. add up (calculation).

awaseru, *vb.* 会わせる introduce people to each other.

awatadashii, *adj.* あわただしい hasty; busy; restless.

awatemono, *n.* あわて者 hasty person.

awateru, *vb.* あわてる be hasty; get confused; be in a panic.

ayabumu, *vb.* 危ぶむ doubt.

ayafuya (na), *adj.* あやふや (な) indecisive; vague; unreliable.

ayamachi, *n.* 過ち fault; error; mistake; blunder.

ayamaru, *vb.* 誤る err; make a mistake.

ayamaru, *vb.* 謝る apologize.

ayamatta, *adj.* 誤つた wrong; misleading.

ayamatte, *adv.* 誤つて by mistake; by accident.

ayame, *n.* あやめ iris (plant).

ayashii, *adj.* 怪しい suspicious; dubious; unreliable.

ayashimu, *vb.* 怪しむ suspect; doubt.

ayasu, *vb.* あやす 1. humor (a baby). 2. amuse; coax.

ayatsuru, *vb.* 操る manipulate; maneuver; handle; control.

ayu, *n.* 鮎 trout.

ayumi, *n.* 歩み 1. walking; step. 2. history; record.

ayumi-yoru, *vb.* 歩み寄る 1. walk up to. 2. compromise.

aza, *n.* あざ birthmark; bruise; black eye.

azakeri, *n.* 嘲り ridicule; mockery.

azakeru, *vb.* 嘲る ridicule; mock; scoff.

azarashi, *n.* あざらし seal (sea animal).

azayaka (na), *adj.* 鮮か (な) 1. colorful; bright; vivid. 2. impressive; beautiful.

azen to suru, *vb.* 啞然とする be dumbfounded.

azukaru, *vb.* 預かる keep; take care of; be in charge of.

azukaru, *vb.* 与かる participate; share; be concerned with.

azukeru, *vb.* 預ける deposit; leave in charge of; check (coat or baggage).

azuki, *n.* 小豆 red bean.

azumaya, *n.* 東屋 bower; arbor.

B

ba, *n.* 場 place; spot; space; occasion.

bā, *n.* バー (E.) bar (place serving liquor).

ba'ai, *n.* 場合 1. case; occasion. 2. circumstance.

bachi, *n.* 罰 punishment; retribution; judgment.

bachiatari (na, no), *adj.* 罰当たり (な、の) spiteful; sinful; cursed.

bachigai (na), *adj.* 場違い (な) out of place.

bāgen(-sēru), *n.* バーゲン (セール) (E.) bargain sale.

bai, *n.* 倍 a double amount; **bai ni naru** to double.

-bai 倍 1. -fold; times; **sanbai** three times. 2. see **-hai.**

baibai, *n.* 売買 buying and selling.

baibai, *interj.* バイバイ (E.) Byebye!

baibai-keiyaku, *n.* 売買契約 sales contract.

baidoku, *n.* 梅毒 syphilis.

baika, *n.* 買価 purchase price.

baikai, *n.* 媒介 carrier; medium; agent.

baikaisha, *n.* 媒介者 carrier (of germs); mediator; agent.

baikai suru, *vb.* 媒介する carry (germs); mediate.

baikin, *n.* ばい菌 germ; virus; bacteria.

baikingu, *n.* バイキング (E. *Viking*)

smorgasbord; buffet-style restaurant meal.

baiku, *n.* バイク (E.) motorbike; motorcycle.

baikyaku suru, *vb.* 売却する sell.

baiorin, *n.* バイオリン (E.) violin.

baiotekunorojī, *n.* バイオテクノロジー (E.) biotechnology.

baipasu, *n.* バイパス (E.) bypass.

baishaku, *n.* 媒酌 matchmaking.

baishakunin, *n.* 媒酌人 matchmaker.

baishin, *n.* 陪審 jury.

baishin'in, *n.* 陪審員 juror.

baishō, *n.* 賠償 compensation; reparation.

baishōkin, *n.* 賠償金 compensation (money); reparation.

baishū suru, *vb.* 買収する purchase; bribe.

baishun, *n.* 売春 prostitution.

baishunfu, *n.* 売春婦 prostitute.

baiten, *n.* 売店 stall; booth; kiosk; stand.

baito, *n.* バイト (G. *Arbeit*) part-time job.

baiu, *n.* 梅雨 rainy season (June and the first half of July).

baiyā, *n.* バイヤー (E.) buyer.

baiyakuzumi, *adj.* 売約済 already sold.

baizō suru, *vb.* 倍増する double.

baka, *n.* 馬鹿 1. stupid person. 2. stupidity; absurdity. 3. **baka ni suru** ridicule; look down on. 4. **baka o miru** make a fool of oneself; **baka o iu** talk nonsense.

baka, *adv.* ばか too much; excessively; extremely; **bakateinei** excessively or ridiculously polite.

bakabakashii, *adj.* 馬鹿馬鹿しい ridiculous; stupid; nonsensical.

bakageta, *adj.* 馬鹿げた ridiculous;

absurd; irrational.

baka (na), *adj.* 馬鹿 (な) foolish; stupid; absurd; impossible.

baka ni, *adv.* 馬鹿に terribly; awfully; very much.

bakarashii, *adj.* 馬鹿らしい ridiculous; absurd; useless.

-bakari ばかり 1. about; **itsukabakari** for about five days. 2. just; **ima tsuitabakari** have just arrived. 3. only; **shigotobakari shiteiru** do nothing but work. 4. almost; **nakanbakari** almost crying.

-bakari de naku, *conj.* ばかりでなく not only ... but.

bakasawagi, *n.* 馬鹿騒ぎ frolicking; revelry; merrymaking.

bakayarō, *interj.* 馬鹿野郎 You fool! Jerk!

bakemono, *n.* 化物 ghost; phantom; monster.

bake no kawa, *n.* 化けの皮 dissemblance; pretense; **bake no kawa ga hagareru** show one's true self.

baketsu, *n.* バケツ (E.) bucket; pail.

bakkin, *n.* 罰金 penalty; fine.

bakku, *n.* バック (E.) back; background.

bakkuappu, *n.* バックアップ (E.) backup; support; help.

bakkuguraundo-myūjikku, *n.* バックグラウンドミュージック (E.) background music.

bakku-mirā, *n.* バックミラー (E.) rearview mirror.

bakku-nanbā, *n.* バックナンバー (E.) back number; back issue.

bakuchi, *n.* 博打 gambling.

bakuchi o suru, *vb.* 博打をする gamble.

bakudai (na), *adj.* 莫大 (な)

enormous; immense; vast.

bakudan, *n.* 爆弾 bomb; **genshi-bakudan** atomic bomb; **chūseishibakudan** neutron bomb; **jigenbakudan** time bomb.

bakufu, *n.* 幕府 shogunate administration.

bakugeki, *n.* 爆撃 bombing; bombardment.

bakugeki suru, *vb.* 爆撃する bomb; bombard.

bakuha, *n.* 爆破 blast (with explosives).

bakuha suru, *vb.* 爆破する blow up; explode.

bakuhatsu, *n.* 爆発 explosion; eruption.

bakuhatsubutsu, *n.* 爆発物 explosive.

bakuhatsu suru, *vb.* 爆発する explode; erupt.

bakuhatsu-teki (na), *adj.* 爆発的 (な) characterized by an explosive increase in (popularity); faddish; voguish.

bakuro suru, *vb.* 暴露する expose; reveal; disclose.

bakushō, *n.* 爆笑 burst of laughter.

bakuteria, *n.* バクテリア (E.) bacteria.

bakuzen to shita, *adj.* 漠然とした ambiguous; uncertain; vague.

bamen, *n.* 場面 scene.

ban, *n.* 晩 evening; night.

ban, *n.* 番 1. watch (guard); **ban o suru** take care of. 2. turn; number; **kimi no ban** your turn; **ichiban** number 1.

banana, *n.* バナナ (E.) banana.

-banare 離れ quitting; stopping (a habit); loss of interest; **chichi-banare** weaning (a baby); **katsujibanare** lose interest in reading.

bancha, *n.* 番茶 lowest quality green tea.

banchi, *n.* 番地 house number; street number.

bando, *n.* バンド (E.) band; belt.

bando-eido, *n.* バンドエイド (E.) Band-Aid.

bane, *n.* ばね spring (elastic).

bangō, *n.* 番号 number; **bangō o utsu** give a number to.

bangōjun ni, *adv.* 番号順に in numerical order.

bangumi, *n.* 番組 TV or radio program.

banji, *n.* 万事 everything; all; **Banji kyūsu da.** It's all over (for me).

bankai suru, *vb.* 挽回する regain; recover; retrieve.

banken, *n.* 番犬 watchdog.

bankoku-hakurankai, *n.* 万国博覧会 international exposition.

bankuruwase, *n.* 番狂わせ unexpected victory or defeat; upset.

-banme (no) 番目 (の) suffix used with a number to form an ordinal; **yonbanme no mondai** the fourth question.

banmeshi, *n.* 晩飯 dinner; supper.

ban'nin, *n.* 番人 guard; watchman; keeper.

ban'nō (na, no), *adj.* 万能 (な、の) almighty; all-around.

banpā, *n.* バンパー (E.) bumper.

bansan, *n.* 晩さん formal dinner; **bansankai** dinner party; banquet.

banshaku, *n.* 晩酌 drink with dinner.

banshū, *n.* 晩秋 late fall.

bansō, *n.* 伴奏 accompaniment (music).

bansōkō, *n.* 絆創膏 medical plaster; Band-Aid.

bansōsha, *n.* 伴奏者 accompanist

(music).

banto, *n.* バント (E.) bunt (baseball).

banzai, *interj.* 万歳 Hurrah!

banzen (no), *adj.* 万全 (の) thorough; sure; unerring; infallible.

bappon-teki (na), *adj.* 抜本的 (な) drastic; radical.

bara, *n.* ばら rose.

barabara ni naru, *vb.* ばらばらに なる be scattered; be disassembled or broken into pieces; be separated from one another.

bara de, *adv.* ばらで separately; loose; not bound together or put in a package.

barakku, *n.* バラック (E.) barracks; shanty.

baramaku, *vb.* ばらまく scatter; strew; throw.

baransu, *n.* バランス (E.) balance; **baransu o toru** to balance; **baransu o nakusu** to lose balance.

baransu no toreta, *adj.* バランス のとれた well-balanced.

barasu, *vb.* ばらす 1. expose (a secret). 2. disassemble. 3. kill.

barē, bare'e, *n.* バレー、バレエ (F.) ballet.

barē(bōru), *n.* バレー(ボール) (E.) volleyball.

barerīna, *n.* バレリーナ (E.) ballerina.

bareru, *vb.* ばれる find out (a secret); reveal; leak.

barikēdo, *n.* バリケード (E.) barricade.

bariki, *n.* 馬力 horsepower; stamina; power; strength.

baromētā, *n.* バロメーター (E.) barometer.

bāsan, *n.* 婆さん old woman; old wife; grandmother.

basho, *n.* 場所 1. place; location; space; seat. 2. position. 3. sumo tournament.

bassoku, *n.* 罰則 penal regulations.

bassui, *n.* 抜すい excerpt; extract.

bassuru, *vb.* 罰する discipline; punish; penalize.

basu, *n.* バス (E.) bus; **basu de** by bus; **basu ni noru** get on a bus; **basu o oriru** get off a bus; **sukūru-basu** school bus.

basu, *n.* バス (E.) bath.

bāsudē, *n.* バースデー (E.) birthday.

bāsudē-kēki, *n.* バースデーケーキ (E.) birthday cake.

bāsudē-pātī, *n.* バースデーパーテ ィー (E.) birthday party.

bāsudē-purezento, *n.* バースデー プレゼント (E.) birthday present.

basue, *n.* 場末 unfrequented area of a town.

basuketto(bōru), *n.* バスケット (ボール) (E.) basketball.

basu-tāminaru, *n.* バスターミナル (E.) bus terminal.

basu-taoru, *n.* バスタオル (E.) bath towel.

basu tei, *n.* バス停 (E.) bus stop.

batā, *n.* バター (E.) butter.

bata-bata suru, *vb.* ばたばたする clatter; bustle about; be frantic.

bāten, *n.* バーテン (E.) bartender.

bateru, *vb.* ばてる get exhausted; get worn out.

batō suru, *vb.* 罵倒する abuse; yell at.

batsu, *n.* 罰 discipline; punishment; penalty.

batsu, *n.* 閥 faction; circle; clique; group.

batsu ga warui, *adj.* 罰が悪い awkward; out of place.

batsugun (na, no), *adj.* 抜群 (な、

の) outstanding; fabulous.

batta, *n.* ばった grasshopper.

battā, *n.* バッター (E.) batter (baseball).

battari, *adv.* ばったり (fall) with a thud; abruptly; accidentally; unexpectedly.

batteki suru, *vb.* 抜的する promote; single out.

batterī, *n.* バッテリー (E.) battery.

batto, *n.* バット (E.) bat (baseball).

bazā, *n.* バザー (E.) bazaar.

bebī, *n.* ベビー (E.) baby.

bebī-kā, *n.* ベビーカー (E.) baby carriage; stroller.

beddo, *n.* ベッド (E.) bed.

beigo, *n.* 米語 American English.

beigun, *n.* 米軍 U.S. armed forces.

beikoku, *n.* 米国 the United States.

beisaku, *n.* 米作 rice-growing; rice crop.

beishoku, *n.* 米食 rice diet.

-bekarazu, *interj.* べからず (imperative use) it is prohibited to...; **Hairu-bekarazu.** Do not enter!

-beki, *parti.* べき should; must; **aubeki** 会うべき should or must meet.

bekka, *n.* 別科 special academic program.

bekkan, *n.* 別館 annex.

bekkasei, *n.* 別科生 student in a special academic program.

bekkō, *n.* べっ甲 tortoiseshell.

bekko ni, *adv.* 別個に separately.

bekkyo, *n.* 別居 separation (of family members or a couple).

bekkyo suru, *vb.* 別居する live separately.

bēkon, *n.* ベーコン (E.) bacon.

ben, *n.* 便 1. convenience. 2. transportation service. 3. feces.

-ben 弁 dialect; **nagoyaben**

Nagoya dialect.

benchi, *n.* ベンチ (E.) bench.

bengi, *n.* 便宜 convenience; assistance; **bengi o hakaru** assist; help.

bengo, *n.* 弁護 defense.

bengoshi, *n.* 弁護士 lawyer.

bengo suru, *vb.* 弁護する defend; plead.

beni, *n.* 紅 red; rouge; lipstick.

ben'i, *n.* 便意 urge to defecate; **ben'i o moyoosu** feel the urge to defecate.

beniya, *n.* ベニヤ (E.) veneer.

benjo, *n.* 便所 bathroom; rest room; toilet.

benkai, *n.* 弁解 excuse; rationalization; justification.

benkai suru, *vb.* 弁解する excuse; rationalize; justify.

benki, *n.* 便器 toilet; urinal.

benkyō, *n.* 勉強 study.

benkyō (o) suru, *vb.* 勉強 (を) する 1. study; learn. 2. give a discount.

benmei suru, *vb.* 弁明する defend oneself.

benpi, *n.* 便秘 constipation.

benri, *n.* 便利 convenience; handiness; usefulness.

benri (na), *adj.* 便利 (な) convenient; handy; useful.

benron, *n.* 弁論 public speaking; debate.

benshō, *n.* 弁償 compensation; restitution.

benshō suru, *vb.* 弁償する compensate; restitute.

bentō, *n.* 弁当 box lunch.

bentsū, *n.* 便通 bowel movement.

benzetsu, *n.* 弁舌 eloquence; persuasiveness.

beppin, *n.* べっぴん good-looking woman.

bera-bera (to), *adv.* べらべら（と） volubly; talkatively.

beranda, *n.* ベランダ (E.) veranda; porch.

beru, *n.* ベル (E.) bell.

bēru, *n.* ベール (E.) veil.

berugī, *n.* ベルギー (E.) Belgium.

besshi, *n.* 別紙 attached sheet of paper (form).

besshitsu, *n.* 別室 another room; separate room.

bessō, *n.* 別荘 summer house; villa; cottage.

bēsu, *n.* ベース (E.) foundation; base.

bēsu, *n.* ベース (E.) bass (singer); double bass (instrument).

bēsu-appu, *n.* ベースアップ (E.) raise in the basic wage.

besuto, *n.* ベスト (E.) the best; **besuto o tsukusu** do one's best.

besuto, *n.* ベスト (E.) vest.

besutoserā, *n.* ベストセラー (E.) bestseller.

beta-beta, *adv.* べたべた all over; thickly; stickily.

beta-beta suru, *vb.* べたべたする be sticky; be clammy; cling to a person (lover).

beteran (no), *adj.* ベテラン（の） (E. *veteran*) experienced; expert; skillful.

betonamu, *n.* ベトナム (E.) Vietnam.

betsu (no), *adj.* 別（の） separate; different; another; other; extra.

betsu-betsu ni, *adv.* 別々に separately.

betsu-betsu (no), *adj.* 別々（の） separate.

betsubin de, *adv.* 別便で under separate cover (mailing).

betsujin, *n.* 別人 different person; some other person.

betsumondai, *n.* 別問題 different issue; another matter.

betsu ni, *adv.* 別に particularly.

betsuri, *n.* 別離 separation.

betto ni, *adv.* 別途に separately.

bi, *n.* 美 beauty.

bibi taru, *adj.* 微々たる minute; trivial; insignificant.

bīchi, *n.* ビーチ (E.) beach.

bichiku, *n.* 備蓄 emergency storage; **sekiyubichiku** emergency oil storage.

bidanshi, *n.* 美男子 good-looking man.

bideo, *n.* ビデオ (E.) videotape; videocassette recorder.

bideo-kamera, *n.* ビデオカメラ (E.) video camera.

bideokasetto, *n.* ビデオカセット (E.) videocassette.

bien, *n.* 鼻炎 rhinitis.

bifu, *n.* ビーフ (E.) beef.

bifuteki, *n.* ビフテキ (E.) beefsteak.

bigaku, *n.* 美学 esthetics.

bihin, *n.* 備品 equipment; fixtures.

bijin, *n.* 美人 beautiful woman; **bijin-kontesuto** beauty contest.

bijinesu, *n.* ビジネス (E.) business.

bijinesu-hoteru, *n.* ビジネスホテル (E. *business hotel*) inexpensive (Western-style) hotel.

bijinesuman, *n.* ビジネスマン (E.) businessman.

bijireiku, *n.* 美辞麗句 florid but insubstantial speech.

bijutsu, *n.* 美術 art; the fine arts.

bijutsugakkō, *n.* 美術学校 art school.

bijutsuhin, *n.* 美術品 work of art.

bijutsuhyōronka, *n.* 美術評論家 art critic.

bijutsuka, *n.* 美術家 artist; painter.

bijutsukan, *n.* 美術館 art museum; gallery.

bijutsuten, *n.* 美術展 art exhibition.

-biki see **-hiki.**

bikkuri saseru, *vb.* びっくりさせ る surprise; shock.

bikkuri suru, *vb.* びっくりする be surprised; be shocked.

bikō suru, *vb.* 尾行する follow; chase; shadow.

biku-biku suru, *vb.* びくびくする feel nervous; be afraid; tremble.

biku to mo shinai, *adj.* びくとも しない composed; secure; stable.

bimei, *n.* 美名 renown; fame.

bimyō (na), *adj.* 微妙 (な) subtle; delicate; ticklish.

bin, *n.* 瓶 bottle; jar; decanter.

-bin 便 1. flight; transportation. 2. mail; **kōkūbin** airmail.

binan, *n.* 美男 good-looking man.

binbō, *n.* 貧乏 poverty; destitution; poor person.

binbō (na), *adj.* 貧乏 (な) poor; destitute.

binbōyusuri, *n.* 貧乏ゆすり nervous habit; fidgeting.

binetsu, *n.* 微熱 slight fever.

binīru, *n.* ビニール (E.) vinyl.

binjō suru, *vb.* 便乗する 1. get a ride in a vehicle. 2. take advantage of. 3. follow the example of others; **binjōneage suru** increase prices (following a competitor).

binkan (na), *adj.* 敏感 (な) sensitive; delicate.

binsen, *n.* 便せん stationery (writing paper).

binshō (na), *adj.* 敏捷 (な)nimble; agile; keen; quick.

binta, *n.* びんた slap on the cheek.

bion, *n.* 鼻音 nasal sound.

bira, *n.* ビラ (E.) handbill.

biri, *n.* びり the last; the bottom.

birōdo, *n.* ビロード (Pg. *vellude*)

velvet.

biru, *n.* ビル (E.) building.

bīru, *n.*ビール(E.) beer; **kan-bīru** canned beer; **nama-bīru** draft beer; **kurobīru** stout (black beer).

bīrusu, *n.* ビールス (G.) virus.

bishin, *n.* 微震 mild earthquake.

bishō, *n.* 微笑 smile.

bishō (na, no), *adj.* 微小 (な、の) minuscule; microscopic.

bishokuka, *n.* 美食家 gourmet.

bishōnen, *n.* 美少年 good-looking young man.

bishonure ni naru, *vb.* びしょぬれ になる get drenched to the skin.

bisuketto, *n.* ビスケット (E.) biscuit; cookie; cracker.

bitamin, *n.* ビタミン (G.) vitamin.

bi-teki (na), *adj.* 美的 (な) aesthetic.

biten, *n.* 美点 good point; merit.

bitoku, *n.* 美徳 virtue.

biwa, *n.* びわ loquat.

biya-hōru, *n.* ビヤホール (E.) beer hall.

biyōgakkō, *n.* 美容学校 beauty school.

biyōin, *n.* 美容院 beauty parlor; beauty shop.

biyōshi, *n.* 美容師 hairdresser; beautician.

biyōtaisō, *n.* 美容体操 exercise to improve one's appearance.

biza, *n.* ビザ (E.) visa.

bō, *n.* 棒 stick; pole; club; bar.

bōbi, *n.* 防備 defense.

bochi, *n.* 墓地 cemetery; graveyard; churchyard.

bōchō suru, *vb.* 膨張する swell; expand.

bōdai na, *adj.* 膨大な huge; enormous; gigantic.

bōdan, *n.* 防弾 bulletproof; **bōdan-chokki** bulletproof vest; **bōdan-**

garasu bulletproof glass.

bodī biru, *n.* ボディービル (E.) bodybuilding.

bodī-chekku, *n.* ボディーチェック (E. *body check*) body search; frisk.

bōdō, *n.* 暴動 riot; fight; scuffle.

bōei, *n.* 防衛 defense.

bōeihi, *n.* 防衛費 defense costs.

bōei suru, *vb.* 防衛する defend; protect.

bōeki, *n.* 貿易 international trade or commerce.

bōekifukinkō, *n.* 貿易不均衡 trade imbalance.

bōekigaisha, *n.* 貿易会社 trading company.

bōekimasatsu, *n.* 貿易摩擦 friction in international trade and business.

bōenkyō, *n.* 望遠鏡 telescope.

bōen-renzu, *n.* 望遠レンズ telephoto lens.

bōfū, *n.* 暴風 windstorm; **bōfū-keihō** windstorm warning.

bōfura, *n.* ぼうふら mosquito larva.

bōfū'u, *n.* 暴風雨 storm; rainstorm.

bōfuzai, *n.* 防腐剤 food preservative.

bōgai, *n.* 妨害 interference; intrusion; disturbance; obstacle.

bōgyo, *n.* 防御 defense; protection.

bōgyo suru, *vb.* 防御する defend; protect.

bōhan, *n.* 防犯 prevention of crime.

bohi, *n.* 墓碑 gravestone; tombstone.

bōi, *n.* ボーイ (E. *boy*) waiter; busboy; bellboy.

bōifurendo, *n.* ボーイフレンド (E.) boyfriend; male friend.

boikotto, *n.* ボイコット (E.) boycott.

boin, *n.* 拇印 thumbprint.

boin, *n.* 母音 vowel; **hanboin** semivowel.

bōka, *n.* 防火 fireproofing; fire prevention.

bōkakōzō, *n.* 防火構造 fireproof structure.

bōkakunren, *n.* 防火訓練 fire drill.

bōkan, *n.* 暴漢 assaulter; thug; ruffian.

bōkansha, *n.* 傍観者 onlooker; bystander; spectator.

bōkan suru, *vb.* 傍観する be an onlooker.

bōkasetsubi, *n.* 防火設備 fire prevention system.

bokashi, *n.* ぼかし shading; blurring; dimness.

bokasu, *vb.* ぼかす shade; blur; dim; obscure.

bokei, *n.* 母系 maternal side.

boken, *n.* 母権 matriarchy; maternal rights; **bokenshakai** matriarchal society.

bōken, *n.* 冒険 adventure; venture; quest.

bokeru, *vb.* ぼける 1. become senile. 2. blur; fade.

boki, *n.* 簿記 bookkeeping.

bokin(undō), *n.* 募金(運動) fundraising (campaign).

bokki, *n.* 勃起 erection (genital).

bokki suru, *vb.* 勃起する have an erection.

bokkō suru, *vb.* 勃興する rise suddenly (in power); spring into existence; grow rapidly.

bokō, *n.* 母校 one's alma mater.

bōkō, *n.* 膀胱 bladder.

bōkō, *n.* 暴行 violence; assault; rape.

bokoku, *n.* 母国 mother country; native land.

bokokugo, *n.* 母国語 mother

tongue; native language.

boku, *n.* 僕 I (used by males).

bokuchiku, *n.* 牧畜 livestock farming.

bokuchikugyō, *n.* 牧畜業 stock farmer.

bōkūgō, *n.* 防空壕 bomb shelter; air-raid shelter.

bokujō, *n.* 牧場 stock farm; ranch; pasture.

bokujū, *n.* 墨汁 Chinese ink.

bokumetsu suru, *vb.* 撲滅する eradicate; exterminate.

bōkun, *n.* 暴君 tyrant; despot.

bokushi, *n.* 牧師 (Christianity) pastor; minister; clergyman.

bokushingu, *n.* ボクシング (E.) boxing.

bōkyaku suru, *vb.* 忘却する forget.

bōkyo, *n.* 暴挙 violence.

bōmei, *n.* 亡命 defection; fleeing from one's country.

bōmeisha, *n.* 亡命者 defector; refugee; fugitive; exile.

bōmei suru, *vb.* 亡命する defect; seek refuge; go into exile.

bon, *n.* 盆 tray.

bon, *n.* 盆 Buddhist summer festival to worship one's ancestors.

-bon see **-hon.**

bōnasu, *n.* ボーナス (E.) bonus.

bonchi, *n.* 盆地 basin (land).

bōnenkai, *n.* 忘年会 end-of-year party or celebration.

bonjin, *n.* 凡人 ordinary person.

bonkei, *n.* 盆景 bonsai (miniature) landscape on a tray.

bonkura, *n.* ぽんくら blockhead.

bon'netto, *n.* ボンネット (E.) bonnet; car hood.

bon'nō, *n.* 煩悩 worldly desire.

bonsai, *n.* 盆栽 bonsai; miniature tree(s) or plant(s) in a pot or a tray.

bon'yari shita (shiteiru), *adj.* ぽんやりした (している) 1. absent-minded; inattentive. 2. dim; vague; hazy.

bon'yari suru, *vb.* ぽんやりする 1. be absent-minded; be inattentive. 2. be idle.

bon'yō (na), *adj.* 凡庸 (な) mediocre; commonplace.

bonyū, *n.* 母乳 mother's milk.

bō'on, *n.* 忘恩 lack of appreciation; ingratitude.

bō'on, *n.* 防音 soundproofing;

bō'onsōchi soundproof device or system.

boppatsu, *n.* 勃発 outbreak.

bōraku, *n.* 暴落 sharp fall in value (currency, stocks).

bōrei, *n.* 亡霊 ghost; spirit.

bōri, *n.* 暴利 excessive profit.

bōringu, *n.* ボーリング (E.) bowling.

bōringu, *n.* ボーリング (E.) drilling.

boro, *n.* ぼろ 1. rag; worn-out thing. 2. hidden fault.

boro-boro (no), *adj.* ぼろぼろ (の) ragged; worn-out.

bōru, *n.* ボール (E.) ball.

bōru, *n.* ボール (E.) bowl.

bōrubako, *n.* ボール箱 cardboard box.

bōrugami, *n.* ボール紙 cardboard.

bōru-pen, *n.* ボールペン (E.) ballpoint pen.

bōryaku, *n.* 謀略 conspiracy; intrigue; plot.

bōryoku, *n.* 暴力 brutality; violence.

bōryokudan, *n.* 暴力団 gang of hoodlums; **bōryokudan'in** gangster.

bōryoku-teki (na), *adj.* 暴力的 (な) brutal; violent.

bōsan, *n.* 坊さん Buddhist priest or monk.

bosei, *n.* 母性 maternity.

boseiai, *n.* 母性愛 maternal love.

boseihon'nō, *n.* 母性本能 maternal instinct.

bosei-teki (na), *adj.* 母性的 (な) motherly.

boseki, *n.* 墓石 tombstone; gravestone.

bōseki, *n.* 紡績 spinning.

bōsekikōjō, *n.* 紡績工場 spinning mill.

boshi, *n.* 母子 mother and her child(ren).

bōshi, *n.* 帽子 hat; cap; **bōshi o kaburu** wear a hat or cap.

bōshi, *n.* 防止 prevention.

boshikatei, *n.* 母子家庭 single-mother family.

bōshitsu, *n.* 防湿 protection against moisture or dampness.

boshū, *n.* 募集 recruitment.

boshūkōkoku, *n.* 募集広告 want ad.

boshū suru, *vb.* 募集する recruit; place a want ad; look for workers or students.

bōshūzai, *n.* 防臭剤 deodorizer.

bōsōzoku, *n.* 暴走族 gang of motorcyclists or hot rodders.

bosshū suru, *vb.* 没収する confiscate; seize; forfeit.

bossuru, *vb.* 没する 1. sink (ship). 2. set (sun). 3. die.

bosu, *n.* ボス (E.) boss.

bōsui, *n.* 防水 waterproofing; **bōsuitokei** waterproof watch.

botai, *n.* 母体 1. condition of a woman at childbirth. 2. nucleus.

bōtakatobi, *n.* 棒高跳 pole vault.

botamochi, *n.* ぼた餅 rice cake covered with sweetened bean paste.

botan, *n.* 牡丹 peony.

botan, *n.* ボタン (E.) button.

botchan, *n.* 坊っちゃん boy; young man; unworldly man; young master; other person's son.

bōto, *n.* ボート (E.) boat.

bōtō, *n.* 暴騰 sudden sharp price increase.

bōtō, *n.* 冒頭 beginning; opening.

bōtoku, *n.* 冒瀆 blasphemy; profanity; impudence; disrespect.

bōtō suru, *vb.* 暴騰する (of prices) increase suddenly and sharply.

botsu-botsu ぽつぽつ 1. *n.* dots; spots. 2. *adv.* gradually; little by little.

botsunyū suru, *vb.* 没入する be absorbed in; be immersed in.

botsuraku, *n.* 没落 decline; downfall.

boya, *n.* ぼや small fire.

bōya, *n.* 坊や boy; son.

boya-boya suru, *vb.* ぼやぼやする be inattentive; be slow to react; dawdle.

boyaku, *vb.* ぼやく complain; grumble.

bōzenjishitsu, *n.* 茫然自失 state of being dumbfounded or petrified.

bōzen to naru/suru, *vb.* 茫然となる／する be dumbfounded or petrified.

bōzu, *n.* 坊主 1. Buddhist priest or monk. 2. boy.

buai, *n.* 歩合 percentage; rate.

buaisō (na), *adj.* 無愛想 (な) unfriendly; aloof; curt.

buatsui, *adj.* 分厚い thick; bulky.

bubun, *n.* 部分 part (of).

bubunhin, *n.* 部分品 parts.

bubun-teki (na), *adj.* 部分的 (な) partial.

bubun-teki ni, *adv.* 部分的に partially.

buchikowasu, *vb.* ぶち壊す
destroy; break; ruin.

buchimakeru, *vb.* ぶちまける
disclose; let out.

buchō, *n.* 部長 section or
department head.

buchōhō (na), *adj.* 不調法 (な)
clumsy; careless; impolite.

budō, *n.* 武道 the way of the
samurai.

budō, *n.* 葡萄 grape.

budōshu, *n.* 葡萄酒 wine.

buenryo (na), *adj.* 無遠慮 (な)
impolite; rude; outspoken;
unreserved.

bugaisha, *n.* 部外者 outsider.

bugaku, *n.* 舞楽 dance and music
of ancient Japan.

bugei, *n.* 武芸 martial arts.

bugu, *n.* 武具 weapons; arms.

bugyō, *n.* 奉行 samurai magistrate.

buin, *n.* 部員 member.

buitiāru, *n.* ブイティーアール (E.)
VTR; videotape recorder; VCR.

buji, *n.* 無事 safety; peace; health;
good condition.

buji ni, *adv.* 無事に safely;
peacefully; well; without problem.

bujoku, *n.* 侮辱 insult; contempt;
disrespect.

bujoku suru, *vb.* 侮辱する insult;
humiliate; disgrace.

buka, *n.* 部下 subordinate staff
member(s); junior officer(s).

bukakkō (na), *adj.* 不格好 (な)
unshapely; ugly; crude.

buke, *n.* 武家 samurai family or
member.

buki, *n.* 武器 weapon; arms.

bukimi (na), *adj.* 不気味 (な)
uncanny; weird; eerie.

bukiryō (na), *adj.* 不器量 (な)
unattractive; ugly.

bukiyō (na), *adj.* 不器用 (な)
clumsy; inept; unskillful.

bukka, *n.* 物価 price.

bukkaku, *n.* 仏閣 Buddhist temple.

bukkashisū, *n.* 物価指数 price
index.

bukka tōsei, *n.* 物価統制 price
control.

bukkirabō (na), *adj.* ぶっきらぼう
(な) curt; blunt; unfriendly.

bukkyō, *n.* 仏教 Buddhism.

bukotsu (na), *adj.* 武骨 (な)
unsophisticated; clumsy; rough;
ill-mannered.

bumon, *n.* 部門 category; class;
division; section; field.

būmu, *n.* ブーム (E.) boom
(increase).

bun, *n.* 文 sentence; composition.

bun, *n.* 分 1. one's share; **Watashi
no bun wa ikura.** How much is
my share (of the bill)? 2.
quantity. 3. one's social status;
bun o wakimaeru recognize or
accept one's social status. 4.
means. 5. state of affairs.

-bun see **-fun.**

bunan (na), *adj.* 無難 (な) safe;
acceptable; tolerable.

bunben, *n.* 分娩 childbirth.

bunbōgu, *n.* 文房具 stationery;
writing materials.

bunbōguya, *n.* 文房具屋 stationery
store.

bunchin, *n.* 文鎮 paperweight.

bundan, *n.* 文壇 literary world;
literary circle.

bungaku, *n.* 文学 literature; **koten
(chūsei, gendai, gaikoku)
bungaku** classical (medieval,
modern, foreign) literature.

bungakubu, *n.* 文学部 Department
of Literature.

bungakuhakushi, *n.* 文学博士
Doctor of Literature.

bungakusakuhin, *n.* 文学作品 literary work.

bungakushi, *n.* 文学士 Bachelor of Arts.

bungei, *n.* 文芸 literature; art and literature.

bungei-hyōron/-hihyō, *n.* 文芸評論／〜批評 literary criticism.

bungeiran, *n.* 文芸欄 literary column.

bungeisakuhin, *n.* 文芸作品 literary work.

bungo, *n.* 文語 classical language; literary language.

bungō, *n.* 文豪 literary giant.

bungyō, *n.* 分業 division of labor.

bunjin, *n.* 文人 writer; man or woman of letters.

bunjō, *n.* 分譲 subdivision; lot; **bunjō-manshon** condominium.

bunka, *n.* 文化 culture.

bunka, *n.* 文科 the humanities; the liberal arts.

bunkaisan, *n.* 文化遺産 cultural legacy.

bunkai suru, *vb.* 分解する take apart; disassemble; disintegrate; fall apart.

bunkasai, *n.* 文化祭 cultural festival.

bunka-teki (na), *adj.* 文化的 (な) cultural; cultured; civilized; sophisticated.

bunkatsubarai, *n.* 分割払い payment on the installment plan.

bunkatsu suru, *vb.* 分割する divide; split.

bunkazai, *n.* 文化財 cultural product; cultural asset.

bunkiten, *n.* 分岐点 crossroads; juncture; watershed; **jinsei no bunkiten** a turning point in one's life.

bunko(bon), *n.* 文庫(本) pocket (-size) book.

bunkō, *n.* 分校 branch school.

bunmei, *n.* 文明 civilization.

bunmeiteki (na), *adj.* 文明的 (な) civilized; cultured; enlightened.

bunmen, *n.* 文面 content (of a written text).

bunmyaku, *n.* 文脈 context.

bun'nō suru, *vb.* 分納する pay in installments.

bunpai, *n.* 分配 distribution; division.

bunpai suru, *vb.* 分配する distribute; divide.

bunpitsu, *n.* 分泌 secretion.

bunpitsu, *n.* 文筆 writing.

bunpitsugyō, *n.* 文筆業 literary profession.

bunpō, *n.* 文法 grammar.

bunpō-ka/-gakusha, *n.* 文法家／〜学者 grammarian.

bunpu, *n.* 分布 distribution.

bunraku, *n.* 文楽 traditional Japanese puppet theater.

bunretsu, *n.* 分裂 division; split; separation.

bunri, *n.* 分離 separation.

bunrui, *n.* 分類 classification; categorization.

bunryō, *n.* 分量 quantity; volume; amount.

bunsan suru, *vb.* 分散する disperse; scatter; split.

bunseki, *n.* 分析 analysis; **seishin-bunseki** psychoanalysis; **seishin-bunseki-gakusha** psychoanalyst.

bunseki suru, *vb.* 分析する analyze.

bunshi, *n.* 分詞 participle; **genzai-bunshi** present participle; **kako-bunshi** past participle.

bunshi, *n.* 分子 1. group; sect. 2. molecule. 3. numerator.

bunsho, *n.* 文書 document; written

material.

bunshō, *n.* 文章 sentence; composition; writing.

bunshū, *n.* 文集 anthology.

bunsū, *n.* 分数 fraction.

buntai, *n.* 文体 literary style.

buntan, *n.* 分担 one's share; allotment; assignment.

buntsū, *n.* 文通 correspondence by mail.

buntsū suru, *vb.* 文通する correspond by mail.

bun'ya, *n.* 分野 field; area; sphere; **kenkyūbun'ya** field of study.

buotoko, *n.* 醜男 ugly man.

buppin, *n.* 物品 article; thing; goods; commodities.

bura-bura suru, *vb.* ぶらぶらする 1. swing (one's legs). 2. swing (in the air). 3. spend time idly; stroll idly. 4. be unemployed.

buraindo, *n.* ブラインド (E.) blind; window shade.

burajā, *n.* ブラジャー (F. *brassière*) brassiere.

burajiru, *n.* ブラジル (E.) Brazil.

burakkurisuto, *n.* ブラックリスト (E.) blacklist.

burandē, *n.* ブランデー (E.) brandy.

burando, *n.* ブランド (E.) brand.

buranko, *n.* ブランコ (Pg. *balanço*) swing.

buranku, *n.* ブランク (E.) blank.

burasagaru, *vb.* ぶら下がる hang down (from).

burasageru, *vb.* ぶら下げる suspend.

burashi, *n.* ブラシ (E.) brush; **ha-burashi** toothbrush.

buratsuku, *vb.* ぶらつく loiter.

burausu, *n.* ブラウス (E.) blouse.

burei (na), *adj.* 無礼 (な) rude; impolite; insolent.

burēki, *n.* ブレーキ (E.) brake (car).

burendo, *n.* ブレンド (E.) blend (coffee).

burezā(kōto), *n.* ブレザー(コート) (E.) blazer (jacket).

-buri ぶり way; attitude; manner; **hanashiburi** the way one talks.

burīfu, *n.* ブリーフ (E.) briefs (underwear).

burīfukēsu, *n.* ブリーフケース (E.) briefcase.

burikaesu, *vb.* ぶり返す come back; return.

buriki, *n.* ブリキ (D. *blik*) tinplate.

-buri ni ぶりに after an interval or absence; **ichinenburi ni** after a year's absence.

burōchi, *n.* ブローチ (E.) brooch.

burōkā, *n.* ブローカー (E.) broker.

burokkorī, *n.* ブロッコリー (E.) broccoli.

-buru ぶる pretend; feign; **ii ko-buru** pretend to be a good person.

burudoggu, *n.* ブルドッグ (E.) bulldog.

burudōzā *n.* ブルドーザー (E.) bulldozer.

burujoa, *n.* ブルジョア (F.) bourgeois(ie).

burūsu, *n.* ブルース (E.) blues (music).

buryoku, *n.* 武力 military power; force.

buryoku-kainyū/-kanshō, *n.* 武力介入／〜干渉 armed intervention.

busahō, *n.* 不作法 bad manners; rudeness; impoliteness.

busahō (na), *adj.* 不作法 (な) ill-mannered; rude; impolite.

busaiku (na), *adj.* 不細工 (な) unattractive; uncouth; clumsy.

bushi, *n.* 武士 warrior; samurai.

bushidō, *n.* 武士道 the way of the

samurai.

bushitsuke (na), *adj.* 不躾 (な) ill-mannered; rude; impolite.

bushō (na), *adj.* 不精 (な) lazy; inactive; **fudebushō** poor correspondent.

busō, *n.* 武装 armament.

busōkaijo, *n.* 武装解除 disarmament.

busshi, *n.* 物資 supplies; goods; materials.

busshienjo, *n.* 物資援助 relief supplies.

busshitsushugi, *n.* 物質主義 materialism.

busshitsushugisha, *n.* 物質主義者 materialist.

busshitsu-teki (na), *adj.* 物質的 (な) materialistic.

bussō (na), *adj.* 物騒 (な) dangerous; unsafe; threatening.

busu, *n.* ぶす ugly woman; hag.

busū, *n.* 部数 number of copies.

busui (na), *adj.* 不粋 (な) unsophisticated; inelegant; clumsy.

buta, *n.* 豚 1. pig; swine. 2. despicable person.

butai, *n.* 舞台 1. stage. 2. setting; scene.

butaigeki, *n.* 舞台劇 stage play.

butaikantoku, *n.* 舞台監督 stage director.

butaisōchi, *n.* 舞台装置 stage setting.

butaniku, *n.* 豚肉 pork.

butō, *n.* 舞踏 dancing.

butsubutsu iu, *vb.* ぶつぶつ言う grumble; complain.

butsudan, *n.* 仏壇 Buddhist altar.

butsukaru, *vb.* ぶつかる crash; collide with; run into; meet with; fall on.

butsuri(gaku), *n.* 物理 (学) physics.

butsurigakusha, *n.* 物理学者 physicist.

butsuzō, *n.* 仏像 Buddhist image or statue.

buttai, *n.* 物体 object; body (in physics).

buttōshi (ni/de), *adv.* ぶっ通し (に、で) without end; at a stretch.

buyōjin (na), *adj.* 不用心 (な) careless; indiscreet.

buzā, *n.* ブザー (E.) buzzer.

buzoku, *n.* 部族 tribe.

byō, *n.* 秒 second (time); **ichibyō** one second.

byō, *n.* 鋲 tack; rivet.

byōbu, *n.* 屏風 folding screen.

byōdō, *n.* 平等 equality.

byōdō (na, no), *adj.* 平等 (な、の) equal; **byōdō no kenri** equal rights.

byōdō ni, *adv.* 平等に equally; evenly.

byōgen, *n.* 病原 cause of illness, sickness, or disease.

byōgenkin, *n.* 病原菌 germ.

byōin, *n.* 病院 hospital.

byōjō, *n.* 病状 patient's condition.

byōketsu, *n.* 病欠 absence owing to illness.

byōki, *n.* 病気 illness; sickness; disease; **byōki ni naru/kakaru** fall ill; **byōki ga naoru** recover from an illness.

byōki (no), *adj.* 病気 (の) ill; sick.

byōnin, *n.* 病人 sick person; invalid.

byōsha suru, *vb.* 描写する describe.

byōshi, *n.* 病死 death resulting from an illness.

byōshin, *n.* 秒針 second hand (of a clock).

byōshitsu, *n.* 病室 hospital room;

sickroom.

byōshō, *n.* 病床 sickbed.

byō-teki (na), *adj.* 病的 (な) sick; morbid; abnormal; repulsive.

C

cha, *n.* 茶 tea.

chachi (na), *adj.* ちゃち (な) cheap; low-quality; petty.

chadō, *n.* 茶道 tea ceremony.

chagashi, *n.* 茶菓子 teacake.

chāhan, *n.* チャーハン fried rice with vegetables and meat.

chairo (na, no), *adj., n.* 茶色 (な、の) brown (color).

chakasu, *vb.* 茶化す ridicule; make fun of.

chakkari shiteiru, *adj.* ちゃっかりしている nimble; adroit; shrewd.

chakkō suru, *vb.* 着工する start (enterprise, construction).

chakku, *n.* チャック zipper; fastener.

-chaku 着 1. arrival; order of arrival (in a race); **narita-chaku no hikōki** an airplane arriving at Narita; **ni-chaku** finishing second. 2. number suffix indicating a counter for clothes; **sebiro ni-chaku** two suits.

chaku-chaku (to), *adv.* 着々と steadily.

chakuchi, *n.* 着地 landing.

chakueki, *n.* 着駅 arrival station.

chakufuku suru, *vb.* 着服する embezzle; pocket.

chakugan, *n.* 着眼 attention.

chakuganten, *n.* 着眼点 viewpoint.

chakujitsu (na), *adj.* 着実な secure; reliable; steady.

chakujitsu ni, *adv.* 着実に securely; reliably; steadily.

chakunan, *n.* 嫡男 heir; eldest son.

chakunin suru, *vb.* 着任する be appointed to a position; arrive at one's new post or office.

chakuriku, *n.* 着陸 landing (aircraft, etc.).

chakuriku suru, *vb.* 着陸する land.

chakuseki, *n.* 着席 taking a seat; sitting down.

chakusekijun ni, *adv.* 着席順に according to seating order.

chakuseki suru, *vb.* 着席する take a seat; sit down.

chakushi, *n.* 嫡子 heir.

chakushu suru, *vb.* 着手する start; launch.

chakusō, *n.* 着想 idea; inspiration.

chame (na), *adj.* 茶目 (な) mischievous (in positive sense); playful.

chāmingu (na), *adj.* チャーミング (な) (E.) charming; attractive.

-chan ちゃん (used after a person's given name to express intimacy and affection): **Toshi-chan**; (also used as a diminutive for children and pets): **neko-chan** (for a cat).

chanbara, *n.* ちゃんばら sword fighting.

chanbaraeiga, *n.* ちゃんばら映画 samurai film.

chankonabe, *n.* ちゃんこ鍋 special meal for sumo wrestlers.

chan'neru, *n.* チャンネル (E.) channel.

chanoma, *n.* 茶の間 family room.

chanomi-tomodachi, *n.* 茶飲み友達 crony.

chanoyu, *n.* 茶の湯 tea ceremony.

chanpion, *n.* チャンピオン (E.) champion.

chanpon, *n.* ちゃんぽん mixture of different things; jumble.

chansu, *n.* チャンス (E.) chance; opportunity; **chansu o tsukamu** embrace an opportunity.

chanto, *adv.* ちゃんと exactly; properly; neatly; clearly; respectably; without fail; fully.

chanto shita, *adj.* ちゃんとした respectable; neat; proper; well-established; **chanto shita hito** a respectable person.

charanporan (na), *adj.* ちゃらんぽらん unreliable; irresponsible.

charenji suru, *vb.* チャレンジする (E.) challenge; try; venture.

charitī, *n.* チャリティー (E.) charity; **charitī-konsāto** charity concert.

chasaji, *n.* 茶さじ teaspoon.

chaseki, *n.* 茶席 seat at a tea ceremony.

chasen, *n.* 茶せん bamboo whisk used in tea ceremony.

chashaku, *n.* 茶杓 teaspoon for scooping powdered tea.

chashitsu, *n.* 茶室 room for a tea ceremony.

chātā-bin, *n.* チャーター便 (E.) chartered flight (bus, boat).

chātā suru, *vb.* チャーターする (E.) charter.

chawan, *n.* 茶碗 teacup; rice bowl.

chawanmushi, *n.* 茶碗蒸し steamed egg curd with meat and vegetables.

chazuke, *n.* 茶漬け green tea poured over a bowl of steamed rice.

che, *interj.* チェ Shucks! Damn!

chekku (no), *adj., n.* チェック (の) check; checkered.

chekku-auto, *n.* チェックアウト (E.) check-out (hotel).

chekku-in, *n.* チェックイン (E.) check-in.

chekku suru, *vb.* チェックする (E.) check; examine.

chēn, *n.* チェーン (E.) chain.

chenji, *n.* チェンジ (E.) change.

chēn-sutoā, *n.* チェーンストアー (E.) chain store.

chero, *n.* チェロ (E.) cello.

chesu, *n.* チェス (E.) chess.

chi, *n.* 地 ground; earth; place; location.

chi, *n.* 血 blood; **chi ga deru** bleed.

chi, *n.* 智、知 intellect; wisdom.

chian, *n.* 治安 safety; public order.

chianbōgai, *n.* 治安妨害 breach of public order.

chi(-chi)banare suru, *vb.* 乳離れする be weaned; become independent.

chibetto, *n.* チベット (E.) Tibet.

chibi, *n.* ちび (derogatory) short person; kid.

chibu, *n.* 恥部 1. private parts (genitals). 2. disgrace; ignominy.

chibusa, *n.* 乳房 female breast.

chichi, *n.* 乳 milk; mother's milk.

chichi, *n.* 父 father; pioneer; originator.

chichū (ni), *adv.* 地中 underground.

chichūkai, *n.* 地中海 the Mediterranean.

chidarake (na, no), *adj.* 血だらけ (な、の)covered in blood.

chidoriashi, *n.* 千鳥足 a reeling movement (from intoxication).

chie, *n.* 知恵 wisdom; intelligence; idea.

chie ga aru, *adj.* 知恵がある wise; smart.

chien, *n.* 遅延 delay.

chieokure (no), *adj.* 知恵遅れ (の) mentally retarded.

chifusu, *n.* チフス (G. *Typhus*) typhus; typhoid.

chigai, *n.* 違い difference.

chigainai 違いない 1. *adj.* sure; **ame ni chigainai** sure to rain. 2. (used postpositively as an *aux. vb.*) must; should; **Sō ni chigainai.** It must be so.

chigau 違う 1. *vb.* differ. 2. *adj.* different; wrong.

chigireru, *vb.* ちぎれる tear off; come off.

chigiri, *n.* 契り vow; pledge.

chigiru, *vb.* ちぎる tear into pieces.

chigo, *n.* 稚児 1. child; page. 2. catamite.

chiguhagu (na, no), *adj.* ちぐはぐ (な、の) mismatched; odd; unbalanced; inconsistent.

chihai, *n.* 遅配 delayed delivery (of goods).

chiheisen, *n.* 地平線 horizon.

chihō, *n.* 痴呆 mental retardation; mentally retarded person.

chihō, *n.* 地方 district; region; countryside.

chihōsaibansho, *n.* 地方裁判所 district court.

chihōshoku, *n.* 地方色 local color.

chihō-teki (na), *adj.* 地方的 (な) regional; local; provincial.

chihōzei, *n.* 地方税 district taxes.

chi'i, *n.* 地位 rank; status; position; **josei no shakai-teki chi'i** women's social status.

chi'iki, *n.* 地域 district; region; area; zone.

chi'iki(kaku)sa, *n.* 地域(格)差 regional difference.

chiisai, *adj.* 小さい 1. small; little; young. 2. trivial; petty. 3. low (sound).

chiisaku naru, *vb.* 小さくなる 1. dwindle; diminish. 2. cringe; be afraid of. 3. become too small for (clothing).

chiji, *n.* 知事 prefectural governor.

chijimeru, *vb.* 縮める shorten; reduce; lessen; abridge.

chijimi, *n.* 縮み crepe (textile).

chijimu, *vb.* 縮む shrink; become short; cringe.

chijin, *n.* 知人 acquaintance; friend.

chijirasu, *vb.* 縮らす frizz (hair).

chijireru, *vb.* 縮れる become frizzled; get wrinkled.

chijō (de, ni), *adv.* 地上 (で、に) above ground; on earth; on land; on the surface of the earth.

chijoku, *n.* 恥辱 shame; humiliation; disgrace.

chika, *n.* 地価 price of land.

chika, *n.* 地下 underground.

chikagai, *n.* 地下街 underground shopping mall.

chikagoro, *adv.* 近頃 recently.

chikai 近い 1. *adj.* near; close (to); intimate; nearsighted (myopic). 2. *adv.* almost.

chikai, *n.* 地階 basement.

chikai, *n.* 誓い vow; pledge.

chikajika, *adv.* 近々 soon; before long.

chikaku, *n.* 近く neighborhood.

chikaku (de, ni, o), *adv.* 近く (で、に、を) 1. (space) in the neighborhood (of); close to; near; around. 2. (time) almost; before long.

chikaku (no), *adj.* 近く (の) nearby; **chikaku no resutoran** a nearby restaurant.

chikamichi, *n.* 近道 shortcut.

chikan, *n.* 痴漢 sexual pervert.

chikara, *n.* 力 1. force; power; energy; ability; talent; skill; **eigo no chikara** skill in English. 2. help; influence.

chikara ga aru, *adj.* 力がある 1. powerful; able; skillful. 2. helpful; influential.

chikaraippai (ni), *adv.* 力一杯 (に) with all one's might; to one's utmost ability.

chikaramakase ni, *adv.* 力任せに with all one's might.

chikaramochi, *n.* 力持ち a powerful or strong person.

chikara ni naru 力になる 1. *vb.* help; support. 2. *adj.* helpful.

chikara o awaseru, *vb.* 力を合わせる cooperate.

chikara o tsukeru, *vb.* 力をつける make progress; become competent; encourage.

chikara o tsukusu, *vb.* 力を尽くす make an effort.

chikarashigoto, *n.* 力仕事 manual labor; blue-collar job.

chikarazoe, *n.* 力添え assistance; help; support.

chikarazukeru, *vb.* 力付ける encourage; cheer up.

chikarazuku de, *adv.* 力ずくで by force.

chikarazuyoi, *adj.* 力強い powerful; encouraging; reassuring.

chikashigen, *n.* 地下資源 underground resources.

chikashitsu, *n.* 地下室 basement.

chikasui, *n.* 地下水 underground water.

chikatetsu, *n.* 地下鉄 subway.

chikau, *vb.* 誓う vow; pledge; swear.

chikayoru, *vb.* 近寄る approach; come up to; go up to.

chikazukeru, *vb.* 近付ける 1. introduce a person to another. 2. draw (something) near to (a thing or person).

chikazuki, *n.* 近付き acquaintance; **chikazuki ni naru** get acquainted.

chikazuku, *vb.* 近付く approach; come up to; go up to; seek to become acquainted.

chiketto, *n.* チケット (E.) ticket.

chiki, *n.* 知己 acquaintance; close friend.

chikin, *n.* チキン (E.) chicken.

chikin-katsu, *n.* チキンカツ (E.) chicken cutlet.

chikin-raisu, *n.* チキンライス (E.) fried rice mixed with chicken, vegetables, and ketchup.

chikoku suru, *vb.* 遅刻する be late (for); be behind time.

chikokutodoke, *n.* 遅刻届け notice of late arrival.

chiku, *n.* 地区 district; area; region; zone.

chiku, *n.* チーク (E.) teak.

chikuba no tomo, *n.* 竹馬の友 childhood friend.

chikubi, *n.* 乳首 nipple; teat.

chiku-chiku suru, *vb.* ちくちくする be prickly; prickle; tingle.

chikudenchi, *n.* 蓄電池 battery (electric).

chikuden suru, *vb.* 蓄電する charge (electricity).

chikugo-teki ni, *adv.* 逐語的に verbatim; word for word.

chikugoyaku, *n.* 逐語訳 verbatim or word-for-word translation; literal translation.

chikuichi, *adv.* 逐一 entirely; fully; minutely.

chikuji, *adv.* 逐次 one by one.

chikusan, *n.* 畜産 livestock farm.

chikusangyō, *n.* 畜産業 livestock farming.

chikuseki, *n.* 蓄積 store; accumulation; buildup.

chikushō, *n.* 畜生 beast; brute; repulsive person or thing; **Chikushō.** Damn it (you, him, her)! Beast!

chikuzai suru, *vb.* 蓄財する save; accumulate wealth.

chikyū, *n.* 地球 the Earth; the globe.

chikyūgi, *n.* 地球儀 globe.

chimame, *n.* 血豆 blood blister.

chimamire (na, no), *adj.* 血まみれ (な、の) covered with blood.

chimanako-de/-ninatte, *adv.* 血眼で／〜になって in a panic; frantically; desperately.

chimata, *n.* 巷 general public; society; street; **chimata no koe** public opinion.

chimayou, *vb.* 血迷う lose control of oneself; become obsessed with; go crazy.

chimei, *n.* 地名 place name.

chimei (na, no), *adj.* 知名 (な、の) famous; well-known.

chimeido, *n.* 知名度 fame.

chimeijin, *n.* 知名人 famous person; celebrity.

chimeishō, *n.* 致命傷 fatal injury; fatal mistake.

chimei-teki (na), *adj.* 致命的 (な) fatal.

chimitsu (na), *adj.* 緻密 (な) elaborate; minute; close.

chīmu, *n.* チーム (E.) team.

chīmuwāku, *n.* チームワーク (E.) teamwork.

chin- 珍 rare; unique; bizarre; absurd; **chinmi** unique food;

chinji bizarre incident; **chinsetsu** absurd opinion.

-chin 賃 wage; pay; rent; fare; **temachin** wage; pay; **yachin** house rent.

chin'age, *n.* 賃上げ wage increase.

chinami ni, *adv.* 因みに in passing; incidentally.

chinamu, *vb.* 因む derive from; be related to.

chin'atsu suru, *vb.* 鎮圧する control (a revolt).

chinbotsu suru, *vb.* 沈没する sink.

chinchaku (na), *adj.* 沈着 (な) composed; calm.

chinchikurin (na, no), *adj.* ちんちくりん (な、の) strange; unmatched; very short.

chinchin, *n.* ちんちん penis.

chinchō suru, *vb.* 珍重する cherish as a rarity.

chinetsu, *n.* 地熱 geothermal heat; **chinetsu-hatsudensho** geothermal power plant.

chingashi suru, *vb.* 賃貸しする lease; rent.

chingin, *n.* 賃金 wage; pay; salary.

chinginkakusa, *n.* 賃金格査 disparity in wages.

chinjō, *n.* 陳情 petition; plea; appeal; request.

chinjōdan, *n.* 陳情団 group of petitioners.

chinjōsho, *n.* 陳情書 petition (letter).

chinjutsu, *n.* 陳述 statement; oral report.

chinka suru, *vb.* 鎮火する extinguish a fire; control a riot.

chinmoku, *n.* 沈黙 silence.

chin'nyūsha, *n.* ちん入者 trespasser; intruder.

chin'nyū suru, *vb.* ちん入する trespass; intrude.

chinō, *n.* 知能 intelligence; intellect.

chinomigo, *n.* 乳呑児 nursing baby.

chinōshisū, *n.* 知能指数 IQ (intelligence quotient).

chinō tesuto, *n.* 知能テスト IQ test.

chinpanjī, *n.* チンパンジー (E.) chimpanzee.

chinpira, *n.* ちんぴら rowdy; punk; hoodlum.

chinpo(ko), *n.* ちんぽ(こ) (vulgar use) penis.

chinpu (na), *adj.* 陳腐 (な) banal; vulgar; insipid.

chinpunkanpun (na), *adj.* ちんぷんかんぷん (な) incomprehensible; unintelligible.

chinretsu, *n.* 陳列 display.

chinretsuhin, *n.* 陳列品 articles on display.

chinretsushitsu, *n.* 陳列室 display room.

chinretsu suru, *vb.* 陳列する display; exhibit.

chinseizai, *n.* 鎮静剤 sedative.

chinsha suru, *vb.* 陳謝する apologize.

chinshi suru, *vb.* 沈思する contemplate; ponder.

chintai, *n.* 賃貸 lease; rental.

chintaikeiyaku, *n.* 賃貸契約 lease contract.

chintairyō, *n.* 賃貸料 rent.

chintai suru, *vb.* 賃貸する lease; rent.

chintsū na, *adj.* 沈痛な poignant; sad.

chintsūzai, *n.* 沈痛剤 painkiller.

chippoke na, *adj.* ちっぽけな tiny; small; petty.

chippu, *n.* チップ (E.) tip (gratuity).

chirabaru, *vb.* 散らばる be scattered (all over); be in disorder.

chira-chira suru, *vb.* ちらちらする flicker.

chirakaru, *vb.* 散らかる be in a mess.

chirakasu, *vb.* 散らかす mess up; litter; scatter.

chirari to, *adv.* ちらりと at a glance; in a moment; **chirari to miru** glimpse; **chirari to kiku** overhear.

chirashi, *n.* 散らし handbill; flier.

chirashizushi, *n.* 散らし寿司 a box of sushi rice topped with raw fish.

chirasu, *vb.* 散らす scatter; sprinkle.

chiratsuku, *vb.* ちらつく fall (rain, snow); flicker; haunt (image).

chiri, *n.* 塵 dust; litter.

chiri, *n.* 地理 geography.

chiri, *n.* チリ (E.) Chile.

chirigami, *n.* 塵紙 toilet paper.

chirijiri(-barabara) ni, *adv.* ちりじり(ばらばら) に in all directions; in pieces (broken); separated (from each other).

chirimen, *n.* 縮緬 crepe (textile).

chiritori, *n.* 塵取 dustpan.

chiru, *vb.* 散る fall; scatter; disperse; **ki ga chiru** be distracted.

chiryō, *n.* 治療 medical treatment.

chiryōhi, *n.* 治療費 medical expenses.

chisei, *n.* 知性 intelligence.

chisei, *n.* 治世 reign.

chisetsu (na), *adj.* 稚拙 (な) unskilled; childish; crude.

chishiki, *n.* 知識 knowledge; learning.

chishikijin, *n.* 知識人 intellectual; learned person.

chishima(rettō), *n.* 千島(列島) the

Kurile Islands.

chissoku, *n.* 窒息 suffocation.

chissokushi, *n.* 窒息死 death from suffocation.

chisuji, *n.* 血筋 bloodline; lineage.

chitai, *n.* 遅滞 delay; arrears.

chitai, *n.* 地帯 zone; area; district.

chi-teki (na), *adj.* 知的 (な) intellectual.

chiten, *n.* 地点 spot; place; point.

chitsu, *n.* 膣 vagina.

chitsujo, *n.* 秩序 order.

chittomo, *adv.* ちっとも not at all.

chiyahoya suru, *vb.* ちやほやする pamper; extol.

chiyu suru, *vb.* 治ゆする recover from; cure.

chizu, *n.* 地図 map.

chīzu, *n.* チーズ (E.) cheese.

chīzubāgā, *n.* チーズバーガー (E.) cheeseburger.

chīzukēki, *n.* チーズケーキ (E.) cheesecake.

-cho 著 book by; **Tanizakicho** book by Tanizaki.

chō, *n.* 腸 intestine; bowel; **daichō** large intestine; **shōchō** small intestine.

chō, *n.* 兆 trillion.

chō- 超 ultra-; super-; over-; **chō-jin-teki (na)** superhuman; **chō-man'in** overcrowded.

-chō 町 town; district; **pontochō** Ponto district.

-chō 庁 agency (government); **bōeichō** Defense Agency.

chōai suru, *vb.* 寵愛する pet; cherish; favor.

chōba, *n.* 嘲罵 derision; mockery.

chōbatsu, *n.* 懲罰 punishment.

chōbo, *n.* 帳簿 account book.

chōbō, *n.* 眺望 view.

chōbun, *n.* 弔文 funeral address.

chochiku, *n.* 貯蓄 saving.

chōchin, *n.* 提灯 lantern.

chōchō, chōcho, *n.* 蝶々 butterfly; **chōchōsan** Madame Butterfly.

chōdai, *vb.* ちょうだい give me (request).

-chōdai ちょうだい please ... (request); **hanashite-chōdai** tell me please.

chōdai suru, *vb.* ちょうだいする 1. receive. 2. eat; drink.

chōda no retsu, *n.* 長蛇の列 long line of people.

chōdo, *adv.* 丁度 exactly.

chōeki, *n.* 懲役 penal servitude.

chōetsu suru, *vb.* 超越する stand out; transcend.

chōfuku suru, *vb.* 重複する repeat; overlap.

chōgenjitsu-teki (na), *adj.* 超現実的 (な) surrealistic.

chōgō suru, *vb.* 調合する prepare medicine.

chōhatsu suru, *vb.* 挑発する instigate; provoke (sexually).

chōhatsu-teki (na), *adj.* 挑発的 (な) instigating; provocative (sexually).

chōhei, *n.* 徴兵 conscription; draft.

chōheiseido, *n.* 徴兵制度 draft system.

chōhen, *n.* 長編 1. novel. 2. long film.

chōhō (na), *adj.* 重宝 (な) helpful; convenient; useful.

chōhōkei, *n.* 長方形 rectangle; oblong.

chōhonnin, *n.* 張本人 ringleader; instigator; provocateur.

choi-choi, *adv.* ちょいちょい frequently.

chōin suru, *vb.* 調印する sign a treaty or contract.

chōja, *n.* 長者 millionaire.

chōjikan, *adv.* 長時間 for long

hours.

chōjin-teki (na), *adj.* 超人的 (な) superhuman.

chōjiri, *n.* 帳尻 balance (bookkeeping).

chōjo, *n.* 長女 eldest daughter.

chōjō, *n.* 頂上 top; summit; pinnacle.

chōju, *n.* 長寿 longevity.

chojutsu, *n.* 著述 writing.

chojutsugyō, *n.* 著述業 literary vocation.

chojutsuka, *n.* 著述家 writer.

chōka, *n.* 超過 excess; **yunyū-chōka** excess of imports.

chōkai, *n.* 懲戒 reprimand; discipline; **chōkai-menshoku** disciplinary dismissal.

chōka kinmu, *n.* 超過勤務 overtime work; **chōkakinmu-teate** overtime pay.

chōkan, *n.* 朝刊 morning newspaper.

chōkan, *n.* 長官 chief; director.

chōkeshi ni suru, *vb.* 帳消しにする cancel; wipe out.

chōki, *n.* 長期 long period of time; **chōkikeikaku** long-range plan; **chōkiyohō** long-range forecast.

chokin, *n.* 貯金 savings.

chokkai o dasu, *vb.* ちょっかいを出す meddle in; interfere with.

chokkaku, *n.* 直角 right angle; **chokkaku-sankakkei** right triangle.

chokkan, *n.* 直感 intuition.

chokkei, *n.* 直径 diameter.

chokkei, *n.* 直系 direct scion of a family; direct disciple.

chokketsu, *n.* 直結 direct connection.

chokki, *n.* チョッキ vest.

chokkō, *n.* 直行 nonstop or direct transportation; **chokkōbin** nonstop flight.

chokkō suru, *vb.* 直行する go directly.

chokkyū, *n.* 直球 line drive (baseball).

choko, *n.* ちょこ sake cup.

chōkō, *n.* 兆候 symptom; sign; harbinger.

chōkoku, *n.* 彫刻 sculpture; carving.

chōkokuka, *n.* 彫刻家 sculptor.

chokorēto, *n.* チョコレート (E.) chocolate.

chōkōsei, *n.* 聴講生 auditor (student).

chōkō suru, *vb.* 聴講する audit; sit in; listen to.

choku-choku, *adv.* ちょくちょく frequently.

chokuei, *n.* 直営 direct management.

chokugo ni, *adv.* 直後に immediately after or behind.

chokumen suru, *vb.* 直面する 1. face; confront with. 2. be involved in.

chokusen, *n.* 直線 straight line.

chokusetsu (ni), *adv.* 直接 (に) directly.

chokusetsu (no), *adj.* 直接 (の) direct; immediate.

chokushanikkō, *n.* 直射日光 direct sunlight.

chokushin suru, *vb.* 直進する go straight.

chokushi suru, *vb.* 直視する look in the face.

chokutsū (no), *adj.* 直通 (の) nonstop; direct; **chokutsū-basu** nonstop bus; **chokutsū-denwa** direct call.

chokuyaku, *n.* 直訳 literal translation.

chokuyunyū, *n.* 直輸入 direct

import.

chokuzen (ni), *adv.* 直前 (に) just before.

chōkyori, *n.* 長距離 long distance; **chōkyoridenwa** long-distance call.

chomei (na), *adj.* 著名 (な) famous; renowned.

chōmei, *n.* 町名 town name; street name.

chōmei, *n.* 長命 long life.

chōmen, *n.* 帳面 notebook.

chōmin, *n.* 町民 townspeople.

chōmiryō, *n.* 調味料 seasoning.

chōnan, *n.* 長男 eldest son.

chō-nekutai, *n.* 蝶ネクタイ bow tie.

chongiru, *vb.* ちょん切る chop off.

chonmage, *n.* ちょんまげ topknot (hair style for a samurai or sumo wrestler).

chōnōryoku, *n.* 超能力 supernatural power.

chōraku, *n.* 凋落 decline; downfall.

chōrei, *n.* 朝礼 morning assembly.

chōri, *n.* 調理 cooking.

chōritsu (no), *adj.* 町立 (の) municipal.

choroi, *adj.* ちょろい easy.

choromakasu, *vb.* ちょろまかす pocket; filch; deceive.

chōrō suru, *vb.* 嘲弄する ridicule.

chōsa, *n.* 調査 investigation; survey; analysis.

chosaku, *n.* 著作 book; writing.

chosakuken, *n.* 著作権 copyright; **chosakuken-shingai** infringement of a copyright.

chōsei, *n.* 調整 adjustment.

chōsen, *n.* 挑戦 challenge.

chōsetsu, *n.* 調節 adjustment; tuning.

chosha, *n.* 著者 writer.

chōshi, *n.* 銚子 earthenware container for sake.

chōshi, *n.* 調子 1. condition (health, thing); **chōshi ga ii** in good condition; harmonious. 2. tune; **chōshi o awaseru** in tune; tune oneself to one's surroundings.

chōshin, *n.* 長針 long hand (watch, clock).

chōshin (no), *adj.* 長身 (の) tall.

chōshisha, *n.* 聴視者 TV viewer; radio listener.

chōshizen (no), *adj.* 超自然 (の) supernatural.

chosho, *n.* 著書 book; writing.

chōsho, *n.* 長所 merit; strong point.

chōsho, *n.* 調書 report of an investigation; record of an interrogation.

chōshō, *n.* 嘲笑 ridicule.

chōshoku, *n.* 朝食 breakfast.

chōshū, *n.* 聴衆 audience.

chōshū suru, *vb.* 徴収する collect (money).

chosuichi, *n.* 貯水池 reservoir.

chosuiryō, *n.* 貯水量 volume of reservoir water.

chōtatsu suru, *vb.* 調達する supply; provide.

chōtei, *n.* 調停 mediation; arbitration.

chōtei, *n.* 朝廷 Imperial Court.

chōten, *n.* 頂点 pinnacle; climax; top.

chōtōha, *n.* 超党派 nonpartisan.

chōtsugai, *n.* 蝶番 hinge.

chotto, *adv.* ちょっと 1. a little. 2. just a moment. 3. not a bit; not very; not easily.

chotto, *interj.* ちょっと Hey you!

chōwa, *n.* 調和 harmony; balance.

chōzei, *n.* 徴税 tax collection.

chōzei, *n.* 町税 town tax.

chōzen-taru/-to shita/-to shiteiru, *adj.* 超然たる／〜とした／〜としている transcendental.

chōzō, *n.* 彫像 statue.

chozō suru, *vb.* 貯蔵する store up.

chū, *n.* 注 annotation; note.

chū, *n.* 忠 faithfulness; loyalty.

chū, *n.* 中 medium; average.

-chū 中 in the middle of; in the process of; during; in; among; **denwachū** (in the middle of speaking) on the phone.

chūbei, *n.* 中米 Central America.

chūbō, *n.* 厨房 kitchen.

chūburarin (na, no), *adj.* 宙ぶらりん (な、の) pending.

chūburu, *n.* 中古 secondhand goods.

chūcho suru, *vb.* ちゅうちょする hesitate.

chūdan suru, *vb.* 中断する discontinue; interrupt; stop.

chūdoku, *n.* 中毒 poisoning; addiction; **fuguchūdoku** blowfish poisoning; **mayaku-chūdoku** drug addiction.

chūdoku(sha), *n.* 中毒(者) addict.

chūgakkō, chūgaku, *n.* 中学校、中学 junior high school.

chūgakusei, *n.* 中学生 junior high school student.

chūgatasha, *n.* 中型車 mid-sized car.

chūgen, *n.* 中元 gift traditionally given in midsummer.

chūgen suru, *vb.* 忠言する admonish; warn.

chūgi, *n.* 忠義 fidelity; loyalty.

chūgoku, *n.* 中国 1. China. 2. western part of Honshū (Hiroshima area).

chūgokugo, *n.* 中国語 Chinese language.

chūgokujin, *n.* 中国人 Chinese person.

chūgurai (na, no), *adj.* 中位 (な、の) medium-size.

chūhen, *n.* 中編 novelette.

chūi, *n.* 注意 attention; caution; advice.

chūi, *n.* 中尉 lieutenant.

chūibukai, *adj.* 注意深い attentive; cautious; careful.

chūihō, *n.* 注意報 weather warning.

chūi jinbutsu, *n.* 注意人物 person of questionable personality, background, or behavior.

chūin-gamu, *n.* チューインガム (E.) chewing gum.

chūi suru, *vb.* 注意する pay attention to; take care of; be careful of.

chūjien, *n.* 中耳炎 middle ear infection.

chūjitsu (na), *adj.* 忠実 (な) faithful; devoted.

chūjun (ni), *adv.* 中旬 (に) around the middle of a month.

chūkagai, *n.* 中華街 Chinatown.

chūkai, *n.* 中介 mediation.

chūkaisha, *n.* 中介者 mediator.

chūkajinmin-kyōwakoku, *n.* 中華人民共和国 People's Republic of China.

chūkan, *n.* 中間 middle; midway.

chūkanabe, *n.* 中華鍋 wok.

chūkankanrishoku, *n.* 中間管理職 middle management.

chūkanshiken, *n.* 中間試験 midterm exam.

chūkaryōri, *n.* 中華料理 Chinese food.

chūkaryōriten, *n.* 中華料理店 Chinese restaurant.

chūkei, *n.* 中継 broadcasting; **terebi-chūkei** TV broadcasting.

chūkeihōsō, *n.* 中継放送 televising.

chūken, *n.* 中堅 mainstay (business).

chūkin, *n.* 忠勤 devotion to one's employer,

chūkintō, *n.* 中近東 the Near and Middle East.

chūkohin, *n.* 中古品 secondhand goods.

chūkoku, *n.* 忠告 advice; admonition.

chūkosha, *n.* 中古車 used car.

chūkyō, *n.* 中共 People's Republic of China.

chūkyū, *n.* 中級 intermediate level; **nihongochūkyū** intermediate Japanese.

chūmoku, *n.* 注目 attention.

chūmon, *n.* 注文 order; request.

chūmonsho, *n.* 注文書 order form.

chūmon suru, *vb.* 注文する order; request.

chūnen (no), *adj.* 中年 (の) middle-aged.

chūnenbutori, *n.* 中年太り middle-age spread.

chū ni, *adv.* 宙に in the air.

chūō, *n.* 中央 center; middle.

chūō, *n.* 中欧 Central Europe.

chūrippu, *n.* チューリップ (E.) tulip.

chūritsu (no), *adj.* 中立 (の) neutral.

chūritsukoku, *n.* 中立国 neutral nation.

chūryū(kaikyū), *n.* 中流(階級) the middle class.

chūsai, *n.* 仲裁 arbitration; mediation.

chūsei, *n.* 忠誠 loyalty; allegiance.

chūsei, *n.* 中世 the Middle Ages; medieval period.

chūsei, *n.* 中性 neuter.

chūseisenzai, *n.* 中性洗剤 neutral detergent.

chūseishi, *n.* 中性子 neutron; **chūseishi-bakudan** neutron bomb.

chūsen, *n.* 抽選 lot; drawing; raffle.

chūsha, *n.* 注射 injection; shot.

chūsha, *n.* 駐車 parking.

chūshaihan, *n.* 駐車違反 parking violation.

chūshajō, *n.* 駐車場 parking lot.

chūshakinshi, *n.* 駐車禁止 No Parking.

chūshaku, *n.* 注釈 annotation; note.

chūsha suru, *vb.* 駐車する park a car.

chūshi, *n.* 注視 attention; **chūshi no mato** center of attention.

chūshin, *n.* 中心 center; core; focus.

chūshin, *n.* 忠信 loyalty; devotion.

chūshinten, *n.* 中心点 central (focal) point.

chūshi suru, *vb.* 中止する suspend; cancel; stop.

chūshō, *n.* 中傷 calumny; defamation.

chūshō, *n.* 抽象 abstraction.

chūshōga, *n.* 抽象画 abstract painting.

chūshōkigyō, *n.* 中小企業 small- and medium-sized companies.

chūshoku, *n.* 昼食 lunch.

chūshōmeishi, *n.* 抽象名詞 abstract noun.

chūshō-teki (na), *adj.* 抽象的 (な) abstract; vague.

chūsū, *n.* 中枢 center; the most important person or thing.

chūtai suru, chūtotaigaku suru, *vb.* 中退する，中途退学する drop out of school; quit school.

chūtō, *n.* 中東 the Middle East.

chūto de, *adv.* 中途で midway; halfway.

chūtohanpa (na, no), *adj.* 中途半端 (な、の) 1. incomplete; fragmentary. 2. halfhearted.

chūtō (no), *adj.* 中等の median; medium.

chūwa suru, *vb.* 中和する neutralize.

chūya, *n.* 昼夜 night and day;

around the clock.

chūyō 中庸 1. *n.* moderation. 2. *adj.* neutral; well-balanced.

chūzai suru, *vb.* 駐在する stay; be stationed in.

chūza suru, *vb.* 中座する leave before an event is over.

chūzetsu, *n.* 中絶 1. interruption; discontinuation; suspension. 2. abortion.

D

daberu, *vb.* だべる chat; gab.

dābī, *n.* ダービー (E. *derby*); horse race.

dabokushō, *n.* 打撲傷 bruise.

dabudabu (no), *adj.* だぶだぶ (の) baggy.

daburu, *adj.* ダブル (E.) double; double-breasted.

daburu, *vb.* ダブる (E. *double*) overlap; duplicate.

dadappiroi, *adj.* だだっ広い extra large; vast; voluminous.

daeki, *n.* 唾液 saliva.

daen(kei), *n.* 楕円(形) oval.

dageki, *n.* 打撃 shock; impact.

daha suru, *vb.* 打破する beat; overcome; overthrow.

dai, *n.* 大 large size.

dai, *n.* 代 1. generation. 2. reign. 3. lifetime. 4. a certain age; **gojūdai no hito** a person in his or her fifties.

dai, *n.* 題 title; topic.

dai, *n.* 台 1. stand; base. 2. a certain amount of space, time, or money.

dai- 第 (ordinal number indicator) **dai-ichi'i** first place.

dai- 大 1. big; serious; **daimondai**

big problem. 2. very (much); **dai-suki** to like very much.

-dai 代 cost; price; **basudai** bus fare; **shokujidai** cost of meal.

daian, *n.* 代案 alternative plan.

daiben, *n.* 大便 feces; bowel movement.

daiben suru, *n.* 代弁する act as a spokesperson.

daibu(n), *adv.* 大分 considerably; quite.

daibubun, *n.* 大部分 major part; majority.

daibutsu, *n.* 大仏 large statue of Buddha.

daichō, *n.* 大腸 large intestine.

daidokoro, *n.* 台所 kitchen.

daietto, *n.* ダイエット (E.) diet.

daietto suru, *vb.* ダイエットする (E.) go on a diet.

daigaku, *n.* 大学 college; university; **kokuritsu (shiritsu, shūritsu, joshi) daigaku** national (private, state, women's) college or university.

daigakude, *n.* 大学出 college or university graduate.

daigakuin, *n.* 大学院 graduate school.

daigakukyōju, *n.* 大学教授 university or college professor.

daigakunyūshi, *n.* 大学入試 college or university entrance examination.

daigakusei, *n.* 大学生 college or university student.

daigishi, *n.* 代議士 politician; congressman; Diet member.

daigomi, *n.* 醍醐味 essential part of a thing or experience.

daihon, *n.* 台本 script (play).

daihyō, *n.* 代表 delegate; representative; representation.

daihyō-teki (na), *adj.* 代表的 (な) representative; exemplary.

dai-ichi (no), *adj.* 第一 (の)the most; the best; first.

dai-ichiji-sekaitaisen, *n.* 第一次 世界大戦 World War I.

daijin, *n.* 大臣 cabinet minister.

daiji (na), *adj.* 大事 (な) important; precious; **(O)daiji ni.** Take care!

daijōbu, *adj.* 大丈夫 all right; safe; fine; **Daijōbu.** I am (it is) all right.

daikibo (na, no), *adj.* 大規模 (な、 の) large-scale.

daikin, *n.* 代金 cost; price; charge.

daikon, *n.* 大根 large white winter radish.

daikō suru, *vb.* 代行する act as a spokesperson or proxy.

daikyū, *n.* 代休 compensatory day(s) off.

daimeishi, *n.* 代名詞 pronoun.

daimyō, *n.* 大名 samurai lord.

dainamikku (na), *adj.* ダイナミッ ク (な) (E.) dynamic; energetic.

dainashi ni suru, *vb.* 台無しにす る mar; ruin.

dai-niji-sekaitaisen, *n.* 第二次世 界大戦 World War II.

dairi, *n.* 代理 agent; proxy; substitute; surrogate; **ryokō-**

dairiten travel agency.

dairibo, *n.* 代理母 surrogate mother.

dairiseki, *n.* 大理石 marble.

daisakusha, *n.* 代作者 ghostwriter.

daishō, *n.* 代償 compensation.

daisotsu, *n.* 大卒 college or university graduate.

daitai, *adv.* 大体 mostly; almost; approximately.

daitan (na), *adj.* 大胆 (な) bold; brave.

daitasū, *n.* 大多数 majority.

daitōryō, *n.* 大統領 (nation's) president; **fukudaitōryō** vice president.

daiya, *n.* ダイヤ (E.) diagram; train schedule.

daiya(mondo), *n.* ダイヤ(モンド) (E.) diamond.

daiyaku, *n.* 代役 substitute; understudy.

daiyaru, daiaru, *n.* ダイヤル, ダイ アル (E.) dial.

daiyō, *n.* 代用 substitute; **daiyō- kyōin** substitute teacher.

daizai, *n.* 題材 subject; topic; theme.

daizu, *n.* 大豆 soybean.

dajare, *n.* 駄洒落 corny joke; **dajare o tobasu** tell a corny joke.

dakai suru, *vb.* 打開する overcome; break through.

dakara, *adv.* だから therefore; so.

dake, *parti.* だけ only; simply; **anata dake** only you; **miru dake no tame ni** just looking.

dakedo, *conj.* だけど although; but.

daketsu suru, *vb.* 打決する reach agreement; settle (a matter).

dakkyaku suru, *vb.* 脱却する come out of (a slump); break through; grow.

daku, *vb.* 抱く hold; embrace; hug.

dāku-hōsu, *n.* ダークホース (E.) dark horse.

dakyō, *n.* 妥協 compromise.

dakyō suru, *vb.* 妥協する compromise.

damaru, *vb.* 黙る keep silent.

damasu, *vb.* だます deceive; cheat.

dame (na), *adj.* だめ (な) 1. bad; wrong. 2. useless; impossible. 3. necessary; **ikanakutewa dame** necessary to go.

damēji, *n.* ダメージ (E.) damage; **damēji o ataeru** to hurt or damage.

damu, *n.* ダム (E.) dam.

dan, *n.* 段 1. stair; step; **dan o agaru** climb steps. 2. (learning or martial art) level; grade; **karate sandan** 3rd grade in karate.

dan, *n.* 壇 platform.

-dan 団 group; party; **kishadan** press group.

dan'atsu, *n.* 弾圧 suppression.

danbō, *n.* 暖房 heating.

danbōru, *n.* 段ボール cardboard.

danbō-setsubi, *n.* 暖房設備 heating equipment or system.

danchi, *n.* 団地 public housing or apartment complex.

danchō, *n.* 団長 group leader.

dan-dan, *adv.* 段々 gradually.

dandori, *n.* 段取り preparation; arrangement; direction.

dangai, *n.* 断崖 precipice; cliff.

dangai suru, *vb.* 弾劾する denounce; accuse.

dangan, *n.* 弾丸 bullet.

dangen suru, *vb.* 断言する allege; assert; declare.

dango, *n.* 団子 dumpling.

dani, *n.* だに 1. tick (insect). 2. scoundrel; scum.

danji, *n.* 男児 male; boy.

danjiki, *n.* 断食 fast.

danjite, *adv.* 断じて 1. (with a negative) definitely not; absolutely not. 2. never.

danjo, *n.* 男女 both sexes.

danjo dōken, *n.* 男女同権 equal rights for the sexes.

danjo kyōgaku, *n.* 男女共学 coeducation.

dankai, *n.* 段階 stage (development); step.

danketsu suru, *vb.* 団結する unite; consolidate.

dankon, *n.* 男根 phallus.

dankotaru, *adj.* 断固たる resolved; determined.

danmen, *n.* 断面 aspect; section.

dan'nasan, *n.* 旦那さん male customer; husband; master.

dan'netsu, *n.* 断熱 insulation.

danpan, *n.* 談判 negotiation.

danpingu, *n.* ダンピング (E.) dumping.

danraku, *n.* 段落 paragraph.

danryoku(sei), *n.* 弾力(性) elasticity; flexibility.

dansei, *n.* 男性 male (person).

dansei-teki (na), *adj.* 男性的 (な) masculine.

danshi, *n.* 男子 boy; male.

danshō, *n.* 男娼 male prostitute.

danshoku, *n.* 男色 male homosexual love.

danson johi, *n.* 男尊女卑 male supremacy.

dansu, *n.* ダンス (E.) dance.

dantai, *n.* 団体 group; organization; **shōhisha dantai** consumer group.

dantei, *n.* 断定 conclusion; affirmation.

dantei suru, *vb.* 断定する conclude.

dan'yū, *n.* 男優 actor.

danzen, *adv.* 断然 by far; prominently.

danzoku-teki (na), *adj.* 断続的 (な) intermittent.

-darake (no) だらけ (の) full of; **hitodarake** full of people.

daraku, *n.* 堕落 depravity; corruption.

darashinai, *adj.* だらしない sloppy; disorganized; undisciplined.

dare, *pron.* 誰 who.

dare demo, *pron.* 誰でも anyone; **Dare demo ii.** Anyone will do.

darehitori, *pron.* 誰ひとり (with a negative) no one; **Darehitori konakatta.** No one came.

dareka, *pron.* 誰か someone.

dare ni, *pron.* 誰に (to) whom.

dare no, *pron.* 誰の whose.

darō *aux. vb.* だろう may; will probably; **kuru darō** will probably come.

darui, *adj.* だるい lethargic; sluggish; dull.

dasaku, *n.* 駄作 worthless (literary, artistic) work.

dasan-teki (na), *adj.* 打算的 (な) calculating; sly; selfish.

dasha, *n.* 打者 batter (baseball).

dashi, *n.* 出し soup stock.

dashin suru, *vb.* 打診する sound out (a person).

dashinuke ni, *adv.* 出し抜けに suddenly; abruptly.

dashi oshimi, *n.* 出し惜しみ stinginess.

dasoku, *n.* 蛇足 unnecessary addition.

dassen, *n.* 脱線 derailment; digression.

dasshimen, *n.* 脱脂綿 absorbent cotton.

dasshoku, *n.* 脱色 bleaching.

dasshu, *n.* ダッシュ (E.) dash (punctuation).

dasshutsu suru, *vb.* 脱出する escape; flee.

dasshūzai, *n.* 脱臭剤 deodorizer.

dassuiki, *n.* 脱水機 spin-dryer.

dassuru, *vb.* 脱する extricate oneself from (crisis, problem).

dasu, *vb.* 出す 1. put forth; produce; issue. 2. draw out; take out. 3. generate. 4. show. 5. mail. 6. hand in. 7. serve (meal).

-dasu 出す start; **hashiri-dasu** start running.

dāsu, *n.* ダース (E.) dozen.

datai, *n.* 堕胎 abortion.

datai suru, *vb.* 堕胎する have an abortion.

-date (no) 建て -storied (building); **nikaidate no** two-storied.

date otoko, *n.* 伊達男 dandy.

datō (na), *adj.* 妥当 (な) right; appropriate; reasonable.

datō suru, *vb.* 打倒する defeat; win.

datsubō suru, *vb.* 脱帽する take one's hat off to; respect.

datsui-sho/-jo, *n.* 脱衣所 changing room; locker room.

datsumō, *n.* 脱毛 hair loss.

datsurakusha, *n.* 脱落者 dropout.

datsuzei, *n.* 脱税 tax evasion.

dattai suru, *vb.* 脱退する secede.

dattō suru, *vb.* 脱党する withdraw (from a political party).

de, *parti.* で 1. (space) at; in; on; **tōkyō de** in Tokyo. 2. (time) in; **gofun de** in five minutes. 3. (means) by; in; on; **inki de** in ink; **denwa de** on the phone. 4. (age) at. 5. (price) at; for. 6. (made) from; of. 7. (cause) because of. 8. per.

deai, *n.* 出会い encounter;

meeting.

dearuku, *vb.* 出歩く walk around; stroll.

deashi, *n.* 出足 1. start; **deashi ga ii** good start. 2. turnout.

deau, *vb.* 出会う encounter; meet.

deban, *n.* 出番 one's turn.

debu, *n.* でぶ (derogatory) fat person.

debushō, *n.* 出不精 homebody; stay-at-home.

debyū, *n.* デビュー (F.) debut.

dedokoro, *n.* 出所 source; origin.

defure, *n.* デフレ (E.) deflation.

deguchi, *n.* 出口 exit.

deiri, *n.* 出入り comings and goings.

deisui suru, *vb.* 泥酔する get dead drunk.

dejitaru, dijitaru, *adj.* デジタル, ディジタル (E.) digital.

deka, *n.* でか (derogatory) policeman; detective.

dekai, *adj.* でかい big; huge.

dekakeru, *vb.* 出掛ける go out; leave.

dekasegi, *n.* 出稼ぎ working temporarily away from home (migrant, seasonal labor).

dekashita, *interj.* でかした Great! Good job! Well done!

deki, *n.* 出来 1. result; product; quality; **deki ga ii** good result (product, quality). 2. ability.

dekiagaru, *vb.* 出来上がる be completed; be ready.

dekiai no, *adj.* 出来合いの ready-made.

dekiai suru, *vb.* 溺愛する dote on; indulge.

dekibae, *n.* 出来栄え result; outcome.

dekigokoro, *n.* 出来心 impulse; **dekigokoro de** impulsively;

thoughtlessly.

dekigoto, *n.* 出来事 occurrence; event.

dekimono, *n.* 出来物 boil; polyp; ulcer.

dekireba, *adv.* 出来れば if possible.

dekiru, *vb.* 出来る 1. be able (to); excel (in); be capable (of). 2. be ready; be finished. 3. be established; be built. 4. be made; be produced.

dekiru-dake/-kagiri, *adv.* 出来るだけ／～限り as (much, many, soon) as possible; to the best of one's ability.

dekiru(koto)nara, *adv.* 出来る(こと)なら if possible.

dekitate (no hoya-hoya), *adj.* 出来たて (のほやほや freshly made; brand-new.

dekoboko (na, no), *adj.* でこぼこ (な、の) uneven or bumpy (surface).

dekuwasu, *vb.* 出くわす bump into; run into.

dema, *n.* デマ (G. *Demagogie*) unsupported rumor; **dema o nagasu** spread a rumor.

demae, *n.* 出前 (food) delivery service; catering service.

demakase ni, *adv.* 出任せに irresponsibly; haphazardly.

demo, *n.* デモ (E.) demonstration.

demo, *conj.* でも however; but.

demo でも 1. *adj.* any; **dare demo** anyone; **Nan demo ii.** Anything will do. 2. *adv.* even; at least; as well; **Boku demo dekiru.** Even I can do that.

demokurashī, *n.* デモクラシー (E.) democracy.

demukaeru, *vb.* 出迎える meet or pick someone up (at an airport, etc.); salute; welcome.

denaosu, *vb.* 出直す come back later; start again.

den'atsu, *n.* 電圧 voltage.

denbun, *n.* 伝聞 hearsay; rumor.

denchi, *n.* 電池 battery.

dendō, *n.* 伝導 proselytizing; preaching.

dendō, *n.* 殿堂 palace; hall.

den'en, *n.* 田園 field (for cultivation); countryside.

dengen, *n.* 電源 electric power source.

dengon, *n.* 伝言 message.

denka, *n.* 殿下 title bestowed on imperial family members.

denka, *n.* 電化 electrification.

denki, *n.* 伝記 biography.

denki, *n.* 電気 electricity; **denkigama (denkimōfu, denkisentakuki, denkisōjiki)** electric rice cooker (blanket, washing machine, vacuum cleaner).

denkiseihin, *n.* 電気製品 electrical appliance; equipment.

denkyū, *n.* 電球 electric bulb.

den'netsuki, *n.* 電熱器 electric heater; radiator.

denpa, *n.* 電波 radio wave.

denpatanchiki, *n.* 電波探知機 radar; radiolocator.

denpō, *n.* 電報 telegram; **denpō o utsu** send a telegram.

denpun, *n.* でんぷん starch.

denpyō, *n.* 伝票 bill; slip; receipt.

denryoku, *n.* 電力 electric power.

denryoku-gaisha/-kaisha, *n.* 電力会社 electric power company.

denryū, *n.* 電流 electric current.

densen, *n.* 電線 electric wire; telephone line; cable.

densen, *n.* 伝染 infection; contagion.

densenbyō, *n.* 伝染病 infectious or contagious disease.

densetsu, *n.* 伝説 legend.

densha, *n.* 電車 train.

denshi, *n.* 電子 electron.

denshikeisanki, *n.* 電子計算機 computer.

denshi kōgaku, *n.* 電子工学 electronics.

denshi-renji, *n.* 電子レンジ microwave oven.

densōshashin, *n.* 電送写真 Wirephoto.

densō suru, *vb.* 電送する transmit by telephone or radio.

dentaku, *n.* 電卓 calculator.

dentatsu, *n.* 伝達 communication; transmission; message; report.

dentō, *n.* 電灯 electric light.

dentō, *n.* 伝統 tradition; heritage.

dentō-teki (na), *adj.* 伝統的 (な) traditional.

denwa, *n.* 電話 telephone; **aka-/kōshū-denwa** public phone; **itazuradenwa** crank call; **kokusaidenwa** international call; **machigaidenwa** wrong number; **denwa o kakeru/suru** make a phone call.

denwabangō, *n.* 電話番号 telephone number.

denwachō, *n.* 電話帳 telephone directory.

denwa-kōkanshu, *n.* 電話交換手 telephone operator.

denwakyoku, *n.* 電話局 telephone company or office.

denwaryō(kin), *n.* 電話料(金) telephone charges.

depāto, *n.* デパート (E.) department store.

derakkusu (na), *adj.* デラックス (な) (E.) deluxe.

deru, *vb.* 出る 1. come out; go out; leave; graduate from. 2. attend;

44

participate. 3. appear. 4. be published.

deshabari, *n.* 出しゃばり nosy person.

deshabaru, *vb.* 出しゃばる poke one's nose into.

deshi, *n.* 弟子 disciple; follower; apprentice.

deshō, *aux. vb.* でしょう 1. will. 2. probably. 3. I think that; I am afraid that; it seems that. 4. Don't you think that ... ?

desuku, *n.* デスク (E.) desk.

dēta, *n.* データ (E.) data.

dēta-banku, *n.* データバンク (E.) data bank.

detarame (na, no), *adj.* でたらめ (な、の) nonsensical; absurd; irresponsible; random.

dēta-shori, *n.* データ処理 (E.) data processing.

detchiageru, *vb.* でっち上げる fake (a story or rumor); fabricate.

dēto, *n.* デート (E.) date (social).

dewa, *interj.* では Now ...; Well ...; Then ...

dezain, *n.* デザイン (E.) design.

dezainā, *n.* デザイナー (E.) designer.

dezāto, *n.* デザート (E.) dessert.

direkutā, *n.* ディレクター (E.) director.

disukasshon, *n.* ディスカッション (E.) discussion.

disukaunto, *n.* ディスカウント (E.) discount.

disuko, *n.* ディスコ (E.) disco.

-do 度 1. degree (temperature, angle, latitude, altitude); **sesshi jūdo** ten degrees Celsius. 2. time (frequency); **sando** three times. 3. proof (alcohol).

dō, *n.* 銅 copper.

dō, *n.* 胴 torso; trunk (body).

dō, *adv.* どう 1. would you like; **Kōhī wa dō.** Would you like coffee? 2. what; what about; **Sore o dō omoimasu ka.** What do you think of that? 3. how; how about; **Ryokō wa dō deshita ka.** How was your trip? 4. **Dō itashimashite.** My pleasure.

doa, *n.* ドア (E.) door; **doa o akeru** open the door; **doa o shimeru** close the door.

dōage (o) suru, *vb.* 胴上げ toss a person in the air (celebrate).

doai, *n.* 度合い degree; extent; intensity.

dobokugishi, *n.* 土木技師 civil engineer.

dobokukōji, *n.* 土木工事 construction project.

dōbutsu, *n.* 動物 animal.

dōbutsuen, *n.* 動物園 zoo.

dochaku (no), *adj.* 土着 (の) aboriginal; indigenous; native.

dochira どちら 1. *pron.* who; which. 2. *adj.* which; what. 3. *adv.* where.

dochira ka, *n.* どちらか one of the two; either ... or ...

dochira mo, *n.* どちらも 1. both. 2. neither of the two; **Dochira mo yokunai.** Neither of them is good.

dodai, *n.* 土台 foundation; basis.

Dō demo ii. どうでもいい It does not matter.

dōdō-taru/-toshita/-toshiteiru, *adj.* 堂々たる／～とした／～としている stately; imposing.

dōfū suru, *vb.* 同封する enclose (in an envelope).

dogaishi suru, *vb.* 度外視する disregard; dismiss.

dōgi, *n.* 道義 morality.

dōgigo, *n.* 同義語 synonym.

dogimagi suru, *vb.* どぎまぎする
feel embarrassed; be abashed.

dogimo o nuku, *vb.* 度肝を抜く
astound; shock.

dogitsui, *adj.* どぎつい 1. gaudy;
garish; loud (color, clothing). 2.
harsh (speech).

dōgu, *n.* 道具 appliance; utensil;
tool.

dōhai, *n.* 同輩 colleague; comrade;
coworker.

dōhan suru, *vb.* 同伴する go
together; accompany.

dōhō, *n.* 同胞 fellow countryman;
comrade.

dohyō, *n.* 土俵 sumo ring.

dōi, *n.* 同意 agreement; consent.

dōigo, *n.* 同意語 synonym.

dōin suru, *vb.* 動員する mobilize.

dōi suru, *vb.* 同意する agree;
consent.

doitsu, *n.* ドイツ (G. *Deutschland*)
Germany.

doitsugo, *n.* ドイツ語 (G. *Deutsch*)
German (language).

doitsujin, *n.* ドイツ人 (G. *Deutsch*)
German (person).

dōitsu (no), *adj.* 同一 (の) same;
alike; equal.

dō iu どう言う 1. *adj.* what sort of;
dō iu hon what sort of book. 2.
adv. **dō iu wake de** why; **dō iu
fū ni** how.

dōjidai (no), *adj.* 同時代 (の)
coeval; contemporary.

dōji ni, *adv.* 同時に
simultaneously.

dōji tsūyaku, *n.* 同時通訳
simultaneous interpretation;
simultaneous interpreter.

dōjō, *n.* 道場 place for practice or
tournament (martial arts).

dōjō, *n.* 同情 sympathy; pity.

dōjō suru, *vb.* 同情する
sympathize; feel pity for.

dōka どうか (used in combination
with a *vb.*) 1. (asking) please; be
so kind as to; **Dōka tetsudatte
kudasai.** Please help me. 2.
(expressing a hope or wish) **Dōka
ki o tsukete kudasai.** Please
take care of yourself. 3. whether
(or not); **Iku ka dōka
wakaranai.** I'm not sure whether
I'll go. 4. disagreement, doubt;
dōka to omou think
questionable.

dōkan suru, *vb.* 同感する have the
same opinion; have the same
feeling (as another).

dokasu, *vb.* どかす remove (a
thing out of one's way).

dōka shiteiru, *vb.* どうかしている
be out of one's mind; be out of
sorts.

dōkaku (no), *adj.* 同格 (の) 1.
equal ability or power. 2.
appositive (grammar).

dōke, *n.* 道化 clown; buffoon.

dōkei, *n.* 憧憬 yearning; adoration;
idolization.

dōkei (no), *adj.* 同系の of the same
bloodline or characteristic;
affiliated; allied.

dōken, *n.* 同権 equal rights.

dokengyō, *n.* 土建業 construction
industry.

doki, *n.* 土器 earthenware.

doki, *n.* 動悸 palpitation; beat (of
the heart).

doki, *n.* 動機 motive.

doki-doki suru, *vb.* どきどきする
feel nervous; have heart
palpitations.

dōkisei, *n.* 同期生 classmate.

doko (ni), *adv.* どこ (に) where.

dōkōkai, *n.* 同好会 circle; league;

clique.

-dokoroka どころか 1. in addition; as well as; **kodomo-dokoroka otona mo** adults as well as children. 2. conversely; on the contrary.

dōkō suru, *vb.* 同行する accompany; go with someone.

doku, *n.* 毒 poison.

doku, *vb.* どく step aside; make way for (someone).

dokudan, *n.* 独断 arbitrary decision.

dokudan-teki (na), *adj.* 独断的 (な) arbitrary; dogmatic.

dokuen, *n.* 独演 one-man or one-woman show.

dokufu, *n.* 毒婦 femme fatale.

dokugaku, *n.* 独学 self-education.

dokuhaku, *n.* 独白 monologue; soliloquy.

dokuji (na, no), *adj.* 独自 (な、の) unique; original.

dokumi, *n.* 毒味 tasting (food).

dokumushi, *n.* 毒虫 poisonous insect.

dokuritsu, *n.* 独立 independence.

dokuritsu suru, *vb.* 独立する become independent.

dokuryoku de, *adv.* 独力で by oneself; independently.

dokusai, *n.* 独裁 dictatorship.

dokusen, *n.* 独占 monopoly.

dokusen kinshi hō, *n.* 独占禁止法 antitrust law.

dokusen'yoku, *n.* 独占欲 possessiveness; **dokusen'yoku no tsuyoi** possessive.

dokusha, *n.* 読者 reader.

dokushin (no), *adj.* 独身 (の) celibate; single; unmarried.

dokushinsha, *n.* 独身者 single person; unmarried person.

dokusho, *n.* 読書 reading.

dokushō, *n.* 独唱 solo singing.

dokusho suru, *vb.* 読書する read (books).

dokushū, *n.* 独習 self-instruction.

dokusō, *n.* 独奏 solo performance on a musical instrument.

dokusō, *n.* 毒草 toxic plant.

dokusō-sei/-ryoku, *n.* 独創性／〜力 creativity; originality; **dokusōsei ga aru** be original.

dokusō-teki (na), *adj.* 独創的 (な) creative; original; unique.

dokutā, *n.* ドクター (E.) doctor of medicine; physician.

dokutoku (na, no), *adj.* 独特 (な、の) unique; characteristic; original.

dōkutsu, *n.* 洞窟 grotto; cave.

dokuzen-teki (na), *adj.* 独善的 (な) self-centered; self-righteous.

dokuzetsu, *n.* 毒舌 sharp tongue; caustic remark.

dokyō, *n.* 度胸 courage; audacity; **dokyō ga aru** be courageous.

dōkyo, *n.* 同居 cohabitation; living together.

dokyumentarī, *n.* ドキュメンタリー (E.) documentary (film).

dōkyūsei, *n.* 同級生 classmate.

dō medaru, *n.* 銅メダル bronze medal.

dōmei, *n.* 同盟 alliance; league; union.

dō mite mo, *adv.* どう見ても definitely; indubitably.

dōmo, *adv.* どうも 1. very much; terribly; **Dōmo arigatō.** Thank you very much. 2. somehow; somewhat. 3. probably; **Dōmo dame darō.** It probably won't (work, happen).

dōmō (na), *adj.* どうもう (な) ferocious; fierce.

domoru, *vb.* 吃る stammer; stutter.

dōmyaku, *n.* 動脈 artery.

donabe, *n.* 土鍋 earthenware pot.

donaru, *vb.* どなる yell at; shout.

donata, *pron.* どなた who.

dōnatsu, *n.* ドーナツ (E.) doughnut.

donburi, *n.* 丼 bowl (for noodles, rice); meal served in such a bowl.

donchansawagi, *n.* どんちゃん騒ぎ uproarious merrymaking; revelry.

don-don どんどん 1. *n.* beating sound; tom-tom. 2. *adv.* progressively; rapidly.

donguri, *n.* どんぐり acorn.

dōnika, *adv.* どうにか somehow; barely.

donkan (na), *adj.* 鈍感 (な) insensitive.

don'na, *adj.* どんな what kind of; what.

don'na ni, *adv.* どんなに however hard; how; **don'na ni hataraite mo** however hard I work.

dono, *adj.* どの 1. which; what. 2. every; any.

dono hen (ni), *adv.* どの辺 (に) where.

dono-kurai/-gurai, *adv.* どの位 how long (many, much, often).

dono yō na, *adj.* どの様な what kind of.

dono yō ni, *adv.* どの様に how; in what way.

don'yoku (na), *adj.* 貪欲 (な) avaricious; greedy.

donzoko, *n.* どん底 depths.

dōon'igigo, *n.* 同音異義語 homonym.

dorai (na), *adj.* ドライ (な) (E.) dry; unemotional.

doraiā, doraiyā, *n.* ドライアー, ドライヤー (E.) hair dryer.

doraibā, *n.* ドライバー (E.) driver.

doraibu, *n.* ドライブ (E.) drive.

dorai-kurīningu, *n.* ドライクリーニング (E.) dry cleaning.

dōraku, *n.* 道楽 1. hobby. 2. dissipation.

dōraku-mono/-sha, *n.* 道楽者／～者 playboy; gambler; idler.

dorama, *n.* ドラマ (E.) drama.

dore, *pron.* どれ which; what.

dore dake, *adv.* どれだけ how many; how much.

dorei, *n.* 奴隷 slave.

dore-kurai/-gurai, *adv.* どれ位 how far (long, many, much).

-dōri 通り street; **aoyamadōri** Aoyama Street.

dōri, *n.* 道理 right; reason; **dōri ni kanau** do the right thing.

dōri de, *adv.* 道理で (it is) no wonder.

doriru, *n.* ドリル (E.) drill.

doro, *n.* 泥 mud.

dōro, *n.* 道路 road.

dorobō, *n.* 泥棒 thief.

dōrochizu, *n.* 道路地図 road map.

dōrojōhō, *n.* 道路情報 traffic information.

dōrokōji, *n.* 道路工事 road construction.

doroppuauto, *n.* ドロップアウト (E.) dropout.

doru, *n.* ドル (E.) dollar.

dōrui (no), *adj.* 同類 (の) of the same kind.

dōryō, *n.* 同僚 pal; colleague; coworker.

doryoku, *n.* 努力 effort.

dōsa, *n.* 動作 movement.

dosakusa, *n.* どさくさ confusion.

dōsan, *n.* 動産 personal property.

dōsatsu(ryoku), tōsatsu(ryoku), *n.* 洞察(力) perspicacity; insight.

dōse, *adv.* どうせ at best; anyway; as supposed.

dōsei, *n.* 同姓 same surname.

dōsei, *n.* 同棲 cohabitation (unmarried couple).

dōsei, *n.* 同性 same sex.

dōseiai, *n.* 同性愛 homosexuality; lesbianism.

dōseiaisha, *n.* 同性愛者 homosexual man or woman.

dōseidōmei, *n.* 同姓同名 same family and given names.

dōshi, *n.* 動詞 verb.

dōshi 同士 1. *n.* peer; member; comrade. 2. *pron.* each other.

doshi-doshi, *adv.* どしどし quantitatively; frequently.

dō shita, *pron., adj.* どうした what; **Dō shita no.** What happened?

dō shite, *adv.* どうして why; how.

dō shite mo, *adv.* どうしても by any means.

dōshitsu (no), *adj.* 同質の of the same quality.

dō shiyō mo nai, *adj.* どうしようもない helpless; impossible.

dōshu (no), *adj.* 同種 (の) of the same type or kind.

dōsō(sei), *n.* 同窓(生) classmate; alumna; alumnus.

dosoku de, *adv.* 土足で with one's shoes on.

dossari (to), *adv.* どっさり (と) abundantly.

dotabata, *n.* どたばた confusion; noise.

dōtai, *n.* 胴体 body; torso.

dotanba, *n.* 土壇場 critical situation; plight.

dotanba de, *adv.* 土壇場で at a crucial moment; at the last moment.

dotchi, *pron.* どっち which.

dotchi mo, *pron.* どっちも 1. both.

2. neither of the two.

dōtei, *n.* 童貞 male virginity; male virgin.

dōten, *n.* 同点 tie (sports).

dōtō (na, no), *adj.* 同等 (な、の) equal.

dōtoku, *n.* 道徳 morality; moral; ethics; **kōshūdōtoku** public morals.

dōtokukyōiku, *n.* 道徳教育 moral education.

dotto, *adv.* どっと in a torrent; suddenly.

dōwa, *n.* 童話 fairy tale.

dowasure suru, *vb.* 度忘れする forget temporarily.

doya-doya (to), *adv.* どやどや (と) boisterously; noisily.

dō yara, *adv.* どうやら probably; somehow.

dō yatte, *adv.* どうやって how.

dōyō, *n.* 童謡 children's song.

dōyō, *n.* 動揺 uneasiness; agitation.

dōyō (na, no), *adj.* 同様 (な、の) similar; same.

doyōbi, *n.* 土曜日 Saturday; **doyōbi ni** on Saturday.

dōyoku (na), *adj.* 胴欲 (な) avaricious; acquisitive.

dōyō suru, *vb.* 動揺する feel uneasy; get agitated; lose composure.

dōzen (no), *adj.* 同然の same; equal.

dōzo, *adv.* どうぞ please; **Dōzo kochira ni.** This way, please. **Dōzo yoroshiku.** Nice to meet you.

dōzō, *n.* 銅像 bronze statue.

dōzoku, *n.* 同族 same stock; same tribe.

E

e, *n.* 絵 painting; drawing.

e, *n.* 柄 handle.

e, *parti.* へ to; for; toward; **nihon e iku** go to Japan.

ē, *adv.* ええ yes.

e', ē, *interj.* えつ、えー 1. (utterance expressing surprise or doubt) Eh? What? 2. (hesitation) Well ...

eakon, *n.* エアコン (E.) air conditioner.

earobikkusu, *n.* エアロビックス (E.) aerobics.

ebi, *n.* 海老 shrimp; prawn.

echiketto, *n.* エチケット (E.) etiquette.

eda, *n.* 枝 bough; branch; twig.

efuemu, *n.* エフエム (E.) FM (radio).

egaku, *vb.* 描く 1. paint; draw. 2. portray; describe.

egao, *n.* 笑顔 smiling face.

ehagaki, *n.* 絵葉書 picture postcard.

ehon, *n.* 絵本 picture book.

eibin (na), *adj.* 鋭敏 (な) sensitive; acute; keen.

eibun, *n.* 英文 English-language text.

eibungaku, *n.* 英文学 English literature.

eibunka, *n.* 英文科 English Department.

eibunpō, *n.* 英文法 English grammar.

eibun wayaku, *n.* 英文和訳 English-to-Japanese translation.

ei-ei jiten, *n.* 英英辞典 English dictionary.

eien, *n.* 永遠 eternity.

eien ni, *adv.* 永遠に eternally; forever.

eien no, *adj.* 永遠の eternal; infinite; undying.

eiga, *n.* 栄華 prosperity; glory.

eiga, *n.* 映画 movie; film; **eiga o miru** watch a movie.

eigahaiyū, *n.* 映画俳優 film star.

eiga-hihyō/-hyōron, *n.* 映画批評／〜評論 movie review.

eigajoyū, *n.* 映画女優 movie actress.

eigakan, *n.* 映画館 movie theater; cinema.

eigakantoku, *n.* 映画監督 film director.

eigakyakuhon, *n.* 映画脚本 film script.

eigo, *n.* 英語 English language.

eigyō, *n.* 営業 business.

eigyōan'nai, *n.* 営業案内 business guide; catalog.

eigyōjikan, *n.* 営業時間 business hours.

eigyōsha, *n.* 営業者 business owner; proprietor.

eigyōsho, *n.* 営業所 business office.

eiji, *n.* 嬰児 infant; baby.

eiji, *n.* 英字 English alphabet; English writing.

eijishinbun, *n.* 英字新聞 English-language newspaper.

eijūsha, *n.* 永住者 permanent resident.

eijū suru, *vb.* 永住する make one's permanent home in.

eikaiwa, *n.* 英会話 English conversation.

eikaiwagakkō, *n.* 英会話学校 English-conversation school.

eikan, *n.* 栄冠 first prize; laurels; glory.

eiki, *n.* 鋭気 energy; stamina; vigor; **eiki o yashinau** to energize oneself.

eikō, *n.* 栄光 glory; eminence.

eikoku, *n.* 英国 England.

eikokujin, *n.* 英国人 English (people).

eikoku no, *adj.* 英国の English (thing[s]).

eikoseisui, *n.* 栄枯盛衰 vicissitudes; rise and fall.

eikyō, *n.* 影響 influence; effect.

eikyū, *n.* 永久 eternity.

eikyū ni, *adv.* 永久に forever; permanently.

eimin, *n.* 永眠 death.

eiri, *n.* 営利 profit; lucre.

eiri no, *adj.* 絵入りの illustrated.

eiri shugi, *n.* 営利主義 commercialism.

eisai, *n.* 英才 gifted or talented person.

eisaikyōiku, *n.* 英才教育 classes for gifted students.

eisakubun, *n.* 英作文 composition in English.

eisei, *n.* 衛生 hygiene; sanitation.

eisei, *n.* 衛星 satellite; **kishōeisei** weather satellite.

eiseihōsō, *n.* 衛星放送 satellite broadcast.

eisei-teki (na), *adj.* 衛生的 (な) hygienic; sanitary.

eiseitoshi, *n.* 衛星都市 satellite city.

eishi, *n.* 英詩 English poetry.

eiten, *n.* 栄転 job transfer with promotion.

ei-wajiten, *n.* 英和辞典 English-Japanese dictionary.

eiyaku, *n.* 英訳 translation (Japanese to English).

eiyo, *n.* 栄誉 honor.

eiyō, *n.* 栄養 nutrition; nourishment.

eiyōshitchō, *n.* 栄養失調 malnutrition.

eiyū, *n.* 英雄 hero.

eizō, *n.* 映像 image; picture (screen).

eizoku suru, *vb.* 永続する continue; last.

eizoku-teki (na), *adj.* 永続的 (な) lasting; enduring.

eizu, *n.* エイズ (E.) AIDS.

eizu-kanja, *n.* エイズ患者 AIDS patient.

ejiki, *n.* えじき prey; victim.

ekaki, *n.* 絵かき painter (artist).

eki, *n.* 駅 railway station.

eki, *n.* 益 usefulness; benefit; profit.

eki, *n.* 液 liquid.

eki, *n.* 易 fortune-telling.

ekiben, *n.* 駅弁 box lunches sold at train stations.

ekibyō, *n.* 疫病 plague; epidemic.

ekichō, *n.* 駅長 railway stationmaster.

eki'in, *n.* 駅員 railway station employee.

ekijō no, *adj.* 液状の liquid.

ekisaito suru, *vb.* エキサイトする (E.) get excited.

ekisha, *n.* 易者 fortuneteller.

ekishō, *n.* 液晶 liquid crystal.

ekisupāto, *n.* エキスパート (E.) expert.

ekitai, *n.* 液体 liquid.

ekkusu-sen, *n.* エックス線 (E.) X-ray.

ekohiiki suru, *vb.* えこひいきする be partial (to a person); favor.

ekubo, *n.* えくぼ dimple.

emakimono, *n.* 絵巻物 scroll painting that tells a story.

emonkake, *n.* 衣紋掛け kimono

stand.

emono, *n.* 獲物 game (hunting); catch (fishing).

en, *n.* 円 1. Japanese yen. 2. circle.

en, *n.* 縁 1. relation; bond; kinship. 2. fate.

enbifuku, *n.* 燕尾服 tailcoat.

enbun, *n.* 塩分 salt or sodium content.

enchaku, *n.* 延着 delay (transportation).

enchaku suru, *vb.* 延着する be delayed.

enchō, *n.* 延長 extension; prolongation.

enchō suru, *vb.* 延長する extend; prolong.

endai, *n.* 演題 topic of a speech.

endai (na), *adj.* 遠大 (な) far-reaching.

endaka, *n.* 円高 appreciation of the yen.

endan, *n.* 演壇 podium.

endan, *n.* 縁談 marriage proposal.

endōi, *adj.* 縁遠い dissociated; unrelated.

en'eki suru, *vb.* 演繹する deduce.

en-en (to), *adv.* 延々 (と) at great length (time).

enerugī, *n.* エネルギー (G. *Energie*) energy.

engan, *n.* 沿岸 coast.

engawa, *n.* 縁側 veranda.

engei, *n.* 演芸 entertainment; performing art.

engei, *n.* 園芸 gardening.

engeki, *n.* 演劇 drama; play.

engi, *n.* 演技 performance (stage).

engi, *n.* 縁起 luck.

engo, *n.* 援護 protection; support.

engo suru, *vb.* 援護する protect; support.

engumi, *n.* 縁組み marriage.

enjin, *n.* エンジン (E.) engine.

enjinia, *n.* エンジニア (E.) engineer.

enjiru, *vb.* 演じる act; perform; play.

enjo, *n.* 援助 support; aid; help; **shikinenjo** financial aid.

enjo suru, *vb.* 援助する support; aid; help.

enjuku, *n.* 円熟 maturity (personality, skill).

enjuku shita, *adj.* 円熟した mature (personality, skill).

enkai, *n.* 演会 party (celebration).

enkatsu (na), *adj.* 円滑な free from hindrances; smooth.

enkatsu ni, *adv.* 円滑に smoothly; **enkatsu ni hakobu** proceed smoothly.

enkei (no), *adj.* 円形 (の) circular.

enki, *n.* 延期 postponement.

enki suru, *vb.* 延期する postpone.

enko, *n.* 縁故 connection (people).

enko suru, *vb.* えんこする break down (car).

enkyoku ni, *adv.* えん曲に indirectly; in a roundabout way.

enkyori, *n.* 遠距離 long distance.

enman (na), *adj.* 円満 (な) 1. harmonious; satisfying. 2. (person) contented.

enmusubi, *n.* 縁結び matchmaking.

en'nichi, *n.* 縁日 religious festival or fair.

enogu, *n.* 絵具 artist's paint; **abura-enogu** oil paint.

e no yō na, *adj.* 絵の様な picturesque.

enpitsu, *n.* 鉛筆 pencil.

enryo, *n.* 遠慮 hesitation; **enryo-naku** without hesitation or reserve.

enryobukai, *adj.* 遠慮深い shy; reserved.

enryogachi (na, no), *adj.* 遠慮がち
(な、の) hesitating; reserved.

enryo suru, *vb.* 遠慮する hesitate;
refrain from; **tabako o enryo
suru** refrain from smoking.

ensei, *n.* 遠征 expedition.

ensen, *n.* 沿線 area alongside a
railway.

enshi, *n.* 遠視 farsightedness.

enshō, *n.* 炎症 inflammation.

enshū, *n.* 演習 1. exercise (study).
2. maneuver (military).

enshutsu, *n.* 演出 direction (stage,
movie).

ensō, *n.* 演奏 performance (music).

ensō-ka/-sha, *n.* 演奏家／～者
performer (music).

ensōkai, *n.* 演奏会 recital; concert.

ensoku, *n.* 遠足 hiking; outing.

entai, *n.* 延滞 delay.

entaikin, *n.* 延滞金 overdue
payment.

entaku kaigi, *n.* 円卓会議 round-
table conference.

enten, *n.* 炎天 very hot weather;
entenka (de, ni) in very hot
weather.

entotsu, *n.* 煙突 chimney.

entsuzuki, *n.* 縁続き people
related by blood or marriage.

en'yasu, *n.* 円安 depreciation of
the yen.

en'yūkai, *n.* 園遊会 garden party.

enzai, *n.* えん罪 false accusation.

enzetsu, *n.* 演説 speech.

episōdo, *n.* エピソード (E.)
episode.

epuron, *n.* エプロン (E.) apron.

erā, *n.* エラー (E.) error.

erabu, *vb.* 選ぶ choose; elect.

erai, *adj.* 偉い 1. eminent (person).
2. awful.

erebētā, *n.* エレベーター (E.)
elevator.

eri, *n.* 襟 collar; lapel.

erigonomi suru, *vb.* 選り好みする
be choosy.

erinuki no, *adj.* 選り抜きの select.

erīto, *n.* エリート (E.) elite.

eriwakeru, *vb.* 選り分ける sort
out.

ero, *n.* エロ (E.) eroticism.

ero(chikku na), *adj.* エロ(チック
な) (E.) erotic.

esa, *n.* 餌 bait; animal feed.

eshaku suru, *vb.* 会釈する salute;
bow.

essē, *n.* エッセー (E.) essay.

esukarētā, *n.* エスカレーター (E.)
escalator.

esukarēto suru, *vb.* エスカレート
する (E.) escalate (expand,
increase).

etai no shirenai, *adj.* 得体の知れ
ない questionable; untrustworthy;
enigmatic.

etchi, *n.* エッチ lecherous person.

ēto, *interj.* えーと Well ...; Let me
see.

etoku suru, *vb.* 会得する
understand; grasp; master.

etsu ni iru, *vb.* 悦に入る be
gratified; be happy.

etsuraku, *n.* 悦楽 pleasure; elation.

etsuransha, *n.* 閲覧者 one who
reads for research or interest.

etsuranshitsu, *n.* 閲覧室 reading
room (of a library).

etsuran suru, *vb.* 閲覧する read
for research or interest.

F

faito, *n.* ファイト (E.) fight; guts.

fakkusu, *n.* ファックス (E.) fax;
  fakkusu de okuru send by fax.

fakushimiri, *n.* ファクシミリ (E.)
  facsimile.

fan, *n.* ファン (E.) fan (admirer).

fasshon, *n.* ファッション (E.)
  fashion.

firumu, *n.* フィルム (E.) film.

fu, *n.* 府 prefecture; **kyōtofu**
  Kyoto Prefecture.

fū, *n.* 封 seal (envelope); **fū o suru**
  seal a letter; **fū o kiru** open a
  letter.

fū, *n.* 風 1. appearance; condition.
  2. style; **wafū** Japanese style.

fuan, *n.* 不安 uneasiness; anxiety.

fuan (na), *adj.* 不安 (な) uneasy;
  anxious.

fubaiundō, *n.* 不買運動 boycott.

fubarai, *n.* 不払い nonpayment.

fuben (na), *adj.* 不便 (な)
  inconvenient.

fubi, *n.* 不備 inadequacy; lack.

fubin (na), *adj.* 不憫 (な) pitiable;
  poignant.

fūbi suru, *vb.* 風びする dominate;
  influence.

fubo, *n.* 父母 parents.

fūbō, *n.* 風貌 appearance (person);
  features.

fubuki, *n.* 吹雪 blizzard.

fubyōdō (na), *adj.* 不平等 (な)
  discriminatory; unequal; unfair.

fuchi, *n.* 縁 1. edge; brim; tip. 2.
  eyeglass frames.

fuchi no, fuji no, *adj.* 不治の
  incurable: **fuchi no yamai**
  incurable disease.

fuchō, *n.* 不調 slump; undesirable
  condition.

fuchō, *n.* 婦長 head nurse.

fūchō, *n.* 風潮 trend.

fuchōwa, *n.* 不調和 disharmony;
  incompatibility.

fuchūi, *n.* 不注意 carelessness;
  inattentiveness.

fuda, *n.* 札 1. label; tag; signboard.
  2. game card. 3. paper talisman.

fudangi, *n.* 普段着 casual clothing.

fudan no, *adj.* 普段の usual;
  casual; everyday.

fude, *n.* 筆 brush for writing or
  painting.

fudebushō, *n.* 筆不精 poor
  correspondent.

fudeki, *n.* 不出来 poor crop; poor
  work.

fudemame, *n.* 筆まめ good
  correspondent.

fūdo, *n.* 風土 natural characteristics
  of an area; climate.

fudō (no), *adj.* 不動 (の) steadfast;
  firm.

fudōsan, *n.* 不動産 real estate.

fudōsangyō, *n.* 不動産業 real
  estate business.

fudōsan-gyōsha/-ya, *n.* 不動産業
  者／〜屋 real estate agency.

fudōtoku (na), *adj.* 不道徳 (な)
  immoral.

fue, *n.* 笛 pipe (music); flute;
  whistle.

fueisei (na), *adj.* 不衛生 (な)
  unsanitary.

fueru, *vb.* 増える increase.

fuete (na), *adj.* 不得手 (な) poor at.

fūfu, *n.* 夫婦 married couple;
  shinkonfūfu newlyweds.

fūfugenka, *n.* 夫婦げんか married

fufuku, *n.* 不服 complaint; dissatisfaction.

fugainai, *adj.* 不甲斐ない gutless; shiftless.

fūgawari (na), *adj.* 風変わり (な) eccentric; odd.

fugi, *n.* 不義 adultery.

fugō, *n.* 富豪 person of great wealth.

fugōkaku, *n.* 不合格 failure (test); **fugōkaku ni naru** fail (an examination).

fugōkakusha, *n.* 不合格者 person who fails an examination.

fugōri (na), *adj.* 不合理 (な) absurd; unreasonable.

fugu, *n.* ふぐ blowfish; puffer.

fugu(sha), *n.* 不具(者) physically handicapped person.

fugū (na, no), *adj.* 不遇 (な、の) ill-starred; unfortunate.

fuhai, *n.* 腐敗 1. decomposition; rot; decay. 2. corruption.

fuhai suru, *vb.* 腐敗する 1. decompose; rot; decay. 2. become corrupt.

fuhaku (na), *adj.* 浮薄 (な) superficial; insincere.

fuharai, fubarai, *n.* 不払い nonpayment.

fuhei, *n.* 不平 complaint; dissatisfaction; **fuhei o iu** complain.

fuhen (no), *adj.* 普遍 (の) constant; unchanging; eternal.

fuhen-teki (na), *adj.* 普遍的 (な) universal.

fuhinkō, *n.* 不品行 immorality; impropriety.

fuhitsuyō (na), *adj.* 不必要 (な) unnecessary.

fuhō (na, no), *adj.* 不法 (な、の) illegal.

fuhōkankin, *n.* 不法監禁 illegal confinement.

fuhōkōi, *n.* 不法行為 illegal conduct.

fuhon'i (na), *adj.* 不本意 (な) unwilling; reluctant.

fuhon'i nagara, *adv.* 不本意ながら against one's will; reluctantly.

fuhōnyūkoku, *n.* 不法入国 illegal entry (into a country).

fuhōnyūkokusha, *n.* 不法入国者 illegal alien.

fuhyō, *n.* 不評 bad reputation or review; unpopularity.

fui ni, *adv.* 不意に suddenly; unexpectedly.

fui ni naru, *vb.* ふいになる become useless; fail.

fui ni suru, *vb.* ふいにする miss (an opportunity); lose.

fui no, *adj.* 不意の sudden; unexpected.

fūin suru, *vb.* 封印する affix a seal (to a letter).

fuirumu, *n.* see **firumu.**

fuitchi, *n.* 不一致 disharmony; disparity; incompatibility.

fuiuchi, *n.* 不意打ち surprise attack; **fuiuchishiken** surprise exam.

fuji, *n.* 藤 wisteria.

fujichaku(riku), *n.* 不時着(陸) emergency landing.

fujimi (no), *adj.* 不死身 (の) immortal; invulnerable.

fujin, *n.* 夫人 wife (of someone other than the speaker).

fujin, *n.* 婦人 woman; lady.

fujinka, *n.* 婦人科 gynecology.

fujinkeikan, *n.* 婦人警官 policewoman.

fuji no, *adj.* see **fuchi no.**

fūjiru, *vb.* 封じる confine (an antagonist); contain; control.

fujitsu (na, no), *adj.* 不実 (な、の) 1. unfaithful; insincere. 2. untrue.

fujiyū (na), *adj.* 不自由 (な) 1. inconvenient; uncomfortable. 2. impecunious. 3. physically handicapped.

fujobōkō, *n.* 婦女暴行 rape.

fujo(shi), *n.* 婦女(子) woman; women.

fujūbun (na), *adj.* 不十分 (な) insufficient.

fujun (na), *adj.* 不順 (な) changeable or unseasonable (weather).

fukahi (no), *adj.* 不可避 (の) unavoidable; inevitable.

fukai, *adj.* 深い 1. deep; profound. 2. dense. 3. intimate.

fukai (na), *adj.* 不快 (な) uncomfortable; offensive.

fukakai (na), *adj.* 不可解 (な) incomprehensible; puzzling; enigmatic.

fukaketsu (na, no), *adj.* 不可欠 (な、の) indispensable.

fukaku, *n.* 不覚 mistake; carelessness; **fukaku ni mo** by mistake; in spite of oneself.

fūkaku, *n.* 風格 style; character.

fukakujitsu (na), *adj.* 不確実 (な) uncertain; unreliable.

fukakutei (na, no), *adj.* 不確定 (な、の) indecisive.

fukameru, *vb.* 深める 1. deepen. 2. elaborate.

fukanō (na), *adj.* 不可能 (な) impossible.

fukanshō, *n.* 不干渉 noninterference.

fukanzen (na), *adj.* 不完全 (な) incomplete; imperfect.

fukasa, *n.* 深さ depth.

fukashigi (na), *adj.* 不可思議 (な) mysterious; magical; miraculous.

fukasu, *vb.* 蒸かす steam (food).

fukasu, *vb.* 吹かす 1. exhale cigarette smoke. 2. rev up (engine).

fukazake, *n.* 深酒 excessive drinking.

fuke, *n.* ふけ dandruff; **fuketori-shanpū** dandruff shampoo.

fukei, *n.* 父兄 parents; guardians.

fukei (no), *n.* 父系 (の) paternal line.

fūkei, *n.* 風景 view; scenery; landscape.

fūkeiga, *n.* 風景画 landscape painting.

fukeiki, *n.* 不景気 recession (economy).

fukeiki (na), *adj.* 不景気 (な) 1. recessionary (economy). 2. glum; uninteresting.

fukeizai (na), *adj.* 不経済 (な) uneconomical.

fuken, *n.* 父権 paternal rights; patriarchy.

fukenkō (na), *adj.* 不健康 (な) unhealthy.

fukenshakai, *n.* 父権社会 patriarchal society.

fukenzen (na), *adj.* 不健全 (な) unwholesome; immoral.

fukeru, *vb.* 老ける age; lose youthful appearance.

fukeru, *vb.* 耽る be absorbed in; indulge in.

fukeru, *vb.* 更ける (time) pass.

fuketsu (na), *adj.* 不潔 (な) 1. unsanitary; filthy. 2. dirty (person); impure; immoral.

fūki, *n.* 風紀 public morals; discipline; **fūki o midasu** corrupt public morals.

fukidasu, *vb.* 吹き出す 1. start to blow (wind); erupt; gush out. 2. burst into laughter.

fukidemono, *n.* 吹き出物 skin eruption; pimple; boil; acne.

fukigen (na), *adj.* 不機嫌 (な) morose; bad-tempered; sullen.

fukikae, *n.* 吹き変え (film) dubbing; stand-in.

fukikaeru, *vb.* 吹き変える (film) dub.

fukikakeru, *vb.* 吹き掛ける sprinkle; spray; blow.

fukikomu, *vb.* 吹き込む 1. blow into. 2. instruct; influence. 3. record (music).

fukin, *n.* 布巾 dish towel.

fukin, *n.* 付近 neighborhood; **kono fukin ni** in this neighborhood; **fukin no resutoran** neighborhood restaurant.

fukinkō, *n.* 不均衡 imbalance; **bōekifukinkō** trade imbalance.

fukinshin (na), *adj.* 不謹慎 (な) indiscreet.

fūkiri, *n.* 封切り first run; new release (movie).

fukisoku (na), *adj.* 不規則 (な) irregular; uneven.

fukiso ni naru, *vb.* 不起訴になる be dropped (legal case); be acquitted.

fukitaosu, *vb.* 吹き倒す blow down.

fukitobu, *vb.* 吹き飛ぶ be blown away.

fukitoru, *vb.* 拭き取る wipe off; mop up.

fukitsu 不吉 1. *n.* ill omen. 2. *adj.* unlucky; ominous.

fukiyamu, *vb.* 吹き止む stop blowing (wind).

fukkatsu, *n.* 復活 revival; resurrection.

fukkatsusai, *n.* 復活祭 Easter.

fukkatsu suru, *vb.* 復活する revive; resurrect; revitalize.

fukki suru, *vb.* 復帰する make a comeback.

fukkō suru, *vb.* 復興する restore; recover; revive.

fukkura shita, *adj.* ふっくらした chubby; plump.

fukkyū, *n.* 復旧 restoration; resumption of service.

fukkyū suru, *vb.* 復旧する restore; resume service.

fukō, *n.* 不幸 1. unhappiness; ill fortune. 2. death.

fukō (na), *adj.* 不幸 (な) unhappy; unfortunate.

fukō (na), *adj.* 不孝 (な) unfaithful; disloyal.

fūkō, *n.* 風光 scene; scenery.

fukōhei (na), *adj.* 不公平 (な) unfair; discriminatory; biased.

fukoku suru, *vb.* 布告する proclaim; declare.

fūkōmeibi (na), *adj.* 風光明媚 (な) scenic.

fuku, *n.* 福 good luck; fortune.

fuku, *n.* 服 clothing; clothes; **fuku o kiru** put on clothes; **fuku o kigaeru** change clothes; **fuku o nugu** undress.

fuku, *vb.* 吹く 1. blow (wind, breath); breathe. 2. whistle; play a wind instrument.

fuku, *vb.* 拭く wipe; mop; dry (dishes).

fuku, *vb.* 噴く (volcano) erupt.

fuku- 副 vice-; **fukudaitōryō** vice president.

fukubiki, *n.* 福引き lottery.

fukubu, *n.* 腹部 belly; abdomen; stomach.

fukubun, *n.* 複文 complex sentence.

fukueki suru, *vb.* 服役する serve time.

fukugaku suru, *vb.* 復学する return to school after a period of absence.

fukugen suru, *vb.* 復元する reconstruct; restore.

fukugō suru, *vb.* 複合する compound.

fukugyō, *n.* 副業 moonlighting; second job.

fukuin, *n.* 復員 demobilization.

fukuji, *n.* 服地 fabric (cloth).

fukujū, *n.* 服従 obedience; submission.

fukujū suru, *vb.* 服従する obey; submit.

fukumen, *n.* 覆面 mask; **fukumen-patokā** unmarked police car.

fukumeru, *vb.* 含める include.

fukumete, *prep.* 含めて including; **kyō o fukumete** including today.

fukumu, *vb.* 含む contain.

fukurama-seru/-su, *vb.* ふくらませる／〜す 1. blow up; **fūsen o fukuramaseru** blow up a balloon. 2. fill; **yume de mune o fukuramaseru** fill one's heart with dreams.

fukuramu, *vb.* ふくらむ swell; bloat; enlarge.

fukureru, *vb.* ふくれる 1. swell; increase. 2. pout; sulk.

fukuri, *n.* 福利 welfare.

fukuri, *n.* 複利 compound interest.

fukuro, *n.* 袋 bag; sack; pack.

fukuro kōji, *n.* 袋小路 dead end.

fukusanbutsu, *n.* 副産物 by-product.

fukusayō, *n.* 副作用 side effect.

fukusha, *n.* 複写 duplicate; reproduction; copy.

fukushaki, *n.* 複写機 copy machine.

fukushi, *n.* 福祉 welfare; **shakai-fukushi** social welfare.

fukushi, *n.* 副詞 adverb.

fukushū, *n.* 復讐 revenge.

fukushū, *n.* 復習 review of lessons.

fukusū, *n.* 複数 plural.

fukusū (no), *adj.* 複数 (の) plural; more than one.

fukutsū, *n.* 腹痛 stomachache.

fukuyō suru, *vb.* 服用する take (medicine).

fukuzatsu (na), *adj.* 複雑 (な) complex; complicated; difficult.

fukyō, *n.* 不況 depression (economic); recession.

fukyū no, *adj.* 不朽の eternal; immortal; **fukyū no meisaku** immortal masterpiece.

fukyū suru, *vb.* 普及する become popular; prevail; become widespread.

fumajime (na), *adj.* 不真面目 (な) inattentive; lazy; insincere.

fuman, *n.* 不満 dissatisfaction; discontent; **fuman ga aru** feel dissatisfied; **fuman o iu** complain; grumble.

fumanzoku (na), *adj.* 不満足 (な) unsatisfying; insufficient.

fumei (na, no), *adj.* 不明 (な、の) unidentified; unclear.

fumeiryō (na), *adj.* 不明瞭 (な) vague; unclear; incomprehensible.

fumeiyo (na), *adj.* 不名誉 (な) disgraceful.

fumetsu (no), *adj.* 不滅 (の) immortal; eternal.

fumikiri, *n.* 踏み切り railroad crossing.

fuminshō, *n.* 不眠症 insomnia.

fumitsukeru, *vb.* 踏みつける trample; insult; victimize.

fumu, *vb.* 踏む 1. step on; tread on. 2. experience; go through; **butai**

o fumu perform on the stage.

fumuki (na, no), *adj.* 不向き (な、の) unsuitable; **kodomo niwa fumuki** unsuitable for children.

-fun, -(p)pun, -bun 分 minute; **i-ppun** one minute; **gofun kan** for five minutes.

funare (na), *adj.* 不慣れ (な) unfamiliar; unaccustomed; inexperienced.

funatsukiba, *n.* 船着場 wharf.

funayoi, *n.* 船酔い seasickness.

funbetsu, *n.* 分別 discretion; thoughtfulness; **funbetsu ga aru** be discreet or thoughtful.

fundakuru, *vb.* ふんだくる 1. snatch away. 2. rip off (steal).

fundan ni, *adv.* ふんだんに abundantly; lavishly.

fundoshi, *n.* ふんどし loincloth.

fune, *n.* 舟、船 ship; boat; **fune ni noru** board or travel on a ship or boat; **Fune ga tsuku.** A ship arrives.

fungai suru, *vb.* 憤慨する be indignant.

funiai (na, no), *adj.* 不似合い (な、の) unbecoming; unsuitable.

fun'iki, *n.* 雰囲気 ambiance; atmosphere; mood.

funin, *n.* 不妊 sterility (woman).

funinjō (na, no), *adj.* 不人情 (な、の) unsympathetic; heartless.

funinki (na), *adj.* 不人気 (な) unpopular.

funinshō (no), *adj.* 不妊症 (の) sterile.

fu ni ochinai, *adj.* 腑に落ちない 1. unacceptable; doubtful. 2. questionable; dissatisfying.

funka, *n.* 噴火 volcanic eruption.

funki suru, *vb.* 奮起する motivate oneself; stir oneself.

funkyū suru, *vb.* 紛糾する result

in argument; become difficult.

funman, *n.* ふんまん indignation; ire; **funman yarukatanai** inability to suppress one's indignation.

funmatsu, *n.* 粉末 powder.

funō, *n.* 不能 impossibility; impotence; sterility (male).

funō (na, no), *adj.* 不能 (な、の) impossible; impotent; sterile (male).

funpatsu suru, *vb.* 奮発する 1. energize oneself; stir oneself. 2. spend money lavishly.

funsai suru, *vb.* 粉砕する crush; defeat; pulverize.

funshitsu suru, *vb.* 紛失する lose (have no longer).

funshitsu todoke, *n.* 紛失届け report of a missing item.

funsō, *n.* 扮装 disguise.

funsō, *n.* 紛争 dispute; fight.

funsui, *n.* 噴水 fountain.

funsuru, *vb.* 扮する portray (drama); disguise oneself as.

funtō suru, *vb.* 奮闘する make one's utmost effort.

funzen to shite, *adv.* 憤然として indignantly.

funzorikaeru, *vb.* ふんぞり返る behave arrogantly.

fuon (na), *adj.* 不穏 (な) disquieting; uneasy; dangerous.

furachi (na), *adj.* 不らち (な) unethical; rude.

fura-fura suru, *vb.* ふらふらする 1. be shaky; be unstable. 2. feel dizzy; stagger. 3. be irresolute. 4. be idle.

fura-fura to, *adv.* ふらふらと unthinkingly; impulsively.

furai, *n.* フライ (E. *fry*) breaded, deep-fried food; **ebi-furai** breaded, deep-fried shrimp.

furansu, *n.* フランス France.

furareru, *vb.* 振られる be spurned (romance).

furari to, *adv.* ふらりと without notice; casually; without planning (outing); **furari to bā ni tachiyoru** drop in at a bar.

furasshu, *n.* フラッシュ (E.) flash attachment (camera); **furasshu o taku** use a flash.

furenzoku (na, no), *adj.* 不連続 (な、の) discontinuous.

fureru, *vb.* 触れる 1. touch; **kokoro ni fureru** touch one's heart. 2. be introduced to; experience; **nihonbunka ni fureru** be introduced to Japanese culture. 3. touch upon; refer to; **jibun no kako ni fureru** touch upon one's past. 4. infringe; violate; **hō ni fureru** violate the law.

furi, *n.* 振り 1. appearance; pretense; **shiranai furi o suru** feign ignorance. 2. choreography.

furi (na), *adj.* 不利 (な) disadvantageous; unfavorable.

furī (na, no), *adj.* フリー (な、の) (E.) free or unoccupied; freelance.

furiageru, *vb.* 振り上げる fling up; raise (hand, thing).

furidasu, *vb.* 降り出す start (raining, snowing).

furieki, *n.* 不利益 disadvantage.

furigana, *n.* 振り仮名 small kana placed to the side of or above kanji to show how they are pronounced.

furikae, *n.* 振り替え alternative; substitute; **furikae-daiya** alternative train schedule; **furikae-kyūjitsu** compensatory holiday.

furikaeru, *vb.* 振り返る look back; turn around.

furikakaru, *vb.* 振りかかる befall.

furikakeru, *vb.* 振りかける sprinkle.

furiko, *n.* 振り子 pendulum (clock).

furikō, *n.* 不履行 breach (of promise); **keiyaku-furikō** breach of contract.

furikomi, *n.* 振り込み transfer; payment (into an account).

furikomu, *vb.* 振り込む transfer; pay (into an account).

furimaku, *vb.* 振りまく sprinkle; scatter; give lavishly.

furimuku, *vb.* 振り向く turn around.

furin, *n.* 不倫 adultery; immorality.

furisode, *n.* 振り袖 kimono with very long sleeves, worn by unmarried women.

furisuteru, *vb.* 振り捨てる abandon.

furitsuke, *n.* 振り付け choreography.

furitsuzuku, *vb.* 降り続く continue to rain or snow.

furiyamu, *vb.* 降り止む stop raining or snowing.

furo, *n.* 風呂 furo; Japanese bath or bathtub; **furo ni hairu** take a bath; **furoya** public bathhouse.

furōsha, *n.* 浮浪者 vagrant.

furoshiki, *n.* 風呂敷 square of cloth used for wrapping.

furu, *vb.* 降る fall (rain, snow).

furu, *vb.* 振る 1. wave; shake; swing. 2. sprinkle. 3. wag (a tail). 4. change kanji into kana. 5. assign; **bangō o furu** assign a number. 6. reject someone's advances; **otoko o furu** reject a man's advances.

furubiru, *vb.* 古びる wear out;

grow old or antiquated.

furudōgu, *n.* 古道具 used object (furniture, tools).

furudōguya, *n.* 古道具屋 curio shop.

furueagaru, *vb.* 震え上がる shudder or shiver violently.

furueru, *vb.* 震える tremble; shake; shiver.

furugi, *n.* 古着 secondhand clothing; **furugiya** secondhand clothing store.

furuhon, *n.* 古本 used book; **furuhon'ya** used bookstore.

furui, *adj.* 古い 1. ancient; old. 2. used; worn-out; stale.

furui ni kakeru, *vb.* ふるいにかける sift; screen; select the best from among many.

furukusai, *adj.* 古臭い outdated or old-fashioned (thing, idea).

furumai, *n.* 振る舞い 1. behavior. 2. treat (of food and/or drink).

furumau, *vb.* 振る舞う 1. behave. 2. treat to food and/or drink.

furumekashii, *adj.* 古めかしい outdated; old-fashioned.

furumono, *n.* 古物 curio; secondhand goods.

furumonoya, *n.* 古物屋 curio shop; secondhand shop.

furusato, *n.* 故郷 hometown; homeland.

furūto, *n.* フルート (E.) flute.

furūtsu, *n.* フルーツ (E.) fruit.

furu'u, *vb.* 振るう 1. wield (weapon); **katana o furu'u** wield a sword. 2. exert; **ude o furu'u** exercise one's ability or skill. 3. be powerful; be active.

furyo, *n.* 俘虜 prisoner of war.

furyō, *n.* 不良 1. delinquent. 2. poor condition; **eiyōfuryō** malnutrition.

furyōhin, *n.* 不良品 defective goods.

fūryoku, *n.* 風力 wind force.

fūryū (na), *adj.* 風流 (な) refined.

fusa, *n.* 房 1. bunch; cluster. 2. tassel.

fusagaru, *vb.* 塞がる 1. be closed up; be clogged up. 2. be occupied.

fusagu, *vb.* 塞ぐ 1. fill up; cover up. 2. block (road). 3. take up (space).

fusai, *n.* 夫妻 married couple.

fusai, *n.* 負債 debt.

fūsai, *n.* 風采 personal appearance; presence.

fusaku, *n.* 不作 poor harvest.

fusansei, *n.* 不賛成 disagreement; disapproval.

fūsa suru, *vb.* 封鎖する blockade.

fusawashii, *adj.* ふさわしい suitable; harmonious.

fusegu, *vb.* 防ぐ prevent; defend.

fusei, *n.* 不正 wrongdoing; unlawfulness; injustice; **fusei torihiki** dishonest dealings.

fuseijitsu (na), *adj.* 不誠実 (な) insincere.

fuseikaku (na), *adj.* 不正確 (な) incorrect; inexact.

fuseikō, *n.* 不成功 failure; **fuseikō ni owaru** end in failure.

fuseiritsu, *n.* 不成立 failure.

fuseiseki, *n.* 不成績 poor results.

fūsen, *n.* 風船 balloon; **fūsen-gamu** bubblegum.

fusenmei (na), *adj.* 不鮮明 (な) unclear; blurred.

fuseru, *vb.* 伏せる 1. lay (an object) facedown. 2. lie down; take to one's bed due to illness. 3. cast down (eyes).

fusessei, *n.* 不節制 overindulgence; intemperance.

fushi, *n.* 節 1. knot (wood). 2.

joint (human body). 3. melody.

fūshi, *n.* 諷刺 satire.

fushiawase, *n.* 不幸せ
unhappiness; misfortune.

fushiawase (na), *adj.* 不幸せ (な)
unhappy; unfortunate.

fushidara (na), *adj.* ふしだら (な)
(person) sloppy; dissolute.

fushigi (na, no), *adj.* 不思議 (な、
の) 1. mysterious; magical. 2.
strange; unintelligible.

fushimatsu, *n.* 不始末 misconduct;
mismanagement; carelessness; **hi
no fushimatsu** carelessness with
fire.

fushin, *n.* 不振 1. slump; lapse;
decline; **eigyōfushin** decline
(business). 2. loss; **shokuyoku-
fushin** loss of appetite.

fushin, *n.* 不信 distrust; disbelief;
fushin no nen o idaku to
distrust.

fushin, *n.* 不審 suspicion; doubt;
fushin ni omou suspect.

fushinjinmon, *n.* 不審尋問
interrogation (police).

fushin na, *adj.* 不審な suspicious;
doubtful.

fushin'nin('an), *n.* 不信任(案)
vote of no confidence.

fushinsetsu (na), *adj.* 不親切 (な)
unkind.

fūshi suru, *vb.* 諷刺する satirize.

fushizen (na), *adj.* 不自然 (な)
unnatural.

fushō, *n.* 負傷 injury; wound.

fushōbushō (ni), *adv.* 不承不承
(に) reluctantly.

fushōchi, *n.* 不承知 disapproval;
disagreement.

fushōjiki (na), *adj.* 不正直 (な)
dishonest.

fushōka, *n.* 不消化 indigestion.

fushoku, *n.* 腐食 corrosion; rust.

fushōnin, *n.* 不承認 disapproval;
disagreement.

fushō suru, *vb.* 負傷する be
injured; be wounded.

fūshū, *n.* 風習 custom; tradition.

fushubi, *n.* 不首尾 blunder; failure;
fushubi ni owaru fail.

fusodenrai (no), *adj.* 父祖伝来
(の) hereditary; ancestral.

fusoku, busoku, *n.* 不足 shortage;
lack; **mizubusoku** water
shortage.

fūsoku, *n.* 風速 wind velocity.

fuson (na), *adj.* 不遜 (な) arrogant.

fusōō (na), *adj.* 不相応 (な)
disproportionate (to one's means
or ability).

fusu, *vb.* see **fuseru.**

fusuma, *n.* 襖 sliding door of paper
on wood frame.

futa, *n.* 蓋 cover; cap (bottle); lid.

futago, *n.* 双子 twins.

futan, *n.* 負担 1. responsibility. 2.
burden. 3. charge.

futari, *n.* 二人 two people.

futashika (na), *adj.* 不確か (な)
unsure; uncertain.

futatabi, *adv.* 再び again.

futatōri, *n.* 二通り two methods or
ways.

futatsu, *n.* 二つ two (things); two
years old.

futegiwa, *n.* 不手際
mismanagement; failure;
clumsiness.

futei (no), *adj.* 不定 (の) uncertain;
unfixed; changeable; **jūshofutei
no hito** a person with no
permanent address.

futeiki (na), *adj.* 不定期 (な)
irregular (schedule).

futeishi, *n.* 不定詞 infinitive
(grammar).

futekinin (na, no), *adj.* 不適任

(な、の) unsuitable (position); unfit.

futekisetsu (na), *adj.* 不適切 (な) improper; inappropriate; unfit.

futekitō (na), *adj.* 不適当 (な) improper; inappropriate; unfit.

futekusareru, *vb.* ふてくされる pout; sulk.

fūten, *n.* ふうてん mental illness; madness.

futettei (na, no), *adj.* 不徹底 (な、の) partial or inadequate; not thorough.

futo, *adv.* ふと accidentally; suddenly; casually.

futō (na, no), *adj.* 不当 (な、の) unjust; unfair.

fūtō, *n.* 封筒 envelope.

futodoki (na), *adj.* 不届き (な) unmannerly; disrespectful; insolent.

futoi, *adj.* 太い 1. thick. 2. boldface (letters). 3. deep (voice). 4. brazen; rude.

futōitsu (na, no), *adj.* 不統一 (な、の) 1. divided; disunited. 2. unharmonious.

futokoro, *n.* 懐 bosom; heart; **futokoro ga hiroi** benevolent; kindhearted.

futokoroguai, *n.* 懐具合 financial condition.

futokui (na), *adj.* 不得意 (な) not good at.

futokuyōryō (na, no), *adj.* 不得要領 (な、の) ambiguous; incoherent.

futōmei (na, no), *adj.* 不透明 (な、の) opaque.

futon, *n.* 布団 futon; Japanese bedding; **futon o shiku** lay out bedding.

futoru, *vb.* 太る gain weight.

futotta, *adj.* 太った fat; plump.

futsū, *n.* 不通 interruption of traffic or telephone service.

futsū, *adv.* 普通 ordinarily; usually; generally.

futsū(no), *adj.* 普通 (の) 1. ordinary; usual; general; **futsū no hito-bito** ordinary people. 2. average.

futsugō (na), *adj.* 不都合 (な) inconvenient; troublesome.

futsukayoi, *n.* 二日酔い hangover.

futsuriai (na, no), *adj.* 不釣り合い (な、の) disproportionate; ill-matched.

futtō suru, *vb.* 沸騰する boil (liquid).

futtsuri (to), *adv.* ふっつり (と) (come) to a complete stop; **tabako o futtsuri yameru** quit smoking (permanently).

fūu, *n.* 風雨 rainstorm; wind and rain.

fu'un, *n.* 不運 misfortune.

fu'un na, *adj.* 不運な unfortunate.

fu'un ni mo, *adv.* 不運にも unfortunately.

fuwa, *n.* 不和 discordant or hostile relationship; **fūfukan no fuwa** discord between a married couple.

fuwa-fuwa-shita/-suru, *adj.* ふわふわした／〜する fluffy; spongy.

fuwataritegata, *n.* 不渡り手形 bounced check.

fuyasu, *vb.* 増やす increase; raise.

fuyō, *n.* 扶養 support; raising (children).

fuyō (na, no), *adj.* 不用 (な、の) unused; useless; unnecessary.

fuyōi (na), *adj.* 不用意 (な) careless; thoughtless.

fuyōi ni, *adv.* 不用意に carelessly; thoughtlessly.

fuyōjin (na), *adj.* 不用心 (な) careless; negligent.

fuyōjō, *n.* 不養生 intemperance; inattention to one's health.

fuyōkazoku, *n.* 扶養家族 dependent family member(s).

fuyōsha, *n.* 扶養者 breadwinner.

fuyō suru, *vb.* 扶養する support dependents; raise (children).

fuyu, *n.* 冬 winter.

fuyukai (na), *adj.* 不愉快 (な) unpleasant.

fuyuyasumi, *n.* 冬休み winter break.

fuzai, *n.* 不在 absence; **anata no fuzaichū ni** during your absence.

fuzakeru, *vb.* ふざける 1. flirt. 2. fool around.

fuzei, *n.* 風情 appeal; attractiveness; **fuzei ga aru** appealing.

fūzoku, *n.* 風俗 manners and customs.

fuzoku (no), *adj.* 付属 (の) affiliated; attached.

fuzoroi (na, no), *adj.* 不揃い (な、の) uneven; irregular.

fuzui suru, *vb.* 付随する accompany; be related to.

G

ga, *n.* 我 self; **ga ga tsuyoi** self-centered; **ga o haru** assert oneself; be selfish.

gabyō, *n.* 画鋲 thumbtack.

-gachi (na, no) がち (な、の) be inclined to; tend to; **yasumigachi** tend to be absent.

gachō, *n.* 鵞鳥 goose.

gai, *n.* 害 harm; damage; **gai ga aru** be harmful; **gai o ataeru** do harm; do damage.

-gai see **-kai, -kkai, gai.**

gaiaku, *n.* 害悪 bad influence; evil.

gaibu, *n.* 外部 1. exterior; outside. 2. others; outside world.

gaido, *n.* ガイド (E.) guide; guidebook.

gaidoku, *n.* 害毒 harm; bad influence.

gaihaku suru, *vb.* 外泊する spend the night away from home.

gaijin, *n.* 外人 foreigner.

gaika, *n.* 外貨 foreign currency.

gaikan, *n.* 外観 surface; exterior.

gaikan, *n.* 概観 overview; outline.

gaiken, *n.* 外見 appearance.

gaikō, *n.* 外交 diplomacy.

gaikōkan, *n.* 外交官 diplomat.

gaikōkankei, *n.* 外交関係 diplomatic relations.

gaikoku, *n.* 外国 foreign country; **gaikoku ni iku** go abroad.

gaikokugo, *n.* 外国語 foreign language.

gaikokugo-gakkō, *n.* 外国語学校 foreign language school.

gaikokujin, *n.* 外国人 foreigner.

gaikokukawase, *n.* 外国為替 foreign exchange.

gaikokuyūbin, *n.* 外国郵便 overseas mail.

gaikōmondai, *n.* 外交問題 foreign affairs.

gaikōseisaku, *n.* 外交政策 foreign policy.

gaikotsu, *n.* 骸骨 skeleton.

gaimen, *n.* 外面 appearance.

gaimu daijin, *n.* 外務大臣 foreign minister.

gaimushō, *n.* 外務省 Ministry of Foreign Affairs.

gainen, *n.* 概念 concept; idea.

gairai (no), *adj.* 外来 (の) from outside; foreign; **gairaikanja** outpatient.

gairo, *n.* 街路 street; avenue.

gairon, *n.* 概論 overview; survey.

gairyaku, *n.* 概略 outline; summary.

gaisan, *n.* 概算 estimate.

gaisen, *n.* 凱旋 triumphal homecoming.

gaisha, *n.* 外車 foreign car.

gaishi, *n.* 外資 foreign capital (investment).

gaishidōnyū, *n.* 外資導入 inflow of foreign capital.

gaishikei-kaisha, *n.* 外資系会社 Japanese company affiliated with a foreign company.

gaishite, *adv.* 概して generally; for the most part.

gaishoku, *n.* 外食 dining out.

gaishutsu suru, *vb.* 外出する go out.

gaisū, *n.* 概数 approximate number.

gaitō, *n.* 街灯 street light.

gaitō, *n.* 街頭 street.

gaitō suru, *vb.* 該当する apply to; correspond to.

gaiya, *n.* 外野 outfield (baseball).

gaiyū suru, *vb.* 外遊する travel abroad.

gaka, *n.* 画家 painter.

-gakari がかり (related to number of people or time) necessary manpower or time; **yonin-gakari (mikkagakari) no shigoto** a job that requires four people (three days).

gake, *n.* 崖 cliff; precipice.

gaki, *n.* 餓鬼 brat; child.

gakka, *n.* 学科 1. subject of study. 2. department; **eibungakka** English Department.

gakka, *n.* 学課 lesson(s) in a textbook.

gakkai, *n.* 学会 academic association; academic conference.

gakkai, *n.* 学界 academic circle.

gakkari suru, *vb.* がっかりする be disappointed; be discouraged.

gakki, *n.* 楽器 musical instrument.

gakki, *n.* 学期 school term; semester; **ichigakki** first term.

gakkimatsu-shiken, *n.* 学期末試験 final examination.

gakkō, *n.* 学校 school; **eikaiwa-gakkō** English conversation school; **gakkō ni hairu** enter a school; **gakkō o deru** graduate from a school.

gakku, *n.* 学区 school district.

gakkyū, *n.* 学級 class.

gaku, *n.* 額 1. picture frame; **shashin o gaku ni ireru** frame a photograph. 2. sum of money.

gaku, *n.* 学 learning; study; **gaku no aru hito** learned person.

gakubu, *n.* 学部 school; college; department; **hōgakubu** law school.

gakubuchi, *n.* 額縁 picture frame.

gakubuchō, *n.* 学部長 dean of a school.

gakuchō, *n.* 学長 college or university president.

gakudan, *n.* 楽団 orchestra.

gakudō, *n.* 学童 schoolchild.

gakuen, *n.* 学園 school.

gakufu, *n.* 楽譜 sheet music.

gakugei, *n.* 学芸 arts and sciences.

gakugyō, *n.* 学業 academic studies.

gakuha, *n.* 学派 academic group sharing common doctrine.

gakuhi, *n.* 学費 tuition.

gakui, *n.* 学位 academic degree.

gakui ronbun, *n.* 学位論文 thesis; dissertation.

gakumen, *n.* 額面 face value; **gakumendōri ni toru** take at face value.

gakumon, *n.* 学問 education; learning; study.

gakunen, *n.* 学年 1. school year. 2. grade; **ichigakunen** first grade.

gakureki, *n.* 学歴 educational background.

gakuryoku, *n.* 学力 academic achievement.

gakuryokushiken, *n.* 学力試験 academic achievement test; proficiency test.

gakusei, *n.* 学生 student.

gakuseishō, *n.* 学生証 student identification card.

gakuseiundō, *n.* 学生運動 student movement.

gakuseki, *n.* 学籍 school register.

gakusetsu, *n.* 学説 academic theory.

gakusha, *n.* 学者 scholar.

gakushi, *n.* 学資 school expenses.

gakushi, *n.* 学士 Bachelor of Arts.

gakushigō, *n.* 学士号 bachelor's degree.

gakushū suru, *vb.* 学習する learn; study.

gakusoku, *n.* 学則 school regulation.

gakuya, *n.* 楽屋 backstage; dressing room.

gakuyōhin, *n.* 学用品 school supplies.

gakuzen to suru, *vb.* 愕然とする be shocked.

gama, *n.* see **kama.**

gaman, *n.* 我慢 patience; endurance; tolerance.

gaman suru, *vb.* 我慢する be patient; put up with; tolerate.

gamen, *n.* 画面 screen; picture (film, TV).

gametsui, *adj.* がめつい stingy.

gan, *n.* 雁 wild goose.

gan, *n.* ガン (E.) gun.

gan, *n.* 癌 cancer; **igan** stomach cancer.

ganbaru, *vb.* 頑張る persevere; do one's best.

ganbō, *n.* 願望 wish; longing.

gangu, *n.* 玩具 toy.

ganjitsu, *n.* 元日 New Year's Day.

ganjō (na), *adj.* 頑丈 (な) sturdy; strong.

ganka, *n.* 眼科 ophthalmology.

gankai, *n.* 眼科医 ophthalmologist.

gankin, *n.* 元金 principal (capital sum).

ganko (na), *adj.* 頑固 (な) stubborn.

gankyō (na), *adj.* 頑強 (な) unyielding; firm.

ganpeki, *n.* 岸壁 pier; wharf.

ganrai (wa), *adv.* 元来 (は) naturally; originally.

gansho, *n.* 願書 application form; **gansho o dasu** submit an application.

ganso, *n.* 元祖 originator; founder.

gantan, *n.* 元旦 New Year's Day.

gan to shite, *adv.* 頑として resolutely; persistently; stubbornly.

gan'yaku, *n.* 丸薬 pill.

gan'yū suru, *vb.* 含有する contain.

ganzō-hin/-butsu, *n.* 贋造品 fake; counterfeit.

ganzō suru, *vb.* 贋造する fake; counterfeit.

gappei suru, *vb.* 合併する incorporate; merge.

gara, *n.* 柄 1. design; pattern. 2. personality; one's nature; **gara ga warui** boorish. 3. physical build.

garakuta, *n.* がらくた junk.

garan to shita, *adj.* がらんとした

empty (space).

garari to, *adv.* がらりと 1. abruptly; **garari to kuzureru** collapse abruptly. 2. completely; **garari to kawaru** change completely or abruptly.

garasu, *n.* ガラス (D. *glas*) glass (material); **garasu no kutsu** glass slippers; **mado-garasu** windowpane.

garasu-bin, *n.* ガラス瓶 glass bottle.

garēji, *n.* ガレージ (E.) garage.

garō, *n.* 画廊 art gallery.

gasatsu (na), *adj.* がさつ (な) coarse; ill-mannered.

gashi suru, *vb.* 餓死する die of starvation.

gasorin, *n.* ガソリン (E.) gasoline; **gasorin o ireru** put gasoline into; **gasorin ga kireru** run out of gas.

gasorin-sutando, *n.* ガソリンスタンド (E. *gasoline stand*) gas station.

gasshō, *n.* 合掌 two hands pressed together; **gasshō(zukuri)** multistoried farmhouse with thatched roof.

gasshō, *n.* 合唱 chorus.

gasshō-dan/-tai, *n.* 合唱団／～隊 chorus group.

gasshuku, *n.* 合宿 training camp.

gassō, *n.* 合奏 ensemble (music).

gasu, *n.* ガス (E.) gas; **ten'nen gasu** natural gas; **gasu-renji** gas range.

gata-gata iu, *vb.* がたがた言う whine; complain.

gata-gata suru, *vb.* がたがたする 1. rattle; quake; tremble. 2. be rickety or shaky (structure).

-gatai 難い difficult to do; **chikayori-gatai** inaccessible.

gatchiri がっちり 1. *adj.* sturdy; firm. 2. *adv.* sturdily; firmly.

gatchi suru, *vb.* 合致する agree.

gat(t)en, *n.* 合点 understanding; agreement; **gaten ga ikanai** do not understand.

gawa, *n.* 側 side; **migigawa** the right-hand side.

gaya-gaya suru, *vb.* がやがやする make noise.

gayōshi, *n.* 画用紙 drawing paper.

gazen, *adv.* 俄然 suddenly.

gazō, *n.* 画像 picture (film, TV).

ge, *n.* 下 1. lower in quality or ranking; **ge no ge** lowest quality or ranking. 2. lower position. 3. latter part.

gebita, *adj.* 下卑た vulgar; indecent.

gedatsu suru, *vb.* 解脱する be emancipated from worldly cares (Buddhism).

gedokuzai, *n.* 解毒剤 antidote.

gehin (na), *adj.* 下品 (な) indecent; coarse; vulgar.

gei, *n.* 芸 1. art or craft; artistic skill or technique. 2. (animal) trick.

gei-bā, *n.* ゲイバー (E.) gay bar.

geigō suru, *vb.* 迎合する flatter; fawn.

geijutsu, *n.* 芸術 art.

geijutsuka, *n.* 芸術家 artist.

geijutsu(saku)hin, *n.* 芸術(作)品 work of art.

geijutsu-teki (na), *adj.* 芸術的 (な) artistic.

geimei, *n.* 芸名 stage name.

geinō, *n.* 芸能 entertainment; performance.

geisha, *n.* 芸者 geisha.

gejun, *n.* 下旬 last third of the month.

geka, *n.* 外科 surgery (medical specialty).

gekai, *n.* 外科医 surgeon.

gekashujutsu, *n.* 外科手術 surgery (operation).

geki, *n.* 劇 play; drama.

gekidan, *n.* 劇団 theatrical company.

gekido, *n.* 激怒 fury; outrage.

gekidō, *n.* 激動 commotion; upheaval.

gekigen, *n.* 激減 sharp decrease.

gekihen, *n.* 激変 drastic change.

gekihyō, *n.* 劇評 review or criticism of a drama.

gekijō, *n.* 劇場 theater.

gekijō, *n.* 激情 intense emotion.

gekika, *n.* 劇化 dramatization.

gekika suru, *vb.* 劇化する dramatize.

gekirei, *n.* 激励 encouragement.

gekirei suru, *vb.* 激励する encourage; inspire.

gekiretsu (na), *adj.* 激烈 (な) violent; intense; frantic.

gekisakka, *n.* 劇作家 dramatist; playwright.

gekisaku, *n.* 劇作 drama; play.

gekisen, *n.* 激戦 (fierce) competition or battle.

gekishō suru, *vb.* 激賞する extol; praise highly.

gekitai suru, *vb.* 撃退する repel; drive away.

gekitotsu suru, *vb.* 激突する collide.

gekitsū, *n.* 激痛 acute pain.

gekkan(shi), *n.* 月刊(紙) monthly (magazine).

gekkei, *n.* 月経 menstruation.

gekkō, *n.* 月光 moonlight.

gekkō suru, *vb.* 激昂する get angry.

gekkyū, *n.* 月給 monthly salary.

gekkyūbi, *n.* 月給日 payday.

gen, *n.* 弦 (musical instrument) bow; string.

gen'an, *n.* 原案 original proposal or plan.

genba, *n.* 現場 site; scene; **kōji-genba** construction site.

genbaku, *n.* 原爆 atomic bomb.

genbun, *n.* 原文 original text.

genchi, *n.* 現地 location; **genchi-jikan** local time.

genchi-chōsa, *n.* 現地調査 field research.

gendai (no), *adj.* 現代 (の) present-day; contemporary; **gendai (no) nihon sakka** contemporary Japanese writer.

gendai-teki (na), *adj.* 現代的 (な) up-to-date; advanced; current.

gendo, *n.* 限度 limit; restriction.

gendō, *n.* 言動 behavior.

gendōryoku, *n.* 原動力 driving force.

gen'eki (no), *adj.* 現役 (の) active nonretired person.

gengai (no), *adj.* 言外 (の) implicit; **gengai no imi** implicit meaning.

gengakki, *n.* 弦楽器 stringed instrument.

gengaku suru, *vb.* 減額する cut (salary or price).

gengi, *n.* 原義 original meaning.

gengo, *n.* 原語 original language.

gengogaku, *n.* 言語学 linguistics; philology.

gengogakusha, *n.* 言語学者 linguist; philologist.

gengoshōgai, *n.* 言語障害 speech problem.

gen'in, *n.* 原因 cause.

gen'inkekka, *n.* 原因結果 cause and effect.

genjiru, *vb.* 減じる decrease; deduct.

genjitsu, *n.* 現実 reality; fact.

genjitsuka, *n.* 現実家 realist.

genjitsushugi, *n.* 現実主義 realism.

genjitsu-teki (na), *adj.* 現実的 (な) practical; realistic.

genjō, *n.* 現状 present condition.

genjū na, *adj.* 厳重な severe; strict.

genjū ni, *adv.* 厳重に severely; strictly; carefully.

genjūsho, *n.* 現住所 present address.

genka, *n.* 原価 original cost.

genkai, *n.* 限界 limit.

genkaku, *n.* 幻覚 hallucination.

genkaku (na), *adj.* 厳格 (な) stern; strict.

genkan, *n.* 玄関 vestibule; entranceway.

genkei, *n.* 原形 original shape or form.

genkei, *n.* 原型 prototype.

genki, *n.* 元気 health; energy; **genki ga aru** energetic; **genki o dasu** cheer up.

genki (na), *adj.* 元気 (な) healthy; fine; energetic; **(O)genki desu ka.** How are you? **Genki desu.** I am fine.

genkin, *n.* 現金 cash; **genkin de harau** pay in cash; **genkinbarai** payment in cash.

genkin, *n.* 厳禁 strict prohibition.

genkin (na), *adj.* 現金 (な) opportunistic; mercenary.

genko, genkotsu, *n.* げんこ、げんこつ fist.

genkō, *n.* 原稿 manuscript; draft.

genkōhan de, *adv.* 現行犯で in flagrante delicto; red-handed.

genkoku, *n.* 原告 plaintiff.

genkō (no), *adj.* 現行 (の) currently practiced or used; existing.

genkōryō, *n.* 原稿料 payment to an author.

genkyū suru, *vb.* 言及する mention; refer to.

genmai, *n.* 玄米 brown rice.

genmei suru, *vb.* 言明する declare; announce.

genmetsu, *n.* 幻滅 disillusionment.

genmetsu suru, *vb.* 幻滅する be disillusioned.

genmitsu (na), *adj.* 厳密 (な) strict; exact; close.

genmitsu ni, *adv.* 厳密に strictly; exactly; closely.

gen'nama, *n.* 現なま cash (slang).

gen ni, *adv.* 現に actually.

genpatsu, *n.* 原発 nuclear power.

genpō, *n.* 減俸 reduction in salary.

genpon, *n.* 原本 original text or copy.

genri, *n.* 原理 principle.

genron, *n.* 言論 speech; **genron no jiyū** freedom of speech.

genryō, *n.* 原料 raw material.

gensaku, *n.* 原作 original work (writing).

gensakusha, *n.* 原作者 original author.

gense, *n.* 現世 this world or life.

gensei (na), *adj.* 厳正 (な) 1. strict. 2. impartial.

genseirin, *n.* 原生林 rain forest.

gensen-kazei, *n.* 源泉課税 withholding tax.

gensen suru, *vb.* 厳選する choose carefully.

genshi, *n.* 原子 atom.

genshibakudan, *n.* 原子爆弾 atomic bomb.

genshirin, *n.* 原始林 virgin forest.

genshiro, *n.* 原子炉 nuclear reactor.

genshiryoku-hatsudensho, *n.* 原子力発電所 nuclear power plant.

genshi-teki (na), *adj.* 原始的 (な) primitive.

gensho, *n.* 原書 text in the original language.

genshō, *n.* 現象 phenomenon.

genshō, *n.* 減少 decrease.

genshoku, *n.* 減食 diet (weight reduction).

genshoku (no), *adj.* 現職 (の) incumbent; current; **genshoku no chiji** current mayor.

genshō suru, *vb.* 減少する decrease; decline.

genshū, *n.* 減収 drop in profit or income.

genshuku (na), *n.* 厳粛 (な) solemn; serious.

genshu suru, *vb.* 厳守する observe strictly (regulations, promises, time).

gensō, *n.* 幻想 fantasy; illusion.

gensoku, *n.* 原則 general rule; principle; **gensoku to shite** in principle.

gensuibaku, *n.* 原水爆 1. atomic bomb. 2. hydrogen bomb.

gentei suru, *vb.* 限定する limit; restrict.

genzai, *n.* 現在 present time.

genzaibunshi, *n.* 現在分詞 present participle.

genzai-kanryōkei, *n.* 現在完了形 present perfect tense.

genzai-shinkōkei, *n.* 現在進行形 present progressive tense.

genzei, *n.* 減税 tax reduction.

genzō, *n.* 現像 film developing.

genzon no, *adj.* 現存の living; existing.

genzon suru, *vb.* 現存する live; exist.

genzō suru, *vb.* 現像する develop (film).

geppō, *n.* 月俸 monthly salary.

geppu, *n.* げっぷ belch; **geppu ga deru** to belch.

geppu, *n.* 月賦 monthly installment; **geppu de kau** buy on the installment plan.

geretsu (na), *adj.* 下劣 (な)

contemptible; base.

geri, *n.* 下痢 diarrhea; **geri o suru** suffer from diarrhea.

gesha suru, *vb.* 下車する get off (vehicle).

geshuku, *n.* 下宿 lodgings; room and board.

geshuku-dai/-ryō, *n.* 下宿代／～料 charges for room and board.

geshukunin, *n.* 下宿人 lodger; boarder.

geshuku suru, *vb.* 下宿する rent a room.

geshukuya, *n.* 下宿屋 rooming house; boarding house.

gessan, *n.* 月産 monthly production.

gessha, *n.* 月謝 monthly tuition fee.

gesshū, *n.* 月収 monthly income.

gesu (na), *adj.* 下司 (な) base; meanspirited.

gesui, *n.* 下水 sewage.

gesuidō, *n.* 下水道 sewage system.

gesuisetsubi, *n.* 下水設備 sewage system; drainage.

geta, *n.* 下駄 Japanese wooden clogs.

getsumatsu, *n.* 月末 end of the month.

getsuyōbi, *n.* 月曜日 Monday; **getsuyōbi ni** on Monday.

gezai, *n.* 下剤 laxative.

gian, *n.* 議案 proposal; bill (legislative); **gian o dasu** propose a bill.

gibo, *n.* 義母 mother-in-law; foster mother; stepmother.

gichō, *n.* 議長 chairperson.

gidai, *n.* 議題 agenda; discussion topics.

gifu, *n.* 義父 father-in-law; foster father; stepfather.

gi'in, *n.* 議員 member of the

legislature; **kokkaigi'in** Diet member.

gijutsu, *n.* 技術 1. skill; technique; **gijutsu ga aru** skilled. 2. technology.

gijutsu-teki (na), *adj.* 技術的 (な) technical.

gijutsu-teki ni, *adv.* 技術的に technically.

gikai, *n.* 議会 national assembly; Congress; Diet.

gikei, *n.* 義兄 brother-in-law.

giketsu, *n.* 議決 (group) resolution; decision.

gikō, *n.* 技巧 technique; skill.

gikochinai, *adj.* ぎこちない stiff; clumsy.

gikyōdai, *n.* 義兄弟 brother-in-law.

gikyoku, *n.* 戯曲 drama; play.

gimei, *n.* 偽名 false name; **gimei o tsukau** give a false name.

gimon, *n.* 疑問 question; doubt; **gimon o idaku** have doubts.

gimu, *n.* 義務 obligation; duty; **gimu o hatasu** discharge one's duties.

gimukyōiku, *n.* 義務教育 compulsory education.

gin, *n.* 銀 silver.

ginen, *n.* 疑念 suspicion; doubt.

gin'iro, *n.* 銀色 silver (color).

ginga, *n.* 銀河 the Milky Way.

ginkō, *n.* 銀行 bank; **nihonginkō** Bank of Japan.

ginkōgōtō, *n.* 銀行強盗 bank robbery; bank robber.

ginkonshiki, *n.* 銀婚式 silver wedding anniversary.

ginmi suru, *vb.* 吟味する check in detail; examine.

ginō, *n.* 技能 technique; (technical) skill.

girei, *n.* 儀礼 protocol; courtesy.

giri, *n.* 義理 moral debt; obligation; duty.

giri no, *adj.* 義理の related by marriage; **giri no chichi** father-in-law.

giron, *n.* 議論 discussion; controversy; argument; **giron no mato** subject of discussion (controversy, argument).

gisei, *n.* 犠牲 victim; sacrifice.

gisei ni naru, *vb.* 犠牲になる suffer; be victimized.

gisei ni suru, *vb.* 犠牲にする victimize; sacrifice.

gishi, *n.* 技師 engineer.

gishiki, *n.* 儀式 ritual; ceremony; formality.

gishiki-teki (na), *adj.* 儀式的 (な) ritualistic; ceremonial; formal.

gishō, *n.* 偽証 false testimony.

gisshiri (to), *adv.* ぎっしり (と) tightly; **gisshiri (to) tsumeru** pack or fill tightly.

giwaku, *n.* 疑惑 suspicion; doubt.

gizen, *n.* 偽善 hypocrisy.

gizen-ka/-sha, *n.* 偽善家／〜者 hypocrite.

gizen-teki (na), *adj.* 偽善的 (な) hypocritical.

gizō, *n.* 偽造 forgery; counterfeit.

go 五 1. *n.* five; **gonin** five people. 2. *adj.* fifth; **gobanme** the fifth.

go, *n.* 碁 Japanese board game played with black and white stones.

go, *n.* 語 language; word; **nihongo** Japanese language.

gōben-kaisha/-kigyō, *n.* 合弁会社／〜企業 joint venture (corporation).

gobihenka, *n.* 語尾変化 word conjugation.

gobu-gobu (no), *adj.* 五分五分 (の) fifty-fifty; even.

gocha-gocha suru, *vb.* ごちゃご
ちゃする be confused; be
disorganized.

gochisō, *n.* 御馳走 delicacy.

gochisō suru, *vb.* 御馳走する treat
someone to food or drink.

gōdō suru, *vb.* 合同する join;
combine.

goei suru, *vb.* 護衛する guard.

gogaku, *n.* 語学 1. language study.
2. study of a foreign language.

gogatsu, *n.* 五月 May.

gogatsu no sekku, *n.* 五月の節句
Boys' Day Festival (May 3).

gogen, *n.* 語源 etymology.

gogo, *n.* 午後 afternoon; p.m.;
gogo rokuji ni at six p.m.

gogo ni, *adv.* 午後に in the
afternoon.

gohan, *n.* 御飯 meal; cooked rice;
asa-(hiru-, ban-)gohan breakfast
(lunch, dinner).

gōhō-teki (na), *adj.* 合法的 (な)
legal; lawful.

goi, *n.* 語彙 vocabulary.

gōi, *n.* 合意 consent; agreement.

gōin (na), *adj.* 強引 (な) high-
handed; pushy.

gōin ni, *adv.* 強引に high-
handedly; pushily; by force.

gōi suru, *vb.* 合意する consent;
agree.

gōjō (na), *adj.* 強情 (な)
bullheaded; stubborn; unyielding.

gojū, *n., adj.* 五十 fifty.

gojū no tō, *n.* 五重の塔 five-storied
pagoda.

gokai, *n.* 誤解 misunderstanding.

gokai suru, *vb.* 誤解する
misunderstand; misconstrue.

gokaku (no), *adj.* 互角 (の) on a
par with.

gōkaku, *n.* 合格 success.

gōkaku suru, *vb.* 合格する pass;
succeed in (examination).

gōkan, *n.* 強姦 rape.

gōkanhan'nin, *n.* 強姦犯人 rapist.

goke(san), *n.* 後家(様) widow.

gokei, *n.* 互恵 mutual benefit;
reciprocity.

gōkei, *n.* 合計 sum; total.

gōkei de, *adv.* 合計で in total.

gōkei suru, *vb.* 合計する add up.

gokiburi, *n.* ごきぶり cockroach.

goku, *n.* 語句 words and phrases.

goku, *adv.* 極く quite; extremely;
very; **goku atarimae** quite
natural or usual.

gokuhi (no), *adj.* 極秘 (の) top-
secret; strictly confidential;
gokuhibunsho top-secret
document.

gokuraku, *n.* 極楽 nirvana
(Buddhism); blissful or ecstatic
sensation.

gokurō(-sama/-san) 御苦労(様)
Thank you for your trouble.

goma, *n.* 胡麻 sesame.

gomakasu, *vb.* ごまかす 1. tell a
lie; falsify; camouflage. 2. cheat.
3. steal money.

gōman (na), *adj.* 傲慢 (な)
insolent; arrogant.

goma o suru, *vb.* 胡麻をする
flatter; fawn.

gomasuri, *n.* 胡麻すり flatterer;
flattery.

gomen (nasai) 御免 (なさい) I am
sorry; excuse me; pardon me.

gomi, *n.* ごみ garbage; rubbish;
dust; waste.

gomibako, *n.* ごみ箱 garbage can;
dustbin; wastebasket.

gōmon, *n.* 拷問 torture.

goraku, *n.* 娯楽 diversion;
recreation; entertainment;
gorakuhi entertainment
expenses; **gorakushitsu**

recreation room.

goran kudasai 御覧下さい Please look at...

gōrei, *n.* 号令 order; command; **gōrei o kakeru** to command.

gōrika, *n.* 合理化 1. streamlining. 2. rationalization

gōrika suru, *vb.* 合理化する 1. streamline. 2. rationalize.

gōri-teki (na), *adj.* 合理的 (な) practical; rational.

-goro 頃 1. sometime around (time); **ichigatsugoro** sometime around January; **ichijigoro** sometime around one o'clock. 2. toward.

gorotsuki, *n.* ごろつき rascal; ruffian.

gorufu, *n.* ゴルフ (E.) golf.

gorufujō, *n.* ゴルフ場 (E.) golf course.

gosai, *n.* 後妻 second wife.

gosan, *n.* 誤算 miscalculation; mistake.

gōsei, *n.* 合成 synthesis.

gōsei (na), *adj.* 豪勢 (な) sumptuous; lavish; luxurious.

gōseisen'i, *n.* 合成繊維 synthetic textile or fiber.

gōshigaisha, *n.* 合資会社 limited partnership.

goshin, *n.* 誤診 misdiagnosis.

goshin, *n.* 護身 self-protection; self-defense.

goshinjutsu, *n.* 護身術 the art of self-defense; **goshinjutsu o mi ni tsukeru** learn how to protect oneself.

gosho, *n.* 御所 Imperial Palace.

gota-gota ごたごた 1. *n.* trouble; chaos; **gota-gota o okosu** cause trouble. 2. *adv.* chaotically; haphazardly; **gota-gota naraberu** arrange haphazardly.

gota-gota suru, *vb.* ごたごたする be chaotic; be complicated; be crowded.

gōtō, *n.* 強盗 burglar; robber.

-goto ni 毎に every; each; **sanjikangoto ni** every three hours; **higoto ni** every day; **au hitogoto ni** every person I meet.

gottagaesu, *vb.* ごった返す be very crowded; be cluttered.

goyaku, *n.* 誤訳 mistranslation.

goza, *n.* ござ straw mat.

gozen, *n.* 午前 morning; a.m.; **gozenchū ni** in the morning; **gozen kuji ni** at nine a.m.

gozonji, *vb.* 御存知 know; **gozonji no yō ni** as you already know (honorific).

guai, *n.* 具合 1. condition; **karada no guai** physical condition. 2. propriety; convenience. 3. the way (to do something); **kon'na guai ni** in this way.

guchi, *n.* 愚痴 complaint.

gūhatsu-teki (na), *adj.* 偶発的 (な) unforeseen; accidental.

gun, *n.* 郡 county.

gun, gunbu, *n.* 軍、軍部 military forces.

gunbi, *n.* 軍備 armaments.

gunbishukushō, *n.* 軍備縮小 arms reduction; disarmament.

gunjihi, *n.* 軍事費 military expenditures.

gunjin, *n.* 軍人 soldier.

gunjuhin, *n.* 軍需品 munitions.

gunkan, *n.* 軍艦 warship.

gunshū, *n.* 群衆 crowd.

gunshuku, *n.* 軍縮 arms reduction; disarmament.

gunsō, *n.* 軍曹 sergeant.

guntai, *n.* 軍隊 military forces.

-gurai, see **-kurai.**

gurasu, *n.* グラス (drinking) glass.

guratsuku, *vb.* ぐらつく jolt; shake.

gurīnsha, *n.* グリーン車 first-class car (train).

guru, *n.* ぐる accomplice; conspirator.

gurūpu, *n.* グループ (E.) group.

gururi to, *adv.* ぐるりと (turning) around.

gussuri (to), *adv.* ぐっすり（と）(sleep) soundly.

gūsū, *n.* 偶数 even number.

gutai-teki (na), *adj.* 具体的（な）concrete (idea, plan); descriptive.

gūzen, *n.* 偶然 coincidence.

gūzen ni, *adv.* 偶然に coincidentally; accidentally.

guzu, *n.* 愚図 slowpoke.

guzu-guzu suru, *vb.* 愚図愚図する waste time; dawdle.

guzutsuku, *vb.* 愚図つく be unsettled (weather).

gyakkyō, *n.* 逆境 hardship; adversity.

gyakukōka, *n.* 逆効果 effect opposite to the one desired.

gyaku ni, *adv.* 逆に 1. on the contrary; antithetically. 2. the other way around; inside out.

gyaku (no), *adj.* 逆（の）contrary; opposite; antithetical.

gyakusatsu, *n.* 虐殺 massacre; slaughter.

gyakusetsu, *n.* 逆説 paradox.

gyakushū suru, *vb.* 逆襲する fight back.

gyakutai, *n.* 虐待 abuse (of a person, animal); **yōjigyakutai** child abuse.

gyakutai suru, *vb.* 虐待する abuse.

gyō, *n.* 行 line; **sangyōme** the third line (text).

gyōgi, *n.* 行儀 conduct; behavior; manners; **gyōgi yoku suru** behave oneself.

gyōgisahō, *n.* 行儀作法 etiquette; good manners.

gyogyō, *n.* 漁業 fishing industry.

gyōji, *n.* 行事 event; **nenjūgyōji** annual event.

gyōkai, *n.* 業界 business world.

gyomin, *n.* 漁民 fishermen.

gyōmu, *n.* 業務 business responsibilities.

gyōretsu, *n.* 行列 march; parade; line of people or animals.

gyōsei, *n.* 行政 government administration.

gyōseki, *n.* 業績 accomplishments; results; performance (business).

gyosen, *n.* 漁船 fishing boat.

gyōten suru, *vb.* 仰天する be astounded.

gyotto suru, *vb.* ぎょっとする be startled.

gyū-gyūzume (no), *adj.* ぎゅうぎゅうづめ（の）jam-packed.

gyūniku, *n.* 牛肉 beef; **yunyū-gyūniku** imported beef.

gyūnyū, *n.* 牛乳 cow's milk.

H

ha, *n.* 歯 tooth; **ha ga itai** have a toothache; **ha o migaku** brush one's teeth.

ha, *n.* 派 group; sect; school.

ha, *n.* 葉 leaf; foliage.

ha, *n.* 刃 blade; edge of a knife.

ha'aku suru, *vb.* 把握する comprehend; understand.

haba, *n.* 幅 width.

habakaru, *vb.* はばかる hesitate; withhold; refrain from.

habamu, *vb.* 阻む block; stop.

habataku, *vb.* はばたく 1. fly; flap (wings). 2. embark on a venture.

habatsu, *n.* 派閥 faction.

habuku, *vb.* 省く 1. omit. 2. cut down (cost); save.

hachi, *n.* 八 eight.

hachi, *n.* 鉢 bowl; flowerpot.

hachi, *n.* 蜂 bee.

hachigatsu, *n.* 八月 August.

hachijū, *n.* 八十 eighty.

hachimitsu, *n.* 蜂蜜 honey.

hachūrui, *n.* 爬虫類 reptile.

hada, *n.* 肌 1. skin. 2. disposition (personality).

hadagi, *n.* 肌着 underwear.

hadaka, *n.* 裸 nudity; nakedness; **hadaka ni naru** disrobe.

hadaka (no), *adj.* 裸 (の) naked; uncovered.

hadashi (no), *adj.* 裸足 (の) barefoot.

hade (na), *adj.* 派手 (な) colorful; gaudy; loud.

hae, *n.* はえ fly (insect).

haeru, *vb.* 生える grow; sprout.

hagaki, *n.* 葉書 postcard; **ehagaki** picture postcard; **hagaki o dasu** send a postcard.

hagasu, hagu, *vb.* 剥がす、剥ぐ 1. strip (the skin, etc.) from something. 2. reveal.

hage, *n.* 禿げ baldness.

hagemasu, *vb.* 励ます encourage; cheer up.

hagemi, *n.* 励み 1. encouragement. 2. incentive; motivation.

hagemu, *vb.* 励む be diligent; make an effort.

hageru, *vb.* 禿げる become bald.

hageru, *vb.* 剥げる come off; peel off.

hageshii, *adj.* 激しい 1. fierce; tempestuous. 2. crowded (traffic). 3. frequent (change).

haguki, *n.* 歯茎 gum (mouth).

hagukumu, *vb.* 育む nourish; nurture.

hagureru, *vb.* はぐれる stray or lose sight of one's companions.

haguruma, *n.* 歯車 gear.

haha, *n.* 母 one's mother; **haha no hi** Mother's Day.

hahen, *n.* 破片 shard; fragment.

hai, *adv.* はい 1. yes. 2. here (roll call).

hai, *n.* 灰 ash.

hai, *n.* 肺 lung.

-hai, -bai, -ppai 杯 number suffix indicating a counter for a glass of; cup of; bowl of; **kōhī ippai** a cup of coffee.

haiboku, *n.* 敗北 defeat.

haibun suru, *vb.* 配分する allot; distribute.

haichi suru, *vb.* 配置する 1. arrange (furniture, decoration). 2. place; station.

haien, *n.* 肺炎 pneumonia.

haifu suru, *vb.* 配布する hand out; distribute.

haigo, *n.* 背後 rear; back; background; **jiken no haigo** circumstances of an incident.

haigō, *n.* 配合 mixture.

haigūsha, *n.* 配偶者 spouse.

haigyō suru, *vb.* 廃業する 1. close one's business. 2. quit one's job.

hai'iro, *n., adj.* 灰色 1. gray (color). 2. dreary; gloomy.

haijin, *n.* 俳人 haiku poet.

haijo suru, *vb.* 排除する eliminate; remove.

haikanryō, *n.* 拝観料 admission fee (for shrines, temples, castles).

haikei 拝啓 Dear (salutation in a letter).

haikei, *n.* 背景 background.

haikekkaku, *n.* 肺結核 tuberculosis.

haiken suru, *vb.* 拝見する read; see (formal).

haiki-gasu, *n.* 排気ガス exhaust gas or fumes.

haikiryō, *n.* 排気量 displacement (car).

haiki suru, *vb.* 廃棄する abolish; eradicate.

haiku, *n.* 俳句 type of Japanese poetry.

haikyo, *n.* 廃墟 remains; ruins.

hainichi-undō, *n.* 排日運動 anti-Japanese movement.

hairu, *vb.* 入る 1. enter; go or come in. 2. join. 3. obtain; get; **okane ga hairu** receive money.

hairyo, *n.* 配慮 1. consideration; attention. 2. support.

haisen, *n.* 敗戦 defeat (in war); loss (in a game).

haisen, *n.* 配線 wiring.

haisha, *n.* 歯医者 dentist.

haiso suru, *n.* 敗訴する lose a lawsuit.

haisui, *n.* 排水 drainage.

haita-teki (na), *adj.* 排他的 (な) exclusive; exclusionary.

haitatsu, *n.* 配達 delivery service; **shinbunhaitatsu** newspaper delivery service.

haitatsu suru, *vb.* 配達する deliver.

haitōkin, *n.* 配当金 dividend.

haiyā, *n.* ハイヤー (E. *hire*) hired car and driver.

haiyū, *n.* 俳優 actor; actress.

haizara, *n.* 灰皿 ashtray.

haji, *n.* 恥 shame; disgrace; **haji o kaku** disgrace oneself; **Haji o shire.** Shame on you!

hajimari, *n.* 始まり beginning; opening (event).

hajimaru, *vb.* 始まる begin; break out; open (event).

hajime, *n.* 初め 1. start; beginning; earlier part (time); **kotoshi-hajime** earlier this year. 2. origin.

hajime kara, *adv.* 初めから from the start.

hajimemashite 初めまして How do you do?

hajime ni, *adv.* 初めに at the start; first.

hajime no, *adj.* 初めの 1. first. 2. former.

hajimete, *adv.* 初めて for the first time.

hajime wa, *adv.* 初めは at first.

hajiru, *vb.* 恥じる feel shame.

hajishirazu (na, no), *adj.* 恥知らず (な、の) shameless.

haka, *n.* 墓 gravestone; graveyard; tomb.

hakadoranai, *vb.* 捗らない make little progress.

hakadoru, *vb.* 捗る develop further; make progress.

hakai, *n.* 破壊 destruction; devastation.

hakai suru, *vb.* 破壊する destroy; devastate.

hakai-teki (na), *adj.* 破壊的 (な) destructive; devastating.

hakaku (no), *adj.* 破格 (の) exceptional; unconventional.

hakama, *n.* 袴 traditional men's trousers resembling culottes.

hakanai, *adj.* はかない 1. ephemeral; fleeting. 2. futile; empty.

hakarau, *vb.* 計らう arrange.

hakari, *n.* 秤 scale (weight).

hakaru, *vb.* 計る、測る measure; gauge.

hakaru, *vb.* 量る weigh.

hakaru, *vb.* 計る time.

hakaru, *vb.* 図る、謀る plot; attempt.

hakase, *n.* 博士 doctoral degree holder.

hakeguchi, *n.* はけ口 outlet (for anger, frustration).

haken suru, *vb.* 派遣する send (a person); dispatch.

haki-haki shita, *adj.* はきはきした lively; clever.

hakike, *n.* 吐き気 nausea; **hakike ga suru** feel nauseated.

hakimono, *n.* 履物 shoes; footwear.

haki suru, *vb.* 破棄する abolish; cancel.

hakka, *n.* 薄荷 mint (herb).

hakkaku suru, *vb.* 発覚する be discovered; be found out.

hakken, *n.* 発見 discovery.

hakken suru, *vb.* 発見する discover.

hakketsubyō, *n.* 白血病 leukemia.

hakkiri shinai, *adj.* はっきりしない unclear; uncertain.

hakkiri shita, *adj.* はっきりした clear; obvious; certain; definite.

hakkiri (to), *adv.* はっきり（と） clearly; obviously; definitely.

hakki suru, *vb.* 発揮する exert or demonstrate (one's ability, skill).

hakkōsha, *n.* 発行者 issuer; publisher.

hakkō suru, *vb.* 発行する issue; publish.

hakkō suru, *vb.* 発酵する ferment.

hakkutsu, *n.* 発掘 excavation.

hakkyō suru, *vb.* 発狂する go mad.

hako, *n.* 箱 box; case.

hakobu, *vb.* 運ぶ 1. convey; transport; carry. 2. make progress.

haku, *vb.* 履く wear (shoes or socks).

haku, *vb.* 掃く sweep.

haku, *vb.* 吐く 1. exhale. 2. vomit; spit. 3. puff.

-haku, -(p)paku 泊 overnight stay; **sanpakuryokō** three-night stay.

hakuaishugi, *n.* 博愛主義 philanthropy.

hakuaishugisha, *n.* 博愛主義者 philanthropist.

hakuboku, *n.* 白墨 white chalk.

hakubutsugaku, *n.* 博物学 natural history.

hakubutsukan, *n.* 博物館 museum (other than art).

hakuchō, *n.* 白鳥 swan.

hakuchū, *n.* 伯仲 fierce competition.

hakuchū, *n., adv.* 白昼 (in the) daytime.

hakuchūmu, *n.* 白昼夢 daydream.

hakudatsu suru, *vb.* 剝奪する deprive of.

hakugai suru, *vb.* 迫害する persecute; victimize.

hakugaku (na, no), *adj.* 博学（な、の）learned; knowledgeable.

hakuhatsu, *n.* 白髪 gray or white hair.

hakui, *n.* 白衣 white uniform.

hakujaku (na), *adj.* 薄弱（な）1. fragile; weak. 2. weak-willed. 3. insubstantial.

hakujin, *n.* 白人 Caucasian.

hakujō, *n.* 白状 confession.

hakujō (na), *adj.* 薄情（な）cruel; heartless; uncaring.

hakujō suru, *vb.* 白状する confess; admit (one's fault, crime).

hakurai no, *adj.* 舶来の imported.
hakurankai, *n.* 博覧会 exposition; exhibition.
hakuryoku, *n.* 迫力 dynamism; power.
hakuryoku ga aru, *adj.* 迫力があ る dynamic; powerful; overwhelming.
hakushi, *n.* 白紙 blank paper.
hakushi, *n.* 博士 holder of a doctorate.
hakushironbun, *n.* 博士論文 doctoral dissertation.
hakusho, *n.* 白書 white paper (official government report).
hakushu, *n.* 拍手 applause.
hakushu suru, *vb.* 拍手する applaud.
hama(be), *n.* 浜(辺) beach; seaside.
hamaguri, *n.* 蛤 clam.
hamaru, *vb.* はまる 1. fall into; be caught. 2. fit in or into.
hame, *n.* 羽目 unwelcome or unfortunate consequence.
hameru, *vb.* はめる 1. put a thing in the right place; fit; mold. 2. deceive; frame. 3. button; fasten; put on (gloves, watch).
hametsu, *n.* 破滅 devastation; ruin.
hamidasu, *vb.* はみ出す stick out.
hamigaki, *n.* 歯磨き toothpaste.
hamon, *n.* 破門 excommunication; expulsion.
hamono, *n.* 刃物 knife; cutting tool.
hamu, *n.* ハム (E.) ham.
han, *n.* 判 signature seal; stamp.
han, *n.* 半 half; **gojihan ni** at five-thirty.
han- 反 anti-; **hansen** antiwar.
hana, *n.* 花 flower; **hana o ikeru** arrange flowers.
hana, *n.* 鼻 nose.

hanabi, *n.* 花火 fireworks.
hanagami, *n.* 鼻紙 facial tissue.
hanagata, *n.* 花形 star; popular person or thing.
hanahada, *adv.* はなはだ terribly; very.
hanaji, *n.* 鼻血 nosebleed.
hanami, *n.* 花見 cherry blossom viewing party.
hanamizu, *n.* 鼻水 runny nose.
hanamuko, *n.* 花婿 bridegroom.
hanareru, *vb.* 離れる move away from; separate from; leave.
hanashi, *n.* 話 1. talk; speech. 2. tale; story. 3. news; rumor.
hanashiau, *vb.* 話し合う talk with; discuss; converse.
hanashikakeru, *vb.* 話しかける address; speak to.
hanashi kotoba, *n.* 話し言葉 spoken language.
hanasu, *vb.* 話す talk; speak; tell.
hanasu, *vb.* 離す set away from; separate.
hanasu, *vb.* 放す set free; loosen.
hanataba, *n.* 花束 bouquet (flowers).
hanatsu, *vb.* 放つ 1. release. 2. fire (a gun); shoot (an arrow). 3. emanate; emit.
hanawa, *n.* 花輪 wreath; garland.
hanaya, *n.* 花屋 florist.
hanayaka (na), *adj.* 華やか（な） dazzling; flamboyant; gorgeous.
hanayome, *n.* 花嫁 bride.
hanbai, *n.* 販売 vending; sale; **jidō-hanbaiki** vending machine.
hanbai'in, *n.* 販売員 salesperson.
hanbaikakaku, *n.* 販売価格 selling price.
hanbai suru, *vb.* 販売する sell.
hanbāgā, *n.* ハンバーガー (E.) hamburger (with bun).
hanbāgu-sutēki, *n.* ハンバーグス

テーキ (E.) hamburger steak.

hanbei, *adj.* 反米 anti-American.

hanboin, *n.* 反母音 semivowel.

hanbun, *n.* 半分 half.

handan, *n.* 判断 conclusion; decision; judgment.

handō, *n.* 反動 reaction.

handoru, *n.* ハンドル (E.) 1. handle; knob.　2. steering wheel.

handō-teki (na), *adj.* 反動的 (な) reactionary.

hane, *n.* 羽、羽根 feather; wing.

hane, *n.* 跳ね splash; **hane o kakeru** make a splash.

han'ei, *n.* 反映 reflection; **mizu no han'ei** reflection on the water.

han'ei, *n.* 繁栄 prosperity.

hanekaeru, *vb.* 跳ね返る rebound.

hanenokeru, *vb.* はね除ける push away.

hanerareru, *vb.* はねられる 1. be run over or be hit (by a car). 2. be rejected; be turned down.

haneru, *vb.* はねる 1. run over or hit (with a car). 2. reject.

haneru, *vb.* 跳ねる 1. spring out; jump; hop; bound.　2. splash.

hanetsukeru, *vb.* はね付ける spurn; turn down; repulse.

hanga, *n.* 版画 woodblock print.

hangaku, *n.* 半額 fifty-percent discount.

hangen suru, *vb.* 半減する decrease by half.

hangyaku, *n.* 反逆 rebellion; treason; betrayal.

han-han, *adv.* 半々、半半 fifty-fifty; half-and-half.

han'i, *n.* 範囲 extent; area; range.

han'igo, *n.* 反意語 antonym.

hanikamiya, *n.* はにかみ屋 shy person.

hanikamu, *vb.* はにかむ be shy.

hanji, *n.* 判事 judge.

hanjō, *n.* 繁盛 success or prosperity (in business).

hankachi, *n.* ハンカチ (E.) handkerchief.

hankagai, *n.* 繁華街 busy shopping area.

hankan, *n.* 反感 ill feelings; animosity; repulsion; **hankan o idaku** have ill feelings.

hankei, *n.* 半径 radius.

hanken, *n.* 版権 copyright.

hanketsu, *n.* 判決 judgment (court).

hanko, *n.* 判こ signature seal; stamp.

hankō, *n.* 犯行 crime.

hankō, *n.* 反抗 rebellion; defiance; resistance.

hankyō, *n.* 反響 1. echo; repercussion.　2. response; reaction; **ii hankyō** a good response or reaction.

hankyū, *n.* 半球 hemisphere; **kita (minami) hankyū** Northern (Southern) Hemisphere.

hanmei suru, *vb.* 判明する 1. prove to be.　2. become clear.

hanmen 反面 1. *n.* the other or opposite side.　2. *adv.* on the other hand.

han'nichi, *adj.* 反日 anti-Japanese.

han'nin, *n.* 犯人 criminal; lawbreaker; offender.

han'nō, *n.* 反応 reaction; response; **kyozetsuhan'nō** rejection reaction (organ transplant).

hanpa (na), *adj.* 半端 (な) 1. insufficient; incomplete.　2. odd. 3. insincere.

hanpatsu suru, *vb.* 反発する 1. defy; resist.　2. repulse; rebound.

hanran, *n.* 反乱 uprising; revolt.

hanran, *n.* 氾濫 inundation; flood.

hanryo, *n.* 伴侶 spouse;

companion; **tabi no hanryo** travel companion.

hansa (na), *adj.* 煩瑣 (な) complicated; troublesome.

hansei, *n.* 反省 1. scrutiny; self-scrutiny. 2. regret.

hansei, *n.* 半生 first half of one's life.

hansen, *adj* 反戦 antiwar.

hansha, *n.* 反射 reflection (of light, sound, heat).

hanshinhangi, *n.* 半信半疑 suspicion; doubt; disbelief.

hanshoku, *n.* 繁殖 proliferation; propagation.

hansode, *n.* 半袖 short-sleeves.

hantai, *n.* 反対 opposition; contrast; reverse.

hantai (no), *adj.* 反対 (の) opposite; contrary; reverse.

hantaisha, *n.* 反対者 opponent; dissenter.

hantai suru, *vb.* 反対する oppose; object.

hantei, *n.* 判定 judgment; decision.

hantō, *n.* 半島 peninsula.

hantsuki, *n.* 半月 half a month.

hanzai, *n.* 犯罪 crime.

hanzaisha, *n.* 犯罪者 criminal.

hanzubon, *n.* 半ズボン shorts.

haori, *n.* 羽織 short jacket worn over kimono.

happi, *n.* 法被 traditional Japanese work jacket.

happyō suru, *vb.* 発表する announce; publish; reveal.

hara, *n.* 腹 1. stomach; abdomen; **hara ga itai** have a stomachache. 2. true feelings.

harabau, *vb.* 腹ばう lie on one's stomach.

harachigai (no), *adj.* 腹違い (の) having the same father but different mothers.

haradatashii, *adj.* 腹立たしい upsetting; irritating.

hara ga suku, *vb.* 腹が空く be hungry.

hara ga tatsu, *vb.* 腹が立つ become angry.

haraguroi, *adj.* 腹黒い wicked; vicious.

hara-hara suru, *vb.* はらはらする worry; feel apprehensive.

haraikomu, *vb.* 払い込む pay through a bank or by mail.

haraimodosu, *vb.* 払い戻す refund.

haraise, *n.* 腹いせ outlet for anger or frustration.

haramu, *vb.* 孕む 1. become pregnant. 2. be filled with (danger).

hara no tatsu, *adj.* 腹の立つ upsetting.

hara o tateru, *vb.* 腹を立てる get angry; get upset.

harau, *vb.* 払う 1. pay (money, attention). 2. brush or sweep off.

harawata, *n.* 腸 intestines; bowels; guts.

hare, *n.* 晴れ fair or fine weather.

haregi, *n.* 晴れ着 one's best clothes.

haremono, *n.* 腫れ物 abscess; swelling; lump.

harenchi (na), *adj.* 破廉恥 (な) shameless; indecent; immoral.

hareru, *vb.* 晴れる 1. clear up (weather). 2. be dispelled (suspicion).

hareru, *vb.* 腫れる swell up.

haretsu suru, *vb.* 破裂する rupture; explode.

hari, *n.* 針 1. needle; pin. 2. hand (clock, watch, dial).

hari, *n.* 鍼 acupuncture.

hariageru, *vb.* 張り上げる raise

(one's voice).

hariau, *vb.* 張り合う compete; contend with.

harigami, *n.* 貼り紙、張り紙 public notice; advertisement; poster.

haritaosu, *vb.* 張り倒す knock down.

haritsumeru, *vb.* 張り詰める be tense; be anxious.

haru, *n.* 春 spring (season).

haru, *vb.* 貼る、張る paste; stick; attach.

haru, *vb.* 張る 1. stretch; spread. 2. become tense. 3. be expensive.

harubaru to, *adv.* はるばると (travel) from afar.

haruka (na, ni), *adj., adv.* 遥か (な、に) 1. far away; way back; **haruka na mukashi ni** very long ago. 2. by far; much (greater); **haruka ni ōkii** much bigger.

harusame, *n.* 春雨 1. spring rain. 2. bean noodles.

haruyasumi, *n.* 春休み spring break or vacation.

hasamareru, *vb.* 挟まれる be caught in between; lie in between.

hasami, *n.* 鋏 scissors; claw (crab).

hasamu, *vb.* 挟む hold or place between; pinch.

hasan, *n.* 破産 bankruptcy.

hasan suru, *vb.* 破産する go bankrupt.

hashi, *n.* 箸 chopsticks.

hashi, *n.* 橋 bridge; **hashi o kakeru** build a bridge.

hashi, *n.* 端 edge; end; border.

hashigo, *n.* 梯子 ladder.

hashika, *n.* はしか measles; **hashika ni kakaru** get the measles.

hashira, *n.* 柱 pillar; post; column.

hashiru, *vb.* 走る run; rush.

hashitanai, *adj.* はしたない indiscreet; shameful.

hason, *n.* 破損 damage; breakage.

hassan suru, *vb.* 発散する discharge; emanate; release.

hassei suru, *vb.* 発生する 1. break out; occur. 2. generate; breed.

hassha, *n.* 発射 firing (firearms); launching (rocket).

hassha, *n.* 発車 departure (train or bus); **hasshajikan** departure time.

hassha suru, *vb.* 発車する depart (train or bus).

hasshin, *n.* 発進 transmission; sending; mailing; **hasshin'nin** sender.

hasshōchi, *n.* 発生地 place of origin; birthplace.

hassō, *n.* 発想 1. idea; inspiration. 2. notion; concept.

hassō suru, *vb.* 発送する send off; ship; dispatch.

hasu, *n.* 蓮 lotus.

hata, *n.* 旗 banner; flag.

hatake, *n.* 畑 1. field (for cultivation). 2. field of expertise.

hataku, *vb.* はたく 1. dust. 2. spend all one's money.

hatan, *n.* 破綻 failure; **hatan o kitasu** break down.

hatarakaseru, *vb.* 働かせる 1. activate; use; **atama o hatarakaseru** use one's brain. 2. put a person to work.

hataraki, *n.* 働き 1. work. 2. function. 3. activity.

hataraku, *vb.* 働く 1. work. 2. function. 3. commit (crime).

hatashite, *adv.* 果たして 1. actually; as imagined. 2. really...?

hatasu, *vb.* 果たす accomplish; realize.

hatchū suru, *vb.* 発注する place an

order.

hate, *n.* 果て most remote point or part; tip; end.

hateru, *vb.* 果てる end; die.

hateshinai, *adj.* 果てしない endless.

hato, *n.* 鳩 dove; pigeon.

hatoba, *n.* 波止場 pier; wharf; quay.

hatsu (no), *adj.* 初 (の) first.

-hatsu 発 leaving; **nyū-yōku-hatsu no hikōki** flight leaving New York.

hatsuan, *n.* 発案 proposal; plan.

hatsubai, *n.* 発売 sale.

hatsubaichū, *adv.* 発売中 on sale; on the market.

hatsubai suru, *vb.* 発売する sell; put on the market.

hatsubyō suru, *vb.* 発病する become ill.

hatsudensho, *n.* 発電所 power plant; **genshiryoku-hatsudensho** nuclear power plant.

hatsugensha, *n.* 発言者 speaker.

hatsugen suru, *vb.* 発言する make a statement.

hatsukoi, *n.* 初恋 first love.

hatsuiku, *n.* 発育 development or growth (physical).

hatsumei, *n.* 発明 invention.

hatsumimi, *n.* 初耳 first time one hears something.

hatsunetsu suru, *vb.* 発熱する have a fever; generate heat.

hatsuon, *n.* 発音 pronunciation.

hatsuonkigō, *n.* 発音記号 phonetic symbol.

hattatsu, *n.* 発達 progress; development; growth.

hattatsu suru, *vb.* 発達する progress; develop; grow.

hatten, *n.* 発展 development;

prosperity.

hatto suru, *vb.* はっとする be startled.

hau, *vb.* 這う creep; crawl.

hayabike/hayabiki suru, *vb.* 早引け／早引きする leave early (from office, school).

hayagat(t)en suru, *vb.* 早合点する jump to a conclusion.

hayai, *adj.* 速い speedy; fast; **hayai norimono** fast vehicle.

hayai, *adj.* 早い early; **hayai jikan** early hours.

hayaimonogachi (ni), *adv.* 早い者勝ち (に) on a first-come, first-served basis.

hayaku, *adv.* 速く speedily; fast; **hayaku hashiru** run fast.

hayaku, *adv.* 早く early; soon; **hayaku okiru** get up early.

hayakuchi, *n.* 早口 speaking quickly.

hayakumo, *adv.* 早くも already.

hayakute (mo), *adv.* 早くて (も) at the earliest.

hayame ni, *adv.* 早目に earlier than expected.

hayameru, *vb.* 早める、速める speed up; hasten.

hayaoki, *n.* 早起き early rising.

hayaru, *vb.* はやる 1. become popular; come into fashion. 2. become successful; prosper.

hayasa, *n.* 速さ speed.

hayashi, *n.* 林 grove; woods.

hayasu, *vb.* 生やす cultivate (plant); grow.

hayasu, *vb.* 囃す jeer; ridicule.

-hazu 筈 1. should; ought; **kekkon suruhazu** due to get married. 2. must; **mitahazu** should have seen. 3. obviously; surely.

-hazu ga nai 筈がない 1. cannot

be. 2. inconceivable; impossible.

hazukashii, *adj.* 恥ずかしい
ashamed; embarrassed; shy.

hazukashigaru, *vb.* 恥ずかしがる
feel ashamed, embarrassed, or
shy.

hazukashimeru, *vb.* 辱める 1.
humiliate; dishonor. 2. rape.

hazumi, *n.* 弾み 1. momentum;
acceleration; **hazumi ga tsuku**
gain momentum. 2. impulse. 3.
bounce.

hazumi de, *adv.* 弾みで on
impulse; on the spur of the
moment.

hazumu, *vb.* 弾む 1. become lively;
become animated. 2. accelerate.
3. bound.

hazureru, *vb.* 外れる 1. fail; lose;
miss; **yosō ga hazureru** fail to
meet one's expectations. 2. come
off; be dislocated. 3. stray.

hazusu, *vb.* 外す 1. remove; take
off. 2. miss. 3. go away.

hebi, *n.* 蛇 snake.

hedatari, *n.* 隔たり distance; gap;
difference.

hei, *n.* 塀 fence; wall.

hei, *n.* 兵 army; soldiers.

heibon (na), *adj.* 平凡 (な)
mediocre; commonplace;
ordinary.

heieki, *n.* 兵役 military service.

heigai, *n.* 弊害 harm; ill effect.

heigen, *n.* 平原 grassland; plain.

heihō, *n., adj.* 平方 square
(measurement).

heijitsu, *n.* 平日 weekday(s).

heijō 平常 1. *n.* usual (state or
time). 2. *adj.* normal; usual;
heijōdōri (ni) as usual.

heika, *n.* 陛下 Emperor; Your
Majesty.

heikai, *n.* 閉会 conclusion (of a

meeting).

heiki, *n.* 兵器 weapon; arms;
kakuheiki nuclear weapon.

heiki (na), *adj.* 平気 (な)
unconcerned; nonchalant.

heikin, *n.* 平均 average; **heikin
shite** on the average.

heikinjumyō, *n.* 平均寿命 average
life span.

heikinten, *n.* 平均点 average
score.

heikō, *n.* 平行 parallel.

heikōsen, *n.* 平行線 parallel lines.

heikō suru, *vb.* 平行する 1.
parallel. 2. take place or exist
simultaneously.

heikō suru, *vb.* 閉口する be
annoyed.

heimen, *n.* 平面 flat surface.

heimin, *n.* 平民 ordinary people.

heion (na), *adj.* 平穏 (な) peaceful;
calm.

heiryoku, *n.* 兵力 military force.

heisa suru, *vb.* 閉鎖する close
down.

heisa-teki (na), *adj.* 閉鎖的 (な)
closed; exclusive.

heisei, *n.* 平静 quietness; placidity;
composure.

heishi, heitai, *n.* 兵士、兵隊
soldier.

heiten, *n.* 閉店 closing (shop,
office, etc.).

heiten jikan, *n.* 閉店時間 closing
time.

heiwa, *n.* 平和 peace; tranquillity.

heiwa (na), *adj.* 平和 (な) peaceful;
tranquil.

heiya, *n.* 平野 vast flatland; plain.

heiyō suru, *vb.* 併用する use
simultaneously.

heizen to, *adv.* 平然と 1.
nonchalantly; calmly. 2. without
compunction; shamelessly.

hekieki suru, *vb.* 辟易する 1. feel discouraged or overwhelmed. 2. get tired of.

hekiga, *n.* 壁画 mural painting.

hekomaseru, hekomasu, *vb.* 凹ませる／凹ます 1. make a dent or hollow in. 2. win over; beat.

hekomu, *vb.* 凹む become dented or hollow; sink.

hema, *n.* へま clumsiness; blunder.

hen, *n.* 偏 radical of a kanji character.

hen, *n.* 辺 side (geometry).

-hen 辺 neighborhood; surroundings; **konohen ni** in this neighborhood.

hen (na), *adj.* 変 (な) funny; strange; clumsy.

hen'atsuki, *n.* 変圧器 electrical transformer.

hendō, *n.* 変動 1. change. 2. commotion; uproar.

henji, *n.* 返事 answer; reply.

henjin, *n.* 変人 eccentric person.

henji o suru, *vb.* 返事をする answer; reply.

henka, *n.* 変化 change; variety; **henka ni tomu** be full of variety.

henka suru, *vb.* 変化する change; vary.

henkei, *n.* 変形 deformity; transformation.

henken, *n.* 偏見 prejudice; bigotry.

henkin, *n.* 返金 refund; repayment.

henkō, *n.* 変更 change; alteration.

henkyaku suru, *vb.* 返却する return something borrowed.

henkyō (na), *adj.* 偏狭 (な) narrow-minded.

henpi (na), *adj.* 辺ぴ (な) far-off; isolated.

henpin, *n.* 返品 returned item.

hensai suru, *vb.* 返済する pay off;

pay back.

hensei suru, *vb.* 編成する organize; constitute; form.

henshin, *n.* 変身 transformation; transmutation.

henshin, *n.* 変心 change of mind.

henshin, *n.* 返信 reply (mail).

henshinyōfūtō, *n.* 返信用封筒 stamped, self-addressed envelope.

henshitsusha, *n.* 変質者 pervert.

henshoku suru, *vb.* 変色する fade; discolor.

henshū, *n.* 編集 editing.

henshūsha, *n.* 編集者 editor.

henshū suru, *vb.* 編集する edit.

hensō, *n.* 変装 disguise.

hensō suru, *vb.* 変装する disguise.

hentai, *n.* 変態 1. pervert; perversion. 2. metamorphosis (insect).

hentōsen, *n.* 扁桃腺 tonsils.

henzōshihei, *n.* 変造紙幣 counterfeit paper currency.

henzō suru, *vb.* 変造する counterfeit; forge.

herasu, *vb.* 減らす lessen; decrease; reduce.

heri, *n.* 縁 border; edge; hem; fringe.

herikudaru, *vb.* へりくだる humble oneself.

heru, *vb.* 減る 1. decrease; lose; **taijū ga heru** lose weight. 2. wear out. 3. **hara ga heru** get hungry.

heru, *vb.* 経る 1. (time) pass. 2. go through. 3. go by way of.

heso, *n.* へそ navel.

hesokuri, *vb.* へそくり secret savings.

heta (na), *adj.* 下手 (な) poor (at); inept; **nihongo ga heta** poor at Japanese.

heto-heto ni naru, *vb.* へとへとに

なる become exhausted.

heya, *n.* 部屋 1. room. 2. sumo barracks.

hi, *n.* 日 1. sun; sunlight; **hi no de** sunrise. 2. day; **aru hi** one day. 3. times; days. 4. daytime.

hi, *n.* 火 fire.

hi, *n.* 灯 light.

hi, *n.* 比 ratio; comparison.

hi- 非 non-; in-; un-; **hikazeihin** nontaxable item; **higōhō** illegal.

-hi 費 cost; expense; **shokuhi** food cost; **gakuhi** school expense.

hiatari ga ii, *adj.* 日当りがいい sunny; sunlit.

hibachi, *n.* 火鉢 hibachi; charcoal brazier.

hibi, *n.* ひび crack; chap (skin, lips).

hibiki, *n.* 響き echo; repercussion; sound.

hibon (na), *adj.* 非凡 (な) unusual; outstanding.

hidari, *n.* 左 1. left; **hidarite** left hand; **hidarigawa ni** on the left side. 2. leftist.

hidari-gitcho/-kiki, *n.* 左ぎっちょ／〜利き left-handed person.

hidoi, *adj.* ひどい 1. inhuman; cruel. 2. bad; absurd. 3. painful. 4. violent.

hidoku, *adv.* ひどく 1. very; badly. 2. hard; violently.

hieru, *vb.* 冷える 1. become chilly or cold. 2. cool.

hifu, *n.* 皮膚 skin.

higaeri, *n.* 日帰り day trip.

higai, *n.* 被害 damage; loss.

higaimōsō (no), *adj.* 被害妄想 (の) paranoid.

higaisha, *n.* 被害者 victim.

higamu, *vb.* 僻む feel inferior; feel sorry for oneself.

higashi, *n.* 東 east.

hige, *n.* 髭 whiskers.

higeki, *n.* 悲劇 tragedy.

hige suru, *vb.* 卑下する humble oneself.

higōhō (na, no), *adj.* 非合法 (な、の) illegal.

higoro no, *adj.* 日頃の usual; everyday.

higoto ni, *adv.* 日毎に day after day.

higure, *n.* 日暮れ nightfall; dusk.

hihan, *n.* 批判 criticism.

hihan suru, *vb.* 批判する criticize.

hihyō, *n.* 批評 review; remark; criticism.

hihyōka, *n.* 批評家 reviewer; critic.

hi'iki, *n.* ひいき favoritism; partiality; patronage.

hi'iki suru, *vb.* ひいきする favor; be partial to; patronize.

hiji, *n.* 肘 elbow.

hijindō-teki (na), *adj.* 非人道的 (な) inhuman.

hijō, *n.* 非常 emergency.

hijōguchi, *n.* 非常口 emergency exit.

hijōkaidan, *n.* 非常階段 fire escape.

hijō na, *adj.* 非常な great; extreme; outstanding.

hijō ni, *adv.* 非常に very much; extremely; outstandingly.

hijōshiki, *n.* 非常識 lack of common sense; thoughtlessness.

hijōshudan, *n.* 非常手段 emergency measure.

hijun suru, *vb.* 批准する ratify.

hikaeme (na, no), *adj.* 控え目 (な、の) moderate; retiring.

hikaeru, *vb.* 控える 1. refrain from. 2. take notes. 3. be imminent (event).

hikaeshitsu, *n.* 控え室 waiting room.

hikagaku-teki (na), *adj.* 非科学的 (な) unscientific.

hikage, *n.* 日陰 shade.

hikaku, *n.* 比較 comparison.

hikaku suru, *vb.* 比較する compare.

hikaku-teki (ni), *adv.* 比較的 (に) comparatively.

hikanshugisha, *n.* 悲観主義者 pessimist.

hikan suru, *vb.* 悲観する be pessimistic; feel hopeless.

hikari, *n.* 光 light; ray; brilliance.

hikaru, *vb.* 光る 1. shine; glitter. 2. stand out.

hikeme, *n.* 引け目 inferiority complex; **hikeme o kanjiru** feel inferior.

hike o toranai, *vb.* 引けをとらない be ahead of others; be superior.

hike o toru, *vb.* 引けをとる be behind others; be inferior.

hikerakasu, *vb.* ひけらかす show off.

hiketsu, *n.* 秘訣 knack; key to (success).

-hiki, -biki, -ppiki 匹 number suffix indicating counter for animals, fish, insects, etc.; **inu ippiki** one dog; **sakana gohiki** five fish.

hikiageru, *vb.* 引き上げる 1. withdraw. 2. raise.

hikidashi, *n.* 引き出し 1. drawer; chest of drawers. 2. (bank) withdrawal.

hikidasu, *vb.* 引き出す 1. draw out. 2. foster (talent).

hikigeki, *n.* 悲喜劇 tragicomedy.

hikihanasu, *vb.* 引き離す 1. separate. 2. surpass; outrun.

hikiiru, *vb.* 率いる lead.

hikikae ni, *adv.* 引き換えに in exchange; **okane to hikikae ni** in exchange for money.

hikikaesu, *vb.* 引き返す go back; turn back.

hikikorosu, *vb.* ひき殺す kill by running over.

hikinige, *n.* ひき逃げ hit-and-run.

hikiniku, *n.* 挽き肉 ground meat.

hikinobasu, *vb.* 引き延ばす enlarge (photograph).

hikiokosu, *vb.* 引き起こす cause (problem); trigger.

hikisaku, *vb.* 引き裂く tear off; separate.

hikitoru, *vb.* 引き取る 1. take over. 2. take charge of. 3. take back. 4. go back.

hikitsugu, *vb.* 引き継ぐ succeed to; take over.

hikitsukeru, *vb.* 引き付ける attract; draw.

hikiukeru, *vb.* 引き受ける take charge of; undertake.

hikiwake, *n.* 引き分け (competition) tie; draw.

hikiwatasu, *vb.* 引き渡す 1. hand over. 2. surrender.

hikizuru, *vb.* 引きずる drag.

hikkaku, *vb.* 引っ掻く scratch.

hikkirinashi ni, *adv.* ひっきりなしに incessantly; constantly; one after another.

hikki shiken, *n.* 筆記試験 written exam.

hikki suru, *vb.* 筆記する write down.

hikkoshi, *n.* 引っ越し moving (household).

hikkosu, *vb.* 引っ越す move (household).

hikkurikaeru, *vb.* ひっくり返る 1. overturn; tip over. 2. collapse.

hikō, *n.* 飛行 flight (airplane); act of flying.

hikōki, *n.* 飛行機 airplane; **hikōki**

de by airplane.

hikoku, *n.* 被告 the defendant; the accused.

hiku, *vb.* 引く 1. attract; draw; pull. 2. subtract. 3. quote. 4. install utilities (gas, electricity, telephone).

hiku, *vb.* ひく run over (with a vehicle); grind.

hiku, *vb.* 弾く play (a stringed instrument).

hikui, *adj.* 低い 1. low. 2. short (person).

hikutsu (na), *adj.* 卑屈 (な) servile; subservient.

hikyō (na), *adj.* 卑怯 (な) sly; sneaky; wily.

hima, *n.* 暇 free time; time; **hima ga aru/nai** have time/have no time; **hima o tsubusu** kill time.

hima (na), *adj.* 暇 (な) 1. unoccupied; idle. 2. (business) slow.

himan, *n.* 肥満 overweight; obesity.

himashi ni, *adv.* 日増しに with each day.

himatsubushi, *n.* 暇つぶし killing (time).

himawari, *n.* ひまわり sunflower.

hime, *n.* 姫 princess.

himei, *n.* 悲鳴 scream; shriek; cry of distress.

himen suru, *vb.* 罷免する dismiss; fire (from a job).

himitsu, *n.* 秘密 secret; **himitsu o mamoru (morasu)** keep (reveal) secret.

himo, *n.* 紐 1. rope; cord; string. 2. procurer.

hin, *n.* 品 gracefulness; refinement; elegance.

hina, *n.* ひな 1. chick; baby bird. 2.

dolls representing courtiers.

hinan, *n.* 非難 criticism; accusation; blame.

hinan suru, *vb.* 非難する criticize; accuse; blame.

hinan suru, *vb.* 避難する evacuate; take refuge.

hinata, *n.* 日向 sunny place.

hinatabokko suru, *vb.* 日向ぼっこする bask in the sun.

hineru, *vb.* ひねる twist; wriggle; turn.

hin'i, *n.* 品位 dignity; gracefulness.

hiniku, *n.* 皮肉 sarcasm; cynicism; irony.

hinin, *n.* 避妊 birth control; contraception.

hinin hō, *n.* 避妊法 contraceptive method.

hininkigu, *n.* 避妊器具 contraceptive device.

hinin suru, *vb.* 避妊する practice birth control.

hinjaku (na), *adj.* 貧弱 (な) poor; dissatisfying; unappealing.

hinketsushō, *n.* 貧血症 anemia.

hinkō hōsei (na), *adj.* 品行方正 (な) good-mannered; virtuous; ethical.

hinkon, *n.* 貧困 poverty.

hinode, *n.* 日の出 sunrise.

hinomaru, *n.* 日の丸 Japanese flag.

hinpan ni, *adv.* 頻繁に frequently; continuously.

hinshi, *n.* 品詞 part of speech.

hinshitsu, *n.* 品質 quality of goods.

hinshitsukanri, *n.* 品質管理 quality control.

hinshu, *n.* 品種 type; kind; category.

hipparu, *vb.* 引っ張る pull; draw.

hiragana, *n.* 平仮名 Japanese syllabary for native words.

hira-hira suru, *vb.* ひらひらする flutter; wave; flap.

hiraku, *vb.* 開く 1. open; unfold. 2. hold (meeting, show, party).

hirame, *n.* 平目 sole (fish).

hirashain, *n.* 平社員 non-management company employee.

hiratai, *adj.* 平たい 1. flat. 2. simple.

hire(niku), *n.* ヒレ(肉) (E.) fillet (meat).

hiretsu (na), *adj.* 卑劣 (な) vicious; contemptible; mean.

hiri-hiri suru, *vb.* ひりひりする ache; (pain) smart.

hiritsu, *n.* 比率 ratio; percentage.

hirō, *n.* 疲労 fatigue.

hiroba, *n.* 広場 plaza; square.

hiro-biro to shita, *adj.* 広々とした spacious; expansive; vast.

hirōen, *n.* 披露宴 wedding reception.

hirogaru, *vb.* 広がる spread; extend; stretch.

hirogeru, *vb.* 広げる spread; unfold; widen.

hiroi, *adj.* 広い large; wide; spacious.

hiroiageru, *vb.* 拾い上げる pick up; select.

hiroku, *adv.* 広く extensively; widely.

hiromaru, *vb.* 広まる pervade; become widespread.

hiromeru, *vb.* 広める publicize; propagate; spread.

hirosa, *n.* 広さ width; expanse.

hirō suru, *vb.* 披露する introduce; show.

hirou, *vb.* 拾う 1. pick up. 2. find. 3. flag down (a taxi).

hiru, *n.* 昼 noon; afternoon; daytime.

hirugohan, *n.* 昼御飯 lunch.

hirumu, *vb.* 怯む be deterred or discouraged; flinch.

hirune, *n.* 昼寝 nap; **hirune o suru** take a nap.

hiruyasumi, *n.* 昼休み lunch break.

hiryō, *n.* 肥料 fertilizer; **kagaku-hiryō** chemical fertilizer; **yūki-hiryō** organic fertilizer.

hisan (na), *adj.* 悲惨 (な) woeful; miserable; pitiable.

hisashiburi, *n.* 久し振り a long interval (time).

hisashiburi ni, *adv.* 久し振りに after a long interval (time).

hisenkyoken, *n.* 被選挙権 eligibility to run for office.

hisho, *n.* 秘書 secretary.

hisoka ni, *adv.* 密かに secretly; behind the scenes.

hissha, *n.* 筆者 writer.

hisshi ni, *adv.* 必死に desperately; frantically.

hisshū, *n.* 必修 required subject.

hissori ひっそり 1. *adj.* quiet; still; motionless. 2. *adv.* quietly; secretly.

hissu (no), *adj.* 必須 (の) imperative; essential; necessary.

hitai, *n.* 額 forehead.

hitei, *n.* 否定 negation; denial.

hitei suru, *n.* 否定する negate; deny.

hitei-teki (na), *adj.* 否定的 (な) negative.

hito 人 1. *n.* person; human being. 2. *pron.* others.

hito-bito, *n.* 人々 people.

hitochigai, *n.* 人違い mistaken identity.

hito de nashi, *adj.* 人でなし inhuman; cruel.

hitogara, *n.* 人柄 personality.

hitogomi, *n.* 人込み crowd.

hitogoroshi, *n.* 人殺し killer; murderer.

hitoiki de/ni, *adv.* 一息で／～に in a single stretch.

hitokire, *n.* 一切れ one slice; one piece.

hitokiwa, *adv.* 一際 conspicuously; prominently; exceptionally.

hitomatome ni, *adv.* 一まとめに in a bundle or bunch.

hitome, *n.* 一目 (one) glance; sight; **hitome aitai** want to get a look at; **hitomebore** love at first sight.

hitome de, *adv.* 一目で at first sight; at a glance.

hitomi, *n.* 瞳 pupil (eye).

hitomukashi ni, *adv.* 一昔に many years (about a decade) ago.

hitonami (na, no), *adj.* 人並み (な、の) average; ordinary.

hitori, *n.* 一人 one person.

hitori, *n.* 独り unmarried person.

hitoriatari, *adv.* 一人当たり per person.

hitori de, *adv.* 一人で by or for oneself.

hitorigoto, *n.* 独り言 talking to oneself.

hitorigurashi, *n.* 一人暮らし living alone.

hitorikko, *n.* 一人っ子 only child.

hitoriyogari (no), *adj.* 独りよがり (の) conceited; self-righteous.

hitori zutsu, *adv.* 一人ずつ one by one (people).

hitosarai, *n.* 人さらい kidnapper; kidnapping.

hitosashi yubi, *n.* 人差し指 index finger.

hitoshii, *adj.* 等しい same; equal.

hitosoroi, *n.* 一揃い complete set; suit (clothes).

hitotsu 一つ 1. *n.* one. 2. *n.* one-year-old. 3. *adj.* same.

hitotsubu, *n.* 一粒 one grain; one drop.

hitotsuzutsu, *adv.* 一つずつ one by one (objects).

hitozuma, *n.* 人妻 married woman; another's wife.

hitsū (na), *adj.* 悲痛 (な) poignant; sorrowful.

hitsugi, *n.* 柩 coffin.

hitsuji, *n.* 羊 sheep.

hitsujuhin, *n.* 必需品 necessity; essential.

hitsuyō (na), *adj.* 必要 (な) necessary; indispensable; integral.

hitsuzensei, *n.* 必然性 inevitability; necessity.

hittakuri, *n.* ひったくり purse-snatcher; **hittakuri ni au** have one's purse snatched.

hitteki suru, *vb.* 匹敵する equal; match.

hitto, *n.* ヒット (E.) hit (baseball, success).

hiwai (na), *adj.* 卑猥 (な) indecent; obscene; lewd.

hiya-hiya suru, *vb.* ひやひやする feel scared; feel nervous.

hiyakasu, *vb.* 冷やかす ridicule; mock; tease.

hiyake, *n.* 日焼け sunburn; suntan.

hiyakedome, *n.* 日焼け止め sunscreen (lotion).

hiyasu, *vb.* 冷やす chill; cool.

hiyō, *n.* 費用 cost; expense.

hiyoko, *n.* ひよこ chick.

hiyorimishugi, *n.* 日和見主義 opportunism.

hiyu, *n.* 比喩 simile; metaphor.

hiza, *n.* 膝 1. knee. 2. lap.

hizuke, *n.* 日付 date (calendar).

hizumi, *n.* 歪み distortion; contortion; warp.

hō, *n.* 頬 cheek.

hō, *n.* 法 1. law. 2. method.

hō 方 1. *n.* direction; side; **migi no hō ni** on the right side. 2. *conj.* (better, bigger, closer, etc.) than; **Kochira no hō ga achira yori ii.** This is better than that.

-ho, -(p)po 歩 step; **ippo** one step; **sanpo** three steps; **goho** five steps.

hōan, *n.* 法案 legislation.

hōbi, *n.* 褒美 reward; **hōbi o ageru (morau)** give (receive) a reward.

hobo, *adv.* ほぼ almost; about.

hōchō, *n.* 包丁 kitchen knife.

hochōki, *n.* 補聴器 hearing aid.

-hōdai 放題 without restriction or control; **tabehōdai** all you can eat.

hodo, *parti.* 程 1. about; **gonin hodo** about five people. 2. (comparison) not as ... as; **Kore wa are hodo yokunai.** This is not as good as that. 3. to (a ... degree); **shinu hodo suki** love someone desperately.

hodō, *n.* 歩道 sidewalk.

hōdō, *n.* 報道 public news or report; **hōdōkikan** the news media.

hodokeru, *vb.* 解ける come loose.

hodoku, *vb.* 解く untie; loosen.

hoeru, *vb.* 吠える howl; bark.

hōfu (na), *adj.* 豊富 (な) abundant; full of.

hōfuku suru, *vb.* 報復する retaliate; revenge.

hōgai (na), *adj.* 法外 (な) exorbitant; outrageous.

hōgaku, *n.* 邦楽 traditional Japanese music.

hōgaku, *n.* 法学 law (study of).

hōgaku, *n.* 方角 route; direction.

hogaraka (na), *adj.* 朗らか (な) happy; cheerful.

hōgen, *n.* 方言 dialect.

hogo, *n.* 保護 protection; care; **shizenhogo** environmental protection.

hogobōeki, *n.* 保護貿易 protectionist trade.

hogosha, *n.* 保護者 protector; guardian.

hogo suru, *vb.* 保護する protect; guard; take care of.

hohei, *n.* 歩兵 infantryman.

hōhige, *n.* 頬髭 whiskers.

hoho, *n.* 頬 cheek.

hōhō, *n.* 方法 method; way; means.

hohoemashii, *adj.* 微笑ましい heartwarming.

hohoemi, *n.* 微笑み smile.

hohoemu, *vb.* 微笑む smile.

hoikuen, *n.* 保育園 day-care center; nursery school.

hojikuru, *vb.* ほじくる 1. dig around in. 2. pry into.

hōjin, *n.* 邦人 Japanese national abroad.

hōjin, *n.* 法人 corporation; **hōjin-zei** corporate tax.

hojo, *n.* 補助 subsidy; aid; support.

hojū suru, *vb.* 補充する supplement; fill up.

hoka, *n.* 他、外 another person, object, or place.

hōka, *n.* 放火 arson.

hōkago (ni), *adv.* 放課後 (に) after school.

hōkai suru, *vb.* 崩壊する fall; collapse.

hokaku suru, *vb.* 捕獲する capture (animal).

hoka ni 他に 1. *adv.* as well as; besides; **kono hoka ni** besides this. 2. *n.* anything or anyone else; **Hoka ni nani ka o-iri desu**

ka. Do you need anything else?

hoka no, *adj.* 他の another; other; some or any other.

hokan suru, *vb.* 保管する keep a close watch over; take good care of.

hōkatsu-teki (na), *adj.* 包括的 (な) inclusive; all-encompassing.

hoka wa, *prep.* 他は other than; except.

hōkei, *n.* 包茎 uncircumcised penis.

hoken, *n.* 保険 insurance; **kokumin-kenkōhoken** national health insurance; **seimei hoken** life insurance.

hōken jidai, *n.* 封建時代 feudal period.

hōken-teki na, *adj.* 封建的 (な) 1. feudalistic. 2. out-of-date.

hoketsu, *n.* 補欠 (person) alternate; substitute.

hōki, *n.* 箒 broom.

hōki, *n.* 法規 law; regulation.

hokinsha, *n.* 保菌者 disease carrier.

hōki suru, *vb.* 放棄する give up; renounce.

hokkinin, *n.* 発起人 initiator; promoter.

hokkyoku, *n.* 北極 Arctic; North Pole.

hokkyokusei, *n.* 北極星 North Star; Polaris; polestar.

hokō, *n.* 歩行 walking.

hōkō, *n.* 方向 direction; **hōkō-kankaku** sense of direction.

hokōki, *n.* 歩行器 walker (for a baby).

hōkoku, *n.* 報告 report.

hōkoku suru, *vb.* 報告する report.

hokori, *n.* 誇り pride; dignity; self-esteem.

hokori, *n.* 埃 dust.

hokoru, *vb.* 誇る take pride in.

hokōsha, *n.* 歩行者 pedestrian.

hokubei, *n.* 北米 North America.

hokui, *n.* 北緯 northern latitudes; **hokui yonjūdo** 40 degrees north latitude.

hokuō, *n.* 北欧 northern Europe.

hokuro, *n.* ほくろ mole (on the skin).

hokusei, *n.* 北西 northwest.

hokutō, *n.* 北東 northeast.

hokyō suru, *vb.* 補強する strengthen; reinforce.

hōkyū, *n.* 俸給 salary.

hokyū suru, *vb.* 補給する supplement; supply; replenish.

homare, *n.* 誉れ honor; distinction.

hōmen, *n.* 方面 area; region; direction.

hōmen suru, *vb.* 放免する acquit; release; let loose.

homeru, *vb.* 褒める、賞める praise; compliment; admire.

hōmon, *n.* 訪問 visit.

hōmu, *n.* ホーム (F. *plateforme*) platform (station).

hōmu ran, *n.* ホームラン (E.) home run.

hōmuru, *vb.* 葬る bury; suppress.

hōmushikku, *n.* ホームシック (E.) homesickness; **hōmushikku ni kakaru/naru** be homesick/ become homesick.

hōmushō, *n.* 法務省 Ministry of Justice.

hōmu-sutei, *n.* ホームステイ (E.) home stay (staying abroad at someone's home).

hon, *n.* 本 book; **hon ni-satsu** two books.

-hon, -bon, -ppon 本 number suffix indicating a counter for long things (bottles, fingers, flowers, neckties, rope, etc.); **bara gohon**

five roses.

honbako, *n.* 本箱 bookcase.

honbu, *n.* 本部 headquarters; main office.

hondana, *n.* 本棚 bookshelf.

hondo, *n.* 本土 mainland.

hone, *n.* 骨 1. bone. 2. rib (umbrella); frame (shoji screen). 3. difficulty.

hone no oreru, *adj.* 骨の折れる arduous.

hone o oru, *vb.* 骨を折る 1. break a bone. 2. toil; make an effort.

hongoku, *n.* 本国 native country.

hōnin suru, *vb.* 放任する give free rein; leave a person to himself or herself.

honjitsu, *n.* 本日 this day; today.

honkaku-teki (na), *adj.* 本格的 (な) 1. authentic; real. 2. full-scale.

honke, *n.* 本家 1. progenitor 2. main branch of a family.

honki de, *adv.* 本気で seriously; earnestly.

honkyo, *n.* 本拠 base; headquarters.

honmō, *n.* 本望 longing; wish.

honmono, *n.* 本物 real or genuine article.

honmyō, *n.* 本名 real name.

hon'ne, *n.* 本音 true feelings.

hon'nin, *n.* 本人 person in question; himself or herself.

hon no, *adj.* ほんの mere; only; just.

hon'nō, *n.* 本能 instinct.

hon'nō-teki ni, *adv.* 本能的に instinctively.

honobono to shita, *adj.* ほのぼのとした heartwarming.

honoka (na), *adj.* 仄か (な) faint; dim; slight.

honomekasu, *vb.* 仄めかす hint;

insinuate; suggest.

hono'o, *n.* 炎 blaze; flame.

honpō (na), *adj.* 奔放 (な) unrestrained; free; wild.

honrai (wa), *adv.* 本来 (は) originally; by nature.

honrō suru, *vb.* 翻弄する toy with; trifle with.

honrui, *n.* 本塁 home plate (baseball).

honryō, *n.* 本領 expertise (talent, skill); **honryō o hakki suru** use one's talent (expertise).

honryū, *n.* 本流 mainstream.

honsai, *n.* 本妻 legal wife.

honsei, *n.* 本姓 real surname.

honsekichi, *n.* 本籍地 permanent address.

honsha, *n.* 本社 head or main office.

honshiki (na, no), *adj.* 本式 (な、の) formal; orthodox.

honshin, *n.* 本心 true intentions; conscience.

honshitsu, *n.* 本質 true nature; essence; substance.

honshitsu-teki (na), *adj.* 本質的 (な) essential; substantial.

honshō, *n.* 本性 one's true character.

honshū, *n.* 本州 Honshu (Japan's main island).

hontō (no), *adj.* 本当 (の) real; true; genuine.

hontō ni, *adv.* 本当に 1. really; truly; genuinely. 2. terribly; **Hontō ni sumimasen.** I am terribly sorry.

hontō wa, *adv.* 本当は in reality; to tell the truth.

hon'ya, *n.* 本屋 bookstore.

hon'yaku, *n.* 翻訳 translation.

honyūbin, *n.* 哺乳瓶 baby's bottle.

hō'ō, *n.* 鳳凰 phoenix (from

ancient Chinese mythology).

hō'ō, *n.* 法王 Pope.

hōpu, *n.* ホープ (E.) hope; plan; aspiration.

hora, *n.* 法螺 exaggeration; tall tale; **hora o fuku** tell a tall tale.

hora, *interj.* ほら Look! See! Listen!

hōrei, *n.* 法令 law.

hōrensō, *n.* ほうれんそう spinach.

horegusuri, *n.* 惚れ薬 love potion; aphrodisiac.

horeru, *vb.* 惚れる fall in love; be attracted to.

hori, *n.* 堀 moat; canal.

hōritsu, *n.* 法律 law.

hōritsu ihan (no), *adj.* 法律違反 (の) illegal.

hōritsu jimusho, *n.* 法律事務所 law firm.

horobiru, *vb.* 滅びる perish; be ruined.

horobosu, *vb.* 滅ぼす ruin; destroy.

hōrō suru, *vb.* 放浪する wander.

horu, *vb.* 掘る dig.

horu, *vb.* 彫る engrave; carve; chisel.

horyo, *n.* 捕虜 prisoner of war; captive.

horyū suru, *vb.* 保留する withhold; suspend.

hōseki, *n.* 宝石 precious; jewel.

hoshakukin, *n.* 保釈金 bail (money).

hoshaku suru, *vb.* 保釈する release on bail.

hōshanō, *n.* 放射能 radioactivity.

hōshanōosen, *n.* 放射能汚染 radioactive contamination.

hōshaseihaikibutsu, *n.* 放射性廃棄物 radioactive waste.

hoshi, *n.* 星 star.

hōshi, *n.* 奉仕 service.

hoshii, *vb.* 欲しい want; yearn for.

hōshiki, *n.* 方式 1. methodology;

method; formula. 2. style.

hōshin, *n.* 方針 policy; principle; direction.

hoshinjutsu, *n.* 保身術 self-defense technique.

hoshi uranai, *n.* 星占い astrology.

hoshō, *n.* 保証 warranty; guarantee; assurance.

hoshō, *n.* 補償 compensation.

hoshōkin, *n.* 補償金 compensation (monetary).

hōshū, *n.* 報酬 1. reward. 2. remuneration.

hoshu-teki (na), *adj.* 保守的 (な) conservative.

hōsō, *n.* 放送 broadcast.

hōsō, *n.* 包装 wrapping.

hosoi, *adj.* 細い 1. thin; narrow; slim. 2. small; flimsy; **hosoi koe** small voice.

hosoku, *n.* 補足 supplement; appendix.

hōsōshi, *n.* 包装紙 wrapping paper.

hossa, *n.* 発作 attack; fit; **shinzō-hossa** heart attack; **hossa o okosu** have a fit (attack).

hossa-teki ni, *adv.* 発作的に fitfully; impulsively.

hossuru, *vb.* 欲する want; crave.

hosu, *vb.* 干す dry; air.

hōtai, *n.* 包帯 bandage.

hotategai, *n.* 帆立て貝 scallop.

hotchikisu, *n.* ホッチキス (E. *Hotchkiss* and Co.) stapler.

hōtei, *n.* 法廷 court of law.

hoteru, *n.* ホテル (E.) hotel.

hōtō, *n.* 放蕩 prodigality; debauchery.

hotoke, *n.* 仏 1. Buddha. 2. deceased person; **hotoke ni naru** die.

hotondo, *adv.* ほとんど almost; nearly; **hotondo owatta** almost finished.

hotteoku, *vb.* ほつておく leave alone; let alone; neglect.

hotto suru, *vb.* ほつとする feel relieved; relax.

hōyōryoku, *n.* 包容力 bigheartedness; magnanimity; **hōyōryoku ga aru** bighearted; magnanimous.

hōyō suru, *vb.* 抱擁する embrace; hug.

hozon, *n.* 保存 preservation.

hyakkajiten, *n.* 百科辞典 encyclopedia.

hyakkaten, *n.* 百貨店 department store.

hyaku, *n.* 百 hundred; **gohyaku** five hundred.

hyakuman, *n.* 百万 million.

hyakushō, *n.* 百姓 farmer.

hyō, *n.* 表 list; chart.

hyō, *n.* 票 vote.

hyōban, *n.* 評判 1. reputation 2. popularity; **hyōban ga ii** popular. 3. rumor.

hyōdai, *n.* 表題、標題 title.

hyōgen, *n.* 表現 expression; **hyōgen no jiyū** freedom of expression.

hyōgen suru, *vb.* 表現する express; describe.

hyōgo, *n.* 標語 slogan; catchphrase.

hyōhakuzai, *n.* 漂白剤 bleach.

hyōhon, *n.* 標本 specimen; sample.

hyōji suru, *vb.* 表示する indicate; express.

hyōjō, *n.* 表情 expression.

hyōjun, *n.* 標準 standard; average.

hyōjungo, *n.* 標準語 standard language.

hyōka, *n.* 評価 assessment; evaluation.

hyōkin (na), *adj.* ひようきん (な) funny; comical.

hyōmen, *n.* 表面 surface; exterior.

hyōmen-teki (na), *adj.* 表面的 (な) superficial; shallow.

hyōron, *n.* 評論 criticism; review.

hyōronka, *n.* 評論家 critic; reviewer; commentator; analyst; **keizai-hyōronka** economic critic or analyst.

hyōsatsu, *n.* 表札 nameplate (outside a residence).

hyōsetsu, *n.* 剽窃 plagiarism.

hyōshi, *n.* 表紙 cover (book, magazine).

hyōshiki, *n.* 標識 sign (board).

hyōteki, *n.* 標的 target.

hyotto, *adv.* ひよつと by chance; without planning or anticipation.

hyotto shitara, *adv.* ひよつとしたら 1. perhaps. 2. by some chance.

hyōzan, *n.* 氷山 iceberg; **hyōzan no ikkaku** tip of the iceberg.

I

i, *n.* 胃 stomach.

-i 位 rank; place (competition); **ichii** first place.

ibaru, *vb.* 威張る 1. be aloof; look down on. 2. brag about.

ibiki, *n.* いびき snoring.

ibiru, *vb.* いびる harass; abuse; treat harshly.

ibitsu (na), *adj.* いびつ (な) warped; distorted.

ibo, *n.* いぼ wart.

ibokyōdai, *n.* 異母兄弟 half-brother or half-sister (by a different mother).

ibukaru, *vb.* 訝かる suspect; doubt.

ichi, *n.* 位置 position; location; situation.

ichi, *n.* 市 fair; market; **kyoei no ichi** *Vanity Fair* (the novel).

ichi, *n.* 一 one; number one; beginning.

ichiba, *n.* 市場 market.

ichiban 一番 1. *n.* the first; the best. 2. *adj.* number one; first; best. 3. *adv.* most; best; **ichiban taisetsu** most precious.

ichibu(bun), *n.* 一部(分) part; section.

ichidan to, *adv.* 一段と better (worse, more, less, etc.) than usual (or before); especially; all the more; **ichidan to kirei** more beautiful than usual (or before).

ichido, *adv.* 一度 once; at one time; **ichido ni** all at once.

ichigatsu, *n.* 一月 January.

ichigo, *n.* 苺 strawberry.

ichi-ichi, *adv.* いちいち 1. one by one. 2. in every case. 3. in detail.

ichijirushii, *adj.* 著しい remarkable; conspicuous.

ichiji-teki (na), *adj.* 一時的 (な) temporary; transient.

ichiji-teki ni, *adv.* 一時的に temporarily; for the moment.

ichimai, *n.* 一枚 one sheet (paper); one slice.

ichimen, *n.* 一面 1. one side. 2. entire surface.

ichimonnashi (no), *adj.* 一文無し (の) penniless.

ichinen, *n.* 一年 one year; **ichinenkan** for one year; **ichinenjū** all year round.

ichinensei, *n.* 一年生 freshman;

first grader.

ichinichi, *n.* 一日 one day; **ichinichijū** all day long.

ichininmae, *n.* 一人前 one serving

ichininmae (no), *adj.* 一人前 (の) grown-up; full-fledged.

-ichi no 一の (superlative indicator) first, best, etc.; **sekaiichi no kanemochi** the richest person in the world.

ichiren, *n.* 一連 series.

ichiryū (no), *adj.* 一流 (の) first-rate.

ichō, *n.* 銀杏 ginkgo (tree).

idai (na), *adj.* 偉大 (な) great; grand.

idaku, *vb.* 抱く 1. embrace; hold. 2. entertain (idea).

iden, *n.* 遺伝 heredity.

idenshi, *n.* 遺伝子 gene.

ideorogī, *n.* イデオロギー (G. *Ideologie*) ideology.

ido, *n.* 井戸 (water) well.

ido, *n.* 緯度 latitude.

idokoro, *n.* 居所 one's whereabouts or address.

idomu, *vb.* 挑む challenge.

idō suru, *vb.* 移動する move.

ie, *n.* 家 1. home; house. 2. family.

iede suru, *vb.* 家出する run away from home.

iedomo いえども 1. *conj.* although; however. 2. *adv.* even.

iegara, *n.* 家柄 one's lineage or family background.

iemoto, *n.* 家元 head or headquarters of a particular school of art.

ifuku, *n.* 衣服 clothing.

-igai 以外 except (for); other than.

igai (na), *adj.* 意外 (な) unexpected.

igai ni, *adv.* 意外に unexpectedly.

igaku, *n.* 医学 medicine.

igan, *n.* 胃癌 stomach cancer.

igata, *n.* 鋳型 mold; cast.

igen, *n.* 威厳 dignity.

igi, *n.* 意義 significance.

igi, *n.* 異議 objection; **igi ga aru** have an objection.

igirisu, *n.* イギリス England.

igirisujin, *n.* イギリス人 English man/woman.

igo, *n.* 囲碁 see **go.**

igo 以後 1. *prep.* after; since. 2. *adv.* from now on.

igokochi, *n.* 居心地 the way one feels in a particular ambience; **igokochi ga ii** cozy.

ihan, *n.* 違反 violation; illegality; offense; **chūshaihan** parking violation.

ihan suru, *vb.* 違反する break the law; commit an offense.

ihen, *n.* 異変 accident; calamity.

ihō (no), *adj.* 違法 (の) illegal.

ii, *adj.* 良い 1. good; fine. 2. appropriate; right. 3. beneficial.

ii いい 1. *adj.* enough. 2. *vb.* can do; may do; **kaette mo ii** can go back. 3. *vb.* would like to do; prefer.

iiai, *n.* 言い合い argument; quarrel.

iiarawasu, *vb.* 言い表わす express; narrate.

iibun, *n.* 言い分 spoken opinion.

iie, *interj.* いいえ No!

iifurasu, *vb.* 言い触らす spread a rumor.

iiharu, *vb.* 言い張る insist.

iikaeru, *vb.* 言い換える paraphrase.

ii kagen (na), *adj.* 好い加減 (な) 1. unreliable; unsubstantial. 2. proper.

iin, *n.* 医院 clinic; physician's office.

iin, *n.* 委員 committee member.

iinazuke, *n.* 許嫁、許婚 fiancé; fiancée.

iinchō, *n.* 委員長 chairperson.

iinkai, *n.* 委員会 committee.

iinogare, *n.* 言い逃れ pretext.

iitsukeru, *vb.* 言いつける 1. tell. 2. teil on; inform.

iitsutae, *n.* 言い伝え legend.

iiwake, *n.* 言い訳 excuse.

iiwake suru, *vb.* 言い訳する make excuses.

iiwatasu, *vb.* 言い渡す deliver (a sentence); order.

iji, *n.* 意地 1. stubbornness; **iji o haru** be stubborn. 2. pride. 3. courage.

iji, *n.* 維持 maintenance.

ijihi, *n.* 維持費 maintenance costs.

ijime, *n.* いじめ bullying; abuse.

ijimeru, *vb.* いじめる bully; abuse.

ijippari, *n., adj.* 意地っ張り stubborn (person).

ijin, *n.* 偉人 exceptional person.

ijiru, *vb.* いじる handle; touch.

iji suru, *vb.* 維持する maintain.

ijiwaru (na, no), *adj.* 意地悪 (な、の) mean; nasty.

ijō 以上 1. *prep.* not less than. 2. *conj.* now that.

ijō (na), *adj.* 異常 (な) abnormal; bizarre.

ijū suru, *vb.* 移住する immigrate; emigrate.

ika, *n.* いか squid; cuttlefish.

ika 以下 1. *adj.* below; less than. 2. *n.* the following; the rest; others.

ikaga, *adv.* 如何 how; how about; would you like; **Ikaga desu ka.** How are you? How do you like it?

ikagawashii, *adj.* いかがわしい 1. indecent. 2. suspicious; dubious.

ikaiyō, *n.* 胃潰瘍 stomach ulcer.

ikameshii, *adj.* いかめしい stern; solemn.

ikan 遺憾 1. *n.* regret. 2. *adj.* regrettable.

ika ni, *adv.* いかに how.

ika ni mo, *adv.* いかにも really; indeed.

ikan nagara, *adv.* 遺憾ながら regrettably.

ikareru, *vb.* いかれる 1. become mentally unbalanced. 2. be obsessed with.

ikari, *n.* 怒り anger; fury.

ikaru, *vb.* 怒る be angry; be furious.

ikasama, *n.* いかさま 1. deception; cheat. 2. fraud.

ikasu, *vb.* 生かす 1. make the most of. 2. keep alive.

ikebana, *n.* 生け花 Japanese flower arrangement.

ikegaki, *n.* 生け垣 hedge.

iken, *n.* 意見 opinion.

ikenai, *adj.* いけない 1. prohibited. 2. bad; unacceptable.

ikeru, *vb.* 生ける、活ける arrange (flowers).

iki, *n.* 息 breath; **iki o hikitoru** die.

iki, *n.* 行き going (outbound).

ikiatari-battari 行き当たりばったり 1. *n.* haphazardness. 2. *adj.* haphazard; aimless; random.

ikigai, *n.* 生き甲斐 reason for living.

iki-iki shita, *adj.* 生き生きした 1. vigorous; lively. 2. lifelike (description).

ikijigoku, *n.* 生き地獄 living hell.

ikikaeru, *vb.* 生き返る revive; be resurrected.

ikimono, *n.* 生き物 living creature.

iki (na), *adj.* 粋 (な) stylish; attractive; vibrant.

ikinari, *adv.* いきなり without notice; suddenly.

iki no ii, *adj.* 生のいい fresh; energetic.

ikinokoru, *vb.* 生き残る survive.

ikinuki, *n.* 息抜き rest; break; diversion.

ikioi, *n.* 勢い power; energy.

iki o suru, *vb.* 息をする breathe.

ikiru, *vb.* 生きる live.

ikisaki, *n.* 行き先 destination.

ikisatsu, *n.* いきさつ background; particulars.

ikita, *adj.* 生きた 1. live.

ikizumari, *n.* 行き詰まり standstill; deadlock.

ikizumaru, *vb.* 行き詰まる reach a standstill; deadlock.

ikizumaru, *vb.* 息詰まる stifle; suffocate.

ikizumaru yō (na), *adj.* 息詰まるような 1. stifling; suffocating. 2. breathtaking; exciting.

ikka, *n.* 一家 family.

ikkai, *n.* 一階 first floor.

ikkai 一回 1. *n.* first time; first round. 2. *adv.* once.

ikkan shite, *adv.* 一貫して consistently.

ikkan shiteiru, *adj.* 一貫している consistent.

ikken, *n.* 一見 a glance; look; **ikken shite** at a glance; **Hyakubun wa ikken ni shikazu.** Seeing is believing.

ikken'ya, *n.* 一軒家 detached house.

ikki ni, *adv.* 一気に at a stretch; in one breath.

ikko, *n.* 一個 one item (a piece, slice, box, etc.).

ikkō, *n.* 一行 a party (of); a group.

ikkō ni, *adv.* 一向に at all; **ikkō ni yokunai** not good at all.

ikkyo ni, *adv.* 一挙に at a stroke; at one stretch.

ikoku, *n.* 異国 foreign country.

ikokujōchō, *n.* 異国情調 exoticism.

ikotsu, *n.* 遺骨 human remains; ashes.

iku, *vb.* 行く go; leave for; visit.

ikubun ka, *adv.* 幾分か to some extent; somehow; somewhat.

ikudo, *adv.* 幾度 how often; how many times.

ikudo mo, *adv.* 幾度も many times; often.

ikuji, *n.* 育児 child rearing.

ikujinashi, *n., adj.* 意気地なし weak-willed (person).

ikuji no nai, *adj.* 意気地のない weak; spineless.

ikura, *n.* イクラ salmon roe.

ikura, *adv.* 幾ら How much?

ikura ka, *adv.* 幾らか somewhat; a little.

ikutsu, *adv.* 幾つ how many; how old.

ikutsu ka, *adj.* 幾つか some; several.

ikutsu mo, *adv.* 幾つも many.

ima, *n.* 居間 family room; living room.

ima 今 1. *n.* present moment. 2. *adv.* now.

ima demo, *adv.* 今でも even now; still.

imagoro wa, *adv.* 今頃は around this time; by now.

ima made, *adv.* 今迄 until now.

ima no tokoro, *adv.* 今の所 up to now; so far.

ima sugu ni, *adv.* 今すぐに immediately; at once.

imi, *n.* 意味 meaning; sense; significance.

imin, *n.* 移民 immigrant; emigrant.

imo, *n.* 芋 sweet potato; taro; potato.

imōto, *n.* 妹 younger sister.

in, *n.* 印 seal; stamp.

-inai ni 以内に (with)in; **go-fun-inai ni** (with)in five minutes.

inaka, *n.* 田舎 1. countryside; rural area. 2. hometown.

inarijinja, *n.* 稲荷神社 shrine for the celebration of harvests.

-inaya いなや as soon as; the moment; **tsuku ya-inaya** as soon as one arrives.

inbō, *n.* 陰謀 plot; conspiracy.

inbun, *n.* 韻文 verse; poetry.

inchiki, *n., adj.* いんちき charlatan; phony; fake.

indo, *n.* インド East India.

ine, *n.* 稲 rice plant.

inemuri, *n.* 居眠り catnap.

infure, *n.* インフレ (E.) inflation.

infuruenza, *n.* インフルエンザ (E.) influenza.

inga, *n.* 因果 cause and effect; destiny.

inga, *n.* 陰画 negative (photograph).

ingenmame, *n.* 隠元豆 string bean; green bean.

inginburei (na), *adj.* いんぎん無礼 (な) disdainfully polite.

ininjō, *n.* 委任状 power of attorney.

inin suru, *vb.* 委任する authorize; commission.

inja, *n.* 隠者 recluse; hermit.

inkan, *n.* 印鑑 signature seal.

inka suru, *vb.* 引火する catch fire.

inkei, *n.* 陰茎 penis.

inken (na), *adj.* 陰険 (な) cunning; sly; crafty.

inki (na), *adj.* 陰気 (な) gloomy; morose; depressing.

inku, *n.* インク (E.) ink.

inkyo, *n.* 隠居 retiree; retirement.

in'nen, *n.* 因縁 1. predestined

course (Buddhism); destiny. 2. pretext for an attack; **in'nen o tsukeru** make a pretext to attack.

inochi, *n.* 命 1. life. 2. most precious possession or person.

inori, *n.* 祈り prayer.

inoru, *vb.* 祈る pray.

inpo, *n.* インポ (E.) impotence.

inryoku, *n.* 引力 gravitation.

inryōsui, *n.* 飲料水 drinking water.

insatsu, *n.* 印刷 printing.

insatsubutsu, *n.* 印刷物 printed matter.

insei (no), *adj.* 陰性 (の) 1. negative. 2. gloomy.

inshō, *n.* 印象 impression.

inshōha, *n.* 印象派 Impressionist; Impressionism.

inshoku, *n.* 飲食 eating and drinking.

inshokubutsu, *n.* 飲食物 food and drink.

inshō-teki (na), *adj.* 印象的 (な) memorable; impressive.

inshu, *n.* 飲酒 drinking (liquor).

inshuunten, *n.* 飲酒運転 drunken driving.

insutanto (no), *adj.* インスタント (の) (E.) instant.

intai suru, *vb.* 引退する retire.

intān, *n.* インターン (E.) intern.

inu, *n.* 犬 1. dog. 2. spy.

in'yōfu, *n.* 引用符 quotation marks.

in'yō suru, *vb.* 引用する quote; refer to.

inzei, *n.* 印税 royalty (publishing).

iō, *n.* 硫黄 sulphur.

ippai 一杯 1. *n.* one cup (glass, spoonful, bowl); **ocha ippai** a cup of tea. 2. *n.* alcoholic drink. 3. *adj.* full of; **hito de ippai** full of people.

ippan (no), *adj.* 一般 (の)

common; general; usual.

ippantaishū, *n.* 一般大衆 general public.

ippan(-teki) ni, *adv.* 一般(的) に commonly; generally; usually.

ippen 一遍 1. *n.* one time. 2. *adv.* once.

ippen de, *adv.* 一遍で the first time.

ippen ni, *adv.* 一遍に at the same time; all at once.

ippō 一方 1. *n.* one side; the other party. 2. *adv.* on the other hand; meanwhile.

ippon, *n.* 一本 one item (long thin object: bottle, necktie, pencil, rope, etc.).

ippō-teki (na), *adj.* 一方的 (な) one-sided; unilateral.

ippō tsūkō, *n.* 一方通行 one-way (street).

ippuku, *n.* 一服 1. puff (tobacco). 2. one dose; one portion.

ippuku suru, *vb.* 一服する 1. smoke. 2. take a break.

ipputasaisei, *n.* 一夫多妻制 polygamy.

iradatsu, *vb.* 苛立つ get irritated; fret.

irai, *n.* 依頼 request; commission.

-irai 以来 since; **areirai** since then.

ira-ira suru, *vb.* いらいらする be testy or irritable; be impatient.

irai suru, *vb.* 依頼する ask; request; consign.

irasshai(mase), *interj.* いらっしゃい(ませ) Welcome!

ireba, *n.* 入れ歯 false tooth.

iremono, *n.* 入れ物 receptacle; box; case.

ireru, *vb.* 入れる 1. put in(to); let in. 2. send someone to. 3. comply with; accept. 4. make (tea, coffee).

irezumi, *n.* 入れ墨、刺青 tattoo.

iriguchi, *n.* 入口 entrance.

iritamago, *n.* いり玉子 scrambled eggs.

iro, *n.* 色 color.

irogami, *n.* 色紙 colored origami paper.

iroha, *n.* いろは 1. Japanese syllabary in poetic form. 2. the basics.

iro-iro (na, no), *adj.* 色々 (な、の) various; manifold.

iroke, *n.* 色気 sexiness.

irokichigai 色気違い 1. *n.* lecher; sex maniac. 2. *adj.* lecherous; lustful.

iron, *n.* 異論 dissenting opinion; different viewpoint.

iro'otoko, *n.* 色男 attractive man; lady-killer.

iroppoi, *adj.* 色っぽい sexy.

irozuri, *n.* 色刷り color printing.

iru, *vb.* 要る need; require.

iru, *vb.* いる、居る 1. be at; be present; exist; there is (are). 2. live in; stay at. 3. have; **koibito ga iru** have a lover, boyfriend, or girlfriend.

iru, *vb.* 射る hit; shoot.

iru, *vb.* 煎る、炒る roast in a dry pan; toast.

-iru, *vb.* いる be in the act of; **hanashiteiru** in the act of speaking.

irui, *n.* 衣類 clothing.

iruka, *n.* いるか dolphin.

iryō, *n.* 医療 medical treatment.

iryoku, *n.* 威力 power; authority.

isagiyoi, *adj.* 潔い 1. unhesitating. 2. ungrudging; wholehearted.

isakai, *n.* いさかい fight; quarrel.

isamashii, *adj.* 勇ましい 1. courageous; spirited; daring. 2. invigorating.

isameru, *vb.* 諌める admonish; warn; remonstrate.

isan, *n.* 遺産 bequest; inheritance; heritage; legacy.

isasaka, *adv.* いささか a little; somewhat; to some extent.

ise'ebi, *n.* 伊勢えび small lobster.

isei, *n.* 異性 opposite sex.

iseisha, *n.* 為政者 administrator; politician.

iseki, *n.* 遺跡 remains; ruins.

isha, ishi, *n.* 医者、医師 physician.

ishi, *n.* 石 pebble; stone.

ishi, *n.* 意志 will; willpower.

ishi, *n.* 意思 mind; intention.

ishiki, *n.* 意識 awareness; consciousness; **ishiki ga nai** have no consciousness or awareness.

ishiki-teki ni, *adv.* 意識的に consciously; on purpose.

ishitsu (na, no), *adj.* 異質 (な、の) different (quality, nature).

ishitsu-butsu/-hin, *n.* 遺失物／〜品 lost article.

ishiwata, *n.* 石綿 asbestos.

isho, *n.* 遺書 will; testament.

ishō, *n.* 衣裳 clothing; costume.

ishoku (na, no), *adj.* 異色 (な、の) unique; eccentric.

isogashii, *adj.* 忙しい busy.

isogu, *vb.* 急ぐ hurry.

isoide, *adv.* 急いで in a hurry.

issai 一切 1. *pron.* everything. 2. *pron.* nothing (with negative). 3. *adv.* never; not at all (with negative).

issakujitsu, *n., adv.* 一昨日 day before yesterday.

issakunen, *n.* 一昨年 year before last.

issatsu, *n.* 一冊 one copy of a book.

issei ni, *adv.* 一斉に at the same

time; all at once; all together.

isshiki, *n.* 一式 complete set.

isshin (furan) ni, *adv.* 一心 (不乱) に avidly; enthusiastically.

isshō, *n.* 一生 lifetime.

isshō kenmei (ni), *adv.* 一生懸命 (に) with all one's might.

issho ni, *adv.* 一緒に together (with); **issho ni iku** go together.

isshū, *n.* 一周 round; tour.

isshūkan 一週間 1. *n.* one week. 2. *adv.* for one week; in a week.

isshun, *n.* 一瞬 moment; instant.

isshu no, *adj.* 一種の a kind of; a type of.

isso, *adv.* いっそ rather; preferably.

issō, *adv.* 一層 all the more; more ... than before.

isu, *n.* 椅子 1. chair; sofa. 2. post; position.

isuraeru, *n.* イスラエル Israel.

isuramukyō, *n.* イスラム教 Islam.

ita, *n.* 板 1. wooden board. 2. metal plate.

itachi, *n.* いたち weasel.

itadaki, *n.* 頂 mountaintop; peak.

itadakimasu 頂きます I am about to partake (civility exchanged before meal).

itadaku, *vb.* 頂く 1. receive. 2. eat; drink. 3. ask to do.

itai, *n.* 遺体 dead body.

itai, *adj.* 痛い painful; aching.

itamae, *n.* 板前 chef (Japanese cuisine).

itamashii, *adj.* 痛ましい poignant; pitiable; tragic.

itameru, *vb.* 炒める stir-fry; sauté.

itameru, *vb.* 痛める injure; hurt.

itami, *n.* 痛み ache; pain.

itamidome, *n.* 痛み止め painkiller; analgesic.

itamu, *vb.* 痛む ache; feel pain; hurt.

itansha, *n.* 異端者 heretic.

itaria, *n.* イタリア Italy.

itaru, *vb.* 至る 1. lead to; reach. 2. result in.

itawaru, *vb.* いたわる take care of; be kind to; console.

itazura, *n.* いたずら prank; mischief.

iten, *n.* 移転 move.

iten suru, *vb.* 移転する move.

ito, *n.* 糸 string; thread.

ito, *n.* 意図 intention; aim.

itoko, *n.* いとこ cousin.

itsu, *adv.* いつ when; what time; **itsu made** until when.

itsuka, *n.* 五日 fifth day of the month.

itsuka, *adv.* いつか 1. some day; in the future. 2. once; before.

itsumo, *adv.* いつも always; usually.

itsu no ma ni ka, *adv.* いつの間にか before one is aware.

itsuwari, *n.* 偽り a lie; deception.

itsuwaru, *vb.* 偽る lie; deceive; pretend.

ittai 一体 1. *n.* one body; a unit. 2. *adv.* how (what, who, etc.) on earth.

ittan, *adv.* 一旦 once; for a moment.

ittō, *n.* 一等 first place; gold award; first class.

ittsui no, *adj.* 一対の pair (e.g., knife and fork).

iu, *vb.* 言う say; tell; speak.

iwa, *n.* 岩 rock.

iwaba, *adv.* いわば as it were; so to speak.

iwai, *n.* 祝い celebration; congratulations.

iwashi, *n.* いわし sardine.

iwau, *vb.* 祝う celebrate; congratulate.

iya, *interj.* いや、嫌 No!

iya (na), *adj.* 嫌 (な) disgusting; disturbing; uncomfortable.

iyagarase, *n.* 嫌がらせ harassment.

iyagaru, *vb.* 嫌がる 1. dislike; resent. 2. hesitate (out of dislike).

iyahon, *n.* イヤホン (E.) earphones.

iya-iya, *adv.* いやいや、嫌々 reluctantly.

iyaringu, *n.* イヤリング (E.) earring.

iyashii, *adj.* 卑しい despicable; mean.

iyasu, *vb.* 癒す 1. cure; heal. 2. quench (thirst).

iyō (na), *adj.* 異様 (な) bizarre; strange.

iyo-iyo, *adv.* いよいよ 1. finally. 2. more and more.

iyoku, *n.* 意欲 aspiration; zeal.

izakaya, *n.* 居酒屋 small bar; tavern.

izen (ni), *adv.* 以前 (に) (long time) ago; before.

izoku, *n.* 遺族 1. surviving family members. 2. the bereaved.

izumi, *n.* 泉 source; spring.

izure いずれ 1. *pron.* which. 2. *adv.* soon; someday. 3. *adv.* in the end.

izure mo, *pron.* いずれも all; every one of them.

J

jā, *interj.* じゃあ Well! Then!

jagaimo, *n.* じゃが芋 potato.

jaguchi, *n.* 蛇口 water faucet.

jajauma, *n.* じゃじゃ馬 shrew; **jajauma narashi** *Taming of the Shrew.*

jaketto, *n.* ジャケット (E.) jacket.

jakkan 若干 1. *adj.* a little; some. 2. *adv.* somehow; somewhat.

jakuten, *n.* 弱点 weak point; weakness.

jama, *n.* 邪魔 burden; disturbance; hindrance.

jama suru, *vb.* 邪魔する hinder; interfere; disturb.

jan-jan, *adv.* じゃんじゃん abundantly; without hesitation.

jari, *n.* 砂利 gravel.

jasui, *n.* 邪推 groundless suspicion.

jettoki, *n.* ジェット機 (E.) jet plane.

ji, *n.* 字 character (letter); handwriting.

-ji 時 o'clock; time; **goji ni** at five o'clock.

jibiki, *n.* 字引き dictionary.

jibun, *n.* 自分 self; oneself; **jibun de** by oneself.

jibunkatte (na, no), *adj.* 自分勝手 (な、の) egoistic; selfish.

jibyō, *n.* 持病 chronic disease.

jichō, *n.* 自嘲 self-ridicule.

jidai, *n.* 時代 era; days; times.

jidaiokure (na, no), *adj.* 時代遅れ (な、の) old-fashioned; out-dated.

jidaisakugo, *n.* 時代錯誤 anachronism.

jidan, *n.* 示談 out-of-court settlement.

jiden, *n.* 自伝 autobiography.

jidō, *n.* 児童 child.

jidōhanbaiki, *n.* 自動販売機 vending machine.

jidō (no), *adj.* 自動 (の) automatic.

jidōsha, *n.* 自動車 car; **jidōsha o unten suru** drive a car.

jidō-teki ni, *adv.* 自動的に automatically.

jieitai, *n.* 自衛隊 Self-Defense Forces.

jiga, *n.* 自我 self.

jigajisan, *n.* 自我自讃 self-praise.

jigazō, *n.* 自画像 self-portrait (painting).

jigen, *n.* 次元 dimension; level; **motto takai jigen** higher level.

-jigen 時限 period (school); **ichi-jigen** first period.

jigenbakudan, *n.* 時限爆弾 time bomb.

jigoku, *n.* 地獄 hell; inferno; **iki-jigoku** living hell.

jigyō, *n.* 事業 business; enterprise.

jihaku, *n.* 自白 confession (to a crime).

jihatsu-teki ni, *adv.* 自発的に willingly; voluntarily; of one's own will.

jihi, *n.* 慈悲 mercy.

jihi de, *adv.* 自費で at one's own expense.

jihitsu, *n.* 自筆 autograph.

jihyō, *n.* 辞表 written resignation; **jihyō o dasu** hand in a resignation.

jihyō, *n.* 時評 commentary on current events.

ji'i, *n.* 自慰 masturbation.

ji'in, *n.* 寺院 temple (Buddhist).

ji'ishiki, *n.* 自意識 self-awareness.

jiji, *n.* 時事 current events.

jijii, *n.* じじい old man; grandfather.

jijitsu, *n.* 事実 fact; truth.

jijo, *n.* 次女 second daughter.

jijō, *n.* 事情 reason; situation; circumstances.

jijoden, *n.* 自叙伝 autobiography.

jika, *n.* 時価 market price.

jikai ni, *adv.* 次回に next time.

jikaku, *n.* 字画 number of strokes (kana, kanji).

jikaku, *n.* 自覚 awareness; consciousness.

jikaku suru, *vb.* 自覚する be aware of; be conscious of.

jikan, *n.* 時間 time; hour; class period; **jikan ga aru (nai)** have (no) time.

jika ni, *adv.* 直に directly.

jikankyū, *n.* 時間給 hourly wage.

jikanwari, *n.* 時間割 schedule.

jikasei (no), *adj.* 自家製 (の) homemade.

jikatsu suru, *vb.* 自活する support oneself.

jiken, *n.* 事件 1. incident; happening. 2. criminal case.

jiketsu, *n.* 自決 suicide.

jiki, *n.* 磁器 chinaware; porcelain.

jiki, *n.* 時期 time; season.

jiki, *n.* 時機 opportunity.

jiki-jiki ni, *adv.* 直々に in person; face to face.

jiki ni, *adv.* 直に before long; soon.

jikka, *n.* 実家 one's parents' family (esp. on wife's side).

jikkan suru, *vb.* 実感する 1. feel keenly. 2. realize.

jikken, *n.* 実験 experiment.

jikkō suru, *vb.* 実行する carry out; realize; implement.

jikkuri (to), *adv.* じっくり (と) thoroughly; over and over again; carefully.

jikkyō(hōsō), *n.* 実況(放送) live broadcast.

jiko, *n.* 事故 accident; **kōtsūjiko o okosu** cause a traffic accident.

jiko, *n.* 自己 self; oneself.

jiko chūshin-teki (na), *adj.* 自己中心的 (な) self-centered.

jikoku, *n.* 時刻 time; hour.

jikokugo, *n.* 自国語 native language.

jikoshōkai, *n.* 自己紹介 self-introduction.

jiku, *n.* 軸 axle; axis; center.

jikyū, *n.* 時給 hourly wage; **jikyū godoru** five dollars per hour.

jikyūjisoku, *n.* 自給自足 self-sufficiency.

jime-jime shita, *adj.* じめじめした damp; humid; gloomy.

jimen, *n.* 地面 ground.

jimi (na), *adj.* 地味 (な) 1. subdued; inconspicuous. 2. unattractive.

jimoto (no), *adj.* 地元 (の) local; hometown.

jimu, *n.* 事務 clerical work; office work.

jimuin, *n.* 事務員 clerk; office worker.

jimusho, *n.* 事務所 office.

jimu-teki na, *adj.* 事務的 (な) businesslike; mechanical.

jinan, *n.* 次男 second son.

jinbunka, *n.* 人文科 Department of Humanities.

jinbutsu, *n.* 人物 person; person of rank, note, or distinction.

jinbutsuga, *n.* 人物画 portrait.

jindōshugi, *n.* 人道主義 humanitarianism.

jindō-teki na, *adj.* 人道的 (な) humanitarian; humane.

jinin suru, *vb.* 辞任する resign (from a position).

jinja, *n.* 神社 Shinto shrine.

jinji, *n.* 人事 personnel concerns; **jinjika** personnel department.

jinkaku, *n.* 人格 personality; character.

jinken, *n.* 人権 human rights.

jinken-hi, *n.* 人件費 labor costs.

jinkō, *n.* 人口 population.

jinkō (no), *adj.* 人工 (の) man-made; artificial.

jinkō eisei, *n.* 人工衛星 artificial satellite.

jinkō-jusei/-jutai, *n.* 人工受精／～受胎 artificial insemination.

jinkō-teki (na), *adj.* 人工的 (な) artificial; man-made.

jinmashin, *n.* じんましん hives; allergic skin rash.

jinmei, *n.* 人命 human life.

jinmei, *n.* 人名 person's name.

jinmin, *n.* 人民 people; citizens.

jinmon suru, *vb.* 尋問する interrogate.

jinrui, *n.* 人類 human race.

jinruiai, *n.* 人類愛 philanthropy.

jinruigaku, *n.* 人類学 anthropology.

jinsei, *n.* 人生 human life.

jinshinkōgeki, *n.* 人身攻撃 criticism of someone for his or her thoughts or actions.

jinshu, *n.* 人種 race (division of humankind).

jintai, *n.* 人体 human body.

jintsū, *n.* 陣痛 labor pains.

jinushi, *n.* 地主 landowner.

jinzai, *n.* 人材 talented (skilled, capable) person.

jinzō, *n.* 腎臓 kidney.

jīpan, *n.* ジーパン jeans.

jirasu, *vb.* 焦らす tantalize; tease.

jirei, *n.* 辞令 official announcement.

jireru, *vb.* 焦れる be impatient.

jiriki de, *adv.* 自力で unassisted; without depending on others.

jiritsu suru, *vb.* 自立する become self-sufficient.

jisa, *n.* 時差 time difference.

jisa boke, *n.* 時差ぼけ jet lag.

jisankin, *n.* 持参金 dowry.

jisan suru, *vb.* 持参する bring; take.

jisatsu, *n.* 自殺 suicide.

jisatsu suru, *vb.* 自殺する commit

suicide.

jisei, *n.* 時制 tense (grammar).

jisei, *n.* 時勢 current times; trend.

jiseishin, *n.* 自制心 self-control.

jishaku, *n.* 磁石 magnet.

jishin, *n.* 地震 earthquake.

jishin, *n.* 自信 self-confidence.

jisho, *n.* 辞書 dictionary.

jishoku suru, *vb.* 辞職する resign (from a position).

jishukisei, *n.* 自主規制 voluntary restraint.

jishu suru, *vb.* 自首する turn oneself in.

jishu-teki (na), *adj.* 自主的 (な) voluntary.

jisoku, *n.* 時速 speed.

jisonshin, *n.* 自尊心 self-esteem.

jissai, *n.* 実際 reality; fact.

jissai ni, *adv.* 実際に in reality; in fact.

jissai no, *adj.* 実際の real; actual.

jisseki, *n.* 実績 accomplishment; achievement.

jisshi suru, *vb.* 実施する carry out; effect.

jisshitsu, *n.* 実質 substance.

jisshitsu-teki (na), *adj.* 実質的 (な) substantive; practical.

jisshū, *n.* 実修 practical training.

jisuberi, *n.* 地滑り landslide.

jisui suru, *vb.* 自炊する cook for oneself.

jita, *n.* 自他 self and others.

jitabata suru, *vb.* じたばたする struggle.

jitai, *n.* 事態 situation; circumstance.

-jitai 自体 oneself; itself; **kono mondaijitai** the problem itself.

jitai suru, *vb.* 辞退する decline.

jitaku, *n.* 自宅 home or house.

jitaku ryōhō, *n.* 自宅療法 home care.

jiten, *n.* 辞典 dictionary.

jitensha, *n.* 自転車 bicycle.

jitsubutsu, *n.* 実物 real thing; real person.

jitsudan, *n.* 実弾 live ammunition.

jitsuen, *n.* 実演 live performance; demonstration.

jitsugen suru, *vb.* 実現する materialize; realize; effect.

jitsugyōka, *n.* 実業家 businessperson.

jitsugyōkai, *n.* 実業界 business world.

jitsumu, *n.* 実務 administrative work.

jitsu ni, *adv.* 実に really; indeed.

jitsu no, *adj.* 実の biological; real; **jitsu no haha** biological mother.

jitsurei, *n.* 実例 example.

jitsuryoku, *n.* 実力 capability; proficiency.

jitsuwa, *n.* 実話 true story.

jitsu wa, *adv.* 実は really; in fact.

jitsuyō, *n.* 実用 usefulness; practicality.

jitsuyōhin, *n.* 実用品 useful or practical thing.

jitsuyō-teki (na), *adj.* 実用的 (な) useful; practical.

jitsuzai no, *adj.* 実在の existing; real.

jittai, *n.* 実体 fact; reality.

jitto, *adv.* じっと 1. without moving; still. 2. intently.

jiwa-jiwa (to), *adv.* じわじわ (と) slowly; gradually.

jiyū, *n.* 自由 liberty; freedom.

jiyū (na, no), *adj.* 自由 (な、の) unfettered; free.

jiyū bōeki, *n.* 自由貿易 free trade.

jiyūka, *n.* 自由化 free market; liberalization.

jiyū keiyaku, *n.* 自由契約 free-agent status.

jiyū ni, *adv.* 自由に freely; as one likes.

jiyūshugisha, *n.* 自由主義者 liberalist.

jizen, *n.* 慈善 charity.

jizendantai, *n.* 慈善団体 charitable organization.

jizenka, *n.* 慈善家 philanthropist.

jizenkatsudō, *n.* 慈善活動 charitable activity.

jizen ni, *adv.* 事前に in advance; beforehand.

jizoku suru, *vb.* 持続する continue; maintain.

jo, *n.* 序 preface; foreword.

jō, *n.* 錠 lock (fastener).

jō, *n.* 情 affection; sensitivity; emotion; **jō ga fukai** affectionate.

jō (no), *adj.* 上 (の) best; upper.

-jō 上 in terms of; **hito no kenkō-jō** in terms of one's health.

-jō 畳 (counter for tatami); **roku-jō** six tatami mats.

jōba, *n.* 乗馬 horseback riding.

jōbu (na), *adj.* 丈夫 (な) healthy; hardy; strong.

jobun, *n.* 序文 preface; foreword.

jōcho, *n.* 情緒 emotion; **jōcho fuantei na** emotionally unstable.

jōchō, *n.* 情調 ambience; atmoshpere.

jochō suru, *vb.* 助長する encourage; foster.

jōdan, *n.* 冗談 joke; humor; **jōdan o iu** make a joke.

jōdan hanbun de/ni, *adv.* 冗談半分で／に half in jest.

jodōshi, *n.* 助動詞 auxiliary verb (grammar).

jōei, *n.* 上映 showing; screening (film).

jōen suru, *vb.* 上演する stage; perform.

jōfu, *n.* 情婦 mistress; kept woman.

jogai suru, *vb.* 除外する exclude; eliminate.

jogakkō, *n.* 女学校 girls' school.

jogakusei, *n.* 女学生 female student.

jōge 上下 1. up and down; top and bottom. 2. upper and lower status (ranking, part, position). 3. first and second volumes (of two).

jogen, *n.* 助言 advice; **jogen o ataeru** advise.

jōgi, *vb.* 定規 measure; ruler.

jōhatsu suru, *vb.* 上達する 1. evaporate. 2. disappear.

jōheki, *n.* 城壁 castle wall.

jōhin (na), *adj.* 上品 (な) elegant; graceful; refined.

jōhō, *n.* 情報 information; news.

jōho suru, *vb.* 譲歩する concede.

johyō suru, *vb.* 除氷する defrost.

joi, *n.* 女医 woman physician.

jōi (no), *adj.* 上位 (の) higher; highest.

jōin, *n.* 上院 Upper House; Senate.

jōji, *n.* 情事 love affair.

jojishi, *n.* 叙事詩 epic.

jo-jo ni, *adv.* 徐々に gradually; step by step.

jojōshi, *n.* 叙情詩 lyric poetry; poem.

jōju, *n.* 成就 achievement; accomplishment; realization.

jōjun, *n.* 上旬 first third of a month.

jōjutsu no, *adj.* 上述の above-mentioned.

joken, *n.* 女権 women's rights.

jōken, *n.* 条件 requirement; condition; **... to iu jōken de** on condition that ... .

jōki, *n.* 蒸気 vapor; steam.

jōkigen (na, no), *adj.* 上機嫌 (な、の) good-humored; cheerful.

jōkin, *n.* 常勤 full-time

employment.

jokō suru, *vb.* 徐行する slow down.

jōkyaku, *n.* 乗客 passenger.

jōkyō, *n.* 状況 circumstance; state.

jokyōju, *n.* 助教授 assistant professor.

jokyoku, *n.* 序曲 overture; prelude.

jōkyū, *n.* 上級 advanced level; **nihongojōkyū** advanced Japanese.

jōmae, *n.* 錠前 lock (fastener).

jomakushiki, *n.* 除幕式 unveiling ceremony.

jomei suru, *vb.* 除名する expel.

jōmuin, *n.* 乗務員 crew member (plane, train, or ship).

jōmyaku, *n.* 静脈 vein (blood vessel).

jōmyakuchūsha, *n.* 静脈注射 intravenous injection.

jōnetsu, *n.* 情熱 enthusiasm; passion.

jōnetsu-teki (na), *adj.* 情熱的 (な) enthusiastic; passionate.

jonin, *n.* 叙任 appointment; investiture.

jōnin, *n.* 常任 permanent member.

jo'ō, *n.* 女王 queen.

jōrei, *n.* 条例 ordinance.

jōren, *n.* 定連 regular customer (guest, visitor, etc.).

joretsu, *n.* 序列 hierarchy; ranking order.

jōriku suru, *vb.* 上陸する 1. land. 2. hit (typhoon).

jōruri, *n.* 浄瑠璃 music for bunraku.

joryoku, *n.* 助力 support; help.

jōryokuju, *n.* 常緑樹 evergreen tree.

joryū (no), *adj.* 女流 (の) woman; **joryū sakka** woman writer.

jōryū (no), *adj.* 上流 (の) upper-class.

josainai, *adj.* 如才ない clever; shrewd.

josanpu, *n.* 助産婦 midwife.

josei, *n.* 女性 woman.

jōsei, *n.* 情勢 situation; circumstances.

joseikin, *n.* 助成金 subsidy.

joseito, *n.* 女生徒 female student.

jōsen suru, *vb.* 乗船する board (ship).

jōshachin, *n.* 乗車賃 train or bus fare.

jōshaken, *n.* 乗車券 train or bus ticket.

jōsha suru, *vb.* 乗車する board (train, bus); get in (car).

joshi, *n.* 女子 girl; woman.

jōshi, *n.* 上司 superior (in a company).

jōshiki, *n.* 常識 common sense; conventional wisdom.

jōshitsu (na, no), *adj.* 上質 (な、の) of high quality.

jōshoku, *n.* 常食 staple food.

jōshō suru, *vb.* 上昇する mount; rise.

joshu, *n.* 助手 assistant.

jōshūsha, *n.* 常習者 habitual user; addict.

jōsō, *n.* 上層 upper class; upper level.

josū, *n.* 序数 ordinal number.

jōtai, *n.* 状態 circumstances; state; condition.

jōtai, *n.* 上体 upper body; torso.

jōtatsu suru, *vb.* 上達する improve.

jōtō (na, no), *adj.* 上等 (な、の) excellent; very good.

jōtōshudan, *n.* 常套手段 old trick.

jōto suru, *vb.* 譲渡する hand over; transfer.

joya, *n.* 除夜 New Year's Eve.

jōyaku, *n.* 条約 treaty; pact.

jōyoku, *n.* 情欲 lust.

jōyōsha, *n.* 乗用車 automobile.

jōyō suru, *vb.* 常用する use regularly; use constantly.

joyū, *n.* 女優 actress.

jōzai, *n.* 錠剤 tablet; pill (medicine).

jōzetsu (na, no), *adj.* じょう舌 (な、の) voluble; talkative.

jōzō suru, *vb.* 醸造する brew; distill.

jōzu (na), *adj.* 上手 (な) good at; skilled; proficient.

jū, *n.* 十 ten.

jū, *n.* 銃 gun.

-jū 中 throughout; **ichinichijū** all day long.

jūatsu, *n.* 重圧 strong pressure.

jūbun (na), *adj.* 十分 (な) enough; ample.

jūbun ni, *adv.* 十分に enough; amply; fully.

jūbyō, *n.* 重病 serious illness or disease.

jūdai, *n.* 十代 teens.

jūdai (na), *adj.* 重大 (な) serious; important.

jūden suru, *vb.* 充電する charge (battery).

judōtai, *n.* 受動体 passive voice (grammar).

jūfuku/chōfuku suru, *vb.* 重複する overlap.

jugaku, *n.* 儒学 Confucianism.

jūgatsu, *n.* 十月 October.

jugyō, *n.* 授業 class.

jugyōryō, *n.* 授業料 tuition.

jūi, *n.* 獣医 veterinarian.

jūichigatsu, *n.* 十一月 November.

jūjika, *n.* 十字架 cross; crucifix.

jūjiro, *n.* 十字路 crossroads.

jūji suru, *vb.* 従事する work in; engage in (profession).

jūjitsu shita, *adj.* 充実した fulfilling.

jūjun (na), *adj.* 従順 (な) obedient.

juken, *n.* 受験 taking of an examination.

jukensha, *n.* 受験者 examinee.

juken suru, *vb.* 受験する take an examination.

jūketsu, *n.* 充血 excessive blood in a body part; **jūketsu shita me** bloodshot eye(s).

jūkinzoku, *n.* 重金属 heavy metal.

jukkō suru, *vb.* 熟考する think over; contemplate.

jūkōgyō, *n.* 重工業 heavy industry.

juku, *n.* 塾 cram school.

jukurensha, *n.* 熟練者 skilled person; expert.

jukuren shita, *adj.* 熟練した skilled; expert.

jukusu, *vb.* 熟す ripen; mature.

jukusui suru, *vb.* 熟睡する sleep well.

jukyō, *n.* 儒教 Confucianism.

jūkyo, *n.* 住居 residence; house.

jukyū, *n.* 需給 supply and demand.

jūman, *n.* 十万 (one) hundred thousand; **nijūman** two hundred thousand.

jūmin, *n.* 住民 resident.

jumyō, *n.* 寿命 life span.

jun, *n.* 順 order; turn.

jun- 準 semi; second-best; **jun-kesshō** semifinal.

jūnan (na), *adj.* 柔軟 (な) flexible.

junban, *n.* 順番 one's turn; order.

junbi, *n.* 準備 preparation.

junbi suru, *vb.* 準備する prepare.

junchō (na), *adj.* 順調 (な) smooth; no problem.

jun'eki, *n.* 純益 net profit.

jun'i, *n.* 順位 ranking; place.

jūnigatsu, *n.* 十二月 December.

jūniji, *n.* 十二時 twelve o'clock; **gozen (gogo) jūniji** twelve a.m.

(p.m.).

junjo, *n.* 順序 order; sequence.

junjō (na), *adj.* 純情 (な) naive; unspoiled; pure.

junkan, *n.* 循環 circulation; circular movement; **akujunkan** vicious circle.

junketsu (na, no), *adj.* 純潔 (な、の) pure; chaste; innocent.

jun'nō suru, *vb.* 順応する adapt to.

junrei, *n.* 巡礼 pilgrimage (Buddhist).

junsa, *n.* 巡査 patrolman.

junshin (na), *adj.* 純心 (な) pure-hearted; innocent.

junsui (na, no), *adj.* 純粋 (な、の) pure; pure-blooded; genuine.

jūoku, *n.* 十億 billion.

jūryō, *n.* 重量 weight.

jūryoku, *n.* 重力 gravity.

jusei, *n.* 受精 fertilization; insemination; **jinkō jusei** artificial insemination.

jūsei, *n.* 銃声 sound of a gunshot.

jushin, *n.* 受信 reception (TV, radio).

jushin, *n.* 受診 examination by a physician.

jūshi suru, *vb.* 重視する emphasize; give priority to.

jūsho, *n.* 住所 address.

jūshō, *n.* 重傷 serious injury.

jūshoku, *n.* 住職 head of a Buddhist temple.

jushō suru, *vb.* 受賞する win an award.

jūsu, *n.* ジュース (E.) juice.

jūtai, *n.* 重態 critical condition.

jūtai, *n.* 渋滞 gridlock (traffic).

jutai suru, *vb.* 受胎する become pregnant; conceive.

jūtaku, *n.* 住宅 residence; house.

jūtan, *n.* じゅうたん carpet; rug.

jūten, *n.* 重点 emphasis; stress; **jūten o oku** emphasize.

jutsugo, *n.* 述語 predicate (grammar).

juwaki, *n.* 受話器 (telephone) receiver.

jūyaku, *n.* 重役 company officer.

jūyō, *n.* 重要 importance.

jūyō (na), *adj.* 重要 (な) 1. important. 2. prominent.

jūyō jinbutsu, *n.* 重要人物 VIP.

juyo suru, *vb.* 授与する confer; award.

K

ka, *n.* 蚊 mosquito.

ka, *parti.* か 1. do (did, is, was, are, etc.) ... ?; **Oishii desu ka.** Does it taste good? 2. or; **are ka kore ka** this or that.

-ka 課 1. office section or department. 2. lesson.

-ka 科 1. academic department; **kokubunka** Department of Japanese Literature. 2. academic course. 3. medical department; medical specialty.

kaban, *n.* 鞄 bag; briefcase; suitcase.

kabau, *vb.* 庇う defend; protect; support.

kabe, *n.* 壁 wall.

kabi, *n.* かび mildew; mold.

kabikusai, *adj.* かび臭い musty.

kabin, *n.* 花瓶 vase.

kabin (na), *adj.* 過敏 (な) oversensitive.

kabocha, *n.* かぼちゃ pumpkin;
squash.

kabu, *n.* かぶ turnip.

kabu, *n.* 株 1. stock. 2. stump.

kabuka, *n.* 株価 stock price.

kabuki, *n.* 歌舞伎 traditional
Japanese drama.

kabunushi, *n.* 株主 stockholder.

kabureru, *vb.* かぶれる 1. be
influenced. 2. develop a rash.

kaburu, *vb.* 被る 1. put something
(on head). 2. be drenched with;
be covered with.

kabuseru, *vb.* 被せる 1. cover. 2.
blame (an innocent person).

kabushiki, *n.* 株式 stock.

kabushiki-gaisha, *n.* 株式会社
corporation.

kabushikishijō, *n.* 株式市場 stock
market.

kabushikisōba, *n.* 株式相場 stock
price or quotation.

kabuto, *n.* かぶと helmet.

kachi, *n.* 価値 value.

kachi, *n.* 勝ち win; victory.

kachiki (na), *adj.* 勝ち気 (な)
strong-minded; unyielding.

kachō, *n.* 課長 section chief;
manager.

kadai, *n.* 課題 1. topic. 2. problem;
issue. 3. assignment.

kadaihyōka suru, *vb.* 過大評価す
る overestimate.

kadan, *n.* 花壇 flower bed.

kado, *n.* 角 corner.

kadō, *n.* 花道 art of flower
arrangement.

-ka dō ka かどうか whether (or
not); **iku-ka dō ka kimerarenai**
unable to decide whether or not
to go.

kaeri, *n.* 帰り going back; coming
back; return.

kaerimiru, *vb.* 顧みる look back

on.

kaeru, *vb.* 帰る go back; come
back; return.

kaeru, *vb.* 返る restore; return.

kaeru, *vb.* 変える change;
transform.

kaeru, *vb.* 替える、換える replace;
exchange.

kaesu, *vb.* 返す 1. give back;
return. 2. invert; reverse.

kaesu, *vb.* かえす hatch.

-kaesu 返す re-; back; **maki-
kaesu** rewind.

kaette, *adv.* かえって 1.
conversely; rather. 2. all the
more.

kagaku, *n.* 科学 science.

kagaku, *n.* 化学 chemistry.

kagakuheiki, *n.* 化学兵器
chemical weapon.

kagami, *n.* 鏡 mirror.

kagamu, *vb.* 屈む squat; crouch.

kagayaki, *n.* 輝き splendor;
radiance; brilliance.

kagayaku, *vb.* 輝く shine; glitter;
sparkle.

kage, *n.* 影 1. shadow. 2.
silhouette.

kage, *n.* 陰 1. shade. 2. gloominess.

kage de, *adv.* 陰で behind one's
back; behind the scenes.

kageguchi, *n.* 陰口 backbiting.

kageki, *n.* 歌劇 opera.

kageki (na), *adj.* 過激 (な)
aggressive; radical.

kagemusha, *n.* 影武者 double
(impersonator).

kagen, *n.* 加減 1. physical
condition. 2. degree; **yu kagen**
temperature of bath water.

kagen suru, *vb.* 加減する
moderate; downgrade.

kagi, *n.* 鍵 1. key. 2. clue.

kagiranai, *vb.* 限らない not

necessarily; not always.

kagiru, *vb.* 限る be limited to.

kago, *n.* 籠 basket; birdcage.

kagu, *n.* 家具 furniture.

kagu, *vb.* 嗅ぐ smell; sniff.

kahansū, *n.* 過半数 majority.

kahei, *n.* 貨幣 currency; money.

kai, *n.* 貝 seashell; shellfish.

kai, *n.* 会 1. meeting; conference. 2. party; gathering. 3. association.

-kai, -kkai 回 (counter) round; time; **jukkai** tenth round; ten times.

-kai, -kkai, -gai 階 counter for floors of a building; stairs; **nikai** second floor; **ikkai** first floor; **hachikai** eighth floor.

kaibatsu, *n.* 海抜 altitude.

kaibō, *n.* 解剖 anatomy; autopsy.

kaibutsu, *n.* 怪物 monster.

kaichō, *n.* 会長 chairman; chairman of the board.

kaichō, *n.* 快調 good form.

kaichū dentō, *n.* 懐中電燈 flashlight.

kaidan, *n.* 階段 steps; stairs.

kaidan, *n.* 会談 consultation; conversation; conference.

kaidan, *n.* 怪談 ghost story.

kaidō, *n.* 街道 highway.

kaifuku suru, *vb.* 回復する recover (from illness); improve.

kaiga, *n.* 絵画 painting.

kaigai 海外 1. *n.* foreign nations. 2. *adj., adv.* overseas.

kaigan, *n.* 海岸 coast; seashore; beach.

kaigara, *n.* 貝殻 seashell.

kaigi, *n.* 会議 meeting; conference; convention.

kaigi-teki (na), *adj.* 懐疑的 (な) skeptical.

kaigun, *n.* 海軍 navy.

kaigyō suru, *vb.* 開業する open

(business).

kaihatsu suru, *vb.* 開発する develop.

kaihi, *n.* 会費 membership fee.

kaihi suru, *vb.* 回避する avoid.

kaihō suru, *vb.* 介抱する take care of (an infirm person); nurse.

kaihō suru, *vb.* 解放する emancipate; liberate; release.

kaihō suru, *vb.* 開放する open; leave open.

kaihyō, *n.* 開票 ballot counting.

kaiin, *n.* 会員 member.

kaiire, *n.* 買入れ purchase.

kaijo, *n.* 解除 lifting (of a ban); removal; cancellation; **keiyaku kaijo** cancellation of a contract.

kaijō, *n.* 会場 site of a gathering or event; venue.

kaijō, *adj.* 海上 marine.

kaika, *n.* 開化 opening; beginning.

kaika (de, ni), *adv.* 階下 (で、に) downstairs.

kai-kaishiki, *n.* 開会式 opening ceremony.

kaikaku, *n.* 改革 reform.

kaikan, *n.* 会館 auditorium.

kaikan suru, *vb.* 開館する open (hall, library, museum, etc.).

kaikatsu (na), *adj.* 快活 (な) lively; cheerful.

kaikei, *n.* 会計 1. account(s). 2. bill; check. 3. payment.

kaikeigaku, *n.* 会計学 accounting (discipline).

kaikeishi, *n.* 会計士 accountant; **kōnin-kaikeishi** Certified Public Accountant.

kaiken, *n.* 会見 1. meeting. 2. interview.

kaiki (na), *adj.* 怪奇 (な) strange; bizarre.

kaikin, *n.* 皆勤 perfect attendance.

kaikin suru, *vb.* 解禁する lift a

ban; lift an embargo.

kaiko, *n.* 回顧 retrospection.

kaiko suru, *vb.* 解雇する dismiss;
ichiji-kaiko suru lay off.

kaikyō, *n.* 海峡 channel; strait.

kaikyō, *n.* 回教 Islam.

kaikyū, *n.* 階級 class; rank; caste.

kaimaku, *n.* 開幕 opening;
beginning.

kaimono, *n.* 買物 shopping;
kaimono ni iku go shopping.

kaimono o suru, *vb.* 買物をする
shop; buy.

kain, *n.* 下院 Lower House; House
of Representatives (U.S.).

kairaku, *n.* 快楽 pleasure.

kairyō, *n.* 改良 improvement;
reform.

kaisan suru, *vb.* 解散する dismiss
(gathering, party, meeting);
dissolve (Diet).

kaisatsuguchi, *n.* 改札口 turnstile;
ticket gate.

kaisei, *n.* 快晴 fair weather.

kaisei suru, *vb.* 改正する reform;
revise; amend.

kaisen suru, *vb.* 開戦する begin a
war.

kaisetsu suru, *vb.* 解説する
explain; comment; interpret.

kaisha, *n.* 会社 corporation;
company; office.

kaisha'in, *n.* 会社員 office worker.

kaishaku, *n.* 解釈 interpretation.

kaishaku suru, *vb.* 解釈する
interpret; explain.

kaishū, *n.* 改修 repair; renovation.

kaishū suru, *vb.* 回収する 1. recall.
2. collect (bills, loans).

kaisō, *n.* 海草 seaweed.

kaisō, *n.* 改装 renovation;
remodeling.

kaisoku(densha), *n.* 快速(電車)
express train; rapid train.

kaisō suru, *vb.* 回送する forward.

kaisū, *n.* 回数 frequency; number
of times.

kaisui, *n.* 海水 sea water.

kaisuiyoku, *n.* 海水浴 swimming
in the ocean.

kaisui-yokujō, *n.* 海水浴場
bathing beach.

kaitakusha, *n.* 開拓者 pioneer.

kaitaku suru, *vb.* 開拓する
develop (wilderness); open up
(new markets, etc.).

kaite, *n.* 買手 buyer.

kaitei-kēburu, *n.* 海底ケーブル
undersea cable.

kaitei-ton'neru, *n.* 海底トンネル
undersea tunnel.

kaiten-doa, *n.* 回転ドア revolving
door.

kaiten suru, *vb.* 回転する revolve;
rotate.

kaiten suru, *vb.* 開店する open
(business: restaurant, store, etc.)
for the day; establish (business:
restaurant, store, etc.).

kaitō, *n.* 解答 answer; response;
reply.

kaitsū suru, *vb.* 開通する go into
service (highway, bridge,
telephone, cable system).

kaiwa, *n.* 会話 conversation;
eikaiwa English conversation.

kaiyaku, *n.* 解約 cancellation of a
contract.

kaiyō, *n.* 海洋 ocean.

kaizen, *n.* 改善 improvement.

kaji, *n.* 家事 household chores.

kaji, *n.* 火事 fire (conflagration).

kaji, *n.* 舵 helm; rudder.

kajiru, *vb.* かじる gnaw; crunch;
bite.

kajō, *n.* 過剰 excess; surplus.

kakaeru, *vb.* 抱える embrace;
hold; employ (person).

kakaku, *n.* 価格 value; price.

kakari, *n.* 係 person in charge.

kakarichō, *n.* 係長 assistant section chief.

kakariin, *n.* 係員 person in charge.

kakaru, *vb.* 罹る contract (an illness).

kakaru, *vb.* かかる 1. take (time); **gofun kakaru** take five minutes. 2. cost; **godoru kakaru** cost five dollars. 3. hang. 4. depend on. 5. consult (a doctor). 6. start moving.

kakasazu (ni) *adv.* 欠かさず（に） without fail; always.

kakato, *n.* 踵 heel (foot, shoe).

kakawarazu, *conj.* かかわらず in spite of; regardless of; although.

kakawaru, *vb.* 係る、関わる be connected with; be involved in.

kake, *n.* 賭け bet; gambling.

kakedasu, *vb.* 駆け出す start running; dash out.

kakegoe, *n.* 掛け声 shout; cheer.

kakehanareru, *vb.* かけ離れる be far apart; be removed from.

kakehiki, *n.* 駆け引き dealing; bargaining.

kakei, *n.* 家系 lineage; genealogy.

kakei, *n.* 家計 household budget.

kakeibo, *n.* 家計簿 household accounts.

kakekin, *n.* 掛け金 1. premium (insurance). 2. (scheduled) payment.

kakeru, *vb.* 欠ける 1. lack. 2. break off.

kakeru, *vb.* 賭ける bet; gamble.

kakeru, *vb.* 駆ける run.

kakeru, *vb.* 掛ける 1. hang. 2. wear (glasses, necklace); cover. 3. sit down. 4. spend (time, money). 5. telephone. 6. keep in mind; care about.

kaketsu suru, *vb.* 可決する approve or pass (a bill).

kaki, *n.* かき oyster.

kaki, *n.* 柿 persimmon.

kaki, *n.* 夏期 summer; **kakikōshū** summer course.

kakine, *n.* 垣根 fence; hedge.

kaki no, *adj.* 下記の the following; mentioned below.

kakitome, *n.* 書留 registered mail.

kakitomeru, *vb.* 書き留める take notes; write down.

kakitori, *n.* 書き取り dictation.

kakkazan, *n.* 活火山 active volcano.

kakki, *n.* 活気 liveliness; activity; **kakki ga aru** be lively or active.

kakki-teki (na), *adj.* 画期的（な） epochmaking.

kakko, *n.* 括弧 parenthesis; bracket.

kakkō, *n.* 格好 1. form; appearance. 2. appropriateness; suitability.

kakko ii, *adj.* かっこいい attractive; good-looking.

kako, *n.* 過去 past.

kakobunshi, *n.* 過去分詞 past participle.

kakōhin, *n.* 加工品 processed goods (esp. food).

kakokanryōkei, *n.* 過去完了形 past perfect participle.

kakokei, *n.* 過去形 past tense.

kakomu, *vb.* 囲む circle; surround.

kaku, *n.* 核 core; nucleus; kernel.

kaku, *n.* 画 stroke (pen or brush) of kana or kanji.

kaku, *vb.* 欠く lack.

kaku, *vb.* 書く write.

kaku, *vb.* 掻く scratch; scrape.

kaku- 各 each; **kakujin** each person.

kaku- 隔 every other; **kaku-jitsu**

(-shū, -nen) every other day (week, year).

kakuheiki, *n.* 核兵器 nuclear weapon.

kakubetsu (na, no), *adj.* 格別 (な、の) special; exceptional.

kakuchō suru, *vb.* 拡張する expand; enlarge; widen.

kakudo, *n.* 角度 angle.

kakueki(teisha), *n.* 各駅(停車) local train.

kakugo suru, *vb.* 覚悟する be prepared (for something unwelcome).

kakuho suru, *vb.* 確保する ensure.

kakuitsu-teki (na), *adj.* 画一的 (な) uniform.

kakuji no, *adj.* 各自の each; (one's) own.

kakujitsu (na), *adj.* 確実 (な) sure; guaranteed; reliable.

kakumei, *n.* 革命 revolution.

kakumei-teki (na), *adj.* 革命的 (な) revolutionary; innovative.

kakū no, *adj.* 架空の imaginary.

kakuri suru, *vb.* 隔離する isolate; quarantine.

kakuryō, *n.* 閣僚 Cabinet member.

kakusage, *n.* 格下げ demotion.

kakusaku, *n.* 画策 plan; stratagem.

kakushiki, *n.* 格式 1. status; class. 2. formality.

kakushikibaru, *vb.* 格式張る be overly formal.

kakushin, *n.* 確信 confidence; conviction.

kakushin, *n.* 核心 1. core; center. 2. central issue.

kakushin, *n.* 革新 reformation; innovation.

kakushinha, *n.* 革新派 reform politician or political group.

kakusu, *vb.* 隠す hide; cover up.

kakutei suru, *vb.* 確定する decide; conclude.

kakutō, *n.* 格闘 match; fight.

kakutoku suru, *vb.* 獲得する win; obtain.

kakuyaku suru, *vb.* 確約する make a firm promise.

kakyū, *n.* 下級 beginner's level; lower rank.

kama, gama, *n.* 釜 pot in which rice is cooked; **denkigama** electric rice cooker.

kamae, *n.* 構え (martial arts) posture.

kamau, *vb.* 構う care about; take care of; pay attention to.

kamawanai, *vb.* 構わない not mind; not care.

kame, *n.* 亀 tortoise; turtle.

kame, *n.* 瓶 earthenware jar.

kamei suru, *vb.* 加盟する join; become a member.

kamen, *n.* 仮面 mask.

kami, *n.* 紙 paper.

kami, *n.* 神 god.

kami, *n.* 髪 hair (head).

kamikaze, *n.* 神風 1. divine wind. 2. name given to suicide pilots in World War II.

kamikuzu, *n.* 紙屑 wastepaper.

kamikuzu-ire/-kago, *n.* 紙屑入れ／〜籠 wastepaper basket.

kaminari, *n.* 雷 lightning; thunder.

kamisori, *n.* 剃刀 razor.

kamo, *n.* 鴨 duck.

kamoku, *n.* 科目 course; subject (school).

kamome, *n.* かもめ seagull.

kamotsu, *n.* 貨物 freight.

kamu, *vb.* 噛む bite; chew.

kan, *n.* 缶 can.

kan, *n.* 勘 intuition; sixth sense.

-kan 間 for; during; **ichi-jikan han** for an hour and a half.

-kan 巻 volume (book).

kana, *n.* 仮名 Japanese syllabary (hiragana; katakana).

kanai, *n.* 家内 one's wife (humble).

kanamono, *n.* 金物 hardware; **kanamonoya** hardware store.

kanarazu, *adv.* 必ず for certain; without fail.

kanarazushimo, *adv.* 必ずしも not necessarily; not always.

kanari, *adv.* かなり fairly; moderately; **kanari ii** fairly good.

kanashii, *adj.* 悲しい sad; sorrowful.

kanashimu, *vb.* 悲しむ feel sad; grieve; lament.

kanashimubeki, *adj.* 悲しむべき lamentable; regrettable.

kanata 彼方 1. *n.* faraway place; yonder. 2. *adv.* faraway.

kanau, *vb.* 叶う (wish, dream) come true; be fulfilled.

kanawanai, *vb.* 適わない 1. be unable to endure. 2. be unable to compete with; be unable to best.

kanazuchi, *n.* 金槌 1. hammer. 2. person who cannot swim.

kanban, *n.* 看板 signboard (shop, movie theater).

kanbashii, *adj.* 芳しい fragrant.

kanbashikunai, *adj.* 芳しくない undesirable; unsatisfactory.

kanbi (na), *adj.* 甘美 (な) sweet.

kanbi shita, *adj.* 完備 (した) fully equipped.

kanbu, *n.* 幹部 executive.

kanbutsuya, *n.* 乾物屋 dry goods store; grocer.

kanbyō suru, *vb.* 看病する care for a sick person.

kanchigai, *n.* 感違い misjudgment; misunderstanding.

kanchi suru, *vb.* 感知する discern; perceive.

kanchō, *n.* 官庁 government office.

kandai (na), *adj.* 寛大 (な) 1. understanding; lenient. 2. generous; broad-minded.

kandenchi, *n.* 乾電池 dry cell (battery).

kandō suru, *vb.* 感動する be touched; be moved.

kane, okane, *n.* 金、お金 money.

kane, *n.* 鐘 bell.

kanemochi, *n.* 金持ち rich person.

kanemōke, *n.* 金儲け money making.

kaneru, *vb.* 兼ねる serve multiple purposes (positions, functions, etc.) at the same time.

kanetsu suru, *vb.* 加熱する heat.

kangae, *n.* 考え idea; thought; view.

kangaechigai, *n.* 考え違い misunderstanding; misconception.

kangaekata, *n.* 考え方 viewpoint; way of thinking.

kangaenaosu, *vb.* 考え直す rethink; reconsider.

kangaeru, *vb.* 考える think; think up; consider.

kangei suru, *vb.* 歓迎する welcome.

kangeki suru, *vb.* 感激する be moved; be touched.

kangengaku, *n.* 管弦楽 orchestral music.

kangen gakudan, *n.* 管弦楽団 orchestra.

kangofu, *n.* 看護婦 nurse.

kango suru, *vb.* 看護する nurse.

kangoku, *n.* 監獄 jail; prison.

kani, *n.* かに crab.

kanja, *n.* 患者 patient.

kanji, *n.* 漢字 Chinese characters used in Japanese writing.

kanji, *n.* 感じ impression; perception; feeling.

kanjin (na, no), *adj.* 肝心 (な、の)

essential; most important; crucial.

kanjiru, *vb.* 感じる feel; sense.

kanjiyasui, *adj.* 感じやすい
sensitive.

kanjō, *n.* 感情 feeling; emotion;
sentiment.

kanjō, *n.* 勘定 1. bill; check. 2.
calculation.

kanjusei, *n.* 感受性 sensitivity.

kankaku, *n.* 感覚 sense;
sensitivity; feeling; **hōkō-
kankaku** sense of direction.

kankaku, *n.* 間隔 interim; interval;
pause; space.

kanka suru, *vb.* 感化する
influence.

kankei, *n.* 関係 relationship;
relation; connection.

kankei-daimeishi, *n.* 関係代名詞
relative pronoun.

kankei ga aru (nai), *vb.* 関係があ
る (ない) be related (unrelated)
to; have something (nothing) to
do with.

kanketsu (na), *adj.* 簡潔 (な)
succinct; crisp.

kanki, *n.* 歓喜 exhilaration; joy.

kanki, *n.* 換気 ventilation.

kankin suru, *vb.* 監禁する
incarcerate; confine.

kankiri, *n.* 缶切り can opener.

kankō, *n.* 観光 sightseeing;
tourism.

kankōan'naisho, *n.* 観光案内所
tourist information office.

kankōchō, *n.* 官公庁 government
and municipal offices.

kankoku, *n.* 勧告
recommendation; advice.

kankoku, *n.* 韓国 South Korea.

kankokugo, *n.* 韓国語 Korean
(language).

kankokujin, *n.* 韓国人 Korean
(person).

kankōkyaku, *n.* 観光客 sightseer;
tourist.

kankyaku, *n.* 観客 audience;
spectator.

kankyō, *n.* 環境 environment;
surroundings.

kankyōhakai, *n.* 環境破壊
destruction of the environment.

kankyōosen, *n.* 環境汚染
environmental pollution.

kanmuri, *n.* 冠 crown.

kan'nen, *n.* 観念 idea; sense.

kan'nen suru, *vb.* 観念する give
up; be resigned to.

kan'nen-teki (na), *adj.* 観念的
(な) abstract; impractical.

kan'ningu, *n.* カンニング (E.
cunning) cheating.

kan'nō-teki (na), *adj.* 官能的 (な)
voluptuous; sensual.

kanojo 彼女 1. *pron.* she; her. 2. *n.*
girlfriend (used by males).

kanojo no, *adj.* 彼女の her;
girlfriend's (used by males).

kanō (na), *adj.* 可能 (な) possible.

kanō na kagiri *adv.* 可能な限り to
the extent possible.

kanōsei, *n.* 可能性 possibility.

kanō suru, *vb.* 化膿する fester.

kanpai, *interj.* 乾杯 Cheers! To
your health! Bottoms up!

kanpai suru, *vb.* 完敗する be
thoroughly defeated.

kanpōyaku, *n.* 漢方薬 traditional
Chinese medicines.

kanrakugai, *n.* 歓楽街
entertainment district.

kanranseki, *n.* 観覧席 spectator or
audience seating.

kanran suru, *vb.* 観覧する watch
(plays, sports, ballet, etc.)

kanrei, *n.* 慣例 custom; common
practice.

kanren (no), *adj.* 関連 (の) related;

associated.

kanri, *n.* 管理 supervision; administration; management.

kanrihi, *n.* 管理費 maintenance fee (for an apartment).

kanryō, *n.* 官僚 government official; bureaucrat.

kanryō suru, *vb.* 完了する finish; complete.

kanryō-teki (na), *adj.* 官僚的 (な) bureaucratic.

kansanki, *n.* 閑散期 off season.

kansanritsu, *n.* 換算率 exchange rate.

kansan suru, *vb.* 換算する exchange; convert.

kansatsu, *n.* 観察 observation.

kansei, *n.* 完成 completion.

kansei suru, *vb.* 完成する accomplish; complete; finish.

kansen, *n.* 感染 contagion; infection.

kansetsu, *n.* 関節 joint (knee, etc.).

kansetsu-teki (na), *adj.* 間接的 (な) indirect.

kansetsu-teki ni, *adv.* 間接的に indirectly.

kansha, *n.* 感謝 gratitude; appreciation.

kansha suru, *vb.* 感謝する appreciate; feel grateful.

kanshi, *n.* 冠詞 article (grammar).

kanshin, *n.* 関心 concern; interest; **kanshin ga aru** be concerned or interested.

kanshin (na), *adj.* 感心 (な) impressive; admirable.

kanshin suru, *vb.* 感心する be impressed; admire.

kanshi suru, *vb.* 監視する supervise; watch over.

kanshite, *prep.* 関して concerning; regarding.

kanshō, *n.* 干渉 interference; intervention.

kanshō suru, *vb.* 鑑賞する appreciate; enjoy listening to (music), viewing (works of art), reading (literature).

kanshō-teki (na), *adj.* 感傷的 (な) sentimental.

kanshū, *n.* 観衆 audience; spectators.

kanshū-teki (na), *adj.* 慣習的 (な) customary; conventional.

kanso (na), *adj.* 簡素 (な) simple.

kansō, *n.* 感想 opinion; impression.

kansōki, *n.* 乾燥機 dryer; clothes dryer.

kansoku, *n.* 観測 observation; survey.

kansō shiteiru/shita, *adj.* 乾燥している／〜した dry.

kansuru 関する 1. *vb.* be related to; concern. 2. *prep.* concerning; about.

kantan (na), *adj.* 簡単 (な) easy; simple; brief.

kantan ni, *adv.* 簡単に easily; simply; briefly.

kantei, *n.* 鑑定 appraisal.

kantoku, *n.* 監督 director; superintendent; manager; **eiga-kantoku** film director.

kanwa suru, *vb.* 緩和する ease; relax.

kan'yō (no), *adj.* 慣用 (の) 1. customary. 2. idiomatic.

kan'yōgoku, *n.* 慣用語句 idiomatic expression.

kanyū suru, *vb.* 加入する join.

kan'yū suru, *vb.* 勧誘する invite or urge to join.

kanzei, *n.* 関税 (customs) duty; tariff.

kanzen (na), *adj.* 完全 (な) perfect; entire.

kanzen (ni), *adv.* 完全 (に) perfectly; entirely.

kanzenshugisha, *n.* 完全主義者 perfectionist.

kanzō, *n.* 肝臓 liver.

kanzume, *n.* 缶詰 canned food.

kao, *n.* 顔 face; look; countenance; **kao o tsubusu** cause someone to lose face.

kaoiro, *n.* 顔色 complexion.

kaori, *n.* 香り、薫り fragrance; scent; smell; aroma.

kappatsu (na), *adj.* 活発 (な) active; vivacious.

kara (no), *adj.* 空 (の) empty; vacant.

-kara から 1. from; since; after. 2. starting at (time). 3. (in passive mode) by; (made) from; (made) of. 4. because; therefore; so.

kara'age, *n.* 空揚げ deep-fried food.

karada, *n.* 体 1. body. 2. health.

karai, *adj.* 辛い 1. bitter; hot (spicy); salty. 2. strict.

karakau, *vb.* からかう ridicule; jeer.

karakuchi (no), *adj.* 辛口 (の) dry (sake).

karamaru, *vb.* 絡まる become entangled in.

karashi, *n.* 辛子、芥子 mustard.

karasu, *n.* 烏 crow.

karate, *n.* 空手 karate.

kare 彼 1. *pron.* he; him. 2. *n.* boyfriend.

karē, *n.* カレー (E.) curry.

karen (na), *adj.* 可憐 (な) lovely or attractive (woman, flower).

kare no, *adj.* 彼の his; boyfriend's.

karera, *pron.* 彼等 they.

kareru, *vb.* 枯れる wither.

kari, *n.* 借り debt.

karikyuramu, *n.* カリキュラム (E.) curriculum.

kari ni, *conj.* 仮に if.

kari no, *adj.* 仮の tentative; temporary.

karinushi, karite, *n.* 借主、借手 borrower; debtor; tenant.

kariru, *vb.* 借りる 1. borrow; rent. 2. use (someone's telephone, rest room, etc.).

karō, *n.* 過労 exhaustion from overwork.

karōjite, *adv.* 辛うじて barely.

karōshi, *n.* 過労死 death from overwork.

karu, *vb.* 刈る reap; mow; cut (hair).

karuhazumi (na), *adj.* 軽はずみ (な) imprudent; indiscreet.

karui, *adj.* 軽い 1. light. 2. easy.

karuta, *n.* カルタ (Pg. *carta*) playing card(s).

kasa, *n.* 傘 umbrella.

kasai, *n.* 火災 fire.

kasaihōchiki, *n.* 火災報知器 fire alarm.

kasaihoken, *n.* 火災保険 fire insurance.

kasanaru, *vb.* 重なる 1. be piled up. 2. be compounded. 3. occur at the same time.

kasaneru, *vb.* 重ねる 1. pile up. 2. repeat.

kasan suru, *vb.* 加算する add.

kasegu, *vb.* 稼ぐ earn.

kasei, *n.* 火星 Mars (planet).

kasei, *n.* 家政 household management.

kasei suru, *vb.* 加勢する help; support.

kaseki, *n.* 化石 fossil.

kasen, *n.* 下線 underscore.

kasen, *n.* 化繊 synthetic fiber.

kashi, *n.* 菓子 confection; cake.

kashi, *n.* 樫 oak.

kashi, *n.* 華氏 Fahrenheit.

kashi, *n.* 歌詞 lyrics.

kashikoi, *adj.* 賢い wise; clever; intelligent.

kashikomari-mashita, *interj.* かしこまりました I understand. Yes, sir! (said by an inferior to a superior).

kashima, *n.* 貸間 room for rent.

kashira, *n.* 頭 1. head. 2. chief; leader.

kashira moji, *n.* 頭文字 initial letter (of a word).

kashitsukeru, *vb.* 貸付ける lend; loan.

kashiya, *n.* 貸家 house for rent.

kasho, *n.* 箇所 place; point.

kashu, *n.* 歌手 singer.

kasō, *n.* 火葬 cremation.

kasoku, *n.* 加速 acceleration; **kasoku ga tsuku** accelerate.

kasōshakai, *n.* 下層社会 lower class.

kasōtekikoku, *n.* 仮想敵国 hypothetical enemy country.

kassai, *n.* 喝采 applause.

kasshoku, *n.* 褐色 brown.

kasu, *vb.* 貸す 1. lend; loan. 2. let someone use something.

kasuka (na), *adj.* 微か (な) faint; vague.

kasumu, *vb.* 霞 blur; be dim; be hazy.

kasurikizu, *n.* かすり傷 scratch; minor injury.

kasutera, *n.* カステラ (Pg. *Castella*) sponge cake.

kata, *n.* 肩 shoulder; **kata ga koru** have stiff shoulders.

kata, *n.* 型 form (martial arts, dance, etc.); posture; style.

kata, *n.* 形 model; type.

kata 方 1. how to; **tsukaikata** how to use. 2. person; **ano kata**

that person.

katachi, *n.* 形 shape; form.

katagaki, *n.* 肩書き title.

katagawatsūkō, *n.* 片側通行 one-way traffic.

katai, *adj.* 固い 1. hard; firm; stiff. 2. upright; conscientious.

katakana, *n.* 片仮名 Japanese syllabary for foreign words.

kataki, *n.* 敵 enemy; rival.

kataki o utsu, *vb.* 敵を討つ revenge; avenge.

katakurushii, *adj.* 堅苦しい 1. rigid; stiff-mannered. 2. overly formal.

katamari, *n.* 固まり lump; mass.

katamaru, *vb.* 固まる 1. coagulate; harden. 2. group together.

katameru, *vb.* 固める 1. harden. 2. solidify. 3. strengthen.

katami, *n.* 形見 keepsake; memento.

katamukeru, *vb.* 傾ける tilt; incline.

katamuku, *vb.* 傾く 1. tilt; incline. 2. decline; go down.

katana, *n.* 刀 Japanese sword.

kataomoi, *n.* 片思い unrequited love.

kataru, *vb.* 語る talk; relate.

katasumi, *n.* 片隅 corner.

katate, *n.* 片手 one hand.

katatsumuri, *n.* かたつむり snail.

katawara (ni), *prep.* 傍ら (に) 1. close by; beside. 2. in addition to; besides.

katazukeru, *vb.* 片付ける 1. tidy up; put things in order. 2. finish; settle. 3. get rid of.

kate, *n.* 糧 food.

katei, *n.* 家庭 home; household.

katei, *n.* 過程 process.

katei, *n.* 課程 course; curriculum.

katei, *n.* 仮定 supposition;

hypothesis; conjecture.

kateihō, *n.* 仮定法 subjunctive mood.

kateikyōshi, *n.* 家庭教師 private tutor.

katei suru, *vb.* 仮定する suppose; hypothesize.

katoki, *n.* 過渡期 period of transition.

katōkyōsō, *n.* 過当競争 excessive competition.

katorikku, *n.* カトリック (Du. *katholiek*) Catholic.

katsu, *n.* カツ breaded, deep-fried cutlet; **tonkatsu** pork cutlet.

katsu, *vb.* 勝 win; defeat.

katsu, *adv., conj.* 且つ and; besides; in addition.

katsudō, *n.* 活動 activity.

katsugu, *vb.* 担ぐ 1. carry; shoulder. 2. trick; dupe.

katsuji, *n.* 活字 type (printing).

katsuo, *n.* 鰹 bonito.

katsura, *n.* かつら wig.

katsute, *adv.* かつて formerly; long ago.

katsuyaku suru, *vb.* 活躍する be active.

katsuyō, *n.* 活用 (grammar) conjugation; inflection.

katsuyō suru, *vb.* 活用する make the most of.

katte, *n.* 勝手 1. selfishness. 2. one's personal concern; one's business; **watashi no katte** my business (none of your business).

katte (na), *adj.* 勝手 (な) 1. selfish. 2. arbitrary. 3. groundless.

katte ni, *adv.* 勝手に 1. selfishly. 2. voluntarily. 3. without permission.

kattō, *n.* 葛藤 conflict; friction.

katto naru, *vb.* かっとなる fly into a rage.

kau, *vb.* 買う 1. buy. 2. appreciate. 3. invite (a mishap).

kau, *vb.* 飼う keep (a pet); raise (cattle).

kawa, *n.* 皮 skin; leather; bark; rind.

kawa, *n.* 川 stream; river.

kawaigaru, *vb.* 可愛がる cherish; dote on.

kawairashii, *adj.* 可愛らしい lovely; cute.

kawaisō (na), *adj.* 可哀そう (な) pitiful; pitiable; poor.

kawaita, *adj.* 乾いた dry.

kawaku, *vb.* 乾く become dry.

kawara, *n.* 瓦 roof tile.

kawari, *n.* 代わり 1. substitute. 2. second helping of food. 3. exchange; return; **sono kawari ni** in exchange or return for that.

kawariyasui, *adj.* 変わりやすい changeable; unstable.

kawaru, *vb.* 変わる change.

kawaru, *vb.* 代わる take the place of.

kawase, *n.* 為替 exchange (currency).

kawasu, *vb.* 交わす exchange.

kawatta, *adj.* 変わった strange; different.

kaya, *n.* 蚊帳 mosquito net.

kayōbi, *n.* 火曜日 Tuesday.

kayōkyoku, *n.* 歌謡曲 Japanese popular song.

kayou, *vb.* 通う commute; frequent.

kayowai, *adj.* か弱い fragile; weak.

kayu, *n.* 粥 rice porridge.

kayui, *adj.* 痒い itchy.

kazan, *n.* 火山 volcano.

kazari, *n.* 飾り decoration; ornament.

kazaru, *vb.* 飾る decorate.

kaze, *n.* 風 breeze; wind; **kaze ga**

fuku the wind blows.

kaze, *n.* 風邪 cold; **kaze o hiku** catch a cold.

kazeihin, *n.* 課税品 taxable item.

kazei suru, *vb.* 課税する tax.

kazetōshi, *n.* 風通し ventilation.

kazoeru, *vb.* 数える count.

kazoku, *n.* 家族 family.

kazu, *n.* 数 number.

ke, *n.* 毛 1. hair. 2. fur; wool.

-ke 家 family; **Wadake** the Wada family.

kebyō, *n.* 仮病 feigned illness.

kechappu, *n.* ケチャップ (E.) ketchup.

kechi (na), *adj.* けち (な) 1. miserly. 2. stingy.

kedakai, *n.* 気高い noble.

kedamono, *n.* 獣 beast.

kega, *n.* 怪我 wound; injury.

kega o suru, *vb.* 怪我をする suffer an injury; get hurt.

kegarawashii, *adj.* 汚らわしい dirty; disgusting; sickening.

kegare, *n.* 汚れ unchastity; impurity; immorality.

kegareru, *vb.* 汚れる become impure or corrupt.

kegasu, *vb.* 汚す sully; disgrace.

kegawa, *n.* 毛皮 fur.

kegen (na), *adj.* 怪訝 (な) suspicious.

kehai, *n.* 気配 harbinger; indication; sign.

kei, *n.* 刑 criminal sentence; punishment.

keiba, *n.* 競馬 horse racing.

keibatsu, *n.* 刑罰 penalty; punishment.

keibetsu suru, *vb.* 軽蔑する disdain; scorn.

keibi, *n.* 警備 guard; watch.

keibu, *n.* 警部 police inspector.

keido, *n.* 経度 longitude.

keido (no), *adj.* 軽度 (の) slight.

keiei, *n.* 経営 management.

keieisha, *n.* 経営者 business owner or manager.

keiei suru, *vb.* 経営する manage; run (business).

keien suru, *vb.* 敬遠する stay away from; avoid.

keifuku suru, *vb.* 敬服する respect; admire.

keigen suru, *vb.* 軽減する reduce; alleviate.

keigo, *n.* 敬語 honorific language.

keigo suru, *vb.* 警護する guard.

keigu 敬具 Yours truly; Yours sincerely.

keihaku (na), *adj.* 軽薄 (な) foolish; shallow.

keihatsu suru, *vb.* 啓発する stimulate; enlighten.

keihi, *n.* 経費 expense.

keihō, *n.* 刑法 criminal law.

keihō, *n.* 警報 warning; alarm.

keii, *n.* 敬意 respect; **keii o hyō suru** express or pay one's respect.

keiji, *n.* 掲示 (written) notice; announcement.

keiji, *n.* 刑事 police detective.

keiji, *n.* 啓示 revelation; enlightenment; inspiration; **keiji o ukeru** become inspired.

keijijō no, *adj.* 形而上の metaphysical.

keika, *n.* 経過 development; progress.

keikai (na), *adj.* 軽快 (な) 1. light. 2. nimble.

keikai suru, *vb.* 警戒する be cautious; watch out.

keikaku, *n.* 計画 project; plan; **keikaku o tateru** make a plan.

keikan, *n.* 警官 police officer.

keika suru, *vb.* 経過する (time) pass.

keiken, *n.* 経験 experience.

keiken suru, *vb.* 経験する experience.

keiki, *n.* 景気 economic situation; business conditions.

keiko, *n.* 稽古 rehearsal; practice; training.

keikō, *n.* 傾向 1. inclination; tendency. 2. trend.

keikoku, *n.* 警告 warning; caution.

keikōtō, *n.* 蛍光灯 fluorescent light.

keimō suru, *vb.* 啓蒙する enlighten.

keimusho, *n.* 刑務所 prison.

keiniku, *n.* 鶏肉 chicken (meat).

keireki, *n.* 経歴 career history.

keiren, *n.* けいれん spasm; cramp.

keiri, *n.* 経理 accounting.

keiryaku, *n.* 計略 plot; trick.

keisai suru, *vb.* 掲載する publish; print.

keisan, *n.* 計算 calculation.

keisan suru, *vb.* 計算する calculate; count.

keisatsu, *n.* 警察 the police.

keisatsusho, *n.* 警察署 police station.

keisei, *n.* 形勢 situation.

keiseki, *n.* 形跡 sign; trace.

keisha suru, *vb.* 傾斜する tilt; slant; slope.

keishiki, *n.* 形式 form; formality.

keishikibatta, *adj.* 形式ばった formal; stiff.

keishi suru, *vb.* 軽視する slight; underestimate; neglect.

keishō, *n.* 軽傷 minor injury.

keishō, *n.* 敬称 honorific.

keishoku, *n.* 軽食 snack; light meal.

keishō suru, *vb.* 継承する succeed to.

keisotsu (na), *adj.* 軽率 (な) thoughtless; hasty.

keitai, *n.* 形態 1. form; shape. 2. system.

keitai suru, *vb.* 携帯する carry.

keitai-yō (no), *adj.* 携帯用 (の) portable.

keito, *n.* 毛糸 woolen yarn.

keitō, *n.* 系統 system.

keiyaku, *n.* 契約 contract; **keiyakuihan** breach of contract.

keiyakusha, *n.* 契約者 party to a contract.

keiyakusho, *n.* 契約書 (written) contract.

keiyōshi, *n.* 形容詞 adjective.

keiyō suru, *vb.* 形容する describe.

keiyū (de), *adv.* 経由 (で) via; by way of.

keizai, *n.* 経済 economy.

keizaigaku, *n.* 経済学 economics.

keizai-teki (na), *adj.* 経済的 (な) economical.

keizoku suru, *vb.* 継続する continue.

keizu, *n.* 系図 lineage; genealogy.

kejime, *n.* けじめ 1. differentiation. 2. solution.

kēki, *n.* ケーキ (E.) cake.

kekka, *n.* 結果 result; consequence.

kekkaku, *n.* 結核 tuberculosis.

kekkan, *n.* 血管 blood vessel.

kekkan, *n.* 欠陥 flaw; defect.

kekkanhin, *n.* 欠陥品 defective product.

kekkansha, *n.* 欠陥車 defective car.

kekkin, *n.* 欠勤 absence from one's place of employment.

kekkō, *n.* 欠航 cancellation of a scheduled flight or sailing.

kekkō (na) 結構 (な) 1. *adj.* good. 2. *adj.* adequate; acceptable. 3. *adv.* rather; adequately.

kekkō desu 結構です No, thank you.

kekkon, *n.* 結婚 marriage.

kekkonshiki, *n.* 結婚式 wedding.

kekkon shiteiru, *adj.* 結婚している married.

kekkon suru, *vb.* 結婚する get married.

kekkyoku, *adv.* 結局 after all; eventually.

kemui, kemutai, *adj.* 煙い, 煙たい 1. smoky. 2. ill at ease.

kemuri, *n.* 煙 smoke.

ken, *n.* 剣 sword.

ken, *n.* 券 ticket.

ken, *n.* 件 matter; case.

ken, *n.* 県 prefecture.

kenasu, *vb.* けなす slander; speak ill of; humiliate.

kenbikyō, *n.* 顕微鏡 microscope.

kenbun, *n.* 見聞 knowledge.

kenbutsu, *n.* 見物 sightseeing; watching (sporting event, etc.).

kenchiku, *n.* 建築 architecture.

kenchikuka, *n.* 建築家 architect.

kencho (na), *adj.* 顕著 (な) conspicuous; remarkable.

kenchō, *n.* 県庁 prefectural office.

kendō, *n.* 剣道 Japanese fencing with bamboo swords.

kenen, *n.* 懸念 apprehension; fear.

ken'etsu, *n.* 検閲 censorship; inspection.

kengaku suru, *vb.* 見学する visit to observe.

kengen, *n.* 権限 power; authority.

kengi, *n.* 嫌疑 suspicion.

ken'i, *n.* 権威 authority.

kenji, *n.* 検事 prosecutor.

kenjō, *n.* 謙譲 humbleness; modesty.

kenjū, *n.* 拳銃 handgun.

kenka, *n.* 喧嘩 fight; quarrel.

kenkai, *n.* 見解 viewpoint.

kenka suru, *vb.* 喧嘩する fight; quarrel.

kenketsu, *n.* 献血 blood donation.

kenkin, *n.* 献金 contribution (money); donation.

kenkō, *n.* 健康 health.

kenkōshindan, *n.* 健康診断 physical examination.

kenkyo, *n.* 謙虚 modesty.

kenkyū, *n.* 研究 study; research.

kenmei (na), *adj.* 賢明 (な) wise.

kenmei ni, *adv.* 懸命に eagerly.

ken'o, *n.* 嫌悪 hatred; disgust.

kenpō, *n.* 憲法 constitution (government).

kenri, *n.* 権利 right.

kenryoku, *n.* 権力 power.

kensa, *n.* 検査 investigation; examination.

kensetsu, *n.* 建設 construction.

kenshiki, *n.* 見識 educated opinion; discernment.

kenshin, *n.* 献身 devotion.

kenshin-teki (na), *adj.* 献身的 (な) devoted; self-sacrificing.

kenshō, *n.* 懸賞 award; prize.

kenshū, *n.* 研修 training.

kenson, *n.* 謙遜 modesty.

kentai, *n.* 倦怠 ennui; tedium.

kentō, *n.* 見当 assumption; speculation.

kentō suru, *vb.* 検討する 1. scrutinize. 2. consider.

ken'yaku suru, *vb.* 倹約する economize; be thrifty.

kenzai (na), *adj.* 健在 (な) 1. healthy. 2. active.

kenzen (na), *adj.* 健全 (な) wholesome; sound.

kenzō, *n.* 建造 construction.

keppaku, *n.* 潔白 innocence.

keppeki (na), *adj.* 潔癖 (な) particular; fastidious.

kerai, *n.* 家来 retainer; subject.

keredo(mo), けれど（も）1. *conj.* although; but. 2. *adv.* nevertheless.

keru, *vb.* 蹴る kick.

kesa, *n., adv.* 今朝 this morning.

keshigomu, *n.* 消しゴム eraser.

keshi'in, *n.* 消し印 postmark.

keshikakeru, *vb.* けしかける instigate; provoke.

keshikaran, *adj.* 怪しからん 1. ill-mannered; rude. 2. disgraceful.

keshiki, *n.* 景色 scenery; view.

keshō, *n.* 化粧 makeup.

keshōshitsu, *n.* 化粧室 dressing room; bathroom.

kessaku, *n.* 傑作 masterpiece.

kessan, *n.* 決算 corporate or government financial report.

kessei suru, *vb.* 結成する organize.

kesseki, *n.* 欠席 absence.

kesseki suru, *vb.* 欠席する be absent.

kessen, kesshō, *n.* 決戦、決勝 deciding match.

kesshin, *n.* 決心 decision; determination.

kesshite, *adv.* 決して never.

kesshō, *n.* 結晶 crystal.

kessuru, *vb.* 決する decide.

kesu, *vb.* 消す 1. wipe out. 2. turn off. 3. extinguish.

ketatamashii, *adj.* けたたましい loud.

ketsuatsu, *n.* 血圧 blood pressure.

ketsubō, *n.* 欠乏 shortage; lack.

ketsueki, *n.* 血液 blood.

ketsugō suru, *n.* 結合する unite; combine.

ketsumatsu, *n.* 結末 ending; result; conclusion.

ketsuretsu suru, *vb.* 決裂する split; break down.

ketsuron, *n.* 結論 conclusion.

ketsuzoku, *n.* 血族 blood relative.

kettaku suru, *vb.* 結託する conspire.

kettei, *n.* 決定 decision; conclusion.

kettei suru, *vb.* 決定する decide; conclude.

ketten, *n.* 欠点 fault; blemish; shortcoming.

kettō, *n.* 血統 blood line; lineage.

kettō, *n.* 決闘 duel.

kewashii, *adj.* 険しい 1. steep. 2. stern.

kezuru, *vb.* 削る 1. shave. 2. sharpen. 3. cut down.

ki, *n.* 木 tree.

ki, *n.* 気 1. spirit; soul. 2. feeling. 3. intention; inclination.

kiatsu, *n.* 気圧 atmospheric pressure.

kiba, *n.* 牙 fang; tusk.

kiban, *n.* 基盤 foundation.

kibarashi, *n.* 気晴らし diversion; pastime.

kibatsu (na), *adj.* 奇抜（な) eccentric; unconventional.

kiben, *n.* 詭弁 sophistry.

kibi-kibi shita, *adj.* きびきびした energetic; witty.

kibin (na), *adj.* 機敏（な) nimble; quick.

kibishii, *adj.* 厳しい stern; rigid.

kibo, *n.* 規模 scale.

kibō, *n.* 希望 hope; wish.

kibō suru, *vb.* 希望する hope; wish.

kibun, *n.* 気分 feeling; mood.

kichi, *n.* 基地 base; **gunji kichi** military base.

kichi, *n.* 機知 wit.

kichi, *n.* 吉 good fortune.

kichigai, *n., adj.* 気違い lunatic; insane.

kichin to, *adv.* きちんと properly; tidily.

kichō (na), *adj.* 貴重 (な) precious.

kichōmen (na), *adj.* 几帳面 (な) scrupulous; meticulous.

kidate, *n.* 気立て disposition; personality.

kidō, *n.* 軌道 orbit.

kidoru, *vb.* 気取る put on airs.

kieru, *vb.* 消える disappear; extinguish.

kifu, *n.* 寄付 contribution; donation.

ki ga au, *vb.* 気が合う feel comfortable or compatible with.

ki ga chiisai, *adj.* 気が小さい timid.

ki ga chiru, *vb.* 気が散る be distracted.

kigaeru, *vb.* 着替える change clothes.

ki ga hikeru, *vb.* 気がひける feel awkward; feel overwhelmed.

ki ga ii, *adj.* 気が良い good-natured.

kigakari, *n.* 気掛かり apprehension; concern.

ki ga kawaru, *vb.* 気が変わる change one's mind.

ki ga ki de nai, *adj.* 気が気でない anxious; uneasy.

ki ga kikanai, *vb.* 気がきかない be insensitive.

ki ga kiku, *vb.* 気がきく be sensitive; be considerate.

ki ga kuru'u, *vb.* 気が狂う go mad.

ki ga mijikai, *adj.* 気が短い short-tempered.

ki ga muku, *vb.* 気が向く feel like doing something.

kigane suru, *vb.* 気がねする hesitate; be reserved.

ki ga omoi, *adj.* 気が重い depressed; discouraged.

ki ga sumu, *vb.* 気がすむ feel satisfied.

ki ga suru, *vb.* 気がする imagine; feel; sense.

ki ga susumanai, *vb.* 気がすすまない be reluctant.

ki ga togameru, *vb.* 気がとがめる feel guilty.

ki ga tsuku, *vb.* 気が付く 1. become aware of; notice. 2. come to; regain consciousness.

ki ga tsuyoi, *adj.* 気が強い strong-willed.

ki ga yowai, *adj.* 気が弱い cowardly; timid.

kigeki, *n.* 喜劇 comedy.

kigen, *n.* 期限 deadline; term.

kigen, *n.* 起源 origin.

kigen, *n.* 機嫌 mood; feeling; humor; **ii kigen** cheerfulness; good-humor.

kigen, *n.* 紀元 era; **seireki kigen 1948** 1948 A.D.

kigenzen, *n.* 紀元前 (year) B.C.

kigō, *n.* 記号 sign; symbol.

kigu, *n.* 器具 equipment; appliance; utensil.

kigurai, *n.* 気位 pride.

kigyō, *n.* 企業 enterprise; company.

kihin, *n.* 気品 grace.

kihon, *n.* 基本 basics.

kihon-teki (na), *adj.* 基本的 (な) basic.

kiiro, *n.* 黄色 yellow.

kiiroi, *adj.* 黄色い yellow.

kiji, *n.* 生地 fabric; textile; cloth.

kiji, *n.* 記事 newspaper article.

kijitsu, *n.* 期日 fixed date.

kijun, *n.* 基準 criterion; standard.

kijutsu suru, *vb.* 記述する describe in writing.

kika, *n.* 帰化 naturalization.

kikagaku, *n.* 幾何学 geometry.

kikai, *n.* 機会 opportunity.

kikai, *n.* 機械 machine.

kikaku, *n.* 企画 project; plan.

kikaku, *n.* 規格 standard.

kikan, *n.* 器官 organ (body).

kikan, *n.* 機関 1. engine. 2. system. 3. agency.

kikan, *n.* 期間 duration; period.

kikanshi, *n.* 機関誌 house organ.

kikazaru, *vb.* 着飾る dress up.

kiken, *n.* 危険 danger; risk.

kiken na, *adj.* 危険な dangerous; risky.

kiki, *n.* 危機 crisis; **sekiyukiki** oil crisis.

kiki-kaesu/-naosu, *vb.* 聞き返す／～直す ask again.

kikin, *n.* 基金 fund.

kikin, *n.* 飢饉 famine.

kikitori, *n.* 聞き取り dictation; listening.

kikitorinikui, *adj.* 聞き取りにくい almost inaudible.

kikitoru, *vb.* 聞き取る hear; understand.

kikkari, *adv.* きっかり exactly.

kikō, *n.* 気候 weather; climate.

kikō, *n.* 機構 structure; system; organization.

kikōbun, *n.* 記行文 written description of a journey.

kikoeru, *vb.* 聞こえる 1. be audible. 2. sound; **hontō ni kikoeru** sound true.

kikoku suru, *vb.* 帰国する return to one's own country.

kikon (no), *adj.* 既婚 (の) married.

kiku, *n.* 菊 chrysanthemum.

kiku, *vb.* 聞く 1. hear; listen. 2. inquire; ask.

kiku, *vb.* 効く be effective.

kikubari, *n.* 気配り consideration.

kikyō, *n.* 帰郷 homecoming.

kimae, *n.* 気前 generosity; **kimae ga ii** generous.

kimagure (na), *adj.* 気紛れ (な) whimsical; capricious.

kimama (na), *adj.* 気まま (な) carefree.

kimari, *n.* 決まり rule.

kimarimonku, *n.* 決まり文句 cliché.

kimaru, *vb.* 決まる be decided.

kimatsushiken, *n.* 期末試験 final examination.

kimazui, *adj.* 気まずい awkward; disagreeable.

kimeru, *vb.* 決める decide.

kimi, *n.* 黄身 egg yolk.

kimi, *pron.* 君 you (informal).

kimi no, *adj.* 君の your (informal).

kimo, *n.* 肝 1. liver. 2. courage.

kimochi, *n.* 気持ち feeling.

kimochi ga ii, *adj.* 気持が良い pleasant; comfortable.

kimono, *n.* 着物 kimono.

kimuzukashii, *adj.* 気難しい difficult (personality); particular.

kimyō (na), *adj.* 奇妙 (な) strange.

kin, *n.* 金 gold.

kin, *n.* 菌 germ; fungus.

kinaga ni, *adv.* 気長に patiently.

kinben (na), *adj.* 勤勉 (な) diligent; hard-working.

kinchō, *n.* 緊張 nervousness; tension.

kindai, *n.* 近代 modern era.

kindai-teki (na), *adj.* 近代的 (な) modern.

kinen, *n.* 記念 memento; memorial; commemoration.

kin'en 禁煙 No Smoking.

kin'enseki, *n.* 禁煙席 nonsmoking seat.

kin'ensha, *n.* 禁煙車 nonsmoking car.

kingaku, *n.* 金額 sum of money.

kingan, *n.* 近眼 nearsightedness.

kingyo, *n.* 金魚 goldfish.

ki ni iranai/kuwanai, *vb.* 気に入らない／～食わない dislike.

ki ni iru, *vb.* 気に入る like; favor.

ki ni naru/suru, *vb.* 気になる／〜する worry about; be concerned about.

kin'itsu (no), *adj.* 均一 (の) equal; uniform.

kinjiru, *vb.* 禁じる prohibit.

kinjo, *n.* 近所 neighborhood.

kinko, *n.* 金庫 safe.

kinkō, *n.* 均衡 balance.

kinkyō, *n.* 近況 latest news; present condition.

kinkyū, *n.* 緊急 emergency.

kinmu suru, *vb.* 勤務する work (at one's place of employment).

kin'nen, *n.* 近年 recent years.

kin'niku, *n.* 筋肉 muscle.

kinō, *n.* 機能 function.

kinō, *n., adv.* 昨日 yesterday.

ki no doku (na), *adj.* 気の毒 (な) pitiful.

ki no hayai, *adj.* 気の早い imprudent; rash.

kinoko, *n.* きのこ mushroom.

ki no nagai, *adj.* 気の長い patient.

kinpaku, *n.* 緊迫 tension; strain.

kinpatsu, *n.* 金髪 blond hair.

kinri, *n.* 金利 interest rate.

kinsei, *n.* 近世 modern times.

kinsei, *n.* 均整 proportion; balance.

kinsei, *n.* 金星 Venus (planet).

kinsen, *n.* 金銭 money.

kinshi, *n.* 禁止 ban; prohibition.

kinshi, *n.* 近視 shortsightedness; nearsightedness.

kinshin, *n.* 近親 close relative.

kinshu, *n.* 禁酒 abstinence from alcohol.

kinu, *n.* 絹 silk.

kin'yōbi, *n.* 金曜日 Friday.

kinyū suru, *vb.* 記入する write in; enter.

kin'yū, *n.* 金融 finance.

kinzoku, *n.* 金属 metal.

kioku, *n.* 記憶 memory.

ki o kubaru, *vb.* 気を配る pay attention.

kioku suru, *vb.* 記憶する remember.

kion, *n.* 気温 (air) temperature.

ki o tsukau, *vb.* 気をつかう worry about.

ki o tsukeru, *vb.* 気をつける be careful.

ki o tsukete, *interj.* 気をつけて Take care! Watch out!

ki o ushinau, *vb.* 気を失う faint; lose consciousness.

kippari (to), *adv.* きっぱり (と) 1. once and for all. 2. point-blank.

kippu, *n.* 切符 ticket; **katamichi-kippu** one-way ticket; **ōfuku-kippu** round-trip ticket.

kirai (na) 嫌い (な) 1. *adj.* distasteful. 2. *vb.* dislike.

kira-kira suru, *vb.* きらきらする glitter; twinkle.

kiraku (na), *adj.* 気楽 (な) easygoing; carefree.

kirasu, *vb.* 切らす run out of; exhaust (supply).

kirau, *vb.* 嫌う dislike.

kirei (na), *adj.* きれい (な) 1. beautiful; pretty. 2. clean. 3. fair.

kireru, *vb.* 切れる 1. cut (well). 2. be disconnected. 3. run out of. 4. expire.

kiri, *n.* 霧 fog; mist.

kirikaeru, *vb.* 切り替える change; switch.

kirin, *n.* きりん giraffe.

kirisageru, *vb.* 切り下げる devalue.

kirisuto, *n.* キリスト (Pg. *Cristo*) Jesus Christ.

kirisutokyō, *n.* キリスト教 Christianity.

kiritaosu, *vb.* 切り倒す cut down

(a tree).

kiritoru, *vb.* 切り取る cut off or out.

kiritsumeru, *vb.* 切り詰める 1. cut down (expense). 2. shorten.

kiritsu suru, *vb.* 起立する stand up.

kiro, *n.* キロ (F. *kilo*) kilogram.

kiroku, *n.* 記録 document; record.

kiru, *vb.* 切る 1. cut. 2. turn off; hang up; stop.

kiru, *vb.* 着る put on; wear (clothes).

kiryō, *n.* 器量 1. looks. 2. ability.

kiryoku, *n.* 気力 willpower; mental energy.

kiryū, *n.* 気流 air current.

kisaku (na), *adj.* 気さく (な) friendly; easygoing.

kisei, *n.* 規制 regulation; restriction.

kisei, *n.* 気勢 vigor; spirit.

kisei, *n.* 帰省 homecoming.

kisei no, *adj.* 既製の ready-made.

kiseki, *n.* 奇蹟 miracle.

kiseru, *vb.* 着せる help someone dress.

kisetsu, *n.* 季節 season.

kisha, *n.* 記者 reporter.

kisha, *n.* 汽車 train with a steam locomotive.

kisha de, *adv.* 汽車で by train.

kisha kaiken, *n.* 記者会見 press conference.

kishi, *n.* 岸 shore.

kishitsu, *n.* 気質 disposition; nature; personality.

kishō, *n.* 気性 nature; temperament; disposition.

kishō, *n.* 気象 weather.

kishu, *n.* 騎手 jockey.

kiso, *n.* 基礎 foundation; base; basics.

kiso, *n.* 起訴 prosecution.

kisoku, *n.* 規則 rule; regulation.

kisou, *vb.* 競う compete with.

kissaten, *n.* 喫茶店 coffee shop.

kissui no, *adj.* 生粋の pure.

kisu, *n.* キス (E.) kiss.

kisū, *n.* 基数 cardinal number.

kisū, *n.* 奇数 odd number.

kisuru, *vb.* 帰する 1. attribute to; originate from. 2. result in.

kita, *n.* 北 north.

kitachōsen, *n.* 北朝鮮 North Korea.

kitaeru, *vb.* 鍛える train; strengthen (oneself).

kitai, *n.* 気体 gas.

kitai, *n.* 期待 expectation.

kitai suru, *vb.* 期待する expect.

kitaku, *n.* 帰宅 returning home; going home.

kitanai, *adj.* 汚い 1. dirty. 2. unjust; mean.

kitchiri (to), *adv.* きっちり (と) 1. exactly. 2. on time. 3. tightly.

kitō, *n.* 祈とう prayer.

kitoku, *n.* 危篤 critical condition (health).

kitsuen, *n.* 喫煙 smoking (tobacco).

kitsuenseki, *n.* 喫煙席 smoking seat.

kitsui, *adj.* きつい 1. laborious; difficult. 2. tight-fitting. 3. stern; harsh.

kitsune, *n.* 狐 fox.

kitte, *n.* 切手 postage stamp.

kitto, *adv.* きっと for sure; without fail.

kiwadatsu, *vb.* 際立つ stand out; be conspicuous.

kiwadoi, *adj.* 際どい 1. precarious; risky. 2. indecent.

kiwameru, *vb.* 極める attain; master.

kiwamete, *adv.* 極めて extremely;

very.

kiyasume, *n.* 気休め insincere reassurance or consolation.

kiyō (na), *adj.* 器用 (な) dexterous; clever.

kiyoi, *adj.* 清い clear; pure.

kiza (na), *adj.* 気障 (な) snobbish; conceited.

kizamu, *vb.* 刻む cut; carve; mince; dice.

kizashi, *n.* 兆し omen.

kizen to shita, *adj.* 毅然とした self-possessed; resolute.

kizetsu suru, *vb.* 気絶する faint.

kizō, *n.* 寄贈 contribution; donation.

kizoku, *n.* 貴族 aristocracy; nobility.

kizu, *n.* 傷 1. scar; wound; injury. 2. defect.

kizuguchi, *n.* 傷口 wound.

kizukau, *vb.* 気遣う care for; worry; pay attention.

kizuku, *vb.* 気付く 1. find out; become aware of. 2. regain consciousness.

kizuku, *vb.* 築く establish; build.

kizuna, *n.* 絆 bond; tie.

kizutsukeru, *vb.* 傷つける hurt; injure; damage.

kizutsuku, *vb.* 傷つく be hurt; be injured; be damaged.

-kkai see **-kai**.

ko, *n.* 子 baby (human, animal); child.

ko, *n.* 弧 arc.

ko- 故 late; deceased; **ko-Ozushi** the late Mr. Ozu.

-ko 個 (counter) **tamago goko** five eggs.

-ko 子 (suffix for woman's given name) **Michiko** Michiko.

kō, *n.* 香 incense.

kō, *adv.* こう this way; like this; so

much like this.

-kō 港 port; **yokohamakō** Port of Yokohama.

kōbai, *n.* 購買 purchase.

kōban, *n.* 交番 police box.

kobetsu-teki ni, *adv.* 個別的に individually.

koboreru, *vb.* こぼれる spill; drop; overflow.

kobosu, *vb.* こぼす spill; drop.

kobu, *n.* こぶ bump; hump; lump.

kōbu, *n.* 後部 rear.

kobun, *n.* 子分 protégé; follower.

kobun, *n.* 古文 classical Japanese literature.

kōbunsho, *n.* 公文書 official document.

kobushi, *n.* 拳 fist.

kōbutsu, *n.* 好物 favorite food.

kōbutsu, *n.* 鉱物 mineral.

kōcha, *n.* 紅茶 black tea; **kōcha o ireru** prepare black tea.

kōchi, *n.* 耕地 cultivated land.

kochira, *pron.* こちら this person; this place; this way.

kōchisho, *n.* 拘置所 detention center.

kōchi suru, *vb.* 拘置する detain.

kochō, *n.* 誇張 exaggeration.

kōchō, *n.* 校長 school principal.

kōchō (na, no), *adj.* 好調 (な、の) in good condition or form.

kodai, *n.* 古代 ancient times.

kōdai (na), *adj.* 広大 (な) vast.

kodai no, *adj.* 古代の ancient.

kodawaru, *vb.* 拘わる be fixated on something; be particular about.

kodō, *n.* 鼓動 beat (drum, heart).

kōdo, *n.* 高度 altitude.

kōdo (na, no), *adj.* 高度 (な、の) high-level; advanced.

kōdō, *n.* 行動 behavior; action.

kōdō, *n.* 講堂 auditorium.

kodoku, *n.* 孤独 solitude; isolation.

kōdoku, *n.* 購読 subscription.

kōdoku suru, *vb.* 購読する subscribe.

kodomo, *n.* 子供 child(ren).

kodomorashii, *adj.* 子供らしい childlike.

koe, *n.* 声 1. voice; **ōkii (chiisai) koe** loud (soft) voice. 2. sound of (animal); **semi no koe** chirping of cicada. 3. opinion.

koeda, *n.* 小枝 twig.

kōei, *n.* 光栄 glory; honor.

kōei no, *adj.* 公営の publicly run.

kōen, *n.* 公園 park.

kōen, *n.* 公演 performance.

kōen, *n.* 講演 speech; lecture.

kōen, *n.* 後援 sponsorship; support.

kōenkai, *n.* 後援会 support group.

kōenkai, *n.* 講演会 lecture.

kōensha, *n.* 講演者 speaker; lecturer.

koeru, *vb.* 越える 1. exceed; surpass. 2. step over; pass; cross.

koeru, *vb.* 肥える put on weight.

koeta, *adj.* 肥えた 1. overweight. 2. fertile.

kofū (na), *adj.* 古風 (な) antiquated; old-fashioned.

kōfuku, *n.* 幸福 happiness.

kōfuku (na, no), *adj.* 幸福 (な、の) happy.

kōfuku ni, *adv.* 幸福に happily.

kōfuku suru, *vb.* 降伏する surrender.

kōfun, *n.* 興奮 excitement.

kōfun suru, *vb.* 興奮する get excited.

kōfu suru, *vb.* 公布する announce; proclaim.

kōfu suru, *vb.* 交付する grant; issue.

kogai, *n.* 戸外 outdoors.

kōgai, *n.* 郊外 suburb.

kōgai, *n.* 公害 environmental pollution.

kogai de/ni, *adv.* 戸外で／～に outdoors.

kogai no, *adj.* 戸外の outdoor.

kōgaku, *n.* 光学 optics.

kōgaku, *n.* 工学 engineering.

kōgan, *n.* 睾丸 testicles.

kogara (na), *adj.* 小柄 (な) short and slim (person).

kogasu, *vb.* 焦がす scorch; burn.

kogata (no), *adj.* 小型 (の) small.

kogata(jidō)sha, *n.* 小型(自動)車 compact car.

kogatana, *n.* 小刀 knife.

kogecha, *n.* 焦茶 dark brown.

kōgei, *n.* 工芸 arts and crafts; industrial art.

kōgeki, *n.* 攻撃 attack; criticism.

kōgeki suru, *vb.* 攻撃する attack; criticize.

kogeru, *vb.* 焦げる be scorched; be burned.

kōgi, *n.* 講義 lecture.

kōgi, *n.* 抗議 protest.

kōgi-demo, *n.* 抗議デモ protest demonstration.

kōgi suru, *vb.* 抗議する protest.

kogitte, *n.* 小切手 check (bank); **kogitte de** by check.

kogo, *n.* 古語 classical language.

kōgo, *n.* 口語 colloquial speech; spoken language.

kōgō, *n.* 皇后 Empress.

kogoeru, *vb.* 凍える be numb from the cold.

kōgo ni, *adv.* 交互に alternately; in turn.

kogoto, *n.* 小言 complaint; scolding.

kogu, *vb.* 漕ぐ row (boat).

kōgu, *n.* 工具 tool.

kōgyō, *n.* 興行 performance; show; production.

kōgyō, *n.* 工業 industry.

kōgyōtoshi, *n.* 工業都市 industrial city.

kōhai, *n.* 後輩 junior (in age, rank, or position).

kōhai, *n.* 荒廃 deterioration; decline; ruin.

kohaku, *n.* 琥珀 amber.

kōhan, *n.* 後半 latter half.

kōhan (na), *adj.* 広範 (な) widespread.

kōhei (na), *adj.* 公平 (な) impartial; fair; unbiased.

kōhi, *n.* 工費 construction costs.

kōhī, *n.* コーヒー (D. *koffie*) coffee.

kōho, *n.* 候補 candidate.

kōhō, *n.* 広報 official report.

kōhyō, *n.* 公表 official announcement.

kōhyō, *n.* 好評 favorable review; good reception.

koi, *n.* 恋 love; **koi o shiteiru** be in love.

koi, *n.* 鯉 carp.

koi, *adj.* 濃い 1. thick. 2. strong; **koi kōhī** strong coffee. 3. dark; deep.

kōi, *n.* 行為 deed; action.

kōi, *n.* 好意 goodwill; kindness.

koibito, *n.* 恋人 lover; boyfriend/girlfriend.

kōin, *n.* 工員 factory worker.

koi ni, *adv.* 故意に intentionally.

koi no, *adj.* 故意の intentional.

koin-randorī, *n.* コインランドリー laundromat.

koinu, *n.* 小犬 puppy.

koishii, *adj.* 恋しい beloved; cherished.

kōishitsu, *n.* 更衣室 changing room.

kōishō, *n.* 後遺症 lingering effects (illness).

koji, *n.* 孤児 orphan.

kōji, *n.* 小路 alley.

kōji, *n.* 公示 public notice.

kōji, *n.* 工事 construction.

kōjichū 工事中 under construction; men at work.

kojiki, *n.* 乞食 beggar.

kojin, *n.* 個人 individual.

kojin, *n.* 故人 deceased person.

kojinkyōju, *n.* 個人教授 private tutoring.

kojinmari shita, *adj.* 小じんまりした small and neat.

kojireru, *vb.* こじれる become complicated; worsen.

koji suru, *vb.* 誇示する show off.

kōjitsu, *n.* 口実 pretext; excuse.

kojitsukeru, *vb.* こじつける distort.

kōjo, *n.* 控除 deduction.

kōjō, *n.* 向上 improvement.

kōjō, *n.* 工場 factory; plant.

kōjō suru, *vb.* 向上する improve.

kōjutsushiken, *n.* 口述試験 oral examination.

kōka, *n.* 硬貨 coin.

kōka, *n.* 効果 effect; **kōka ga aru (nai)** effective (ineffective).

kōka, *n.* 工科 engineering department.

kōka (na), *adj.* 高価 (な) expensive.

kōkai, *n.* 航海 sailing; (ocean) voyage.

kōkai, *n.* 公海 open sea.

kōkai, *n.* 後悔 regret.

kōkaidō, *n.* 公会堂 public hall.

kōkai suru, *vb.* 後悔する regret.

kōkai suru, *vb.* 公開する open or make available to the public.

kōkan, *n.* 好感 good impression; **kōkan o idaku** feel favorably disposed toward someone.

kōkan, *n.* 交換 exchange.

kōkan-ryūgakusei, *n.* 交換留学生 exchange student.

kōkanshu, *n.* 交換手 telephone operator.

kōkan suru, *vb.* 交換する exchange.

kōka-teki (na), *adj.* 効果的 (な) effective.

kōkatsu (na), *adj.* 狡猾 (な) cunning; sneaky.

koke, *n.* 苔 moss.

kokei (no), *adj.* 固形 (の) solid.

kōkei, *n.* 光景 scene; sight.

kōkeiki, *n.* 好景気 booming economy.

kōkeisha, *n.* 後継者 successor.

kōken, *n.* 貢献 contribution.

kōken'nin, *n.* 後見人 guardian; patron.

kōken suru, *vb.* 貢献する contribute.

kōketsu (na, no), *adj.* 高潔 (な、の) noble-minded.

kōketsuatsu, *n.* 高血圧 high blood pressure.

kōki, *n.* 後期 second half (of a period).

kōki, *n.* 好機 opportunity; **kōki o tsukamu** take advantage of an opportunity; **kōki o nogasu** miss an opportunity.

kōki (na, no), *n.* 高貴 (な、の) noble; aristocratic.

kōkiatsu, *n.* 高気圧 high atmospheric pressure.

kōkishin, *n.* 好奇心 curiosity.

kokka, *n.* 国家 nation; country.

kokka, *n.* 国歌 national anthem.

kokkai, *n.* 国会 Diet (legislative assembly).

kokkaigijidō, *n.* 国会議事堂 Diet Building.

kokkei (na), *adj.* 滑稽 (な) funny; comical.

kokki, *n.* 国旗 national flag.

kokko, *n.* 国庫 national treasury.

kokku, *n.* コック (E.) cook.

kokkyō, *n.* 国境 border (between nations).

kokkyō, *n.* 国教 state religion.

koko, *n.* ここ this place; here.

kōkō, *n.* 高校 senior high school.

kōkō, *n.* 孝行 filial piety.

kokoku, *n.* 故国 homeland.

kōkoku, *n.* 広告 advertisement; **kyūjinkōkoku** help-wanted advertisement.

koko no, *adj.* 個々の individual.

kokonotsu, *n.* 九つ nine; nine years old.

kokoro, *n.* 心 spirit; heart; mind; **kokoro no soko kara** from the bottom of one's heart.

kokoroatari, *n.* 心当たり some information; **kokoroatari ga aru** have something in mind; have some information.

kokorobosoi, *adj.* 心細い downhearted; forlorn.

kokoroe, *n.* 心得 1. knowledge; readiness. 2. guideline.

kokoroeru, *vb.* 心得る be aware of; be ready.

kokorogakeru, *vb.* 心掛ける keep in mind.

kokorogawari, *n.* 心変わり change of mind or heart.

kokorogurushii, *adj.* 心苦しい emotionally painful.

kokoromi, *n.* 試み venture; trial.

kokoromiru, *vb.* 試みる experiment; try.

kokoronarazu mo, *adv.* 心ならずも against one's will.

kokoroyoi, *adj.* 快い pleasant; comfortable.

kokoroyoku, *adv.* 快く gladly.

kokoroyuku made, *adv.* 心行くまで to one's heart's content.

kokorozashi, *n.* 志 ambition; wish;

goal.

kokorozasu, *vb.* 志す aspire; wish.

kokorozukai, *n.* 心遣い thoughtfulness.

koku (na), *adj.* 酷 (な) harsh; cruel.

kōkū, *n.* 航空 aviation.

kokuban, *n.* 黒板 blackboard.

kokubetsushiki, *n.* 告別式 wake.

kōkūbin, *n.* 航空便 airmail; **kōkūbin de** via airmail.

kokubō, *n.* 国防 national defense.

kokubun, *n.* 国文 Japanese literature.

kokudo, *n.* 国土 country; nation; land.

kokudō, *n.* 国道 national highway.

kokuei (no), *adj.* 国営 (の) government-run.

kokufuku suru, *vb.* 克服する overcome; conquer.

kokugai de/ni, *adv.* 国外で／〜に abroad.

kōkūgaisha, *n.* 航空会社 airline.

kokugo, *n.* 国語 Japanese language; national language.

kokugojiten, *n.* 国語辞典 Japanese dictionary.

kokuhaku, *n.* 告白 confession.

kokuhaku suru, *vb.* 告白する confess.

kokuhatsu suru, *vb.* 告発する accuse; indict.

kokuhi, *n.* 国費 national expenditure.

kokuhō, *n.* 国宝 national treasure.

kokui, *n.* 黒衣 black clothing.

kokuji, *n.* 告示 announcement.

kokujin, *n.* 黒人 black person.

kokumei (na), *adj.* 克明 (な) detailed; minute.

kokumin, *n.* 国民 people of a nation; citizen.

kokumin-kenkōhoken, *n.* 国民健康保険 national health insurance.

kokumin-sōseisan, *n.* 国民総生産 gross national product.

kokumotsu, *n.* 穀物 grain; cereal.

kokunai (no), *adj.* 国内 (の) domestic.

kokuō, *n.* 国王 king; monarch.

kokuren, *n.* 国連 United Nations.

kokurengun, *n.* 国連軍 United Nations forces.

kokuritsu (no), *adj.* 国立 (の) national.

kōkūryōkin, *n.* 航空料金 airfare.

kokusai, *n.* 国債 government bond.

kokusaikankei, *n.* 国際関係 international relations.

kokusaikūkō, *n.* 国際空航 international airport.

kokusairengō, *n.* 国際連合 United Nations.

kokusai-teki (na), *adj.* 国際的 (な) international.

kokusaitoshi, *n.* 国際都市 cosmopolitan city.

kokusan (no), *adj.* 国産 (の) domestic; made in Japan.

kokusanhin, *n.* 国産品 domestic product.

kokusei, *n.* 国政 government.

kokuseichōsa, *n.* 国勢調査 national census.

kokuseki, *n.* 国籍 nationality.

kokushi, *n.* 酷使 abuse.

kōkūshokan, *n.* 航空書簡 aerogramme; air letter.

kokuso suru, *vb.* 告訴する sue; accuse.

kokusui-shugisha, *n.* 国粋主義者 ultranationalist; extreme rightist.

kokuyū (no), *adj.* 国有 (の) government-owned.

kokuzei, *n.* 国税 national tax.

kokyō, *n.* 故郷 hometown.

kōkyo, *n.* 皇居 Imperial Palace.

kōkyō, *n.* 好況 economic boom.

kōkyō (no), *adj.* 公共 (の) public.

kōkyōgaku, *n.* 交響楽 symphony.

kōkyōgakudan, *n.* 交響楽団 symphony orchestra.

kokyū, *n.* 呼吸 breathing; respiration; **jinkōkokyū** artificial respiration.

kōkyū, *n.* 高給 high salary.

kōkyūbi, *n.* 公休日 legal holiday.

kōkyū (na), *adj.* 高級 (な) high-quality; high-class.

kokyū suru, *vb.* 呼吸する breathe; respire.

koma, *n.* こま top (toy).

komakai, *adj.* 細かい 1. small; minute. 2. meticulous; detailed.

komakaku, *adv.* 細かく minutely; in detail.

kōman (na), *adj.* 高慢 (な) arrogant; haughty.

komaru, *vb.* 困る 1. be in trouble; be annoyed; be at a loss. 2. be short of money.

komayaka (na), *adj.* こまやか (な) sensitive; considerate.

kome, *n.* 米 uncooked white rice.

komekami, *n.* こめかみ temple (forehead).

komeru, *vb.* 込める put into; include.

komichi, *n.* 小道 alley; lane.

komochi, *n.* 子持ち parent.

komoji, *n.* 小文字 small letter; lowercase letter.

komon, *n.* 顧問 adviser; counselor.

kōmon, *n.* 肛門 anus.

komori, *n.* 子守 baby-sitter; baby-sitting.

kōmorigasa, *n.* こうもり傘 umbrella.

komu, *vb.* 込む 1. be crowded. 2. be intricate.

komugi, *n.* 小麦 wheat.

komugiko, *n.* 小麦粉 wheat flour.

kōmuin, *n.* 公務員 civil servant.

kōmuru, *vb.* 被る 1. suffer. 2. receive.

kōmuten, *n.* 工務店 construction company.

kōmyō (na), *adj.* 巧妙 (な) adroit; adept.

kona, *n.* 粉 1. powder. 2. flour.

kōnai, *n.* 構内 grounds; premises.

kona-miruku, *n.* 粉ミルク powdered milk.

konasekken, *n.* 粉せっけん soap powder.

konban, *n.* 今晩 this evening; tonight.

konban wa, *interj.* 今晩は Good evening!

konbu, *n.* 昆布 kelp.

konchū, *n.* 昆虫 insect.

kondan, *n.* 懇談 meeting; talk.

kondate, *n.* 献立 menu.

kondo, *n., adv.* 今度 1. this time. 2. next time.

kondō, *n.* 混同 confusion; mixup.

kondo wa, *adv.* 今度は 1. this time. 2. next time.

kone, *n.* コネ (E.) connection.

koneko, *n.* 子猫 kitten.

kōnetsu, *n.* 高熱 high fever.

kōnetsuhi, *n.* 光熱費 utility charges.

kongan suru, *vb.* 懇願する entreat.

kongaragaru, *vb.* こんがらがる become complicated; become entangled.

kongetsu, *n.* 今月 this month.

kongo, *adv.* 今後 hereafter.

kongō, *n.* 混合 mixture.

kon'i (na), *adj.* 懇意 (な) intimate; close (human relationship).

konimotsu, *n.* 小荷物 parcel; small package.

kon'in, *n.* 婚姻 marriage.

kōninkaikeishi, *n.* 公認会計士 certified public accountant.

kōnin no, *adj.* 公認の (publicly) authorized; approved.

kōnin(sha), *n.* 後任(者) successor; replacement.

kōnin suru, *vb.* 公認する (publicly) authorize; approve.

kon(iro), *n.* 紺(色) navy blue.

konjō, *n.* 根性 1. will power. 2. character.

konkai, *n.* 今回 this time.

konketsu, *n.* 混血 miscegenation.

konki, *n.* 婚期 marriageable age.

konki, *n.* 根気 patience; perseverance.

konkizuyoi, *adj.* 根気強い patient; tenacious.

konkyo, *n.* 根拠 source or basis (of a rumor, debate, reasoning, etc.).

konkyū, *n.* 困窮 poverty.

konmake suru, *vb.* 根負けする give up; give in.

kon'na, *adj.* こんな such; this kind of.

kon'nan (na), *n.* 困難 (な) difficult.

kon'nichi, *n.* 今日 today.

kon'nichi no, *adj.* 今日の today's.

kon'nichi wa, *interj.* 今日は Good afternoon! Good morning!

kono, *adj.* この this.

kono aida, konaida, *adv.* この間, こないだ the other day; recently.

kono goro, *adv.* この頃 these days; currently.

kono-gurai/-kurai no, *adj.* この位の about this much.

kono hen ni, *adv.* この辺に in this neighborhood.

kono mae, *n.* この前 the last time; the other day.

kono mama ni suru, *vb.* このままにする leave (something) as it is.

konomashii, *adj.* 好ましい pleasant; desirable.

konomashikunai, *adj.* 好ましくない unpleasant; undesirable.

konomi, *n.* 木の実 nut; fruit.

konomi, *n.* 好み taste; preference.

konomu, *vb.* 好む like; favor.

kono tabi, *n.* この度 this time.

kono tsugi (no) この次 (の) 1. *adj.* next. 2. *adv.* next time.

kono yo, *n.* この世 this world.

kono yō ni, *adv.* このように in this way; like this.

konpon, *n.* 根本 base; foundation.

konpyūta, *n.* コンピュータ (E.) computer.

konran, *n.* 混乱 confusion; chaos.

konrei, *n.* 婚礼 marriage ceremony; wedding.

konsen, *n.* 混線 crossed wires.

konsento, *n.* コンセント electrical outlet.

konshū, *n.* 今週 this week.

konton, *n.* 混沌 chaos.

konwaku, *n.* 困惑 embarrassment; perplexity.

kon'ya, *n.* 今夜 this evening; tonight.

kon'yaku, *n.* 婚約 engagement.

kon'yakusha, *n.* 婚約者 fiancé; fiancée.

kon'yaku suru, *vb.* 婚約する become engaged; betrothed.

kon'yoku, *n.* 混浴 mixed bathing.

kōnyū, *n.* 購入 purchase.

konzatsu, *n.* 混雑 crowdedness; congestion.

konzetsu suru, *vb.* 根絶する exterminate.

kōon, *n.* 高温 high temperature.

koppu, *n.* コップ (D. *kop*) cup; glass.

koraeru, *vb.* 堪える endure.

korashimeru, *vb.* こらしめる

punish.

korasu, *vb.* 凝らす focus on.

kore, *pron.* これ this (object).

kōrei (no), *adj.* 高齢 (の) elderly; old.

kōrei (no), *adj.* 恒例 (の) customary.

kore kara, *adv.* これから from now on.

kore made, *adv.* これまで until now.

korera, *pron.* これら these (objects).

kōri, *n.* 氷 ice.

kōri, *n.* 高利 high interest rate.

koriru, *vb.* こりる learn a lesson; get sick of.

kōri-teki (na), *adj.* 功利的 (な) utilitarian; pragmatic.

koritsu, *n.* 孤立 isolation.

kōritsu, *n.* 効率 efficiency.

kōritsu (no), *adj.* 公立 (の) public.

koritsu suru, *vb.* 孤立する be isolated.

-koro 頃 1. (time) when; **chiisai-koro** when I was small. 2. variant of **-goro**; about (time).

kōro, *n.* 航路 route (air, sea).

korobu, *vb.* 転ぶ stumble; fall down.

korogaru, *vb.* 転がる roll over; lie around.

korogasu, *vb.* 転がす roll; knock down.

kōrogi, *n.* こうろぎ cricket (insect).

korokke, *n.* コロッケ (F.) potato croquette.

koromo, *n.* 衣 1. coating; breading (food). 2. clothes.

kōron, *n.* 口論 argument; quarrel.

korosu, *vb.* 殺す murder; kill.

koru, *vb.* 凝る 1. be obsessed with; be absorbed in. 2. become stiff (neck).

kōru, *vb.* 凍る freeze.

kōryo, *n.* 考慮 consideration.

kōryo suru, *vb.* 考慮する think about; consider.

kōryoku, *n.* 効力 effect.

kōryū, *n.* 交流 interchange.

kōryū suru, *vb.* 興隆する prosper.

kōsai suru, *vb.* 交際する 1. associate with. 2. be friendly with; date.

kōsaku, *n.* 耕作 cultivation (of land).

kōsaku suru, *vb.* 工作する manipulate; maneuver.

kosame, *n.* 小雨 light rain.

kōsan suru, *vb.* 降参する surrender; give up.

kōsa suru, *vb.* 交差する intersect; cross.

kōsaten, *n.* 交差点 intersection; crossing.

kōsatsu suru, *n.* 考察する consider; examine; ponder.

kosei, *n.* 個性 individuality; personality.

kōsei, *n.* 厚生 public welfare.

kōsei, *n.* 構成 structure; composition.

kōsei, *n.* 後世 future; posterity.

kōsei, *n.* 校正 proofreading.

kōsei, *n.* 更生 rebirth.

kōsei (na), *adj.* 公正 (な) just; fair.

kōseibusshitsu, *n.* 抗生物質 antibiotic.

kosei-teki (na), *adj.* 個性的 (な) unique; individualistic.

koseki, *n.* 戸籍 family register.

kōseki, *n.* 功績 achievement.

kōseki, *n.* 鉱石 ore.

kōsha, *n.* 校舎 school building.

kōsha, *n.* 後者 the latter.

koshi, *n.* 腰 waist; back; hip.

kōshi, *n.* 講師 lecturer; instructor.

kōshi, *n.* 公使 minister (of state).

kōshi, *n.* 格子 latticework; grille.

koshikake, *n.* 腰掛け chair; seat; stool.

kōshiki, *n.* 公式 formula.

kōshiki (na, no), *adj.* 公式 (な、の) official.

kōshiki ni, *adv.* 公式に officially.

kōshin, *n.* 行進 march.

kōshin, *vb.* 更新 renewal.

kōshin suru, *vb.* 更新する renew.

koshinuke, *n.* 腰し抜け coward.

koshi o kakeru, *vb.* 腰を掛ける sit down; take a seat.

kōshi suru, *vb.* 行使する use; exercise.

koshitsu, *n.* 個室 private room (hospital); single room (hotel).

kōshitsu, *n.* 皇室 imperial family.

koshitsu suru, *vb.* 固執する stick to; be persistent.

koshō, *n.* 胡椒 pepper (condiment).

koshō, *n.* 故障 breakdown (mechanical); malfunction.

kōshō, *n.* 交渉 1. negotiation; bargaining. 2. contact.

kōshō (na), *adj.* 高尚 (な) highbrow; high-class; noble.

kōshoku (na), *adj.* 好色 (な) amorous; erotic; lecherous.

kōshokubungaku, *n.* 好色文学 pornographic literature.

kōshōnin, *n.* 公証人 notary.

koshō suru, *vb.* 故障する break down (mechanical).

koshu, *n.* 戸主 head of a family.

kōshū, *n.* 公衆 general public; the masses.

kōshūbenjo, *n.* 公衆便所 public toilet.

kōshūdōtoku, *n.* 公衆道徳 public morality.

kōshūkai, *n.* 講習会 classes; lessons; course; **kiruto no**

kōshūkai classes in quilting.

koshu suru, *vb.* 固守する stick to; stand firm.

kōsō, *n.* 構想 plan; blueprint; concept; **kōsō o tateru** make an outline or plan.

kōsō, *n.* 抗争 strife; dispute.

kosodate, *n.* 子育て child raising.

kōsō-kenchiku/-biru, *n.* 高層建築／〜ビル skyscraper.

koso-koso suru, *vb.* こそこそする behave sneakily.

kōsoku, *n.* 拘束 restraint; restriction.

kōsoku, *n.* 校則 school regulations.

kōsoku, *n.* 高速 high speed.

kōsokudōro, *n.* 高速道路 highway; freeway.

kōsoku suru, *vb.* 拘束する restrain; restrict.

kossetsu suru, *vb.* 骨折する break a bone.

kossori (to), *adv.* こっそり (と) secretly; sneakily.

kosu, *vb.* 越す 1. exceed. 2. pass; cross. 3. move (residence).

kosu, *vb.* 漉す strain; filter.

kōsui, *n.* 香水 perfume.

kōsui, *n.* 硬水 hard water.

kosuru, *vb.* 擦る rub; scrub.

kotae, *n.* 答え answer; solution.

kotaeru, *vb.* 答える answer.

kotaeru, *vb.* 応える 1. respond. 2. affect.

kotai, *n.* 個体 solid.

kōtai, *n.* 交代 shift; alternation.

kōtai de, *adv.* 交代で in shifts; in turn.

kōtaigō, *n.* 皇太后 Empress Dowager.

kōtaishi, *n.* 皇太子 Crown Prince.

kōtai suru, *vb.* 交代する take one's shift or turn.

kōtai suru, *vb.* 後退する recede;

retreat.

kōtaku, *n.* 光沢 luster.

kotatsu, *n.* こたつ Japanese room heater covered with a quilt.

kōtei, *n.* 行程 process.

kōtei, *n.* 校庭 schoolyard.

kōtei, *n.* 皇帝 emperor.

kōteibuai, *n.* 公定歩合 official bank rate.

kotei suru, *vb.* 固定する rivet; fix; stabilize.

kōtei suru, *vb.* 肯定する affirm; answer positively; admit.

kōteki (na), *adj.* 好適 (な) suitable.

koten, *n.* 個展 individual exhibition.

koten, *n.* 古典 classical work; classic.

kōten, *n.* 好天 good weather.

kōten, *n.* 荒天 rough weather.

kōten suru, *vb.* 好転する improve.

kōten-teki (na), *adj.* 後天的 (な) acquired (after birth).

kōtetsu, *n.* 鋼鉄 steel.

koto, *n.* 事 1. thing. 2. matter; affair. 3. event; occurrence.

koto, *n.* 古都 former capital (esp. Kyoto).

koto, *n.* 琴 Japanese thirteen-stringed musical instrument.

kōto, *n.* コート (E.) coat.

kōtō (na), *adj.* 高等 (な) advanced; higher.

kōtō (no), *adj.* 口頭 (の) oral.

kotoba, *n.* 言葉 language; word.

-koto ga aru ことがある have done; **yonda-koto ga aru** have read.

kōtōgakkō, *n.* 高等学校 senior high school.

kotogotoku, *adv.* ことごとく without exception; entirely.

kotogara, *n.* 事柄 matter.

kōtokushin, *n.* 公徳心 public

spirit.

kōtō kyōiku, *n.* 高等教育 higher education.

kōtōmukei (na, no), *adj.* 荒唐無稽 (な、の) nonsensical; absurd.

kotonaru, *vb.* 異なる differ.

kotonatta, *adj.* 異なつた different.

kotoni, *adv.* 殊に especially; above all.

kotori, *n.* 小鳥 small bird.

kōtōsaibansho, *n.* 高等裁判所 high court.

kotoshi, *n.* 今年 this year.

kōtōshiken, *n.* 口頭試験 oral exam.

kotowari, *n.* 断り 1. refusal. 2. notice.

kotowaru, *vb.* 断る decline; refuse.

kotowaza, *n.* ことわざ proverb.

kotozuke, *n.* 言付け message.

kotsu, *n.* こつ knack; **kotsu o oboeru** get a feel for.

kōtsū, *n.* 交通 traffic; transportation.

kōtsugō (na, no), *adj.* 好都合 (な、の) convenient.

kōtsūjiko, *n.* 交通事故 traffic accident.

kōtsūjūtai, *n.* 交通渋滞 traffic jam.

kōtsūshingō, *n.* 交通信号 traffic light.

kottō(hin), *n.* 骨董(品) antique; curio.

kou, *vb.* 乞う beg; ask.

kouma, *n.* 小馬 pony; colt.

kōun, *n.* 幸運 good luck.

kōun (na, no), *adj.* 幸運 (な、の) lucky; fortunate.

kōun ni mo, *adv.* 幸運にも luckily; fortunately; happily.

kouri, *n.* 小売り retail.

kourikakaku, *n.* 小売り価格 retail price.

kouriten, *n.* 小売り店 retail shop.

koushi, *n.* 子牛 calf; **koushi no niku** veal.

kowagaru, *vb.* 怖がる feel scared (afraid, nervous).

kowai, *adj.* 怖い scared; afraid; **hito ga kowai** afraid of people.

kōwajōyaku, *n.* 講和条約 peace treaty.

kowareru, *vb.* 壊れる break; be broken.

kowasu, *vb.* 壊す break; damage; destroy.

koya, *n.* 小屋 cabin; hut; shed.

kōya, *n.* 荒野 wilderness; the wild.

kōyaku, *n.* 公約 public pledge.

koyō, *n.* 雇用 employment.

kōyō, *n.* 効用 effectiveness.

kōyō, *n.* 公用 official business.

kōyōgo, *n.* 公用語 official language.

koyoi, *n.* 今宵 tonight; this evening.

koyomi, *n.* 暦 calendar.

kōyū, *n.* 交友 friend(s).

kōyū, *n.* 校友 schoolmate.

koyubi, *n.* 小指 little finger; little toe.

koyūmeishi, *n.* 固有名詞 proper noun (grammar).

koyū no, *adj.* 固有の unique; distinctive.

kōyū no, *adj.* 公有の public.

kōza, *n.* 講座 academic course; lecture.

kōza, *n.* 口座 bank account; **kōza o hiraku** open a bank account.

kōzabangō, *n.* 口座番号 (bank) account number.

kōzan, *n.* 鉱山 mine.

kozara, *n.* 小皿 saucer; small plate.

kozeni, *n.* 小銭 coin; small change.

kōzen no, *adj.* 公然の open; public.

kōzen to, *adv.* 公然と openly; publicly.

kozō, *n.* 小僧 1. boy. 2. novice priest.

kōzō, *n.* 構造 structure.

kōzu, *n.* 構図 composition (graphics).

kozue, *n.* 梢 twig.

kōzui, *n.* 洪水 inundation; flood.

kozukai, *n.* 小遣 pocket money; allowance.

kozutsumi, *n.* 小包 parcel (sent by mail).

ku, *n.* 句 1. phrase. 2. haiku.

ku, *n.* 苦 1. agony; pain. 2. anxiety; worry; **ku ni suru** to worry.

ku, *n.* 区 district; zone.

ku, *n.* 九 nine.

-ku 区 ward; **shinjukuku** Shinjuku Ward.

kubaru, *vb.* 配る 1. distribute; hand out. 2. deliver.

kubetsu, *n.* 区別 distinction; differentiation.

kubetsu suru, *vb.* 区別する distinguish; differentiate.

kubi, *n.* 首 neck; head.

kubikazari, *n.* 首飾り necklace.

kubikiri, *n.* 首切り 1. dismissal (from a job). 2. beheading; decapitation.

kubi o kiru, *vb.* 首を切る 1. dismiss from a job. 2. behead; decapitate.

kubomi, *n.* 凹み hollow; crevice; depression.

kubomu, *vb.* 凹む sink.

kubun, *n.* 区分 classification; division.

kuchi, *n.* 口 1. mouth. 2. taste (sense of). 3. position (employment).

kuchibashi, *n.* くちばし beak; bill.

kuchibeni, *n.* 口紅 lipstick.

kuchibeta (na), *adj.* 口下手 (な)

inept in expressing oneself; inarticulate.

kuchibiru, *n.* 唇 lip(s).

kuchibue, *n.* 口笛 whistling; **kuchibue o fuku** to whistle.

kuchidome o suru, *vb.* 口止めを する bind someone to secrecy.

kuchi ga karui, *adj.* 口が軽い talkative; indiscreet.

kuchi ga umai, *adj.* 口がうまい glib.

kuchi ga warui, *adj.* 口が悪い foul-mouthed.

kuchigenka, *n.* 口喧嘩 argument.

kuchigomoru, *vb.* 口ごもる mumble.

kuchihige, *n.* 口髭 mustache.

kuchikiki, *n.* 口利き mediator; mediation.

kuchikomi de, *adv.* 口コミで by word of mouth.

kuchiku, *n.* 駆逐 expulsion.

kuchimane, *n.* 口真似 imitating someone's voice or speech.

kuchinashi, *n.* くちなし gardenia.

kuchi o dasu, *vb.* 口を出す interrupt; mind someone else's business.

kuchi o kiku, *vb.* 口をきく speak; talk.

kuchiru, *vb.* 朽ちる rot; decay.

kuchisaki dake, *n.* 口先だけ mere words; lip service.

kuchiurusai, *adj.* 口うるさい nagging; scolding.

kuchiyakusoku, *n.* 口約束 oral promise.

kuchizuke, *n.* 口づけ kiss.

kūchū ni, *adv.* 空中に in midair.

kuda, *n.* 管 tube; pipe.

kudakeru, *vb.* 砕ける be broken; be smashed.

kudaku, *vb.* 砕く break; smash.

kudamono, *n.* 果物 fruit.

kudaranai, *adj.* 下らない 1. ridiculous; stupid. 2. worthless; petty.

kudari, *n.* 下り 1. descent; going down. 2. train from Tokyo.

kudarizaka, *n.* 下り坂 downward slope.

kudaru, *vb.* 下る 1. descend; go down.

kudasai, *adv.* 下さい please; **Michi o oshiete kudasai.** Please show me the way. **Ocha kudasai.** Tea, please. **Sushi kudasai.** Sushi, please.

kudoi, *adj.* くどい repetitious; tedious; persistent.

kudoku, *vb.* 口説く 1. persuade. 2. seduce; make advances.

kufū, *n.* 工夫 ingenuity.

kūfuku, *n.* 空腹 empty stomach; hunger.

kugatsu, *n.* 九月 September.

kugi, *n.* 釘 nail; peg.

kuginuki, *n.* 釘抜き nail puller.

kugiri, *n.* 区切り ending; stop; pause; **kugiri o tsukeru** leave off (work).

kugiru, *vb.* 区切る divide; mark off.

kūgun, *n.* 空軍 air force.

kūgunkichi, *n.* 空軍基地 air force base.

kuguru, *vb.* 潜る pass under or through.

kūhaku, *n.* 空白 blank.

kui, *n.* 杭 stake.

kui, *n.* 悔い regret; **kui ga nokoru** have regrets.

kuichigai, *n.* 食い違い disparity; conflict (of opinion).

kuichigau, *vb.* 食い違う clash.

kuidōraku, *n.* 食い道楽 gastronomy; gourmet.

kuiki, *n.* 区域 area; zone.

kuimono, *n.* 食い物 eats; grub.

kuinokoshi, *n.* 食い残し leftovers.

kuiru, *vb.* 悔いる regret; repent.

kuisugi, *n.* 食い過ぎ overeating.

kuitomeru, *vb.* 食い止める hold back; stop.

kujaku, *n.* 孔雀 peacock; peahen.

kuji, *n.* くじ lottery; raffle.

kujikeru, *vb.* 挫ける lose heart; be discouraged.

kujiku, *vb.* 挫く 1. sprain (ankle, etc.). 2. discourage.

kujira, *n.* 鯨 whale.

kujo, *n.* 駆除 extermination.

kujō, *n.* 苦情 complaint.

kujō o iu, *vb.* 苦情を言う complain.

kukaku, *n.* 区画 division; block.

kūkan, *n.* 空間 space.

kuki, *n.* 茎 stem; stalk.

kūki, *n.* 空気 air; atmosphere.

kukkiri (to), *adv.* くっきり（と） clearly.

kūkō, *n.* 空港 airport.

kuku, *n.* 九九 multiplication table.

kukuru, *vb.* 括る bind; bundle.

kukyō, *n.* 苦境 adversity; misfortune; trouble; **kukyō ni ochiiru** fall into adversity, misfortune, or trouble.

kūkyo (na), *adj.* 空虚（な） empty.

kuma, *n.* 熊 bear.

kumen suru, *vb.* 工面する contrive.

kumi, *n.* 組 1. group; team. 2. class (school).

kumiai, *n.* 組合 union; association.

kumiawase, *n.* 組み合わせ combination; pairing.

kumiawaseru, *vb.* 組み合わせる combine; pair.

kumifuseru, *vb.* 組み伏せる hold down.

kumitateru, *vb.* 組み立てる build; assemble.

kumitsuku, *vb.* 組み付く grapple with; tackle.

kumo, *n.* 蜘蛛 spider.

kumo, *n.* 雲 cloud.

kumo no su, *n.* 蜘蛛の巣 cobweb.

kumori, *n.* 曇り cloudy weather.

kumoru, *vb.* 曇る 1. become cloudy. 2. be in a gloomy mood.

kumu, *vb.* 汲む 1. get water (by scooping, pumping, etc.). 2. comprehend; discern.

kumu, *vb.* 組む 1. assemble. 2. unite; pair. 3. fold (arms); cross (legs). 4. make (a plan).

-kun 君 Mr.; Ms. (used in addressing younger people or colleagues in place of **-san** or **-sama**).

kunan, *n.* 苦難 hardship; adversity.

kuneru, *vb.* くねる twist; wind around.

kuni, *n.* 国 1. nation; country. 2. hometown.

kunō, *n.* 苦悩 agony; anguish.

kunren, *n.* 訓練 training; drilling.

kunren suru, *vb.* 訓練する train; drill.

kunsei, *n.* 薫製 smoked food.

kunshō, *n.* 勲章 medal; decoration.

kunshu, *n.* 君主 monarch; ruler.

kun(yomi), *n.* 訓(読み) Japanese reading of a Chinese character.

kuppuku suru, *vb.* 屈服する surrender; succumb.

kura, *n.* 蔵、倉 storehouse.

kūrā, *n.* クーラー (E. *cooler*) air conditioner.

kuraberu, *vb.* 比べる compare.

kuragari, *n.* 暗がり darkness.

kurage, *n.* くらげ jellyfish.

kurai, *n.* 位 rank.

kurai, *adj.* 暗い 1. dark. 2. gloomy; depressing.

-kurai, -gurai くらい、ぐらい 1.

about; approximately; almost. 2. something like. 3. as ... as.

kura-kura suru, *vb.* くらくらする feel giddy or dizzy.

kuramasu, *vb.* 晦ます disappear.

kuramu, *vb.* 眩む be dazzled; be blinded.

kurashi, *n.* 暮らし living; life.

kurasu, *vb.* 暮らす live; make a living.

kurasu, *n.* クラス (E.) class.

kurayami, *n.* 暗闇 darkness.

kure, *n.* 暮れ 1. year-end. 2. nightfall.

kuregure mo, *adj.* くれぐれも sincere; **Kuregure mo minasama ni yoroshiku.** Be sure to give (my) sincere regards to everyone.

kureru, *vb.* 呉れる 1. give. 2. do a favor for.

kureru, *vb.* 暮れる get dark; end; be absorbed in.

kuri, *n.* 栗 chestnut.

kurikaeshi, *n.* 繰り返し repetition; refrain.

kurikaeshi(te), *adv.* 繰り返し(て) repeatedly; again.

kurikaesu, *vb.* 繰り返す repeat.

kurīningu, *n.* クリーニング (E.) dry cleaning; **kurīningu ni dasu** send (clothes) to the dry cleaner.

kurinuku, *vb.* くり抜く hollow.

kuro, *n.* 黒 black.

kurō, *n.* 苦労 hardship; suffering; trouble.

kūro, *n.* 空路 flight (route).

kuroi, *adj.* 黒い black.

kuroji, *n.* 黒字 being in the black.

kurō suru, *vb.* 苦労する suffer hardship.

kurōto, *n.* 玄人 expert; professional.

kuru, *vb.* 来る 1. come; arrive. 2.

derive (from).

kuru-kuru, *adv.* くるくる round and round.

kuruma, *n.* 車 1. automobile; car; taxi; **kuruma o unten suru** drive a car; **kuruma o oriru** get out of a car. 2. wheel.

kuruma isu, *n.* 車椅子 wheelchair.

kurumi, *n.* 胡桃 walnut.

kurumu, *vb.* くるむ wrap.

kurushii, *adj.* 苦しい 1. painful. 2. difficult; laborious.

kurushimeru, *vb.* 苦しめる harass; torture.

kurushimi, *n.* 苦しみ pain; agony.

kurushimu, *vb.* 苦しむ feel pain; suffer; struggle.

kuru'u, *vb.* 狂う 1. go mad. 2. be obsessed with. 3. go wrong.

kusa, *n.* 草 grass.

kusabi, *n.* くさび wedge.

kusai, *adj.* 臭い 1. smelly; stinking. 2. suspicious.

kusakari, *n.* 草刈り mowing.

kusami, *n.* 臭み bad odor.

kusamura, *n.* 草むら grassy area.

kusari, *n.* 鎖 chain.

kusaru, *vb.* 腐る rot; spoil; be corrupted.

kuse, *n.* 癖 1. habit; **kuse ga tsuku** acquire a habit. 2. idiosyncratic behavior.

kūseki, *n.* 空席 1. vacant seat. 2. vacant position.

kūsha, *n.* 空車 available taxi.

kusha-kusha (na, no), *adj.* くしゃくしゃ (な、の) wrinkled; crumpled.

kushami, *n.* くしゃみ sneeze.

kushami o suru, *vb.* くしゃみをする sneeze.

kushi, *n.* 櫛 comb.

kushi, *n.* 串 skewer.

kushin, *n.* 苦心 painful effort;

struggle.

kushin suru, *vb.* 苦心する struggle.

kushi suru, *vb.* 駆使する make the most of; use to advantage.

kushiyaki, *n.* 串焼き skewered and grilled food.

kūshū, *n.* 空襲 air raid.

kuso くそ 1. *n.* feces. 2. *interj.* Damn it! Shit!

kūso (na), *adj.* 空疎 (な) insubstantial.

kūsō, *n.* 空想 fantasy; imagination.

kūsō(-jō) no, *adj.* 空想(上) の imaginary.

kūsōka, *n.* 空想家 dreamer; visionary.

kūsōkagaku-shōsetsu, *n.* 空想科学小説 science fiction novel.

kūsō suru, *vb.* 空想する fantasize; imagine.

kussuru, *vb.* 屈する bend; yield to.

kusuguru, *vb.* くすぐる tickle.

kusuguttai, *adj.* くすぐったい ticklish.

kusu-kusu warai, *n.* くすくす笑い giggle.

kusu-kusu warau, *vb.* くすくす笑う giggle.

kusunda, *adj.* くすんだ dark; drab.

kusuri, *n.* 薬 1. medicine; pill; drug. 2. ointment. 3. good lesson; **Kusuri ni natta.** (I) learned a good lesson.

kusuriya, *n.* 薬屋 pharmacy.

kusuri yubi, *n.* 薬指 third finger; ring finger.

kutabaru, *vb.* くたばる die (pejorative usage).

kutabireru, *vb.* くたびれる 1. be fatigued. 2. become worn.

kutō suru, *vb.* 苦闘する struggle.

kutōten, *n.* 句読点 punctuation marks; **kutōten o utsu/tsukeru**

to use punctuation marks.

kutsu, *n.* 靴 shoe(s); **kutsu o haku** wear shoes; **kutsu o nugu** remove one's shoes.

kutsū, *n.* 苦痛 pain; agony; anguish.

kutsugaesu, *vb.* 覆す overturn; overthrow.

kutsu himo, *n.* 靴紐 shoelace.

kutsujoku, *n.* 屈辱 humiliation; disgrace.

kutsujoku-teki (na), *adj.* 屈辱的 (な) humiliating; disgraceful.

kutsumigaki, *n.* 靴磨き shoe shine; shoeshine boy.

kutsurogu, *vb.* 寛ぐ relax; make oneself at home.

kutsushita, *n.* 靴下 sock(s); **kutsushita nisoku** two pairs of socks.

kutsuzumi, *n.* 靴墨 shoe polish.

kuttsuku, *vb.* くっ付く adhere to.

ku'u, *vb.* 食う 1. eat; bite; consume (vulgar). 2. support oneself; live. 3. cheat.

kuwadate, *n.* 企て attempt; plot.

kuwadateru, *vb.* 企てる attempt; plot.

kuwaeru, *vb.* 加える add; include; **X o Y ni kuwaeru** add X to Y.

kuwaeru, *vb.* くわえる hold in one's mouth.

kuwaete, *adv.* 加えて on top of; in addition to.

kuwashii, *adj.* 詳しい 1. detailed; fully explained. 2. versed; knowledgeable; **kabuki ni kuwashii** versed in Kabuki.

kuwawaru, *vb.* 加わる join; **hanashi ni kuwawaru** join in a conversation.

(o)kuyami, *n.* (お)悔やみ condolence(s).

kuyamu, *vb.* 悔やむ regret; repent.

kuyashii, *adj.* 悔やしい mortifying.

kuyashigaru, *vb.* 悔やしがる feel mortified or bitter.

kuyo-kuyo suru, *vb.* くよくよする brood.

kūyu suru, *vb.* 空輸する send by air.

kūzen no, *adj.* 空前の unprecedented.

kuzu, *n.* 屑 rubbish; waste.

kuzukago, *n.* 屑籠 wastebasket.

kuzureru, *vb.* 崩れる 1. collapse; be destroyed. 2. lose shape.

kuzusu, *vb.* 崩す 1. dismantle; pull down; destroy. 2. make change (money).

kyabetsu, *n.* キャベツ cabbage.

kyakkanshi suru, *vb.* 客観視する regard objectively.

kyakkan-teki (na), *adj.* 客観的 (な) objective.

kyakkō, *n.* 脚光 spotlight; attention; **kyakkō o abiru** be in the spotlight.

kyaku, *n.* 客 1. customer; client; guest; visitor. 2. passenger.

kyakuhon, *n.* 脚本 screenplay; script.

kyakuhonka, *n.* 脚本家 scriptwriter.

kyakuinkyōju, *n.* 客員教授 visiting professor.

kyakuma, *n.* 客間 parlor; drawing room.

kyakuseki, *n.* 客席 seat in the audience; passenger seat.

kyakusen, *n.* 客船 passenger ship.

kyakusha, *n.* 客車 passenger car (train).

kyakushitsu, *n.* 客室 hotel room.

kyasha (na), *adj.* 華奢 (な) fragile; slender; delicate.

kyō, *n.* 今日 today.

kyōaku (na), *adj.* 凶悪 (な) brutal;
inhuman.

kyōbai, *n.* 競売 auction.

kyōben, *n.* 教鞭 teaching; **kyōben o toru** to teach.

kyōbō, *n.* 共謀 conspiracy.

kyōbō (na), *adj.* 凶暴 (な) savage; ferocious.

kyōcho, *n.* 共著 coauthorship.

kyōchō, *n.* 強調 emphasis.

kyōchō, *n.* 協調 cooperation; coordination.

kyōchō suru, *vb.* 強調する emphasize.

kyōchō suru, *vb.* 協調する cooperate; coordinate.

kyodai (na), *adj.* 巨大 (な) huge; colossal; enormous.

kyōdai, *n.* 鏡台 dressing table.

kyōdai, *n.* 兄弟 brother(s); sister(s).

kyōdai (na), *adj.* 強大 (な) powerful; mighty.

kyōdan, *n.* 教壇 rostrum.

kyodō, *n.* 挙動 conduct; behavior.

kyōdo, *n.* 郷土 hometown; homeland.

kyōdō, *n.* 協同 cooperation.

kyōdo (no), *adj.* 強度 (の) strong; powerful.

kyōdō (no), *adj.* 共同 (の) 1. cooperative. 2. communal.

kyōdō suru, *vb.* 協同する cooperate; work together.

kyoeishin, *n.* 虚栄心 vanity.

kyōen, *n.* 饗宴 banquet.

kyōfu, *n.* 恐怖 fear; horror.

kyōgaku, *n.* 共学 coeducation.

kyōgen, *n.* 狂言 1. comic-relief interlude in Noh presentations. 2. hoax.

kyōgenjisatsu, *n.* 狂言自殺 faked suicide.

kyogi, *n.* 虚偽 deception; lie.

kyōgi, *n.* 教義 doctrine; teaching.

kyōgi, *n.* 協議 discussion; conference.

kyōgi, *n.* 競技 athletic competition.

kyōgijō, *n.* 競技場 athletic field; sports arena.

kyōgi suru, *vb.* 協議する discuss.

kyōhaku, *n.* 脅迫 threat; blackmail.

kyōhaku suru, *vb.* 脅迫する threaten; blackmail.

kyōhan, *n.* 共犯 complicity.

kyōhansha, *n.* 共犯者 accomplice.

kyohi, *n.* 拒否 rejection; refusal.

kyohi suru, *vb.* 拒否する reject; refuse.

kyōi, *n.* 脅威 menace; peril; threat.

kyōi, *n.* 驚異 miracle; marvel.

kyōiku, *n.* 教育 education.

kyōiku-ka/-sha, *n.* 教育家、〜者 educator; teacher.

kyōiku no aru, *adj.* 教育のある educated; learned.

kyōiku suru, *vb.* 教育する educate; teach.

kyōin, *n.* 教員 teacher.

kyōi-teki (na), *n.* 驚異的 (な) miraculous; marvelous.

kyojin, *n.* 巨人 giant.

kyōjin, *n.* 狂人 lunatic.

kyojū, *n.* 居住 residence.

kyōju, *n.* 教授 1. professor. 2. teaching.

kyojūsha, *n.* 居住者 resident.

kyōju suru, *vb.* 享受する enjoy.

kyoka, *n.* 許可 permission; approval; **kyoka o ataeru** give permission or approval.

kyōka, *n.* 教科 subject; course of study.

kyōkai, *n.* 教会 church.

kyōkai, *n.* 協会 association; organization.

kyōkai, *n.* 境界 boundary; border.

kyōkaisen, *n.* 境界線 borderline.

kyōkan, *n.* 共感 sympathy; **kyōkan o yobu** arouse sympathy.

kyokashō, *n.* 許可証 license; permit.

kyōkasho, *n.* 教科書 textbook.

kyoka suru, *vb.* 許可する permit; approve; allow.

kyōka suru, *vb.* 強化する fortify; reinforce; strengthen.

kyōkatsu suru, *vb.* 恐喝する blackmail; threaten.

kyōki, *n.* 狂気 lunacy; madness.

kyōki, *n.* 凶器 lethal weapon.

kyokkai suru, *vb.* 曲解する distort.

kyokō, *n.* 虚構 fabrication.

kyōko (na), *adj.* 強固 (な) stable; firm.

kyōkō, *n.* 教皇 Pope.

kyōkō, *n.* 恐慌 panic; **kyōkō o kitasu** cause a panic.

kyōkōha, *n.* 強行派 hard-liner.

kyōkoku, *n.* 峡谷 canyon; ravine.

kyōkō suru, *vb.* 挙行する hold; perform.

kyoku, *n.* 曲 musical composition; song.

kyoku, *n.* 局 office; **denwa kyoku** telephone exchange; **yūbin kyoku** post office.

kyokuchi, *n.* 極致 culmination.

kyokugei, *n.* 曲芸 acrobatics.

kyokugen, *n.* 極限 limit.

kyokumen, *n.* 局面 phase; situation.

kyōkun, *n.* 教訓 moral; teaching; lesson.

kyokuryoku, *adv.* 極力 as much as possible; to the best of one's ability; **kyokuryoku sakeru** avoid as much as possible.

kyokusen, *n.* 曲線 curved line.

kyokutan (na), *adj.* 極端 (な)

extreme.

kyokutan ni, *adv.* 極端に
extremely.

kyokutō, *n.* 極東 Far East.

kyōkyū, *n.* 供給 supply.

kyōkyū suru, *vb.* 供給する supply;
provide.

kyōmei suru, *vb.* 共鳴する 1.
resonate. 2. sympathize.

kyōmi, *n.* 興味 interest (in); **nihon
bunka ni kyōmi ga aru** have an
interest in Japanese culture.

kyōmibukai, *adj.* 興味深い very
interesting.

kyonen, *n.* 去年 last year.

kyōraku, *n.* 享楽 pleasure.

kyōretsu (na), *adj.* 強烈 (な)
intense; stunning; powerful.

kyori, *n.* 距離 distance.

kyōri, *n.* 郷里 hometown.

kyoro-kyoro suru, *vb.* きょろきょ
ろする look around anxiously.

kyōryoku (na), *adj.* 強力 (な)
powerful; mighty.

kyōryoku suru, *vb.* 協力する
cooperate; collaborate.

kyōryū, *n.* 恐竜 dinosaur.

kyōsanshugi, *n.* 共産主義
communism.

kyōsanshugisha, *n.* 共産主義者
Communist.

kyōsei, *n.* 強勢 emphasis; **kyōsei o
oku** emphasize.

kyōsei, *n.* 矯正 correction.

kyōsei, *n.* 強制 compulsion; duress.

kyōsei suru, *vb.* 強制する compel;
force.

kyōsei suru, *vb.* 矯正する correct.

kyōsei-teki (na), *adj.* 強制的 (な)
compulsory.

kyōsei-teki ni, *adv.* 強制的に
compulsorily.

kyōshi, *n.* 教師 teacher.

kyoshiki, *n.* 挙式 ceremony;

wedding; **kyoshiki o toriokonau**
hold a (wedding) ceremony.

kyōshitsu, *n.* 教室 classroom.

kyoshō, *n.* 巨匠 master;
preeminent person.

kyoshoku, *n.* 虚飾 vanity.

kyōshū, *n.* 郷愁 nostalgia;
homesickness.

kyōshuku suru, *vb.* 恐縮する 1.
feel grateful. 2. feel embarrassed.

kyōsō, *n.* 競走 footrace.

kyōsō, *n.* 競争 competition;
contest; rivalry.

kyōsoku-hon/-bon, *n.* 教則本
methods book (music).

kyōsōkyoku, *n.* 協奏曲 concerto.

kyōsō suru, *vb.* 競争する compete
against; contest.

kyōtei, *n.* 協定 pact; agreement;
kyōtei o musubu conclude a
pact or agreement.

kyōteki, *n.* 強敵 powerful enemy.

kyoten, *n.* 拠点 base (location).

kyotō, *n.* 巨頭 leader; magnate.

kyōto, *n.* 教徒 adherent (religion).

kyotōkaidan, *n.* 巨頭会談 summit
conference.

kyōtsū (no), *adj.* 共通 (の)
common; mutual.

kyōtsū suru, *vb.* 共通する be
common (to).

kyōwakoku, *n.* 共和国 republic.

kyōyō, *n.* 教養 education; learning.

kyōyō, *n.* 共用 common use.

kyōyō ga aru, *adj.* 教養がある
cultured; learned.

kyōyō gakubu, *n.* 教養学部
college of liberal arts.

kyoyō suru, *vb.* 許容する accept;
tolerate.

kyōyō suru, *vb.* 強要する compel;
force.

kyōyū (no), *adj.* 共有 (の) jointly
owned.

kyōzai, *n.* 教材 teaching materials.

kyōzame (na), *adj.* 興醒め (な) disappointing.

kyozetsu, *n.* 拒絶 refusal.

kyozetsu suru, *vb.* 拒絶する refuse.

kyōzon, *n.* 共存 coexistence.

kyū, *n.* 九 nine.

kyū, *n.* 球 ball; sphere.

kyū, *n.* 級 class; level; grade.

kyū (na), *adj.* 急 (な) 1. urgent. 2. sudden; unexpected. 3. steep; **kyū na sakamichi** steep slope. 4. rapid.

kyūbyō, *n.* 急病 sudden illness.

kyūchi, *n.* 窮地 plight; adversity; **kyūchi ni ochiiru** fall into adversity.

kyūdai suru, *vb.* 及第する pass an examination.

kyūdan, *n.* 糾弾 denunciation.

kyūdan, *n.* 球団 baseball team.

kyūden, *n.* 宮殿 palace.

kyūdō, *n.* 弓道 archery.

kyūen, *n.* 救援 rescue.

kyūgeki (na), *adj.* 急激 (な) 1. abrupt. 2. rapid.

kyūgyō suru, *vb.* 休業する close temporarily (business).

kyūhen, *n.* 急変 sudden change.

kyūji, *n.* 給仕 1. service (meal). 2. waiter; waitress.

kyūjin, *n.* 求人 employment opportunity.

kyūjinkōkoku, *n.* 求人広告 help-wanted advertisement.

kyūjitsu, *n.* 休日 holiday.

kyūjo, *n.* 救助 rescue; relief.

kyūjotai, *n.* 救助隊 rescue team.

kyūjū, *n.* 九十 ninety.

kyūka, *n.* 休暇 vacation day(s); **kyūka o toru** take vacation or take day(s) off.

kyūkaku, *n.* 嗅覚 sense of smell.

kyūkanbi, *n.* 休館日 day closed (at museums, libraries, etc.).

kyūkei, *n.* 休憩 rest; break.

kyūkei suru, *vb.* 休憩する take a rest; take a break.

kyūketsuki, *n.* 吸血鬼 vampire.

kyūkō, *n.* 急行 express train.

kyūkō, *n.* 休講 canceled class.

kyūkon, *n.* 球根 bulb (plant).

kyūkon, *n.* 求婚 marriage proposal.

kyūkonsha, *n.* 求婚者 suitor.

kyūkon suru, *vb.* 求婚する propose marriage.

kyūkutsu (na), *adj.* 窮屈 (な) 1. cramped; narrow; tight. 2. ill at ease.

kyūkyoku no tokoro, *adv.* 究極の ところ in the end; after all.

kyūkyūbako, *n.* 救急箱 first-aid kit.

kyūkyūsha, *n.* 救急車 ambulance.

kyūmei suru, *vb.* 究明する examine; investigate.

kyūrei, *n.* 旧例 precedent.

kyūri, *n.* きゅうり cucumber.

kyūryō, *n.* 給料 salary; pay; wages.

kyūryōbi, *n.* 給料日 pay day.

kyūsai, *n.* 救済 help; rescue; relief.

kyūsai suru, *vb.* 救済する help; rescue.

kyūsei, *n.* 旧姓 former name; maiden name.

kyūseishu, *n.* 救世主 savior.

kyūseki, *n.* 旧跡 historic site.

kyūsen, *n.* 休戦 cease-fire; armistice; truce.

kyūshi, *n.* 休止 pause or stoppage.

kyūshiki (na, no), *adj.* 旧式 (な、の) old-fashioned; outdated.

kyūshin-teki (na), *adj.* 急進的 (な) extreme; radical.

kyūsho, *n.* 急所 1. key point; weak point; **kyūsho o tsuku** attack someone's weak point. 2. groin.

kyūshoku, *n.* 求職 job-hunting.

kyūshoku, *n.* 休職 leave of absence (employment).

kyūshū, *n.* 旧習 old custom.

kyūshū suru, *vb.* 吸収する absorb; digest.

kyūshutsu, *n.* 救出 rescue.

kyūsoku ni, *adv.* 急速に rapidly; promptly.

kyūtei, *n.* 宮廷 royal palace; court.

kyūtō, *n.* 急騰 sharp rise (price).

kyūyakuseisho, *n.* 旧約聖書 Old Testament.

kyūyō, *n.* 急用 urgent business.

kyūyō suru, *vb.* 休養する rest; recuperate.

kyūyu, *n.* 給油 refueling.

kyūyusho, *n.* 給油所 gas station.

kyūyū, *n.* 旧友 old friend.

kyūzō, *n.* 急増 sudden increase.

M

ma, *n.* 間 1. interval; pause; time. 2. space. 3. room.

mā, *interj.* まあ 1. Oh! Wow! 2. Well!

ma'atarashii, *adj.* 真新しい fresh; brand-new.

mabara (na), *adj.* 疎ら（な）sparse.

mabataki, *n.* まばたき blink.

mabayui, *adj.* 眩い dazzling.

maboroshi, *n.* 幻 illusion; chimera.

mabushii, *adj.* 眩しい dazzling; blinding.

mabuta, *n.* まぶた eyelid.

machi, *n.* 町 town.

machiaishitsu, *n.* 待合室 waiting room.

machiawaseru, *vb.* 待ち合わせる rendezvous.

machibuseru, *vb.* 待ち伏せる ambush.

machidōshii, *vb.* 待ち遠しい long for; be impatient for; look forward to; **ryokō ga machidōshii** look forward to a trip.

machigaeru, *vb.* 間違える make a mistake.

machigai, *n.* 間違い mistake.

machigainai, *adj.* 間違いない unmistakable; unquestionable.

machigatta, *adj.* 間違った 1. mistaken. 2. wrong.

machigatte, *adv.* 間違って by mistake.

machigau, *vb.* 間違う make a mistake.

machikaneru, *vb.* 待ち兼ねる wait eagerly for; look forward to.

mada, *adv.* 未だ 1. as yet; still. 2. not yet (with negative).

made, *art.* 迄 1. till; until; **ashita made** until tomorrow. 2. as far as; up to.

made ni, *art.* 迄に by (time); **ashita made ni** by tomorrow.

mado, *n.* 窓 window.

mado-garasu, *n.* 窓ガラス 1. windowpane. 2. window glass.

madoguchi, *n.* 窓口 ticket window.

madowasu, *vb.* 惑わす 1. delude. 2. seduce.

mae 前 1. *n.* front; **ie no mae ni** in front of the house. 2. *prep., conj.* before; **goji mae ni** before five o'clock; **kare ga iku mae ni** before he leaves. 3. *adj.* ago; **mikka mae** three days ago.

mae (no), *adj.* 前（の）1. former;

preceding. 2. facing.

-mae 前 order of (food); **sushi ichinin-mae** one order of sushi.

maebure, *n.* 前触れ advance notice; sign; harbinger.

maemotte, *adv.* 前以って beforehand; in advance.

mae ni, *adv.* 前に formerly; before.

maeuriken, *n.* 前売り券 advance ticket sale.

mafuyu, *n.* 真冬 midwinter.

magari, *n.* 間借り renting a room.

magarikado, *n.* 曲がり角 street corner.

māgarin, *n.* マーガリン (E.) margarine.

magarinin, *n.* 間借り人 lodger.

magaru, *vb.* 曲がる 1. turn; **kado o magaru** turn at the corner. 2. bend; warp.

mageru, *vb.* 曲げる 1. twist. 2. falsify.

magirasu, *vb.* 紛らす 1. elude; avoid. 2. divert; distract.

magirawashii, *adj.* 紛らわしい confusing; misleading.

magireru, *vb.* 紛れる 1. be diverted. 2. be confused.

magiwa ni 間際に 1. *adv.* at the last moment. 2. *prep.* just before.

mago, *n.* 孫 grandchild.

magokoro, *n.* 真心 sincerity; heart and soul.

mago-mago suru, *vb.* まごまごする be bewildered; be embarrassed.

magure(atari), *n.* まぐれ(当たり) good luck; fluke.

maguro, *n.* 鮪 tuna.

mahadaka (no), *adj.* 真裸 (の) stark naked.

mahi, *n.* 麻痺 numbness; paralysis.

mahiru, *n.* 真昼 broad daylight; midday.

mahi suru, *vb.* 麻痺する be numbed; be paralyzed.

mahō, *n.* 魔法 magic; witchcraft.

mahōbin, *n.* 魔法びん thermos.

mahōtsukai, *n.* 魔法使い magician; wizard; **ozu no mahōtsukai** The Wizard of Oz.

mai, *n.* 舞 dance.

mai- 毎 each; every; **maiasa** every morning; **maiban** every evening (night).

-mai 枚 number suffix indicating counter for flat and thin items; **kami nimai** two pieces of paper.

maido 毎度 1. *n.* each time; every time. 2. *adv.* always.

maigo, *n.* 迷子 lost person.

maikai, *n.* 毎回 each time; every time.

mainen, *n., adv.* 毎年 every year.

mainichi, *n., adv.* 毎日 every day.

mairu, *n.* マイル (E.) mile.

mairu, *vb.* 参る go; come.

mairu, *vb.* 詣る make a pilgrimage; visit a sacred place.

mairu, *vb.* 参る 1. be defeated; surrender. 2. be fed up with.

maishū, *n., adv.* 毎週 every week.

maisō, *n.* 埋葬 burial.

maitoshi, *n., adv.* 毎年 every year.

maitsuki, *n., adv.* 毎月 every month.

majime (na), *adj.* 真面目 (な) 1. sincere; honest. 2. industrious. 3. serious.

majinai, *n.* 呪い incantation.

majiwari, *n.* 交わり friendship; association.

majiwaru, *vb.* 交わる 1. keep company with; mix with. 2. intersect.

majo, *n.* 魔女 witch.

makaseru, *vb.* 任せる entrust.

makasu, *vb.* 負かす defeat; beat.

make, *n.* 負け defeat.

makeru, *vb.* 負ける 1. be defeated; lose. 2. give a discount. 3. succumb to.

maki, *n.* 薪 firewood.

makiba, *n.* 牧場 meadow; pasture.

makie, *n.* 蒔絵 gold lacquer.

makikomu, *vb.* 巻き込む involve in; entangle in.

makimono, *n.* 巻き物 scroll painting.

makka (na), *adj.* 真赤 (な) 1. crimson. 2. downright.

makkura (na), *adj.* 真暗 (な) pitch dark.

makkuro (na), *adj.* 真黒 (な) jet-black.

makoto, *n.* 真 1. truth. 2. sincerity.

makoto ni, *adv.* 真に truly; really; very.

maku, *n.* 膜 membrane; film.

maku, *n.* 幕 1. theater curtain. 2. act of a play.

maku, *vb.* 撒く sprinkle; scatter.

maku, *vb.* 巻く roll; wind.

maku, *vb.* 蒔く sow.

makura, *n.* 枕 pillow.

makuru, *vb.* まくる roll up.

mama, *adv.* まま as is; **sono mama ni suru** leave as is.

mā-mā (no), *adj.* まあまあ (の) so-so; passable.

mamahaha, *n.* 継母 stepmother.

mamako, *n.* 継子 stepchild.

mame, *n.* 豆 bean; pea.

mame, *n.* まめ blister; **mame ga dekiru** develop a blister.

mame (na), *adj.* まめ (な) 1. hardworking; industrious. 2. meticulous.

mametsu suru, *vb.* 摩滅する wear out.

mamonaku, *adv.* 間もなく before long; soon.

mamoru, *vb.* 守る 1. protect. 2. observe (rules); keep (promises).

mamukai, *n.* 真向い a place (location) right across (from).

mamukai ni, *adv.* 真向いに directly opposite.

man, *n.* 万 ten thousand; **niman** twenty thousand.

manabu, *vb.* 学ぶ learn; study.

manaita, *n.* まないた cutting board.

manatsu, *n.* 真夏 midsummer.

manazashi, *n.* 眼差し gaze.

manbiki, *n.* 万引き shoplifting; shoplifter.

manchō, *n.* 満潮 high tide.

mane, *n.* 真似 imitation; mimicry.

maneki, *n.* 招き invitation.

maneku, *vb.* 招く invite.

maneru, *vb.* 真似る imitate; mimic.

manga, *n.* 漫画 cartoon; comic strip.

mangetsu, *n.* 満月 full moon.

ma ni au, *vb.* 間に合う 1. be in time for. 2. suffice.

man'ichi, *adv.* 万一 unlikely event.

man'in (no), *adj.* 満員 (の) filled to capacity.

manjōitchi de, *adv.* 満場一致で unanimously.

mankai (no), *adj.* 満開 (の) in full bloom.

man'naka, *n.* 真中 center; middle.

man'naka (no), *adj.* 真中 (の) central; middle.

man'nenhitsu, *n.* 万年筆 fountain pen.

manpuku, *n.* 満腹 full stomach.

mansei (no), *adj.* 慢性 (の) chronic.

manshon, *n.* マンション (E. *mansion*) condominium; apartment; apartment building.

manten, *n.* 満点 perfect score.

manugareru, *vb.* 免れる be exempted from; avoid.

manuke, *n.* 間抜け fool.

manuke (na), *adj.* 間抜け (な) foolish.

manzara, *adv.* 満更 not entirely (with negative).

manzoku, *n.* 満足 satisfaction.

manzoku suru, *vb.* 満足する be satisfied.

mare (na), *adj.* 稀 (な) unusual; rare.

mare ni, *adv.* 稀に seldom.

mari, *n.* まり ball.

maru, *n.* 丸 circle.

maru de まるで 1. *adv.* absolutely. 2. *conj.* just like.

marui, *adj.* 丸い circular; globular; round.

maryoku, *n.* 魔力 magical power.

masaka, *interj.* まさか Impossible! That can't be!

masa ni 正に 1. *adv.* exactly; really. 2. *prep.* on the point of (doing).

masaru, *vb.* 勝る outclass; outdo.

masashiku, *adv.* 正しく undoubtedly.

masatsu, *n.* 摩擦 friction; rubbing.

mashi (na), *adj.* まし (な) better; preferable.

mashita, *n.* 真下 the place directly below.

mashita ni, *adv.* 真下に directly underneath.

mashite, *adv.* まして let alone; not to mention.

massaichū ni, *adv.* 真最中に at the height of.

massaki ni, *adv.* 真先に first of all.

massao (na), *adj.* 真青 (な) pallid.

massatsu suru, *vb.* 抹殺する obliterate.

masshiro (na), *adj.* 真白 (な) pure white.

massugu (na), *adj.* 真っ直ぐ (な) 1. straight. 2. honest.

massugu ni, *adv.* 真っ直ぐに 1. straight. 2. directly.

masu, *n.* ます trout.

masu, *vb.* 増す increase.

masui, *n.* 麻酔 anesthesia.

masu-komi, *n.* マスコミ (E.) mass media.

masu-masu, *adv.* ますます increasingly.

mata, *n.* 股 thigh; groin.

mata また 1. *adv.* again; also. 2. *conj.* and; as well as.

matagaru, *vb.* またがる sit astride; extend (over).

matagiki, *n.* 又聞き hearsay.

matagiki suru, *vb.* 又聞きする hear about.

matagu, *vb.* またぐ straddle.

mataseru, *vb.* 待たせる keep someone waiting.

matataki, *n.* 瞬き blink.

matataku, *vb.* 瞬く blink; twinkle.

matataku ma ni, *adv.* 瞬く間に in an instant.

mata wa, *conj.* または or; either ... or.

matcha, *n.* 抹茶 powdered green tea.

mato, *n.* 的 1. target. 2. center (of attention).

matomeru, *vb.* まとめる 1. bundle together; compile. 2. finish; settle. 3. summarize.

matomete, *adv.* まとめて all together.

matomo (na), *adj.* まとも (な) 1. honest. 2. decent.

matsu, *n.* 松 pine tree.

matsu, *vb.* 待つ wait for; expect.

matsuge, *n.* まつげ eyelashes.

matsuri, *n.* 祭 festival.

matsuru, *vb.* 祭る deify; worship.

mattaku, *adv.* 全く indeed; really; utterly.

mau, *vb.* 舞う dance.

maue, *n.* 真上 the place directly above.

maue ni, *adv., prep.* 真上に directly above.

maushiro, *n.* 真後ろ the place directly behind.

maushiro ni, *adv., prep.* 真後ろに directly behind.

mawari, *n.* 周り、回り circumference.

mawarimichi, *n.* 回り道 detour; roundabout way.

mawari ni, *prep.* まわりに around.

mawaru, *vb.* 回る 1. turn; reel; spin. 2. circulate.

mawasu, *vb.* 回す 1. turn; wind; spin. 2. circulate. 3. refer.

mayaku, *n.* 麻薬 narcotic.

mayonaka, *n.* 真夜中 midnight.

mayou, *vb.* 迷う 1. lose (direction); **michi ni mayou** lose one's way. 2. vacillate. 3. be captivated.

mayu, *n.* まゆ cocoon.

mayu(ge), *n.* 眉(毛) eyebrow.

maza-maza to, *adv.* まざまざと graphically; explicitly.

mazeru, *vb.* 混ぜる mix.

mazo, *n.* マゾ (E.) masochism; masochist.

mazu, *adv.* 先ず 1. first of all. 2. possibly.

mazui, *adj.* まずい 1. bad tasting. 2. inadvisable.

mazushii, *adj.* 貧しい destitute; poor.

me, *n.* 芽 sprout.

me, *n.* 目 eye; discernment.

meate, *n.* 目当て prospect; aim.

mebae, *n.* 芽生え budding; awakening.

meboshi, *n.* 目星 expectation; guess.

meboshii, *adj.* めぼしい conspicuous; leading.

meboshi o tsukeru, *vb.* 目星をつける aim at.

mechakucha (na), *adj.* めちゃくちゃ (な) 1. chaotic. 2. irrational; nonsensical.

medama, *n.* 目玉 eyeball.

medatsu, *vb.* 目立つ stand out.

medetai, *adj.* めでたい 1. auspicious. 2. stupid.

me ga kuramu, *vb.* 目がくらむ be dazzled; feel dizzy.

megami, *n.* 女神 goddess.

megane, *n.* 眼鏡 eyeglasses.

me ga sameru, *vb.* 目が覚める wake up.

megumi, *n.* 恵み blessing; bounty.

megumu, *vb.* 恵む 1. give alms. 2. show mercy to.

meguriai, *n.* 巡り合い encounter.

meguriau, *vb.* 巡り会う encounter.

meguru, *vb.* 巡る go or come around; surround.

megusuri, *n.* 目薬 eye drops.

mei, *n.* 姪 niece.

meian, *n.* 名案 good idea; **meian ga aru** have a good idea.

meibo, *n.* 名簿 directory; list of names.

meibutsu, *n.* 名物 attraction.

meichū suru, *vb.* 命中する hit (a target); strike.

meiga, *n.* 名画 masterpiece (painting, drawing, film).

meigara, *n.* 銘柄 brand name.

meigijō (no), *adj.* 名義上 (の) nominal.

meihaku (na), *adj.* 明白 (な) obvious.

meijin, *n.* 名人 expert; master.

meijiru, *vb.* 命じる 1. command; order. 2. appoint.

meiji suru, *vb.* 明示する show clearly.

meikai (na), *adj.* 明快 (な) clear; explicit.

meikaku (na), *adj.* 明確 (な) clear-cut; precise.

meikyū, *n.* 迷宮 labyrinth.

meimei suru, *vb.* 命名する christen; name.

meimetsu, *n.* 明滅 blinking; flickering.

meimokujō (no), *adj.* 名目上 (の) nominal.

meimon (no), *adj.* 名門の renowned; prestigious.

meirei, *n.* 命令 command; order.

meireihō, *n.* 命令法 imperative mood.

meirei suru, *vb.* 命令する command; order.

meirō-kaikatsu (na), *adj.* 明朗快活 (な) good-humored; cheerful.

meiru, *vb.* 滅入る feel depressed.

meiryō (na), *adj.* 明瞭 (な) obvious; clear.

meisai, *n.* 明細 detail; particulars.

meisaku, *n.* 名作 masterpiece.

meisatsu, *n.* 明察 insight.

meisei, *n.* 名声 renown.

meiseki (na), *adj.* 明晰 (な) clear; distinct.

meisha, *n.* 目医者 ophthalmologist.

meishi, *n.* 名刺 calling card; business card.

meishi, *n.* 名詞 noun.

meishi, *n.* 名士 celebrity; renowned person.

meishin, *n.* 迷信 superstition.

meisho, *n.* 名所 historic site; place of interest.

meishō, *n.* 名称 name; title.

meishu, *n.* 名手 expert; master.

meishu, *n.* 名酒 sake renowned for its high quality.

meisō, *n.* 瞑想 meditation.

meisō suru, *vb.* 瞑想する meditate.

meitō, *n.* 名刀 fine sword.

meiwaku, *n.* 迷惑 annoyance; nuisance; trouble; **meiwaku o kakeru** inconvenience.

meiwaku (na), *adj.* 迷惑 (な) annoying; troublesome.

meiyo, *n.* 名誉 honor; glory.

mejirushi, *n.* 目印 landmark; sign.

mekake, *n.* 妾 mistress.

mekakushi, *n.* 目隠し blindfold.

mekasu, *vb.* めかす dress up.

mekata, *n.* 目方 weight.

mekki, *n.* めっき gilding; plating.

mekkiri, *adv.* めっきり considerably.

mekubase, *n.* 目配せ wink.

mekura, *n.* 盲 1. blindness; blind person (not in polite use). 2. ignorance.

mekuru, *vb.* めくる turn over; turn (page).

memagurushii, *adj.* 目まぐるしい bewildering; hectic.

memai, *n.* めまい dizziness; giddiness.

men, *n.* 面 1. mask; face; **men to mukatte** face to face. 2. surface. 3. aspect. 4. page (newspaper).

men, *n.* 綿 cotton.

men, *n.* めん noodles.

menbō, *n.* 綿棒 cotton swab.

menboku, *n.* 面木 reputation.

mendan, *n.* 面談 interview.

mendō, *n.* 面倒 1. annoyance; difficulty. 2. care; **mendō o miru** take care of (someone).

mendōkusai, *adj.* 面倒臭い annoying; tiresome.

mendori, *n.* 雌鳥 hen.

men'eki, *n.* 免疫 immunity.

menjo, *n.* 免除 exemption.

menjō, *n.* 免状 1. diploma. 2.

license.

menjo suru, *vb.* 免除する exempt.

menkai, *n.* 面会 interview; meeting.

menkyo, *n.* 免許 license.

menmitsu (na), *adj.* 綿密 (な) detailed; meticulous.

me no kataki, *n.* 目の仇 archenemy.

me no mae de/ni, *adv.* 目の前で、 ～に before one's very eyes.

menseki, *n.* 面積 area.

mensetsu, *n.* 面接 interview.

menshiki, *n.* 面職 acquaintance; **menshiki ga aru** be acquainted.

menshoku, *n.* 免職 dismissal from a position.

mentsu, *n.* メンツ face; honor; **mentsu o ushinau** lose face.

menzei, *n.* 免税 tax exemption.

menzeihin, *n.* 免税品 duty-free item.

me o miharu, *vb.* 目を見張る stare.

me o samasu, *vb.* 目を覚ます awake.

me o tōsu, *vb.* 目を通す look over.

me o tsukeru, *vb.* 目を付ける notice; keep an eye on.

merikenko, *n.* メリケン粉 flour.

meshi, *n.* 飯 rice; food; meal (used by males).

meshiagaru, *vb.* 召し上がる eat; drink (polite).

meshita, *n.* 目下 subordinate.

messuru, *vb.* 滅する die; perish.

mesu, *n.* 雌 female (animal).

metoru, *vb.* めとる marry (a woman).

mētoru, *n.* メートル (F.) meter.

metsubō, *n.* 滅亡 extinction; ruin.

metta ni, *adv.* 滅多に rarely; seldom.

meue, *n.* 目上 superior; one's

senior.

meushi, *n.* 雌牛 cow.

meyasu, *n.* 目安 gauge; standard.

mezamashii, *adj.* 目覚ましい outstanding; striking.

mezamashi(-dokei), *n.* 目覚まし (時計) alarm clock.

mezameru, *vb.* 目覚める wake up.

mezasu, *vb.* 目指す aim at.

mezawari, *n.* 目障り eyesore.

mezurashii, *adj.* 珍しい rare; unusual.

mezurashiku, *adv.* 珍しく unusually; unexpectedly.

mezurashisō ni, *adv.* 珍しそうに curiously.

mi, *n.* 身 1. body. 2. person; **hitori mi** single person. 3. flesh; meat.

mi, *n.* 実 fruit; nut; **mi ga naru** bear fruit.

miageru, *vb.* 見上げる look upward.

miai, *n.* 見合い arranged marriage meeting.

miakiru, *vb.* 見飽きる tire of seeing.

miawasu, *vb.* 見合わす look at each other.

mibōjin, *n.* 未亡人 widow.

mibun, *n.* 身分 social status.

mibunshōmeisho, *n.* 身分証明書 identification card.

miburi, *n.* 身振り gesture.

miburui, *n.* 身震い shudder.

michi, *n.* 道 1. road; way. 2. means. 3. doctrine. 4. career.

michi (no), *adj.* 未知 (の) unknown.

michibiku, *vb.* 導く direct; guide; lead.

michijun, *n.* 道順 route; way.

michinori, *n.* 道のり distance.

michiru, *vb.* 満ちる become full.

michisū, *n.* 未知数 unknown

quantity.

michizure, *n.* 道連れ traveling companion.

midara (na), *adj.* 淫ら (な) indecent.

midareru, *vb.* 乱れる 1. become chaotic; become disrupted. 2. be windblown (hair).

midasu, *vb.* 乱す disrupt; disturb.

midori, *n.* 緑 green.

mie, *n.* 見栄 vanity; pretentiousness.

mie o haru, *vb.* 見栄を張る be vain; pretend to be important.

mieru, *vb.* 見える 1. be able to see. 2. appear.

migaku, *vb.* 磨く 1. brush; shine; polish; **ha o migaku** brush one's teeth. 2. improve (a skill).

migamae, *n.* 身構え defensive posture (martial arts).

migamaeru, *vb.* 身構える assume a defensive position.

migaru (na), *adj.* 身軽 (な) 1. light; agile 2. unburdened; without obligation.

migatte (na), *adj.* 身勝手 (な) selfish.

migawari, *n.* 身代わり substitute (person).

migi, *n.* 右 right-hand side or direction; **migi ni** on the right.

migigawa, *n.* 右側 right side.

migikiki (no), *adj.* 右利き (の) right-handed.

migite, *n.* 右手 right hand.

migiude, *n.* 右腕 right arm.

migomoru, *vb.* 身ごもる get pregnant.

migoto (na), *adj.* 見事 (な) wonderful; marvelous.

migurushii, *adj.* 見苦しい 1. unsightly. 2. shameful.

mihanasu, *vb.* 見放す forsake.

miharai, *n.* 未払い unpaid (bill, rent).

miharashi, *vb.* 見晴らし view; **miharashi ga ii** have a good view.

mihari, *n.* 見張り guard; watchman.

miharu, *vb.* 見張る stand guard; watch.

mihon, *n.* 見本 sample; example.

mi'idasu, *vb.* 見い出す discover; detect.

mijika (na, no), *adj.* 身近 (な、の) close at hand; closely related.

mijikai, *adj.* 短い short.

mijime (na), *adj.* 惨め (な) miserable.

mijitaku, *n.* 身支度 act of dressing.

mijuku (na), *adj.* 未熟 (な) immature; inexperienced.

mikado, *n.* 帝 emperor.

mikaesu, *vb.* 見返す 1. look back. 2. strike back (at an enemy).

mikai (no), *adj.* 未開 (の) undeveloped; uncivilized.

mikaiketsu (no), *adj.* 未解決 (の) unsolved.

mikake, *n.* 見掛け appearance; facade.

mikakeru, *vb.* 見掛ける catch sight of.

mikaku, *n.* 味覚 taste; palate.

mikan, *n.* みかん mandarin orange.

mikan (no), *adj.* 未刊 (の) unpublished.

mikan (no), *adj.* 未完 (の) unfinished.

mikata, *n.* 味方 supporter; ally; **mikata o suru** take someone's side.

mikata, *n.* 見方 viewpoint; **mikata o kaeru** change one's viewpoint.

mikazuki, *n.* 三日月 crescent moon.

mikeiken (na, no), *adj.* 未経験 (な、の) inexperienced.

miki, *n.* 幹 tree trunk.

mikiri, *n.* 見切り abandonment.

mikiri o tsukeru, *vb.* 見切りをつける abandon; forsake.

mikka, *n.* 三日 the third day of the month; three days.

mikkai, *n.* 密会 secret meeting.

mikkō, *n.* 密航 smuggling (by boat).

mikkōsha, *n.* 密航者 smuggler (by boat).

mikkyō, *n.* 密教 esoteric Buddhism.

mikomi, *n.* 見込み prospect.

mikon (no), *adj.* 未婚 (の) unmarried.

mikonsha, *n.* 未婚者 unmarried person.

mikubiru, *vb.* 見くびる slight; underestimate.

mikudasu, *vb.* 見下す scorn.

mimai, *n.* 見舞い visit (to a sick or injured person).

mimamoru, *vb.* 見守る 1. watch over; protect; support. 2. follow (event).

-miman 未満 under; less than.

mimawaru, *vb.* 見回る patrol.

mimi, *n.* 耳 ear.

mimikazari, *n.* 耳飾り earring.

mimitabu, *n.* 耳たぶ earlobe.

mimiuchi suru, *vb.* 耳打ちする whisper (in someone's ear).

mimizawari (na), *adj.* 耳障り (な) annoying (sound).

mimoto, *n.* 身元 identity; lineage.

mina, *pron.* 皆 all; everyone; everything.

minage, *n.* 身投げ suicide by jumping into a river, ocean, or volcano, or from a high place.

minami, *n.* 南 south.

minamoto, *n.* 源 origin; source.

minaosu, *vb.* 見直す reexamine; reconsider.

minarai, *n.* 見習い apprentice; apprenticeship.

minareta, *adj.* 見慣れた familiar.

minari, *n.* 身なり 1. clothes. 2. appearance.

minashigo, *n.* みなしご orphan.

minasu, *vb.* 見なす regard as; presume.

minato, *n.* 港 harbor; port.

mine, *n.* 峰 mountain peak.

min'ei, *n.* 民営 private management.

mingei, *n.* 民芸 folk art.

minikui, *adj.* 醜い ugly.

minikui, *adj.* 見にくい hard to see; obscure.

mi ni tsukeru, *vb.* 身につける learn.

minka, *n.* 民家 private house.

minkan (no), *adj.* 民間 (の) private.

minkandenshō, *n.* 民間伝承 folklore.

min'na de, *adv.* 皆で 1. all told; in sum. 2. all together.

minō, *n.* 未納 non-payment.

minogasu, *vb.* 見逃す 1. overlook. 2. turn a blind eye to.

minori, *n.* 実り harvest.

minoru, *vb.* 実る bear fruit; ripen.

minoshirokin, *n.* 身代金 ransom.

minoue-banashi, *n.* 身上話 life history.

minpō, *n.* 民法 civil law.

minshū, *n.* 民衆 people; populace.

minshuku, *n.* 民宿 private home providing food and lodging for travelers.

minshushugi, *n.* 民主主義

democracy.

minshushugisha, *n.* 民主主義者 democrat.

minshu-teki (na), *adj.* 民主的 (な) democratic.

minshutō, *n.* 民主党 Democratic Party.

minuku, *vb.* 見抜く see through (someone).

minwa, *n.* 民話 folklore.

minyō, *n.* 民謡 folk song.

minzoku, *n.* 民族 ethnic group; race.

minzokugaku, *n.* 民族学 ethnology.

mioboe, *n.* 見覚え recognition; recollection.

mioboe ga aru, *vb.* 見覚えがある recognize; remember.

miokuri, *n.* 見送り 1. seeing a person off; send-off. 2. shelving.

miokuru, *vb.* 見送る see a person off.

miorosu, *vb.* 見下ろす overlook (scenery).

miotosu, *vb.* 見落とす overlook.

mirai, *n.* 未来 future.

miren, *n.* 未練 attachment; regret; **mada miren ga aru** still feel affection for.

miru, *vb.* 見る 1. look; see; watch. 2. take care of.

-miru みる try; **tabetemiru** try food.

miruku, *n.* ミルク (E.) milk.

miryoku, *n.* 魅力 attractiveness; charm.

miryoku-teki (na), *adj.* 魅力的 (な) fascinating; charming.

misaki, *n.* 岬 cape; promontory.

misao, *n.* 操 1. fidelity. 2. chastity.

mise, *n.* 店 shop; store.

misebirakasu, *vb.* 見せびらかす show off; flaunt.

miseinensha, *n.* 未成年者 minor (person).

misemono, *n.* 見世物 attraction; show.

miseru, *vb.* 見せる show.

mishin, *n.* ミシン (E.) sewing machine.

mishiranu, *adj.* 見知らぬ unfamiliar.

miso, *n.* みそ fermented bean paste.

misogi, *n.* みそぎ purification; exorcism.

misokonau, *vb.* 見損なう 1. misjudge. 2. fail to see.

misomeru, *vb.* 見初める fall in love with.

misoshiru, *n.* みそ汁 miso soup.

missetsu (na), *adj.* 密接 (な) closely related; intimate.

misuborashii, *adj.* みすぼらしい shabby; tattered.

misugosu, *vb.* 見過ごす overlook.

misui, *n.* 未遂 failed attempt.

misuteru, *vb.* 見捨てる abandon; forsake.

-mitai みたい resembling; seeming; **bakamitai** seeming silly.

mitasu, *vb.* 満たす fill (up); fulfill.

mitei (no), *adj.* 未定 (の) undecided.

mitomeru, *vb.* 認める recognize; admit.

mitoreru, *vb.* 見とれる be fascinated by; admire.

mitōshi, *n.* 見通し perspective; outlook.

mitsubachi, *n.* 蜜蜂 honeybee.

mitsudo, *n.* 密度 density.

mitsukaru, *vb.* 見つかる be found; be caught.

mitsukeru, *vb.* 見つける find out; locate.

mitsumeru, *vb.* 見つめる gaze at.

mitsumori, *n.* 見積もり estimate.

mitsumoru, *vb.* 見積もる estimate.

mitsuyunyū, *n.* 密輸入 smuggling.

mittomonai, *adj.* みっともない disgraceful; shameful.

mittsu, *n.* 三つ three; three years old.

mittsū, *n.* 密通 adultery.

miuchi, *n.* 身内 relative.

miushinau, *vb.* 身失う lose sight of.

miwake, *n.* 見分け differentiation; distinction; **miwake ga tsukanai** unable to differentiate.

miwakeru, *vb.* 見分ける distinguish.

miwaku, *n.* 魅惑 enchantment; allure; charm.

miwatasu, *vb.* 見渡す look out (over, across).

miyage, *n.* みやげ souvenir; present.

miyako, *n.* 都 capital.

miyori, *n.* 身寄 relative.

mizen ni, *adv.* 未然に beforehand.

mizo, *n.* 溝 ditch; groove; gap.

mizore, *n.* みぞれ sleet.

mizu, *n.* 水 water.

mizugi, *n.* 水着 bathing suit.

mizuiro, *n.* 水色 light blue.

mizukara, *adv.* 自ら personally; on one's own initiative.

mizuke, *n.* 水気 moisture.

mizu-mizushii, *adj.* みずみずしい juicy.

mizumushi, *n.* 水虫 athlete's foot.

mizusashi, *n.* 水差し water pitcher.

mizuumi, *n.* 湖 lake.

mo, *n.* 喪 mourning.

mo, *parti.* も 1. also; and. 2. even.

mō もう 1. *adv.* already; before long. 2. *adj.* another; more; **mō sannin** three more people.

mochi, *n.* もち Japanese rice cake.

mochiageru, *vb.* 持ち上げる lift up.

mochidasu, *vb.* 持ち出す bring up; run away with.

mochihakobu, *vb.* 持ち運ぶ carry.

mochiiru, *vb.* 用いる use.

mochikomu, *vb.* 持ち込む bring in.

mochimono, *n.* 持ち物 belongings.

mochinushi, *n.* 持ち主 owner.

mochiron, *adv.* もちろん needless to say; of course.

mochisaru, *vb.* 持ち去る carry away; make off with.

mōchōen, *n.* 盲腸炎 appendicitis.

mochū, *n.* 喪中 mourning period.

modaeru, *vb.* 悶える agonize; writhe (in pain).

modoru, *vb.* 戻る return; revert.

modosu, *vb.* 戻す return; put back.

moeru, *vb.* 燃える burn.

mōfu, *n.* 毛布 blanket.

mogu, *vb.* もぐ pick; pluck.

moguru, *vb.* 潜る dive; hide.

mohan, *n.* 模範 example; model.

mohan-teki (na), *adj.* 模範的 (な) model.

mohaya, *adv.* 最早 1. by now. 2. no longer (with negative).

mohō, *n.* 模倣 imitation.

moji, *n.* 文字 character; letter.

moji-moji suru, *vb.* もじもじする fidget.

mōjin, *n.* 盲人 blind person.

mōjū, *n.* 猛獣 beast of prey.

mōjū suru, *vb.* 盲従する obey blindly.

mōkaru, *vb.* 儲かる make a profit; be profitable.

mōke, *n.* 儲け profit.

mokei, *n.* 模型 model (train, etc.).

mōkeru, *vb.* 儲ける profit (from).

mōkeru, *vb.* 設ける set up.

mokka, *adv.* もつか now; at this moment.

mokudoku, *n.* 黙読 reading silently.

mokugekisha, *n.* 目撃者 witness.

mokugeki suru, *vb.* 目撃する witness.

mokuhanga, *n.* 木版画 woodblock print.

mokuhyō, *n.* 目標 goal; aim.

mokuji, *n.* 目次 table of contents.

mokuren, *n.* 木蓮 magnolia.

mokuroku, *n.* 目録 catalog.

mokuromu, *vb.* もくろむ plan.

mokusei, *n.* 木星 Jupiter (planet).

mokusei (no), *adj.* 木製 (の) wooden.

mokuteki, *n.* 目的 purpose.

mokutekigo, *n.* 目的語 object (grammar).

mokuyōbi, *n.* 木曜日 Thursday.

mokuzai, *n.* 木材 lumber.

mokuzō (no), *adj.* 木造 (の) wooden.

momen, *n.* 木綿 cotton.

momeru, *vb.* 揉める be at odds.

momiji, *n.* 紅葉 maple.

momikesu, *vb.* もみ消す 1. extinguish. 2. hush up.

momo, *n.* 桃 peach.

momo, *n.* 腿 thigh.

momoiro, *n.* 桃色 pink.

mōmoku, *n.* 盲目 blindness.

momu, *vb.* 揉む rub; massage.

mon, *n.* 門 gate.

mon, *n.* 紋 family crest (heraldic).

mondai, *n.* 問題 question; problem.

mondō, *n.* 問答 questions and answers.

mongen, *n.* 門限 curfew.

monko, *n.* 門戸 door.

monku, *n.* 文句 1. phrase; words. 2. complaint.

monmō, *n.* 文盲 illiteracy.

mono, *n.* 者 person.

mono, *n.* 物 thing; object.

monogatari, *n.* 物語 story; tale.

monogoto, *n.* 物事 a matter; things.

monomane, *n.* 物真似 mimicry; takeoff.

mono'omoi, *n.* 物思い pondering; reflection; thinking; **mono'omoi ni fukeru** be lost in thought.

mono'oshimi, *n.* 物惜しみ stinginess.

mono'oto, *n.* 物音 noise; sound.

monosashi, *n.* 物差し gauge; scale.

monoshiri, *n.* 物知り knowledgeable person; well-informed person.

monosugoi, *adj.* ものすごい 1. exceptional; unusual. 2. awful.

monosugoku, *adv.* ものすごく extremely; horribly.

monotarinai, *adj.* 物足りない unsatisfying.

monozuki (na), *adj.* 物好き (な) curious; peculiar.

monshō, *n.* 紋章 crest (heraldic).

montsuki, *n.* 紋付き kimono bearing a family crest (heraldic).

moppara, *adv.* 専ら exclusively; chiefly.

moraite, *n.* 貰い手 receiver.

morasu, *vb.* 漏らす 1. let out. 2. omit.

morau, *vb.* 貰う 1. receive. 2. (as auxiliary verb) have something done for you.

moreru, *vb.* 漏れる leak.

mōretsu (na), *adj.* 猛烈 (な) fierce; fervent.

mori, *n.* 森 woods; grove.

moriagaru, *vb.* 盛り上がる swell; rise.

moridakusan (na, no), *adj.* 盛り

沢山 (な、の) plenty; a lot.

moroi, *adj.* 脆い fragile.

mōroku suru, *vb.* もうろくする become senile.

moro ni, *adv.* もろに altogether.

moru, *vb.* 盛る fill; pile up.

moru, *vb.* 漏る leak.

mosaku suru, *vb.* 模索する search; inquire; probe.

mosha, *n.* 模写 copy (reproduction).

moshi もし 1. *adv.* providing. 2. *conj.* if; in case.

mōshiageru, *vb.* 申し上げる say; speak; tell (humble).

mōshiawaseru, *vb.* 申し合わせる agree.

mōshideru, *vb.* 申し出る offer; volunteer.

mōshikomi, *n.* 申し込み application.

mōshikomisho, *n.* 申し込み書 application form.

mōshikomu, *vb.* 申し込む apply for.

moshiku wa, *conj.* もしくは or.

moshi-moshi, *interj.* もしもし 1. Hello. (telephone). 2. Excuse me. (to get someone's attention).

mōshiwake, *n.* 申し訳 apology; excuse.

mōshiwake arimasen, *adj.* 申し訳 ありません (I'm) sorry.

mōsō, *n.* 妄想 fantasy; delusion.

mōsōkyō, *n.* 妄想狂 paranoia.

mōsu, *vb.* 申す say; speak; tell (humble).

mō sukoshi, *adj.* もう少し a little bit more.

motarasu, *vb.* もたらす bring about; yield.

motareru, *vb.* もたれる lean on.

moteamasu, *vb.* 持て余す be beyond control.

moteasobu, *vb.* 弄ぶ trifle with.

mōten, *n.* 盲点 blind spot.

motenashi, *n.* もてなし hospitality; entertainment.

motenasu, *vb.* もてなす entertain.

moteru, *vb.* もてる be popular.

moto, *n.* 元、本 1. base; origin; source. 2. principal (money).

moto, *adv.* 元 formerly.

moto (no), *adj.* 元の original; former.

motode, *n.* 元手 capital.

motome, *n.* 求め request.

motomeru, *vb.* 求める 1. ask; request. 2. buy.

moto-moto, *adv.* 元々 originally; from the outset.

motone, *n.* 元値 cost price.

moto wa, *adv.* 元は formerly; before.

moto yori, *adv.* 元より from the first.

motozuku, *vb.* 基く be based on; derive from.

motsu, *vb.* 持つ 1. have; hold; own. 2. last.

motsureru, *vb.* もつれる tangle; become complicated.

mottai-buru, *vb.* 勿体振る put on airs.

mottainai, *adj.* 勿体ない 1. wasteful. 2. too good for.

-motte もって with; by way of; owing to.

motteiku, *vb.* 持って行く take along; take away.

motto, *adv.* もっと more.

mottomo, *interj.* もっとも Indeed!

mottomo, *adv.* 最も most; **mottomo kirei** most beautiful; **mottomo ōkii** biggest.

mottomo (na) もっとも (な) 1. *adj.* logical; rational; true. 2. *conj.* however; of course.

mottomorashii, *adj.* もっともらしい plausible.

moya, *n.* もや haze; mist.

moyashi, *n.* もやし bean sprout.

moyasu, *vb.* 燃やす burn.

moyō, *n.* 模様 design; pattern.

moyo'oshi, *n.* 催し event; meeting.

moyo'osu, *vb.* 催す hold an event.

moyori (no), *adj.* 最寄り (の) nearest.

mozō, *n.* 模造 imitation; copy.

mu, *n.* 無 nothing.

mucha (na), *adj.* 無茶 (な) reckless; absurd; immoderate.

muchi, *n.* 鞭 whip.

muchi (na), *adj.* 無知 (な) ignorant.

muchitsujo, *n.* 無秩序 chaos; disorder.

muchū, *n.* 夢中 absorption; rapture.

muchū de, *adv.* 夢中で 1. madly; intently. 2. desperately.

muda (na), *adj.* 無駄 (な) useless; wasteful.

mudan de, *adv.* 無断で without permission.

mufunbetsu (na), *adj.* 無分別 (な) thoughtless; indiscreet.

muga, *n.* 無我 selflessness.

mugai (na), *adj.* 無害 (な) harmless.

mugen, *n.* 無限 eternity; infinity.

mugen (no), *adj.* 無限 (の) eternal; endless; infinite.

mugoi, *adj.* 酷い cruel; brutal.

mugon (no), *adj.* 無言 (の) speechless; silent.

muhō (na, no), *adj.* 無法 (な、の) 1. unlawful. 2. outrageous.

muhon, *n.* 謀反 mutiny; rebellion.

muhōshin (na, no), *adj.* 無方針 (な、の) planless.

muhyōjō (na, no), *adj.* 無表情 (な、の) expressionless; poker-faced.

muichimon (no), *adj.* 無一文 (の) penniless.

muimi (na), *adj.* 無意味 (な) meaningless; purposeless.

muishiki, *n.* 無意識 unconscious.

muishiki ni, *adv.* 無意識に unconsciously.

mujaki (na), *adj.* 無邪気 (な) innocent; ingenuous.

mujihi (na), *adj.* 無慈悲 (な) merciless.

mujitsu, *n.* 無実 innocence (crime).

mujō, *n.* 無常 impermanence.

mujō (na), *adj.* 無情 (な) heartless; unfeeling.

mujōken de/ni, *adv.* 無条件で、～に unconditionally.

mujun, *n.* 矛盾 inconsistency.

mujun suru, *vb.* 矛盾する be inconsistent.

mukae, *n.* 迎え meeting an arriving passenger.

mukae ni iku, *vb.* 迎えに行く go to meet an arriving passenger.

mukaeru, *vb.* 迎える meet; welcome.

mukai (no), *prep.* 向かい (の) across the street; **mukai no mise** store across the street.

muka-muka suru, *vb.* むかむかする 1. feel nauseated. 2. feel disgusted.

mukankei (na), *adj.* 無関係 (な) unrelated.

mukanshin, *n.* 無関心 indifference.

mukashi, *n.* 昔 old days; ancient times.

mukashi (no), *adj.* 昔 (の) old; ancient; former.

mukashibanashi, *n.* 昔話 1.

legend. 2. reminiscences.

mukau, *vb.* 向かう 1. head for. 2. face.

mukeiken (na, no), *adj.* 無経験 (な、の) inexperienced.

mukeru, *vb.* 向ける direct; project; turn.

mukidō (na), *adj.* 無軌道 (な) reckless; aberrant.

mukigen ni, *adv.* 無期限に indefinitely.

mukimei (no), *adj.* 無記名 (の) unsigned.

mukiryoku, *n.* 無気力 lethargy.

muko, *n.* 婿 bridegroom; son-in-law.

mukō, *n.* 無効 invalidity.

mukō, *n.* 向こう 1. opposite side. 2. foreign country. 3. the other or opposite party.

mukōmizu (na, no), *adj.* 向こう見ず (な、の) reckless.

mukō ni, *adv.* 向こうに over there.

muku, *vb.* 向く 1. look; turn to. 2. be suitable.

muku, *vb.* 剥く peel.

mukuchi, *n.* 無口 reticence; taciturnity.

mukui, *n.* 報い reward; retribution.

mukuiru, *vb.* 報いる reward; repay.

mukumu, *vb.* むくむ swell.

mumei (no), *adj.* 無名 (の) anonymous; unknown.

mumenkyo (no), *adj.* 無免許 (の) unlicensed.

munashii, *adj.* 空しい empty; fruitless.

mune, *n.* 胸 chest; breast.

munō (na), *adj.* 無能 (な) incompetent.

mura, *n.* 村 village.

muragaru, *vb.* 群がる flock; throng.

murahachibu, *n.* 村八分 ostracism.

murasaki, *n.* 紫 purple.

mure, *n.* 群れ crowd; group; hoard.

muri, *n.* 無理 1. impossibility. 2. unreasonableness.

muri (na), *adj.* 無理 (な) 1. impossible. 2. unreasonable.

muri ni, *adv.* 無理に by force.

muryō (no), *adj.* 無料 (の) free of charge.

muryoku, *n.* 無力 powerlessness.

musaboru, *vb.* むさぼる devour.

musakurushii, *adj.* むさ苦しい 1. untidy. 2. shabby.

musebu, *vb.* むせぶ be choked by (smoke, tears).

museifushugi, *n.* 無政府主義 anarchism.

museigen (no), *adj.* 無制限 (の) without bounds; limitless.

musekinin (na), *adj.* 無責任 (な) irresponsible.

musen, *n.* 無線 wireless (electronics).

mushi, *n.* 虫 1. insect. 2. worm.

mushi (no), *adj.* 無私 (の) selfless; impartial.

mushiatsui, *adj.* 蒸し暑い hot and humid.

mushiba, *n.* 虫歯 decayed tooth.

mushibamu, *vb.* むしばむ spoil; eat away at.

mushimegane, *n.* 虫眼鏡 magnifying glass.

mushin, *n.* 無心 1. innocence; honesty. 2. request for money.

mushinkei (na, no), *adj.* 無神経 (な、の) insensitive; indifferent.

mushiro, *adv.* むしろ rather.

mushiru, *vb.* むしる tear; pull out.

mushi suru, *vb.* 無視する ignore; disregard.

mushiyaki, *n.* 蒸し焼き baking in

a covered pot.

mushō de, *adv.* 無償で without compensation.

mushoku (no), *adj.* 無色 (の) colorless.

mushoku (no), *adj.* 無職 (の) unemployed.

mushozoku, *n.* 無所属 independent (unaffiliated with a political party).

musō suru, *vb.* 夢想する dream; daydream.

musu, *vb.* 蒸す 1. steam. 2. be hot and humid.

musū (no), *adj.* 無数の countless; innumerable.

musubu, *vb.* 結ぶ 1. bind; connect; tie. 2. conclude. 3. form; organize.

musuko, *n.* 息子 son.

musume, *n.* 娘 daughter; girl.

muteki (no), *adj.* 無敵 (の) invincible; unrivaled.

mutonchaku (na), *adj.* 無頓着 (な) nonchalant; indifferent.

mutto suru, *vb.* むっとする 1. take offense. 2. be muggy.

muttsu, *n.* 六つ 1. six (counter).

2. six years old.

muttsuri shita, *adj.* むっつりした sullen.

muyami ni, *adv.* 無暗に indiscriminately; recklessly.

muyō (no), *adj.* 無用の useless.

muzai, *n.* 無罪 innocence (crime).

muzan (na), *adj.* 無残 (な) 1. heartless. 2. tragic.

muzōsa, *n.* 無雑作 nonchalance; indifference.

muzukashii, *adj.* 難しい difficult.

muzu-muzu suru, *vb.* むずむずする feel itchy.

myaku, *n.* 脈 pulse; vein.

myō (na), *adj.* 妙 (な) 1. odd; strange. 2. unique.

myōban, *n., adv.* 明晩 tomorrow evening; tomorrow night.

myōchō, *n., adv.* 明朝 tomorrow morning.

myōgo-nichi, *n.* 明後日 day after tomorrow.

myōji, *n.* 名字 family name.

myō ni *adv.* 妙に strangely; without reason.

myōnichi, *n., adv.* 明日 tomorrow.

N

na, *n.* 名 1. name. 2. fame.

-na な don't (do); **Miruna.** Don't look.

nabe, *n.* 鍋 pan; pot.

nabiku, *vb.* なびく 1. wave (in the wind). 2. be seduced; succumb.

nadakai, *adj.* 名高い famous.

nadameru, *vb.* なだめる calm down; soothe.

nadare, *n.* 雪崩 avalanche.

naderu, *vb.* 撫でる rub; stroke.

nado, *parti.* など 1. et cetera. 2.

for instance. 3. such as.

nae, *n.* 苗 seedling.

nafuda, *n.* 名札 name tag.

nagagutsu, *n.* 長靴 knee-high boots (rubber or leather).

nagai, *adj.* 長い long.

naga'iki, *n.* 長生き longevity.

nagaku, *adv.* 長く long; for a long time; **nagaku ikiru** live long.

nagame, *n.* 眺め view; **nagame no yoi heya** room with a good view.

nagameru, *vb.* 眺める gaze; look at.

-nagara ながら 1. while; at the same time. 2. although; nevertheless.

nagare, *n.* 流れ flow; stream; **ishiki no nagare** stream of consciousness.

nagareboshi, *n.* 流れ星 meteor.

nagareru, *vb.* 流れる 1. flow; be washed away. 2. pass (time). 3. be called off.

nagasa, *n.* 長さ length.

nagashi, *n.* 流し kitchen sink.

nagasode, *n.* 長袖 long-sleeved garment.

nagasu, *vb.* 流す 1. drain; pour; flush. 2. shed (tears). 3. wash away.

nageki, *n.* 嘆き lament; sorrow.

nageku, *vb.* 嘆く lament; grieve.

nageru, *vb.* 投げる 1. throw. 2. give up.

nagesuteru, *vb.* 投げ捨てる throw away.

nagetobasu, *vb.* 投げ飛ばす fling away.

nagisa, *n.* 渚 beach.

nagori, *n.* 名残 traces; remnants.

nagorioshii, *adj.* 名残惜しい reluctant to depart.

nagoyaka (na), *adj.* 和やか (な) gentle; peaceful.

naguru, *vb.* 殴る beat up; punch; slap.

nagusame, *n.* 慰め consolation; diversion.

nagusameru, *vb.* 慰める console; divert.

nai, *adv.* ない no; not.

naibu, *n.* 内部 inside; insider.

naika, *n.* 内科 internal medicine.

naika'i, *n.* 内科医 internist.

naikaku, *n.* 内閣 Cabinet.

naikaku-sōridaijin, *n.* 内閣総理大臣 (Japanese) prime minister.

naikō-teki (na), *adj.* 内向的 (な) introverted.

naimitsu (no), *adj.* 内密 (の) secret; confidential.

nairan, *n.* 内乱 civil war.

naisei, *n.* 内政 domestic affairs (of a nation).

naisen, *n.* 内線 extension (telephone).

naisen, *n.* 内戦 civil war.

naishin, *n.* 内心 innermost thoughts or feelings.

naisho, *n.* 内緒 secret.

naishoku, *n.* 内職 side job.

naisō, *n.* 内装 interior decoration.

naiya, *n.* 内野 infield (baseball).

naiyō, *n.* 内容 1. content. 2. substance; **naiyō ga nai** have no substance.

naizō, *n.* 内臓 internal organs.

najimi (no), *adj.* 馴染み (の) familiar; regular (customer).

najimu, *vb.* 馴染む 1. adapt. 2. become accustomed to.

naka, *n.* 中 1. inside. 2. middle.

naka, *n.* 仲 relationship; **naka ga ii** be on good terms.

nakaba 半ば 1. *n.* middle. 2. *adv.* halfway; in-between. 3. *adv.* partially.

naka de, *prep.* 中で among; in.

nakama, *n.* 仲間 colleague; friend; partner.

nakami, *n.* 中身 content; substance.

naka-naka, *adv.* 中々 1. (with negative) not easily; not in the way one wishes. 2. quite.

nakanaori, *n.* 仲直り reconciliation.

nakaniwa, *n.* 中庭 courtyard.

nakatagai, *n.* 仲違い

disagreement.

-nakattara なかったら if not; if it had not been for.

nakayoshi, *n.* 仲良し close friend.

nakayubi, *n.* 中指 middle finger.

-nakereba-naranai なければならない see **-nakutewa-naranai.**

nakidasu, *vb.* 泣き出す start crying.

nakigara, *n.* 亡骸 corpse.

nakigoe, *n.* 泣き声 (human) weeping; sobbing; crying.

nakigoe, *n.* 鳴き声 (animal) howling; crying; chirping.

nakigoto, *n.* 泣き言 complaint; whining.

nakimushi, *n.* 泣き虫 crybaby.

nakitsuku, *vb.* 泣きつく appeal to; implore.

nakōdo, *n.* 仲人 go-between; matchmaker.

naku, *vb.* 泣く (human) cry; weep.

naku, *vb.* 鳴く (animal) bark; chirp; cry.

nakunaru, *vb.* 亡くなる die.

nakunaru, *vb.* 無くなる run out; disappear.

nakusu, *vb.* 無くす lose.

-nakutewa-naranai なくてはならない 1. must; should; **Ika-nakutewa-naranai.** (I) must leave. 2. indispensable.

namae, *n.* 名前 name.

namahōsō, *n.* 生放送 live broadcast.

namaiki (na), *adj.* 生意気 (な) conceited.

namakemono, *n.* 怠け者 lazy person.

namakeru, *vb.* 怠ける be lazy.

namamekashii, *adj.* なまめかしい charming; bewitching.

nama-namashii, *adj.* 生々しい graphic; vivid.

nama no, *adj.* 生の 1. raw; uncooked. 2. live (performance).

namari, *n.* 鉛 lead (mineral).

namari, *n.* 訛 accent (pronunciation).

namazu, *n.* なまず catfish.

nameraka (na), *adj.* 滑らか (な) smooth; mellow.

nameru, *vb.* なめる 1. lick. 2. underestimate; insult.

nami, *n.* 波 wave.

namida, *n.* 涙 tears.

namihazureta, *adj.* 並外れた extraordinary; exceptional.

namiki, *n.* 並木 trees lining a street.

nami-nami to, *adv.* なみなみと fully.

nami no, *adj.* 並の ordinary; usual.

nami taitei (no), *adj.* 並大抵 (の) ordinary; usual.

nan 何 1. *adj.* what. 2. *pron.* what.

naname (no), *adj.* 斜め (の) diagonal; oblique.

nanatsu, *n.* 七つ 1. seven. 2. seven years old.

nanban, *n.* 何番 1. What number? 2. What ranking?

nanboku, *n.* 南北 north and south.

nan da, *interj.* 何だ 1. Is this all? 2. It's nothing!

nan da ka, *adv.* 何だか somehow.

nandemo 何でも *pron.* anything.

nan demo nai, *interj.* 何でもない It's nothing!

nando, *n.* 何度 how many times.

nandomo, *adv.* 何度も many times.

nani, *pron.* 何 what.

nanika, *pron.* 何か 1. something. 2. anything.

nanimo, *pron.* 何も (with negative) nothing.

nanimokamo, *pron.* 何もかも

everything.

nani shiro, *adv.* 何しろ anyway.

nani yori (mo), *adv.* 何より（も）
more than anything.

nanji *n.* 何時 what time.

nankai *n.* 何回 how many times.

nankai mo *adv.* 何回も many
times.

nankō, *n.* 軟膏 ointment.

nankyoku, *n.* 南極 South Pole.

nanmin, *n.* 難民 refugee.

nannen *n.* 何年 what year; how
many years; what grade (in
school).

nannichi *n.* 何日 what day.

nannin, *n.* 何人 how many people.

-nanode なので because.

nanoka, *n.* 七日 seventh day of the
month.

nansai, *adv.* 何歳 how old.

nanto, *adv.* 何と what; how.

nantoka, *adv.* 何とか somehow;
some way or other.

nantonaku, *adv.* 何となく
somehow.

nanto shitemo, *adv.* 何としても at
any cost.

nao, *adv.* 尚 1. further; in addition.
2. still.

naoru, *vb.* 直る 1. be corrected. 2.
be repaired; be restored.

naoru, *vb.* 治る be cured; heal.

naosu, *vb.* 治す cure; heal.

naosu, *vb.* 直す correct; repair;
alter.

-naosu なおす redo; do again.

-nara(ba) ならば if; in that case.

naraberu, *vb.* 並べる align; place
side by side.

narabu, *vb.* 並ぶ form a line.

narasu, *vb.* 慣らす 1. train. 2.
accustom.

narasu, *vb.* 馴らす tame.

narasu, *vb.* 鳴らす sound.

narasu, *vb.* 均す level.

narau, *vb.* 習う learn; study.

narau, *vb.* 倣う follow; imitate.

narawashi, *n.* 習わし custom;
tradition.

nareru, *vb.* 慣れる become
accustomed to.

nareta, *adj.* 慣れた experienced.

nariagari, *n.* 成り上がり upstart.

narikin, *n.* 成金 nouveau riche.

-nari ni なりに in one's own way.

naritatsu, *vb.* 成り立つ 1. consist
of. 2. materialize.

nariyuki, *n.* 成り行き course of
events.

naru, *vb.* なる 1. become; **sensei
ni naru** become a teacher. 2.
turn out; result in.

naru, *vb.* 生る bear fruit.

naru, *vb.* 鳴る chime; ring; sound.

naru, *vb.* 成る consist of.

narubeku, *adv.* なるべく as ... as
possible; **narubeku hayaku** as
soon as possible.

naruhodo, *adv.* なるほど indeed.

nasake, *n.* 情 compassion;
kindness.

nasakebukai, *adj.* 情深い
compassionate; kind.

nasakenai, *adj.* 情無い 1.
disappointing; regrettable. 2.
shameful.

nashi, *n.* 梨 pear.

-nashi de 無しで without.

nashitogeru, *vb.* 成し遂げる
accomplish; complete.

nasu, *vb.* 成す 1. achieve. 2. effect.

nasu(bi), *n.* なす(び) eggplant.

natsu, *n.* 夏 summer.

natsukashii, *adj.* 懐かしい
nostalgic; evocative of times past.

natsukashigaru, *vb.* 懐かしがる
feel nostalgic; miss.

natsuyasumi, *n.* 夏休み summer

vacation.

nattō, *n.* 納豆 fermented soybeans.

nattoku suru, *vb.* 納得する acquiesce; agree.

nawa, *n.* 縄 rope.

nawabari, *n.* 縄張り territory; turf.

nayamasu, *vb.* 悩ます annoy; worry.

nayami, *n.* 悩み distress; worry.

nayamu, *vb.* 悩む be troubled; be worried.

naze, *adv.* なぜ why.

nazeka, *adv.* なぜか somehow.

naze nara(ba), *conj.* なぜなら（ば） because.

nazo, *n.* 謎 enigma; riddle; **nazo o kakeru** pose a riddle.

nazo no, *adj.* 謎の enigmatic; mysterious.

nazukeoya, *n.* 名付け親 godfather; godmother.

nazukeru, *vb.* 名付ける name.

ne, *n.* 根 root.

ne, *n.* 値 price.

neagari, *n.* 値上がり price increase.

neage suru, *vb.* 値上げする raise (price).

neba-neba suru, *vb.* ねばねばする be sticky.

nebaru, *vb.* 粘る 1. persist. 2. be sticky.

nebiki, *n.* 値引き discount; **nebiki suru** give a discount.

nebusoku, *n.* 寝不足 lack of sleep.

nedan, *n.* 値段 price.

nedoko, *n.* 寝床 bed; futon.

negai, *n.* 願い hope; prayer; request.

negau, *vb.* 願う ask; hope; pray; request.

negi, *n.* ねぎ green onion.

negiru, *vb.* 値切る bargain.

neiro, *n.* 音色 timbre.

neji, *n.* ねじ screw.

nejireru, *vb.* ねじれる be twisted.

nejiru, *vb.* ねじる twist.

nekki, *n.* 熱気 hot air; intensity; zeal.

nekkyō, *n.* 熱狂 enthusiasm; excitement.

neko, *n.* 猫 cat.

nekutai, *n.* ネクタイ (E.) necktie.

nemaki, *n.* 寝巻き pajamas; nightclothes.

nemui, *adj.* 眠い sleepy.

nemuri, *n.* 眠り sleep.

nemuru, *vb.* 眠る sleep.

-nen 年 1. year. 2. grade (in school).

nendai, *n.* 年代 1. age; generation. 2. date; period.

nendo, *n.* 年度 fiscal year.

nendo, *n.* 粘土 clay.

nengajō, *n.* 年賀状 New Year's card.

nengan, *n.* 念願 desire.

nen'iri (na), *adj.* 念入り（な） elaborate; minute; meticulous.

nenjū 年中 1. *n.* the whole year. 2. *adv.* throughout the year; always.

nenkan, *n.* 年鑑 yearbook.

nenkan 年間 1. *n.* era; period. 2. *n.* the whole year. 3. *adj.* annual.

nenkin, *n.* 年金 annuity; pension.

nenmatsu, *n.* 年末 year end.

nenpai, *n.* 年輩 age.

nenpō, *n.* 年俸 annual salary.

nenrei, *n.* 年齢 age.

nenryō, *n.* 燃料 fuel.

nenshi, *n.* 年始 1. New Year's Day.

nenza, *n.* 捻挫 sprain.

nerau, *vb.* 狙う aim at; target.

neru, *vb.* 寝る sleep; go to bed.

neru, *vb.* 練る 1. knead. 2. plan carefully.

nesagari, *n.* 値下がり price decrease.

nesage suru, *vb.* 値下げする

reduce a price.

nēsan, *n.* 姉さん elder sister; Miss (familiar form of address).

nesshin, *n.* 熱心 ardor; enthusiasm.

nesshin (na), *adj.* 熱心 (な) ardent; enthusiastic.

nesshin ni, *adv.* 熱心に ardently; enthusiastically.

nessuru, *vb.* 熱する heat.

nesugosu, *vb.* 寝過ごす oversleep.

netamu, *vb.* 妬む be jealous; envy.

netchū suru, *vb.* 熱中する be absorbed in; be enthusiastic about.

netsu, *n.* 熱 1. heat. 2. fever; **netsu ga aru** have a fever. 3. obsession; zeal.

netsui, *n.* 熱意 ardor.

netsujō, *n.* 熱情 passion.

netsuke, *n.* 根付け small carved toggle used to suspend pouch (for tobacco, etc.) from kimono sash.

netsuretsu (na), *adj.* 熱烈 (な) passionate.

netsuzō suru, *vb.* 捏造する fake; fabricate.

nettai, *n.* 熱帯 tropics.

nettō, *n.* 熱湯 boiling water.

neuchi, *n.* 値打ち value; merit.

neuchi no aru, *adj.* 値打ちのある worthy; valuable.

nezumi, *n.* ねずみ mouse; rat.

nezumi'iro, *n.* ねずみ色 gray color.

ni, *n.* 二 two (number).

ni, *parti.* に 1. at; by; for; from; in; on; to. 2. per.

niau, *vb.* 似合う become; suit.

nibai, *adv.* 二倍 twice; twofold.

niban, *n.* 二番 second place.

nibui, *adj.* 鈍い dull; dim-witted.

nibun no ichi, *n.* 二分の一 half.

-nichi 日 day; date.

nichibotsu, *n.* 日没 sunset.

nichiji, *n.* 日時 date.

nichi-yōbi, *n.* 日曜日 Sunday.

nichiyōhin, *n.* 日用品 everyday necessities.

nichiyō no, *adj.* 日用の everyday.

nido, *adv.* 二度 twice; a second time.

nieru, *vb.* 煮える boil.

nigai, *adj.* 苦い bitter.

nigasu, *vb.* 逃がす let loose; lose.

nigate, *n.* 苦手 weak point; tough customer.

nigatsu, *n.* 二月 February.

nigeru, *vb.* 逃げる escape; run away.

nigiru, *vb.* 握る grasp; hold tight.

nigiwau, *vb.* 賑わう be active; be lively; be crowded.

nigiyaka (na), *adj.* 賑やか (な) lively; crowded.

nigoru, *vb.* 濁る be unclear; be muddy.

nigotta, *adj.* 濁った unclear; muddy.

nihon, *n.* 日本 Japan.

nihonbungaku, *n.* 日本文学 Japanese literature.

nihonga, *n.* 日本画 Japanese painting.

nihongo, *n.* 日本語 Japanese language.

nihonjin, *n.* 日本人 Japanese person/people.

nihon ryōri, *n.* 日本料理 Japanese cuisine.

nihonshu, *n.* 日本酒 Japanese wine; sake.

niisan, *n.* 兄さん elder brother.

niji, *n.* 虹 rainbow.

niji (no), *adj.* 二次 (の) second.

nijimu, *vb.* にじむ blur; run.

nijū, *n.* 二十 twenty.

nijū no, *adj.* 二重の double.

nikai, *n.* 二階 second floor.

nikibi, *n.* にきび acne; pimple.

nikka, *n.* 日課 daily schedule.

nikkan(shi), *n.* 日刊(紙) daily paper.

nikki, *n.* 日記 diary; **nikki o tsukeru** keep a diary.

nikkō, *n.* 日光 sunlight.

nikkori suru, *vb.* にっこりする smile.

nikkyū, *n.* 日給 daily wage.

niko-niko suru, *vb.* にこにこする smile.

nikoyaka (na), *adj.* にこやか (な) sunny; beaming.

niku, *n.* 肉 1. meat. 2. flesh.

nikui, *adj.* 憎い hateful.

-nikui にくい difficult (to do); **kikinikui** difficult to hear.

nikumu, *vb.* 憎む hate; loathe.

nikurashii, *adj.* 憎らしい detestable; disgusting.

nikushimi, *n.* 憎しみ hatred.

nikushin, *n.* 肉親 blood relative.

nikutai, *n.* 肉体 human body.

nikutairōdō, *n.* 肉体労働 manual labor.

nikuya, *n.* 肉屋 butcher shop.

nimaime, *n.* 二枚目 good-looking man.

nimono, *n.* 煮物 boiled food.

nimotsu, *n.* 荷物 baggage; cargo; load.

-nin 人 person; people; **sannin** three people.

ninau, *vb.* 担う carry; bear.

ninensei, *n.* 二年生 sophomore; second-grader.

ningen, *n.* 人間 human being.

ningyo, *n.* 人魚 mermaid.

ningyō, *n.* 人形 doll.

ninja, *n.* 忍者 spy; secret agent.

ninjin, *n.* にんじん carrot.

ninjō, *n.* 人情 sympathy; human feelings.

ninka, *n.* 認可 permission; sanction.

ninki, *n.* 任期 term of office.

ninki, *n.* 人気 popularity.

ninmei, *n.* 任命 appointment.

ninmu, *n.* 任務 duty.

nin'niku, *n.* にんにく garlic.

ninpu, *n.* 妊婦 pregnant woman.

ninshiki, *n.* 認識 awareness; recognition; knowledge.

ninshin, *n.* 妊娠 pregnancy.

ninshinchūzetsu, *n.* 妊娠中絶 abortion.

ninshin suru, *vb.* 妊娠する become pregnant.

ninsō, *n.* 人相 looks; (facial) features.

nintai, *n.* 忍耐 patience.

nintaizuyoi, *adj.* 忍耐強い patient.

nintei suru, *vb.* 認定する recognize; authorize.

ninzū, *n.* 人数 number of people.

nioi, *n.* 臭い、匂い smell; scent.

niou, *vb.* 臭う、匂う smell of.

nippon, *n.* 日本 Japan.

niramu, *vb.* にらむ glare at.

niru, *vb.* 似る resemble; look like.

niru, *vb.* 煮る boil; cook.

nisan (no), *adj.* 二、三 (の) two or three.

nise (no), *adj.* 偽 (の) fake; forged.

nisei, *n.* 二世 1. Junior. 2. the Second (in royal line).

nisemono, *n.* 偽物 counterfeit; fake.

nisesatsu, *n.* 偽札 counterfeit banknote.

nishi, *n.* 西 west.

nishi kaigan, *n.* 西海岸 west coast.

nisshi, *n.* 日誌 diary.

nitchū, *n.* 日中 daytime.

nittei, *n.* 日程 daily schedule.

niwa, *n.* 庭 garden; yard.

niwatori, *n.* 鶏 chicken.

nizukuri, *n.* 荷作り packing;
  crating.

no, *n.* 野 field.

no, *parti.* の at; for; in; of; on; from.

nō, *n.* 脳 brain.

nō, *n.* 能 old-style Japanese theater
  (Noh).

nobasu, *vb.* 延ばす 1. extend. 2.
  postpone.

nobasu, *vb.* 伸ばす 1. enlarge;
  lengthen; stretch. 2. develop;
  cultivate. 3. straighten up.

noberu, *vb.* 述べる tell; state.

nobi, *n.* 伸び growth.

nobiru, *vb.* 伸びる 1. develop;
  grow. 2. be postponed. 3. be
  exhausted; collapse.

nobori, *n.* 上り ascent.

noboru, *vb.* 上る rise; ascend.

noboru, *vb.* 登る climb.

nochi (no), *adj.* 後 (の) later;
  future.

nochihodo, *adv.* 後程 afterward;
  later.

-node ので because.

nodo, *n.* 喉 throat.

nodo ga kawaku, *vb.* 喉が渇く be
  thirsty.

nodoka (na), *adj.* のどか (な)
  peaceful.

nōdōtai, *n.* 能動態 active voice
  (grammar).

nōdō-teki (na), *adj.* 能動的 (な)
  active.

nōen, *n.* 農園 farm.

nōfu, *n.* 農夫 farmer.

nōgaku, *n.* 能楽 see **nō.**

nōgakudō, *n.* 能楽堂 Noh theater
  (building or space).

nogareru, *vb.* 逃れる escape.

nogasu, *vb.* 逃す let go; let escape.

nōgyō, *n.* 農業 agriculture.

nohara, *n.* 野原 field.

nōka, *n.* 農家 farmer; farmhouse.

nokeru, *vb.* 退ける remove.

noki, *n.* 軒 eaves.

nōkin, *n.* 納金 payment.

nōkō, *n.* 農耕 agriculture.

noko(giri), *n.* 鋸 hand or electric
  saw.

nokorazu, *adv.* 残らず entirely.

nokori, *n.* 残り remainder;
  balance.

nokoru, *vb.* 残る stay behind;
  remain.

nokosu, *vb.* 残す leave; leave
  behind.

noku, *vb.* 退く step aside.

nomi, *n.* のみ chisel.

nomi, *n.* 蚤 flea.

-nomi のみ only.

nomikomu, *vb.* 飲み込む 1.
  swallow. 2. understand.

nomimono, *n.* 飲み物 beverage.

nōmin, *n.* 農民 farmer.

-nominarazu のみならず not only
  ... but also.

nomisugi, *n.* 飲み過ぎ excessive
  drinking.

nomiya, *n.* 飲み屋 bar.

nomu, *vb.* 飲む 1. drink; swallow;
  take (pills). 2. smoke.

nonbiri suru, *vb.* のんびりする be
  relaxed; be unhurried.

-noni のに 1. although; on the
  other hand. 2. if only; **Motto
  yasui to ii-noni.** If only it were
  cheaper.

nonki (na), *adj.* のんき (な)
  easygoing; nonchalant.

noren, *n.* のれん shop curtain.

nori, *n.* 糊 starch.

nori, *n.* 海苔 dried seaweed sold in
  sheets.

noriba, *n.* 乗り場 taxi stand; train
  platform; bus stop.

norikae, *n.* 乗り換え transfer point
  (transportation).

norikaeru, *vb.* 乗り換える transfer.

norikumi'in, *n.* 乗組員 crew member.

norimono, *n.* 乗り物 vehicle.

noriokureru, *vb.* 乗り遅れる miss (a train, bus, airplane).

nōritsu, *n.* 能率 efficiency.

noritsugi, *n.* 乗り継ぎ connection (transportation).

nōritsu-teki (na), *adj.* 能率的 (な) efficient.

noroi, *n.* 呪い curse; **noroi o kakeru** put a curse on (someone).

noroi, *adj.* のろい 1. slow (movement). 2. slow-witted.

noroma, *n.* のろま slow-witted person.

norou, *vb.* 呪う curse.

noru, *vb.* 乗る get on; ride; take (a train, taxi, etc.).

noru, *vb.* 載る 1. be printed. 2. be placed on.

nōryoku, *n.* 能力 ability; competence; skill.

nōsanbutsu, *n.* 農産物 agricultural product.

noseru, *vb.* 乗せる 1. carry. 2. load. 3. transport.

noseru, *vb.* 載せる 1. put on top of. 2. publish (in a newspaper or journal).

nōson, *n.* 農村 farming village.

nō sotchū, *n.* 脳卒中 stroke; apoplexy.

nōto, *n.* ノート (E.) notebook.

nōyaku, *n.* 農薬 agricultural chemical; pesticide.

nōzei, *n.* 納税 payment of taxes.

nozoite, *prep.* 除いて except.

nozoku, *vb.* 除く eliminate; remove.

nozoku, *n.* 覗く snoop.

nozomi, *n.* 望み hope; dream; wish; **nozomi ga kanau** dream comes true.

nozomu, *n.* 望む hope; dream; wish.

nozomu, *vb.* 臨む 1. attend. 2. look out upon.

nugu, *vb.* 脱ぐ remove (clothing).

nugu'u, *vb.* 拭う wipe.

nukarumi, *n.* ぬかるみ mire.

nukasu, *vb.* 抜かす omit; overlook; skip.

nukemenai, *adj.* 抜け目ない smart; cunning.

nukemichi, *n.* 抜け道 1. byway. 2. loophole.

nukeru, *vb.* 抜ける 1. come off; fall out. 2. escape. 3. go through. 4. lack.

nukitoru, *vb.* 抜き取る pull out.

nuku, *vb.* 抜く 1. pull out. 2. outrun; surpass. 3. skip; eliminate. 4. open (a bottle).

nukumeru, *vb.* ぬくめる warm.

numa, *n.* 沼 swamp.

numachi, *n.* 沼地 marshland.

nuno, *n.* 布 cloth.

nurasu, *vb.* 濡らす wet.

nureru, *vb.* 濡れる get wet.

nuru, *vb.* 塗る paint; spread (butter).

nurui, *adj.* ぬるい lukewarm; tepid.

nusubito, *n.* 盗人 thief; robber.

nusumareru, *vb.* 盗まれる be stolen.

nusumu, *vb.* 盗む steal.

nu'u, *vb.* 縫う sew.

nyō, *n.* 尿 urine.

nyōbō, *n.* 女房 one's wife.

nyūeki, *n.* 乳液 lotion.

nyūgaku, *n.* 入学 enrollment (school); matriculation.

nyūgakugansho, *n.* 入学願書 application for admission (school).

nyū(gaku)shi(ken), *n.* 入(学)試(験) entrance examination.

nyūgan, *n.* 乳癌 breast cancer.

nyūin, *n.* 入院 hospitalization.

nyūin suru, *vb.* 入院する be hospitalized.

nyūji, *n.* 乳児 infant.

nyūjō, *n.* 入場 admission (to theater, arena, auditorium, etc.).

nyūjōken, *n.* 入場券 ticket of admission.

nyūjōryō, *n.* 入場料 admission fee.

nyūkin, *n.* 入金 receipt of money.

nyūkoku, *n.* 入国 immigration; entrance into a country.

nyūmon suru, *vb.* 入門する become a disciple or student.

nyūnen ni, *adv.* 入念に elaborately; meticulously.

nyūryoku, *n.* 入力 computer input; data entry.

nyūryoku suru, *vb.* 入力する input; enter (computer data).

nyūsha, *n.* 入社 joining a company.

nyūshō, *n.* 入賞 winning a prize.

nyūshu suru, *vb.* 入手する obtain.

nyūsu, *n.* ニュース (E.) news.

nyūtai suru, *vb.* 入隊する join the military.

nyūyoku suru, *vb.* 入浴する take a bath.

O

o, *n.* 尾 tail; **o o furu** wag a tail.

o-, *pref.* attached to nouns: (1) indicates that the object in question belongs to someone other than the speaker; (2) shows politeness; or (3) has become inseparable from certain nouns, such as **ocha** (tea).

ō, *n.* 王 king.

ōame, *n.* 大雨 heavy rain.

ōatari, *n.* 大当たり great success.

oba(san), *n.* 伯母(さん) aunt; middle-aged woman.

ōbā, *n.* オーバー (E.) overcoat.

obake, *n.* お化け ghost; monster.

obāsan, *n.* お婆さん grandmother; elderly woman.

ōbei, *n.* 欧米 Europe and the U.S.; the West.

obi, *n.* 帯 kimono sash.

obieru, *vb.* 怯える be frightened.

obitadashii, *adj.* おびただしい immense; abundant.

obiyakasu, *vb.* 脅かす menace; threaten.

ōbo, *n.* 応募 application; subscription.

ōbō (na), *adj.* 横暴 (な) oppressive; tyrannical.

oboeru, *vb.* 覚える 1. memorize; remember. 2. learn. 3. feel.

oboreru, *vb.* 溺れる drown.

oboroge ni, *adv.* おぼろげに vaguely.

ōbo suru, *vb.* 応募する apply for.

ocha, *n.* お茶 tea.

ōchaku (na), *adj.* 横着 (な) 1. impudent. 2. lazy.

ochiba, *n.* 落ち葉 fallen leaves.

ochibureru, *vb.* 落ちぶれる decline; be ruined.

ochiiru, *vb.* 陥る fall into; be trapped in.

ochikomu, *vb.* 落ち込む feel depressed.

ochiru, *vb.* 落ちる 1. come off; fall.

2. fail. 3. go downhill.

ochitsuki, *n.* 落ち着き 1. composure. 2. calmness; serenity.

ochitsuki no aru, *adj.* 落ち着きの ある 1. self-possessed. 2. calm; serene.

ochitsuku, *vb.* 落ち着く 1. become calm; relax. 2. be settled.

ōchō, *n.* 王朝 dynasty.

odaiji ni, *interj.* Take care!

ōdanhodō, *n.* 横断歩道 pedestrian crossing; crosswalk.

ōdan suru, *vb.* 横断する traverse.

odateru, *vb.* おだてる flatter.

odayaka (na), *adj.* 穏やか (な) calm; peaceful.

odeki, *n.* おでき swelling; eruption (skin).

ōdio, *n.* オーディオ (E.) audio.

odokasu, *vb.* 脅かす 1. frighten. 2. threaten.

odokeru, *vb.* おどける joke; play the fool.

odo-odo suru, *vb.* おどおどする be fearful; be nervous.

odori, *n.* 踊り dance.

ōdōri, *n.* 大通り main street.

odorokasu, *vb.* 驚ろかす surprise.

odoroki, *n.* 驚ろき surprise.

odoroku, *vb.* 驚ろく be surprised.

odorokubeki, *adj.* 驚ろくべき surprising; remarkable.

odoru, *vb.* 踊る dance.

odoshi, *n.* 脅し menace; threat.

odosu, *vb.* 脅す menace; threaten.

ōen, *n.* 応援 support.

ōen suru, *vb.* 応援する support.

oeru, *vb.* 終える finish.

ōeru, *n.* オーエル (E. *office lady*) female office worker.

oetsu, *n.* 嗚咽 sobbing.

ōfuku, *n.* 往復 round trip.

ōfukukippu, *n.* 往復切符 round-trip ticket.

ofukuro(san), *n.* お袋(さん) mother.

ogamu, *vb.* 拝む 1. pray. 2. worship; revere.

ōgata, *n.* 大型 large size.

ogawa, *n.* 小川 brook.

ōgesa (na), *adj.* 大げさ (な) exaggerated.

ōgi, *n.* 扇 folding fan.

oginau, *vb.* 補う supplement; compensate for.

ōgoe, *n.* 大声 loud voice; **ōgoe de** in a loud voice.

ōgon, *n.* 黄金 gold.

ogori, *n.* 奢り treat; **Watashi no ogori desu.** It's my treat.

ogoru, *vb.* 奢る provide free food, drink, or entertainment.

ogosoka (na), *adj.* 厳か (な) solemn.

ohayō (gozaimasu), *interj.* おはよ う (ございます) Good morning!

ōhei (na), *adj.* 横柄 (な) arrogant; patronizing.

ōhi, *n.* 王妃 queen.

oi, *n.* 甥 nephew.

oi, *n.* 老い old age.

oi, *interj.* おい Hey!

ōi, *n.* 王位 throne; **ōi ni tsuku** ascend to the throne.

ōi, *adj.* 多い 1. many; much. 2. frequent.

ōi, *n.* 覆い cover; **ōi o kakeru** put a cover on.

oidasu, *vb.* 追い出す expel; evict.

oiharau, *vb.* 追い払う drive away.

oikakeru, *vb.* 追いかける pursue; chase after.

oikomu, *vb.* 追い込む drive (into).

oikosu, *vb.* 追い越す 1. overtake. 2. surpass.

oimawasu, *vb.* 追い回す chase about.

oime, *n.* 負い目 debt.

oimotomeru, *vb.* 追い求める
pursue; seek after; long for.

ōi ni, *adv.* 大いに very.

oinuku, *vb.* 追い抜く surpass; pass.

oiru, *vb.* 老いる grow old.

oishii, *adj.* おいしい delicious;
tasty.

oishisō (na), *adj.* おいしそう (な)
mouth-watering; appetizing.

ō'isogi de, *adv.* 大急ぎで in a great
hurry.

oisore to (wa), *adv.* おいそれと
(は) easily.

oitachi, *n.* 生立ち personal history.

oitateru, *vb.* 追い立てる hurry
(someone); chase away.

oitoma, *n.* お暇 leave-taking;
parting.

oitoma suru, *vb.* お暇する depart;
leave.

oitsuku, *vb.* 追い付く catch up
with; overtake.

ōja, *n.* 王者 king; victor.

oji(san), *n.* 伯父(さん) uncle.

ōji(sama), *n.* 王子(様) prince.

ojigi, *n.* お辞儀 bow (polite
gesture).

ojikeru, *vb.* 怖じける fear.

ōjiru, *vb.* 応じる respond; comply
with.

ojiisan, *n.* お爺さん grandfather;
old man.

ōjo(sama), *n.* 王女(様) princess.

ojōsan, *n.* お嬢さん 1. young girl.
2. (someone else's) daughter.

oka, *n.* 丘、岡 hill.

oka, *n.* 陸 land; shore.

okage(sama) de おかげ(さま)で 1.
adv. thanks to; owing to. 2. *conj.*
because.

ōkakumaku, *n.* 横隔膜
diaphragm.

ōkan, *n.* 王冠 crown.

ōkare sukunakare, *adv.* 多かれ少
なかれ more or less.

okāsan, *n.* お母さん mother.

okashi, *n.* お菓子 confection; cake.

okashii, *adj.* おかしい 1. funny. 2.
wrong; suspicious. 3. unusual;
odd.

okasu, *vb.* 侵す invade.

okasu, *vb.* 犯す 1. infringe. 2.
violate; commit a crime; rape.

okasu, *vb.* 冒す 1. brave. 2. afflict.

ōkata, *adv.* 大方 1. almost. 2.
probably.

okawari, *n.* お代わり second
helping.

okazu, *n.* おかず side dishes
(served with rice).

oke, *n.* 桶 bucket; pail.

okeru, *prep.* おける at; in; on.

oki'agaru, *vb.* 起き上がる get up;
stand up.

okiba, *n.* 置き場 storage space.

okidokei, *n.* 置き時計 clock.

ōkii, *adj.* 大きい 1. big; large. 2.
loud (voice).

okikaeru, *vb.* 置き換える replace;
substitute.

-oki ni おきに every other; **ichi-
nichi-oki ni** every other day.

okini'iri, *n.* お気に入り favorite
thing or person.

okiru, *vb.* 起きる 1. get up; wake
up. 2. happen.

ōkisa, *n.* 大きさ size.

okite, *n.* 掟 rule; law.

okiwasureru, *vb.* 置き忘れる
mislay.

okkū, *adj.* 億劫 bothersome.

ōkoku, *n.* 王国 kingdom.

okonai, *n.* 行い act; behavior.

okonau, *vb.* 行う perform;
conduct.

okoraseru, *vb.* 怒らせる offend;
anger.

okori, *n.* 起こり origin.

okorippoi, *adj.* 怒りっぽい short-tempered.

okoru, *vb.* 起こる 1. originate; start. 2. happen; break out.

okoru, *vb.* 怒る get upset; get angry.

okosu, *vb.* 起こす 1. wake someone up. 2. start. 3. generate; cause; make (a fire).

ōkō suru, *vb.* 横行する be rampant.

okotaru, *vb.* 怠る be lazy; neglect; overlook.

oku, *n.* 奥 back; depths.

oku, *n.* 億 a hundred million.

oku, *vb.* 置く 1. put; place. 2. leave (as it is).

ōku 多く 1. *n.* most. 2. *adv.* mainly.

okuba, *n.* 奥歯 back tooth.

okubyō (na), *adj.* 臆病 (な) timid.

okugai, *n.* 屋外 outdoors.

okujō, *n.* 屋上 rooftop.

okunai, *n.* 屋内 interior (house).

ōkurashō, *n.* 大蔵省 Finance Ministry.

okureru, *vb.* 遅れる 1. be behind schedule; be late for. 2. lag behind others. 3. (watch) lose time.

okureta, *adj.* 遅れた belated.

okuridasu, *vb.* 送り出す send out; see (someone) out.

okurikaesu, *vb.* 送り返す send back.

okurimono, *n.* 贈り物 present; gift.

okurisaki, *n.* 送り先 receiver; destination.

okuru, *vb.* 贈る give a present; confer an award.

okuru, *vb.* 送る 1. send. 2. see off. 2. lead (a life); spend (time).

okusama, *n.* 奥様 1. (someone else's) wife. 2. married woman.

okusoko, *n.* 奥底 bottom.

okusoku, *n.* 憶測 guess; assumption.

ōkute (mo), *adv.* 多くて (も) at most.

okuyukashii, *adj.* 奥床しい elegant; refined.

ōkyū, *n.* 応急 emergency.

ōkyū-shochi/-teate, *n.* 応急処置、〜手当 emergency measures; first-aid treatment.

omae, *pron.* お前 you (informal).

ōmaka (na), *adj.* 大まか (な) broad; rough.

omamori, *n.* お守り amulet; talisman.

omatsuri, *n.* お祭り festival.

omawari(san), *n.* おまわり(さん) policeman.

omedeta, *n.* おめでた happy event; marriage; pregnancy.

omedetō (gozaimasu), *interj.* おめでとう (ございます) Congratulations! Happy ... !; **Kekkon omedetō.** Congratulations on your marriage! **Tanjōbi omedetō.** Happy Birthday!

ome ni kakaru, *vb.* お目にかかる see (a person).

ōme ni miru, *vb.* 大目に見る be understanding; overlook.

ōmisoka, *n.* 大晦日 New Year's Eve.

o-miyage, *n.* お土産 souvenir; present.

ōmizu, *n.* 大水 flood.

omocha, *n.* おもちゃ toy.

omochaya, *n.* おもちゃ屋 toy store.

omoi, *n.* 思い 1. idea; thought; sentiment. 2. love.

omoi, *adj.* 重い 1. heavy. 2.

175

serious; weighty.

omoidasu, *vb.* 思い出す recall; remember.

omoide, *n.* 思い出 recollection; memory.

omoidōri ni, *adv.* 思い通りに to one's satisfaction.

omoigakenai, *adj.* 思いがけない unexpected.

omoigakenaku, *adv.* 思いがけなく 1. unexpectedly. 2. without notice; suddenly.

omoikiri 思い切り 1. *n.* decision. 2. *adv.* to the utmost; to one's heart's content.

omoitsuki, *n.* 思い付き notion; brainstorm.

omoitsuku, *vb.* 思い付く hit upon an idea.

omoitsumeru, *vb.* 思い詰める brood over.

omoiyari, *n.* 思い遣り empathy; consideration.

omoiyaru, *vb.* 思い遣る empathize; identify with; care about.

ōmoji, *n.* 大文字 capital letter.

omokurushii, *adj.* 重苦しい gloomy; oppressive; stuffy.

omomi, *n.* 重み weight.

omomuki, *n.* 趣 effect; taste; **omomuki ga aru** tasteful.

omomuku, *vb.* 赴く go; tend toward.

omo na, *adj.* 主な main; chief.

omoni, *n.* 重荷 burden.

omo ni, *adv.* 主に mainly; chiefly.

omonjiru, *vb.* 重んじる esteem; prize.

ōmono, *n.* 大物 1. trophy. 2. magnate; important figure.

omo-omoshii, *adj.* 重々しい grave; solemn.

omosa, *n.* 重さ weight.

omoshirogaru, *vb.* 面白がる enjoy; be amused by.

omoshirohanbun ni, *adv.* 面白半分に for the fun of; for sport.

omoshiroi, *adj.* 面白い interesting; enjoyable; funny.

omoshirokunai, *adj.* 面白くない boring; uninteresting.

omote, *n.* 表 1. surface. 2. front. 3. outdoors.

omotedōri, *n.* 表通り main street.

omotemuki, *adv.* 表向き openly; publicly; officially.

omou, *vb.* 思う think; feel; intend.

omou zonbun, *adv.* 思う存分 to one's heart's content.

omowaku, *n.* 思惑 speculation; calculation; **omowaku ga hazureru** have one's calculations go wrong.

omowareru, *vb.* 思われる 1. seem. 2. be considered. 3. be loved.

omowazu, *adv.* 思わず unintentionally.

ōmu, *n.* おうむ parrot.

ōmukashi, *n.* 大昔 ages ago.

ōmune, *adv.* 概ね 1. mostly. 2. generally speaking.

omuretsu, *n.* オムレツ (F.) omelette.

omutsu, *n.* おむつ diaper.

on, *n.* 恩 indebtedness; obligation; gratitude; **on ni kiru** feel indebted/grateful; **on ni kiseru** make someone feel indebted.

onaji, *adj.* 同じ same; equivalent to.

onajiku, *adv.* 同じく similarly.

onaka, *n.* お腹 belly; stomach; **onaka ga ōkii** be pregnant; be full.

onboro (no), *adj.* おんぼろ (の) worn-out; tattered.

onbu, *n.* おんぶ piggyback ride.

ondan (na), *adj.* 温暖 (な) mild (weather).

ondo, *n.* 温度 temperature.

ondokei, *n.* 温度計 thermometer.

onēsan, *n.* お姉さん elder sister.

ongaeshi, *n.* 恩返し returning a favor.

ongaku, *n.* 音楽 music.

ongakuka, *n.* 音楽家 musician.

ongakukai, *n.* 音楽会 classical music concert.

oni, *n.* 鬼 1. devil. 2. cruel person.

oniisan, *n.* お兄さん elder brother.

onjin, *n.* 恩人 benefactor; patron.

onkei, *n.* 恩恵 1. favor. 2. benefit.

onken (na), *adj.* 穏健 (な) moderate.

onkyō, *n.* 音響 sound.

onkyū, *n.* 恩給 pension.

on'na, *n.* 女 woman.

on'nagata, *n.* 女方 female impersonator (kabuki).

on'na no ko, *n.* 女の子 girl.

ono, *n.* 斧 ax.

onore, *pron.* 己 oneself.

onozukara, *adv.* 自ずから involuntarily.

onsen, *n.* 温泉 hot spring.

onsetsu, *n.* 音節 syllable.

onshin, *n.* 音信 correspondence; news.

onshirazu (no), *adj.* 恩知らず (の) ungrateful.

onshitsu, *n.* 温室 greenhouse.

onwa (na), *adj.* 温和 (な) mild; calm; gentle.

ō'ō ni shite, *adv.* 往々にして sometimes; frequently.

o'oshii, *adj.* 雄々しい 1. manly. 2. brave.

ō'otoko, *n.* 大男 giant; very tall man.

oppai, *n.* おっぱい 1. breast. 2. breast milk.

ōppira (na), *adj.* 大つぴら (な) open.

ōppira ni, *adv.* 大つぴらに openly.

ōrai, *n.* 往来 traffic.

ōraka (na), *adj.* おおらか (な) easygoing; bighearted.

oranda, *n.* オランダ Holland.

orandajin, *n.* オランダ人 Dutch (person).

ore, *n.* 俺 I (male, informal).

orei, *n.* お礼 gratitude; thanks.

oreru, *vb.* 折れる 1. be broken. 2. give in.

ori, *n.* 檻 cage; cell.

ori, *n.* 折り occasion; opportunity; time.

oriai, *n.* 折り合い relationship; terms; **oriai ga warui** on bad terms.

origami, *n.* 折り紙 Japanese paper folding.

orikaesu, *vb.* 折り返す 1. turn back. 2. go back; return.

orimageru, *vb.* 折り曲げる bend; fold down.

orimono, *n.* 織り物 textile.

oriru, *vb.* 降りる get off; descend; go or come down.

oritatami-shiki (no), *adj.* 折り畳み式 (の) collapsible; folding.

oroka (na), *adj.* 愚か (な) foolish.

oroshi(uri), *n.* 卸し(売り) wholesale.

orosoka ni suru, *vb.* 疎かにする neglect.

orosu, *vb.* 下ろす 1. bring down. 2. draw out (money).

oru, *vb.* 折る break.

oru, *vb.* 織る weave.

ōryō, *n.* 横領 embezzlement.

osaeru, *vb.* 押える 1. press down. 2. apprehend. 3. comprehend; master.

osaeru, *vb.* 抑える suppress;

control.

Osaki ni dōzo. お先にどうぞ After you.

Osaki ni (shitsurei shimasu). お先に (失礼します) Please forgive my going first.

osamaru, *vb.* 収まる、納まる 1. be settled; be solved; **maruku osamaru** be settled satisfactorily. 2. be satisfied. 3. calm down.

osameru, *vb.* 収める、納める 1. put away (in a closet, chest, etc.). 2. conclude. 3. pay a bill or pay for merchandise.

osameru, *vb.* 修める learn; master.

osameru, *vb.* 治める reign; administer.

osan, *n.* お産 childbirth.

osanai, *adj.* 幼い 1. very young. 2. childish.

osarai, *n.* おさらい review.

osarai o suru, *vb.* おさらいをする review.

ōsawagi, *n.* 大騒ぎ fuss; uproar.

ōsei (na), *adj.* 旺盛 (な) flourishing; active.

oseibo, *n.* お歳暮 year-end gift.

oseji, *n.* お世辞 flattery.

oseji o iu, *vb.* お世辞を言う flatter.

osekkai, *n.* お節介 busybody.

osen, *n.* 汚染 pollution.

ōsetsu-ma/-shitsu, *n.* 応接間／〜室 drawing room.

oshaberi, *n.* おしゃべり 1. chatting. 2. talkative person; rumormonger.

oshaburi, *n.* おしゃぶり teething ring.

oshare (na), *adj.* お洒落 (な) fashion-conscious.

oshi, *n.* おし mute (person).

oshidasu, *vb.* 押し出す push out.

oshie, *n.* 教え teaching; dogma; doctrine.

oshieru, *vb.* 教える 1. teach. 2. show; tell.

oshii, *adj.* 惜しい unfortunate; regrettable.

oshi'ire, *n.* 押し入れ closet.

oshimai, *n.* お仕舞い ending; conclusion.

oshimu, *vb.* 惜しむ 1. regret. 2. begrudge.

ōshin, *n.* 往診 house call.

oshinagasu, *vb.* 押し流す wash away.

oshinokeru, *vb.* 押し退ける jostle; elbow.

oshiroi, *n.* おしろい face powder.

oshitaosu, *vb.* 押し倒す knock down; push down.

oshitōsu, *vb.* 押し通す persist; persevere.

ōshitsu, *n.* 王室 royal family.

oshitsubusu, *vb.* 押し潰す crush; squash.

oshitsuke-gamashii, *adj.* 押しつけがましい pushy.

oshitsukeru, *vb.* 押しつける coerce; push.

oshō, *n.* 和尚 Buddhist priest.

oshoku, *n.* 汚職 corruption (by officials).

ōshū, *n.* 欧州 Europe.

ōshū suru, *vb.* 押収する confiscate.

osoi, *adj.* 遅い 1. late. 2. slow.

osoku tomo, *adv.* 遅くとも at the latest.

osomatsu (na), *adj.* お粗末 (な) crude; clumsy.

osoraku, *adv.* 恐らく perhaps; probably.

osore, *n.* 恐れ fear.

osore'iru, *vb.* 恐れ入る appreciate; feel grateful; feel ashamed.

Osore'irimasu. 恐れ入ります I appreciate it. I am sorry.

osoreru, *vb.* 恐れる fear; be

apprehensive.

osoroi de, *adv.* お揃いで all together.

osoroshii, *adj.* 恐ろしい frightening; terrible.

osoroshiku, *adv.* 恐ろしく terribly.

osou, *vb.* 襲う attack.

osowaru, *vb.* 教わる be taught.

ossharu, *vb.* おっしゃる say; tell (polite).

osu, *n.* 雄 male animal.

osu, *vb.* 押す 1. press; push. 2. force.

osu, *vb.* 推す recommend.

ōsuji, *n.* 大筋 outline.

ōsutoraria, *n.* オーストラリア (E.) Australia.

otafukukaze, *n.* お多福風邪 mumps.

otagai, *pron.* お互い each other; one another.

ōtai suru, *vb.* 応待する receive or wait on people.

otaku お宅 1. *pron.* you (polite). 2. *n.* your house; your home.

otamajakushi, *n.* おたまじゃくし tadpole.

oteage, *n.* お手上げ helplessness; hopeless situation.

otearai, *n.* お手洗い bathroom; restroom.

otenba, *n.* お転婆 tomboy.

ōte no, *adj.* 大手の major (company).

oto, *n.* 音 sound.

ōtō, *n.* 応答 response; reply.

ōtobai, *n.* オートバイ motorcycle.

otogibanashi, *n.* お伽話 fairy tale.

otoko, *n.* 男 male; man.

otoko no ko, *n.* 男の子 boy.

otokoyamome, *n.* 男やもめ widower.

otome, *n.* 乙女 maiden.

otomo suru, *vb.* お供する accompany.

otona, *n.* 大人 adult; grown-up.

otonashii, *adj.* 大人しい 1. quiet. 2. submissive.

otoroeru, *vb.* 衰える become infirm; decline.

otoru, *vb.* 劣る be inferior.

otōsan, *n.* お父さん father.

otoshidama, *n.* お年玉 New Year's present.

otosu, *vb.* 落とす 1. drop. 2. lose. 3. decrease.

otōto, *n.* 弟 younger brother.

ototoi, *n.* おととい day before yesterday.

ototoshi, *n.* おととし year before last.

otozure, *n.* 訪れ visit; arrival.

otozureru, *vb.* 訪れる visit; arrive.

otsukai, *n.* お使い errand.

otto, *n.* 夫 husband.

ou, *vb.* 追う chase after; follow; pursue.

ou, *vb.* 負う 1. carry on one's back. 2. bear (responsibility); be indebted to. 3. sustain (injury).

ōu, *vb.* 覆う cover.

ō'uridashi, *n.* 大売り出し (bargain) sale.

oushi, *n.* 雄牛 bull.

owari, *n.* 終り ending; finale; closing.

owaru, *vb.* 終る end; finish; be over.

oya, *n.* 親 parent.

ōya, *n.* 大家 landlord.

oyabaka, *n.* 親馬鹿 doting parent.

oyabun, *n.* 親分 boss.

oyagoroshi, *n.* 親殺し patricide; matricide.

ōyake (no), *adj.* 公 (の) public; open.

oyako, *n.* 親子 parent and child.

oyasumi(nasai), *interj.* お休み（な

さい) Good night!

oyayubi, *n.* 親指 thumb.

ōyō, *n.* 応用 application.

ōyō (na), *adj.* おうよう (な) easygoing; generous.

oyobi, *conj.* 及び and.

oyobosu, *vb.* 及ぼす affect; influence.

oyobu, *vb.* 及ぶ reach; extend to.

oyogi, *n.* 泳ぎ swimming.

oyogu, *vb.* 泳ぐ swim.

oyoso 凡そ 1. *n.* estimate; outline. 2. *adv.* approximately.

ōyō suru, *vb.* 応用する apply; put into practice.

ōyuki, *n.* 大雪 heavy snow.

ōzei, *n.* 大勢 crowd (of people).

ōzora, *n.* 大空 sky.

ōzume, *n.* 大詰め final phase; conclusion.

P

pachinko, *n.* パチンコ Japanese pinball game.

pai, *n.* パイ (E.) pie.

painappuru, *n.* パイナップル (E.) pineapple.

pairotto, *n.* パイロット (E.) pilot.

pajama, *n.* パジャマ (E.) pajamas.

pākingu, *n.* パーキング (E.) parking; parking lot.

pakkēji, *n.* パッケージ (E.) package.

pāma, *n.* パーマ permanent wave; **pāma o kakeru** get a permanent.

pan, *n.* パン (Pg. *pāo*) bread.

panda, *n.* パンダ (E.) panda.

panfuretto, *n.* パンフレット (E.) pamphlet.

panikku, *n.* パニック (E.) panic; **panikku ni ochi'iru** to panic.

pan-ko/-kuzu, *n.* パン粉、～屑 breadcrumbs.

panku, *n.* パンク (E.) puncture; flat tire.

panku suru, *vb.* パンクする get a flat tire.

pansuto, *n.* パンスト (E.) pantyhose.

pantī, *n.* パンティー (E.) panties.

pantsu, *n.* パンツ (E.) briefs; men's underpants.

pan'ya, *n.* パン屋 bakery; baker.

papa, *n.* パパ (E.) papa.

para-para furu, *vb.* ぱらぱら降る rain lightly.

pari-pari suru, *vb.* ぱりぱりする crunch (cracker, etc.).

pāsento, *n.* パーセント (E.) percent.

pasokon, *n.* パソコン (E.) personal computer.

pasu, *n.* パス (E.) pass; commuter pass; free ticket.

pasupōto, *n.* パスポート (E.) passport.

pasu suru, *vb.* パスする pass.

pata-pata suru, *vb.* ぱたぱたする flap; flutter.

pātī, *n.* パーティー (E.) party.

pāto, *n.* パート (E.) part-timer; part-time job.

patokā, *n.* パトカー (E.) patrol car.

pātonā, *n.* パートナー (E.) partner.

patto, *adv.* ぱっと instantly; suddenly; in a flash.

patto shinai, *vb.* ぱっとしない be mediocre; be unspectacular.

pea, *n.* ペア (E.) pair; couple.

180

pedaru, *n.* ペダル (E.) pedal.

pēji, *n.* ページ (E.) page; **ichipēji** one page; page one.

peko-peko suru, *vb.* ぺこぺこする 1. flatter; fawn. 2. cringe.

pen, *n.* ペン (E.) pen.

penchi, *n.* ペンチ pliers.

pendanto, *n.* ペンダント (E.) pendant.

penki, *n.* ペンキ (D. *pek*) paint.

penshon, *n.* ペンション (F. *pension*) small hotel.

pēpā-tesuto, *n.* ペーパーテスト written exam.

pera-pera, *adv.* ぺらぺら fluently; volubly.

pera-pera shaberu, *vb.* ぺらぺらしゃべる chatter.

peten, *n.* ぺてん fraud.

petenshi, *n.* ぺてん師 impostor; swindler.

piano, *n.* ピアノ (It.) piano; **piano o hiku** play the piano.

picha-picha suru, *vb.* ぴちゃぴちゃする splash; lap.

pika-pika suru, *vb.* ぴかぴかする glisten; sparkle.

piku-piku suru, *vb.* ぴくぴくする twitch.

pīman, *n.* ピーマン (F. *piment*) green pepper.

pīnattsu, *n.* ピーナッツ (E.) peanut.

pin-boke, *n.* ピンぼけ out-of-focus photograph.

pinhane, *n.* ピンはね kickback.

pin-pin shite iru, *adj.* ぴんぴんしている healthy.

pin-pon, *n.* ピンポン (E.) Ping-Pong.

pinto, *n.* ピント (D. *brandpunt*) focus (camera).

piri-piri suru, *vb.* ぴりぴりする smart; sting.

pittari, *adv.* ぴったり 1. tightly. 2. exactly.

pittari suru, *vb.* ぴったりする fit perfectly.

piza(pai), *n.* ピザ(パイ) (It. *pizza*) pizza.

poketto, *n.* ポケット (E.) pocket.

pondo, *n.* ポンド (E.) pound.

poro-shatsu, *n.* ポロシャツ (E.) polo shirt.

poruno, *n.* ポルノ (E.) pornography.

posutā, *n.* ポスター (E.) poster.

posuto, *n.* ポスト (E. *post*) mailbox.

poteto, *n.* ポテト potato.

potto naru, *vb.* ぽっとなる blush.

-ppai see **-hai.**

-ppiki see **-hiki.**

-ppon see **-hon.**

pun-pun suru, *vb.* ぷんぷんする 1. be indignant. 2. reek.

puran, *n.* プラン (E.) plan; **puran o tateru** form a plan.

purasuchikku, *n.* プラスチック (E.) plastic.

purattohōmu, *n.* プラットホーム (E.) platform (train).

purezento, *n.* プレゼント (E. *present*) gift.

purin, *n.* プリン (E. *pudding*) caramel custard; flan.

purintā, *n.* プリンター (E.) printer.

purinto, *n.* プリント (E. *print*) printed material; copy.

puroguramu, *n.* プログラム (E.) program.

pūru, *n.* プール (E.) pool.

pusshu-hon, *n.* プッシュホン (E.) touch-tone phone.

puro, *n.* プロ (E.) professional.

pyon-pyon haneru, *vb.* ぴょんぴょんはねる hop; skip.

R

-ra 等 plural indicator; and so on; **karera** they.

raden, *n.* 螺鈿 mother-of-pearl.

ragubī, *n.* ラグビー (E.) rugby.

raigetsu, *n.* 来月 next month.

raihin, *n.* 来賓 guest; visitor.

raihō, *n.* 来訪 visit.

raikyaku, *n.* 来客 guest; visitor.

rainichi suru, *vb.* 来日する visit Japan.

raisan, *n.* 礼讃 glorification.

raise, *n.* 来世 afterlife (Buddhism).

raishū, *n.* 来週 next week.

raisu, *n.* ライス (E.) rice (when served with Western-style dishes).

raisu-karē, *n.* ライスカレー curry and rice.

raitā, *n.* ライター (E.) lighter.

raito, *n.* ライト (E.) light.

raito, *n.* ライト (E.) right.

rajio, *n.* ラジオ (E.) radio.

rakkan, *n.* 楽観 optimism.

rakkanshugi, *n.* 楽観主義 optimism.

rakkanshugisha, *n.* 楽観主義者 optimist.

rakkan-teki (na), *adj.* 楽観的 (な) optimistic.

rakkī (na), *adj.* ラッキー (な) (E.) lucky.

raku, *n.* 楽 comfort; pleasure; relief.

rakuchaku, *n.* 落着 solution; settlement.

rakuda, *n.* ラクダ camel.

rakudai, *n.* 落第 failure in an examination.

rakugaki, *n.* 落書き graffiti.

rakugo suru, *vb.* 落伍する drop out.

raku (na), *adj.* 楽 (な) comfortable; easy.

raku ni naru, *vb.* 楽になる 1. feel at ease. 2. be relieved (from pain).

rakunō, *n.* 酪農 dairy farming.

raku-raku (to), *adv.* 楽々 (と) easily.

rakutan suru, *vb.* 落胆する be disappointed.

rāmen, *n.* ラーメン Chinese style noodles in broth.

ran, *n.* 蘭 orchid.

ran, *n.* 欄 column (newspaper).

ran, *n.* 乱 war; riot; rebellion.

ranbō (na), *adj.* 乱暴 (な) violent; disorderly.

ranchi, *n.* ランチ (E.) lunch.

ranpi, *n.* 乱費 extravagance.

ranpu, *n.* ランプ (E.) lamp.

ranyō, *n.* 乱用 misuse; abuse.

ranzatsu (na), *adj.* 乱雑 (な) chaotic; disorderly.

-rashii らしい 1. seem; appear; sound. 2. I hear (that). 3. befitting; **otokorashii** befitting a man.

rasshu-awā, *n.* ラッシュアワー (E.) rush hour.

ratai, *n.* 裸体 naked body; nudity.

ratai (no), *adj.* 裸体 (の) nude; naked.

rei, *n.* 霊 1. soul. 2. ghost.

rei, *n.* 零 zero.

rei, *n.* 礼 1. bow; salute. 2. gratitude; thanks; **rei o noberu** express gratitude.

rei, *n.* 例 example; **rei o ageru** give an example.

reibō, *n.* 冷房 air conditioning.

reigai, *n.* 例外 exception.

reigi, *n.* 礼儀 civility; etiquette.

reigi tadashii, *adj.* 礼儀正しい polite; well-mannered.

reihai, *n.* 礼拝 worship.

reiji, *n.* 零時 twelve o'clock midnight.

reijō, *n.* 礼状 thank-you note.

reikoku (na), *adj.* 冷酷 (な) cruel; heartless; inhuman.

reikon, *n.* 霊魂 spirit; soul.

reikyaku suru, *vb.* 冷却する cool.

reinendōri, *adv.* 例年通り as usual; as in years past.

rei no, *adj.* 例の usual.

rei o suru, *vb.* 礼をする 1. bow; salute. 2. thank; express gratitude.

reisei (na), *adj.* 冷静 (な) calm; composed; level-headed.

reisei ni, *adv.* 冷静に calmly.

reishō suru, *n.* 冷笑する sneer.

reitan (na), *adj.* 冷淡 (な) cool; indifferent.

reitōshokuhin, *n.* 冷凍食品 frozen food.

reitō suru, *vb.* 冷凍する freeze.

reizōko, *n.* 冷蔵庫 refrigerator.

reji, *n.* レジ (E.) register; cashier.

rekishi, *n.* 歴史 history.

rekishi, *n.* 轢死 death (from being hit by car or train).

rekishijō (no), *adj.* 歴史上 (の) historical.

rekishika, *n.* 歴史家 historian.

rekishi-teki (na), *adj.* 歴史的 (な) historic; epoch-making.

rekōdo, *n.* レコード (E.) record; **rekōdo o kakeru** play a record.

remon, *n.* レモン (E.) lemon.

ren'ai, *n.* 恋愛 romantic love.

renchū, *n.* 連中 group of people; crowd (social).

renga, *n.* 煉瓦 brick.

renga, *n.* 連歌 Japanese linked verse.

rengō, *n.* 連合 alliance; federation; coalition.

rengō suru, *vb.* 連合する unite.

renji, *n.* レンジ (E.) range (kitchen).

renketsu suru, *vb.* 連結する connect.

renkon, *n.* 蓮根 lotus root.

renkyū, *n.* 連休 consecutive days off (esp. three-day weekend).

renpō, *n.* 連邦 federation.

renraku, *n.* 連絡 1. contact; **Kare to renraku o toru.** (I) will contact him. 2. communication.

renraku suru, *vb.* 連絡する contact; inform.

rensa han'nō, *n.* 連鎖反応 chain reaction.

renshū, *n.* 練習 practice; exercise; drill.

renshū suru, *vb.* 練習する practice; exercise; drill.

rensō, *n.* 連想 association (ideas).

rensō suru, *vb.* 連想する associate; be reminded of.

rentai, *adj.* 連帯 joint; **rentai sekinin** joint responsibility.

renta-kā, *n.* レンタカー (E.) rental car.

rentogen, *n.* レントゲン (G. *Röntgen*) x-ray.

renzoku, *n.* 連続 series.

renzoku-teki (na), *adj.* 連続的 (な) continuous; consecutive.

renzoku-teki ni, *adv.* 連続的に continuously.

reshīto, *n.* レシート (E.) receipt.

ressha, *n.* 列車 train.

ressun, *n.* レッスン (E.) lesson.

resutoran, *n.* レストラン (F.) restaurant.

retsu, *n.* 列 row; line.

rettō, *n.* 列島 archipelago.

rettōkan, *n.* 劣等感 inferiority complex.

richigi (na), *adj.* 律儀 (な) conscientious.

richi-teki (na), *adj.* 理知的 (な) intelligent.

ridatsu suru, *vb.* 離脱する secede.

rieki, *n.* 利益 profit.

rien, *n.* 離縁 divorce.

rifujin (na), *adj.* 理不尽 (な) unfair; absurd.

rigai, *n.* 利害 advantages and disadvantages; interests.

rihatsuten, *n.* 理髪店 barber shop.

riji, *n.* 理事 director; member of the board.

rijun, *n.* 利潤 profit.

rika, *n.* 理科 science (course).

rikai, *n.* 理解 understanding.

rikisetsu suru, *vb.* 力説する emphasize.

rikkōho, *n.* 立候補 candidacy.

rikkōho suru, *vb.* 立候補する run for; be a candidate for.

rikō (na), *adj.* 利口 (な) clever; smart.

rikon, *n.* 離婚 divorce.

rikon suru, *vb.* 離婚する obtain a divorce.

rikoshugi, *n.* 利己主義 (の) egotism; selfishness.

rikoshugisha, *n.* 利己主義者 egotist.

riko-teki (na), *adj.* 利己的 (な) egotistic; self-centered.

riku, *n.* 陸 land.

rikugun, *n.* 陸軍 army.

rikutsu, *n.* 理屈 1. argument. 2. theory. 3. pretext.

rikutsu o iu, *vb.* 理屈を言う 1. argue. 2. theorize.

rimen, *n.* 裏面 reverse; inside.

ringo, *n.* りんご apple.

rinji (no), *adj.* 臨時 (の) 1. temporary. 2. extraordinary. 3. emergency.

rinjin, *n.* 隣人 neighbor.

rinjū, *n.* 臨終 deathbed.

rinkaku, *n.* 輪郭 outline.

rinri, *n.* 倫理 ethics.

rippa (na), *adj.* 立派 (な) admirable; splendid; respectable.

rippa ni, *adv.* 立派に admirably; wonderfully.

rippuku suru, *vb.* 立腹する become angry.

rirekisho, *n.* 履歴書 resume; curriculum vitae.

ririku suru, *vb.* 離陸する take off (flight).

riritsu, *n.* 利率 interest rate.

riron, *n.* 理論 theory.

riron-teki (na), *adj.* 理論的 (な) theoretical.

risei, *n.* 理性 reasoning power.

risei-teki (na), *adj.* 理性的 (な) rational.

rishi, *n.* 利子 interest (money).

rishū suru, *vb.* 履修する complete a course (of study).

risō, *n.* 理想 ideal.

risō-ka/-shugisha, *n.* 理想家、～ 主義者 idealist.

risō-teki (na), *adj.* 理想的 (な) ideal.

risshō, *n.* 立証 proof.

risshō suru, *vb.* 立証する prove.

risu, *n.* りす squirrel.

ritsu, *n.* 率 percentage; proportion; rate.

rittai, *n.* 立体 solid.

rittai-teki (na), *adj.* 立体的 (な) three-dimensional.

riyō suru, *vb.* 利用する use; utilize.

riyū, *n.* 理由 reason; excuse.

ro, *n.* 炉 fireplace; furnace.

rō, *n.* ろう wax.

roba, *n.* ろば donkey.

rōbai suru, *vb.* 狼狽する be disconcerted; panic.

robotto, *n.* ロボット (E.) robot.

rōden, *n.* 漏電 short circuit.

rōdō, *n.* 労働 manual labor.

rōdoku, *n.* 朗読 recitation; reading aloud.

rōdōkumiai, *n.* 労働組合 labor union.

rōdōsha, *n.* 労働者 laborer.

rōgan, *n.* 老眼 farsightedness due to aging.

rōgankyō, *n.* 老眼鏡 reading glasses.

rōgo, *n.* 老後 old age.

rōhi, *n.* 浪費 1. dissipation. 2. waste.

rōhi suru, *vb.* 浪費する 1. squander; dissipate. 2. waste.

rōhō, *n.* 朗報 good news.

roji, *n.* 路地 alley.

rōjin, *n.* 老人 elderly person.

rōjin-hōmu, *n.* 老人ホーム nursing home for the aged.

rōka, *n.* 廊下 corridor; hallway.

roka suru, *vb.* 濾過する filter.

roketto, *n.* ロケット (E.) rocket.

rokkotsu, *n.* 肋骨 rib.

rōkō (na), *adj.* 老巧 (な) skilled; seasoned; experienced.

rokotsu (na), *adj.* 露骨 (な) 1. bare; uncovered. 2. frank.

roku, *n.* 六 six.

rokuga, *n.* 録画 video recording.

rokuga suru, *vb.* 録画する videotape.

rokugatsu, *n.* 六月 June.

rokujū, *n.* 六十 sixty.

roku ni, *adv.* ろくに (not) satisfactorily (used with negative).

rokuon, *n.* 録音 sound recording.

rōmaji, *n.* ローマ字 Roman letter.

ron, *n.* 論 1. theory. 2. opinion; argument.

ronbun, *n.* 論文 essay; research paper; thesis; dissertation.

rongi, *n.* 論議 debate; discussion.

rōnin, *n.* 浪人 1. masterless samurai. 2. unemployed person. 3. high school graduate who has not yet passed a college entrance examination.

ronjiru, *vb.* 論じる argue; discuss.

ronkyo, *n.* 論拠 basis (for argument).

ronkyū, *n.* 論及 reference; comment.

ronri, *n.* 論理 logic.

ronri-teki (na), *adj.* 論理的 (な) logical.

ronsetsu, *n.* 論説 editorial.

ronsō, *n.* 論争 controversy; argument.

rōren (na, no), *adj.* 老練 (な、の) skilled; experienced; seasoned.

rōryoku, *n.* 労力 labor force.

rosen, *n.* 路線 route (transportation).

rōshi, *n.* 老死 death (from old age).

roshia, *n.* ロシア Russia.

roshiago, *n.* ロシア語 Russian language.

roshiajin, *n.* ロシア人 Russian (person).

roshutsu, *n.* 露出 exposure.

roshutsukyō, *n.* 露出狂 exhibitionist.

roshutsu suru, *vb.* 露出する expose.

rōsoku, *n.* ろうそく candle; **rōsoku o tsukeru** light a candle.

rōsu, *n.* ロース (E.) roast (meat).

rōsui, *n.* 老衰 senility.

roten, *n.* 露店 street vendor's stall.

rotenburo, *n.* 露店風呂 open-air bath.

rōya, *n.* 牢屋 prison; jail.

rui, *n.* 類 category; class; type.

ruigo, *n.* 類語 synonym.

ruiji (no), *adj.* 類似 (の) similar.

ruijihin, *n.* 類似品 imitation.

rusu, *n.* 留守 absence (from home).

rusu (no), *adj.* 留守 (の) away (from home).

rusuban, *n.* 留守番 caretaker (during one's absence).

rusubandenwa, *n.* 留守番電話 answering machine.

rusu ni suru, *vb.* 留守にする be absent; be away (from home).

ryaku, *n.* 略 abbreviation; abridgement; omission.

ryakudatsu, *n.* 略奪 looting.

ryaku suru, *vb.* 略する abbreviate; abridge; omit.

ryō, *n.* 猟 hunting.

ryō, *n.* 漁 fishing.

ryō, *n.* 寮 dormitory.

ryō, *n.* 量 quantity.

ryōdo, *n.* 領土 territory.

ryōgae, *n.* 両替 1. making change (money). 2. foreign currency exchange.

ryōga suru, *vb.* 凌駕する surpass.

ryōgawa, *n.* 両側 both sides.

ryohi, *n.* 旅費 travel expenses.

ryōhō 両方 1. *pron.* both. 2. *n.* both sides; both parties.

ryōji, *n.* 領事 consul.

ryōjikan, *n.* 領事館 consulate; **amerika-ryōjikan** American consulate.

ryōjū, *n.* 猟銃 hunting rifle.

ryōkai, *n.* 了解 agreement; consent; understanding.

ryōkai suru, *vb.* 了解する agree; consent; understand.

ryokaku, *n.* 旅客 passenger; traveler.

ryokakuki, *n.* 旅客機 passenger airplane.

ryokan, *n.* 旅館 Japanese-style inn.

ryoken, *n.* 旅券 passport.

ryōkin, *n.* 料金 fare; fee; price.

ryokō, *n.* 旅行 travel; trip; tour.

ryokōgaisha, *n.* 旅行会社 travel agency.

ryokō suru, *vb.* 旅行する travel; take a trip; tour.

ryokucha, *n.* 緑茶 green tea.

ryōri, *n.* 料理 cooking; cuisine.

ryōri suru, *vb.* 料理する cook; prepare a meal.

ryōsei, *n.* 両性 both sexes.

ryōshi, *n.* 漁師 fisherman.

ryōshiki, *n.* 良識 sound judgment.

ryōshin, *n.* 良心 conscience.

ryōshin, *n.* 両親 parents.

ryōshitsu, *n.* 良質 good quality.

ryōshūsho, *n.* 領収書 receipt.

ryōte, *n.* 両手 both hands.

ryotei, *n.* 旅程 itinerary.

ryōtei, *n.* 料亭 exclusive Japanese restaurant.

ryōyō suru, *vb.* 療養する receive medical treatment; recuperate.

ryū, *n.* 竜 dragon.

ryūchijō, *n.* 留置場 lockup.

ryūchō (na), *adj.* 流暢な fluent; **ryūchō na nihongo** fluent Japanese.

ryūchō ni, *adv.* 流暢に fluently; **ryūchō ni hanasu** speak fluently.

ryūgaku, *n.* 留学 study abroad.

ryūgaku-sei, *n.* 留学生 foreign student.

ryūi suru, *vb.* 留意する keep in mind.

ryūkō, *n.* 流行 vogue; fashion.

ryūkō'okure (no), *adj.* 流行遅れ outdated.

ryūkō suru, *vb.* 流行する 1. be in vogue; be popular. 2. be prevalent; be rampant.

ryūkyūshotō, *n.* 琉球諸島 Ryukyu

Islands; Okinawa.

ryūtsū, *n.* 流通 distribution.

ryūtsūkikō, *n.* 流通機構

distribution system.

ryūzan, *n.* 流産 1. miscarriage. 2. failure.

S

sa, *n.* 差 difference; gap; **nichibei no sa** difference between Japan and the U.S.

saba, *n.* 鯖 mackerel.

sabaku, *n.* 砂漠 desert.

sabaku, *vb.* さばく settle; pass judgment on.

sabetsu, *n.* 差別 discrimination; **sei sabetsu** sex discrimination.

sabetsu suru, *vb.* 差別する discriminate.

sabi, *n.* 錆 rust.

sabi, *n.* 寂 antiquated elegance (aesthetic concept).

sabireru, *vb.* 寂れる decline; deteriorate.

sabiru, *vb.* 錆びる rust.

sabishii, *adj.* 寂しい 1. lonely. 2. desolate.

sabishigaru, *vb.* 寂しがる feel lonely; miss (a person).

sabishisa, *n.* 寂しさ loneliness.

sābisu, *n.* サービス (E.) service (assistance).

saboru, *vb.* さぼる 1. neglect (one's job or duty). 2. cut class.

saboten, *n.* サボテン cactus.

sadamaru, *vb.* 定まる be decided; be regulated.

sadame, *n.* 定め 1. decision; law. 2. destiny.

sadameru, *vb.* 定める decide; prescribe.

sadō, *n.* 茶道 tea ceremony.

-sae さえ 1. even; **kodomo-sae** even a child. 2. if only; **Okane-**

sae areba. If only I had money.

saegiru, *vb.* 遮る block; interrupt.

saeru, *vb.* 冴える be clear; be lucid.

saezuru, *vb.* さえずる chirp; warble (birds).

sagaru, *vb.* 下がる 1. hang (from). 2. go down; step backward. 3. drop.

sagasu, *vb.* 捜す look for.

sageru, *vb.* 下げる 1. hang. 2. lower. 3. reduce. 4. remove; **sara o sageru** clear the table (remove the plates).

sagesumu, *vb.* 蔑む look down on.

sagi, *n.* さぎ heron.

sagi, *n.* 詐欺 fraud; hoax.

sagishi, *n.* 詐欺師 fraud; swindler.

saguru, *vb.* 探る grope; look for; probe.

sagyō, *n.* 作業 work; operation.

sahō, *n.* 作法 etiquette; manners.

sahodo, *adv.* さほど (with negative) not very; not so much.

sai, *n.* 才 ability; talent.

sai- 再 re-; **saikon** remarriage.

-sai 歳、才 age; years old; **rokusai** six years old.

sai'ai (no), *adj.* 最愛 (の) most cherished.

sai'aku (no), *adj.* 最悪 (の) worst; **sai'aku no bāi ni wa** in the worst case.

saibai, *n.* 栽培 cultivation (plants).

saiban, *n.* 裁判 trial; judgment.

saibankan, *n.* 裁判官 judge.

saibansho, *n.* 裁判所 court of law.

saibō, *n.* 細胞 cell (biology).

saibu, *n.* 細部 details.

saichū *prep.* 最中 in the midst of; during.

saidai (no), *adj.* 最大 (の) 1. biggest; largest; maximum; **nihon saidai no otera** biggest temple in Japan. 2. best.

saidan, *n.* 祭壇 altar.

saido, *adv.* 再度 again.

saifu, *n.* 財布 wallet; purse.

saigai, *n.* 災害 disaster.

saigen, *n.* 際限 end; limit; bounds; **saigen ga nai** without bounds.

saigen'naku, *adv.* 際限無く endlessly.

saigetsu, *n.* 歳月 time; years.

saigi, *n.* 猜疑 suspicion.

saigo, *n.* 最後 end.

saigo (no), *adj.* 最後 (の) last; final.

saigo ni, *adv.* 最後に in the end; finally.

saigunbi, *n.* 再軍備 rearmament.

saihakkō, *n.* 再発行 reissue.

saihō, *n.* 裁縫 sewing.

saihōsō, *n.* 再放送 rerun (broadcasting).

saijin, *n.* 才人 talented person.

saijitsu, *n.* 祭日 holiday.

saijō (no), *adj.* 最上 (の) best.

saikai suru, *vb.* 再開する reopen; resume.

saikai suru, *vb.* 再会する meet again.

saikeikoku-taigū, *n.* 最恵国待遇 most-favored-nation treatment.

saiken, *n.* 債券 bond (finance).

saiken, *n.* 債権 credit; claim.

saikenkoku, *n.* 債権国 creditor nation.

saiken suru, *vb.* 再建する rebuild; revive; re-establish.

saiketsu, *n.* 採決 vote.

saiki, *n.* 才気 talent; ingenuity.

saiki, *n.* 再起 comeback.

saikin, *n.* 細菌 bacterium; germ.

saikin, *adv.* 最近 recently; these days.

saikin (no), *adj.* 最近 (の) 1. recent. 2. latest; up-to-date.

saikō (no), *adj.* 最高 (の) best; highest; supreme.

saikon, *n.* 再婚 remarriage.

saikon suru, *vb.* 再婚する remarry.

saikoro, *n.* さいころ die; dice.

saikō suru, *vb.* 再考する reconsider; reexamine.

saikō suru, *vb.* 再興する revive; re-establish.

saiku, *n.* 細工 1. craft; craftsmanship. 2. device.

saiku suru, *vb.* 細工する 1. devise. 2. manipulate.

saiminjutsu, *n.* 催眠術 hypnotism.

saimu, *n.* 債務 debt.

sain, *n.* サイン (E.) sign; signature; autograph.

sainan, *n.* 災難 misfortune; disaster.

sainō, *n.* 才能 ability; talent.

sainō ga aru, *adj.* 才能がある able; gifted; talented; **sainō ga aru hito** gifted or talented person.

sain (o) suru, *vb.* サイン (を) する sign; autograph.

sainyū, *n.* 歳入 annual revenue.

sairei, *n.* 祭礼 religious festival.

sairyō no, *adj.* 最良の best.

saisan, *n.* 採算 profit; surplus; **saisan ga au** profitable.

saisan, *adv.* 再三 many times; again and again.

saisei, *n.* 再生 1. recycling. 2. rebirth; regeneration.

saiseishi, *n.* 再生紙 recycled paper.

saisei suru, *vb.* 再生する 1. recycle. 2. be reborn; revive.

saisen, *n.* さい銭 monetary offering

(at temples and shrines).

saisenbako, *n.* さい銭箱 receptacle for monetary offerings.

saishi, *n.* 妻子 family; wife and children.

saishin (no), *adj.* 細心 (の) careful; scrupulous; **saishin no chūi o harau** pay scrupulous attention.

saishin (no), *adj.* 最新 (の) latest; newest; **saishin no fasshon** latest fashion.

saisho, *n.* 最初 beginning.

saisho (no), *adj.* 最初 (の) first; earliest; original.

saisho kara, *adv.* 最初から from the outset.

saishō (no), *adj.* 最少 (の) fewest; minimum.

saishokushugi, *n.* 菜食主義 vegetarianism.

saishoku-shugisha, *n.* 菜食主義者 vegetarian.

saisho ni, *adv.* 最初に 1. first; at the outset. 2. first of all.

saishū, *n.* 採集 collection.

saishū (no), *adj.* 最終 (の) last; **saishūdensha** last train of the day.

saishū suru, *vb.* 採集する collect.

saisoku suru, *vb.* 催促する demand; urge.

saitei (no), *adj.* 最低 (の) 1. lowest; minimum. 2. worst.

saiteichingin, *n.* 最低賃金 minimum wage.

saiteki (na), *adj.* 最適 (な) most suitable; optimum.

saiten, *n.* 祭典 festival.

saiten, *n.* 採点 grading; marking.

saiten suru, *vb.* 採点する grade; mark.

saiwai, *n.* 幸い happiness; good luck.

saiwai (na), *adj.* 幸い (な) lucky; happy.

saiwai (ni), *adv.* 幸い (に) fortunately; luckily.

saiyō, *n.* 採用 1. adoption; acceptance. 2. employment.

saiyō suru, *vb.* 採用する 1. adopt; accept. 2. employ.

saizen, *n.* 最善 best effort; **saizen o tsukusu** put forth one's best effort.

saizen (no), *adj.* 最善 (の) best.

saji, *n.* さじ spoon.

saji o nageru, *vb.* さじを投げる give up.

saka, *n.* 坂 slope; hill.

sakaba, *n.* 酒場 bar; pub.

sakaeru, *vb.* 栄える prosper; thrive.

sakai, *n.* 境 1. border; frontier. 2. boundary.

sakan (na), *adj.* 盛ん (な) 1. active; enthusiastic; energetic. 2. popular; thriving.

sakana, *n.* 肴 appetizer.

sakana, *n.* 魚 fish.

sakanaya, *n.* 魚屋 fish store.

sakan ni, *adv.* 盛んに 1. actively; enthusiastically; energetically. 2. often. 3. lavishly.

sakanoboru, *vb.* 遡る 1. date back. 2. go upstream.

sakarau, *vb.* 逆らう oppose; disobey.

sakari, *n.* 盛り prime; height.

sakariba, *n.* 盛り場 entertainment district; restaurant and bar district.

sakasama (no), *adj.* 逆さま (の) reverse; upside-down; topsy-turvy.

sakaya, *n.* 酒屋 1. liquor store. 2. sake maker.

sakazuki, *n.* 杯 sake cup.

sake, *n.* 酒 1. Japanese rice wine. 2. alcoholic drink.

sake, *n.* 鮭 salmon.

sakebi, *n.* 叫び scream; shout.

sakebu, *vb.* 叫ぶ scream; shout.

sakeru, *vb.* 避ける avoid.

sakeru, *vb.* 裂ける split; tear.

saki, *n.* 先 1. tip; point. 2. first. 3. future.

saki (no), *adj.* 先 (の) 1. former (position). 2. future.

sakigake, *n.* 先駆け harbinger.

sakihodo, *adv.* 先程 a short time ago.

saki ni 先に 1. *adv.* ahead; formerly; **saki ni iku** precede. 2. *prep.* before; beyond.

sakiyuki, *n.* 先行き future; outlook.

sakka, *n.* 作家 writer.

sakkaku, *n.* 錯覚 illusion; misunderstanding.

sakki, *adv.* さっき a short time ago.

sakkin, *n.* 殺菌 sterilization; pasteurization.

sakkyokuka, *n.* 作曲家 composer.

sakkyoku suru, *vb.* 作曲する compose (music).

sakoku, *n.* 鎖国 self-imposed isolation of a nation.

sakokushugi, *n.* 鎖国主義 isolationism.

saku, *n.* 策 1. plan; scheme. 2. device.

saku, *n.* 柵 fence.

saku, *vb.* 割く spare; **jikan o saku** make time for.

saku, *vb.* 裂く split; tear.

saku, *vb.* 咲く blossom; flower.

sakuban, *n., adv.* 昨晩 last night.

sakubun, *n.* 作文 composition (writing).

sakugen, *n.* 削減 curtailment; reduction.

sakuhin, *n.* 作品 creation; opus.

sakuin, *n.* 索引 index.

sakui-teki (na), *adv.* 作為的 (な) intentional; deliberate.

sakujitsu, *n.* 昨日 yesterday.

sakujo suru, *vb.* 削除する delete; eliminate.

sakumotsu, *n.* 作物 crops.

sakunen, *n., adv.* 昨年 last year.

sakura, *n.* 桜 cherry tree; cherry blossom.

sakuranbo, *n.* 桜ん坊 cherry.

sakusei suru, *vb.* 作製する draw up; prepare.

sakusen, *n.* 作戦 1. plan; strategy; **sakusen o tateru** devise a plan or strategy. 2. military operation.

sakusha, *n.* 作者 writer; author; creator.

sakushu, *n.* 搾取 exploitation.

sakuya, *n., adv.* 昨夜 last night; yesterday evening.

sakyū, *n.* 砂丘 dune.

-sama 様 Mr.; Mrs.; Ms.(formal).

samasu, *vb.* 冷ます cool.

samasu, *vb.* 覚ます awake.

samatageru, *vb.* 妨げる hinder; obstruct.

samazama (na, no), *adj.* 様々 (な、の) various; **samazama na jinshu** various (human) races.

same, *n.* 鮫 shark.

sameru, *vb.* 覚める 1. wake up. 2. become sober.

sameru, *vb.* 冷める cool off; become cold.

sameru, *vb.* 褪める lose color.

samonai to, *adv.* さもないと otherwise; if not.

samui, *adj.* 寒い chilly; cold.

samuke, *n.* 寒気 chill.

samurai, *n.* 侍 Japanese warrior.

san, *n.* 三 three.

san, *n.* 酸 acid.

-san 様 Mr.; Mrs.; Ms.

sanba(san), *n.* 産婆 (さん) midwife.

sanbi suru, *vb.* 賛美する laud; praise.

sanbun, *n.* 散文 prose.

sanbutsu, *n.* 産物 product.

sanchō, *n.* 山頂 mountaintop.

sandoitchi, *n.* サンドイッチ (E.) sandwich.

sanfujinka, *n.* 産婦人科 obstetrics and gynecology.

sangatsu, *n.* 三月 March.

sango, *n.* さんご coral.

sangoshō, *n.* さんご礁 coral reef.

sangyō, *n.* 産業 industry.

sangyōkakumei, *n.* 産業革命 industrial revolution.

sanji, *n.* 惨事 disaster; tragedy.

sanjiseigen, *n.* 産児制限 birth control.

sanjū, *n.* 三十 thirty.

sanka, *n.* 参加 participation.

sankaku, *n.* 三角 triangle.

sankakukankei, *n.* 三角関係 love triangle.

sanka suru, *vb.* 参加する participate.

sankō, *n.* 参考 reference.

sankō ni suru, *vb.* 参考にする refer to.

sankōsho, *n.* 参考書 reference book.

sanmyaku, *n.* 山脈 mountain range; **arupusu-sanmyaku** the Alps.

sanpatsu, *n.* 散髪 haircut.

sanpo, *n.* 散歩 walk.

sanpo suru, *vb.* 散歩する go for a walk.

sanretsu suru, *vb.* 参列する attend; participate.

sansei, *n.* 酸性 acidity.

sansei, *n.* 賛成 agreement.

sanseiken, *n.* 参政権 right to vote.

sansei suru, *vb.* 賛成する agree.

sansen, *n.* 参戦 participation in or entry into a war.

sanshō suru, *vb.* 参照する refer to; consult (dictionary).

sanso, *n.* 酸素 oxygen.

sansū, *n.* 算数 arithmetic.

santakurōsu, *n.* サンタクロース (E.) Santa Claus.

sanzan (na) 散々 (な) 1. *adj.* devastating; terrible. 2. *adv.* devastatingly; severely.

sao, *n.* 竿 pole; rod.

sappari, *adv.* さっぱり not at all; **Sappari wakaranai.** (I) don't understand it at all.

sappari shita, *adj.* さっぱりした 1. neat. 2. plain. 3. frank.

sappari suru, *vb.* さっぱりする feel refreshed.

sappūkei (na), *adj.* 殺風景 (な) bleak; insipid.

sara, *n.* 皿 dish; plate; saucer; **sara ichimai** one dish, plate, or saucer.

sara'araiki, *n.* 皿洗い機 automatic dishwasher.

sarada, *n.* サラダ (E.) salad.

saraigetsu, *n.* 再来月 the month after next.

sarainen, *n.* 再来年 the year after next.

saraishū, *n.* 再来週 the week after next.

sarakedasu, *vb.* さらけ出す expose; reveal.

sara ni, *adv.* 更に 1. again. 2. further; in addition.

sararī, *n.* サラリー (E.) salary.

sararīman, *n.* サラリーマン (E.) male salaried worker.

sarasu, *vb.* 晒す expose.

sarau, *vb.* さらう 1. kidnap. 2. dredge. 3. review.

saru, *n.* 猿 monkey.

saru, *vb.* 去る depart; leave.

sasa, *n.* 笹 bamboo grass.

sasae, *n.* 支え support; prop.

sasaeru, *vb.* 支える 1. support; bolster. 2. maintain.

sasageru, *vb.* 捧げる dedicate; devote; offer; **inochi o sasageru** offer one's life; devote oneself.

sasai (na), *adj.* 些細 (な) trivial; insignificant.

sasayaka (na), *adj.* ささやか (な) modest; small.

sasayaki, *n.* ささやき whisper.

sasayaku, *vb.* ささやく whisper.

sasen suru, *vb.* 左遷する demote.

-saseru let one do; make one do; have one do; **hanasaseru** let someone speak.

sashi'ageru, *vb.* 差し上げる give; offer (polite).

sashi'atari, *adv.* 差し当たり for the present.

sashidashinin, *n.* 差し出し人 sender (of mail).

sashidasu, *vb.* 差し出す 1. offer; present. 2. send.

sashie, *n.* 挿絵 illustration.

sashihiki, *n.* 差し引き deduction; balance (accounting).

sashikomu, *vb.* 差し込む 1. insert; plug in. 2. come in (sunlight).

sashikorosu, *vb.* 刺し殺す stab to death.

sashimi, *n.* 刺し身 sliced raw fish or seafood.

sashinoberu, *vb.* 差し伸べる offer; extend (a hand).

sashisawari, *n.* 差し障り obstacle; nuisance; **sashisawari ga aru** offensive.

sashisemaru, *vb.* 差し迫る be imminent.

sashizu, *n.* 指図 1. direction; instruction. 2. command; order.

sashō, *n.* 査証 visa.

sasoi, *n.* 誘い 1. invitation. 2.

enticement.

sasou, *vb.* 誘う 1. invite. 2. entice. 3. incite.

sassa to, *adv.* さっさと quickly; swiftly.

sassoku, *adv.* 早速 immediately; at once.

sassuru, *vb.* 察する guess; imagine; sympathize.

sasu, *vb.* 指す point at; point to; indicate.

sasu, *vb.* 差す 1. hold up; **kasa o sasu** hold up an umbrella. 2. rise. 3. fill; insert.

sasu, *vb.* 刺す stab; sting; bite (insect).

sasuga (ni), *adv.* さすが (に) indeed; as expected.

sasurai, *n.* さすらい wandering.

sasurau, *vb.* さすらう wander.

sasuru, *vb.* さする rub; stroke.

satchi suru, *vb.* 察知する perceive.

sate, *interj.* さて Well! Now!

sato, *n.* 里 1. hometown. 2. village.

satō, *n.* 砂糖 sugar.

satogaeri, *n.* 里帰り married woman's visit to her family.

satogo, *n.* 里子 foster child.

sato'oya, *n.* 里親 foster parent.

satori, *n.* 悟り enlightenment.

satoru, *vb.* 悟る realize; fathom; be enlightened.

satosu, *vb.* 諭す warn; advise.

satsu, *n.* 札 paper currency.

-satsu 冊 (counter for books) **ni-satsu** two books.

satsuei, *n.* 撮影 filming; photographing.

satsueikinshi, *n.* 撮影禁止 photography prohibited.

satsugai suru, *vb.* 殺害する kill; murder.

satsujin, *n.* 殺人 murderer.

satsumaimo, *n.* さつま芋 sweet potato.

sattō suru, *vb.* 殺到する rush at; surge.

sawagashii, *adj.* 騒がしい clamorous; noisy.

sawagasu, *vb.* 騒がす disturb; trouble.

sawagi, *n.* 騒ぎ 1. noise. 2. chaos; trouble; tumult.

sawagu, *vb.* 騒ぐ 1. make noise; be clamorous; be riotous. 2. make a fuss.

sawaru, *vb.* 触る touch; feel.

sawaru, *vb.* 障る harm; annoy.

sawayaka (na), *adj.* さわやか (な) refreshing; pleasant.

sayō, *n.* 作用 1. action. 2. effect; **fukusayō** side effect.

sayoku, *n.* 左翼 left wing.

sayōnara, *interj.* さようなら Goodbye.

sayō suru, *vb.* 作用する act on; work on.

sayu, *n.* 白湯 hot water (for drinking).

sayū, *n.* 左右 right and left sides.

sayū suru, *vb.* 左右する influence.

sazukaru, *vb.* 授かる be endowed with; be blessed with.

sazukeru, *vb.* 授ける give; grant.

se, *n.* 背 1. back (body). 2. height (person); **Se ga takai.** (He) is tall.

sebiro, *n.* 背広 man's suit.

sebone, *n.* 背骨 backbone; spine.

sedai, *n.* 世代 generation; **sedai no sa** generation gap.

segamu, *vb.* せがむ nag; implore.

segare, *n.* 倅 my son.

sehyō, *n.* 世評 public opinion.

sei, *n.* 生 life.

sei, *n.* 性 1. gender; sex. 2. sexual act. 3. nature; personality.

sei, *n.* 姓 family name; surname.

sei, *n.* 精 1. spirit; sprite. 2. vigor; energy; **sei o dasu** apply oneself.

sei, *n.* 背 height.

sei, *n.* 聖 1. holiness; sacredness. 2. Saint; **sei Pōru ji'in** St. Paul's Cathedral.

sei, *n.* せい fault; responsibility.

-sei 生 suffix indicating student level; **sannensei** third grader; junior; **daigaku-ichinensei** university freshman.

-sei 製 made in; made of; **nihon-sei** made in Japan.

seiatsu suru, *vb.* 制圧する conquer; control.

seibetsu, *n.* 性別 gender.

seibi, *n.* 整備 adjustment; maintenance; repair.

seibo, *n.* 生母 biological mother.

seibo, *n.* 歳暮 year-end gift.

seibo, *n.* 聖母 Virgin Mary.

seibu, *n.* 西部 western region.

seibugeki, *n.* 西部劇 western (movie).

seibun, *n.* 成分 ingredient; component.

seibutsu, *n.* 生物 living creature.

seibutsuga, *n.* 静物画 still life (painting).

seibutsugaku, *n.* 生物学 biology.

seibyō, *n.* 性病 venereal disease.

seichi, *n.* 生地 birthplace.

seichō, *n.* 成長 growth.

seichō suru, *n.* 成長する grow; become mature.

seidai (na), *adj.* 盛大 (な) 1. grandiose; pompous. 2. thriving; successful; **seidai na pātī** successful party.

sei de, *prep.* せいで because of; owing to; **taifū no sei de** because of the typhoon.

seido, *n.* 制度 system; regime.

seidō, *n.* 青銅 bronze.

sei'ei, *n.* 精鋭 elite.

sei'eki, *n.* 精液 sperm.

sei'en, *n.* 声援 cheering; encouragement; support; **seien o okuru** cheer on.

seifu, *n.* 政府 government.

seifuku, *n.* 制服 uniform.

seifuku, *n.* 征服 conquest.

seifukusha, *n.* 征服者 conqueror.

seifuku suru, *vb.* 征服する conquer.

seigaku, *n.* 声楽 vocal music.

seigan suru, *vb.* 請願する petition.

seigen, *n.* 制限 limit; restriction; **seigensokudo** speed limit.

seigen suru, *vb.* 制限する limit; restrict.

seigi, *n.* 正義 justice.

seihantai (no), *adj.* 正反対 (の) diametrically opposite.

seiheki, *n.* 性癖 proclivity; propensity.

seihen, *n.* 政変 political upheaval; political change.

seihin, *n.* 製品 product.

seihirei, *n.* 正比例 direct proportion; **... ni seihirei shite** in direct proportion to.

seihō, *n.* 製法 manufacturing method; recipe.

seihōkei, *n.* 正方形 square (geometry).

seihoku, *n.* 西北 northwest.

sei'i, *n.* 誠意 sincerity.

sei'iku, *n.* 生育 growth.

sei'in, *n.* 成員 member.

sei'i no aru, *adj.* 誠意のある sincere.

sei'ippai, *adv.* 精一杯 with all one's might.

seijaku, *n.* 静寂 silence; stillness.

seiji, *n.* 青磁 celadon.

seiji, *n.* 政治 1. politics. 2. administration; government.

seijigaku, *n.* 政治学 political science.

seijihan, *n.* 政治犯 political prisoner.

seijika, *n.* 政治家 politician; statesman.

seijin, *n.* 聖人 saint.

seijin, *n.* 成人 adult; grownup.

seijineiga, *n.* 成人映画 adult film.

seijitsu (na), *adj.* 誠実 (な) sincere; faithful.

seijō (na), *adj.* 正常 (な) normal.

seijōki, *n.* 星条旗 Stars and Stripes (flag).

seijuku, *n.* 成熟 maturity; ripeness.

seijuku shita, *adj.* 成熟した mature; ripe.

seijuku suru, *vb.* 成熟する mature; ripen.

seijun (na), *adj.* 清純 (な) pure; innocent.

seika, *n.* 正価 net price.

seika, *n.* 成果 product; result (of one's efforts).

seika, *n.* 聖歌 hymn.

seikagaku, *n.* 生化学 biochemistry.

seikai, *n.* 正解 correct answer.

seikai, *n.* 政界 political arena.

seikaku, *n.* 性格 personality; disposition.

seikaku (na), *adj.* 正確 (な) accurate; exact.

seikaku ni, *adv.* 正確に accurately; exactly.

seikatai, *n.* 聖歌隊 church choir.

seikatsu, *n.* 生活 life; livelihood.

seikatsuhi, *n.* 生活費 cost of living.

seikatsu-suijun, *n.* 生活水準 living standard.

seikatsu suru, *vb.* 生活する live; make a living.

seikei, *n.* 生計 livelihood; living.

seikei(-shujutsu), *n.* 整形(手術) plastic surgery; orthopedic surgery.

seiken, *n.* 政権 1. political power; reign. 2. government.

seiketsu (na), *adj.* 清潔 (な) clean.

seiki, *n.* 世紀 century; **jūnana-seiki** seventeenth century.

seiki, *n.* 生気 vigor; liveliness.

seiki, *n.* 性器 sex organ.

seiki (no), *adj.* 正規 (の) 1. regular. 2. formal.

seikō, *n.* 成功 success.

seikō, *n.* 性向 disposition; proclivity.

seikō, *n.* 性交 sexual intercourse.

seikō (na), *adj.* 精巧 (な) complex; elaborate.

seikōgyō, *n.* 製鋼業 steel industry.

seikō suru, *vb.* 成功する succeed.

seiku, *n.* 成句 idiomatic expression.

seikyō, *n.* 盛況 popularity; success.

seikyōiku, *n.* 性教育 sex education.

seikyo suru, *vb.* 逝去する die.

seikyū, *n.* 請求 claim; demand; request.

seikyū (na), *adj.* 性急 (な) impatient; impetuous.

seikyūsho, *n.* 請求書 bill; invoice; written application.

seikyū suru, *vb.* 請求する demand; request.

seimei, *n.* 姓名 full name.

seimei, *n.* 声明 public announcement or statement.

seimei, *n.* 生命 life.

seimeihoken, *n.* 生命保険 life insurance; **seimeihoken o kakeru** insure someone's life.

seimitsu (na), *adj.* 精密 (な) 1. detailed; precise. 2. thorough.

seinan, *n.* 西南 southwest.

seinaru, *adj.* 聖なる holy; sacred.

seinen, *n.* 成年 adulthood; **seinen ni tassuru** come of age.

seinen, *n.* 青年 young adult.

seinengappi, *n.* 生年月日 date of birth.

seinō, *n.* 性能 performance; efficiency.

seinō ga yoi/ii, *adj.* 性能が良い efficient.

seiō, *n.* 西欧 Western Europe; the West.

seirai, *adv.* 生来 by nature; inherently.

seireki, *n.* 西暦 Anno Domini; A.D. (Christian calendar).

seiren suru, *vb.* 精錬する refine (metals).

seiretsu suru, *vb.* 正列する form a line.

seiri, *n.* 生理 1. physiology. 2. menstruation.

seiri, *n.* 整理 arrangement; consolidation.

seiri suru, *vb.* 整理する 1. arrange; consolidate; put in order. 2. retrench.

seiritsu suru, *vb.* 成立する be formed; be created; be established.

seiryaku, *n.* 政略 strategy; political maneuver.

seiryō-inryōsui, *n.* 清涼飲料水 soft drink.

seiryoku, *n.* 勢力 power; influence.

seiryoku, *n.* 精力 energy; vigor; vitality.

seiryoku-teki (na), *adj.* 精力的 (な) energetic; vigorous.

seisabetsu, *n.* 性差別 sexual discrimination.

seisai, *n.* 正妻 legal wife.

seisai, *n.* 制裁 punishment; sanction.

seisai o kuwaeru, *vb.* 制裁を加える punish; apply sanctions against.

seisaku, *n.* 政策 policy.

seisaku, *n.* 制作 manufacture; production.

seisakusha, *n.* 制作者 manufacturer; producer.

seisaku suru, *vb.* 制作する manufacture; make; produce.

seisan, *n.* 生産 production.

seisan, *n.* 清算 adjustment (financial).

seisan suru, *vb.* 清算する settle (an account); clear a debt.

seisei dōdō to, *adv.* 正々堂々と aboveboard; openly; fairly and squarely.

sei-sei suru, *vb.* せいせいする feel relieved; feel refreshed.

seiseki, *n.* 成績 1. achievement; result; showing. 2. school grades.

seiseki-shōmeisho, *n.* 成績証明書 transcript.

seisenshokuhin, *n.* 生鮮食品 perishables.

seishi, *n.* 生死 life and death.

seishiki (na, no), *adj.* 正式 (な、の) 1. formal. 2. official.

seishin, *n.* 精神 mind; soul; spirit.

seishinanteizai, *n.* 精神安定剤 tranquilizer.

seishinbunseki, *n.* 精神分析 psychoanalysis.

seishinbyō, *n.* 精神病 mental illness.

seishinbyōin, *n.* 精神病院 mental hospital.

seishinka, *n.* 精神科 psychiatry.

seishin-teki (na), *adj.* 精神的 (な) spiritual; mental.

seishi suru, *vb.* 制止する control; halt; stop.

seishi suru, *vb.* 静止する stand still.

seishitsu, *n.* 性質 nature; character.

seisho, *n.* 聖書 Bible.

seishoku, *n.* 生殖 reproduction; procreation.

seishokuki, *n.* 生殖器 genitals.

seishokusha, *n.* 聖職者 priest; clergyman.

seishōnen, *n.* 青少年 juveniles; young people.

seishun, *n.* 青春 adolescence; youth.

seishun-jidai/-ki, *n.* 青春時代／〜期 adolescence; youth.

seisō, *n.* 清掃 cleaning.

seisō, *n.* 正装 full dress.

seisoku, *n.* 棲息 habitation.

seisokuchi, *n.* 棲息地 habitat; habitation.

seisō suru, *vb.* 盛装する dress up.

seitai, *n.* 声帯 vocal cords.

seitaigaku, *n.* 生態学 ecology.

seitan, *n.* 生誕 birth.

seitei suru, *vb.* 制定する enact; institute.

sei-teki (na), *adj.* 性的 (な) sexual; **sei-teki na iyagarase** sexual harassment.

seiten, *n.* 晴天 fair weather.

seitetsu, *n.* 製鉄 iron or steel production.

seito, *n.* 生徒 pupil; student.

seitō, *n.* 政党 political party.

seitō (na, no), *adj.* 正当 (な、の) 1. orthodox; legitimate. 2. just.

seiton suru, *vb.* 整頓する organize; tidy up.

sei'ukei, *n.* 晴雨計 barometer.

seiyaku, *n.* 制約 restriction.

seiyaku, *n.* 誓約 pledge; vow.

seiyakusho, *n.* 誓約書 written pledge.

seiyō, *n.* 西洋 the West.

seiyō (no), *adj.* 西洋 (の) occidental; Western.

seiyōjin, *n.* 西洋人 Westerner.

seiyō suru, *vb.* 静養する rest;

recuperate.

seiyu, *n.* 精油 refined oil.

seiza, *n.* 星座 constellation.

seiza, *n.* 正座 traditional Japanese way of sitting on tatami (e.g., for tea ceremony).

seizei, *adv.* せいぜい at best; at most.

seizen to shita, *adj.* 整然とした orderly; systematic.

seizō, *n.* 製造 manufacture; production.

seizōmoto, *n.* 製造元 manufacturer; producer.

seizon, *n.* 生存 1. existence. 2. survival.

seizoroi suru, *vb.* 勢揃いする get together.

seizō suru, *vb.* 製造する manufacture; produce.

seizu, *n.* 製図 mechanical drawing; drafting.

seizui, *n.* 精髄 essence; gist; quintessence.

sekai, *n.* 世界 world; society; **sekai-ryokō** trip around the world.

sekasu, *vb.* 急かす hurry; urge on.

seken, *n.* 世間 1. society. 2. other people. 3. way of the world.

sekenbanashi, *n.* 世間話 gossip; small talk.

seki, *n.* 籍 1. family register. 2. membership.

seki, *n.* 席 1. seat; **seki ni tsuku** take a seat. 2. occasion.

seki, *n.* 咳 cough.

sekidō, *n.* 赤道 equator.

sekidome, *n.* 咳止め cough medicine.

sekigaisen, *n.* 赤外線 infrared rays.

sekihanga, *n.* 石版画 lithograph.

sekijūji, *n.* 赤十字 Red Cross.

sekimen suru, *vb.* 赤面する blush.

sekinin, *n.* 責任 responsibility; **sekinin o toru** take responsibility.

sekinin ga aru, *adj.* 責任がある responsible; in charge.

sekininsha, *n.* 責任者 person in charge.

seki o suru, *vb.* 咳をする cough.

sekitan, *n.* 石炭 coal.

sekitsui, *n.* 脊椎 spine.

sekiyu, *n.* 石油 petroleum; oil; kerosene.

sekiyu-sutōbu, *n.* 石油ストーブ kerosene heater.

sekizui, *n.* 脊髄 spinal cord.

sekkachi (na), *adj.* せっかち（な） headlong; impatient; impetuous.

sekkaku, *adv.* せっかく 1. at great pains. 2. kindly.

sekkei, *n.* 設計 design; plan.

sekkeisha, *n.* 設計者 designer.

sekken, *n.* せっけん soap.

sekki, *n.* 石器 1. stoneware. 2. stone tool.

sekkijidai, *n.* 石器時代 Stone Age.

sekkin suru, *vb.* 接近する approach.

sekkō, *n.* 石膏 plaster.

sekkyō, *n.* 説教 admonishment; preaching; sermon.

sekkyoku-teki (na), *adj.* 積極的（な） 1. aggressive. 2. positive.

sekkyō suru, *vb.* 説教する admonish; preach.

semai, *adj.* 狭い narrow; small.

semaru, *vb.* 迫る 1. draw near; come close. 2. urge.

semento, *n.* セメント (E.) cement.

semeru, *vb.* 責める 1. accuse; reproach. 2. torment.

semeru, *vb.* 攻める attack; invade.

semete, *adv.* せめて at least.

semi, *n.* 蟬 cicada.

sen, *n.* 線 1. line; **sen o hiku** draw

a line. 2. tranportation line or track.

sen, *n.* 栓 bottle cap; cork; stopper.

sen, *n.* 千 thousand.

senaka, *n.* 背中 back (body).

senbatsu, *n.* 選抜 selection.

senbei, *n.* せんべい rice cracker.

senbetsu, *n.* せんべつ farewell present.

senbō, *n.* 羨望 envy.

senchaku jun ni, *adv.* 先着順に on a first-come, first-served basis.

senchō, *n.* 船長 captain (ship).

senden, *n.* 宣伝 advertisement; propaganda; publicity.

sendo, *n.* 鮮度 freshness.

sendō, *n.* 扇動 agitation; instigation.

sendōsha, *n.* 扇動者 agitator; instigator.

sengen, *n.* 宣言 proclamation; declaration.

sengetsu, *n., adv.* 先月 last month.

sengo, *n.* 戦後 postwar period.

sengyō, *n.* 専業 profession; full-time job.

sen'i, *n.* 繊維 fiber.

sen'ihin, *n.* 繊維品 textile; cloth.

sen'in, *n.* 船員 sailor; seaman; crew.

senjitsu *n., adv.* 先日 yesterday; the other day.

senjō, *n.* 戦場 battlefield.

senjō-teki (na), *adj.* 扇情的 (な) suggestive; sensational.

senjūmin(zoku), *n.* 先住民(族) aborigine.

senjutsu, *n.* 戦術 tactics; strategy.

senken, *n.* 先見 foresight.

senkō, *n.* 専攻 major; specialty;
    Senkō wa nan desu ka. What is your major?

senkō, *n.* 選考 selection.

senkō, *n.* 線香 incense.

senkoku, *n.* 宣告 sentence; judgment.

senkō suru, *vb.* 専攻する major; specialize; **bijinesu o senkō suru** major in business.

senkō suru, *vb.* 先行する precede.

senkusha, *n.* 先駆者 originator; pioneer.

senkyaku, *n.* 先客 preceding visitor.

senkyo, *n.* 選挙 election.

senkyō, *n.* 宣教 missionary work.

senkyoken, *n.* 選挙権 right to vote.

senkyōshi, *n.* 宣教師 missionary.

senkyo suru, *vb.* 占拠する occupy; take over (a place).

senkyo-undō, *n.* 選挙運動 election campaign.

senmei (na), *n.* 鮮明 (な) bright; clear; vivid.

senmenjo, *n.* 洗面所 restroom; bathroom.

senmon, *n.* 専門 specialty.

senmonka, *n.* 専門家 specialist; expert.

senmonten, *n.* 専門店 specialty store.

sen'nen suru, *vb.* 専念する concentrate; devote oneself to; focus on.

sen'nin (no), *adj.* 専任 (の) full-time.

sen'nō, *n.* 洗脳 brainwashing.

sen'nō suru, *vb.* 洗脳する brainwash.

sen'nuki, *n.* 栓抜き corkscrew; bottle opener.

sen'nyūkan, *n.* 先入感 1. prejudice; preconception. 2. bias.

senobi suru, *vb.* 背伸びする stretch; stand on tiptoe.

senpai, *n.* 先輩 senior; elder; predecessor.

senpaku, *n.* 船舶 ship.

senpan, *n.* 戦犯 war criminal.

senpi, *n.* 戦費 war expenditure.

senpō, *n.* 先方 other person or party.

senpu, *n.* 先夫 ex-husband; former husband.

senpū, *n.* 旋風 1. whirlwind. 2. excitement; sensation; **senpū o okosu** cause a sensation.

senpūki, *n.* 扇風機 electric fan.

senran, *n.* 戦乱 war; strife.

senrei, *n.* 洗礼 baptism.

senrei, *n.* 先例 precedent.

senren, *n.* 洗練 refinement.

senren sareta, *adj.* 洗練された refined.

senrihin, *n.* 戦利品 war trophy or booty.

senritsu, *n.* 旋律 melody.

senritsu, *n.* 戦慄 shiver; shudder.

senro, *n.* 線路 track; rail (train).

senryaku, *n.* 戦略 strategy; tactics.

senryō, *n.* 染料 dye.

senryōgun, *n.* 占領軍 occupation army.

senryoku, *n.* 戦力 military power.

senryō suru, *n.* 占領する occupy; seize.

senryū, *n.* 川柳 satiric poem.

sensai, *n.* 先妻 ex-wife; former wife.

sensai (na), *adj.* 繊細 (な) delicate; fragile; sensitive.

sensaku suru, *vb.* 詮索する nose about; inquire.

sensakuzuki (na), *adj.* 詮索好き (な) nosy; inquisitive.

sensei, *n.* 先生 1. teacher; master. 2. doctor (M.D.). 3. title used when speaking of or to members of certain professions (lawyers, politicians).

sensei, *n.* 宣誓 oath; vow.

sensei, *n.* 専制 autocracy; tyranny.

senseisho, *n.* 宣誓書 affidavit.

sensen, *n.* 戦線 battle line or front.

sensen, *n.* 宣戦 declaration of war.

sensha, *n.* 戦車 tank (military vehicle).

senshi, *n.* 戦士 warrior.

senshi, *n.* 戦死 death in action.

senshinkoku, *n.* 先進国 advanced nation.

senshin suru, *vb.* 専心する concentrate on; devote oneself to.

senshitsu, *n.* 船室 cabin; stateroom.

senshoku, *n.* 染色 dyeing.

senshu, *n.* 選手 athlete; athletic team member.

senshū, *n., adv.* 先週 last week.

senshuken, *n.* 選手権 championship.

senshūraku, *n.* 千秋楽 last day (tournament or show).

senshutsu suru, *vb.* 選出する elect.

sensō, *n.* 戦争 battle; war.

sensu, *n.* 扇子 folding fan.

sensui, *n.* 潜水 diving.

sensuikan, *n.* 潜水艦 submarine.

sentaku, *n.* 洗濯 washing (laundry).

sentaku, *n.* 選択 choice; selection.

sentakuki, *n.* 洗濯機 washing machine.

sentaku suru, *vb.* 選択する choose; select.

sentakuya, *n.* 洗濯屋 laundry; dry cleaner.

sentan, *n.* 先端 1. tip; end. 2. vanguard.

sentan o iku, *vb.* 先端を行く be a front runner.

senten-teki (na), *adj.* 先天的 (な) congenital; inherent.

sento, *n.* セント (E.) cent.

sentō, *n.* 先頭 lead; first place;
  sentō ni tatsu be in the lead.
sentō, *n.* 銭湯 public bath.
sentō, *n.* 戦闘 battle.
sen'yaku, *n.* 先約 previous
  engagement; **sen'yaku ga aru**
  have a previous engagement.
sen'yō (no), *adj.* 専用 (の)
  exclusive; private.
senzai, *n.* 洗剤 detergent.
senzai-teki (na), *adj.* 潜在的 (な)
  latent; potential.
senzen, *n.* 戦前 prewar period.
senzo, *n.* 先祖 ancestor.
senzoku, *n.* 専属 exclusive
  contract.
seou, *vb.* 背負う 1. carry on one's
  back. 2. shoulder (burden).
seppuku, *n.* 切腹 Japanese ritual
  suicide; harakiri.
seri, *n.* 競り auction; **seri ni
  kakeru** put up for auction.
serifu, *n.* 台詞 lines (stage play).
seron, *n.* 世論 public opinion.
serori, *n.* セロリ (E.) celery.
sēru, *n.* セール (E.) sale.
sērusuman, *n.* セールスマン (E.)
  salesperson.
seshū (no), *adj.* 世襲 (の)
  inherited; hereditary.
seshūzaisan, *n.* 世襲財産
  inheritance.
sessei, *n.* 節制 temperance; self-
  control.
sessen, *n.* 接戦 close contest.
sesse to, *adv.* せっせと diligently;
  industriously.
sesshi, *n.* 摂氏 Celsius; **sesshi
  sanjūnido** thirty-two degrees
  Celsius.
sesshoku suru, *vb.* 接触する 1.
  touch. 2. contact.
sesshoku suru, *vb.* 節食する eat
  sparingly.

sesshō suru, *vb.* 折衝する
  negotiate.
sesshu, *n.* 接種 inoculation;
  vaccination.
sesshu suru, *vb.* 摂取する 1.
  ingest; absorb. 2. assimilate.
sessuru, *vb.* 接する 1. border on;
  adjoin. 2. encounter.
sētā, *n.* セーター (E.) sweater.
setai, *n.* 世帯 family; household;
  setai o motsu/kamaeru
  establish a household.
setake, *n.* 背丈 height.
setchakuzai, *n.* 接着剤 glue.
setchi suru, *vb.* 設置する install;
  set up.
setogiwa, *n.* 瀬戸際 1. last
  moment; **setogiwa de** at the last
  moment. 2. brink; **setogiwa ni
  tatsu** be on the brink of.
setomono, *n.* 瀬戸物 china;
  pottery.
setsu, *n.* 説 theory; opinion.
setsu, *n.* 節 1. clause (grammar);
  paragraph. 2. occasion; season.
setsubi, *n.* 設備 equipment;
  facility.
setsubiji, *n.* 接尾辞 suffix
  (grammar).
setsudan suru, *vb.* 切断する cut;
  sever.
setsudo, *n.* 節度 1. decency;
  propriety. 2. moderation.
setsuei, *n.* 設営 setting up;
  construction.
setsugen, *n.* 節減 reduction;
  cutback.
setsugō, *n.* 接合 fusing; linking.
setsujitsu (na), *adj.* 切実 (な)
  keen; acute; sincere.
setsumei, *n.* 説明 explanation;
  illustration.
setsumei suru, *vb.* 説明する
  explain; illustrate.

setsuritsu suru, *vb.* 設立する establish; found.

setsuyaku, *n.* 節約 economy; thrift.

setsuyaku suru, *vb.* 節約する economize; save.

setsuzoku, *n.* 接続 connection.

setsuzokushi, *n.* 接続詞 conjunction (grammar).

setsuzoku suru, *vb.* 接続する join; connect.

settai suru, *vb.* 接待する receive (guest); welcome; entertain.

settei suru, *vb.* 設定する set up.

settō, *n.* 窃盗 theft.

settōgo, *n.* 接頭語 prefix (grammar).

settoku, *n.* 説得 persuasion.

settoku suru, *vb.* 説得する persuade.

sewa, *n.* 世話 1. care; **sewa o suru** take care of (person). 2. inconvenience; trouble; **sewa o kakeru** cause inconvenience or trouble.

sezoku-teki (na), *adj.* 世俗的 (な) mundane; common.

shaberu, *vb.* しゃべる talk; chat; chatter.

shaburu, *vb.* しゃぶる suck.

shachō, *n.* 社長 company president.

shadō, *n.* 車道 road; drive.

shagamu, *vb.* しゃがむ squat.

shagaregoe, *n.* しゃがれ声 husky or hoarse voice.

shageki, *n.* 射撃 firing; shooting.

sha'in, *n.* 社員 employee.

shajitsushugi, *n.* 写実主義 realism.

shajitsu-teki (na), *adj.* 写実的 (な) realistic; graphic.

shaka, *n.* 釈迦 Buddha.

shakai, *n.* 社会 society.

shakaifukushi, *n.* 社会福祉 social welfare.

shakaigaku, *n.* 社会学 sociology.

shakaishugi, *n.* 社会主義 socialism.

shakkin, *n.* 借金 debt; **shakkin o suru** incur a debt.

shakkuri, *n.* しゃっくり hiccup.

shako, *n.* 車庫 garage.

shakō, *n.* 社交 socializing.

shakō-teki (na), *adj.* 社交的 (な) social; sociable.

shaku (na, no), *adj.* 癪 (な、の) annoying; offensive.

shakudo, *n.* 尺度 measure; criterion.

shakumei, *n.* 釈明 apology; vindication.

shakuya, *n.* 借家 rented house.

shakuyōgo, *n.* 借用語 loanword.

shakuyō suru, *vb.* 借用する borrow.

shamen, *n.* 斜面 slope.

shamen, *n.* 赦免 pardon.

shamisen, *n.* 三味線 Japanese string instrument.

shamoji, *n.* しゃもじ rice ladle.

shanikusai, *n.* 謝肉祭 carnival (season).

shanpū, *n.* シャンプー (E.) shampoo.

share, *n.* しゃれ joke.

sharei, *n.* 謝礼 1. reward. 2. fee.

shareta, *adj.* しゃれた stylish.

sharin, *n.* 車輪 wheel.

sharyō, *n.* 車輌 vehicle.

shasatsu, *n.* 射殺 shooting to death.

shasei, *n.* 写生 sketching.

shasei, *n.* 射精 ejaculation.

shasen, *n.* 斜線 oblique line.

shasetsu, *n.* 社説 editorial.

shashi, *n.* 奢侈 luxury.

shashihin, *n.* 奢侈品 luxury item.

shashin, *n.* 写真 photograph;

shashin o toru take a photograph.

shashō, *n.* 車掌 bus or train conductor.

shatai, *n.* 車体 body (car).

shatsu, *n.* シャツ (E.) shirt.

shazai suru, *vb.* 謝罪する apologize.

shi, *n.* 四 four.

shi, *n.* 死 death.

shi, *n.* 詩 poem.

shi, *n.* 師 teacher; master.

shi, *n.* 市 city.

-shi 氏 Mr.; Mrs.; Ms.

shiage, *n.* 仕上げ completion.

shiageru, *vb.* 仕上げる complete; finish.

shiai, *n.* 試合 competition; game; match.

shiatsu, *n.* 指圧 Japanese massage using finger pressure.

shiawase (na), *adj.* 幸せ (な) happy.

shibafu, *n.* 芝生 lawn; turf.

shibai, *n.* 芝居 drama; play.

shibaraku, *adv.* 暫く 1. for a while. 2. for a long time.

shibaru, *vb.* 縛る tie; bind.

shiba-shiba, *adv.* しばしば frequently.

shibireru, *vb.* 痺れる become paralyzed; be numbed.

shibō, *n.* 死亡 death.

shibō, *n.* 脂肪 fat.

shibō, *n.* 志望 hope; wish.

shibomu, *vb.* しぼむ wither away; fade.

shibori, *n.* 絞り 1. tie-dyed fabric. 2. shutter (camera).

shiboru, *vb.* 絞る 1. wring. 2. narrow down.

shibu, *n.* 支部 subdivision; branch (office).

shibui, *adj.* 渋い 1. astringent. 2.

chic. 3. sullen.

shiburu, *vb.* 渋る hesitate; be reluctant.

shibu-shibu, *adv.* 渋々 reluctantly.

shibutoi, *adj.* しぶとい persistent; stubborn.

shibutsu, *n.* 私物 personal belongings.

shichaku suru, *vb.* 試着する try on clothes.

shichi, *n.* 七 seven.

shichigatsu, *n.* 七月 July.

shichijū, *n.* 七十 seventy.

shichimenchō, *n.* 七面鳥 turkey.

shichō, *n.* 市長 mayor.

shichō, *n.* 市庁 city office.

shichōsha, *n.* 視聴者 TV viewer; audience.

shichū, *n.* 支柱 prop; support.

shidai ni, *adv.* 次第に gradually; by and by.

shidarezakura, *n.* しだれ桜 weeping cherry tree.

shidashi, *n.* 仕出し catering.

shidō, *n.* 指導 guidance; direction; advice.

shidōsha, *n.* 指導者 leader; adviser.

shiekidōshi, *n.* 使役動詞 causative verb.

shien, *n.* 支援 support.

shifuku, *n.* 私服 civilian clothes.

shigai, *n.* 死骸 corpse.

shigai, *n.* 市街 city; city street.

shigai, *n.* 市外 suburbs.

shigaidenwa, *n.* 市外電話 long-distance call.

shigaisen, *n.* 紫外線 ultraviolet ray.

shigamitsuku, *vb.* しがみ付く cling to.

shigansha, *n.* 志願者 1. applicant. 2. volunteer.

shigan suru, *vb.* 志願する 1. apply

for. 2. volunteer.

shigatsu, *n.* 四月 April.

shigeki, *n.* 刺激 stimulation.

shigeki-teki (na), *adj.* 刺激的 (な) stimulating; inspiring.

shigemi, *n.* 繁み bush.

shigen, *n.* 資源 resources.

shigeru, *vb.* 繁る grow luxuriant.

shigo, *n.* 私語 private conversation in a public setting (classroom, etc.)

shigoku, *adv.* 至極 quite; very.

shigoto, *n.* 仕事 job; work.

shigoto o suru, *vb.* 仕事をする work.

shigusa, *n.* しぐさ gesture; mannerism.

shigyōshiki, *n.* 始業式 opening ceremony.

shihai, *n.* 支配 control; rule.

shihai-nin, *n.* 支配人 manager.

shihai suru, *vb.* 支配する control; rule.

shiharai, *n.* 支払い payment.

shiharau, *vb.* 支払う pay.

shihatsu, *n.* 始発 first train or bus.

shihei, *n.* 紙幣 paper money; bank note.

shihō, *n.* 四方 all directions.

shihō, *n.* 司法 administration of justice.

shihon, *n.* 資本 capital.

shihonkin, *n.* 資本金 capital.

shihonshugi, *n.* 資本主義 capitalism.

shihonshugisha, *n.* 資本主義者 capitalist.

shi'in (shion), *n.* 子音 consonant.

shi'ire, *n.* 仕入れ purchasing; laying in (stock).

shi'ire kakaku, *n.* 仕入れ価格 purchase price.

shi'ireru, *vb.* 仕入れる purchase; stock.

shi'iru, *vb.* 強いる force.

shi'itageru, *vb.* 虐げる persecute; oppress.

shi'itake, *n.* しいたけ Japanese mushroom.

shiji, *n.* 私事 personal affairs.

shiji, *n.* 指示 instruction; direction.

shiji, *n.* 支持 support.

shijin, *n.* 詩人 poet.

shiji suru, *vb.* 支持する support.

shiji suru, *vb.* 指示する direct; indicate.

shijitsu, *n.* 史実 historical fact.

shijō, *n.* 市場 market.

shijō (de), *adv.* 史上 (で) historically.

shijū, *n.* 四十 forty.

shijū, *adv.* 始終 always; constantly.

shijūsō, *n.* 四重奏 quartet.

shika, *n.* 市価 market price.

shika, *n.* 歯科 dentistry; dental clinic.

shika, *n.* 鹿 deer.

-shika しか only; **mizu-shika nomanai** drink only water.

shikaeshi, *n.* 仕返し revenge; **shikaeshi o suru** take revenge.

shikai, *n.* 視界 field of vision.

shikai, *n.* 歯科医 dentist.

shikai(sha), *n.* 司会(者) 1. chairperson. 2. master of ceremonies.

shikaku, *n.* 視覚 eyesight.

shikaku, *n.* 資格 credentials; qualifications.

shikaku, *n.* 四角 square; rectangle.

shikakui, *adj.* 四角い square; rectangular.

shikameru, *vb.* しかめる **(kao o) shikameru** frown.

shikamo *adv.* しかも on top of that; in addition; besides.

shikaneru, *vb.* しかねる 1. hesitate. 2. be unable to do.

shikarareru, *vb.* 叱られる get

scolded.

shikaru, *vb.* 叱る scold.

shikashi, *conj.* しかし however; but.

shikata, *n.* 仕方 way; method; **unten no shikata** the way to drive.

shikata ga nai, *vb.* 仕方がない 1. cannot be helped. 2. cannot help (doing).

shike, *n.* 時化 stormy seas.

shikei, *n.* 死刑 death penalty.

shiken, *n.* 試験 examination; test; **shiken o ukeru** take an examination.

shiki, *n.* 式 1. ceremony; rite. 2. style; **nihonshiki** Japanese style.

shiki, *n.* 士気 morale.

shiki, *n.* 四季 the four seasons.

shiki, *n.* 指揮 conducting; direction; command.

shikibetsu, *n.* 識別 differentiation; identification.

shikibuton, *n.* 敷布団 bottom futon; futon mattress.

shikichi, *n.* 敷地 location; site.

shikifu, *n.* 敷布 bedsheet.

shikijō, *n.* 式場 hall where ceremonies are held.

shikikin, *n.* 敷金 security deposit (rent).

shikin, *n.* 資金 capital; funds.

shikinseki, *n.* 試金石 touchstone.

shikiri, *n.* 仕切り divider; partition.

shikiri ni, *adv.* しきりに 1. often; frequently. 2. eagerly.

shikiru, *vb.* 仕切る divide; partition.

shikisai, *n.* 色彩 coloration.

shikisha, *n.* 指揮者 conductor; commander.

shikitari, *n.* しきたり convention; tradition; custom.

shikiten, *n.* 式典 ceremony.

shikkaku, *n.* 失格 elimination; disqualification.

shikkari, *adv.* しっかり firmly; tightly; strongly.

shikkari shita, *adj.* しっかりした 1. firm; stable. 2. reliable.

shikkari suru, *vb.* しっかりする 1. become strong. 2. get a hold on oneself.

shikke, *n.* 湿気 dampness; humidity.

shikkei (na), *adj.* 失敬 (な) impudent; rude.

shikki, *n.* 漆器 lacquerware.

shikkō suru, *vb.* 執行する carry out; execute.

shikkui, *n.* 漆喰 mortar; plaster.

shikkyaku suru, *vb.* 失却する fall from power.

shikō, *n.* 嗜好 taste; liking.

shikō, *n.* 思考 consideration; thought.

shikomu, *vb.* 仕込む 1. train. 2. stock (merchandise).

shikō suru, *vb.* 思考する think; ponder.

shikō suru, *vb.* 施行する enact; enforce; carry out.

shiku, *n.* 詩句 verse.

shiku, *vb.* 敷く 1. lay out; spread. 2. enact.

shiku hakku suru, *vb.* 四苦八苦する suffer.

shikujiri, *n.* しくじり blunder; mistake.

shikumi, *n.* 仕組み mechanism; device.

shikumu, *vb.* 仕組む plot; plan.

shikyū, *n.* 子宮 uterus; womb.

shikyū, *adv.* 至急 immediately; urgently.

shikyū suru, *vb.* 支給する supply; provide.

shima, *n.* 島 island.

shima, *n.* 縞 stripe.

shimai, *n.* 姉妹 sisters.

shimai, *n.* 仕舞い end; conclusion.

shimaru, *vb.* 締まる tighten.

shimaru, *vb.* 閉まる close; shut.

shimatsu, *n.* 始末 1. circumstances. 2. disposal.

shimatsu suru, *vb.* 始末する 1. settle; dispose of. 2. clear.

shimatta, *interj.* しまった Damn!

shimau, *vb.* 仕舞う 1. put away. 2. close.

-shimau, *vb.* しまう finish (doing something); **tabeteshimau** finish eating (something).

shimedasu, *vb.* 締め出す shut out.

shimei, *n.* 氏名 full name.

shimei, *n.* 使命 mission; assignment.

shimei suru, *vb.* 指名する appoint; nominate.

shimei-tehainin, *n.* 指名手配人 wanted criminal.

shimekiri, *n.* 締め切り closing; deadline.

shimekiribi, *n.* 締め切り日 closing date; deadline.

shimekiru, *vb.* 締め切る close.

shimekorosu, *vb.* 締め殺す kill by strangulation.

shimeppoi, *adj.* 湿っぽい 1. damp; humid. 2. depressing.

shimeru, *vb.* 閉める close; shut.

shimeru, *vb.* 締める fasten (seat belt); tie (necktie); strangle; tighten.

shimeru, *vb.* 占める occupy.

shimesu, *vb.* 示す show; point out.

shimetsu, *n.* 死滅 extinction.

shimetsukeru, *vb.* 締め付ける tighten.

shimi, *n.* 染み stain.

shimijimi (to), *adv.* しみじみ (と) thoroughly; keenly.

shimin, *n.* 市民 citizen.

shimiru, *vb.* 染みる penetrate.

shimizu, *n.* 清水 clear water.

shimo, *n.* 霜 frost.

shimon, *n.* 指紋 fingerprint.

shin, *n.* 芯 core; heart; center.

shin (no), *adj.* 真 (の) true; genuine; real.

shin- 新 new; **shinsekai** New World.

shina, *n.* 品 1. goods. 2. quality.

shinabiru, *vb.* しなびる wither.

shinagire, *adj.* 品切れ out of stock.

shinai, *n.* 市内 city limits.

shinai, *n.* 竹刀 bamboo sword.

shinamono, *n.* 品物 1. merchandise. 2. article.

shinan (no), *adj.* 至難 (の) extremely difficult.

shinaosu, *vb.* しなおす do over again; try again.

shinasadame, *n.* 品定め assessment; estimation.

shinayaka (na), *adj.* しなやか (な) pliant; supple.

shinbishugi, *n.* 審美主義 aestheticism.

shinbishugisha, *n.* 審美主義者 aesthete.

shinbō, *n.* 辛抱 endurance; patience.

shinbokukai, *n.* 親睦会 social gathering.

shinbōzuyoi, *adj.* 辛抱強い patient.

shinbun, *n.* 新聞 newspaper.

shinbunkiji, *n.* 新聞記事 newspaper article.

shinbunsha, *n.* 新聞社 newspaper publisher.

shinbun'uriba, *n.* 新聞売り場 newsstand.

shinchiku (no), *adj.* 新築 (の) newly built.

shinchintaisha, *n.* 新陳代謝 metabolism.

shinchō, *n.* 身長 a person's height.

shinchō (na), *adj.* 慎重 (な) cautious; prudent.

shinchū, *n.* 真ちゅう brass.

shinchū, *n.* 心中 innermost thoughts.

shindai, *n.* 寝台 bed.

shindaisha, *n.* 寝台車 sleeping car.

shindan, *n.* 診断 diagnosis.

shindo, *n.* 進度 progress.

shindo, *n.* 震度 magnitude of an earthquake (Japanese scale).

shindo, *n.* 深度 depth (water).

shindō, *n.* 震動 quaking; oscillation; trembling.

shinfonī, *n.* シンフォニー (E.) symphony.

shingai, *n.* 侵害 violation; infringement.

shingai (na), *adj.* 心外 (な) 1. unexpected. 2. regrettable.

shingaku, *n.* 神学 theology.

shingaku, *n.* 進学 entrance into a school of a higher level (e.g., university from high school).

shingao, *n.* 新顔 newcomer; new face.

shingetsu, *n.* 新月 new moon.

shingi, *n.* 真偽 truth.

shingi, *n.* 審議 discussion; scrutiny.

shingin suru, *vb.* 呻吟する groan.

shingo, *n.* 新語 newly coined word.

shingō, *n.* 信号 traffic light; signal.

shingu, *n.* 寝具 futon; bedding.

shinguru, *n.* シングル (E.) single.

shin'i, *n.* 真意 true feeling.

shinin, *n.* 死人 dead person.

shin'in, *n.* 真因 true cause.

shin'iri, *n.* 新入り newcomer.

shinise, *n.* 老舗 established shop.

shinja, *n.* 信者 religious believer; member of a religious sect.

shinjin, *n.* 信心 religious belief.

shinjin, *n.* 新人 newcomer.

shinjinbukai, *adj.* 信心深い devout.

shinjinikui, *adj.* 信じにくい doubtful.

shinjirarenai, *adj.* 信じられない unbelievable.

shinjitsu, *n.* 真実 fact; truth.

shinjō, *n.* 心情 feeling.

shinju, *n.* 真珠 pearl.

shinjū, *n.* 心中 double suicide.

shinka, *n.* 真価 true value.

shinka, *n.* 進化 progress.

shinkan, *n.* 新館 annex.

shinkansen, *n.* 新幹線 bullet train.

shinkaron, *n.* 進化論 theory of evolution.

shinkei, *n.* 神経 nerve (anatomy).

shinkeikabin (na), *adj.* 神経過敏 (な) oversensitive.

shinkeishitsu (na), *adj.* 神経質 (な) nervous; high-strung.

shinken, *n.* 親権 parental authority.

shinken (na), *adj.* 真剣 (な) earnest; sincere.

shinkinkan, *n.* 親近感 feeling of intimacy.

shinkiroku, *n.* 新記録 new record (in competition).

shinkō, *n.* 信仰 belief; religion.

shinkō, *n.* 進行 progress.

shinkō, *n.* 親交 friendship.

shinkoku (na), *adj.* 深刻 (な) serious; grave.

shinkoku suru, *vb.* 申告する 1. report. 2. submit.

shinkokyū, *n.* 深呼吸 deep breathing.

shinkon, *n.* 新婚 newlywed.

shinkonryokō, *n.* 新婚旅行 honeymoon.

shinkū, *n.* 真空 vacuum.

shinkyō, *n.* 心境 mind; feeling.

shinkyō, *n.* 新教 Protestantism.

shinkyū suru, *vb.* 進級する be promoted; advance.

shinmai, *n.* 新米 1. new rice. 2. novice.

shinme, *n.* 新芽 bud; sprout.

shinmi ni, *adv.* 親身に kindly.

shinmin, *n.* 臣民 royal subject.

shinmitsu (na), *adj.* 親密 (な) intimate; close.

shin'nen, *n.* 新年 new year; **Shin'nen akemashite omedetō gozaimasu.** Happy New Year!

shin'nen, *n.* 信念 conviction; faith.

shin'ninjō, *n.* 信任状 credentials.

shin'nin suru, *vb.* 信任する trust.

shin'nyū, *n.* 侵入 invasion.

shin'nyū-sei, *n.* 新入生 new student; freshman.

shinobu, *vb.* 忍ぶ endure.

shinogu, *vb.* 凌ぐ surpass.

shinpai, *n.* 心配 anxiety; worry.

shinpai suru, *vb.* 心配する be anxious; worry.

shinpan, *n.* 審判 refereeing; judgment.

shinpi, *n.* 神秘 mystery.

shinpishugi, *n.* 神秘主義 mysticism.

shinpo, *n.* 進歩 progress.

shinpo-teki (na), *adj.* 進歩的 (な) progressive; advanced.

shinpu, *n.* 新婦 bride.

shinpu, *n.* 神父 Christian priest.

shinpyōsei, *n.* 信ぴょう性 credibility.

shinrai, *n.* 信頼 trust; confidence.

shinrai suru, *vb.* 信頼する trust; rely on.

shinri, *n.* 真理 truth.

shinri, *n.* 審理 judicial inquiry.

shinri, *n.* 心理 state of mind.

shinrigaku, *n.* 心理学 psychology.

shinrigakusha, *n.* 心理学者 psychologist.

shinrin, *n.* 森林 forest; woods.

shinro, *n.* 進路 course; route.

shinrō, *n.* 新郎 bridegroom.

shinrui, *n.* 親類 relative.

shinryaku, *n.* 侵略 aggression; invasion.

shinryō, *n.* 診療 medical treatment.

shinryōjo, *n.* 診療所 clinic.

shinsa, *n.* 審査 screening; examination.

shinsa'in, *n.* 審査員 judge; examiner.

shinsatsu, *n.* 診察 medical examination.

shinsei (na), *adj.* 神聖 (な) holy; sacred.

shinsei suru, *vb.* 申請する apply.

shinseki, *n.* 親戚 relative.

shinsen (na), *adj.* 新鮮 (な) fresh.

shinsetsu (na), *adj.* 親切 (な) kind.

shinshi, *n.* 紳士 gentleman.

shinshiki, *n.* 新式 new model; new style; new technique.

shinshitsu, *n.* 寝室 bedroom.

shinshuku-sei (no), *adj.* 伸縮性 (の) elastic.

shinshun, *n.* 新春 new year.

shinshutsu suru, *vb.* 進出する enter; branch out into; progress.

shinsoko, *n.* 心底 bottom of one's heart; **shinsoko kara** from the bottom of one's heart.

shinsui suru, *vb.* 浸水する be inundated; be flooded.

shintai, *n.* 身体 (human) body.

shintaku, *n.* 信託 trust (finance).

shintakuginkō, *n.* 信託銀行 trust bank.

shinten, *adj.* 親展 confidential; personal (on an envelope, etc.).

shinto, *n.* 信徒 member of a religious organization.

shintō, *n.* 神道 Japanese religion based on animism and ancestor worship.

shintsū, *n.* 心痛 mental anguish.

shinu, *vb.* 死ぬ die.

shinwa, *n.* 神話 mythology.

shin'ya, *n.* 深夜 dead of the night.

shin'yakuseisho, *n.* 新約聖書 New Testament.

shin'yō, *n.* 信用 trust; faith.

shin'yōkumiai, *n.* 信用組合 credit union.

shin'yū, *n.* 親友 close friend.

shinzen, *n.* 親善 friendship.

shinzō, *n.* 心臓 heart.

shinzōhossa, *n.* 心臓発作 heart attack.

shinzui, *n.* 真髄 essence; gist.

shio, *n.* 塩 salt.

shio, *n.* 潮 1. tide. 2. sea water.

shiokarai, *adj.* 塩辛い salty.

shiomizu, *n.* 塩水 salt water.

shioreru, *vb.* しおれる 1. wilt; wither; droop. 2. feel depressed.

shiori, *n.* しおり 1. bookmark. 2. guidebook.

shippai, *n.* 失敗 mistake; failure.

shippai suru, *vb.* 失敗する make a mistake; fail.

shippitsu suru, *vb.* 執筆する write (for a publication).

shippo, *n.* しっぽ tail.

shippō(yaki), *n.* 七宝(焼き) cloisonné.

shippu, *n.* 湿布 compress.

shippū, *n.* 疾風 gale.

shiraberu, *vb.* 調べる 1. investigate; check. 2. consult; look up.

shiraga, *n.* 白髪 gray hair; white hair.

shirase, *n.* 知らせ notification; news.

shiraseru, *vb.* 知らせる notify; inform.

shiren, *n.* 試練 trial; ordeal.

shiri, *n.* 尻 1. buttocks. 2. bottom.

shiri, *n.* 私利 self-interest.

shiriau, *vb.* 知り合う meet; get acquainted.

shirigomi suru, *vb.* 尻込みする hesitate; shy away from.

shirimetsuretsu (na), *adj.* 支離滅裂 (な) inconsistent; incoherent.

shiritsu (no), *adj.* 市立 (の) municipal.

shiritsu (no), *adj.* 私立 (の) private.

shirizokeru, *vb.* 退ける 1. chase away; repel. 2. reject.

shirizoku, *vb.* 退く retreat.

shiro, *n.* 城 castle.

shiroi, *adj.* 白い white.

shiromi, *n.* 白身 white meat or fish.

shiromono, *n.* 代物 article; item.

shirōto, *n.* 素人 amateur.

shiru, *n.* 汁 1. soup. 2. juice.

shiru, *vb.* 知る know.

shirushi, *n.* 印 sign; symbol; indication.

shirusu, *vb.* 記す record; write.

shiryo, *n.* 思慮 discretion.

shiryō, *n.* 資料 data; material.

shiryō, *n.* 史料 historical records.

shiryoku, *n.* 視力 eyesight.

shiryoku, *n.* 資力 funds; financial resources.

shisa, *n.* 示唆 implication; suggestion.

shisai, *n.* 司祭 Christian priest.

shisai, *n.* 仔細 details.

shisaku, *n.* 思索 contemplation; reflection.

shisan, *n.* 資産 assets.

shisanka, *n.* 資産家 wealthy

person.

shisatsu, *n.* 視察 inspection.

shisei, *n.* 姿勢 posture; stance.

shisei, *n.* 施政 administration.

shiseiji, *n.* 私生児 illegitimate child.

shiseikatsu, *n.* 私生活 private life.

shiseki, *n.* 史跡 historic site.

shisen, *n.* 視線 gaze.

shisetsu, *n.* 施設 1. equipment. 2. facility; institution.

shisetsu, *n.* 使節 delegate.

shisha, *n.* 死者 deceased.

shisha, *n.* 使者 emissary; envoy.

shisha, *n.* 支社 branch office.

shisha, *n.* 試写 preview.

shishi, *n.* 獅子 lion.

shishin, *n.* 指針 guideline.

shisho, *n.* 司書 librarian.

shishō, *n.* 師匠 master; teacher.

shishō, *n.* 支障 hindrance; **shishō o kitasu** hinder.

shishobako, *n.* 私書箱 post office box.

shishōsha, *n.* 死傷者 casualty.

shishū, *n.* 刺しゅう embroidery.

shishunki, *n.* 思春期 adolescence; puberty.

shishutsu, *n.* 支出 expenditure.

shiso, *n.* 始祖 founder.

shisō, *n.* 思想 thought; idea.

shisokonau, *vb.* しそこなう fail; make a mistake.

shison, *n.* 子孫 descendant.

shisshin, *n.* 失神 fainting.

shisshin suru, *vb.* 失神する faint.

shisso (na), *adj.* 質素 (な) 1. plain; simple. 2. frugal.

shisū, *n.* 指数 index; **keizaishisū** economic index.

shisugiru, *vb.* し過ぎる overdo.

shita, *n.* 舌 tongue.

shita, *n.* 下 bottom.

shitagatte, *adv.* 従って therefore.

shitagau, *vb.* 従う obey; follow.

shitagi, *n.* 下着 underwear.

shitai, *n.* 死体 dead body.

shitaku, *n.* 私宅 private home.

shitaku, *n.* 支度 preparation.

shitamachi, *n.* 下町 downtown.

shitamawaru, *vb.* 下回る be less than.

shitami, *n.* 下見 preliminary inspection.

shita ni, *adv.* 下に below; beneath; under.

shitashii, *adj.* 親しい intimate; friendly.

shitashimi, *n.* 親しみ intimacy; friendliness.

shitashimu, *vb.* 親しむ become intimate with; make friends with.

shitashirabe, *vb.* 下調べ preliminary research.

shitataka (na), *adj.* したたか (な) tough; severe; heavy.

shitataka ni, *adv.* したたかに severely; heavily.

shitataru, *vb.* 滴る drip.

shitateru, *vb.* 仕立てる 1. tailor; sew. 2. prepare; set up. 3. train.

shitau, *vb.* 慕う 1. adore. 2. yearn for.

shitauke, *n.* 下受け subcontract.

shitchō, *n.* 失調 imbalance.

shitei, *n.* 子弟 children.

shitei suru, *vb.* 指定する appoint; designate.

shi-teki (na), *adj.* 詩的 (な) poetic.

shiteki suru, *vb.* 指摘する point out.

shiten, *n.* 支店 branch (office, store).

shiten, *n.* 視点 viewpoint; **josei no shiten kara** from a woman's viewpoint.

shitetsu, *n.* 私鉄 private railroad.

shīto, *n.* シート (E.) seat.

shīto, *n.* シート (E.) tarpaulin.

shīto-beruto, *n.* シートベルト (E.) seat belt.

shitogeru, *vb.* し遂げる accomplish; complete.

shitsu, *n.* 質 quality.

shītsu, *n.* シーツ (E.) bedsheet.

-shitsu 室 room; **kaigishitsu** conference room.

shitsubō, *n.* 失望 disappointment.

shitsubō suru, *vb.* 失望する be disappointed.

shitsudo, *n.* 湿度 humidity.

shitsugai, *n.* 室外 outdoors.

shitsugen, *n.* 失言 slip of the tongue.

shitsugiōtō, *n.* 質疑応答 question-and-answer session.

shitsugyō, *n.* 失業 unemployment.

shitsugyōchū (no), *adj.* 失業中 (の) unemployed.

shitsugyōhoken, *n.* 失業保険 unemployment insurance.

shitsui, *n.* 失意 disappointment.

shitsuke, *n.* 躾 1. discipline; training. 2. manners.

shitsukeru, *vb.* 躾ける 1. train. 2. teach manners.

shitsu(k)koi, *adj.* しつ(つ)こい persistent; obstinate.

shitsumon, *n.* 質問 question; **shitsumon ga aru** have a question.

shitsumon suru, *vb.* 質問する ask a question.

shitsunai, *n.* 室内 indoors.

shitsurei (na), *adj.* 失礼 (な) rude; discourteous.

shitsurei (shimasu), *vb.* 失礼 (します) 1. Excuse me. 2. I must be going.

shitsurei suru, *vb.* 失礼する excuse oneself.

shitsuren, *n.* 失恋 unrequited love;

lost love.

shitto, *n.* 嫉妬 jealousy.

shittobukai, *adj.* 嫉妬深い jealous.

shiuchi, *n.* 仕打ち treatment.

shiwa, *n.* しわ wrinkle.

shiwadarake (no), *adj.* しわだらけ (の) wrinkled.

shiwasu, *n.* 師走 December.

shiwaza, *n.* 仕業 deeds; acts.

shiya, *n.* 視野 scope; vision; view.

shiyakusho, *n.* 市役所 city office; city hall.

shiyō, *n.* 仕様 means; method; way.

shiyō, *n.* 使用 use; employment.

shiyō (no), *adj.* 私用 (の) private.

shiyō suru, *vb.* 使用する use.

shiyū (no), *adj.* 私有 (の) privately owned.

shizen, *n.* 自然 nature.

shizen (na, no), *adj.* 自然 (な、の) natural; spontaneous; **shizen-shokuhin** natural foods.

shizenkagaku, *n.* 自然科学 natural science.

shizenshugi, *n.* 自然主義 naturalism.

shizuka (na), *adj.* 静か (な) 1. quiet; silent. 2. calm.

shizumaru, *vb.* 鎮まる 1. subside. 2. be suppressed.

shizumaru, *vb.* 静まる become calm; become quiet.

shizumeru, *vb.* 静める calm; quiet.

shizumeru, *vb.* 鎮める alleviate; suppress.

shizumeru, *vb.* 沈める sink; submerge.

shizumu, *vb.* 沈む 1. set (sun, moon). 2. sink. 3. feel depressed.

sho, *n.* 書 1. calligraphy. 2. book.

shō, *n.* 賞 prize.

shō, *n.* 性 disposition; nature; personality; **shō ni au** be suited to one's nature.

shō, *n.* 章 chapter.

shō, *n.* 省 ministry; **hōmushō** Ministry of Justice.

shōbai, *n.* 商売 business; commerce.

shobatsu suru, *vb.* 処罰する penalize.

shōben, *n.* 小便 urine.

shōbō, *n.* 消防 firefighting.

shōbōshi, *n.* 消防士 firefighter.

shōbōsho, *n.* 消防署 firehouse.

shōbu, *n.* 勝負 game; fight; match.

shobun, *n.* 処分 1. disposal. 2. expulsion; punishment.

shobun suru, *vb.* 処分する 1. get rid of; clear away. 2. expel; punish.

shochi, *n.* 処置 measures; treatment.

shōchi, *n.* 承知 1. acceptance; consent. 2. understanding.

shochi suru, *vb.* 処置する deal with; treat.

shōchi suru, *vb.* 承知する 1. accept; consent. 2. understand.

shochō, *n.* 所長 director.

shōchō, *n.* 小腸 small intestine.

shōchō, *n.* 象徴 symbol.

shōchōshugi, *n.* 象徴主義 symbolism.

shōchō-teki (na), *adj.* 象徴的 (な) symbolic.

shōdaku, *n.* 承諾 compliance; approval; consent.

shōdaku suru, *vb.* 承諾する comply; approve; consent.

shodana, *n.* 書棚 bookshelf.

shodō, *n.* 書道 calligraphy (using a brush).

shōdō, *n.* 衝動 impulse.

shōdoku, *n.* 消毒 sterilization.

shōdō-teki (na), *adj.* 衝動的 (な) impulsive.

shoen, *n.* 初演 premiere; **sekai-shoen** world premiere.

shō-ene, *n.* 省エネ energy conservation.

shōfuda, *n.* 正札 price tag.

shōga, *n.* 生姜 ginger.

shōgai, *n.* 障害 obstacle.

shōgai, *n.* 傷害 injury.

shōgai, *n.* 生涯 life; career.

shōgakkō, *n.* 小学校 elementary school.

shōgakukin, *n.* 奨学金 fellowship; scholarship; stipend.

shōgakusei, *n.* 小学生 elementary school student.

shōgatsu, *n.* 正月 New Year; New Year's Day.

shōgeki, *n.* 衝撃 impact; shock.

shōgen, *n.* 証言 testimony.

shōgen suru, *vb.* 証言する testify; give evidence.

shogeru, *vb.* しょげる be dejected; be depressed.

shōgi, *n.* 将棋 Japanese chess.

shōgo, *n.* 正午 noon.

shōgō, *n.* 称号 title.

shōgun, *n.* 将軍 general; head of samurai government.

shōgyō, *n.* 商業 business; commerce.

shōgyōeigo, *n.* 商業英語 business English.

shōgyōshugi, *n.* 商業主義 commercialism.

shōhi, *n.* 消費 consumption.

shōhisha, *n.* 消費者 consumer.

shōhisha kakaku, *n.* 消費者価格 consumer price.

shōhizei, *n.* 消費税 sales tax.

shōhin, *n.* 商品 goods; merchandise.

shōhin, *n.* 賞品 prize.

shoho, *n.* 初歩 1. introductory level. 2. basics.

shoho (no), *adj.* 初歩 (の) elementary.

shohōsen, *n.* 処方せん prescription (medical).

shōhyō, *n.* 商標 trademark.

shoikomu, *vb.* しよい込む 1. take on a burden. 2. be burdened with.

shōji, *n.* 障子 Japanese paper and wood door or screen.

shojihin, *n.* 所持品 personal possessions.

shōjiki (na), *adj.* 正直 (な) honest.

shōjin, *n.* 精進 1. dedication; devotion. 2. vegetarianism.

shōjinryōri, *n.* 精進料理 vegetarian meal (originally for monks).

shōjin suru, *vb.* 精進する devote oneself to.

shōjiru, *vb.* 生じる 1. arise; occur. 2. bring about.

shoji suru, *vb.* 所持する carry; possess.

shojo, *n.* 処女 virgin.

shōjo, *n.* 少女 girl.

shōjō, *n.* 症状 1. condition of a patient. 2. symptom.

shōjō, *n.* 賞状 certificate of merit.

shōjū, *n.* 小銃 rifle.

shojun, *n.* 初旬 first ten days of a month.

shoka, *n.* 初夏 early summer.

shōka, *n.* 消火 the extinguishing of a fire.

shōka, *n.* 消化 digestion (food and information).

shōkafuryō, *n.* 消化不良 indigestion.

shōkaki, *n.* 消火器 fire extinguisher.

shōkai, *n.* 商会 trading company.

shōkai, *n.* 照会 reference; inquiry.

shōkai, *n.* 紹介 introduction.

shōkaijō, *n.* 紹介状 letter of introduction.

shōkai suru, *vb.* 照会する refer; inquire.

shōkai suru, *vb.* 紹介する introduce.

shokan, *n.* 書簡 letter.

shōkan suru, *vb.* 召喚する summon.

shōka suru, *vb.* 消化する digest (food and information).

shokei, *n.* 処刑 punishment; execution (of a criminal).

shōkeimoji, *n.* 象形文字 hieroglyph.

shoken, *n.* 所見 opinion; view.

shōken, *n.* 証券 stocks; securities.

shōkengaisha, *n.* 証券会社 securities firm.

shoki, *n.* 書記 secretary; clerk.

shoki, *n.* 初期 beginning; initial stage.

shōki, *n.* 正気 sanity.

shōkin, *n.* 賞金 cash prize.

shokkaku, *n.* 触覚 sense of touch.

shokken, *n.* 食券 meal coupon.

shokki, *n.* 食器 tableware (dishes; cups; flatware; chopsticks).

shokkidana, *n.* 食器棚 cupboard.

shokku, *n.* ショック (E.) shock.

shoko, *n.* 書庫 library stacks.

shōko, *n.* 証拠 evidence; proof; testimony.

shōkō, *n.* 症候 symptom (medical).

shōkō, *n.* 将校 commissioned officer.

shōkōgyō, *n.* 商工業 commerce and industry.

shōkō kaigisho, *n.* 商工会議所 chamber of commerce.

shokon, *n.* 初婚 first marriage.

shoku, *n.* 食 appetite; food.

shoku, *n.* 職 employment; job;
   shoku o sagasu look for a job.

shokuba, *n.* 職場 workplace.

shokubutsu, *n.* 植物 plant; vegetation.

shokubutsuen, *n.* 植物園 botanical garden.

shokuchūdoku, *n.* 食中毒 food poisoning.

shokudō, *n.* 食堂 dining room; restaurant.

shokudō, *n.* 食道 esophagus.

shokuen, *n.* 食塩 table salt.

shokugyō, *n.* 職業 occupation; profession.

shokugyō-anteisho, *n.* 職業安定所 public office for employment referral.

shokuhi, *n.* 食費 (food) expenses.

shokuhin, *n.* 食品 food products.

shokuin, *n.* 職員 staff; personnel.

shokuji, *n.* 植字 typesetting.

shokuji, *n.* 食事 meal.

shokuji o suru, *vb.* 食事をする dine.

shokujiryōhō, *n.* 食餌療法 diet; regimen.

shokuminchi, *n.* 植民地 colony.

shokuminchishugi, *n.* 植民地主義 colonialism.

shokumotsu, *n.* 食物 food.

shokumu, *n.* 職務 duty; office.

shokun, *pron.* 諸君 everyone (informal).

shokunin, *n.* 職人 craftsperson; artisan.

shokupan, *n.* 食パン bread.

shokureki, *n.* 職歴 career history.

shokurin, *n.* 植林 tree planting.

shokuryō(hin), *n.* 食料(品) food.

shokuryōhinten, *n.* 食料品店 grocery store.

shokutaku, *n.* 食卓 dining table.

shokuyō (no), *adj.* 食用 (の) edible.

shokuyoku, *n.* 食欲 appetite;

shokuyoku ga aru have an appetite.

shokuzen, *n.* 食膳 dining table.

shōkyoku-teki (na), *adj.* 消極的 (な) 1. passive. 2. negative.

shokyū, *n.* 初級 beginners' level.

shōkyū, *n.* 昇給 pay raise.

shomei, *n.* 署名 signature.

shomei, *n.* 書名 book title.

shōmei, *n.* 照明 lighting.

shōmei, *n.* 証明 proof; identification.

shōmeisho, *n.* 証明書 certificate; credential.

shomei undō, *n.* 署名運動 signature-collecting campaign.

shōmen, *n.* 正面 front.

shōmetsu, *n.* 消滅 disappearance; extinction.

shomin, *n.* 庶民 people; the masses.

shōmō, *n.* 消耗 1. consumption; exhaustion. 2. fatigue.

shōmon, *n.* 証文 instrument (bond, deed).

shōmō suru, *vb.* 消耗する 1. consume. 2. use up; deplete.

shomotsu, *n.* 書物 book.

shomu, *n.* 庶務 general affairs.

shonbori suru, *vb.* しょんぼりする be disheartened; be dejected.

shōnen, *n.* 少年 boy.

shōni, *n.* 小児 infant; child.

shonichi, *n.* 初日 opening day; first day.

shōnika, *n.* 小児科 pediatrics.

shōnika'i, *n.* 小児科医 pediatrician.

shoninkyū, *n.* 初任給 starting salary.

shōnimahi, *n.* 小児麻痺 polio.

shōnin, *n.* 商人 shopkeeper; merchant.

shōnin, *n.* 承認 approval; recognition; sanction.

shōnin, *n.* 証人 witness.

shōnindai, *n.* 証人台 witness stand.

shōnin suru, *vb.* 承認する approve; recognize; sanction.

shō'ō, *n.* 照応 correspondence; agreement.

shōrai, *n.* 将来 future; **shōrai ga aru** have a (bright) future.

shōrei, *n.* 奨励 encouragement; promotion.

shori, *n.* 処理 1. handling; treatment. 2. elimination.

shōri, *n.* 勝利 victory.

shōrisha, *n.* 勝利者 victor; winner.

shori suru, *vb.* 処理する 1. handle; treat. 2. get rid of; dispose of.

shorui, *n.* 書類 document.

shōryaku, *n.* 省略 abbreviation; omission.

shōryaku suru, *vb.* 省略する abbreviate; omit.

shōryō, *n.* 少量 small amount.

shōryō (no), *adj.* 少量 (の) a bit of; a little.

shosai, *n.* 書斎 1. library (home). 2. study.

shōsai, *n.* 小細 detail.

shosan, *n.* 所産 1. product. 2. outcome.

shōsan, *n.* 賞讃、称讃 exaltation; praise.

shōsan, *n.* 硝酸 nitric acid.

shōsan, *n.* 勝算 possibility of winning.

shōsei, *n.* 招請 invitation.

shoseki, *n.* 書籍 book.

shosen, *adv.* 所詮 after all.

shōsetsu, *n.* 小説 novel.

shōsetsuka, *n.* 小説家 novelist.

shōsha, *n.* 商社 trading company.

shoshi, *n.* 庶子 legitimate child.

shoshiki, *n.* 書式 form; format (written).

shoshin, *n.* 所信 opinion; belief.

shoshin, *n.* 初診 first visit to a doctor.

shoshin, *n.* 傷心 heartbreak; grief.

shoshin, *n.* 昇進 promotion.

shōshin (na), *adj.* 小心 (な) cowardly; timid.

shoshinsha, *n.* 初心者 beginner; novice.

shōshinshōmei (no), *adj.* 正真正銘 (の) genuine; authentic.

shōshitsu suru, *vb.* 焼失する be destroyed by fire.

shōsho, *n.* 証書 1. written instrument. 2. certificate.

shōshō 少々 1. *adv.* a bit; a little; **shōshō takai** a bit expensive. 2. *n.* a moment; **Shōshō omachi kudasai.** Please wait a moment.

shōshū suru, *vb.* 召集する 1. convene; summon. 2. draft (military).

shōsoku, *n.* 消息 1. news. 2. letter. 3. whereabouts.

shōso suru, *vb.* 勝訴する win a court case.

shōsū, *n.* 少数 small number; minority.

shōsū, *n.* 小数 decimal.

shōsui, *n.* 憔悴 exhaustion.

shōsū no, *adj.* 小数の a small number of; a few.

shō suru, *vb.* 称する 1. name. 2. be called.

shotai, *n.* 所帯 household; family.

shōtai, *n.* 正体 1. true nature or self; **shōtai o arawasu** reveal one's true nature. 2. consciousness.

shōtai, *n.* 招待 invitation.

shōtaijō, *n.* 招待状 invitation (letter, card); **shōtaijō o dasu** send invitations.

shotaimen, *n.* 初対面 first meeting.

shotai o motsu, *vb.* 所帯を持つ get married and establish a household.

shōtchū, *adv.* しょっちゅう always; constantly.

shoten, *n.* 書店 1. bookstore. 2. publishing company.

shōten, *n.* 焦点 focus; central issue; **(ni) shōten o awaseru** focus (on).

shōten, *n.* 商店 store; shop.

shotō, *n.* 諸島 archipelago; islands.

shotō, *n.* 初等 elementary level.

shotoku, *n.* 所得 income.

shōtotsu, *n.* 衝突 1. crash; collision. 2. conflict.

shōtotsu suru, *vb.* 衝突する 1. crash; collide. 2. conflict.

shoya, *n.* 初夜 wedding night.

shōyo, *n.* 賞与 reward; bonus.

shōyō de, *adv.* 商用で on business.

shōyu, *n.* しょう油 soy sauce.

shoyū, *n.* 所有 possession.

shoyūbutsu, *n.* 所有物 belongings; property.

shoyū suru, *vb.* 所有する possess.

shozai, *n.* 所在 location; whereabouts.

shōzōga, *n.* 肖像画 portrait.

shozoku suru, *vb.* 所属する belong to.

shōzō suru, *vb.* 所蔵する own.

shu, *n.* 主 1. the Lord (God). 2. master; lord.

shu, *n.* 種 species.

shū, *n.* 週 week; **konshū** this week.

shū, *n.* 州 province; state; **Yuta-shū** state of Utah.

shubi yoku, *adv.* 首尾良く successfully.

shūbun, *n.* 秋分 autumnal equinox.

shūbun, *n.* 醜聞 scandal.

shūchaku, *n.* 執着 attachment; persistence.

shūchakueki, *n.* 終着駅 terminal (railroad).

shūchi, *n.* 羞恥 shame.

shūchi (no), *adj.* 周知 (の) well-known.

shūchishin, *n.* 羞恥心 sense of shame.

shuchō, *n.* 主張 assertion; claim.

shuchō suru, *vb.* 主張する assert; claim.

shūchū, *n.* 集中 concentration.

shūchū suru, *vb.* 集中する concentrate.

shudai, *n.* 主題 theme; topic.

shudan, *n.* 手段 means; way.

shūdan, *n.* 集団 group.

shūdensha, *n.* 終電車 last train.

shudōken, *n.* 主動権 1. domination. 2. leadership.

shudōsha, *n.* 主動者 leader.

shuei, *n.* 守衛 doorman; guard.

shūeki, *n.* 収益 revenue; profit.

shuen suru, *vb.* 主演する play a title role.

shufu, *n.* 主婦 housewife.

shufu, *n.* 首府 capital city.

shūfuku, *n.* 修復 restoration.

shūgakuryokō, *n.* 修学旅行 school trip.

shugei, *n.* 手芸 handicraft.

shūgeki, *n.* 襲撃 attack.

shūgeki suru, *vb.* 襲撃する attack; assault.

shūgen, *n.* 祝言 wedding.

shugi, *n.* 主義 belief; ism; principle.

shūgi, *n.* 祝儀 1. celebration; wedding. 2. gratuity.

shūgi'in, *n.* 衆議院 House of Representatives (Japan).

shugo, *n.* 主語 subject (grammar).

shugo suru, *vb.* 守護する protect.

shūgō suru, *vb.* 集合する gather;

congregate.

shugyō, *n.* 修業 1. training. 2. apprenticeship.

shūgyō, *n.* 就業 employment.

shūgyō, *n.* 終業 closing.

shūha, *n.* 宗派 religious sect.

shūhai, *n.* 集配 mail collection and delivery.

shūhasū, *n.* 周波数 frequency.

shūhen, *n.* 周辺 1. neighborhood; vicinity. 2. circumference.

shuhin, *n.* 主賓 guest of honor.

shuhō, *n.* 手法 technique; style.

shui, *n.* 首位 first place.

shuin, *n.* 主因 main cause.

shūji, *n.* 習字 calligraphy.

shuji'i, *n.* 主治医 attending physician.

shujin, *n.* 主人 1. husband. 2. owner. 3. master; mistress.

shūjin, *n.* 囚人 prisoner.

shujinkō, *n.* 主人公 protagonist; hero; heroine.

shūjitsu, *n.* 週日 weekday.

shuju (no), *adj.* 種々 (の) various.

shujū, *n.* 主従 master and servant.

shujūkankei, *n.* 主従関係 master-servant relationship.

shujutsu, *n.* 手術 surgery.

shujutsu suru, *vb.* 手術する perform surgery.

shūkai, *n.* 集会 meeting.

shukaku, *n.* 主格 nominative case.

shūkaku, *n.* 収穫 harvest; crop.

shukan, *n.* 主観 subjectivity.

shūkan, *n.* 習慣 custom; habit.

-shūkan 週間 week(s); **nishūkan** two weeks.

shūkanshi, *n.* 週刊紙 weekly magazine.

shukan-teki (na), *adj.* 主観的 (な) subjective.

shuken, *n.* 主権 sovereignty.

shūketsu, *n.* 終結 ending.

shūketsu suru, *vb.* 終結する end.

shuki, *n.* 手記 memorandum; memoirs.

shūki, *n.* 臭気 odor.

shūki, *n.* 周期 cycle.

shūkin, *n.* 集金 bill collection.

shūki-teki (na), *adj.* 周期的 (な) cyclical; periodic.

shukka suru, *vb.* 出荷する ship; send.

shukketsu, *n.* 出血 bleeding.

shukketsu, *n.* 出欠 roll call; **shukketsu o toru** call the roll.

shukkin suru, *vb.* 出勤する go to work.

shukkoku, *n.* 出国 departure from a country.

shukōgyōhin, *n.* 手工業品 handicraft.

shukudai, *n.* 宿題 homework; assignment.

shukugakai, *n.* 祝賀会 celebration.

shukugan, *n.* 宿願 wish.

shukuhai, *n.* 祝杯 toast; celebration; **shukuhai o ageru** drink a toast.

shukuhakuryō, *n.* 宿泊料 hotel bill.

shukuhaku suru, *vb.* 宿泊する stay (hotel).

shukuji, *n.* 祝辞 congratulatory speech.

shukujitsu, *n.* 祝日 holiday.

shukujo, *n.* 淑女 lady.

shukumei, *n.* 宿命 destiny; fate.

shukusha, *n.* 宿舎 lodging.

shukushō, *n.* 縮小 reduction; cutback.

shukuteki, *n.* 宿敵 archenemy; nemesis.

shukuzu, *n.* 縮図 microcosm.

shūkyō, *n.* 宗教 religion.

shūkyū, *n.* 週休 regular days off.

shūkyū, *n.* 週給 weekly wage.

shūmai, *n.* シューマイ steamed Chinese dumpling.

shūmatsu, *n.* 週末 weekend.

shumi, *n.* 趣味 1. hobby; diversion. 2. taste.

shumoku, *n.* 種目 category.

shun (no), *adj.* 旬 (の) seasonal.

shunbun, *n.* 春分 vernal equinox.

shūnen, *n.* 周年 anniversary.

shūnenbukai, *adj.* 執念深い 1. persistent; tenacious. 2. unforgiving.

shunga, *n.* 春画 erotic picture.

shuniku, *n.* 朱肉 red ink used for seals.

shunin, *n.* 主任 director; head.

shūnin, *n.* 就任 1. assumption of office. 2. inauguration.

shūnin suru, *vb.* 就任する be appointed; be inaugurated.

shunkan, *n.* 瞬間 second; moment.

shunkan-teki ni, *adv.* 瞬間的に momentarily.

shunō, *n.* 首脳 leader; top executive.

shūnyū, *n.* 収入 income.

shuppan, *n.* 出版 publication.

shuppansha, *n.* 出版社 publisher.

shuppan suru, *vb.* 出版する publish.

shuppatsu, *n.* 出発 departure; start.

shuppatsu suru, *vb.* 出発する depart; start out.

shuppei suru, *vb.* 出兵する dispatch troops.

shuppi, *n.* 出費 expenditure.

shūri, *n.* 修理 repair.

shūri suru, *vb.* 修理する repair.

shurui, *n.* 種類 type; kind.

shuryō, *n.* 狩猟 hunting.

shūryō, *n.* 終了 ending; termination.

shūryō, *n.* 修了 completion.

shuryū, *n.* 主流 mainstream.

shūsai, *n.* 秀才 1. outstanding student. 2. able person; gifted person.

shusai suru, *vb.* 主宰する preside.

shusai suru, *vb.* 主催する sponsor.

shūsei, *n.* 修正 correction; revision.

shūsei suru, *vb.* 修正する correct; revise.

shuseki, *n.* 首席 head; chief.

shūsekikairo, *n.* 集積回路 integrated circuit.

shūsen, *n.* 終戦 termination of a war.

shushi, *n.* 主旨 1. purpose. 2. gist; tenor.

shūshi, *n.* 収支 income and expenditures.

shūshi 終始 1. *n.* beginning and ending. 2. *adv.* from beginning to end; all the while.

shūshi(gō), *n.* 修士(号) master's degree.

shūshifu, *n.* 終止符 period; ending; **shūshifu o utsu** put an end to.

shūshin, *n.* 終身 lifetime.

shūshinkei, *n.* 終身刑 life imprisonment.

shūshin koyōsei, *n.* 終身雇用制 lifetime employment.

shushō, *n.* 首相 prime minister.

shushō, *n.* 主将 team captain.

shushoku, *n.* 主食 staple food.

shūshoku, *n.* 就職 employment.

shūshoku suru, *vb.* 就職する find employment.

shūshoku suru, *vb.* 修飾する 1. modify. 2. ornament.

shūshōrōbai, *n.* 周章狼狽 panic.

shūshū, *n.* 収集 collection.

shūshū suru, *vb.* 収集する collect; gather.

shūshū suru, *vb.* 収拾する control; manage.

shūshuku suru, *vb.* 収縮する contract; shrink.

shūsoku, *n.* 終息 end.

shussan, *n.* 出産 childbirth.

shussan suru, *vb.* 出産する give birth.

shusse, *n.* 出世 success; promotion; **shusse suru** succeed.

shussei, *n.* 出生 birth.

shusseichi, *n.* 出生地 birthplace.

shusseki, *n.* 出席 attendance; **shusseki o toru** take attendance.

shusseki suru, *vb.* 出席する attend; be present.

shussha suru, *vb.* 出社する go to one's office.

shusshi, *n.* 出資 investment.

shusshikin, *n.* 出資金 capital investment.

shusshin, *n.* 出身 1. birthplace; hometown. 2. former affiliation; alma mater.

shusshisha, *n.* 出資者 investor.

shussho, *n.* 出所 source; origin.

shutaisei, *n.* 主体性 1. identity; **shutaisei ni kakeru** lack identity. 2. autonomy; independence.

shutchō, *n.* 出張 business trip.

shūten, *n.* 終点 last stop.

shuto, *n.* 首都 capital city.

shūto, *n.* しゅうと father-in-law.

shutoku suru, *vb.* 取得する acquire; obtain.

shūtoku suru, *vb.* 習得する master a subject or skill.

shūtome, *n.* 姑 mother-in-law.

shu to shite, *adv.* 主として chiefly; mainly.

shutsuba suru, *vb.* 出馬する run for office.

shutsuensha, *n.* 出演者 actor; performer.

shutsuen suru, *vb.* 出演する act (in a film or play).

shutsugan, *n.* 出願 application.

shutsugen suru, *vb.* 出現する appear.

shutsujō suru, *vb.* 出場する participate; enter (a competition).

shutsuryoku, *n.* 出力 output.

shuttei suru, *vb.* 出廷する appear in court.

shutten, *n.* 出典 source (literary).

shuwa, *n.* 手話 sign language.

shūwaijiken, *n.* 収賄事件 bribery case.

shuwan, *n.* 手腕 ability; skill.

shuyaku, *n.* 主役 leading role.

shuyō (na), *adj.* 主要 (な) chief; major.

shūyōsho, *n.* 収容所 1. asylum. 2. internment camp.

shūyō suru, *vb.* 収容する accommodate; take in.

shūyō suru, *vb.* 修養する improve oneself.

shuzai suru, *vb.* 取材する collect information; do research.

shūzen, *n.* 修繕 repair.

shūzen suru, *vb.* 修繕する repair.

shuzoku, *n.* 種族 race; tribe.

shūzoku, *n.* 習俗 custom.

sō, *n.* 層 1. layer. 2. class.

sō, *n.* 僧 monk; priest.

sō そう 1. *adj.* so. 2. *adv.* yes; so; in that way.

-sō そう seem; I hear (that); **yasashisō** seems easy.

soaku (na), *adj.* 粗悪 (な) crude.

sōan, *n.* 草案 draft.

soba, *n.* そば buckwheat; buckwheat noodles.

soba, *n.* 側 neighborhood; vicinity.

sōba, *n.* 相場 market; market price.

sobakasu, *n.* そばかす freckles.

soba ni 側に 1. *prep.* beside. 2. *adv.* close to; in the neighborhood of.

sōbetsukai, *n.* 送別会 farewell party.

sōbi, *n.* 装備 equipment.

sobieru, *vb.* 聳える tower.

sobieto, *n.* ソビエト Soviet Union; USSR.

sobo, *n.* 祖母 grandmother.

soboku (na), *adj.* 素朴 (な) simple; naive; unpretentious.

soburi, *n.* 素振り 1. bearing; manner. 2. indication.

sochi, *n.* 措置 action; **sochi o toru** take action.

sōchi, *n.* 装置 equipment; device.

sochira そちら 1. *pron.* you. 2. *n.* over there.

sōchō, *n.* 総長 university president.

sōchō, *n.* 早朝 early morning.

sōchō (na), *adj.* 荘重 (な) solemn.

-sō da そうだ I hear (that); **Ame ga furusō da.** I hear that it's going to rain.

sodachi, *n.* 育ち upbringing.

sōdai (na), *adj.* 壮大 (な) imposing; magnificent.

sōdan, *n.* 相談 advice; consultation.

sōdan suru, *vb.* 相談する consult; ask for advice.

sodateru, *vb.* 育てる raise; rear (child, plant, etc.).

sodatsu, *vb.* 育つ grow up; be brought up.

sode, *n.* 袖 sleeve.

sodeguchi, *n.* 袖口 cuff (sleeve).

sōdō, *n.* 騒動 turmoil; uproar.

soeru, *vb.* 添える attach to.

sofu, *n.* 祖父 grandfather.

sōfu suru, *vb.* 送付する send; ship.

sofuto-kurīmu, *n.* ソフトクリーム (E.) soft ice cream.

sofuto(ueā), *n.* ソフトウエアー (E.) software.

sogai suru, *vb.* 阻害する block; hinder.

sōgaku, *n.* 総額 total amount.

sōgankyō, *n.* 双眼鏡 binoculars.

sōgen, *n.* 草原 prairie.

sōgi, *n.* 葬儀 funeral.

sōgo 相互 1. *pron.* each other; one another. 2. *n.* mutuality.

sōgō, *n.* 総合 total; whole.

sōgon (na), *adj.* 荘厳 (な) solemn.

sōgo no, *adj.* 相互の mutual; reciprocal; **sōgo no rikai** mutual understanding.

sōgō suru, *vb.* 総合する synthesize; integrate.

sogu, *vb.* 削ぐ 1. shave off; slice. 2. diminish. 3. spoil.

sōgu, *n.* 装具 outfit; equipment.

sōgū, *n.* 遭遇 encounter.

soguwanai, *adj.* そぐわない inappropriate; unsuitable.

sōgyō suru, *vb.* 操業する operate; run.

sōhaku (na, no), *adj.* 蒼白 (な、の) pale.

sōhō, *n.* 相方 both sides.

sōi, *n.* 創意 originality.

sōi, *n.* 相違 difference.

sōi nai, *adj.* 相違ない assured; unquestionable.

sōji, *n.* 相似 similarity.

sōji, *n.* 掃除 cleaning; dusting; sweeping.

sōji (no), *adj.* 相似 (の) analogous; similar.

sōjiki, *n.* 掃除機 vacuum cleaner.

sōji (o) suru, *vb.* 掃除 (を) する clean; dust; sweep.

sōjite, *adv.* 総じて in general; on the whole.

sōjū, *n.* 操縦 management; handling; operation.

sōjuku (na, no), *adj.* 早熟 (な、の) precocious.

sōjūseki, *n.* 操縦席 cockpit.

sōjū suru, *vb.* 操縦する handle; operate.

sōkai (na), *adj.* そう快 (な) refreshing.

sōkan, *n.* 壮観 magnificent view.

sōkan kankei, *n.* 相関関係 correlation.

sōkatsu suru, *vb.* 総括する generalize; summarize.

sōkei, *n.* 総計 sum; total.

sōken (na), *adj.* 壮健 (な) healthy.

sōki, *n.* 早期 early stage.

sōkin, *n.* 送金 remittance.

sokkenai, *adj.* そっけない 1. blunt. 2. unfriendly.

sokki, *n.* 速記 shorthand; stenography.

sokkin, *n.* 即金 cash; **sokkin de harau** pay in cash.

sokkoku, *adv.* 即刻 immediately.

sokkuri そっくり 1. *n.* all. 2. *adj.* identical. 3. *adv.* altogether.

sokkusu, *n.* ソックス (E.) socks.

sokkyō, *n.* 即興 improvisation.

soko, *n.* 底 1. bottom; **kokoro no soko kara** from the bottom of one's heart. 2. shoe sole.

soko, *n.* そこ there; that place.

sōko, *n.* 倉庫 warehouse.

sōkō, *n.* 草稿 draft; manuscript.

soko de そこで 1. *conj.* then. 2. *adv.* therefore; thereupon.

sokoku, *n.* 祖国 native country.

sokonau, *vb.* 損なう injure; mar; spoil.

-sokonau 損なう fail to do something; **yomisokonau** fail to read.

sokoneru, *vb.* 損ねる injure; offend.

sokora そこら 1. *adv.* thereabouts; around there. 2. *prep.* about.

soko-soko, *adv.* そこそこ barely; at most.

-soku 足 suffix indicating a pair (footwear); **kutsushita sansoku** three pairs of socks.

sokubaku, *n.* 束縛 restraint; restriction.

sokudo, *n.* 速度 speed.

sokuji (ni), *adv.* 即時 (に) without delay; instantly.

sokujitsu, *n.* 即日 same day.

sokumen, *n.* 側面 side; aspect.

sokuryō, *n.* 測量 measurement; survey.

sokuryoku, *n.* 速力 speed.

sokuseki, *n.* 足跡 footprint.

sokuseki (no), *adj.* 即席 (の) 1. instant. 2. improvised.

sokushi, *n.* 即死 instantaneous death.

sokushin, *n.* 促進 propagation; promotion.

sokutatsu, *n.* 速達 special delivery.

sokutei suru, *vb.* 測定する measure.

sokuza ni, *adv.* 即座に immediately.

sōkyū ni, *adv.* 早急に immediately; as soon as possible.

somaru, *vb.* 染まる 1. be dyed or stained. 2. be influenced.

somatsu (na), *adj.* 粗末 (な) cheap; poor; shabby.

sōmei (na), *adj.* 聡明 (な) intelligent; wise.

sōmen, *n.* そうめん fine noodles.

someru, *vb.* 染める dye; tint.

somo-somo, *adv.* そもそも to begin with.

somukeru, *vb.* 背ける avert (eyes).

somuku, *vb.* 背く 1. rebel against; disobey. 2. violate.

son, *n.* 損 disadvantage; damage; loss.

sonaeru, *vb.* 供える offer (at an altar).

sonaeru, *vb.* 備える 1. prepare. 2. have; be equipped with.

sonaetsukeru, *vb.* 備え付ける install; provide.

sōnan, *n.* 遭難 accident; disaster.

sonawaru, *vb.* 備わる have; be equipped with.

sonchō suru, *vb.* 尊重する respect; value.

sondai (na), *adj.* 尊大 (な) arrogant.

sōnen, *n.* 壮年 prime of life.

songai, *n.* 損害 damage; loss.

sonkei, *n.* 尊敬 respect.

sonkei suru, *vb.* 尊敬する respect.

son'na, *adj.* そんな that; that kind of; such.

sono, *adj.* その that; those.

sonoba de, *adv.* その場で on the spot.

sonogo, *adv.* その後 after that; afterward.

sono hen ni, *adv.* その辺に in the vicinity of.

sono hi, *n.* その日 that day.

sono hito, *n.* その人 that person.

sono hoka, *n.* その他 the rest; others.

sono hoka (no), *adj.* その他 (の) other.

sono hoka ni, *adv.* その他に besides that; in addition to that.

sono kawari ni, *adv.* その代わりに instead.

sono kuse ni, *adv.* そのくせに nevertheless; yet.

sono mama, *adv.* そのまま as is.

sono uchi ni, *adv.* その内に 1. soon. 2. in the meantime.

sono ue (ni) その上 (に) 1. *prep.* besides. 2. *adv.* in addition; on top of that.

sonshitsu, *n.* 損失 loss.

son suru, *vb.* 損する lose (money).

sōnyū suru, *vb.* 挿入する insert.

sonzai, *n.* 存在 1. existence. 2. presence.

sonzai suru, *vb.* 存在する exist.

sō'ō (na, no), *adj.* 相応 (な、の) appropriate; suitable.

sō'on, *n.* 騒音 noise.

soppo o muku, *vb.* そっぽを向く ignore.

sora, *n.* 空 1. sky. 2. weather.

sora, *interj.* そら Hey!; Look!

sorasu, *vb.* 外らす 1. dodge. 2. turn away.

sore, *pron.* それ that.

sore de, *adv.* それで and then.

sore dewa それでは 1. *adv.* so; then. 2. *interj.* Well.

sore hodo, *adv.* それほど so much; **sore hodo takakunai** not so expensive.

sore kara それから 1. *conj.* and. 2. *adv.* afterward; since then.

sore made, *adv.* それまで till then.

soren, *n.* ソ連 Soviet Union.

sore ni それに 1. *prep.* besides. 2. *adv.* in addition; moreover.

soreru, *vb.* 逸れる 1. digress; deviate from. 2. miss.

sore to mo, *conj.* それとも or.

sore to naku, *adv.* それとなく indirectly; casually.

sorezore, *adv.* それぞれ individually; respectively.

sori, *n.* そり sleigh.

sōridaijin, *n.* 総理大臣 prime minister.

sorikaeru, *vb.* 反り返る bend back; warp.

sōritsu suru, *vb.* 創立する establish.

soroban, *n.* 算盤 abacus.

soroeru, *vb.* 揃える 1. arrange; prepare. 2. put in order; make complete. 3. make uniform.

soro-soro, *adv.* そろそろ 1. soon; now; **Soro-soro shitsurei shimasu.** I must be going. 2. slowly; **soro-soro aruku** walk slowly.

sorou, *vb.* 揃う 1. be complete. 2. be equal; be the same. 3. assemble.

soru, *vb.* 剃る shave.

soru, *vb.* 反る bend; warp.

sōryo, *n.* 僧侶 monk; priest.

sōryō, *n.* 送料 shipping charge; postage.

sōsa, *n.* 捜査 police investigation.

sōsa, *n.* 操作 operation (machine).

sōsai, *n.* 総裁 president.

sōsaku, *n.* 捜索 investigation; search.

sōsaku, *n.* 創作 creation; creative writing.

sōsaku suru, *n.* 捜索する investigate; search.

sōsaku suru, *n.* 創作する create; write.

sōsa suru, *vb.* 操作する operate a machine.

sōseiji, *n.* 双生児 twin(s).

sōseiki, *n.* 創生記 Genesis (Bible).

sosei suru, *vb.* 組成する constitute.

sosei suru, *vb.* 蘇生する revive.

sōsēji, *n.* ソーセージ (E.) sausage.

sosen, *n.* 祖先 ancestor.

sōsenkyo, *n.* 総選挙 general election.

sōsetsu suru, *vb.* 創設する found; establish.

sōsha, *n.* 走者 runner.

soshi, *n.* 阻止 obstruction; hindrance.

sōshihainin, *n.* 総支配人 general manager.

soshiki, *n.* 組織 organization; system.

sōshiki, *n.* 葬式 funeral.

sōshin, *n.* 送信 transmission.

sōshingu, *n.* 装身具 accessories (personal).

sōshisha, *n.* 創始者 founder; originator.

soshi suru, *vb.* 阻止する obstruct; hinder.

soshite そして 1. *conj.* and. 2. *adv.* consequently.

soshitsu, *n.* 素質 potential; talent.

sōshitsu, *n.* 喪失 loss.

soshō, *n.* 訴訟 lawsuit.

soshō jiken, *n.* 訴訟事件 legal case.

sōshoku, *n.* 装飾 decoration.

sosō, *n.* 粗相 carelessness; mistake.

sōsō (ni), *adv.* 早々 (に) 1. immediately. 2. early.

sosogu, *vb.* 注ぐ 1. pour. 2. devote.

sosokkashii, *adj.* そそっかしい hasty; rash.

sosonokasu, *vb.* そそのかす instigate; agitate.

sosoru, *vb.* そそる induce; excite; stimulate.

sōsōtaru, *adj.* そうそうたる distinguished.

sossen suru, *vb.* 率先する take the lead.

sōsu, *n.* ソース (E.) sauce.

sōsū, *n.* 総数 total number.

sōtai-teki ni, *adv.* 総体的に relatively.

sotchi そっち 1. *pron.* you (informal). 2. *n.* over there.

sotchinoke ni suru, *vb.* そっちのけにする neglect one's duties.

sotchoku (na), *adj.* 率直 (な) candid; frank; straightforward.

sotchū, *n.* 卒中 stroke (seizure).

sōtei suru, *vb.* 想定する assume; suppose.

soto, *n.* 外 exterior; outside; outdoors.

sōtō (na, no), *adj.* 相当 (な、の) 1. appropriate. 2. considerable; very large.

sotogawa, *n.* 外側 exterior; outside.

sōtō suru, *vb.* 相当する be the equivalent (of); be comparable (to).

sotsugyō, *n.* 卒業 graduation.

sotsugyōshiki, *n.* 卒業式 graduation ceremony.

sotsugyōshōsho, *n.* 卒業証書 diploma.

sotsugyō suru, *vb.* 卒業する graduate.

sotsu no nai, *adj.* そつのない 1. careful. 2. faultless.

sotte 沿って 1. *prep.* along. 2. *adv.* in line with.

sotto, *adv.* そっと 1. softly; quietly. 2. secretly.

sotto shite oku, *vb.* そっとしておく leave alone; leave as is.

sottō suru, *vb.* 卒倒する faint; swoon.

sou, *vb.* 添う 1. accompany. 2. marry. 3. satisfy; **kitai ni sou** satisfy one's expectations.

sou, *vb.* 沿う follow.

sowa-sowa to, *adv.* そわそわと restlessly; uneasily.

soya (na), *adj.* 粗野 (な) crude; boorish.

soyō, *n.* 素養 skill; accomplishment.

soyo kaze, *n.* そよ風 breeze.

sozai, *n.* 素材 ingredient; material.

sōzaiya, *n.* 総菜屋 delicatessen.

sozatsu (na), *adj.* 粗雑 (な) rough; crude.

sozei, *n.* 租税 taxation.

sōzen, *n.* 騒然 commotion; turmoil.

sōzō, *n.* 創造 creation.

sōzō, *n.* 想像 imagination.

sōzōjō no, *adj.* 想像上の imaginary.

sōzoku, *n.* 相続 inheritance; succession.

sōzokunin, *n.* 相続人 heir; heiress.

sōzoku suru, *vb.* 相続する inherit; succeed to.

sōzokuzaisan, *n.* 相続財産 inheritance; legacy.

sōzōryoku, *n.* 想像力 imagination.

sōzōryoku, *n.* 創造力 creativity.

sōzōshii, *adj.* 騒々しい noisy.

sōzō suru, *vb.* 想像する imagine.

su, *n.* 酢 vinegar.

su, *n.* 巣 animal habitat: nest, cobweb, den, honeycomb.

sū, *n.* 数 number.

suashi, *n.* 素足 bare feet.

subarashii, *adj.* 素晴らしい wonderful; superb.

subayai, *adj.* 素早い nimble; speedy.

suberidai, *n.* 滑り台 sliding board.

suberu, *vb.* 滑る 1. slip; slide. 2. fail (an examination).

subete, *n.* 全て all; everything.

subete (no), *adj.* 全て (の) all.

subomeru, *vb.* すぼめる make narrower.

sude de, *adv.* 素手で barehanded.

sude ni, *adv.* 既に already.

sue, *n.* 末 1. tip; end. 2. future.

suekko, *n.* 末っ子 youngest child.

sueoku, *vb.* 据え置く defer; freeze (price).

sueru, *vb.* 据える 1. place. 2. install; set up.

suetsukeru, *vb.* 据え付ける install; set up.

sūgaku, *n.* 数学 mathematics.

sugao, *n.* 素顔 1. true self. 2. unmade-up face.

sugaru, *vb.* すがる cling to; depend on.

suga-sugashii, *adj.* すがすがしい refreshing.

sugata, *n.* 姿 1. appearance; figure; features. 2. condition.

sugata o arawasu, *vb.* 姿を現す appear; show oneself.

sugi, *n.* 杉 cedar.

-sugi 過ぎ past; over; **gojisugi** past five o'clock; **hatachisugi** over twenty years old.

sugiru, *vb.* 過ぎる 1. pass by. 2. exceed. 3. expire.

-sugiru 過ぎる to excess; **nomi-sugiru** drink to excess.

sugoi, *adj.* すごい 1. amazing; wonderful. 2. awful; terrifying.

sugoku, *adv.* すごく very; awfully.

sugosu, *vb.* 過ごす (time) spend; pass.

sugu (ni), *adv.* すぐ (に) 1. immediately. 2. easily. 3. very; **sugu chikaku ni** very near to.

sugureru, *vb.* 優れる excel.

sugureta, *adj.* 優れた excellent.

suhada, *n.* 素肌 bare skin.

sūhai, *n.* 崇拝 adoration; worship.

sūhaisha, *n.* 崇拝者 adorer; worshiper.

sūhai suru, *vb.* 崇拝する adore; worship.

suiageru, *vb.* 吸い上げる pump up; suck up.

suibaku, *n.* 水爆 hydrogen bomb.

suibun, *n.* 水分 moisture; water.

suichoku (na), *adj.* 垂直 (な) perpendicular; vertical.

suichoku ni, *adv.* 垂直に vertically.

suichū de/ni, *adv.* 水中で、〜に under water.

suiden, *n.* 水田 rice paddy.

suidō, *n.* 水道 water supply.

suidōsui, *n.* 水道水 tap water.

suiei, *n.* 水泳 swimming.

suifu, *n.* 水夫 sailor.

suigai, *n.* 水害 flood damage.

suigara, *n.* 吸い殻 cigarette butt.

suigin, *n.* 水銀 mercury.

suihanki, *n.* 炊飯器 rice cooker.

suihei (na, no), *adj.* 水平 (な、の) horizontal.

suihei ni, *adv.* 水平に horizontally.

suiheisen, *n.* 水平線 horizon.

sui'i, *n.* 水位 water level.

sui'i, *n.* 推移 change; evolution.

suijaku suru, *vb.* 衰弱する become weak.

suiji, *n.* 炊事 cooking.

suijun, *n.* 水準 standard; level.

suika, *n.* 西瓜 watermelon.

suikomu, *vb.* 吸い込む inhale; absorb.

suikō suru, *vb.* 遂行する execute; perform.

suimen, *n.* 水面 surface of water.

suimin, *n.* 睡眠 sleep.

suiminbusoku, *n.* 睡眠不足 lack of sleep.

suimin o toru, *vb.* 睡眠を取る get some sleep.

suimin'yaku, *n.* 睡眠薬 sleeping pill.

suimono, *n.* 吸い物 Japanese-style soup.

suion, *n.* 水温 water temperature.

suiren, *n.* 水蓮 water lily.

suiri, *n.* 推理 speculation; inference.

suiri suru, *vb.* 推理する speculate; infer.

suiryokudenki, *n.* 水力電気 hydroelectricity.

suiryoku-hatsuden, *n.* 水力発電 hydroelectric power.

suisaiga, *n.* 水彩画 watercolor painting.

suisatsu, *n.* 推察 conjecture; guess.

suisei, *n.* 水星 Mercury (planet).

suisei, *n.* 彗星 comet.

suisen, *n.* 推薦 recommendation.

suisen, *n.* 水仙 daffodil; narcissus.

suisenbenjo, *n.* 水洗便所 flush toilet.

suisenjō, *n.* 推薦状 letter of recommendation.

suisen suru, *vb.* 推薦する recommend.

suisha, *n.* 水車 waterwheel.

suishinryoku, *n.* 推進力 driving force.

suishin suru, *vb.* 推進する promote.

suishō, *n.* 水晶 crystal.

suiso, *n.* 水素 hydrogen.

suisō, *n.* 水槽 water tank.

suisoku, *n.* 推測 assumption; guess.

suisoku suru, *vb.* 推測する assume; guess.

suisu, *n.* スイス Switzerland.

suitchi, *n.* スイッチ (E.) switch; ignition.

suitei suru, *vb.* 推定する assume; estimate.

suitō, *n.* 出納 accounts.

suitō, *n.* 水筒 water bottle.

suitoru, *vb.* 吸い取る absorb; soak up.

suiun, *n.* 衰運 decline.

suiyōbi, *n.* 水曜日 Wednesday.

suizokukan, *n.* 水族館 aquarium.

suji, *n.* 筋 1. streak (line). 2. fiber; muscle; tendon. 3. story line; logic. 4. lineage.

sūji, *n.* 数字 number; figure.

sujigaki, *n.* 筋書き outline; story line.

sujimichi, *n.* 筋道 rationality; reason; logic.

sukasazu, *adv.* すかさず immediately.

sukasu, *vb.* 透かす look through.

sukebe(i), *n.* 助平 lecher.

sukejūru, *n.* スケジュール (E.) schedule.

sukeru, *vb.* 透ける be transparent.

sukēto, *n.* スケート (E.) skates; skating.

suki, *n.* 鋤 plow.

suki, *n.* 隙 1. gap; opening. 2. carelessness; inattentiveness.

suki 好き 1. *n.* fondness; love. 2. *adj.* favorite; fond. 3. *vb.* like; love.

suki (na), *adj.* 好き (な) favorite; **watashi no sukina mono** my favorite things.

sukī, *n.* スキー skiing.

sukima, *n.* 隙間 gap; hole.

sukimakaze, *n.* 隙間風 draft (air current).

sukitōtta, *adj.* 透き通った transparent; clear.

sukiyaki, *n.* すき焼き Japanese meat dish.

sukkari, *adv.* すっかり completely; thoroughly.

sukkiri suru, *vb.* すっきりする be satisfied; feel refreshed.

sūkō (na), *adj.* 崇高 (な) sublime; lofty.

sukoburu, *adv.* すこぶる very.

sukoshi 少し 1. *n.* a small amount. 2. *adv.* a little bit; slightly; for a short time.

sukoshi mo, *adv.* 少しも not at all (with negative).

sukoshi zutsu, *adv.* 少しずつ little by little.

suku, *vb.* 透く 1. thin out. 2. be transparent.

suku, *vb.* 空く become empty.

sukui, *n.* 救い help; hope.

sukumeru, *vb.* すくめる 1. shrug. 2. duck.

sukunai, *adj.* 少ない few.

sukunaku tomo, *adv.* 少なくとも

at least.

suku'u, *vb.* 救う rescue.

suku'u, *vb.* 掬う scoop up.

sumai, *n.* 住まい residence; house.

sumanai, *adj.* 済まない inexcusable.

sumasu, *vb.* 済ます finish.

sumāto (na), *adj.* スマート（な）(E. *smart*) 1. stylish. 2. well-proportioned; slim.

sumi, *n.* 墨 Chinese ink.

sumi, *n.* 炭 charcoal.

sumi, *n.* 隅 corner; nook.

sumika, *n.* 住み家 home; residence.

sumimasen, *interj.* すみません 1. I am sorry! Excuse me! 2. Thank you!

sumire, *n.* 菫 violet (plant).

sumiyaka (na), *adj.* 速やか（な） swift.

sumō, *n.* 相撲 Japanese wrestling.

sumomo, *n.* 李 Japanese plum.

sumu, *vb.* 住む reside.

sumu, *vb.* 済む 1. end. 2. manage; do without.

sumu, *vb.* 澄む be clear.

suna, *n.* 砂 sand.

sunahama, *n.* 砂浜 sandy beach.

sunao (na), *adj.* 素直（な）1. docile. 2. honest.

sunawachi 即ち 1. *conj.* or; that is. 2. *adv.* namely; in other words.

sundan suru, *vb.* 寸断する cut into pieces.

sune, *n.* すね shin.

suneru, *vb.* すねる sulk.

sunpō, *n.* 寸法 measurement.

sunzen de/ni, *prep.* 寸前で、〜に just before (time or place).

sūpā(māketto), *n.* スーパー（マーケット）(E.) supermarket.

supagettī, *n.* スパゲッティー (It.) spaghetti.

supein, *n.* スペイン (E.) Spain.

superu, superingu, *n.* スペル、スペリング (E.) spelling.

supīdo, *n.* スピード (E.) speed.

supīdo-ihan, *n.* スピード違反 speeding violation.

suponsā, *n.* スポンサー (E.) sponsor.

supōtsu, *n.* スポーツ (E.) sport(s).

suppai, *adj.* 酸っぱい sour.

suppanuku, *vb.* すっぱ抜く divulge (a secret); reveal.

suppokasu, *vb.* すっぽかす neglect (work); break (promise).

sūpu, *n.* スープ (E.) soup.

supūn, *n.* スプーン (E.) spoon.

sura, *parti.* すら even; **Hiragana sura yomenai.** (He) cannot even read hiragana.

sura-sura (to), *adv.* すらすら（と） fluently; easily; **nihongo o sura-sura hanasu** speak Japanese fluently.

sureru, *vb.* 擦れる 1. rub (against). 2. wear down. 3. become jaded.

sure-sure, *adj.* すれすれ extremely close (location).

sure-sure ni, *adv.* すれすれに barely; almost.

suri, *n.* すり pickpocket.

suriherasu, *vb.* 磨り減らす wear down; exhaust.

suriheru, *vb.* 磨り減る be worn down; be exhausted.

surikireru, *vb.* 擦り切れる wear out.

surikizu, *n.* 擦り傷 scratch (injury).

surimuku, *vb.* 擦りむく abrade; scrape.

surinukeru, *vb.* 擦り抜ける squeeze through.

suriotosu, *vb.* 擦り落とす scrape off.

surippa, *n.* スリッパ (E.) slippers.

surippu, *n.* スリップ (E.) 1. slip; skid. 2. slip (lingerie).

suritsubusu, *vb.* 磨りつぶす grind down; mash.

suru, *vb.* する 1. do; play (games, sports, etc.). 2. make (into); **Kimi o shiawase ni suru.** (I'll make you happy. 3. choose; decide on; **kore ni suru** choose or decide on this. 4. cost; **hyaku en suru** cost 100 yen. 5. have; get.

suru, *vb.* 刷る print.

suru, *vb.* 磨る grind.

suru, *vb.* 擦る chafe; rub.

surudoi, *adj.* 鋭い 1. acute; sharp. 2. insightful; keen.

suru-suru to, *adv.* するすると smoothly.

suru to, *conj.* すると and then.

susamajii, *adj.* すさまじい amazing; horrible.

susamu, *vb.* 荒む grow wild; go to waste.

sushi, *n.* 寿司 raw fish slices on rice.

suso, *n.* 裾 1. hem. 2. foot (of a mountain).

susu, *n.* 煤 soot.

susugu, *vb.* すすぐ rinse.

susumeru, *vb.* 進める advance; promote.

susumeru, *vb.* 勧める advise; recommend.

susumi, *n.* 進み progress.

susumu, *vb.* 進む advance; make progress.

susunde, *adv.* 進んで voluntarily; willingly.

susurinaku, *vb.* すすり泣く sob.

susuru, *vb.* すする sip.

sutajiamu, *n.* スタジアム (E.) stadium.

sutajio, *n.* スタジオ (E.) studio.

sutando, *n.* スタンド (E.) stand; stands.

sutareru, *vb.* 廃れる decline; become obsolete; become outdated.

suteki (na), *adj.* 素敵 (な) great; wonderful.

sutēki, *n.* ステーキ (E.) steak.

sutereo, *n.* ステレオ (E.) stereo.

suteru, *vb.* 捨てる throw away; abandon.

sutōbu, *n.* ストーブ (E.) stove; heater.

sutokkingu, *n.* ストッキング (E.) stockings.

sutokku, *n.* ストック (E.) stock (inventory).

suto(raiki), *n.* スト(ライキ) (E.) (labor) strike.

sutoresu, *vb.* ストレス (E.) stress.

sūtsu, *n.* スーツ (E.) suit (clothing).

sūtsukēsu, *n.* スーツケース (E.) suitcase.

su'u, *vb.* 吸う 1. breathe in; inhale; smoke. 2. absorb; suck up.

suwaru, *vb.* 座る sit down; take a seat.

suzu, *n.* 鈴 small bell.

suzu, *n.* 錫 tin.

suzume, *n.* 雀 sparrow.

suzuran, *n.* 鈴蘭 lily of the valley.

suzuri, *n.* 硯 inkstone for calligraphy.

suzushii, *adj.* 涼しい cool.

T

ta, *n.* 田 rice field.

ta (no), *adj.* 他 (の) other; another.

taba, *n.* 束 bunch; bundle.

tabako, *n.* タバコ (Pg. *tabaco*) cigarette; **tabako o nomu/su'u** smoke a cigarette.

tabaneru, *vb.* 束ねる bundle.

tabemono, *n.* 食べ物 food.

taben (na), *adj.* 多弁 (な) talkative.

tabenokoshi, *n.* 食べ残し leftover food.

taberu, *vb.* 食べる eat.

tabesugi, *n.* 食べ過ぎ overeating.

tabi, *n.* 足袋 Japanese-style socks.

tabi, *n.* 旅 traveling; trip; **tabi o suru** take a trip; travel.

tabikasanaru, *vb.* 度重なる happen repeatedly.

-tabi ni 度に each time; **kare ni au-tabi ni** each time I see him.

tabi-tabi, *adv.* 度々 repeatedly; frequently.

tabō (na), *adj.* 多忙 (な) very busy.

tabun, *adv.* 多分 perhaps; probably.

tachi, *n.* 質 personality; nature; **tachi no warui** bad natured.

-tachi 達 (plural indicator) **kodomotachi** children.

tachiagaru, *vb.* 立ち上がる stand up.

tachiau, *vb.* 立ち合う witness; attend.

tachiba, *n.* 立場 position; situation.

tachigiki, *n.* 立ち聞き eavesdropping.

tachi'iru, *vb.* 立ち入る 1. enter. 2. meddle; be nosy.

tachimachi, *adv.* たちまち instantly; on the spot.

tachimiseki, *n.* 立ち見席 standing room.

tachimukau, *vb.* 立ち向かう oppose; confront.

tachinoku, *vb.* 立ち退く evacuate; vacate.

tachiōjō suru, *vb.* 立ち往生する be stuck; come to a standstill.

tachisaru, *vb.* 立ち去る leave.

tachiuchi, *n.* 太刀打ち contest; fight.

tachiuchi dekinai, *adj.* 太刀打ちできない unbeatable.

tachiyoru, *vb.* 立ち寄る drop in; stop by; **bā ni tachiyoru** drop in at a bar.

tada ただ 1. *adv.* only. 2. *conj.* but; however.

tada (no), *adj.* 只 (の) 1. free of charge. 2. ordinary.

tadachi ni, *adv.* 直ちに immediately.

tada de, *adv.* 只で free of charge.

tadai (na, no), *adj.* 多大 (な、の) enormous.

tadaima, *adv.* 只今 1. at present. 2. soon.

tadaima, *interj.* ただいま I'm home!

tadashi, *conj.* ただし but; however.

tadashii, *adj.* 正しい correct; right.

tadayou, *vb.* 漂う drift.

tadoru, *vb.* 辿る follow; trace.

tadōshi, *n.* 他動詞 transitive verb.

taegatai, *adj.* 耐え難い intolerable; unbearable.

taemanai, *adj.* 絶え間ない constant; incessant.

taemanaku, *adv.* 絶え間なく constantly; incessantly.

taenaru, *adj.* 妙なる exquisite.

taeru, *vb.* 絶える discontinue; cease.

taeru, *vb.* 耐える endure.

tagai 互い *pron.* each other; one another.

tagai ni, *adv.* 互いに with (at, to, etc.) each other; reciprocally; mutually.

tagayasu, *vb.* 耕す till; cultivate (land).

tagiru, *vb.* たぎる boil.

taguru, *vb.* 手操る 1. pull in. 2. retrace.

tahata, *n.* 田畑 field (crops).

tahatsu suru, *vb.* 多発する occur frequently.

tahō 他方 1. *n.* the other side. 2. *adv.* on the other hand.

tahōmen, *n.* 多方面 multifariousness.

tai, *n.* 鯛 sea bream.

tai, *n.* 隊 group; party.

tai, *n.* タイ Thailand.

-tai たい want to (do); **nihon ni ikitai** want to go to Japan.

taiatari suru, *vb.* 体当りする 1. throw oneself at. 2. throw oneself into.

taibatsu, *n.* 体罰 corporal punishment.

taibō (no), *adj.* 待望の wished-for; eagerly awaited.

taibyō, *n.* 大病 serious illness.

taida (na), *adj.* 怠惰 (な) lazy.

taidan, *n.* 対談 conversation; dialogue.

taido, *n.* 態度 attitude.

taifū, *n.* 台風 typhoon.

taigai, *adv.* 大概 mostly.

taigai (no), *adj.* 大概 (の) most.

taigai bōeki, *n.* 対外貿易 foreign trade.

taigū, *n.* 待遇 1. (customer) service; treatment. 2. salary and benefits.

taihai, *n.* 退廃 decline; decay; degeneration.

taihan, *n.* 大半 majority.

taiheiyō, *n.* 太平洋 Pacific Ocean.

taihen 大変 1. *adj.* difficult. 2. *adv.* very; extremely.

taihi suru, *vb.* 対比する compare; contrast.

taiho suru, *vb.* 逮捕する arrest.

tai'iku, *n.* 体育 physical training.

tai'ikukan, *n.* 体育館 gymnasium.

tai'in suru, *vb.* 退院する be discharged from a hospital.

taiji, *n.* 胎児 fetus.

taijin suru, *vb.* 退陣する withdraw; retire.

taiji suru, *vb.* 退治する conquer; eliminate.

taijū, *n.* 体重 weight (of a person).

taika, *n.* 大家 master; great man.

taika, *n.* 耐火 fire resistance.

taikai, *n.* 大会 convention.

taikaku, *n.* 体格 physical build.

taika suru, *vb.* 退化する regress; retrogress.

taikei, *n.* 体型 system.

taiken, *n.* 体験 experience.

taiken suru, *vb.* 体験する experience.

taiketsu suru, *vb.* 対決する confront.

taiki, *n.* 大気 air; atmosphere.

taiki suru, *vb.* 待機する stand by.

taiko, *n.* 太鼓 drum.

taikō suru, *vb.* 対抗する oppose; fight.

taikutsu (na), *adj.* 退屈 (な) boring.

taikyaku suru, *vb.* 退却する retreat.

taikyū-ryoku/-sei, *n.* 耐久力／～性 durability.

taiman (na), *adj.* 怠慢 (な)

negligent.

taimen, *n.* 体面 reputation.

taimen, *n.* 対面 meeting.

tainō, *n.* 滞納 delinquency (payment).

taiō, *n.* 対応 handling; treatment.

taion, *n.* 体温 body temperature; **taion o hakaru** take one's temperature.

taionkei, *n.* 体温計 thermometer (clinical).

taiō suru, *vb.* 対応する deal with.

taipuraitā, *n.* タイプライター (E.) typewriter.

taira (na), *adj.* 平ら (な) flat; level.

tairiku, *n.* 大陸 continent.

tairitsu, *n.* 対立 dispute; antagonism; confrontation.

tairitsu suru, *vb.* 対立する confront.

tairu, *n.* タイル (E.) tile.

tairyaku, *n.* 大略 summary.

tairyō, *n.* 大量 large amount.

tairyoku, *n.* 体力 stamina.

taisaku, *n.* 対策 1. measures (actions). 2. strategy; **taisaku o tateru** plan a strategy.

taisei, *n.* 体制 1. power; government. 2. social or economic structure.

taiseiyō, *n.* 大西洋 Atlantic Ocean.

taisen, *n.* 大戦 world war.

taisetsu (na), *adj.* 大切 (な) 1. important. 2. beloved.

taisha, *n.* 退社 1. resignation; retirement (from one's job). 2. leaving the office (for the day).

taishi, *n.* 大使 ambassador.

taishikan, *n.* 大使館 embassy.

taishita, *adj.* 大した 1. great. 2. not very significant (with negative).

taishite, *adv.* 大して not very (with negative).

taishite, *prep.* 対して 1. against. 2. in contrast to; as opposed to. 3. toward.

taishitsu, *n.* 体質 disposition; nature.

taishō, *n.* 対象 object.

taishō, *n.* 大将 1. leader; head. 2. general.

taishoku, *n.* 退職 retirement (from one's job).

taishokukin, *n.* 退職金 severance pay.

taishoku suru, *vb.* 退職する resign, retire (from one's job).

taisho suru, *vb.* 対処する deal with.

taishō-teki (na), *adj.* 対照的 (な) diametrically opposite.

taishō-teki (na), *adj.* 対称的 (な) symmetrical.

taishū, *n.* 体臭 body odor.

taishū, *n.* 大衆 populace; the masses.

taishū-teki (na), *adj.* 大衆的 (な) mass; popular.

taisō, *n.* 体操 gymnastics; exercise.

taisō, *adv.* 大層 very.

taisui, *adj.* 耐水 waterproof.

taitō (na, no), *adj.* 対等 (な、の) equal; fair.

taitoku suru, *vb.* 体得する master.

taitō ni, *adv.* 対等に equally; impartially.

taiwa, *n.* 対話 conversation; dialogue.

taiwan, *n.* 台湾 Taiwan; Republic of China.

taiya, *n.* タイヤ (E.) tire.

taiyō, *n.* 太陽 sun.

taiyō, *n.* 大洋 ocean.

taizai, *n.* 滞在 stay; sojourn.

taizai suru, *vb.* 滞在する stay.

tajirogu, *vb.* たじろぐ flinch; recoil.

taka, *n.* 鷹 hawk.

takabisha (na), *adj.* 高飛車 (な) high-handed; haughty.

takai, *adj.* 高い 1. high. 2. expensive. 2. loud (sound).

takai suru, *vb.* 他界する die.

takakukeiei, *n.* 多角経営 diversified management.

takamaru, *vb.* 高まる increase; rise.

takameru, *vb.* 高める raise.

takara, *n.* 宝 treasure.

takarakuji, *n.* 宝くじ lottery.

takasa, *n.* 高さ height.

take, *n.* 竹 bamboo.

take, *n.* 丈 size; height.

takenoko, *n.* 竹の子 bamboo shoot.

takeru, *vb.* 長ける excel in.

taki, *n.* 滝 waterfall; cascade.

takken, *n.* 卓見 insight.

takkyū, *n.* 卓球 table tennis.

tako, *n.* たこ callus.

tako, *n.* 凧 kite; **tako o ageru** fly a kite.

tako, *n.* 蛸 octopus.

takoku, *n.* 他国 foreign country.

taku, *n.* 宅 1. my husband. 2. house; home.

taku, *vb.* 炊く boil; cook.

taku, *vb.* 焚く burn (wood).

takuan, *n.* たくあん pickled Japanese radish.

takuchi, *n.* 宅地 residential site.

takujisho, *n.* 託児所 day-care center; nursery school.

takumashii, *adj.* たくましい 1. strong. 2. dependable.

takumi (na), *adj.* 巧みな skillful.

takumi ni, *adv.* 巧みに skillfully.

takuramu, *vb.* 企む plot; scheme.

takusan, *n.* 沢山 1. many; much. 2. more than enough.

takushī, *n.* タクシー (E.) taxi.

taku suru, *vb.* 託する entrust.

takuwae, *n.* 蓄え 1. savings. 2. provisions.

takuwaeru, *vb.* 蓄える store; save.

tama, *n.* 玉 1. ball; bead. 2. bullet.

tamago, *n.* 卵 1. egg. 2. fish roe.

tamamono, *n.* 賜物 1. gift. 2. outcome; fruit.

tamanegi, *n.* 玉ねぎ onion.

tama ni, *adv.* たまに occasionally.

tamaranai, *adj.* たまらない 1. intolerable. 2. exciting.

tamaru, *vb.* 溜まる 1. accumulate; heap up. 2. be overdue.

tamashii, *n.* 魂 soul.

tama-tama, *adv.* たまたま by chance.

tamatsuki, *n.* 玉突き billiards.

tame, *n.* 為 benefit; sake.

tame (ni), *conj.* 為 (に) 1. in order to; **eizu-bōshi no tame ni** in order to prevent AIDS; **kazoku o yashinau tame ni** in order to support one's family. 2. because of; owing to.

tame ni naru, *vb.* 為になる be beneficial; be useful.

tamerau, *vb.* ためらう hesitate.

tameru, *vb.* 貯める save; store.

tameshi ni, *adv.* 試しに tentatively.

tamesu, *vb.* 試す test; attempt.

tamotsu, *vb.* 保つ keep; maintain.

tan, *n.* たん phlegm.

tana, *n.* 棚 shelf.

tanabata, *n.* 七夕 Japanese festival (July 7).

tanan (na), *adj.* 多難 (な) full of difficulties.

tanbo, *n.* 田んぼ rice field.

tanchō (na), *adj.* 単調 (な) monotonous.

tandoku de, *adv.* 単独で alone; independently.

tane, *n.* 種 1. seed. 2. source; cause.

tangan suru, *vb.* 嘆願する appeal; entreat.

tango, *n.* 単語 word.

tani, *n.* 谷 valley; ravine.

tan'i, *n.* 単位 1. (school course) credit; **tan'i o toru** earn credits. 2. unit.

tanin, *n.* 他人 1. stranger. 2. other people.

tan'itsu (no), *adj.* 単一 (の) single; one.

tanjō, *n.* 誕生 birth.

tanjōbi, *n.* 誕生日 birthday.

tanjun (na), *adj.* 単純 (な) simple.

tanjunka suru, *vb.* 単純化する simplify.

tanka, *n.* 短歌 traditional Japanese poetry (31 syllables).

tanka, *n.* 担架 stretcher.

tanken, *n.* 短剣 dagger.

tanken, *n.* 探険 exploration; expedition.

tanki, *n.* 短期 short term.

tanki, *n.* 短気 short temper; **tanki o okosu** lose one's temper.

tanki (na), *adj.* 短気 (な) short-tempered.

tankidaigaku, *n.* 短期大学 junior college.

tankō, *n.* 炭鉱 coal mine.

tankōbon, *n.* 単行本 book.

tankyū, *n.* 探究 pursuit; quest; research.

tanmono, *n.* 反物 cloth; textile.

tan naru, *adj.* 単なる mere.

tan'nen (na), *adj.* 丹念 (な) precise; meticulous.

tan ni, *adv.* 単に merely; only.

tan'nō (na), *adj.* 堪能 (な) skillful.

tanō (na), *adj.* 多能 (な) versatile.

tanomi, *n.* 頼み 1. request. 2. reliance.

tanomi ni naru, *vb.* 頼みになる be reliable.

tanomi ni suru, *vb.* 頼みにする depend on; rely on.

tanomoshii, *adj.* 頼もしい reliable; promising.

tanomu, *vb.* 頼む ask; request.

tanoshii, *adj.* 楽しい enjoyable; pleasant.

tanoshimaseru, *vb.* 楽しませる amuse; entertain.

tanoshimi, *n.* 楽しみ enjoyment; pleasure.

tanoshimi ni suru, *vb.* 楽しみにする look forward to; anticipate.

tanoshimu, *vb.* 楽しむ enjoy.

tanpa, *n.* 短波 shortwave.

tanpaku (na), *adj.* 淡泊 (な) 1. simple (tastes). 2. nonchalant.

tanpaku(shitsu), *n.* 蛋白(質) protein.

tanpen(shōsetsu), *n.* 短編(小説) short story.

tanpo, *n.* 担保 mortgage; security.

tanpopo, *n.* たんぽぽ dandelion.

tanren suru, *vb.* 鍛練する train.

tanri, *n.* 単利 simple interest.

tansei, *n.* 丹精 devotion.

tansei (na), *adj.* 端正 (な) correct.

tanseki, *n.* 胆石 gallstone.

tanshin, *n.* 単身 being alone; being separated (from one's family).

tanshinfunin, *n.* 単身赴任 job transfer (to new location) made without one's family.

tanshuku suru, *vb.* 短縮する curtail; shorten.

tansoku, *n.* 嘆息 sigh.

tansu, *n.* たんす Japanese chest of drawers.

tansū, *n.* 単数 singular (grammar).

tansui, *n.* 淡水 fresh water.

tansuigyo, *n.* 淡水魚 freshwater fish.

tansuikabutsu, *n.* 炭水化物 carbohydrate.

tan-tan to shita, *adj.* 淡々とした disinterested.

tantei, *n.* 探偵 detective work.

tanteishōsetsu, *n.* 探偵小説 detective story.

tanteki (na), *adj.* 端的 (な) direct; incisive.

tanteki ni, *adv.* 端的に directly; to the point.

tantō, *n.* 短刀 dagger.

tantō, *n.* 担当 charge (duty).

tantōchokunyū (na), *adj.* 単刀直入 (な) point-blank; direct.

tantōchokunyū ni, *adv.* 単刀直入に point-blank; directly.

tanuki, *n.* 狸 raccoon-like animal indigenous to Japan.

taoreru, *vb.* 倒れる 1. fall; faint. 2. become bankrupt.

taoru, *n.* タオル (E.) towel.

tappitsu, *n.* 達筆 good penmanship.

tappuri, *adv.* たっぷり 1. abundantly. 2. as much as one likes.

tara, *n.* たら codfish.

tarai, *n.* たらい washbasin.

tarako, *n.* たら子 codfish roe.

tarappu, *n.* タラップ (D. *trap*) movable stairs.

tarasu, *vb.* 垂らす suspend; drop.

tareru, *vb.* 垂れる hang down; sag.

tariki, *n.* 他力 the help of others.

tarinai, *vb.* 足りない be insufficient.

tariru, *vb.* 足りる be sufficient.

taru, *n.* 樽 barrel; cask.

tarumu, *vb.* 弛む become loose; sag.

taryō, *n.* 多量 large quantity.

tasai (na), *adj.* 多才 (な) versatile.

tasai (na), *adj.* 多彩 (な) colorful.

tasan (na), *adj.* 多産 (な) prolific; productive.

tashi, *n.* 足し supplement.

tashika (na), *adj.* 確か (な) 1. sure; secure. 2. reliable.

tashikameru, *vb.* 確かめる make sure; confirm.

tashika ni, *adv.* 確かに definitely.

tashinameru, *vb.* たしなめる admonish; warn.

tashinami, *n.* たしなみ 1. self-control. 2. accomplishments.

tashō (no), *adj.* 多少 (の) a little.

tasogare, *n.* たそがれ twilight.

tassei, *n.* 達成 achievement.

tassei suru, *vb.* 達成する achieve.

tassha (na), *adj.* 達者 (な) 1. skillful. 2. healthy.

tassuru, *vb.* 達する reach; become; **seinen ni tassuru** become an adult.

tasu, *vb.* 足す add.

tasū, *n.* 多数 majority; large number.

tasuke, *n.* 助け help; support.

tasukeru, *vb.* 助ける help; support.

tataeru, *vb.* 賛える praise.

tatakai, *n.* 戦い battle; fight.

tatakau, *vb.* 戦う battle; fight.

tataku, *vb.* 叩く beat; strike.

tatami, *n.* 畳 Japanese straw floor mat.

tatamu, *vb.* 畳む fold.

tatari, *n.* たたり curse.

tataru, *vb.* たたる curse; haunt.

tate, *n.* 盾 shield.

tate, *n.* 縦 length; height; **tate no sen** vertical line.

tategaki, *n.* 縦書き vertical writing.

tategami, *n.* たてがみ mane.

tatekaeru, *vb.* 建て替える remodel (a building); rebuild.

tatekaeru, *vb.* 立て替える make a payment (for someone).

tatekakeru, *vb.* 立て掛ける rest (something) against.

tatemono, *n.* 建物 building.

tateru, *vb.* 建てる 1. build. 2. put upright.

tatetsuzuke ni, *adv.* 立て続けに in succession; one after another.

tatoe, *n.* たとえ example.

tatoeba, *adv.* 例えば for example.

tatoeru, *vb.* たとえる compare to.

tatsu, *vb.* 立つ 1. stand. 2. be built.

tatsu, *vb.* 絶つ、断つ cut off; discontinue.

tatsu, *vb.* 裁つ cut (cloth).

tatsu, *n.* 竜 dragon.

tatsujin, *n.* 達人 expert; master.

tatsumaki, *n.* 竜巻 tornado.

tatta (no), *adv.* たった (の) only.

taue, *n.* 田植え rice-planting.

tawainai, *adj.* たわいない 1. insignificant. 2. absurd.

tawamureru, *vb.* 戯れる play; sport.

tayasui, *adj.* たやすい easy.

tayori, *n.* 便り news; letter.

tayori, *n.* 頼り reliance.

tayorinai, *adj.* 頼りない unreliable.

tayori ni suru, *vb.* 頼りにする rely on.

tayoru, *vb.* 頼る rely on.

tazuneru, *vb.* 尋ねる 1. ask; inquire. 2. search for.

tazuneru, *vb.* 訪ねる visit.

tazusaeru, *vb.* 携える carry with; bring or take with.

tazusawaru, *vb.* 携わる engage (in).

te, *n.* 手 1. hand. 2. means; way. 3. kind; type.

tearai, *n.* 手洗い restroom.

teara (na), *adj.* 手荒 (な) rough; harsh.

teashi, *n.* 手足 hands and feet; limbs.

teatari-shidai ni, *adv.* 手当り次第に haphazardly; at random.

teate, *n.* 手当て 1. allowance. 2. medical treatment.

teatsui, *adj.* 手厚い attentive.

tebanasu, *vb.* 手離す part with.

tebayaku, *adv.* 手早く quickly.

tebiki, *n.* 手引き instruction; manual.

tebukuro, *n.* 手袋 gloves.

tēburu, *n.* テーブル (E.) table.

techō, *n.* 手帳 pocket notebook.

tedashi (o) suru, *vb.* 手出し(を)する 1. meddle. 2. make advances to.

tedori, *n.* 手取り income after taxes.

tegakari, *n.* 手掛かり clue.

tegakeru, *vb.* 手掛ける manage; handle.

tegaki, *n.* 手書き handwriting.

tegaki (no), *adj.* 手書き (の) handwritten.

tegami, *n.* 手紙 letter; **tegami o dasu** mail a letter.

tegara, *n.* 手柄 exploit; credit.

tegaru (na), *adj.* 手軽 (な) easy; quick.

tegata, *n.* 手形 bill; check.

tegatai, *adj.* 手固い solid and steady; reliable.

tegiwa yoi, *adj.* 手際良い skillful.

tegoro (na), *adj.* 手頃 (な) 1. handy. 2. affordable.

tegotae, *n.* 手応え response; ii **tegotae ga aru** get a good response.

tegowai, *adj.* 手ごわい difficult to deal with or overcome.

teguchi, *n.* 手口 method; trick.

tehai suru, *vb.* 手配する 1. arrange; prepare. 2. institute a search.

tehajime ni, *adv.* 手始めに to begin with; in the first place.

tehodoki, *n.* 手ほどき guidance; initiation.

tehon, *n.* 手本 example; model.

tei'an, *n.* 提案 proposal.

teibō, *n.* 堤防 1. embankment. 2. dike.

teichaku suru, *vb.* 定着する settle; take root.

teichingin, *n.* 低賃金 low wages.

teichō (na), *adj.* 低調 (な) low-keyed; inactive.

teichō (na), *adj.* 丁重 (な) polite.

teichō ni, *adv.* 丁重に politely.

teiden, *n.* 停電 power failure.

teido, *n.* 程度 1. criterion; standard; **teido ga takai** high standard. 2. extent; **sono teido made** to that extent.

teien, *n.* 庭園 garden.

teigaku, *n.* 停学 suspension from school.

teigi, *n.* 定義 definition.

teihaku suru, *vb.* 停泊する drop anchor (ship).

teihen, *n.* 底辺 base; bottom.

teihyō, *n.* 定評 1. reputation. 2. notoriety.

tei'in, *n.* 定員 capacity (people).

teiji, *n.* 定時 regular time.

teiji suru, *vb.* 提示する show; present.

teijū suru, *vb.* 定住する settle; reside permanently.

teika, *n.* 定価 list price.

teikanshi, *n.* 定冠詞 definite article.

teika suru, *vb.* 低下する drop; decrease.

teikei suru, *vb.* 提携する cooperate; form a partnership.

teiketsuatsu, *n.* 低血圧 low blood

pressure.

teiki, *n.* 定期 routine; regularity.

teikibin, *n.* 定期便 scheduled flight.

teikiken, *n.* 定期券 commutation ticket.

teikinri, *n.* 低金利 low interest.

teikiyokin, *n.* 定期預金 time deposit.

teikō, *n.* 抵抗 resistance; defiance.

teikoku, *n.* 定刻 appointed time.

teikoku, *n.* 帝国 empire.

teikokushugi, *n.* 帝国主義 imperialism.

teikō suru, *vb.* 抵抗する resist; rebel.

teikyō suru, *vb.* 提供する offer; provide; sponsor.

teikyūbi, *n.* 定休日 regular day off.

teinei (na), *adj.* 丁寧 (な) 1. polite; courteous. 2. careful.

teinei ni, *adv.* 丁寧に 1. politely; courteously. 2. carefully.

teinen, *n.* 停年 retirement age.

teinen-taishokusha, *n.* 定年退職者 retiree.

teiō, *n.* 帝王 emperor.

teion, *n.* 低温 low temperature.

te'ire, *n.* 手入れ 1. care. 2. police raid.

te'ire suru, *vb.* 手入れする take care of.

teiryū, *n.* 底流 undercurrent.

teiryūjo, *n.* 停留所 bus stop.

teisai, *n.* 体裁 appearance; looks.

teisei, *n.* 訂正 correction.

teisei suru, *vb.* 訂正する correct.

teisen, *n.* 停戦 cease-fire.

teisetsu, *n.* 定説 established theory.

teisetsu (na), *adj.* 貞節 (な) faithful (woman).

teisha, *n.* 停車 stopping (vehicle).

teishi suru, *vb.* 停止する stop;

suspend.

teishoku, *n.* 定職 permanent job;
  teishoku ni tsuku get a
  permanent job.

teishoku, *n.* 定食 set meal; table
  d'hôte.

teishoku suru, *vb.* 抵触する
  conflict with.

teishō suru, *vb.* 提唱する propose.

teishu, *n.* 亭主 husband.

teishukanpaku, *n.* 亭主関白
  tyrannical husband.

teishuku (na), *adj.* 貞淑 (な)
  virtuous (woman).

teishūnyū, *n.* 定収入 steady
  income.

teishutsu suru, *vb.* 提出する hand
  in; submit.

teiso, *n.* 提訴 (court) suit; appeal.

teisō, *n.* 貞操 chastity (female).

teitai, *n.* 停滞 paralysis; slump;
  stagnation.

teitaku, *n.* 邸宅 mansion;
  residence.

teitō, *n.* 抵当 mortgage.

teitoku, *n.* 提督 admiral.

teizoku (na), *adj.* 低俗 (な) vulgar.

tejika (na, no), *adj.* 手近 (な、の)
  1. nearby. 2. familiar.

tejina, *n.* 手品 magic trick.

tejō, *n.* 手錠 handcuffs.

tejun, *n.* 手順 process;
  arrangement.

teki, *n.* 敵 enemy; opponent.

-teki (na) 的 (な) (adjectival suffix)
  -ic; -ing; -ish; -like, etc.; **shinbi-
  teki na** aesthetic.

tekido (na, no), *adj.* 適度 (な、の)
  appropriate; moderate.

tekigō suru, *vb.* 適合する adapt;
  fit; suit.

tekihatsu suru, *vb.* 摘発する
  expose; disclose.

teki'i, *n.* 敵意 hostility.

tekikaku (na), *adj.* 的確 (な)
  accurate; precise.

tekikaku (na), *adj.* 適格 (な)
  qualified.

tekikaku ni, *adv.* 的確に
  accurately; precisely.

tekimen (no), *adj.* てきめん (の)
  1. noticeable; evident. 2. quick.

tekininsha, *n.* 適任者 qualified
  person.

tekiō suru, *vb.* 適応する adapt
  oneself to.

tekipaki (to), *adv.* てきぱき (と) 1.
  efficiently. 2. quickly.

tekireiki, *n.* 適齢期 marriageable
  age.

tekisei, *n.* 適正 aptitude.

tekisetsu (na), *adj.* 適切 (な)
  proper; fitting.

teki suru, *vb.* 適する fit; be
  suitable.

tekisuto, *n.* テキスト (E.)
  textbook.

tekitai suru, *vb.* 敵対する oppose;
  fight.

tekitō (na), *adj.* 適当 (な) 1.
  appropriate; suitable. 2.
  reasonable.

tekiyō suru, *vb.* 適用する apply.

tekkai suru, *vb.* 撤回する
  withdraw; retract.

tekkin-konkurīto, *n.* 鉄筋コンク
  リート reinforced concrete.

tekkō, *n.* 鉄鋼 steel.

tekkyō, *n.* 鉄橋 iron bridge.

tekkyo suru, *vb.* 撤去する remove.

teko, *n.* てこ lever.

tekozuru, *vb.* てこずる have
  difficulty dealing with.

tekubi, *n.* 手首 wrist.

tema, *n.* 手間 (a lot of) time;
  trouble; **tema ga kakaru** require
  a lot of time and trouble.

tēma, *n.* テーマ (E.) theme; topic.

temachin, *n.* 手間賃 wage.

temae, *n.* 手前 1. front. 2. this side. 3. social propriety.

temane, *n.* 手真似 gesture.

temaneki suru, *vb.* 手招きする beckon.

temari, *n.* 手まり Japanese handball.

temawarihin, *n.* 手回り品 personal belongings.

temawashi, *n.* 手回し preparations; arrangements.

temijika ni, *adv.* 手短かに briefly.

temiyage, *n.* 手土産 present.

-temo ても even if; **okane ga nakutemo** even if (I) don't have any money.

temoto ni, *adv.* 手元に at hand.

ten, *n.* 天 sky; heaven.

ten, *n.* 点 1. dot; period; point. 2. grade; mark; score. 3. item.

tenaoshi, *n.* 手直し correction; touching up.

tenareta, *adj.* 手馴れた skillful; experienced.

tenbō, *n.* 展望 1. prospect. 2. vista.

tendon, *n.* 天丼 tempura on rice.

tengoku, *n.* 天国 paradise; heaven.

tengyō, *n.* 転業 career change.

te ni amaru, *vb.* 手に余る be unmanageable.

te ni ireru, *vb.* 手に入れる obtain.

tenimotsu, *n.* 手荷物 carry-on baggage.

ten'in, *n.* 店員 store clerk; salesperson.

tenji, *n.* 展示 display; exhibition.

tenjō, *n.* 天井 ceiling.

tenka, *n.* 天下 world; an entire nation.

tenka, *n.* 点火 ignition; lighting.

tenkai, *n.* 展開 development.

tenkan, *n.* てんかん epilepsy.

tenkan suru, *vb.* 転換する change; convert.

tenka suru, *vb.* 点火する ignite; light; fire up.

tenka suru, *vb.* 転化する change.

tenkei, *n.* 典型 pattern; model; example.

tenkei-teki (na), *adj.* 典型的 (な) typical.

tenken, *n.* 点検 inspection.

tenken suru, *vb.* 点検する inspect.

tenki, *n.* 転機 turning point.

tenki, *n.* 天気 weather; good weather.

tenkin, *n.* 転勤 job transfer.

tenkiyohō, *n.* 天気予報 weather forecast.

tenko, *n.* 点呼 roll call.

tenkō, *n.* 天候 weather.

tenkyo, *n.* 転居 move; change of address.

tenkyo, *n.* 典拠 authority; source.

tenmado, *n.* 天窓 skylight.

tenmetsu suru, *vb.* 点滅する go on and off; blink.

tenmongaku, *n.* 天文学 astronomy.

ten'nen (no), *adj.* 天然 (の) natural; **ten'nenshigen** natural resources.

ten'nō, *n.* 天皇 emperor of Japan.

tenohira, *n.* 掌 palm (hand).

tenpo, *n.* 店舗 store.

tenpuku suru, *vb.* 転覆する capsize; overturn.

tenpu (no), *adj.* 天賦 (の) inborn.

tenpura, *n.* 天ぷら tempura (Japanese deep-fried dish).

tenraku, *n.* 転落 fall; decline.

tenrankai, *n.* 展覧会 exhibition.

tensai, *n.* 天才 genius.

tensai, *n.* 天災 natural disaster.

tensaku, *n.* 添削 correction.

tensen, *n.* 点線 dotted line.

tenshi, *n.* 天使 angel.

tenshoku, *n.* 転職 job or career change.

tenshu, *n.* 店主 shop owner.

tenshutsu, *n.* 転出 transfer.

tensū, *n.* 点数 points; score.

tentai, *n.* 天体 heavenly body.

tenteki, *n.* 点滴 intravenous drip.

tentōmushi, *n.* てんとう虫 ladybug.

tenugui, *n.* 手拭い Japanese-style towel.

tenurui, *adj.* 手ぬるい permissive.

teochi, *n.* 手落ち oversight; negligence.

te o dasu, *vb.* 手を出す 1. get involved in. 2. meddle.

teokure, *n.* 手遅れ occurring too late.

te o musubu, *vb.* 手を結ぶ cooperate; unite with.

te o tsukusu, *vb.* 手をつくす do everything possible.

teppai, *n.* 撤廃 abolition.

teppan'yaki, *n.* 鉄板焼き food grilled on iron griddle.

teppei, *n.* 撤兵 evacuation (military).

teppen, *n.* てっぺん top; summit.

teppō, *n.* 鉄砲 gun.

tēpu, *n.* テープ (E.) tape.

tera, *n.* 寺 temple.

terasu, *vb.* 照らす illuminate; light.

terebi, *n.* テレビ (E.) television set.

terebi-bangumi, *n.* テレビ番組 television program.

terehon-kādo, *n.* テレホンカード (E.) telephone card.

teriyaki, *n.* 照り焼き teriyaki.

teru, *vb.* 照る shine.

tesage, *n.* 手提げ 1. shopping bag. 2. briefcase.

tesaguri suru, *vb.* 手探りする grope.

tesei (no), *adj.* 手製 (の) handmade; homemade.

tesō(mi), *n.* 手相(見) palm reading.

tesū, *n.* 手数 pains; trouble.

tesuri, *n.* 手すり handrail.

tesūryō, *n.* 手数料 handling fee; commission.

tesuto, *n.* テスト (E.) test; examination.

tetsu, *n.* 鉄 iron.

tetsubō, *n.* 鉄棒 iron bar.

tetsudai, *n.* 手伝い 1. helper. 2. help.

tetsudau, *vb.* 手伝う help.

tetsudō, *n.* 鉄道 railroad.

tetsugaku, *n.* 哲学 philosophy.

tetsuke(kin), *n.* 手付け(金) deposit (money).

tetsuya de, *adv.* 徹夜で all night.

tetsuya suru, *vb.* 徹夜する stay up all night.

tetsuzuki, *n.* 手続き procedure.

tettai suru, *vb.* 撤退する withdraw.

tettei suru, *vb.* 徹底する be thorough.

tettei-teki ni, *adv.* 徹底的に completely; thoroughly.

tettoribayai, *adj.* 手っ取り早い quick; easy.

tewatasu, *vb.* 手渡す hand to; submit.

tezawari, *n.* 手触り touch; feel.

tezukuri (no), *adj.* 手作り (の) handmade; homemade.

to, *n.* 戸 door.

to, *parti.* と 1. *conj.* and; **anata to watashi** you and me. 2. *prep.* with; **haha to** with my mother. 3. *conj.* when; **uchi ni kaeru to** when I came back home. 4. *conj.* if; **ame ga furu to** if it rains.

tō, *n.* 十 ten; ten years old.

tō, *n.* 藤 rattan.

tō, *n.* 塔 pagoda; tower.

tō, *n.* 党 group; political party.

-tō 等 1. etc.; **sushi, sashimitō** sushi, sashimi, etc. 2. place (competition); **nitō** second place.

tōan, *n.* 答案 answer sheet (used during examination).

tobaku, *n.* 賭博 gambling.

tōban, *n.* 当番 being on duty.

tobasu, *vb.* 飛ばす 1. fly; speed. 2. skip over.

tōben, *n.* 答弁 response; answer.

tobiagaru, *vb.* 飛び上がる jump; leap.

tobidasu, *vb.* 飛び出す jump out.

tobikakaru, *vb.* 飛びかかる jump at.

tobikiri (no), *adj.* とびきり (の) exceptional; outstanding.

tobikomi, *n.* 飛び込み diving.

tobikomu, *vb.* 飛び込む dive into; jump into.

tobikosu, *vb.* 飛び越す leap; fly over; jump over.

tobimawaru, *vb.* 飛び回る jump around; fly around.

tobinoru, *vb.* 飛び乗る jump into (vehicle).

tobinukete, *adv.* 飛び抜けて by far.

tobiokiru, *vb.* 飛び起きる jump up; get up.

tobioriru, *vb.* 飛び降りる jump down.

tobira, *n.* 扉 1. door. 2. title page.

tobisaru, *vb.* 飛び去る fly away.

tobitatsu, *vb.* 飛び立つ take flight.

tobitsuku, *vb.* 飛び付く jump at.

tōbō, *n.* 逃亡 escape; flight.

tobokeru, *vb.* とぼける feign innocence or ignorance.

tōbōsha, *n.* 逃亡者 fugitive.

toboshii, *adj.* 乏しい scarce.

tobu, *vb.* 飛ぶ 1. fly. 2. skip (number, page).

tobu, *vb.* 跳ぶ jump; leap.

tōbu, *n.* 頭部 head.

tōbu, *n.* 東部 eastern region.

tōbun, *n.* 糖分 sugar.

tōbun, *adv.* 当分 for the moment; for a while.

tōbun suru, *vb.* 等分する divide equally.

tōchaku, *n.* 到着 arrival.

tōchaku suru, *vb.* 到着する arrive.

tochi, *n.* 土地 1. land; soil. 2. locality.

tōchi, *n.* 当地 this place; this town.

tōchi suru, *vb.* 統治する govern; control.

tochū, *adv.* 途中 halfway.

tochū de, *adv.* 途中で 1. en route. 2. in the middle.

todaeru, *vb.* 途絶える cease; end.

tōdai, *n.* 灯台 lighthouse.

todana, *n.* 戸棚 cupboard.

todokeru, *vb.* 届ける 1. deliver. 2. notify.

todoku, *vb.* 届く reach; be received.

todomaru, *vb.* 留まる stay.

todomeru, *vb.* 止める 1. put an end to. 2. detain.

todoroki, *n.* とどろき roar; thunder.

todoroku, *vb.* とどろく 1. roar; thunder. 2. resound; spread (fame). 3. throb.

tōei suru, *vb.* 投影する project.

tōen, *n.* 遠縁 distant relative.

tōfu, *n.* 豆腐 tofu; bean curd.

togameru, *vb.* 咎める blame.

tōgarashi, *n.* 唐辛子 hot pepper.

togarasu, *vb.* 尖らす sharpen.

togaru, *vb.* 尖る be pointed.

togatta, *adj.* 尖った pointed.

toge, *n.* とげ thorn.

tōge, *n.* 峠 1. mountain pass or peak. 2. crucial point.

tōgei, *n.* 陶芸 ceramic art.

tōgeika, *n.* 陶芸家 potter.

togeru, *vb.* 遂げる accomplish.

tōgi, *n.* 討議 discussion.

tōgi, *n.* 闘技 competition (strength or skill).

togireru, *vb.* 途切れる discontinue; halt.

tōgoku suru, *vb.* 投獄する imprison.

tōgō suru, *vb.* 統合する combine; unite.

togu, *vb.* 研ぐ 1. sharpen. 2. wash (rice).

toguchi, *n.* 戸口 doorway.

tōgyū, *n.* 闘牛 bullfighting.

tōhi, *n.* 当否 right or wrong.

tōhi, *n.* 逃避 escape; evasion.

toho, *n.* 徒歩 walking.

tōhō, *pron.* 当方 I; we.

toho de, *adv.* 徒歩で on foot.

tōhoku, *n.* 東北 northeast.

tohō mo nai, *adj.* 途方もない absurd; unreasonable.

tohō ni kureru, *vb.* 途方に暮れる be at a loss.

tōhyō, *n.* 投票 vote; voting.

tōhyōsha, *n.* 投票者 voter.

toi, *n.* 問い question.

toi, *n.* 樋 rain gutter.

tōi, *adj.* 遠い distant; far.

toi'awaseru, *n.* 問い合わせる inquire; refer to.

toiki, *n.* 吐息 sigh.

tōin, *n.* 党員 party member.

toire, toiretto, *n.* トイレ、トイレット (E.) toilet; restroom.

toiretto pēpā, *n.* トイレットペーパー (E.) toilet paper.

toitadasu, *vb.* 問い質す inquire; question.

tōitsu, *n.* 統一 1. standardization. 2. unification.

-to iu という named; called; **Keiji-**

to iu hito a person called Keiji.

-to iu no ni というのに although; **ikuna-to iu noni** although I say "don't go."

tōji, *n.* 当時 old days; those days; **tōji wa** in those days.

tōji, *n.* 冬至 winter solstice.

tōji, *n.* 湯治 stay at a hot spring resort.

tōjiba, *n.* 湯治場 hot spring resort.

tōjiki, *n.* 陶磁器 chinaware.

tojikomeru, *vb.* 閉じ込める confine; shut up.

tojikomoru, *vb.* 閉じこもる shut oneself up.

tojimari suru, *vb.* 戸締りする lock the door(s) and window(s).

tojiru, *vb.* 閉じる 1. close; shut. 2. end.

tojiru, *vb.* 綴じる bind (books).

tōjiru, *vb.* 投じる 1. throw into. 2. invest.

tōjitsu, *n.* 当日 that day; designated day; **tōjitsukagiri** valid only for that day; **tōjitsuken** ticket sold on the day of the performance.

tōjō, *n.* 登場 entrance (stage, story).

tōjō, *n.* 搭乗 boarding (ship, plane).

tōjōin, *n.* 搭乗員 crew member.

tōjōjinbutsu, *n.* 登場人物 cast; characters (play, story).

tōjōken, *n.* 搭乗券 boarding pass.

tōjō suru, *vb.* 搭乗する board (ship, plane).

tōka, *n.* 十日 tenth day of the month.

tokai, *n.* 都会 city.

tōkan suru, *vb.* 投函する mail.

tokasu, *vb.* 溶かす melt; dissolve; liquefy.

tokasu, *vb.* 梳かす comb (hair).

tōka suru, *vb.* 投下する 1. drop;

discharge. 2. invest.

tokei, *n.* 時計 clock; watch.

tōkei, *n.* 統計 statistics.

tōkeigaku, *n.* 統計学 statistics (the science).

tokekomu, *vb.* 溶け込む adjust; blend in with.

tōken, *n.* 刀剣 swords.

tokeru, *vb.* 溶ける melt; dissolve.

tokeru, *vb.* 解ける 1. untie; undo. 2. solve.

tōketsu, *n.* 凍結 freezing.

toki, *n.* 時 1. time. 2. opportunity; timing.

-toki とき when; **kare ga nihon ni itta-toki** when he visited Japan.

tōki, *n.* 陶器 chinaware; pottery.

tōki, *n.* 登記 registration.

tōki, *n.* 投機 investment; speculation.

tōki, *n.* 冬期 winter; **tōki-orinpikku** Winter Olympic Games.

tōkibi, *n.* とうきび corn (food).

tokidoki, *adv.* 時々 sometimes; now and then.

tokifuseru, *vb.* 説き伏せる persuade; convince.

tokimeku, *vb.* ときめく throb.

toki ni wa, *adv.* 時には sometimes.

tokitama, *adv.* 時たま now and then.

tokkahin, *n.* 特価品 item sold at a bargain price.

tokken, *n.* 特権 privilege.

tokkun, *n.* 特訓 crash course.

tokku ni, *adv.* とっくに a long time ago; already.

tokkuri, *n.* 徳利 earthenware container for sake.

tokkyo, *n.* 特許 patent.

tokkyū, *n.* 特急 express train.

toko, *n.* 床 1. floor. 2. bed.

tōkō, *n.* 陶工 potter.

tōkō, *n.* 登校 attendance at school.

tōkō, *n.* 投稿 written contribution (to a journal).

tokonoma, *n.* 床の間 alcove (for hanging scrolls or for ikebana).

tokoro, *n.* 所 1. place. 2. part. 3. address; house.

-tokoro ところ 1. on the point of; almost; **shinu-tokoro** on the point of death. 2. just when; **tabeteiru-tokoro** just when (I) was eating.

tokoro de, *adv.* ところで by the way.

tokoro ga, *conj.* ところが but.

tokoya, *n.* 床屋 barbershop.

toku, *n.* 徳 virtue.

toku, *n.* 得 benefit; profit.

toku, *vb.* 解く 1. solve. 2. undo. 3. dismiss. 4. absolve.

tokubetsu (na, no), *adj.* 特別 (な、の) special; exceptional.

tokuchō, *n.* 特徴 characteristic; special feature.

tokuchō, *n.* 特長 strong point.

tokudai, *n.* 特大 extra-large size.

tokudane, *n.* 特種 scoop (journalism).

tokugi, *n.* 特技 one's special talent.

tokuhyō, *n.* 得票 number of votes obtained.

tokui (na), *adj.* 得意 (な) 1. skillful. 2. elated.

tokui (na), *adj.* 特異 (な) peculiar; unique.

tokui(saki), *n.* 得意(先) good customer.

tokumei, *n.* 匿名 anonymity.

tokumei (no), *adj.* 匿名 (の) anonymous.

toku ni, *adv.* 特に especially; particularly.

tokusaku, *n.* 得策 good idea; wise

plan.

tokusan-butsu/-hin, *n.* 特産物、
～品 special product of a particular
location.

tokusei, *n.* 特性 special quality;
idiosyncrasy.

tokusha, *n.* 特赦 amnesty.

tokushitsu, *n.* 特質 peculiarity;
characteristic.

tokushoku, *n.* 特色 distinguishing
characteristic.

tokushu (na), *adj.* 特殊 (な)
unique; peculiar; special.

tokusokujō, *n.* 督促状 dunning
notice.

toku suru, *vb.* 得する benefit;
profit.

tokutei (no), *adj.* 特定 (の)
particular; specific.

tokuten, *n.* 特典 advantage;
privilege.

tokuten, *n.* 得点 marks; score.

tokutō (no), *adj.* 特等 (の) special;
top-grade.

tokuyō (no), *adj.* 徳用 (の)
economical.

tokuyū (na, no), *adj.* 特有 (な、
の) unique; peculiar; **nihon ni
tokuyū no** peculiar to Japan.

tōkyō, *n.* 東京 Tokyo.

tōkyoku, *n.* 当局 authorities.

tōkyū, *n.* 等級 grade; ranking.

tomadoi, *n.* とまどい
disorientation.

tomadou, *vb.* とまどう be
disoriented; be bewildered.

tomarikyaku, *n.* 泊まり客
overnight guest.

tomaru, *vb.* 止まる stop.

tomaru, *vb.* 留まる 1. stay (on);
perch. 2. be fastened.

tomaru, *vb.* 泊まる stay overnight
(house, hotel).

tomato, *n.* トマト (E.) tomato.

tōmawari suru, *vb.* 遠回りする
make a detour; go a roundabout
way.

tōmawashi ni, *adv.* 遠回しに
indirectly; in a roundabout way.

tōmei (na), *adj.* 透明 (な)
transparent; **tōmeiningen**
invisible man.

tōmen (no), *adj.* 当面 (の) urgent.

tomeru, *vb.* 止める stop;
discontinue; turn off.

tomeru, *vb.* 留める fasten; button;
attach.

tomeru, *vb.* 泊める lodge someone
overnight.

tomi, *n.* 富 wealth.

tōmin, *n.* 冬眠 hibernation.

tōmin, *n.* 島民 islander(s).

tomo, *n.* 友 friend.

tomo, *n.* 供 attendant.

-tomo 共 both; **futari-tomo** both
(of us).

-tomo とも even though; whatever
(whoever, whichever, etc.) may
...; **nani ga okorō-tomo**
whatever may happen.

tomodachi, *n.* 友達 friend.

tomokaku, *adv.* ともかく 1.
anyway; in any case. 2. aside
from.

tomonau, *vb.* 伴う take with; be
accompanied by.

tomo ni 共に 1. *adj.* both. 2. *adv.*
together.

tōmorokoshi, *n.* とうもろこし
corn (food).

tomosu, *vb.* 灯す light (candle,
etc.).

tomu, *vb.* 富む be rich; be wealthy;
prosper.

tomurai, *n.* 弔い funeral;
mourning.

tomurau, *vb.* 弔う 1. mourn the
dead. 2. hold a funeral.

ton, *n.* トン (E.) ton; tonnage.

tonaeru, *vb.* 唱える 1. advocate. 2. recite.

tonaeru, *vb.* 称える name.

tōnan, *n.* 盗難 burglary; robbery.

tōnan, *n.* 東南 southeast.

tōnan-ajia, *n.* 東南アジア Southeast Asia.

tōnansha, *n.* 盗難車 stolen car.

tonari, *n.* 隣 next-door neighbor; house next door.

tonari (no), *adj.* 隣 (の) next-door; next.

tonbo, *n.* とんぼ dragonfly.

tonchaku suru, *vb.* 頓着する care about; mind.

tondemonai とんでもない 1. *adj.* horrible; surprising. 2. *adj.* unreasonable. 3. *interj.* My pleasure! 4. *interj.* Not a chance!

tō ni, *adv.* とうに already; a long time ago.

tonikaku, *adv.* とにかく 1. anyway. 2. really; indeed.

tōnin, *n.* 当人 the person in question.

tonkatsu, *n.* 豚カツ pork cutlet.

ton'neru, *n.* トンネル (E.) tunnel.

tono, *n.* 殿 lord; master.

tonogata, *n.* 殿方 gentleman.

ton'ya, *n.* 問屋 wholesaler.

tōnyōbyō, *n.* 糖尿病 diabetes.

toppa suru, *vb.* 突破する break through.

toppatsu suru, *vb.* 突発する break out.

toppatsu-teki (na), *adj.* 突発的 (な) unpredictable; unexpected.

toppi (na), *adj.* 突飛 (な) reckless; extraordinary.

toppu, *n.* トップ (E.) top.

toppū, *n.* 突風 gust of wind.

tora, *n.* 虎 tiger.

toraburu, *n.* トラブル (E.) trouble.

toraeru, *vb.* 捕える、捉える 1. arrest; capture. 2. understand.

tōrai suru, *vb.* 到来する arrive.

torakku, *n.* トラック (E.) truck.

torakku, *n.* トラック (E.) track.

toranpu, *n.* トランプ playing cards; card game.

toreru, *vb.* とれる 1. be caught (fish, etc.); be harvested. 2. come off. 3. go away; vanish.

tori, *n.* 鳥 1. bird. 2. poultry.

tōri, *n.* 通り 1. street; avenue. 2. understanding.

-tōri (ni) とおりに as; **Watashi no iu-tōri ni shiro.** Do as I say! **sensei no ossharu-tōri ni** as the teacher says.

toriaezu, *adv.* とりあえず for the moment.

toriageru, *vb.* 取り上げる 1. take up; feature. 2. adopt. 3. take away. 4. pick up.

toriatsukai, *n.* 取り扱い handling; treatment.

toriatsukau, *vb.* 取り扱う handle; treat.

toriawase, *n.* 取り合わせ assortment; combination.

torichigaeru, *vb.* 取り違える misunderstand.

toridasu, *vb.* 取り出す take out; extract.

toride, *n.* 砦 fortress.

torie, *n.* 取り柄 good point; merit.

torihada, *n.* 鳥肌 goose pimples; **torihada ga tatsu** get goose pimples.

torihazusu, *vb.* 取り外す take off; remove.

torihiki, *n.* 取り引き transaction; business deal.

torihiki-kakaku, *n.* 取り引き価格 market price.

tori'i, *n.* 鳥居 shrine gate.

tori'ireru, *vb.* 取り入れる 1. take in; take up; use. 2. harvest.

torikaeru, *vb.* 取り替える change; exchange; replace.

torikaesu, *vb.* 取り返す recover; take back.

torikago, *n.* 鳥籠 birdcage.

torikakaru, *vb.* 取り掛かる launch; start.

torikakomu, *vb.* 取り囲む surround.

torikesu, *vb.* 取り消す cancel; repeal.

toriko, *n.* 虜 captive; prisoner.

tōrikosu, *vb.* 通り超す go beyond.

torikowasu, *vb.* 取り壊す raze; tear down.

torikumu, *vb.* 取り組む 1. wrestle with. 2. deal with.

torimaku, *vb.* 取り巻く surround.

tōrimichi, *n.* 通り道 road; pathway.

torimidasu, *vb.* 取り乱す lose control; be confused.

torimodosu, *vb.* 取り戻す get back.

torimotsu, *vb.* 取り持つ mediate.

torinaosu, *vb.* 取り直す recover; **ki o torinaosu** cheer up.

torinasu, *vb.* 取りなす mediate.

torinozoku, *vb.* 取り除く eliminate; remove.

tōrinukeru, *vb.* 通り抜ける pass through.

torisageru, *vb.* 取り下げる withdraw.

torishimaru, *vb.* 取り締まる control; oversee.

torishiraberu, *vb.* 取り調べる investigate.

tōrisugiru, *vb.* 通り過ぎる pass by; pass over.

toritome ga nai, *adj.* とりとめがない meandering; incoherent.

toritsugi-nin/-sho, *n.* 取り次ぎ人、～所 agent; agency.

toritsugu, *vb.* 取り次ぐ convey; transmit.

toritsukeru, *vb.* 取り付ける install; equip.

toriwake, *adv.* とりわけ above all; especially.

toriwakeru, *vb.* 取り分ける divide; distribute.

toriyameru, *vb.* 取り止める cancel.

toriyoseru, *vb.* 取り寄せる order.

toro, *n.* tuna meat prized for its oil content (sushi).

torō, *n.* 徒労 vain attempt.

tōrō, *n.* 灯籠 lantern.

tōroku-hi/-ryō, *n.* 登録費、～料 registration fee.

tōroku suru, *vb.* 登録する register; enroll.

tōron, *n.* 討論 debate; discussion.

tōron suru, *vb.* 討論する debate; discuss.

toru, *vb.* 取る 1. get; take; pick up. 2. eat; take (food, medicine, etc.). 3. take (course). 4. steal; rob. 5. subscribe.

toru, *vb.* 撮る take (a photograph).

toru, *vb.* 採る 1. hire. 2. adopt. 3. collect; pick up.

toru, *vb.* 捕る catch.

tōru, *vb.* 通る 1. pass through or by. 2. pass (examination).

toruko, *n.* トルコ Turkey.

toryō, *n.* 塗料 paint.

tōsaku, *n.* 倒錯 perversion.

tōsaku, *n.* 盗作 plagiarism.

tōsan, *n.* 父さん one's father (daddy).

tōsan, *n.* 倒産 bankruptcy.

tōsatsu(ryoku), *n.* 洞察力 insight.

tōsei, *n.* 統制 control.

tōsei, *n.* 陶製 earthenware.

tōsei (no), *adj.* 当世 (の) current;

contemporary.

tōseifū (no), *adj.* 当世風 (の) up-to-date; current; in vogue.

tōseikakaku, *n.* 統制価格 price controls.

tōseikeizai, *n.* 統制経済 controlled economy.

tōsen suru, *vb.* 当選する win an election.

tōsha, *n.* 投射 projection.

toshi, *n.* 年 age; year.

toshi, *n.* 都市 city.

tōshi, *n.* 投資 investment.

tōshi, *n.* 闘士 activist.

tōshi, *n.* 闘志 fighting spirit.

tōshibangō, *n.* 通し番号 serial number.

toshigoro, *n.* 年頃 1. marriageable age. 2. puberty.

toshin, *n.* 都心 city center.

tōshindai (no), *adj.* 等身大 (の) life-size.

toshishita (no), *adj.* 年下 (の) younger.

toshitsuki, *n.* 年月 time; years.

toshiue (no), *adj.* 年上 (の) senior; older.

toshiyori, *n.* 年寄り elderly person.

toshiyori (no), *adj.* 年寄り (の) elderly.

tosho, *n.* 図書 books.

tōsho, *n.* 当初 beginning.

tōsho, *n.* 投書 letter to the editor.

toshokan, *n.* 図書館 library.

tōshu, *n.* 党首 leader (political party).

tōshu, *n.* 投手 pitcher (baseball).

tōshū suru, *vb.* 踏襲する follow.

tosō, *n.* 塗装 coat of paint.

tōsō, *n.* 闘争 1. fight. 2. labor strike.

tōsō, *n.* 逃走 escape; flight.

tōsotsu suru, *vb.* 統率する command; lead.

tossa (no), *adj.* とっさ (の) instantaneous.

tossa ni, *adv.* とっさ (に) on the spot; impromptu.

tosshin suru, *vb.* 突進する rush at.

tōsu, *vb.* 通す 1. let someone pass; pass (an object) through. 2. admit; show in. 3. penetrate.

tōsui, *n.* 陶酔 intoxication; ecstasy.

tōsui suru, *vb.* 陶酔する be intoxicated; be in ecstasy.

tōsuto, *n.* トースト (E.) toast (bread).

tōta, *n.* 淘汰 selection.

totan ni, *adv.* 途端に at the very moment.

tōtatsu suru, *vb.* 到達する reach; attain.

totei, *n.* 徒弟 apprentice.

tōtei, *adv.* 到底 (with negative) not by any means; not at all.

totemo, *adv.* とても very.

tōtō, *adv.* とうとう at last; after all.

tōtobu, *vb.* 尊ぶ respect; esteem highly.

tōtoi, *adj.* 尊い 1. sacred. 2. important; valuable.

totonoeru, *vb.* 整える 1. put in order; organize. 2. prepare; arrange.

totonou, *vb.* 整う、調う 1. be in order. 2. be ready.

tōtotsu (na), *adj.* 唐突 (な) sudden; abrupt.

totsugeki, *n.* 突撃 charge; assault.

totsugu, *vb.* 嫁ぐ get married (bride).

totsunyū suru, *vb.* 突入する enter; rush into.

totsuzen (ni), *adv.* 突然 (に) abruptly; suddenly.

totsuzen (no), *adj.* 突然 (の) abrupt; sudden.

totte, *n.* 取っ手 doorknob; handle.

-totte とって for; to; **watashi ni-totte** to me.

tottekawaru, *vb.* 取って代わる replace; supplant.

totteoku, *vb.* 取って置く set aside.

tou, *vb.* 問う ask; inquire.

tōwaku, *n.* 当惑 embarrassment.

tōyō, *n.* 東洋 East; Orient.

tōyōjin, *n.* 東洋人 Oriental (person).

tōyō suru, *vb.* 登用する employ; promote.

tōyu, *n.* 灯油 kerosene.

tōza, *n.* 当座 the time being.

tōza (no), *adj.* 当座 (の) temporary.

tōzai, *n.* 東西 east and west; East and West.

tōzainanboku, *n.* 東西南北 four directions; north, south, east, and west.

tōzakaru, *vb.* 遠ざかる withdraw; recede.

tōzakeru, *vb.* 遠ざける alienate; keep away from.

tozan, *n.* 登山 mountain climbing.

tozasu, *vb.* 閉ざす shut; lock.

tōzayokin, *n.* 当座預金 checking account.

tōzen, *adv.* 当然 naturally.

tōzen (no), *adj.* 当然 (の) natural; rightful.

tōzoku, *n.* 盗賊 robber; burglar.

tsū, *n.* 通 connoisseur; expert.

tsuā, *n.* ツアー (E.) tour.

tsuba(ki), *n.* 唾 saliva.

tsubaki, *n.* 椿 camellia.

tsubame, *n.* つばめ swallow (bird).

tsubasa, *n.* 翼 wing.

tsubo, *n.* 壺 jar; pot; urn.

tsubomi, *n.* つぼみ bud.

tsubu, *n.* 粒 grain.

tsubureru, *vb.* つぶれる 1. be crushed. 2. go bankrupt.

tsuburu, *vb.* つぶる close (eyes).

tsubusu, *vb.* つぶす 1. crush; mash. 2. kill (time). 3. wreck.

tsubuyaku, *vb.* 呟く mumble; mutter.

tsuchi, *n.* 土 soil; earth.

tsūchi, *n.* 通知 notification.

tsuchikau, *vb.* 培う nourish; cultivate.

tsūchi suru, *vb.* 通知する notify.

-tsudo つど every time; **unten suru sono-tsudo** every time (I) drive.

tsudoi, *n.* 集い gathering; meeting.

tsudou, *vb.* 集う gather; meet.

tsue, *n.* 杖 walking stick; cane.

tsūgaku suru, *vb.* 通学する attend school.

tsugeru, *vb.* 告げる tell; inform.

tsugi, *n.* 次 next.

tsugi (no), *adj.* 次 (の) next; following.

tsugime, *n.* 継ぎ目 seam; joint.

tsugi ni, *adv.* 次に next (to).

tsugi-tsugi to/ni, *adv.* 次々と、〜に one after another.

tsugō, *n.* 都合 convenience.

tsugō ga warui, *adj.* 都合が悪い inconvenient.

tsugō ga yoi/ii, *adj.* 都合が良い、〜いい convenient.

tsugō suru, *vb.* 都合する manage (to do something).

tsugu, *vb.* 継ぐ succeed to; inherit.

tsugu, *vb.* 注ぐ pour (tea, coffee, etc.).

tsugu, *vb.* 接ぐ graft; join.

tsugumu, *vb.* つぐむ shut (mouth).

tsugunai, *n.* 償い compensation.

tsugunau, *vb.* 償う compensate.

tsui, *n.* 対 pair.

tsui, *adv.* つい 1. accidentally; in spite of oneself. 2. just; only.

-tsuide 次いで second to; **nihon**

ni-tsuide second to Japan.

tsuide ni, *adv.* ついでに 1.
incidentally. 2. in passing; while
(I'm) on the subject.

tsuihō suru, *vb.* 追放する expel;
banish.

tsuika, *n.* 追加 addition.

tsuika suru, *vb.* 追加する add.

tsuikyū suru, *vb.* 追求する pursue;
chase.

tsuikyū suru, *vb.* 追究する seek;
explore; investigate.

tsuikyū suru, *vb.* 追及する press
(for an answer).

tsuin, *n.* ツイン (E.) twin room.

tsui ni, *adv.* 遂に finally; in the
end; after all.

tsuioku, *n.* 追憶 recollection.

tsuiraku, *n.* 墜落 1. plane crash. 2.
fall.

tsuiseki suru, *vb.* 追跡する chase.

tsuishin, *n.* 追伸 postscript.

tsuitachi, *n.* 一日 first day of the
month.

-tsuite ついて about; on; **kabuki
ni-tsuite hanasu** talk about
kabuki.

tsuite'iku, *vb.* ついて行く 1.
follow. 2. keep up with. 3.
accompany.

tsuiteiru, *adj.* ついている lucky.

tsuitekuru, *vb.* ついて来る 1.
come along with. 2. follow.

tsuitotsujiko, *n.* 追突事故 rear-
end collision.

tsuitotsu suru, *vb.* 追突する
collide.

tsuiyasu, *vb.* 費やす spend.

tsuizui suru, *vb.* 追随する follow.

tsūjiru, *vb.* 通じる 1. lead to. 2.
reach by telephone. 3.
communicate; make oneself
understood. 4. be knowledgeable.

tsūjite, *prep.* 通じて 1. by way of.

2. through; throughout.

tsūjō, *adv.* 通常 usually.

tsūjō (no), *adj.* 通常 (の) usual.

tsūjōdōri, *adv.* 通常通り as usual.

tsūka, *n.* 通貨 currency.

tsūka, *n.* 通過 transit; passage.

tsukaeru, *vb.* 仕える serve.

tsukaeru, *vb.* 使える be usable.

tsukaeru, *vb.* つかえる be clogged;
be congested.

tsukai, *n.* 使い 1. errand; **tsukai ni
iku** go on an errand. 2.
messenger.

tsūkai (na), *adj.* 痛快 (な) thrilling;
pleasing.

tsukaihatasu, *vb.* 使い果たす use
up.

tsukaikata, *n.* 使い方 the way to
use.

tsukaikonasu, *vb.* 使いこなす
master; use skillfully.

tsukaisute (no), *adj.* 使い捨て (の)
disposable; **tsukaisute kamera**
disposable camera.

tsukamaeru, *vb.* 捕まえる capture;
catch.

tsukamaru, *vb.* 捕まる be caught.

tsukamaru, *vb.* つかまる hold
tight.

tsukamu, *vb.* つかむ grasp; grip.

tsuka no ma, *n.* 束の間 moment.

tsuka no ma (no), *adj.* 束の間 (の)
momentary; brief; ephemeral.

tsūkan suru, *vb.* 痛感する feel
keenly.

tsukare, *n.* 疲れ fatigue.

tsukareru, *vb.* 疲れる get tired;
become fatigued.

tsukareta, *adj.* 疲れた 1. tired;
fatigued. 2. worn-out.

tsukaru, *vb.* 浸かる be soaked in.

tsūka suru, *vb.* 通過する pass; go
through.

tsukau, *vb.* 使う 1. use. 2. employ

(person). 3. spend; **hyakuen tsukau** spend one hundred yen.

tsukawasu, *vb.* 遣わす dispatch.

tsuke de, *vb.* 付けで on credit.

tsukeiru, *vb.* 付け入る impose upon.

tsukekaeru, *vb.* 付け替える replace; renew.

tsukekuwaeru, *vb.* 付け加える add.

tsukemono, *n.* 漬物 pickled vegetables.

tsukene, *n.* 付け値 bid.

tsukenerau, *vb.* 付け狙う hunt; pursue.

tsukeru, *vb.* 付ける 1. attach. 2. install. 3. follow; pursue. 4. make an entry.

tsukeru, *vb.* 着ける wear (clothing, accessories).

tsukeru, *vb.* 点ける light; turn on.

tsukeru, *vb.* 漬ける 1. soak. 2. marinate.

tsuketasu, *vb.* 付け足す add.

tsuki, *n.* 月 1. moon. 2. month.

tsukiai, *n.* 付き合い association; friendship.

tsukiataru, *vb.* 突き当たる 1. hit against; bump into. 2. come to the end of (street).

tsukiau, *vb.* 付き合う associate with.

tsukiawaseru, *vb.* 付き合わせる compare with.

tsukidashi, *n.* 突き出し 1. appetizer. 2. pushing opponent out of ring (sumo).

tsukidasu, *vb.* 突き出す push out; thrust out.

tsukideru, *vb.* 突き出る stick out; protrude.

tsukihanasu, *vb.* 突き放す 1. abandon. 2. push off.

tsukihi, *n.* 月日 time; years.

tsukikaesu, *vb.* 突き返す 1. push back. 2. send back; turn down.

tsukimatou, *vb.* 付きまとう 1. follow; shadow. 2. haunt.

tsukimi, *n.* 月見 moon-viewing party.

tsūkin, *n.* 通勤 commuting.

tsukinami (na, no), *adj.* 月並 (な、の) commonplace; clichéd.

tsūkindensha, *n.* 通勤電車 commuter train.

tsūkinsha, *n.* 通勤者 commuter.

tsukiotosu, *vb.* 突き落とす push over.

tsukiru, *vb.* 尽きる be used up.

tsukisasu, *vb.* 突き刺す stab; pierce; skewer.

tsukisoi, *n.* 付き添い attendant; nurse.

tsukisou, *vb.* 付き添う 1. accompany. 2. take care of.

tsukitaosu, *vb.* 突き倒す push down.

tsukitobasu, *vb.* 突き飛ばす push away; send flying.

tsukitomeru, *vb.* 突き止める find out; locate; ascertain.

tsukitōsu, *vb.* 突き通す penetrate.

tsukitsumeru, *vb.* 突き詰める investigate thoroughly.

tsukiyo, *n.* 月夜 moonlit night.

tsukizuki (no), *adj.* 月々 (の) monthly.

tsukkendon (na), *adj.* つっけんどん (な) brusque; blunt.

tsukkomu, *vb.* 突っ込む 1. thrust into. 2. jump into.

tsūkō, *n.* 通行 traffic.

tsūkōdome, *n.* 通行止め road closed (sign).

tsūkoku suru, *vb.* 通告する notify.

tsūkōnin, *n.* 通行人 passer(s)by.

tsuku, *vb.* 着く 1. arrive. 2. come in contact with.

tsuku, *vb.* 点く 1. be lit; be ignited. 2. be turned on (television, lights).

tsuku, *vb.* 付く 1. adhere; stick. 2. be added; come along with.

tsuku, *vb.* 突く 1. poke; push; thrust. 2. use (for support).

tsuku, *vb.* 就く 1. start; set out. 2. obtain a position.

tsuku, *vb.* 即く be inaugurated; be enthroned.

tsukue, *n.* 机 desk.

tsukuri, *n.* 造り、作り structure.

tsukuriageru, *vb.* 作り上げる 1. complete. 2. fake.

tsukuribanashi, *n.* 作り話 fiction; lie.

tsukuridasu, *vb.* 作り出す produce; devise.

tsukurikaeru, *vb.* 作り替える remodel; remake.

tsukurikata, *n.* 作り方 recipe.

tsukurinaosu, *vb.* 作り直す remodel; remake.

tsukurou, *vb.* 繕う mend; repair.

tsukuru, *vb.* 作る 1. make; produce. 2. prepare (food). 3. build. 4. grow (plants).

tsukusu, *vb.* 尽くす 1. use up. 2. exert oneself.

tsukuzuku, *adv.* つくずく 1. keenly. 2. carefully.

tsuma, *n.* 妻 one's own wife.

tsumami, *n.* つまみ 1. knob. 2. pinch; **shio hito tsumami** a pinch of salt. 3. appetizer.

tsumamidasu, *vb.* つまみ出す 1. throw out. 2. pick out.

tsumamu, *vb.* つまむ 1. pick up (with the fingers). 2. eat (with the fingers).

tsumaranai, *adj.* つまらない 1. dull; uninspiring. 2. petty; unimportant.

tsumari, *adv.* つまり namely; in short.

tsumaru, *vb.* 詰まる 1. be full; be congested. 2. be at a standstill.

tsumasaki de, *adv.* 爪先で on tiptoe.

tsumayōji, *n.* 爪揚子 toothpick.

tsumazuku, *vb.* つまずく 1. stumble; trip. 2. blunder.

tsume, *n.* 爪 nail; claw.

tsume, *n.* 詰め end game.

tsumekiri, *n.* 爪切り nail clipper.

tsumekomu, *vb.* 詰め込む cram; stuff.

tsumeru, *vb.* 詰める fill; stuff; pack into.

tsumetai, *adj.* 冷たい 1. chilly; cold. 2. cold-hearted.

tsumi, *n.* 罪 sin; crime.

tsumiageru, *vb.* 積み上げる pile up; accumulate.

tsumidasu, *vb.* 積み出す ship.

tsumikasaneru, *vb.* 積み重ねる stack; amass.

tsumori, *n.* つもり intention; expectation.

tsumoru, *vb.* 積る pile up.

tsumu, *vb.* 積む 1. heap up; accumulate. 2. load.

tsumu, *vb.* 摘む pick (tea, cotton, etc.).

tsumugu, *n.* 紡ぐ spin.

tsuna, *n.* 綱 rope.

tsunagari, *n.* つながり link; relationship.

tsunagaru, *vb.* つながる be linked; be related.

tsunagu, *vb.* つなぐ 1. connect; link. 2. fasten; tie.

tsunami, *n.* 津波 tidal wave.

tsūnen, *n.* 通念 widely accepted idea.

tsune ni, *adv.* 常に always; continually.

tsuneru, *vb.* つねる pinch.

tsuno, *n.* 角 1. horn; antler. 2. feeler.

tsunoru, *vb.* 募る 1. advertise. 2. recruit. 3. intensify; increase.

tsura, *vb.* 面 face (slang).

tsurai, *adj.* 辛い tormenting; painful.

tsuranaru, *vb.* 連なる stand in a row; range.

tsuranuku, *vb.* 貫く 1. penetrate. 2. accomplish.

tsurara, *n.* 氷柱 icicle.

tsure, *n.* 連れ companion.

tsuredasu, *vb.* 連れ出す lure (a person) out.

-tsurete つれて as; **nihon ga tomu ni-tsurete** as Japan becomes more prosperous.

tsureteiku, *vb.* 連れて行く usher; take (a person) with one.

tsurezure, *n.* つれづれ tedium; ennui.

tsuri, *n.* 釣り fishing.

tsuriageru, *vb.* 吊り上げる 1. lift up. 2. suspend.

tsuriai, *n.* 釣り合い balance; harmony.

tsuriau, *vb.* 釣り合う balance; be well matched.

tsuribashi, *n.* 吊り橋 suspension bridge.

tsuri(sen), *n.* 釣り(銭) change (money).

tsurizao, *n.* 釣竿 fishing rod.

tsūro, *n.* 通路 passageway.

tsuru, *n.* 鶴 crane (bird).

tsuru, *n.* 蔓 tendril; vine.

tsuru, *vb.* 吊る suspend; hang up.

tsuru, *vb.* 釣る fish.

tsurugi, *n.* 剣 sword.

tsurusu, *vb.* 吊るす suspend; hang up.

tsūsanshō, *n.* 通産省 MITI (Ministry of International Trade and Industry).

tsūsetsu (na), *adj.* 痛切 (な) acute.

tsūsetsu ni, *adv.* 痛切に acutely.

tsūshin, *n.* 通信 correspondence; communication.

tsūshinran, *n.* 通信欄 letters-to-the-editor column.

tsūshō, *n.* 通称 1. pseudonym. 2. nickname.

tsushō, *n.* 通商 trade; commerce.

tsuta, *n.* 蔦 ivy.

tsutaeru, *vb.* 伝える 1. tell; inform; convey. 2. hand down. 3. transmit.

tsutanai, *adj.* 拙い clumsy; unskillful.

tsūtatsu, *n.* 通達 notice; notification.

tsutawaru, *vb.* 伝わる 1. be handed down; be transmitted. 2. reach; spread.

tsute, *n.* 伝手 connection; intermediary.

tsutome, *n.* 勤め、務め 1. job. 2. responsibility.

tsutomeguchi, *n.* 勤め口 position; job.

tsutomenin, *n.* 勤め人 office worker.

tsutomeru, *vb.* 勤める work for a company.

tsutomeru, *vb.* 務める discharge one's duty.

tsutomeru, *vb.* 努める make an effort.

tsutomesaki, *n.* 勤め先 place of employment.

tsutsu, *n.* 筒 cylinder.

tsutsuji, *n.* つつじ azalea.

tsutsuku, *vb.* つつく peck; poke.

tsutsumashii, *adj.* 慎ましい 1. shy; modest. 2. frugal.

tsutsumi, *n.* 堤 embankment.

tsutsumi, *n.* 包み package.

tsutsumigami, *n.* 包み紙 wrapping paper.

tsutsumikakusu, *vb.* 包み隠す hide.

tsutsumu, *vb.* 包む wrap.

tsutsushimu, *vb.* 慎しむ 1. be discreet. 2. refrain from.

tsūwa, *n.* 通話 telephone call.

tsuwari, *n.* つわり morning sickness.

tsuya, *n.* 通夜 wake (for the deceased).

tsuya, *n.* 艶 luster.

tsūyaku, *n.* 通訳 interpreter; interpretation.

tsuyoi, *adj.* 強い strong.

tsuyomeru, *vb.* 強める 1. strengthen. 2. emphasize.

tsuyosa, *n.* 強さ strength; power.

tsūyō suru, *vb.* 通用する be valid; be useful; be acceptable; be used.

tsuyu, *n.* 梅雨 rainy season.

tsuyu, *n.* 汁 Japanese-style soup or sauce.

tsuyu, *n.* 露 dew.

tsūzoku-teki (na), *adj.* 通俗的 (な) popular; appealing to the masses.

tsuzukeru, *vb.* 続ける continue.

tsuzuki, *n.* 続き continuation.

tsuzuku, *vb.* 続く 1. be continued. 2. adjoin.

tsuzuri, *n.* 綴り spelling.

tsuzuru, *vb.* 綴る spell; write.

U

u, *n.* 鵜 cormorant.

uba, *n.* 乳母 wet nurse.

ubaguruma, *n.* 乳母車 baby carriage; stroller.

ubai'au, *vb.* 奪い合う fight over.

ubau, *vb.* 奪う 1. rob. 2. fascinate.

ubu (na), *adj.* うぶ (な) innocent; naive.

uchi, *n.* 内 1. inside; insider. 2. one's family; one's organization.

uchi, *n.* 家 house; home.

uchi うち 1. *prep.* in; among; within; **kazoku no uchi de** within one's family. 2. *conj.* while; **atsui uchi ni** while it is hot.

uchiageru, *vb.* 打ち上げる 1. wash ashore. 2. launch; shoot off. 3. finish; close (a performance).

uchiakeru, *vb.* 打ち明ける confide in.

uchiawase, *n.* 打ち合わせ preliminary arrangements.

uchiawaseru, *vb.* 打ち合わせる make preliminary arrangements.

uchigawa, *n.* 内側 inside.

uchikaesu, *vb.* 打ち返す strike back.

uchiki (na), *adj.* 内気 (な) shy.

uchikin, *n.* 内金 partial payment.

uchikiru, *vb.* 打ち切る discontinue; break off.

uchimaku, *n.* 内幕 inside story.

uchitaosu, *vb.* 打ち倒す strike down.

uchitokeru, *vb.* 打ち解ける cast off one's reserve.

uchitsukeru, *vb.* 打ち付ける hammer.

uchiwa, *n.* うちわ nonfolding fan.

uchiwa, *n.* 内輪 family or inner circle.

uchiwa (no), *adj.* 内輪 (の) private; internal.

uchiwake, *n.* 内訳 details.

uchiyaburu, *vb.* 打ち破る 1. break.
2. conquer.

uchōten, *n.* 有頂天 ecstasy.

uchū, *n.* 宇宙 universe; outer
space.

uchūeisei, *n.* 宇宙衛星 space
satellite.

uchūhikōshi, *n.* 宇宙飛行士
astronaut.

ude, *n.* 腕 1. arm. 2. skill.

udedokei, *n.* 腕時計 wristwatch.

udekiki (no), *adj.* 腕利き (の)
competent; skilled.

udemae, *n.* 腕前 skill.

udezuku de, *adv.* 腕ずくで by
force.

udon, *n.* うどん Japanese noodles.

ue 上 1. *n.* top; surface; **tsukue no
ue ni** on (top of) the desk. 2. *n.*
upper part; person ranking above
others. 3. *prep.* above; on; over.
4. *adv.* up.

ue, *n.* 飢え hunger; starvation.

uedingu, *n.* ウエディング (E.)
wedding.

uedingu-doresu, *n.* ウエディング
ドレス (E.) wedding dress.

uedingu-kēki, *n.* ウエディング
ケーキ (E.) wedding cake.

ueitā, *n.* ウエイター (E.) waiter.

ueitoresu, *n.* ウエイトレス (E.)
waitress.

ueki, *n.* 植木 garden plant or tree;
potted plant.

uekibachi, *n.* 植木鉢 flowerpot.

ueru, *vb.* 飢える starve.

ugai, *n.* うがい gargling.

ugatsu, *vb.* 穿つ drill; excavate; dig.

ugokasu, *vb.* 動かす 1. move. 2.
operate (machinery). 3.
influence.

ugoki, *n.* 動き movement; trend.

ugoku, *vb.* 動く 1. move; stir. 2.

change; vary. 3. operate.

uguisu, *n.* うぐいす Japanese bush
warbler.

uha, *n.* 右派 right wing.

uisukī, *n.* ウイスキー (E.) whiskey.

ukaberu, *vb.* 浮かべる set afloat.

ukabu, *vb.* 浮かぶ 1. float. 2.
surface.

ukagau, *vb.* 伺う 1. visit. 2. ask.

ukagau, *vb.* 窺う observe; watch.

ukai, *n.* 迂回 detour.

ukaru, *vb.* 受かる pass (exam).

ukatsu (na), *adj.* うかつ (な)
inattentive; thoughtless.

ukeau, *vb.* 請け合う guarantee;
endorse.

ukeireru, *vb.* 受け入れる accept.

ukemi, *n.* 受身 1. passivity. 2.
passive voice.

ukeou, *vb.* 請け負う contract.

ukeru, *vb.* 受ける 1. catch; get;
receive. 2. take (exam, class, etc.).
3. be affected; suffer from.

uketamawaru, *vb.* 承る 1. hear.
2. be told.

uketomeru, *vb.* 受け止める
receive; catch.

uketori, *n.* 受け取り receipt.

uketoru, *vb.* 受け取る 1. receive.
2. interpret.

uketsugu, *vb.* 受け継ぐ inherit;
succeed to.

uketsuke, *n.* 受け付け 1.
acceptance. 2. receptionist;
reception desk.

uketsukeru, *vb.* 受け付ける
accept; receive.

ukibori, *n.* 浮き彫り relief
(carving).

uki-uki suru, *vb.* うきうきする be
excited.

ukiyo, *n.* 浮世 1. transitory world.
2. fleeting life.

ukiyobanare shita, *adj.* 浮世離れ

した unworldly.

ukiyoe, *n.* 浮世絵 premodern Japanese woodblock print.

ukkari, *adv.* うっかり carelessly.

uku, *vb.* 浮く float.

uma, *n.* 馬 horse.

umai, *adj.* うまい 1. delicious. 2. skillful. 3. promising; successful.

umaku, *adv.* うまく well; dexterously.

ūman-ribu, *n.* ウーマンリブ (E.) women's liberation.

umare, *n.* 生まれ birth; birthplace.

umareru, *vb.* 生まれる be born.

umaretsuki, *adv.* 生まれつき by birth; by nature.

umaru, *vb.* 埋る be buried in; be filled with; **hana de umaru** be filled with flowers.

ume, *n.* 梅 plum.

umeawase, *n.* 埋め合わせ amends; compensation.

umeboshi, *n.* 梅干し pickled Japanese plum.

umeku, *vb.* 呻く groan; moan.

umeru, *vb.* 埋める bury.

umi, *n.* 海 sea; ocean.

umibe, *n.* 海辺 beach; seashore.

umi no oya, *n.* 生みの親 1. biological mother. 2. originator.

umoreru, *vb.* 埋もれる be buried in.

umu, *vb.* 産む、生む give birth; produce; lay (egg).

un, *n.* 運 luck; fortune; **un ga ii** lucky; **un ga warui** unlucky.

un, *interj.* うん Yes! That's right!

unagasu, *vb.* 促す urge.

unagi, *n.* うなぎ eel.

una(gi)don(buri), *n.* うな(ぎ)丼 grilled eel served over rice.

unajū, *n.* うな重 grilled eel served over rice in a lacquer box.

unaru, *vb.* 唸る groan; roar.

unazuku, *vb.* 頷く 1. nod. 2. agree.

unchin, *n.* 運賃 fare (transportation).

undō, *n.* 運動 1. exercise; sport. 2. action; movement. 3. campaign.

undōgutsu, *n.* 運動靴 athletic shoes; sneakers.

un'ei suru, *vb.* 運営する manage; operate.

unga, *n.* 運河 canal; **panama-unga** Panama Canal.

uni, *n.* うに sea urchin (sushi).

unkō, *n.* 運行 1. revolution (planet). 2. operation. 3. transportation.

unmei, *n.* 運命 destiny.

unsei, *n.* 運勢 fate; fortune.

unsō, *n.* 運送 shipment; transportation.

unten, *n.* 運転 operation of an automobile or machinery.

untenshu, *n.* 運転手 driver.

unten suru, *vb.* 運転する drive a car; operate a machine.

unubore, *n.* うぬぼれ conceit.

unuboreru, *vb.* うぬぼれる be conceited.

un waruku, *adv.* 運悪く unfortunately.

un yoku, *adv.* 運良く luckily; fortunately.

un'yō suru, *vb.* 運用する use; operate.

un'yu, *n.* 運輸 transportation.

unzari suru, *vb.* うんざりする get disgusted with; become fed up with.

uo, *n.* 魚 fish.

uogashi, *n.* 魚河岸 (riverside) fish market.

uoichiba, *n.* 魚市場 fish market.

uppun, *n.* うっぷん anger; frustration; **uppun o harasu** vent one's anger.

ura, *n.* 裏 1. back; rear. 2. reverse. 3. hidden aspect.

uradōri, *n.* 裏通り back street.

uragaesu, *vb.* 裏返す turn over; turn inside out.

uragawa, *n.* 裏側 reverse side.

uragiru, *vb.* 裏切る betray; deceive.

urami, *n.* 恨み grudge; animosity.

uramu, *vb.* 恨む bear a grudge.

uranai, *n.* 占い fortune-telling.

uraniwa, *n.* 裏庭 backyard.

urayamashii, *adj.* 羨ましい envious.

urayamu, *vb.* 羨む envy.

urei, *n.* 憂い、愁い melancholy; sorrow.

ureru, *vb.* 売れる sell; be in demand.

ureru, *vb.* 熟れる ripen.

ureshii, *adj.* 嬉しい happy.

uriage, *n.* 売り上げ sales.

uriba, *n.* 売り場 counter; box office; department; **bunbōgu uriba** stationery department.

urikireru, *vb.* 売り切れる be sold out.

urikomu, *vb.* 売り込む promote; advertise.

urimono, *n.* 売り物 item for sale.

urine, *n.* 売り値 selling price.

urite, *n.* 売り手 seller.

uroko, *n.* うろこ scale (fish).

urotaeru, *vb.* うろたえる be at a loss.

urotsuku, *vb.* うろつく loiter; hover.

uru, *vb.* 売る sell.

ūru, *n.* ウール (E.) wool.

urumu, *vb.* 潤む moisten; be blurred.

uruoi, *n.* 潤い 1. charm. 2. profit. 3. moisture.

uruou, *vb.* 潤う 1. profit. 2.

become moist.

urusai, *adj.* うるさい 1. annoying. 2. noisy. 3. fussy; meticulous. 4. inquisitive.

urushi, *n.* 漆 lacquer; lacquerware.

uruwashii, *adj.* 麗しい beautiful; charming.

usabarashi, *n.* 憂さ晴らし diversion; distraction.

usagi, *n.* 兎 rabbit.

usankusai, *adj.* うさん臭い suspicious; shady.

ushi, *n.* 牛 cow; bull.

ushinau, *vb.* 失う lose.

ushiro, *n.* 後ろ back; rear.

ushiro ni/de 後ろに、～で 1. *prep.* behind. 2. *adv.* at the back.

uso, *n.* 嘘 lie.

uso (no), *adj.* 嘘 (の) false.

uso (o) tsuku, *vb.* 嘘 (を) 吐く tell a lie.

usotsuki, *n.* 嘘吐き liar.

usu- 薄 1. thin; light; **usuaoi** light blue. 2. somewhat.

usugurai, *adj.* 薄暗い dim.

usui, *adj.* 薄い thin; light; weak.

usu-kimiwarui, *adj.* 薄気味悪い eerie.

usumeru, *vb.* 薄める thin; weaken; dilute (drink).

usuppera (na), *adj.* 薄っぺら (な) 1. thin. 2. superficial.

usureru, *vb.* 薄れる abate; dwindle; wane.

usuwarai, *n.* 薄笑い sneer.

uta, *n.* 歌 song.

uta, *n.* 詩 poem.

utagai, *n.* 疑い doubt; suspicion.

utagaibukai, *adj.* 疑い深い distrustful; suspicious.

utagau, *vb.* 疑う doubt; suspect.

utagawashii, *adj.* 疑わしい doubtful; dubious.

utau, *vb.* 歌う sing.

uten, *n.* 雨天 rainy weather.

utoi, *adj.* 疎い ignorant; estranged from.

uto-uto suru, *vb.* うとうとする doze.

utsu, *vb.* 打つ 1. beat; hit; strike. 2. impress; touch (the heart).

utsu, *vb.* 撃つ fire (gun).

utsubuse, *n.* うつぶせ lying on one's stomach.

utsukushii, *adj.* 美しい beautiful.

utsumuku, *vb.* うつむく look down; hang one's head.

utsuri, *n.* 映り、写り reflection; image (on screen).

utsurikawaru, *vb.* 移り変わる change.

utsuro (na), *adj.* 虚ろ (な) empty; vacant.

utsuru, *vb.* 移る 1. change; move. 2. be infected with.

utsuru, *vb.* 映る、写る be shown (on screen); be reflected.

utsushi, *n.* 写し copy.

utsusu, *vb.* 移す 1. move; transmit. 2. infect.

utsusu, *vb.* 映す 1. project (on screen). 2. reflect.

utsusu, *vb.* 写す take (photograph); copy.

utsuwa, *n.* 器 1. container (bowl, plate, etc.); receptacle. 2. ability.

uttae, *n.* 訴え lawsuit; appeal.

uttaeru, *vb.* 訴える 1. sue; appeal. 2. complain of.

uttetsuke (no), *adj.* 打って付け (の) most suitable.

uttori suru, *vb.* うっとりする be spellbound.

uttōshii, *adj.* うっとうしい gloomy; depressing.

uwabe, *n.* 上べ appearance; surface.

uwagi, *n.* 上着 jacket.

uwaki, *n.* 浮気 extramarital affair; infidelity.

uwamawaru, *vb.* 上回る surpass; exceed.

uwamuki (no), *adj.* 上向き (の) upward.

uwa no sora de, *adv.* 上の空で absent-mindedly.

uwasa, *n.* 噂 rumor; gossip.

uwasa (o) suru, *vb.* 噂(を)する spread a rumor; gossip.

uwate, *n.* 上手 upper hand; superiority; **uwate o toru** get the upper hand.

uyamau, *vb.* 敬う respect; venerate.

uyamuya (na), *adj.* うやむや (な) noncommittal.

uya-uyashii, *adj.* 恭々しい deferential.

uyoku, *n.* 右翼 right wing.

uzu, *n.* 渦 whirlpool.

uzuku, *vb.* 疼く ache; throb.

uzukumaru, *vb.* うずくまる crouch.

uzumaki, *n.* 渦巻き whirlpool.

uzumakijō (no), *adj.* 渦巻き状 (の) spiral.

uzumeru, *vb.* 埋める fill up; bury (face).

uzu-uzu suru, *vb.* うずうずする be impatient.

W

wa, *n.* 和 1. harmony. 2. total.

wa, *n.* 輪 round shape (ring, circle, wheel, etc.).

wabi, *n.* 詫び apology.

wabi, *n.* わび stillness or loneliness (aesthetic concept).

wabiru, *vb.* 詫びる apologize.

wabishii, *adj.* わびしい dreary; lonely.

wabun, *n.* 和文 Japanese text.

wadai, *n.* 話題 topic.

wadakamari, *n.* わだかまり ill feeling; grudge.

waeijiten, *n.* 和英辞典 Japanese-English dictionary.

wafū, *n.* 和風 Japanese style.

wafuku, *n.* 和服 Japanese clothing; kimono.

waga- 我が one's (my, our, etc.); **wagasha** our company; **wagaya** my house.

wagamama (na), *adj.* 我がまま (な) selfish; spoiled.

wa-gomu, *n.* 輪ゴム rubber band.

wahei, *n.* 和平 peace.

waheikōshō, *n.* 和平交渉 peace negotiation.

waikyoku suru, *vb.* 歪曲する distort; falsify.

wain, *n.* ワイン (E.) wine.

waipā, *n.* ワイパー (E.) windshield wiper.

wairo, *n.* 賄賂 bribe.

waisetsu (na), *adj.* わいせつ (な) obscene.

wai-shatsu, *n.* ワイシャツ (E.) dress shirt.

waka, *n.* 和歌 31-syllable Japanese poem.

wakaba, *n.* 若葉 young leaf.

wakachiau, *vb.* 分かち合う share.

wakagaeru, *vb.* 若返る be rejuvenated.

wakai, *adj.* 若い young; immature.

wakai, *n.* 和解 reconciliation.

wakai suru, *vb.* 和解する come to terms with.

wakajini, *n.* 若死に premature death.

wakame, *n.* 若芽 bud; sprout.

wakamono, *n.* 若者 young person.

wakaranai, *vb.* 分からない not understand.

wakarazuya, *n.* 分からず屋 obdurate or obstinate person.

wakare, *n.* 別れ separation; parting.

wakareru, *vb.* 別れる separate from; divorce; leave.

wakareru, *vb.* 分かれる branch off.

wakari, *n.* 分かり understanding.

wakarikitta, *adj.* 分かりきった obvious.

wakarinikui, *adj.* 分かりにくい puzzling; incomprehensible.

wakariyasui, *adj.* 分かりやすい easy to understand.

wakaru, *vb.* 分かる understand; know; recognize.

wakasa, *n.* 若さ youth; youthfulness.

wakasu, *vb.* 沸かす 1. boil; simmer. 2. excite.

wakate (no), *adj.* 若手 (の) young.

waka-wakashii, *adj.* 若々しい youthful.

wakazō, *n.* 若僧、若造 upstart; youngster.

wake, *n.* 訳 1. reason. 2. meaning.

wakemae, *n.* 分け前 share.

wakenai, *adj.* 訳ない easy.

wakeru, *vb.* 分ける 1. divide. 2. share. 3. categorize.

waki, *n.* 脇 side.

wakiagaru, *vb.* 沸き上がる come or go up; rise.

wakikaeru, *vb.* 沸き返る 1. boil up. 2. arise.

wakimaeru, *vb.* 弁える discern; understand.

wakimichi, *n.* 脇道 side road.

waki ni 脇に 1. *prep.* at the side of; beside. 2. *adv.* alongside.

wakiyaku, *n.* 脇役 supporting role.

waku, *n.* 枠 1. frame; framework. 2. limit.

waku, *vb.* 沸く 1. boil. 2. be enthusiastic.

wakuchin, *n.* ワクチン (G. *Vakzin*) vaccine.

wakusei, *n.* 惑星 planet.

waku-waku suru, *vb.* わくわくする be excited.

wameku, *vb.* 喚く yell; shriek.

wan, *n.* 湾 gulf; bay.

wan, *n.* 腕 bowl.

wana, *n.* 罠 snare; trap.

wana ni kakaru, *vb.* 罠にかかる be caught in a trap.

wani, *n.* わに crocodile; alligator.

wanpaku (na), *adj.* 腕白 (な) naughty.

wāpuro, *n.* ワープロ (E.) word processor.

wara, *n.* わら straw.

warai, *n.* 笑い laughter; smile.

waraimono, *n.* 笑い者 laughingstock.

warau, *vb.* 笑う laugh; smile.

ware, *pron.* 我、吾 self.

wareme, *n.* 割れ目 crack.

waremono, *n.* 割れ物 fragile article.

warera, *pron.* 我ら we.

wareru, *vb.* 割れる break; crack; split.

ware-ware, *pron.* 我々 we.

wari, *n.* 割 rate; percent; ten percent; **gowari** fifty percent.

wariai, *n.* 割合 ratio; percentage; proportion.

wariai (ni), *adv.* 割り合い (に) comparatively.

wariate, *n.* 割り当て allotment; allocation.

waribashi, *n.* 割りばし disposable wooden chopsticks.

waribiki, *n.* 割り引き discount.

waribiku, *vb.* 割り引く discount.

warikan, *n.* 割り勘 Dutch treat.

warikirenai 割りきれない 1. indivisible. 2. unconvincing; unsatisfactory.

warikiru, *vb.* 割りきる give a logical explanation.

warikomu, *vb.* 割り込む break into; cut in.

warimashiryōkin, *n.* 割り増し料金 surcharge.

wari ni 割に 1. *adv.* comparatively; proportionately. 2. *prep.* considering; **toshi no wari ni** considering (his) age.

waru, *n.* 悪 scoundrel.

waru, *vb.* 割る 1. break; split. 2. divide. 3. go below (score, value).

warui, *adj.* 悪い bad; wrong.

warukuchi, *n.* 悪口 slander; abuse.

warumono, *n.* 悪者 scoundrel.

wasabi, *n.* わさび Japanese horseradish.

washi, *n.* わし eagle.

washi, *n.* 和紙 Japanese paper.

washitsu, *n.* 和室 Japanese-style room.

washoku, *n.* 和食 Japanese meal.

wasuremono, *n.* 忘れ物 lost item; item left behind.

wasureppoi, *adj.* 忘れっぽい
  forgetful.

wasure-rarenai, *adj.* 忘れられない
  unforgettable.

wasureru, *vb.* 忘れる 1. forget. 2.
  leave behind.

wata, *n.* 綿 cotton.

watagashi, *n.* 綿菓子 cotton candy.

watakushi, *pron.* 私 I.

watakushigoto, *n.* 私事 personal
  matter.

watakushiritsu (no), *adj.* 私立
  (の) private (establishment).

wataridori, *n.* 渡り鳥 migratory
  bird.

wataru, *vb.* 渡る 1. cross; pass. 2.
  be given; be obtained.

wataru, *vb.* 亘る 1. extend; span.
  2. continue; stretch.

watashi, *pron.* 私 I.

watashi (no), *adj.* 私 (の) my.

watashitachi, *pron.* 私達 we.

watashitachi (no), *adj.* 私達 (の)
our.

watasu, *vb.* 渡す 1. pass; hand
  over. 2. carry across.

watto, *n.* ワット (E.) watt.

wayaku, *n.* 和訳 translation into
  Japanese.

waza, *n.* 技 skill; technique.

waza to, *adv.* わざと intentionally.

wazawai, *n.* 災い calamity;
  disaster.

waza-waza, *adv.* わざわざ
  purposely.

wazuka (ni), *adv.* わずか (に) 1.
  barely; slightly. 2. only.

wazuka (no), *adj.* わずか (の) very
  few; very little.

wazurau, *vb.* 患う suffer (from
  illness).

wazurau, *vb.* 煩らう worry about.

wazurawashii, *adj.* 煩らわしい
  complicated; troublesome.

wazurawasu, *vb.* 煩らわす bother;
  trouble.

Y

ya, *n.* 矢 arrow.

ya や and; **hanaya tori** flowers
  and birds.

-ya 屋 shop; **hanaya** florist.

yā, *interj.* やー Hi!

yaban (na), *adj.* 野蛮 (な)
  barbarous; uncivilized.

yabo (na), *adj.* 野暮 (な) 1.
  unsophisticated. 2. senseless.

yabu, *n.* やぶ bush; thicket.

yabuku, *vb.* 破く tear; rip.

yabure, *n.* 破れ crack; hole; rent.

yabureru, *vb.* 破れる 1. be torn; be
  ripped. 2. be broken. 3. fail.

yabureru, *vb.* 敗れる be defeated;
  lose.

yaburu, *vb.* 破る 1. tear; break. 2.
  violate.

yachin, *n.* 家賃 house rent; room
  rent.

yado, *n.* 宿 lodging; hotel; inn.

yadoru, *vb.* 宿る lodge; dwell.

yadosu, *vb.* 宿す 1. be pregnant.
  2. conceive.

yadoya, *n.* 宿屋 inn.

yagai, *n.* 野外 outdoors; **yagai-
  konsāto** outdoor concert.

yagaku, *n.* 夜学 evening class.

yagate, *adv.* やがて before long;
  soon.

yagi, *n.* 山羊 goat.

yagu, *n.* 夜具 futon; bedding.

yahari, *adv.* やはり 1. after all. 2. again.

yaji, *n.* 野次 jeering.

yajiru, *vb.* 野次る jeer.

yajirushi, *n.* 矢印 arrow (on map or sign).

yajiuma, *n.* 野次馬 mob; curious crowd.

yajū, *n.* 野獣 wild animal.

yakamashii, *adj.* やかましい 1. noisy. 2. controversial; **yakamashī jiken** controversial case. 3. particular.

yakan, *n.* やかん kettle.

yakan, *n.* 夜間 nighttime.

yake, *n.* やけ desperation; **yake o okosu** surrender to desperation.

yakedo, *n.* 火傷 burn (injury).

yakei, *n.* 夜景 night view.

yakei, *n.* 夜警 night watch.

yake ni, *adv.* やけに 1. awfully. 2. desperately.

yake ni naru, *vb.* やけになる become desperate; become reckless.

yakeru, *vb.* 焼ける 1. be burned or charred (grilled or roasted). 2. be suntanned.

-yaki 焼き pottery; **hagiyaki** Hagi pottery.

yakimeshi, *n.* 焼き飯 fried rice.

yakimochi, *n.* 焼きもち jealousy.

yakimono, *n.* 焼き物 chinaware; earthenware; pottery.

yakin, *n.* 夜勤 night work.

yakiniku, *n.* 焼き肉 broiled (grilled, roasted) meat.

yakisoba, *n.* 焼きそば fried noodles.

yakitori, *n.* 焼き鳥 grilled skewered chicken and vegetables.

yakitsukeru, *vb.* 焼き付ける print (photograph).

yakkai (na), *adj.* 厄介 (な) troublesome; awkward.

yakkyoku, *n.* 薬局 drugstore; pharmacy.

yaku, *n.* 益 benefit; usefulness.

yaku, *n.* 役 1. role. 2. job; position. 3. helpfulness; usefulness.

yaku, *n.* 訳 translation.

yaku, *vb.* 焼く 1. burn or char (broil, grill, toast, etc.). 2. get a suntan. 3. print (photograph). 4. bake (pottery).

yaku, *vb.* 妬く be jealous.

yaku, *adv.* 約 about; approximately.

yakudatsu, *vb.* 役立つ be useful; be helpful.

yakudō-teki (na), *adj.* 躍動的 (な) active; exciting.

yakuhin, *n.* 薬品 medicine; drug.

yakuin, *n.* 役員 director; officer.

yakume, *n.* 役目 responsibility; function; role.

yakumi, *n.* 薬味 spice.

yaku-nin, *n.* 役人 bureaucrat.

yaku ni tatanai, *vb.* 役に立たない be useless.

yaku ni tatsu, *vb.* 役に立つ be useful; be helpful.

yakusha, *n.* 役者 actor; actress.

yakusha, *n.* 訳者 translator.

yakushin, *n.* 躍進 progress.

yakushin suru, *vb.* 躍進する make progress.

yakusho, *n.* 役所 public office.

yakusō, *n.* 薬草 medicinal herb.

yakusoku, *n.* 約束 1. promise; **yakusoku o mamoru** keep one's promise. 2. appointment; **hoka no yakusoku ga aru** have another appointment.

yakusu, *vb.* 訳す translate; **nihongo ni yakusu** translate into Japanese.

yakuwari, *n.* 役割り role.

yakuyō (no), *adj.* 薬用 (の) medicinal.

yakuza, *n.* やくざ hoodlum; gangster.

yakuzai, *n.* 薬剤 medicine; drug.

yakuzaishi, *n.* 薬剤師 pharmacist.

yakyū, *n.* 野球 baseball.

yakyūsenshu, *n.* 野球選手 baseball player.

yama, *n.* 山 1. mountain; hill; pile. 2. speculation. 3. crisis; climax.

yamabiko, *n.* 山彦 echo.

yamaba, *n.* 山場 climax.

yamai, *n.* 病 disease; sickness.

yamamori (no), *adj.* 山盛り (の) abundant; heaping.

yamanobori, *n.* 山登り mountain climbing.

yamashii, *adj.* やましい remorseful; penitent.

yameru, *vb.* 止める stop; give up.

yameru, *vb.* 辞める resign; quit.

yami, *n.* 闇 darkness.

yamitsuki, *n.* 病み付き passion; obsession.

yamome, *n.* やもめ widow.

yamu, *vb.* 止む stop; cease.

yamu, *vb.* 病む fall ill.

yamu o enai, *adj.* やむを得ない inevitable; unavoidable.

yamu o ezu, *adv.* やむを得ず out of necessity.

yanagi, *n.* 柳 willow.

yancha (na), *adj.* やんちゃ (な) mischievous.

yane, *n.* 屋根 roof.

yanushi, *n.* 家主 landlady; landlord.

yaoya, *n.* 八百屋 store selling vegetables and fruit; produce stand.

yappari, *adv.* やっぱり 1. after all. 2. again.

yare-yare, *interj.* やれやれ 1.

Thank goodness that's over! 2. Good grief!

yari, *n.* 槍 spear.

yarikake (no), *adj.* やりかけ (の) unfinished.

yarikata, *n.* やり方 way of doing something; procedure.

yarikirenai, *vb.* やりきれない be unbearable.

yarikuri, *n.* やりくり managing (time or money); contrivance.

yarinaosu, *vb.* やり残す redo.

yarisokonau, *vb.* やり損なう fail.

yaritogeru, *vb.* やり遂げる accomplish.

yarō, *n.* 野郎 1. man; guy (slang). 2. rascal.

yaru, *vb.* やる 1. give (informal). 2. do. 3. get along.

yaruki, *n.* やる気 determination.

yasai, *n.* 野菜 vegetable.

yasashii, *adj.* 易しい easy.

yasashii, *adj.* 優しい 1. kind; gentle. 2. graceful.

yasei (no), *adj.* 野性 (の) wild (animal, plant).

yaseru, *vb.* やせる 1. lose weight; become thin. 2. become barren.

yaseta, *adj.* やせた 1. slender; thin. 2. barren.

yashi, *n.* 椰子 palm tree; coconut palm.

yashiki, *n.* 屋敷 mansion.

yashin, *n.* 野心 ambition.

yashinaigo, *n.* 養い子 foster child(ren).

yashinaioya, *n.* 養い親 foster parent(s).

yashinau, *vb.* 養う feed; nourish; support; cultivate.

yasui, *adj.* 安い cheap; inexpensive.

-yasui 易い 1. easy (to do); **tsukai-yasui** easy to use. 2. easily; **okoriyasui** easily angered.

yasumeru, *vb.* 休める allow to rest.

yasumi, *n.* 休み 1. rest; break; recess. 2. day(s) off; holiday; **yasumi o toru** take a day (or days) off. 3. absence. 4. sleep.

yasumono, *n.* 安物 cheap item.

yasumu, *vb.* 休む 1. take a break or rest; relax. 2. be absent from. 3. sleep.

yasuppoi, *adj.* 安っぽい cheap.

yasuragu, *vb.* 安らぐ feel at peace.

yasuraka (na), *adj.* 安らか (な) peaceful.

yasuraka ni, *adv.* 安らかに peacefully.

yasuri, *n.* やすり file (tool).

yasu'uri, *n.* 安売り (bargain) sale.

yasu-yasu to, *adv.* やすやすと easily.

yatai, *n.* 屋台 street food vendor.

yatara (ni, to), *adv.* やたら (に、と) 1. at random. 2. excessively.

yatō, *n.* 野党 opposition party.

yatoinushi, *n.* 雇い主 employer.

yatou, *vb.* 雇う employ; hire.

yatsu 奴 (slang) 1. *pron.* he; she. 2. *n.* that person. 3. *n.* fellow.

yatsuatari suru, *vb.* 八つ当りする vent one's anger at random.

yatsugibaya ni, *adv.* 矢継ぎ早に one after another; rapidly.

yatsura, *pron.* 奴ら they (slang).

yatsureru, *vb.* やつれる become haggard.

yatsureta, *adj.* やつれた worn-out.

yatteiku, *vb.* やって行く manage; get along.

yattekuru, *vb.* やって来る 1. arrive. 2. turn up.

yattemiru, *vb.* やってみる try; make an attempt.

yatto, *adv.* やっと 1. barely; somehow. 2. finally.

yattsu, *n.* 八つ eight; eight years old.

yattsukeru, *vb.* やっつける beat; defeat.

yawarageru, *vb.* 和らげる soften; mitigate.

yawaragu, *vb.* 和らぐ soften; become less severe.

yawarakai, *adj.* 柔らかい soft; tender.

yaya, *adv.* やや somewhat; a little bit.

yayakoshii, *adj.* ややこしい complicated; difficult.

yo, *n.* 夜 night.

yo, *n.* 世 1. world; society. 2. life. 3. epoch; reign.

yō, *n.* 陽 yang; positive.

yō, *n.* 用 1. business; job. 2. errand.

yō 様 look like; sound like; **Hontō no yō desu.** (It) sounds true.

-yō 用 for the use of; **kodomoyō** for the use of children.

yoake, *n.* 夜明け daybreak.

yobi (no), *adj.* 予備 (の) 1. extra; spare; **yobi no denchi** spare batteries. 2. preliminary.

-yōbi 曜日 day of the week; **sui-yōbi** Wednesday.

yobidasu, *vb.* 呼び出す call; summon.

yobigoe, *n.* 呼び声 call; cry.

yobikakeru, *vb.* 呼び掛ける call to; appeal.

yobikō, *n.* 予備校 cram school (special school to prepare high-school students for college entrance examinations).

yobimono, *n.* 呼び物 attraction; main event.

yobina, *n.* 呼び名 name; alias.

yobirin, *n.* 呼び鈴 doorbell; buzzer.

yobō, *n.* 予防 prevention.

yōbo, *n.* 養母 foster mother.

yōbō, *n.* 要望 demand; request.

yōbō, *n.* 容貌 face; features; looks.

yobōchūsha, *n.* 予防注射 vaccination.

yobōsesshu, *n.* 予防接種 inoculation.

yobō suru, *vb.* 予防する prevent.

yobu, *vb.* 呼ぶ 1. call. 2. send for. 3. invite.

yobun, *n.* 余分 surplus; extra.

yobun (no), *adj.* 余分 (の) extra; spare.

yōbun, *n.* 養分 nutriment.

yobun ni, *adv.* 余分に extra; too much.

yochi, *n.* 余地 room; space.

yōchi, *n.* 用地 site.

yōchi (na), *adj.* 幼稚 (な) childish; puerile.

yōchien, *n.* 幼稚園 kindergarten.

yochi suru, *vb.* 予知する predict; foresee.

yōdai, *n.* 容体 condition of a patient.

yodare, *n.* 涎 saliva; drool.

yodomu, *vb.* 淀む become stagnant or sluggish.

yodōshi de, *adv.* 夜通しで all night.

yōen (na), *adj.* 妖艶 (な) sexy.

yōfu, *n.* 養父 foster father.

yōfū (no), *adj.* 洋風 (の) Western-style.

yofukashi suru, *vb.* 夜更かしする stay up late.

yofuke, *n.* 夜更け late night; after midnight.

yōfuku, *n.* 洋服 Western-style clothes.

yōfukudansu, *n.* 洋服だんす wardrobe (piece of furniture).

yōfukuya, *n.* 洋服屋 clothing store.

yoga, *n.* ヨガ (Hindi) yoga.

yōga, *n.* 洋画 1. foreign film. 2. Western-style painting.

yōgaku, *n.* 洋学 Western music.

yōgan, *n.* 溶岩 lava.

yogen, *n.* 予言 prediction.

yoginaku, *adv.* 余儀なく unavoidably; necessarily.

yōgisha, *n.* 容疑者 suspect.

yōgo, *n.* 擁護 protection.

yōgo, *n.* 用語 (technical) terminology; jargon.

yogore, *n.* 汚れ dirt; stain.

yogoremono, *n.* 汚れ物 dirty clothes.

yogoreru, *vb.* 汚れる get dirty; be stained.

yogosu, *vb.* 汚す soil; stain.

yōgu, *n.* 用具 equipment; tool.

yōguruto, *n.* ヨーグルト (E.) yogurt.

yoha, *n.* 余波 aftereffect.

yohaku, *n.* 余白 blank space; margin (page).

yōhin, *n.* 用品 1. supplies. 2. utensils.

yohō, *n.* 予報 forecast.

yōhō, *n.* 用法 directions (for use).

yohodo, *adv.* 余程 considerably.

yoi, *n.* 酔い drunkenness; intoxication.

yoi, *n.* 宵 evening.

yoi, *adj.* 良い good.

yōi, *n.* 用意 preparation.

yōi (na), *adj.* 容易 (な) easy.

yōiku, *n.* 養育 child rearing.

yōikuhi, *n.* 養育費 expense of raising a child.

yōiku suru, *vb.* 養育する raise; bring up.

yōin, *n.* 要因 factor.

yōi ni, *adv.* 容易に easily.

yōi suru, *vb.* 用意する prepare.

yoitsubureru, *vb.* 酔い潰れる pass out (from excessive drinking).

yōji, *n.* 用事 business; errand.

yōji, *n.* 幼児 young child.

yōji, *n.* 幼時 childhood.

yōjin, *n.* 用心 caution.

yōjinbō, *n.* 用心棒 bodyguard.

yōjinbukai, *adj.* 用心深い careful; cautious.

yojinoboru, *vb.* よじ登る climb; scale.

yōjin suru, *vb.* 用心する be careful; be cautious.

yojireru, *vb.* よじれる become twisted.

yōjo, *n.* 養女 adopted daughter.

yōjō suru, *vb.* 養生する recuperate.

yoka, *n.* 余暇 free time; leisure time.

yōka, *n.* 八日 eighth day of the month; eight days.

yōkai, *n.* 妖怪 ghost; phantom.

yokan, *n.* 予感 premonition; presentiment.

yokei (na), *adj.* 余計 (な) excessive; unnecessary.

yokei ni, *adv.* 余計に 1. excessively; unnecessarily. 2. all the more.

yōken, *n.* 用件 business.

yokeru, *vb.* 避ける avoid.

yoki, *n.* 予期 expectation; prediction.

yōki, *n.* 容器 receptacle; container.

yōki, *n.* 陽気 comfortable weather.

yōki (na), *adj.* 陽気 (な) merry; happy-go-lucky.

yokin, *n.* 預金 bank deposit.

yokka, *n.* 四日 fourth day of the month; four days.

yokkyū, *n.* 欲求 desire.

yokkyūfuman, *n.* 欲求不満 frustration.

yoko, *n.* 横 side; width.

yōkō, *n.* 要項 outline.

yokodori suru, *vb.* 横取りする steal; snatch away.

yokogao, *n.* 横顔 profile.

yokogiru, *vb.* 横切る cross; cut across.

yokoku, *n.* 予告 advance notice.

yokokuhen, *n.* 予告編 preview.

yokoku suru, *vb.* 予告する give advance notice.

yokomichi, *n.* 横道 side road.

yoko ni suru, *vb.* 横にする lay down.

yōkoso, *interj.* ようこそ Welcome!

yokosu, *vb.* よこす give; send.

yokotaeru, *vb.* 横たえる lay down.

yokotawaru, *vb.* 横たわる lie down.

yokozuna, *n.* 横綱 grand champion (sumo).

yoku, *n.* 欲 greed.

yoku, *adv.* よく 1. well. 2. often. 3. thoroughly.

yoku- 翌 the next; the following; **yokushū** the following week.

yokuatsu suru, *vb.* 抑圧する oppress; suppress.

yokubari (na), *adj.* 欲張り (な) greedy.

yokubaru, *vb.* 欲張る be greedy.

yokubō, *n.* 欲望 ambition; desire.

yoku ga nai, *adj.* 欲が無い generous; unselfish.

yokujitsu, *n.* 翌日 the next day.

yokunaru, *vb.* 良くなる improve.

yokusei suru, *vb.* 抑制する control; curb.

yokushitsu, *n.* 浴室 bathroom.

yokuyō, *n.* 抑揚 intonation; inflection.

yōkyoku, *n.* 謡曲 Noh song.

yōkyū, *n.* 要求 request; demand.

yōkyū suru, *vb.* 要求する request; demand.

yōma, *n.* 洋間 Western-style room.

yome, *n.* 嫁 bride; daughter-in-law (used by husband's parents).

yomeiri, *n.* 嫁入り marriage.

yomigaeru, *vb.* 蘇る revive; rise from the dead.

yomikaesu, *vb.* 読み返す reread.

yomikaki, *n.* 読み書き reading and writing.

yomimono, *n.* 読み物 reading material.

yomise, *n.* 夜店 makeshift store open only at night.

yomite, *n.* 読み手 reader.

yōmō, *n.* 羊毛 wool.

yomu, *vb.* 読む read.

yō (na, ni) 様 (な、に) as; like; sounding like; resembling; **yume no yō na hanashi** story resembling a dream (unlikely story); **anata no iu yō ni** as you say.

yon, *n.* 四 four.

yonaka, *n.* 夜中 middle of the night.

yonareta, *adj.* 世慣れた worldly wise; sophisticated.

yōnenjidai, *n.* 幼年時代 childhood.

yonensei, *n.* 四年生 fourth grader; college senior.

yō ni ように in order to; **seikō suru yō ni** in order to succeed.

yōnin suru, *vb.* 容認する approve; acknowledge.

yonjū, *n.* 四十 forty.

yo no naka, *n.* 世の中 life; society; world.

yopparai, *n.* 酔っ払い drunkard.

yopparaiunten, *n.* 酔っ払い運転 drunken driving.

yopparau, *vb.* 酔っ払う get drunk.

yoppodo, *adv.* よっぽど considerably.

yōrei, *n.* 用例 example; illustration.

yore-yore (no), *adj.* よれよれ (の) ragged; tattered.

yori より 1. *conj.* than; **are yori ii** better than that. 2. *prep.* from; since. 3. *adv.* more; **yori tanoshiku naru** become more enjoyable.

yorikakaru, *vb.* 寄り掛かる lean on.

yorimichi, *n.* 寄り道 stopping off; breaking of a journey.

yorinuki (no), *adj.* 選り抜き (の) carefully selected.

yori o modosu, *vb.* よりを戻す renew old ties.

yorisou, *vb.* 寄り添う lean on someone; draw near to someone (physically).

yoritsukanai, *vb.* 寄り付かない stay away from.

yoritsuku, *vb.* 寄り付く approach; come or go closer.

yoriwakeru, *vb.* 選り分ける select; sort out.

yoroi, *n.* 鎧 armor.

yōrōin, *n.* 養老院 nursing home.

yorokeru, *vb.* よろける stagger; reel.

yorokoba-seru/-su, *vb.* 喜ばせる／〜す please; make happy.

yorokobashii, *adj.* 喜ばしい delightful.

yorokobi, *n.* 喜び joy; delight.

yorokobu, *vb.* 喜ぶ be happy; be delighted.

yorokonde, *adv.* 喜んで with pleasure.

yoromeku, *vb.* よろめく stagger; wobble.

yoron, *n.* 世論 public opinion.

yōroppa, *n.* ヨーロッパ (Pg. *Europa*) Europe.

yoroshii, *adj.* よろしい good.

yoroshiku よろしく 1. *adv.* well. 2. *interj.* Pleased to meet you.

yoru, *n.* 夜 night.

yoru, *vb.* 寄る 1. go closer. 2. drop

in at. 3. gather.

yoru, *vb.* 因る be caused by.

yoru, *vb.* 依る depend on.

yoru, *vb.* よる twist.

yoru to よると according to; **nyūsu ni yoru to** according to the news.

yōryō, *n.* 用量 dosage.

yōryō, *n.* 容量 capacity.

yōryō, *n.* 要領 1. main point; **yōryō o enai** fail to get to the point. 2. dexterity; cleverness.

yōryō ga ii, *adj.* 要領がいい clever; smart; dexterous.

yōryō ga warui, *adj.* 要領が悪い clumsy.

yosa, *n.* 良さ merit; virtue.

yōsai, *n.* 洋裁 sewing (Western-style clothes).

yōsai, *n.* 要塞 citadel; fortress.

yosan, *n.* 予算 budget.

yoseatsumeru, *vb.* 寄せ集める collect.

yosei, *n.* 余生 rest of one's life.

yōsei, *n.* 妖精 elf; fairy.

yōsei (no), *adj.* 陽性 (の) 1. cheerful. 2. positive.

yōsei suru, *vb.* 要請する demand; request.

yōsei suru, *vb.* 養成する educate; nourish; train.

yōseki, *n.* 容積 volume; capacity.

yosen, *n.* 予選 heat; preliminary contest.

yoseru, *vb.* 寄せる 1. bring closer; gather. 2. send.

yōshanaku, *adv.* 容赦なく mercilessly; strictly.

yōsha suru, *vb.* 容赦する forgive.

yoshi, *interj.* よし Good!

yōshi, *n.* 養子 adopted child.

yōshi, *n.* 容姿 looks.

yōshi, *n.* 要旨 gist; main idea.

yōshi, *n.* 用紙 blank printed form.

yōshiki, *n.* 洋式 Western style.

yōshiki, *n.* 様式 style.

yoshin, *n.* 余震 aftershock.

yōshitsu, *n.* 洋室 Western-style room.

yōsho, *n.* 洋書 foreign (Western) book.

yōsho, *n.* 要所 main point.

yōshō, *n.* 幼小 childhood; infancy.

yōshoku, *n.* 容色 looks; facial features.

yōshoku, *n.* 洋食 Western-style meal.

yōshoku, *n.* 要職 important position or job.

yōshoku, *n.* 養殖 fish or pearl farming.

yoshū, *n.* 予習 preparation.

yōshu, *n.* 洋酒 imported liquor.

yoso, *n.* よそ another place.

yosō, *n.* 予想 expectation; speculation; **yosō ni hanshite** contrary to one's expectation.

yōso, *n.* 要素 element; factor.

yosōgai (no), *adj.* 予想外 (の) unexpected.

yosōgai ni, *adv.* 予想外に unexpectedly.

yosoku, *n.* 予測 prediction; supposition.

yosomono, *n.* よそ者 stranger.

yoso'ou, *vb.* 装う 1. wear; dress up. 2. pretend.

yoso-yososhii, *adj.* よそよそしい distant; unfriendly.

yosu, *vb.* 止す stop; desist from.

yōsu, *n.* 様子 condition; state.

yōsuru, *vb.* 要する require.

yōsuru ni, *adv.* 要するに in short.

yotei, *n.* 予定 schedule; plan; **yoteidōri** on schedule.

yōten, *n.* 要点 emphasis; main point.

yōto, *n.* 用途 usage; application.

yotō, *n.* 与党 governing party.

yotsugi, *n.* 世続ぎ heir; heiress; successor.

yotsukado, *n.* 四つ角 intersection (road).

yotte, *adv.* よって therefore.

yotto, *n.* ヨット (E.) yacht.

yottsu, *n.* 四つ four; four years old.

you, *vb.* 酔う 1. get drunk; get intoxicated. 2. suffer from motion sickness.

yowai, *adj.* 弱い weak.

yowaki, *n.* 弱気 timidity.

yowameru, *vb.* 弱める reduce (force, speed).

yowami, *n.* 弱み weak point.

yowamushi, *n.* 弱虫 coward.

yowane, *n.* 弱音 complaining.

yowaru, *vb.* 弱る 1. become weak. 2. be dejected.

yowa-yowashii, *adj.* 弱々しい fragile.

yoyaku, *n.* 予約 appointment; reservation; **yoyaku o toru/suru** make an appointment; make a reservation.

yōyaku, *adv.* 漸く 1. finally. 2. barely; somehow.

yoyakuseki, *n.* 予約席 reserved seat.

yoyū, *n.* 余裕 1. room; space. 2. composure.

yu, *n.* 湯 hot water.

yūbe, *n.* 夕べ 1. evening. 2. yesterday evening.

yūben (na), *adj.* 雄弁 (な) eloquent.

yubi, *n.* 指 finger; toe.

yūbin, *n.* 郵便 mail.

yūbinbako, *n.* 郵便箱 mailbox.

yūbinbangō, *n.* 郵便番号 zip code.

yūbinhagaki, *n.* 郵便葉書 postcard.

yūbinhaitatsu, *n.* 郵便配達 mail delivery; mail carrier.

yūbinkozutsumi, *n.* 郵便小包 small parcel sent by mail.

yūbinkyoku, *n.* 郵便局 post office.

yūbin-posuto, *n.* 郵便ポスト mailbox.

yūbinryōkin, *n.* 郵便料金 postage.

yubisaki, *n.* 指先 fingertip.

yubisasu, *vb.* 指差す point to (with a finger).

yubiwa, *n.* 指輪 ring (jewelry); **kekkonyubiwa** wedding ring.

yūbō (na), *adj.* 有望 (な) promising.

yubune, *n.* 湯舟 bathtub.

yuchaku, *n.* 癒着 1. adhesion. 2. union.

yūchi suru, *vb.* 誘致する invite; draw; lure.

yūdachi, *n.* 夕立 shower (rain).

yūdai (na), *adj.* 雄大 (な) grand; grandiose.

yudaneru, *vb.* 委ねる entrust.

yudan suru, *vb.* 油断する be inattentive; be off guard.

yudayajin, *n.* ユダヤ人 Jew.

yudayakyō, *n.* ユダヤ教 Judaism.

yuden, *n.* 油田 oil field.

yuderu, *vb.* ゆでる boil.

yudetamago, *n.* ゆで玉子 boiled egg.

yūdō, *n.* 誘導 guidance; induction.

yūdoku (na), *adj.* 有毒 (な) poisonous.

yue 故 because of; **anata yue** because of you.

yue ni, *adv.* 故に therefore.

yūeki (na), *adj.* 有益 (な) beneficial; useful.

yūenchi, *n.* 遊園地 amusement park.

yūetsu, *n.* 優越 superiority.

yūetsukan, *n.* 優越感 superiority complex.

yūetsu suru, *vb.* 優越する be superior.

yūfuku (na), *adj.* 裕福 (な) wealthy.

yūga (na), *adj.* 優雅 (な) elegant.

yūgai (na), *adj.* 有害 (な) harmful.

yugaku, *vb.* ゆがく parboil.

yugameru, *vb.* 歪める bend; distort.

yugamu, *vb.* 歪む be bent; be distorted.

yūgata, *n.* 夕方 evening.

yuge, *n.* 湯気 steam.

yūgen (na), *adj.* 幽玄 (な) mysterious.

yūgen (no), *adj.* 有限 (の) limited.

yūgi, *n.* 遊戯 game; amusement.

yūgō, *n.* 融合 blending; fusion.

yūgū suru, *vb.* 優遇する favor.

yūgure, *n.* 夕暮れ early evening; twilight.

yūhei suru, *vb.* 幽閉する imprison.

yūhi, *n.* 夕日 setting sun.

yūi, *n.* 優位 upper hand; superiority.

yuibutsuron, *n.* 唯物論 materialism.

yūigi (na), *adj.* 有意義 (な) meaningful; useful.

yuigon, *n.* 遺言 will; deathbed instructions.

yui'itsu (no), *adj.* 唯一 (の) only; exclusive.

yūin, *n.* 誘因 motive.

yuisho, *n.* 由緒 1. history. 2. fame.

yūjin, *n.* 友人 friend.

yūjo, *n.* 遊女 courtesan; prostitute.

yūjō, *n.* 友情 friendship.

yūjūfudan (na), *adj.* 優柔不断 (な) indecisive; irresolute.

yuka, *n.* 床 floor.

yukai (na), *adj.* 愉快 (な) pleasant; cheerful.

yūkai, *n.* 誘拐 abduction.

yūkai suru, *vb.* 誘拐する abduct.

yūkan, *n.* 夕刊 evening paper.

yūkan (na), *adj.* 勇敢 (な) brave.

yukari, *n.* ゆかり connection.

yukata, *n.* 浴衣 informal summer kimono.

yūkei (no), *adj.* 有形 (の) material; physical.

yūkensha, *n.* 有権者 voter.

yuketsu, *n.* 輸血 blood transfusion.

yuki, *n.* 雪 snow.

-yuki (no) 行き bound for (transportation); **Narayuki no densha** train bound for Nara.

yūki, *n.* 勇気 courage; **yūki o dasu** get up one's courage.

yukiatari-battari (no), *adj.* 行き当たりばったり (の) haphazard.

yūkibutsu, *n.* 有機物 organic substance.

yukidaruma, *n.* 雪だるま snowman.

yukidomari, *n.* 行き止まり dead end.

yuki ga furu, *vb.* 雪が降る snow.

yukiguni, *n.* 雪国 snow country.

yukikai, *n.* 行き交い traffic.

yūkikagaku, *n.* 有機化学 organic chemistry.

yukisugiru, *vb.* 行き過ぎる go beyond; overdo.

yukitodoku, *vb.* 行き届く be thorough; pay attention to.

yukizumari, *n.* 行き詰まり impasse; deadlock.

yukkuri, *adv.* ゆっくり 1. slowly. 2. leisurely.

yukkuri suru, *vb.* ゆっくりする 1. relax; rest. 2. take one's time.

yūkō, *n.* 友好 friendship.

yūkō (na), *adj.* 有効 (な) valid; effective.

yuku, *vb.* 行く go.

yukue, *n.* 行方 whereabouts.

267

yukuefumei, *adj.* 行方不明 missing (person).

yūkyūkyūka, *n.* 有給休暇 paid vacation.

yūkyū (no), *adj.* 悠久 (の) eternal.

yume, *n.* 夢 dream; **yume ga aru** have a dream.

yūmei (na), *adj.* 有名 (な) famous.

yumi, *n.* 弓 bow (archery).

yumigata, *n.* 弓形 arch shape.

yūmoa, *n.* ユーモア (E.) humor.

yūnō (na), *adj.* 有能 (な) able; competent.

yunyū, *n.* 輸入 import.

yunyūchōka, *n.* 輸入超過 excess of imports (over exports).

yunyūhin, *n.* 輸入品 imported goods.

yuragu, *vb.* 揺らぐ sway; swing.

yurai, *n.* 由来 origin.

yūran-basu, *n.* 遊覧バス tour bus.

yūrei, *n.* 幽霊 ghost.

yureru, *vb.* 揺れる sway; shake.

yūretsu, *n.* 優劣 superiority and inferiority; relative merits.

yuri, *n.* 百合 lily.

yūri (na), *adj.* 有利 (な) advantageous; favorable.

yūri suru, *vb.* 遊離する separate.

yurikago, *n.* 揺りかご cradle; bassinet.

yurugasu, *vb.* 揺るがす shake.

yurui, *adj.* 緩い 1. lax; loose. 2. slow.

yurumeru, *vb.* 緩める relax; loosen.

yurumu, *vb.* 緩む abate; become loose.

yurushi, *n.* 許し 1. forgiveness. 2. acceptance; permission.

yurusu, *vb.* 許す 1. forgive. 2. accept; permit.

yuruyaka (na), *adj.* 緩やか (な) 1. loose. 2. lenient. 3. slow.

yūryō (na), *adj.* 優良 (な) excellent.

yūryō (no), *adj.* 有料 (の) pay (TV, phone, toilet, etc.); toll (road).

yūryoku (na), *adj.* 有力 (な) influential; powerful.

yūsei (na), *adj.* 優勢 (な) dominant.

yūsen, *n.* 優先 priority.

yūsen, *n.* 有線 wire; cable (communication).

yūsen suru, *vb.* 優先する give priority to.

yūsen-terebi, *n.* 有線テレビ cable TV.

yushi, *n.* 油脂 oil; fat.

yūshi, *n.* 融資 financing.

yūshi suru, *vb.* 融資する finance.

yūshō, *n.* 優勝 championship; victory.

yūshoku, *n.* 夕食 evening meal.

yūshoku (no), *adj.* 有色 (の) colored.

yūshōsha, *n.* 優勝者 champion; winner.

yūshō suru, *vb.* 優勝する win (first place).

yūshū (na), *adj.* 優秀 (な) outstanding; prominent.

yushutsu, *n.* 輸出 export.

yusō, *n.* 輸送 shipment; transportation.

yūsō, *n.* 郵送 mailing.

yūsō (na), *adj.* 勇壮 (な) brave; heroic.

yūsū (no), *adj.* 有数 (の) prominent.

yusuburu, *vb.* 揺すぶる shake.

yusugu, *n.* ゆすぐ rinse.

yusuri, *n.* 強請り 1. extortion. 2. blackmail.

yusuru, *vb.* 強請る blackmail.

yusuru, *vb.* 揺する shake.

yutaka (na), *adj.* 豊か (な) rich.

yūtō (na, no), *adj.* 優等 (な、の)

excellent; outstanding.

yutori, *n.* ゆとり 1. space; room. 2. ease.

yūtō-sei, *n.* 優等生 honor student.

yū'utsu, *n.* 憂うつ depression; melancholy.

yū'utsu (na), *adj.* 憂うつ (な) depressing; gloomy.

yūwa, *n.* 融和 harmony.

yuwakashi, *n.* 湯沸かし teakettle.

yūwaku, *n.* 誘惑 seduction; temptation.

yūwaku suru, *vb.* 誘惑する seduce; tempt.

yūyake, *n.* 夕焼け sunset.

yūyo suru, *vb.* 猶予する 1. grant a postponement. 2. reprieve.

yūzai (no), *adj.* 有罪 (の) guilty (criminal).

yūzen(zome), *n.* 有禅(染め) method of textile dyeing originated in Kyoto.

yuzuriukeru, *vb.* 譲り受ける inherit.

yuzuriwatasu, *vb.* 譲り渡す hand over; transfer.

yuzuru, *vb.* 譲る 1. give way. 2. hand over. 3. sell. 4. bequeath.

yūzū suru, *vb.* 融通する finance; lend money.

Z

za, *n.* 座 1. seat; **za ni tsuku** take a seat. 2. post; position; **sōri no za ni tsuku** assume the position of prime minister.

zabuton, *n.* 座布団 floor cushion.

zadan, *n.* 座談 talk; conversation.

zai, *n.* 財 wealth; **zai o nasu** make a fortune.

zai'aku, *n.* 罪悪 1. crime. 2. sin; vice.

zai'akukan, *n.* 罪悪感 guilt feelings.

zaibatsu, *n.* 財閥 financial combine.

zaidan, *n.* 財団 foundation (institution).

zaigaku, *n.* 在学 school enrollment.

zaigaku-shōmeisho, *n.* 在学証明書 school registration certificate.

zaigen, *n.* 財源 financial resources.

zaihō, *n.* 財宝 treasure; wealth.

zaijū, *n.* 在住 residence.

zaikai, *n.* 財界 business world.

zaiko, *n.* 在庫 stock; inventory.

zaimoku, *n.* 材木 lumber; timber.

zaimu, *n.* 財務 financial matters.

zainin, *n.* 罪人 criminal; sinner.

zairyō, *n.* 材料 material; ingredient.

zairyoku, *n.* 財力 1. financial power. 2. assets; wealth.

zaisan, *n.* 財産 assets; fortune; property.

zaisei, *n.* 財政 public finance.

zaiseichū ni, *adv.* 在世中に during one's lifetime.

zaiseikiki, *n.* 財政危機 financial crisis.

zaitaku, *n.* 在宅 being at home.

zakkaten, *n.* 雑貨店 variety store.

zakkubaran (na, no), *adj.* ざっくばらん (な、の) frank; straightforward.

zakuro, *n.* ざくろ pomegranate.

zakyō, *n.* 座興 fun; entertainment.

zandaka, *n.* 残高 outstanding balance.

zangai, *n.* 残骸 wreckage; ruin.

zangaku, *n.* 残額 outstanding balance.

zange, *n.* ざんげ contrition; confession.

zangyaku (na), *adj.* 残虐 (な) cruel; inhuman.

zangyō, *n.* 残業 overtime work.

zankin, *n.* 残金 remaining balance.

zankoku (na), *adj.* 残酷 (な) brutal; atrocious.

zanmuseiri, *n.* 残務整理 liquidation.

zan'nen (na), *adj.* 残念 (な) disappointing; regrettable.

zan'nin (na), *adj.* 残忍 (な) inhuman; atrocious.

zanshin (na), *adj.* 斬新 (な) creative; original.

zantei-teki ni, *adv.* 暫定的に for the moment; tentatively.

zappi, *n.* 雑費 miscellaneous expenses.

zara-zara suru, *vb.* ざらざらする 1. feel rough. 2. be sandy.

zarigani, *n.* ざりがに crayfish.

zaru, *n.* ざる bamboo colander.

zaseki, *n.* 座席 seat (transportation, theater).

zaseki-shiteiken, *n.* 座席指定券 reserved-seat ticket.

zasetsu, *n.* 挫折 failure; setback.

zasetsu suru, *vb.* 挫折する be frustrated; collapse; fail.

zashiki, *n.* 座敷 Japanese-style room with tatami flooring.

zasshi, *n.* 雑誌 magazine; periodical.

zasshu, *n.* 雑種 mongrel; mixed breed.

zassō, *n.* 雑草 weeds.

zatsu (na), *adj.* 雑 (な) crude; sloppy.

zatsudan, *n.* 雑談 chat.

zatsunen, *n.* 雑念 1. distraction. 2. worldly thoughts.

zatsuon, *n.* 雑音 noise; static.

zatsuyō, *n.* 雑用 miscellaneous duties; chores.

zatta (na, no), *adj.* 雑多 (な、の) miscellaneous.

zatto, *adv.* ざっと 1. roughly; approximately. 2. briefly.

zattō, *n.* 雑踏 crowd; congestion.

zawameku, *vb.* ざわめく rustle; be noisy.

zawatsuku, *vb.* ざわつく be noisy.

zazen, *n.* 座禅 Zen meditation.

zehi, *adv.* 是非 by all means; definitely; really.

zei, *n.* 税 tax; duty.

zeigen, *n.* 税源 tax resources.

zeijaku (na), *adj.* 脆弱 (な) fragile; weak.

zeikan, *n.* 税関 customs office.

zeikin, *n.* 税金 tax; duty.

zeikomi de, *adv.* 税込みで including tax.

zeimusho, *n.* 税務署 tax office.

zeiniku, *n.* 贅肉 body fat.

zeiritsu, *n.* 税率 tax rate.

zeitaku, *n.* 贅沢 extravagance; luxury.

zeitaku (na), *adj.* 贅沢 (な) extravagant; luxurious.

zekkō (no), *adj.* 絶好 (の) propitious; ideal; wished-for.

zekkō suru, *vb.* 絶交する break off a relationship.

zekku suru, *vb.* 絶句する be speechless.

zekkyō, *n.* 絶叫 scream; shriek.

zemi(nā), *n.* ゼミ(ナー) (G. *Zeminar*) seminar.

zen, *n.* 禅 Zen Buddhism.

zen, *n.* 善 good; right; virtue.

zen 前 1. *adj.* ex-; former; **zendaigishi** former Diet member.

2. *prep.* before; in front of; **ganzen de** before my eyes.

zen- 全 all; whole; **zensekai** the whole world.

-zen 膳 counter for bowls of cooked rice; **gohan ichizen** a bowl of cooked rice.

zenbu 全部 1. *pron.* all; everything. 2. *adj.* all.

zenbu de, *adv.* 全部で in all; everything included.

zenbun, *n.* 前文 preface.

zenchishi, *n.* 前置詞 preposition.

zenchō, *n.* 前兆 premonition; omen.

zendo, *n.* 全土 whole country; whole area.

zen'ei, 前衛 1. *n.* forward (sports). 2. *adj.* avant-garde (art, theater).

zen'ei-teki (na), *adj.* 前衛的 (な) avant-garde; experimental (art).

zengaku, *n.* 全額 entire amount (money).

zengo, *n.* 前後 1. front and rear. 2. time before and after. 3. sequence.

zengo (ni), *adv.* 前後 (に) 1. in front and behind; back and forth. 2. about; **hyaku-doru zengo** about one hundred dollars.

zenhan, *n.* 前半 first half.

zen'i, *n.* 善意 goodwill.

zen'in, *n.* 全員 all members; everyone.

zenin suru, *vb.* 是認する approve.

zenji, *adv.* 漸次 gradually.

zenjitsu, *n.* 前日 previous day.

zenjutsu (no), *adj.* 前述 (の) above-mentioned.

zenka, *n.* 前科 previous criminal record.

zenkai, *n.* 前回 last time.

zenkai suru, *vb.* 全快する recover (one's health) completely.

zenkei, *n.* 前景 foreground.

zenki, *n.* 前期 first term.

zenki (no), *adj.* 前記 (の) above-mentioned.

zenkoku, *n.* 全国 entire nation.

zenmen-teki ni, *adv.* 全面的に entirely; wholly.

zenmetsu suru, *vb.* 全滅する be destroyed; be eliminated.

zen'nen, *n.* 前年 previous year.

zen'nin, *n.* 善人 good person.

zen'nō, *n.* 全納 payment in full.

zenpai suru, *vb.* 全廃する abolish.

zenpan, *n.* 全般 the whole.

zenpan ni, *adv.* 全般に as a whole; in general.

zenpō ni, *adv.* 前方に in front; ahead; forward.

zenra (no), *adj.* 全裸 (の) stark naked.

zenrei, *n.* 前例 precedent.

zenreki, *n.* 前歴 personal history.

zenryaku, *n.* 前略 salutation in a letter indicating that the writer is dispensing with formalities.

zenryō (na), *adj.* 善良 (な) good-hearted.

zenryoku o tsukusu, *vb.* 全力を尽くす do one's utmost.

zensai, *n.* 前菜 appetizer; hors d'oeuvre.

zense, *n.* 前世 previous incarnation.

zensei, *n.* 全盛 culmination; heyday; peak.

zensekai, *n.* 全世界 the whole world.

zensen, *n.* 前線 front line.

zensha, *n.* 前者 the former.

zenshin, *n.* 全身 the entire body (human).

zenshinmasui, *n.* 全身麻酔 general anesthesia.

zenshin suru, *vb.* 前進する 1.

move forward. 2. make progress.

zensho suru, *vb.* 善処する make an effort to solve a problem; make the best of.

zenshū, *n.* 禅宗 Zen (religion).

zenshū, *n.* 全集 complete literary works.

zensoku, *n.* ぜん息 asthma.

zensokuryoku de, *adv.* 全速力で at full speed.

zensōkyoku, *n.* 前奏曲 prelude.

zentai, *n.* 全体 whole.

zentai de, *adv.* 全体で in all; all told.

zentaishugi, *n.* 全体主義 totalitarianism.

zentai to shite, *adv.* 全体として as a whole; in general.

zentei, *n.* 前提 premise; prerequisite.

zento, *n.* 前途 future prospects.

zen'ya, *n.* 前夜 previous evening or night; eve.

zen'yaku, *n.* 全訳 complete translation.

zen-zen, *adv.* ぜんぜん 1. entirely. 2. (with negative) never; not at all; **Sake o zen-zen nomanai.** (I) never drink sake.

zeppan, *adj.* 絶版 out-of-print.

zeppeki, *n.* 絶壁 precipice.

zero, *n.* ゼロ (E.) zero.

zesei suru, *vb.* 是正する correct.

zessan, *n.* 絶賛 acclaim; high praise.

zessan suru, *vb.* 絶賛する acclaim; praise highly.

zessei (no), *adj.* 絶世 (の) matchless; peerless.

zesshoku, *n.* 絶食 fast.

zetchō, *n.* 絶頂 culmination; peak.

zetsubō, *n.* 絶望 despair.

zetsudai (na), *adj.* 絶大 (な) great; immense.

zetsumei, *n.* 絶命 death.

zetsumetsu, *n.* 絶滅 extinction.

zetsumyō (na), *adj.* 絶妙 (な) exquisite; outstanding.

zettai (ni), *adv.* 絶対 (に) 1. absolutely; definitely. 2. by any means.

zō, *n.* 象 elephant.

zō, *n.* 像 image; portrait; statue.

zōdai suru, *vb.* 増大する enlarge; increase.

zōen, *n.* 造園 landscaping.

zōgan, *n.* 象眼 inlay; inlaid enamel or lacquer.

zōge, *n.* 象牙 ivory.

zōgo, *n.* 造語 coined word.

zōin, *n.* 増員 personnel increase.

-zoi ni 沿いに along; **kawazoi ni** along the river.

zōka, *n.* 造花 artificial flowers.

zōka suru, *vb.* 増加する increase.

zōkei, *n.* 造詣 knowledge; mastery.

zōki, *n.* 臓器 internal organ.

zōkin, *n.* 雑巾 dustcloth; cleaning cloth.

zokka, *n.* 俗化 popularization.

zokkō suru, *vb.* 続行する continue.

zoku, *n.* 賊 burglar; robber.

-zoku 族 1. family; class; race; tribe; **kizoku** noble family or class.

zoku (na), *adj.* 俗 (な) mundane; vulgar; common.

zokuaku (na), *adj.* 俗悪 (な) vulgar.

zokubutsu, *n.* 俗物 1. mediocre person. 2. snob. 3. worldly person.

zokugo, *n.* 俗語 slang.

zokuhen, *n.* 続編 sequel.

zoku ni, *adv.* 俗に generally; commonly.

zokusei, *n.* 属性 attribute.

zokusetsu, *n.* 俗説 commonly accepted opinion.

zokushin, *n.* 俗信 common belief; superstition.

zokushū, *n.* 俗習 convention; custom.

zoku suru, *vb.* 属する belong; **kyōsan tō ni zoku suru** belong to the Communist Party.

zoku-zoku (to), *adv.* 続々 (と) one after another.

zoku-zoku suru, *vb.* ぞくぞくする 1. feel chilly. 2. be excited.

zonbun (ni), *adv.* 存分 (に) fully; to one's heart's content.

zonjiru, *vb.* 存じる know.

zonmei suru, *vb.* 存命する be alive.

zonzai (na), *adj.* ぞんざい (な) impolite; coarse.

zō'o, *n.* 憎悪 abhorrence; hatred.

zōri, *n.* 草履 Japanese sandals.

zōsan, *n.* 増産 increase in production.

zōsen, *n.* 造船 shipbuilding.

zōsensho, *n.* 造船所 shipyard.

zōsetsu, *n.* 増設 increase of buildings or equipment.

zōshin suru, *vb.* 増進する increase; promote.

zōsho, *n.* 蔵書 book collection; library.

zōshū, *n.* 増収 income or profit increase.

zōsui suru, *vb.* 増水する rise (water level).

zōtei suru, *vb.* 贈呈する donate; present.

zōtōhin, *n.* 贈呈品 gift; present.

zotto suru, *vb.* ぞっとする shudder; be scared; be disgusted.

zōwai, *n.* 贈賄 bribery.

zōzei, *n.* 増税 tax increase.

zu, *n.* 図 drawing; illustration; picture.

zuan, *n.* 図案 design.

zubanukeru, *vb.* ずば抜ける excel; be outstanding.

zubon, *n.* ズボン (F. *Jupon*) pants; trousers.

zubon-tsuri, *n.* ズボン吊り suspenders.

zubora (na), *adj.* ずぼら (な) lazy; sloppy.

zubu (no), *adj.* ずぶ (の) utter; rank.

zubunure (no), *adj.* ずぶ濡れ (の) soaking wet.

zubutoi, *adj.* 図太い audacious; brazen.

zuga, *n.* 図画 drawing; painting.

zugaikotsu, *n.* 頭蓋骨 skull.

zuhyō, *n.* 図表 chart; diagram.

zui, *n.* 髄 marrow.

zuibun, *adv.* 随分 very.

zuihitsu, *n.* 随筆 essay.

zuihitsuka, *n.* 随筆家 essayist.

zui'ichi (no), *adj.* 随一 (の) number one; top.

zui'i ni, *adv.* 随意に as one likes.

zuikōin, *n.* 随行員 retinue; attendant.

zuikō suru, *vb.* 随行する accompany.

zujō ni, *adv.* 頭上に overhead.

zukai, *n.* 図解 illustration.

zukan, *n.* 図鑑 picture book.

zukei, *n.* 図形 drawing; figure.

zuki-zuki suru, *vb.* ずきずきする smart; throb.

-zukume ずくめ full of; **ii koto-zukume** full of good things.

zumen, *n.* 図面 blueprint; design.

zunguri shita, *adj.* ずんぐりした short and stocky.

zunō, *n.* 頭脳 brains; head.

zurari to, *adv.* ずらりと in a row.

zurasu, *vb.* ずらす move or shift

(location, schedule).

zure, *n.* ずれ gap.

zureru, *vb.* ずれる shift out of place; deviate; stray.

zuriochiru, *vb.* ずり落ちる slip down.

zurui, *adj.* ずるい dishonest; sly.

zusan (na), *adj.* ずさん (な) sloppy; neglectful.

zushi suru, *vb.* 図示する illustrate.

zūtai, *n.* 図体 frame (human body).

-zutsu, *parti.* ずつ 1. by (one by one, little by little, etc.); **hitori zutsu** one by one (people). 2. (for) each; **ringo futatsu zutsu** two apples (for) each (person).

zutsū, *n.* 頭痛 headache; **zutsū ga suru** have a headache.

zutto, *adv.* ずっと 1. always; all the while; all the way. 2. very much; far more; **zutto omoshiroi** far more interesting.

zū-zūshii, *adj.* 図々しい brazen; shameless.

English-Japanese
Dictionary

辞典

A

a, *art.* 1. hitotsu (no) 一つ (の) (one thing); hitori (no) 一人 (の) (one person). 2. aru 或る (a certain).

abacus, *n.* soroban 算盤.

abalone, *n.* awabi あわび.

abandon, *vb.* 1. akirameru あきらめる; yameru 止める (give up). 2. misuteru 見捨る (forsake).

abase, *vb.* 1. hige suru 卑下する (humble oneself). 2. sageru 下げる (degrade).

abate, *vb.* 1. osamaru 治まる (calm). 2. herasu 減らす; sageru 下げる (decrease).

abbreviate, *vb.* shōryaku suru 省略する.

abbreviation, *n.* shōryakukei 省略形.

abdicate, *vb.* tai'i suru 退位する; shirizoku 退く.

abdomen, *n.* fukubu 腹部; onaka お腹.

abduct, *vb.* yūkai suru 誘拐する.

abduction, *n.* yūkai 誘拐.

aberration, *n.* 1. itsudatsu 逸脱; dassen 脱線 (deviation). 2. seishin sakuran 精神錯乱 (mental disorder).

abet, *vb.* sosonokasu そそのかす; keshikakeru けしかける.

abeyance, *n.* ichijichūshi 一時中止; horyū 保留.

abhor, *vb.* nikumu 憎む.

abhorrence, *n.* nikushimi 憎しみ.

abhorrent, *adj.* iya de tamaranai 嫌でたまらない; daikirai (na) 大嫌い (な).

abide, *vb.* 1. nokoru 残る; iru 居る (stay). 2. sumu 住む (reside).

abiding, *adj.* eizoku-teki (na) 永続

的 (な).

ability, *n.* 1. nōryoku 能力 (competence). 2. sainō 才能 (talent).

abject, *adj.* mijime (na) 惨め (な); nasakenai 情無い (wretched).

ablaze, *adj.* 1. moeteiru 燃えている (on fire). 2. kōfun shiteiru 興奮している (excited).

able, *adj.* 1. yūnō (na) 有能 (な) (competent). 2. dekiru 出来る (able to do); **able to speak** hanasu koto ga dekiru.

abnegation, *n.* jisei 自制.

abnormal, *adj.* ijō (na) 異常 (な).

aboard, *adv.* ... ni notte ... に乗って (bus, train, ship).

abode, *n.* 1. ie 家 (house); jūtaku 住宅 (residence). 2. taizai 滞在 (extended stay).

abolish, *vb.* haishi suru 廃止する.

aborigine, *n.* genjūmin 原住民.

abort, *vb.* 1. (ninshin) chūzetsu suru (妊娠) 中絶する (end pregnancy). 2. ryūzan suru 流産する (miscarry). 3. shippai suru 失敗する (fail). 4. chūdan suru 中断する (discontinue).

abortion, *n.* 1. (ninshin)chūzetsu (妊娠)中絶. 2. ryūzan 流産. 3. shippai 失敗. 4. chūdan 中断.

abound, *vb.* hōfu (na) 豊富 (な); takusan (no) 沢山 (の).

about, 1. *adv.* daitai 大体; oyoso 凡そ; yaku 約; -gurai/-kurai -位 (approximately); **about five people** gonin-gurai 五人位. 2. *prep.* -goro -頃 (around); **about five o'clock** goji-goro; ... ni tsuite ... について (concerning); **about**

this book kono hon ni tsuite この本について.

above, *adv., prep.* (...yori, no) ue ni (...より、の) 上に.

aboveboard, *adv.* dō-dō to 堂々と.

abrade, *vb.* suriheru 磨り減る (wear off); suriherasu 磨り減らす (cause to wear off).

abrasion, *n.* 1. mametsu 磨滅 (wearing down). 2. surikizu 擦り傷 (injury, scratch).

abrasive, *adj.* 1. suriherasu 磨り減らす (causing abrasion). 2. iya (na) 嫌 (な); kan ni sawaru 癇にさわる (annoying).

abreast, *adv.* narande 並んで; tomo ni 供に; **keep abreast of** ...ni tsuite iku ...について行く.

abridge, *vb.* tanshuku suru 短縮する (shorten); herasu 減らす (decrease).

abroad, *adv.* gaikoku de/ni 外国で／に; kaigai de/ni 海外で／に.

abrogate, *vb.* haishi suru 廃止する.

abrupt, *adj.* kyū (na) 急 (な); totsuzen (no) 突然 (の).

abscess, *n.* nōyō 膿瘍.

abscond, *vb.* tōbō suru 逃亡する; nigeru 逃げる.

absence, *n.* rusu 留守 (from office, home); kesseki 欠席 (from class, meeting).

absent, *adj.* inai いない; rusu (no) 留守 (の) (out for a while from office, home); **be absent** rusu ni suru 留守にする; yasumu 休む.

absent-minded, *adj.* bon'yari shita ぼんやりした.

absolute, *adj.* zettai-teki (na) 絶対的 (な); zettai (no) 絶対 (の).

absolutely, *adv.* zettai ni 絶対に (definitely); kanzen ni 完全に (completely).

absolve, *vb.* yurusu 許す (forgive);

menjo suru 免除する (release).

absorb, *vb.* kyūshū suru 吸収する; nomikomu 飲み込む; **be absorbed (in)** ...ni bottō suru ...に没頭する.

absorption, *n.* 1. kyūshū 吸収 (soaking up). 2. bottō 没頭 (enthusiasm).

abstain, *vb.* hikaeru 控える; tsutsushimu 慎む.

abstinence, *n.* 1. jisei 自制 (self-restraint). 2. kinshu 禁酒 (from drinking).

abstract, 1. *n.* chūshōgainen 抽象概念 (abstract idea); yōyaku 要約 (summary). 2. *adj.* chūshō-teki (na) 抽象的 (な).

absurd, *adj.* fugōri (na) 不合理 (な); bakageta 馬鹿げた.

absurdity, *n.* fugōri 不合理; baka(-rashisa) 馬鹿(らしさ).

abundance, *n.* taryō 多量 (large amount); tasū 多数 (large number).

abundant, *adj.* hōfu (na) 豊富 (な); takusan (no) 沢山 (の).

abuse, 1. *n.* gyakutai 虐待 (maltreatment); akuyō 悪用 (misuse). 2. *vb.* gyakutai suru 虐待する; akuyō suru 悪用する.

abusive, *adj.* 1. ranbō na 乱暴な (cruel). 2. kuchigitanai 口汚ない (scurrilous).

abut (on), *vb.* sessuru 接する.

abyss, *n.* shin'en 深淵; naraku 奈落.

academic, *adj.* 1. akademikku (na) アカデミック (な); gakumon (no) 学問 (の) (scholastic). 2. daigaku (no) 大学 (の) (of a university).

academy, *n.* akademī アカデミー; gakuen 学園.

accede, *vb.* 1. dōi suru 同意する (agree). 2. ...ni tsuku ...に就く

(assume title).

accelerate, *vb.* kasoku suru 加速する.

accelerator, *n.* akuseru アクセル.

accent, *n.* 1. akusento アクセント; kyōchō 強調 (emphasis). 2. namari 訛 (local speech).

accentuate, *vb.* kyōchō suru 強調する (emphasize).

accept, *vb.* ukeireru 受け入れる; shōdaku suru 承諾する (agree to); uketoru 受け取る (receive).

acceptable, *adj.* 1. ii いい; kekkō (na) 結構 (な) (agreeable). 2. mā-mā (no) まあまあ (の) (bearable).

acceptance, *n.* ukeire 受け入れ; shōdaku 承諾.

access, *n.* sekkin 接近 (approach); chikazuku hōhō 近づく方法 (means of approach); **have access to** te ni hairu 手に入る.

accessible, *adj.* chikazuki-yasui 近づき易い; te ni ire-yasui 手に入れ易い.

accessory, *n.* akusesarī アクセサリー; sōshingu 装身具.

accident, *n.* jiko 事故; **by accident** gūzen ni 偶然に (coincidental); fui ni 不意に (unintentional).

accidental, *adj.* gūzen (no) 偶然 (の); fui (no) 不意 (の).

accidentally, *adv.* gūzen ni 偶然に; fui ni 不意に.

acclaim, 1. *n.* shōsan 賞讃. 2. *vb.* shōsan suru 賞讃する.

acclamation, *n.* shōsan 賞讃; kassai 喝采.

acclimate, *vb.* nareru 慣れる; jun'nō suru 順応する.

accommodate, *vb.* 1. bengi o hakaru 便宜を図る (oblige). 2. tomeru 泊める (lodge). 3. tekiō saseru 適応させる (adapt).

accommodating, *adj.* shinsetsu (na) 親切 (な).

accommodation, *n.* 1. bengi 便宜 (convenience). 2. shukuhakusho 宿泊所 (lodge); shisetsu 施設 (facilities). 3. tekiō 適応 (adaptation).

accompaniment, *n.* 1. fuzokubutsu 付属物 (attached item). 2. bansō 伴奏 (music).

accompanist, *n.* bansōsha 伴奏者.

accompany, *vb.* 1. otomo suru お供する; dōkō suru 同行する (go with). 2. tsuite kuru ついて来る (come with). 3. bansō suru 伴奏する (music).

accomplice, *n.* kyōhansha 共犯者.

accomplish, *vb.* nashitogeru 成し遂げる; kansei suru 完成する.

accomplished, *adj.* kansei shita 完成した (completed); sugureta 勝れた (superb).

accomplishment, *n.* 1. gyōseki 業績 (achievement). 2. kyōyō 教養; tashinami たしなみ (abilities).

accord, 1. *n.* itchi 一致; chōwa 調和 (harmony); kyōtei 協定 (agreement); **of one's own accord** jihatsu-teki ni 自発的に. 2. *vb.* itchi suru 一致する; chōwa suru 調和する.

according to, *prep.* ...ni yoruto/yoreba ...によると／よれば (quotation). 2. ...ni shitagatte ...に従って (based on).

accordingly, *adv.* shitagatte 従って; sorede それで.

accordion, *n.* akōdion アコーディオン.

accost, *vb.* hanashikakeru 話しかける.

account, 1. *n.* riyū 理由 (reason); hanashi 話 (narration); hōkoku 報告 (report); yokinkōza 預金口座

(bank account); kanjō 勘定 (bill).
2. *vb.* kazoeru 数える (calculate);
hanasu 話す (narrate); **account
for** setsumei suru 説明する
(explain).

accountable, *adj.* 1. sekinin ga aru
責任がある(responsible). 2.
setsumei dekiru 説明出来る
(explicable).

accountant, *n.* kaikei-shi/-gakari
会計士/〜係.

accounting, *n.* kaikei 会計.

accumulate, *vb.* tameru/tamaru 溜
める／溜まる; tsumoru 積もる.

accuracy, *n.* seikakusa 正確さ.

accurate, *adj.* seikaku (na) 正確
(な).

accuse, *vb.* semeru 責める.

accustom, *vb.* narasu 慣らす; **get
accustomed to** ...ni nareru.

ace, *n.* ēsu エース.

ache, 1. *n.* itami 痛み. 2. *vb.* itamu
痛む.

achieve, *vb.* tassei suru 達成する.

achievement, *n.* tassei 達成.

acid, 1. *n.* san 酸. 2. *adj.* sansei (no)
酸性 (の) (acidic); suppai 酸っぱい
(sour).

acknowledge, *vb.* mitomeru 認め
る; shōnin suru 承認する.

acknowledgment, *n.* zenin 是認;
shōnin 承認 (recognition); **in
acknowledgment of** ...ni/o
kansha shite ...に／を感謝して.

acorn, *n.* donguri どんぐり.

acoustics, *n.* akōsutikkusu アコー
スティックス; onkyō 音響.

acquaint, *vb.* shiraseru 知らせる;
be acquainted with (...o) shitteiru (...を) 知っている; **get
acquainted with** (...to) shiriai ni
naru (...と) 知り合いになる
(person); ...ni nareru ...に慣れる
(get accustomed to).

acquaintance, *n.* shiriai 知り合い;
chijin 知人.

acquiesce, *vb.* fukujū suru 服従す
る.

acquire, *vb.* 1. eru 得る (get). 2.
shūtoku suru 習得する (learn).

acquisition, *n.* shutokubutsu 取得
物 (obtainment); kaimono 買物
(purchase).

acquit, *vb.* 1. menjiru 免じる
(release). 2. furumau ふるまう
(behave).

acquittal, *n.* menjo 免除; shakuhō
釈放.

acre, *n.* ēkā エーカー.

acrimonious, *adj.* tsūretsu (na) 痛
烈 (な).

acrobat, *n.* akurobatto アクロバッ
ト; kyokugei 曲芸.

across, *adv., prep.* (...o) yokogitte
(...を) 横切って; (...no) mukō ni
(...の) 向こうに; **go across**
yokogiru.

act, 1. *n.* okonai 行ない; kōdō 行動
(behavior); maku 幕 (theater). 2.
vb. suru する (do); furumau ふる
まう (behave); engi suru 演技する
(theater).

acting, 1. *n.* engi 演技; shibai 芝居.
2. *adj.* dairi (no) 代理 (の)
(substitute).

action, *n.* ugoki 動き; katsudō 活
動.

activate, *vb.* ugokasu 動かす;
katsudō saseru 活動させる.

active, *adj.* kappatsu (na) 活発
(な); katsudō-teki (na) 活動的
(な).

activity, *n.* katsudō 活動; undō 運
動.

actor, *n.* haiyū 俳優 (male,
female); danyū 男優 (male).

actress, *n.* joyū 女優.

actual, *adj.* 1. genjitsu (no) 現実

(の) (real). 2. ima (no) 今 (の)
(present).

actuality, *n.* genjitsu 現実.

actually, *adv.* genjitsu ni 現実に;
jitsu wa 実は.

acumen, *n.* dōsatsuryoku 洞察力.

acupuncture, *n.* hari (chiryō) 針
(治療).

acute, *adj.* 1. surudoi 鋭い (sharp);
hageshii 激しい (intense). 2.
setsujitsu (na) 切実 (な) (critical).
3. kyūsei (no) 急性 (の) (disease).

adage, *n.* kakugen 格言; kotowaza
諺.

adamant, *adj.* 1. ganko (na) 頑固
(な) (stubborn). 2. katai 堅い
(hard).

adapt, *vb.* 1. tekiō saseru 適応させ
る (make fit). 2. kyakushoku suru
脚色する (rewrite).

adaptable, *adj.* jun'nō dekiru 順応
出来る.

adaptation, *n.* 1. tekiō 適応 (fit).
2. kyakushoku 脚色 (rewriting).

adapter, *n.* adaputā アダプター.

add, *vb.* tasu 足す; kuwaeru 加え
る; **add up** gōkei suru 合計する.

addict, *n.* chūdoku(sha) 中毒(者);
drug addict mayaku-chūdoku.

addiction, *n.* chūdoku 中毒.

addition, *n.* tsuika 追加 (extra);
tashizan 足し算 (mathematics); **in
addition** sono ue ni その上に; **in
addition to** ...ni kuwaete ...に加
えて; mata また.

additional, *adj.* tsuika (no) 追加
(の); sono hoka (no) その他 (の).

additive, n. tenkabutsu 添加物
(food).

address, 1. *n.* jūsho 住所
(location); enzetsu 演説 (speech).
2. *vb.* jūsho o kaku 住所を書く
(address a letter); hanashikakeru
話しかける (speak to); torikumu

取り組む (handle).

addressee, *n.* uketorinin 受け取り
人.

adept, *adj.* takumi (na) 巧み (な).

adequate, *adj.* jūbun (na) 十分
(な).

adhere, *vb.* 1. kuttsuku くっつく
(glue). 2. yaritōsu やり通す;
mamoritōsu 守り通す (be
faithful).

adhesive, *adj.* nenchakusei (no) 粘
着性 (の).

adhesive tape, *n.* nenchaku-tēpu
粘着テープ.

adjacent, *adj.* tonari (no) 隣 (の);
chikaku (no) 近く (の).

adjective, *n.* keiyōshi 形容詞.

adjoining, *adj.* tonari (no) 隣 (の).

adjourn, *vb.* enki suru 延期する.

adjunct, *adj.* fuzoku (no) 付属
(の).

adjust, *vb.* 1. chōsetsu suru 調節す
る; awaseru 合わせる (tune,
regulate). 2. totonoeru 整える
(organize).

adjustment, *n.* 1. chōsetsu 調節
(regulation). 2. seiri 整理 (putting
in order).

administer, *vb.* 1. kanri suru 管理
する (manage); osameru 治める
(govern). 2. shikō suru 施行する
(put into practice).

administration, *n.* 1. kanri 管理
(management); keiei 経営
(business); gyōsei 行政
(governing). 2. shikō 施行
(practice).

administrative, *adj.* kanri (no) 管
理 (の) (management); gyōsei (no)
行政 (の) (government).

administrator, *n.* kanrishoku 管理
職; gyōseisha 行政者.

admirable, *adj.* subarashii 素晴ら
しい.

admiral, *n.* teitoku 提督.

admiration, *n.* shōsan 賞賛.

admire, *vb.* shōsan suru 賞賛する; tataeru 称える (praise); kanshin suru 感心する (be impressed); miageru 見上げる (look up to).

admirer, *n.* shōsansha 賞賛者; sūhaisha 崇拝者.

admission, *n.* 1. nyūjōkyoka 入場許可 (entrance admission); nyūgakukyoka 入学許可 (school admission). 2. nyūjōryō 入場料 (admission fee).

admit, *vb.* 1. ukeireru 受け入れる (allow). 2. mitomeru 認める (confess).

admittance, *n.* nyūjō 入場 (entrance); **No admittance.** Nyūjōkinshi 入場禁止; Tachi'iri-kinshi 立入り禁止.

admonish, *vb.* chūi suru 注意する; isameru 諫める.

adolescence, *n.* seinenki 青年期.

adolescent, *n., adj.* seinen (no) 青年 (の).

adopt, *vb.* 1. saiyō suru 採用する (use). 2. yōshi ni suru 養子にする (adopt a child).

adopted, adoptive, *adj.* yōshi (no) 養子 (の) (of a child).

adoption, *n.* 1. saiyō 採用 (use). 2. yōshiengumi 養子縁組 (child adoption).

adorable, *adj.* kawaii 可愛い.

adore, *vb.* 1. sūhai suru 崇拝する (honor). 2. netsuai suru 熱愛する (love).

adorn, *vb.* kazaru 飾る.

adornment, *n.* kazari 飾り.

adrift, *adv.* samayotte さまよって.

adroit, *adj.* 1. kiyō (na) 器用 (な) (dexterous). 2. kibin (na) 機敏 (な) (nimble).

adulate, *vb.* goma o suru 胡麻をす

る; hetsurau へつらう.

adulation, *n.* gomasuri 胡麻すり; hetsurai へつらい.

adult, *n., adj.* otona (no) 大人 (の); seijin (no) 成人 (の).

adulterate, *vb.* shitsu o sageru 質を下げる.

adultery, *n.* kantsū 姦通; fugi 不義.

advance, 1. *n.* shinpo 進歩 (progress); zenshin 前進 (moving forward); shōshin 昇進 (promotion); maekin 前金 (money); **in advance** maemotte 前もって. 2. *vb.* shinpo suru 進歩する (progress); susumu 進む (move forward); shōshin suru 昇進する (promote).

advanced, *adj.* susunda 進んだ (progressed); jōkyū (no) 上級 (の) (at higher level).

advancement, *n.* 1. shinpo 進歩 (progress). 2. zenshin 前進 (moving forward). 3. shōshin 昇進 (promotion).

advantage, *n.* yūri 有利; **take advantage of** (...o) riyō suru (...を) 利用する (utilize).

advantageous, *adj.* tsugō ga ii 都合がいい; yūri (na) 有利 (な).

advent, *n.* tōrai 到来.

adventure, *n.* bōken 冒険.

adventurer, *n.* bōkenka 冒険家.

adventuresome, adventurous, *adj.* bōken-teki (na) 冒険的 (な).

adverb, *n.* fukushi 副詞.

adversary, *n.* teki 敵 (enemy); kyōsōaite 競争相手 (rival).

adverse, *adj.* 1. hantai (no) 反対 (の); gyaku (no) 逆 (の) (opposite). 2. furi (na) 不利 (な) (disadvantageous).

adversity, *n.* gyakkyō 逆境.

advertise, *vb.* senden suru 宣伝する; kōkoku o dasu 広告を出す

(promote).

advertisement, *n.* 1. senden 宣伝; kōkoku 広告 (promotion). 2. tsūkoku 通告 (notice).

advertiser, *n.* kōkokusha 広告者.

advertising agency, *n.* kōkoku-dairiten 広告代理店.

advice, *n.* adobaisu アドバイス; jogen 助言.

advisable, *adj.* nozomashii 望ましい (desirable); kenmei (na) 賢明 (な).

advise, *vb.* adobaisu suru アドバイスする; jogen suru 助言する.

advisement, *n.* jukuryo 熟慮; **take under advisement** jukuryo suru.

adviser, advisor, *n.* kaunserā カウンセラー; jogensha 助言者; sōdansha 相談者.

advocate, 1. *n.* shijisha 支持者 (supporter); yōgosha 擁護者 (defender). 2. *vb.* shiji suru 支持する; yōgo suru 擁護する.

aerial, 1. *n.* antena アンテナ. 2. *adj.* kūki (no) 空気 (の) (air); kōkūki (no) 航空機 (の) (airplane).

aesthetic, *adj.* bi (no) 美 (の); bi-teki (na) 美的 (な).

aesthetics, *n.* bigaku 美学.

afar, *adv.* tōku ni 遠くに; **from afar** tōku kara 遠くから.

affable, *adj.* shitashimi-yasui 親しみ易い.

affair, *n.* 1. shigoto 仕事; yōji 用事 (business). 2. jiken 事件 (event). 3. **love affair** ren'ai 恋愛.

affect, *vb.* 1. eikyō suru 影響する (influence). 2. kandō saseru 感動させる (move). 3. furi o suru 振りをする (pretend).

affectation, *n.* furi 振り; kidori 気取り.

affected, *adj.* 1. eikyō sareta 影響された (influenced). 2. kidotta 気取った (pretentious). 3. misekake (no) 見せかけ (の) (feigned).

affection, *n.* aichaku 愛着.

affectionate, *adj.* aijōbukai 愛情深い.

affiliate, 1. *n.* kankeisha 関係者 (affiliated person); kankeidantai 関係団体 (affiliated organization). 2. *vb.* kankei saseru/suru 関係させる／する (associate); kanyū saseru 加入させる (join).

affiliation, *n.* kankei 関係 (connection); kanyū 加入 (joining).

affinity, *n.* 1. shinkinkan 親近感; shitashimi 親しみ (liking). 2. ruijisei 類似性 (similarity).

affirm, *vb.* kōtei suru 肯定する; dangen suru 断言する.

affirmative, 1. *n.* kōteibun 肯定文 (sentence). 2. *adj.* kōtei-teki (na) 肯定的 (な); dantei-teki (na) 断定的 (な).

affix, *vb.* 1. haritsukeru 張りつける (adhere). 2. soeru 添える (append).

afflict, *vb.* kurushimeru 苦しめる; **be afflicted with** ...de kurushimu ...で苦しむ.

affliction, *n.* 1. kurushimi 苦しみ (pain). 2. byōki 病気 (sickness).

affluence, *n.* 1. tomi 富 (wealth). 2. yutakasa 豊かさ (abundance).

affluent, *adj.* 1. yūfuku (na) 裕福 (な) (wealthy). 2. yutaka (na) 豊か (な) (abundant).

afford, *vb.* 1. (okane, jikan ga) aru (お金、時間が) 有る (have money, time). 2. yoyū ga aru 余裕が有る (handle). 3. ataeru 与える (supply).

affront, 1. *n.* bujoku 侮辱. 2. *vb.*

bujoku suru 侮辱する.

afield, *adv.* 1. kokyō kara tōku hanarete 故郷から遠く離れて (away from home); **far afield** haruka tōku ni 遥か遠くに. 2. mayotte 迷つて (astray).

afire, *adj.* 1. moete 燃えて (on fire). 2. kōfun shite 興奮して (excited).

aflame, *adj.* 1. moete 燃えて (on fire). 2. akarande 赤らんで (blushed).

afraid, *adj.* 1. kowai 怖い; osoroshii 恐ろしい (frightened); **be afraid of** ...ga kowai/shinpai ...が怖い／心配. 2. shinpai (na) 心配 (な) (worried). 3. zan'nen (na) 残念 (な) (sorry).

after, 1. *adv.* ato de/ni 後で／に (afterward, later); ushiro de/ni 後ろで／に (behind). 2. *prep.* (...no) ato de/ni (...の)後で／に (later than); (...no) ushiro de/ni (...の)後ろで／に (behind); ...ni naratte に倣つて (following). 3. *conj.* sorekara それから; (...shita) ato de (...した) 後で.

afterlife, *n.* 1. raise 来世 (next life). 2. ban'nen 晩年 (later years).

aftermath, *n.* sainan no kekka 災難の結果 (result of tragedy); yoha 余波(effects).

afternoon, *n.* gogo 午後; **good afternoon** kon'nichiwa 今日は.

afterward, *adv.* ato de/ni 後で／に.

again, *adv.* mata 又; futatabi 再び.

against, *prep.* 1. ...ni taishite ...に対して (in competition with). 2. ...ni sakaratte ...に逆らつて (in opposition to). 3. mukatte 向かつて (toward). 4. ...ni motarete ....にもたれて (lean upon).

agape, *adv.* akirete あきれて; azen to shite 啞然として.

age, 1. *n.* toshi 年; nenrei 年齢 (of a man or animal); nensū 年数 (of inanimate objects); jidai 時代 (era); **of age** seijin 成人; **old age** rōnen 老年. 2. *vb.* toshi o toru 年をとる (advance in years); fukeru 老ける (get old); jukusuru 熟する (mature).

aged, *adj.* toshi totta 年とつた (elderly); fuketa 老けた (old); furui 古い (antiquated).

ageless, *adj.* furō (no) 不老 (の); towa (no) とわ (の).

agency, *n.* 1. dairiten 代理店 (agent company); **travel agency** ryokōdairiten. 2. jimusho 事務所 (office). 3. hataraki 働き (function).

agenda, *n.* kyōgijikō 協議事項.

agent, *n.* 1. dairi(nin) 代理(人) (acting person); dairiten 代理店 (firm). 2. daihyōsha 代表者 (representative). 3. yakunin 役人 (government agent). 4. dōin 導因 (cause).

aggrandize, *vb.* 1. tsuyomeru 強める (strengthen). 2. masu 増す (increase).

aggravate, *vb.* 1. akka saseru 悪化させる (exacerbate). 2. ira-ira saseru いらいらさせる (annoy).

aggravation, *n.* 1. akka 悪化 (exacerbation). 2. iradachi 苛立ち (annoyance).

aggregate, 1. *n.* atsumari 集まり (mass); gōkei 合計 (total). 2. *vb.* atsumeru 集める; gōkei suru 合計する. 3. *adj.* sōkei (shita, no) 総計 (した、の).

aggression, *n.* shinryaku 侵略; kōgeki 攻撃.

aggressive, *adj.* 1. kōgeki-teki (na)

攻撃的 (な) (quarrelsome). 2.
sekkyoku-teki (na) 積極的 (な)
(active).

aggressor, *n.* shinryakusha 侵略者;
kōgekisha 攻撃者.

aghast, *adj.* zotto shite ぞっとして
(horrified); bōzen to shite 茫然と
して (stunned).

agile, *adj.* kibin (na) 機敏 (な);
keikai (na) 軽快 (な).

agility, *n.* kibinsa 機敏さ; keikaisa
軽快さ.

agitate, *vb.* 1. yuriugokasu 揺り動
かす (move). 2. dōyō saseru 動揺
させる (perturb). 3. uttaeru 訴え
る (argue). 4. sendō suru 扇動す
る (manipulate).

agitator, *n.* sendōsha 扇動者.

ago, *adj., adv.* mae ni 前に; **two
days ago** futsuka mae ni.

agonize, *vb.* kurushimu 苦しむ.

agony, *n.* kurushimi 苦しみ; kutsū
苦痛.

agrarian, *adj.* nōgyō (no) 農業
(の).

agree, *vb.* 1. dōi suru 同意する;
sansei suru 賛成する (consent). 2.
itchi suru 一致する (concur).

agreeable, *adj.* kokochi yoi 心地良
い; tanoshii 楽しい.

agreement, *n.* 1. dōi 同意; sansei
賛成 (consensus). 2. itchi 一致
(concurrence).

agricultural, *adj.* nōgyō (no) 農業
(の); nōkō (no) 農耕 (の).

agriculture, *n.* nōgyō 農業.

ahead, *adv.* mae ni 前に; saki ni 先
に; **straight ahead** massugu saki
ni まっすぐ先に; **Go ahead.**
Osaki ni dōzo お先にどうぞ.
(After you.).

aid, 1. *n.* enjo 援助. 2. *vb.* enjo
suru 援助する.

AIDS, *n.* eizu エイズ.

ail, *vb.* 1. itamu 痛む (pain). 2.
komaru 困る (trouble). 3.
wazurau 患う (ill).

ailing, *adj.* byōki (no) 病気 (の)
(ill).

ailment, *n.* byōki 病気.

aim, 1. *n.* mokuteki 目的
(purpose); mato 的 (goal). 2. *vb.*
nerau 狙う (point); mezasu 目指す
(intend).

aimless, *adj.* mokuteki ga nai 目的
がない.

air, 1. *n.* kūki 空気 (gas); yōsu 様
子; fūsai 風采(impression); sora 空
(sky); merodī メロディー (tune);
in the open air soto de/ni 外で／
に. 2. *vb.* kaze o tōsu 風を通す
(dry).

air base, *n.* kūgunkichi 空軍基地.

air-conditioned, *adj.* reidanbō
(tsuki) (no) 冷暖房(付) (の).

air-conditioner, *n.* eakon エアコ
ン; reidanbōki 冷暖房機.

air-conditioning, *n.* reidanbō 冷暖
房.

aircraft, *n.* hikōki 飛行機; kōkūki
航空機.

aircraft carrier, *n.* kōkūbokan 航
空母艦.

air force, *n.* kūgun 空軍.

airline, *n.* kōkū(gaisha) 航空(会社)
(company).

airmail, *n.* kōkūbin 航空便.

airplane, *n.* hikōki 飛行機.

airport, *n.* kūkō 空港.

air raid, *n.* kūshū 空襲.

air raid shelter, *n.* bōkūgō 防空壕.

airsick, *adj.* hikōkiyoi 飛行機酔い.

aisle, *n.* tsūro 通路.

ajar, *adj.* hanbiraki (no) 半開き
(の).

akin, *adj.* 1. ketsuen (no) 血縁 (の)
(by blood). 2. nita 似た (by
nature).

alarm, 1. *n.* keihō 警報 (signal); osore 恐れ (fear). 2. *vb.* keihō o dasu 警報を出す (signal); odorokaseru 驚ろかせる (scare).

alarm clock, *n.* mezamashi-dokei 目覚まし時計.

alas, *interj.* aa ああ.

album, *n.* arubamu アルバム; -chō -帳; **picture album** shashin-chō 写真帳.

alchemy, *n.* renkinjutsu 錬金術.

alcohol, *n.* arukōru アルコール; sake 酒.

alcoholic, 1. *adj.* arukōru-chūdoku (no) アルコール中毒 (の) (addicted); sake (no) 酒 (の) (of alcohol). 2. *n.* aru(kōru) chū(doku) アル(コール)中(毒).

alcove, *n.* tokonoma 床の間 (in a traditional Japanese room).

alert, 1. *n.* keihō 警報 (alarm); yōjin 用心 (vigilance). 2. *adj.* nukeme nai 抜け目ない (thoroughly attentive); yōjinbukai 用心深い (vigilant). 3. *vb.* yōjin saseru 用心させる; keikoku suru 警告する.

algebra, *n.* daisūgaku 代数学.

alias, *n.* betsumei 別名.

alien, 1. *adj.* gaikoku (no) 外国 (の) (of a foreign country); awanai 合わない (strange); hantai (no) 反対 (の) (adverse). 2. *n.* gaikokujin 外国人 (foreigner); yosomono よそ者 (outsider).

alienate, *vb.* sogai suru 疎外する; tōzakeru 遠ざける.

alight, *vb.* oriru 降りる; chakuchi suru 着地する.

align, *vb.* naraberu 並べる; soroeru 揃える.

alike, *adj.* 1. nita 似た; niteiru 似ている (similar). 2. onaji 同じ (same).

alimentary, *adj.* eiyō (no) 栄養 (の) (nutritional); tabemono (no) 食べ物 (の) (of food).

alimony, *n.* bekkyoteate 別居手当; rikonteate 離婚手当.

alive, *adj.* ikiteiru 生きている (living); iki-iki shiteiru 生き生きしている (lively).

all, 1. *pron.* subete 全て; min'na 皆; zenbu 全部; **after all** kekkyoku 結局; **Not at all.** Dōitashimashite. どういたしまして (Don't mention it.). 2. *adj.* subete (no) 全て (の); min'na (no) 皆 (の); zenbu (no) 全部 (の). 3. *adv.* sukkari すっかり; mattaku 全く; **all of a sudden** totsuzen 突然.

all-around, *adj.* 1. tasai (na) 多才 (な); ban'nō (na, no) 万能 (な、の) (extremely capable). 2. kanzen (na) 完全 (な) (complete).

allay, *vb.* shizumeru 静める; yawarageru 和らげる.

allegation, *n.* 1. dangen 断言 (affirmation). 2. shuchō 主張 (assertion). 3. mōshitate 申し立て (legal).

allege, *vb.* 1. dangen suru 断言する. 2. shuchō suru 主張する. 3. mōshitateru 申し立てる.

allegiance, *n.* 1. chūsei 忠誠 (loyalty). 2. gimu 義務 (duty).

allegory, *n.* tatoebanashi 譬話; gūwa 寓話.

allergic, *adj.* arerugīsei (no) アレルギー性 (の).

allergy, *n.* arerugī アレルギー; kyozetsuhan'nō 拒絶反応.

alleviate, *vb.* yawarageru 和らげる; shizumeru 静める.

alley, *n.* yokochō 横町; komichi 小道.

alliance, *n.* dōmei 同盟; engumi 縁組.

alligator, *n.* wani わに.

allocate, *vb.* (wari)ateru (割)当てる.

allocation, *n.* wariate 割り当て.

allot, *vb.* bunpai suru 分配する (distribute); ateru 当てる (allocate).

allotment, *n.* bunpai 分配; wariate 割り当て.

all-out, *adj.* tettei-teki (na) 徹底的 (な).

allow, *vb.* 1. yurusu 許す (permit). 2. ataeru 与える (give). 3. mitomeru 認める (admit).

allowance, *n.* 1. kyoka 許可 (permission). 2. hiyō 費用; teate 手当て (expense). 3. wariate 割り当て (allotment). 4. kozukai 小遣い (spending money). 5. **make allowance for** (...o) kōryo suru (...を) 考慮する.

alloy, *n.* gōkin 合金.

all right, 1. *adj.* yoroshii よろしい (good); daijōbu (na) 大丈夫 (な) (safe, OK). 2. *interj.* ii いい; daijōbu 大丈夫.

allude, *vb.* honomekasu ほのめかす; genkyū suru 言及する.

allure, 1. *n.* miwaku 魅惑 (fascination). 2. *vb.* hikitsukeru 引き付ける (attract); obikidasu 誘き出す (bait).

alluring, *adj.* miwaku-teki (na) 魅惑的 (な).

allusion, *n.* honomekashi ほのめかし; genkyū 言及.

ally, 1. *n.* dōmeikoku 同盟国 (allied nation); kyōryokusha 協力者 (supporter). 2. *vb.* dōmei suru 同盟する; en o musubu 縁を結ぶ (establish relations).

almanac, *n.* koyomi 暦 (calendar); nenkan 年鑑 (yearbook).

almond, *n.* āmondo アーモンド.

almost, *adv.* hotondo ほとんど; daitai 大体.

alms, *n.* hodokoshi 施し; kifu 寄付.

aloft, *adv.* kūchū de/ni 空中で／に (mid-air); ue de/ni 上で／に (upward).

alone, 1. *adj.* hitori (no) 一人 (の) (person); ...nomi ....のみ (only). 2. *adv.* hitori de 一人で; **leave alone** hitori ni shiteoku (person); hotte oku 放っておく.

along, 1. *adv.* issho ni 一緒に (together); **all along** zutto ずっと; **get along with** (...to) umaku yatte iku (...と) うまくやっていく. 2. *prep.* ...ni sotte ...に沿って (over the length of); ...ni awasete ...に合わせて (in accordance with).

alongside, *adv., prep.* (...to) narande (...と) 並んで; (...no) soba ni (...の) 側に.

aloof, *adj.* reitan (na) 冷淡 (な).

aloud, *adv.* koe o dashite 声を出して.

alphabet, *n.* arufabetto アルファベット.

alphabetical, *adj.* arufabetto(jun) (no) アルファベット(順) (の).

Alps, *n.* arupusu アルプス.

already, *adv.* mō もう; sude ni 既に.

also, *adv.* mo も; mata 又.

altar, *n.* saidan 祭壇 (Christianity); butsudan 仏壇 (Buddhism).

alter, *vb.* 1. kaeru 変える (change). 2. naosu 直す (alter size).

altercation, *n.* kuchigenka 口げんか; kōron 口論.

alternate, 1. *adj.* kōgo (no) 交互 (の) (by turns); hitotsuoki (no) 一つおき (の) (every other). 2. *n.* kawari 代わり (substitute). 3. *vb.* kaeru 代える; kawaru 代わる (change); kōtai de suru 交代です

る (do by turns).

alternative, 1. *adj.* kawari (no) 代わり (の). 2. *n.* kawari 代わり (substitute); sentaku 選択 (choice).

although, *conj.* ...desuga ...ですが; ...dakedo ...だけど.

altitude, *n.* kōdo 高度; takasa 高さ.

altogether, *adv.* 1. zenbu de 全部で (in all). 2. mattaku 全く (completely). 3. zentai ni 全体に (as a whole).

altruism, *n.* ritashugi 利他主義.

aluminum, *n.* arumi(niumu) アルミ(ニウム).

alumna, *n.* joshi-sotsugyōsei 女子卒業生.

alumni, *n.* sotsugyōsei 卒業生.

alumnus, *n.* danshi-sotsugyōsei 男子卒業生.

always, *adv.* itsumo いつも.

a.m., gozen 午前; **nine a.m.** gozen kuji.

amalgamate, *vb.* mazeru 混ぜる (mix); musubu 結ぶ (unite).

amass, *vb.* tsumu 積む (pile); atsumeru 集める (collect).

amateur, *n.* amachua アマチュア; shirōto 素人.

amaze, *vb.* odorokaseru 驚ろかせる; **be amazed at** ...ni odoroku に驚ろく.

amazement, *n.* odoroki 驚ろき.

amazing, *adj.* odoroku beki 驚くべき; subarashii 素晴らしい.

ambassador, *n.* taishi 大使.

amber, 1. *adj.* kohaku(iro) (no) 琥珀(色) (の). 2. *n.* kohaku 琥珀.

ambiguous, *adj.* aimai (na) 曖昧 (な); bon'yari shita ぼんやりした.

ambition, *n.* yashin 野心; iyoku 意欲.

ambitious, *adj.* yashin-teki (na) 野心的 (な); iyoku-teki (na) 意欲的

ambivalent, *adj.* kimochi ga sadamaranai 気持が定まらない.

ambulance, *n.* kyūkyūsha 救急車.

ambush, 1. *n.* machibuse 待ち伏せ; fui'uchi 不意打ち. 2. *vb.* machibuse suru 待ち伏せする.

amenable, *adj.* jūjun (na) 従順 (な); shitagai-yasui 従い易い.

amend, *vb.* kaisei suru 改正する; aratameru 改める.

amendment, *n.* kaisei 改正.

amends, *n.* 1. kaisei 改正 (improvement). 2. tsugunai 償い (compensation); **make amends** tsugunau 償う.

amenity, *n.* reigi 礼儀 (courtesy).

America, *n.* amerika アメリカ (U.S.).

American, 1. *n.* amerikajin アメリカ人. 2. *adj.* amerika (no) アメリカ (の) (of the U.S.); amerikajin (no) アメリカ人 (の) (of an American).

amiable, *adj.* shinsetsu (na) 親切 (な) (kind); yūkō-teki (na) 友好的 (な) (friendly).

amicable, *adj.* yūkō-teki (na) 友好的 (な).

amiss, 1. *adj.* hazure (no) 外れ (の); machigai (no) 間違い (の). 2. *adv.* hazurete 外れて; machigatte 間違って; **take amiss** waruku toru 悪くとる; gokai suru 誤解する.

amity, *n.* yūkō 友好.

amnesia, *n.* kioku sōshitsu 記憶喪失; kenbōshō 健忘症.

amnesty, 1. *n.* onsha 恩赦. 2. *vb.* onsha o ataeru 恩赦を与える.

amok, *adv.* see **amuck.**

among, *prep.* (...no) aida de/ni (...の) 間で/に (between); (...no) naka de/ni (...の) 中で/に (in the midst of).

amorous, *adj.* 1. aijōbukai 愛情深
い (affectionate). 2. ren'aichū
(no) 恋愛中 (の) (in love). 3.
kōshoku (na) 好色 (な)
(lecherous).

amortize, *vb.* bunkatsu de harau
分割で払う.

amount, 1. *n.* gōkei 合計. 2. *vb.*
amount to ...ni tassuru ...に達す
る; ...ni naru ...になる.

amp, ampere, *n.* anpea アンペア.

amphitheater, *n.* enkei-gekijō/
-tōgijō 円形劇場／～闘技場.

ample, *adj.* jūbun (na) 十分 (な).

amplify, *vb.* kakudai suru 拡大す
る; hirogeru 拡げる.

amputate, *vb.* kiru 切る; setsudan
suru 切断する.

amuck, *adv.* **run amuck**
abarekuru'u 暴れ狂う.

amulet, *n.* omamori お守り.

amuse, *vb.* tanoshimaseru 楽しま
せる; **amuse oneself** tanoshimu
楽しむ.

amusement, *n.* tanoshimi 楽しみ;
goraku 娯楽.

amusing, *adj.* tanoshii 楽しい;
okashii おかしい.

an, *art.* see **a.**

anachronism, *n.* jidaisakugo 時代
錯誤.

anal, *adj.* kōmon (no) 肛門 (の).

analogous, *adj.* ruiji (no) 類似 (の);
nita 似た.

analogy, *n.* ruiji 類似.

analysis, *n.* bunseki 分析.

analyst, *n.* bunsekisha 分析者;
kaisetsusha 解説者.

analytical, *adj.* bunseki-teki (na)
分析的 (な).

analyze, *vb.* bunseki suru 分析す
る.

anarchism, *n.* museifu shugi 無政

府主義.

anatomy, *n.* shikumi 仕組み
(system); kaibō 解剖 (dissect);
bunseki 分析 (analysis).

ancestor, *n.* sosen 祖先; senzo 先
祖.

ancestral, *adj.* sosen (no) 祖先
(の); senzo (no) 先祖 (の).

ancestry, *n.* 1. iegara 家柄
(lineage). 2. sosen 祖先
(ancestor).

anchor, 1. *n.* ankā アンカー; ikari
錨. 2. *vb.* tomeru 留める (fasten);
teihaku suru 停泊する (anchor
boat); ikari o orosu 錨を下ろす
(lower anchor).

ancient, 1. *n.* kodaijin 古代人. 2.
adj. kodai (no) 古代 (の);
ōmukashi (no) 大昔 (の) (of
ancient times); rōjin (no) 老人
(の) (of an elderly person).

and, *conj.* soshite そして; ...to ...と.

anecdote, *n.* itsuwa 逸話.

anemia, *n.* hinketsu(shō) 貧血(症).

anemic, *adj.* hinketsu(shō) (no) 貧
血(症) (の).

anesthetic, *n.* masui 麻酔.

anew, *adv.* arata ni 新たに;
atarashiku 新しく.

angel, *n.* enjeru エンジェル; tenshi
天使.

angelic, *adj.* tenshi noyō (na) 天使
のよう (な).

anger, 1. *n.* ikari 怒り. 2. *vb.*
okoraseru 怒らせる (provoke);
okoru 怒る (get angry).

angle, *n.* kakudo 角度; **right angle**
chokkaku 直角.

angry, *adj.* okkotteiru 怒っている;
get/be angry okoru 怒る.

anguish, *n.* kurushimi 苦しみ;
kunō 苦悩.

anguished, *adj.* kurushii 苦しい;
kunō shite iru 苦悩している.

animal, *n.* dōbutsu 動物.

animate, 1. *adj.* ikiteiru 生きてい
る (live); iki-iki shiteiru 生き生き
している (lively). 2. *vb.*
kakkizukeru 活気づける.

animated, *adj.* iki-iki shita 生き生
きした; kappatsu (na) 活発 (な).

animation, *n.* 1. animēshon アニ
メーション; mangaeiga 漫画映画
(animated film). 2. kakki 活気
(liveliness).

animosity, *n.* hankan 反感; teki'i
敵意.

ankle, *n.* kurubushi くるぶし;
ashikubi 足首.

annex, 1. *n.* anekkusu アネックス;
bekkan 別館. 2. *vb.* tsuketasu 付
け足す.

annihilate, *vb.* zenmetsu saseru 全
滅させる.

anniversary, *n.* kinenbi 記念日.

annotation, *n.* chūshaku 注釈.

announce, *vb.* kōhyō suru 公表す
る; shiraseru 知らせる.

announcement, *n.* happyō 発表;
shirase 知らせ; kokuji 告示.

announcer, *n.* anaunsā アナウンサ
ー.

annoy, *vb.* ira-ira saseru いらいら
させる; **be annoyed** ira-ira suru
いらいらする.

annoyance, *n.* meiwaku 迷惑.

annoying, *adj.* meiwaku (na) 迷惑
(な); yakkai (na) 厄介 (な).

annual, 1. *adj.* (ichi)nen (no) (一)
年 (の) (yearly); maitoshi (no) 毎
年 (の) (recurring yearly). 2. *n.*
nenkan 年鑑 (publication).

annuity, *n.* nenkin 年金.

annul, *vb.* haishi suru 廃止する.

anomalous, *adj.* kimyō (na) 奇妙
(な); ijō (na) 異状 (な).

anomaly, *n.* reigai 例外; ijō 異状.

anonymity, *n.* mumei 無名

(unknown name); tokumei 匿名
(withheld name).

anonymous, *adj.* mumei (no) 無名
(の); tokumei (no) 匿名 (の).

another, *adj.*, *pron.* mō hitori (no)
もう一人 (の) (person); mō hitotsu
(no) もう一つ (の) (thing).

answer, 1. *n.* kotae 答え (reply to a
question); henji 返事 (response).
2. *vb.* kotaeru 答える; henji suru
返事する.

ant, *n.* ari 蟻.

antagonism, *n.* teki'i 敵意
(hostility); hankō 反抗
(rebellion).

antagonist, *n.* tairitsusha 対立者;
hankōsha 反抗者.

antagonistic, *adj.* tairitsu-teki (na)
対立的 (な); hankō-teki (na) 反抗
的 (な).

antagonize, *vb.* teki ni mawasu 敵
に回す (make enemy); tairitsu
suru 対立する (oppose).

Antarctica, *n.* nankyoku(tairiku)
南極(大陸).

antecedent, *n.* 1. senrei 先例
(forerunner). 2. sosen 祖先
(ancestor).

antenna, *n.* antena アンテナ
(equipment); shokkaku 触角
(insect).

anthem, *n.* 1. kokka 国歌 (national
anthem). 2. seika 聖歌 (church
music).

anthology, *n.* senshū 選集.

anthropologist, *n.* jinruigakusha
人類学者.

anthropology, *n.* jinruigaku 人類
学.

anti-, han- 反; **han-shakai-teki**
antisocial.

antibiotic, *n.* kōseibusshitsu 抗生
物質.

anticipate, *vb.* 1. kitai suru 期待す

る (expect). 2. yoki suru 予期する (foresee).

antics, *n.* hyōkin ひょうきん.

antidote, *n.* kaidokuzai 解毒剤.

antipathy, *n.* hankan 反感.

antiquated, *adj.* jidai okure (no) 時代遅れ (の) (behind times); furukusai 古くさい (old).

antique, *n.* kottō(hin) 骨董(品).

antiquity, *n.* 1. furusa 古さ (ancientness). 2. kodai 古代; mukashi 昔 (ancient times).

antithesis, *n.* taishō 対照; hantai 反対.

antler, *n.* tsuno 角.

anus, *n.* kōmon 肛門.

anxiety, *n.* 1. shinpai 心配 (worry). 2. setsubō 切望 (longing).

anxious, *adj.* 1. shinpai (na) 心配 (な) (worried). 2. nesshin (na) 熱心 (な) (eager).

any, 1. *adj., pron.* (affirmative sentence) nandemo 何でも (anything at all); subete 全て (everything); daredemo 誰でも (anyone, everyone); (negative sentence) nanimo 何も (not anything); daremo 誰も (not anybody); (interrogative, conditional sentence) nanika 何か (anything, something); dareka 誰か (anyone, someone). 2. *adv.* **any longer/more** mohaya (... nai) 最早 (...ない); mō (...nai) もう (...ない).

anybody, *pron.* 1. (affirmative sentence) daredemo 誰でも. 2. (negative sentence) daremo 誰も. 3. (interrogative, conditional sentence) dareka 誰か.

anyhow, *adv.* 1. tonikaku とにかく (in any case). 2. zehi 是非 (under any circumstances).

anyone, *pron.* see **anybody**.

anything, 1. *pron.* (affirmative sentence) nandemo 何でも; (negative sentence) nanimo 何も; (interrogative, conditional sentence) nanika 何か. 2. *adv.* (affirmative sentence) sukoshiwa 少しは; (negative sentence) sukoshimo 少しも.

anyway, *pron.* see **anyhow**.

anywhere, *adv.* 1. (affirmative sentence) doko demo どこでも. 2. (interrogative, conditional sentence) doko ka どこか. 3. (negative sentence) doko nimo (...nai) どこにも (...ない).

apart, *adv.* 1. bara-bara ni ばらばら に (into pieces); **take apart** bara-bara ni suru ばらばらにする; bunkai suru 分解する. 2. hanarete 離れて (away from). 3. kobetsu ni 個別に (individually).

apartment, *n.* apāto アパート.

apathetic, *adj.* 1. mukanjō (na, no) 無感情 (な、の) (emotionless). 2. mukanshin (na) 無関心 (な) (indifferent).

apathy, *n.* 1. mukanjō 無感情. 2. mukanshin 無関心.

ape, 1. *n.* saru 猿. 2. *vb.* mane suru 真似する.

apéritif, *n.* aperitifu アペリティフ; shokuzenshu 食前酒.

aphorism, *n.* keiku 警句.

aphrodisiac, *n.* biyaku 媚薬; seiryoku-kyōsōzai 精力強壮剤.

apiece, *adv.* 1. hitotsu (ni tsuki) 一 つ (に付き) (per piece). 2. hitori (ni tsuki) 一人 (に付き) (per person).

apologetic, *adj.* shazai (no) 謝罪 (の); ayamari (no) 誤り (の) (regretful). 2. benmei (no) 弁明 (の) (defensive).

apologize, *vb.* 1. ayamaru 誤る. 2. benmei suru 弁明する.

apology, *n.* 1. shazai 謝罪. 2. benmei 弁明.

apoplexy, *n.* sotchū 卒中.

appall, *vb.* **be appalled** 1. zotto suru ぞっとする (be scared). 2. akireru あきれる (be dismayed).

apparatus, *n.* 1. kikai 器械; sōchi 装置 (instrument). 2. kikō 機構; kikan 機関 (system).

apparel, *n.* fuku 服.

apparent, *adj.* akiraka (na) 明らか (な).

apparition, *n.* 1. yūrei 幽霊 (ghost). 2. shutsugen 出現 (appearance).

appeal, 1. *n.* uttae 訴え; yōsei 要請 (entreaty); miryoku 魅力 (attraction); kōso 控訴 (court petition). 2. *vb.* uttaeru 訴える; yōsei suru 要請する; hikitsukeru 引き付ける (attract); kōso suru 控訴する.

appear, *vb.* 1. arawareru 現れる; deru 出る (show up, come into sight). 2. (...no yō ni) mieru (...の ように) 見える (seem).

appearance, *n.* 1. tōjō 登場; shutsugen 出現 (showing up). 2. gaiken 外見; yōsu 様子 (outward show).

appease, *vb.* nadameru なだめる; iyasu 癒す.

append, *vb.* tsukeru 付ける; tsuketasu 付け足す.

appendage, *n.* fuzokubutsu 付属 物.

appendectomy, *n.* chūsui setsujo 虫垂切除.

appendicitis, *n.* mōchōen 盲腸炎; chūsuien 虫垂炎.

appendix, *n.* 1. tsuika 追加; tsuiho 追ほ (supplement). 2.

fuzokubutsu 付属物 (appendage). 3. chūsui 虫垂 (vermiform appendix).

appetite, *n.* shokuyoku 食欲.

appetizer, *n.* apetaizā アペタイザ ー; zensai 前菜.

appetizing, *adj.* oishisō (na) おい しそう (な).

applaud, *vb.* kassai suru 喝采する; hakushu suru 拍手する.

applause, *n.* kassai 喝采; hakushu 拍手.

apple, *n.* ringo りんご.

appliance, *n.* kigu 器具; kikai 器械.

applicant, *n.* mōshikomisha 申し 込み者; ōbosha 応募者.

application, *n.* 1. mōshikomi 申し 込み; ōbo 応募 (request). 2. shiyō 使用 (use). 3. ōyō 応用 (derived use). 4. mōshikomi yōshi 申し込 み用紙; mōshikomisho 申し込み書 (form).

applied, *adj.* ōyō (no) 応用 (の).

apply, *vb.* 1. tsukeru 付ける (put on). 2. tsukau 使う (use). 3. **apply to** ōyō suru 応用する. 4. **apply for** mōshikomu 申し込む; ōbo suru 応募する.

appoint, *vb.* 1. ninmei suru 任命す る (name). 2. shitei suru 指定する (set).

appointment, *n.* 1. ninmei 任命. 2. shitei 指定. 3. yakusoku 約束; yoyaku 予約 (meeting).

apportion, *vb.* bunpai suru 分配す る.

appraisal, *n.* hyōka 評価; kantei 鑑 定.

appraise, *vb.* hyōka suru 評価する; kantei suru 鑑定する.

appreciable, *adj.* kanari (no) かな り (の).

appreciate, *vb.* 1. kansha suru 感 謝する (thank). 2. (takaku) hyōka suru (高く) 評価する; kanshō suru 鑑賞する(value). 3. sassuru 察する (be aware). 4. kachi o ageru 価値を上げる (raise value).

appreciation, *n.* 1. kansha 感謝. 2. hyōka 評価; kanshō 鑑賞. 3. ninshiki 認識 (recognition). 4. kachi no zōka 価値の増加.

apprehend, *vb.* 1. sassuru 察する; kizuku 気づく (perceive). 2. shinpai suru 心配する (worry). 3. taiho suru 逮捕する (arrest).

apprehension, *n.* 1. shinpai 心配; fuan 不安 (worry). 2. taiho 逮捕 (arrest).

apprehensive, *adj.* shinpai (na) 心配 (な); fuan (na) 不安 (な) (uneasy).

apprentice, *n.* deshi 弟子; minarai 見習い.

approach, 1. *n.* sekkin 接近; chikazuki 近づき (coming near); hōhō 方法 (method); shudan 手段 (means). 2. *vb.* sekkin suru 接近する; chikazuku 近づく; kōshō suru 交渉する (discuss); torikakaru 取り掛かる (begin).

appropriate, 1. *adj.* fusawashii ふさわしい (suitable). 2. *vb.* ateru 当てる (set aside); nusumu 盗む (steal).

approval, *n.* shōnin 承認; sansei 賛成.

approve, *vb.* shōnin suru 承認する; sansei suru 賛成する.

approximate, *adj.* daitai (no) 大体 (の); chikai 近い.

apricot, *n.* anzu 杏.

April, *n.* shi-gatsu 四月.

apron, *n.* epuron エプロン; maekake 前掛け.

apropos, *adv.* tekisetsu na 適切な (appropriate); ...ni tsuite ...につい て (concerning).

apt, *adj.* 1. -yasui 易い; (...no) keikō ga aru (...の) 傾向がある (inclined, tending); **apt to get upset** okori-yasui. 2. tekisetsu (na) 適切 (な) (fitting).

aptitude, *n.* 1. keikō 傾向 (tendency). 2. sainō 才能 (ability).

aquarium, *n.* suisō 水槽 (fishbowl); suizokukan 水族館 (fish museum).

aquatic, *adj.* suisei (no) 水棲 (の); suichū (no) 水中 (の).

aqueduct, *n.* suiro 水路.

Arab, *n.* arabiajin アラビア人.

Arabia, *n.* arabia アラビア.

Arabian, *adj.* 1. arabia (no) アラビ ア (の) (of Arabia). 2. arabiajin (no) アラビア人 (の) (of an Arabian).

Arabic, *n.* arabiago アラビア語.

arable, *adj.* hatake ni tekishita 畑に 適した; hatake (no) 畑 (の).

arbiter, *n.* chūsaisha 仲裁者.

arbitrary, *adj.* 1. shukan-teki (na) 主観的 (な) (subjective). 2. katte (na) 勝手 (な) (unreasonable).

arbitrate, *vb.* chōtei suru 調停する; chūsai suru 仲裁する.

arbitration, *n.* chōtei 調停; chūsai 仲裁.

arbitrator, *n.* chōtei-nin 調停人.

arbor, *n.* kokage 木陰.

arc, *n.* enko 円弧.

arcade, *n.* ākēdo アーケード; shōtengai 商店街.

arch, *n.* āchi アーチ; yumigata 弓 形.

archaeologist, *n.* kōkogakusha 考 古学者.

archaeology, *n.* kōkogaku 考古学.

archaic, *adj.* sutareta 廃れた (no longer used); mukashi (no) 昔

(の) (old, ancient).

archer, *n.* ite 射手.

archetype, *n.* genkei 原型.

archipelago, *n.* rettō 列島; guntō 群島.

architect, *n.* 1. kenchikuka 建築家 (building designer). 2. kōsōsha 構想者 (planner).

architectural, *adj.* kenchiku (no) 建築 (の).

architecture, *n.* 1. kenchikugaku 建築学 (profession, study). 2. kenchiku 建築 (building, construction). 3. kenchiku-yōshiki 建築様式 (style).

archives, *n.* 1. kiroku 記録. 2. kiroku(hozon)sho 記録(保存)書.

arctic, 1. *n.* **Arctic** hokkyoku 北極. 2. *adj.* hokkyoku (no) 北極 (の).

ardent, *adj.* nesshin (na) 熱心 (な).

ardor, *n.* netsui 熱意.

arduous, *adj.* taihen (na) 大変 (な); kitsui きつい.

area, *n.* 1. chiku 地区; chi'iki 地域 (region). 2. bun'ya 分野 (field). 3. tokoro 所 (section, space).

area code, *n.* shigaikyokuban 市外局番.

arena, *n.* kyōgijō 競技場.

argue, *vb.* 1. giron suru 議論する; noberu 述べる (debate, state). 2. iiarasou 言い争う (dispute). 3. shuchō suru 主張する (reason).

argument, *n.* 1. giron 議論; tōron 討論 (debate). 2. ii arasoi 言い争い (dispute). 3. shuchō 主張 (reasoning).

arid, *adj.* kawaita 乾いた (dry).

arise, *vb.* 1. okoru 起こる; shōjiru 生じる (occur). 2. tachiagaru 立ち上がる (get up).

aristocracy, *n.* 1. kizoku(kaikyū) 貴族(階級) (class). 2. kizoku seiji 貴族政治 (government).

aristocrat, *n.* kizoku 貴族.

aristocratic, *adj.* kizoku (no) 貴族 (の); kizoku-teki (na) 貴族的 (な).

arithmetic, *n.* sansū 算数 (study); keisan 計算 (figuring).

arm, 1. *n.* ude 腕 (limb); buki 武器 (weapon). 2. *vb.* busō suru 武装する.

armament, *n.* 1. heiki 兵器 (weapons). 2. busō 武装; gunbi 軍備 (arming).

armchair, *n.* hijikakeisu 肘掛け椅子.

armed forces, *n.* gun(tai) 軍(隊).

armful, *n.* ude ippai 腕一杯.

armistice, *n.* kyūsen 休戦.

armor, *n.* yoroi 鎧.

armory, *n.* bukikakunōko 武器格納庫.

armpit, *n.* waki no shita 脇の下.

army, *n.* rikugun 陸軍.

aroma, *n.* kaori 香り.

around, 1. *adv.* shūi ni 周囲に; gururi to ぐるりと (in a circle); shihō ni 四方に (on every side); fukin ni 付近に (nearby); daitai 大体; yaku 約 (approximately). 2. *prep.* ...no mawari ni ...のまわりに (surrounding); ...no fukin ni ...の付近に (near); -goro -頃 (time);

around noon jūniji-goro.

arouse, *vb.* 1. shigeki suru 刺激する (stir). 2. okosu 起こす; mezamesaseru 目覚めさせる (awaken).

arraign, *vb.* kokuhatsu suru 告発する (accuse).

arrange, *vb.* 1. seiri suru 整理する (put in order). 2. yōi suru 用意する; junbi suru 準備する (prepare). 3. ikeru 生ける (flowers).

arrangement, *n.* 1. seiri 整理. 2. yōi 用意; junbi 準備.

arrest, 1. *n.* taiho 逮捕 (seizure);

soshi 阻止 (stoppage). 2. *vb.* taiho
suru 逮捕する; soshi suru 阻止す
る.

arrival, *n.* tōchaku 到着.

arrive, *vb.* tsuku 着く; tōchaku
suru 到着する.

arrogance, *n.* gōman 傲慢.

arrogant, *adj.* gōman (na) 傲慢
(な).

arrow, *n.* 1. ya 矢. 2. yajirushi 矢
印 (figure).

arson, *n.* hōka 放火.

art, *n.* 1. geijutsu 芸術; bijutsu 美
術; **art gallery** āto-gyararī アート
ギャラリー; garō 画廊. 2. gijutsu
技術 (skill).

artery, *n.* dōmyaku 動脈.

artful, *adj.* 1. zurugashikoi ずる賢
い (cunning). 2. kōmyō (na) 巧妙
(な) (ingenious).

arthritis, *n.* kansetsuen 関節炎.

article, *n.* 1. kiji 記事 (writing). 2.
mono 物 (thing). 3. kanshi 冠詞
(grammar).

articulate, 1. *vb.* hakkiri-iu/-
hanasu はっきり言う／～話す
(speak clearly). 2. *adj.* meikaku
(na) 明確 (な) (clear).

artifice, *n.* sakuryaku 策略 (clever
trick).

artificial, *adj.* 1. jinkō (no) 人工
(の); jinkō-teki (na) 人工的 (な)
(man-made). 2. nisemono (no) 偽
物 (の) (fake).

artillery, *n.* taihō 大砲.

artisan, *n.* shokunin 職人; kōgeika
工芸家.

artist, *n.* āchisuto アーチスト;
geijutsuka 芸術家.

artistic, *adj.* geijutsu-teki (na) 芸術
的 (な).

artistry, *n.* geijutsusei 芸術性.

artless, *adj.* shizen (na) 自然 (な);
soboku (na) 素朴 (な).

as, 1. *adv.* onaji kurai 同じくらい;
as much as ...to onaji kurai ...と
同じくらい; **as yet** ima made no
tokoro 今までのところ; **as well**
mata また. 2. *prep.* ...no yōni ...の
ように (like); ...toshite ...として
(in the role of); **as for** ...ni tsuite
wa ...については; **as of** ...kara ...か
ら. 3. *conj.* yō ni ように (in the
way that); toki とき (when);
nanode なので; dakara だから
(because); dakedo だけど
(though); **as if** marude...no yō ni
まるで...ように; **as well as** ...to
onajiku ...と同じく; **as long as**
...kagiri ...かぎり; **as soon as** ...to
sugu ni ...とすぐに.

ascend, *vb.* noboru 上る; agaru 上
がる.

ascendance, ascendancy, *n.* yūi
優位; shihai 支配.

ascent, *n.* 1. jōshō 上昇. 2. nobori
kaidan 上り階段 (stair); nobori
michi 上り道 (slope).

ascertain, *vb.* tashikameru 確かめ
る.

ash, *n.* hai 灰.

ashamed, *adj.* hazukashii 恥ずかし
い; **be ashamed of** (o) hajiru (を)
恥じる.

ashen, *adj.* massao (na) 真っ青 (な)
(pallid).

ashore, *adv.* kishi/riku de 岸／陸で
(on shore); kishi/riku ni 岸／陸に
(to shore); **go ashore** jōriku suru
上陸する.

ashtray, *n.* haizara 灰皿.

Asia, *n.* ajia アジア.

Asian, 1. *n.* ajiajin アジア人. 2.
adj. ajia (no) アジア (の) (of Asia);
ajiajin (no) アジア人 (の) (of an
Asian).

aside, 1. *n.* bōhaku 傍白 (in a
play). 2. *adv.* waki ni 脇に (to one

side); hanashite 離して (separate);
aside from (o/wa) nozoite (を／
は) 除いて (except for); sono ue ni
その上に (besides).

ask, *vb*. 1. kiku 聞く; tazuneru 尋ね
る; shitsumon suru 質問する
(question, inquire). 2. tanomu 頼
む; motomeru 求める (request).
3. maneku 招く (invite).

askance, *adv*. 1. utagatte 疑って
(with mistrust). 2. yokome de 横
目で (sideways glance).

asleep, *adj*. nemutteiru 眠ってい
る; **fall asleep** nemuru 眠る.

aspect, *n*. 1. mikake 見かけ; yōsu
様子 (appearance). 2. jōtai 状態
(condition). 3. kyokumen 局面
(phase). 4. mikata 見方 (view).

aspersion, *n*. chūshō 中傷.

asphyxiate, *vb*. chissoku saseru 窒
息させる.

aspiration, *n*. yashin 野心; yume
夢.

aspire, *vb*. akogareru 憧れる;
mezasu 目指す.

ass, *n*. roba ろば (donkey).

assail, *vb*. kōgeki suru 攻撃する;
hinan suru 非難する.

assassin, *n*. ansatsusha 暗殺者.

assassinate, *vb*. ansatsu suru 暗殺
する.

assassination, *n*. ansatsu 暗殺.

assault, 1. *n*. kōgeki 攻撃 (attack);
bōkō 暴行 (violence); gōkan 強姦
(rape). 2. *vb*. kōgeki suru 攻撃す
る; bōkō o kuwaeru 暴行を加える;
gōkan suru 強姦する.

assay, *vb*. bunseki suru 分析する.

assemblage, *n*. atsumari 集まり.

assemble, *vb*. atsumeru 集める
(bring together); atsumaru 集まる
(come together); kumitateru 組立
てる (put together).

assembly, *n*. shūkai 集会

(meeting).

assembly line, *n*. nagaresagyō 流
れ作業.

assent, 1. *n*. dōi 同意. 2. *vb*. dōi
suru 同意する.

assert, *vb*. 1. dangen suru 断言する
(declare). 2. shuchō suru 主張す
る (claim).

assertion, *n*. 1. dangen 断言. 2.
shuchō 主張.

assess, *vb*. 1. kazeihyōka suru 課税
評価する (for tax). 2. hyōka suru
評価する (evaluate).

asset, *n*. 1. riten 利点 (valuable
quality). 2. zaisan 財産 (valuable
item).

assets, *n*. zaisan 財産; shisan 資産.

assiduous, *adj*. nesshin (na) 熱心
(な).

assign, *vb*. 1. wariateru 割り当てる
(allocate). 2. shitei suru 指定する
(designate time, place, etc.). 3.
ninmei suru 任命する (designate a
person).

assignment, *n*. 1. ninmu 任務
(job). 2. ninmei 任命 (act of
assigning). 3. shukudai 宿題
(homework).

assimilate, *vb*. tokekomu 溶け込む
(become part); kyūshū suru 吸収
する (absorb).

assist, *vb*. tasukeru 助ける; enjo
suru 援助する.

assistance, *n*. enjo 援助.

assistant, *n*. ashisutanto アシスタ
ント; joshu 助手.

associate, 1. *n*. nakama 仲間;
kyōdōsha 共同者. 2. *vb*. rensō
suru 連想する (relate). 2. te o
musubu 手を結ぶ (unite). 3.
tsukiau 付き合う (keep company).

association, *n*. 1. kai 会; dantai 団
体 (organization). 2. kankei 関係
(relationship).

assorted, *adj.* iro-iro (na, no) いろいろ (な、の).

assortment, *n.* toriawase 取り合わせ.

assuage, *vb.* yawarageru 和らげる; shizumeru 静める.

assume, *vb.* 1. katei suru 仮定する (suppose). 2. hikiukeru 引き受ける (undertake). 3. (...no) furi o suru (...の) 振りをする (pretend).

assumption, *n.* 1. katei 仮定; suitei 推定 (supposition). 2. hikiuke 引き受け (undertaking).

assurance, *n.* 1. dangen 断言 (declaration). 2. hoshō 保障 (guarantee).

assure, *vb.* 1. dangen suru 断言する. 2. hoshō suru 保障する. 3. tashikameru 確かめる (make sure).

asthma, *n.* zensoku ぜん息.

astigmatism, *n.* ranshi 乱視.

astonish, *vb.* odorokaseru 驚かせる; **be astonished** odoroku 驚ろく.

astonishment, *n.* odoroki 驚ろき.

astound, *vb.* bikkuri(gyōten) saseru びっくり(仰天) させる.

astray, *adv.* mayotte 迷って; **lead astray** mayowasu 迷わす.

astringent, *adj.* 1. shūshukusei (no) 収縮性 (の) (contracting). 2. kibishii 厳しい (severe).

astrology, *n.* hoshi uranai 星占い.

astronaut, *n.* uchūhikōshi 宇宙飛行士.

astronomical, *adj.* 1. tenmongaku (no) 天文学 (の) (of astronomy). 2. tenmongaku-teki (na) 天文学的 (な); bakudai (na) 莫大 (な) (very large).

astronomy, *n.* tenmongaku 天文学.

astute, *adj.* nukeme ga nai 抜けめがない.

asunder, *adv.* hanarete 離れて; bara-bara ni ばらばらに.

asylum, *n.* ryōyōsho 療養所 (sanitarium); shūyōsho 収容所 (mental institution).

at, *prep.* de で; ni に; e へ.

atheist, *n.* mushinronsha 無神論者.

athlete, *n.* undōsenshu 運動選手; kyōgisha 競技者.

athletic, *adj.* asurechikku (na) アスレチック (な); undō (no) 運動 (の).

athletics, *n.* undō 運動; kyōgi 競技.

Atlantic, 1. *adj.* taiseiyō (no) 大西洋 (の). 2. *n.* taiseiyō 大西洋.

atlas, *n.* chizuchō 地図帳.

atmosphere, *n.* 1. taiki 大気 (air). 2. fun'iki 雰囲気 (mood).

atom, *n.* atomu アトム; genshi 原子.

atomic, *adj.* genshi (no) 原子 (の).

atomic bomb, *n.* genshibakudan 原子爆弾; genbaku 原爆.

atomic energy, *n.* genshiryoku 原子力.

atone, *vb.* tsugunau 償う.

atrocious, *adj.* zangyaku (na) 残虐 (な) (brutal); hidoi ひどい (terrible).

atrocity, *n.* zangyaku 残虐.

atrophy, 1. *vb.* suijaku suru 衰弱する. 2. *n.* suijaku 衰弱.

attach, *vb.* tsukeru 付ける (join); musubu 結ぶ (tie).

attaché, *n.* taishikan'in 大使館員 (embassy personnel).

attached, *adj.* 1. suki (na) 好き (な); aichaku ga aru 愛着がある (feel affection for). 2. fuzoku (no) 付属 (の) (connected to)

attachment, *n.* 1. toritsuke 取り付

け (fastening). 2. toritsukehin 取
り付け品 (fastened item). 3. aijō
愛情; aichaku 愛着 (fondness).

attack, 1. *n.* kōgeki 攻撃 (assault);
hossa 発作 (seizure); bōkō 暴行
(assault). 2. *vb.* kōgeki suru 攻撃
する; torikakaru 取り掛かる (set
about doing).

attain, *vb.* 1. tassuru 達する (arrive
at). 2. nashitogeru 成し遂げる
(accomplish).

attainment, *n.* tassei 達成.

attempt, 1. *n.* kokoromi 試み. 2.
vb. kokoromiru 試みる.

attend, *vb.* 1. shusseki suru 出席す
る (be present at); kayou 通う
(frequent). 2. tomonau 伴う (go
with). 3. sewa o suru 世話をする
(take care of). 4. ki o tsukeru 気
を付ける (take heed).

attendance, *n.* 1. shusseki 出席
(presence). 2. shussekisha 出席者
(people present).

attendant, 1. *adj.* fuzui (no) 付随
(の) (connected); (o)tomo (no) お
供 (の) (accompanying); shusseki
(no) 出席 (の) (present). 2. *n.*
tsukisoinin 付き添い人 (attending
person); otomo お供 (person
accompanying); shussekisha 出席
者 (person present); an'naigakari
案内係り (public helper).

attention, *n.* 1. chūmoku 注目
(directing mind); chūi 注意
(careful notice); **pay attention**
chūmoku/chūi suru. 2. omoiyari
思い遣り; hairyo 配慮
(consideration, care).

attentive, *adj.* 1. chūibukai 注意深
い (observant). 2. omoiyari ga
aru 思い遣りがある (considerate).

attenuate, *vb.* 1. yowameru 弱め
る (weaken). 2. hosomeru 細める
(make thin).

attest (to), *vb.* shōmei suru 証明す
る.

attic, *n.* yaneurabeya 屋根裏部屋.

attire, 1. *n.* (i)fuku (衣)服. 2. *vb.*
kikazaru 着飾る.

attitude, *n.* 1. taido 態度
(orientation, manner). 2. shisei 姿
勢 (posture).

attorney, *n.* bengoshi 弁護士
(lawyer).

attract, *vb.* hikitsukeru 引き付ける
(draw, charm).

attraction, *n.* 1. miryoku 魅力
(attractive quality). 2. hikitsukeru
chikara 引き付ける力 (attractive
power). 3. inryoku 引力
(attracting force). 4. yobimono 呼
び物 (spectacle).

attractive, *adj.* miryoku-teki (na)
魅力的 (な) (fascinating); kakkoii
かっこいい (good-looking).

attribute, 1. *n.* zokusei 属性;
tokushitsu 特質 (characteristic).
2. *vb.* ...ni yoru to kangaeru ...によ
ると考える (assign to).

attune, *vb.* narasu 馴らす; awaseru
合わせる.

auction, *n.* ōkushon オークション;
kyōbai 競売.

auctioneer, *n.* kyōbainin 競売人.

audacious, *adj.* 1. daitan (na) 大胆
(な) (bold). 2. atsukamashii 厚か
ましい; burei (na) 無礼 (な)
(insolent).

audible, *adj.* kikoeru 聞こえる.

audience, *n.* chōshū 聴衆
(listener); kankyaku 観客
(theatergoer); kanshū 観衆
(viewer); dokusha 読者 (reader).

audit, 1. *n.* kaikeikensa 会計検査
(examination). 2. *vb.* kaikeikensa
o suru 会計検査をする; chōkō
suru 聴講する (attend a class).

audition, *n.* ōdishon オーディショ

ン.

auditor, *n.* 1. kaikei kensain 会計検査員 (accountant).　2. chōkōsei 聴講生 (student).

auditorium, *n.* kōdō 講堂; kaikan 会館.

augment, *vb.* fuyasu 増やす.

August, *n.* hachigatsu 八月.

aunt, *n.* oba(san) 伯母(さん).

auspicious, *adj.* 1. saisaki ga ii 幸先がいい (fortunate).　2. yūbō (na) 有望 (な) (promising).

austere, *adj.* 1. kibishii 厳しい (stern).　2. kanso (na) 簡素 (な) (plain).　3. mazushii 貧しい (frugal).

austerity, *n.* 1. kibishisa 厳しさ.　2. kanso 簡素.　3. mazushisa 貧しさ.

Australia, *n.* ōsutoraria オーストラリア.

Australian, 1. *n.* ōsutorariajin オーストラリア人.　2. *adj.* ōsutoraria (no) オーストラリア (の) (of Australia); ōsutorariajin (no) オーストラリア人 (の) (of an Australian).

authentic, *adj.* 1. tashika (na) 確か (な) (reliable).　2. honmono (no) 本物 (の) (genuine).

author, *n.* sakusha 作者; chosha 著者.

authority, *n.* ken'i 権威 (power to judge); ken'isha 権威者 (person with power); tōkyoku 当局 (legal power).

authorize, *vb.* 1. kengen o ataeru 権限を与える (give authority).　2. kōnin suru 公認する (sanction formally).

authorship, *n.* 1. chojutsugyō 著述業 (occupation).　2. sakusha 作者; dedokoro 出所 (personal origin).

autobiography, *n.* ji(jo)den 自(叙)伝.

autocratic, *adj.* dokusai(sei) (no) 独裁(政) (の).

autograph, 1. *n.* sain サイン; shomei 署名.　2. *vb.* sain suru サインする; shomei suru 署名する.

automatic, *adj.* ōtomachikku (no) オートマチック (の); jidō (no) 自動 (の).

automation, *n.* ōtomēshon オートメーション; jidōsōchi 自動装置.

automobile, *n.* jidōsha 自動車.

automotive, *adj.* jidōsha (no) 自動車 (の).

autonomy, *n.* jichi 自治.

autopsy, *n.* kaibō 解剖.

autumn, *n.* aki 秋.

auxiliary, *adj.* hojo (no) 補助 (の).

auxiliary verb, *n.* jodōshi 助動詞.

avail, 1. *n.* kōka 効果; rieki 利益; **to no avail** muda ni owaru 無駄に終わる.　2. *vb.* yaku ni tatsu 役にたつ (be useful); **avail oneself of** riyō suru 利用する.

available, *adj.* 1. te ni hairu 手に入る; aru 有る (obtainable, at hand).　2. au koto ga dekiru 会う事が出来る (ready to be seen); jikan ga aru 時間がある (not busy).

avalanche, *n.* nadare 雪崩.

avant-garde, *adj.* zen'ei-teki (na) 前衛的 (な); zen'ei (no) 前衛 (の).

avarice, *n.* don'yoku 貪欲.

avaricious, *adj.* don'yoku (na) 貪欲 (な).

avenge, *vb.* fukushū suru 復讐する.

avenger, *n.* fukushūsha 復讐者.

avenue, *n.* 1. ōdōri 大通り; ...gai ...街 (street); **Fifth Avenue** gobangai.　2. (sekkin)shudan (接近)手段 (approach).

average, 1. *n.* heikin 平均.　2. *adj.* heikin (no) 平均 (の) (of an average); futsū (no) 普通 (の)

(ordinary). 3. *vb.* heikin ...ni naru
平均...になる.

averse, *adj.* 1. ki ga mukanai 気が
向かない (unwilling). 2. hantai
(no) 反対 (の) (opposed).

aversion, *n.* ken'o 嫌悪.

avert, *vb.* 1. sorasu 逸らす (turn
away). 2. fusegu 防ぐ (prevent).

aviation, *n.* hikōjutsu 飛行術;
kōkūjutsu 航空術.

avid, *adj.* nesshin (na) 熱心 (な)
(enthusiastic); hoshigaru 欲しがる
(desiring).

avocation, *n.* fukugyō 副業.

avoid, *vb.* 1. nogareru 逃れる
(escape). 2. sakeru 避ける (keep
away).

await, *vb.* matsu 待つ; matteiru
待っている.

awake, 1. *adj.* okiteiru 起きている
(not sleeping). 2. kizuiteiru 気づ
いている (conscious). 2. *vb.*
mezameru 目覚める (wake up).

awaken, *vb.* 1. mezamesaseru 目覚
めさせる (rouse from sleep). 2.
kizukaseru 気付かせる (cause to
understand).

award, 1. *n.* shō 賞 (prize);
baishōkin 賠償金 (by judicial
decree). 2. *vb.* ataeru 与える.

aware, *adj.* kizuiteiru 気付いている.

awareness, *n.* jikaku 自覚; ishiki
意識.

away, 1. *adv.* yoso/hoka ni 余所／
他に (from this or that place, in
another direction, in another
place); hanarete 離れて (at a
distance, apart); kiete 消えて (to
nothing). 2. *adj.* rusu (no) 留守
(の) (absent); hanareteiru 離れて
いる (distant).

awe, *n.* ikei 畏敬.

awesome, *adj.* sōgon (na) 荘厳
(な).

awful, *adj.* 1. kowai 怖い; osoroshii
恐ろしい(dreadful). 2. hidoi ひど
い; warui 悪い (bad).

awfully, *adv.* taihen 大変 (very).

awhile, *adv.* shibaraku 暫く.

awkward, *adj.* 1. gikochinai ぎこ
ちない; bukakkō (na) 無格好 (な)
(clumsy). 2. muzukashii 難しい
(difficult). 3. kimazui 気まずい
(embarrassing).

awning, *n.* hiyoke 日除け.

awry, *adv.* 1. magatta 曲がった;
nejireta ねじれた (twisted). 2.
machigatta 間違った (wrong).

ax, axe, *n.* ono 斧.

axiom, *n.* genri 原理; shinri 真理.

axis, *n.* jiku 軸; chūshinsen 中心
線.

axle, *n.* shinbō 心棒; shajiku 車軸.

azalea, *n.* tsutsuji つつじ.

azure, *adj.* aoi 青い; sorairo (no) 空
色 (の).

B

babble, 1. *n.* oshaberi おしゃべり
(excessive talk). 2. *vb.*
makushitateru まくしたてる
(speak fast); shaberu しゃべる
(talk excessively).

baby, *n.* aka-chan 赤ちゃん; nyūji

乳児.

babysitter, *n.* komori 子守り.

bachelor, *n.* dokushindansei 独身
男性.

back, 1. *n.* se(naka) 背(中) (of
person, animal, chair); ura 裏

(reverse side); oku 奥 (farthest from front); **in back of** (...no) ushiro ni/de (...の) 後ろに／で. 2. *vb.* shiji suru 支持する (sponsor); atomodori/bakku suru 後戻り／バックする (move backward). 3. *adj.* ushiro no 後ろの (in the rear); mukashi/mae (no) 昔／前 (の) (of the past). 4. *adv.* ushiro ni/de 後ろに／で (at the rear); mukashi 昔 (in the past).

backbone, *n.* 1. sebone 背骨; sekitsui 脊椎 (spine). 2. kikotsu 気骨 (strength of character). 3. daikokubashira 大黒柱 (main support).

background, *n.* 1. haikei 背景 (backdrop, background circumstance). 2. keireki 経歴 (personal background); umare 生まれ (person's origin). 3. rekishi 歴史 (historical background).

backing, *n.* shien 支援 (support).

backlash, *n.* 1. hanekaeri 跳返り (backward movement). 2. hantai-undō 反対運動 (reaction to social or political change).

backlog, *n.* yarinokoshi やり残し (unfinished tasks).

backpack, *n.* ryukkusakku リュックサック; nappusakku ナップサック.

backside, *n.* oshiri お尻 (buttocks).

backtalk, *n.* kuchigotae 口答え.

backtrack, *vb.* 1. hikikaesu 引き返す (return). 2. hikisagaru 引き下がる (retreat).

backup, *n.* bakkuappu バックアップ (computers).

backward, 1. *adj.* ushiromuki (no) 後ろ向き (の) (toward the rear); gyaku (no) 逆 (の) (reversed); okureta 遅れた (behind in time or development). 2. *adv.* ushiro no

hō ni 後ろの方に (toward the rear); ushiro kara 後ろから (from behind); kako ni 過去に (in the past); hantai ni 反対に (reverse of).

backyard, *n.* uraniwa 裏庭.

bacon, *n.* bēkon ベーコン.

bad, *adj.* warui 悪い (not good, wicked, harmful); akushitsu (na, no) 悪質 (な、の) (wicked nature); machigai (no) 間違い (の) (incorrect); kusatta 腐った (spoiled).

badge, *n.* bajji バッジ; kishō 記章.

badger, 1. *n.* anaguma 穴熊. 2. *vb.* shitsukoku iu しつこく言う.

badly, *adv.* waruku 悪く; hidoku ひどく.

baffle, *vb.* magotsukaseru まごつかせる.

bag, 1. *n.* baggu バッグ; fukuro 袋; tesage 手下げ; kaban 鞄. 2. *vb.* fukuro ni ireru 袋に入れる (put in a bag).

baggage, *n.* sūtsukēsu スーツケース; tenimotsu 手荷物.

baggy, *adj.* dabu-dabu shita だぶだぶした.

bail, 1. *n.* hoshakukin 保釈金; **go bail for** hoshakukin o dasu. 2. *vb.* kumidasu 汲み出す (water); **bail out** tobioriru 飛び降りる (jump); tasukeru 助ける (rescue).

bait, 1. *n.* esa 餌 (food); otori おとり (allurement). 2. *vb.* esa o tsukeru 餌を付ける (food); obikiyoseru 誘き寄せる (entice).

bake, *vb.* yaku 焼く.

baker, *n.* panya パン屋.

bakery, *n.* bēkarī ベーカリー; panya パン屋.

baking powder, *n.* bēkingu-paudā ベーキングパウダー; fukurashiko ふくらし粉.

balance, 1. *n.* hakari 秤 (scale); baransu バランス ; tsuriai 釣合 (equilibrium); sashihiki-zandaka 差引き残高 (account balance). 2. *vb.* hakaru 計る (weigh, value); tsuriawaseru 釣合わせる (make equal); sōsai suru 相殺する (offset); shūshi o kessan suru 収支を決算する (adjust account).

balance sheet, *n.* taishaku-taishōhyō 貸借対照表.

balcony, *n.* terasu テラス; barukonī バルコニー.

bald, *adj.* hageta 禿げた; hage (no) 禿げ (の).

baldness, *n.* hage 禿.

ball, *n.* 1. bōru ボール; kyū 球; tama 玉 (spherical object). 2. butōkai 舞踏会 (dance).

ballad, *n.* barādo バラード; min'yō 民謡.

ballerina, *n.* barerīna バレリーナ.

ballet, *n.* barē バレー.

balloon, *n.* fūsen 風船 (toy); kikyū 気球 (hot air).

ballot, 1. *n.* tōhyōyōshi 投票用紙 (form); sōtōhyō(sū) 総投票(数) (total votes). 2. *vb.* tōhyō suru 投票する (vote).

ballpoint pen, *n.* bōru-pen ボールペン.

balm, *n.* 1. kōyu 香油 (fragrant ointment) 2. hōkō 芳香 (fragrance). 3. nagusame 慰め (emotional comfort).

bamboo, *n.* take 竹.

bamboo shoot, *n.* takenoko 竹の子.

ban, 1. *n.* kinshi 禁止. 2. *vb.* kinshi suru 禁止する.

banal, *adj.* heibon (na) 平凡 (な); chinpu (na) 陳腐 (な).

banana, *n.* banana バナナ.

band, 1. *n.* bando バンド , himo 紐 (material for binding); gurūpu グループ ; dan 団 (group); bando バンド (music group); gakudan 楽団 (orchestra). 2. *vb.* **band together** danketsu suru 団結する.

bandage, 1. *n.* hōtai 包帯. 2. *vb.* hōtai o suru 包帯をする.

bang, 1. *n.* batan/ban/doshin/don ばたん／ばん／どしん／どん (loud noise); maegami 前髪 (hair bangs). 2. *vb.* oto o tateru 音をたてる (make noise); (gatan to) butsukeru (がたんと) ぶつける (hit against); tsuyoku utsu 強く打つ (strike).

banish, *vb.* 1. tsuihō suru 追放する (exile). 2. oidasu 追い出す (drive away).

bank, 1. *n.* ginkō 銀行 (financial institution); kishi 岸; tsutsumi 堤 (river bank); moritsuchi 盛り土 (heap or mass). 2. *vb.* yokin suru 預金する (deposit).

bank account, *n.* ginkōkōza 銀行口座.

bankbook, *n.* ginkōtsūchō 銀行通帳.

bank clerk, *n.* ginkōin 銀行員.

bankrupt, 1. *n.* hasansha 破産者 (person). 2. *adj.* hasan shita 破産した (insolvent); **go bankrupt** hasan suru 破産する.

bankruptcy, *n.* hasan 破産; tōsan 倒産.

banner, *n.* hata 旗.

banquet, *n.* utage 宴; enkai 宴会.

banter, 1. *n.* fuzakebanashi ふざけ話し. 2. *vb.* fuzakeru ふざける.

bar, 1. *n.* bō 棒 (long object); katamari 塊 (piece of solid material); shōgai 障害 (obstacle); kan'nuki 閂 (bolt); bā バー ; sakaba 酒場 (barroom); cauntā カウンター (counter); suji 筋

(stripe). 2. *vb.* shimeru 締める (close); samatageru 妨げる (block); shimedasu 締め出す (exclude).

barbarian, *n.* yabanjin 野蛮人.

barbecue, 1. *n.* bābekyū バーベキュー. 2. *vb.* bābekyū o suru バーベキューをする.

barber, *n.* tokoya 床屋.

barbershop, *n.* tokoya 床屋; rihatsuten 理髪店.

bare, 1. *adj.* hadaka (no) 裸 (の) (uncovered); (...no) nai (...の)ない (empty); kōzen (no) 公然 (の) (unconcealed); tatta (no) たった (の) (mere). 2. *vb.* sarasu 曝す; arawa ni suru あらわにする (lay bare).

barefoot, *adj.* hadashi (no) はだし (の).

barely, *adv.* karōjite 辛うじて; nantoka 何とか.

bargain, 1. *n.* baibai-keiyaku 売買契約 (commercial agreement); kōshō 交渉 (negotiation); bāgen バーゲン; okaidoku(hin) お買い得 (品) (advantageous purchase). 2. *vb.* torihiki/kōshō suru 取り引き／交渉する (negotiate).

barge, 1. *n.* kogatanimotsu-unpansen 小形荷物運搬船. 2. *vb.* **barge into** warikomu 割り込む.

bark, 1. *n.* juhi 樹皮 (tree); hoegoe 吠え声(dog). 2. *vb.* hoeru 吠える (dog).

barley, *n.* ōmugi 大麦.

barn, *n.* naya 納屋; kachikugoya 家畜小屋.

barometer, *n.* baromētā バロメーター; kiatsukei 気圧計.

baron, *n.* danshaku 男爵.

baroness, *n.* danshaku fujin 男爵夫人.

baroque, 1. *adj.* barokku (no) バロ

ック (の). 2. *n.* barokku バロック.

barracks, *n.* heisha 兵舎.

barrel, *n.* taru 樽.

barren, *adj.* 1. funin (no) 不妊 (の) (sterile). 2. fumō (na, no) 不毛 (な、の); hinjaku (na) 貧弱 (な) (unfruitful). 3. kaketeiru 欠けている (devoid).

barrier, *n.* 1. shōgai 障害 (obstacle). 2. saku 柵 (fence).

bartender, *n.* bāten バーテン.

barter, 1. *n.* butsu-butsu kōkan 物々交換. 2. *vb.* butsu-butsu kōkan suru 物々交換する.

base, 1. *n.* moto 元, soko 底 (bottom); kiso 基礎 (foundation); fumoto 麓 (foot of mountain); konkyo 根拠 (basis); kichi 基地 (military). 2. *adj.* iyashii 卑しい (despicable); tsumaranai つまらない (worthless). 3. *vb.* motozuku 基づく; **be based on** ...ni motozuku.

baseball, *n.* yakyū 野球; bēsubōru ベースボール.

basement, *n.* chika(shitsu) 地下 (室); chikai 地階.

bash, 1. *n.* ichigeki 一撃 (heavy blow); pātī パーティー (party). 2. *vb.* naguru 殴る.

bashful, *adj.* hazukashii 恥ずかしい; uchiki (na) 内気 (な).

basic, *adj.* kihon-teki (na) 基本的 (な).

basin, *n.* tarai たらい; hachi 鉢; sen'menki 洗面器.

basis, *n.* kihon 基本; kiso 基礎.

basket, *n.* basuketto バスケット; kago 籠.

basketball, *n.* basuketto-bōru バスケットボール.

bass, *n.* 1. suzuki すずき (fish). 2. basu/bēsu バス／ベース (music).

bastard, *n.* 1. shiseiji 私生児

(illegitimate child). 2. yarō 野郎 (despicable person).

bat, *n.* 1. kōmori こうもり (animal). 2. batto バット (baseball).

bath, *n.* (o)furo (お)風呂; basu バ ス.

bathe, *vb.* 1. (o)furo ni hairu (お) 風呂に入る (take a bath). 2. abiru 浴びる; tsukaru 浸かる (immerse).

bathing cap, *n.* suieibō 水泳帽.

bathing suit, *n.* mizugi 水着.

bathrobe, *n.* basurōbu バスローブ.

bathroom, *n.* 1. furoba 風呂場 (for bathing). 2. otearai お手洗い (rest room).

bathtub, *n.* furo'oke 風呂桶.

batter, 1. *n.* koromo 衣 (food coating). 2. *vb.* tsuzukete utsu 続 けて打つ (beat); tsubusu 潰す; uchikowasu 打ち壊す (damage).

battery, *n.* batterī バッテリー (for vehicles); denchi 電池 (for appliances).

battle, 1. *n.* sentō 戦闘; tatakai 戦 い. 2. *vb.* tatakau 戦う.

battlefield, *n.* senjō 戦場.

battleship, *n.* senkan 戦艦; gunkan 軍艦.

bauble, *n.* yasumono no kazari 安 物の飾り.

bawl, *vb.* 1. wameku 喚く (cry out); donaru どなる (yell). 2. **bawl out** shikaru 叱る.

bay, *n.* wan 湾 (water).

bazaar, *n.* bazā バザー; ichi 市.

be, *vb.* iru/imasu 居る／居ます; aru/arimasu 有る／有ります; dearu/desu である／です.

beach, *n.* hama 浜; kishibe 岸辺.

beacon, *n.* kagaribi かがり火.

bead, *n.* bīzu ビーズ (decoration); tama 玉 (drop).

beak, *n.* kuchibashi くちばし.

beam, 1. *n.* hari 梁 (structure);

kōsen 光線 (light). 2. *vb.* hikaru 光る (emit light); hohoemu 微笑 む (smile).

bean, *n.* mame 豆.

bear, 1. *n.* kuma 熊. 2. *vb.* umu 産 む (bear a child); sasaeru 支える (support); hakobu 運ぶ (carry); taeru 耐える (endure); **bear down** osaetsukeru 押さえつける; **bear in mind** oboete oku 覚えて おく; **bear out** jisshō suru 実証す る; **bear up** ganbaru 頑張る.

bearable, *adj.* gaman dekiru 我慢 出来る.

beard, *n.* ago hige あご髭.

bearer, *n.* unpannin 運搬人.

bearing, *n.* 1. monogoshi 物腰; taido 態度 (manner). 2. kankei 関 係 (relation). 3. gaman 我慢 (patience). 4. bearingu ベアリン グ (ball bearing).

beast, *n.* ke(da)mono 獣; dōbutsu 動物.

beastly, *adj.* 1. kemono no yō (na) 獣のよう (な) (like a beast). 2. hidoi ひどい (nasty).

beat, 1. *n.* kodō 鼓動 (heartbeat); hyōshi 拍子 (rhythm); junkai 巡回 (patrol route). 2. *vb.* utsu 打つ (strike, dash against); butsu 打つ (hit a person); tataku 叩く (hit repeatedly); kakimazeru 掻き混ぜ る (stir); hyōshi o toru 拍子を取る (rhythm); uchimakasu 打ち負かす (defeat).

beating, *n.* 1. tatakinomeshi 叩き のめし (violent hitting). 2. haiboku 敗北 (defeat).

beautiful, *adj.* utsukushii 美しい; kirei (na) きれい (な).

beauty, *n.* 1. bi 美. 2. bijin 美人 (woman). 3. **beauty parlor** biyōin 美容院.

because, *conj.* nazenara なぜな

ら...; node ので; (...da)kara (...だ) から; **because of** (...no) tame ni (...の) 為に.

beckon, *vb.* temaneki suru 手招き する.

become, *vb.* 1. ...ni naru ...になる (come to be). 2. (ni)au (に)合う (suit).

becoming, *adj.* niau 似合う (attractive); fusawashii ふさわしい (suitable).

bed, *n.* beddo ベッド; shindai 寝台.

bedroom, *n.* shinshitsu 寝室.

bedspread, *n.* beddo-kake ベッド 掛.

bee, *n.* mitsubachi 密蜂 (honeybee); hachi 蜂 (bee).

beef, *n.* gyūniku 牛肉; bīfu ビーフ.

beefsteak, *n.* bifuteki ビフテキ; sutēki ステーキ.

beehive, *n.* hachi no su 蜂の巣.

beer, *n.* bīru ビール.

beet, *n.* akakabu 赤蕪.

beetle, *n.* kōchū 甲虫.

before, 1. *adv.* mae ni 前に (in front, previously); izen 以前 (previously). 2. *prep.* (...no) mae ni/de (...の) 前に／で (in front of, in the presence of); (...yori) mae ni (...より) 前に (previous to). 3. *conj.* (...suru) mae ni (...する) 前に.

beforehand, *adv.* maemotte 前も って.

befriend, *vb.* tomo ni naru 友に成 る.

beg, *vb.* 1. kou 請う (ask for charity). 2. tanomu 頼む (ask).

beget, *vb.* 1. mōkeru 儲ける (father). 2. umu 生む (produce).

beggar, *n.* kojiki 乞食.

begin, *vb.* hajimeru 始める (cause to start); hajimaru 始まる (start to move or act).

beginner, *n.* shoshinsha 初心者.

beginning, *n.* hajime 初め.

behalf, *n.* **in/on one's behalf** (...no) tame ni (...の)為に (for someone); **on behalf of** (...o) daihyō shite (...を) 代表して (as representative); ...ni kawatte ...に 代わって (as proxy).

behave, *vb.* 1. furumau ふるまう (conduct oneself). 2. gyōgi yoku suru 行儀良くする (act properly).

behavior, *n.* 1. furumai ふるまい (conduct, manners); taido 態度 (attitude). 2. kōdō 行動 (actions).

behead, *vb.* kubi o kiru 首を切る.

behind, 1. *adv.* ushiro/ato ni 後 ろ／後に (at the back); okurete 遅 れて (slow); **be behind** okurete- iru. 2. *prep.* (...no) ushiro ni (...の) 後ろに (at the back of); (...no) ato de (...の) 後で (later than). 3. *n.* (o)shiri (お)尻 (buttocks).

behold, 1. *vb.* miru 見る. 2. *interj.* miyo 見よ.

beige, 1. *adj.* bēju (no) ベージュ (の). 2. *n.* bēju ベージュ.

being, *n.* 1. sonzai 存在 (existence). 2. seimei 生命 (life). 3. **human being** ningen 人間.

belated, *adj.* okureta 遅れた.

belch, *n.* geppu げっぷ.

belief, *n.* 1. shin'nen 信念 (conviction). 2. shinrai 信頼 (trust). 3. shinjin 信心 (religious tenet).

believable, *adj.* shinjirareru 信じら れる.

believe, *vb.* shinjiru 信じる (accept as true, trust). 2. (...to) kangaeru (...と) 考える (suppose). 3. **make believe** (...no) furi o suru (...の) 振りをする.

believer, *n.* 1. shinpōsha 信奉者; shinja 信者.

belittle, *vb.* mikubiru 見くびる.

bell, *n.* 1. kane 鐘; beru ベル. 2. doaberu ドアベル; chaimu チャイム (doorbell). 3. suzu 鈴 (small bell).

bellboy, *n.* bōi(san) ボーイ(さん).

belligerent, *adj.* kenkagoshi (no) けんか腰 (の); sentō-teki (na) 戦闘的 (な).

bellow, 1. *n.* hoegoe 吠え声; todoroki とどろき. 2. *vb.* hoeru 吠える; todoroku とどろく.

bellows, *n.* fuigo ふいご.

bell tower, *n.* kanetsukidō 鐘撞堂.

belly, *n.* onaka お腹; hara 腹.

belong to, *vb.* ...ni zokusuru ...に属する.

belongings, *n.* shojihin 所持品.

beloved, *adj.* aisuru 愛する; taisetsu (na) 大切 (な).

below, 1. *adv.* shita ni/de 下に／で. 2. *prep.* (...no/yori) shita ni/de (...の／より) 下に／で; (...yori) hikui (...より) 低い.

belt, *n.* beruto ベルト; obi 帯.

bench, *n.* benchi ベンチ; nagaisu 長椅子.

bend, 1. *n.* magari 曲がり (curve). 2. *vb.* magaru 曲がる (become curved); mageru 曲げる (curve something); makasu 負かす (cause to submit).

beneath, *prep.* (...no) shita ni/de (...の) 下に／で; (...yori) hikui (...より) 低い (lower than, under, unworthy of).

benefactor, -tress, *n.* onjin 恩人.

beneficial, *adj.* tame ni naru 為になる; rieki ni naru 利益になる.

beneficiary, *n.* uketorinin 受け取り人.

benefit, 1. *n.* jizen 慈善 (kind act); rieki 利益 (advantage); teate 手当て (payment). 2. *vb.* tame ni naru 為になる (do good for); toku suru 得する (gain advantage).

benevolence, *n.* zen'i 善意; jizen 慈善.

benevolent, *adj.* zen'i ni michita 善意に満ちた.

bent, 1. *adj.* magatta 曲がった (not straight); hinekureta ひねくれた (crooked attitude); **bent on** kesshin shiteiru 決心している (resolved). 2. *n.* keikō 傾向 (inclination); sainō 才能 (talent).

bequeath, *vb.* (isan o) nokosu (遺産を) 残す.

bequest, *n.* isan 遺産.

berate, *vb.* shikaru 叱る.

berry, *n.* **mulberry** kuwa no mi 桑の実; **raspberry** ki'ichigo 木苺; **strawberry** ichigo 苺.

berth, *n.* 1. shindai 寝台 (bed). 2. teihakuichi 停泊位置 (dock).

beseech, *vb.* kongan suru 懇願する.

beside, *prep.* 1. (...no) soba ni/de (...の) 側に／で (at the side of). 2. (...to) kurabete (...と) 比べて (compared with).

besides, 1. *adv.* soreni それに (also); sono ue ni その上に (in addition). 2. *prep.* (...no) hoka ni (...の) 他に (other than). 3. (...ni) kuwaete (...に) 加えて (in addition to).

besiege, *vb.* hōi suru 包囲する; torikakomu 取り囲む (surround).

best, 1. *adj., adv.* ichiban ii 一番良い; sairyō (no) 最良 (の); **at best** yokutemo 良くても. 2. *n.* saizen 最善; **do one's best** saizen o tsukusu 最善を尽くす.

bestow, *vb.* ataeru 与える.

bet, 1. *n.* kakekin 掛金 (money). 2. *vb.* kakeru 賭ける (risk money or thing); **I bet...** kitto ... dearu きっと...である.

betray, *vb.* 1. uragiru 裏切る (be unfaithful). 2. bakuro suru 暴露する (disclose).

betrayal, *n.* uragiri 裏切り.

betrothal, *n.* kon'yaku 婚約.

betrothed, 1. *n.* kon'yakusha 婚約者 (fiancé, fiancée). 2. *adj.* kon'yaku shiteiru 婚約している.

better, 1. *adj.* motto ii もっと良い (of superior quality); kibun ga ii 気分が良い (healthy). 2. *vb.* kairyō suru 改良する.

between, 1. *adv.* aida ni 間に. 2. *prep.* (...no) aida/naka de (ni, o) (...の) 間／中で (に、を).

beverage, *n.* nomimono 飲物.

beware, 1. *vb.* yōjin suru 用心する; ki o tsukeru 気を付ける. 2. *interj.* Ki o tsukete/tsukenasai 気を付けて／付けなさい.

bewilder, *vb.* rōbai saseru 狼狽させる.

bewitch, *vb.* mahō ni kakeru 魔法にかける.

beyond, 1. *n.* anoyo あの世; raise 来世 (afterlife). 2. *adv.* mukō ni 向こうに (farther away). 3. *prep.* (...no) mukō ni (...の) 向こうに (on the farther side of); (...o) sugite (...を)過ぎて (past); (...o) koete (...を) 超えて (outside the limits of); te no todokanai 手の届かない (outside the reach of); (...no) ue ni (...の)上に (surpassing).

bias, 1. *n.* henken 偏見 (prejudice); shasen 斜線 (slanted line); **on the bias** naname ni 斜めに. 2. *vb.* henken o motaseru 偏見をもたせる.

bib, *n.* yodarekake 涎掛け.

bibliography, *n.* 1. tosho-mokuroku 図書目録 (book list); sankō-bunken-mokuroku 参考文献目録 (research references). 2.

shoshigaku 書誌学 (science).

bicycle, *n.* jitensha 自転車.

bid, 1. *n.* nyūsatsu 入札 (offer); meirei 命令 (command). 2. *vb.* nyūsatsu suru 入札する; meirei suru 命令する; iu 言う (say).

bifocal, *adj.* enkinryōyō (no) 遠近両用 (の).

big, *adj.* 1. ōkii 大きい (large, loud). 2. jūyō (na) 重要 (な) (important). 3. hijō na 非常な (outstanding).

bigamy, *n.* jūkon 重婚.

bigger, *adj.* motto ōkii もっと大きい.

biggest, *adj.* ichiban ōkii 一番大きい; saidai (no) 最大 (の).

bigot, *n.* henken ni michita hito 偏見に満ちた人; henkutsusha 偏屈者.

bigoted, *adj.* henken ni michita 偏見に満ちた; henkutsu (na) 偏屈 (な).

bigotry, *n.* henken 偏見; henkutsu 偏屈.

big shot, *n.* ōmono 大物.

big toe, *n.* (ashi no) oyayubi (足の) 親指.

bikini, *n.* bikini ビキニ.

bilateral, *adj.* ryōhō/sōhō (no) 両方／双方 (の).

bilingual, *adj.* nikakokugo (no) ニか国語 (の).

bilk, *vb.* 1. damashitoru だましとる (defraud). 2. fumitaosu 踏み倒す (evade payment).

bill, 1. *n.* seikyūsho 請求書; kanjō 勘定 (statement of money owed); satsu 札; shihei 紙幣 (money); hōan 法案 (proposed law); kōkoku 広告 (notice); kuchibashi くちばし (beak). 2. *vb.* seikyūsho o okuru 請求書を送る.

billboard, *n.* kōkokuban 広告板.

billfold, *n.* saifu 財布; satsuire 札入

れ.

billiards, *n.* biriyādo ビリヤード; tamatsuki 玉突き.

billion, *n.* 1. (U.S.) jūoku 十億 (a thousand million). 2. (Brit.) chō 兆 (a million million).

bimonthly, *adj.* nikagetsu ni ichido (no) 二か月に一度 (の).

bin, *n.* hako 箱 (container); chozōsho 貯蔵所 (granary).

binary, *adj.* nishinhō (no) 二進法 (の) (mathematics).

bind, *vb.* 1. musubu 結ぶ; tsunagu つなぐ; shibaru 縛る (unite, tie). 2. maku 巻く (encircle). 3. seihon suru 製本する (make book).

binding, *adj.* gimu-teki (na) 義務的 (な).

binoculars, *n.* sōgankyō 双眼鏡.

biodegradable, *adj.* shizenbunkai dekiru 自然分解出来る.

biography, *n.* denki 伝記.

biologist, *n.* seibutsu-gakusha 生物学者.

biology, *n.* seibutsugaku 生物学.

bird, *n.* tori 鳥.

birth, *n.* 1. tanjō 誕生 (fact of being born); shussan 出産 (act of being born); **by birth** umaretsuki 生まれつき; **give birth to** (...o) umu (...を) 産む. 2. umare 生まれ (lineage).

birth certificate, *n.* shusshō-/ shussei shōmeisho 出生証明書.

birth control, *n.* sanjiseigen 産児制限.

birthday, *n.* tanjōbi 誕生日.

birthplace, *n.* shusshōchi 出生地.

birthrate, *n.* shusshōritsu 出生率.

bisect, *vb.* nitōbun suru 二等分する.

bishop, *n.* shikyō 司教.

bit, *n.* 1. shōryō 少量; **a bit** sukoshi 少し; chotto ちょっと. 2. kiri 錐

(drill). 3. bitto ビット (computers).

bitch, *n.* 1. mesuinu 雌犬 (dog). 2. abazureon'na あばずれ女 (woman).

bite, 1. *n.* kamitsuki 噛みつき (act of biting); sashikizu 刺し傷 (insect); hitokuchi 一口 (food). 2. *vb.* kamu 噛む (with teeth); sasu 刺す (insect).

bitter, *adj.* 1. nigai 苦い (of harsh taste). 2. kurushii 苦しい; tsurai 辛い (unbearable). 3. kibishii 厳しい (severe).

bizarre, *adj.* kimyō (na) 奇妙 (な).

black, 1. *adj.* kuroi 黒い (color); hada no kuroi 肌の黒い (having dark skin); kurai 暗い (without light, gloomy). 2. *n.* kuro(iro) 黒 (色) (color); kokujin 黒人 (black race or person).

blackberry, *n.* ki'ichigo 木苺.

blackboard, *n.* kokuban 黒板.

blacken, *vb.* 1. kuroku suru 黒くする (make black). 2. kuraku suru 暗くする (make dark).

black eye, *n.* (me no mawari no) aza (目のまわりの) 痣.

black hole, *n.* burraku-hōru ブラックホール.

black list, *n.* burraku-risuto ブラックリスト.

blackmail, 1. *n.* yusuri 強請. 2. *vb.* yusuru 強請る.

black market, *n.* yami'ichi 闇市.

blackout, *n.* 1. teiden 停電 (electricity). 2. kioku-sōshitsu 記憶喪失 (amnesia).

blacksmith, *n.* kajiya 鍛冶屋.

bladder, *n.* bōkō 膀胱.

blade, *n.* 1. ha 刃 (knife). 2. ha 葉 (leaf).

blame, 1. *n.* hinan 非難 (censure); sekinin 責任 (responsibility). 2.

vb. semeru 責める; togameru 咎める (censure); **be to blame for** (...no) sekinin ga aru.

bland, *adj.* 1. odayaka (na) 穏やか (な) (agreeable). 2. ajikenai 味気ない (insipid).

blank, 1. *n.* kūhaku 空白 (space to be filled in); hakushi 白紙 (paper without writing). 2. *adj.* kūhaku (no) 空白 (の); hakushi (no) 白紙 (の); muhyōjō (na) 無表情 (な) (no facial expression); garanto shita がらんとした (emotionless, empty).

blanket, *n.* mōfu 毛布.

blare, 1. *n.* yakamashii hibiki 喧しい響き. 2. *vb.* yakamashiku hibiku 喧しく響く.

blasphemy, *n.* bōtoku 冒瀆.

blast, 1. *n.* toppū 突風 (wind); bakuhatsu 爆発 (explosion); hibiki 響き(horn); **full blast** zen'ryoku de 全力で. 2. *vb.* uchikowasu 打ち壊す (destroy); bakuha suru 爆破する (blow up).

blast-off, *n.* hassha 発射.

blatant, *adj.* kore miyogashi (no) これみよがし (の) (obvious).

blaze, 1. *n.* hono'o 炎 (flame); kagayaki 輝き (glow). 2. *vb.* moeru 燃える (burn); kagayaku 輝く (shine).

bleach, 1. *n.* hyōhakuzai 漂白剤. 2. *vb.* hyōhaku suru 漂白する.

bleak, *adj.* 1. kurai 暗い (dreary). 2. sabishii 寂しい (desolate). 3. samui 寒い (cold).

bleed, *vb.* shukketsu suru 出血する.

blemish, *n.* kizu 傷; ketten 欠点.

blend, 1. *n.* burendo ブレンド; kongō 混合. 2. *vb.* mazeru 混ぜる.

bless, *vb.* 1. (shukufuku o) inoru (祝福を) 祈る (request divine favor for). 2. (megumi o) sazukeru (恵みを) 授ける (endow). 3. tataeru 賛える (praise).

blessed, *adj.* 1. megumareta 恵まれた (favored). 2. shinsei (na) 神聖 (な) (holy).

blessing, *n.* 1. shukufuku 祝福 (God's favor). 2. kami no megumi 神の恵み (God's gift).

blight, *n.* 1. byōki 病気 (disease). 2. hametsu 破滅 (ruin).

blind, 1. *n.* buraindo ブラインド; hiyoke 日除け (window shade). 2. *adj.* mō(moku) (no) 盲(目) (の) (unable to see). 3. *vb.* mienaku suru 見えなくする (cause to not see).

blind alley, *n.* ikidomari 行き止まり.

blindfold, 1. *n.* mekakushi 目隠し. 2. *vb.* mekakushi o suru 目隠しをする.

blink, 1. *n.* matataki 瞬き (blinking, glimmer). 2. *vb.* mabataki suru 瞬きする (wink).

bliss, *n.* shifuku 至福.

blister, *n.* mizubukure 水ぶくれ.

blithe, *adj.* yukai (na) 愉快 (な).

blizzard, *n.* fubuki 吹雪.

bloat, *vb.* fukureru 膨れる.

bloc, *n.* ken 圏.

block, 1. *n.* burokku ブロック; katamari 塊 (solid mass); shōgai 障害 (obstacle); -chōme -丁目 (city block); tsumiki 積み木 (toy). 2. *vb.* fusagu 塞ぐ; samatageru 妨げる (obstruct).

blockade, 1. *n.* fūsa 封鎖. 2. *vb.* fūsa suru 封鎖する.

blond, *adj.* burondo (no) ブロンド (の); kinpatsu (no) 金髪 (の).

blood, *n.* 1. chi 血; ketsueki 血液 (liquid). 2. ketsuen 血縁 (family relation); kettō 血統 (lineage).

bloodless, *adj.* 1. muketsu (no) 無血 (の) (without blood, without killing). 2. tsumetai 冷たい (without feeling).

blood pressure, *n.* ketsuatsu 血圧.

bloodshed, *n.* satsugai 殺害.

bloodshot, *adj.* jūketsu 充血.

bloodthirsty, *adj.* sakkidatta 殺気立った.

blood type, *n.* ketsuekigata 血液型.

blood vessel, *n.* kekkan 血管.

bloody, *adj.* chimamire (no) 血まみれ (の) (blood-covered).

bloom, 1. *n.* hana 花 (flower); kaika 開花 (blossoming). 2. *vb.* hana saku 花咲く; kaika suru 開花する.

blossom, 1. *n.* hana 花. 2. *vb.* hana saku 花咲く.

blot, 1. *n.* shimi しみ; oten 汚点 (stain, fault). 2. *vb.* yogosu 汚す (stain).

blotch, *n.* shimi しみ.

blouse, *n.* burausu ブラウス.

blow, 1. *n.* tsuyoi kaze 強い風 (blast of wind); dageki 打撃 (stroke, shock). 2. *vb.* fuku 吹く (wind); narasu 鳴らす (instrument); **blow one's nose** hana o kamu 鼻をかむ; **blow up** kanshaku o okosu 癇癪を起こす (lose temper); bakuha suru 爆破する (explode); hikinobasu 引き伸す (enlarge photograph).

blowfish, *n.* fugu ふぐ.

blowout, *n.* panku パンク (puncture).

blowup, *n.* 1. bakuha 爆破 (explosion). 2. kanshaku 癇癪 (emotional outburst). 3. hikinobashi 引き伸し (photograph).

bludgeon, 1. *n.* konbō 棍棒. 2. *vb.* uchinomesu 打ちのめす (strike); odosu 脅す (coerce).

blue, 1. *adj.* aoi 青い (color); yū'utsu (na) 憂うつ (な) (melancholy). 2. *n.* ao(iro) 青(色) (color).

blueprint, *n.* aojashin 青写真 (drawing); keikaku 計画 (plan).

blunder, 1. *n.* shikujiri しくじり; machigai 間違い. 2. *vb.* shikujiru しくじる.

blunt, 1. *adj.* nibui 鈍い (dull); sotchoku (na) 率直 (な) (frank). 2. *vb.* nibuku suru 鈍くする.

blur, 1. *n.* fusenmei 不鮮明; kasumi 霞 (indistinctness). 2. *vb.* bokasu ぼかす (obscure); kasumu 霞む (become indistinct).

blush, 1. *n.* sekimen 赤面. 2. *vb.* akaku naru 赤くなる (redden); haji'iru 恥じ入る (feel shame).

board, 1. *n.* ita 板 (timber, sheet of wood); i'inkai 委員会 (managing group); **room and board** makanaitsuki-geshuku 賄い付き下宿. 2. *vb.* noru 乗る (go aboard); geshuku saseru 下宿させる (take in boarder).

boarder, *n.* geshukunin 下宿人.

boarding house, *n.* geshuku 下宿.

boarding pass, *n.* tōjōken 搭乗券.

boarding school, *n.* ryōsei-gakkō 寮制学校.

boast, 1. *n.* jiman 自慢. 2. *vb.* jiman suru 自慢する.

boat, *n.* bōto ボート; kobune 小船.

bob, *vb.* 1. jōge ni ugoku 上下に動く (move). 2. mijikaku suru 短くする (cut short).

bobby pin, *n.* hea-pin ヘアピン.

bodily, *adj.* karada (no) 体 (の); nikutai (no) 肉体 (の).

body, *n.* 1. karada 体 (physical

structure); shitai 死体 (corpse). 2. hontai 本体 (main mass). 3. dantai 団体 (group).

bodyguard, *n.* yōjinbō 用心棒.

bog, 1. *n.* numa 沼. 2. *vb.* **bog down** ugoki ga torenaku-naru 動きが取れなくなる.

boil, 1. *n.* futtō 沸騰 (water); dekimono 出来物 (sore). 2. *vb.* futtō suru 沸騰する (reach boiling point); niru 煮る (cause to boil); ikaru 怒る (be angry).

boiler, *n.* boirā ボイラー.

boisterous, *adj.* 1. sawagashii 騒がしい (noisy). 2. ara-arashii 荒々しい (rough).

bold, *adj.* 1. daitan (na) 大胆 (な) (daring). 2. atsukamashii 厚かましい (immodest). 3. medatsu 目立つ (conspicuous). 4. futoji (no) 太字 (の) (boldface type).

bolster, *vb.* sasaeru 支える.

bolt, 1. *n.* boruto ボルト (pin); kan'nuki 閂 (bar); inazuma 稲妻 (thunderbolt); tōsō 逃走 (flight). 2. *vb.* shimeru 締める (fasten); nigeru 逃げる (run away).

bomb, 1. *n.* bakudan 爆弾 (missile); shippai 失敗 (failure). 2. *vb.* bakugeki suru 爆撃する (attack); shippai suru 失敗する (fail).

bombard, *vb.* bakugeki suru 爆撃する.

bombastic, *adj.* ōgesa (na) 大げさ (な).

bomber, *n.* bakugekiki 爆撃機 (plane).

bombing, *n.* bakugeki 爆撃.

bombshell, *n.* bakudan 爆弾.

bond, *n.* 1. kizuna 絆 (tie between people). 2. setchakuzai 接着剤 (glue). 3. saiken 債券 (financial).

bondage, *n.* sokubaku 束縛.

bone, 1. *n.* hone 骨. 2. *vb.* hone o toru 骨を取る.

bonfire, *n.* takibi 焚き火.

bonsai, *n.* bonsai 盆栽.

bonus, *n.* bōnasu ボーナス; shōyokin 賞与金.

bony, *adj.* 1. hone ga ōi 骨が多い (full of bones). 2. yasekoketa やせこけた (thin).

book, 1. *n.* hon 本 (bound); kaikeibo 会計簿 (account book). 2. *vb.* kinyū suru 記入する (record); yoyaku suru 予約する (reserve).

bookbinding, *n.* seihon 製本.

bookcase, *n.* honbako 本箱.

bookkeeper, *n.* bokigakari 簿記係.

bookkeeping, *n.* boki 簿記.

booklet, *n.* panfuretto パンフレット.

book review, *n.* shohyō 書評.

bookseller, *n.* honya 本屋; shoten 書店.

bookshelf, *n.* hondana 本棚.

bookstore, *n.* honya 本屋; shoten 書店.

bookworm, *n.* 1. dokushoka 読書家 (reader). 2. shimi 紙魚 (insect).

boom, *n.* 1. gō'on 轟音 (sound). 2. būmu ブーム; kōkeiki 好景気 (growth).

boon, *n.* megumi 恵み; onkei 恩恵.

boor, *n.* busahōmono 無作法者.

boost, 1. *n.* oshiage 押し上げ (upward push); ato'oshi 後押し (aid); jōshō 上昇 (increase, rise). 2. *vb.* mochiageru 持ち上げる (lift); ato'oshi suru 後押しする (aid); neage suru 値上げする (raise price); ageru 上げる (increase).

boot, *n.* būtsu ブーツ; nagagutsu 長靴.

bootblack, *n.* kutsu migaki 靴磨き.

booth, *n.* 1. koshitsu 小室 (compartment). 2. yatai 屋台 (street vendor).

border, 1. *n.* kokkyō 国境 (national border); sakai (boundary). 2. fuchi 縁 (margin). 2. *vb.* fuchi o tsukeru 縁を付ける; **border on** sessuru 接する.

borderline, 1. *n.* sakai 境. 2. *adj.* kiwadoi 際どい (almost unacceptable); dotchi tsukazu (no) どっちつかず (の) (uncertain).

bore, 1. *n.* ana 穴 (hole); tsumaranai hito つまらない人 (person). 2. *vb.* ana o akeru 穴を開ける (hole); taikutsu saseru 退屈させる (weary).

bored, *adj.* unzari shiteiru うんざりしている; akita 飽きた.

boredom, *n.* taikutsu 退屈.

boring, *adj.* taikutsu (na) 退屈 (な); tsumaranai つまらない.

born, *adj.* umaretsuki (no) 生まれつき (の) (by nature); **be born** umareru 生まれる.

borrow, *vb.* kariru/karu 借りる／借る.

bosom, *n.* 1. mune 胸 (breast). 2. kokoro 心 (center of feelings).

boss, *n.* 1. jōshi 上司 (superior). 2. bosu ボス; oyabun 親分 (group leader).

bossy, *adj.* ibatteiru 威張っている.

botanical, *adj.* shokubutsu (no) 植物 (の); **botanical garden** shokubutsuen.

botany, *n.* shokubutsugaku 植物学.

botch, 1. *n.* futegiwa 不手際; hema へま. 2. *vb.* yarisokonau やり損なう.

both, 1. *pron.* dochira mo どちらも; ryōhō tomo 両方とも. 2. *adj.*
ryōhō (no) 両方 (の).

bother, 1. *n.* yakkai 厄介 (trouble); meiwaku 迷惑 (annoyance). 2. *vb.* nayamaseru 悩ませる (trouble); meiwaku o kakeru 迷惑をかける (annoy).

bothersome, *adj.* yakkai/mendō (na) 厄介／面倒 (な).

bottle, 1. *n.* bin 瓶. 2. *vb.* bin ni tsumeru 瓶につめる.

bottom, *n.* 1. soko 底. 2. (o)shiri (お)尻 (buttocks).

bough, *n.* ōeda 大枝.

boulevard, *n.* ōdōri 大通り.

bounce, 1. *n.* hanekaeri 跳ね返り (spring); baundo バウンド (ball bounce). 2. *vb.* hanekaeru 跳ね返る (spring back); tobiagaru 飛び上がる (jump up).

bound, *adj.* shibararete-iru 縛られている (tied up); gimu ga aru 義務がある (obligated); tojita 綴じた (fastened); **bound for** (...) iki (no) (...) 行き (の).

boundary, *n.* 1. sakai 境; kyōkai 境界 (border). 2. genkai 限界 (limit).

bountiful, *adj.* takusan (no) 沢山 (の); hōfu (na) 豊富 (な).

bounty, *n.* 1. kandaisa 寛大さ (generosity). 2. okurimono 贈り物 (gift).

bouquet, *n.* hanataba 花束.

bourgeois, *adj.* burujowa (no) ブルジョワ (の).

bout, *n.* 1. shōbu 勝負 (contest). 2. kikan 期間 (period).

bow, 1. *n.* ojigi お辞儀 (salutation); hesaki 舳先 (ship); yumi 弓 (archery, violin); chōmusubi 蝶結び (ribbon). 2. *vb.* atama o sageru 頭を下げる (bend down); ojigi o suru お辞儀をする (salute); mageru 曲げる (curve).

bowels, *n.* chō 腸 (intestine);
bowel movement bentsū 便通.

bowl, 1. *n.* (o)wan (お)椀 (round
dish); chawan 茶碗 (rice bowl);
donburi 丼 (big round dish); bōru
ボール (mixing bowl). 2. *vb.*
bōringu o suru ボーリングをする
(sport).

bowlegged, *adj.* ganimata (no) が
に股 (の).

bowling, *n.* bōringu ボーリング.

bow tie, *n.* chō-nekutai 蝶ネクタ
イ.

box, 1. *n.* hako 箱 (container);
sajikiseki 桟敷席 (in theater). 2.
vb. hako ni ireru 箱に入れる (put
into a box); naguru 殴る (strike);
bokushingu o suru ボクシングを
する (sport).

boxer, *n.* bokusā ボクサー.

boxing, *n.* bokushingu ボクシング;
kentō 拳闘.

box office, *n.* kippu'uriba 切符売
場.

boy, *n.* otoko no ko 男の子; shōnen
少年.

boycott, 1. *n.* boikotto ボイコット;
fubaiundō 不買運動. 2. *vb.*
boikotto suru ボイコットする;
kawanai 買わない.

boyfriend, *n.* kare(shi) 彼(氏);
koibito 恋人; bōifurendo ボーイフ
レンド.

brace, *n.* sasae支え (support). 2.
vb. hokyō suru 補強する
(reinforce).

bracelet, *n.* buresuretto ブレスレ
ット; udewa 腕輪.

bracket, 1. *n.* kakko 括弧;
kakugakko 角括弧 (sign); sasae 支
え; dai 台 (wall support); gurūpu
グループ (class or grouping). 2.
vb. kakko ni ireru 括弧に入れる;
dōitsu gurūpu ni ireru 同一グルー

プに入れる (class together).

brag, 1. *n.* jiman 自慢. 2. *vb.* jiman
suru 自慢する.

braggart, *n.* unubore 自惚れ.

braid, 1. *n.* kumihimo 組み紐
(rope); osagegami おさげ髪;
mitsuami 三つ編み (hair). 2. *vb.*
kumu 組む; amu 編む.

brain, *n.* 1. nō 脳. 2. chisei 知性;
zunō 頭脳 (intelligence).

brainwashing, *n.* sen'nō 洗脳.

brake, 1. *n.* burēki ブレーキ. 2. *vb.*
burēki o kakeru ブレーキをかけ
る.

branch, 1. *n.* koeda 小枝 (tree);
bumon 部門 (division); shiryū 支
流 (river); **branch office**
shisha/shiten 支社／支店. 2. *vb.*
wakareru 分かれる; **branch out**
te o hirogeru 手を広げる.

brand, 1. *n.* burando ブランド;
shōhyō 商標 (trademark); yaki'in
焼き印 (burned mark). 2. *vb.*
yakitsuku 焼き付く (impress
indelibly); omei o kiseru 汚名を着
せる (stigmatize).

brandish, *vb.* furimawasu 振り回
す.

brand-new, *adj.* ma'atarashii 真新
しい.

brandy, *n.* burandē ブランデー.

brash, *adj.* 1. mukōmizu (na, no)
向こう見ず (な、の) (hasty). 2.
namaiki (na) 生意気 (な) (rude).

brass, *n.* shinchū 真ちゅう (metal).

brassiere, *n.* burajā ブラジャー.

brat, *n.* gaki 餓鬼.

bravado, *n.* kyosei 虚勢.

brave, *adj.* yūkan (na) 勇敢 (な).

bravery, *n.* yūki 勇気.

brawl, 1. *n.* kenka けんか. 2. *vb.*
kenka suru けんかする.

brawn, *n.* 1. kin'niku 筋肉
(muscles). 2. kinryoku 筋力

(strength).

brazen, *adj.* 1. atsukamashii 厚かましい; haji shirazu (na, no) 恥知らず (な、の) (shameless). 2. shinchū (no) 真ちゅう (の) (of brass).

Brazil, *n.* burajiru ブラジル.

Brazilian, 1. *n.* burajirujin ブラジル人. 2. *adj.* burajiru (no) ブラジル (の) (of Brazil); burajirujin (no) ブラジル人 (の) (of a Brazilian).

breach, 1. *n.* furikō 不履行 (infraction); ihan 違犯 (violation). 2. *vb.* yaburu 破る (violate).

bread, *n.* 1. pan パン (food). 2. seikei 生計 (livelihood).

bread crumb, *n.* panko パン粉.

breaded, *adj.* panko o mabushita パン粉をまぶした.

breadth, *n.* haba 幅; hirosa 広さ.

break, 1. *n.* yabure 破れ (rupture); sakeme 裂け目 (gap); kyūkei 休憩 (rest). 2. *vb.* waru 割る; kudaku 砕く (separate into parts); kowasu 壊す(make useless); yaburu 破る (violate, tear); oru 折る (fracture, break off); sakeru 裂ける; kudakeru 砕ける (become ruptured or separated); wareru 割れる (become cracked); kowareru 壊れる (become useless); yabureru 破れる(become torn); oreru 折れる (become fractured or broken off).

breakable, *adj.* kowareyasui 壊れ易い.

breakdown, *n.* 1. koshō 故障 (failure to operate). 2. suijaku 衰弱 (physical collapse).

breakfast, 1. *n.* asagohan 朝御飯; chōshoku 朝食. 2. *vb.* asa gohan o taberu 朝御飯を食べる.

breakthrough, *n.* 1. toppa 突破 (movement). 2. hakken 発見

(discovery).

breakup, *n.* 1. wakare 別れ (end of relationship). 2. kaitai 解体 (disintegration).

breakwater, *n.* bōhatei 防波堤.

breast, *n.* 1. mune 胸 (chest). 2. chichi 乳 (milk gland). 3. kyōchū 胸中 (feelings).

breast-feed, *vb.* bonyū de sodateru 母乳で育てる.

breath, *n.* iki 息; **catch one's breath** iki o nomu; **hold one's breath** iki o tomeru; **out of breath** iki ga kireru.

breathe, *vb.* iki o suru 息をする.

breather, *n.* kyūkei 休憩 (short rest).

breathing, *n.* kokyū 呼吸; ikizukai 息遣い.

breed, 1. *n.* hinshu 品種; shuzoku 種族 (sort); kettō 血統 (lineage). 2. *vb.* umu 産む (produce); kau 飼う; sodateru 育てる (raise).

breeder, *n.* shi'ikusha 飼育者.

breeding, *n.* 1. yōiku 養育 (producing). 2. sodachi 育ち (upbringing).

breeze, *n.* soyokaze そよ風.

brevity, *n.* mijikasa 短さ (shortness). 2. kanketsusa 簡潔さ (conciseness).

brew, 1. *n.* jōzō 醸造. 2. *vb.* jōzō suru 醸造する (beer); ireru 入れる (tea).

brewer, *n.* tsukurizakaya 造り酒屋 (sake maker).

brewery, *n.* jōzōsho 醸造所.

bribe, 1. *n.* wairo 賄賂. 2. *vb.* baishū suru 買収する.

brick, *n.* renga 煉瓦.

bride, *n.* shinpu 新婦; hanayome 花嫁.

bridegroom, *n.* shinrō 新郎; hanamuko 花婿.

bridge, *n.* 1. hashi 橋. 2. burijji ブリッジ (game).

bridle, *vb.* seigyo suru 制御する (control).

brief, 1. *adj.* mijikai 短い (short); kanketsu (na) 簡潔 (な) (concise). 2. *n.* yōshi/yōyaku 要旨／要約 (outline, concise statement); burīfu ブリーフ (underwear). 3. *vb.* temijika ni iu 手短に言う (inform in advance).

briefcase, *n.* burīfukēsu ブリーフケース; kaban 鞄.

briefing, *n.* jizensetsumei 事前説明.

brier, *n.* ibara 茨.

bright, *adj.* 1. akarui 明るい (filled with light, happy); hikaru 光る; kagayaku 輝く (shining). 2. kagayakashii 輝かしい (glorious). 3. atama ga ii 頭が良い (clever, intelligent, wise). 4. azayaka (na) 鮮やか (な) (bright color).

brighten, *vb.* akaruku suru 明るくする (make bright); akaruku naru 明るくなる (become bright).

brilliance, *n.* kagayaki 輝き (splendor).

brilliant, *adj.* 1. kagayaiteiru 輝いている (bright). 2. subarashii 素晴らしい (splendid).

brim, *n.* 1. fuchi 縁. 2. tsuba つば (hat).

brine, *n.* shiomizu 塩水.

bring, *vb.* 1. tsuretekuru 連れて来る (a person); mottekuru 持って来る (a thing). 2. michibiku 導く (lead). 3. **bring about** motarasu もたらす; **bring up** sodateru 育てる.

brink, *n.* 1. fuchi 縁; hashi 端 (edge). 2. setogiwa 瀬戸際 (verge).

brisk, *adj.* 1. kakki ga aru 活気があ

る (quick and active). 2. sawayaka (na) さわやか (な) (sharp and stimulating).

Britain, *n.* igirisu イギリス; eikoku 英国.

British, 1. *n.* igirisujin イギリス人; eikokujin 英国人. 2. *adj.* igirisu (no) イギリス (の) (of Britain); igirisujin (no) イギリス人 (の) (of a British person).

brittle, *adj.* wareyasui 割れ易い; moroi 脆い.

broach, 1. *n.* burōchi ブローチ. 2. *vb.* kiridasu 切り出す.

broad, *adj.* 1. (haba)hiroi (幅)広い (wide, vast). 2. ōmaka (na) 大まか (な) (general). 3. kandai (na) 寛大 (な) (tolerant).

broadcast, 1. *n.* hōsō 放送. 2. *vb.* hōsō suru 放送する (radio, TV); hiromeru 広める (make known).

broaden, *vb.* hirogeru 広げる.

broadminded, *adj.* kandai (na) 寛大 (な); kokoro ga hiroi 心が広い.

broccoli, *n.* burokkorī ブロッコリー.

brochure, *n.* panfuretto パンフレット.

broil, *vb.* aburu あぶる.

broken, *adj.* 1. kowareta 壊れた (out of order). 2. wareta 割れた (in fragments); oreta 折れた (fractured); yabureta 破れた (torn, disrupted).

broken-hearted, *adj.* shitsubō shita 失望した.

broker, *n.* burōkā ブローカー; nakagainin 仲買人.

brokerage, *n.* shōkengaisha 証券会社.

bronchitis, *n.* kikanshien 気管支炎.

bronze, *n.* seidō 青銅; buronzu ブロンズ.

brooch, *n.* burōchi ブローチ.

brood, 1. *n.* hina ひな (chicks). 2. *vb.* kangaekomu 考え込む (ponder).

brook, *n.* ogawa 小川.

broom, *n.* hōki 箒.

broth, *n.* dashi だし; sūpu スープ.

brother, *n.* 1. kyōdai 兄弟. 2. ani 兄; oniisan お兄さん (older brother). 3. otōto 弟 (younger brother).

brother-in-law, *n.* giri no kyōdai 義理の兄弟.

brow, *n.* 1. hitai 額 (forehead). 2. mayu まゆ (eyebrow).

browbeat, *vb.* odosu 脅す.

brown, 1. *adj.* chairoi 茶色い. 2. *n.* chairo 茶色.

browse, *vb.* 1. hiroiyomi suru 拾い読みする (read). 2. miaruku 見歩く (look at goods leisurely).

bruise, 1. *n.* uchikizu 打ち傷; aza 痣. 2. *vb.* utsu 打つ; aza ga dekiru 痣ができる.

brunt, *n.* shuryoku 主力; **bear the brunt of** (...no) yaomote ni tatsu (...の) 矢面に立つ.

brush, 1. *n.* burashi ブラシ (for brushing); fude 筆 (for painting). 2. *vb.* burashi o kakeru ブラシを掛ける (clean with brush); kasumeru 掠める (touch lightly); **brush up** benkyō shinaosu 勉強し直す (knowledge).

brusque, *adj.* buaisō (na) 無愛想 (な).

brutal, *adj.* 1. zan'nin/zankoku (na) 残忍／残酷 (な) (cruel). 2. muchakucha (na) むちゃくちゃ (な) (unreasonable).

brutality, *n.* 1. zan'ninsei 残忍性 (brutal quality). 2. zankoku na kōi 残酷な行為 (brutal action).

brutalize, *vb.* zankoku ni atsukau 残酷に扱う.

brute, *n.* 1. kedamono 獣 (animal, beastly person). 2. hitodenashi 人でなし (cruel person).

bubble, 1. *n.* awa 泡 (foam); shabondama シャボン玉 (soap bubble). 2. *vb.* awadatsu 泡立つ.

bucket, *n.* baketsu バケツ.

buckle, 1. *n.* bakkuru バックル; tomegu 留め具. 2. *vb.* shimeru 締める; tomeru 留める; **buckle down** torikakaru 取り掛かる.

buckwheat, *n.* soba そば (grain); sobako そば粉 (flour).

bud, 1. *n.* tsubomi つぼみ; me 芽. 2. *vb.* tsubomi/me ga deru つぼみ／芽が出る.

Buddhism, *n.* bukkyō 仏教.

Buddhist, *n.* bukkyōto 仏教徒.

buddy, *n.* nakama 仲間.

budget, 1. *n.* yosan 予算. 2. *vb.* yosan o kumu 予算を組む.

buffer, 1. *n.* baffā バッファアー (computer). 2. *vb.* fusegu 防ぐ; kanwa suru 緩和する.

buffet, *n.* 1. byuffe ビュッフェ (food). 2. shokkidana 食器棚 (furniture).

buffoon, *n.* dōke(mono) 道化(者).

bug, *n.* mushi 虫 (insect).

bugle, *n.* rappa らっぱ.

build, 1. *n.* tsukuri 造り (structure). 2. *vb.* tateru 建てる (construct); kizuku 築く (base, develop).

builder, *n.* kenchikusha 建築者.

building, *n.* tatemono 建物; biru ビル.

built-in, *n.* tsukuritsuke (no) 造り付け (の) (furniture); naizō (no) 内蔵 (の) (mechanics).

bulb, *n.* 1. denkyū 電球 (light bulb). 2. kyūkon 球根 (root).

bulge, 1. *n.* fukurami 膨らみ. 2.

vb. fukureru 膨れる; tsukideru 突き出る.

bulk, *n.* 1. ōkisa 大きさ (amount). 2. daibubun 大部分 (main mass).

bulky, *adj.* kasabatta 嵩張った.

bull, *n.* oushi 牡牛.

bulldozer, *n.* burudōzā ブルドーザー.

bullet, *n.* dangan 弾丸; teppō no tama 鉄砲の玉.

bulletin, *n.* hōkoku 報告; tsūchi 通知.

bulletin board, *n.* keijiban 掲示板.

bulletproof, *adj.* bōdan (no) 防弾 (の).

bullfighting, *n.* tōgyū 闘牛.

bull's-eye, *n.* mato 的.

bully, 1. *n.* ijimekko いじめっこ. 2. *vb.* ijimeru いじめる (abuse); ibaru 威張る (be arrogant).

bump, 1. *n.* shōtotsu 衝突 (blow); kobu 瘤 (swelling). 2. *vb.* butsukaru ぶつかる; utsu 打つ (strike); **bump into** ...ni dekuwasu ...に出くわす (come across).

bumper, *n.* banpā バンパー.

bun, *n.* 1. kashi-pan 菓子パン (sweet bread); rōrupan ロールパン (roll). 2. sokuhatsu 束髪 (hair).

bunch, *n.* 1. taba 束; fusa 房 (cluster). 2. mure 群れ (group of people).

bundle, 1. *n.* taba 束; tsutsumi 包み (package). 2. *vb.* tabaneru 束ねる (bind); tsutsumu 包む (wrap); **bundle up** kikomu 着込む (dress); matomeru まとめる (gather).

bungle, 1. *n.* hema へま; shikujiri しくじり. 2. *vb.* hema o suru へまをする; shikujiru しくじる.

bunk, *n.* shindai 寝台.

bunny, *n.* (ko)usagi (子)兎.

buoy, *n.* 1. bui ブイ (navigation marker). 2. kyūmeigu 救命具 (life buoy).

buoyant, *adj.* 1. ukiagaru 浮き上がる (tending to float). 2. akarui 明るい (cheerful).

burden, 1. *n.* omoni 重荷 (spiritual or material burden); yakkai 厄介 (trouble). 2. *vb.* omoni o owaseru 重荷を負わせる (load); wazurawasu 煩わす (trouble).

burdensome, *adj.* yakkai (na) 厄介 (な).

bureau, *n.* 1. tansu たんす (furniture). 2. ka 課 (department); jimusho 事務所 (office).

bureaucracy, *n.* kanryōseido 官僚制度 (government).

bureaucrat, *n.* kanryō 官僚.

bureaucratic, *adj.* kanryō shugi (no) 官僚主義.

burglar, *n.* gōtō 強盗.

burglar alarm, *n.* tōnankeihōki 盗難警報機.

burglarize, *vb.* oshi'iru 押し入る.

burglary, *n.* tōnan 盗難.

burial, *n.* maisō 埋葬.

burlesque, 1. *n.* parodī パロディー (parody); nūdo-baraetī-shō ヌードバラエティーショー (vulgar show). 2. *vb.* chakasu 茶化す.

burly, *adj.* ganjō (na) 頑丈 (な); takumashii 逞しい.

burn, 1. *n.* yakedo 火傷 (injury). 2. *vb.* moeru 燃える (be on fire, be excited); moyasu 燃やす (consume with fire); yaku 焼く (broil, grill); kogasu 焦がす (scorch); yakedo suru 火傷する (injure).

burp, 1. *n.* geppu げっぷ. 2. *vb.* geppu o suru げっぷをする.

burst, 1. *n.* haretsu 破裂 (rupture); bakuhatsu 爆発 (explosion). 2. *vb.* haretsu suru 破裂する (break violently); bakuhatsu suru 爆発する (explode); **burst into** totsuzen/issei ni shidasu 突然／いっせいにしだす.

bury, *vb.* umeru 埋める (in the ground); hōmuru 葬る (in a grave).

bus, *n.* basu バス; **catch a bus** basu ni maniau.

bush, *n.* shigemi 茂み; yabu やぶ (shrub, thicket).

business, *n.* 1. bijinesu ビジネス; shōbai 商売; eigyō 営業 (commerce, trade); **business hours** eigyōjikan 営業時間. 2. shigoto 仕事 (profession, work). 3. yōken 用件 (personal concern).

businessman, *n.* bijinesuman ビジネスマン; jitsugyōka 実業家.

businesswoman, *n.* josei-jitsugyōka 女性実業家.

bust, *n.* 1. mune 胸 (bosom). 2. kyōzō 胸像 (sculpture).

bustle, *n.* zawameki ざわめき; kakki 活気.

busy, 1. *adj.* isogashii 忙しい (actively employed); kōtsū ga ōi 交通が多い (street); hanashichū (no) 話し中 (の) (telephone). 2. *vb.* **busy oneself** isoshimu いそしむ.

busybody, *n.* deshabari でしゃばり.

but, 1. *prep.* (...o) nozoite (...を) 除いて (other than). 2. *conj.* dakedo だけど; shikashi しかし; ga が (however).

butcher shop, *n.* nikuya 肉屋.

butler, *n.* shitsuji 執事.

butt, *n.* 1. moto 元 (end); suigara 吸殻 (cigarette end). 2. (o)shiri (お)尻 (buttocks).

butter, *n.* batā バター.

butterfly, *n.* chōcho 蝶々.

buttocks, *n.* (o)shiri (お)尻.

button, 1. *n.* botan ボタン. 2. *vb.* botan o kakeru ボタンを掛ける.

buttonhole, *n.* botan ana ボタン穴.

buttress, 1. *n.* sasae 支え (support). 2. *vb.* sasaeru 支える (support); hokyō suru 補強する (strengthen).

buxom, *adj.* hōman (na) 豊満 (な).

buy, 1. *vb.* kau 買う. 2. *n.* kaimono 買物.

buyer, *n.* kaite 買い手; kōbaisha 購買者.

buzz, 1. *n.* bun-bun to iu oto ぶんぶんという音 (bee); zawameki ざわめき (voices). 2. *vb.* bun-bun suru ぶんぶんする; zawameku ざわめく; buzā o osu ブザーを押す (signal with buzzer).

by, 1. *prep.* ...ni yotte ...によって; de で (by means of); (...no) chikaku/soba ni (...の) 近く／側に (near to); made ni までに (not later than); ... o tōshite ...を通して (through); ...zutsu ...ずつ (after); **little by little** sukoshi zutsu; **by oneself** hitori de 一人で. 2. *adv.* soba ni 側に (near); sugite 過ぎて (past); **by and by** yagate やがて; **by and large** ippan ni 一般に.

bye-bye, *interj.* sayonara さよなら; bai-bai バイバイ.

bygone, *adj.* sugita 過ぎた; mukashi (no) 昔 (の).

bylaw, *n.* naiki 内規.

bypass, 1. *n.* baipasu バイパス; ukairo 迂回路. 2. *vb.* ukai suru 迂回する.

by-product, *n.* fukusanbutsu 副産

物.

bystander, *n.* bōkansha 傍観者;

kenbutsunin 見物人.

byte, *n.* baito バイト (computers).

C

cab, *n.* takushī タクシー (taxi).

cabaret, *n.* kyabarē キャバレー.

cabbage, *n.* kyabetsu キャベツ.

cabin, *n.* 1. koya 小屋 (small house). 2. kyabin キャビン (ship, plane).

cabinet, *n.* 1. kyabinetto キャビネット; todana 戸棚 (furniture). 2. naikaku 内閣 (government).

cable, *n.* 1. futozuna 太綱 (hawser). 2. kēburu ケーブル (cablegram).

cable television, *n.* yūsen-terebi 有線テレビ.

cache, *n.* kakushibasho 隠し場所 (hiding place).

cactus, *n.* saboten サボテン.

cadaver, *n.* shitai 死体.

cadence, *n.* hyōshi 拍子 (beat); yokuyō 抑揚 (intonation).

cadet, *n.* shikankōhosei 士官候補生 (military or naval student).

café, *n.* 1. kissaten 喫茶店 (tea or coffee parlor). 2. keishokudō 軽食堂 (restaurant).

cafeteria, *n.* kafeteria カフェテリア.

caffeine, *n.* kafein カフェイン.

cage, *n.* torikago 鳥籠 (bird cage); ori 檻 (large cage).

cajole, *vb.* odateru おだてる.

cake, *n.* 1. kēki ケーキ. 2. **piece of cake** kantan na koto 簡単な事.

calamity, *n.* sanji 惨事.

calcium, *n.* karushiumu カルシウム.

calculate, *vb.* 1. keisan suru 計算

する (compute). 2. **be calculated to ...** o neratte iru ... を狙っている.

calculation, *n.* 1. keisan 計算 (computation). 2. dasan 打算 (cunning).

calculator, *n.* dentaku 電卓 (pocket calculator).

calendar, *n.* karendā カレンダー; koyomi 暦.

calf, *n.* 1. fukurahagi ふくら脛 (part of leg). 2. koushi 子牛 (young cow or bull).

caliber, *n.* 1. kōkei 口径 (caliber of gun). 2. shitsu 質 (quality).

calisthenics, *n.* biyōtaisō 美容体操.

call, 1. *n.* denwa 電話 (phone call); hōmon 訪問 (visit); shōshū 召集 (summons); yobigoe 呼び声 (shout); nakigoe 鳴き声 (call of a bird). 2. *vb.* denwa suru 電話する (phone); hōmon suru 訪問する (visit); yobu 呼ぶ (summon); nazukeru 名付ける (name); **call back** ato de mata denwa suru (phone); **call on ...** o hōmon suru (visit); **call off** kyanseru suru キャンセルする (cancel).

caller, *n.* hōmonsha 訪問者 (visitor).

calling, *n.* shokugyō 職業 (profession).

callous, *adj.* tsumetai 冷たい (cold).

callus, *n.* tako たこ.

calm, 1. *adj.* heisei (na) 平静 (な)

319

(undisturbed); odayaka (na) 穏や
か (な) (not windy, not rough). 2.
vb. nadameru 宥める (make calm,
as a baby, etc.); shizumeru 静める
(make quiet or peaceful); **calm
down** shizuka ni naru 静かになる
(become quiet).

calorie, *n.* karorī カロリー.

camel, *n.* rakuda ラクダ.

camellia, *n.* tsubaki 椿.

cameo, *n.* kameo カメオ (jewelry).

camera, *n.* kamera カメラ.

camp, 1. *n.* kyanpujō キャンプ場
(campground); kichi 基地
(military camp); habatsu 派閥
(faction). 2. *vb.* kyanpu o suru キ
ャンプをする (go camping).

campaign, 1. *n.* undō 運動
(political action); senkyoundō 選
挙運動 (electioneering); gunjikōdō 軍事行動 (military
operation). 2. *vb.* undō suru 運動
する.

camping, *n.* kyanpu キャンプ
(recreation).

campus, *n.* kyanpasu キャンパス.

can, *vb.* 1. dekiru 出来る (be able);
can do suru koto ga dekiru する
ことが出来る. 2. shitemo ii して
もいい (be allowed to do).

can, 1. *n.* kan 缶; **canned food**
kanzume 缶詰め; **can opener**
kankiri 缶切り. 2. *vb.* kanzume ni
suru 缶詰めにする.

Canada, *n.* kanada カナダ.

Canadian, 1. *n.* kanadajin カナダ
人 (person). 2. *adj.* kanada (no)
カナダ (の) (of Canada);
kanadajin (no) カナダ人 (の) (of
the Canadians).

canal, *n.* unga 運河.

canary, *n.* kanaria カナリア.

cancel, *vb.* kyanseru suru キャンセ
ルする.

cancellation, *n.* kyanseru キャン
セル.

cancer, *n.* gan 癌.

candid, *adj.* sotchoku (na) 率直
(な).

candidacy, *n.* kōho 候補.

candidate, *n.* kōhosha 候補者.

candle, *n.* kyandoru キャンドル;
rōsoku 臘燭.

candleholder, *n.* rōsokutate 臘燭
立て.

candor, *n.* sotchokusa 率直さ.

candy, *n.* kyandē キャンデー; ame
飴.

cane, 1. *n.* kuki 茎 (stalk); satōkibi
砂糖きび (sugarcane); take 竹
(bamboo); tsue 杖 (for walking).
2. *vb.* muchiutsu 鞭打つ (beat).

canine, 1. *n.* inu 犬 (dog); inuka 犬
科 (animal of the family Canidae).
2. *adj.* inu (no) 犬 (の) (of dogs).

canister, *n.* kan 缶 (food
container).

canned goods, *n.* kanzume
shokuhin 缶詰め食品.

cannibal, *n.* hitokui 人食い.

cannon, *n.* taihō 大砲 (gun).

cannot, *vb.* dekinai 出来ない.

canoe, *n.* kanū カヌー.

canopy, *n.* tengai 天蓋.

cantaloupe, *n.* meron メロン.

canvas, *n.* kyanbasu キャンバス
(cloth, painting, etc.).

canyon, *n.* kyōkoku 峡谷.

cap, 1. *n.* bōshi 帽子 (head
covering); futa 蓋 (lid). 2. *vb.* ōu
覆う (cover); shinogu 凌ぐ
(surpass).

capability, *n.* 1. sainō 才能
(ability); shōraisei 将来性
(potential).

capable, *adj.* 1. yūnō (na) 有能
(な) (competent). 2. **be capable
of** ... ga dekiru ...が出来る (can

do); ... kanōsei ga aru ... 可能性が
ある (be disposed to).

capacity, *n.* 1. shūyōnōryoku 収容
能力 (amount contained). 2.
seisanryoku 生産力 (amount
produced). 3. nōryoku 能力
(ability). 4. shikaku 資格
(position).

cape, *n.* 1. kēpu ケープ (coat). 2.
misaki 岬 (geography).

caper, *vb.* tobimawaru 飛び回る.

capital, *n.* 1. shuto 首都 (capital
city). 2. shihonkin 資本金
(money). 3. ōmoji 大文字 (capital
letter).

capitalism, *n.* shihonshugi 資本主
義.

capitalist, *n.* shihonshugisha 資本
主義者.

capitalize, *vb.* ōmoji de kaku 大文
字で書く (write in capitals);
capitalize on ... o riyō suru ... を
利用する (take advantage of).

capitulate, *vb.* kōfuku suru 降伏す
る.

caprice, *n.* kimagure 気紛れ.

capricious, *adj.* kimagure (na) 気
紛れ(な).

capsize, *vb.* tenpuku suru 転覆す
る.

capsule, *n.* kapuseru カプセル
(medicine, spacecraft).

captain, *n.* 1. kyaputen キャプテン
(group leader, ship master, etc.).
2. taii 大尉; taisa 大佐 (military
officer).

caption, *n.* setsumeibun 説明文.

captivate, *vb.* miwaku suru 魅惑す
る.

captive, *n.* horyo 捕虜 (war
prisoner).

captivity, *n.* kankin 監禁.

capture, *vb.* toraeru 捕える (seize,
record).

car, *n.* 1. kuruma 車 (automobile).
2. sharyō 車両 (train car).

caramel, *n.* kyarameru キャラメ
ル.

carat, *n.* karatto カラット.

caravan, *n.* kyaraban キャラバン.

carbohydrate, *n.* tansuikabutsu 炭
水化物.

carbon, *n.* tanso 炭素; **carbon
paper** kābonshi カーボン紙.

carbonated, *adj.* tansan iri (no) 炭
酸入り (の); **carbonated water**
tansansui 炭酸水.

carbon dioxide, *n.* nisankatanso
二酸化炭素.

carburetor, *n.* kyaburetā キャブレ
ター.

carcass, *n.* shigai 死骸.

card, *n.* 1. kādo カード (index). 2.
meishi 名刺 (calling card). 3.
toranpu トランプ (playing card);
play cards toranpu o suru トラン
プをする.

cardboard, *n.* bōru-gami ボール紙.

cardiac, *adj.* shinzō (no) 心臓 (の);
heart disease shinzōbyō 心臓病.

cardinal, *adj.* shuyō (na) 主要 (な)
(principal); **cardinal number**
kisū 基数.

care, 1. *n.* shinpai 心配 (worry);
chūi 注意 (caution); kantoku 監督
(supervision); hogo 保護
(protection); **Take care!** Ki o
tsukete. 気をつけて. 2. *vb.* **care
(about)** (... o) ki ni suru (... を) 気
にする (mind); (... o) shinpai suru
(... を) 心配する (worry); **care for**
... ga suki ... が好き (like); **take
care of** ... no mendō o miru ... の
面倒を見る (look after, be
responsible for).

career, *n.* kyaria キャリア;
shokugyō 職業.

carefree, *adj.* shinpai ga nai 心配が

ない.

careful, *adj.* chūibukai 注意深い;
be careful chūi suru 注意する.

careless, *adj.* 1. fuchūi (na) 不注意
(な) (inattentive). 2. iikagen (na)
いい加減 (な) (sloppy).

carelessness, *n.* fuchūi 不注意.

caress, 1. *n.* aibu 愛撫. 2. *vb.* aibu
suru 愛撫する.

caretaker, *n.* 1. hogosha 保護者
(guardian). 2. kanrinin 管理人 (of
a building).

cargo, *n.* tsumini 積荷.

caricature, *n.* fūshiga 風刺画;
karikachua カリカチュア.

carnal, *adj.* nikutai (no) 肉体 (の).

carnation, *n.* kānēshon カーネー
ション.

carnival, *n.* kānibaru カーニバル.

carnivorous, *adj.* nikushoku (no)
肉食 (の).

carouse, *vb.* donchan sawagi o
suru どんちゃん騒ぎをする.

carousel, *n.* kaiten mokuba 回転木
馬.

carpenter, *n.* daiku 大工.

carpentry, *n.* daiku shigoto 大工仕
事.

carpet, *n.* kāpetto カーペット;
jūtan 絨毯.

carriage, *n.* 1. basha 馬車 (horse
drawn carriage). 2. mi no konashi
身のこなし (deportment).

carrier, *n.* 1. un'yugaisha 運輸会社
(of goods). 2. hokinsha 保菌者 (of
a disease).

carrot, *n.* ninjin 人参.

carry, *vb.* 1. hakobu 運ぶ
(transport). 2. tazusaeru 携える
(take with one). 3. tomonau 伴う
(entail, involve). 4. **carry the
weight of** ...sasaeru ...支える
(support); **be carried away** ware
o wasureru 我を忘れる (lose

control); **carry on** tsuzukeru 続け
る (continue); **carry out** jikkō
suru 実行する (put into action).

cart, *n.* teoshiguruma 手押し車
(handcart).

cartel, *n.* karuteru カルテル.

cartilage, *n.* nankotsu 軟骨.

carton, *n.* bōru-bako ボール箱.

cartoon, *n.* manga 漫画 (drawing);
anime アニメ (animated cartoon).

cartoonist, *n.* mangaka 漫画家.

cartridge, *n.* 1. kātorijji カートリッ
ジ (interchangeable part). 2.
dan'yakutō 弾楽とう
(ammunition casing).

carve, *vb.* 1. horu 彫る (wood). 2.
kiriwakeru 切り分ける (meat).

carving, *n.* chōkoku 彫刻
(sculpture).

cascade, *n.* taki 滝 (waterfall).

case, *n.* 1. kēsu ケース (container).
2. jitsurei 実例 (instance). 3. ba'ai
場合 (situation). 4. jiken 事件
(event). 5. kanja 患者 (medical
patient). 6. soshō 訴訟 (lawsuit).
7. kaku 格 (grammar). 8. **in any
case** tonikaku とにかく; **just in
case** ... ni sonaete... に備えて; **in
case of** ... no ba'ai niwa... の場合
には.

cash, 1. *n.* genkin 現金; **in cash**
genkin de; **cash register** reji レジ.
2. *vb.* genkinka suru 現金化する
(convert into cash); **cash in on**
...riyō suru ...利用する (take
advantage of).

cashew, *n.* kashū-nattsu カシュー
ナッツ (nut).

cashier, *n.* reji-gakari レジ係;
kaikei-gakari 会計係.

cashmere, *n.* kashimia カシミア.

casino, *n.* kajino カジノ.

cask, *n.* taru 樽.

casket, *n.* 1. hitsugi 柩 (coffin). 2.

hōsekibako 宝石箱 (jewel box).

casserole, *n.* kaserōru カセロール.

cassette, *n.* kasetto カセット.

cast, 1. *n.* kyasuto キャスト (performers); igata 鋳型 (mold); gibusu ギブス (orthopedic). 2. *vb.* nageru 投げる (throw); yaku ni tsukeru 役につける (hire to perform); igata ni ireru 鋳型に入れる (mold); tōhyō suru 投票する (cast a vote).

caste, *n.* kāsuto カースト; kaikyū 階級.

castigate, *n.* bassuru 罰する (punish); kokuhyō suru 酷評する (criticize severely).

castle, *n.* shiro 城.

castor oil, *n.* himashiyu ひまし油.

castrate, *vb.* kyosei suru 去勢する.

casual, *adj.* 1. kajuaru (na) カジュアル (な) (informal). 2. kiraku (na) 気楽 (な) (not caring, not serious). 3. gūzen (no) 偶然 (の) (accidental).

casualty, *n.* 1. jiko 事故 (accident). 2. giseisha 犠牲者 (victim). 3. fushōsha 負傷者 (wounded person).

cat, *n.* neko 猫.

catalog, *n.* katarogu カタログ.

catalyst, *n.* shokubai 触媒.

cataract, *n.* 1. bakufu 瀑布 (water). 2. hakunaishō 白内障 (eye).

catastrophe, *n.* hakyoku 破局; sainan 災難.

catch, *vb.* 1. toraeru 捕らえる (get hold of, capture). 2. toru 捕る (fish). 3. ... ni kakaru ... にかかる (contract, as an illness). 4. ... ni ma ni au ... に間に合う (get aboard on time). 5. hiku 引く (attract). 6. wakaru 分かる (grasp mentally). 7. kikoeru 聞こえる (hear correctly). 8. **catch cold**

kaze o hiku 風邪を引く; **catch sight of** ... o mikakeru ... を見かける; **catch up with** ... ni oitsuku ...に追いつく.

category, *n.* kategorī カテゴリー.

cater, *vb.* 1. shidashi o suru 仕出しをする (food). 2. **cater to** ... ni awaseru ... に合わせる.

caterpillar, *n.* imomushi 芋虫 (not furry); kemushi 毛虫 (furry).

catfish, *n.* namazu なまず.

catharsis, *n.* katarushisu カタルシス.

cathedral, *n.* katedoraru カテドラル; daiseidō 大聖堂.

Catholic, 1. *n.* katorikku-shinja カトリック信者 (person). 2. *adj.* katorikku (no) カトリック (の) (of Catholicism).

Catholicism, *n.* katorikku カトリック.

cattle, *n.* kachiku 家畜.

cauliflower, *n.* karifurawā カリフラワー.

cause, 1. *n.* gen'in 原因 (basis); riyū 理由 (reason); shin'nen 信念 (strong belief). 2. *vb.* hikiokosu 引き起こす.

caustic, *adj.* 1. fushokusei (no) 腐食性 (の) (corrosive). 2. hiniku tappuri (no) 皮肉たっぷり (の) (sarcastic).

caution, 1. *n.* keikoku 警告 (warning); yōjin 用心 (carefulness). 2. *vb.* keikoku suru 警告する (warn).

cautious, *adj.* yōjinbukai 用心深い.

cave, cavern, *n.* dōkutsu 洞窟.

caviar, *n.* kyabia キャビア.

cavity, *n.* 1. ana 穴 (hole). 2. mushiba (no ana) 虫歯 (の穴) (dental).

cease, *vb.* yameru やめる.

ceasefire, *n.* teisen 停戦.

cedar, *n.* sugi 杉.

cede, *vb.* yuzuriwatasu 譲り渡す.

ceiling, *n.* tenjō 天井.

celebrate, *vb.* iwau 祝う.

celebration, *n.* iwai 祝い (party); shikiten 式典 (commemoration).

celebrity, *n.* yūmeijin 有名人.

celery, *n.* serori セロリ.

celestial, *adj.* 1. tentai (no) 天体 (の) (of the sky or space). 2. tengoku-teki (na) 天国的 (な) (of heaven).

celibacy, *n.* 1. dokushin 独身 (unmarried state). 2. kin'yoku 禁欲 (sexual abstinence).

cell, *n.* 1. rōya 牢屋 (prison). 2. saibō 細胞 (biology).

cellar, *n.* chika sōko 地下倉庫.

cello, *n.* chero チェロ.

cellophane, *n.* serohan セロハン.

cement, 1. *n.* semento セメント (clay-lime mixture); setchakuzai 接着剤 (adhesive). 2. *vb.* tsuyomeru 強める (strengthen).

cemetery, *n.* bochi 墓地.

censor, 1. *n.* ken'etsukan 検閲官 (official). 2. *vb.* ken'etsu suru 検閲する.

censorship, *n.* ken'etsu 検閲.

censure, *vb.* hinan suru 非難する.

census, *n.* kokuseichōsa 国政調査.

cent, *n.* sento セント.

centennial, *n.* hyakushūnen 百周年.

center, 1. *n.* chūshin 中心 (middle point, chief person); sentā センター (group of buildings). 2. *vb.* chūshin ni sueru 中心にすえる (place in middle).

centigrade, *n.* sesshi 摂氏.

centimeter, *n.* senchi (mētoru) センチ (メートル).

central, *adj.* 1. chūshin (no) 中心 (の) (of or at center). 2. saijūyō (na) 最重要 (な) (most important).

centralize, *vb.* shūchū suru 集中する.

century, *n.* seiki 世紀; **nineteenth century** jūkyū seiki.

ceramic, *adj.* tōsei (no) 陶製 (の).

ceramics, *n.* tōki 陶器.

cereal, *n.* 1. kokumotsu 穀物 (grain). 2. shiriaru シリアル (breakfast cereal).

ceremony, *n.* shiki 式 (act); gishiki 儀式 (ritual).

certain, *adj.* 1. tashika (na) 確か (な) (sure); **make certain** tashikameru. 2. ikubun ka (no) 幾分か (の) (some).

certainly, *adv.* 1. tashika ni 確かに (without doubt). 2. mochiron もちろん (of course).

certificate, *n.* shōmeisho 証明書.

certify, *vb.* 1. shōmei suru 証明する (vouch for in writing). 2. hoshō suru 保証する (guarantee). 3. shikaku o ataeru 資格を与える (permit to practice a profession).

chafe, *vb.* surimuku 擦りむく.

chagrin, *n.* kuyashisa 悔しさ.

chain, *n.* 1. kusari 鎖 (connected rings); renzoku 連続 (series). 2. *vb.* kusari de tsunagu 鎖でつなぐ (fasten).

chain reaction, *n.* rensahannō 連鎖反応.

chain store, *n.* chēnsutoā チェーンストアー.

chair, 1. *n.* isu 椅子 (furniture); gakubuchō 学部長 (university department head); i'inchō 委員長 (committee leader). 2. *vb.* i'inchō o tsutomeru 委員長を勤める (preside over committee).

chalet, *n.* yamagoya 山小屋.

chalk, *n.* chōku チョーク.

challenge, 1. *n.* charenji チャレン

ジ; chōsen 挑戦. 2. *vb.* ... ni
chōsen suru ... に挑戦する.

challenger, *n.* chōsensha 挑戦者.

chamber, *n.* 1. heya 部屋 (room).
2. kaigisho 会議所 (assembly
room). 3. giin 議員 (legislative
body).

chamber of commerce, *n.*
shōgyō-kaigisho 商業会議所.

chameleon, *n.* kamereon カメレオ
ン.

champagne, *n.* shanpen シャンペ
ン.

champion, *n.* chanpion チャンピ
オン; yūshōsha 優勝者.

championship, *n.* chanpionshippu
チャンピオンシップ.

chance, 1. *n.* kikai 機会
(opportunity); un 運; gūzen 偶然
(fate, luck); kanōsei 可能性
(possibility); kake 賭 (risk); **by
chance** gūzen ni. 2. *adj.* gūzen
(no) 偶然 (の) (accidental). 3. *vb.*
kakeru 賭ける (risk).

chancellor, *n.* 1. daijin 大臣
(government official). 2. gakuchō
学長 (university official).

chandelier, *n.* shanderia シャンデ
リア.

change, 1. *n.* henka 変化 (in
condition); henkō 変更
(alteration); kōkan 交換
(exchange); (o)tsuri (お)釣り
(from bill payment); kozeni 小銭
(small change); kigae 着替え (of
clothes); **for a change** kibun
tenkan ni 気分転換に (change of
mood). 2. *vb.* kawaru/kaeru 変わ
る／変える (alter/cause to alter in
condition); kōkan suru 交換する
(exchange); ryōgae suru 両替する
(currency); kigaeru 着替える
(clothes).

changeable, *adj.* kawariyasui 変わ

り易い.

channel, 1. *n.* kaikyō 海峡
(geography); suiro 水路 (for liquid);
michi 道 (route); chan'neru チャ
ンネル (TV). 2. *vb.* furimukeru ふ
り向ける (direct); tsukisusumu 突
き進む (clear a way).

chant, *vb.* tonaeru 唱える.

chaos, *n.* konton 混沌; muchitsujo
無秩序.

chaotic, *adj.* mechakucha (na) め
ちゃくちゃ (な); muchitsujo (no)
無秩序 (の).

chap, 1. *n.* yatsu 奴 (fellow). 2. *vb.*
akagire suru あかぎれする
(roughen and redden).

chapter, *n.* 1. shō 章 (book). 2.
shibu 支部 (branch of a society).

char, *vb.* kogeru/kogasu 焦げる／
焦がす (burn/cause to burn).

character, *n.* 1. seikaku 性格
(personal nature). 2. tōjōjinbutsu
登場人物 (in play, novel, etc.). 3.
hinsei 品性 (moral strength). 4.
hito 人 (person). 5. moji 文字
(written or printed symbol).

characteristic, 1. *adj.* tokuchō-teki
(na) 特徴的 (な). 2. *n.* tokuchō 特
徴.

characterize, *vb.* 1. ... no tokuchō
de aru ... の特徴である
(distinguish). 2. ... no tokuchō o
egaku ... の特徴を描く (describe).

charcoal, *n.* sumi 炭.

charge, 1. *n.* ryōkin 料金 (price);
sekinin 責任 (responsibility);
hihan 批判 (accusation); kōgeki 攻
撃 (attack); kokuso 告訴 (legal);
be in charge of ... no sekinin ga
aru. 2. *vb.* kōgeki suru 攻撃する
(attack); kokuso suru 告訴する
(legal); jūden suru 充電する
(charge a battery).

charge account, *n.* kurejitto-kōza

クレジット口座.

charisma, *n.* karisuma カリスマ.

charity, *n.* 1. charitī チャリティー; jizen 慈善 (aid); kifu 寄付 (donation). 2. jihishin 慈悲心 (benevolence); yasashisa 優しさ (kindness). 3. jizendantai 慈善団体 (benevolent organization).

charm, 1. *n.* miryoku 魅力 (fascination); mayoke 魔よけ (amulet, talisman); jumon 呪文 (incantation). 2. *vb.* miwaku suru 魅惑する (fascinate).

charming, *adj.* miryoku-teki (na) 魅力的 (な) (fascinating).

chart, 1. *n.* chāto チャート; zu 図; hyō 表 (diagram, map, table); gurafu グラフ (graph). 2. *vb.* zushi suru 図示する.

charter, 1. *n.* tokkyojō 特許状 (commission); chātā チャーター (contract); **charter flight** chātā-bin. 2. *vb.* kyoka suru 許可する (grant permission); chātā suru チャーターする (hire).

chase, 1. *n.* tsuiseki 追跡. 2. *vb.* tsuiseki suru 追跡する (go after); **chase away** oiharau 追い払う (drive away).

chasm, *n.* wareme 割れ目.

chaste, *adj.* junketsu (na) 純潔 (な).

chastise, *vb.* korashimeru 懲らしめる.

chastity, *n.* junketsu 純潔.

chat, 1. *n.* zatsudan 雑談. 2. *vb.* zatsudan o suru 雑談をする.

chatter, 1. *n.* oshaberi おしゃべり. 2. *vb.* shaberimakuru しゃべりまくる (talk); gaku-gaku naru がくがく鳴る (teeth).

chatterbox, *n.* oshaberiya おしゃべり屋.

chauffeur, *n.* okakae-untenshu お

抱え運転手.

chauvinism, *n.* chō-aikoku-shugi 超愛国主義 (extreme patriotism); **male chauvinism** danseiyūi-shugi 男性優位主義 (ideology of male supremacy); joseibesshi 女性蔑視 (woman-hating).

cheap, *adj.* 1. yasui 安い (inexpensive). 2. yasuppoi 安っぽい (of low quality).

cheapen, *vb.* yasuppoku suru 安っぽくする.

cheat, *vb.* 1. damasu だます (deceive). 2. kan'ningu o suru カンニングをする (cheat on examination).

check, 1. *n.* tenken 点検 (test or inspection); yokusei 抑制 (control); kogitte 小切手 (bank); shōgō no shirushi 商号の印 (mark); kōshimoyō 格子模様 (pattern). 2. *vb.* shiraberu 調べる; chekku suru チェックする (examine, verify); yokusei suru 抑制する (control); shirushi o tsukeru 印をつける (mark); **check in/out** chekku-in/-auto suru チェックイン／～アウトする (hotel).

checking account, *n.* tōzayokin 当座預金.

checkup, *n.* kenkōshindan 健康診断 (medical).

cheek, *n.* hoho 頬.

cheer, 1. *n.* seien 声援 (shout of encouragement); yorokobi 喜び (gladness). 2. *vb.* kansei o okuru 歓声を送る (shout encouragement); yorokobaseru 喜ばせる (gladden).

cheerful, *adj.* tanoshii 楽しい.

Cheers! *interj.* Kanpai! 乾杯. (when drinking).

cheese, *n.* chīzu チーズ.

chef, *n.* shefu シェフ.

chemical, 1. *n.* kagakubusshitsu 化学物質. 2. *adj.* kagaku (no) 化学 (の) (of chemistry).

chemistry, *n.* kagaku 化学.

chemotherapy, *n.* kagakuryōhō 化学療法.

cherish, *vb.* daiji ni suru 大事にする.

cherry, *n.* 1. sakuranbo 桜ん坊 (fruit). 2. sakura 桜 (tree).

chess, *n.* chesu チェス.

chest, *n.* 1. mune 胸 (body). 2. hako 箱 (box); **chest of drawers** tansu たんす.

chestnut, *n.* kurumi くるみ.

chew, *vb.* kamu 噛む (food).

chewing gum, *n.* chūingamu チューインガム.

chic, *adj.* shikku (na) シック (な).

chicken, *n.* 1. keiniku 鶏肉 (meat). 2. niwatori 鶏 (bird).

chide, *vb.* shikaru 叱る.

chief, 1. *n.* -chō 長 (head); shūchō 酋長 (head of tribe). 2. *adj.* shuyō (na) 主要 (な) (most important); daiichi (no) 第一 (の) (ranked highest).

chiefly, *adv.* omo ni 主に.

chieftain, *n.* shūchō 酋長.

child, *n.* ko(domo) 子(供).

childbirth, *n.* shussan 出産.

childhood, *n.* kodomojidai 子供時代.

childish, *adj.* yōchi (na) 幼稚 (な).

chili pepper, *n.* chiri チリ; tōgarashi 唐辛子.

chill, 1. *n.* hie 冷え (coldness); samuke 寒気 (feeling of coldness). 2. *vb.* hiyasu 冷やす.

chilly, *adj.* 1. samui 寒い (cold). 2. hiyayaka (na) 冷ややか (な) (unfriendly).

chime, 1. *n.* chaimu チャイム (musical bells); chaimu no oto チャイムの音 (sound made by chime). 2. *vb.* chaimu ga naru チャイムが鳴る (sound); **chime in** warikomu 割り込む (interrupt).

chimney, *n.* entotsu 煙突.

chimpanzee, *n.* chinpanjī チンパンジー.

chin, *n.* ago あご.

china, *n.* tōjiki 陶磁器 (ceramic ware).

China, *n.* chūgoku 中国.

Chinese, *n.* 1. chūgokujin 中国人 (person); chūgokugo 中国語 (language). 2. *adj.* chūgoku (no) 中国 (の) (of China); chūgokujin (no) 中国人 (の) (of the Chinese).

chip, 1. *n.* kakera 欠けら (small piece); kakeato 欠け跡 (broken piece); chippu チップ (computer). 2. *vb.* kakeru 欠ける (dent, break off); kizutsukeru 傷つける (make dent, cause to break off).

chirp, 1. *n.* saezuri さえずり. 2. *vb.* saezuru さえずる.

chisel, 1. *n.* nomi のみ (tool). 2. *vb.* nomi de horu のみで彫る (cut, carve); damashitoru だまし取る (deceive).

chive, *n.* asatsuki あさつき.

chlorine, *n.* enso 塩素.

chloroform, *n.* kurorohorumu クロロホルム.

chock-full, *adj.* manpai (no) 満杯 (の).

chocolate, *n.* chokorēto チョコレート.

choice, 1. *n.* sentaku 選択 (preference); eranda hito 選んだ人 (chosen person); eranda mono 選んだ物 (chosen thing); **make one's choice** erabu; **have no choice** shikata ga nai 仕方がない. 2. *adj.* yorinuki (no) 選り抜き (の)

(picked).

choir, *n.* gasshōtai 合唱隊 (group).

choke, *vb.* 1. musebu 咽ぶ (struggle to breathe). 2. chissoku suru 窒息する (be unable to breathe). 3. iki o tomeru 息を止める (stop breathing); shimekorosu 絞め殺す (kill). 4. fusagu 塞ぐ (block).

choking, *adj.* ikigurushii 息苦しい (suffocating).

cholera, *n.* korera コレラ.

cholesterol, *n.* koresuterōru コレ ステロール.

choose, *vb.* 1. erabu 選ぶ (pick). 2. kimeru 決める (decide).

chop, 1. *n.* choppu チョップ (meat). 2. *vb.* waru 割る (cut with blows); kizamu 刻む (cut in pieces).

choppy, *adj.* shiketeiru しけている (sea).

chopsticks, *n.* hashi 箸.

chorale, *n.* gasshōkyoku 合唱曲.

chord, *n.* kōdo コード; waon 和音.

chore, *n.* zatsuyō 雑用.

choreography, *n.* furitsuke 振り付け.

chorus, *n.* kōrasu コーラス; gasshō 合唱.

Christ, *n.* iesu(-kirisuto) イエス (-キリスト); kirisuto キリスト.

Christian, 1. *n.* kurisuchan クリスチャン. 2. *adj.* kirisuto-kyō (no) キリスト教 (の).

Christianity, *n.* kirisuto-kyō キリスト教.

Christmas, *n.* kurisumasu クリスマス; **Christmas eve** kurisumasu-ibu; **Merry Christmas!** Merī kurisumasu.

chromosome, *n.* senshokutai 染色体.

chronic, *adj.* mansei-teki (na) 慢性 的 (な) (illness, problem).

chronicle, *n.* nendaiki 年代記.

chronological, *adj.* nendaijun (no) 年代順 (の).

chrysalis, *n.* sanagi さなぎ.

chubby, *adj.* kobutori (no) 小太り (の).

chuck, *vb.* nageru 投げる (throw); nagesuteru 投げ捨てる (throw away); oidasu 追い出す (eject).

chuckle, 1. *n.* kusu-kusu warai く すくす笑い. 2. *vb.* kusu-kusu warau くすくす笑う.

chum, *n.* shin'yū 親友.

chunk, *n.* 1. taihan 大半 (big portion). 2. ōkii katamari 大きい 塊 (big lump).

church, *n.* kyōkai 教会.

churn, *vb.* kakitateru かき立てる; **churn out** tairyōseisan suru 大量 生産する.

cicada, *n.* semi 蟬.

cider, *n.* ringoshu りんご酒.

cigar, *n.* hamaki 葉巻.

cigarette, *n.* tabako 煙草; **cigarette case** tabakoire; **cigarette lighter** raitā ライター.

cinder, *n.* moegara 燃え殻.

cinema, *n.* eiga 映画.

cinnamon, *n.* shinamon シナモン

cipher, *n.* 1. zero ゼロ (number). 2. angō 暗号 (code).

circle, 1. *n.* sākuru サークル (group); wa 輪; en 円; maru 丸 (shape). 2. *vb.* wa de kakomu 輪 で囲む (enclose); mawaru 回る (go around).

circuit, *n.* 1. kairo 回路 (electrical path). 2. isshū 一周 (journey around).

circuitous, *adj.* magari-kunetteiru 曲がりくねっている.

circular, *adj.* marui 丸い.

circulate, *vb.* 1. nagareru 流れる

(flow). 2. ugokimawaru 動き回る (move around). 3. hiromaru 広まる (spread).

circulation, *n.* 1. junkan 循環 (blood, water, etc.). 2. hakkō-busū 発行部数 (book, magazine circulation).

circumcision, *n.* katsurei 割礼.

circumference, *n.* 1. enshū 円周 (outer boundary of a circular area). 2. enshū no nagasa 円周の長さ (length of outer boundary).

circumscribe, *vb.* 1. maru de kakomu 丸で囲む (encircle). 2. gentei suru 限定する (confine).

circumstance, *n.* 1. jōkyō 状況 (condition). 2. koto 事 (fact). 3. **depend on the circumstances** jōkyō ni yoru; **under the circumstances** sonna jōkyō dewa; **under no circumstances** nani ga attemo 何があっても.

circumvent, *vb.* kaihi suru 回避する (evade).

circus, *n.* sākasu サーカス.

cistern, *n.* suisō 水槽.

citation, *n.* in'yō 引用 (quotation).

cite, *vb.* in'yō suru 引用する (quote).

citizen, *n.* 1. shimin 市民 (of a city or nation); kokumin 国民 (a nation). 2. jūnin 住人 (inhabitant, resident).

citizenship, *n.* shiminken 市民権.

citrus, *adj.* kankitsurui (no) かんきつ類 (の).

city, *n.* 1. shi 市 (large town). 2. tokai 都会 (metropolis).

city council, *n.* shigikai 市議会.

city hall, *n.* shiyakusho 市役所.

civic, *adj.* 1. shi (no) 市 (の) (of a city). 2. shimin (no) 市民 (の) (of a citizen).

civil, *adj.* 1. shimin (no) 市民 (の) (of all citizens); minkan (no) 民間 (の) (of the general population). 2. teichō (na) 丁重 (な) (polite). 3. minji (no) 民事 (の) (legal). 4. **civil law** minpō 民法; **civil rights** kōminken 公民権; **civil servant** kōmuin 公務員; **civil war** naisen 内戦.

civilian, *n.* minkanjin 民間人.

civility, *n.* reigi tadashisa 礼儀正しさ.

civilization, *n.* bunmei 文明.

civilize, *vb.* 1. bunmeika suru 文明化する (convert from barbaric state). 2. senren suru 洗練する (make sophisticated).

claim, 1. *n.* yōkyū 要求 (demand); shuchō 主張 (assertion); shinkoku 申告 (insurance claim); kenri 権利 (right, title). 2. *vb.* yōkyū suru 要求する (demand); shuchō suru 主張する (assert); shinkoku suru 申告する (make insurance claim).

clairvoyant, *n.* yochi-nōryokusha 予知能力者.

clam, *n.* kai 貝; hamaguri 蛤.

clamber, *vb.* yojinoboru よじ登る.

clamor, 1. *n.* kensō 喧騒 (loud noise); fuhei 不平 (complaint). 2. *vb.* sawagitateru 騒ぎ立てる (make noise).

clamorous, *adj.* sawagashii 騒がしい (noisy).

clamp, 1. *n.* koteikigu 固定器具. 2. *vb.* kotei suru 固定する; **clamp down on** ... o torishimaru ... を取り締まる.

clan, *n.* ichizoku 一族.

clandestine, *adj.* himitsu (no) 秘密 (の).

clang, *vb.* naru 鳴る (make a sound); narasu 鳴らす (cause to sound).

clannish, *adj.* haita-teki (na) 排他

的 (な).

clap, *vb.* hakushu suru 拍手する (applaud).

clarification, *n.* setsumei 説明.

clarify, *vb.* akiraka ni naru/suru 明らかになる／する (become/make clear).

clarinet, *n.* kurarinetto クラリネット.

clarity, *n.* 1. meiryōsa 明瞭さ (clearness). 2. tōmeisa 透明さ (transparency).

clash, 1. *n.* fuitchi 不一致 (disagreement); arasoi 争い (fight). 2. *vb.* awanai 合わない (disagree); arasou 争う (fight).

clasp, 1. *n.* tomegane 留め金 (fastener); hōyō 抱擁 (hug); nigiru koto 握ること (act of gripping). 2. *vb.* tomeru 留める (fasten); daku 抱く (hug); nigiru 握る (grip).

class, *n.* 1. kaikyū 階級 (rank, caste); **class struggle** kaikyūtōsō 階級闘争. 2. burui 部類 (group). 3. kurasu クラス (students, course). 4. tō(kyū) 等(級) (level of quality).

classic, 1. *n.* koten 古典 (established classic); meisaku 名作 (masterpiece). 2. *adj.* ichiryū (no) 一流 (の) (superior); tenkei-teki (na) 典型的 (な) (model).

classical, *adj.* 1. kurashikku (na, no) クラシック (な、の); koten (no) 古典 (の) (of an established classic); **classical music** kurasshikku ongaku クラシック音楽. 2. koten-teki (na) 古典的 (な) (classic in nature).

classification, *n.* bunrui 分類.

classify, *vb.* bunrui suru 分類する.

classmate, *n.* dōkyūsei 同級生.

classroom, *n.* kyōshitsu 教室.

clatter, *vb.* kata-kata naru カタカ

タ鳴る.

clause, *n.* setsu 節 (grammar); kajō 箇条 (of law, treaty).

claw, *n.* tsume 爪.

clay, *n.* nendo 粘土.

clean, 1. *adj.* kirei (na) きれい (な) (free from dirt); seiketsu (na) 清潔 (な) (sanitary); kiyoraka (na) 清らか (な) (free from vice); meikaku (na) 明確 (な) (trim). 2. *vb.* kirei ni naru/suru きれいになる／する (become/make clean); sōji suru 掃除する (tidy up).

cleaner, *n.* 1. sōjinin 掃除人 (occupation). 2. dorai-kurīningu-ya ドライクリーニング屋 (owner of a dry-cleaning store). 3. senzai 洗剤 (detergent).

cleaning, *n.* sōji 掃除 (a room).

cleanse, *vb.* 1. kiyomeru 清める (make clean or pure). 2. shōdoku suru 消毒する (sterilize).

cleanser, *n.* kurenzā クレンザー.

clear, 1. *adj.* sundeiru 澄んでいる (sky, water, eyes); hare (no) 晴れ (の) (weather); tōmei (na) 透明 (な) (transparent); meihaku (na) 明白 (な) (evident); meikai (na) 明快 (な) (easily perceived); hakkiri shiteiru はっきりしている (clear-cut). 2. *vb.* hareru 晴れる (weather); katazukeru 片付ける (clear away); kansai suru 完済する (pay in full); koeru 超える (pass beyond).

clear-cut, *adj.* hakkiri shiteiru はっきりしている (well-defined, trim); meikai (na) 明解 (な) (obvious).

clearing, *n.* akichi 空き地 (land).

clemency, *n.* jihi 慈悲 (mercy); onjō 温情 (leniency).

clergyman, *n.* bokushi 牧師.

clerical, *adj.* 1. jimu (no) 事務 (の) (of a clerk). 2. seishoku (no) 聖職

(の) (of a religion).

clerk, *n.* 1. jimuin 事務員 (office employee). 2. ten'in 店員 (store employee).

clever, *adj.* rikō (na) 利口 (な).

cliché, *n.* kimarimonku 決まり文句.

click, *n.* kachiri to iu oto かちりという音.

client, *n.* 1. irainin 依頼人 (legal). 2. kyaku 客 (customer).

clientele, *n.* kokyaku 顧客.

cliff, *n.* gake 崖.

climate, *n.* 1. kikō 気候 (weather). 2. jōkyō 状況 (condition).

climax, *n.* kuraimakkusu クライマックス.

climb, *vb.* noboru 登る; agaru 上がる.

clinch, *vb.* ... no ketchaku o tsukeru ... の決着をつける (settle decisively).

cling, *vb.* shigamitsuku しがみつく (hold on firmly).

clinic, *n.* kurinikku クリニック; shinryōsho 診療所.

clink, *vb.* chirin to naru チリンと鳴る.

clip, 1. *n.* kurippu クリップ (metal clasp); **paper clip** kamibasami 紙鋏. 2. *vb.* kurippu de tomeru クリップで留める (fasten with a clip); kiru 切る (cut paper, cloth, etc.); karu 刈る (cut hair, wool, etc.).

clique, *n.* nakama 仲間; ichimi 一味.

cloak, 1. *n.* manto マント. 2. *vb.* kakusu 隠す (conceal).

clock, *n.* tokei 時計; **alarm clock** mezamashi-dokei 目覚まし時計; **around the clock** nijūyojikan 二十四時間.

clockwise, *adv.* migimawari ni 右回りに; **counterclockwise**

hidarimawari ni 左回りに.

clog, 1. *n.* kigutsu 木靴 (wooden shoe); geta 下駄 (Japanese wooden shoe). 2. *vb.* tsumaru 詰まる (become blocked).

cloisonné, *n.* shippō-yaki 七宝焼.

close, 1. *n.* owari 終わり (end). 2. *vb.* shimeru 閉める (shut); shimaru 閉まる (be shut); oeru 終える (bring to an end); **close down** heisa suru 閉鎖する; **close in** torikakomu 取り囲む. 3. *adj.* chikai 近い (near); shitashii 親しい (intimate); **be close to** ... ni chikai. 4. *adv.* chikaku ni 近くに (near); **close to** hotondo ほとんど (almost).

closed, *adj.* shimatteiru 閉まっている.

closet, *n.* oshiire 押入れ (small room); tansu たんす (cabinet).

clot, *n.* katamari 塊 (mass).

cloth, *n.* nuno 布.

clothe, *vb.* fuku o kiseru 服を着せる.

clothes, clothing, *n.* fuku 服.

cloud, *n.* kumo 雲.

cloudburst, *n.* gōu 豪雨.

cloudiness, *n.* kumori 曇り.

cloudy, *adj.* 1. kumori (no) 曇り (の) (full of clouds). 2. nigotteiru 濁っている (not clear).

clove, *n.* chōji チョウジ (spice).

clover, *n.* kurōbā クローバー.

clown, *n.* dōkeshi 道化師.

club, *n.* 1. kurabu クラブ (organization). 2. konbō 棍棒 (stick).

clue, *n.* itoguchi 糸口.

clump, *n.* katamari 塊.

clumsy, *adj.* 1. bukiyō (na) 不器用 (な) (unskillful). 2. bukakkō (na) 不格好 (な) (ungraceful).

cluster, 1. *n.* atsumari 集まり

(group, bunch). 2. *vb.* atsumaru 集まる (gather).

clutch, 1. *n.* kuratchi クラッチ (car); tsukamari つかまり (tight hold). 2. *vb.* tsukamu つかむ (hold tight).

clutter, *vb.* chirakasu 散らかす.

coach, 1. *n.* basha 馬車 (horse-drawn carriage); basu バス (bus); ekonomī-kurasu エコノミークラス (economy class); kōchi コーチ (sports). 2. *vb.* shidō suru 指導する (advise).

coagulate, *vb.* katamaru 固まる.

coal, *n.* sekitan 石炭.

coalesce, *vb.* gattai suru 合体する.

coalition, *n.* renmei 連盟.

coarse, *adj.* 1. arai 粗い (rough). 2. soya (na) 粗野 (な) (vulgar).

coast, *n.* kaigan 海岸.

coast guard, *n.* engan-keibitai 沿岸警備隊.

coat, 1. *n.* kōto コート (outer garment); kegawa 毛皮 (fur); maku 膜 (coating). 2. *vb.* ōu 覆う (cover).

coax, *vb.* settoku suru 説得する (persuade).

cobweb, *n.* kumo no su 蜘蛛の巣.

cocaine, *n.* kokain コカイン.

cock, *n.* ondori 雄鶏 (rooster).

cockpit, *n.* sōjūshitsu 操縦室 (of plane).

cockroach, *n.* gokiburi ごきぶり.

cocktail, *n.* kakuteru カクテル.

cocky, *adj.* unubore (no) うぬぼれ (の).

cocoa, *n.* kokoa ココア.

coconut, *n.* kokonattsu ココナッツ; **coconut palm** yashi no ki やしの木.

cocoon, *n.* mayu まゆ.

cod, *n.* tara たら.

coddle, *vb.* amayakasu 甘やかす.

code, *n.* 1. angō 暗号 (secret words); fugō 符号 (signals). 2. hōten 法典 (collection of laws).

cod-liver oil, *n.* kan'yu 肝油.

coerce, *vb.* kyōsei suru 強制する.

coexist, *vb.* kyōzon suru 共存する.

coffee, *n.* kōhī コーヒー.

coffee pot, *n.* kōhī-potto コーヒーポット.

coffin, *n.* hitsugi 棺.

coherence, *n.* ikkansei 一貫性.

coherent, *adj.* ikkansei ga aru 一貫性がある.

cohesion, *n.* danketsu 団結 (of group).

coil, 1. *n.* wa 輪 (ring); koiru コイル (electrical). 2. *vb.* maku 巻く.

coin, 1. *n.* koin コイン; kōka 硬貨 (money). 2. *vb.* chūzō suru 鋳造する (coin money); tsukuru 創る (invent).

coincide, *vb.* 1. dōji ni okoru 同時に起こる (occur at same time). 2. au 合う (agree).

coincidence, *n.* gūzen no itchi 偶然の一致.

coincidental, *adj.* gūzen (no) 偶然 (の).

coitus, *n.* seikō 性交.

colander, *n.* zaru ざる; mizukoshi 水こし.

cold, 1. *n.* samusa 寒さ (absence of heat); kaze 風邪 (illness); **catch cold** kaze o hiku 風邪を引く. 2. *adj.* samui 寒い (cold weather, low temperature); tsumetai 冷たい (cold to the touch, unfriendly).

coldblooded, *adj.* reikoku (na) 冷酷 (な) (callous).

coldness, *n.* 1. samusa 寒さ (weather, room). 2. tsumetasa 冷たさ (water, person).

colic, *n.* fukutsū 腹痛.

collaborate, *vb.* kyōryoku suru 協

力する (work together); gassaku suru 合作する (write or produce together).

collaboration, *n.* kyōryoku 協力; **in collaboration** kyōryoku shite 協力して.

collapse, *vb.* 1. kowareru 壊れる; hōkai suru 崩壊する (fall or cave in). 2. taoreru 倒れる (faint). 3. shippai suru 失敗する (fail). 4. oritatameru 折りたためる (fold together compactly).

collar, *n.* 1. eri 襟 (garment). 2. kubiwa 首輪 (dog).

collarbone, *n.* sakotsu 鎖骨.

collate, *vb.* junjoyoku naraberu 順序良く並べる (arrange).

collateral, *n.* tanpo 担保.

colleague, *n.* dōryō 同僚.

collect, *vb.* 1. atsumeru 集める (accumulate); atsumaru 集まる (come together). 2. shūkin suru 集金する (receive or compel payment). 3. shūhai suru 集配する (mail).

collect call, *n.* korekuto-kōru コレクトコール.

collected, *adj.* reisei (na) 冷静 (な) (calm).

collection, *n.* korekushon コレクション; shūshū 収集 (of paintings, etc.).

collective, *adj.* 1. kyōdō (no) 共同 (の) (joint). 2. dantai (no) 団体 (の); shūdan (no) 集団 (の) (by a group); **collective bargaining** dantaikōshō 団体交渉.

collector, *n.* shūshūka 収集家 (of paintings, etc.).

college, *n.* daigaku 大学; karejji カレッジ.

collide, *vb.* shōtotsu suru 衝突する.

collision, *n.* shōtotsu 衝突.

colloquial, *adj.* kōgo (no) 口語

(の).

collusion, *n.* kyōbō 共謀.

cologne, *n.* ōdekoron オーデコロン.

colon, 1. *n.* daichō 大腸 (anatomy). 2. koron コロン (punctuation).

colonel, *n.* taisa 大佐.

colonial, *adj.* shokuminchi (no) 植民地 (の).

colonize, *vb.* shokuminchika suru 植民地化する.

colony, *n.* shokuminchi 植民地.

color, 1. *n.* iro 色 (hue); enogu 絵の具 (for painting); kaoiro 顔色 (complexion). 2. *vb.* iro o tsukeru 色をつける (give color to); irozuku 色づく (take on color); akaku naru 赤くなる (blush); yugameru 歪める (distort in telling).

colorblind, *adj.* shikimō 色盲.

colorful, *adj.* 1. shikisai yutaka (na) 色彩豊か (な) (full of color). 2. azayaka (na) 鮮やか (な) (bright, vivid). 3. hanayaka (na) 華やか (な) (vibrant, exciting).

colorless, *adj.* 1. mushoku (no) 無色 (の) (without color). 2. taikutsu (na) 退屈 (な) (dull).

colossal, *adj.* kyodai (na) 巨大 (な).

colt, *n.* osu no kouma 雄の子馬.

column, *n.* 1. hashira 柱 (pillar). 2. ran 欄 (area of print). 3. koramu コラム (regular journalistic piece).

columnist, *n.* koramunisuto コラムニスト.

coma, *n.* konsui 昏睡.

comb, 1. *n.* kushi 櫛. 2. *vb.* kushi de toku 櫛でとく.

combat, 1. *n.* sentō 戦闘 (warfare); tatakai 戦い (battle). 2. *vb.* tatakau 戦う (fight, battle).

combatant, *n.* sentōin 戦闘員.

combination, *n.* 1. gōdō 合同 (alliance). 2. kumiawase 組み合わせ (matching, pairing). 3. kumiawase-bangō 組み合わせ番号 (number for a lock).

combine, *vb.* 1. musubi-tsuku/tsukeru 結びつく／〜つける (become/make united). 2. mazeru 混ぜる (mix). 3. kumiawaseru 組み合わせる (match, pair).

combustible, *adj.* kanensei (no) 可燃性 (の).

combustion, *n.* nenshō 燃焼.

come, *vb.* 1. kuru 来る (approach). 2. tsuku 着く (arrive). 3. naru なる (become). 4. **come about** okoru 起こる (happen); **come across** dekuwasu 出くわす (meet, find); **come back** kaeru 帰る (return); fukki suru 復帰する (revert; return to a former position, prosperity, etc.); **come down** oriru 降りる (descend); **come from** ...kara kuru; **come in** ... ni hairu ... に入る (enter); **Come in!** Dōzo ohairi kudasai; **come out** deru 出る (appear, be published); **come to** ... ni tassuru ... に達する (total); **come up** wadai ni noboru 話題にのぼる (be referred to).

comeback, *n.* fukki 復帰.

comedy, *n.* komedī コメディー; kigeki 喜劇.

comely, *adj.* kirei (na) きれい (な).

comet, *n.* suisei 彗星.

comfort, 1. *n.* nagusami 慰み (consolation); kaiteki 快適; anraku 安楽 (ease). 2. *vb.* nagusameru 慰める (console, cheer).

comfortable, *adj.* 1. kaiteki (na) 快適 (な) (cozy, complacent). 2. raku (na) 楽 (な) (easy,

untroubled). 3. jūbun (na) 十分 (な) (affluent).

comforter, *n.* uwabuton 上布団 (quilt).

comic, 1. *n.* manga 漫画 (book); kigekihaiyū 喜劇俳優 (comedian). 2. *adj.* kokkei (na) 滑稽 (な) (funny).

comical, *adj.* kokkei (na) 滑稽 (な) (funny).

comic strip, *n.* sūkomamanga 数コマ漫画.

comma, *n.* konma コンマ.

command, 1. *n.* meirei 命令 (order); tōsotsu 統率 (leadership, authority); nōryoku 能力 (facility, ability). 2. *vb.* meirei suru 命令する (order); ... o tōsotsu suru ... を統率する (have authority over); kontorōru suru コントロールする (control).

commander, *n.* shireikan 司令官; **commander in chief** shirei chōkan 司令長官.

commemorate, *vb.* kinen suru 記念する.

commemoration, *n.* kinen 記念; **in commemoration of** ... o kinen shite.

commence, *vb.* hajimeru 始める.

commencement, *n.* 1. kaishi 開始 (beginning). 2. sotsugyōshiki 卒業式 (graduation ceremony).

commend, *vb.* homeru ほめる.

comment, 1. *n.* komento コメント. 2. *vb.* komento suru コメントする.

commentary, *n.* 1. chūshaku 注釈. 2. kaisetsu 解説 (broadcast commentary).

commerce, *n.* shōgyō 商業 (business); bōeki 貿易 (foreign trade).

commercial, 1. *n.* komāsharu コマ

ーシャル (advertisement). 2. *adj.* shōgyō (no) 商業 (の) (of commerce); bōeki (no) 貿易 (の) (of foreign trade).

commercialize, *vb.* shōgyōka suru 商業化する.

commission, 1. *n.* komisshon コミッション (fee for services); i'inkai 委員会 (group); itaku 委託 (act of giving authority); **be out of commission** kowareteiru 壊れている (out of order). 2. *vb.* ... ni itaku suru ... に委託する (consign).

commissioner, *n.* chōkan 長官 (government official).

commit, *vb.* 1. okasu 犯す (perform, do); **commit a crime** tsumi o okasu; **commit suicide** jisatsu suru 自殺する. 2. yudaneru 委ねる (entrust). 3. **commit oneself (to do)** (... suru to) chikau (...すると) 誓う (pledge oneself); **commit oneself (to something)** ... ni uchikomu ... に打ち込む (devote oneself).

commitment, *n.* 1. sekinin 責任 (responsibility). 2. chikai 誓い (pledge). 3. kenshin 献身 (devotion).

committee, *n.* iinkai 委員会.

commodity, *n.* shōhin 商品.

common, *adj.* 1. kyōtsū (no) 共通 (の) (shared by all). 2. arifureteiru ありふれている (ordinary); futsū (no) 普通 (の) (usual). 3. kōkyō (no) 公共 (の) (public). 4. gehin (na) 下品 (な) (vulgar).

commoner, *n.* shomin 庶民.

commonplace, *adj.* futsū (no) 普通 (の) (usual); arifureteiru ありふれている (ordinary).

common sense, *n.* jōshiki 常識.

commonwealth, *n.* renpō 連邦

(association of nations).

commotion, *n.* 1. dōyō 動揺 (tumult). 2. sōdō 騒動 (upheaval).

communal, *adj.* 1. kyōdō (no) 共同 (の) (used by members of a community). 2. kyōyū (no) 共有 (の) (marked by common ownership).

commune, 1. *n.* komyūn コミューン (close-knit community of people). 2. *vb.* danwa suru 談話する (converse).

communicable, *adj.* kansen shiyasui 感染しやすい (of disease).

communicate, *vb.* 1. komyunikēto suru コミュニケートする; tsutaeru 伝える (make known). 2. hanasu 話す (talk).

communication, *n.* 1. komyunikēshon コミュニケーション; dentatsu 伝達 (act of communicating); renraku 連絡 (getting in touch). 2. ishisōtsū 意志疎通 (interchange of thoughts). 3. messēji メッセージ (message).

communiqué, *n.* kōshikihappyō 公式発表.

communism, *n.* kyōsanshugi 共産主義.

communist, 1. *n.* kyōsanshugisha 共産主義者. 2. *adj.* kyōsanshugi (no) 共産主義 (の) (of communism).

community, *n.* 1. komyuniti コミュニティ; kyōdōtai 共同体 (social group). 2. kinjo 近所 (neighborhood); chiiki 地域 (area). 3. shakai 社会 (the public).

commute, *vb.* 1. kayou 通う (travel). 2. genkei suru 減刑する (commute a penalty).

commuter, *n.* tsūkinsha 通勤者.

compact, 1. *n.* konpakuto コンパクト (cosmetic case). 2. *adj.* tsumatte iru 詰まっている (packed together); konpakuto (na) コンパクト (な) (small in size).

companion, *n.* 1. tomo 友 (comrade). 2. nakama 仲間 (associate). 3. tsure 連れ (traveling companion). 4. katahō 片方 (one of a pair).

companionship, *n.* nakamazukiai 仲間付き合い (camaraderie); kōyū 交友 (friendly relationship).

company, *n.* 1. kaisha 会社 (corporation, enterprise). 2. nakamazukiai 仲間付き合い (camaraderie, companionship). 3. tsukiai aite 付き合い相手 (companions). 4. **keep/part company with** ... to tsukiau/wakareru ... と付き合う／別れる.

comparative, *adj.* hikaku (no) 比較 (の).

comparatively, *adv.* hikaku-teki ni 比較的に.

compare, *vb.* 1. hikaku suru 比較する (contrast). 2. tatoeru たとえる (liken).

comparison, *n.* hikaku 比較.

compartment, *n.* konpātomento コンパートメント (room).

compass, *n.* 1. konpasu コンパス (drafting tool). 2. rashinban 羅針盤 (tool for finding directions).

compassion, *n.* dōjō 同情.

compassionate, *adj.* omoiyari ga aru 思いやりがある.

compatriot, *n.* dōkokujin 同国人.

compel, *vb.* kyōsei suru 強制する.

compensate, *vb.* 1. tsugunau 償う (make up for). 2. ... ni hoshō suru

... に補償する (make payment to); baishō suru 賠償する (make amends).

compensation, *n.* 1. tsugunai 償い (act of making up for). 2. hoshō 補償 (payment); baishō 賠償 (reparation).

compete, *vb.* kisou 競う.

competence, *n.* nōryoku 能力.

competent, *adj.* yūnō (na) 有能 (な).

competition, *n.* 1. kyōsō 競争 (rivalry). 2. kyōgikai 競技会 (match, race, tournament); konkūru コンクール (music or art contest).

competitor, *n.* kyōsōsha 競争者.

compile, *vb.* henshū suru 編集する; matomeru まとめる (put together in one book or work).

complacency, *n.* jikomanzoku 自己満足.

complacent, *adj.* jikomanzoku shite iru 自己満足している.

complain, *vb.* 1. fuhei o iu 不平を言う (express discontent); kujō o iu 苦情を言う (remonstrate). 2. uttaeru 訴える (accuse, report).

complaint, *n.* 1. fuhei 不平 (discontent); kujō 苦情 (remonstrance). 2. fuhei no tane 不平の種 (cause of discontent). 3. uttae 訴え (accusation).

complement, 1. *n.* kakkō no toriawase 格好の取り合わせ (ideal counterpart); hojū 補充 (supplement); hogo 補語 (grammar). 2. *vb.* tsuriau 釣り合う (counterbalance); hojū suru 補充する (supplement).

complete, 1. *adj.* kanzen (na) 完全 (な) (perfect); mattaku (no) 全く (の) (entire). 2. *vb.* kanzen ni suru 完全にする (make perfect);

kansei suru 完成する (achieve, finish); owaraseru 終わらせる (bring to an end).

completion, *n.* 1. kansei 完成 (achievement). 2. owari 終わり (end).

complex, 1. *n.* konpurekkusu コンプレックス (fixation); shūgō 集合 (compound); **inferiority complex** rettōkan 劣等感. 2. *adj.* fukuzatsu (na) 複雑 (な) (complicated).

complexion, *n.* kaoiro 顔色.

complexity, *n.* fukuzatsusa 複雑さ.

compliance, *n.* fukujū 服従 (obedience).

complicate, *vb.* fukuzatsu ni suru 複雑にする (make complex). 2. muzukashiku suru 難しくする (make difficult).

complicated, *adj.* 1. fukuzatsu (na) 複雑 (な) (complex). 2. muzukashii 難しい (difficult).

complication, *n.* 1. mō hitotsu no mondai もう一つの問題 (another problem). 2. heihatsushō 併発症 (medical condition).

complicity, *n.* kyōbō 共謀 (partnership in wrongdoing).

compliment, 1. *n.* sanji 賛辞 (expression of praise); aisatsu 挨拶 (regards). 2. *vb.* homeru ほめる (express praise).

complimentary, *adj.* 1. sanji (no) 賛辞 (の) (of praise). 2. muryō (no) 無料 (の) (given free).

comply, *vb.* **comply with** ... ni shitagau ... に従う (obey); ... o mamoru ... を守る (observe).

component, *n.* bubun 部分.

compose, *vb.* 1. kumitateru 組み立てる (make by uniting parts). 2. kōsei suru 構成する (be a part of);

be composed of ... kara naru ... から成る. 3. kaku 書く (write a literary work); sakkyoku suru 作曲する (write music). 4. **compose oneself** ochitsuku 落ち着く.

composer, *n.* sakkyokuka 作曲家 (music).

composite, *adj.* 1. fukugō (no) 複合 (の) (combined). 2. gōsei (no) 合成 (の) (synthesized).

composition, *n.* 1. kumitate 組み立て (combination). 2. sakubun 作文 (short essay); sakkyoku 作曲 (act of writing music); kyoku 曲 (music).

composure, *n.* ochitsuki 落ち着き.

compound, 1. *n.* fukugōbutsu 複合物 (combined parts). 2. *adj.* fukugō (no) 複合 (の) (made of parts). 3. *vb.* kumiawaseru 組み合わせる (combine); fuyasu 増やす (increase).

compound interest, *n.* fukuri 複利.

comprehend, *vb.* rikai suru 理解する.

comprehension, *n.* 1. rikai 理解 (act of understanding). 2. rikairyoku 理解力 (ability to understand).

comprehensive, *adj.* hōkatsu-teki (na) 包括的 (な) (inclusive).

compress, *vb.* 1. asshuku suru 圧縮する (press together). 2. chijimeru 縮める (abridge, reduce).

comprise, *vb.* ... kara naru ... から成る (consist of).

compromise, *n.* dakyō 妥協 (agreement by mutual concession). 2. *vb.* dakyō suru 妥協する (agree).

compulsion, *n.* 1. kyōsei 強制

(compelling force). 2. osaerarenai shōdō 抑えられない衝動 (irresistible impulse).

compulsive, *adj.* osaerarenai 抑えられない.

compulsory, *adj.* 1. kyōsei-teki (na) 強制的 (な). 2. hisshū (no) 必修 (の) (of a school subject).

compute, *vb.* keisan suru 計算する.

computer, *n.* konpyūtā コンピューター.

computerize, *vb.* konpyūtāka suru コンピューター化する.

computer science, *n.* konpyūtā-kagaku コンピューター科学.

comrade, *n.* 1. nakama 仲間 (close companion). 2. dōshi 同志 (fellow member).

concave, *adj.* ōmen no 凹面の; kubonda 凹んだ.

conceal, *vb.* kakusu 隠す.

concede, *vb.* 1. mitomeru 認める (acknowledge). 2. yuzuru 譲る (yield).

conceit, *n.* 1. unubore うぬぼれ (excessive self-esteem). 2. kisō 奇想 (fanciful idea).

conceited, *adj.* unubore ga tsuyoi うぬぼれが強い.

conceivable, *adj.* kangaerareru 考えられる.

conceive, *vb.* 1. kangaetsuku 考えつく (form plan or idea); **conceive of** ... koto o kangaeru (think of). 2. ninshin suru 妊娠する (become pregnant).

concentrate, *vb.* 1. ... ni shūchū suru ... に集中する (give full attention). 2. nōshuku suru 濃縮する (make denser).

concentration, *n.* shūchū 集中 (fixed attention, gathering in one place).

concentration camp, *n.* kyōsei-shūyōsho 強制収容所.

concept, *n.* gainen 概念 (general idea).

conception, *n.* 1. chakusō 着想 (act of conceiving an idea). 2. kangae 考え (idea). 3. ninshin 妊娠 (inception of pregnancy).

concern, 1. *n.* kanshinji 関心事 (matter that concerns); shinpai 心配 (worry); jigyō 事業 (business). 2. *vb.* ... ni kansuru ... に関する (relate to); ... ni eikyō o ataeru ... に影響を与える (have an effect on); shinpai saseru 心配させる (worry); **concern oneself with** ... ni kankei suru ... に関係する.

concerned, *adj.* 1. kankei ga aru 関係がある (related, involved). 2. **be concerned about** ...ni kanshin ga aru ...に関心がある (be interested in); ... ga shinpai de aru ... が心配である (be worried about). 3. **as far as I am concerned** watashi ni kansuru kagiri.

concerning, *prep.* ... ni tsuite wa ... については.

concert, *n.* konsāto コンサート; ensōkai 演奏会.

concerto, *n.* koncheruto コンチェルト; kyōsōkyoku 協奏曲.

concession, *n.* 1. jōho 譲歩 (act of yielding). 2. tokken 特権 (right yielded).

conciliate, *vb.* 1. uchikatsu 打ち勝つ (overcome distrust or hostility). 2. kachieru 勝ち得る (win regard or favor).

concise, *adj.* konsaisu (na) コンサイス (な); kanketsu (na) 簡潔 (な).

conclude, *vb.* 1. oeru 終える (end). 2. torikimeru 取り決める (settle). 3. ketsuron o kudasu 結論を下す

(judge, infer). 4. kimeru 決める
(decide, determine).

conclusion, *n.* 1. ketsuron 結論
(final decision). 2. owari 終わり
(ending); **in conclusion** owari ni.
3. teiketsu 定結 (final agreement
or settlement).

concoct, *vb.* 1. tsukuriageru 作り上
げる (make, invent). 2.
detchiageru でっち上げる (fake,
fabricate).

concoction, *n.* 1. chōgōbutsu 調合
物 (blend). 2. detchiage でっち上
げ (fake, fabrication).

concord, *n.* 1. yūkō 友好
(friendship). 2. itchi 一致
(agreement). 3. heiwa 平和
(peace).

concrete, 1. *n.* konkurīto コンクリ
ート (building material). 2. *adj.*
konkurīto (no) コンクリート (の)
(made of concrete); gutai-teki
(na) 具体的 (な) (not abstract).

concubine, *n.* (o)mekake(san) (お)
妾(さん).

concur, *vb.* itchi suru 一致する
(agree); dōi suru 同意する (agree
in opinion).

concurrent, *adj.* 1. dōji ni okoru
同時に起こる (simultaneous). 2.
onaji (no) 同じ (の) (same, in
agreement).

concussion, *n.* nōshintō 脳震盪
(brain).

condemn, *vb.* 1. hinan suru 非難す
る (denounce). 2. yūzai o
senkoku suru 有罪を宣告する
(find guilty). 3. futekitō to
handan suru 不適当と判断する
(judge unfit).

condemnation, *n.* hinan 非難
(denunciation).

condense, *vb.* 1. yōyaku suru 要約
する (summarize). 2. ekika suru

液化する (change vapor to liquid).
3. koku suru 濃くする
(concentrate).

condescend, *vb.* **condescend to
do** ...otakaku tomatte ... suru お高
くとまって... する (do arrogantly);
onkisegamashiku ... suru 恩着せが
ましく... する (do patronizingly).

condescending, *adj.* 1.
onkisegamashii 恩着せがましい
(patronizing). 2. herikudatte-iru
へり下っている (self-humbling).

condiment, *n.* yakumi 薬味.

condition, *n.* 1. jōtai 状態 (state of
being); kenkōjōtai 健康状態;
chōshi 調子 (state of health); **out
of condition** chōshi ga warui. 2.
jōken 条件 (requirement); **on
condition that** ... no jōken de.

conditional, *adj.* jōkentsuki (no)
条件付き (の) (not absolute).

condolence, *n.* (o)kuyami (お)悔
やみ (on occasion of death).

condom, *n.* kondōmu コンドーム.

condominium, *n.* bunjō-manshon
分譲マンション.

condone, *vb.* 1. mokunin suru 黙
認する (approve tacitly). 2.
yurusu 許す (forgive). 3.
minogasu 見のがす (overlook).

conducive, *adj.* **be conducive to**
... ni tsunagaru ... につながる.

conduct, 1. *n.* furumai 振るまい
(behavior); un'ei 運営
(management). 2. *vb.* un'ei suru
運営する (manage, run);
michibiku 導く; hiki'iru 率いる
(direct, lead); dendō suru 伝道す
る (transfer heat, electricity, etc.);
shiki suru 指揮する (act as musical
conductor); okonau 行う (carry
on); **conduct oneself** furumau.

conductor, *n.* 1. shikisha 指揮者
(music). 2. shashō 車掌 (bus,

train). 3. dendōtai 伝導体 (substance).

cone, *n.* 1. ensuikei 円錐形 (form). 2. aisukurīmu-ire アイスクリーム入れ (ice cream cone). 3. matsukasa 松かさ (pine cone).

confection, *n.* (o)kashi (お)菓子.

confederacy, *n.* 1. renmei 連盟 (alliance). 2. kyōbō 共謀 (conspiracy).

confederate, 1. *n.* renmeiin 連盟員 (member); kyōbōsha 共謀者 (accomplice). 2. *vb.* renmei o musubu 連盟を結ぶ (unite).

confer, *vb.* 1. hanashiau 話し合う (discuss). 2. ataeru 与える (give).

conference, *n.* kaigi 会議.

confess, *vb.* 1. kokuhaku suru 告白する (reveal one's secret). 2. jihaku suru 自白する (admit one's crime). 3. mitomeru 認める (admit).

confession, *n.* 1. kokuhaku 告白 (revelation of one's secret). 2. jihaku 自白 (admission of one's crime).

confetti, *n.* kamifubuki 紙吹雪.

confidant, *n.* fukushin no tomo 腹心の友 (bosom friend).

confide, *vb.* 1. uchiakeru 打ち明ける (impart secrets or private matters). 2. shin'yō suru 信用する (place trust in).

confidence, *n.* 1. shin'yō 信用 (trust). 2. jishin 自信 (self-confidence). 3. himitsu 秘密 (secret); **in confidence** naisho de 内緒で.

confident, *adj.* 1. kakushin shite-iru 確信している (sure). 2. jishin ga aru 自信がある (sure of oneself).

confidential, *adj.* 1. naimitsu (no) 内密 (の) (secret, private). 2.

shinten (no) 親展 (の) (of letter).

confine, *vb.* tojikomeru 閉じ込める (shut or lock up); gentei suru 限定する (limit).

confinement, *n.* kankin 監禁 (imprisonment).

confines, *n.* han'i 範囲 (region); genkai 限界 (limit[s]).

confirm, *vb.* 1. kakunin suru 確認する (make certain). 2. tsuyomeru 強める (strengthen).

confirmation, *n.* kakunin 確認 (act of making certain).

confiscate, *vb.* bosshū suru 没収する (seize by public authority).

conflagration, *n.* taika 大火.

conflict, 1. *n.* tatakai 戦い (battle); sensō 戦争 (war); kenka 喧嘩 (quarrel); tairitsu 対立 (antagonism, discord). 2. *vb.* arasou 争う (fight); tairitsu suru 対立する (oppose); kuichigau 食い違う (differ, disagree).

conform, *vb.* 1. shitagau 従う (obey). 2. itchi suru 一致する; (be in agreement); itchi saseru 一致させる (bring into agreement). 3. au 合う (be in accord or harmony); awaseru 合わせる (bring into agreement or harmony).

confound, *vb.* tomadowaseru 戸惑わせる (bewilder); magotsukaseru まごつかせる (perplex, confuse).

confront, *vb.* 1. tachimukau 立ち向かう (face courageously, make effort). 2. tairitsu suru 対立する (face hostilely). 3. chokumen suru 直面する (encounter).

confrontation, *n.* tairitsu 対立 (opposition, clash).

confuse, *vb.* 1. kondō suru 混同する (mix up). 2. konran saseru 混乱させる (throw into disorder). 3.

tomadowaseru 戸惑わせる (bewilder).

confusion, *n.* 1. kondō 混同 (mix-up). 2. konran 混乱 (disorder). 3. tomadoi 戸惑い (bewilderment).

con game, *n.* damashi だまし; sagi 詐欺.

congenial, *adj.* 1. kimochi ga ii 気持ちが良い (pleasant). 2. tekishite iru 適している (suitable).

congenital, *adj.* seirai (no) 生来 (の).

congested, *adj.* 1. kondeiru 混んでいる (crowded). 2. tsumatte iru 詰まっている; fusagatte iru 塞がっている (stuffed, blocked).

congestion, *n.* 1. kōtsūjūtai 交通渋滞 (traffic). 2. hanazumari 鼻づまり (nasal).

conglomerate, *n.* konguromaritto コングロマリット (business).

congratulate, *vb.* iwai no kotoba o noberu 祝いの言葉を述べる (express sympathetic joy).

congratulations, 1. *n.* iwai no kotoba 祝いの言葉. 2. *interj.* Omedetō おめでとう.

congregate, *vb.* atsumaru 集まる (come together); atsumeru 集める (bring together).

congregation, *n.* 1. atsumari 集まり (assembly). 2. shūkai 集会 (meeting).

congress, *n.* 1. kaigi 会議 (meeting). 2. kokkai 国会 (national legislative body); gikai 議会 (U.S. Congress).

congressional, *adj.* kokkai (no) 国会 (の) (of national legislative body); gikai (no) 議会 (の) (of U.S. Congress).

congressman, -woman, *n.* kokkaigiin 国会議員 (member of national legislature); kaingiin 下院議員 (member of U.S. House of Representatives).

conjecture, 1. *n.* suisoku 推測 (guess). 2. *vb.* suisoku suru 推測する.

conjugal, *adj.* kekkon (no) 結婚 (の).

conjugate, *vb.* katsuyō saseru 活用させる (grammar).

conjugation, *n.* dōshikatsuyō 動詞活用 (verb conjugation).

conjunction, *n.* 1. setsuzokushi 接続詞 (grammar). 2. renketsu 連結 (act of conjoining); **in conjunction with** ... to tomo ni ... と共に (together with).

conjure, *vb.* 1. mahō de toridasu 魔法で取り出す (produce by magic). 2. **conjure up** omoiegaku 思い描く (imagine); yobiokosu 呼び起こす (recall); mahō de yobidasu 魔法で呼び出す (bring into existence by magic or spell).

con man, *n.* sagishi 詐欺師.

connect, *vb.* 1. tsunagu 繋ぐ (link, establish telephone communication). 2. renraku suru 連絡する (buses, trains, etc.). 3. kanrenzukeru 関連づける (associate).

connected, *adj.* 1. tsunagatte iru 繋がっている (linked). 2. kanren (no) 関連 (の) (related); **be related to** ... to kankei ga aru ... と関係がある.

connection, *n.* 1. renketsu 連結 (link). 2. renraku 連絡 (buses, trains, etc.). 3. tsunagari 繋がり (relationship). 4. kone コネ (powerful person). 5. **in connection with** ... ni kanren shite ... に関連して (in association with).

connive, *vb.* kyōbō suru 共謀する.

connoisseur, *n.* kurōto 玄人; tsū 通.

connotation, *n.* gengai no imi 言外の意味.

connote, *vb.* imi suru 意味する.

conquer, *vb.* seifuku suru 征服する.

conqueror, *n.* seifukusha 征服者.

conquest, *n.* seifuku 征服.

conscience, *n.* ryōshin 良心.

conscientious, *adj.* ryōshin-teki (na) 良心的 (な).

conscious, *adj.* 1. ishiki ga aru 意識がある (aware). 2. ishiki-teki (na) 意識的 (な) (intentional).

consciousness, *n.* ishiki 意識 (awareness).

conscript, 1. *n.* chōshūhei 徴集兵. 2. *vb.* chōhei suru 徴兵する.

conscription, *n.* chōheiseido 徴兵制度.

consecrate, *vb.* 1. shinseika suru 神聖化する (make sacred). 2. sasageru 捧げる (devote).

consecutive, *adj.* renzoku (no) 連続 (の).

consensus, *n.* gōi 合意.

consent, 1. *n.* gōi 合意 (agreement); kyoka 許可 (permission). 2. *vb.* gōi suru 合意する (agree); kyoka suru 許可する (permit).

consequence, *n.* 1. kekka 結果 (result). 2. jūyōsei 重要性 (importance); **of consequence** jūyō (na); **of little consequence** jūyō de nai.

consequently, *adv.* sono kekka その結果 (as a result); yue ni 故に (therefore).

conservation, *n.* 1. hozon 保存 (preservation). 2. setsuyaku 節約 (controlled utilization).

conservationist, *n.* shizenhogo

shugisha 自然保護主義者.

conservatism, *n.* hoshushugi 保守主義.

conservative, 1. *n.* hoshuha 保守派. 2. *adj.* hoshu-teki (na) 保守的 (な) (favoring existing conditions); shinchō (na) 慎重 (な) (cautious); hikaeme (na) 控え目 (な) (modest).

conservatory, *n.* 1. ongakugakkō 音楽学校 (music school); engeki-gakkō 演劇学校 (acting school). 2. onshitsu 温室 (hothouse).

conserve, *vb.* 1. hozon suru 保存する (keep intact). 2. setsuyaku suru 節約する (save).

consider, *vb.* 1. jukkō suru 熟考する (think over); kangaeru 考える (think about). 2. kentō suru 見当する (examine). 3. ... to minasu ... と見なす; ... to omou と思う (deem); **consider expensive** takai to omou 高いと思う.

considerable, *adj.* kanari no かなりの.

considerate, *adj.* omoiyari ga aru 思いやりがある.

consideration, *n.* 1. omoiyari 思いやり (kindness, thoughtfulness). 2. kōryo 考慮 (thought). 3. **in consideration of** ... o kōryo shite; **take into consideration** kōryo ni ireru; **show consideration for** kōryo suru.

considering, *prep., conj.* ... o kōryo sureba ...を考慮すれば.

consign, *vb.* 1. okuru 送る (ship). 2. yudaneru 委ねる (entrust). 3. hikiwatasu 引き渡す (hand over).

consignment, *n.* itaku 委託 (goods).

consist, *vb.* **consist of** ... kara naru ... からなる.

consistency, *n.* 1. ikkansei 一貫性

(constancy). 2. katasa 固さ (degree of firmness); kosa 濃さ (degree of density).

consistent, *adj.* ikkan shite iru 一貫している.

consolation, *n.* nagusame 慰め.

console, *vb.* nagusameru 慰める.

consolidate, *vb.* 1. tsuyomeru 強める (make firm); tsuyomaru 強まる (become firm). 2. gappei suru 合併する (unite, as companies).

consonant, *n.* shi'in 子音.

consort, *n.* haigūsha 配偶者.

conspicuous, *adj.* medatsu 目立つ.

conspiracy, *n.* inbō 陰謀.

conspirator, *n.* kyōbōsha 共謀者.

conspire, *vb.* 1. kyōbō suru 共謀する (plot together). 2. kyōryoku suru 協力する (act together).

constant, *adj.* 1. ittei (no) 一定 (の) (fixed). 2. taemanai 絶え間ない (uninterrupted). 3. seijitsu (na) 誠実 (な) (faithful).

constellation, *n.* seiza 星座.

consternation, *n.* gyōten 仰天.

constipation, *n.* benpi 便秘.

constituency, *n.* 1. senkyomin 選挙民 (voter[s]). 2. senkyoku 選挙区 (district).

constituent, *n.* 1. senkyomin 選挙民 (voter). 2. kōseibubun 構成部分 (component); seibun 成分 (element).

constitute, *vb.* 1. kōsei suru 構成する (form). 2. ninmei suru 任命する (appoint to an office). 3. seitei suru 制定する (establish, as law).

constitution, *n.* 1. sosei 組成 (makeup). 2. taishitsu 体質 (physical condition). 3. kenpō 憲法 (law).

constitutional, *adj.* 1. taishitsujō (no) 体質上 (の) (of one's physical

condition). 2. kenpōjō (no) 憲法上 (の) (of law).

constrain, *vb.* seigen suru 制限する.

constraint, *n.* 1. seigen 制限 (restriction). 2. yokusei 抑制 (repression of natural feelings). 3. kyūkutsusa 窮屈さ (unnatural restraint in manner).

constrict, *vb.* 1. sebameru 狭める (make narrower). 2. shimetsukeru 締め付ける (compress).

constricted, *adj.* semai 狭い (narrow).

construct, *vb.* 1. kensetsu suru 建設する (build). 2. kumitateru 組み立てる (form).

construction, *n.* 1. kensetsu 建設 (act of constructing); **under construction** kensetsuchū (no) 建設中 (の). 2. tatemono 建て物 (building). 3. kōzō 構造 (structure). 4. kensetsugyō 建設業 (industry).

constructive, *adj.* kensetsu-teki (na) 建設的 (な).

construe, *vb.* kaishaku suru 解釈する.

consul, *n.* ryōji 領事.

consulate, *n.* ryōjikan 領事館.

consult, *vb.* 1. ... ni sōdan suru ... に相談する (ask advice of). 2. (isha ni) mite morau (医者に) 見てもらう (be checked by, e.g., doctor). 3. shiraberu 調べる (refer to, e.g., dictionary).

consultant, *n.* konsarutanto コンサルタント.

consultation, *n.* 1. sōdan 相談 (act of consulting); **in consultation with** ... to sōdan no ue de ... と相談の上で. 2. kyōgikai 協議会 (meeting). 3. shinsatsu 診察

(medical).

consume, *vb.* 1. tsukaihatasu 使い
果たす (use up). 2. taberu 食べる
(eat); nomu 飲む (drink). 3. shōhi
suru 消費する (buy goods, etc.).
4. rōhi suru 浪費する (waste).

consumer, *n.* shōhisha 消費者.

consumer price index, *n.*
shōhisha-bukkashisū 消費者物価
指数.

consummate, 1. *adj.* kanzen (na)
完全 (な) (perfect). 2. *vb.* kanzen
ni suru 完全にする (make
perfect); mitasu 満たす (fulfill);
nikutai-teki ni musubareru 肉体的
に結ばれる (consummate a
marriage).

consumption, *n.* 1. shōhi 消費
(act of consuming goods). 2.
shōhidaka 消費高 (amount
consumed). 3. kekkaku 結核
(tuberculosis).

contact, 1. *n.* sesshoku 接触
(touching); renraku 連絡
(communication); **make contact
with** ... to renraku o toru. 2. *vb.*
... to sesshoku suru ... と接触する
(touch); ... to renraku o toru ... と
連絡をとる (communicate with).

contact lens, *n.* kontakuto-renzu
コンタクトレンズ.

contagious, *adj.* 1. densensei (no)
伝染性 (の) (transmittable). 2.
kansen shiyasui 感染し易い
(infectious).

contain, *vb.* 1. ... ga haitteiru ... が
入っている (have within). 2.
fukumu 含む (include). 3. osaeru
抑える (hold back).

container, *n.* 1. yōki 容器
(receptacle). 2. kontenā コンテナ
ー (for cargo).

contaminate, *vb.* osen suru 汚染す
る.

contemplate, *vb.* 1. kangaeru 考え
る (think about). 2. yoku
kangaeru よく考える (consider
thoroughly). 3. yoku miru よく見
る (look at with attention). 4.
keikaku suru 計画する (intend).

contemporary, 1. *n.* dōjidaijin 同
時代人. 2. *adj.* dōjidai (no) 同時代
(の) (of same period); gendai (no)
現代 (の) (modern).

contempt, *n.* keibetsu 軽蔑.

contemptible, *adj.* iyashii 卑しい.

contemptuous, *adj.* keibetsu ni
michiteiru 軽蔑に満ちている.

contend, *vb.* 1. kisou 競う
(compete). 2. tatakau 戦う
(fight). 3. giron suru 議論する
(dispute). 4. shuchō suru 主張す
る (assert).

contender, *n.* kyōgisha 競技者 (in
a contest).

content, *n.* naiyō 内容 (subject);
nakami 中身 (what is contained);
table of contents mokuji 目次.

content, 1. *n.* **to one's heart's
content** omouzonbun ni 思う存
分に. 2. *adj.* **be content (with)**
(... de) manzoku shiteiru (... で)
満足している. 3. *vb.* manzoku
saseru 満足させる; **content
oneself (with)** (... de) manzoku
suru (... で) 満足する.

contented, *adj.* **be contented**
manzoku shite iru 満足している.

contention, *n.* 1. ronsō 論争
(controversy). 2. kyōsō 競争
(contest). 3. shuchō 主張 (claim).

contest, 1. *n.* kontesuto コンテス
ト; konkūru コンクール
(competition for a prize); tatakai
戦い (struggle); giron 議論
(dispute). 2. *vb.* kisou 競う
(compete with); arasou 争う (fight
for); ... ni igi o tonaeru ... に異議

を唱える (argue about).

contestant, *n.* sankasha 参加者 (in a competition).

context, *n.* 1. bunmyaku 文脈 (surrounding words). 2. mawari no jōkyō 周りの状況 (surrounding circumstances).

continence, *n.* 1. jisei 自制 (self-restraint). 2. kin'yoku 禁欲 (abstinence).

continent, *n.* tairiku 大陸 (major land mass).

continental, *adj.* 1. tairiku (no) 大陸 (の) (of a continent). 2. tairiku-teki (na) 大陸的 (な) (of the nature of a continent).

contingency, *n.* fusoku no jiko 不測の事故 (unpredictable accident).

contingent, *adj.* **contingent on ...** shidai ...次第 (dependent on).

continual, *adj.* taemanai 絶え間ない (very frequent, continuous in time).

continuation, *n.* 1. zokkō 続行 (act of continuing). 2. tsuzuki 続き (extension, sequel).

continue, *vb.* tsuzuku 続く (go on); tsuzukeru 続ける (carry on, extend).

continuity, *n.* renzokusei 連続性.

continuous, *adj.* togireru koto ga nai 途切れる事がない.

contort, *vb.* yugamu 歪む (become twisted); yugameru 歪める (twist something).

contortion, *n.* yugami 歪み (state of being twisted).

contour, *n.* rinkaku 輪郭.

contraband, *n.* mitsuyuhin 密輸品.

contraception, *n.* hinin 避妊.

contraceptive, *n.* hiningu 避妊具 (device); hinin'yaku 避妊薬 (pill).

contract, 1. *n.* keiyaku 契約 (agreement); keiyakusho 契約書 (written form). 2. *vb.* keiyaku suru 契約する (agree); chijimu 縮む (become smaller or shorter); chijimeru 縮める (cause to become smaller or shorter); ... ni kakaru ... にかかる (catch, as disease).

contraction, *n.* 1. shūshuku 収縮 (act of contracting). 2. tanshukukei 短縮形 (shortened form of a word).

contractor, *n.* ukeoinin 請負人.

contradict, *vb.* 1. ... ni hantai suru ... に反対する (assert the opposite of). 2. hitei suru 否定する (deny). 3. ... to kuichigau ... と食い違う (be inconsistent).

contradiction, *n.* 1. hantai 反対 (opposition). 2. hitei 否定 (denial). 3. mujun 矛盾 (inconsistency).

contradictory, *adj.* **be contradictory to ...** to kuichigau ... と食い違う (be inconsistent with).

contraption, *n.* shikake 仕掛け.

contrary, *n.* hantai 反対 (opposite); **on the contrary** hantai ni 反対に; kaette かえって; **to the contrary** chigau fū ni 違う風に (differently). 2. *adj.* hantai (no) 反対 (の); gyaku (no) 逆 (の) (opposite); hinekurete-iru ひねくれている (perverse); **contrary to** ... ni hanshite ... に反して.

contrast, 1. *n.* chigai 違い (difference). 2. *vb.* kuraberu 比べる (compare); chigau 違う (differ).

contribute, *vb.* 1. kifu suru 寄付する (donate). 2. kikō suru 寄稿する (write a work under contract). 3. **contribute to ...** ni kōken suru ... に貢献する (to be an important factor in).

contribution, *n.* 1. kifu 寄付 (donation). 2. kikō 寄稿 (work written under contract). 3. kōken 貢献 (great help).

contributor, *n.* 1. kifusha 寄付者 (donor). 2. kōkensha 貢献者 (participant, supporter). 3. kikōsha 寄稿者 (writer under contract).

contrition, *n.* kaigo 悔悟.

contrive, *vb.* nashitogeru 成し遂げる.

contrived, *adj.* fushizen (na) 不自然 (な).

control, 1. *n.* shihai 支配 (domination); kanri 管理 (management); yokusei 抑制 (restraint); **get under control** seigyo suru 制御する. 2. *vb.* shihai suru 支配する (dominate); kanri suru 管理する (manage); yokusei suru 抑制する (restrain); **control oneself** jibun o osaeru 自分を抑える.

controversial, *adj.* giron o yobu 議論を呼ぶ.

controversy, *n.* ronsen 論戦 (dispute); giron 議論 (argument).

convalesce, *vb.* kaifuku suru 回復する.

convalescent, *n.* kaifukuki no byōnin 回復期の病人.

convene, *vb.* atsumaru 集まる (assemble); shōshū suru 招集する (convoke).

convenience, *n.* 1. benri 便利 (handiness). 2. tsugō 都合 (personal suitableness); **at one's convenience** tsugō no ii toki ni.

convenient, *adj.* 1. benri (na) 便利 (な) (handy). 2. kōtsugō (na) 好都合 (な) (favorable).

convention, *n.* 1. shūkan 習慣

(accepted usage). 2. taikai 大会 (meeting).

conventional, *adj.* 1. inshūteki (na) 因習的 (な) (customary). 2. dentōteki (na) 伝統的 (な) (traditional).

converge, *vb.* shūchū suru 集中する (concentrate); shūsoku suru 収束する (mathematics).

conversant, *adj.* **be conversant with** ... o yoku shitteiru ... をよく知っている.

conversation, *n.* kaiwa 会話.

converse, 1. *n.* hantai 反対 (opposite). 2. *adj.* hantai (no) 反対 (の). 3. *vb.* hanasu 話す (talk).

conversion, *n.* 1. henkan 変換 (change). 2. kaishū 改宗 (religion).

convert, 1. *n.* kaishūsha 改宗者 (religion). 2. *vb.* kaishū suru 改宗する (become a convert); kaishū saseru 改宗させる (cause to convert); kaeru 変える (change); kaesaseru 変えさせる (cause to change).

converter, *n.* konbātā コンバーター (electricity).

convertible, 1. *n.* konbātiburu コンバーティブル (car). 2. *adj.* henkan dekiru 変換できる (able to be converted).

convex, *adj.* totsumen (no) 凸面 (の).

convey, *vb.* 1. hakobu 運ぶ (carry). 2. tsutaeru 伝える (transmit).

convict, 1. *n.* shūjin 囚人. 2. *vb.* yūzai o iiwatasu 有罪を言い渡す (find guilty).

conviction, *n.* 1. shin'nen 信念 (firm belief). 2. yūzai no hanketsu 有罪の判決 (legal guilt).

convince, *vb.* 1. settoku suru 説得する (persuade). 2. shinji saseru

信じさせる (cause to believe).

convincing, *adj.* settokuryoku ga aru 説得力がある.

convoluted, *adj.* fukuzatsu (na) 複雑 (な).

convulsion, *n.* keiren けいれん.

coo, *vb.* yasashiku sasayaku 優しくささやく (person); kū-kū naku くーくー鳴く (bird).

cook, 1. *n.* kokku コック (of western-style meal); ryōrishi 料理師 (of Japanese-style meal). 2. *vb.* ryōri suru 料理する (prepare by heating); **cook up** detchiageru でっち上げる (fabricate).

cookbook, *n.* ryōri no hon 料理の本.

cookie, *n.* kukkī クッキー.

cooking, *n.* ryōri 料理.

cool, 1. *adj.* suzushii 涼しい (temperature); tsumetai 冷たい (unaffectionate or unfriendly); reisei (na) 冷静 (な) (detached). 2. *vb.* hieru 冷える (become chilled); hiyasu 冷やす (make chilled); sameru 冷める (become cooler); samasu 冷ます (make cooler).

coop, *n.* torigoya 鳥小屋 (chicken coop).

co-op, *n.* see **cooperative.**

cooperate, *vb.* kyōryoku suru 協力する.

cooperation, *n.* kyōryoku 協力.

cooperative, 1. *n.* kyōdōkanri-bunjō-manshon 共同管理分譲マンション (apartment); kyōdō-kumiai 協同組合 (business). 2. *adj.* kyōdō (no) 協同 (の) (working together); kyōryoku-teki (na) 協力的 (な) (helpful).

coordinate, *vb.* awaseru 合わせる.

coordination, *n.* chōwa 調和.

coordinator, *n.* kōdinētā コー

ディネーター.

cop, *n.* keikan 警官.

cope, *vb.* **cope with** ... o umaku shori suru ... をうまく処理する.

copier, *n.* kopī-kikai コピー機械 (photocopier).

copious, *adj.* takusan (no) たくさん (の).

copper, *n.* dō 銅.

copulate, *vb.* sekkusu o suru セックスをする.

copy, 1. *n.* kopī コピー (duplicate); -bu -部 (newspaper, magazine); -satsu -冊 (book); **two copies of a book** hon nisatsu. 2. *vb.* kopī o suru コピーをする (make copy); mohō suru 模倣する (imitate); kakiutsusu 書き写す (transcribe).

copyright, *n.* chosakuken 著作権.

coquettish, *adj.* adappoi あだっぽい.

coral, *n.* sango 珊瑚.

cord, *n.* 1. kōdo コード (electric wire). 2. himo ひも (string).

cordial, 1. *n.* rikyūru リキュール (liqueur). 2. *adj.* atatakai 暖かい (friendly).

corduroy, *n.* kōruten コールテン.

core, *n.* 1. shin 芯 (of fruit). 2. kakushin 核心 (essential part).

cork, *n.* 1. koruku コルク (tree bark). 2. korukusen コルク栓 (stopper).

corkscrew, *n.* sen'nuki 栓抜き.

corn, *n.* 1. tōmorokoshi とうもろこし (food). 2. uonome 魚の目 (growth on foot).

cornea, *n.* kakumaku 角膜.

corned beef, *n.* kōnbīfu コーンビーフ.

corner, 1. *n.* kado 角 (intersection; angle); hashi 端 (margin); sumi 隅 (niche, nook); **cut corners** tettoribayaku sumaseru てっとり

早く済ませる (do a quick job). 2. *vb.* oitsumeru 追い詰める (trap).

cornerstone, *n.* kiban 基盤.

cornet, *n.* korunetto コルネット.

cornflakes, *n.* kōnfurēku コーンフレーク.

cornstarch, *n.* kōnsutāchi コーンスターチ.

corollary, *n.* kekka 結果 (result).

coronation, *n.* taikanshiki 戴冠式.

corporal, *adj.* nikutai (no) 肉体 (の); **corporal punishment** taibatsu 体罰.

corporate, *adj.* 1. kigyō (no) 企業 (の) (of a corporation). 2. dantai (no) 団体 (の) (of a group).

corporation, *n.* kigyō 企業 (business organization).

corps, *n.* 1. gundan 軍団 (military). 2. dantai 団体 (group).

corpse, *n.* shitai 死体.

corpulent, *adj.* futotte iru 太っている.

corpuscle, *n.* kekkyū 血球.

corral, 1. *n.* kakoi 囲い. 2. *vb.* kakoi ni ireru 囲いに入れる (put in a corral); kakutoku suru 獲得する (seize).

correct, 1. *adj.* tadashii 正しい (right); seikaku (na) 正確 (な) (accurate). 2. *vb.* tadasu 正す (make right).

correction, *n.* 1. teisei 訂正 (act of making right). 2. korashime 懲らしめ (chastisement).

correctness, *n.* seikakusa 正確さ.

correlation, *n.* sōgo kankei 相互関係.

correspond, *vb.* 1. itchi suru 一致する (match). 2. sōtō suru 相当する (be analogous). 3. buntsū suru 文通する (communicate by letters).

correspondence, *n.* 1. itchi 一致

(agreement). 2. sō'ō 相応 (analogy). 3. buntsū 文通 (communication by letters).

correspondent, *n.* 1. buntsūsha 文通者 (letter writer). 2. tokuhain 特派員 (reporter).

corresponding, *adj.* 1. itchi suru 一致する (identical). 2. sō'ō (no) 相応 (の) (matching).

corridor, *n.* rōka 廊下.

corroborate, *vb.* urazukeru 裏付ける.

corrode, *vb.* fushoku suru/saseru 腐食する／させる.

corrosion, *n.* fushoku 腐食.

corrugated, *adj.* namigata (no) 波型 (の).

corrupt, 1. *adj.* daraku shiteiru 堕落している (depraved); kusatte-iru 腐っている (decayed). 2. *vb.* daraku suru/saseru 堕落する／させる (become/make depraved); kusareru 腐れる (become decayed); kusaraseru 腐らせる (make decayed); baishū suru 買収する (bribe); kegareru 汚れる (become tainted).

corruption, *n.* 1. daraku 堕落 (depravity). 2. oshoku 汚職 (acceptance of bribery). 3. fuhai 腐敗 (decay).

corsage, *n.* kosāju コサージュ.

corset, *n.* korusetto コルセット.

cosmetic, 1. *n.* keshōhin 化粧品 (powder, lotion, etc.). 2. *adj.* hyōmen-teki (na) 表面的 (な) (superficial).

cosmic, *adj.* uchū (no) 宇宙 (の).

cosmopolitan, *adj.* sekai-teki (na) 世界的 (な) (global); kokusai-teki (na) 国際的 (な) (international).

cosmos, *n.* uchū 宇宙.

cost, 1. *n.* hiyō 費用 (expenditure); kakaku 価格 (price paid); **cost of**

living seikatsuhi 生活費; **at all costs** dōshitemo どうしても; **at the cost of** ... o gisei ni shite ... を犠牲にして. 2. *vb*. ... ga kakaru ...がかかる (require payment of); yōsuru 要する (require effort, time).

costly, *adj*. 1. takai 高い (expensive). 2. takaku tsuku 高くつく (resulting in great loss).

costume, *n*. ishō 衣装.

cot, *n*. kan'i beddo 簡易ベッド.

cottage, *n*. koya 小屋.

cottage cheese, *n*. kattēji-chīzu カッテージチーズ.

cotton, *n*. 1. wata 綿 (plant, wadding). 2. momen 木綿 (cloth).

couch, *n*. sofā ソファー.

cough, 1. *n*. seki 咳. 2. *vb*. seki o suru 咳をする.

council, *n*. i'inkai 委員会 (committee); kaigi 会議 (assembly).

councilman, -woman, *n*. hyōgi'in 評議員 (assembly member).

counsel, 1. *n*. bengoshi 弁護士 (lawyer); sōdan 相談 (advice); chūkoku 忠告 (caution). 2. *vb*. jogen o ataeru 助言を与える (give advice); sōdan suru 相談する (get advice); chūkoku suru 忠告する (caution).

counselor, *n*. 1. kaunserā カウンセラー (adviser). 2. bengoshi 弁護士 (lawyer).

count, 1. *n*. keisan 計算 (act of counting); sōsū 総数 (total number); hakushaku 伯爵 (title). 2. *vb*. kazoeru 数える (determine number); taisetsu de aru 大切である (be important); fukumu 含む (include); ... to minasu ... とみなす (consider); **count on** ... o ate ni suru ... を当てにする.

countdown, *n*. byō yomi 秒読み.

countenance, 1. *n*. kaotsuki 顔付き (facial expression); kaodachi 顔立ち (facial features). 2. *vb*. yurusu 許す (allow).

counter, 1. *n*. kauntā カウンター (sales or food); **under the counter** ura de 裏で (secretly). 2. *vb*. hantai suru 反対する (oppose); hangeki suru 反撃する (return a blow). 3. *adv*. **counter to** ... no gyaku ni ... の逆に (contrary to); ... ni hanshite ... に反して (in opposition to).

counteract, *vb*. chūwa suru 中和する.

counterattack, *vb*. hangeki suru 反撃する.

counterbalance, 1. *n*. tsuriai 釣り合い. 2. *vb*. tsuriai o toru 釣り合いを取る.

counterfeit, 1. *n*. nisemono 偽せ物 (a fake). 2. *vb*. gizō suru 偽造する (fake).

countermand, *vb*. tekkai suru 撤回する.

counterpart, *n*. sōtō suru hito 相当する人 (person); sōtōbutsu 相当物 (thing).

countess, *n*. hakushakufujin 伯爵夫人.

countless, *adj*. musū (no) 無数 (の).

country, *n*. 1. kuni 国 (nation; homeland). 2. kokumin 国民 (people of a country). 3. inaka 田舎 (rural district).

countryman, -woman, *n*. dōkokujin 同国人 (from the same country).

countryside, *n*. inaka 田舎.

county, *n*. gun 郡.

coup, *n*. ōtegara 大手柄 (masterstroke).

coup d'état, *n.* kūdetā クーデター.

couple, 1. *n.* kappuru カップル (lovers); fūfu 夫婦 (married couple); futari 二人 (two people); futatsu 二つ (two things). 2. *vb.* tsunagu つなぐ (connect, fasten); hitotsu ni naru/suru 一つになる／する (become/make united).

coupon, *n.* kūpon クーポン; ken 券 (ticket).

courage, *n.* yūki 勇気.

courageous, *adj.* yūki ga aru 勇気がある.

courier, *n.* kyūshi 急使.

course, 1. *n.* kōsu コース; michi 道 (route); hōkō 方向 (direction); kōza 講座 (set of lectures); **in the course of** ... no aida ni ... の間に. 2. *adv.* **of course** mochiron もちろん (needless to say).

court, 1. *n.* nakaniwa 中庭 (patio); kōto コート (level area for games); ōkyū 王宮 (palace); hōtei 法廷 (law court); **settle out of court** jidan ni suru 示談にする; **take into court** saibanzata ni suru 裁判沙汰にする. 2. *vb.* ... no kigen o toru ... の機嫌をとる (flatter); kyūai suru 求愛する (woo).

courteous, *adj.* 1. reigi tadashii 礼儀正しい (good-mannered). 2. teinei (na) 丁寧 (な) (polite).

courtesy, *n.* 1. reigi 礼儀 (good manners). 2. teineisa 丁寧さ (politeness).

courthouse, *n.* saibansho 裁判所.

courtyard, *n.* nakaniwa 中庭.

cousin, *n.* itoko いとこ.

cove, *n.* irie 入り江.

covenant, *n.* seiyaku 誓約.

cover, 1. *n.* kabā カバー (anything that covers); futa 蓋 (lid, top). 2. *vb.* ōu 覆う (place something on, spread over); ... ni futa o suru ... に蓋をする (put a lid on); kurumu くるむ (wrap); **cover up** kakusu 隠す (hide).

coverage, *n.* hōdō 報道 (journalism).

cover charge, *n.* kabā-chāji カバーチャージ; nyūjōryō 入場料 (for a show).

covering, *n.* ōi 覆い.

covert, *adj.* hisoka (na) 密か (な).

covet, *vb.* hoshigaru 欲しがる.

covetous, *adj.* don'yoku (na) 貪欲 (な).

cow, *n.* 1. mesu 雌 (female animal). 2. nyūgyū 乳牛 (female bovine animal).

coward, *n.* okubyōmono 臆病者.

cowardice, *n.* okubyō 臆病.

cowboy, *n.* kaubōi カウボーイ.

cower, *vb.* ojikezuku 怖じ気づく.

coy, *adj.* uchikisō na soburi (no) 内気そうな素振り (の).

cozy, *adj.* igokochi ga ii 居心地がいい.

crab, *n.* kani 蟹 (crustacean).

crabby, *adj.* kimuzukashii 気難しい (peevish).

crack, 1. *n.* hibi ひび (crevice); sakeme 裂け目 (opening); wareme 割れ目 (chink); wareru oto 割れる音 (noise). 2. *vb.* hibi ga hairu ひびが入る (fracture); waru 割る (break something); wareru 割れる (break open); **crack down** torishimaru 取り締まる.

cracker, *n.* kurakkā クラッカー (food).

crackle, *n.* pachi-pachi to iu oto パチパチという音 (sound).

cradle, *n.* yurikago ゆりかご.

craft, *n.* 1. gijutsu 技術 (skill). 2. kōgei 工芸 (industrial arts). 3. shokugyō 職業 (profession). 4.

fune 船 (boat).

craftsman, *n.* shokunin 職人.

craftsmanship, *n.* 1. shokuningei 職人芸 (expertise). 2. gijutsu 技術 (skill).

crafty, *adj.* zurugashikoi ずる賢い.

crag, *n.* kewashii iwa 険しい岩.

cram, *vb.* tsumekomu 詰め込む (stuff, prepare for examination).

cramp, *n.* keiren けいれん (spasm); ikeiren 胃けいれん (stomach spasm).

cranberry, *n.* kuranberī クランベリー.

crane, *n.* 1. kurēn クレーン (machine). 2. tsuru 鶴 (bird).

cranium, *n.* zugaikotsu 頭蓋骨.

crank, *n.* kuranku クランク.

cranny, *n.* wareme 割れ目.

crash, 1. *n.* tsuiraku 墜落 (fall); shōtotsu 衝突 (collision); tōsan 倒産 (bankruptcy); gachan to iu oto がちゃんという音 (sound of breaking). 2. *vb.* tsuiraku suru 墜落する (fall); shōtotsu suru 衝突する (collide); hasan suru 破産する (go bankrupt).

crass, *adj.* soya (na) 粗野 (な).

crate, *n.* hako 箱.

crater, *n.* kurētā クレーター.

crave, *vb.* hoshigaru 欲しがる.

craving, *n.* netsubō 熱望.

crawfish, *n.* zarigani ざりがに.

crawl, 1. *n.* noroi ugoki のろい動き (slow movement); kurōru クロール (swimming stroke). 2. *vb.* hau 這う (move slowly, creep).

crayfish, *n.* zarigani ざりがに.

crayon, *n.* kureyon クレヨン.

craze, 1. *n.* dairyūkō 大流行 (fad). 2. *vb.* kuruwaseru 狂わせる (make insane); nekkyō saseru 熱狂させる (make excited).

craziness, *n.* kyōki 狂気.

crazy, *adj.* 1. nekkyō (no) 熱狂 (の) (insane). 2. baka (na) 馬鹿 (な) (silly). 3. **crazy about** ... ni muchū (no) ... に夢中 (の).

creak, 1. *n.* kishiru oto きしる音. 2. *vb.* kishiru きしる.

cream, *n.* 1. kurīmu クリーム (food, cosmetic, medicament). 2. besuto ベスト (best part of anything).

creamy, *adj.* kurīmu no yō (na) クリームのよう (な).

crease, 1. *n.* shiwa しわ (wrinkle); orime 折り目 (fold). 2. *vb.* shiwa ni suru しわにする (wrinkle); shiwa ni naru しわになる (become wrinkled); oru 折る (fold).

create, *vb.* 1. sōzō suru 創造する (cause to exist). 2. hikiokosu 引き起こす (cause to happen).

creation, *n.* 1. sōzō 創造 (act of creating). 2. sōzōbutsu 創造物 (something created).

creative, *adj.* sōzō-teki (na) 創造的 (な).

creative writing, *n.* 1. sakubun 作文 (composition). 2. shōsetsu 小説 (fiction).

creativity, *n.* sōzōryoku 創造力.

creator, *n.* seisakusha 制作者.

creature, *n.* 1. dōbutsu 動物 (animal). 2. hito 人 (person).

credence, *n.* shin'yō 信用; **give credence to** ... o shinjiru ... を信じる.

credentials, *n.* shikaku-shōmeisho 資格証明書.

credibility, *n.* kakujitsusei 確実性.

credible, *adj.* 1. shinjirareru 信じられる (trustworthy). 2. kakujitsu (na) 確実 (な) (reliable).

credit, 1. *n.* kurejitto クレジット; tsuke 付け (for buying); tan'i 単位

(for a degree); shin'yō 信用
(belief); shōsan 賞賛
(commendation); hokori 誇り
(honor); **on credit** kurejitto de;
tsuke de; **give credit to** ... o
shinjiru ... を信じる; **do credit to**
... no hokori to naru. 2. *vb.*
shinjiru 信じる (believe); kurejitto
ni suru クレジットにする (credit
an account); **credit to** ... no yue
de aru to suru ... の故であるとす
る (ascribe to); **credit (someone)
with** ... o sonaeteiru ... を備えて
いる.

credit card, *n.* kurejitto-kādo クレ
ジットカード.

creditor, *n.* saikensha 債権者.

creed, *n.* kyōgi 教議.

creek, *n.* ogawa 小川.

creep, *vb.* 1. hau 這う (crawl). 2.
shinobiyoru 忍び寄る (sneak).

cremate, *vb.* kasō ni suru 火葬にす
る.

crescent, *n.* mikazuki 三日月
(moon).

crest, *n.* 1. tosaka とさか (bird). 2.
itadaki 頂 (top). 3. mon 紋
(heraldic device).

crestfallen, *adj.* ikishōchin shiteiru 意気消沈している.

crevice, *n.* wareme 割れ目.

crew, *n.* 1. norikumiin 乗組員
(ship, airplane, etc.). 2. kurū-han
クルー班 (group of workers).

crib, *n.* bebī-beddo ベビーベッド
(bed).

cricket, *n.* 1. kuriketto クリケット
(game). 2. kōrogi こおろぎ
(insect).

crime, *n.* 1. hanzai 犯罪 (unlawful
act); **commit a crime** hanzai o
okasu. 2. tsumi 罪 (sin).

criminal, 1. *n.* hanzaisha 犯罪者.
2. *adj.* hanzai (no) 犯罪 (の) (of a

crime); **criminal law** keihō 刑法.

crimson, 1. *adj.* shinku (no) 真紅
(の). 2. *n.* shinku 真紅.

cringe, *vb.* ishuku suru 畏縮する.

cripple, 1. *n.* shitai-fujiyūsha 肢体
不自由者. 2. *vb.* fugu ni suru 不具
にする (make lame); funō ni suru
不能にする (disable).

crisis, *n.* kiki 危機.

crisp, *adj.* 1. tekipaki to shiteiru て
きぱきとしている (brisk, decided).
2. meikai (na) 明解 (な) (lively,
pithy). 3. pari-pari shiteiru ぱりぱ
りしている (hard but easily
breakable). 4. shaki-shaki shiteiru しゃきしゃきしている (firm
and fresh).

criterion, *n.* kijun 基準.

critic, *n.* 1. hihyōka 批評家
(reviewer). 2. hihansha 批判者
(antagonist).

critical, *adj.* 1. kibishii 厳しい
(severe in judgment). 2. hihyō
(no) 批評 (の) (involving
judgment). 3. kitoku (no) 危篤
(の) (medical condition). 4. jūyō
(na) 重要 (な) (essential).

criticism, *n.* 1. hihyō 批評
(critique). 2. hihan 批判
(reproach).

criticize, *vb.* 1. hihyō suru 批評す
る (critique). 2. hihan suru 批判
する (reproach).

critique, *n.* hihyō 批評.

croak, *vb.* 1. kā-kā naku かーかー
鳴く (crow); kero-kero naku けろ
けろ鳴く (frog). 2. shagaregoe de
iu しゃがれ声で言う (speak with a
hoarse voice).

crochet, *n.* kagibariami かぎ針編
み.

crocodile, *n.* wani わに.

crony, *n.* nakama 仲間.

crook, 1. dorobō 泥棒 (thief). 2.

kagi 鍵 (hook).

crooked, *adj.* 1. fushōjiki (na) 不正直 (な) (dishonest). 2. magatteiru 曲がっている (curved).

crop, 1. *n.* sakumotsu 作物 (produce); shūkaku 収穫 (yield). 2. *vb.* karikomu 刈り込む (cut short); **crop up** shōjiru 生じる (appear).

croquette, *n.* korokke コロッケ.

cross, 1. *n.* jūji 十字 (cross symbol); jūjika 十字架 (the cross of Christianity). 2. *adj.* fukigen (na) 不機嫌 (な) (ill-humored). 3. *vb.* yokogiru 横切る (go or pass across); majiwaru 交わる (intersect); hantai suru 反対する (oppose); **cross out** sen o hiite kesu 線をひいて消す; **cross one's arms** ude o kumu 腕を組む; **cross oneself** jūji o kiru 十字をきる.

crossbreed, *n.* kōhaishu 交配種.

cross-examine, *vb.* hantaijinmon suru 反対尋問する.

cross-eyed, *adj.* yorime (no) 寄り目 (の).

crossing, *n.* 1. kōsaten 交差点 (intersection). 2. ōdanhodō 横断歩道 (crosswalk).

crossroads, *n.* jūjiro 十字路.

cross section, *n.* danmen 断面.

crosswalk, *n.* ōdanhodō 横断歩道.

crossword puzzle, *n.* kurosuwādo pazuru クロスワードパズル.

crotch, *n.* mata 股.

crouch, *vb.* mi o kagameru 身をかがめる.

crow, *n.* karasu 烏.

crowbar, *n.* kanateko かなてこ.

crowd, 1. *n.* gunshū 群衆 (large group of people). 2. *vb.* muragaru 群がる (throng); oshikomu 押し込む (push forward); mitasu 満たす (fill).

crowded, *adj.* kondeiru 混んでいる.

crown, 1. *n.* ōkan 王冠 (coronet); ōken 王権 (sovereignty); chōten 頂点 (top); atama 頭 (head); shikan 歯冠 (of tooth). 2. *vb.* sokui saseru 即位させる (invest with sovereignty); ōu 覆う (cover).

crucial, *adj.* 1. jūdai (na) 重大 (な) (important). 2. kettei-teki (na) 決定的 (な) (determining).

crucify, *vb.* haritsuke ni suru はりつけにする.

crude, *adj.* 1. bukiyō (na) 不器用 (な) (clumsy). 2. soya (na) 粗野 (な) (coarse). 3. mikakō (no) 未加工 (の) (unprocessed).

crudeness, *n.* bukiyōsa 不器用さ.

crude oil, *n.* gen'yu 原油.

crudity, *n.* bukiyōsa 不器用さ.

cruel, *adj.* zankoku (na) 残酷 (な) (heartless). 2. hidoi ひどい (causing pain).

cruelty, *n.* 1. zankokusa 残酷さ (heartlessness). 2. hidosa ひどさ (painfulness).

cruise, 1. *n.* funatabi 船旅 (voyage). 2. *vb.* junkō suru 巡航する (sail, fly).

crumb, *n.* pankuzu パン屑 (bread crumb); kuzu 屑 (morsel).

crumble, *vb.* 1. hōkai suru 崩壊する (collapse). 2. konagona ni suru 粉々にする (break into pieces).

crumple, *vb.* shiwadarake ni naru しわだらけになる (become wrinkled).

crunch, *vb.* kamikudaku 噛み砕く (chew noisily).

crusade, *n.* 1. undō 運動 (political campaign). 2. jūjigun 十字軍 (Christian military expedition).

crush, 1. *n.* hitogomi 人混み (crowd); **have a crush on** ... ni muchū ni naru ... に夢中になる. 2. *vb.* oshitsubusu 押し潰す (break by pressing); tsumekakeru 詰め掛ける (crowd).

crust, *n.* 1. kawa 皮 (bread, pie). 2. chikaku 地殻 (surface of the earth).

crutch, *n.* matsubazue 松葉杖.

crux, *n.* chūshinten 中心点.

cry, 1. *n.* sakebi 叫び (scream); nakigoe 泣き声 (weeping); nakigoe 鳴き声 (animal cry). 2. *vb.* sakebu 叫ぶ (scream); naku 泣く (weep); naku 鳴く (animal cry).

crypt, *n.* 1. chikashitsu 地下室 (subterranean vault). 2. chika-nōkotsudō 地下納骨堂 (burial place).

cryptic, *adj.* 1. himitsu (no) 秘密 (の) (secret). 2. nazo ni michiteiru 謎に満ちている (mysterious).

crystal, *n.* 1. kurisutaru クリスタル (glass). 2. suishō 水晶 (mineral).

cub, *n.* 1. ko 子 (young animal).

cube, *n.* 1. sanjō 三乗 (mathematics). 2. rippōtai 立方体 (solid bounded by six squares).

cubic, *adj.* rippō (no) 立方 (の).

cuckold, *n.* netorare-otoko 寝取られ男.

cuckoo, *n.* kakkō かっこう (bird).

cucumber, *n.* kyūri きゅうり.

cuddle, *vb.* dakishimeru 抱き締める.

cue, *n.* 1. aizu 合図 (signal). 2. kyū キュー (for playing pool).

cuff, *n.* sodeguchi 袖口 (sleeve); orikaeshi 折り返し (pants).

cufflinks, *n.* kafusu-botan カフスボタン.

cuisine, *n.* ryōri 料理.

culinary, *adj.* ryōri (no) 料理 (の).

culminate, *vb.* 1. chōten ni tassuru 頂点に達する (reach the highest point). 2. **culminate in** ... ni owaru ... に終わる (result in).

culmination, *n.* chōten 頂点.

culpable, *adj.* 1. semerubeki 責めるべき (deserving blame). 2. tsumi ga aru 罪がある (guilty).

culprit, *n.* hanzainin 犯罪人.

cult, *n.* 1. shūkyō 宗教 (religion). 2. ryūkō 流行 (faddish devotion).

cultivate, *vb.* 1. tagayasu 耕す (till, plow). 2. kaihatsu suru 開発する (develop).

cultivation, *n.* kōsaku 耕作 (agriculture).

cultural, *adj.* 1. kyōyō-teki (na) 教養的 (な) (nourishing to the mind). 2. bunka-teki (na) 文化的 (な) (cultured). 3. bunmei-teki (na) 文明的 (な) (civilized).

culture, *n.* 1. kyōyō 教養 (cultivation of the mind). 2. bunmei 文明; bunka 文化 (civilization, arts, etc.).

cultured, *adj.* kyōyō ga aru 教養がある.

cumbersome, *adj.* ōkisugiru 大き過ぎる (too big).

cumulative, *adj.* ruiseki (no) 累積 (の).

cunning, *adj.* 1. zurugashikoi ずる賢い (clever). 2. zurui ずるい (sly).

cup, *n.* kappu カップ (china, measurement); koppu コップ (mug).

cupboard, *n.* shokkidana 食器棚.

cupidity, *n.* gōyoku 強欲.

curator, *n.* kanchō 館長 (head of museum, etc).

curb, 1. *n.* yokusei 抑制 (restraint). 2. *vb.* yokusei suru 抑制する

(restrain).

cure, 1. *n.* chiryō 治療 (remedy); kaifuku 回復 (restoration to health). 2. *vb.* chiryō suru 治療する (treat a patient); naosu 治す (restore to health).

curfew, *n.* 1. mongen 門限 (home, dormitory). 2. yakangaishutsu-kinshirei 夜間外出禁止令 (governmental).

curio, *n.* kottōhin 骨董品.

curiosity, *n.* kōkishin 好奇心.

curious, *adj.* 1. kōkishin ni michiteiru 好奇心に満ちている (eager to know). 2. sensakuzuki (na) 詮索好き (な) (prying). 3. hen (na) 変 (な) (strange).

curl, 1. *n.* kāru カール (ringlet). 2. *vb.* kāru ni suru カールにする (form ringlets); maku 巻く (coil).

curler, *n.* kārā カーラー.

curly, *adj.* kāru shiteiru カールしている.

currency, *n.* 1. tsūka 通貨 (money). 2. tsūyō 通用 (prevalence); **gain currency** tsūyō suru.

current, 1. *n.* nagare 流れ (stream); suiryū 水流 (water); denryū 電流 (electricity). 2. *adj.* genzai (no) 現在 (の) (of today); tsūyō shiteiru 通用している (prevailing); **current events** jiji 時事.

curriculum, *n.* karikyuramu カリキュラム.

curriculum vitae, *n.* rirekisho 履歴書.

curry, *n.* karē カレー (hot sauce or powder). 2. *vb.* hetsurau へつらう (seek favor).

curse, 1. *n.* noroi 呪い (wish that evil befall someone); nonoshiri ののしり (profane oath). 2. *vb.*

norou 呪う (wish evil upon); nonoshiru ののしる (swear).

cursed, *adj.* norowarete iru 呪われている.

cursory, *adj.* iikagen (na) 好い加減 (な).

curt, *adj.* bukkirabō (na) ぶっきらぼう (な).

curtail, *vb.* kiritsumeru 切り詰める.

curtain, *n.* kāten カーテン (drape); maku 幕 (theater).

curve, *n.* kābu カーブ; kyokusen 曲線 (line). 2. *vb.* magaru/mageru 曲がる／曲げる (bend/cause to bend).

cushion, 1. *n.* kusshon クッション (pad). 2. *vb.* yawarageru 和らげる (mitigate).

custard, *n.* purin プリン (caramel custard); kasutādo カスタード (custard in general).

custodian, *n.* 1. hogosha 保護者 (guardian). 2. kanrinin 管理人 (caretaker).

custody, *n.* 1. hogo 保護 (guardianship). 2. kanri 管理 (care). 3. kōryū 拘留 (imprisonment).

custom, *n.* shūkan 習慣.

customary, *adj.* 1. futsū 普通 (usual). 2. itsumo no いつもの (habitual).

customer, *n.* (o)kyaku (お)客.

customs, *n.* 1. zeikan 税関 (office). 2. kanzei 関税 (tax).

cut, 1. *n.* kirikizu 切り傷 (wound); sakugen 削減 (reduction). 2. *vb.* kiru 切る (wound, divide); kireru 切れる (be sharp); mijikaku suru 短くする (shorten); **cut across** yokogiru 横切る.

cutback, *n.* sakugen 削減.

cute, *adj.* kawaii 可愛い.

cutlet, *n.* katsu(retsu) カツ(レツ).

cutter, *n.* kattā カッター.

cutting, *n.* 1. kiru koto 切ること (act of cutting). 2. kirinuki 切り抜き (clipping). 3. kirieda 切り枝 (cut stem).

cycle, *n.* 1. saikuru サイクル; shūki 周期 (regular occurrence, recurring time). 2. jitensha 自転車 (bicycle).

cyclical, *adj.* shūki-teki (na) 周期的 (な) (occurring regularly).

cycling, *n.* saikuringu サイクリング.

cyclist, *n.* saikurisuto サイクリスト.

cyclone, *n.* saikuron サイクロン.

cylinder, *n.* 1. entō 円筒; enchūkei 円柱形 (round elongated solid). 2. shirindā シリンダー (machine part).

cymbal, *n.* shinbaru シンバル.

cynical, *adj.* shinikaru (na) シニカル (な); hinikuppoi 皮肉っぽい (distrustful, skeptical).

cynicism, *n.* reishō-teki na taido 冷笑的な態度 (cynical disposition).

cypress, *n.* itosugi 糸杉.

D

dab, *vb.* karuku ateru 軽く当てる.

dabble in, *vb.* omoshirohanbun de suru 面白半分でする.

dad, *n.* otōsan お父さん; papa パパ.

dagger, *n.* tantō 短刀.

daily, 1. *n.* nikkanshi 日刊紙 (newspaper). 2. *adj.* mainichi (no) 毎日 (の). 3. *adv.* mainichi 毎日.

dainty, *adj.* kyasha (na) 華奢 (な).

dairy, *n.* 1. nyūseihinten 乳製品店 (store). 2. rakunōjō 酪農場 (farm).

daisy, *n.* deijī デイジー; hinagiku ひな菊.

dally, *vb.* 1. guzu-guzu suru ぐずぐずする (delay). 2. tawamureru 戯れる (flirt).

dam, *n.* damu ダム.

damage, 1. *n.* damēji ダメージ; songai 損害. 2. *vb.* songai o ataeru 損害を与える.

dame, *n.* 1. on'na no hito 女の人 (woman). 2. kifujin 貴婦人 (woman of rank).

damn, 1. *vb.* jigoku ni otosu 地獄に落とす (condemn to hell); kokuhyō suru 酷評する (declare bad). 2. *interj.* Chikushō 畜生.

damned, 1. *adj.* mattaku (no) 全く (の) (utter); norowarete iru 呪われている (cursed); **damned fool** mattaku no baka. 2. *adv.* mattaku 全く (extremely).

damp, *adj.* shimeppoi 湿っぽい.

dampen, *vb.* shimerasu 湿らす (make moist); shimeru 湿る (become moist).

dampness, *n.* shikke 湿気.

dance, 1. *n.* dansu ダンス; odori 踊り (dancing); dansu pātī ダンスパーティー (party with dancing). 2. *vb.* odoru 踊る.

dancer, *n.* dansā ダンサー; odorite 踊り手.

dandelion, *n.* tanpopo たんぽぽ.

dandruff, *n.* fuke ふけ.

dandy, *n.* dandī ダンディー.

danger, *n.* 1. kiken 危険 (exposure to harm); kiki 危機 (threat). 2. **be in danger of** (... no) osore ga aru

(... の) 恐れがある; **in danger** kitoku 危篤 (critically ill); **out of danger** kiki o dassuru 危機を脱する.

dangerous, *adj.* kiken (na) 危険 (な).

dangle, *vb.* 1. burasagaru/ burasageru ぶら下がる／ぶら下げる (hang/cause to hang). 2. bura-bura suru/saseru ぶらぶらする／させる (swing/cause to swing).

dare, *vb.* 1. idomu 挑む (face boldly); unagasu 促す (challenge a person). 2. (... suru) yūki ga aru (... する) 勇気がある (have courage).

daredevil, *n.* mukōmizu na ningen 向こう見ずな人間.

daring, 1. *adj.* yūkan (na) 勇敢 (な) (brave); daitan (na) 大胆 (な) (bold). 2. *n.* yūki 勇気 (bravery).

dark, 1. *n.* kurayami 暗闇 (absence of light); yūgure 夕暮 (nightfall); **after dark** yūgure no ato; **in the dark** shiranai 知らない (ignorant). 2. *adj.* kurai 暗い (having no light); kuroppoi 黒っぽい (blackish); iroguro (no) 色黒 (の) (swarthy); **Dark Ages** ankokujidai 暗黒時代; **dark horse** dāku-hōsu ダークホース.

darken, *vb.* kuraku naru/suru 暗くなる／する (become/make dark).

darkroom, *n.* anshitsu 暗室.

darling, 1. *n.* anata あなた (wife addressing husband); itoshii hito 愛しい人 (loved one). 2. *adj.* itoshii 愛しい (beloved).

darn, *vb.* tsukurou 繕う.

dart, 1. *n.* nageya 投げ矢 (arrow); tosshin 突進 (dash). 2. *vb.* tosshin suru 突進する (walk or run swiftly); satto ... suru さっと... する (act suddenly and quickly).

dash, 1. *n.* tosshin 突進 (run); dasshu ダッシュ (punctuation); **a dash of** shō-shō (no) 少々 (の). 2. *vb.* isogu 急ぐ (hurry); nagetsukeru 投げつける (throw violently against); kudaku 砕く (destroy).

dashboard, *n.* keikiban 計器盤 (car).

data, *n.* 1. dēta データ; jōhō 情報 (information). 2. **data processing** dēta-shori データ処理.

date, 1. *n.* nengappi 年月日; hizuke 日付 (particular time); yakusoku 約束 (appointment); dēto デート (with member of opposite sex); **date of birth** seinengappi; **out of date** jidaiokure 時代おくれ (old-fashioned); kigengire 期限切れ (invalid); **to date** ima made no tokoro 今までのところ. 2. *vb.* hi o kimeru 日を決める (fix the date for); hizuke ga aru 日付がある (show the date of); hizuke o kaku 日付を書く (write the date on); furuku naru 古くなる (become out of date); dēto suru デートする (go on a date).

daub, *vb.* nuritsukeru 塗り付ける (cover with mud, paint, etc.).

daughter, *n.* musume 娘.

daughter-in-law, *n.* yome 嫁.

daunt, *vb.* 1. iki o kujiku 意気を挫く (dishearten). 2. kowagaraseru 怖がらせる (frighten).

dauntless, *adj.* yūkan (na) 勇敢 (な).

dawdle, *vb.* 1. bura-bura suru ぶらぶらする (waste time). 2. guzu-guzu suru 愚図愚図する (be slow).

dawn, 1. *n.* yoake 夜明け. 2. *vb.* yo ga akeru 夜が明ける (begin to grow light); kizuku 気付く

(notice, realize); **It dawned on me that ...** ni kizuita.

day, *n.* 1. hi 日 (24 hours). 2. hiru(ma) 昼(間) (daytime). 3. **all day** ichinichijū 一日中; **day after day** mainichi 毎日; **day after tomorrow** asatte あさって; **day before yesterday** ototoi おととい; **every day** mainichi 毎日; **every other day** ichinichi oki ni 一日おきに; **the next day** yokujitsu 翌日; **one day** itsuka いつか (someday); ichinichi 一日 (single day); **the other day** senjitsu 先日; **these days** konogoro この頃.

daybreak, *n.* yoake 夜明け.

day-care center, *n.* hoikusho 保育所.

daydream, *n.* hakuchūmu 白昼夢; musō 夢想.

daylight, *n.* hi no hikari 日の光; nikkō 日光.

daylight saving time, *n.* samā-taimu サマータイム.

daytime, *n.* hiru (ma) 昼 (間).

daze, *vb.* azen to saserareru 啞然とさせられる (stun).

dazzle, *vb.* 1. me o kuramaseru 目を眩ませる (blind). 2. miwaku suru 魅惑する (fascinate).

dead, *adj.* 1. shindeiru 死んでいる (no longer alive or active). 2. sutareteiru すたれている (obsolete, in decline). 3. mukankaku (no) 無感覚 (の) (bereft of sensation). 4. kireteiru きれている (without power or charge); ugokanai 動かない (no longer functioning).

deaden, *vb.* osaeru 抑える; yowameru 弱める (lower intensity).

dead end, *n.* ikidomari 行き止ま

り.

deadline, *n.* shimekiri 締め切り; kigen 期限.

deadlock, *n.* ikizumari 行き詰まり.

deadly, *adj.* 1. chimei-teki (na) 致命的 (な) (fatal); shi o motarasu 死をもたらす (lethal). 2. tsūretsu (na) 痛烈 (な) (unrelenting).

deaf, *adj.* 1. mimi ga kikoenai 耳が聞こえない. 2. **turn a deaf ear to ...** ni mimi o kasanai に耳を貸さない.

deaf-mute, *n.* rōasha 聾唖者.

deal, 1. *n.* torihiki 取り引き (commerce); **a good/great deal** ii kaimono 買い物 (a bargain). 2. *vb.* kubaru 配る (distribute); **deal with ...** ni taisho suru ... に対処する (handle, treat); ... **to** torihiki o suru ... と取り引きをする (commerce); **deal in ...** o atsukau ... を扱う (commerce).

dealer, *n.* dīrā ディーラー (commerce).

dear, *adj.* 1. taisetsu (na) 大切 (な) (precious). 2. takai 高い (expensive). 3. haikei 拝啓 (salutation in letters).

death, *n.* 1. shi 死 (end of life); **death certificate** shibō-shōmeishō; **death penalty** shikei. 2. owari 終わり (end).

debacle, *n.* hōkai 崩壊.

debase, *vb.* hinshitsu o sageru 品質を下げる (reduce quality); kachi o sageru 価値を下げる (devalue).

debate, 1. *n.* tōron 討論. 2. *vb.* hanashiau 話し合う; tōron suru 討論する.

debauch, *vb.* daraku saseru 堕落させる.

debauchery, *n.* hōtō 放蕩.

debilitate, *vb.* suijaku saseru 衰弱させる.

debit, *n.* kari'iregaku 借入額 (borrowed money).

debris, *n.* gareki がれき (rubble); zangai 残骸 (ruins).

debt, *n.* 1. shakkin 借金; fusai 負債 (money); **be in debt** shakkin ga aru. 2. ongi 恩義 (obligation).

debtor, *n.* fusaisha 負債者.

debunk, *vb.* uso o bakuro suru 嘘を暴露する.

debut, 1. *n.* debyū デビュー. 2. *vb.* debyū suru デビューする.

decade, *n.* jūnenkan 十年間.

decadence, *n.* taihai 退廃.

decadent, *adj.* taihai-teki (na) 退廃的 (な).

decaffeinated, *adj.* dekafe デカフェ; kafein'nuki (no) カフェイン抜き (の).

decapitate, *vb.* kubi o haneru 首をはねる.

decay, 1. *n.* otoroe 衰え (decline); mushiba 虫歯 (teeth); fuhai 腐敗 (rot). 2. *vb.* otoroeru 衰える (decline); mushiba ni naru 虫歯になる (teeth); areru 荒れる (crumble); fuhai suru 腐敗する (rot).

deceased, *adj.* shibō shita 死亡した.

deceit, *n.* 1. itsuwari 偽り (deception). 2. sagi 詐欺 (fraud).

deceitful, *adj.* uso (no) 嘘 (の); itsuwari (no) 偽り (の).

deceive, *vb.* damasu だます.

December, *n.* jūnigatsu 十二月.

decency, *n.* 1. reigi tadashisa 礼儀正しさ (courteousness). 2. jōhinsa 上品さ (propriety).

decent, *adj.* 1. reigi tadashii 礼儀正しい (respectable, courteous). 2. jōhin (na) 上品 (な) (not obscene). 3. ii いい (good). 4. shinsetsu (na) 親切 (な) (kind).

decentralize, *vb.* bunsan suru 分散する.

deception, *n.* 1. uso 嘘 (lie); damashi だまし (act of deceiving). 2. sagi 詐欺 (fraud).

deceptive, *adj.* 1. itsuwari (no) 偽り (の) (deceiving). 2. magirawashii 紛らわしい (misleading).

decide, *vb.* 1. kimeru 決める; kettei suru 決定する (conclude, settle, etc.); kesshin suru 決心する (make up one's mind). 2. hanketsu o kudasu 判決を下す (law). 3. kaiketsu suru 解決する (solve).

decimal, *adj.* 1. shōsū (no) 小数 (の) (of tenths); **decimal point** shōsūten. 2. jusshinhō (no) 十進法 (の) (of tens).

decipher, *vb.* kaidoku suru 解読する.

decision, *n.* 1. kettei 決定; ketsuron 結論 (conclusion, settlement); kesshin 決心 (making up one's mind); **reach a decision** ketsuron ni tassuru. 2. hanketsu 判決 (law).

decisive, *adj.* 1. kettei-teki (na) 決定的 (な) (determining). 2. dankotaru 断固たる (resolute).

deck, *n.* dekki デッキ (of ship, patio).

declaration, *n.* 1. sengen 宣言 (proclamation). 2. shinkoku 申告 (at Customs, etc.).

declare, *vb.* 1. sengen suru 宣言する (proclaim). 2. shinkoku suru 申告する (at Customs, etc.). 3. dangen suru 断言する (affirm).

declension, *n.* kakuhenka 格変化.

decline, 1. *n.* genshō 減少 (decrease); suitai 衰退; botsuraku 没落 (downfall); suijaku 衰弱 (of health). 2. *vb*. jitai suru 辞退する (refuse); otoroeru 衰える (diminish, weaken); sagaru 下がる (drop).

decompose, *vb*. 1. kusaru 腐る (become rotten). 2. bunkai suru 分解する (separate into parts).

décor, *n*. kazaritsuke 飾りつけ (decoration); shitsunai-sōshoku 室内装飾 (interior decoration).

decorate, *vb*. 1. kazaru 飾る (adorn). 2. naisō o suru 内装をする (house). 3. kunshō o ataeru 勲章を与える (military).

decoration, *n*. 1. kazari 飾り (adornment). 2. kunshō 勲章 (military).

decorum, *n*. 1. shakaikihan 社会規範 (social propriety). 2. reigi 礼儀 (conventions of polite behavior).

decoy, *n*. otori おとり.

decrease, 1. *n*. genshō 減少 (decreasing). 2. *vb*. heru/herasu 減る／減らす (become/make less in quantity); sagaru/sageru 下がる／下げる (become/make less in quality or degree).

decree, 1. *n*. meirei 命令 (command). 2. *vb*. meijiru 命じる.

decrepit, *adj*. yobo-yobo (no) よぼよぼ (の) (infirm); gata-gata (no) がたがた (の) (run-down).

decry, *vb*. kenasu けなす.

dedicate, *vb*. sasageru 捧げる (devote, give, inscribe in honor of someone); **dedicate oneself to** ... ni mi o sasageru (devote oneself to); ... ni sen'nen suru ... に専念する (be absorbed in).

dedication, *n*. 1. kenshin 献身 (devotion). 2. kenji 献辞 (book).

deduce, *vb*. suitei suru 推定する.

deduct, *vb*. sashihiku 差し引く.

deduction, *n*. 1. suitei 推定 (inference). 2. kōjo 控除 (what is subtracted).

deed, *n*. 1. okonai 行い (action). 2. shōsho 証書 (legal title).

deem, *vb*. ... to minasu/omou ... と見なす／思う (consider/think).

deep, *adj*. 1. fukai 深い (extending far down, profound); okuyuki ga aru 奥行きがある (extending far into the rear). 2. koi 濃い (dark). 3. **in deep** hamarikonde はまり込んで; **in deep water** hijō ni komatte 非常に困って.

deepen, *vb*. 1. fukameru 深める (make deep); fukaku naru 深くなる (become deep). 2. koku suru/naru 濃くする／なる (make/become darker).

deer, *vb*. shika 鹿.

deface, *vb*. sokonau 損う (mar).

defamation, *n*. chūshō 中傷 (slander); meiyokison 名誉毀損 (attacking of reputation).

defame, *vb*. chūshō suru 中傷する (slander).

default, 1. *n*. taiman 怠慢 (neglect); furikō 不履行 (failure to meet legal obligation); **win by default** fusenshō suru 不戦勝する. 2. *vb*. okotaru 怠る (fail to meet obligation).

defeat, 1. *n*. haiboku 敗北 (act of losing). 2. *vb*. makasu 負かす (overthrow).

defect, 1. *n*. kekkan 欠陥 (imperfection); ketten 欠点 (fault). 2. *vb*. bōmei suru 亡命する (forsake one's country).

defective, *adj*. kekkan ga aru 欠陥がある.

defend, *vb*. 1. mamoru 守る (protect). 2. benmei suru 弁明する (justify). 3. bengo suru 弁護す

る (law).

defendant, *n*. hikoku 被告.

defense, *n*. 1. bōei 防衛 (resistance to attack). 2. bengo 弁護 (defending argument).

defenseless, *adj*. mubōbi (no) 無防備 (の).

defensive, *adj*. 1. bōeiyō (no) 防衛用 (の) (used for defending). 2. benkaigamashii 弁解がましい (attitude). 2. **be on the defensive** mamori ni mawaru 守りに回る.

defer, *vb*. enki suru 延期する (postpone).

deference, *n*. kei'i 敬意.

defiance, *n*. hankō 反抗 (bold resistance); **in defiance of** ... ni sakaratte ... に逆らって.

defiant, *adj*. hankō-teki (na) 反抗的 (な) (rebellious).

deficiency, *n*. 1. ketsubō 欠乏 (lack). 2. kekkan 欠陥 (defect).

deficient (in), *adj*. 1. (... ga) tarinai (... が) 足りない (insufficient, lacking). 2. ... ni kakeru ... に欠ける (defective).

deficit, *n*. akaji 赤字 (deficiency of funds).

defile, *vb*. 1. kegasu 汚す (befoul). 2. bōtoku suru 冒涜する (desecrate).

define, *vb*. 1. teigi suru 定義する (state meaning of). 2. meikaku ni suru 明確にする (clarify).

definite, *adj*. meikaku (na) 明確 (な) (clear).

definition, *n*. 1. teigi 定義 (statement that defines). 2. meikakusa 明確さ (clearness).

definitive, *adj*. saigo (no) 最後 (の) (final); kettei-teki (na) 決定的 (な) (conclusive).

deflect, *vb*. soreru/sorasu それる／

そらす (turn/cause to turn from true course).

deform, *vb*. 1. kuzusu 崩す (disfigure). 2. sokonau 損う (spoil).

deformity, *n*. 1. fugu 不具 (physical impairment). 2. kikei 奇形 (abnormally formed part).

defraud, *vb*. (... kara) sakushu suru (... から) 搾取する.

defray, *vb*. shiharau 支払う.

defrost, *vb*. 1. shimo o tokasu 霜を溶かす (de-ice). 2. kaitō suru 解凍する (unfreeze).

deft, *adj*. takumi (na) 巧み (な).

defunct, *adj*. 1. shindeiru 死んでいる (dead). 2. sutareteiru すたれている (not in use).

defy, *vb*. teikō suru 抵抗する (challenge).

degenerate, 1. *adj*. daraku shiteiru 堕落している (corrupt). 2. *vb*. daraku suru 堕落する (become corrupt); akka suru 悪化する (deteriorate).

degrade, *vb*. 1. otoshimeru 貶める (humiliate). 2. sageru 下げる (debase, lower).

degrading, *adj*. kutsujoku-teki (na) 屈辱的 (な) (humiliating).

degree, *n*. 1. do 度 (intensity, angle, temperature). 2. teido 程度 (extent); **to a certain degree** aru teido; **by degrees** jojo ni 徐々に. 3. gakui 学位 (academic achievement).

dehydrate, *vb*. dassui suru 脱水する.

deify, *vb*. shinkakuka suru 神格化する.

deign, *vb*. **deign to do** shite kudasaru して下さる (condescend to do).

deity, *n*. kami 神.

dejected, *adj.* rakutan shiteiru 落胆している.

dejection, *n.* rakutan 落胆.

delay, 1. *n.* okure 遅れ. 2. *vb.* enki suru 延期する (postpone); temadoraseru 手間取らせる (hinder).

delegate, 1. *n.* daihyō 代表 (representative); dairi 代理 (proxy). 2. *vb.* daihyō to shite okuru 代表として送る (send as a representative); inin suru 委任する (commit to another).

delegation, *n.* 1. haken 派遣 (act of sending). 2. daihyōdan 代表団 (group).

delete, *vb.* kesu 消す.

deletion, *n.* sakujo 削除.

deliberate, 1. *adj.* koi (no) 故意 (の) (intentional); shinchō (na) 慎重 (な) (cautious); yūchō (na) 悠長 (な) (unhurried). 2. *vb.* shingi suru 審議する (discuss); jukkō suru 熟考する (reflect).

delicacy, *n.* 1. sensaisa 繊細さ (fineness). 2. chinmi 珍味 (food).

delicate, *adj.* 1. derikēto (na) デリケート (な); sensai (na) 繊細 (な) (dainty and fragile). 2. bimyō (na) 微妙 (な) (requiring tact).

delicatessen, *n.* derikatessen デリカテッセン.

delicious, *adj.* oishii おいしい.

delight, 1. *n.* yorokobi 喜び. 2. *vb.* tanoshimaseru 楽しませる; **delight in ...** o tanoshimu.

delightful, *adj.* tanoshii 楽しい.

delineate, *vb.* egaku 描く (describe, sketch).

delinquency, *n.* hikō 非行 (wrongdoing by youth).

delinquent, 1. *n.* furyō 不良 (young wrongdoer). 2. *adj.* miharai (no) 未払い (の) (past due on debt).

delirious, *adj.* seishinsakuran (no) 精神錯乱 (の) (deranged).

delirium, *n.* seishinsakuran 精神錯乱.

deliver, *vb.* 1. haitatsu suru 配達する (convey); tewatasu 手渡す (hand over). 2. kaihō suru 解放する (free). 3. enzetsu suru 演説する (speak in public). 4. motarasu もたらす (produce). 5. osan o tasukeru お産を助ける (deliver a baby).

delivery, *n.* haitatsu 配達 (act of conveying). 2. osan お産 (childbirth). 3. kaihō 解放 (liberation). 4. enzetsu no shikata 演説の仕方 (style of public speaking).

delta, *n.* deruta デルタ.

delude, *vb.* damasu だます.

deluge, *n.* 1. kōzui 洪水 (flood). 2. gōu 豪雨 (heavy rain).

delusion, *n.* sakkaku 錯覚 (misconception).

deluxe, *adj.* derakkusu (na) デラックス (な).

delve, *vb.* saguru 探る.

demagogue, *n.* sendōsha 扇動者.

demagoguery, *n.* sendō 扇動.

demand, 1. *n.* yōkyū 要求 (requirement); shuchō 主張 (claim); juyō 需要 (commerce); **be in great demand** juyō ga ōi. 2. *vb.* yōkyū suru 要求する; shuchō suru 主張する.

demanding, *adj.* taihen (na) 大変 (な) (difficult).

demeaning, *adj.* kutsujoku-teki (na) 屈辱的 (な).

demeanor, *n.* furumai ふるまい.

demented, *adj.* kichigai (no) 気違い (の).

demise, *n.* shi 死.

democracy, *n.* 1. demokurashī デモクラシー; minshushugi 民主主義 (social equality). 2. minshushugi kokka 民主主義国家 (democratic country).

democrat, *n.* 1. minshushugisha 民主主義者 (believer in democracy). 2. **Democrat** minshutōin 民主党員 (member of party).

democratic, *adj.* minshu-teki (na) 民主的 (な) (of democracy).

demolish, *n.* torikowasu 取り壊す (tear down); tsubusu つぶす (crush).

demon, *n.* akurei 悪霊.

demonstrate, *vb.* 1. shimesu 示す (show); arawasu 表わす (express). 2. shōmei suru 証明する (prove); setsumei suru 説明する (explain). 3. demo o suru デモをする (parade).

demonstration, *n.* 1. jitsuen 実演 (display, exhibition). 2. setsumei 説明 (explanation). 3. demo デモ (political).

demoralize, *vb.* 1. ikishōchin saseru 意気消沈させる (discourage). 2. daraku saseru 堕落させる (corrupt).

demote, *vb.* chii o sageru 地位を下げる.

demur, *vb.* hantai suru 反対する (object).

demure, *adj.* 1. hikaeme (na) 控え目 (な) (shy and modest). 2. torisumashite-iru とりすましている (coyly sedate).

den, *n.* 1. dōkutsu 洞窟 (home of wild animal or criminal). 2. gorakushitsu 娯楽室 (family room).

denial, *n.* 1. hitei 否定 (negation). 2. kyohi 拒否 (refusal).

denim, *n.* denimu デニム.

Denmark, *n.* denmāku デンマーク.

denomination, *n.* 1. kaheikachi 貨幣価値 (value of monetary unit). 2. meishō 名称 (name). 3. shūha 宗派 (religion).

denominator, *n.* bunbo 分母.

denote, *vb.* shimesu 示す (indicate); imi suru 意味する (mean).

denounce, *vb.* hinan suru 非難する.

dense, *adj.* 1. misshū shiteiru 密集している (crowded). 2. koi 濃い (thick). 3. nibui 鈍い (slow).

density, *n.* mitsudo 密度.

dent, 1. *n.* hekomi 凹み; kubomi 窪み (depression). 2. *vb.* hekomaseru 凹ませる.

dental, *adj.* ha (no) 歯 (の).

dentist, *n.* haisha 歯医者.

dentistry, *n.* shikaigaku 歯科医学.

denture, *n.* ireba 入れ歯.

denunciation, *n.* hinan 非難.

deny, *vb.* 1. kyozetsu suru 拒絶する (refuse to agree or give). 2. hitei suru 否定する (negate).

deodorant, *n.* bōshūzai 防臭剤 (deodorizer); deodoranto デオドラント (for human body).

depart, *vb.* 1. saru 去る; iku 行く (go away); deru 出る (train, etc.). 2. shinu 死ぬ (die).

department, *n.* ka 課 (business, etc.); gakubu 学部 (university).

department store, *n.* depāto デパート.

departure, *n.* shuppatsu 出発 (act of leaving).

depend, *vb.* **depend on** 1. ... ni tayoru ... に頼る (rely on); ... o ate ni suru ... を当てにする (count on). 2. shin'yō suru 信用する

(trust). 3. ... shidai de aru ... 次第
である (be contingent on).

dependable, *adj.* shin'yō dekiru 信
用できる (trustworthy); ate ni
naru 当てになる (reliable).

dependence, *n.* izon 依存 (state of
being supported).

dependent, 1. *n.* fuyōkazoku 扶養
家族 (family). 2. *adj.* ... shidai
(no) ... 次第 (の) (contingent);
izon shiteiru 依存している
(supported).

depict, *vb.* egaku 描く.

depiction, *n.* byōsha 描写.

deplete, *vb.* herasu 減らす
(lessen); kara ni suru 空にする
(empty).

deplore, *vb.* kanashimu 悲しむ
(lament).

deploy, *vb.* haichi suru 配置する
(military).

deport, *vb.* kyōseisōkan suru 強制
送還する.

deposit, 1. *n.* yokin 預金 (bank);
tetsukekin 手付け金; hoshōkin 保
証金 (for purchasing something);
shikikin 敷金 (for renting an
apartment). 2. *vb.* oku 置く
(place); yokin suru 預金する.

depositor, *n.* yokinsha 預金者
(bank).

depot, *n.* 1. eki 駅 (station). 2.
sōko 倉庫 (storehouse).

depraved, *adj.* ja'aku (na) 邪悪
(な).

deprecate, *vb.* 1. hantai suru 反対
する (protest). 2. hinan suru 非難
する (express disapproval).

depreciate, *vb.* geraku suru 下落す
る (decline in value).

depress, *vb.* 1. ochikomaseru 落ち
込ませる (make despondent). 2.
yowameru 弱める (weaken). 3.
osu 押す (press inward).

depressed, *adj.* 1. ochikondeiru 落
ち込んでいる (despondent). 2.
fukeiki (no) 不景気 (の)
(economy).

depression, *n.* 1. yū'utsu 憂うつ
(despondence). 2. fukyō 不況
(economy). 3. kubomi 凹み
(hollow).

deprive, *vb.* ubaitoru 奪い取る
(divest).

depth, *n.* 1. fukasa 深さ (distance
down); okuyuki 奥行き (distance
to the back). 2. fukami 深み
(profundity). 3. **in depth** tettei-
teki ni 徹底的に (thoroughly).

deputy, *n.* dairi 代理 (proxy).

derail, *vb.* dassen suru/saseru 脱線
する／させる (run/cause to run
off rails).

derange, *vb.* ki o kuruwaseru 気を
狂わせる (make insane); **be
deranged** kurutteiru 狂っている.

derelict, 1. *n.* furōsha 浮浪者
(vagrant). 2. *adj.* misuterareta 見
捨てられた (abandoned);
arehateta 荒れ果てた (left to
decay).

deride, *vb.* azawarau あざ笑う.

derision, *n.* azawarai あざ笑い.

derivative, *n.* 1. haseigo 派生語
(word). 2. haseibutsu 派生物
(something derived).

derive from, *vb.* 1. ... ni yurai suru
... に由来する (originate from). 2.
... kara kuru ... から来る (come or
stem from). 3. ... kara eru ... から
得る (obtain from).

derogatory, *adj.* chūshō-teki (na)
中傷的 (な).

descend, *vb.* 1. kudaru 下る; oriru
降りる (move down); shizumu 沈
む (settle, sink). 2. **descend
from** (... no) shison de aru (... の)
子孫である (be a descendant of).

descendant, *n.* shison 子孫.

descent, *n.* 1. kudarizaka 下り坂 (slope). 2. kakei 家系 (lineage).

describe, *vb.* byōsha suru 描写する (depict); setsumei suru 説明する (explain).

description, *n.* byōsha 描写 (depiction); setsumei 説明 (explanation).

descriptive, *adj.* byōsha-teki (na) 描写的 (な) (vivid).

desecrate, *vb.* bōtoku suru 冒瀆する (profane).

desert, 1. *n.* sabaku 砂漠 (sand). 2. *vb.* misuteru 見捨てる (abandon); dassō suru 脱走する (military).

deserter, *n.* dassōhei 脱走兵 (military).

deserve, *vb.* ... ni atai suru ... に値する (be worthy of).

design, 1. *n.* dezain デザイン (art of designing); sekkei 設計 (blueprint); keikaku 計画 (plan, project); ito 意図 (intention); keiryaku 計略 (plot). 2. *vb.* dezain suru デザインする; sekkei suru 設計する; keikaku suru 計画する; ito suru 意図する.

designate, *vb.* 1. shimesu 示す (indicate). 2. ninmei suru 任命する (appoint).

designation, *n.* 1. shitei 指定 (stipulation). 2. ninmei 任命 (appointment).

designer, *n.* dezainā デザイナー (of a dress, etc.); sekkeisha 設計者 (of a house, machine, etc.).

desirable, *adj.* nozomashii 望ましい.

desire, 1. *n.* netsubō 熱望 (strong wish); yokubō 欲望 (lust, greed). 2. *vb.* netsubō suru 熱望する (wish strongly); yokubō suru 欲望する (lust, be greedy).

desist, *vb.* yameru 止める (stop); **desist from doing** ... suru koto o yameru ... することを止める.

desk, *n.* 1. tsukue 机 (furniture). 2. desuku デスク (where a person in charge sits); **front desk** furonto-desuku フロントデスク.

desolate, *adj.* 1. kōryōtaru 荒涼たる (bleak); in'utsu (na) 陰うつ (な) (dismal). 2. uchihishigarete-iru 打ちひしがれている (dejected).

desolation, *n.* wabishisa わびしさ (bleakness, loneliness).

despair, 1. *n.* zetsubō 絶望. 2. *vb.* zetsubō suru 絶望する.

desperado, *n.* kyōakuhan 凶悪犯 (reckless criminal).

desperate, *adj.* 1. zetsubō-teki (na) 絶望的 (な) (hopeless). 2. hisshi (no) 必死 (の) (frantic); **be desperate for** hisshi ni ... o motomeru 必死に... を求める.

desperation, *n.* zetsubō 絶望.

despicable, *adj.* iyashii 卑しい.

despise, *vb.* keibetsu suru 軽蔑する.

despite, *prep.* ... nimo kakawarazu ... にもかかわらず.

despoil, *vb.* ryakudatsu suru 略奪する.

despondent, *adj.* ochikondeiru 落ち込んでいる (dejected); hikan-teki (na) 悲観的 (な) (pessimistic).

despot, *n.* bōkun 暴君.

dessert, *n.* dezāto デザート.

destination, *n.* mokutekichi 目的地 (trip); atesaki 宛先 (mail).

destined, *adj.* sadamerarete-iru 定められている.

destiny, *n.* unmei 運命.

destitute, *adj.* 1. gokuhin (no) 極貧 (の) (extreme poverty). 2. nai 無い (deprived).

destroy, *vb.* 1. hakai suru 破壊する (ruin, end). 2. korosu 殺す (kill).

destruction, *n.* hakai 破壊.

destructive, *adj.* hakai-teki (na) 破壊的 (な).

detach, *vb.* hazusu 外す (separate).

detail, 1. *n.* shōsai 詳細; **in detail** kuwashiku 詳しく. 2. *vb.* kuwashiku hanasu 詳しく話す (relate in detail).

detain, *vb.* 1. horyū suru 保留する (keep from proceeding). 2. tojikomeru 閉じ込める (confine).

detect, *vb.* 1. mitsukeru 見つける (discover). 2. satchi suru 察知する (perceive).

detective, *n.* tantei 探偵 (investigator); keibu 警部 (police); **detective novel** tanteishōsetsu.

detector, *n.* tanchiki 探知器.

detention, *n.* kōryū 拘留.

deter, *vb.* samatageru 妨げる.

detergent, *n.* senzai 洗剤.

deteriorate, *vb.* akka suru 悪化する.

determination, *n.* 1. ketsui 決意 (fortitude). 2. kettei 決定 (conclusion).

determine, *vb.* kimeru 決める (decide, conclude, resolve, intend).

detest, *vb.* ken'o suru 嫌悪する.

detonate, *vb.* bakuhatsu suru/saseru 爆発する／させる (erupt/cause to erupt).

detour, *n.* ukairo 迂回路; mawarimichi 回り道.

detract, *vb.* sokonau 損う (spoil); **detract from** ... o sokonau.

detriment, *n.* gai 害 (harm); **to the detriment of** ... o gai shite ... を害して.

detrimental, *adj.* **detrimental to** ... ni gai ga aru ... に害がある (harmful to).

devalue, *vb.* 1. kachi o sageru 価値を下げる (reduce in value). 2. heika o kirisageru 平価を切り下げる (currency).

devastate, *vb.* uchinomesu 打ちのめす.

devastating, *adj.* 1. kaimetsu-teki (na) 壊滅的 (な) (completely destructive). 2. shokku (na) ショック (な) (shocking).

develop, *vb.* 1. sodatsu/sodateru 育つ／育てる (grow/cause to grow); hatten suru/saseru 発展する／させる (evolve or advance/cause to evolve or advance). 2. genzō suru 現像する (photo).

development, *n.* 1. seichō 成長 (growth). 2. hatten 発展 (advance, new event). 3. genzō 現像 (photo).

deviate, *vb.* itsudatsu suru 逸脱する (depart from an accepted course).

deviation, *n.* itsudatsu 逸脱.

device, *n.* 1. kufū 工夫 (contrivance). 2. keikaku 計画 (plan).

devil, *n.* akuma 悪魔.

devilish, *adj.* akuma no yō (na) 悪魔のよう (な).

devious, *adj.* 1. magarikunette-iru 曲がりくねっている (circuitous). 2. kōkatsu (na) 狡猾 (な) (underhanded).

devise, *vb.* kangaetsuku 考えつく (form a plan, contrive).

devoid, *adj.* **be devoid of** ... ga nai ... が無い.

devote, *vb.* 1. sasageru 捧げる (consecrate, commit). 2. ateru 充てる (set aside). 3. **devote oneself to** ... ni sen'nen suru ... に専念する (immerse oneself in);

... ni mi o sasageru ... に身を捧げる (commit oneself to).

devotee, *n.* shinpōsha 信奉者.

devotion, *n.* 1. sasageru koto 捧げること; kenshin 献身 (consecration, act of consigning). 2. aichaku 愛着 (attachment). 3. shinjin 信心 (religious faith).

devour, *vb.* musaboru 貪る.

devout, *adj.* 1. nesshin (na) 熱心 (な) (ardent). 2. shinjinbukai 信心深い (pious).

dew, *n.* tsuyu 露.

dexterity, *n.* kiyōsa 器用さ; takumisa 巧みさ.

diabetes, *n.* tōnyōbyō 糖尿病.

diabolic, *adj.* akuma-teki (na) 悪魔的 (な).

diagnose, *vb.* shindan suru 診断する.

diagnosis, *n.* shindan 診断.

diagonal, *adj.* taikakusen 対角線.

diagram, *n.* zuhyō 図表 (chart, plan).

dial, 1. *n.* mojiban 文字盤 (clock, watch); tsumami つまみ (knob); daiyaru ダイヤル (phone, radio). 2. *vb.* daiyaru o awaseru ダイヤルを合わせる (radio); denwa suru 電話する (phone).

dialect, *n.* hōgen 方言.

dialogue, *n.* taiwa 対話.

diameter, *n.* chokkei 直径.

diamond, *n.* daiyamondo ダイヤモンド.

diaper, *n.* omutsu おむつ.

diaphragm, *n.* ōkakumaku 横隔膜 (muscle).

diarrhea, *n.* geri 下痢.

diary, *n.* nikki 日記; **keep a diary** nikki o tsukeru 日記をつける.

dice, *n.* saikoro さいころ.

dichotomy, *n.* nibun 二分.

dictate, *vb.* 1. kakitoraseru 書き取らせる (say something to be written down). 2. meirei suru 命令する (command).

dictation, *n.* kakitori 書き取り (act of writing down); dikutēshon ディクテーション (test).

dictator, *n.* dokusaisha 独裁者.

dictatorship, *n.* dokusaiseiji 独裁政治.

diction, *n.* hanashikata 話し方 (style of speaking).

dictionary, *n.* jiten 辞典; jisho 辞書.

didactic, *adj.* kyōkun-teki (na) 教訓的 (な).

die, 1. *n.* saikoro さいころ (singular of dice); daisu ダイス (machining). 2. *vb.* shinu 死ぬ (person, animal); kareru 枯れる (plant); owaru 終わる (cease); **die away** jojo ni kieteiku 徐々に消えて行く; **be dying for/to** ... ga totemo hoshii/shitai ... がとても欲しい／したい; **die of** ... de shinu; **die down** yowamaru 弱まる; **die out** shinitaeru.

diet, *n.* 1. tabemono 食べ物 (food); daietto (shokuhin) ダイエット(食品) (food chosen for health, etc.); **go on a diet** daietto o suru. 2. **Diet** kokkai 国会 (Japanese legislative assembly).

differ, *vb.* 1. kotonaru 異なる (be unlike). 2. iken ga kotonaru 意見が異なる (disagree).

difference, *n.* 1. chigai 違い (unlikeness). 2. iken no shōtotsu 意見の衝突 (disagreement, quarrel). 3. sa 差 (amount separating two quantities).

different, *adj.* 1. chigau 違う (unlike). 2. iro-iro (na) 色々 (な) (various).

differentiate, *vb.* 1. kubetsu suru

区別する (distinguish). 2. sabetsu suru 差別する (discriminate).

difficult, *adj.* 1. muzukashii 難しい (hard to do). 2. kimuzukashii 気難しい (unfriendly).

difficulty, *n.* kon'nan 困難 (trouble, predicament); mondai 問題 (problem).

diffuse, 1. *adj.* bunsan-teki (na) 分散的 (な) (spread out). 2. *vb.* bunsan suru/saseru 分散する／させる (spread out/cause to spread out).

dig, *vb.* 1. horu 掘る (shovel, excavate); **dig up** horiokosu (excavate). 2. sagashidasu 捜し出す (find out).

digest, 1. *n.* daijesuto ダイジェスト (summary). 2. *vb.* shōka suru 消化する (absorb, comprehend).

digestion, *n.* shōka 消化 (absorption, comprehension).

digit, *n.* 1. keta 桁 (number). 2. yubi 指 (finger, toe).

digital, *adj.* dejitaru (no) デジタル (の).

dignified, *adj.* igen ga aru 威厳がある (stately); kihin ga aru 気品がある (noble).

dignitary, *n.* meishi 名士.

dignity, *n.* igen 威厳 (stateliness); kihin 気品 (nobleness).

digress, *vb.* itsudatsu suru 逸脱する; soreru それる (diverge).

digression, *n.* itsudatsu 逸脱.

dike, *n.* 1. teibō 堤防 (bank, wall). 2. mizo 溝 (ditch).

dilapidated, *adj.* onboro (no) おんぼろ (の).

dilate, *vb.* hirogaru/hirogeru 広がる／広げる (expand/cause to expand).

dilemma, *n.* jirenma ジレンマ.

diligent, *adj.* kinben (na) 勤勉

(な).

dilute, *vb.* 1. usumeru 薄める (thin). 2. yowameru 弱める (weaken).

dim, 1. *adj.* usugurai 薄暗い (not bright); fumeiryō (na) 不明瞭 (な) (indistinct). 2. *vb.* usuguraku naru/suru 薄暗くなる／する (become/make dim).

dimension, *n.* 1. sunpō 寸法 (measurement). 2. ōkisa 大きさ (magnitude, size).

diminish, *vb.* 1. heru/herasu 減る／減らす (decrease/cause to decrease). 2. yowamaru/yowameru 弱まる／弱める (wane/cause to wane).

diminutive, 1. *n.* aishō 愛称 (name). 2. *adj.* chiisai 小さい (small).

dimple, *n.* ekubo えくぼ.

din, *n.* sō'on 騒音.

dine, *vb.* shokuji o suru 食事をする; **dine out** gaishoku suru 外食する.

diner, *n.* 1. kyaku 客 (customer). 2. keishokudō 軽食堂 (restaurant). 3. shokudōsha 食堂車 (dining car).

dingy, *adj.* misuborashii みすぼらしい.

dining car, *n.* shokudōsha 食堂車.

dining room, *n.* shokudō 食堂.

dinner, *n.* 1. shokuji 食事 (meal); chūshoku 昼食 (lunch); yūshoku 夕食 (evening meal). 2. seisan 正餐 (formal dinner).

dinosaur, *n.* kyōryū 恐竜.

dip, 1. *n.* kudarizaka 下り坂 (slope). 2. *vb.* ireru 入れる; tsukeru 浸ける (plunge); sukuiageru すくい上げる (scoop); sagaru 下がる (slope down).

diphtheria, *n.* jifuteria ジフテリア.

diploma, *n.* sotsugyō shōsho 卒業証書.

diplomacy, *n.* 1. gaikō 外交 (politics). 2. gaikōjutsu 外交術 (tact).

diplomat, *n.* gaikōkan 外交官.

diplomatic, *adj.* 1. gaikōjō (no) 外交上 (の) (of diplomacy). 2. josainai 如才ない (tactful).

dire, *adj.* 1. setsujitsu (na) 切実 (な) (acute, desperate). 2. osoroshii 恐ろしい (terrible).

direct, 1. *adj.* massugu (na, no) 真っ直ぐ (な、の) (straight); chokusetsu (no) 直接 (の) (immediate, nothing in between); chokkō (no) 直行 (の) (transportation); sotchoku (na) 率直 (な) (straightforward). 2. *vb.* hōkō o oshieru 方向を教える (guide, tell the way to); kantoku suru 監督する (control, manage); shiji suru 指示する (command); mukeru 向ける (turn).

direction, *n.* 1. hōkō 方向 (course). 2. shiji 指示 (instruction[s]); adobaisu アドバイス (advice). 3. kantoku 監督 (movies). 4. enshutsu 演出 (theater). 5. **in all directions** shihō ni 四方に; **under the direction of** (... no) shiji no moto ni.

directive, *n.* kunji 訓示.

director, *n.* 1. direkutā ディレクター; kantoku 監督 (movies). 2. jūyaku 重役 (business). 3. kanrisha 管理者 (one who directs).

directory, *n.* jūshoroku 住所録 (addresses); meibo 名簿 (names); denwachō 電話帳 (telephone numbers).

dirge, *n.* aitōka 哀悼歌.

dirt, *n.* 1. yogore 汚れ (filth). 2. tsuchi 土 (earth).

dirty, *adj.* 1. kitanai 汚ない (unclean, ignoble); **dirty trick[s]** kitanai teguchi. 2. hiwai (na) 卑猥 (な) (indecent).

disability, *n.* shintai shōgai 身体障害 (physical); seishin shōgai 精神障害 (mental).

disable, *vb.* 1. dekinaku suru 出来なくする (make impossible). 2. fugu ni suru 不具にする (cripple).

disabled, *n.* shintai shōgaisha 身体障害者 (people).

disadvantage, *n.* furi 不利; **be at a disadvantage** furi de aru.

disagree, *vb.* 1. iken ga awanai 意見が合わない (disagree with). 2. itchi shinai 一致しない (differ).

disagreeable, *adj.* fuyukai (na) 不愉快 (な).

disagreement, *n.* fuitchi 不一致 (discrepancy).

disappear, *vb.* 1. kieru 消える (go out of sight). 2. nakunaru なくなる (become lost).

disappearance, *n.* shōshitsu 消失; mienakunaru koto 見えなくなること.

disappoint, *vb.* gakkari saseru がっかりさせる (fail to fulfill a hope).

disappointed, *adj.* **be disappointed with** ... ni gakkari suru ... にがっかりする.

disappointment, *n.* rakutan 落胆 (failure to fulfill a hope).

disapproval, *n.* 1. hinin 否認 (rejection); (... e no) hantai (... への) 反対 (objection). 2. hihan 批判 (criticism).

disapprove, *vb.* 1. hinin suru 否認する; ... ni hantai suru ... に反対する. 2. hihan suru 批判する.

disarm, *vb.* 1. buki o toriageru 武器を取り上げる (take away weapon). 2. busōkaijo suru 武装解除する (military).

disarmament, *n.* busōkaijo 武装解除.

disarray, *n.* midare 乱れ (clothing); ranzatsu 乱雑 (room, house, etc.); **in disarray** midarete.

disassemble, *vb.* bunkai suru 分解する.

disaster, *n.* sainan 災難 (great misfortune); daisaigai 大災害 (catastrophe, natural disaster).

disastrous, *adj.* kaimetsu-teki (na) 壊滅的 (な) (devastating).

disavow, *vb.* hitei suru 否定する (deny).

disband, *vb.* kaisan suru 解散する.

disbelief, *n.* utagai 疑い.

disburse, *vb.* shiharau 支払う.

discard, *vb.* suteru 捨てる (thing); misuteru 見捨てる (person).

discern, *vb.* 1. mitomeru 認める (notice). 2. shikibetsu suru 識別する (distinguish).

discerning, *adj.* handanryoku ni tondeiru 判断力に富んでいる (judicious).

discharge, 1. *n.* rikō 履行 (fulfillment); hensai 返済 (act of paying); hōshutsu 放出 (emission); happō 発砲 (gunshot); jotai 除隊 (military); shakuhō 釈放 (jail, camp); tai'in 退院 (hospital). 2. *vb.* hatasu 果たす (fulfill duty, etc.); hensai suru 返済する (pay); hōshutsu suru 放出する (emit); happō suru 発砲する (fire gun); jotai saseru 除隊させる (military); tai'in saseru 退院させる (hospital); shakuhō suru 釈放する (prisoner).

disciple, *n.* deshi 弟子.

discipline, 1. *n.* tanren 鍛錬 (training in rules); kiritsu 規律 (subjection to rules); chōbatsu 懲罰 (punishment); senmonbun'ya 専門分野 (specialty). 2. *vb.* kunren suru 訓練する (train); bassuru 罰する (punish).

disclaim, *vb.* hitei suru 否定する (deny).

disclose, *vb.* akiraka ni suru 明らかにする (reveal); bakuro suru 暴露する (expose); shiraseru 知らせる (make known).

disclosure, *n.* bakuro 暴露 (exposure); shiraseru koto 知らせること (act of making known).

discolor, *vb.* henshoku suru 変色する.

discomfort, *n.* fukaikan 不快感 (uncomfortable sensation); fukai 不快 (lack of comfort).

disconcert, *vb.* tomadowaseru 戸惑わせる; urotaesaseru うろたえさせる.

disconnect, *vb.* 1. kirihanasu 切り放す (separate). 2. kiru 切る (cut off telephone, etc.). 3. tatsu 絶つ (cut off).

discontent, *n.* fuman 不満.

discontented, *adj.* **be discontented with** ... ni fuman de aru ... に不満である.

discontinue, *vb.* yameru 止める.

discord, *n.* 1. fuitchi 不一致 (disagreement); fuwa 不和 (strife). 2. fukyō waon 不協和音 (music).

discordant, *adj.* 1. itchi shinai 一致しない (conflicting). 2. fukyō waon (no) 不協和音 (の) (music).

discotheque, *n.* disuko ディスコ.

discount, 1. *n.* disukaunto ディスカウント; waribiki 割引. 2. *vb.* waribiki suru 割引する.

discourage, *vb.* 1. kujikesaseru 挫

けさせる (deprive of will);
rakutan saseru 落胆させる
(dishearten). 2. kinjiru 禁じる
(prohibit). 3. omoi todomaraseru
思いとどまらせる (dissuade).

discourse, *n.* 1. kōen 講演
(lecture). 2. giron 議論
(discussion).

discourtesy, *n.* shitsurei 失礼;
burei 無礼.

discover, *vb.* hakken suru 発見す
る.

discoverer, *n.* hakkensha 発見者.

discovery, *n.* hakken 発見.

discredit, *vb.* 1. shin'yō o nakusu
信用を無くす (injure reputation
of). 2. hitei suru 否定する
(reject).

discreet, *adj.* 1. kenmei (na) 賢明
(な) (wise). 2. shiryobukai 思慮深
い (careful).

discrepancy, *n.* 1. kuichigai 食い
違い (difference). 2. mujun 矛盾
(inconsistency).

discretion, *n.* funbetsu 分別;
kenmeisa 賢明さ.

discriminate, *vb.* 1. **discriminate
against** ... o sabetsu suru ... を差
別する. 2. kubetsu suru 区別する
(distinguish).

discrimination, *n.* sabetsu 差別.

discuss, *vb.* giron suru 議論する
(debate); hanashiau 話し合う
(talk about).

discussion, *n.* giron 議論 (debate);
hanashiai 話し合い (talk).

disdain, 1. *n.* keibetsu 軽蔑. 2. *vb.*
keibetsu suru 軽蔑する.

disease, *n.* byōki 病気.

disembark, *vb.* jōriku suru 上陸す
る.

disengage, *vb.* kirihanasu 切り離
す.

disentangle, *vb.* hodoku ほどく.

disfavor, *n.* 1. fukō 不興
(displeasure). 2. ken'o 嫌悪
(dislike).

disfigure, *vb.* sokonau 損う (mar);
minikuku suru 醜くする (make
ugly).

disgorge, *vb.* haku 吐く (vomit).

disgrace, 1. *n.* haji 恥 (shame);
fumeiyo 不名誉 (infamy). 2. *vb.*
meiyo o kegasu 名誉を汚す
(dishonor); haji o kakaseru 恥をか
かせる (humiliate).

disgraceful, *adj.* fumeiyo (na) 不名
誉 (な).

disguise, 1. *n.* hensō 変装
(costume); misekake 見せかけ
(pretense); **in disguise** hensō
shite. 2. *vb.* hensō suru 変装する
(conceal by costume); kakusu 隠
す (hide).

disgust, 1. *n.* ken'o no nen 嫌悪の
念. 2. *vb.* ken'o saseru 嫌悪させる
(cause to dislike); mukatsukaseru
むかつかせる (nauseate).

disgusting, *adj.* iya (na) 嫌 (な).

dish, *n.* 1. sara 皿 (plate). 2. ryōri
料理 (particular food).

disharmony, *n.* fuchōwa 不調和.

dishearten, *vb.* rakutan saseru 落
胆させる.

disheveled, *adj.* midareteiru 乱れ
ている.

dishonest, *adj.* fushōjiki (na) 不正
直 (な).

dishonesty, *n.* fushōjikisa 不正直
さ.

dishonor, 1. *n.* fumeiyo 不名誉. 2.
vb. meiyo o kegasu 名誉を汚す.

dishonorable, *adj.* fumeiyo (na) 不
名誉 (な).

dishwasher, *n.* sara'araiki 皿洗い
機 (machine); sara'arai 皿洗い
(person).

disillusion, *vb.* genmetsu saseru 幻

滅させる.

disinfect, *vb.* shōdoku suru 消毒する.

disinfectant, *n.* shōdokuzai 消毒剤.

disinherit, *vb.* kandō suru 勘当する.

disintegrate, *vb.* bunkai suru 分解する.

disinterested, *adj.* 1. mushimuyoku (na, no) 無私無欲 (な、の) (unselfish). 2. chūritsu (no) 中立 (の) (neutral).

disjointed, *adj.* bara-bara (na) ばらばら (な) (in pieces); shirimetsuretsu (na) 支離滅裂 (な) (disorganized).

disk, *n.* disuku ディスク (flat plate); **floppy disk** furoppī フロッピー.

diskette, *n.* disuketto ディスケット (computer).

dislike, 1. *n.* ken'o 嫌悪. 2. *vb.* kirau 嫌う.

dislocate, *vb.* dakkyū saseru 脱臼させる (bone).

dislodge, *vb.* oidasu 追い出す (chase out); dokeru どける (move from original place).

dismal, *adj.* 1. in'utsu (na) 陰うつ (な) (gloomy). 2. saki ga kurai 先が暗い (gloomy outlook).

dismantle, *vb.* torihazusu 取り外す.

dismay, 1. *n.* gyōten 仰天; shokku ショック (astonishment); rakutan 落胆 (discouragement). 2. *vb.* rakutan saseru 落胆させる (discourage).

dismember, *vb.* teashi o setsudan suru 手足を切断する.

dismiss, *vb.* 1. kaiko suru 解雇する (from employment). 2. kaisan saseru 解散させる (from meeting, class, etc). 3. shirizokeru 退ける (reject).

dismount, *vb.* oriru 降りる.

disobedient, *adj.* hankō-teki (na) 反抗的 (な).

disobey, *vb.* shitagawanai 従わない (not obey); hankō suru 反抗する (rebel).

disorder, *n.* 1. byōki 病気 (illness or disease). 2. konran 混乱 (confusion); ranzatsu 乱雑 (untidiness). 3. sōdō 騒動 (riot).

disorderly, *adj.* 1. ranzatsu (na) 乱雑 (な) (untidy). 2. ranbō (na) 乱暴 (な) (rowdy).

disorganized, *adj.* mechakucha (na) 滅茶苦茶 (な) (chaotic); shirimetsuretsu (na) 支離滅裂 (な) (disjointed).

disoriented, *adj.* tohō ni kureteiru 途方に暮れている (bewildered).

disown, *vb.* 1. kobamu 拒む (refuse). 2. kandō suru 勘当する (disinherit).

disparage, *vb.* kenasu けなす.

disparate, *adj.* konpon-teki ni kotonaru 根本的に異なる.

disparity, *n.* chigai 違い (difference).

dispassionate, *adj.* kōhei (na) 公平 (な) (impartial).

dispatch, 1. *n.* messēji メッセージ (message); supīdo スピード (speed). 2. *vb.* okuru 送る; hassō suru 発送する (send off something); haken suru 派遣する (send off a representative, messenger, etc.).

dispel, *vb.* shizumeru 静める (allay); chirasu 散らす (cause to dissipate).

dispense, *vb.* 1. kubaru 配る (distribute). 2. jisshi suru 実施する (administer). 3. **dispense**

with nashi de sumasu 無しで済ます (do without).

dispersal, dispersion, *n.* bunsan 分散.

disperse, *vb.* chirabaru/chirasu 散らばる／散らす (scatter/cause to scatter).

displace, *vb.* 1. ... ni tottekawaru ... に取って代わる (take the place of). 2. oidasu 追い出す (force out of place); **displaced person** nanmin 難民.

display, 1. *n.* tenji 展示 (at a show or exhibition); disupurē ディスプレー; chinretsu 陳列 (store display); hyōgen 表現 (expression). 2. *vb.* tenji suru 展示する (exhibit); chinretsu suru 陳列する (lay out goods); miseru 見せる (show).

displease, *vb.* okoraseru 怒らせる; **be displeased with** ... ni okoru.

disposable, *adj.* tsukaisute (no) 使い捨て (の).

disposal, *n.* 1. shobun 処分 (riddance). 2. **at someone's disposal** (... no) zui'i ni tsukaeru (... の) 随意に使える.

dispose, *vb.* 1. haichi suru 配置する (place in good order). 2. **dispose of** ... o shobun suru ... を処分する (get rid of); ... o suteru ... を捨てる (discard).

disposition, *n.* 1. seishitsu 性質 (personality). 2. keikōsei 傾向性 (tendency).

dispossess, *vb.* toriageru 取り上げる.

disproportionate, *adj.* 1. ōsugiru 多過ぎる (too much); sukunasugiru 少な過ぎる (too little). 2. futsuriai (na, no) 不釣り合い (な、の) (unbalanced); **disproportionate to** ... ni

taishite futsuriai (na).

disprove, *vb.* hanshō suru 反証する.

dispute, 1. *n.* giron 議論 (argument); kōron 口論 (quarrel). 2. *vb.* giron suru 議論する (argue); iiarasou 言い争う (quarrel); gimonshi suru 疑問視する (doubt).

disqualify, *vb.* shikkaku saseru 失格させる; shikaku o toriageru 資格を取り上げる (make ineligible); **be disqualified** shikaku o nakusu (lose eligibility).

disregard, 1. *n.* mushi 無視 (neglect). 2. *vb.* mushi suru 無視する (ignore).

disrepair, *n.* **fall into disrepair** areru 荒れる.

disreputable, *adj.* hyōban ga warui 評判が悪い.

disrespect, *n.* burei 無礼; shitsurei 失礼 (rudeness, insolence).

disrespectful, *adj.* burei (na) 無礼 (な); shitsurei (na) 失礼 (な).

disrobe, *vb.* fuku o nugu 服を脱ぐ.

disrupt, *vb.* 1. samatageru 妨げる (interrupt, disturb). 2. konran saseru 混乱させる (cause disorder in).

dissatisfaction, *n.* fuman 不満.

dissatisfied, *adj.* fuman (na) 不満 (な).

dissect, *vb.* kaibō suru 解剖する.

dissemble, *vb.* kakusu 隠す.

disseminate, *vb.* hiromeru 広める (spread).

dissent, 1. *n.* hantai 反対 (objection). 2. *vb.* hantai suru 反対する (disagree).

dissertation, *n.* ronbun 論文 (treatise); hakushironbun 博士論文 (treatise for a doctoral degree).

disservice, *n.* gai 害; **do a**

disservice gai o oyobosu.

dissident, *n.* hantaisha 反対者.

dissimilar, *adj.* kotonaru 異なる.

dissipate, *vb.* 1. chiru/chirasu 散る／散らす (scatter/cause to scatter). 2. muda ni suru 無駄にする (waste). 3. tsukaihatasu 使い果たす (use up).

dissociate, *vb.* hanasu 離す (separate); **dissociate from** ... kara hanareru (separate from); ... to kōsai o tatsu ... と交際を絶つ (cut off contact with).

dissolute, *adj.* fushidara (na) ふしだら (な).

dissolve, *vb.* 1. tokeru/tokasu 溶ける／溶かす (become/make liquid). 2. kaisan suru/saseru 解散する／させる (break up/cause to break up).

dissuade, *vb.* omoi todomaraseru 思い留まらせる.

distance, *n.* 1. kyori 距離 (space between); hedatari 隔り (time in between; remoteness in any respect, as in a relationship). 2. tōsa 遠さ (remoteness); **in the distance** tōku de/ni 遠くで／に (far away). 3. yoso-yososhisa よそよそしさ (aloofness, unfriendliness); **keep one's distance** yoso-yososhiku suru よそよそしくする.

distant, *adj.* 1. tōi 遠い; haruka (na) 遥か (な) (remote). 2. yoso-yososhii よそよそしい (unfriendly).

distaste, *n.* ken'o 嫌悪.

distasteful, *adj.* fuyukai (na) 不愉快 (な).

distill, *vb.* jōryū suru 蒸留する.

distillery, *n.* shuzōsho 酒造所.

distinct, *adj.* 1. meihaku (na) 明白 (な) (clear). 2. kotonaru 異なる (different, separate).

distinction, *n.* 1. kubetsu 区別 (differentiation). 2. sabetsu 差別 (discrimination). 3. chigai 違い (point of difference). 4. meisei 名声 (eminence, fame).

distinctive, *adj.* dokutoku (no) 独特 (の) (characteristic).

distinguish, *vb.* 1. kubetsu suru 区別する (identify as different). 2. wakaru 分かる (identify, perceive). 3. **distinguish oneself** meisei o eru 名声を得る (make oneself eminent).

distinguished, *adj.* yūmei (na) 有名 (な) (famous); tataerarete-iru 賛えられている (acclaimed).

distort, *vb.* 1. mageru 曲げる; yugameru 歪める (twist). 2. waikyoku suru 歪曲する (falsify).

distortion, *n.* 1. yugami 歪み (twist). 2. waikyoku 歪曲 (falsification).

distract, *vb.* 1. ki o chiraseru 気を散らせる (divert attention of); **be distracted by** ... de ki ga chiru. 2. nayamaseru 悩ませる (worry).

distracted, *adj.* konwaku shiteiru 困惑している (troubled, worried).

distraction, *n.* 1. ki o chirasu koto 気を散らすこと (thing that prevents concentration). 2. kibarashi 気晴らし (diversion, amusement). 3. seishinsakuran 精神錯乱 (mental derangement).

distraught, *adj.* 1. hōshinjōtai (no) 放心状態 (の) (absent-minded). 2. ki mo kuruwan bakari (no) 気も狂わんばかり (の) (crazed with anxiety).

distress, 1. *n.* kurushimi 苦しみ (agony, pain); nayami 悩み (anxiety, trouble); kiki 危機 (crisis); **be in distress** kiki ni

ochi'itte. 2. *vb.* kurushimeru 苦し
める (afflict with agony or pain);
nayamaseru 悩ませる (worry).

distribute, *vb.* 1. wakeru 分ける
(divide in shares). 2. maku 撒く
(spread out). 3. kubaru 配る
(circulate, disperse).

distribution, *n.* 1. bunpai 分配
(act of dividing). 2. sanpu 散布
(act of spreading out). 3. shōhin
ryūtsū 商品流通 (commerce).

district, *n.* chiku 地区; chi'iki 地域.

district attorney, *n.* chihōkenji 地
方検事.

distrust, 1. *n.* fushin 不信. 2. *vb.*
utagau 疑う.

disturb, *vb.* 1. jama suru 邪魔する
(interrupt). 2. iradataseru 苛立た
せる (irritate). 3. midasu 乱す
(unsettle).

disturbance, *n.* 1. bōgai 妨害
(interruption). 2. sawagi 騒ぎ
(commotion). 3. meiwaku 迷惑
(annoyance).

ditch, *n.* mizo 溝.

dive, 1. *n.* tobikomi 飛び込み (act
of jumping into water, etc.);
sensui 潜水 (submergence);
kyūkōka 急降下 (sharp descent of
airplane). 2. *vb.* tobikomu 飛び込
む (jump into); moguru 潜る
(plunge deeply); kyūkōka suru 急
降下する (plunge through the air).

diver, *n.* daibā ダイバー.

diverge, *vb.* 1. wakareru 別れる
(separate, split). 2. soreru それる
(deviate).

diverse, *adj.* tayō (na, no) 多様
(な、の) (various).

diversify, *vb.* tayōka suru 多様化す
る (vary).

diversion, *n.* 1. ii kibarashi 良い気
晴らし (amusing distraction,
pastime); goraku 娯楽

(amusement, entertainment). 2.
ukairo 迂回路 (detour). 3.
mondai kaihi 問題回避
(intentional digression).

diversity, *n.* tayōsei 多様性.

divert, *vb.* 1. tanoshimaseru 楽しま
せる (entertain). 2. ukai saseru 迂
回させる (road). 3. sorasu そらす
(turn aside).

divest, *vb.* toriageru 取り上げる
(deprive).

divide, *vb.* wakeru 分ける
(apportion, share, separate into
parts); wakareru 別れる (be
separated into parts); **divide into
two** futatsu ni wakeru.

dividend, *n.* haitōkin 配当金
(profit share).

divine, 1. *adj.* kami (no) 神 (の) (of
God or a god); shinsei (na) 神聖
(な) (sacred); kōgōshii 神々しい
(glorious). 2. *vb.* yogen suru 予言
する (prophesy).

diving board, *n.* tobikomidai 飛び
込み台.

divinity, *n.* 1. shinsei 神聖 (divine
nature). 2. kami 神 (god).

division, *n.* 1. bunpai 分配
(distribution). 2. bunkatsu 分割
(separation); bunkatsuten 分割点
(point that separates). 3. bubun
部分 (section). 4. shibu 支部
(branch); bumon 部門
(department). 5. bunretsu 分裂
(disagreement). 6. warizan 割り
算 (math).

divorce, 1. *n.* rikon 離婚. 2. *vb.*
rikon suru 離婚する.

divorcé -cée, *n.* rikonsha 離婚者.

divulge, *vb.* akasu 明かす.

dizziness, *n.* memai めまい.

dizzy, *adj.* **feel dizzy** memai ga
suru めまいがする.

do, *vb.* 1. suru する (perform,

execute, behave). 2. oeru 終える
(finish). 3. taru 足る (be enough).
4. au 合う (be suitable). 5.
maniau 間に合う (suffice). 6. **do
away with** ... ... o korosu ... を殺
す (kill); haishi suru 廃止する
(abolish); **do without** ... nashi de
sumasu ... なしで済ます; **have
something to do with** ... to
kankei ga aru ... と関係がある;
have nothing to do with ... to
nan no kankei mo nai.

docile, *adj.* sunao (na) 素直 (な).

dock, *n.* 1. dokku ドック (where
ship is repaired). 2. hatoba 波止場
(wharf).

doctor, *n.* 1. isha 医者 (medical
doctor). 2. hakushi 博士 (holder
of highest degree).

doctorate, *n.* hakushigō 博士号.

doctrinaire, *adj.* kyōjōshugi (no)
教条主義 (の).

doctrine, *n.* 1. kyōgi 教義
(teachings). 2. shugi 主義
(principle).

document, 1. *n.* shorui 書類
(paper); kiroku 記録 (record). 2.
vb. shōmei suru 証明する (prove);
kiroku suru 記録する (record).

documentary, *n.* dokyumentarī ド
キュメンタリー.

dodge, *vb.* 1. mi o kawasu 身をか
わす (elude). 2. kaihi suru 回避す
る (avoid).

doe, *n.* mejika 雌鹿.

dog, *n.* inu 犬.

dogma, *n.* doguma ドグマ; kyōgi
教義 (doctrine); shinjō 信条
(belief).

dogmatic, *adj.* dokudan-teki (na)
独断的 (な).

dole, *vb.* **dole out** wakeataeru 分
け与える (distribute).

doll, *n.* ningyō 人形.

dollar, *n.* doru ドル.

dolphin, *n.* iruka いるか.

dolt, *n.* baka 馬鹿.

domain, *n.* 1. shihaichi 支配地
(land under the control of a
ruler); shoyūchi 所有地 (private
estate); ryōdo 領土 (territory). 2.
senmonbun'ya 専門分野
(specialty).

dome, *n.* dōmu ドーム; maruyane
丸屋根 (roof).

domestic, *adj.* 1. kokunai (no) 国
内 (の) (of a country); **domestic
flight** kokunaisen. 2. kokusan
(no) 国産 (の) (produced locally);
domestic car kokusansha. 3.
katei (no) 家庭 (の) (of the home
or family). 4. hitonare shiteiru 人
慣れしている (domesticated,
tame); kachiku (no) 家畜 (の) (of
cattle).

domesticate, *vb.* 1. kainarasu 飼い
慣らす (tame). 2. katei-teki ni
suru 家庭的にする (make
someone family-oriented).

domicile, *n.* jūkyo 住居.

dominant, *adj.* 1. shihai-teki (na)
支配的 (な) (controlling). 2.
shuyō (na) 主要 (な) (main). 3.
attō-teki (na) 圧倒的 (な)
(overpowering).

dominate, *vb.* 1. shihai suru 支配
する (control, rule). 2. sobietatsu
そびえ立つ (tower above). 3. attō
suru 圧倒する (overpower).

domineering, *adj.* ōbō (na) 横暴
(な).

dominion, *n.* 1. shihaiken 支配権
(power of governing). 2. ryōdo 領
土 (territory governed).

donate, *vb.* kifu suru 寄付する.

donation, *n.* kifu 寄付; **make a
donation** kifu suru.

done, *adj.* 1. owatta 終わった

(finished). 2. **be done for** oshimai de aru お仕舞いである; **be done in** kutakuta ni tsukarete iru くたくたに疲れている.

donkey, *n.* roba ろば.

donor, *n.* kizōsha 寄贈者.

doom, 1. *n.* fu'un 不運. 2. *vb.* **be doomed to do** ... suru sadame de aru ... する定めである.

doomed, *adj.* norowareteiru 呪われている (cursed).

door, *n.* doa ドア; to 戸.

doorbell, *n.* doaberu ドアベル.

doorman, *n.* doaman ドアマン.

doormat, *n.* doamatto ドアマット.

doorway, *n.* iriguchi 入口.

dope, *n.* 1. mayaku 麻薬 (narcotic). 2. baka 馬鹿 (idiot).

dormant, *adj.* 1. nemutteiru 眠っている (asleep). 2. kyūshi shite-iru 休止している (temporarily inactive). 3. mukiryoku (na) 無気力 (な) (lethargic).

dormitory, *n.* ryō 寮.

dosage, *n.* 1. tōyaku 投薬 (administration of medicine). 2. fukuyōryō 服用量 (amount of medicine given).

dose, *n.* 1. ippuku 一服; ikkaibun 一回分 (quantity of medicine taken). 2. ryō 量 (quantity).

dossier, *n.* kiroku 記録; bunsho 文書 (set of documents).

dot, 1. *n.* ten 点; **on the dot** jikandōri 時間通り. 2. *vb.* ten o utsu 点を打つ (mark with dot or dots); ten-ten to saseru 点々とさせる (stud with dots); **be dotted with** ... ga ten-ten to shiteiru ... が点々としている.

dote on, *vb.* ... o dekiai suru ... を溺愛する.

dotted line, *n.* tensen 点線.

double, 1. *adj.* daburu (no) ダブル

(の); nijū (no) 二重 (の) (of two parts); nibai (no) 二倍 (の) (twice as great); futariyō (no) 二人用 (の) (for two people). 2. *vb.* nijū ni suru 二重にする (bend, fold); nibai ni naru/suru 二倍になる／する (become/make double). 3. *adv.* nibai ni 二倍に (twice).

double bed, *n.* daburu-beddo ダブルベッド.

double-cross, *vb.* uragiru 裏切る.

doubt, 1. *n.* gimon 疑問 (uncertainty); kenen 懸念 (apprehension); **without doubt** machigainaku 間違いなく. 2. *vb.* gimonshi suru 疑問視する (be uncertain); **doubt that** ... to omowanai ... と思わない (consider unlikely).

doubtful, *adj.* 1. ayafuya (na) あやふや (な) (uncertain). 2. utagawashii 疑わしい; shinjirarenai 信じられない (unlikely).

doubtlessly, *adv.* machigainaku 間違いなく (without doubt).

dough, *n.* neriko 練り粉.

doughnut, *n.* dōnattsu ドーナッツ.

douse, *vb.* 1. mizu o kakeru 水をかける (throw water over). 2. kesu 消す (extinguish).

dove, *n.* hato 鳩.

down, 1. *n.* umō 羽毛 (feather[s]). 2. *adv.* shita de/ni 下で／に (at, in/to a lower place); kami ni 紙に (on paper). 3. *prep.* (... no) shita de/ni (... の) 下で／に (in/to a descent).

downcast, *adj.* unadarete-iru うなだれている.

downfall, *n.* botsuraku 没落; suitai 衰退 (decline).

downhearted, *adj.* gakkari shiteiru がっかりしている.

downhill, *adv.* kudatte 下って; shita ni 下に (in downward direction); **go downhill** akka suru 悪化する (deteriorate).

downpour, *n.* gōu 豪雨.

downright, *adj.* mattaku (no) 全く (の).

downstairs, *adv.* shita de/ni 下で／に.

downstream, *adv.* karyū de/ni 下流で／に.

downtown, *n.* dauntaun ダウンタウン; shōgyōkuiki 商業区域 (business section); shōtengai 商店街 (shopping district).

downward, 1. *adj.* shita (no) 下 (の). 2. *adv.* shita de/ni 下で／に.

doze, 1. *n.* inemuri 居眠り. 2. *vb.* inemuri suru 居眠りする.

dozen, *n.* dāsu ダース; jūni 十二; **one dozen** ichidāsu 一ダース.

drab, *adj.* tsumaranai つまらない (dull).

draft, 1. *n.* zuan 図案 (sketch); sōan 草案 (preliminary version); kawase 為替 (money order); sukimakaze すき間風 (current of air); tegata 手形 (commercial bill); chōhei 徴兵 (military). 2. *vb.* keikaku suru 計画する (plan); sōan o kaku 草案を書く (write a draft); chōhei suru 徴兵する (military).

draft beer, *n.* nama-bīru 生ビール.

draftsman, *n.* 1. ritsuansha 立案者 (planner). 2. seizuka 製図家 (person who draws a draft).

drag, 1. *n.* hikizuru koto 引きずること (act of dragging); jama 邪魔 (hindrance); taikutsu 退屈 (boredom); josō 女装 (female impersonation). 2. *vb.* hikizuru 引きずる (trail on ground, pull

heavily); guzu-guzu suru ぐずぐずする (lag behind).

dragon, *n.* ryū 竜.

dragonfly, *n.* tonbo とんぼ.

drain, 1. *n.* haisui setsubi 排水設備 (drain pipe, ditch, etc.). 2. *vb.* haisui suru 排水する (draw off liquid); hirōkonbai suru 疲労困ばいする (be exhausted); tsukaihatasu 使い果たす (use up).

drainage, *n.* 1. haisui 排水 (act of draining). 2. haisui setsubi 排水設備 (system of drains).

drain pipe, *n.* haisuikan 排水管.

drama, *n.* dorama ドラマ; geki 劇 (play).

dramatic, *adj.* doramachikku (na) ドラマチック (な); geki-teki (na) 劇的 (な).

dramatist, *n.* geki sakka 劇作家.

dramatize, *vb.* gekika suru 劇化する.

drapes, *n.* kāten カーテン.

drastic, *adj.* 1. kyokutan (na) 極端 (な) (extreme). 2. kageki (na) 過激 (な) (radical).

draw, 1. *n.* kujibiki くじ引き (lottery); hikiwake 引き分け (sports); yobimono 呼び物 (attraction). 2. *vb.* hiku 引く (pull, attract); hipparu 引っ張る (pull strongly); hikidasu 引き出す (take out); hikitsukeru 引きつける (attract); e o kaku 絵を描く; suketchi o suru スケッチをする (sketch); hikiwake ni naru 引き分けになる (sports); **draw up** sakusei suru 作成する (prepare).

drawback, *n.* nanten 難点.

drawer, *n.* hikidashi 引き出し.

drawing, *n.* e 絵 (picture); suketchi スケッチ (sketch).

dread, 1. *n.* kyōfu 恐怖. 2. *vb.* osoreru 恐れる.

dreadful, *adj.* 1. osoroshii 恐ろしい (horrifying). 2. hidoi ひどい (very bad).

dream, 1. *n.* yume 夢. 2. *vb.* yumemiru 夢見る; **dream of** ... o yumemiru.

dreamer, *n.* 1. yumemiru hito 夢見る人 (person who dreams). 2. musōka 夢想家 (day-dreamer).

dreary, *adj.* inki (na) 陰気 (な).

dredge, *vb.* 1. sarau 浚う; shunsetsu suru 浚渫する (use a dredge).

drench, *vb.* **be drenched** zubunure ni naru ずぶ濡れになる.

dress, 1. *n.* doresu ドレス (formal wear); wanpīsu ワンピース (woman's outer garment); fuku 服 (attire). 2. *vb.* fuku o kiru/kiseru 服を着る／着せる (clothe oneself/someone); seisō o suru 正装をする (dress oneself up); ...no fukusō o suru ...の服装をする (be dressed in); teate o suru 手当てをする (wound).

dresser, *n.* doressā ドレッサー; kagamidansu 鏡だんす (chest of drawers with mirror).

dressing, *n.* 1. hōtai 包帯 (wound). 2. doresshingu ドレッシング (salad). 3. fuku o kiru koto 服を着ること (act of putting on clothing).

dressing gown, *n.* gaun ガウン.

dressing table, *n.* keshōdai 化粧台.

drift, *n.* keikō 傾向 (tendency); fukidamari 吹き溜まり (snow, sand, ash); imi 意味 (meaning). 2. *vb.* hyōryū suru 漂流する (be carried by currents); samayou 彷徨う (wander); fukidamari ni naru 吹き溜まりになる (pile up); **drift apart** hanarebanare ni naru 離れ離れになる.

drifter, *n.* nagaremono 流れ者.

drill, 1. *n.* doriru ドリル (exercise); kunren 訓練 (training); doriru ドリル (tool). 2. *vb.* doriru o suru ドリルをする (exercise); kunren suru 訓練する (train); **drill a hole** doriru de ana o akeru ドリルで穴を開ける.

drink, 1. *n.* nomimono 飲み物 (liquid); sake 酒 (liquor). 2. *vb.* nomu 飲む (swallow); sake o nomu 酒を飲む (drink liquor).

drip, 1. *n.* shitatari 滴り (act of dripping); shitataru oto 滴る音 (sound of dripping). 2. *vb.* shitataru 滴る.

drive, 1. *n.* doraibu ドライブ (ride); yaruki やる気 (motivation, enthusiasm); undō 運動 (campaign); shadō 車道 (roadway). 2. *vb.* unten suru 運転する (car); kuruma ni noseru 車に乗せる (give a ride); oiyaru 追いやる (chase away); ugokasu 動かす (move); karitateru 駆り立てる (force to work); uchikomu 打ち込む (nail).

driver, *n.* doraibā ドライバー; untensha 運転者 (car); untenshu 運転手 (bus, taxi, etc.); **driver's license** untenmenkyo 運転免許.

driveway, *n.* kojin no shadō 個人の車道.

drizzle, *n.* kirisame 霧雨.

drone, 1. *n.* unaru oto 唸る音 (sound). 2. *vb.* bun-bun unaru ぶんぶん唸る (make humming sound); en-en to shaberu えんえんとしゃべる (babble).

drool, *vb.* yodare o tarasu 涎を垂らす (salivate).

droop, *vb.* 1. shioreru しおれる (wilt, wither); tareru 垂れる (sag, hang down). 2. ikishōchin suru 意気消沈する (lose spirit).

drop, 1. *n.* shizuku しずく (droplet); shōryō 少量 (small quantity); rakka 落下 (fall). 2. *vb.* ochiru/otosu 落ちる／落とす (fall/let fall); sagaru/sageru 下がる／下げる (decrease/cause to decrease in price, etc.); yameru 止める (cease); otosu/nukasu 落とす／抜かす (leave out); **drop in** ... ni tachiyoru ... に立ち寄る; **drop off** orosu 降ろす (someone from vehicle); **drop out** yameru 止める (leave).

dropper, *n.* supoito スポイト.

drought, *n.* kanbatsu 干ばつ.

drove, *n.* mure 群れ.

drown, *vb.* 1. oboreshinu 溺れ死ぬ (death); oboreru 溺れる (be drowned). 2. oboresaseru 溺れさせる (drown someone). 3. **drown out** attō suru 圧倒する (overpower).

drowsy, *adj.* nemui 眠い (sleepy).

drug, *n.* 1. kusuri 薬 (medicine). 2. mayaku 麻薬 (narcotic).

drug addict, *n.* mayaku-chūdokusha 麻薬中毒者.

druggist, *n.* yakuzaishi 薬剤師.

drugstore, *n.* doraggusutoa ドラッグストアー; yakkyoku 薬局 (pharmacy).

drum, *n.* doramu ドラム; taiko 太鼓.

drummer, *n.* doramā ドラマー; taikouchi 太鼓打ち.

drumstick, *n.* bachi ばち (for drum).

drunk, 1. *n.* yopparai 酔払い. 2. *adj.* yopparatteiru 酔っ払っている; **get drunk** yopparau 酔払う.

drunkard, *n.* yopparai 酔払い.

drunkenness, *n.* yoi 酔い.

dry, 1. *adj.* kawaiteiru 乾いている (not wet); ame ga furanai 雨が降らない (rainless); nodo ga kawaku 喉が乾く (thirsty); dorai (na) ドライ (な) (sarcastic); karakuchi (no) 辛口 (の) (not sweet); taikutsu (na) 退屈 (な) (boring). 2. *vb.* kawaku/kawakasu 乾く／乾かす (become/make dry); fuku 拭く (wipe dry).

dry-cleaning, *n.* dorai-kurīningu ドライクリーニング.

dryer, *n.* 1. kansōki 乾燥機 (for clothes). 2. **hair dryer** hea-doraiyā ヘアドライヤー.

dryness, *n.* kansō 乾燥.

dual, *adj.* nijū (no) 二重 (の).

dub, *vb.* 1. fukikaeru 吹き替える (film). 2. dabingu suru ダビングする (copy tape). 3. adana o tsukeru あだ名をつける (give nickname).

dubious, *adj.* 1. mayotteiru 迷っている (uncertain). 2. ayashii 怪しい (doubtful).

duchess, *n.* kōshakufujin 公爵婦人.

duck, 1. *n.* ahiru あひる (domestic duck); kamo 鴨 (wild duck). 2. *vb.* moguru 潜る (plunge under water); mi o kagameru 身をかがめる (stoop, bend); kaihi suru 回避する (avoid).

duct, *n.* 1. sen 線; kan 管 (tube in the body). 2. kuda/kan 管 (pipe).

due, *adj.* 1. shiharau beki (no) 支払うべき (の) (payable). 2. tekitō (na) 適当 (な) (suitable); seitō (na) 正当 (な) (just). 3. yotei (no) 予定 (の) (scheduled). 4. **due to** ... ga gen'in de ... が原因で (caused by); ... no okage de ... のおかげで (owing to); **in due time** yagate やがて.

duel, *n.* kettō 決闘.

dues, *n.* kaihi 会費 (membership).

duet, *n.* dyuetto デュエット.

duke, *n.* kōshaku 公爵.

dull, 1. *adj.* kusundeiru くすんでいる (not bright in color); taikutsu (na) 退屈 (な) (tedious); nibui 鈍い (not sharp, blunt). 2. *vb.* nibuku naru/suru 鈍くなる／する (become/make blunt).

dumb, *adj.* 1. kuchi ga kikenai 口がきけない (unable to speak). 2. baka (na) 馬鹿 (な) (stupid).

dumbfound, *vb.* azen to saseru 啞然とさせる.

dummy, *n.* 1. manekin'ningyō マネキン人形 (mannequin). 2. mokei 模型 (copy, model). 3. baka 馬鹿 (idiot).

dump, 1. *n.* gomisuteba ごみ捨場 (dumping site); gomitame ごみ溜め (dirty place). 2. *vb.* suteru 捨てる (discard).

dune, *n.* sakyū 砂丘.

dung, *n.* fun 糞.

dungeon, *n.* chikarō 地下牢.

dunk, *vb.* hitasu 浸す (immerse).

dupe, 1. *n.* kamo かも. 2. *vb.* damasu だます.

duplicate, 1. *n.* kopī コピー; fukusei 複製 (copy). 2. *vb.* fukusei o tsukuru 複製を作る (copy a key, etc.); kopī o suru コピーをする (copy using copy machine).

duplicity, *n.* inchiki いんちき (deceit).

durable, *adj.* 1. nagamochi suru 長持ちする (long-wearing, sturdy). 2. nagatsuzuki suru 長続きする (long-lasting).

duration, *n.* aida 間; kikan 期間.

duress, *n.* kyōhaku 強迫.

during, *prep.* (... no) aida ni (... の) 間に.

dusk, *n.* yūgure 夕暮れ.

dust, 1. *n.* hokori 埃 (fine particles). 2. *vb.* hokori o toru 埃をとる (clean); maku 撒く (sprinkle).

dusty, *adj.* hokorippoi 埃っぽい.

Dutch, 1. *n.* orandajin オランダ人 (person); orandago オランダ語 (language). 2. *adj.* oranda (no) オランダ (の) (of Holland); orandajin (no) オランダ人 (の) (of the Dutch).

duty, *n.* 1. gimu 義務 (obligation); sekinin 責任 (responsibility); shigoto 仕事 (function); **on duty** shigotochū; **off duty** yasumi 休み. 2. zeikin 税金 (tax).

duty-free, *adj.* hikazei (no) 非課税 (の).

dwarf, *n.* kobito 小人.

dwell, *vb.* 1. ... ni sumu ... に住む (live). 2. **dwell on** ... ni tsuite kangaeru ... について考える.

dwelling, *n.* jūkyo 住居.

dwindle, *vb.* yowamaru 弱まる (weaken); heru 減る (decrease).

dye, 1. *n.* senryō 染料. 2. *vb.* someru 染める.

dying, *adj.* shinikaketeiru 死にかけている.

dynamic, *adj.* dainamikku (na) ダイナミック (な).

dynamite, *n.* dainamaito ダイナマイト.

dynasty, *n.* ōchō 王朝.

dysentery, *n.* sekiri 赤痢.

E

each, 1. *pron.* sorezore それぞれ; **each other** otagai (o, ni) お互い (を、に). 2. *adj.* sorezore no それぞれの.

eager, *adj.* nesshin (na) 熱心 (な); **be eager to do ...** nesshin ni ... o shitagatte-iru.

eagerness, *n.* netsui 熱意.

eagle, *n.* washi 鷲.

ear, *n.* 1. mimi 耳. 2. ho 穂 (of corn).

eardrum, *n.* komaku 鼓膜.

early, 1. *adj.* hayai 早い (early in time; premature); shoki (no) 初期 (の) (of an initial stage); wakai koro (no) 若い頃 (の) (of a person's youth). 2. *adv.* hayaku 早く.

earn, *vb.* 1. eru 得る (acquire). 2. kasegu 稼ぐ (earn money).

earnest, *adj.* 1. nesshin (na) 熱心 (な) (zealous). 2. seijitsu (na) 誠実 (な) (sincere).

earnings, *n.* shūnyū 収入.

earphone, *n.* iyahōn イヤホーン.

earplugs, *n.* mimisen 耳栓.

earring, *n.* iaringu イアリング; mimikazari 耳飾り.

earth, *n.* 1. chikyū 地球 (planet). 2. tsuchi 土 (soil). 3. tochi 土地 (land); jimen 地面 (ground).

earthquake, *n.* jishin 地震.

earthworm, *n.* mimizu みみず.

ease, 1. *n.* anraku 安楽 (comfort); raku 楽 (coziness, relief); kantan 簡単 (absence of difficulty); **be at ease** ochitsuite-iru 落着いている; **be ill at ease** ochitsukanai 落ち着かない. 2. *vb.* yawarageru 和らげる (mitigate); raku ni suru 楽にす

る (make comfortable); **ease (someone's) mind** anshin saseru 安心させる.

easel, *n.* īzeru イーゼル.

east, *n.* higashi 東; **the East** tōyō 東洋 (the Orient).

eastern, *adj.* 1. higashi no 東の (of the east); higashi kara no 東からの (from the east). 2. tōbu (no) 東部 (の) (of the eastern part). 3. tōyō (no) 東洋 (の) (of the Orient); higashi yōroppa (no) 東ヨーロッパ (の) (of Eastern Europe).

easy, *adj.* 1. yasashii 易しい (not difficult). 2. raku (na) 楽 (な) (relieved, comfortable).

easygoing, *adj.* kiraku (na) 気楽 (な).

eat, *vb.* taberu 食べる.

eaves, *n.* noki 軒.

ebb, 1. *n.* hikishio 引き潮 (ebb tide); suitai 衰退 (decline). 2. *vb.* hiku 引く (flow away); otoroeru 衰える (decline).

eccentric, *adj.* fūgawari (na) 風変わり (な).

echo, 1. *n.* ekō エコー; kodama こだま; hibiki 響き. 2. *vb.* kodama suru こだまする; hibiku 響く.

eclipse, *n.* 1. nisshoku 日食 (sun); gesshoku 月食 (moon). 2. suitai 衰退 (decline).

ecology, *n.* ekorojī エコロジー; kankyō 環境.

economic, *adj.* keizai (no) 経済 (の) (pertaining to economy).

economical, *adj.* keizai-teki (na) 経済的 (な) (not wasteful).

economics, *n.* keizaigaku 経済学.

economist, *n.* keizaigakusha 経済

学者.

economize, *vb.* setsuyaku suru 節
約する.

economy, *n.* 1. keizai 経済
(system). 2. ken'yaku 倹約
(thrifty management).

ecstasy, *n.* ekusutashī エクスタシ
ー; kōkotsu 恍惚.

edge, *n.* 1. hashi 端; fuchi 縁
(border). 2. ha/yaiba 刃 (cutting
edge).

edible, *adj.* taberareru 食べられる.

edict, *n.* meirei 命令 (command);
seirei 政令 (official order).

edifice, *n.* kyodai kenchiku 巨大建
築.

edit, *vb.* henshū suru 編集する.

editing, *n.* henshū 編集.

edition, *n.* 1. hakkō busū 発行部数
(one printing of a book). 2. -ban
-版 (format); **deluxe edition**
gōka-ban.

editor, *n.* editā エディター;
henshūsha 編集者.

editorial, 1. *n.* shasetsu 社説 (of
newspaper). 2. *adj.* henshūjō (no)
編集上 (の) (related to editing).

educate, *vb.* kyōiku suru 教育する;
oshieru 教える.

education, *n.* kyōiku 教育.

educational, *adj.* kyōiku-teki (na)
教育的 (な).

eel, *n.* unagi うなぎ (freshwater
eel); anago 穴子 (marine eel).

efface, *vb.* keshisaru 消し去る.

effect, 1. *n.* kōka 効果 (result);
kekka 結果 (outcome); jisshi 実施
(operation); imi 意味 (intent); **in
effect** jisshitsu-teki ni 実質的に
(virtually); yōsuru ni 要するに
(essentially); **take effect** jisshi
sareru. 2. *vb.* ... no kōka o
motarasu ... の効果をもたらす.

effective, *adj.* 1. kōka-teki (na) 効

果的 (な) (producing results). 2.
jisshi sareru 実施される
(operative).

effeminate, *adj.* on'na no yō (na)
女のよう (な).

efficiency, *n.* kōritsu 効率; nōritsu
能率.

efficient, *adj.* kōritsu-teki (na) 効
率的 (な); nōritsu-teki (na) 能率的
(な).

effort, *n.* doryoku 努力; **make an
effort** doryoku suru.

egg, 1. *n.* tamago 卵; **egg shell**
tamago no kara; **egg white**
shiromi 白身; **egg yolk** kimi 黄身;
fried egg medamayaki 目玉焼;
lay eggs tamago o umu. 2. *vb.*
egg on susumeru 勧める.

eggplant, *n.* nasu(bi) なす(び).

ego, *n.* 1. jiga 自我 (self). 2. ego エ
ゴ (self-importance).

egocentric, *adj.* jikochūshin-teki
(na) 自己中心的 (な).

egoist, *n.* egoisuto エゴイスト;
rikoshugisha 利己主義者.

egotism, *n.* 1. jiko chūshin shugi
自己中心主義 (self-centeredness).
2. unubore うぬぼれ (self-
conceit).

Egypt, *n.* ejiputo エジプト.

eight, *n.* hachi 八; yattsu 八つ.

eighteen, *n.* jūhachi 十八.

eighteenth, *adj.* jūhachibanme
(no) 十八番目 (の).

eighth, *adj.* hachibanme (no) 八番
目 (の).

eight hundred, *n.* happyaku 八百.

eightieth, *adj.* hachijūbanme (no)
八十番目 (の).

eighty, *n.* hachijū 八十.

either, 1. *pron.*, *adj.* dochiraka (no)
どちらか (の) (one or the other);
sōhō (no) 双方 (の) (each of two).
2. *adv.* ... mo (mata) ... も (また).

3. *conj.* **either ... or** ... ka ... ka ... か... か.

ejaculate, *vb.* 1. hōshutsu suru 放出する (discharge). 2. sakebu 叫ぶ (exclaim).

eject, *vb.* hōridasu 放り出す.

elaborate, 1. *adj.* kotta 凝った (painstaking, ornate); tan'nen (na) 丹念 (な) (precise, meticulous). 2. *vb.* tema o kakeru 手間をかける (take pains to do); kuwashiku setsumei suru 詳しく説明する (expand on).

elapse, *vb.* sugiru 過ぎる.

elastic, *adj.* shinshukusei (no) 伸縮性 (の); nobiru 伸びる.

elate, *vb.* yorokobaseru 喜ばせる; **be elated** kanki suru 歓喜する.

elbow, 1. *n.* hiji 肘. 2. *vb.* hiji de tsuku 肘で突く.

elder, 1. *n.* toshiue no hito 年上の人. 2. *adj.* toshiue (no) 年上 (の).

elderly, *adj.* toshiyori (no) 年寄り (の).

eldest, *adj.* sainenchō (no) 最年長 (の).

elect, *vb.* senkyo suru 選挙する; erabu 選ぶ.

election, *n.* senkyo 選挙.

electric, electrical, *adj.* denki (no) 電気 (の).

electrician, *n.* denkigishi 電気技師.

electricity, *n.* denki 電気.

electrify, *vb.* 1. denki o tōsu 電気を通す (charge with electricity). 2. kōfun saseru 興奮させる (excite).

electrocute, *vb.* **be electrocuted** kandenshi suru 感電死する.

electronic, *adj.* denshi (no) 電子 (の).

electronics, *n.* erekutoronikkusu エレクトロニックス; denshi-kōgaku 電子工学.

elegance, *n.* eregansu エレガンス; yūgasa 優雅さ.

elegant, *adj.* ereganto (na) エレガント (な); yūga (na) 優雅 (な).

element, *n.* 1. yōso 要素 (component part). 2. kiso 基礎 (rudiment). 3. genso 元素 (chemical).

elementary, *adj.* 1. shoho no 初歩の (rudimentary); **elementary school** shōgakkō 小学校. 2. kihon-teki (na) 基本的 (な) (fundamental).

elephant, *n.* zō 象.

elevate, *vb.* ageru 上げる (cause to go up).

elevation, *n.* 1. takai tokoro 高い所 (elevated place). 2. takasa 高さ (height). 3. kaibatsu 海抜 (altitude).

elevator, *n.* erebētā エレベーター.

eleven, *n.* jūichi 十一.

eleventh, *adj.* jūichibanme (no) 十一番目 (の).

elicit, *vb.* hikidasu 引き出す (draw out).

eligible, *adj.* 1. shikaku ga aru 資格がある; atehamaru 当てはまる (qualified). 2. nozomashii 望ましい (desirable).

eliminate, *vb.* 1. nozoku 除く (remove, omit). 2. korosu 殺す (kill).

elite, *n.* erīto エリート.

elm, *n.* nire no ki 楡の木.

elongate, *vb.* nagaku suru 長くする.

elope, *vb.* kakeochi suru 駆け落ちする.

eloquence, *n.* yūben 雄弁.

eloquent, *adj.* yūben (na) 雄弁 (な).

else, *adj.* hoka (no) 他 (の); **someone else** hoka no hito;

something else hoka no mono;
anything else hoka ni nanika;
no one else hoka ni daremo ...
nai; **nothing else** hoka ni nanimo
... nai. 2. *adv.* **or else**
sōdenakereba そうでなければ (if
not).

elsewhere, *adv.* yoso ni よそに.

elucidate, *vb.* hakkiri setsumei
suru はっきり説明する.

elude, *vb.* 1. sakeru 避ける
(evade); ... kara nigeru ...から逃げ
る (escape from ...). 2. wakaranai
わからない (be incomprehen-
sible); **elude one's memory**
omoidasenai 思い出せない.

elusive, *adj.* wakarinikui わかりに
くい (hard to understand);
keiyōshigatai 形容し難い (hard to
define).

emaciated, *adj.* yaseotoroete iru や
せ衰えている.

emanate, *vb.* (... kara) hassuru (...
から) 発する; (... kara) detekuru
(...から) 出て来る.

emancipate, *vb.* kaihō suru 解放す
る.

emasculate, *vb.* kyosei suru 去勢す
る.

embankment, *n.* teibō 堤防;
tsutsumi 堤.

embargo, *n.* 1. teishi meirei 停止命
令 (ban). 2. seigen 制限
(restriction); kinshi 禁止
(prohibition).

embark, *vb.* 1. (... ni) noru (...に)
乗る (board a ship, etc.). 2.
embark on ... o hajimeru ...を始
める.

embarkation, *n.* 1. jōsen 乗船 (on
a ship, etc.). 2. kaishi 開始 (start).

embarrass, *vb.* 1. haji'iraseru 恥じ
入らせる (make ashamed);
tomadowaseru 戸惑わせる

(fluster). 2. komaraseru 困らせる
(disconcert, complicate). 3. **be
embarrassed** hazukashii 恥ずか
しい (feel ashamed); tomadou 戸
惑う (feel flustered); komaru 困る
(feel disconcerted or helpless).

embarrassment, *n.* 1. haji 恥
(shame). 2. tomadoi 戸惑い
(mortification).

embassy, *n.* taishikan 大使館
(building).

embed, *vb.* umekomu 埋め込む.

embellish, *vb.* kazaru 飾る.

ember, *n.* moenokori 燃え残り.

embezzle, *vb.* ōryō suru 横領する.

embezzlement, *n.* ōryō 横領.

embitter, *vb.* **be embittered** nigai
omoi o suru 苦い思いをする.

emblem, *n.* shinboru シンボル;
shirushi 徴; shōchō 象徴.

embody, *vb.* 1. taigen suru 体現す
る (personify, exemplify). 2.
arawasu 表わす (express).

embrace, 1. *n.* hōyō 包容
(hugging). 2. *vb.* daku 抱く (hug);
ukeireru 受け入れる (accept);
fukumu 含む (contain).

embroider, *vb.* shishū o suru 刺繍
をする.

embroidery, *n.* shishū 刺繍.

embryo, *n.* taiji 胎児 (of animals or
humans). 2. hai 胚 (of plants).

emerald, *n.* emerarudo エメラル
ド.

emerge, *vb.* arawareru 現れる
(appear); dete kuru 出て来る
(come forth).

emergence, *n.* shutsugen 出現.

emergency, *n.* hijōjitai 非常事態;
emergency exit hijōguchi 非常口.

emigrant, *n.* ijūsha 移住者.

emigrate, *vb.* kaigai'ijū suru 海外
移住する.

émigré, *n.* 1. ijūsha 移住者. 2.

bōmeisha 亡命者 (political).

eminent, *adj.* 1. nadakai 名高い
(distinguished). 2. saidai (no) 最
大の (utmost). 3. kōi no 高位の
(highly ranked).

emissary, *n.* 1. shisetsu 使節. 2.
misshi 密使 (on secret mission).

emission, *n.* 1. hōshutsu 放出 (act
of emitting). 2. hōshutsubutsu 放
出物 (something emitted).

emit, *vb.* hōshutsu suru 放出する
(send forth).

emotion, *n.* kanjō 感情.

emotional, *adj.* 1. kanjō no 感情の
(of the emotions). 2. kanjō-teki
(na) 感情的 (な) (high strung,
stirring).

empathy, *n.* dōkan 同感.

emperor, *n.* 1. kōtei 皇帝. 2.
ten'nō 天皇 (Japanese emperor).

emphasis, *n.* kyōchō 強調; rikiten
力点.

emphasize, *vb.* kyōchō suru 強調
する.

emphatic, *adj.* kyōchō shita 強調し
た; tsuyoi 強い (strongly
expressive).

empire, *n.* teikoku 帝国.

employ, *vb.* yatou 雇う (hire);
tsukau 使う (use).

employee, *n.* jūgyōin 従業員.

employer, *n.* koyōsha 雇用者;
yatoinushi 雇い主.

employment, *n.* 1. koyō 雇用 (act
or state of employing). 2. shigoto
仕事 (work, occupation).

empower, *vb.* kengen o ataeru 権
限を与える.

empress, *n.* kōgō 皇后.

emptiness, *n.* 1. kara no jōtai 空の
状態 (being empty). 2. munashisa
空しさ (empty feeling).

empty, 1. *adj.* kara (no) 空 (の)
(containing nothing); aiteiru 空い

ている (unoccupied); munashii 空
しい (meaningless). 2. *vb.* kara ni
suru 空にする (make empty);
akeru 空ける (discharge contents);
kara ni naru 空になる (become
empty).

empty-headed, *adj.* baka (na, no)
馬鹿 (な、の).

emulate, *vb.* maneru 真似る
(imitate).

enable, *vb.* (... o) kanō ni suru (...
を) 可能にする; (... ga) dekiru
yōni suru (...が) 出来るようにす
る.

enact, *vb.* hō(ritsu) ni sadameru 法
(律) に定める (make into law).

enactment, *n.* hōritsu(ka) 法律
(化) (law).

enamel, *n.* 1. enameru エナメル
(glassy substance). 2. enameru
shitsu エナメル質 (tooth enamel).

enamored, *adj.* daisuki 大好き.

encampment, *n.* yaei 野営.

enchant, *vb.* 1. miwaku suru 魅惑
する (captivate). 2. mahō o
kakeru 魔法をかける (bewitch).

enchantment, *n.* 1. miwaku 魅惑
(fascination). 2. mahō 魔法
(magic).

encircle, *vb.* kakomu 囲む.

enclave, *n.* tobichi 飛び地.

enclose, *vb.* 1. kakomu 囲む. 2.
dōfū suru 同封する (letter).

enclosure, *n.* 1. kakoikomi 囲い込
み. 2. dōfū no mono 同封の物
(letter).

encompass, *vb.* 1. kakomu 囲む
(surround). 2. fukumu 含む
(contain).

encore, *n.* ankōru アンコール.

encounter, 1. *n.* deai 出会い
(meeting). 2. *vb.* (... ni) deau (...
に) 出会う (meet); (... to) tatakau
(...と) 戦う (combat).

encourage, *vb*. 1. hagemasu 励ます (inspire, cheer up). 2. susumeru 勧める (promote, stimulate).

encouragement, *n*. 1. hagemashi 励まし (inspiration). 2. susume 勧め (promotion, stimulation).

encroach, *vb*. shin'nyū suru 進入する.

encumber, *vb*. 1. samatageru 妨げる (hinder). 2. seoikomu 背負い込む (burden). 3. fusagu 塞ぐ (block).

encumbrance, *n*. 1. omoni 重荷 (burden). 2. jama 邪魔 (hindrance).

encyclopedia, *n*. hyakkajiten 百科辞典.

end, 1. *n*. owari 終り (close, conclusion); hashi 端; saki 先 (extremity); mokuteki 目的 (purpose); kekka 結果 (result); **in the end** tsui ni 遂に (finally); **come to an end** owaru 終わる; **on end** tsuzukete 続けて. 2. *vb*. owaru 終わる; **end up (in)** ... ni itaru ...に至る.

endanger, *vb*. kiken ni sarasu 危険にさらす.

endear, *vb*. itoshiku omowaseru 愛しく思わせる.

endearment, *n*. aijō 愛情.

endeavor, 1. *n*. doryoku 努力. 2. *vb*. doryoku suru 努力する.

ending, *n*. endingu エンディング; owari 終わり.

endless, *adj*. mugen (no) 無限 (の); saigen ga nai 際限が無い.

endorse, *vb*. 1. shiji suru 支持する (support). 2. shomei suru 署名する (authorize).

endorsement, *n*. 1. shiji 支持 (support); ninka 認可 (approval). 2. shomei 署名 (signature).

endow, *vb*. ataeru 与える; kifu suru 寄付する (donate).

endowment, *n*. kifu 寄付 (donation).

endurance, *n*. nintai 忍耐; shinbō 辛抱 (fact of bearing pain, adversity, etc.).

endure, *vb*. 1. taeru 耐える; shinbō suru 辛抱する (tolerate). 2. motsu もつ (last).

enema, *n*. kanchō 灌腸.

enemy, *n*. teki 敵.

energetic, *adj*. enerugisshu (na) エネルギッシュ (な); seiryoku-teki (na) 精力的 (な).

energy, *n*. enerugī エネルギー; seiryoku 精力.

enfold, *vb*. tsutsumu 包む.

enforce, *vb*. 1. oshitsukeru 押しつける (compel, impose). 2. shikkō suru 執行する (law).

engage, *vb*. 1. hiki'ireru 引き入れる (involve). 2. yatou 雇う (hire); tehai suru 手配する (secure a room, etc.). 3. hikitsukeru 引き付ける (attract). 4. **engage in** ... ni tazusawaru ...に携わる.

engaged, *adj*. 1. isogashii 忙しい (busy). 2. torikundeiru 取り組んでいる (involved, committed). 3. kon'yaku shiteiru 婚約している (betrothed); **get engaged** kon'yaku suru.

engagement, *n*. 1. yoyaku 予約 (appointment). 2. kon'yaku 婚約 (betrothal). 3. shigoto 仕事 (employment).

engine, *n*. 1. enjin エンジン; mōtā モーター (machine). 2. kikansha 機関車 (locomotive).

engineer, *n*. enjiniā エンジニアー; gishi 技師.

engineering, *n*. enjiniaringu エンジニアリング; kōgaku 工学.

England, *n.* igirisu イギリス.

English, 1. *n.* igirisujin イギリス人 (person); eigo 英語 (language). 2. *adj.* igirisu (no) イギリス (の) (of England); igirisujin (no) イギリス人 (の) (of the English).

Englishman, -woman, *n.* igirisujin イギリス人.

engrave, *vb.* horu 掘る (cut into something).

engraving, *n.* hanga 版画 (printing).

engross, *vb.* **be engrossed in** ... ni bottō shiteiru ...に没頭している.

enhance, *vb.* takameru 高める.

enigma, *n.* nazo 謎.

enigmatic, *adj.* fushigi (na) 不思議 (な); nazo no yō (na) 謎のよう (な).

enjoy, *vb.* tanoshimu 楽しむ; **enjoy dinner** bangohan o tanoshimu; **enjoy oneself** tanoshimu.

enjoyment, *n.* yorokobi 喜び.

enkindle, *vb.* kakitateru 掻き立てる.

enlarge, *vb.* kakudai suru 拡大する.

enlargement, *n.* kakudai 拡大.

enlighten, *vb.* keimō suru 啓蒙する; keihatsu suru 啓発する.

enlightenment, *n.* keimō 啓蒙; keihatsu 啓発 (act of enlightening).

enlist, *vb.* nyūtai suru 入隊する (in army, etc.).

enliven, *vb.* kakkizukeru 活気付ける.

enmesh, *vb.* **be enmeshed in** ... ni hamarikomu ...にはまり込む.

enormous, *adj.* kyodai (na) 巨大 (な); bōdai (na) 膨大 (な).

enough, *adj., adv.* jūbun (na, ni) 十分 (な、に).

enrage, *vb.* okoraseru 怒らせる.

enrich, *vb.* 1. yutaka ni suru 豊かにする (make rich). 2. jūjitsu saseru 充実させる (add greater value); yoku suru 良くする (improve).

enroll, *vb.* 1. tōroku suru 登録する (register). 2. nyūgaku suru 入学する (enroll in school).

enrollment, *n.* 1. tōroku 登録 (registration). 2. tōrokushasū 登録者数 (number of people enrolled).

enslave, *vb.* dorei ni suru 奴隷にする.

ensue, *vb.* tsuzuku 続く.

entail, *vb.* yōsuru 要する (require).

entangle, *vb.* **be entangled in** ... ni karamaru ...に絡まる.

enter, *vb.* 1. hairu 入る (come or go in, be admitted into). 2. ireru 入れる (put into). 3. hajimeru 始める (begin). 4. kinyū suru 記入する (record). 5. shutsujō suru 出場する (enter a competition).

enterprise, *n.* 1. jigyō 事業 (project). 2. kigyō 企業 (business firm). 3. yaru ki やる気 (initiative).

enterprising, *adj.* yaru ki ni michita やる気に満ちた (energetic).

entertain, *n.* 1. tanoshimaseru 楽しませる (amuse). 2. motenasu もてなす; kangei suru 歓迎する (have as a guest). 3. idaku 抱く (have in mind).

entertainer, *n.* geinōjin 芸能人; entāteinā エンターテイナー.

entertainment, *n.* 1. goraku 娯楽 (amusement). 2. geinō 芸能 (public performance); yokyō 余興 (hobby). 3. motenashi もてなし (hospitality).

enthrall, *vb.* toriko ni suru 虜にする (enslave); miryō suru 魅了する (captivate).

enthusiasm, *n.* nekkyō 熱狂.

enthusiastic, *adj.* nekkyō-teki (na) 熱狂的 (な).

entice, *vb.* 1. hikitsukeru 引き付ける (attract). 2. yūwaku suru 誘惑する (seduce).

enticement, *n.* 1. miryoku 魅力 (attraction). 2. yūwaku 誘惑 (seduction).

entire, *adj.* subete (no) 全て (の); zenbu (no) 全部 (の).

entirely, *adv.* sukkari すっかり; kanzen ni 完全に.

entirety, *n.* subete 全て; zenbu 全部.

entitle, *vb.* 1. kenri o ataeru 権利を与える; **be entitled to do ...** suru kenri ga aru. 2. (... to) dai o tsukeru (...と) 題をつける (entitle a book, etc.).

entity, *n.* 1. sonzai 存在 (existence). 2. jittai 実態 (reality).

entourage, *n.* torimaki no hitobito 取り巻きの人々.

entrails, *n.* naizō 内臓.

entrance, 1. *n.* nyūjō 入場 (act of entering); nyūgaku 入学 (entrance to school); iriguchi 入口 (doorway, etc.); nyūjōkyoka 入場許可 (permission to enter). 2. *vb.* miwaku suru 魅惑する (charm).

entreat, *vb.* kongan suru 懇願する.

entreaty, *n.* kongan 懇願.

entrée, *n.* antore アントレ; mein kōsu メインコース (main dish).

entrepreneur, *n.* kigyōka 企業家.

entrust, *vb.* azukeru 預ける; yudaneru 委ねる (commit in trust).

entry, *n.* 1. nyūjō 入場 (act of entering a place). 2. kinyū 記入

(record). 3. sanka 参加 (participation); sankasha 参加者 (participant, competitor). 4. kōmoku 項目 (entry in dictionary, etc.).

enumerate, *vb.* rekkyo suru 列挙する.

enunciate, *vb.* 1. kōhyō suru 公表する (proclaim). 2. hatsuon suru 発音する (pronounce).

envelop, *vb.* 1. tsutsumu 包む (wrap). 2. kakomu 囲む (surround).

envelope, *n.* fūtō 封筒.

envious, *adj.* urayamashii 羨ましい.

environment, *n.* kankyō 環境.

environmental, *adj.* kankyō (no) 環境 (の); **environmental pollution** kankyō'osen 環境汚染.

envision, *vb.* omoiegaku 思い描く.

envoy, *n.* 1. kōshi 公使; shisetsu 使節 (diplomat). 2. shisha 使者 (agent, representative).

envy, 1. *n.* senbō 羨望; urayamashisa 羨ましさ. 2. *vb.* urayamu 羨む.

enzyme, *n.* kōso 酵素.

ephemeral, *adj.* hakanai はかない.

epic, *n.* jojishi 叙事詩 (poetry).

epidemic, *n.* densenbyō 伝染病.

epigram, *n.* keiku 警句.

epilepsy, *n.* tenkan てんかん.

epilogue, *n.* musubi no kotoba 結びの言葉.

episode, *n.* episōdo エピソード; dekigoto 出来事 (incident).

epitaph, *n.* bohimei 墓碑銘.

epithet, *n.* 1. keiyōshi 形容詞 (adjective). 2. batō 罵倒 (abusive words).

epitome, *n.* kakkō no mihon 格好の見本 (typical specimen).

epoch, *n.* epokku エポック; jidai 時

代.

equal, 1. *n.* hittekisha 匹敵者 (person that is equal). 2. *adj.* hitoshii 等しい; onaji 同じ (same, alike); byōdō (no) 平等 (の) (having the same right); jūbun dekiru 十分出来る (adequate in ability). 2. *vb.* ... ni hitoshii ...に等しい.

equality, *n.* byōdō 平等.

equalize, *vb.* onaji ni suru 同じにする.

equally, *adv.* 1. hitoshiku 等しく (in an equal manner). 2. onajiku 同じく (to an equal degree).

equanimity, *n.* ochitsuki 落ち着き.

equate, *vb.* onaji mono to minasu 同じものと見なす (consider equal).

equation, *n.* 1. hōteishiki 方程式 (algebra). 2. hikaku 比較 (comparison).

equator, *n.* sekidō 赤道.

equilibrium, *n.* 1. baransu バランス; heikō 平衡 (balance). 2. ochitsuki 落ち着き (equanimity).

equip, *vb.* 1. sōbi suru 装備する (fit out). 2. sonaetsukeru 備え付ける (furnish). 3. **be equipped with** ... ga aru ...がある.

equipment, *n.* sōchi 装置; dōgu 道具 (implements).

equitable, *adj.* kōhei (na) 公平 (な) (just and fair).

equity, *n.* kōhei(sa) 公平(さ) (fairness).

equivalent, 1. *n.* sōtō suru mono 相当するもの. 2. *adj.* (... ni) hitoshii (...に) 等しい (equal); (... ni) sōtō suru (...に) 相当する (corresponding).

equivocal, *adj.* imi ga aimai (na) 意味があいまい (な).

era, *n.* jidai 時代.

eradicate, *vb.* zetsumetsu saseru 絶滅させる (destroy utterly); nozoku 除く (remove).

erase, *vb.* kesu 消す.

eraser, *n.* kokubanfuki 黒板拭き (blackboard); keshi-gomu 消しゴム (rubber).

erect, 1. *adj.* tatte iru 立っている (upright). 2. *vb.* tateru 立てる (put upright); tateru 建てる (build).

erection, *n.* 1. kenchiku 建築 (act of building). 2. bokki 勃起 (genital).

erode, *vb.* fushoku suru 腐食する (of metal); shinshoku suru 侵食する (of land); surikireru 擦り切れる (wear away).

erosion, *n.* fushoku 腐食 (of metal); shinshoku 侵食 (of sea); suitai 衰退 (decline).

erotic, *adj.* erochikku (na) エロチック (な); sei-teki (na) 性的 (な); kōshoku (na) 好色 (な).

err, *vb.* machigau 間違う (be mistaken).

errand, *n.* yōji 用事; (o)tsukai (お) 使い.

erratic, *adj.* 1. yosoku dekinai 予測できない (unpredictable). 2. kawariyasui 変わり易い (changeable). 3. fukisoku (na) 不規則 (な) (irregular).

erroneous, *adj.* machigatta 間違った.

error, *n.* erā エラー; machigai 間違い.

erudite, *adj.* gakushiki yutaka (na) 学識豊か (な).

erudition, *n.* gakushiki 学識.

erupt, *vb.* 1. funka suru 噴火する (volcano). 2. boppatsu suru 勃発する (incident).

eruption, *n.* 1. funka 噴火 (volcano). 2. boppatsu 勃発

(outburst).

escalator, *n.* esukarētā エスカレーター.

escapade, *n.* toppi na kōi 突飛な行為.

escape, 1. *n.* tōbō 逃亡 (flight); genjitsu tōhi 現実逃避 (avoidance of reality); more 漏れ (leakage). 2. *vb.* nigeru 逃げる (get away); sakeru 避ける (avoid); moreru 漏れる (leak).

eschew, *vb.* sakeru 避ける.

escort, 1. *n.* tsukisoi 付き添い (companion, attendant); goei 護衛 (guard). 2. *vb.* tsukisou 付き添う.

esoteric, *adj.* 1. nankai (na) 難解 (な) (abstruse). 2. himitsu (no) 秘密 (の) (secret).

especially, *adv.* toku ni 特に.

espionage, *n.* supai-katsudō スパイ活動.

espouse, *vb.* 1. saiyō suru 採用する (adopt). 2. shiji suru 支持する (advocate).

essay, *n.* 1. shōronbun 小論文 (short thesis); essē エッセー; zuihitsu 随筆 (composition); kokoromi 試み (attempt). 2. *vb.* kokoromiru 試みる (attempt).

essence, *n.* 1. essensu エッセンス; honshitsu 本質 (intrinsic nature). 2. shinzui 真髄 (gist).

essential, *adj.* 1. mottomo hitsuyō (na) 最も必要 (な) (most necessary). 2. honshitsu-teki (na) 本質的 (な) (central).

establish, *vb.* 1. setsuritsu suru 設立する (found). 2. kakuritsu suru (settle) 確立する. 3. shōmei suru 証明する (prove).

establishment, *n.* 1. setsuritsu 設立する (institution). 2. **the Establishment** ken'i 権威 (institutional authority). 3. kigyō

企業 (business).

estate, *n.* 1. tochiyashiki 土地屋敷 (land and house). 2. zaisan 財産 (property).

esteem, 1. *n.* sonkei 尊敬 (respect). 2. *vb.* sonkei suru 尊敬する (respect); ... to minasu ...と見なす (regard as ...).

estimate, 1. *n.* mitsumori 見積り (calculation); iken 意見; handan 判断 (opinion). 2. *vb.* mitsumoru 見積もる (calculate); handan suru 判断する (form an opinion).

estimation, *n.* 1. mitsumori 見積り. 2. iken 意見; handan 判断.

estrange, *vb.* 1. wakaresaseru わかられる (keep at a distance). 2. **be estranged** naka ga waruku naru 仲が悪くなる (become hostile).

etch, *vb.* horu 彫る.

etching, *n.* etchingu エッチング.

eternal, *adj.* eien (no) 永遠 (の).

eternity, *n.* eien 永遠.

ether, *n.* ēteru エーテル.

ethereal, *adj.* 1. konoyo naranu この世ならぬ (heavenly). 2. reimyō (na) 霊妙な (delicate).

ethic, *n.* 1. rinri 倫理. 2. **ethics** rinrigaku 倫理学 (philosophy).

ethical, *adj.* rinri-teki (na) 倫理的 (な).

ethnic, *adj.* esunikku (no) エスニック (の); shōsūminzoku (no) 少数民族 (の).

etiquette, *n.* echiketto エチケット; manā マナー; reigi 礼儀.

etymology, *n.* gogen 語源.

eulogy, *n.* 1. sanbi 賛美 (praise). 2. chōji 弔辞 (for a deceased person).

eunuch, *n.* kangan 宦官.

euphemism, *n.* enkyoku-teki na hyōgen 婉曲的な表現.

euphoria, *n.* kōfukukan 幸福感.

Europe, *n.* yōroppa ヨーロッパ.

European, 1. *n.* yōroppajin ヨーロッパ人 (person). 2. *adj.* yōroppa (no) ヨーロッパ (の) (of Europe); yōroppajin (no) ヨーロッパ人 (の) (of the Europeans).

evacuate, *vb.* 1. kara ni suru 空にする (vacate). 2. hinan saseru 逃難させる (remove a person for safety).

evade, *vb.* 1. sakeru 避ける (avoid, escape). 2. gomakasu ごまかす (avoid answering directly).

evaluate, *vb.* hyōka suru 評価する.

evaluation, *n.* hyōka 評価.

evaporate, *vb.* jōhatsu suru 蒸発する.

evasion, *n.* 1. kaihi 回避 (act of avoiding or escaping). 2. gomakashi ごまかし (subterfuge).

evasive, *adj.* kaihi teki na 回避的な (tending to avoid); hakkiri shinai はっきりしない (unclear).

eve, *n.* zen'ya 前夜 (evening before).

even, 1. *adj.* nameraka (na) 滑らか (な) (smooth); taira (na) 平ら (な) (level); ichiyō (na) 一様 (な) (unchanging); hitoshii 等しい; gokaku (no) 互角 (の) (equal); gūsū no 偶数の (of a number); **break even** shūshi ga zero de aru 収支がゼロである; **get even** shikaeshi suru 仕返しする. 2. *adv.* ... sae mo ...さえも (unlikely or extreme case); sara ni さらに (still, yet); **even now** ima demo 今でも; **even so** sore demo それでも. 3. *vb.* **even up** hitoshiku suru.

evening, *n.* yūgata 夕方; ban 晩; **Good evening.** Konban wa. 今晩は.

event, *n.* 1. ibento イベント; dekigoto 出来事 (something that happens). 2. kekka 結果 (result).

3. shiai 試合 (competition). 4. **in any event** tonikaku とにかく; **in the event of** ... no bāi niwa ...の場合には.

eventful, *adj.* 1. jūyō (na) 重要 (な) (momentous). 2. haran ni tomu 波乱に富む (full of events).

eventual, *adj.* saishū (no) 最終 (の) (ultimate).

eventually, *adv.* saigo ni 最後に; kekkyoku 結局.

ever, *adv.* 1. itsuka いつか (at some time); itsumo いつも (always); moshimo もしも (at any time); mae ni 前に (at any time up to the present). 2. tsune ni 常に (always). 3. man ga ichi 万が一 (by any chance). 4. **ever since** ... irai zutto ...以来ずっと; **ever so ...** taihen ... 大変; **than ever** mae yori 前より.

every, *adj.* 1. (dekiru kagiri) subete no (出来る限り) 全ての (all possible). 2. sorezore no それぞれの; mai- 毎; dono ... mo どの...も (each). 3. **every month** mai-tsuki; **every country** dono kuni mo; **every now and then** tokidoki 時々; **every other day** ichinichi oki ni 一日おきに.

everybody, everyone, *pron.* min'na 皆; subete no hito 全ての人.

everyday, *adj.* 1. mainichi (no) 毎日 (の) (of every day). 2. fudan (no) 普段 (の) (of ordinary days).

everything, *pron.* subete (no koto/mono) 全て (のこと／もの).

everywhere, *adv.* itaru tokoro (de, ni) 至るところ (で、に); doko demo どこでも.

evict, *vb.* tachinokaseru 立ち退かせる.

eviction, *n.* tachinoki 立ち退き.

evidence, *n.* shōko 証拠.

evident, *adj.* akiraka (na) 明らか (な).

evidently, *adv.* akiraka ni 明らかに.

evil, 1. *n.* aku 悪. 2. *adj.* warui 悪い (bad); ja'aku (na) 邪悪 (な) (wicked).

evoke, *vb.* 1. hikidasu 引き出す (draw out). 2. yobiokosu 呼び起こす (memory, etc.).

evolution, *n.* 1. hatten 発展 (development). 2. shinka 進化 (biological concept).

evolve, *vb.* 1. hatten saseru 発展させる (cause to develop); hatten suru 発展する (come forth into being). 2. shinka suru 進化する (evolve biologically).

exacerbate, *vb.* akka saseru 悪化させる.

exact, 1. *adj.* seikaku (na) 正確 (な) (accurate, precise). 2. *vb.* kyōyō suru 強要する (force).

exaggerate, *vb.* kochō suru 誇張する.

exaggeration, *n.* kochō 誇張.

exalt, *vb.* 1. shōshin saseru 昇進させる (elevate in rank). 2. tataeru 賛える (extol).

examination, *n.* shiken 試験 (test); kensa 検査 (inspection, checking). 2. chōsa 調査 (investigation). 3. shinsatsu 診察 (medical).

examine, *vb.* shiken o suru 試験をする (test). 2. chōsa suru 調査する; shiraberu 調べる (check, interrogate, investigate). 3. shinsatsu o suru 診察をする (give a medical examination).

example, *n.* rei 例; tatoe 例え; **for example** tatoeba 例えば.

exasperate, *vb.* okoraseru 怒らせる

る.

excavate, *vb.* hakkutsu suru 発掘する.

excavation, *n.* hakkutsu 発掘.

exceed, *vb.* 1. koeru 越える (go beyond). 2. shinogu 凌ぐ (surpass).

exceedingly, *adv.* hijō ni 非常に; taihen 大変.

excel, *vb.* (... ni) masaru (...に) 優る; (... o) shinogu (...を) 凌ぐ.

excellence, *n.* subarashisa 素晴らしさ.

excellent, *adj.* subarashii 素晴らしい; yūshū (na) 優秀 (な).

except, 1. *vb.* nozoku 除く (exclude). 2. *prep.* ... o nozoite ... を除いて.

exception, *n.* reigai 例外.

exceptional, *adj.* 1. reigai-teki (na) 例外的 (な) (unusual). 2. kiwadatteiru 際立っている (outstanding).

excerpt, *n.* bassui 抜粋.

excess, 1. *n.* chōka 超過; kajō 過剰 (surplus); ikisugi 行き過ぎ; yarisugi やり過ぎ (lack of moderation). 2. *adj.* chōka (no) 超過 (の) (superfluous).

excessive, *adj.* do o sugiteiru 度を過ぎている.

exchange, 1. *n.* kōkan 交換 (reciprocal exchange); torikae 取り替え (act of replacing); ryōgae 両替 (currency exchange); torihikisho 取引所 (place for exchange); **exchange rate** ryōgaeritsu; kawase-rēto 為替レート; **in exchange for** ... to hikikae ni ...と引き替えに; **stock exchange** shōken-torihikisho 証券取引所; **telephone exchange** denwa-kōkankyoku 電話交換局. 2. *vb.* kōkan suru 交換する (give and receive); torikaeru 取り替える (replace); ryōgae suru 両替えする (exchange currencies).

excite, *vb.* 1. kōfun saseru 興奮させる (stir up the emotions); **be excited** kōfun shiteiru. 2. shigeki suru 刺激する (stimulate).

excitement, *n.* kōfun 興奮.

exciting, *adj.* kōfun saseru (yō na) 興奮させる (ような).

exclaim, *vb.* sakebu 叫ぶ.

exclamation, *n.* sakebi 叫び.

exclamation mark, *n.* kantanfu 感嘆符.

exclude, *vb.* jogai suru 除外する.

exclusion, *n.* jogai 除外.

exclusive, *adj.* 1. sen'yō (no) 専用 (の) (for private use). 2. yui'itsu (no) 唯一 (の) (sole). 3. haita-teki (na) 排他的 (な) (not admitting others). 3. kōkyū (na) 高級 (な) (expensive and chic). 4. **exclusive of** ... o nozoite ...を除いて.

excrement, *n.* haisetsubutsu 排泄物; ben 便.

excruciating, *adj.* kakoku (na) 苛酷 (な).

excursion, *n.* 1. yusan 遊山 (short journey for pleasure). 2. kakuyasu-tsuā 格安ツアー (trip at a reduced rate).

excuse, 1. *n.* benkai 弁解 (reasons for being excused). 2. *vb.* yurusu 許す (pardon); ayamaru 謝る (apologize for); benkai suru 弁解する (justify); menjo suru 免除する (release from obligation); **Excuse me.** Sumimasen. すみません.

execute, *vb.* 1. jisshi suru 実施する (carry out, make effective). 2. okonau 行う (do, perform). 3. shokei suru 処刑する (put to death).

execution, *n.* 1. jisshi 実施. 2. okonai 行い. 3. shokei 処刑.

executive, 1. *n.* kanrishoku 管理職; jūyaku 重役 (in business); gyōseisha 行政者 (in government). 2. *adj.* keiei (no) 経営 (の) (of business administration); gyōsei (no) 行政 (の) (of government administration).

exemplary, *adj.* mohan-teki (na) 模範的 (な) (worthy of imitation).

exempt, 1. *adj.* menjo sareta 免除された. 2. *vb.* menjo suru 免除する.

exemption, *n.* menjo 免除.

exercise, 1. *n.* undō 運動 (bodily exercise); kunren 訓練 (training); renshūmondai 練習問題 (set of practice questions); shiyō 使用 (putting to use). 2. *vb.* undō suru 運動する (do exercise); kunren suru 訓練する (train); tsukau 使う (use, activate).

exert, *vb.* 1. tsukau 使う (use); furu'u ふるう (use vigorously). 2. **exert oneself** jibun no chikara o hakki suru 自分の力を発揮する.

exertion, *n.* doryoku 努力 (effort).

exhale, *vb.* haku 吐く.

exhaust, 1. *n.* haiki-gasu 排気ガス (waste gases); haikikō 排気口 (pipe). 2. *vb.* tsukare saseru 疲れさせる (fatigue); tsukaihatasu 使い果たす (use up).

exhausted, *adj.* tsukarekitte-iru 疲れ切っている (fatigued).

exhausting, *adj.* tsukare saseru 疲れさせる.

exhaustion, *n.* hirō 疲労.

exhaustive, *adj.* tettei-teki (na) 徹底的 (な) (thorough).

exhibit, 1. *n.* tenji 展示

(exhibition); tenjihin 展示品 (something exhibited). 2. *vb.* tenji suru 展示する (place on show); miseru 見せる (offer to view).

exhibition, *n.* 1. tenji 展示 (presenting to view). 2. tenrankai 展覧会 (public show).

exhilarate, *vb.* hogaraka ni suru 朗らかにする (make cheerful).

exhort, *vb.* nesshin ni toku 熱心に説く.

exile, 1. *n.* ruzai 流罪 (expulsion); bōmei 亡命 (refuge abroad); bōmeisha 亡命者 (voluntary exile, refugee). 2. *vb.* ruzai ni suru 流罪にする (expel); **exile oneself** bōmei suru 亡命する.

exist, *vb.* 1. sonzai suru 存在する; aru/iru ある／いる (be). 2. ikite-iku 生きて行く (continue to live).

existence, *n.* 1. sonzai 存在 (being). 2. seikatsu 生活 (way of living).

existent, *adj.* sonzai shite iru 存在している.

existentialism, *n.* jitsuzonshugi 実存主義.

exit, 1. *n.* deguchi 出口 (way out); taishutsu 退出 (departure). 2. *vb.* deru 出る.

exodus, *n.* dasshutsu 脱出.

exonerate, *vb.* 1. mi no akashi o tateru 身の証しをたてる (free of blame). 2. menjiru 免じる (relieve from obligation).

exorbitant, *adj.* 1. takasugiru 高過ぎる (too expensive). 2. hōgai (na) 法外 (な) (outrageous).

exorcise, *vb.* harau 払う.

exorcism, *n.* (o)harai (お)払い.

exotic, *adj.* ekizochikku (na) エキゾチック (な); ikoku-teki (na) 異国的 (な) (foreign).

expand, *vb.* 1. hirogaru 広がる

(grow larger, spread out); hirogeru 広げる (cause to grow large or spread out). 2. fueru 増える (increase in quantity); fuyasu 増やす (cause to increase). 3. hatten suru 発展する (develop); hatten saseru 発展させる (cause to develop).

expanse, *n.* hirogari 広がり.

expansion, *n.* 1. kakudai 拡大 (act of expanding). 2. hatten 発展 (development).

expatriate, 1. *n.* kokugai-tsuihōsha 国外追放者 (exile); kokugai-zaijūsha 国外在住者 (person dwelling in foreign land). 2. *vb.* kokugai ni tsuihō suru 国外に追放する (banish); kokugai ni ijū suru 国外に移住する (leave one's country).

expect, *vb.* 1. kitai suru 期待する (anticipate). 2. matsu 待つ (wait). 3. omou 思う (suppose). 4. shussan o matsu 出産を待つ (anticipate a baby); **be expecting** ninshinchū 妊娠中 (be pregnant).

expectation, *n.* kitai 期待 (anticipation).

expedient, *adj.* 1. kenmei (na) 懸命 (な) (advisable). 2. kōtsugō (na) 好都合 (な) (advantageous).

expedite, *vb.* hayameru 速める.

expel, *vb.* tsuihō suru 追放する.

expend, *vb.* tsukaihatasu 使い果たす.

expenditure, *n.* 1. shōhi 消費 (spending). 2. hiyō 費用 (expense).

expense, *n.* 1. hiyō 費用 (cost). 2. shōhi 消費 (expenditure). 3. **at the expense of** ... o gisei ni shite ... を犠牲にして.

expensive, *adj.* takai 高い.

experience, 1. *n.* keiken 経験. 2.

vb. keiken suru 経験する.

experienced, *adj.* keiken yutaka (na) 経験豊か (な); jukuren shita 熟練した (skilled).

experiment, 1. *n.* jikken 実験. 2. *vb.* jikken suru 実験する; tamesu 試す.

experimental, *adj.* jikken-teki (na) 実験的 (な).

expert, 1. *n.* ekisupāto エキスパート; senmonka 専門家. 2. *adj.* senmonka (no) 専門家 (の) (of an expert); jukuren shita 熟練した (skillful).

expertise, *n.* senmonchishiki 専門知識 (expert knowledge).

expiration, *n.* shūryō 終了.

expire, *vb.* owaru 終わる; kigen ga kireru 期限が切れる (come to an end).

explain, *vb.* setsumei suru 説明する.

explanation, *n.* setsumei 説明.

explanatory, *adj.* setsumei-teki (na) 説明的 (な).

explicable, *adj.* setsumeikanō (na) 説明可能 (な).

explicit, *adj.* akiraka (na) 明らか (な).

explode, *vb.* bakuhatsu suru 爆発する (of an explosive or feeling).

exploit, 1. *n.* tegara 手柄 (notable act). 2. *vb.* sakushu suru 搾取する (use another person selfishly).

exploitation, *n.* sakushu 搾取 (selfish manipulation of another person).

explore, *vb.* 1. tanken suru 探検する (go on an expedition). 2. saguru 探る; shiraberu 調べる (investigate).

explorer, *n.* tankenka 探検家 (person who explores).

explosion, *n.* 1. bakuhatsu 爆発

(burst, eruption). 2. bakuhatsuon 爆発音 (sound).

explosive, *n.* bakuhatsubutsu 爆発物.

export, 1. *n.* yushutsu 輸出 (trade); yushutsuhin 輸出品 (things exported). 2. *vb.* yushutsu suru 輸出する.

exporter, *n.* yushutsugyōsha 輸出業者.

expose, *vb.* 1. sarasu 曝す (bare, endanger). 2. bakuro suru 暴露する (reveal). 3. miseru 見せる (show).

exposition, *n.* 1. hakurankai 博覧会; tenjikai 展示会 (public exhibition). 2. setsumei 説明 (explanation).

exposure, *n.* 1. sarasu koto 曝すこと (act of exposing). 2. roshutsu 露出 (photograph). 3. bakuro 暴露 (disclosure).

express, 1. *n.* kyūkō(densha) 急行 (電車) (train); sokutatsu 速達 (express mail). 2. *vb.* noberu 述べる (put into words); arawasu 表わす; hyōgen suru 表現する (show); tsutaeru 伝える (communicate).

expression, *n.* 1. hyōgen 表現 (act of expressing); hyōgenryoku 表現力 (power of expressing). 2. hyōjō 表情 (facial look). 3. kotoba 言葉 (words).

expulsion, *n.* tsuihō 追放.

exquisite, *adj.* 1. subarashii 素晴らしい (excellent). 2. ereganto (na) エレガント (な) (elegant).

extemporaneous, *adj.* sokkyō (no) 即興 (の).

extend, *vb.* 1. nobiru 伸びる (stretch); nobasu 伸ばす (cause to stretch). 2. hirogeru 広げる (stretch to limit). 3. sashinoberu 差し伸べる (offer).

extension, *n.* 1. enchō 延長 (act of extending). 2. tsuika 追加 (addition); zōchiku 増築 (additional construction). 3. naisen 内線 (telephone).

extensive, *adj.* 1. hiroi 広い (wide); habahiroi 幅広い (broad, far-reaching). 2. ōkii 大きい (large).

extent, *n.* 1. teido 程度 (degree of extension). 2. han'i 範囲 (range); hirosa 広さ (area); nagasa 長さ (length); ōkisa 大きさ (volume). 3. **to a certain extent** aru teido made; **to the extent that** ... (suru) teido made.

extenuate, *vb.* jōjōshakuryō suru 情状酌量する (lessen); **extenuating circumstances** shakuryō subeki jijō.

exterior, 1. *n.* sotogawa 外側 (outside). 2. *adj.* sotogawa (no) 外側 (の) (of the outside).

exterminate, *vb.* zetsumetsu saseru 絶滅させる.

extermination, *n.* zetsumetsu 絶滅.

external, *adj.* 1. soto (no) 外 (の); gaibu (no) 外部 (の) (of the outside). 2. gaiyō (no) 外用 (の) (for use on the outside of the body). 3. gaikoku (no) 外国 (の) (foreign).

extinct, *adj.* sonzai shinai 存在しない; horonda 滅んだ.

extinction, *n.* 1. zetsumetsu 絶滅 (of a species). 2. shōmetsu 消滅 (dying out).

extinguish, *n.* 1. kesu 消す (put out). 2. owaraseru 終わらせる (end).

extinguisher, *n.* shōkaki 消火器.

extort, *vb.* kyōyō suru 強要する; yusuru 強請る.

extortion, *n.* kyōyō 強要; yusuri 強請り.

extra, 1. *n.* yobun na mono 余分なもの (surplus); tokubetsu na mono 特別なもの (special thing); tsuikaryōkin 追加料金 (additional charge); ekisutora エキストラ (actor). 2. *adj.* yobun (na, no) 余分 (な、の) (spare, superfluous); tsuika ryōkin (no) 追加料金 (の) (added charge); tokubetsu (no) 特別 (の) (special, exceptional).

extract, 1. *n.* bassui 抜粋 (excerpt); ekisu エキス (extracted essence). 2. *vb.* nuku 抜く (draw out); hikidasu 引き出す (draw forth); eru 得る (obtain); bassui suru 抜粋する (copy out excerpts).

extradite, *vb.* hikiwatasu 引き渡す.

extradition, *n.* sōkan 送還.

extraneous, *adj.* mukankei (na, no) 無関係 (な、の) (irrelevant).

extraordinary, *adj.* 1. hijō (na) 非常 (な) (extreme, outstanding). 2. ijō (na) 異常 (な) (very strange).

extravagant, *adj.* 1. rōhi (no) 浪費 (の) (spending too much); zeitaku 贅沢 (costly). 2. hōgai (na) 法外 (な) (exorbitant, outrageous). 3. kabi (na) 華美 (な) (showy).

extreme, *n.* kyokutan 極端; kyokudo 極度; **opposite extreme** seihantai 正反対.

extremely, *adv.* hijō ni 非常に.

extremity, *n.* 1. hashi 端 (edge). 2. **extremities** teashi 手足 (limbs). 3. konkyū 困窮 (extreme distress).

extricate, *vb.* kyūjo suru 救助する.

extrovert, *n.* gaikō-teki na hito 外向的な人.

exuberant, *adj.* 1. yorokobi ni michita 喜びに満ちた

(enthusiastic). 2. sei'iku ga yutaka (na) 生育が豊か (な) (growing profusely).

exude, *vb.* nijimidasu 滲み出す (ooze out); hassan saseru 発散させる (radiate).

exult, *vb.* yorokobu 喜ぶ.

eye, *n.* me 眼.

eyeball, *n.* medama 目玉.

eyebrow, *n.* mayuge 眉毛.

eyeglasses, *n.* megane 眼鏡.

eyelash, *n.* matsuge 睫毛.

eyelid, *n.* mabuta 瞼.

eye shadow, *n.* aishadō アイシャドー.

eyesight, *n.* shiryoku 視力.

eyewitness, *n.* mokugekisha 目撃者.

F

fable, *n.* gūwa 寓話 (short moral story).

fabric, *n.* nuno 布 (cloth).

fabricate, *vb.* 1. tsukuru 作る (make, construct). 2. detchiageru でっちあげる (forge).

fabrication, *n.* detchiage でっちあげ (falsehood).

fabulous, *adj.* 1. subarashii 素晴らしい (wonderful). 2. shinjirarenai 信じられない (incredible).

façade, *n.* shōmen 正面 (front).

face, 1. *n.* kao 顔 (of a head); kaotsuki 顔付き (facial expression); omote 表 (surface); mikake 見かけ (appearance); menboku 面目 (dignity); **face to face** men to mukatte 面と向かって; **in the face of** ... nimo kakawarazu ...にもかかわらず (despite); **lose/save face** menboku o ushinau/ hodokosu; **make faces** shikameru しかめる. 2. *vb.* (... ni) men suru (...に) 面する (look toward); chokumen suru 直面する (confront); **face up to** ... ni tachimukau ...に立ち向かう.

facelift, *n.* seikei-shujutsu 整形手術.

facet, *n.* (soku)men (側)面.

facetious, *adj.* warufuzake (no) 悪ふざけ (の).

facial, *adj.* kao (no) 顔 (の).

facile, *adj.* 1. tayasui たやすい (easy). 2. keihaku (na) 軽薄 (な) (shallow).

facilitate, *vb.* yōi ni suru 容易にする.

facility, *n.* 1. setsubi 設備 (in a building). 2. nōryoku 能力 (ability). 3. bengi 便宜 (convenience).

facsimile, *n.* fakushimiri ファクシミリ; fukusha 複写.

fact, *n.* 1. shinjitsu 真実 (truth). 2. jijitsu 事実 (real story); jissai 実際 (reality). 3. **in fact** hontō wa 本当は; jissai wa 実際は (really, actually).

factor, *n.* yōso 要素 (element).

factory, *n.* kōjō 工場.

factual, *adj.* jijitsu ni motozuku 事実に基づく (based on fact).

faculty, *n.* 1. kinō 機能 (ability). 2. gakubu 学部 (academic department). 3. kyōin 教員 (teachers).

fad, *n.* ryūkō 流行.

fade, *vb.* 1. kieru 消える (disappear). 2. shioreru しおれる

(wither). 3. aseru 焦る (discolor).

fail, 1. *n.* **without fail** kanarazu 必ず. 2. *vb.* shippai suru 失敗する (be unsuccessful); ochiru 落ちる (fail a test); otosu 落とす (fail a student); kinō shinai 機能しない (cease to function); yowaru 弱る (become weaker).

failure, *n.* 1. shippai 失敗 (blunder). 2. rakugosha 落伍者 (person).

faint, 1. *adj.* kasuka (na) 幽か (な) (indistinct, slight); yowai 弱い (feeble). 2. *vb.* kizetsu suru 気絶する (lose consciousness).

fair, 1. *n.* feā フェアー (show, exhibition); ichi 市 (market). 2. *adj.* kōsei (na) 公正 (な) (just); kōhei 公平 (unbiased); mā-mā (no) まあまあ (の) (so-so); irojiro (no) 色白 (の) (fair-skinned); kinpatsu (no) 金髪 (の) (blond); hare (no) 晴れ (の) (weather).

fairly, *adv.* 1. kanari かなり (rather). 2. kōhei ni 公平に (honestly, equally).

fairy, *n.* yōsei 妖精; **fairy tale** otogibanashi おとぎ話.

faith, *n.* 1. shinrai 信頼 (trust). 2. yakusoku 約束 (promise). 3. shinkō 信仰 (religious belief).

faithful, *adj.* chūjitsu (na) 忠実 (な) (true to fact, loyal).

faithfulness, *n.* chūjitsusa 忠実さ.

fake, 1. *n.* nisemono 贋物. 2. *adj.* nise (no) 贋 (の). 3. *vb.* detchiageru でっちあげる (counterfeit).

falcon, *n.* taka 鷹.

fall, 1. *n.* rakka 落下 (act of falling); kōka 降下 (decrease); taki 滝 (waterfall); aki 秋 (autumn); haiboku 敗北 (defeat). 2. *vb.* ochiru 落ちる (drop); taoreru 倒れ

る (fall down); sagaru 下がる (decline in degree); **fall back on** ... ni tayoru ...に頼る; **fall behind** okureru 遅れる; **fall due** kigen ga kuru 期限が来る; **fall flat** shippai suru 失敗する (fail); **fall for** damasareru 騙される (be deceived by); **fall ill** byōki ni naru 病気になる; **fall in love** koi o suru 恋をする; **fall off** heru 減る (decline).

fallacy, *n.* 1. itsuwari 偽り (deception). 2. goshin 誤信 (misconception).

fallible, *adj.* ayamachi o okashiyasui 過ちを犯し易い.

fallout, *n.* shi no hai 死の灰 (radioactive fallout).

fallow, *adj.* horikaeshita dake (no) 堀り返しただけ (の).

false, *adj.* 1. machigatteiru 間違っている (incorrect). 2. itsuwari (no) 偽り (の) (not truthful); nise (no) 偽せ (の) (spurious); **false teeth** ireba 入れ歯. 3. fujitsu (na) 不実 (な) (unfaithful).

falsehood, *n.* itsuwari 偽り; uso 嘘.

falsify, *vb.* itsuwaru 偽る.

falter, *vb.* 1. yoromeku よろめく (in walking). 2. motatsuku もたつく (in speaking).

fame, *n.* meisei 名声.

famed, *adj.* nadakai 名高い.

familiar, *adj.* 1. shitashii 親しい (intimate); yoku shitte iru よく知っている (well-known, versed in); **be familiar with** ... to shitashii (be intimate with); ... o yoku shitte iru ...をよく知っている (know well, be versed in). 2. (o)najimi (no) (お)馴染み (の) (well-acquainted).

familiarize, *vb.* naresaseru 慣れさせる (someone); ... ni nareru ...に

慣れる (oneself).

family, *n.* 1. kazoku 家族 (parent[s] and children). 2. shinseki 親戚 (relative[s]). 3. zoku 族; nakama 仲間 (group).

family name, *n.* myōji 名字; sei 姓.

famine, *n.* kikin 飢饉.

famished, *adj.* uete iru 飢えている.

famous, *adj.* yūmei (na) 有名 (な).

fan, 1. *n.* ōgi 扇 (folding fan); senpūki 扇風機 (electric fan); fan ファン (enthusiast). 2. *vb.* aogu 扇ぐ (send air); aoru 煽る (instigate).

fanatic, *n.* kyōshinsha 狂信者.

fanatical, *adj.* kyōshin-teki (na) 狂信的 (な).

fanaticism, *n.* kyōshin 狂信.

fanciful, *adj.* 1. kūsō yutaka (na) 空想豊か (な) (full of imagination). 2. sōzōjō (no) 想像上 (の) (imaginary).

fancy, 1. *n.* kūsō 空想 (imagination); kūsōryoku 空想力 (imaginative power); musō 夢想 (daydream); **take a fancy to** ...ga ki ni iru ...が気に入る. 2. *adj.* kazari no ōi 飾りの多い (decorative). 3. *vb.* kūsō suru 空想する (imagine); hoshigaru 欲しがる (crave).

fanfare, *n.* fanfāre ファンファーレ.

fang, *n.* kiba 牙.

fantastic, *adj.* 1. higenjitsu-teki (na) 非現実的 (な) (unrealistic). 2. kikai (na) 奇怪 (な) (bizarre). 3. subarashii 素晴らしい (wonderful).

fantasy, *n.* 1. yume 夢 (dream). 2. sōzō 想像 (imagination).

far, 1. *adj.* tōi 遠い (remote). 2. *adv.* tōku ni 遠くに (at or to a distant place); haruka ni 遥かに (very much); **as far as I know** watashi ga shitte iru kagiri 私が知っている限り; **how far** dono kurai どの位 (to what extent); **so far** kore made no tokoro これまでのところ (until now).

farce, *n.* chabangeki 茶番劇.

fare, 1. *n.* ryōkin 料金 (fee); tabemono 食べ物 (food). 2. *vb.* yatte ikku やって行く (get along).

Far East, *n.* kyokutō 極東.

farewell, 1. *n.* wakare 別れ (leavetaking); **bid farewell to** wakare o tsugeru 2. *interj.* Sayonara. さよなら.

farfetched, *adj.* kojitsuke (no) こじつけ (の).

farm, 1. *n.* nōjō 農場. 2. *vb.* tagayasu 耕す (cultivate).

farmer, *n.* nōgyōkeieisha 農業経営者 (farm operator).

farmhouse, *n.* nōka 農家.

farming, *n.* nōgyō 農業.

fascinate, *vb.* miwaku suru 魅惑する.

fascinating, *adj.* miwaku-teki (na) 魅惑的 (な).

fascination, *n.* miwaku 魅惑.

fascism, *n.* fashizumu ファシズム; zentaishugi 全体主義.

fascist, 1. *n.* fashisuto ファシスト. 2. *adj.* fashisuto (no) ファシスト (の).

fashion, 1. *n.* fasshon ファッション; ryūkō 流行 (prevailing style); yarikata やり方 (manner); **in fashion** ryūkōchū (no). 2. *vb.* tsukuru 作る (make).

fashionable, *adj.* ryūkō (no) 流行 (の).

fast, 1. *n.* danjiki 断食 (abstinence from food). 2. *adj.* hayai 速い (rapid); shikkari shiteiru しっかりしている (firm); susundeiru 進ん

でいる (ahead of correct time). 3. *vb.* danjiki suru 断食する (abstain from food). 4. *adv.* hayaku 速く (rapidly); shikkari しっかり (tightly).

fasten, *vb.* tomeru 留める; shimeru 閉める (fix); tomaru 留まる; shimaru 閉まる (become fixed).

fastener, *n.* fasunā ファスナー; chakku チャック.

fast food, *n.* fāsuto fūdo ファースト・フード.

fastidious, *adj.* kimuzukashii 気難しい.

fat, 1. *n.* shibō 脂肪 (grease). 2. *adj.* futotteiru 太っている (plump).

fatal, *adj.* chimei-teki (na) 致命的 (な) (causing death or ruin).

fatality, *n.* shibō 死亡.

fate, *n.* 1. shukumei 宿命 (destiny). 2. shi 死 (death); hametsu 破滅 (ruin).

fateful, *adj.* jūdai (na) 重大 (な) (important).

father, *n.* chichi 父; otōsan お父さん; papa パパ.

father-in-law, *n.* gifu 義父.

fathom, *vb.* wakaru わかる (understand).

fatigue, 1. *n.* hirō 疲労. 2. *vb.* tsukaresaseru 疲れさせる.

fatten, *vb.* futoraseru 太らせる.

fatuous, *adj.* kudaranai くだらない.

faucet, *n.* jaguchi 蛇口.

fault, 1. *n.* kashitsu 過失 (mistake); kekkan 欠陥 (defect); **at fault** warui 悪い; **be one's fault** ... no sekinin de aru ...の責任である. 2. *vb.* ... no arasagashi o suru ...の荒捜しをする.

faulty, *adj.* 1. kekkan (no) 欠陥 (の) (defective). 2. ayamatta 誤った (erroneous).

favor, 1. *n.* kōi 好意 (good will, high regard); onegai お願い (a favor to ask); shinsetsu 親切 (kind act); ekohiiki えこひいき (partiality); **ask a favor** onegai suru; **be in favor** kōi o motareteiru; **Can you do me a favor?** Onegai ga arimasu; **in favor of** ... no tame ni ...の為に (to the advantage of); ... ni sansei ...に賛成 (in support of). 2. *vb.* konomu 好む (prefer); ekohiiki suru えこひいきする (treat with partiality).

favorable, *adj.* 1. kōi-teki (na) 好意的 (な) (approving). 2. yūri (na) 有利 (advantageous).

favorite, *adj.* oki ni iri (no) お気に入り (の); suki (na) 好き (な).

favoritism, *n.* ekohiiki えこひいき.

fawn, 1. *n.* kojika 子鹿 (deer). 2. *vb.* hetsurau へつらう (seek favor).

fear, 1. *n.* kyōfu 恐怖; **in fear of** ... o osorete ...を恐れて. 2. *vb.* osoreru 恐れる (be afraid of); shinpai suru 心配する (worry).

fearful, *adj.* osoroshii 恐ろしい (afraid, frightening).

fearless, *adj.* osore shirazu (no) 恐れ知らず (の).

feasible, *adj.* kanō (na) 可能 (な).

feast, 1. *n.* gochisō 御馳走 (meal); enkai 宴会 (party); saijitsu 祭日 (holiday). 2. *vb.* gochisō o taberu 御馳走を食べる (eat); **feast on** ... o tanoshimu ...を楽しむ (relish).

feat, *n.* tegara 手柄.

feather, *n.* hane 羽.

feature, *n.* tokuchō 特徴 (characteristic); medatsu bubun 目立つ部分 (noticeable part); chōhen-eiga 長編映画 (full-length movie); tokubetsukiji 特別記事

(feature article).

February, *n.* nigatsu 二月.

feces, *n.* ben 便.

fecund, *adj.* minori yutaka (na) 実り豊か (な) (fruitful).

fed, *adj.* **fed up** unzari shita うんざりした.

federal, *adj.* 1. renpō (no) 連邦 (の) (of a union of states). 2. kuni (no) 国 (の) (of the U.S. government).

federation, *n.* renpō 連邦; renmei 連盟.

fee, *n.* 1. ryōkin 料金 (charge). 2. jugyōryō 授業料 (tuition).

feeble, *adj.* yowai 弱い.

feed, 1. *n.* esa 餌 (for an animal). 2. *vb.* tabesaseru 食べさせる (give food to); taberu 食べる (eat); ataeru 与える (supply, provide); **feed on** ... o tabete ikiru ...を食べて生きる.

feedback, *n.* fīdobakku フィードバック.

feel, 1. *n.* kanshoku 感触 (touch); kanji 感じ (sensation). 2. *vb.* sawaru 触る (touch); kanjiru 感じる (experience, perceive); tesaguri suru 手探りする (search for by touching); omou 思う (think); **feel as if** marude ... no yō da to omou まるで...のようだと思う. **feel like doing** ... shitai ...したい (want to do).

feeling, *n.* 1. ishiki 意識 (awareness). 2. kanjō 感情; kimochi 気持ち (emotion). 3. kanji 感じ (impression). 4. shokkaku 触覚; kankaku 感覚 (capacity to perceive by touching).

feign, *vb.* furi o suru ふりをする.

feline, *adj.* 1. nekoka (no) 猫科 (の) (of the cat family). 2. neko no yō (na) 猫のよう (な)

(resembling a cat).

fell, *vb.* uchitaosu 打ち倒す (knock down).

fellow, *n.* 1. otoko 男 (man); yatsu 奴 (guy). 2. kai'in 会員 (member). 3. nakama 仲間 (comrade).

fellowship, *n.* 1. kai 会 (society). 2. shinkō 親交 (companionship). 3. shōgakukin 奨学金 (money); kenkyūin 研究員 (academic position).

felony, *n.* jūzai 重罪.

felt, *n.* feruto フェルト.

female, *n.* josei 女性; on'na 女 (human); mesu 雌 (animal, plant).

feminine, *adj.* 1. josei (no) 女性 (の) (of a woman). 2. joseirashii 女性らしい (womanly). 3. josei-teki (na) 女性的 (な) (effeminate).

femininity, *n.* joseirashisa 女性らしさ.

feminism, *n.* feminizumu フェミニズム.

feminist, *n.* feminisuto フェミニスト.

fence, 1. *n.* saku 柵; kakoi 囲い (barrier). 2. *vb.* kakomu 囲む (surround).

fencing, *n.* fenshingu フェンシング (sport).

fender, *n.* fendā フェンダー (car).

ferment, *n.* 1. kōbo 酵母 (yeast). 2. sōran 騒乱 (agitation).

fern, *n.* shida しだ.

ferocious, *adj.* kyōaku (na) 凶悪 (な); mugoi 惨い.

ferry, ferryboat, *n.* ferī フェリー.

fertile, *adj.* 1. tasan (na) 多産 (な) (productive). 2. hiyoku (na) 肥沃 (な) (soil). 3. kodomo ga umeru 子供が産める (capable of bearing young).

fertility, *n.* 1. hanshokuryoku 繁殖

力 (ability to reproduce). 2. yutakasa 豊かさ (profuseness).

fertilize, *vb.* 1. hiryō o yaru 肥料をやる (feed with fertilizer). 2. jusei saseru 受精させる (impregnate).

fertilizer, *n.* hiryō 肥料.

fervent, *adj.* jōnetsu-teki (na) 情熱的 (な).

fervor, *n.* jōnetsu 情熱.

fester, *vb.* 1. kanō suru 化膿する (form pus). 2. mushibamu 蝕む (rot).

festival, *n.* 1. (o)matsuri (お)祭り; saiten 祭典 (program of festive activities, gaiety). 2. saijitsu 祭日 (time of celebration).

festive, *adj.* 1. (o)matsuri (no) (お)祭り (の) (of a festival). 2. tanoshii 楽しい (joyous).

festivity, *n.* (o)iwai (お)祝い.

festoon, 1. *n.* hanazuna 花づな (garland). 2. *vb.* kazaru 飾る (decorate).

fetch, *vb.* 1. tsurete kuru 連れて来る (person); totte kuru 取って来る (thing). 2. ... ni ureru ...に売れる (be sold for ...).

fete, *n.* (o)matsuri (お)祭り.

fetid, *adj.* kusai 臭い.

fetish, *n.* fetisshu フェティッシュ.

fetter, *n.* ashikase 足かせ.

fetus, *n.* taiji 胎児.

feud, *n.* arasoi 争い.

feudal, *adj.* 1. hōkenseido (no) 封建制度 (の) (of feudalism). 2. **feudal age** hōkenjidai; **Japanese feudal lord** daimyō 大名; **feudal system** hōkenseido.

feudalistic, *adj.* hōken-teki (na) 封建的 (な).

fever, *n.* 1. netsu 熱 (high temperature). 2. nekkyō 熱狂 (craze).

feverish, *adj.* 1. netsu ga aru 熱が

ある (having a high temperature). 2. nekkyō-teki (na) 熱狂的 (な) (fervent).

few, 1. *n.* **a few** ikutsu ka 幾つか (things); ikunin ka 幾人か (people); **quite a few** tasū 多数. 2. *adj.* sukunai 少ない (not enough); shōsū (no) 少数 (not many); **no fewer than** sukunakutemo.

fiancé, -cée, *n.* fianse フィアンセ; kon'yakusha 婚約者.

fiasco, *n.* daishippai 大失敗.

fiat, *n.* meirei 命令.

fib, *n.* uso 嘘.

fiber, *n.* sen'i 繊維 (threadlike piece).

fiberglass, *n.* faibāgurasu ファイバーグラス.

fickle, *adj.* kimagure (na) 気紛れ (な).

fiction, *n.* 1. fikushon フィクション; shōsetsu 小説 (literature). 2. detchiage でっちあげ (fabrication).

fictional, *adj.* kakū (no) 架空 (の) (imaginary).

fictitious, *adj.* 1. uso (no) 嘘 (の) (fabricated). 2. kakū (no) 架空 (の) (imaginary).

fiddle, 1. *n.* baiorin バイオリン. 2. *vb.* baiorin o hiku バイオリンを弾く (play a fiddle); **fiddle with** ijikuru いじくる (toy with).

fidelity, *n.* chūsei 忠誠 (faithfulness).

fidget, *vb.* sowa-sowa suru そわそわする.

field, *n.* 1. fīrudo フィールド; kyōgijō 競技場 (sports). 2. nohara 野原 (grassland); hatake 畑 (farmland). 3. bun'ya 分野 (area of interest). 4. **fieldwork** fīrudowāku フィールドワーク.

fiend, *n.* akuma 悪魔; oni 鬼 (demon).

fierce, *adj.* 1. kyōretsu (na) 強烈 (な) (intense). 2. dōmō (na) 獰猛 (な) (ferocious).

fiery, *adj.* 1. hi no yō (na) 火のよう (な) (resembling fire). 2. hageshii 激しい (fervent).

fifteen, *n.* jūgo 十五.

fifteenth, *adj.* jūgobanme (no) 十 五番目 (の).

fifth, *adj.* gobanme (no) 五番目 (の).

fifty, *n.* gojū 五十.

fifty-fifty, *adj.* gobu-gobu (no) 五 分五分 (の).

fig, *n.* ichijiku いちじく.

fight, 1. *n.* kenka 喧嘩 (quarrel); tatakai 戦い (battle, confrontation, war); tōshi 闘志 (fighting spirit). 2. *vb.* (... to) kenka suru (...と) 喧 嘩する (quarrel); (... to) tatakau (...と) 戦う (do battle).

fighter, *n.* 1. senshi 戦士 (warrior); bokusā ボクサー (boxer). 2. sentōki 戦闘機 (plane).

figment, *n.* **a figment of one's imagination** omoisugoshi 思い過 ごし.

figurative, *adj.* hiyu-teki (na) 比喩 的 (な).

figure, 1. *n.* sūji 数字 (numerical symbol, amount); jinbutsu 人物 (person); katachi 形 (shape); zu 図 (illustration, diagram); **figure of speech** hiyu 比喩. 2. *vb.* keisan suru 計算する (compute); omou 思う (consider); **figure on** ... o ate ni suru ...を当てにする (count on); **figure out** wakaru わかる (understand); mitsukedasu 見つけ 出す (find out).

figurehead, *n.* namae dake no hito 名前だけの人.

filament, *n.* firamento フィラメン ト.

file, 1. *n.* fairu ファイル; shorui 書 類 (documents); fairu-ire ファイル 入れ (file box, folder, etc.); yasuri やすり (tool); retsu 列 (row); **file cabinet** fairu-kabinetto. 2. *vb.* fairu ni ireru ファイルに入れる (place in a file); teishutsu suru 提 出する (submit); yasuri o kakeru やすりをかける (grind with a file).

fill, *vb.* 1. michiru 満ちる (become full); mitasu 満たす (make full). 2. michiru 満ちる (occupy to capacity). 3. tsumeru 詰める (stuff, pack). 4. shimeru 占める (position). 5. **fill in** kakikomu 書 き込む (write in); daiyaku o suru 代役をする (substitute for someone).

fillet, *n.* hire(niku) ヒレ(肉) (meat); kirimi 切り身 (fish).

filling, *n.* tsumemono 詰め物.

film, 1. *n.* firumu フィルム (photographic film); eiga 映画 (movie); maku 幕 (coating). 2. *vb.* eiga o toru 映画を撮る (film a movie).

filter, 1. *n.* firutā フィルター (screen, strainer). 2. *vb.* kosu 漉す (strain).

filth, *n.* 1. yogore 汚れ (dirt). 2. hiwai na mono 卑猥なもの (obscenity).

filthy, *adj.* 1. kitanai 汚い (dirty). 2. hiwai (na) 卑猥 (な) (obscene).

fin, *n.* hire ひれ (fish).

final, 1. *n.* kimatsushiken 期末試験 (final exam); kesshōsen 決勝戦 (decisive match). 2. *adj.* saigo 最 後; saishū 最終 (last).

finale, *n.* fināre フィナーレ.

finalist, *n.* kesshō shutsujōsha 決勝 出場者.

finally, *adv.* 1. tsui ni 遂に (at last). 2. saishū-teki ni 最終的に (conclusively).

finance, 1. *n.* zaisei 財政 (money matters); zaigen 財源 (funds). 2. *vb.* yūshi suru 融資する (supply with money).

financial, *adj.* 1. kinsen-teki (na) 金銭的 (な) (monetary). 2. kin'yū (no) 金融 (の) (of banking).

financier, *n.* shihonka 資本家.

financing, *n.* yūshikin 融資金 (monetary backing).

find, 1. *n.* mekkemono めっけもの (discovery). 2. *vb.* mitsukeru 見つける (discover, come across); **find out** mitsukedasu 見つけ出す.

fine, 1. *n.* bakkin 罰金 (penalty). 2. *adj.* rippa (na) 立派 (な) (excellent); hosoi 細い (thin); sensai (na) 繊細 (な) (delicate); komakai 細かい (minute); hare (no) 晴れ (の) (weather); genki 元気 (healthy). 3. *vb.* bakkin o kasu 罰金を課す. 4. *adv.* yoku 良く (well); komakaku 細かく (thinly).

fine arts, *n.* bijutsu 美術.

finery, *n.* haregi 晴れ着 (clothes).

finesse, *n.* udemae 腕前 (skill).

finger, *n.* yubi 指; **fingertip** yubisaki 指先; **keep one's fingers crossed** kōun o inoru 幸運を祈る (pray for good luck).

fingernail, *n.* tsume 爪.

fingerprint, *n.* shimon 指紋.

finicky, *adj.* kimuzukashii 気難しい.

finish, 1. *n.* owari 終わり (end); shiage 仕上げ (surface coating or treatment). 2. *vb.* owaru 終わる (end); oeru 終える (bring to an end); shiageru 仕上げる (give a desired coating to); sumaseru 済ませる (finish eating, studying, etc.).

finite, *adj.* yūgen (no) 有限 (の).

fir, *n.* momi no ki もみの木.

fire, 1. *n.* hi 火 (flame, burning); kaji 火事 (burning of a building, etc.); netsui 熱意 (ardor); **on fire** moete 燃えて; **catch fire** hi ga tsuku; **set on fire** hi o tsukeru; **fire alarm** kasai keihōki 火災警報器; **fire engine** shōbōsha 消防車; **fire escape** hijōguchi 非常口; **fire extinguisher** shōkaki 消火器. 2. *vb.* takitsukeru 焚き付ける (ignite); happō suru 発砲する (shoot); kaiko suru 解雇する (dismiss).

firearm, *n.* teppō 鉄砲.

firecracker, *n.* bakuchiku 爆竹.

firefighter, *n.* shōbōshi 消防士.

firefly, *n.* hotaru 蛍.

fireplace, *n.* danro 暖炉.

fireproof, *adj.* taikasei (no) 耐火製 (の).

firewood, *n.* maki 薪.

fireworks, *n.* hanabi 花火.

firm, 1. *n.* kaisha 会社 (company). 2. *adj.* katai 硬い (hard); tsuyoi 強い (strong); kotei shiteiru 固定している (fixed, unchanging); ketsui ga katai 決意が固い (resolute).

first, *adj.* 1. saisho (no) 最初 (の); hajime (no) 初め (の) (earliest, initial, primary). 2. ichiban (no) 一番 (の) (leading, best, earliest, initial). 3. **first floor** ikkai 一階; **first of all** mazu まず; **at first** hajime wa 初めは; **for the first time** hajimete.

first aid, *n.* ōkyū teate 応急手当て.

first-class, *adj.* ittō (no) 一等 (の).

fiscal, *adj.* zaisei (no) 財政 (の); kaikei (no) 会計 (の); **fiscal year** kaikei nendo 会計年度.

fish, 1. *n.* sakana 魚. 2. *vb.* tsuru 釣る.

fish bowl, *n.* kingyobachi 金魚鉢.

fisherman, *n.* ryōshi 漁師.

fishhook, *n.* tsuribari 釣り針.

fishing, *n.* tsuri 釣り.

fish market, *n.* uoichiba 魚市場.

fishmonger, *n.* sakanaya 魚屋.

fishy, *adj.* 1. sakana kusai 魚臭い (having a fishy smell or taste). 2. ayashii 怪しい (dubious).

fission, *n.* bunretsu 分裂.

fissure, *n.* sakeme 裂け目.

fist, *n.* kobushi 拳.

fit, 1. *n.* hossa 発作 (spasm, paroxysm); bakuhatsu 爆発 (emotional explosion); **have a fit** bakuhatsu suru (explode). 2. *adj.* fusawashii ふさわしい (suitable); kenkō (na) 健康 (な) (healthy). 3. *vb.* ... ni au ...に合う (be suitable for, be the right size for); ... ni awaseru ...に合わせる (make suitable for); tsukeru 付ける (equip).

fitful, *adj.* 1. ochitsukanai 落ち着かない (disturbed). 2. hossa-teki (na) 発作的 (な) (spasmodic).

fitness, *n.* 1. fittonesu フィットネス (health, exercise). 2. tekiōsei 適応性 (suitableness).

fitting, *adj.* fusawashii ふさわしい.

five, *n.* go 五; itsutsu 五つ.

five hundred, *n.* gohyaku 五百.

fix, 1. *n.* kyūchi 窮地 (predicament). 2. *vb.* kotei suru 固定する (fasten, make steady); naosu 直す (repair, correct); tsukuru 作る (cook); kimeru 決める (determine).

fixed, *adj.* kotei shiteiru 固定している (fastened, unchangeable).

fixture, *n.* setsubi 設備.

fizzle out, *vb.* shirisubomi ni owaru 尻すぼみに終わる.

flabby, *adj.* gunya-gunya (no) ぐにゃぐにゃ (の).

flaccid, *adj.* gunya-gunya (no) ぐにゃぐにゃ (の).

flag, *n.* hata 旗.

flagellate, *vb.* muchiutsu 鞭打つ.

flagpole, *n.* hatazao 旗竿.

flagrant, *adj.* me ni amaru 目に余る (brazen); hajishirazu (no) 恥知らず (の) (shameless).

flair, *n.* sainō 才能 (talent).

flake, *n.* hakuhen 薄片; hitohira 一片.

flamboyant, *adj.* hade (na) 派手 (な) (flashy); daitan (na) 大胆 (な) (bold).

flame, 1. *n.* hono'o 炎 (blaze). 2. *vb.* moeru 燃える.

flamingo, *n.* furamingo フラミンゴ.

flammable, *adj.* moeyasui 燃え易い.

flank, 1. *n.* wakibara 脇腹 (of a body); yoko 横 (side). 2. *vb.* (... no) yoko ni aru (...の) 横にある (be at the side of).

flannel, *n.* furan'neru フランネル.

flap, *vb.* habatakaseru 羽ばたかせる (wings); hirugaeru 翻る (flag).

flare, 1. *n.* yureru hono'o 揺れる炎 (swaying flame); shōmeidan 照明弾 (signal). 2. *vb.* yura-yura moeru ゆらゆら燃え上がる (burn); **flare up** moeagaru 燃え上がる.

flash, 1. *n.* senkō 閃光 (lightning); kirameki きらめき (spark); furasshu フラッシュ (camera); isshun 一瞬 (instant); nyūsu-furasshu ニュースフラッシュ (news); **in a flash** tachimachi たちまち. 2. *vb.* isshun hikaru 一瞬光る (sparkle); hikaraseru 光らせる (make sparkle).

flashback, *n.* furasshubakku フ

ラッシュバック.

flash bulb, *n.* furasshu-barubu フラッシュバルブ.

flashlight, *n.* furasshuraito フラッシュライト.

flashy, *adj.* hade (na) 派手 (な).

flask, *n.* furasuko フラスコ.

flat, 1. *n.* panku パンク (flat tire); furatto フラット (music). 2. *adj.* taira (na) 平ら (な) (level); hiratai 平たい (not thick); panku shita パンクした (of a tire); tsumaranai つまらない (dull); furatto (no) フラット (の) (music).

flatten, *vb.* taira ni suru 平らにする (make flat); taira ni naru 平らになる (become flat).

flatter, *n.* 1. oseji o iu お世辞を言う (praise insincerely); hetsurau へつらう (be subservient). 2. **be flattered** ureshigaru 嬉しがる; **flatter oneself** unuboreru うぬぼれる.

flattery, *n.* oseji お世辞 (praise).

flaunt, *vb.* misebirakasu 見せびらかす.

flavor, 1. *n.* aji 味 (taste). 2. *vb.* aji o tsukeru 味をつける.

flaw, *n.* kizu 傷; kekkan 欠陥.

flawless, *adj.* mukizu (no) 無傷 (の); kanpeki (na) 完璧 (な).

flax, *n.* ama 亜麻.

flea, *n.* nomi 蚤.

flea market, *n.* nomi no ichi 蚤の市.

fleck, *n.* hanten 斑点 (speck).

fledgling, *n.* hinadori ひな鳥 (bird); shinmai 新米; kakedashi 駆け出し (person).

flee, *vb.* nigeru 逃げる (escape).

fleece, 1. *n.* yōmō 羊毛 (wool). 2. *vb.* damashitoru 騙し取る (swindle).

fleet, *n.* sentai 船隊 (ships); kantai 艦隊 (navy).

fleeting, *adj.* 1. mijikai 短い (not lasting). 2. hayaku sugiru 速く過ぎる (quick).

flesh, *n.* 1. niku 肉 (muscle and fat). 2. nikutai 肉体 (human body). 3. **in the flesh** jitsubutsu (o, ni, wa) 実物 (を、に、は) (in person).

flex, *vb.* magenobashi suru 曲げ伸ばしする.

flexible, *adj.* jūnan (na) 柔軟 (な) (elastic, adaptable).

flick, 1. *n.* keida 軽打 (light stroke). 2. *vb.* karuku utsu 軽く打つ (strike lightly).

flicker, *vb.* chira-chira hikaru/moeru ちらちら光る／燃える (glow/burn unsteadily).

flier, *n.* chirashi 散らし; bira ビラ (handbill).

flight, *n.* 1. hikō 飛行 (flying); furaito フライト; hikō 飛行 (flying by airplane); **flight attendant** jōkyakugakari 乗客係. 2. tōsō 逃走 (fleeing). 3. kaidan 階段 (steps).

flighty, *adj.* utsurigi (na) 移り気 (な).

flimsy, *adj.* 1. moroi 脆い (feeble). 2. konkyo no hakujaku (na) 根拠の薄弱 (な) (unconvincing).

flinch, *vb.* tajirogu たじろぐ; shirigomi suru 尻込みする (shrink).

fling, *vb.* nagetsukeru 投げつける.

flint, *n.* hiuchi ishi 火打石 (stone).

flip, *vb.* 1. hajiku 弾く (toss by snapping finger). 2. hikkurikaesu ひっくり返す (turn over).

flippant, *adj.* keisotsu (na) 軽卒 (な).

flirt, 1. *n.* purēbōi プレーボーイ (playboy); purēgāru プレーガール

(playgirl). 2. *vb.* ichatsuku いちゃ
つく (trifle in love).

float, *vb.* ukabu 浮かぶ (bob,
hover); ukaberu 浮かべる (cause
to float).

flock, 1. *n.* mure 群れ (group);
gunshū 群衆 (crowd). 2. *vb.*
muretsudou 群れ集う (gather in
flock).

flog, *vb.* muchiutsu 鞭打つ.

flood, 1. *n.* kōzui 洪水; hanran 氾
濫 (inundation); sattō 殺到
(overflow). 2. *vb.* hanran suru 氾
濫する (inundate); sattō suru 殺到
する (surge).

floor, 1. *n.* furoā フロアー; yuka 床
(surface); kai 階 (story). 2. *vb.*
yuka o haru 床を張る (cover);
uchinomesu 打ちのめす (knock
down).

flop, 1. *n.* daishippai 大失敗
(failure). 2. *vb.* daishippai suru 大
失敗する (fail).

floppy, *adj.* funya-funya shiteiru
ふにゃふにゃしている.

floppy disk, *n.* furoppī-disuku フ
ロッピーディスク.

floral, *adj.* hana (no) 花 (の) (of
flowers).

florid, *adj.* 1. sōshokukata (no) 装
飾過多 (の) (ornate). 2. kesshoku
ga ii 血色が良い (ruddy).

florist, *n.* hanaya 花屋.

flounce, *vb.* okotte tobidasu 怒って
飛び出す.

flounder, 1. *n.* hirame 平目 (fish).
2. *vb.* mogaku もがく (struggle
clumsily); magotsuku まごつく
(falter in speaking).

flour, *n.* komugiko 小麦粉 (wheat
flour).

flourish, 1. *n.* hade na yōsu 派手な
様子 (bravado). 2. *vb.* sakaeru 栄
える (thrive); yoku sodatsu 良く育

つ (grow well); furimawasu 振り
回す (brandish).

flout, *vb.* mikudasu 見下す.

flow, 1. *n.* nagare 流れ (stream);
ryūshutsu 流出 (outpouring). 2.
vb. nagareru 流れる (move in
stream); nagarederu 流れ出る
(pour out).

flower, 1. *n.* hana 花. 2. *vb.* hana
ga saku 花が咲く.

flowerbed, *n.* kadan 花壇.

flowerpot, *n.* uekibachi 植木鉢.

flowery, *adj.* 1. hana ippai (no) 花
一杯 (の) (full of flowers). 2.
hanagara (no) 花柄 (の) (flower-
patterned). 3. hanayaka (na) 華や
か (な) (florid).

flu, *n.* infuruenza インフルエンザ.

fluctuate, *vb.* hendō suru 変動する
(change); jōge suru 上下する
(shift up and down).

fluent, *adj.* ryūchō (na) 流暢 (な)
(in writing and speaking); tan'nō
(na) 堪能 (な) (in a foreign
language).

fluff, *n.* watage 綿毛.

fluffy, *adj.* fuwa-fuwa shite iru ふ
わふわしている.

fluid, 1. *n.* ekitai 液体 (liquid); kitai
気体 (gas). 2. *adj.* ekijō (no) 液状
(の) (liquid); kitai (no) 気体 (の)
(gaseous); ryūdō-teki (na) 流動的
(な) (changeable).

fluke, *n.* magure まぐれ.

flunk, *vb.* ochiru 落ちる (fail
examination); otosu 落とす (cause
to fail).

fluorescent, *adj.* keikōsei (no) 蛍
光性 (の); **fluorescent light**
keikōtō 蛍光灯.

flurry, *n.* 1. niwakayuki にわか雪
(snow); toppū 突風 (wind). 2.
arashi 嵐; dōyō 動揺 (sudden
excitement, commotion, etc.).

flush, 1. *n.* kōchō 紅潮 (rosy glow). 2. *adj.* suisen(shiki no) 水洗(式の) (toilet); onaji takasa (no) 同じ高さ (の) (even with surrounding surface); yutaka (na) 豊か (な) (rich). 3. *vb.* akaku naru 赤くなる (become red); mizu de oshinagasu 水で押し流す(wash out with water).

fluster, *vb.* magotsukaseru まごつかせる.

flute, *n.* furūto フルート.

flutter, 1. *n.* kōfun 興奮 (agitation). 2. *vb.* habataku 羽ばたく (wave in the air).

flux, *n.* 1. nagare 流れ (flowing). 2. eien no henka 永遠の変化 (continuous change).

fly, 1. *n.* hae 蝿 (insect); chakku チャック (of pants). 2. *vb.* tobu 飛ぶ (move or travel through the air); sōjū suru 操縦する (operate an airplane).

flying saucer, *n.* sora tobu enban 空飛ぶ円盤.

foam, 1. *n.* awa 泡. 2. *vb.* awa o tateru 泡を立てる.

focus, 1. *n.* shōten 焦点 (focal point); chūshin 中心 (center); **in/out of focus** shōten ga atte/hazurete. 2. *vb.* (... ni) shōten o awaseru (...に) 焦点を合わせる.

fodder, *n.* kaiba 飼葉.

foe, *n.* teki 敵.

fog, *n.* kiri 霧.

foggy, *adj.* kiri ga ōi 霧が多い.

foible, *n.* kiheki 奇癖.

foil, 1. *n.* haku 箔 (metallic sheet); hikitate-yaku/-mono 引き立て役／～もの (supporting role/thing); **aluminum** アルミニウム **foil** arumi-hoiru アルミホイル. 2. *vb.* habamu 阻む (frustrate).

foist, *vb.* oshitsukeru 押し付ける

(impinge).

fold, 1. *n.* orime 折り目 (crease); hida ひだ (pleat); shiwa しわ (wrinkle); kakoi 囲い (for sheep). 2. *vb.* oru 折る (paper, handkerchief, etc.); tsutsumu 包む (wrap); kumu 組む (limbs); oru 折る (collapse).

folder, *n.* hōrudā ホールダー.

foliage, *n.* ha 葉.

folk, 1. *n.* hitobito 人々 (people); kokumin 国民 (nation); minzoku 民族 (race). 2. *adj.* minkan (no) 民間 (の) (of people).

folklore, *n.* minkandensetsu 民間伝説.

follow, *vb.* 1. ... ni tsuite kuru/iku ...について来る／行く (come/go after). 2. tsugi ni kuru 次に来る (come next). 3. bikō suru 尾行する (chase). 4. ... ni shitagau ...に従う (conform, observe). 5. ... ni sotte iku ...に沿って行く (move along over or beside). 6. chūmoku suru 注目する (pay attention to). 7. wakaru わかる (understand). 8. **as follows** tsugi no tōri 次の通り; **follow up** tsuikyū suru 追求する (pursue).

follower, *n.* 1. shijisha 支持者 (supporter); fan ファン (fan). 2. buka 部下 (subordinate); deshi 弟子 (disciple).

following, 1. *n.* tsugi no koto 次の事 (what follows). 2. *adj.* tsugi (no) 次 (の).

folly, *n.* gukō 愚行.

fond, *adj.* 1. suki 好き (having affection); ai ni afureta 愛に溢れた (full of love); **be fond of** ... ga suki de aru. 2. dekiai (no) 溺愛 (の) (doting).

fondle, *vb.* aibu suru 愛撫する.

food, *n.* tabemono 食べ物.

foodstuffs, *n.* shokuryō 食料.

fool, 1. *n.* baka 馬鹿; **make a fool of** ... o baka ni suru. 2. *vb.* damasu 騙す (deceive); jōdan o iu 冗談を言う (joke); **fool around** fuzakemawaru ふざけ回る.

foolhardy, *adj.* mucha (na) 無茶 (な).

foolish, *adj.* baka (na) 馬鹿 (な); oroka (na) 愚か (な).

foot, *n.* 1. ashi 足 (part of body); **on foot** aruite 歩いて. 2. fīto フィート (unit of length). 3. moto もと (lowest part); fumoto 麓 (mountain foot).

football, *n.* futtobōru フットボール.

foothold, *n.* ashiba 足場.

footing, *n.* kiban 基盤 (foundation); ashiba 足場 (foothold).

footlights, *n.* futtoraito フットライト.

footnote, *n.* kyakuchū 脚注.

footprint, *n.* ashiato 足跡.

footstep, *n.* ashioto 足音.

footwear, *n.* hakimono 履物.

for, 1. *prep.* ... no tame ni ...の為に (with the purpose of, in the interest of, in favor of); ... no kawari ni ...の代わりに (in place of); ... no aida ...の間; -kan -間 (during); ... ni mukatte ...に向かって (toward); ... to shite ...として (as being). 2. *conj.* naze nara 何故 なら (because). 3. **for five hours** gojikan 五時間; **as for** ... ni tsuite wa ...については; **for all** ... nimo kakawarazu にもかかわらず (despite); **for good** eikyū ni 永久 に (forever); **for once** ichido dake 一度だけ; **if it were not for** ... ga (i)nakereba ...が (い)なければ.

forage, *vb.* sagasu 捜す.

foray, *n.* totsugeki 突撃.

forbearance, *n.* 1. nintai 忍耐 (patience). 2. kandaisa 寛大さ (tolerance, mercy).

forbid, *vb.* kinjiru 禁じる.

force, 1. *n.* chikara 力 (power, strength, influence); bōryoku 暴力 (violence); kenryoku 権力 (political power); guntai 軍隊 (military units); **by force** bōryoku de (using violence); **force of arms** buryoku 武力; **in force** ōzei de 大勢で (in large numbers). 2. *vb.* kyōsei suru 強制する (impose upon a person); muri ni ... saseru 無理に...させる (compel to do...); oshiakeru 押し開ける (break open by force).

forceful, *adj.* chikarazuyoi 力強い (powerful).

forcible, *adj.* 1. chikarazuku (no) 力づく (の) (using one's physical force). 2. chikarazuyoi 力強い (forceful); yūryoku (na) 有力 (な) (influential).

ford, *n.* asase 浅瀬.

fore, *n.* zenmen 前面; **to the fore** zenmen ni.

forearm, *n.* maeude 前腕.

forebear, *n.* senzo 先祖.

foreboding, *n.* warui yokan 悪い予 感.

forecast, 1. *n.* yohō 予報. 2. *vb.* yosoku suru 予測する.

forefather, *n.* senzo 先祖.

forefinger, *n.* hitosashi yubi 人差 し指.

forefront, *n.* saizensen 最前線.

foreground, *n.* zenmen 前面.

forehead, *n.* hitai 額.

foreign, *adj.* 1. gaikoku (no) 外国 (の) (of or related to a foreign country). 2. ishitsu (no) 異質 (の) (incompatible). 3. soto kara (no)

外から (の) (from outside). 4.
foreign affairs gaikōmondai 外交
問題; **foreign exchange**
gaikokukawase.

foreigner, *n.* gaikokujin 外国人.

foreman, *n.* genba kantoku 現場監
督.

foremost, *adj.* ichiban (no) 一番
(の).

forensic, *adj.* hōtei (no) 法廷 (の);
  forensic medicine hōigaku 法医
学.

forerunner, *n.* senkusha 先駆者.

foresee, *vb.* yosoku suru 予測する.

foreseeable, *adj.* yosoku kanō (na)
予測可能 (な).

foreshadow, *vb.* ... no maebure to
naru ...の前触れとなる.

foresight, *n.* senken no mei 先見の
明.

forest, *n.* mori 森.

forestall, *vb.* dashinuku 出し抜く.

forestry, *n.* sanrinkanri 山林管理.

foretell, *vb.* yogen suru 予言する.

forever, *adv.* 1. itsu made mo いつ
までも; eien ni 永遠に (eternally).
2. itsumo いつも (always).

forewarn, *vb.* keikoku suru 警告す
る.

foreword, *n.* maegaki 前書き.

forfeit, *vb.* bosshū sareru 没収され
る (have taken away); nakusu な
くす (lose).

forge, 1. *n.* ro 炉 (furnace, smithy).
2. *vb.* gizō suru 偽造する (imitate
fraudulently); tsukuru 作る
(make).

forgery, *n.* gizō 偽造 (act of
counterfeiting); gizōhin 偽造品
(counterfeit).

forget, *vb.* wasureru 忘れる.

forgetful, *adj.* wasureppoi 忘れっ
ぽい.

forgive, *vb.* yurusu 許す.

forgiveness, *n.* yōsha 容赦;
yurushi 許し.

forgo, *vb.* ... nashi de sumasu ... な
しで済ます.

fork, *n.* 1. fōku フォーク (for
eating). 2. kumade 熊手 (for
farming). 3. wakaremichi 別れ道
(in a road); mata 股 (of a tree).

forlorn, *adj.* kodoku (na, no) 孤独
(な、の) (solitary); sabishii 寂しい
(lonely).

form, 1. *n.* katachi 形 (shape, sort);
kata 型 (mold); yōshi 用紙
(document); hōshiki 方式
(standard practice). 2. *vb.*
katachizukuru 形作る (shape);
tsukuru 作る (build, make).

formal, *adj.* 1. seishiki (na) 正式
(な) (appropriate, official); kōrei
(no) 恒例 (の) (customary). 2.
gishiki-teki (na) 儀式的 (な)
(ceremonious). 3. katakurushii 固
苦しい (stiff).

formality, *n.* 1. keishiki 形式
(ceremony). 2. keishiki-teki
tetsuzuki 形式的手続き (formal
procedure). 3. keishikisonchō 形
式尊重 (observance of
convention).

format, *n.* teisai 体裁 (in printed
matter); fōmatto フォーマット (in
computers).

formation, *n.* keisei 形成
(generation, development, etc.).

former, *adj.* mae (no) 前 (の); **the
former** zensha 前者.

formerly, *adv.* mae ni/wa 前に／
は.

formidable, *adj.* 1. osore ōi 恐れ多
い (awesome). 2. te ni oenai 手に
負えない (difficult).

formula, *n.* 1. kōshiki 公式
(scientific description). 2. kimarimonku 決まり文句 (set form of

words). 3. tsukurikata 作り方 (recipe).

formulate, *vb.* junjoyoku noberu 順序良く述べる (state systematically).

fornicate, *vb.* shitsū suru 私通する (commit illicit intercourse).

forsake, *vb.* suteru 捨てる (give up something); misuteru 見捨てる (abandon someone).

forswear, *vb.* chikatte yameru 誓って止める.

fort, *n.* toride 砦.

forte, *n.* tsuyomi 強み.

forth, *adv.* saki ni 先に (forward); soto ni 外に (out); ato ni 後に (onward); **and so forth** ... nado ... など; **go forth** susumu 進む; **back and forth** ittari kitari 行ったり来たり.

forthcoming, *adj.* chikaku okonawareru/kuru 近く行われる／来る (about to happen/appear).

forthright, *adj.* sotchoku (na) 卒直 (な).

fortieth, *adj.* yonjūbanme (no) 四十番目 (の).

fortify, *vb.* tsuyomeru 強める.

fortitude, *n.* fukutsu 不屈.

fortnight, *n.* nishūkan 二週間.

fortress, *n.* yōsai 要塞.

fortuitous, *adj.* gūzen (no) 偶然 (の).

fortunate, *adj.* kōun (na) 幸運 (な).

fortune, *n.* **good fortune** kōun 幸運.

fortuneteller, *n.* uranaishi 占い師.

forty, *n.* yonjū 四十.

forum, *n.* fōramu フォーラム.

forward, 1. *adj.* mae (no) 前 (の) (toward the front); ato (no) 後 (の) (future); susunde iru 進んでいる (advanced). 2. *vb.* kaisō suru

回送する (forward a letter). 3. *adv.* mae ni 前に (toward the front); ato ni 後に (toward the future).

fossil, *n.* kaseki 化石.

foster, 1. *adj.* **foster parent** sato-oya 里親. 2. *vb.* sodateru 育てる (promote growth).

foul, 1. *adj.* kitanai 汚い (dirty); kusai 臭い (bad smelling); areru 荒れる (stormy); akushitsu (na) 悪質 (な) (bad); iya (na) 嫌 (な) (abominable). 2. *vb.* yogosu 汚す (make impure); yogoreru 汚れる (become impure).

foul-mouthed, *adj.* kuchi ga warui 口が悪い.

found, *vb.* setsuritsu suru 設立する (establish).

foundation, *n.* 1. kiso 基礎 (base). 2. zaidan 財団; kikin 基金 (organization).

founder, 1. *n.* setsuritsusha 設立者 (person who founds). 2. *vb.* chinbotsu suru 沈没する (sink).

foundry, *n.* izōkōjō 鋳造工場.

fountain, *n.* izumi 泉 (spring); funsui 噴水 (mechanical jet).

four, *n.* yon 四; yottsu 四つ; **on all fours** yotsunbai de 四つん這いで (crawling).

four hundred, *n.* yonhyaku 四百.

fourteen, *n.* jūyon 十四.

fourteenth, *adj.* jūyonbanme 十四番目.

fourth, *adj.* yonbanme 四番目.

fowl, *n.* tori 鳥 (bird); niwatori 鶏 (chicken).

fox, *n.* kitsune 狐.

fox trot, *n.* fokkusu-torotto フォックストロット.

foxy, *adj.* 1. kitsune no yō (na) 狐のよう (な) (resembling a fox). 2. zurui ずるい (cunning). 3. sekushī (na) セクシー (な) (sexy).

foyer, *n.* genkan 玄関 (entrance); robī ロビー (lobby).

fracas, *n.* kenka 喧嘩.

fraction, *n.* 1. ichibubun 一部分 (small part). 2. bunsū 分数 (math).

fracture, 1. *n.* kossetsu 骨折 (breaking of bone). 2. *vb.* oreru/oru 折れる／折る (break/cause to break bone, etc.).

fragile, *adj.* 1. moroi 脆い; kowareyasui 壊れ易い (easily damaged). 2. hiyowa (na) ひ弱 (な) (weak).

fragment, *n.* danpen 断片 (of a story, etc.); hahen 破片 (of glass, etc.).

fragmentary, *adj.* danpen-teki (na) 断片的 (な).

fragrance, *n.* kaori 香り.

fragrant, *adj.* kaguwashii かぐわしい.

frail, *adj.* kayowai か弱い (physically weak).

frame, 1. *n.* furēmu フレーム; gaku 額 (for a painting, etc); waku 枠 (enclosing border); taikaku 体格 (bodily build); kokkaku 骨格 (skeleton); kōzō 構造 (structure); **frame of mind** shinjō 心情. 2. *vb.* gaku ni ireru 額に入れる (painting).

framework, *n.* honegumi 骨組み.

France, *n.* furansu フランス.

franchise, *n.* 1. senkyoken 選挙権 (right to vote). 2. furanchaizu フランチャイズ (right to do business).

frank, *adj.* sotchoku (na) 卒直 (な) (candid).

frankness, *n.* sotchokusa 卒直さ (candidness).

frantic, *adj.* kōfun shiteiru 興奮している.

fraternal, *adj.* 1. kyōdai (no) 兄弟 (の) (of brothers). 2. kyōdai no yō (na) 兄弟のよう (な) (like brothers).

fraternity, *n.* danshishakō-kurabu 男子社交クラブ.

fraud, *n.* sagi 詐欺.

fraudulent, *adj.* 1. sagi (no) 詐欺 (の) (characterized by fraud). 2. fusei (na) 不正 (な) (dishonest).

fray, 1. *n.* kenka 喧嘩 (fight). 2. *vb.* suriheru 磨り減る (wear out by rubbing).

freak, *n.* 1. kikei 奇形 (unnatural form). 2. kichigai 気違い (enthusiast). 3. henjin 変人 (eccentric person).

freckle, *n.* sobakasu そばかす.

free, 1. *adj.* jiyū (na, no) 自由 (な、の) (liberated, emancipated); hima (na) 暇 (な) (not busy); tada (no) 只 (の) (without charge); aiteiru 空いている (not occupied); **for free** tada de; **free from** ... o manugarete ...を免れて. 2. *vb.* kaihō suru 解放する (emancipate, make free).

freedom, *n.* jiyū 自由.

freeway, *n.* furīwei フリーウェイ.

free will, *n.* jiyūishi 自由意志.

freeze, *vb.* 1. kōru/kōraseru 凍る／凍らせる (harden/cause to harden into ice). 2. kogoeru 凍える (feel extremely cold). 3. reitō suru 冷凍する (freeze food). 4. tachitsukusu 立ち尽くす; ugokanai 動かない (stand still). 5. tōketsu suru 凍結する (freeze prices, wages, etc.).

freezer, *n.* furīzā フリーザー.

freight, *n.* 1. yusō 輸送 (conveyance of goods). 2. kamotsu 貨物 (thing conveyed). 3. yusōryō 輸送料 (charges).

freighter, *n.* kamotsusen 貨物船.

French, 1. *n.* furansujin フランス人 (person); furansugo フランス語 (language). 2. *adj.* furansu (no) フランス (の) (of France); furansujin (no) フランス人 (の) (of the French).

French fries, *n.* furenchi-furai フレンチフライ.

Frenchman -woman, *n.* furansujin フランス人.

frenzy, *n.* gyakujō 逆上 (hysteria); kyōran 狂乱 (hysteria, outburst, madness); hossa 発作 (fit, attack).

frequency, *n.* 1. shūhasū 周波数 (radio). 2. hindo 頻度 (rate of recurrence).

frequent, 1. *adj.* hinpan (na) 頻繁 (な). 2. *vb.* hinpan ni otozureru 頻繁に訪れる.

fresh, *adj.* 1. furesshu (na) フレッシュ (な); shinsen (na) 新鮮 (な) (air, food, flower, etc.). 2. mamizu (no) 真水 (の) (freshwater). 3. atarashii 新しい (new). 4. betsu (no) 別 (の) (another). 5. namaiki (na) 生意気 (な) (cheeky).

freshen, *vb.* atarashiku naru/suru 新しくなる／する (become/make new).

fret, *vb.* 1. yakimoki suru やきもきする (worry). 2. iratsuku 苛つく (irritate).

friar, *n.* shūdōshi 修道士.

friction, *n.* masatsu 摩擦.

Friday, *n.* kin'yōbi 金曜日.

fried, *adj.* 1. furai (no) フライ (の). 2. **fried potato** furaido-poteto フライドポテト; poteto-furai ポテトフライ; **fried egg** medamayaki 目玉焼き; **fried rice** yakimeshi 焼飯.

friend, *n.* tomodachi 友達; **make friends with** ... to tomodachi ni naru.

friendly, *adj.* 1. shinsetsu (na) 親切 (な) (kind, helpful). 2. hito natsukkoi 人なつっこい (fond of people); aisō ga ii 愛想が良い (affable, sociable). 3. yūkō-teki (na) 友好的 (な) (amicable); **friendly nation** yūkōkoku 友好国.

friendship, *n.* yūjō 友情.

frigate, *n.* furigēto-kan フリゲート艦.

fright, *n.* kyōfu 恐怖; obie 怯え (fear); **in a fright** obiete 怯えて.

frighten, *vb.* obiyakasu 脅かす.

frightful, *adj.* 1. osoroshii 恐ろしい (dreadful). 2. hidoi ひどい (ugly, tasteless).

frigid, *adj.* 1. tsumetai 冷たい (cold, unfriendly). 2. fukanshō (no) 不感症 (の) (lacking sexual appetite).

frill, *n.* 1. furiru フリル (of a curtain, dress, etc.). 2. yokei na kazari 余計な飾り (unnecessary ornament).

fringe, *n.* 1. fuchidori 縁取り (border). 2. hashikko 端っこ; katasumi 片隅 (farthest end); **fringe of society** shakai no katasumi.

frisky, *adj.* genki ippai (no) 元気一杯 (の).

frivolous, *adj.* 1. fuzake hanbun (no) ふざけ半分 (の) (not serious). 2. keihaku (na) 軽薄 (な) (flippant).

frock, *n.* doress ドレス.

frog, *n.* kaeru 蛙.

frogman, *n.* sensuifu 潜水夫.

frolic, 1. *n.* ukaresawagi 浮かれ騒ぎ. 2. *vb.* asobimawaru 遊び回る.

from, *prep.* 1. ...kara ...から (out of, starting at, given by); **from**

America amerika kara; **from nine o'clock** kuji kara. 2. ...de ... で (because of); **die from** ... de shinu ...で死ぬ.

front, 1. *n.* mae 前; zenmen 前面 (foremost part); shōmen 正面 (of a building); hyōmen 表面 (foremost surface); misekake 見せかけ (outward appearance); zensen 前線 (military, weather); **in front** mae de/ni; **in front of** ... no mae de/ni. 2. *adj.* mae (no) 前 (の) (of, situated in, or at the front); shōmen (no) 正面 (の) (of a bulding).

frontal, *adj.* zenmen (no) 前面 (の) (of, in, or at the front).

frontier, *n.* 1. kokkyō 国境 (border of a country). 2. henkyō 辺境 (outer edge of civilization).

frost, *n.* shimo 霜.

frostbite, *n.* shimoyake 霜焼け.

frosty, *adj.* 1. samui 寒い (cold). 2. shimofuri (no) 霜降り (の) (covered with frost). 3. reitan (na) 冷淡 (な) (unfriendly).

froth, *n.* awa 泡.

frown, 1. *n.* shikamettsura しかめつ面. 2. *vb.* kao o shikameru 顔をしかめる.

frugal, *adj.* 1. ken'yaku (no) 倹約 (の) (thrifty). 2. shisso (na) 質素 (な) (scanty).

fruit, *n.* 1. furūtsu フルーツ; kudamono 果物 (food). 2. seika 成果 (result).

fruitful, *adj.* minori yutaka (na) 実り豊か (な).

fruition, *n.* jitsugen 実現 (realization).

fruitless, *adj.* muda (na) 無駄 (な) (useless).

frustrate, *vb.* 1. habamu 阻む (thwart). 2. yokkyūfuman ni

ochi'iraseru 欲求不満に陥らせる (cause frustration).

frustration, *n.* yokkyūfuman 欲求不満 (dissatisfaction).

fry, *vb.* ageru 揚げる (deep-fry); itameru 炒める (stir-fry); yaku 焼く (fry lightly).

frying pan, *n.* furai-pan フライパン.

fuel, *n.* nenryō 燃料.

fugitive, *n.* tōbōsha 逃亡者.

fulcrum, *n.* shiten 支点.

fulfill, *vb.* 1. mitasu 満たす (satisfy requirement, etc.). 2. hatasu 果たす (carry out, achieve, finish, succeed).

fulfillment, *n.* 1. kansei 完成 (achievement). 2. manzoku 満足 (contentment).

full, *adj.* 1. ippai haitteiru 一杯入っている (filled completely); man'in (no) 満員 (の) (filled with people). 2. takusan (no) たくさん (の) (abundant). 3. zenbu (no) 全部 (の) (entire); kanzen (na) 完全 (な) (complete). 4. onaka ga ippai (no) お腹が一杯 (の) (having a full stomach). 5. **full of** ... de ippai.

full moon, *n.* mangetsu 満月.

full-time, *adj.* 1. seishain (no) 正社員 (の) (of a worker); sen'nin (no) 専任 (の) (of a teacher); seiki no gakusei (no) 正規の学生 (の) (of a student). 2. **work full-time** seishain de hataraku

fumble, *vb.* 1. tesaguri suru 手探りする (grope). 2. hema o suru へまをする (bungle, botch).

fume, *vb.* gekido suru 激怒する.

fumigate, *vb.* funmushōdoku suru 噴霧消毒する.

fun, *n.* 1. yukai na koto 愉快なこと; tanoshii koto 楽しいこと

(enjoyment, playfulness). 2. **have fun** tanoshimu 楽しむ; **make fun of** ... o karakau ...をからかう; **in fun** jōdan de 冗談で.

function, 1. *n.* kinō 機能; hataraki 働き (fitting or assigned activity); gyōji 行事 (formal social gathering). 2. *vb.* kinō suru 機能する (perform a function); ugoku 動く (work, operate).

functional, *adj.* kinō-teki (na) 機能的 (な).

fund, *n.* kikin 基金 (supply of money).

fundamental, *adj.* kihon-teki (na) 基本的 (な).

funeral, *n.* sōshiki 葬式.

fungus, *n.* 1. kabi かび (mold). 2. kinoko きのこ (mushroom).

funnel, *n.* 1. jōgo じょうご (utensil). 2. entotsu 煙突 (smokestack).

funny, *adj.* 1. okashii おかしい (amusing). 2. hen (na) 変 (な) (strange).

fur, *n.* kegawa 毛皮 (skin, garment).

furious, *adj.* 1. ikarikuru'u 怒り狂う (angry). 2. arekuru'u 荒れ狂う (violent).

furlough, *n.* 1. kyūka 休暇 (leave of absence). 2. ichijikaiko 一時解雇 (temporary layoff).

furnace, *n.* 1. yōkōro 溶鉱炉 (for smelting ores). 2. danbōro 暖房炉 (for heating a house).

furnish, *vb.* kagu o sonaetsukeru 家具を備え付ける (fit out with furniture). 2. kyōkyū suru 供給する (supply).

furniture, *n.* kagu 家具.

furor, *n.* nekkyō 熱狂.

furrow, *n.* 1. unema 畝間 (trench made by plow). 2. shiwa しわ (wrinkle).

furry, *adj.* 1. kegawa (no) 毛皮 (の) (of fur). 2. kegawa de ōwareteiru 毛皮で覆われている (covered with fur).

further, 1. *adj.* sore ijō (no) それ以上 (の) (more); hoka (no) 他 (の) (other). 2. *adv.* sara ni 更に; motto もっと (more); motto tōku made もっと遠くまで (to a greater distance). 3. *vb.* sokushin suru 促進する (promote).

furthermore, *adv.* sore ni それに.

furtive, *adj.* koso-koso shiteiru こそこそしている.

fury, *n.* gekido 激怒 (anger).

fuse, 1. *n.* dōkasen 導火線 (for a bomb); hyūzu ヒューズ (for a circuit breaker). 2. *vb.* tokeru 溶ける (melt); tokasu 溶かす (cause to melt); tokeau 溶け合う (blend).

fusion, *n.* fyūjon フュージョン; yūgō 融合 (blending, union).

fuss, 1. *n.* torikoshigurō 取り越し苦労 (needless concern); ōsawagi 大騒ぎ (overreaction); fuhei 不平 (complaint); **make a fuss** ōsawagi o suru. 2. *vb.* sawagi tateru 騒ぎ立てる (overreact).

fussy, *adj.* komakai 細かい (fastidious); urusai うるさい (particular, meticulous).

futile, *adj.* muda (na) 無駄 (な).

future, *n.* mirai 未来; shōrai 将来.

fuzz, *n.* watage 綿毛 (fluff).

fuzzy, *adj.* 1. kebadatteiru 毛ば立っている (fluffy). 2. hakkiri shinai はっきりしない (vague).

G

gable, *n.* kirizuma 切妻.

gadget, *n.* 1. kufū 工夫 (device). 2. benri na mono 便利なもの (ingenious article).

gag, *n.* 1. sarugutsuwa 猿轡 (restraint). 2. jōdan 冗談; gyagu ギャグ (joke).

gaiety, *n.* yōkisa 陽気さ; tanoshisa 楽しさ (merriment).

gain, 1. *n.* mōke 儲け; rieki 利益 (profit); zōka 増加 (increase). 2. *vb.* eru 得る (obtain); fueru 増える (increase); mōkeru 儲ける (gain profit); kachieru 勝ち得る (win); oiageru 追い上げる (in a race); susumu 進む (of a watch); **gain weight** taijū ga fueru 体重が増える.

gait, *n.* ashidori 足取り.

gala, *n.* iwai 祝い; shukuten 祝典.

galaxy, *n.* 1. ginga 銀河; **Galaxy** amanogawa 天の川 (Milky Way). 2. kagayakashii ichidan 輝かしい一団 (brilliant group).

gall bladder, *n.* tan'nō 胆のう.

gallant, *adj.* 1. gyaranto (na) ギャラント (な); isamashii 勇ましい (brave); kedakai 気高い (noble). 2. shinshi-teki na 紳士的な (gentlemanly); kishi no yō (na) 騎士のよう (な) (chivalrous).

gallery, *n.* 1. gyararī ギャラリー; garō 画廊 (for art exhibition); bijutsukan 美術館 (art museum). 2. tenjishitsu 展示室 (exhibition room). 3. rōka 廊下 (hallway).

galley, *n.* 1. gera ゲラ (galley proof). 2. chōrishitsu 調理室 (ship kitchen).

gallon, *n.* garon ガロン.

gallop, 1. *n.* gyaroppu ギャロップ. 2. *vb.* hayaku hashiru 速く走る.

gallows, *n.* kōshudai 絞首台.

galore, *adv.* tappuri たっぷり; takusan たくさん.

galvanize, *vb.* 1. aenmekki o suru 亜鉛めっきをする (coat with zinc). 2. denki o nagasu 電気を流す (conduct electric current). 3. karitateru 駆り立てる (startle into action).

gamble, 1. *n.* gyanburu ギャンブル; kake 賭け. 2. *vb.* gyanburu o suru ギャンブルをする; kakeru 賭ける.

gambler, *n.* gyanburā ギャンブラー.

gambling, *n.* gyanburu ギャンブル; kake 賭け.

game, *n.* 1. asobi 遊び (pastime). 2. shiai 試合; kyōgi 競技; gēmu ゲーム (match, contest). 3. emono 獲物 (hunted animal).

gamut, *n.* zenbu 全部; zen'iki 全域 (full range).

gang, *n.* ichimi 一味; bōryokudan 暴力団 (group of gangsters).

gangster, *n.* gangu ギャング; bōryokudan'in 暴力団員.

gap, *n.* 1. gyappu ギャップ; mizo 溝 (disparity). 2. ana 穴; sukima 隙間 (opening). 3. kūhaku 空白 (blank space).

gape, *vb.* 1. kuchi o akeru 口を開ける (open one's mouth). 2. pokan to shite mitsumeru ぽかんとして見つめる (stare with open mouth).

garage, *n.* garēji ガレージ; shako 車庫.

garb, *n.* fukusō 服装.

garbage, *n.* gomi ゴミ; kuzu 屑.

garble, *n.* 1. torichigaeru 取り違える (confuse unintentionally). 2. waikyoku suru 歪曲する (distort).

garden, *n.* niwa 庭 (private); teien 庭園 (public); **botanical garden** shokubutsuen 植物園.

gardener, *n.* niwashi 庭師; zōenka 造園家.

gardening, *n.* niwashigoto 庭仕事; zōen 造園.

gargle, 1. *n.* ugai うがい. 2. *vb.* ugai o suru うがいをする.

garland, *n.* hanawa 花輪.

garlic, *n.* gārikku ガーリック; nin'niku にんにく.

garment, *n.* fuku 服.

garnish, 1. *n.* kazari 飾り (decoration); ryōri no soemono 料理の添え物 (food). 2. *vb.* kazaru 飾る (decorate).

garret, *n.* yaneurabeya 屋根裏部屋.

garrulous, *adj.* oshaberi (na) おしゃべり (な).

garter, *n.* gātā ガーター (elastic band).

gas, *n.* 1. gasu ガス; kitai 気体 (fluid). 2. gasorin ガソリン (gasoline); **gas station** gasorin-sutando.

gash, *n.* fukai kirikizu 深い切り傷 (deep wound).

gasp, 1. *n.* iki o nomu koto 息を飲む事 (intake of breath); aegi あえぎ (convulsive effort to breathe). 2. *vb.* iki o nomu 息を飲む (catch one's breath); aegu あえぐ (struggle for breath); aeide iu あえいで言う (say while gasping).

gastronomy, *n.* bishokuhō 美食法.

gate, *n.* mon 門.

gather, *vb.* 1. atsumeru 集める (bring together); atsumaru 集まる (get together). 2. suisoku suru 推測する (infer). 3. tori'ireru 取り入れる (harvest).

gathering, *n.* tsudoi 集い; atsumari 集まり.

gaudy, *adj.* keba-kebashii けばけばしい; hade (na) 派手 (な).

gauge, 1. *n.* hakari 計り (measurement); keiryōki 計量器 (measuring instrument); hyōka 評価 (appraisal); kijun 基準 (criterion). 2. *vb.* hakaru 計る (measure); hyōka suru 評価する (appraise).

gaunt, *adj.* yasekokete iru やせこけている.

gauze, *n.* 1. sha 紗 (fabric). 2. gāze ガーゼ (medical).

gay, 1. *n.* gei ゲイ; homo ホモ; dōseiaisha 同性愛者 (homosexual). 2. *adj.* yōki (na) 陽気 (な); hade (na) 派手 (な) (bright, showy); gei/homo (no) ゲイ／ホモ (の).

gaze, 1. *n.* gyōshi 凝視. 2. *vb.* mitsumeru 見つめる.

gear, *n.* 1. gia ギア; haguruma 歯車 (cogwheel). 2. dōgu 道具 (tools).

gelatin, *n.* zerachin ゼラチン.

gem, *n.* hōseki 宝石.

gender, *n.* sei 性; **gender discrimination** seisabetsu.

gene, *n.* idenshi 遺伝子.

genealogy, *n.* keizu 系図; kakei 家系.

general, 1. *n.* rikugunshōkan 陸軍将官 (military). 2. *adj.* ippan no 一般の (usual); zentai-teki (na) 全体的 (な) (of entirety); daitai no 大体の (approximate).

generalization, *n.* 1. ippanka 一般化 (act of generalizing). 2. ippan-hōsoku 一般法則 (general principle).

generalize, *vb.* ippanka suru 一般化する; hōsokuka suru 法則化する.

generally, *adv.* 1. ippan ni 一般に (in general). 2. futsū wa 普通は (usually). 3. taitei 大抵 (for the most part).

generate, *vb.* umidasu 生み出す (produce).

generation, *n.* 1. sedai 世代 (of people); **generation gap** sedaisa. 2. seisan 生産 (production); hatsuden 発電 (generation of electricity).

generator, *n.* jenerētā ジェネレーター; hatsudenki 発電機 (electrical).

generosity, *n.* kandaisa 寛大さ; kimae no yosa 気前の良さ (magnanimity).

generous, *adj.* 1. kandai (na) 寛大 (な) (magnanimous); kimae ga ii 気前が良い (giving freely). 2. tappuri (no) たっぷり (の) (abundant).

genesis, *n.* hajimari 始まり; hassei 発生 (beginning, origin).

genetic, *adj.* 1. idengaku (no) 遺伝学 (の) (pertaining to genetics). 2. idenshi (no) 遺伝子 (の) (pertaining to genes).

genetics, *n.* idengaku 遺伝学.

genial, *adj.* 1. yūkō-teki (na) 友好的 (な); yasashii 優しい (person). 2. kaiteki (na) 快適 (な) (weather).

genitals, *n.* seiki 性器.

genius, *n.* tensai 天才.

genocide, *n.* minzoku-bokumetsu 民族撲滅.

genre, *n.* 1. janru ジャンル; burui 部類; ha 派 (class). 2. yōshiki 様式 (style).

genteel, *adj.* 1. jōhin (na) 上品 (な) (elegant). 2. kidotta 気取った (affected).

gentle, *adj.* 1. yasashii 優しい (kindly). 2. odayaka (na) 穏やかな (mild, moderate). 3. yuruyaka (na) 緩やか (な) (gradual). 4. shizuka (na) 静か (な) (quiet).

gentleman, *n.* shinshi 紳士.

gentleness, *n.* 1. yasashisa 優しさ (kindness). 2. odayakasa 穏やかさ (mildness, moderateness). 3. yuruyakasa 緩やかさ (being gradual). 4. shizukesa 静けさ (quietness).

genuine, *adj.* 1. honmono (no) 本物 (の) (authentic, real). 2. kokoro no komotta 心の込もった (sincere).

genus, *n.* shurui 種類.

geography, *n.* chirigaku 地理学.

geological, *adj.* chishitsugaku-teki (na) 地質学的 (な).

geology, *n.* chishitsugaku 地質学.

geometry, *n.* kikagaku 幾何学.

geranium, *n.* zeraniumu ゼラニウム.

germ, *n.* saikin 細菌; baikin ばい菌.

German, 1. *n.* doitsujin ドイツ人 (person); doitsugo ドイツ語 (language). 2. *adj.* doitsu (no) ドイツ (の) (of Germany); doitsujin (no) ドイツ人 (の) (of the Germans).

Germany, *n.* doitsu ドイツ.

germinate, *vb.* mebaeru 芽生える.

gestation, *n.* kaininkikan 懐妊期間.

gesture, *n.* jesuchā ジェスチャー; dōsa 動作; miburi 身振り.

get, *vb.* 1. eru 得る; te ni ireru 手に入れる (obtain). 2. uketoru 受け取る (receive). 3. ... ni naru ...になる (become). 4. ... te morau ...てもらう; ... saseru ...させる

(cause to do); **get hair cut** kami o kitte morau. 5. kasegu 稼ぐ (earn). 6. mottekuru 持って来る (fetch). 7. kikoeru 聞こえる (hear clearly). 8. wakaru わかる (understand). 9. ... ni kakaru ...に かかる (suffer from an illness). 10. **get around** ugokimawaru 動き回る (move around); **get along** saru 去る (leave); yatteiku やっていく (go on); **get away** nigeru 逃げる; **get off** (... o) oriru (...を) 降りる; **get on** ... ni noru ... に乗る; **get over** kaifuku suru 回復する; **get to** ... ni tsuku ...に着く (arrive); **get together** atsumaru 集まる (congregate, meet); atsumeru 集める (gather); **get up** okiru 起きる; **have got to do** ... shinakereba-naranai ...しなければ ならない.

getaway, *n.* tōbō 逃亡 (fleeing).

get-together, *n.* atsumari 集まり.

ghastly, *adj.* 1. osoroshii 恐ろしい (dreadful). 2. obake no yō (na) お 化けのよう (な) (spectral).

ghetto, *n.* suramu スラム.

ghost, *n.* obake お化け; yūrei 幽霊.

giant, 1. *n.* kyojin 巨人; jaianto ジャイアント. 2. *adj.* kyodai (na) 巨大 (な).

gibberish, *n.* tawagoto たわ言.

gibe, 1. *n.* azakeri 嘲り. 2. *vb.* azakeru 嘲る.

giddy, *adj.* me no kuramu (yō na) 目の眩む (ような) (dizzy).

gift, *n.* 1. okurimono 贈り物; gifuto ギフト; purezento プレゼント (present). 2. sainō 才能 (talent).

gifted, *adj.* sainō yutaka (na) 才能 豊か (な).

gigantic, *adj.* kyodai (na) 巨大 (な).

giggle, 1. *n.* kusu-kusu warai くす

くす笑い. 2. *vb.* kusu-kusu warau くすくす笑う.

gild, *vb.* kinmekki o suru 金めっき をする.

gills, *n.* era えら.

gimmick, *n.* 1. shikake 仕掛け (device). 2. tejina no tane 手品の 種 (of magic).

gin, *n.* jin ジン (drink).

ginger, *n.* shōga 生姜.

giraffe, *n.* kirin きりん.

gird, *vb.* beruto o shimeru ベルト を締める (bind with a belt).

girdle, *n.* gādoru ガードル.

girl, *n.* 1. on'na no ko 女の子; shōjo 少女 (female child). 2. wakai josei 若い女性 (young woman). 3. musume 娘 (one's daughter).

girlfriend, *n.* gārufurendo ガール フレンド; kanojo 彼女.

gist, *n.* honshitsu 本質.

give, *vb.* 1. ataeru 与える; ageru 上 げる. 2. **give back** kaesu 返す (return); **give in** makeru 負ける (yield); **give off** hanatsu 放つ (emanate); **give out** kubaru 配る (distribute); happyō suru 発表する (make public); **give up** akirameru あきらめる (abandon hope); yameru 止める (desist from, stop); hikiwatasu 引き渡す (surrender).

glacier, *n.* hyōga 氷河.

glad, *adj.* 1. ureshii 嬉しい (happy). 2. **be glad to do** yorokonde... suru 喜んで...する.

gladly, *adv.* yorokonde 喜んで.

glamour, *n.* miryoku 魅力 (fascination).

glamorous, *adj.* miryoku-teki (na) 魅力的 (な).

glance, 1. *n.* ichibetsu 一べつ. 2. *vb.* chotto miru; ちょっと見る ichibetsu suru 一べつする (look briefly).

gland, *n.* sen 腺; **endocrine gland** naibunpisen 内分泌腺.

glare, 1. *n.* giratsuku hikari ぎらつく光り (dazzling light); nirami にらみ (stare). 2. *vb.* giratsuku ぎらつく (shine); niramitsukeru にらみつける (stare).

glaring, *adj.* mabushii 眩しい (dazzling).

glass, *n.* 1. garasu ガラス (material). 2. koppu コップ (drinking glass).

glasses, *n.* megane 眼鏡.

glaze, 1. *n.* uwagusuri うわ薬 (pottery). 2. *vb.* garasu o hameru ガラスをはめる (insert glass); uwagusuri o kakeru うわ薬をかける (coat pottery); tsuya o kakeru つやをかける (gloss).

gleam, 1. *n.* hikari 光. 2. *vb.* hikaru 光る.

glee, *n.* yorokobi 喜び.

glide, *vb.* suberu 滑る; nameraka ni ugoku 滑らかに動く.

glimmer, 1. *n.* kasuka na hikari 微かな光. 2. *vb.* kasuka ni hikaru 微かに光る.

glimpse, 1. *n.* ichibetsu 一べつ. 2. *vb.* chirari to mieru ちらりと見える (catch a glimpse of); chirari to miru ちらりと見る (look briefly).

glisten, *vb.* matataku またたく; kirameku きらめく.

glitter, 1. *n.* kagayaki 輝き. 2. *vb.* kagayaku 輝く.

gloat, *vb.* manzokuge ni miru 満足気に見る.

global, *adj.* sekai-teki (na) 世界的 (な) (worldwide).

globe, *n.* chikyū 地球.

gloom, *n.* 1. usugurasa 薄暗さ (darkness). 2. yū'utsu 憂うつ (depression); kanashimi 悲しみ

(sadness).

gloomy, *adj.* 1. usugurai 薄暗い (dark). 2. yū'utsu (na) 憂うつ (な) (depressed); kanashii 悲しい (sad); unadareteiru うなだれている (dejected).

glorify, *vb.* homeageru ほめあげる.

glorious, *adj.* kagayakashii 輝かしい; eikō ni michita 栄光に満ちた.

glory, *n.* kagayakashisa 輝かしさ; eikō 栄光; homare 誉れ.

gloss, *n.* kōtaku 光沢.

glossary, *n.* shiyōgo-ichiranhyō 使用語一覧表; yōgojiten 用語辞典.

glossy, *adj.* kōtaku ga aru 光沢がある.

glove, *n.* gurōbu グローブ; tebukuro 手袋.

glow, *vb.* 1. moeru 燃える (burn). 2. hikaru 光る (shine). 3. hoteru 火照る (feel hot).

glue, 1. *n.* setchakuzai 接着剤; nori 糊. 2. *vb.* setchaku suru 接着する; tsukeru 付ける.

glum, *adj.* fukigen (na) 不機嫌 (な) (sullen); fusagikondeiru 塞ぎ込んでいる (silently gloomy).

glut, 1. *n.* kyōkyūkajō 供給過剰 (excessive supply). 2. *vb.* akiru made taberu 飽きるまで食べる (eat to excess); ... de michiafure-saseru ...で満ちあふれさせる (overfill).

glutton, *n.* ōgui 大食い; taishokukan 大食漢.

gnash, *vb.* hagishiri suru 歯ぎしりする.

gnat, *n.* buyo 蚋.

gnaw, *vb.* kajiru かじる.

go, *vb.* 1. iku 行く (move from one place to another). 2. ugoku 動く (function). 3. ... ni naru ...になる (become). 4. **be going to do** ... suru tsumori ...するつもり (intend to do); ... suru tokoro ...するところ (be about to do); **go around** hiromaru 広まる (be pervasive); **go after** motomeru 求める (try to win); **go ahead** hajimeru 始める (begin); **go away** saru 去る (leave); **go back** kaeru 帰る (return); **go by** sugiru 過ぎる (pass); **go down** sagaru 下がる (decrease); kudaru 下る (descend); shizumu 沈む (sink); **go on** aru ある (take place); tsuzukeru 続ける (continue); **go out** dekakeru 出掛ける (leave); kieru 消える (burn out); **go over** shiraberu 調べる (examine); kurikaesu 繰り返す (repeat); **go through** keiken suru 経験する (experience); tsūka suru 通過する (pass through); **go up** agaru 上がる (rise); noboru 上る (ascend).

goal, *n.* 1. gōru ゴール (target). 2. mokuteki 目的 (purpose).

goat, *n.* yagi 山羊.

God, god, *n.* kami 神.

godchild, *n.* nazukego 名付け子.

goddess, *n.* megami 女神.

godfather, godmother, *n.* nazukeoya 名付け親.

godsend, *n.* ten no tasuke 天の助け.

going, *n.* shuppatsu 出発 (departure).

gold, *n.* 1. kin 金; ōgon 黄金 (metal). 2. kin'iro 金色 (color).

golden, *adj.* 1. kin (no) 金 (の) (of gold). 2. kin'iro (no) 金色 (の) (gold-colored).

goldfish, *n.* kingyo 金魚.

goldsmith, *n.* kinzaikushi 金細工師.

golf, *n.* gorufu ゴルフ; **play golf** gorufu o suru.

gong, *n.* dora どら.

gonorrhea, *n.* rinbyō 淋病.

good, 1. *n.* eki 益 (benefit); zen 善 (moral excellence); **goods** shōhin 商品 (merchandise); shoyūhin 所有品 (possession[s]); **for good** eikyū ni 永久に. 2. *adj.* ii/yoi いい／良い; zenryō (na) 善良 (な) (morally excellent); jōshitsu (no) 上質 (の) (of good quality); jōzu (na) 上手 (な) (skillful); shinsetsu (na) 親切 (な) (kind); **a good deal** takusan たくさん (abundant); **no good** muda 無駄 (be useless).

good afternoon, *interj.* kon'nichi wa 今日は.

good-bye, *interj.* sayōnara さようなら; bai-bai バイバイ.

good evening, *interj.* konban wa 今晩は.

good-hearted, *adj.* shinsetsu (na) 親切 (な).

good-humored, *adj.* akarui 明るい.

good morning, *interj.* ohayō gozaimasu おはようございます.

good-natured, *adj.* seikaku ga ii 性格が良い.

good night, *interj.* oyasuminasai お休みなさい.

good-looking, *adj.* 1. kao ga ii 顔が良い; kakko ii かっこ良い. 2. hansamu (na) ハンサム (な) (man); kirei (na) きれい (な) (woman).

goodness, *n.* 1. zenryō 善良 (state of being good). 2. bitoku 美徳 (virtue). 3. yasashisa 優しさ (kindly feeling). 4. **Thank goodness!** Yare-yare. やれやれ.

goodwill, *n.* zen'i 善意.

goose, *n.* gachō 鵞鳥.

gore, 1. *n.* chinori 血糊; satsugai 殺害 (bloodshed). 2. *vb.* tsuku 突く

(pierce).

gorge, 1. *n.* kyōkoku 峡谷 (canyon). 2. *vb.* musaborikū 貪り食う (stuff with food).

gorgeous, *adj.* 1. gōka (na) 豪華 (な); gōjasu (na) ゴージャス (な) (luxurious). 2. subarashii 素晴らしい (splendid). 3. kirei (na) きれい (な) (very beautiful).

gorilla, *n.* gorira ゴリラ.

gory, *adj.* chimamire (no) 血まみれ (の).

gosh, *interj.* oya mā おやまあ.

gossip, 1. *n.* uwasa 噂; goshippu ゴシップ (rumor); oshaberiya おしゃべり屋 (person). 2. *vb.* uwasabanashi o suru 噂話しをする.

Gothic, *adj.* goshikku-yōshiki (no) ゴシック様式 (の) (architectural style).

gourd, *n.* hyōtan ひょうたん.

gourmand, *n.* ōgui 大食い; taishokukan 大食漢.

gourmet, *n.* shokutsū 食通; gurume グルメ.

govern, *vb.* tōchi suru 統治する; osameru 治める.

governess, *n.* josei-kateikyōshi 女性家庭教師.

government, *n.* seiji 政治 (system of rule). 2. seifu 政府 (governing body).

governor, *n.* 1. shūchiji 州知事 (in the U.S.). 2. chiji 知事 (province ruler).

gown, *n.* gaun ガウン.

grab, *vb.* tsukamu つかむ; toraeru 捕える (seize).

grace, *n.* 1. yūgasa 優雅さ; jōhinsa 上品さ (elegance). 2. biten 美点 (attractive quality). 3. megumi 恵み (favor, mercy); **in someone's good graces** (... no) okiniiri de

(...の) お気に入りで.

graceful, *adj.* yūga (na) 優雅 (な); jōhin (na) 上品 (な).

gracious, *adj.* 1. shinsetsu (na) 親切 (な) (kind). 2. michitarita 満ち足りた (pleasant).

gradation, *n.* dankai 段階.

grade, 1. *n.* tōkyū 等級 (degree of quality, rank); dankai 段階 (step); gakunen 学年 (scholastic division); seiseki 成績 (rating in school). 2. *vb.* tōkyū ni wakeru 等級に分ける (categorize); seiseki o tsukeru 成績をつける (assign a grade).

gradual, *adj.* sukoshi zutsu (no) 少しずつ (の).

graduate, 1. *n.* sotsugyōsei 卒業生. 2. *vb.* sotsugyō suru 卒業する.

graduate school, *n.* daigakuin 大学院.

graduation, *n.* sotsugyō 卒業.

graft, 1. *n.* tsugiki 接ぎ木 (of plant); ishoku 移植 (surgical); oshoku 汚職 (political). 2. *vb.* tsugiki suru 接ぎ木する; ishoku suru 移植する; oshoku o okosu 汚職を起こす.

grain, *n.* 1. kokumotsu 穀物 (seed). 2. tsubu 粒 (hard particle); **a grain of** hitotsubu (no). 3. mokume 木目 (wood grain). 4. seishitsu 性質 (one's nature).

gram, *n.* guramu グラム.

grammar, *n.* guramā グラマー; bunpō 文法.

grammatical, *adj.* bunpō-teki (na) 文法的 (な).

grand, *adj.* 1. sōdai (na) 壮大 (な) (impressive in size); dō-dōtaru 堂々たる (stately); subarashii 素晴らしい (splendid). 2. ōkii 大きい (large, major).

granddaughter, *n.* magomusume

孫娘.

grandeur, *n.* sōdaisa 壮大さ.

grandfather, *n.* sofu 祖父; ojiisan おじいさん.

grandiose, *adj.* sōrei (na) 壮麗 (な).

grandmother, *n.* sobo 祖母; obāsan おばあさん.

grandparents, *n.* sofubo 祖父母.

grandson, *n.* magomusuko 孫息子.

grandstand, *n.* sutando スタンド; kankyakuseki 観客席.

granite, *n.* mikageishi 御影石.

grant, 1. *n.* joseikin 助成金 (subsidy); shōgakukin 奨学金 (scholarship fund). 2. *vb.* ataeru 与える (confer, give); mitomeru 認める (admit); **take for granted** atarimae to kangaeru 当たり前と 考える (assume without question); keishi suru 軽視する (treat indifferently).

granular, *adj.* tsubujō (no) 粒状 (の).

granulate, *vb.* tsubu ni suru 粒にす る.

grape, *n.* budō 葡萄.

grapefruit, *n.* gurēpufurūtsu グレ ープフルーツ.

graph, *n.* gurafu グラフ; zuhyō 図 表.

graphic, *adj.* 1. zushi sareta 図示さ れた (pertaining to graphs or diagrams). 2. nama-namashii 生々しい (vivid). 3. gurafikku (no) グラフィック (の) (pertaining to the graphic arts).

grapple, *vb.* **grapple with** ... ni torikumu ...に取り組む (try to overcome); ... to momiau ...揉み合 う (wrestle with).

grasp, 1. *n.* haaku 把握 (hold); rikai 理解 (comprehension). 2. *vb.* haaku suru 把握する; rikai suru 理 解する (understand); tsukamu つ かむ (seize).

grass, *n.* 1. kusa 草. 2. shibafu 芝生 (lawn).

grasshopper, *n.* batta ばった.

grate, *vb.* 1. kan ni sawaru 癇に触 る (irritate). 2. kishiraseru きしら せる (make harsh sound). 3. suru 擦る (grind into small pieces).

grateful, *adj.* kansha shiteiru 感謝 している; arigatai 有難い.

gratification, *n.* manzoku 満足.

gratify, *vb.* manzoku saseru 満足さ せる.

grating, 1. *n.* kōshi 格子 (latticework). 2. *adj.* iratsukaseru 苛つかせる (irritating).

gratitude, *n.* kansha 感謝.

gratuitous, *adj.* 1. muryō/tada (no) 無料／只 (の) (without charge). 2. futō (na) 不当 (な) (without reasonable cause).

gratuity, *n.* chippu チップ.

grave, 1. *n.* haka 墓 (for burial). 2. *adj.* omo-omoshii 重々しい (weighty, solemn); jūyō (na) 重要 (な) (critical).

gravel, *n.* jari 砂利; koishi 小石.

gravestone, *n.* hakaishi 墓石.

graveyard, *n.* bochi 墓地.

gravitate, *vb.* hikiyoserareru 引き 寄せられる.

gravity, *n.* 1. jūryoku 重力 (terrestrial force). 2. omo-omoshisa 重々しさ (solemnity).

gravy, *n.* gurēbī グレービー; nikujū 肉汁.

gray, 1. *adj.* haiiro (no) 灰色 (の). 2. *n.* haiiro 灰色 (color).

graze, *vb.* 1. kasuru 擦る (scrape). 2. kusa o taberu 草を食べる (feed on grass).

grease, *n.* gurīsu グリース; abura

油 (oily matter); shibō 脂肪 (fat).

greasy, *adj.* aburakkoi 油っこい; beto-beto shita べとべとした.

great, *adj.* 1. ōkii 大きい (large). 2. idai (na) 偉大 (な) (distinguished); yūmei (na) 有名 (な) (famous). 3. jūyō (na) 重要 (な) (important).

Great Britain, *n.* igirisu イギリス.

great-grandchild, *n.* himago ひ孫.

great-grandfather, *n.* hisofu ひ祖父.

great-grandmother, *n.* hisobo ひ祖母.

greatly, *adv.* taihen 大変.

Greece, *n.* girisha ギリシャ.

greed, *n.* don'yoku 貪欲.

greedy, *adj.* don'yoku (na) 貪欲 (な).

Greek, 1. *n.* girishajin ギリシャ人 (person); girishago ギリシャ語 (language). 2. *adj.* girisha (no) ギリシャ (の) (of Greece); girishajin (no) ギリシャ人 (の) (of the Greeks).

green, 1. *adj.* midori(iro no) 緑(色の). 2. *n.* midori (color).

greenery, *n.* midori 緑.

greengrocer, *n.* yasaiya 野菜屋; yaoya 八百屋.

greenhouse, *n.* onshitsu 温室.

greet, *vb.* 1. aisatsu suru 挨拶する (salute). 2. kangei suru 歓迎する (welcome).

greeting, *n.* 1. aisatsu 挨拶. 2. **greetings** kangei 歓迎.

gregarious, *adj.* 1. shakō-teki (na) 社交的 (な) (sociable). 2. hitozuki (na) 人好き (な) (companionable).

grenade, *n.* shuryūdan 手榴弾.

grief, *n.* kanashimi 悲しみ.

grievance, *n.* fufuku no moto 不服の元 (cause for complaint).

grill, 1. *n.* guriru グリル (utensil, restaurant); yakimono 焼き物 (grilled food). 2. *vb.* yaku 焼く (broil).

grim, *adj.* 1. kibishii 厳しい (stern); ganko (na) 頑固 (な) (unyielding). 2. zotto saseru yō (na) ぞっとさせるよう (な) (ghastly). 3. zankoku (na) 残酷 (な) (cruel).

grimace, 1. *n.* shikamettsura しかめっ面. 2. *vb.* kao o shikameru 顔をしかめる.

grime, *n.* yogore 汚れ.

grin, 1. *n.* usuwarai 薄笑い. 2. *vb.* usuwarai o suru 薄笑いをする.

grind, *vb.* 1. hiku 挽く (grind flour). 2. togu 研ぐ (grind a knife). 3. (ha o) kishiraseru (歯を) きしらせる (grind teeth).

grip, 1. *n.* tsukamu koto つかむこと (grasp); shihai 支配 (control); totte 取っ手 (handle). 2. *vb.* nigiru 握る; tsukamu つかむ (grasp).

gripe, 1. *n.* guchi 愚痴 (complaint). 2. *vb.* guchi o iu 愚痴を言う (complain).

grisly, *adj.* zotto suru yō na ぞっとするような.

grit, *n.* 1. jari 砂利 (gravel). 2. yūki 勇気 (courage).

grizzled, grizzly, *adj.* haiirogakkata 灰色がかった.

groan, 1. *n.* umeki 呻き. 2. *vb.* umeku 呻く.

grocer, *n.* shokuryōhinten 食料品店 (dealer).

grocery, *n.* 1. shokuryōhin 食料品 (goods). 2. shokuryōhinten 食料品店 (store).

groggy, *adj.* yoromeite-iru よろめいている.

groin, *n.* mata 股.

groom, *n.* shinrō 新郎 (bridegroom).

groove, *n.* mizo 溝.

grope, *vb.* 1. tesaguri suru 手探り する (feel about with hands). 2. mosaku suru 模索する (search blindly).

gross, 1. *n.* sōshūnyū 総収入 (total income). 2. *adj.* zentai (no) 全体 (の) (total); hanahadashii はなは だしい (extreme); gehin (na) 下品 (な) (indecent); soya (na) 粗野 (な) (coarse); futoi 太い (thick); **gross national product** kokumin-sōseisan 国民総生産.

grotesque, *adj.* gurotesuku (na) グ ロテスク (な); kimi ga warui 気味 が悪い.

grotto, *n.* dōkutsu 洞窟.

ground, *n.* 1. jimen 地面 (earth); tsuchi 土 (soil). 2. gurando グラン ド (playground). 3. **grounds** konkyo 根拠 (reason).

groundless, *adj.* konkyo no nai 根 拠のない.

group, 1. *n.* gurūpu グループ; dantai 団体. 2. *vb.* atsumeru 集め る.

groupie, *n.* torimaki 取り巻き; fan ファン.

grove, *n.* hayashi 林.

grovel, *vb.* 1. hige suru 卑下する (humble oneself). 2. hirefusu ひ れ伏す (prostrate oneself).

grow, *vb.* 1. sodatsu 育つ (increase in size); fueru 増える (increase in quantity); sodateru 育てる (raise plants, etc.). 2. haeru 生える (sprout). 3. ... ni naru ...になる (develop).

grower, *n.* saibaisha 栽培者.

growl, 1. *n.* unarigoe 唸り声. 2. *vb.* unaru 唸る.

grownup, *n.* otona 大人; seijin 成 人.

growth, *n.* 1. seichō 成長 (act of

growing). 2. hattatsu 発達 (development).

grubby, *adj.* kitanai 汚い.

grudge, 1. *n.* urami 恨み (resentment); **bear a grudge** uramu. 2. *vb.* iya-iya ataeru いや いや与える (give unwillingly).

gruesome, *adj.* minoke ga/no yodatsu 身の毛が／のよだつ (horrible and repugnant).

gruff, *adj.* 1. bukkirabō (na) ぶっき らぼう (な) (surly). 2. damigoe (no) だみ声 (の) (hoarse).

grumble, *vb.* guchi o iu 愚痴を言 う.

grumpy, *adj.* buaiso (na) 無愛想 (な); fukigen (na) 不機嫌 (な).

grunt, *vb.* 1. bū-bū naku ぶーぶー 鳴く (a hog). 2. guchi o iu 愚痴を 言う (grumble).

guarantee, 1. *n.* hoshō 保証 (security); hoshōsho 保証書 (written assurance). 2. *vb.* hoshō suru 保証する.

guard, 1. *n.* gādoman ガードマン; ban'nin 番人 (person); kanshi 監 視 (close watch); bōgyo 防御 (safeguard). 2. *vb.* hogo suru 保護 する; mamoru 守る (protect); miharu 見張る (keep watch); yōjin suru 用心する (take precautions).

guardian, *n.* 1. kōken'nin 後見人 (patron); hogosha 保護者 (protector). 2. kanshisha 監視者 (person who watches over).

guerrilla, *n.* gerira ゲリラ.

guess, 1. *n.* suisoku 推測 (conjecture). 2. *vb.* suisoku suru 推測する (conjecture); iiateru 言い 当てる (guess right); ... to omou ... と思う (think).

guesswork, *n.* atezuppō 当てずっ ぽう; suisoku 推測 (conjecture).

guest, *n.* gesuto ゲスト; (o)kyaku(san) (お)客(さん).

guffaw, *n.* bakawarai 馬鹿笑い.

guidance, *n.* 1. jogen 助言; adobaisu アドバイス (advice). 2. an'nai 案内 (information).

guide, 1. *n.* gaido ガイド; an'nainin 案内人 (person); hyōji 表示 (mark, tab, sign); tebiki 手引き (instruction). 2. *vb.* an'nai suru 案内する (show, introduce); michibiku 導く (direct, lead).

guidebook, *n.* (ryokō-)gaidobukku (旅行)ガイドブック.

guided missile, *n.* yūdōdan 誘導弾.

guild, *n.* girudo ギルド; kumiai 組合.

guile, *n.* zurugashikosa ずる賢さ.

guillotine, *n.* girochin ギロチン.

guilt, *n.* 1. tsumi 罪 (blame). 2. hanzai 犯罪 (criminal conduct). 3. tsumi no ishiki 罪の意識 (guilty conscience).

guilty, *adj.* 1. ushirometai 後ろめたい (feeling culpable). 2. yūzai (no) 有罪 (の) (criminal).

guinea pig, *n.* 1. jikkendōbutsu 実験動物 (subject of experiment). 2. morumotto モルモット (animal).

guise, *n.* 1. mikake 見かけ (appearance). 2. misekake 見せかけ (assumed appearance).

guitar, *n.* 1. gitā ギター. 2. ereki-gitā エレキギター (electric).

guitarist, *n.* gitarisuto ギタリスト.

gulf, *n.* wan 湾 (water).

gull, *n.* kamome かもめ.

gullet, *n.* nodo 喉; shokudō 食道.

gullible, *adj.* damasareyasui だまされ易い.

gulp, *vb.* nomu 飲む (swallow); **gulp down** nomikomu 飲み込む (gobble).

gum, *n.* 1. gomu ゴム (material for rubber). 2. gamu ガム (chewing gum). 3. haguki 歯ぐき (of teeth).

gun, *n.* teppō 鉄砲; kenjū 拳銃; pisutoru ピストル (handgun); raifuru ライフル (rifle).

gunfire, *n.* happō 発砲.

gunman, *n.* ganman ガンマン.

gunpoint, *n.* **at gunpoint** teppō o tsukitsuke-rarete 鉄砲を突きつけられて.

gunpowder, *n.* kayaku 火薬.

gunshot, *n.* shageki 射撃.

gurgle, 1. *n.* mizu no oto 水の音 (sound of water). 2. *vb.* goku-goku oto o tateru ごくごく音を立てる (drink noisily).

gush, 1. *n.* hotobashiri ほとばしり (sudden flow). 2. *vb.* hotobashiru ほとばしる (flow out).

gust, *n.* toppū 突風 (wind).

gut, *n.* 1. chō 腸 (intestine, bowel). 2. **guts** harawata 腸 (intestines, bowels); yūki 勇気 (courage).

gutsy, *adj.* yūki ga aru 勇気がある; tsuyoi 強い.

gutter, *n.* 1. mizo 溝 (along road). 2. amadoi 雨樋 (along roof).

guttural, *adj.* 1. nodo no 喉の (of the throat). 2. nodo kara deru 喉から出る (pronounced in the throat). 3. shiwagaregoe (no) しわがれ声 (の) (throaty).

guy, *n.* otoko 男; yatsu 奴.

guzzle, *vb.* gatsu-gatsu taberu/nomu がつがつ食べる／飲む (eat/drink).

gym, *n.* jimu ジム; tai'ikukan 体育館.

gymnast, *n.* taisōkyōgisha 体操競技者.

gymnastic, *adj.* taisō (no) 体操 (の).

gymnastics, *n.* taisō 体操.

gynecology, *n.* fujinka 婦人科.

gyp, *vb.* damashitoru だまし取る.

gypsy, *n.* jipushī ジプシー.

gyrate, *vb.* mawaru 回る.

H

habit, *n.* 1. shūkan 習慣 (customary practice). 2. kuse 癖 (acquired behavior).

habitable, *adj.* sumeru 住める.

habitat, *n.* seisokuchi 生息地.

habitation, *n.* jūkyo 住居 (dwelling).

habitual, *adj.* 1. shūkan-teki (na) 習慣的 (な) (resulting from habit). 2. itsumo (no) いつも (の) (customary).

hack, 1. *n.* buttagiri ぶった切り (cut); kizami 刻み (notch). 2. *adj.* chinpu (na) 陳腐 (な) (trite). 3. *vb.* kiru 切る (cut); **hack down** kiritaosu 切り倒す.

hacker, *n.* hakkā ハッカー.

hackneyed, *adj.* chinpu (na) 陳腐 (な).

hag, *n.* baba ばば.

haggard, *adj.* yatsurete iru やつれている.

haggle, *vb.* negiru 値切る.

hail, 1. *n.* arare あられ; hyō ひょう (ice); kansei 歓声 (shout); aisatsu 挨拶 (salutation). 2. *vb.* arare/hyō ga furu あられ／ひょうが降る (pour down hail); kangei suru 歓迎する (welcome); aisatsu suru 挨拶する (salute); yobu 呼ぶ (call out to); **hail from** ... shusshin de aru ...出身である.

hailstone, *n.* arare あられ; hyō ひょう.

hair, *n.* kami(noke) 髪(の毛) (head hair); ke 毛 (body hair, fur).

haircut, *n.* heakatto ヘアカット;

sanpatsu 散髪.

hairdo, *n.* heasutairu ヘアスタイル; kamigata 髪型.

hairdresser, *n.* biyōshi 美容師.

hairpin, *n.* heapin ヘアピン.

hair-raising, *adj.* zotto suru (yō na) ぞっとする (ような).

hair spray, *n.* hea-supurē ヘアスプレー.

hairy, *adj.* kebukai 毛深い (covered with hair).

hale, *adj.* genki (na) 元気 (な) (healthy).

half, 1. *n.* han(bun) 半(分); nibun no ichi 二分の一; **in half** hanbun ni 半分に; **half a year** hantoshi 半年; **half an hour** hanjikan 半時間. 2. *adj.* hanbun (no) 半分 (の). 3. *adv.* hanbun ni 半分に.

half brother/sister, *n.* ibo(ifu) kyōdai/-shimai 異母(異父)兄弟／～姉妹.

half-cooked, *adj.* namanie (no) 生煮え (の).

half-hearted, *adj.* ki ga noranai 気が乗らない.

half-opened, *adj.* hanbiraki (no) 半開き (の).

half-price, *adj.* hangaku (no) 半額 (の).

halfway, *adv.* 1. nakaba de/made 半ばで／まで (at/to the midway point). 2. hotondo ほとんど (almost).

half-wit, *n.* manuke (na) まぬけ (な).

hall, *n.* 1. hōru ホール (large room, auditorium, building). 2. rōka 廊

下 (corridor). 3. genkan 玄関; robī ロビー (entrance, lobby).

hallmark, *n.* 1. ken'in 検印 (official mark or stamp). 2. tokushitsu 特質 (distinguishing feature).

hallucination, *n.* genkaku 幻覚.

hallway, *n.* 1. rōka 廊下 (corridor). 2. genkan 玄関 (entrance).

halt, 1. *n.* teishi 停止 (stop). 2. *vb.* tomaru 止まる (stop); tomeru 止める (cause to stop); tsumazuku つまずく (stumble). 3. *interj.* Tomare. 止まれ.

halve, *vb.* 1. hanbun ni wakeru 半分に分ける (divide, share). 2. hanbun ni suru 半分にする (reduce to half).

ham, *n.* hamu ハム (meat).

hamburger, *n.* hanbāgā ハンバーガー.

hamlet, *n.* chiisai mura 小さい村.

hammer, 1. *n.* kanazuchi 金槌; hanmā ハンマー. 2. *vb.* uchikomu 打ち込む; tataku 叩く (pound).

hamper, 1. *n.* kago 籠 (basket). 2. *vb.* samatageru 妨げる (impede); jama o suru 邪魔をする (interfere with).

hand, 1. *n.* te 手 (physical); hatarakite 働き手 (worker); hari 針 (of clock); tasuke 助け (assistance); hisseki 筆跡 (handwriting); gawa 側 (side); kekkonseiyaku 結婚誓約 (pledge of marriage); **at hand** tejika ni 手近に; **by hand** te de 手で; **hands down** tayasuku たやすく; **hand in hand** tomo ni 共に; **on the other hand** sono ippō その一方; **shake hands** akushu suru 握手する; **out of hand** te ni oenai 手に負えない. 2. *adj.* te (no) 手 (の) (of the hand); tesei (no) 手製 (の)

(handmade); shudō (no) 手動 (の) (operated by hand). 3. *vb.* tewatasu 手渡す (pass); te o kasu 手を貸す (help, guide); **hand in** teishutsu suru 提出する; **hand out** kubaru 配る.

handbag, *n.* handobaggu ハンドバッグ.

handball, *n.* handobōru ハンドボール.

handbook, *n.* manyuaru マニュアル; tebikisho 手引書.

handcuffs, *n.* tejō 手錠.

handful, *n.* 1. hitonigiri 一握り (amount). 2. shōsū 少数 (small number).

handicap, *n.* handī ハンディー; furi 不利 (disadvantage).

handicapped, *adj.* shintai-shōgaisha (no) 身体障害者 (の) (person).

handicraft, *n.* shukōgeihin 手工芸品 (craft).

handiwork, *n.* teshigoto 手仕事 (work done by hand).

handkerchief, *n.* hankachi ハンカチ.

handle, 1. *n.* handoru ハンドル; totte 取っ手. 2. *vb.* atsukau 扱う (feel, deal with, manipulate).

handlebar, *n.* handoru ハンドル.

handmade, *adj.* tesei (no) 手製 (の).

handshake, *n.* akushu 握手.

handsome, *adj.* 1. hansamu (na) ハンサム (な) (good-looking). 2. kimae ga ii 気前が良い (generous).

handwriting, *n.* tegaki 手書き.

handy, *adj.* 1. te ni ireyasui 手に入れ易い (accessible). 2. benri (na) 便利 (な) (convenient). 3. kiyō (na) 器用 (な) (dexterous).

hang, *vb.* kakeru 掛ける; sageru 下

げる (suspend); kubi o tsuru 首を
吊る (die by hanging); **hang
around** buratsuku ぶらつく;
hang on shigamitsuku しがみつ
く (cling to); ganbaru 頑張る
(persevere); matsu 待つ
(telephone); **hang up** kakeru か
ける (suspend on hook); denwa o
kiru 電話を切る (telephone).

hanger, n. emonkake 衣紋掛け;
hangā ハンガー.

hanging, n. kubitsuri 首吊り;
kōshukei 絞首刑 (execution);
hangings kakemono 掛け物
(decorations on wall).

hangover, n. futsukayoi 二日酔い.

hanker, vb. (...) ni akogareru ... に
憧れる.

hankering, n. akogare 憧れ.

haphazard, adj. detarame (na) で
たらめ (な).

happen, vb. 1. okoru 起こる (take
place). 2. gūzen ... suru 偶然 ...す
る (come by chance).

happening, n. hapuningu ハプニ
ング; dekigoto 出来事.

happiness, n. shiawase 幸せ;
kōfuku 幸福.

happy, adj. shiawase (na) 幸せ
(な); kōfuku (na) 幸福 (な);
ureshii 嬉しい.

happy-go-lucky, adj. rakuten-teki
(na) 楽天的 (な).

harangue, 1. n. netsuben 熱弁. 2.
vb. netsuben o furuu 熱弁をふる
う.

harass, vb. nayamasu 悩ます.

harassment, n. iyagarase 嫌がら
せ; **sexual harassment** sei-teki
iyagarase 性的嫌がらせ; sekuhara
セクハラ.

harbinger, n. maebure 前触れ.

harbor, 1. n. minato 港 (port);
hinansho 避難所 (shelter). 2. vb.

kakumau かくまう (give shelter).

hard, 1. adj. katai 固い (solid);
muzukashii 難しい (difficult);
nesshin (na) 熱心 (な) (energetic,
persistent); kibishii 厳しい
(severe). 2. adv. nesshin ni 熱心に
(earnestly, with vigor); kataku 固
く (firmly, solidly); tsuyoku 強く
(violently); **be hard up** (o)kane
ga nai (お)金がない; **be hard hit**
itade o ukeru 痛手を受ける.

hard-boiled, adj. katayude (no) 固
ゆで (の) (egg).

hard disk, n. hādo-disuku ハード
ディスク.

harden, vb. 1. kataku naru 固くな
る (become hard); kataku suru 固
くする (make hard). 2. mujihi ni
naru 無慈悲になる (become
pitiless); mujihi ni suru 無慈悲に
する (make pitiless).

hard-headed, adj. 1. reitetsu (na)
冷徹 (な) (not easily moved). 2.
ganko (na) 頑固 (な) (stubborn).

hard-hearted, adj. mujihi (na) 無
慈悲 (な).

hardly, adv. 1. hotondo ... nai ほと
んど...ない (almost not). 2.
mattaku ... nai 全く...ない (not at
all).

hardness, n. katasa 固さ.

hardship, n. kon'nan 困難; kurō
苦労.

hardware, n. 1. kanamono 金物
(metalware). 2. hādouea ハード
ウエア (computers).

hardy, adj. ganjō (na) 頑丈 (な)
(sturdy, strong).

hare, n. usagi うさぎ.

harem, n. hāremu ハーレム.

harm, 1. n. gai 害 (damage); kega
怪我 (injury). 2. vb. kizu tsukeru
傷つける (damage, injure).

harmful, adj. yūgai (na) 有害 (な).

harmless, *adj.* mugai (na) 無害 (な).

harmonica, *n.* hāmonika ハーモニカ.

harmonious, *adj.* 1. chōwa ni tomu 調和に富む (blending well). 2. ki ga au 気が合う (agreeing in feeling).

harmonize, *vb.* 1. chōwa saseru 調和させる (bring into agreement). 2. chōwa suru 調和する (be in accord).

harmony, *n.* 1. chōwa 調和 (accord). 2. hāmonī ハーモニー (music).

harness, 1. *n.* bagu 馬具 (horse). 2. *vb.* tsukaikonasu 使いこなす (control and use).

harp, *n.* hāpu ハープ; tategoto 竪琴.

harpoon, *n.* mori 銛.

harpsichord, *n.* hāpushikōdo ハープシコード.

harry, *vb.* 1. sainamu 苛む (torment). 2. hakai suru 破壊する (devastate).

harsh, *adj.* 1. arai 荒い (rough). 2. fukai (na) 不快 (な) (unpleasant). 3. kibishii 厳しい (severe).

harshness, *n.* 1. ara-arashisa 荒々しさ (roughness). 2. kibishisa 厳しさ (severity).

harvest, 1. *n.* shūkaku 収穫; tori'ire 取り入れ (gathering of crops); shūkakubutsu 収穫物 (crop). 2. *vb.* shūkaku suru 収穫する; tori'ireru 取り入れる (reap).

hassle, *n.* 1. kuchigenka 口喧嘩 (dispute). 2. mendō 面倒 (trouble).

haste, *n.* isogi 急ぎ (speed); **make haste** isogu 急ぐ. 2. seikyūsa 性急さ (unnecessary haste).

hasten, *vb.* 1. isogu 急ぐ (hurry).

2. hayameru 早める (cause to hurry).

hasty, *adj.* 1. subayai 素早い (hurried, speedy). 2. seikyū (na) 性急 (な) (impetuous).

hat, *n.* bōshi 帽子.

hatch, 1. *n.* hatchi ハッチ (boat or airplane). 2. *vb.* (tamago o) kaesu (卵を) かえす (hatch an egg); (tamago ga) kaeru (卵が) かえる (egg hatches).

hatchet, *n.* teono 手斧.

hate, 1. *n.* nikushimi 憎しみ. 2. *vb.* nikumu 憎む (detest); kirau 嫌う (dislike).

hateful, *adj.* nikurashii 憎らしい (repulsive).

hatred, *n.* nikushimi 憎しみ (aversion); teki'i 敵意 (hostility).

haughty, *adj.* kōman (na) 高慢 (な).

haul, 1. *n.* yusōhin 輸送品 (transported load). 2. *vb.* hiku 引く (pull); yusō suru 輸送する (transport).

haunch, *n.* koshi 腰.

haunt, 1. *n.* najimi no tokoro 馴染みの所 (place of frequent visits). 2. *vb.* kayou 通う (frequent); shutsubotsu suru 出没する (of a ghost); tsukimatou 付きまとう (recur).

haunted, *adj.* toritsukarete iru 取りつかれている; **haunted house** yūreiyashiki 幽霊屋敷.

have, 1. *vb.* aru ある; motteiru 持っている (possess); nomu 飲む (drink); taberu 食べる (eat); uketoru 受け取る (receive); idaku 抱く (hold in mind). 2. *aux. vb.* (used with past participle) ... shita koto ga aru ...したことがある (have experienced); mō ... shita もう...した; ... shite shimatta ...して

しまった (have finished doing).
3. **have been doing** zutto ... shite iru ずっと ... している; **have (something) done** ... shite morau ...してもらう; **have to do** ... shinakereba-naranai ...しなければならない; **had better do** ... shita hō ga ii ...したほうがいい; **have on** ... o kite iru ...を着ている (be clothed in); **have to do with** ... to kankei ga aru ...と関係がある (have dealings with); **have had it** mō takusan もうたくさん.

haven, *n.* anzen no chi 安全の地; hinansho 避難所 (shelter).

havoc, *n.* sōdō 騒動 (ruinous confusion); **play havoc with** ... o dame ni suru ...をだめにする (ruin).

hawk, *n.* taka 鷹.

hay, *n.* hoshikusa 干し草.

hay fever, *n.* kafunshō 花粉症.

haystack, *n.* hoshikusa no yama 干し草の山.

haywire, *adj.* mechakucha (na) めちゃくちゃ (な) (out of control).

hazard, 1. *n.* kiken 危険 (danger); kikenbutsu 危険物 (object causing hazard). 2. *vb.* kaketemiru 賭けてみる (risk).

hazardous, *adj.* kiken (na) 危険 (な) (dangerous).

haze, *n.* 1. kasumi 霞 (mistlike obscurity). 2. mōrō もうろう (vagueness of mind).

hazy, *adj.* 1. kasundeiru 霞んでいる (full of haze). 2. mōrō to shiteiru もうろうとしている (vague).

he, *pron.* kare (ga/wa) 彼 (が／は).

head, 1. *n.* atama 頭 (part of body, brain); chō 長 (chief); saki 先 (topmost part); **heads or tails** omote ka ura ka 表か裏か. 2. *vb.*

hiki'iru 率いる (lead); mukau 向かう (move); **head for** ... ni mukau ...に向かう.

headache, *n.* zutsū 頭痛.

headfirst, *adv.* 1. atama kara saki ni 頭から先に (starting with head). 2. asette あせって (rashly). 3. muteppō ni 無鉄砲に (without deliberation).

heading, *n.* taitoru タイトル; dai 題 (title).

headlight, *n.* heddoraito ヘッドライト.

headline, *n.* heddorain ヘッドライン; midashi 見出し.

headlong, *adv.* see **headfirst**.

head-on, *adj.* shōmen (no) 正面 (の) (with head foremost); **head-on collision** shōmen-shōtotsu 正面衝突.

headquarters, *n.* 1. honbu 本部. 2. sōshireibu 総司令部 (military).

headstone, *n.* bohyō 墓標; hakaishi 墓石.

headstrong, *adj.* ganko (na) 頑固 (な).

headway, *n.* zenshin 前進 (movement forward).

heady, *adj.* 1. seikyū (na) 性急 (な) (impetuous). 2. yowaseru 酔わせる (intoxicating).

heal, *vb.* naosu 治す (restore to health); naoru 治る (get well).

health, *n.* kenkō 健康 (soundness, vigor).

healthful, *adj.* kenkō ni ii 健康に良い (good for health).

healthy, *adj.* 1. kenkō (na) 健康 (な) (vigorous). 2. kenkō ni ii 健康に良い (good for health).

heap, 1. *n.* yamazumi 山積み (pile); **a heap of** takusan (no) たくさん (の) (a lot of). 2. *vb.* tsumiageru 積み上げる (pile up);

yama to ataeru 山と与える (give abundantly); yama to tsumekomu 山と詰め込む(fill).

hear, *vb.* kiku 聞く (listen, be informed); kikoeru 聞こえる (audible); **hear from** ... kara tayori/tegami ga aru ...から便り／手紙がある; **hear about/of** ... no koto o kiku ...のことを聞く.

hearing, *n.* 1. chōkaku 聴覚 (sense). 2. chōmonkai 聴聞会 (legal session).

hearsay, *n.* matagiki 又聞き; uwasa 噂 (rumor).

hearse, *n.* reikyūsha 霊柩車.

heart, *n.* 1. shinzō 心臓 (organ); **heart attack** shinzō hossa 心臓発作; **heart disease** shinzōbyō 心臓病. 2. kokoro 心 (seat of emotion). 3. jō 情 (sympathy). 4. yūki 勇気 (courage); yaruki やる気 (enthusiasm). 5. chūshin 中心 (central part). 6. **at heart** kihon-teki ni 基本的に (fundamentally); **by heart** sora de そらで; **from the bottom of one's heart** kokoro kara 心から; **lose heart** yaruki o nakusu やる気を無くす; **set one's heart on** kesshin suru 決心する; **take to heart** meiki suru 銘記する (take seriously); kanji'iru 感じ入る (be deeply affected).

heartache, *n.* shintsū 心痛; kanashimi 悲しみ.

heartbreak, *n.* shitsui 失意; hitsū 悲痛.

heartbreaking, *adj.* hitsū (na) 悲痛 (な).

heartbroken, *adj.* shitsui (no) 失意 (の); hitsū (na) 悲痛 (な).

heartburn, *n.* muneyake 胸焼け.

hearth, *n.* irori いろり; danro 暖炉.

heartsick, *adj.* shitsui ni kureru 失意に暮れる.

hearty, *adj.* 1. kokoro no atatakai 心の暖かい (cordial). 2. shin (no) 真 (の) (genuine). 3. kokoro kara (no) 心から (の) (heartfelt). 4. genki (na) 元気 (な) (vigorous). 5. ōkii 大きい (substantial).

heat, 1. *n.* netsu 熱 (hot); nekkyō 熱狂 (ardor). 2. *vb.* atatameru 暖める (warm); atatamaru 暖まる (become warm); nekkyō suru 熱狂する (excite).

heater, *n.* hītā ヒーター; danbōki 暖房器.

heating, *n.* danbō 暖房.

heatstroke, *n.* nesshabyō 熱射病.

heat wave, *n.* neppa 熱波.

heave, *vb.* 1. mochiageru 持ち上げる (raise). 2. nageru 投げる (throw). 3. (koe o) tateru (声を) たてる (utter); **heave a sigh** tameiki o tsuku ため息を吐く. 4. jōge suru 上下する (rise and fall).

heaven, *n.* 1. tengoku 天国. 2. **heavens** sora 空; ten 天 (sky).

heavenly, *adj.* 1. tengoku (no) 天国 (の) (of heaven). 2. sora (no) 空 (の); ten (no) 天 (の) (of the heavens). 3. subarashii 素晴らしい (delightful).

heavy, *adj.* 1. omoi 重い (weighty, burdensome, oppressive); futotte-iru 太っている (overweight). 2. takusan (no) たくさん (の) (large amount); ōkii 大きい (of great size, substantial). 3. hageshii 激しい (intense, violent, crowded); **heavy rain** hageshii ame 激しい雨; **heavy traffic** hageshii kōtsū 激しい交通. 4. jūdai (na) 重大 (な) (serious). 5. kitsui きつい (trying). 6. dai (no) 大 (の) (excessive); **heavy drinker** dai no sakenomi 大の酒飲み;

ōzakenomi 大酒飲み. 7. futoi 太
い (broad). 8. atsui 厚い (thick).
9. arai 粗い (coarse). 10. fukai 深
い (deep); **heavy slumber** fukai
nemuri 深い眠り. 11. **heavy
industry** jūkōgyō 重工業; **heavy
metal** jūkinzoku 重金属; **heavy
heart** omoi kokoro 重い心.

heckle, *vb.* yajiru 野次る.

hectic, *adj.* awatadashii あわただし
い.

hedge, *n.* ikegaki 生け垣.

hedonism, *n.* kairakushugi 快楽主
義; kyōrakushugi 享楽主義.

heed, 1. *n.* chūi 注意 (notice). 2.
vb. ... ni chūi suru ... に注意する
(notice); kiki'ireru 聞き入れる
(pay serious attention to).

heedless, *adj.* ... ni mutonchaku
(na) ...に無頓着 (な).

heel, *n.* kakato 踵 (of foot or shoe).

hefty, *adj.* 1. omoi 重い (heavy).
2. ōkii 大きい (big). 3. ganjō (na)
頑丈 (な) (sturdy).

height, *n.* 1. takasa 高さ. 2.
shinchō 身長 (height of a person).
3. kōdo 高度 (altitude). 4. chōten
頂点(apex, peak). 5. **heights** oka
丘、岡; takadai 高台.

heighten, *vb.* 1. takaku suru 高く
する (make higher); takaku naru
高くなる (become higher). 2.
takameru 高める (cause to
increase); takamaru 高まる
(increase).

heir, heiress, *n.* sōzokunin 相続人.

helicopter, *n.* herikoputā ヘリコプ
ター.

helium, *n.* heriumu ヘリウム.

hell, *n.* jigoku 地獄.

hellish, *adj.* jigoku no yō (na) 地獄
のよう (な) (like hell).

hello, *interj.* 1. konnichi wa 今日は
(greeting). 2. moshi-moshi もしも

し (answering telephone).

helmet, *n.* herumetto ヘルメット.

helmsman, *n.* kajitorinin 舵取り
人.

help, 1. *n.* tasuke 助け (aid,
assistance); tetsudai 手伝い
(helper). 2. *vb.* tetsudau 手伝う;
tasukeru 助ける (aid); (... no)
tasuke ni naru (...の) 助けになる
(be of service to); **Please help
yourself.** Gojiyū ni dōzo. 御自由
にどうぞ; **help oneself to** jiyū ni
... o taberu/nomu 自由に... を食べ
る／飲む (eat/drink); ... o ōryō
suru ...を横領する
(misappropriate, embezzle); **help
out** sukuu 救う. 3. *interj.*
Tasukete. 助けて.

helper, *n.* herupā ヘルパー;
tetsudai 手伝い.

helpful, *adj.* yaku ni tatsu 役に立
つ (useful).

helpless, *adj.* muryoku (na, no) 無
力 (な、の) (powerless).

hem, 1. *n.* heri 縁 (hemmed edge).
2. *vb.* heri o tsukeru 縁を付ける
(sew down the edge); kakomu 囲
む (enclose).

hemisphere, *n.* hankyū 半球.

hemorrhage, *n.* shukketsu 出血.

hemorrhoids, *n.* ji 痔.

hemp, *n.* asa 麻.

hen, *n.* mendori 雌鳥.

hence, *adv.* 1. sore de それで; yue
ni 故に (therefore). 2. ima kara 今
から (from this time).

henceforth, *adv.* kongo 今後 (from
now on).

henchman, *n.* kobun 子分.

hepatitis, *n.* kan'en 肝炎.

her, 1. *adj.* kanojo (no) 彼女 (の).
2. *pron.* kanojo o/ni 彼女を／に.

herald, *n.* shisha 使者 (messenger).

herb, *n.* yakusō 薬草.

herbivorous, *adj.* sōshoku (no) 草食 (の).

herd, *n.* mure 群れ (flock, mass).

here, *adv.* 1. koko de (e/ni) ここで (へ／に).

hereafter, *adv.* 1. raise de 来世で (in the life to come). 2. kongo 今後 (from now on).

hereby, *adv.* kore ni yotte これによって (as a result of this).

hereditary, *adj.* 1. sōzoku (no) 相続 (の) (passing from parents to offspring). 2. iden-teki (na) 遺伝的 (な) (genetic).

heredity, *n.* iden 遺伝.

heresy, *n.* itan 異端.

heretic, *n.* itansha 異端者.

heritage, *n.* isan 遺産 (inheritance, traditions).

hermit, *n.* inja 隠者.

hernia, *n.* herunia ヘルニア.

hero, *n.* 1. hīrō ヒーロー; eiyū 英雄 (man of valor). 2. shujinkō 主人公 (main character).

heroic, *adj.* eiyū-teki (na) 英雄的 (な) (of or like a hero).

heroin, *n.* heroin ヘロイン.

heroine, *n.* 1. joketsu 女傑 (female hero). 2. hiroin ヒロイン; on'nashujinkō 女主人公 (main character).

heron, *n.* sagi 鷺.

herring, *n.* nishin 鯡.

hers, *pron.* kanojo no mono 彼女のもの.

herself, *pron.* kanojojishin 彼女自身; **by herself** kanojojishin de 彼女自身で.

hesitant, *adj.* tameraigachi (na) ためらいがち (な).

hesitate, *vb.* tamerau ためらう.

hesitation, *n.* tamerai ためらい.

heterosexual, 1. *n.* iseiaisha 異性愛者. 2. *adj.* iseiai (no) 異性愛

(の).

heyday, *n.* sakari 盛り; zenseiki 全盛期.

hibernate, *vb.* tōmin suru 冬眠する.

hiatus, *n.* 1. chūdan 中断 (interruption). 2. ketsuraku 欠落 (gap).

hiccup, 1. *n.* shakkuri しゃっくり. 2. *vb.* shakkuri o suru しゃっくりをする.

hidden, *adj.* kakusareta 隠された.

hide, 1. *n.* kawa 皮 (animal skin). 2. *vb.* kakusu 隠す (conceal); kakureru 隠れる (conceal oneself); himitsu ni suru 秘密にする (keep secret).

hideous, *adj.* osoroshii 恐ろしい; minikui 醜い.

hideout, hiding place, *n.* kakurega 隠れ家.

hierarchy, *n.* hierarukī ヒエラルキー; kaisōsei 階層制 (system).

hieroglyphic, *n., adj.* shōkeimoji (no) 象形文字 (の).

high, *adj.* 1. takai 高い (tall, lofty, expensive). 2. kōon (no) 高音 (の) (shrill). 3. jōkyū (no) 上級 (の); jōryū (no) 上流 (の) (high in position or status); **high official** jōkyūkanryō 上級官僚; **high society** jōryūshakai 上流社会. 4. **high speed** kōsoku 高速; **high living** zeitaku (na) seikatsu 贅沢 (な) 生活.

highbrow, *adj.* interi-butteiru インテリぶっている.

high-class, *adj.* hai-kurasu (no) ハイクラス (の); ikkyū (no) 一級 (の) (first rate).

high fidelity, *n.* kōseinō 高性能.

highland, *n.* kōchi 高地; sangakuchi 山岳地.

highlight, 1. *n.* hairaito ハイライ

ト; mein-ibento メインイベント (main event). 2. *vb.* kyōchō suru 強調する (emphasize).

highly, *adv.* 1. hijō ni 非常に (extremely). 2. yoku よく (admiringly).

high school, *n.* kō(tōgak)kō 高(等学)校.

highway, *n.* haiuē ハイウエー; kōsokudōro 高速道路.

hijack, *vb.* haijakku suru ハイジャックする; nottoru 乗っ取る.

hijacker, *n.* nottorihan 乗っ取り犯.

hijacking, *n.* haijakku ハイジャック; nottori 乗っ取り.

hike, 1. *n.* haikingu ハイキング (walk). 2. *vb.* haikingu suru ハイキングする (walk).

hilarious, *adj.* 1. yukai (na) 愉快 (な) (merry). 2. okashii おかしい (funny).

hill, *n.* oka 丘、岡; yama 山.

hilt, *n.* 1. tsuka 塚. 2. **to the hilt** kanzen ni 完全に.

him, *pron.* kare o/ni 彼を/に.

himself, *pron.* karejishin wa (o/ni) 彼自身は (を/に); **by himself** kare jishin de 彼自身で.

hind, *adj.* ushiro (no) 後ろ (の).

hinder, *vb.* samatageru 妨げる.

hindrance, *n.* shōgai 障害.

hinge, 1. *n.* chōtsugai 蝶番. 2. *vb.* chōtsugai o tsukeru 蝶番を付ける (furnish with a hinge).

hint, 1. *n.* hinto ヒント; anji 暗示. 2. *vb.* hinto o ataeru ヒントを与える; anji suru 暗示する.

hinterland, *n.* nairikuchi 内陸地.

hip, *n.* koshi 腰 (haunch); (o)shiri (お)尻 (buttock).

hippopotamus, *n.* kaba 河馬.

hire, 1. *n.* yatoichin 雇い賃 (price of hiring a person); kashichin 貸し

賃 (price of hiring an item); chingashi 賃貸し (act of hiring an item). 2. *vb.* yatou 雇う (employ a person); chingari suru 賃借りする (purchase services or use of); chingashi suru 賃貸しする (offer services or use of).

his, 1. *pron.* kare no mono 彼のもの. 2. *adj.* kare no 彼の.

hiss, 1. *n.* shī/shū しーっ／しゅーっ. 2. *vb.* shī to iu しーっと言う (make a sound); hantai suru 反対する (disapprove).

historian, *n.* rekishika 歴史家.

historical, historic, *adj.* 1. rekishijō (no) 歴史上 (の) (existed in history). 2. rekishi-teki (na) 歴史的 (な) (important). 3. rekishi ni motozuku 歴史に基づく (based on history).

history, *n.* rekishi 歴史.

hit, 1. *n.* hitto ヒット; shōtotsu 衝突 (collision); dageki 打撃 (blow); seikō 成功 (success); **hit or miss** noru ka soru ka のるかそるか. 2. *vb.* utsu 打つ (strike); shōtotsu suru 衝突する (collide with); ... ni dekuwasu ...に出くわす(come upon); omoitsuku 思い付く (get a good idea).

hit-and-run, *adj.* hikinige (no) 轢き逃げ (の).

hitch, 1. *n.* musubime 結び目 (knot); shōgai 障害 (obstruction); hippari 引っ張り (pull). 2. *vb.* tsunagu つなぐ (fasten); hikiageru 引き上げる (raise).

hive, *n.* hachi no subako 蜂の巣箱 (beehive).

hives, *n.* jinmashin じんましん.

hoard, 1. *n.* takuwae 貯え. 2. *vb.* tameru 溜める.

hoarse, *adj.* shagaregoe (no) しゃがれ声 (の) (voice).

hoax, 1. *n.* tsukuribanashi 作り話 (deception). 2. *vb.* damasu だます.

hobby, *n.* shumi 趣味.

hobbyhorse, *n.* 1. mokuba 木馬 (rocking horse). 2. ohako おはこ (pet idea).

hockey, *n.* hokkē ホッケー.

hodgepodge, *n.* gotamaze ごたまぜ (mixture).

hoe, *n.* kuwa くわ.

hog, *n.* buta 豚 (pig).

hoist, *vb.* hikiageru 引き上げる.

hold, 1. *n.* tsukamu koto 摑む事 (grasp); **get a hold on** ... o tsukamu ...を摑む (grasp). 2. *vb.* motsu 持つ; nigiru 握る (have in hand); motteiru 持っている (possess); tamotsu 保つ (retain); hikitomeru 引き止める (detain); (... to) omou (...と) 思う (consider, think); shinjiru 信じる (believe); okonau 行う (hold a meeting, ceremony, etc.); shimeru 占める (occupy); **hold back** osaeru 抑える; **hold down** osaeru 抑える (keep under control); **hold on** tsukamu 摑む (grip); tsuzukeru 続ける (continue); **Hold on, please.** Chotto matte kudasai. ちょっと待って下さい (telephone); **hold out** sashidasu 差し出す (offer); motsu 持つ (last); **hold up** sasaeru 支える (support); okuraseru 遅らせる (delay); mochikotaeru 持ちこたえる (persevere).

holdings, *n.* 1. shoyūbutsu 所有物 (possessions). 2. shoyūchi 所有地 (land); mochikabu 持ち株 (stocks).

hold-up, *n.* 1. okure 遅れ (delay). 2. gōtō 強盗 (robbery).

hole, *n.* ana 穴.

holiday, *n.* 1. shukujitsu 祝日 (public holiday). 2. kyūjitsu 休日; yasumi 休み (exemption from work/school). 3. saijitsu 祭日 (religious holiday).

Holland, *n.* oranda オランダ.

hollow, 1. *n.* ana 穴 (hole); tani 谷 (valley). 2. *adj.* utsuro (na) 虚ろ (な) (empty, sounding hollow); kubonde iru 窪んでいる (sunken); kudaranai 下らない (without worth); munashii 空しい (having an empty feeling). 3. *vb.* ana o akeru 穴を開ける.

holocaust, *n.* daisanji 大惨事; **Holocaust** yudayajin daigyakusatsu ユダヤ人大虐殺.

holy, *adj.* 1. shinsei (na) 神聖 (な) (sacred); kiyoraka (na) 清らか (な) (pure). 2. kami ni sasagerareta 神に捧げられた (dedicated to God).

homage, *n.* kei'i 敬意 (reverence); **pay homage to** ... ni kei'i o harau ....に敬意を払う.

home, *n.* 1. ie 家 (residence); katei 家庭 (place of domestic affections). 2. furusato 故郷 (native area). 3. shisetsu 施設 (institution). 4. **be at home** uchi ni iru うちにいる (be in one's own house); kutsurogu くつろぐ (be at ease); yoku shitte iru よく知っている (be well-informed); **bring home** akiraka ni suru 明らかにする (clarify).

homebody, *n.* debushō 出不精; gaishutsugirai 外出嫌い.

homeland, *n.* sokoku 祖国.

homeless, *adj.* hōmuresu (no) ホームレス (の); yadonashi (no) 宿無し (の).

homely, *adj.* 1. heibon (na) 平凡 (な) (unattractive). 2. soboku (na) 素朴 (な) (simple).

homemade, *adj.* jikasei (no) 自家製 (の).

homemaker, *n.* shufu 主婦 (housewife).

home office, *n.* hōmu-ofisu ホームオフィス.

homesick, *adj.* hōmushikku (no) ホームシック (の).

hometown, *n.* furusato 故郷; inaka 田舎.

homeward, *adv.* ie ni mukatte 家に向かって.

homework, *n.* 1. shukudai 宿題 (school work). 2. junbi 準備 (preparation).

homicide, *n.* satsujin 殺人 (murder); satsujinhan 殺人犯 (murderer).

homogeneous, *adj.* 1. tan'itsu (no) 単一 (の); kin'itsu (no) 均一 (の) (same kind); 2. tan'itsuminzoku 単一民族 (same race).

homogenize, *vb.* kinshitsuka suru 均質化する.

homosexual, 1. *n.* dōseiaisha 同性愛者 (homosexual person); gei ゲイ; homo ホモ (man); rezubian レズビアン (woman). 2. *adj.* dōseiai (no) 同性愛 (の).

homosexuality, *n.* dōseiai 同性愛.

hone, *vb.* togu 研ぐ.

honest, *adj.* 1. shōjiki (na) 正直 (な) (upright). 2. seijitsu (na) 誠実 (な) (sincere). 3. sotchoku (na) 率直 (な) (frank).

honesty, *n.* 1. shōjikisa 正直さ. 2. seijutsusa 誠実さ. 3. sotchokusa 率直さ (frankness).

honey, *n.* hanī ハニー; hachimitsu 蜂蜜.

honeycomb, *n.* mitsubachi no su 蜜蜂の巣.

honeymoon, *n.* hanemūn ハネムーン; shinkonryokō 新婚旅行.

honeysuckle, *n.* suikazura 忍冬.

honk, 1. *n.* kurakushon no oto クラクションの音 (sound of car horn). 2. *vb.* kurakushon o narasu クラクションを鳴らす.

honor, 1. *n.* meisei 名声 (public esteem, reputation); meiyo 名誉 (high ethical character, source of distinction); sonkei 尊敬 (respect); **do honor to** ... ni keii o harau ... に敬意を払う. 2. *vb.* tataeru 賛える (revere); meiyo o ataeru 名誉を与える (confer honor); **I am honored.** Kōei desu 光栄です.

honorable, *adj.* 1. meiyo ni atai suru 名誉に値する (worthy of honor). 2. rippa (na) 立派 (な) (good).

honorarium, *n.* sharei 謝礼.

honorary, *adj.* meiyo(shoku) (no) 名誉(職) (の).

hood, *n.* 1. fūdo フード (head covering). 2. bon'netto ボンネット (car).

hoodlum, *n.* chinpira ちんぴら; gorotsuki ごろつき.

hoodwink, *vb.* damasu だます.

hoof, *n.* hizume ひづめ.

hook, 1. *n.* hokku ホック; kagi 鉤 (curved piece of metal); yōfukukake 洋服掛け (for clothing); tsuribari 釣り針 (fishhook). 2. *vb.* kakeru 掛ける (suspend); toraeru 捕える (catch); magaru 曲がる (curve); **hook up** tomeru 留める (fasten); **be off the hook** juwaki ga hazurete iru 受話器が外れている (telephone); kirinukeru 切り抜ける (be released from difficulty).

hoop, *n.* wa 輪.

hoot, 1. *n.* yaji 野次 (jeer). 2. *vb.* yajiru 野次る.

hop, *vb.* tobu 跳ぶ (leap); kataashi de tobu 片足で跳ぶ (leap on one foot).

hope, 1. *n.* kibō 希望; nozomi 望み. 2. *vb.* kitai suru 期待する; nozomu 望む.

hopeful, *adj.* 1. kibō ni michita 希望に満ちた (full of hope). 2. kitai dekiru 期待できる (has potential).

hopefully, *adv.* negawaku wa 願わくは (it is hoped).

hopeless, *adj.* 1. zetsubō-teki (na) 絶望的 (な) (desperate, without hope). 2. yaku ni tatanai 役に立たない (useless).

horde, *n.* mure 群れ.

horizon, *n.* suiheisen 水平線 (sea); chiheisen 地平線 (land).

horizontal, *adj.* suihei (na) 水平 (な).

hormone, *n.* horumon ホルモン.

horn, *n.* 1. tsuno 角 (animal). 2. kurakushon クラクション (car). 3. horun ホルン (musical instrument).

hornet, *n.* suzumebachi 雀蜂.

horoscope, *n.* hoshiuranai 星占い.

horrendous, *adj.* 1. osoroshii 恐ろしい (horrible). 2. susamajii すさまじい (shocking).

horrible, *adj.* 1. osoroshii 恐ろしい (dreadful). 2. fuyukai (na) 不愉快 (な) (unpleasant); hidoi ひどい (disgusting).

horrid, *adj.* 1. osoroshii 恐ろしい (dreadful). 2. ijiwaru (na) いじ悪 (な) (nasty).

horrify, *vb.* zotto saseru ぞっとさせる (cause to fear).

horror, *n.* 1. kyōfu 恐怖 (fear). 2. ken'o 嫌悪 (repugnance).

horse, *n.* uma 馬; **ride a horse** uma ni noru 馬に乗る.

horseback, *adv.* uma ni notte 馬に乗って.

horseman, *n.* kishu 騎手.

horsepower, *n.* bariki 馬力.

horseradish, *n.* wasabi わさび.

horseshoe, *n.* teitetsu 蹄鉄.

horsewoman, *n.* joseikishu 女性騎手.

horticulture, *n.* engei 園芸.

hose, *n.* 1. hōsu ホース. 2. sutokkingu ストッキング (stockings); kutsushita 靴下 (socks).

hospital, *n.* byōin 病院.

hospitality, *n.* kantai 歓待; kokoro kara no motenashi 心からのもてなし.

hospitalize, *vb.* nyūin saseru 入院させる; **be hospitalized** nyūin suru 入院する.

host, *n.* 1. shujin 主人; hosuto ホスト (person who receives guests). 2. shikaisha 司会者 (master of ceremonies). 3. **a host of** takusan (no) たくさん (の).

hostage, *n.* hitojichi 人質.

hostess, *n.* 1. on'nashujin 女主人 (female host). 2. josei-shikaisha 女性司会者 (female master of ceremonies). 3. hosutesu ホステス (nightclub).

hostile, *adj.* 1. tekii ga aru 敵意がある (unfriendly). 2. teki (no) 敵 (の) (of an enemy).

hostility, *n.* teki'i 敵意 (hostile attitude).

hot, *adj.* 1. atsui 熱い (high temperature); **hot water** (o)yu (お)湯. 2. atsui 熱い (feeling great heat). 3. karai 辛い (peppery). 4. hageshii 激しい (violent). 5. nesshin (na) 熱心 (な) (earnest).

hot-blooded, *adj.* kanjō-teki (na) 感情的 (な) (excitable); jōnetsu-teki (na) 情熱的 (な) (passionate).

hot cake, *n.* hotto-kēki ホットケーキ.

hot dog, *n.* hotto-doggu ホットドッグ.

hotel, *n.* hoteru ホテル.

hot-headed, *adj.* 1. tanki (na) 短気 (な) (short-tempered). 2. sekkachi (na) せっかち (な) (hasty).

hothouse, *n.* onshitsu 温室.

hot line, *n.* hotto-rain ホットライン.

hound, 1. *n.* ryōken 猟犬 (hunting dog); haundo-ken ハウンド犬 (hound dog). 2. *vb.* ou 追う (track); semesainamu 責め苛む (harass).

hour, *n.* 1. jikan 時間 (any specific time or period of day). 2. ichijikan 一時間 (sixty minutes).

hourglass, *n.* sunadokei 砂時計.

hourly, 1. *adj.* ichijikan goto (no) 一時間毎 (の) (of each successive hour); ichijikan (no) 一時間 (の) (calculated by the hour); **hourly wage** (ichi)jikankyū (一)時間給. 2. *adv.* ichijikan goto ni 一時間毎に (at every hour); ichijikan ni tsuki 一時間につき(per hour).

house, 1. *n.* ie 家; uchi うち (home); gekijō 劇場 (theater). 2. *vb.* jūkyo o ataeru 住居を与える (provide with a dwelling); shūyō suru 収容する (receive into a shelter); motteiru 持っている (contain).

household, *n.* kazoku 家族 (family); ie 家; uchi うち (house).

housekeeper, *n.* kaseifu 家政婦.

housekeeping, *n.* kasei 家政.

housemaid, *n.* otetsudai お手伝い.

housewarming, *n.* hikkoshi-pātī 引越しパーティ.

housewife, *n.* shufu 主婦.

housework, *n.* kaji 家事.

housing, *n.* 1. jūkyo 住居 (dwelling place, houses). 2. jūtakukyōkyū 住宅供給 (providing houses).

housing project, *n.* jūtakudanchi 住宅団地.

hovel, *n.* hottategoya 掘っ建て小屋.

hover, *vb.* 1. ukabu 浮かぶ (hover in the air). 2. urotsuku うろつく (linger about). 3. samayou さまよう (stay uncertain).

how, 1. *adv.* dōyatte どうやって (by what means); dono gurai どの位 (to what extent); dō どう (in what condition); dōshite どうして (why); nanto 何と (used as an intensifier); **how about** ... wa dō/ikaga desu ka ...はどう／いかがですか; **How are you?** Genki desu ka 元気ですか; **how come** dōshite どうして; **how far** dono gurai tōi desu ka どの位遠いですか; **how long** dono gurai どの位; **how much** ikura いくら (what is the cost); dono gurai どの位 (in what quantity); **how many** nan'nin 何人 (how many people); ikutsu いくつ (how many things); **How old (are you)?** Nansai desu ka. 何歳ですか; **How pretty!** Nanto kawaii. 何とかわいい. 2. *conj.* shikata 仕方; dōyatte どうやって (way in which); **how to drive** unten no shikata 運転の仕方.

however, 1. *adv.* don'na ni ... temo/demo どんなに...ても／でも. 2. *conj.* shikashi しかし.

howl, 1. *n.* hoegoe 吠え声 (cry of a wolf, etc.); nakisakebi 泣き叫び (wail of a person). 2. *vb.* hoeru 吠える (dog, wolf, etc.); nakisakebu 泣き叫ぶ (person).

hub, *n.* 1. habu ハブ (center of wheel). 2. chūshin 中心 (center).

huddle, 1. *n.* ranzatsu 乱雑 (confused pile). 2. *vb.* (people) mi o yoseau 身を寄せ合う (gather together); (objects) tsumekomu 詰め込む (cause to crowd together).

hue, *n.* shikichō 色調 (color).

huff, *n.* ikari 怒り (anger); **in a huff** okotte 怒って.

hug, 1. *n.* dakishime 抱き締め. 2. *vb.* dakishimeru 抱き締める.

huge, *adj.* kyodai (na) 巨大 (な).

hull, *n.* 1. kawa 皮 (grain, seeds). 2. sentai 船体 (ship).

hum, 1. *n.* hamingu ハミング (song); bun-bun ぶんぶん (droning sound). 2. *vb.* hamingu suru ハミングする (sing); bun-bun unaru ぶんぶん唸る (make a droning sound).

human, 1. *adj.* ningen (no) 人間 (の) (of human beings); ningen-teki (na) 人間的 (な) (sympathetic). 2. *n.* ningen 人間.

human being, *n.* ningen 人間.

humane, *adj.* ningen-teki (na) 人間的 (な); nasakebukai 情深い.

humanitarian, *adj.* jindō-teki (na) 人道的 (な).

humanities, *n.* jinbunkagaku 人文科学.

humanity, *n.* 1. hūmanitī ヒューマニティー; ningensei 人間性 (human state or quality). 2. jinrui 人類 (humankind).

humankind, *n.* jinrui 人類.

humble, 1. *adj.* kenkyo (na) 謙虚 (な) (not arrogant); hige shite iru 卑下している (feeling inferior); hikui 低い (low). 2. *vb.* hige suru 卑下する (abase oneself); otoshimeru おとしめる (humble someone).

humbug, *n.* 1. inchiki いんちき (fraud). 2. ikasamashi いかさま師 (impostor).

humdrum, *adj.* taikutsu (na) 退屈 (な).

humid, *adj.* shitsudo no takai 湿度の高い.

humidify, *vb.* shimeraseru 湿らせる.

humidity, *n.* shikke 湿気.

humiliate, *vb.* hazukashimeru 辱める; otoshimeru おとしめる.

humiliation, *n.* haji 恥.

humility, *n.* kenkyo 謙虚.

humor, 1. *n.* yūmoa ユーモア; jōdan 冗談 (funniness); kishitsu 気質 (mental disposition); kimagure 気紛れ (whim). 2. *vb.* kigen o toru 機嫌を取る.

humorous, *adj.* okashii おかしい; kokkei (na) 滑稽 (な) (funny).

hump, *n.* 1. kobu こぶ (of a camel). 2. koyama 小山 (small hill).

humpback, hunchback, *n.* semushi せむし.

hunch, *n.* 1. kobu こぶ (hump). 2. yokan 予感 (premonition).

hundred, 1. *n.* hyaku 百. 2. *adj.* hyaku (no) 百 (の).

hundredth, *adj.* hyakubanme (no) 百番目 (の).

Hungary, *n.* hangarī ハンガリー.

hunger, 1. *n.* ue 飢え (starvation); kūfuku 空腹 (empty stomach). 2. *vb.* ueru 飢える (starve); onaka ga suku お腹が空く (become hungry); **hunger for** ... ni ueru ... に飢える.

hungry, *adj.* 1. **hungry (for)** (...) ni uete iru (...) に飢えている. 2. onaka ga suiteiru お腹が空いている (in need of food).

hunt, 1. *n.* kari 狩り (hunting

game); sagashi 捜し (search). 2. *vb.* kari o suru 狩りをする (chase game); sagasu 捜す (search for); **hunt down** oitsumeru 追い詰める; **hunt out** sagashidasu 捜し出す; **hunt for a house** ie o sagasu 家を捜す.

hunter, -tress, *n.* hantā ハンター; ryōshi 猟師.

hunting, *n.* 1. kari 狩り (hunting game). 2. sagashi 捜し (search); **job-hunting** shokusagashi 職捜し.

hurdle, *n.* 1. hādoru ハードル (in a race). 2. shōgai 障害 (obstacle).

hurl, *vb.* nagetsukeru 投げつける (throw, utter).

hurricane, *n.* harikēn ハリケーン; ōarashi 大嵐.

hurried, *adj.* ōisogi (no) 大急ぎ (の).

hurry, 1. *n.* isogi 急ぎ (haste); **(be) in a hurry** isoide (iru) 急いで (いる). 2. *vb.* isogu 急ぐ (act with speed); isogasu 急がす (hasten); **hurry up** isogu 急ぐ (do faster); isogaseru 急がせる (make someone act faster).

hurt, 1. *n.* kizu 傷 (wound); kutsū 苦痛 (pain). 2. *vb.* kizutsukeru 傷つける (cause bodily or mental pain); kibun o gaisuru 気分を害する (offend); itamu 痛む (suffer from pain).

husband, *n.* otto 夫; shujin 主人.

hush, 1. *n.* chinmoku 沈黙 (silence); shizukesa 静けさ (stillness). 2. *vb.* shizuka ni naru 静かになる (become silent); shizuka ni suru 静かにする (make silent). 3. *interj.* shizuka ni 静かに.

husk, *n.* kawa 皮 (of corn, seeds, etc.).

husky, *adj.* hasukī (na) ハスキー (な); shagaregoe (no) しゃがれ声 (の) (of voice).

hustle, 1. *n.* kakki 活気 (energetic activity); oshinoke 押しのけ (jostling); **hustle and bustle** zattō 雑踏. 2. *vb.* seiryoku-teki ni hataraku 精力的に働く (work energetically); oshinokeru 押しのける (push one's way); ... ni oshikomu ...に押し込む (force someone into).

hustler, *n.* 1. seiryokuka 精力家 (active person). 2. sagishi 詐欺師 (swindler). 3. baishunfu 売春婦 (prostitute).

hut, *n.* koya 小屋.

hyacinth, *n.* hiashinsu ヒアシンス.

hybrid, *adj.* haiburiddo (no) ハイブリッド (の); kōhaishu (no) 交配種 (の).

hydrangea, *n.* ajisai あじさい.

hydrant, *n.* shōkasen 消火栓.

hydroelectric, *adj.* suiryoku-hatsuden (no) 水力発電 (の).

hydrogen, *n.* suiso 水素.

hyena, *n.* haiena ハイエナ.

hygiene, *n.* eisei 衛生.

hygienic, *adj.* eisei-teki (na) 衛生的 (な).

hymn, *n.* 1. sanbika 賛美歌 (religious). 2. sanka 賛歌 (song of praise).

hyperbole, *n.* kochō 誇張.

hypertension, *n.* kōketsuatsu 高血圧 (elevation of blood pressure).

hypertensive, *n.* kōketsuatsu kanja 高血圧患者.

hyphen, *n.* haifun ハイフン.

hyphenate, *vb.* haifun de tsunagu/wakeru ハイフンでつなぐ／分ける (join/divide by a hyphen).

hypnosis, *n.* saiminjōtai 催眠状態

(hypnotic state).

hypnotic, *adj.* 1. saiminjutsu (no) 催眠術 (の) (of hypnotism); saimin (no) 催眠 (の) (of hypnosis). 2. nemuke o sasou 眠気を誘う (inducing sleep).

hypnotism, *n.* saiminjutsu 催眠術 (practice of inducing sleep).

hypnotize, *vb.* saimin o kakeru 催眠をかける (put to sleep by hypnotism).

hypochondriac, *n.* hipokonderī kanja ヒポコンデリー患者; shinkishō kanja 心気症患者.

hypocrisy, *n.* gizen 偽善.

hypocrite, *n.* gizensha 偽善者.

hypocritical, *adj.* gizen-teki (na) 偽善的 (な).

hypodermic, *adj.* hika (no) 皮下 (の).

hypothesis, *n.* 1. katei 仮定 (proposition, guess). 2. kasetsu 仮説 (provisional theory).

hypothetical, *adj.* katei-teki (na) 仮定的 (な).

hysteria, *n.* hisuterī ヒステリー.

hysterical, *adj.* hisuterikku (na) ヒステリック (な).

I

I, *pron.* watashi (ga, wa) 私 (が、は).

ice, 1. *n.* kōri 氷. 2. *vb.* kōraseru 凍らせる (freeze); kōri de hiyasu 氷で冷やす (cool with ice).

iceberg, *n.* hyōzan 氷山.

ice cream, *n.* aisukurīmu アイスクリーム.

iced, *adj.* kōtte iru 凍っている (frozen); tsumetai 冷たい (chilled).

icicle, *n.* tsurara つらら.

icon, *n.* 1. shirushi 印 (symbol). 2. zō 像 (image). 3. seizō 聖像 (sacred image).

iconoclast, *n.* 1. kyūshūhakaisha 旧習破壊者 (attacker of cherished beliefs). 2. gūzōhakaisha 偶像破壊者 (destroyer of images).

icy, *adj.* 1. kōri ga hatteiru 氷が張っている (covered with ice). 2. tsumetai 冷たい (cold).

idea, *n.* 1. aidea アイデア; kangae 考え (concept in mind, thought); **good idea** ii kangae 良い考え. 2.

chishiki 知識 (knowledge). 3. inshō 印象 (impression). 4. iken 意見 (opinion). 5. keikaku 計画 (plan). 6. rikai 理解 (understanding); **have no idea** sappari wakaranai さっぱりわからない.

ideal, *adj.* risō-teki (na) 理想的 (な).

idealism, *n.* risōshugi 理想主義.

idealist, *n.* aidearisuto アイデアリスト; risōshugisha 理想主義者.

idealize, *vb.* risōka suru 理想化する.

identical, *adj.* 1. onaji (no) 同じ (の) (same). 2. niteiru 似ている (resembling).

identification, *n.* 1. kakunin 確認 (act of identifying). 2. mimoto kakuninsho 身元確認書 (something that identifies a person); mibun shōmeisho 身分証明書 (identification card).

identify, *vb.* 1. mitomeru 認める (recognize). 2. onaji to shōmei suru 同じと証明する (prove to be identical). 3. dōitsushi suru 同一視する (consider as same).

identity, *n.* 1. dōitsu 同一 (state of being the same). 2. hontō no jibun 本当の自分 (true self); mimoto 身元 (origin, background).

ideology, *n.* ideorogī イデオロギー; shisō 思想; kangae 考え.

idiom, *n.* idiomu イディオム; kanyōku 慣用句 (phrase).

idiomatic, *adj.* idiomu (no) イディオム (の); kan'yō-teki (na) 慣用的 (な).

idiosyncrasy, *n.* tokuchō 特長 (individual trait).

idiot, *n.* baka 馬鹿.

idiotic, *adj.* bakagete iru 馬鹿げている; baka (na) 馬鹿 (な).

idle, 1. *adj.* hima (na) 暇 (な) (not active, not busy); bushō (na) 無精 (な) (lazy); kudaranai 下らない (of no worth); **idle talk** kudaranai hanashi 下らない話; oshaberi おしゃべり. 2. *vb.* nani mo shinai 何もしない (do nothing); bura-bura suru ぶらぶらする (saunter aimlessly, idle away).

idleness, *n.* bushō 無精.

idol, *n.* 1. aidoru アイドル (admired person). 2. gūzō 偶像 (image).

idolize, *vb.* 1. sūhai suru 崇拝する (admire). 2. gūzōka suru 偶像化する (make idol of).

if, *conj.* 1. moshi(mo) ... naraba もし(も) ...ならば (in case that). 2. tatoe ... demo たとえ...でも (even though). 3. ... ka dōka ...かどうか (whether). 4. **if only** ... nara ii noni ...ならいいのに; **even if** tatoe ... demo/temo たとえ...でも／ても; **as if** marude ... no yō ni

まるで...のように; **if you like** moshi yokereba もしよければ.

ignite, *vb.* hi o tsukeru 火を点ける (set on fire); hi ga tsuku 火が点く (catch fire).

ignition, *n.* tenka 点火 (act of igniting).

ignoble, *adj.* 1. kokoro no iyashii 心の卑しい (base). 2. mibun no hikui 身分の低い (of humble descent).

ignominious, *adj.* 1. kutsujoku-teki (na) 屈辱的 (な) (humiliating). 2. hazubeki 恥ずべき (contemptible).

ignorance, *n.* 1. muchi 無知 (lack of knowledge). 2. mugaku 無学 (lack of learning).

ignorant, *adj.* 1. shiranai 知らない (lacking knowledge). 2. ki ga tsukanai 気がつかない (unaware).

ignore, *vb.* mushi suru 無視する.

ill, 1. *adj.* byōki (no) 病気 (の) (sick); warui 悪い (evil, faulty, unfavorable); **ill at ease** igokochi ga warui 居心地が悪い. 2. *n.* byōki 病気 (ailment); aku 悪 (evil). 3. *adv.* waruku 悪く (badly, unfavorably); **speak ill of** ... o waruku iu ...を悪く言う.

illegal, *adj.* fuhō (na) 不法 (な).

illegible, *adj.* yomenai 読めない.

illegitimate, *adj.* 1. shoshi (no) 庶子 (の) (born out of wedlock). 2. fuhō (na) 不法 (な) (unlawful).

ill-fated, *adj.* fu'un (na) 不運 (な).

illicit, *adj.* 1. fuhō (na) 不法 (な) (unlawful). 2. fudōtoku (na) 不道徳 (な) (immoral).

illiteracy, *n.* monmō 文盲.

illiterate, *adj.* monmō (no) 文盲 (の).

ill-mannered, *adj.* gyōgi ga warui 行儀が悪い.

illness, *n.* byōki 病気.

illogical, *adj.* fugōri (na) 不合理 (な).

illuminate, *vb.* terasu 照らす; akari o tsukeru 明りをつける (supply with light).

illumination, *n.* shōmei 照明 (lighting); iruminēshon イルミネーション(decorative lighting).

illusion, *n.* 1. genkaku 幻覚 (false optical impression). 2. sakkaku 錯覚 (confusion, false impression). 3. giman 欺瞞 (deception).

illusory, *adj.* 1. genkaku-teki (na) 幻覚的 (な) (causing illusion). 2. machigawase-yasui 間違わせ易い (misleading). 3. jittai ga nai 実体がない (unsubstantial).

illustrate, *vb.* 1. rei o ageru 例を挙げる (give example); zushi suru 図示する (provide charts, etc.). 2. sashie o tsukeru 挿絵を付ける (furnish with pictures).

illustration, *n.* 1. irasutorēshon イラストレーション; sashie 挿絵 (picture in a book, etc.). 2. rei 例 (example); zuhyō 図表 (chart, diagram).

illustrator, *n.* irasutorētā イラストレーター (artist).

illustrious, *adj.* chomei (na) 著名 (な) (famous).

ill will, *n.* tekii 敵意 (enmity); ken'o 嫌悪 (hatred).

image, *n.* 1. imēji イメージ; shinzō 心像(idea, mental representation, impression). 2. zō 像; sugata 姿 (physical representation or likeness, image in mirror).

imagery, *n.* hiyu 比喩 (use of figures of speech).

imaginary, *adj.* sōzōjō (no) 想像上 (の); kakū (no) 架空 (の) (fancied).

imagination, *n.* 1. sōzō 想像 (creation of the mind). 2. sōzōryoku 想像力 (creative talent); hassōryoku 発想力 (resourcefulness).

imaginative, *adj.* sōzōryoku ni michita 想像力に満ちた.

imagine, *vb.* 1. sōzō suru 想像する (form mental images). 2. omou 思う (think, guess).

imbalance, *n.* fukinkō 不均衡.

imbecile, *n.* 低能者 (person of low intelligence); 馬鹿 (fool).

imbibe, *vb.* nomu 飲む (drink).

imbue, *vb.* 1. fukikomu 吹き込む (inspire). 2. afuresaseru 溢れさせる (saturate).

imitate, *vb.* mane suru 真似する.

imitation, *n.* mane 真似; mohō 模倣 (copy); mozōhin 模造品 (counterfeit).

imitator, *n.* mohōsha 模倣者.

immaculate, *adj.* 1. shimihitotsu nai 染み一つない (spotlessly clean). 2. kiyoraka (na) 清らか (な) (morally pure). 3. kanpeki (na) 完璧 (な) (flawless).

immaterial, *adj.* 1. jūyō de nai 重要でない (unimportant). 2. hibusshitsu-teki (na) 非物質的 (な) (not material).

immature, *adj.* mijuku (na) 未熟 (な) (unripe, childish).

immediate, *adj.* 1. sokuji (no) 即時 (の) (instant). 2. ichiban chikai 一番近い (nearest). 3. mokka (no) 目下 (の) (present).

immediately, *adv.* 1. tadachi ni 直ちに (at once). 2. chokusetsu ni 直接に(directly).

immense, *adj.* bōdai (na) 膨大 (な) (vast).

immerse, *vb.* 1. hitasu 浸す; tsukeru 浸ける (dip). 2. bottō saseru 没頭させる (cause to be engrossed); **be immersed in** ... ni bottō suru ...に没頭する.

immigrant, *n.* imin 移民.

immigrate, *vb.* ijū suru 移住する (settle in a foreign country).

imminent, *adj.* sashisematte-iru 差し迫っている (impending).

immobile, *adj.* fudō (no) 不動 (の).

immoral, *adj.* fudōtoku-teki (na) 不道徳的 (な).

immorality, *n.* fudōtoku 不道徳.

immortal, *adj.* 1. fushi (no) 不死 (の) (not mortal). 2. eien (no) 永遠 (の) (everlasting).

immortality, *n.* fushi 不死 (unending life).

immortalize, *vb.* eienka suru 永遠化する (perpetuate).

immune, *adj.* 1. men'ekisei ga aru 免疫性がある (protected from a disease). 2. teikōryoku ga aru 抵抗力がある (not susceptible). 3. manugarete-iru 免れている (exempt).

immunity, *n.* 1. men'eki 免疫 (protection from a disease). 2. teikōryoku 抵抗力 (resistance). 3. menjo 免除 (exemption).

immunize, *vb.* men'eki o suru 免疫をする.

impact, *n.* 1. shōgeki 衝撃 (force, collision). 2. eikyō 影響 (influence).

impair, *vb.* sokonau 損う (damage).

impart, *vb.* 1. uchiakeru 打ち明ける (disclose). 2. ataeru 与える (bestow); wakeataeru 分け与える (give a share of).

impartial, *adj.* kōhei (na) 公平 (な).

impasse, *n.* 1. ikizumari 行き詰まり (deadlock). 2. ikidomari 行き止まり (road).

impassioned, *adj.* nesshin (na) 熱心 (な).

impassive, *adj.* mukanjō (no) 無感情 (の) (unemotional).

impatient, *adj.* 1. **be impatient (to do)** (... suru koto ga) matenai (...することが) 待てない (be unable to wait, be eager). 2. gaman dekinai 我慢出来ない (intolerant).

impeach, *vb.* hihan suru 批判する (criticize); dangai suru 弾劾する (accuse official).

impeachment, *n.* hihan 批判 (criticism); dangai 弾劾 (political).

impeccable, *adj.* kanpeki (na) 完璧 (な) (flawless).

impede, *vb.* jama o suru 邪魔をする.

impediment, *n.* jama 邪魔; bōgai 妨害.

impel, *vb.* unagasu 促す.

impending, *adj.* sashisematte-iru 差し迫っている.

impenetrable, *adj.* tsukiyabure-nai 突き破れない(incapable of being penetrated). 2. fukakai (na) 不可解 (な) (incomprehensible).

imperative, 1. *n.* meireikei 命令形 (grammar). 2. *adj.* hitsuyō (na) 必要 (な) (necessary); meirei (no) 命令 (の) (expressing a command).

imperceptible, *adj.* 1. kanjirarenai 感じられない (not perceived by the senses). 2. komakai 細かい (slight).

imperfect, *adj.* fukanzen (na) 不完全 (な).

imperfection, *n.* fukanzen 不完全.

imperial, *adj.* 1. teikoku (no) 帝国 (の) (empire). 2. ōshitsu (no) 王室 (の) (king); kōshitsu (no) 皇室 (の) (emperor).

imperialism, *n.* teikokushugi 帝国主義.

impersonal, *adj.* 1. kyakkan-teki (na) 客観的 (な) (objective). 2. ippan-teki (na) 一般的 (な) (general).

impersonate, *vb.* 1. ... no furi o suru ... のふりをする (pretend to be). 2. ... no mane o suru ... の真似をする (mimic). 3. ... ni funsuru ...に扮する (perform the role of).

impertinent, *adj.* burei (na) 無礼 (な).

impervious, *adj.* 1. futōsei (no) 不透性 (の) (impenetrable). 2. okasarenai 冒されない (incapable of being injured).

impetuous, *adj.* seikyū (na) 性急 (な).

impetus, *n.* 1. shigeki 刺激 (stimulus). 2. ikioi 勢い (force of motion).

impinge, *vb.* 1. eikyō suru 影響する (have an effect). 2. shingai suru 侵害する (infringe). 3. butsukaru ぶつかる (collide).

implacable, *adj.* 1. nadame-rarenai なだめられない (cannot calm). 2. mujihi (na) 無慈悲 (な) (merciless).

implant, *vb.* 1. uetsukeru 植え付ける (instill, plant). 2. ishoku suru 移植する (graft).

implement, 1. *n.* dōgu 道具. 2. *vb.* jikkō ni utsusu 実行に移す (carry out).

implicate, *vb.* kanren saseru 関連させる (relate); eikyō suru 影響する (affect).

implication, *n.* 1. honomekashi 仄めかし (act of implying). 2. kankei 関係 (connection).

implicit, *adj.* 1. gengai (no) 言外 (の) (implied). 2. zettai-teki (na) 絶対的 (な) (unquestioning).

implore, *vb.* kongan suru 懇願する.

imply, *vb.* 1. honomekasu 仄めかす (suggest). 2. imi suru 意味する (signify).

impolite, *adj.* shitsurei (na) 失礼 (な).

import, 1. *n.* yunyū 輸入 (act of importing); yunyūhin 輸入品 (something imported); imi 意味 (meaning). 2. *vb.* yunyū suru 輸入する (ship); imi suru 意味する (signify).

importance, *n.* jūyōsa 重要さ (great significance).

important, *adj.* jūyō (na) 重要 (な); daiji (na) 大事 (な) (of great significance).

importation, *n.* 1. yunyū 輸入 (act of importing). 2. yunyūhin 輸入品 (something imported).

importune, *vb.* segamu せがむ.

impose, *vb.* 1. kasu 課す (set as an obligation). 2. oshitsukeru 押し付ける (force oneself on others). 3.

impose on tsukekomu 付け込む (take advantage of); damasu だます (deceive).

imposing, *adj.* attō sareru (yō na) 圧倒される (ような).

imposition, *n.* 1. futan 負担 (burden); gimu 義務 (obligation). 2. kyōsei 強制 (act of imposing).

impossible, *adj.* 1. fukanō (na) 不可能 (な) (cannot be done or effected). 2. arienai あり得ない (cannot exist or happen).

impostor, *n.* petenshi ぺてん師; ikasamashi いかさま師.

impotent, *adj.* 1. muryoku (na) 無力 (な) (lacking power). 2. inpo (no) インポ (の); funō (na, no) 不

能 (な、の) (lacking sexual powers).

impound, *vb.* bosshū suru 没収する (seize by law).

impoverish, *vb.* mazushiku suru 貧しくする (make poor); **be impoverished** mazushiku naru 貧しくなる.

impregnate, *vb.* 1. ninshin saseru 妊娠させる (make pregnant). 2. shimikomaseru 染み込ませる (cause to be infused).

impress, *vb.* 1. kanshin saseru 感心させる (cause respect). 2. inshōzukeru 印象付ける (fix in mind). 3. osu 押す (press).

impression, *n.* 1. inshō 印象 (effect on the mind). 2. kanji 感じ (vague awareness). 3. shirushi 印 (stamped mark).

Impressionism, *n.* inshōshugi 印象主義.

impressive, *adj.* migoto (na) 見事 (な) (admirable).

imprison, *vb.* keimusho ni ireru 刑務所に入れる.

imprisonment, *n.* tōgoku 投獄.

improbable, *adj.* arisō ni nai ありそうにない.

impromptu, *adj.* sokkyō (no) 即興 (の).

improper, *adj.* futekitō (na) 不適当 (な) (not suitable).

improve, *vb.* 1. kaizen suru 改善する; yoku suru 良くする (make better). 2. yoku naru 良くなる (become better).

improvement, *n.* kaizen 改善; kōjō 向上.

improvise, *vb.* sokkyō de suru 即興でする.

impudent, *adj.* atsukamashii 厚かましい.

impulse, *n.* 1. shigeki 刺激;

shōgeki 衝撃 (stimulus). 2. shōdō 衝動 (sudden inclination).

impulsive, *adj.* shōdō-teki (na) 衝動的 (な).

impunity, *n.* mubatsu 無罰.

impure, *adj.* 1. fujun (na) 不純 (な) (not pure). 2. 2. fudōtoku (na) 不道徳 (な) (immoral).

impute, *vb.* **impute to** ... no sei ni suru ...のせいにする.

in, 1. *prep.* ... no naka de/ni ...の中で／に (inside, within, among); ... no aida ni ...の間に (while, during); ... de ...で (by way of, within a space of time); ... no tame ni ...のために (for the purpose of). 2. *adv.* naka de/ni 中で／に (inside, within); iru いる ([be] in one's house, office, etc.).

inaccessible, *adj.* chikazukenai 近づけない (unapproachable).

inaccurate, *adj.* fuseikaku (na) 不正確 (な).

inane, *adj.* oroka (na) 愚か (な).

inasmuch as, *conj.* ... node ...ので;... kara ...から.

inaugurate, *vb.* 1. shūnin saseru 就任させる (induct into office). 2. hajimeru 始める (begin).

inauguration, *n.* 1. shūninshiki 就任式 (ceremony). 2. kaishi 開始 (beginning).

inborn, *adj.* umaretsuki (no) 生まれつき (の).

incandescent, *adj.* kagayaku 輝く (radiant).

incantation, *n.* jumon 呪文.

incapable, *adj.* **be incapable of** ... ga dekinai ...ができない.

incapacitate, *vb.* dekinaku suru できなくする (make unable).

incarcerate, *vb.* tōgoku suru 投獄する.

incarnate, *adj.* nikutaika (shita) 肉

体化 (した) (embodied in flesh); keshin (no) 化身 (の) (disguised in flesh).

incarnation, *n.* nikutaika 肉体化; keshin 化身 (embodiment).

incense, 1. *n.* senkō 線香. 2. *vb.* gekido saseru 激怒させる (infuriate).

incentive, *n.* 1. dōki 動機 (motive). 2. shigeki 刺激 (stimulus).

inception, *n.* kaishi 開始.

incessant, *adj.* hikkirinashi (no) ひっきりなし (の).

incessantly, *adv.* hikkirinashi ni ひっきりなしに.

incest, *n.* kinshinsōkan 近親相姦.

inch, *n.* inchi インチ.

incidence, *n.* 1. hindo 頻度 (rate of occurrence). 2. hassei 発生 (occurrence).

incident, *n.* 1. jiken 事件; jihen 事変 (riotous incident). 2. dekigoto 出来事 (happening, event).

incidental, *adj.* 1. fuzui-teki (na) 付随的 (な) (subordinate). 2. sonota (no) その他 (の) (additional).

incidentally, *adv.* 1. tokoro de ところで (by the way). 2. gūzen ni 偶然に (by chance).

incinerate, *vb.* yaku 焼く; hai ni suru 灰にする.

incipient, *adj.* shoki (no) 初期 (の) (beginning).

incision, *n.* kirikomi 切り込み (cut); sekkai 切開 (surgery).

incisive, *adj.* surudoi 鋭い (acute).

incite, *vb.* karitateru 駆り立てる (stir up); sosonokasu そそのかす (instigate).

inclination, *n.* 1. katamuki 傾き (slope, tilt). 2. konomi 好み (liking). 3. keikō 傾向 (tendency).

incline, 1. *n.* shamen 斜面 (inclined surface); sakamichi 坂道 (of a road). 2. *vb.* katamuku 傾く (slope, tilt); katamukeru 傾ける (cause to slope or tilt); mageru 曲げる (bend or bow one's head, etc.); **be inclined to** ... shitai ki ga suru ...したい気がする (feel like doing); ... shigachi de aru ...しがちである (have a tendency to do).

include, *vb.* fukumu 含む.

including, *prep.* (... o) fukumete (...を) 含めて.

inclusion, *n.* hōkatsu 包括.

inclusive, *adj.* fukumete 含めて; **inclusive of** ... o fukumete ...を含めて.

incognito, *n., adj., adv.* tokumei/henmei (no, de) 匿名／変名 (の、で).

income, *n.* shotoku 所得; shūnyū 収入; **income tax** shotokuzei 所得税.

incongruous, *adj.* chiguhagu (na) ちぐはぐ (な); fuchōwa (na) 不調和 (な) (not harmonious).

inconvenience, *n.* fuben 不便; mendō 面倒.

inconvenient, *adj.* fuben (na) 不便 (な); mendō (na) 面倒 (な).

incorporate, *vb.* kumikomu 組み込む (form as a part).

increase, 1. *n.* zōka 増加; jōshō 上昇. 2. *vb.* fuyasu 増やす (make more numerous or greater); fueru 増える (become more numerous or greater).

incredible, *adj.* shinjirarenai 信じられない.

incredulous, *adj.* fushin (na, no) 不審 (な、の).

increment, *n.* zōkaryō 増加量; jōshōryō 上昇量.

incriminate, *vb.* kokuhatsu suru 告発する (charge); makikomu 巻き込む (involve).

incubator, *n.* hoikuki 保育機 (for baby).

inculcate, *vb.* oshiekomu 教え込む.

incumbent, 1. *n.* genshokusha 現職者; gen'eki 現役 (holder of an office). 2. *adj.* genshoku (no) 現職 (の); gen'eki (no) 現役 (の) (holding an indicated office); gimu (no) 義務 (の) (obligatory).

incur, *vb.* 1. maneku 招く; hikiokosu 引き起こす (bring upon oneself). 2. seoikomu 背負い込む (become liable for).

indebted, *adj.* **be indebted to** ... ni kari ga aru ...に借りがある (owing money to); ... ni on ga aru ...に恩がある (owing gratitude to).

indeed, *adv.* hontō ni 本当に; jitsu ni 実に; mattaku 全く.

indefinite, *adj.* 1. futei (no) 不定 (の) (without fixed limit, not clearly determined). 2. fumeiryō (na) 不明瞭 (な) (uncertain).

indelible, *adj.* kesu koto ga dekinai 消すことができない.

indemnify, *vb.* baishō suru 賠償する (compensate). 2. hoshō suru 補償する (insure).

indemnity, *n.* 1. sonshitsuhoshō 損失補償 (security for loss). 2. baishō 賠償 (compensation).

indent, *vb.* 1. hekomi o tsukeru 凹みを付ける (form recess). 2. kakidashi o zurasu 書き出しをずらす (set back from margin).

independence, *n.* 1. dokuritsu 独立 (not dependent on others); dokuritsudoppo 独立独歩 (self-reliance). 2. jiyū 自由 (freedom).

independent, *adj.* 1. dokuritsu shiteiru 独立している (not dependent on others); dokuritsudoppo (no) 独立独歩 (の) (not influenced by others). 2. jiyū (na) 自由 (な) (free).

index, 1. *n.* indekkusu インデックス; sakuin 索引 (list); shihyō 指標 (indication); **index card** sakuin-kādo 索引カード; **index finger** hitosashiyubi 人差し指. 2. *vb.* sakuin o tsukeru 索引を付ける (provide with index).

India, *n.* indo インド.

Indian, 1. *n.* indojin インド人 (Indian); indian インディアン (American Indian). 2. *adj.* indo (no) インド (の) (of India); indojin (no) インド人 (の) (of an Indian); indian (no) インディアン (の) (of an American Indian).

indicate, *vb.* 1. imi suru 意味する (mean); shisa suru 示唆する (be a sign of). 2. sashishimesu 指し示す (point to).

indication, *n.* 1. shirushi 印 (sign). 2. shiji 指示 (act of pointing out).

indicative, *adj.* **be indicative of** ... o imi/shisa suru ...を意味／示唆する.

indicator, *n.* indikētā インディケーター; hyōjiki 表示器.

indict, *vb.* kiso suru 起訴する.

indictment, *n.* 1. kiso 起訴 (legal action). 2. hinan 非難 (criticize).

indifferent, *adj.* 1. mukanshin (na) 無関心 (な) (without interest). 2. nami (no) 並 (の) (not particularly good).

indigenous, *adj.* 1. dochaku (no) 土着 (の); genjū (no) 原住 (の) (people). 2. gensei (no) 原生 (の) (plants).

indigent, *adj.* mazushii 貧しい.

indigestion, *n.* shōkafuryō 消化不

良.

indignant, *adj.* rippuku shiteiru 立腹している.

indignation, *n.* ikari 怒り.

indignity, *n.* kutsujoku 屈辱.

indigo, *n.* ai 藍 (dye).

indirect, *adj.* kansetsu-teki (na) 間接的 (な).

indiscreet, *adj.* keisotsu (na) 軽率 (な) (not prudent).

indiscriminate, *adj.* 1. teatari-battari (no) 手当りばつたり (の) (haphazard). 2. musabetsu (no) 無差別 (の) (lacking in selectivity).

indispensable, *adj.* fukaketsu (na, no) 不可欠 (な、の).

indisposed, *adj.* 1. kibun ga warui 気分が悪い (slightly ill). 2. ki ga noranai 気が乗らない (not willing).

individual, 1. *n.* kojin 個人; hito 人 (person). 2. *adj.* kojin (no) 個人 (の) (of person); ko-ko (no) 個々 (の) (of item).

indivisible, *adj.* fukabun (no) 不可分 (の).

indoctrinate, *vb.* tatakikomu 叩き込む.

indolent, *adj.* namakemono (no) 怠け者 (の).

indoor, 1. *adj.* okunai (no) 屋内 (の). 2. *adv.* **indoors** okunai de/ni 屋内で／に.

induce, *vb.* 1. sono ki ni suru その気にする (persuade). 2. motarasu もたらす (bring about, produce).

induct, *vb.* 1. shūnin saseru 就任させる (bring into office). 2. michibiku 導く (introduce).

indulge, *vb.* 1. amayakasu 甘やかす (spoil); mankitsu saseru 満喫させる (gratify). 2. **indulge in** ... ni fukeru ...に耽る; ... o omou zonbun ni suru ...を思う存分にする.

indulgence, *n.* 1. amayakashi 甘やかし (leniency). 2. omou mama 思うまま (gratification); tandeki 耽溺 (excessive gratification).

indulgent, *adj.* 1. amai 甘い (lenient). 2. omou mama (no) 思うまま (の) (gratifying).

industrial, *adj.* kōgyō (no) 工業 (の); sangyō (no) 産業 (の).

industrialize, *vb.* kōgyōka suru 工業化する; sangyōka suru 産業化する.

industrious, *adj.* kinben (na) 勤勉 (な).

industry, *n.* 1. kōgyō 工業; sangyō 産業 (trade or manufacture). 2. kinben 勤勉 (diligence).

inebriate, *vb.* yowaseru 酔わせる; **inebriated** yotteiru 酔っている.

inept, *adj.* 1. bukiyō (na) 不器用 (な) (clumsy). 2. chikara ga nai 力が無い (incompetent).

inequity, *n.* 1. fukōhei 不公平 (unfairness). 2. fusei 不正 (injustice).

inert, *adj.* 1. fukappatsu (na) 不活発 (な) (without inherent power to move, etc.). 2. noroi のろい (slow moving); bushō (na) 無精 (な) (lazy).

inertia, *n.* 1. fukappatsu 不活発 (inactivity). 2. bushō 無精 (laziness).

inevitable, *adj.* sakerarenai 避けられない.

inexpensive, *adj.* yasui 安い.

inexperienced, *adj.* keikenbusoku (no) 経験不足 (の).

inexplicable, *adj.* setsumei dekinai 説明できない.

inextricable, *adj.* 1. tokenai 解けない (incapable of being disentangled). 2. nogare-rarenai 逃れられない (incapable of being freed).

infallible, *adj.* 1. zettai ni machigai ga nai 絶対に間違いがない (exempt from liability to error). 2. kakujitsu (na) 確実 (な) (sure).

infamous, *adj.* 1. akumyōdakai 悪名高い (having a bad reputation). 2. hidoi ひどい (detestable).

infamy, *n.* 1. akumyō 悪名 (bad reputation). 2. hazubeki kōi 恥ずべき行為 (infamous act).

infancy, *n.* nyūjiki 乳児期 (babyhood); yōjiki 幼児期 (early childhood).

infant, *n.* akachan 赤ちゃん; nyūji 乳児.

infantile, *adj.* yōchi (na) 幼稚 (な).

infantry, *n.* hoheitai 歩兵隊.

infatuated, *adj.* **be infatuated with** ... ni nobosete iru ... にのぼせている.

infect, *vb.* 1. kansen saseru 感染させる (afflict with disease). 2. eikyō o ataeru 影響を与える (affect). 3. **be infected with** ... ni kansen suru ... に感染する (be afflicted with disease); ... ni eikyō sareru ... に影響させる (be affected).

infection, *n.* 1. kansen 感染 (act of infecting). 2. densenbyō 伝染病 (disease).

infectious, *adj.* 1. kansen shiyasui 感染し易い (disease). 2. utsuriyasui 移り易い (tending to affect others).

infer, *vb.* 1. suisoku suru 推測する (surmise). 2. ketsuronzukeru 結論付ける (conclude).

inference, *n.* 1. suisoku 推測. 2. ketsuron 結論.

inferior, *adj.* 1. ototteiru 劣っている (lower in quality). 2. shita (no) 下 (の) (lower in rank).

inferiority complex, *n.* rettōkan 劣等感.

infernal, *adj.* jigoku (no) 地獄 (の) (of hell); jigoku no yō (na) 地獄のよう (な) (hellish).

inferno, *n.* jigoku 地獄 (hell).

infest, *vb.* habikoru はびこる (overrun).

infidel, *n.* mushinjinsha 無信心者.

infidelity, *n.* fujitsu 不実; uwaki 浮気 (extramarital affair).

infiltrate, *vb.* 1. shimikomu 染み込む (filter into). 2. sen'nyū suru 潜入する (move into surreptitiously).

infinite, *adj.* 1. mugen (no) 無限 (の) (endless). 2. bakudai (na) 莫大 (な) (immeasurably great).

infinitesimal, *adj.* kyokushō (no) 極小 (の).

infinitive, *n.* futeishi 不定詞.

infinity, *n.* mugen 無限 (infinite space or quantity); eien 永遠 (infinite time).

infirm, *adj.* yowai 弱い (weak, faltering).

infirmity, *n.* kyojaku 虚弱 (weakness); byōki 病気 (ailment).

inflame, *vb.* 1. moyasu 燃やす (set afire). 2. okoraseru 怒らせる (anger). 3. **be inflamed** enshō o okosu 炎症をおこす (be affected with inflammation).

inflammable, *adj.* kanensei (no) 可燃性 (の) (capable of being set on fire).

inflammation, *n.* enshō 炎症 (redness and swelling).

inflate, *vb.* fukuramaseru 膨らませる (cause to swell with gas).

inflation, *n.* infure インフレ (economic).

inflection, *n.* gobihenka 語尾変化; gokeihenka 語形変化 (grammar).

inflict, *vb.* 1. ataeru 与える

(impose harmfully). 2. oshitsukeru 押し付ける (force).

influence, 1. *n.* eikyō 影響 (influential power). 2. *vb.* eikyō o ataeru 影響を与える.

influential, *adj.* eikyōryoku no aru 影響力のある.

influenza, *n.* infuruenza インフルエンザ (specific disease); kaze 風邪 (cold).

influx, *n.* nagarekomi 流れ込み.

inform, *vb.* shiraseru 知らせる; tsugeru 告げる.

informal, *adj.* 1. hikōshiki (na) 非公式 (な) (unofficial); gishiki nuki (no) 儀式抜き (の) (without ceremony). 2. kajuaru (na) カジュアル (な) (casual); katakurushiku nai 堅苦しくない (relaxed).

informant, *n.* 1. tsūkokusha 通告者 (informer). 2. jōhōteikyōsha 情報提供者 (person who supplies cultural or social data).

information, *n.* infomēshon インフォメーション; jōhō 情報.

informative, *adj.* tame ni naru 為になる.

infraction, *n.* ihan 違反.

infrared rays, *n.* sekigaisen 赤外線.

infringe, *vb.* okasu 犯す.

infringement, *n.* ihan 違反.

infuriate, *vb.* kan-kan ni okoraseru かんかんに怒らせる.

infusion, *n.* chūnyū 注入 (act of infusing).

ingenious, *adj.* 1. hassō yutaka (na) 発想豊か (な) (characterized by originality). 2. rikō (na) 利口 (な) (cleverly inventive); kōmyō (na) 巧妙 (な) (cleverly skillful).

ingenuity, *n.* 1. hassō 発想 (inventiveness). 2. kōmyōsa 巧妙

さ (cleverness).

ingenuous, *adj.* 1. seijitsu (na) 誠実 (な) (sincere). 2. junshin (na) 純心 (な) (artless, naive).

ingest, *vb.* sesshu suru 摂取する.

ingot, *n.* ingotto インゴット.

ingrained, *adj.* nebukai 根深い (deep-rooted).

ingratiate, *vb.* **ingratiate oneself with** ... ni omoneru ...におもねる.

ingratitude, *n.* onshirazu 恩知らず.

ingredient, *n.* 1. zairyō 材料 (element of a mixture). 2. seibun 成分 (constituent).

inhabit, *vb.* sumu 住む.

inhabitant, *n.* jūnin 住人 (resident).

inhale, *vb.* su'u 吸う; suikomu 吸い込む.

inherent, *adj.* 1. naizai-teki (na) 内在的 (な) (innate). 2. kirihanasenai 切り離せない (inseparable).

inherit, *vb.* 1. sōzoku suru 相続する (be an heir to). 2. uketsugu 受け継ぐ (receive).

inheritance, *n.* isan 遺産 (heritage, legacy, property). 2. iden 遺伝 (heredity).

inhibit, *vb.* osaeru 抑える (restrain).

inhibition, *n.* yokusei 抑制.

inhuman, *adj.* hiningen-teki (na) 非人間的 (な).

iniquity, *n.* aku 悪.

initial, 1. *n.* inisharu イニシャル (initial letter). 2. *adj.* hajime (no) 始め (の).

initiate, *vb.* 1. hajimeru 始める (begin). 2. michibiku 導く; tehodoki o suru 手ほどきをする (introduce some knowledge). 3. nyūkai saseru 入会させる (admit into a group).

initiation, *n.* 1. nyūkai 入会 (acceptance into a group); nyūkaishiki 入会式 (initiation ceremony). 2. tehodoki 手ほどき (introduction).

initiative, *n.* 1. sossen 率先 (leading action); **take the initiative** sossen suru 率先する. 2. sossenryoku 率先力 (ability to initiate action). 3. ishi 意志 (one's decision); **on one's own initiative** jibun no ishi de 自分の意志で.

inject, *vb.* 1. chūsha suru 注射する (inject with syringe). 2. ireru 入れる (add).

injection, *n.* chūsha 注射 (shot).

injunction, *n.* meirei 命令 (command); kinshi 禁止 (prohibition).

injure, *vb.* 1. kizutsukeru 傷付ける (hurt); sokonau 損う (impair). 2. gai suru 害する (offend, do wrong).

injurious, *adj.* gai ga aru 害がある (harmful).

injury, *n.* kega 怪我; kizu 傷 (wound).

ink, *n.* 1. inki インキ. 2. **Chinese ink** sumi 墨.

inkling, *n.* 1. honomekashi 仄めかし (suggestion). 2. nantonaku kanzuku koto 何となく感付くこと (vague idea).

inkwell, *n.* inki-ire インキ入れ.

inland, *adj.* nairiku (no) 内陸 (の).

inlet, *n.* irie 入江.

inmate, *n.* nyūinkanja 入院患者 (in hospital); shūjin 囚人 (in prison).

inn, *n.* ryokan 旅館 (Japanese style); chiisai hoteru 小さいホテル (Western style).

innate, *adj.* umaretsuki (no) 生まれつき (の).

inner, *adj.* 1. naka (no) 中 (の) (interior). 2. seishin-teki (na) 精神的 (な); kokoro (no) 心 (の) (emotional).

inner tube, *n.* chūbu チューブ.

innocence, *n.* 1. mujaki 無邪気; junshin 純心 (naive quality). 2. mujitsu 無実 (freedom from guilt).

innocent, *adj.* 1. mujaki (na) 無邪気 (な); junshin (na) 純真 (な) (naive). 2. mujitsu (no) 無実 (の) (free from guilt).

innocuous, *adj.* mugai (na) 無害 (な).

innovate, *vb.* kaikaku suru 改革する (bring in something new).

innuendo, *n.* iyami 嫌味; atetsuke 当てつけ.

innumerable, *adj.* musū (no) 無数 (の) (cannot be counted); takusan (no) たくさん (の) (numerous).

inoculate, *vb.* yobōsesshu o suru 予防接種をする (immunization).

input, *n.* 1. inputto インプット (computer). 2. nyūryoku 入力 (power, energy). 3. dēta データ (data, information).

inquest, *n.* kenshi 検死 (inquiry by coroner).

inquire, *vb.* 1. chōsa suru 調査する (conduct investigation). 2. tazuneru 尋ねる (ask). 3. toiawaseru 問い合わせる (seek information).

inquiry, *n.* 1. chōsa 調査 (investigation). 2. shitsumon 質問 (question). 3. toiawase 問い合わせ (seeking information).

inquisition, *n.* jinmon 尋問.

inquisitive, *adj.* kōkishin ga tsuyoi 好奇心が強い (very curious); sensakuzuki (na, no) 詮索好き

(な、の) (prying).

inroads, *n.* 1. dageki 打撃 (damaging encroachment). 2. shūgeki 襲撃 (raid).

insane, *adj.* kurutteiru 狂っている; kichigai (no) 気違い (の); **insane asylum** seishin byōin 精神病院.

insanity, *n.* kyōki 狂気.

inscribe, *vb.* 1. kakikomu 書き込む (write); horikomu 彫り込む (engrave). 2. sasageru 捧げる (dedicate).

inscription, *n.* 1. hibun 碑文 (engraved/written text). 2. kenji 献辞 (dedication).

insect, *n.* konchū 昆虫; mushi 虫.

insecticide, *n.* satchūzai 殺虫剤.

insemination, *n.* jusei 受精.

insensitive, *adj.* nibui 鈍い; mushinkei (na) 無神経 (な).

insert, *vb.* ireru 入れる.

insertion, *n.* sōnyū 挿入.

inside, 1. *n.* naka 中; uchigawa 内側 (inner side, interior). 2. *adj.* naka (no) 中 (の) (internal, interior); naibu (no) 内部 (の) (confidential). 3. *adv.* naka de/e/ni/o 中で／に／を (within, indoors); **inside out** uragaeshi ni 裏返しに (with the inner side turned out). 4. *prep.* ...no naka de/e/ni ...の中で／へ／に.

insidious, *adj.* 1. giman (no) 欺瞞 (の) (deceitful). 2. senkōsei (no) 潜行性 (の) (proceeding unnoticed).

insight, *n.* dōsatsuryoku 洞察力.

insignia, *n.* 1. kunshō 勲章 (badge). 2. shirushi 印 (sign).

insignificant, *adj.* tsumaranai つまらない; toru ni tarinai 取るに足りない.

insincere, *adj.* fushōjiki (na) 不正直 (な) (dishonest).

insinuate, *vb.* honomekasu 仄めかす.

insipid, *adj.* tsumaranai つまらない (dull); mumikansō (na) 無味乾燥 (な) (without flavor).

insist, *vb.* iiharu 言い張る; shuchō suru 主張する (declare firmly, be persistent).

insistence, *n.* dangen 断言; shuchō 主張.

insistent, *adj.* shitsukoi しつこい.

insolent, *adj.* ōhei (na) 横柄 (な).

insomnia, *n.* fuminshō 不眠症.

inspect, *vb.* kensa suru 検査する; shiraberu 調べる.

inspection, *n.* kensa 検査; chōsa 調査.

inspector, *n.* 1. kensakan 検査官 (person who inspects). 2. keibu 警部 (police official).

inspiration, *n.* insupirēshon インスピレーション; hirameki 閃き (inspiring influence, good idea).

inspire, *vb.* 1. insupirēshon o ataeru インスピレーションを与える (be a source of a good result). 2. furui-tataseru 奮い立たせる (encourage, arouse). 3. fukikomu 吹き込む(fill with a feeling, etc.).

instability, *n.* fuantei 不安定.

install, *vb.* 1. sonaetsukeru 備え付ける (set up apparatus). 2. shūnin saseru 就任させる (establish in office).

installment, *n.* ikkaibun no shiharai 一回分の支払い (payment); **installment plan** bunkatsubarai 分割払い.

instance, *n.* 1. baai 場合 (occasion). 2. rei 例 (example); **for instance** tatoeba 例えば.

instant, 1. *n.* shunkan 瞬間 (moment). 2. *adj.* shunkan (no) 瞬間 (の) (immediate); insutanto (no) インスタント (の); sokuseki (no) 即席 (の) (short preparation time); **instant coffee** insutanto-kōhī インスタントコーヒー; kinkyū (no) 緊急 (の) (urgent).

instantaneous, *adj.* shunkan-teki (na) 瞬間的 (な).

instead, *adv.* sono kawari ni その代わりに; **instead of** ... no kawari ni ...の代わりに.

instigate, *vb.* keshikakeru けしかける; sendō suru 扇動する (incite to action).

instill, *vb.* sosogikomu 注ぎ込む (infuse).

instinct, *n.* hon'nō 本能.

instinctive, *adj.* hon'nō-teki (na) 本能的 (な).

institute, 1. *n.* kyōkai 協会 (society); senmongakkō 専門学校 (specialized school). 2. *vb.* setsuritsu suru 設立する (establish); hajimeru 始める (start).

institution, *n.* 1. setsuritsu 設立 (establishment). 2. kōkyōdantai 公共団体; kyōkai 協会 (organization with public purpose). 3. seido 制度 (established tradition, etc.). 4. shisetsu 施設 (home, asylum, etc.)

instruct, *vb.* 1. oshieru 教える (teach). 2. meijiru 命じる (order).

instruction, *n.* 1. kyōiku 教育 (teaching). 2. shikata 仕方 (information on method).

instructor, *n.* sensei 先生 (teacher).

instrument, *n.* 1. dōgu 道具 (tool). 2. shudan 手段 (means). 3. **musical instrument** gakki 楽器.

insular, *adj.* 1. shima (no) 島 (の) (of an island). 2. shimagunikonjō (no) 島国根性 (の) (narrow-

minded).

insulation, *n.* bōon 防音 (act of insulating for sound); dan'netsu 断熱 (heat); zetsuen 絶縁 (electricity).

insulator, *n.* zetsuenbutsu 絶縁物 (material of low conductivity).

insulin, *n.* inshurin インシュリン.

insult, 1. *n.* bujoku 侮辱. 2. *vb.* bujoku suru 侮辱する.

insuperable, *adj.* kokufuku dekinai 克服できない.

insurance, *n.* hoken 保険; **insurance policy** hoken-keiyakusho 保険契約書; **life insurance** seimeihoken 生命保険.

insure, *vb.* 1. hoken o kakeru 保険をかける (obtain insurance). 2. hoshō suru 保証する (ensure).

insurgent, *adj.* hanran (no) 反乱 (の) (rebellious).

insurrection, *n.* bōdō 暴動; hanran 反乱.

intact, *adj.* kawaranai 変わらない; moto no mama (no) 元のまま (の) (not altered).

integral, *adj.* kakasenai 欠かせない (necessary).

integrate, *vb.* 1. kumikomu 組み込む (incorporate into whole). 2. tokekomu 溶け込む (become part of a group); tokekomaseru 溶け込ませる (make part of a group).

integrity, *n.* seijitsusa 誠実さ (sincerity).

intellect, *n.* chisei 知性.

intellectual, 1. *n.* interi インテリ. 2. *adj.* chisei-teki (na) 知性的 (な) (of the intellect).

intelligence, *n.* 1. chinō 知能 (capacity for reasoning, etc.). 2. chishiki 知識 (knowledge); jōhō 情報 (information).

intelligent, *adj.* atama ga ii 頭が良

い.

intelligible, *adj.* wakariyasui わかり易い.

intend, *vb.* 1. **intend to do** ... suru tsumori ...するつもり (plan to do). 2. **be intended for** ... no tame (no) ...のため (の) (be designed for).

intense, *adj.* kyōryoku (na) 強力 (な) (strong).

intensify, *vb.* tsuyomeru 強める.

intensity, *n.* hageshisa 激しさ.

intensive, *adj.* 1. hageshii 激しい (strong). 2. shūchū-teki (na) 集中的 (な) (thorough); **intensive care** shūchūchiryō 集中治療.

intent, 1. *n.* mokuteki 目的; ito 意図 (purpose). 2. *adj.* **intent on** ... ni muchū (no) ...に夢中 (の) (firmly concentrated on).

intention, *n.* 1. ishi 意志 (determination). 2. mokuteki 目的 (purpose). 3. imi 意味 (meaning).

intentional, *adj.* ishiki-teki (na) 意識的 (な); koi (no) 故意 (の).

inter, *vb.* maisō suru 埋葬する.

intercede, *vb.* torinasu 取りなす.

interchange, 1. *n.* kōkan 交換 (exchange). 2. *vb.* torikaeru 取り替える; kōkan suru 交換する.

interchangeable, *adj.* gokansei (no) 互換性 (の); kōkan dekiru 交換できる.

intercourse, *n.* 1. kōsai 交際 (dealings between people, etc.) 2. seikō 性交 (sexual intercourse).

interdict, *vb.* kinshi meirei o dasu 禁止命令を出す (prohibit).

interest, 1. *n.* kyōmi 興味; kanshin 関心 (concern, curiosity); kabu 株 (shares); rieki 利益 (profit); rishi 利子 (payment for use of money). 2. *vb.* kyōmi o motaseru 興味を持たせる; **be interested in** ... ni kyōmi ga aru ...に興味がある.

interesting, *adj.* omoshiroi おもしろい.

interface, *n.* intāfeisu インターフェイス (computer).

interfere, *vb.* 1. bōgai suru 妨害する (obstruct). 2. kanshō suru 干渉する (meddle).

interference, *n.* 1. bōgai 妨害 (obstruction). 2. kanshō 干渉 (meddling).

interim, 1. *n.* aida 間; **in the interim** sono aida ni その間に. 2. *adj.* ima no tokoro (no) 今のところ (の).

interior, 1. *n.* naibu 内部; naka 中 (the internal or inner part, inside); interia インテリア; naisō 内装 (interior decoration). 2. *adj.* naibu (no) 内部 (の); naka (no) 中 (の); interia (no) インテリア (の); naisō (no) 内装 (の).

interjection, *n.* sakebi 叫び (exclamation).

interlude, *n.* 1. aima 合間 (intervening time). 2. makuaikyōgen 幕間狂言 (performance).

intermediary, 1. *n.* chūkaisha 仲介者 (intermediate agent). 2. *adj.* chūkan (no) 中間 (の) (being between); chūkai (no) 仲介 (の) (acting as an intermediary).

intermediate, *adj.* chūkan (no) 中間 (の) (being between two points); **intermediate Japanese course** chūkyūnihongo-kōsu 中級日本語コース.

interment, *n.* maisō 埋葬.

intermission, *n.* kyūkei 休憩 (break, interval).

intermittent, *adj.* danzoku-teki (na) 断続的 (な).

intern, 1. *n.* kenshūsei 研修生 (trainee); intān インターン (medical). 2. *vb.* kōsoku suru 拘束する (keep as hostage).

internal, *adj.* 1. naibu (no) 内部 (の) (interior, inner); **internal medicine** naika 内科. 2. kokunai (no) 国内 (の) (domestic).

international, *adj.* intānashonaru (no) インターナショナル (の); kokusai-teki (na) 国際的 (な).

interpret, *vb.* 1. kaishaku suru 解釈する (construe). 2. tsūyaku suru 通訳する (translate).

interpretation, *n.* 1. kaishaku 解釈 (clarification). 2. tsūyaku 通訳 (oral translation).

interpreter, *n.* 1. kaishakusha 解釈者 (person who explains). 2. tsūyaku 通訳 (oral translator).

interrogate, *vb.* shitsumon suru 質問する.

interrogation, *n.* shitsumon 質問.

interrogative, *adj.* shitsumon (no) 質問 (の); gimon (no) 疑問 (の).

interrupt, *vb.* 1. saegiru 遮る; jama suru 邪魔する (break in). 2. chūdan suru 中断する (stop).

interruption, *n.* 1. jama 邪魔 (interference). 2. chūdan 中断 (cessation).

intersect, *vb.* kōsa suru 交差する.

intersection, *n.* kōsaten 交差点.

intersperse, *vb.* baramaku ばらまく.

intertwine, *vb.* karamaseru 絡ませる (entangle); karamaru 絡ませる (be tangled).

interval, *n.* aima 合間 (of time); kankaku 間隔 (of space); **at intervals** tokidoki 時々 (now and then).

intervene, *vb.* 1. aida ni hairu 間に入る (come between); aida ni okoru 間に起こる (happen between). 2. kainyū suru 介入する (mediate).

intervention, *n.* kainyū 介入 (mediation).

interview, 1. *n.* intabyū インタビュー (meeting for questions and answers); mensetsu 面接 (meeting for evaluation); kaiken 会見 (journalism). 2. *vb.* intabyū o suru インタビューをする (meet to ask questions); mensetsu o suru 面接をする (meet to evaluate); kaiken o suru 会見をする (journalism).

intestine, *n.* chō 腸.

intimacy, *n.* 1. shinmitsusei 親密性 (state of being close). 2. shitashimi 親しみ (friendship, familiarity).

intimate, 1. *n.* shin'yū 親友 (intimate friend). 2. *adj.* shitashii 親しい (close); shitashimi afureru 親しみ溢れる (friendly); kojin-teki (na) 個人的 (な) (private). 3. *vb.* honomekasu 仄めかす.

intimidate, *vb.* 1. odosu 脅す (scare). 2. ojike-zukaseru 怖じけづかせる (make timid).

into, *prep.* ... no naka e/ni ...の中へ／に (to the inside of).

intolerable, *adj.* taerarenai 耐えられない.

intolerant, *adj.* 1. ta o mitomenai 他を認めない (not tolerating opposing beliefs). 2. gaman dekinai 我慢できない (unable to tolerate).

intonation, *n.* intonēshon イントネーション; yokuyō 抑揚.

intoxicate, *vb.* yowaseru 酔わせる; **be intoxicated by** ... ni you ...に酔う.

intoxication, *n.* 1. yoi 酔い

(drunkenness). 2. tōsui 陶酔 (excitement).

intractable, *adj.* 1. ganko (na) 頑固 (な) (stubborn). 2. te ni oenai 手に負えない (uncontrollable).

intransitive verb, *n.* jidōshi 自動詞.

intravenous, *adj.* jōmyakuchūsha (no) 静脈注射 (の).

intrepid, *adj.* daitanfuteki (na) 大胆不敵 (な).

intricate, *adj.* fukuzatsu (na) 複雑 (な).

intrigue, 1. *n.* keiryaku 計略 (plot). 2. *vb.* takuramu 企む (plot); kyōmi o sosoru 興味をそそる (interest by puzzling).

intrinsic, *adj.* 1. naizai-teki (na) 内在的 (な) (inherent). 2. honshitsu-teki (na) 本質的 (な) (basic).

introduce, *vb.* 1. shōkai suru 紹介する (present a person to another; bring in something for the first time). 2. tehodoki o suru 手ほどきをする (give a person first experience of). 3. hajimeru 始める (begin, preface).

introduction, *n.* 1. shōkai 紹介 (of a person). 2. dōnyū 導入 (of a new idea or thing). 3. jobun 序文 (of a book).

introductory, *adj.* dōnyū (no) 導入 (の) (preliminary).

introspection, *n.* naisei 内省.

introvert, *n.* 1. uchiki na hito 内気な人 (shy person). 2. naisei-teki na hito 内省的な人 (introspective person).

intrude, *vb.* 1. warikomu 割り込む (thrust in without welcome). 2. jama suru 邪魔する (come in without welcome).

intruder, *n.* shingaisha 侵害者.

intuition, *n.* chokkan 直感.

inundate, *vb.* **be inundated** 1. kōzui ni naru 洪水になる (be flooded). 2. ... de afureru ...で溢れる (be full). 3. ... ni attō sareru ...に圧倒される (be overwhelmed).

invade, *vb.* shinryaku suru 侵略する.

invader, *n.* shinryakusha 侵略者.

invalid, 1. *n.* byōnin 病人 (sick person). 2. *adj.* byōjaku (na) 病弱 (な) (infirm); byōnin (no) 病人 (の) (of invalids); mukō (no) 無効 (の) (void of legal force).

invariable, *adj.* kawaranai 変わらない.

invariably, *adv.* itsumo いつも.

invasion, *n.* shinryaku 侵略.

invective, *n.* tsūretsu na hinan 痛烈な非難.

invent, *vb.* 1. hatsumei suru 発明する (originate). 2. kangaedasu 考え出す (create with imagination). 3. detchiageru でっち上げる (fabricate).

invention, *n.* 1. hatsumei 発明 (act of originating). 2. hatsumeihin 発明品 (something invented).

inventor, *n.* hatsumeisha 発明者 (originator).

inventory, *n.* mokuroku 目録 (list); tanaoroshi 棚卸し (yearly check).

inverse, *adj.* gyaku (no) 逆 (の) (opposite, reversed); sakasama (no) 逆さま (の) (upside down).

invert, *vb.* gyaku ni suru 逆にする (reverse); sakasama ni suru 逆さまにする (turn upside down).

invertebrate, *n.* musekitsui-dōbutsu 無脊椎動物.

invest, *vb.* 1. tōshi suru 投資する (spend money for future return).

2. tsugikomu 注ぎ込む (make effort for future return). 3. kiseru 着せる (clothe).

investigate, *vb.* 1. shiraberu 調べる (examine). 2. torishirabe o suru 取り調べをする (search).

investigation, *n.* 1. chōsa 調査. 2. torishirabe 取り調べ (of crime).

investigator, *n.* chōsakan 調査官 (examiner).

investment, *n.* tōshi 投資 (investing of money or effort).

investor, *n.* tōshika 投資家.

inveterate, *adj.* jōshū-teki (na) 常習的 (な).

invidious, *adj.* 1. ima-imashii 忌ま忌ましい (causing animosity). 2. sabetsu-teki (na) 差別的 (な) (unfairly discriminating).

invigorate, *vb.* genkizukeru 元気付ける; yūkizukeru 勇気付ける.

invincible, *adj.* muteki (no) 無敵 (の).

invisible, *adj.* mienai 見えない.

invitation, *n.* shōtai 招待.

invite, *vb.* 1. shōtai suru 招待する (invite to dinner, etc.). 2. maneku 招く (cause; ask for participation). 3. onegai suru お願いする (ask politely).

invoice, *n.* seikyūsho 請求書.

invoke, *vb.* 1. kongan suru 懇願する (implore). 2. inoru 祈る (call on a deity, muse, etc.). 3. mochiiru 用いる (put into effect).

involve, *vb.* 1. tomonau 伴う (include as necessary). 2. makikomu 巻き込む (cause others to become concerned; implicate). 3. ... ni kan'yo shiteiru ... に関与している (be related to). 4. **be involved in** ... de isogashii ... で忙しい (be busy with).

inward, 1. *adj.* naka (no) 中 (の);

uchi (no) 内 (の). 2. *adv.* naka e/ni 中へ／に.

iodine, *n.* yōso 沃素; yōdo ヨード.

ion, *n.* ion イオン.

I.O.U., *n.* shakuyōsho 借用書.

I.Q., *n.* aikyū アイキュー; chinōshisū 知能指数.

Iran, *n.* iran イラン.

Iraq, *n.* iraku イラク.

irascible, *adj.* okoriyasui 怒り易い.

irate, *adj.* okotte iru 怒っている.

ire, *n.* ikari 怒り.

Ireland, *n.* airurando アイルランド.

iridescent, *adj.* nijiiro (no) 虹色 (の) (rainbow-like glow).

iris, *n.* 1. ayame あやめ (plant). 2. kōsai 虹彩 (eye).

irk, *vb.* komaraseru 困らせる (annoy); iradataseru 荷立たせる (irritate).

iron, 1. *n.* tetsu 鉄 (metallic element); airon アイロン (press). 2. *vb.* airon o kakeru アイロンをかける (press clothes).

ironic, *adj.* aironikku (na) アイロニック (な); hiniku (na) 皮肉 (な).

irony, *n.* aironī アイロニー; hiniku 皮肉.

irrational, *adj.* fugōri (na) 不合理 (な).

irreconcilable, *adj.* oriawanai 折り合わない.

irregular, *adj.* 1. fukisoku (na) 不規則 (な) (not conforming to rule). 2. fuzoroi (no) 不揃い (の) (not symmetrical).

irrelevant, *adj.* kankeinai 関係ない.

irreparable, *adj.* torikaeshi ga tsukanai 取り返しがつかない.

irresistible, *adj.* teikō dekinai 抵抗できない.

irrespective (of), *adj.* ... ni

kankeinaku ... に関係なく.

irresponsible, *adj.* musekinin (na) 無責任 (な).

irrigation, *n.* kangai 灌漑.

irritable, *adj.* okorippoi 怒りっぽい.

irritate, *vb.* iradataseru 苛立たせる.

Islam, *n.* isuramu-kyō イスラム教 (religion).

island, *n.* shima 島.

islander, *n.* shimabito 島人.

isolate, *vb.* 1. koritsu saseru 孤立させる (cause to be separated from others). 2. kakuri suru 隔離する (quarantine).

isolation, *n.* koritsu 孤立.

Israel, *n.* isuraeru イスラエル.

issuance, *n.* hakkō 発行 (act of issuing).

issue, 1. *n.* hakkō 発行 (act of issuing); mondaiten 問題点 (point in question); shison 子孫 (offspring); gō 号 (one of a series of periodicals); kekka 結果 (result); **at issue** giron no mato 議論の的 (being disputed). 2. *vb.* hakkō suru 発行する (publish); haikyū suru 配給する (distribute); dasu 出す (send out, emit); deru 出る (emerge, go); **issue from** ... ni yurai suru ... に由来する (result from).

it, *pron.* (often omitted in Japanese) sore (ga, wa, o, ni) それ (が、は、を、に).

Italian, 1. *n.* itariajin イタリア人 (person); itariago イタリア語 (language). 2. *adj.* itaria (no) イタリア (の) (of Italy); itariajin (no) イタリア人 (の) (of the Italians).

italic, *n.* itarikku-tai イタリック体; shatai 斜体.

italicize, *vb.* itarikku-tai o tsukau イタリック体を使う; shatai ni suru 斜体にする.

Italy, *n.* itaria イタリア.

itch, 1. *n.* kayumi 痒み (skin irritation); yokkyū 欲求 (desire). 2. *vb.* kayui 痒い (feel skin irritation); muzu-muzu suru むずむずする (desire).

itchy, *adj.* muzugayui むず痒い (feeling skin irritation).

item, *n.* 1. kōmoku 項目; mokuroku 目録 (separate article). 2. kiji 記事 (news). 3. mono 物 (thing).

itemize, *vb.* kōmokubetsu ni ageru 項目別に挙げる (list by items).

itinerary, *n.* ryokōnittei 旅行日程.

its, *adj.* sono その; sore no それの.

itself, *pron.* sono mono そのもの.

ivory, *n.* zōge 象牙 (elephant tusk); **ivory tower** zōge no tō 象牙の塔.

ivy, *n.* tsuta 蔦.

J

jab, 1. *n.* tsuki 突き. 2. *vb.* tsuku 突く; tsukisasu 突き刺す.

jabber, 1. *n.* hayakuchi 早口. 2. *vb.* hayakuchi de shaberu 早口でしゃべる.

jack, *n.* 1. jakki ジャッキ (tool). 2.

jakku ジャック (playing card). 3. sashikomi 差し込み (electrical).

jackass, *n.* ton'ma とんま; baka 馬鹿.

jacket, *n.* uwagi 上着; jaketto ジャケット.

jackknife, *n.* jakkunaifu ジャックナイフ.

jade, *n.* hisui ひすい.

jagged, *adj.* giza-giza (no) ぎざぎざ (の).

jail, 1. *n.* rōya 牢屋; kangoku 監獄; keimusho 刑務所. 2. *vb.* rō/keimusho ni ireru 牢／刑務所に入れる.

jailer, *n.* kanshu 看守.

jalopy, *n.* ponkotsu-/onboro-guruma ぽんこつ～／おんぼろ車.

jam, 1. *n.* jamu ジャム (preserve); konzatsu 混雑 (crowded state); **traffic jam** kōtsūjūtai 交通渋滞. 2. *vb.* tsumekomu 詰め込む (squeeze into).

janitor, *n.* kanrinin 管理人.

January, *n.* ichigatsu 一月.

Japan, *n.* nihon/nippon 日本／日本.

Japanese, 1. *n.* nihonjin 日本人 (person); nihongo 日本語 (language). 2. *adj.* nihon (no) 日本 (の) (of Japan); nihonjin (no) 日本人 (の) (of the Japanese).

jar, 1. *n.* jā ジャー; bin 瓶; tsubo 壷 (container); hageshii shindō 激しい震動 (jolt). 2. *vb.* hageshiku shindō saseru 激しく震動させる (jolt).

jargon, *n.* nakamakotoba 仲間言葉 (informal); senmon'yōgo 専門用語 (specialized vocabulary).

jaundice, *n.* ōdan 黄疸.

jaunt, *n.* ryokō 旅行 (trip); ensoku 遠足 (day excursion).

javelin, *n.* nageyari 投げ槍.

jaw, *n.* ago あご.

jealous, *adj.* 1. shittobukai 嫉妬深い (fearful of losing love). 2. netamibukai 妬み深い (resentful and envious); urayamashigaru 羨ましがる (envious).

jealousy, *n.* 1. shitto 嫉妬. 2. netami 妬み.

jeans, *n.* jīpan ジーパン; jīnzu ジーンズ.

jeep, *n.* jīpu ジープ.

jeer, 1. *n.* azakeri 嘲けり; karakai からかい. 2. *vb.* azakeru 嘲ける; karakau からかう.

jelly, *n.* zerī ゼリー.

jellyfish, *n.* kurage くらげ.

jeopardize, *vb.* abunaku suru 危なくする; kiki ni sarasu 危機にさらす.

jeopardy, *n.* kiki 危機; kon'nan 困難.

jerk, 1. *n.* gui to hiku koto ぐいと引くこと (pull); totsuzen no ugoki 突然の動き (sudden movement). 2. *vb.* gui to hiku ぐいと引く; totsuzen ugoku 突然動く.

jest, 1. *n.* jōdan 冗談 (joke). 2. *vb.* jōdan o iu 冗談を言う.

jester, *n.* fuzake/odoke mono ふざけ／おどけ者.

jet, *n.* 1. funsha 噴射 (gas stream). 2. **jet plane** jettoki ジェット.

jet-black, *adj.* makkura (na, no) 真っ暗 (な、の).

jetty, *n.* 1. bōhatei 防波堤 (harbor protection). 2. sanbashi 桟橋 (pier).

Jew, *n.* yudayajin ユダヤ人; isuraerujin イスラエル人.

jewel, *n.* hōseki 宝石.

jeweler, *n.* hōseki-shō/-ten 宝石商／～店.

jewelry, *n.* hōseki 宝石 (precious stones); sōshingu 装身具 (adornments).

Jewish, *adj.* yudayajin (no) ユダヤ人 (の).

jigsaw puzzle, *n.* jigusō-pazuru ジグソーパズル.

jilt, *vb.* koibito o suteru 恋人を捨て

る; **be jilted** furareru 振られる.

jingle, 1. *n.* rin-rin りんりん. 2. *vb.* rin-rin to naru りんりんと鳴る.

jinx, 1. *n.* engi no warui koto 縁起の悪いこと. 2. *vb.* aku'un o motarasu 悪運をもたらす.

job, *n.* shigoto 仕事.

jockey, *n.* kishu 騎手.

jocular, *adj.* kokkei (na) 滑稽 (な); okashii おかしい.

jog, *vb.* 1. chotto tsuku ちょっと突く (nudge); chotto yusuru ちょっと揺する (shake). 2. hashiru 走る; jogingu suru ジョギングする (run).

join, *vb.* 1. musubu 結ぶ (put together). 2. hitotsu ni naru 一つになる (unite). 3. kuwawaru 加わる (become member of).

joint, 1. *n.* setsugō-ten/-bu 接合点／〜部 (connection); kansetsu 関節 (movable joint). 2. *adj.* kyōdō (no) 共同 (の).

joke, 1. *n.* jōdan 冗談; jōku ジョーク. 2. *vb.* jōdan o iu 冗談を言う.

jolly, *adj.* tanoshii 楽しい; yukai (na) 愉快 (な).

jolt, 1. *n.* yure 揺れ (shaking); shokku ショック (shock). 2. *vb.* yuriugokasu 揺り動かす (shake).

jostle, *vb.* 1. oshinokeru 押し退ける (shove). 2. tsukiataru 突き当たる (bump).

jot down, *vb.* kakitomeru 書き留める.

journal, *n.* 1. shinbun 新聞 (newspaper). 2. nisshi 日誌 (daily record). 3. zasshi 雑誌 (periodical).

journalism, *n.* jānarizumu ジャーナリズム.

journalist, *n.* jānarisuto ジャーナリスト; kisha 記者.

journey, 1. *n.* tabi 旅; ryokō 旅行.

2. *vb.* tabi/ryokō suru 旅／旅行する.

jovial, *adj.* yōki (na) 陽気 (な); tanoshii 楽しい.

jowl, *n.* ago あご; hoho 頬.

joy, *n.* kōfuku 幸福; yorokobi 喜び.

joyful, *adj.* shiawase (na) 幸せ (な); tanoshii 楽しい.

jubilant, *adj.* yorokobi ni michita 喜びに満ちた; ōyorokobi (no) 大喜び (の).

jubilee, *n.* 1. kinensai 記念祭 (anniversary). 2. shukuten 祝典 (celebration).

Judaism, *n.* yudaya-kyō ユダヤ教.

judge, 1. *n.* saibankan 裁判官 (law); shinpan 審判 (sports); shinsain 審査員 (competition). 2. *vb.* sabaku 裁く (pass legal judgment); handan suru 判断する (form judgment); shinsa suru 審査する (in competition).

judgment, *n.* 1. hanketsu 判決 (official decision). 2. handan 判断 (opinion). 3. handanryoku 判断力 (judging ability).

judicial, *adj.* shihō/saiban (no) 司法／裁判 (の).

judicious, *adj.* rikō (na) 利口 (な); handanryoku ga aru 判断力がある.

judo, *n.* jūdō 柔道.

jug, *n.* mizusashi 水差し.

juice, *n.* 1. jūsu ジュース (of fruit). 2. shiru 汁 (liquid).

juicy, *adj.* shiruke ga ōi 汁気が多い.

jujitsu, *n.* jūjutsu 柔術.

July, *n.* shichigatsu 七月.

jumble, 1. *n.* gotamaze ごた混ぜ (mixture); konran 混乱 (confusion). 2. *vb.* gotamaze ni suru ごた混ぜにする (mix); hikkurikaesu ひっくり返す

(topple).

jump, 1. *n.* janpu ジャンプ. 2. *vb.* tobu 飛ぶ.

jumpy, *adj.* ochitsukanai 落ち着かない (nervous).

junction, *n.* 1. setsuzokuten 接続点 (connection). 2. kōsaten 交差点 (crossroads).

juncture, *n.* 1. jiten 時点 (point of time). 2. kiki 危機 (crisis).

June, *n.* rokugatsu 六月.

jungle, *n.* janguru ジャングル; mitsurin 密林.

junior, 1. *n.* san'nensei 三年生 (college student); toshishita 年下 (younger person). 2. *adj.* toshishita (no) 年下 (の).

junk, *n.* garakuta がらくた (rubbish); jankusen ジャンク船 (ship).

jurisdiction, *n.* 1. shihōken 司法権 (legal authority). 2. kanrikuiki 管理区域 (area).

jurisprudence, *n.* hōgaku 法学 (science of law).

jurist, *n.* hōgakusha 法学者.

juror, *n.* 1. baishin'in 陪審員 (in court). 2. shinsain 審査員 (in competition).

jury, *n.* 1. baishin'in(dan) 陪審員(団) (in court). 2. shinsain(dan) 審査員(団) (in competition).

just, 1. *adj.* kōsei (na) 公正 (な) (fair); tadashii 正しい (right); datō (na) 妥当 (な) (proper); seikaku (na) 正確 (な) (exact). 2. *adv.* chōdo 丁度 (exactly); tatta たった (only); **just now** tatta ima たった今.

justice, *n.* 1. seigi 正義; kōsei 公正 (fairness). 2. saiban 裁判 (administration of law). 3. saibankan 裁判官 (judge).

justification, *n.* seitōsei 正当性; benmei 弁明.

justify, *vb.* seitōka suru 正当化する; benmei suru 弁明する.

jut out, *vb.* tsukideru 突き出る.

juvenile, *adj.* seishōnen (no) 青少年 (の) (youth); jidō (no) 児童 (の) (child); shōnen (no) 少年 (の) (boy); shōjo (no) 少女 (の) (girl).

juxtapose, *vb.* heichi suru 併置する.

K

kangaroo, *n.* kangarū カンガルー.

karate, *n.* karate 空手.

keel over, *vb.* tenpuku suru 転覆する (boat); kizetsu suru 気絶する (faint).

keen, *adj.* 1. surudoi 鋭い (sharp). 2. kibishii 厳しい (biting). 3. eibin (na) 鋭敏 (な) (sensitive). 4. hageshii 激しい (fierce). 5. nesshin (na) 熱心 (な) (eager).

keep, *vb.* 1. tsuzukeru 続ける (continue to do). 2. tamotsu 保つ (maintain). 3. motsu 持つ (have). 4. yashinau 養う (support). 5. mamoru 守る (observe, guard). 6. **keep on** tsuzukeru 続ける; **keep up with** ... ni tsuite iku ...について行く.

keepsake, *n.* kinenhin 記念品; katami 形見.

keg, *n.* chiisai taru 小さい樽.

kennel, *n.* inugoya 犬小屋.

kept woman, *n.* (o)mekake(san) (お)妾(さん).

kerchief, *n.* nekkachīfu ネッカチーフ (for head, neck); hankachi ハンカチ (handkerchief).

kernel, *n.* tsubu 粒 (grain); kaku 核 (center).

kerosene, *n.* tōyu 灯油.

ketchup, *n.* kechappu ケチャップ.

kettle, *n.* yakan やかん.

key, 1. *n.* kī キー; kagi 鍵 (for a lock, clue); chō 調 (principal music key); ken 鍵 (piano). 2. *adj.* jūyō (na) 重要 (な) (important).

keyboard, *n.* kenban 鍵盤; kībōdo キーボード.

key ring, *n.* kī-ringu キーリング.

kick, *vb.* keru 蹴る.

kid, 1. *n.* koyagi 子山羊 (young goat); kodomo 子供 (child). 2. *vb.* karakau からかう (fool); jōdan o iu 冗談を言う (jest).

kidnap, *vb.* yūkai suru 誘拐する.

kidnapper, *n.* yūkaihan'nin 誘拐犯人.

kidnapping, *n.* yūkai 誘拐.

kidney, *n.* jinzō 腎臓.

kill, *vb.* 1. korosu 殺す (end life, murder). 2. hakai suru 破壊する (destroy). 3. **kill time** jikan o tsubusu 時間をつぶす.

killer, *n.* satsujinhan'nin 殺人犯人.

killing, *n.* koroshi 殺し (act of killing); satsujin 殺人 (killing a person).

kill-joy, *n.* kyōzame 興醒め.

kiln, *n.* kama 釜; ro 炉.

kilo, *n.* kiro キロ.

kilogram, *n.* kiroguramu キログラム.

kilohertz, *n.* kiroherutsu キロヘルツ.

kilometer, *n.* kiromētoru キロメートル.

kilowatt, *n.* kirowatto キロワット.

kin, *n.* shinseki 親戚; ketsuen(sha) 血縁(者) (relatives).

kind, 1. *adj.* shinsetsu (na) 親切 (な) (gentle, kind-hearted); ii 良い (good); yasashii 優しい (tender). 2. *n.* shurui 種類 (type); tokushitsu 特質 (nature); **a kind of** isshu (no) 一種 (の); **kind of** chotto ちょっと; yaya やや.

kindergarten, *n.* yōchien 幼稚園.

kindle, *vb.* 1. hi o tsukeru 火を点ける (set afire). 2. kakitateru 掻き立てる (rouse feelings).

kindly, *adv.* shinsetsu ni 親切に; yasashiku 優しく.

kindness, *n.* omoiyari 思い遣り; shinsetsu 親切.

kindred, 1. *adj.* tsunagari ga aru つながりがある (related); dōrui (no) 同類 (の) (similar). 2. *n.* shinseki 親戚; ketsuen(sha) 血縁(者) (relatives).

kinfolk, *n.* kazoku 家族.

king, *n.* ō(sama) 王(様); kokuō 国王.

kingdom, *n.* ōkoku 王国.

king-size, *adj.* kingu-saizu (no) キングサイズ (の); tokudai (no) 特大 (の).

kink, *n.* nejire ねじれ (twist).

kinky, *adj.* nejireta ねじれた (twisted); hentai (no) 変態 (の) (sexually perverted).

kinship, *n.* 1. shinzokukankei 親族関係; tsunagari つながり (family relationship). 2. ruijisei 類似性 (affinity).

kiosk, *n.* baiten 売店; kiosuku キオスク.

kiss, 1. *n.* kisu キス; kuchizuke 口づけ. 2. *vb.* kisu suru キスする; kuchizukeru 口づける.

kit, *n.* 1. dōguisshiki 道具一式 (set of tools). 2. zairyōisshiki 材料一式 (set of materials).

kitchen, *n.* daidokoro 台所; kitchin キッチン.

kite, *n.* tako 凧.

kitten, *n.* koneko 子猫.

Kleenex, *n.* tisshu ティッシュ.

knack, *n.* kotsu こつ; gijutsu 技術.

knapsack, *n.* nappusakku ナップ サック; ryukkusakku リュック サック.

knead, *vb.* neru 練る; koneru こね る.

knee, *n.* hiza 膝.

kneecap, *n.* hizagashira 膝頭.

kneel, *vb.* hizamazuku 膝跪く.

knickknack, *n.* komamono 小間 物.

knife, *n.* naifu ナイフ; hōchō 包丁 (for cutting); kogatana 小刀 (dagger).

knight, *n.* kishi 騎士.

knit, *vb.* amu 編む.

knitting, *n.* amimono 編み物.

knob, *n.* totte 取っ手 (handle).

knock, 1. *n.* nokku ノック. 2. *vb.* nokku suru ノックする; tataku 叩 く; utsu 打つ.

knot, 1. *n.* musubime 結び目. 2. *vb.* musubu 結ぶ (tie); motsureru もつれる (become entangled).

know, *vb.* 1. shiru 知る (get knowledge); shitteiru 知っている (have knowledge, be acquainted). 2. wakaru わかる (understand).

know-how, *n.* yarikata やり方; gijutsu 技術.

know-it-all, *n.* shittakaburi 知った かぶり.

knowledge, *n.* chishiki 知識.

knuckle, *n.* yubikansetsu 指関節.

knuckle down, *vb.* sei o dasu 精を 出す.

knuckle under, *vb.* kōsan suru 降 参する; makeru 負ける.

Korea, *n.* kitachōsen 北朝鮮 (North Korea); kankoku 韓国 (South Korea).

Korean, 1. *n.* kitachōsenjin 北朝鮮 人 (North Korean person); kankokujin 韓国人 (South Korean person); kankokugo 韓国語 (language). 2. *adj.* kitachōsen (no) 北朝鮮 (の) (of North Korea); kankoku (no) 韓国 (の) (of South Korea); kitachōsenjin (no) 北朝鮮 人 (の) (of the North Koreans); kankokujin (no) 韓国人 (の) (of the South Koreans).

L

label, 1. *n.* raberu ラベル. 2. *vb.* raberu o haru ラベルを貼る.

labor, 1. *n.* shigoto 仕事; rōdō 労働 (work); osan お産 (childbirth). 2. *vb.* hataraku 働く.

laboratory, *n.* kenkyūjo 研究所 (place for scientific work); jikkenshitsu 実験室 (room for experiments).

laborer, *n.* rōdōsha 労働者.

laborious, *adj.* tema ga kakaru 手

間がかかる.

labor union, *n.* rōdōkumiai 労働組 合.

labyrinth, *n.* meikyū 迷宮; meiro 迷路.

lace, *n.* 1. rēsu レース (fabric). 2. kutsuhimo 靴紐 (shoelace).

lacerate, *vb.* hikisaku 引き裂く (tear).

laceration, *n.* 1. hikisaki 引き裂き (act of tearing). 2. sakikizu 裂き傷

(wound).

lack, 1. *n.* fusoku 不足; ketsubō 欠乏. 2. *vb.* kaku 欠く; (... ga) nai (...が) 無い.

lackadaisical, *adj.* mukiryoku (na) 無気力 (な) (listless).

lackey, *n.* gomasuri ごますり; tsuishōsha 追従者.

lackluster, *adj.* 1. don'yori shita どんよりした (lacking brilliance). 2. kakki ga nai 活気がない (lacking vitality).

lacquer, *n.* 1. wanisu ワニス; rakkā ラッカー (varnish). 2. urushi 漆 (Japanese lacquer); shikki 漆器 (Japanese lacquerware).

lad, *n.* shōnen 少年; wakamono 若者.

ladder, *n.* hashigo 梯子.

laden, *adj.* mansai shita 満載した.

ladle, *n.* hishaku 柄杓 (for dipping water); shakushi 杓子 (soup).

lady, *n.* 1. redī レディー; shukujo 淑女 (woman of refinement). 2. fujin 婦人 (woman).

ladybug, *n.* tentōmushi 天道虫.

lag, 1. *n.* okure 遅れ. 2. *vb.* okureru 遅れる (delay, fail to maintain speed).

lair, *n.* su 巣.

lake, *n.* mizuumi 湖; -ko -湖; **Lake Biwa** biwako 琵琶湖.

lamb, *n.* 1. kohitsuji 小羊 (young sheep). 2. ramuniku ラム肉 (meat).

lame, *adj.* 1. bikko (no) びっこ (の) (crippled). 2. heta (na) 下手 (な) (inadequate).

lament, 1. *n.* nageki 嘆き. 2. *vb.* nageki-kanashimu 嘆き悲しむ.

lamp, *n.* ranpu ランプ; akari 明り.

lampoon, 1. *n.* fūshi 諷刺. 2. *vb.* fūshi suru 諷刺する.

lance, *n.* yari 槍.

land, 1. *n.* riku 陸 (dry part of earth's surface); tochi 土地 (a portion of land); kuni 国 (country); tsuchi 土 (soil); **native land** sokoku 祖国. 2. *vb.* chakuriku suru 着陸する (plane); jōriku suru 上陸する (ship).

landing, *n.* 1. chakuriku 着陸 (plane); jōriku 上陸 (ship). 2. odoriba 踊り場 (stairs).

landing gear, *n.* chakurikusōchi 着陸装置.

landlady, *n.* 1. yanushi 家主 (house, apartment, etc.). 2. okami(san) おかみ(さん) (inn, etc.).

landlord, *n.* 1. yanushi 家主 (house, apartment, etc.). 2. teishu 亭主 (inn, etc.).

landmark, *n.* 1. mejirushi 目印 (prominent object serving as guide). 2. kakki-teki na koto 画期的なこと (landmark event).

landowner, *n.* jinushi 地主.

landscape, *n,* 1. keshiki 景色 (scenery). 2. fūkeiga 風景画 (picture).

landslide, *n.* 1. jisuberi 地滑り (fall of earth or rock). 2. asshō 圧勝 (victory).

lane, *n.* 1. komichi 小道; yokochō 横丁 (narrow road). 2. shasen 車線 (car lane).

language, *n.* kotoba 言葉; -go -語; **Japanese language** nihongo 日本語; **national language** kokugo 国語.

languid, *adj.* 1. darui だるい (drooping from fatigue). 2. genki ga nai 元気がない (without vigor).

languish, *vb.* 1. otoroeru 衰える (become feeble). 2. kogareru 焦がれる (pine with desire). 3. kurushimu 苦しむ (suffer).

languor, *n.* 1. darusa だるさ (sluggishness). 2. mukiryoku 無気力 (lack of interest).

lanky, *adj.* hyoronagai ひょろ長い.

lantern, *n.* chōchin 提灯.

lap, 1. *n.* hiza 膝 (body); kasanari 重なり (overlapping part); isshū 一周 (racecourse). 2. *vb.* tsutsumu 包む (wrap); uchiyoseru 打ち寄せる (wash against); nameru なめる (lick).

lapel, *n.* raperu ラペル; eri 襟.

lapse, 1. *n.* chiisana machigai 小さな間違い (small error); kashitsu 過失 (failure); keika 経過 (slow passing). 2. *vb.* ochiiru 陥る (fall); keika suru 経過する (pass).

laptop, *n.* rapputoppu ラップトップ.

larceny, *n.* settōzai 窃盗罪.

lard, *n.* rādo ラード.

large, *adj.* ōkii 大きい (great in number or size); hiroi 広い (spacious).

largely, *adv.* omo ni 主に; shutoshite 主として (in great part).

largeness, *n.* ōkisa 大きさ; hirosa 広さ.

large-scale, *adj.* daikibo (na, no) 大規模 (な、の).

lark, *n.* hibari ひばり (bird).

larva, *n.* yōchū 幼虫.

larynx, *n.* kōtō 喉頭.

lascivious, *adj.* kōshoku (na) 好色 (な); midara (na) 淫ら (な).

laser, *n.* rēzā レーザー.

lash, 1. *n.* muchihimo 鞭紐 (part of whip); muchiuchi 鞭打ち (whipping); matsuge まつげ (eyelash). 2. *vb.* muchiutsu むち打つ (whip); shibaru 縛る (bind); **lash out** kōgeki suru 攻撃する (attack).

lass, *n.* otome 乙女; shōjo 少女.

last, 1. *n.* saigo 最後; **at last** tsui ni 遂に. 2. *adj.* saigo no 最後の (final); saikin no 最近の (most recent); mae no 前の (latest); sen- 先-; saku- 昨-; **last month** sengetsu 先月; **last week** senshū 先週; **last year** sakunen 昨年. 3. *adv.* saikin 最近 (most recently); saigo ni 最後に (in the end). 4. *vb.* tsuzuku 続く (continue); motsu 持つ (remain useful).

lasting, *adj.* 1. nagaku tsuzuku 長く続く (continuing). 2. nagamochi suru 長持ちする (durable).

last name, *n.* myōji 名字; sei 姓.

latch, *n.* kakegane 掛け金; kan'nuki 閂.

late, 1. *adj.* osoi 遅い; okureteiru 遅れている (after the usual time); (... no) owarigoro (no) (...の) 終わり頃 (の) (at the end of a day, season, etc.); **late April** shigatsu no owarigoro 四月の終わり頃; saikin no 最近の (recent); ko 故 (deceased). 2. *adv.* osoku 遅く; okurete 遅れて (occurring after the proper time); osoku made 遅くまで (until a late hour).

lately, *adv.* saikin 最近; konogoro この頃.

latent, *adj.* senzai-teki (na) 潜在的 (な).

later, *adj.* 1. ato no hō (no) 後の方 (の). 2. *adv.* ato de 後で; **See you later.** Ato de aimashō. 後で会いましょう.

lateral, *adj.* yoko no 横の (of the side); yoko kara no 横からの (from the side).

lathe, *n.* senban 旋盤.

lather, *n.* sekken no awa 石けんの泡 (detergent foam).

Latin, 1. *n.* ratengo ラテン語
(language). 2. *adj.* ratengo (no) ラ
テン語 (の) (of the language).

Latin America, *n.* minami-
amerika 南アメリカ; nanbei 南米.

latitude, *n.* ido 緯度.

latrine, *n.* kyōdō-toire 共同トイレ.

latter, *adj.* kōsha (no) 後者 (の)
(second); **the latter** kōsha 後者.

lattice, *n.* kōshi 格子.

laud, *vb.* homeru ほめる; tataeru
称える、賛える.

laudable, *adj.* rippa (na) 立派 (な).

laugh, 1. *n.* warai 笑い. 2. *vb.*
warau 笑う; **laugh at** azakeri-
warau 嘲り笑う; baka ni suru 馬
鹿にする.

laughable, *adj.* 1. okashii おかしい
(funny). 2. bakarashii 馬鹿らしい
(ridiculous).

laughingstock, *n.* monowarai no
tane 物笑いの種.

laughter, *n.* warai 笑い.

launch, 1. *n.* shinsui 進水 (floating
a boat). 2. *vb.* hajimeru 始める
(start); shinsui saseru 進水させる
(float); hassha saseru 発車させる
(send forth a spacecraft).

launder, *vb.* sentaku suru 洗濯する
(wash).

laundromat, *n.* koin-randorī コイ
ンランドリー.

laundry, *n.* 1. sentakumono 洗濯
物 (clothes, etc.). 2. sentakuba
洗濯場 (place for doing the family
wash). 3. sentakuya 洗濯屋
(commercial establishment).

laureate, *n.* 1. jushōsha 受賞者;
Nobel laureate nōberu-shō
jushōsha ノーベル賞受賞者. 2.
poet laureate keikanshijin 桂冠
詩人.

laurel, *n.* gekkeiju 月桂樹 (tree);
gekkeikan 月桂冠 (wreath).

lava, *n.* yōgan 溶岩.

lavatory, *n.* keshōshitsu 化粧室;
otearai お手洗; toire(tto) トイレ
(ット).

lavender, *n.* rabendā ラベンダー.

lavish, 1. *adj.* takusan (no) たくさ
ん (の) (abundant); kimae ga ii 気
前が良い (giving). 2. *vb.*
kimaeyoku ataeru (tsukau) 気前良
く与える (使う) (give or spend
lavishly).

law, *n.* 1. hō 法 (rule); hōritsu 法律
(legal rules). 2. hō(ritsu)gaku 法
(律)学 (study). 3. soshō 訴訟
(legal action). 4. hōsoku 法則
(principle).

lawful, *adj.* 1. gōhō (na) 合法 (な)
(allowed by law). 2. hōritsujō
(no) 法律上 (の); hōtei (no) 法定
(の) (sanctioned by law).

lawless, *adj.* 1. fuhō (na) 不法 (な)
(contrary to the law). 2. muhō
(na) 無法 (な) (unruly).

lawn, *n.* shibafu 芝生; **lawn
mower** shibakariki 芝刈り機.

lawsuit, *n.* soshō 訴訟.

lawyer, *n.* bengoshi 弁護士.

lax, *adj.* 1. taiman (na) 怠慢 (な)
(careless). 2. yurui 緩い (not
strict, slack).

laxative, *n.* gezai 下剤.

lay, 1. *adj.* zokujin (no) 俗人 (の)
(of the laity); shiroto (no) 素人
(の) (not professional). 2. *vb.* oku
置く (put down, place); taosu 倒す
(knock down); tateru 立てる
(devise, as a plan); (tamago o)
umu (卵を) 産む (produce eggs);
lay aside totteoku とっておく
(save for future use); **lay off**
ichijikaiko suru 一時解雇する; **lay
out** hirogeru 広げる (spread out);
haichi suru 配置する (arrange
well).

layer, *n.* sō 層 (one thickness). 2. nuri 塗り (of paint, lacquer, etc.).

layman, *n.* 1. zokujin 俗人 (member of the laity). 2. shiroto 素人 (non-professional).

layout, *n.* reiauto レイアウト; haichi 配置 (arrangement). 2. sekkei 設計; keikaku 計画 (plan).

lazy, *adj.* 1. taiman (na) 怠慢 (な); namakemono (no) 怠け者 (の) (disliking effort). 2. noroi のろい (slow moving).

lead, *n.* namari 鉛 (metal).

lead, 1. *n.* rīdo リード; sentō 先頭 (foremost place); sendō 先導 (act of leading); tegakari 手掛かり (clue); rīdāshippu リーダーシップ (leadership); shuensha 主演者 (principal performer). 2. *vb.* rīdo suru リードする; sentō o iku 先頭を行く (be ahead); michibiku 導く (guide); ... yō ni naru ...ようになる (induce); **lead to** ... ni itaru ...に至る (result in).

leaden, *adj.* 1. namari (no) 鉛 (の) (of lead). 2. namari'iro (no) 鉛色 (の) (of a leaden color). 3. omoi 重い (heavy); omogurushii 重苦しい (gloomy).

leader, *n.* rīdā リーダー; shidōsha 指導者 (person who guides). 2. sentō 先頭 (person who is ahead of others).

leadership, *n.* rīdāshippu リーダーシップ; shidōryoku 指導力.

leaf, *n.* 1. ha 葉 (plant). 2. pēji ページ (book).

leaflet, *n.* chirashi 散らし.

league, *n.* 1. rīgu リーグ; renmei 連盟. 2. rīgu リーグ (measure).

leak, 1. *n.* ana 穴 (hole); more 漏れ (leaking gas, etc.). 2. *vb.* moreru 漏れる (pass through leak); morasu 漏らす (make known, let pass through leak).

lean, 1. *adj.* yaseteiru やせている (not fat); shibō ga sukunai 脂肪が少ない (meat). 2. *vb.* katamuku 傾く (incline); katamukeru 傾ける (cause to lean); (... ni) motareru (...に) もたれる (rest against); **lean on** tayoru 頼る (rely on).

leap, 1. *n.* chōyaku 跳躍 (jump); yakushin 躍進 (advancement); jōshō 上昇 (increase). 2. *vb.* tobiagaru 飛び上がる (spring through the air); tobu 飛ぶ (jump); **leap at** ... ni tobitsuku ...に飛びつく.

leap year, *n.* uruudoshi うるう年.

learn, *vb.* 1. narau 習う; manabu 学ぶ (learn skill). 2. oboeru 覚える (memorize). 3. shiru 知る (be informed).

learned, *adj.* gakushiki yutaka (na) 学識豊か (な).

learning, *n.* gakumon 学問.

lease, 1. *n.* rīsu リース; shakuyō-shōsho 借用証書 (lease contract). 2. *vb.* kasu 貸す (grant lease); kariru 借りる (hold by lease).

leash, *n.* himo 紐 (cord).

least, 1. *n.* **at least** sukunakutomo 少くとも. 2. *adj.* ichiban chiisai 一番小さい (smallest in size); ichiban sukunai 一番少ない (smallest in amount).

leather, *n.* kawa 皮; rezā レザー.

leave, 1. *n.* kyoka 許可 (permission); wakare 別れ (farewell); kyūka 休暇 (furlough). 2. *vb.* saru 去る (depart); deru 出る (go out); itomagoi o suru 暇乞いをする (say good-bye); yameru 止める (stop); nokosu 残す (leave behind, bequeath); (... no mama ni) shiteoku (...のままに) しておく (leave unchanged); wasureru

忘れる (forget); **leave for** ... e
tabidatsu ...へ旅立つ; **leave off**
yameru 止める; **leave out**
habuku 省く.

leaven, *n.* kōbo 酵母 (leavening
substance).

lecherous, *adj.* midara (na) 淫ら
(な); kōshoku (na) 好色 (な).

lechery, *n.* kōshoku 好色.

lecture, 1. *n.* kōgi 講義 (discourse);
sekkyō 説教 (reprimand). 2. *vb.*
kōgi o suru 講義をする; sekkyō
suru 説教する.

lecturer, *n.* kōshi 講師 (academic
rank). 2. kōensha 講演者
(speaker).

ledger, *n.* daichō 台帳.

leech, *n.* hiru 蛭.

leek, *n.* nira にら.

leer, *n.* 1. irome 色目 (lascivious
look). 2. inken na metsuki 陰険な
目付き (sly look).

leery, *adj.* keikai shiteiru 警戒して
いる.

leeway, *n.* yochi 余地.

left, 1. *n.* hidari 左 (direction);
sayoku 左翼 (political). 2. *adj.*
hidari (no) 左 (の). 3. *adv.* hidari
ni/e 左に／へ.

left-handed, *adj.* hidarikiki (no)
左利き (の).

leftist, *n., adj.* sayoku (no) 左翼
(の).

leftovers, *n.* nokorimono 残り物.

leg, *n.* ashi 足.

legacy, *n.* isan 遺産.

legal, *adj.* 1. gōhō (na) 合法 (な)
(lawful). 2. hōritsu (no) 法律 (の)
(of law).

legalize, *vb.* gōhōka suru 合法化す
る.

legation, *n.* 1. kōshi 公使
(minister); kōshikan'in 公使館員
(staff). 2. kōshikan 公使館

(headquarters).

legend, *n.* densetsu 伝説 (story).

legendary, *adj.* densetsu-teki (na)
伝説的 (な).

legible, *adj.* wakariyasui 分かり易
い (easy to understand);
yomiyasui 読み易い (easy to
read).

legion, *n.* 1. butai 部隊 (military
unit). 2. tasū 多数 (multitude).

legislate, *vb.* hō o sadameru 法を
定める (make laws).

legislation, *n.* hōteika 法定化;
rippō 立法.

legislative, *adj.* rippō (no) 立法
(の).

legislator, *n.* rippōsha 立法者.

legislature, *n.* rippōkikan 立法機関
(law-making body).

legitimacy, *n.* gōhō 合法; seitō 正
当 (lawful).

legitimate, *adj.* 1. gōhō (na) 合法
(な); seitō (na) 正当 (な) (lawful).
2. mottomo (na) 最も (な) (valid,
logical). 3. chakushutsu (no)
嫡出 (の) (born to a married
couple).

legitimize, *vb.* gōhōka suru 合法化
する (make lawful).

legume, *n.* mame 豆 (peas or
beans).

leisure, *n.* hima 暇; rejā レジャー;
at one's leisure hima na toki ni
暇な時に.

leisurely, *adj.* yukkuri shita ゆっく
りした.

lemon, *n.* remon レモン.

lemonade, *n.* remonēdo レモネー
ド.

lend, *vb.* kasu 貸す.

length, *n.* nagasa 長さ (size or
extent from end to end); **at
length** sukkari すっかり (fully);
tsui ni 遂に (at last).

lengthen, *vb.* nagaku suru 長くする (make longer); nagaku naru 長くなる (become longer).

lengthwise, *adv.* tate ni 縦に.

lengthy, *adj.* naga-nagashii 長々しい.

lenient, *adj.* kan'yō (na) 寛容 (な); amai 甘い.

lens, *n.* renzu レンズ.

leopard, *n.* hyō ひょう.

leprosy, *n.* hansenshi-byō ハンセン氏病.

lesbian, *n.* rezu(bian) レズ(ビアン); dōseiaisha 同性愛者.

less, 1. *adj.* ... yori sukunai ...より少ない (less in amount); ... yori chiisai ...より小さい (smaller); **less expensive than this** kore yori yasui. 2. *adv.* ... yori sukunaku ...より少なく; ... yori chiisaku ...より小さく; **less and less** dan-dan sukunaku だんだん少なく.

lessee, *n.* karinushi 借主.

lessen, *vb.* sukunaku naru 少なくなる (become less); herasu 減らす (make less).

lesser, *adj.* hikaku-teki chiisai/sukunai 比較的小さい／少ない.

lesson, *n.* 1. ressun レッスン; kurasu クラス; jugyō 授業 (session). 2. ka 課 (unit of a book). 3. benkyō 勉強 (something to be learned, useful experience). 4. imashime 戒め (reproof).

lessor, *n.* kashinushi 貸主.

lest, *conj.* ... (shi)nai tame/yō ni ...(し)ないため／ように.

let, *vb.* 1. yurusu 許す (permit). 2. tōsu 通す (allow to pass). 3. saseru させる (make). 4. kasu 貸す (rent out). 5. **let down**

gakkari saseru がっかりさせる (disappoint); **let on** morasu 漏らす (tell a secret); **let up** owaru 終わる (cease); **let's** ... -mashō ...-ましょう; **let us do** ... sasete kudasai ...させてください (allow us to).

letdown, *n.* kiochi 気落ち; gakkari suru koto がっかりすること (disappointment).

lethal, *adj.* chimei-teki (na) 致命的 (な).

lethargic, *adj.* mukiryoku (na) 無気力 (な) (apathetic).

lethargy, *n.* mukiryoku 無気力 (apathy).

letter, *n.* 1. tegami 手紙 (written communication). 2. moji 文字 (alphabet).

lettuce, *n.* retasu レタス.

leukemia, *n.* hakketsubyō 白血病.

level, 1. *n.* reberu レベル (standard, amount); takasa 高さ (height); heimen 平面 (flat surface). 2. *adj.* taira (na) 平ら (な) (even and flat); suihei (na) 水平 (な) (horizontal); ichiyō (no) 一様 (の) (uniform).

lever, *n.* rebā レバー; teko 挺子.

levity, *n.* fuzake ふざけ; fumajime 不真面目.

levy, 1. *n.* zeikin 税金 (tax); chōhei 徴兵 (conscription); chōshū 徴収 (collection). 2. *vb.* kazei suru 課税する (tax); chōhei suru 徴兵する (conscript); sensō o hajimeru 戦争を始める (start war).

lewd, *adj.* midara (na) 淫ら (な); hiwai (na) 卑猥 (な).

lexicon, *n.* jiten 辞典 (dictionary).

liability, *n.* 1. **liabilities** shakkin 借金; fusai 負債 (debt). 2. furi 不利 (disadvantage). 3. sekinin 責任 (state of being liable).

liable, *adj.* 1. sekinin ga aru 責任がある (responsible); harau beki 払うべき (responsible for payment). 2. ... shigachi (na) ...しがち (な) (likely to do).

liaison, *n.* 1. renkei 連携 (contact to ensure cooperation). 2. furin 不倫 (illicit sexual relationship).

liar, *n.* usotsuki 嘘吐き.

libel, 1. *n.* chūshō 中傷. 2. *vb.* chūshō suru 中傷する.

liberal, *adj.* 1. riberaru (na) リベラル (な); jiyūshugi (no) 自由主義 (の) (political). 2. kan'yō (na) 寛容 (な); kandai (na) 寛大 (な) (tolerant). 3. kimae ga ii 気前がいい (generous).

liberalize, *vb.* jiyūka suru 自由化する.

liberate, *vb.* kaihō suru 解放する.

liberation, *n.* kaihō 解放.

liberator, *n.* kaihōsha 解放者.

libertine, *n.* asobinin 遊び人; hōtōmono 放蕩者 (unrestrained person).

liberty, *n.* jiyū 自由.

libido, *n.* 1. ribidō リビドー. 2. seihon'nō 性本能 (sexual instinct).

librarian, *n.* shisho 司書 (professional librarian); toshokan'in 図書館員 (library worker).

library, *n.* 1. toshokan 図書館 (communal library); dokushobeya 読書部屋 (home library). 2. zōsho 蔵書 (collection).

license, *n.* 1. kyoka 許可 (permission). 2. raisensu ライセンス; menkyo 免許 (certificate); **driver's license** unten menkyo 運転免許.

licentious, *adj.* kōshoku (na) 好色 (な); hōshō (na) 放縦 (な).

lick, *vb.* 1. nameru なめる (pass the tongue over). 2. katsu 勝つ (overcome, defeat).

lid, *n.* 1. futa 蓋 (cover). 2. mabuta まぶた (eyelid).

lie, 1. *n.* uso 嘘 (false statement). 2. *vb.* uso o tsuku 嘘を吐く (tell a lie); yokotawaru 横たわる (be in a flat position); (... ni) aru (... に) ある (be placed).

lieu, *n.* **in lieu of** ... no kawari ni ...の代わりに.

lieutenant, *n.* chūi 中尉.

life, *n.* 1. inochi 命 (animation). 2. jinsei 人生; shōgai 生涯 (period of one's being alive); jumyō 寿命 (lifespan). 3. seikatsu 生活 (mode of existence). 4. seibutsu 生物 (living things).

lifeboat, *n.* kyūmei-bōto 救命ボート.

life expectancy, *n.* heikinjumyō 平均寿命.

lifeguard, *n.* raifugādo ライフガード; kyūmei'in 救命員.

life insurance, *n.* seimeihoken 生命保険.

lifeless, *adj.* 1. inochi ga nai 命が無い (inanimate). 2. seibutsu ga inai 生物がいない (destitute of living things). 3. shindeiru 死んでいる (dead).

lifelong, *adj.* isshō no 一生の.

life preserver, *n.* kyūmeigu 救命具.

lifestyle, *n.* raifusutairu ライフスタイル; ikikata 生き方.

lift, 1. *n.* rifuto リフト (apparatus for lifting); ageru koto 上げること (act of lifting); **give a lift** nosete iku 乗せて行く. 2. *vb.* ageru 上げる (raise, bring upward); haishi suru 廃止する (end).

ligament, *n.* jintai 靭帯 (band of tissue).

light, 1. *n.* raito ライト; akari 明り (illumination); hikari 光 (natural light); **bring to light** shiraseru 知らせる; **come to light** shirareru yō ni naru 知られるようになる. 2. *adj.* akarui 明るい (bright); karui 軽い (not heavy, not serious, easy); usui 薄い (color). 3. *vb.* akari o tsukeru 明りを点ける (illuminate); hi o tsukeru 火を点ける (ignite).

light bulb, *n.* denkyū 電球.

lighten, *vb.* 1. akaruku suru 明るくする (make brighter); akaruku naru 明るくなる (become brighter). 2. karuku suru 軽くする (make less heavy); karuku naru 軽くなる (become less heavy).

lighter, *n.* raitā ライター.

lightheaded, *adj.* 1. furatsuite-iru ふらついている (giddy). 2. asahaka (na) 浅はか (な) (silly, thoughtless).

lighthouse, *n.* tōdai 灯台.

lighting, *n.* shōmei 照明 (theater, etc.).

lightning, *n.* inazuma 稲妻.

lightning rod, *n.* hiraishin 避雷針.

light-year, *n.* kōnen 光年.

likable, *adj.* sukareru 好かれる.

like, 1. *adj.* (... ni) niteiru (... に) 似ている (similar); onaji yō na 同じような (alike). 2. *conj.* ... yō ni ... ように (just as, as if). 3. *prep.* (... no) yō ni (...の) ように (similar to); (... no) yō na (...の) ような (such as); ... rashii ...らしい (characteristic of). 4. *vb.* konomu 好む; (... ga) suki (de aru) (...が) 好き(である); **would like to** ... (shi)tai ... (し)たい.

likelihood, *n.* kanōsei 可能性.

likely, *adj.* 1. arisō (na) ありそう (な) (probable, believable). 2. mikomi ga aru 見込みがある (promising).

liken, *vb.* (... ni) tatoeru (...に) 例える.

likeness, *n.* 1. shōzōga 肖像画 (portrait). 2. niteiru koto 似ていること (state of being similar).

likewise, *adv.* dōyō ni 同様に.

lilac, *n.* rira リラ; rairakku ライラック.

lily, *n.* yuri 百合.

limb, *n.* 1. teashi 手足 (body). 2. eda 枝 (branch).

limber, 1. *adj.* yawarakai 柔らかい (supple); jūnan (na) 柔軟 (な) (flexible). 2. *vb.* **limber up** karada o hogusu 体をほぐす (make oneself limber).

lime, *n.* 1. sekkai 石灰 (quicklime). 2. raimu ライム (fruit).

limelight, *n.* chūmoku no mato 注目の的 (center of interest).

limestone, *n.* sekkaigan 石灰岩.

limit, 1. *n.* genkai 限界 (farthest extent); kyōkai 境界 (boundary); **off limits** tachi'iri kinshi 立入禁止. 2. *vb.* kagiru 限る.

limitation, *n.* genkai 限界.

limousine, *n.* rimujin リムジン.

limp, 1. *n.* bikko びっこ. 2. *adj.* gunya-gunya shiteiru ぐにゃぐにゃしている (not firm). 3. *vb.* bikko o hiku びっこを引く (walk with a limp).

limpid, *adj.* sumikitta 澄み切った (clear).

line, 1. *n.* rain ライン; sen 線 (thin mark, string, cord); denwa 電話 (telephone); shiwa しわ (wrinkle); retsu 列 (row). 2. *vb.* sen o hiku 線を引く (mark with a line); uraji o tsukeru 裏地を付ける (cover inner side of); **line up** narabu 並

ぶ (form a row).

lineage, *n.* kakei 家系; kettō 血統 (ancestry).

linear, *adj.* 1. sen (no) 線 (の) (lines). 2. tate (no) 縦 (の) (length).

linen, *n.* 1. rinen リネン. 2. shikifu 敷布 (sheets); napukin ナプキン (napkins).

linger, *vb.* 1. inokoru 居残る (stay on). 2. kangaekomu 考え込む (dwell in thought). 3. nagabiku 長引く (persist).

lingerie, *n.* ranjerī ランジェリー.

linguistic, *adj.* 1. kotoba (no) 言葉 (の) (of languages). 2. gengogaku (no) 言語学 (の) (of linguistics).

linguistics, *n.* gengogaku 言語学.

lining, *n.* uraji 裏地.

link, 1. *n.* wa 輪 (section of a chain); tsunagari つながり (bond). 2. *vb.* tsunagu つなぐ (unite).

linkage, *n.* tsunagari つながり; kankei 関係.

linoleum, *n.* rinoriumu リノリウム.

lint, *n.* itokuzu 糸屑.

lion, *n.* raion ライオン; shishi 獅子.

lioness, *n.* mesu-raion 雌ライオン.

lip, *n.* kuchibiru 唇.

lipstick, *n.* kuchibeni 口紅.

liqueur, *n.* rikyūru リキュール.

liquid, *n.* ekitai 液体.

liquidate, *vb.* 1. hensai suru 返済する (pay a debt). 2. heiten/heisa suru 閉店／閉鎖する (dissolve a business). 3. genkinka suru 現金化する (convert into cash).

liquor, *n.* arukōru アルコール; sake 酒.

lisp, 1. *n.* shitatarazu 舌足らず. 2. *vb.* shitatarazu ni hanasu 舌足らずに話す.

list, 1. *n.* risuto リスト; ichiranhyō

一覧表; meibo 名簿. 2. *vb.* risuto ni ageru リストに挙げる.

listen (to), *vb.* (... o) kiku (...を) 聞く.

listener, *n.* 1. kikite 聞き手. 2. chōshusha 聴取者 (radio).

listless, *adj.* mukanshin (na) 無関心 (な); monoui 物憂い.

liter, *n.* rittoru リットル.

literacy, *n.* shikiji 識字.

literal, *adj.* mojidōri (no) 文字通り (の); chikugo-teki (na) 逐語的 (な) (following the original words).

literally, *adv.* 1. genmitsu ni 厳密に (strictly). 2. mojidōri ni 文字通りに (word for word).

literary, *adj.* bungaku (no) 文学 (の) (of literature).

literate, *adj.* moji ga wakaru 文字がわかる (able to read and write). 2. gakumon ga aru 学問がある (educated).

literature, *n.* 1. bungaku 文学 (prose, poetry, etc.). 2. bunken 文献 (entire body of writings on a specific subject).

litigation, *n.* soshō 訴訟.

litter, 1. *n.* gomi ごみ (rubbish). 2. *vb.* chirakasu 散らかす (strew, scatter).

little, 1. *n.* **a little** sukoshi 少し. 2. *adj.* chiisai 小さい (size, mind); sukunai 少ない (quantity); mijikai 短い (time). 3. *adv.* sukoshi 少し (slightly); **little by little** sukoshi zutsu 少しずつ.

live, 1. *adj.* ikiteiru 生きている (alive); kakki ga aru 活気がある (energetic); jitsuen (no) 実演 (の) (performance). 2. *vb.* ikiru 生きる (have life); sumu 住む (reside); ikiteiru 生きている (be alive); seikatsu suru 生活する (maintain a lifestyle); nokoru 残る (endure in reputation).

livelihood, *n.* seikei 生計.

lively, *adj.* 1. kappatsu (na) 活発 (な); nigiyaka (na) にぎやか (な) (active). 2. kakki ni michita 活気 に満ちた (spirited). 3. waku-waku suru わくわくする (exciting).

liver, *n.* rebā レバー; kimo 肝.

livery, *n.* seifuku 制服.

livestock, *n.* kachiku 家畜 (domestic farm animals).

livid, *adj.* 1. aoguroi 青黒い (dull blue). 2. ikidōtteiru 憤っている (furious).

living, 1. *n.* seikatsu 生活 (lifestyle); seikatsuhi 生活費 (livelihood); **earn a living** seikatsuhi o eru 生活費を得る. 2. *adj.* ikiteiru 生きている (alive); tsukawarete-iru 使われている (in active use).

living room, *n.* ima 居間.

lizard, *n.* tokage とかげ.

load, 1. *n.* ni(motsu) 荷(物) (cargo, anything carried). 2. *vb.* ni o tsumu 荷を積む (put a load in or on); tama o tsumeru 弾を詰める (charge a gun).

loaf, *n.* pan パン (bread).

loafer, *n.* namakemono 怠け者 (idle person).

loan, 1. *n.* rōn ローン; kashitsuke 貸し付け. 2. *vb.* kasu 貸す.

loath, *adj.* iyagaru 嫌がる; **be loath to do** ... suru koto o iyagaru ...することを嫌がる.

loathe, *vb.* kirau 嫌う.

loathsome, *adj.* iya (na) 嫌 (な).

lobby, *n.* 1. robī ロビー (entrance hall). 2. atsuryoku dantai 圧力団 体 (political group).

lobbyist, *n.* robīsuto ロビースト.

lobe, *n.* mimitabu 耳たぶ (earlobe).

lobster, *n.* iseebi 伊勢えび.

local, 1. *n.* kakuekiteisha 各駅停車 (local train). 2. *adj.* chihō (no) 地 方 (の); tōchi (no) 当地 (の); **local color** chihōshoku 地方色.

locale, *n.* basho 場所 (place, setting).

locality, *n.* tokoro 所; basho 場所 (place, area).

locate, *vb.* 1. mitsukeru 見つける (find). 2. **be located at** ... ni aru/iru ...にある／いる.

location, *n.* basho 場所.

lock, 1. *n.* rokku ロック; jō 錠 (security device); makige 巻毛 (curl); **locks** kami 髪 (hair). 2. *vb.* kagi o kakeru 鍵を掛ける (secure with a lock); **lock in** tojikomeru 閉じ込める (confine); **lock out** heisa suru 閉鎖する.

locker, *n.* rokkā ロッカー.

locket, *n.* roketto ロケット.

locksmith, *n.* kagiya 鍵屋.

locomotive, *n.* kikansha 機関車.

locust, *n.* inago 蝗.

lodge, 1. *n.* koya 小屋 (hut); rojji ロッジ (inn); (himitsu)kessha (秘 密)結社 (secret society). 2. *vb.* tomaru 泊まる (stay at an inn); geshuku suru 下宿する (live in rented quarters); tsukaeru つかえ る (clog at a particular position); umaru 埋まる (be implanted); mōshitateru 申し立てる (lodge a complaint).

lodger, *n.* geshukunin 下宿人 (roomer).

lodging, *n.* 1. yado 宿 (temporary housing). 2. **lodgings** geshukubeya 下宿部屋 (rooms).

loft, *n.* rofuto ロフト.

lofty, *adj.* 1. kōshō (na) 高尚 (な) (exalted in dignity). 2. takai 高い (high). 3. kōman (na) 高慢 (な)

(arrogant).

log, *n.* 1. maruta 丸太 (tree). 2. nisshi 日誌 (nautical).

logger, *n.* kikori 樵 (lumberjack).

logic, *n.* rojikku ロジック; ronri 論理.

logical, *adj.* rojikaru (na) ロジカル (な); ronri-teki (na) 論理的 (な).

logistics, *n.* keikaku 計画 (planning).

loin, *n.* 1. **loins** koshi 腰 (hips and groin); seiki 性器 (genitalia). 2. koshiniku 腰肉 (of meat).

loincloth, *n.* fundoshi ふんどし.

loiter, *vb.* buratsuku ぶらつく (linger).

lollipop, *n.* pero-pero kyandē ぺろぺろキャンデー.

London, *n.* rondon ロンドン.

lone, *adj.* 1. hitori dake no 一人だけの (person). 2. hitotsu dake no 一つだけの (thing).

loneliness, *n.* kodoku 孤独; sabishisa 寂しさ.

lonely, lonesome, *adj.* 1. kodoku (na, no) 孤独 (な、の) (alone). 2. sabishii 寂しい (wishing for company). 3. koritsu shita 孤立した (isolated).

long, 1. *adj.* nagai 長い. 2. *adv.* nagaku 長く. 3. *vb.* **long for** ... o koimotomeru ...をこい求める. 4. **long ago** zutto mae ni ずっと前に; **long live!** banzai 万歳; **a long time** nagai aida 長い間; **as long as** ... (suru) kagiri ... (する) 限り (provided that); ... node ...ので (since); ... no aida ...の間 (while); **before long** sugu ni すぐに; mamonaku 間もなく; **How long?** Dono gurai. どの位; **no longer** mohaya ... (dewa) nai もはや... (では) ない; **so long** dewa mata ではまた; sayōnara さようなら.

long-distance, *adj.* chōkyori (no) 長距離 (の).

longevity, *n.* 1. chōju 長寿 (long life). 2. jumyō 寿命 (length of life).

longing, *n.* setsubō 切望.

longitude, *n.* keido 経度.

long-term, *adj.* chōki no 長期の.

look, 1. *n.* miru koto 見ること (act of looking); mikake 見かけ (appearance); **take a look** miru 見る; **looks** yōbō 容貌. 2. *vb.* miru 見る (direct the eyes); (...no yō ni) mieru (...のように) 見える (seem); **look after** sewa o suru 世話をする; **look at** ... o miru ...を見る; **look for** ... o sagasu ...を捜す; **look forward to** ... o tanoshimi ni suru ...を楽しみにする; **look into** ... o shiraberu ...を調べる; **look like** ... ni niteiru ...に似ている (resemble); ... no yō da ...のようだ (seem); **look out** (... ni) ki o tsukeru (...に) 気をつける; **look up** miageru 見上げる (see upward); shiraberu 調べる (check); **look up to** ... o sonkei suru ...を尊敬する.

loom, 1. *n.* hataoriki 機織機. 2. *vb.* hata o oru 機を織る (weave); ōkiku ukabiagaru 大きく浮かび上がる (appear).

loop, *n.* wa 輪 (circle).

loophole, *n.* 1. ana 穴 (opening). 2. nigemichi 逃げ道 (means of escape).

loose, *adj.* 1. jiyū (na) 自由 (な) (free). 2. tokareta 解かれた (released from binding). 3. yurui 緩い (not tight). 4. ōmaka (na) 大まか (な) (not exact, broad). 5. fushidara (na) ふしだら (な) (promiscuous).

loosen, *vb.* yurumeru 緩める

(make less tight, relax in severity).

loot, 1. *n.* ryakudatsu-hin 略奪品 (spoils). 2. *vb.* ryakudatsu suru 略奪する (plunder).

looting, *n.* ryakudatsu 略奪.

lopsided, *adj.* katamuita 傾いた.

loquacious, *adj.* oshaberi (no) おしゃべり (の).

lord, *n.* 1. shihaisha 支配者 (ruler). 2. kunshu 君主 (monarch, master, etc.). 3. kizoku 貴族 (nobleman); -kyō -卿 (British title); **Lord Byron** baironkyō バイロン卿. 4. **Lord** shu 主 (Christ).

lose, *vb.* 1. nakusu 無くす; ushinau 失う (fail to keep, fail to find, cease to have, be bereaved of). 2. wasureru 忘れる (misplace). 3. heru 減る; hikuku naru 低くなる (become less or lower); **lose weight** taijū ga heru 体重が減る. 4. makeru 負ける (fail to win). 5. okureru 遅れる (become slower by). 6. **lose oneself** (... de) ware o wasureru (...で) 我を忘れる (become engrossed in); **lose one's way** michi ni mayou 道に迷う.

loser, *n.* haibokusha 敗北者.

loss, *n.* 1. nakusu koto 無くすこと (deprivation); sonshitsu 損失 (disadvantage); sōshitsu 喪失 (deprivation through death). 2. funshitsu 紛失 (act of losing something); funshitsubutsu 紛失物 (something lost). 3. make 負け (losing by defeat). 4. **be at a loss** tohō ni kureru 途方に暮れる (be bewildered).

lost, *adj.* 1. nakushita 無くした (no longer possessed or found). 2. maigo (no) 迷子 (の) (having gone astray); **lost dog** maigo no inu 迷子の犬.

lost cause, *n.* makeikusa 負け戦.

lot, *n.* 1. kuji くじ (object drawn to decide); **draw lots** kuji o hiku くじを引く. 2. wariate 割当て (allocation). 3. sadame 定め (fortune). 4. basho 場所; -jō -場 (piece of land); **parking lot** chūshajō 駐車場. 5. **a lot (of), lots (of)** takusan (no) たくさん (の).

lotion, *n.* rōshon ローション; nyūeki 乳液.

lottery, *n.* takarakuji 宝くじ.

loud, 1. *adj.* ōgoe (no) 大声 (の) (strong voice); oto ga ōkii 音が大きい (making loud sound); urusai うるさい (clamorous); hade (na) 派手 (な) (loud color). 2. *adv.* ōgoe de 大声で (in a loud voice).

loudspeaker, *n.* supīkā スピーカー.

lounge, 1. *n.* raunji ラウンジ; robī ロビー. 2. *vb.* motareru もたれる (recline); buratsuku ぶらつく (saunter).

louse, *n.* shirami しらみ (insect).

lousy, *adj.* 1. hiretsu (na) 卑劣 (な) (contemptible). 2. mijime (na) 惨め (な) (miserable).

love, 1. *n.* koi 恋 (romantic attachment); ai 愛 (passionate attachment, affection); seiai 性愛 (sexual love); koibito 恋人 (sweetheart); **fall in love** ai/koi suru 愛／恋する; **be in love** ren'aichū (no) 恋愛中 (の); **make love** neru 寝る. 2. *vb.* ai suru 愛する (have love or affection, have a strong liking).

lovely, *adj.* 1. kawaii 可愛い (charming); kirei (na) きれい (な) (beautiful). 2. tanoshii 楽しい (delightful).

lover, *n.* 1. koibito 恋人 (girlfriend, boyfriend, sweetheart). 2. aijin 愛

人 (mistress). 3. aikōka 愛好家 (devotee).

low, *adj.* 1. hikui 低い (not high or tall, humble in status, not loud). 2. ototta 劣つた (inferior); warui 悪い (bad). 3. shizunda 沈んだ (depressed).

lower, *vb.* sageru 下げる (reduce, diminish, make lower).

lowly, *adj.* 1. misuborashii みすぼらしい (humble in condition). 2. hikui 低い (low in growth or position).

loyal, *adj.* chūjitsu (na) 忠実 (な); seijitsu (na) 誠実 (な).

loyalty, *n.* chūjitsu 忠実; seijitsu 誠実.

lubricant, *n.* junkatsuzai 潤滑剤.

lubricate, *vb.* abura o sasu 油を注す (oil).

lucid, *adj.* 1. meikai (na) 明解 (な) (intelligible). 2. shōki (no) 正気 (の) (sane).

luck, *n.* un 運; **bad luck** aku'un 悪運; **good luck** kōun 幸運; **Good luck!** Ganbatte. がんばって.

lucky, *adj.* un ga ii 運が良い; kōun (na, no) 幸運 (な、の).

luckily, *adv.* un'yoku 運良く.

lucrative, *adj.* (okane ga) mōkaru (お金が) 儲かる.

ludicrous, *adj.* bakarashii 馬鹿らしい.

lug, *vb.* hikizuru 引きずる (drag).

luggage, *n.* ryokōkaban 旅行鞄 (traveling bag); sūtsukēsu スーツケース (suitcase); toranku トランク (trunk).

lukewarm, *adj.* 1. namanurui 生ぬるい (tepid). 2. ozanari (na, no) おざなり (な、の) (having little zeal).

lull, 1. *n.* kyūshi 休止 (temporary calm). 2. *vb.* nekasetsukeru 寝か

せつける (soothe to sleep).

lullaby, *n.* komoriuta 子守り歌.

lumber, *n.* zaimoku 材木.

lumberjack, *n.* kikori 樵.

luminous, *adj.* 1. kagayaku 輝く (giving light). 2. meikai (na) 明解 (な) (easily understood).

lump, *n.* 1. katamari 塊 (mass); **a lump of sugar** kakuzatō hitotsu 角砂糖一つ. 2. hare 腫れ (swelling).

lunacy, *n.* kyōki 狂気 (insanity).

lunar, *adj.* tsuki no 月の.

lunatic, 1. *n.* kichigai 気違い (insane or foolish person). 2. *adj.* kichigai (no) 気違い (の).

lunch, 1. *n.* ranchi ランチ; hirugohan 昼御飯. 2. *vb.* hirugohan o taberu 昼御飯を食べる.

luncheon, *n.* ranchi-pātī ランチーパーティー (lunch party).

luncheonette, *n.* keishokukissa 軽食喫茶.

lung, *n.* hai 肺.

lunge, 1. *n.* hitotsuki 一突き (thrust). 2. *vb.* tobikakaru 飛びかかる.

lure, 1. *n.* yūwaku 誘惑 (enticement); otori おとり (decoy, bait). 2. *vb.* yūwaku suru 誘惑する (entice); obikiyoseru 誘き寄せる (bait).

lurid, *adj.* 1. susamajii すさまじい (horrible). 2. shokkingu (na) ショッキング (な) (shocking). 3. makka (na) 真赤 (な) (garishly red).

lurk, *vb.* hisomu 潜む (lie hidden, exist unperceived).

luscious, *adj.* 1. oishii おいしい (tasty); ii nioi (no) 良い匂い (の) (sweet smelling). 2. miryoku-teki (na) 魅力的 (な) (attractive).

lush, *adj.* 1. oishigetteiru 生い茂つ

ている (growing abundantly). 2. mizu-mizushii みずみずしい (tender and juicy).

lust, *n.* yokubō 欲望 (desire).

luster, *n.* kōtaku 光沢; tsuya 艶.

lustful, *adj.* 1. yokubō ni karareteiru 欲望に駆られている (motivated by lust).

lusty, *adj.* genki (na) 元気 (な) (vigorous).

luxurious, *adj.* 1. gōka (na) 豪華 (な) (characterized by luxury). 2. zeitaku (na) 贅沢 (な) (fond of luxury).

luxury, *n.* zeitaku 贅沢; zeitakuhin 贅沢品 (indulgence).

lymph, *n.* rimpa リンパ.

lynch, *vb.* rinchi o suru リンチをする.

lyre, *n.* tategoto 竪琴.

lyric, *n.* jojōshi 叙情詩; **lyrics** kashi 歌詞.

M

macabre, *adj.* 1. shi (no) 死 (の) (of death). 2. kimi ga warui 気味が悪い (gruesome).

macaroni, *n.* makaroni マカロニ.

machination, *n.* keiryaku 計略 (crafty plot).

machine, *n.* kikai 機械 (apparatus, instrument).

machine gun, *n.* mashingan マシンガン; kikanjū 機関銃.

machinery, *n.* 1. kikai 機械 (machines). 2. kikō 機構 (system).

mackerel, *n.* saba 鯖.

mad, *adj.* 1. kichigai (no) 気違い (の) (lunatic). 2. okotteiru 怒っている (furious).

madam, *n.* madamu マダム; okusama 奥様.

madden, *vb.* okoru 怒る (become angry); okoraseru 怒らせる (make angry).

madman, -woman, *n.* kichigai 気違い.

madness, *n.* kyōki 狂気 (lunacy).

magazine, *n.* magajin マガジン; zasshi 雑誌.

maggot, *n.* ujimushi 蛆虫.

magic, *n.* majikku マジック; mahō 魔法 (mystical charm or power). 2. tejina 手品 (art of causing illusions).

magical, *adj.* mahō (no) 魔法 (の) (mystical power).

magician, *n.* 1. mahōtsukai 魔法使い; majutsushi 魔術師 (enchanter, sorcerer). 2. tejinashi 手品師 (illusionist, conjuror).

magistrate, *n.* hanji 判事.

magnanimous, *adj.* kandai (na) 寛大 (な).

magnate, *n.* yūryokusha 有力者.

magnesium, *n.* maguneshiumu マグネシウム.

magnet, *n.* jishaku 磁石.

magnetic, *adj.* 1. jishaku (no) 磁石 (の) (magnet). 2. miryoku-teki (na) 魅力的 (な) (attractive).

magnificent, *adj.* subarashii 素晴らしい (splendid).

magnify, *vb.* 1. kakudai suru 拡大する (increase the size of). 2. kochō suru 誇張する (cause to seem greater).

magnifying glass, *n.* mushi-megane 虫眼鏡.

magnitude, *n.* magunichūdo マグニチュード; shindo 震度.

magnolia, *n.* mokuren 木蓮.

magpie, *n.* kasasagi 鵲.

mahogany, *n.* mahoganī マホガニー.

maid, *n.* 1. otome 乙女 (young girl). 2. meido メイド (female servant).

maiden, 1. *n.* otome 乙女 (young girl). 2. *adj.* mikon (no) 未婚 (の) (unmarried); **maiden name** kyūsei 旧姓.

mail, 1. *n.* yūbin 郵便 (postal system); yūbinbutsu 郵便物 (things sent by mail); tegami 手紙 (correspondence). 2. *vb.* yūsō suru 郵送する (post).

mailbox, *n.* yūbinbako 郵便箱.

mailman, *n.* yūbinhaitatsu 郵便配達.

mail order, *n.* tsūshinhanbai 通信販売.

maim, *vb.* fugu ni suru 不具にする.

main, 1. *n.* honkan 本管 (principal pipe); **in the main** daitai 大体. 2. *adj.* shuyō (na) 主要 (な) (chief).

mainland, *n.* hondo 本土.

mainstay, *n.* daikoku-bashira 大黒柱 (person).

mainstream, *n.* shuryū 主流 (dominant tendency).

mainstreet, *n.* ōdōri 大通り.

maintain, *vb.* 1. tamotsu 保つ (keep in existence, keep unimpaired); iji suru 維持する (keep in good condition). 2. shuchō suru 主張する (assert, insist). 3. sasaeru 支える (support).

maintenance, *n.* 1. iji 維持 (act of maintaining). 2. seikatsuhi 生活費 (livelihood).

majestic, *adj.* igen ga aru 威厳があ
る; dōdōtaru 堂々たる.

majesty, *n.* 1. igen 威厳 (dignity). 2. saikōken'i 最高権威 (supreme authority). 3. **Majesty** heika 陛下.

major, 1. *n.* shōsa 少佐 (military); senkō 専攻 (study). 2. *adj.* ōkii 大きい; omo (na) 主 (な) (great in size, extent, or importance). 3. *vb.* **major in** ... o senkō suru ...を専攻する.

majority, *n.* 1. daitasū 大多数 (greater number). 2. kahansū 過半数 (more than half). 3. seinen 青年 (adulthood).

make, *vb.* 1. tsukuru 作る (produce, prepare). 2. saseru させる (force). 3. kasegu 稼ぐ (earn). 4. naru なる (become, add up). 5. **make away with** nusumu 盗む (steal); **make believe** ... no furi o suru ...のふりをする; **make for** ... ni iku ...に行く (approach); **make it** yaritogeru やり遂げる (achieve); ma ni au 間に合う (be in time); **make out** wakaru 分かる (comprehend); umaku yaru うまくやる (succeed); **make over** kaeru 変える (alter); **make up** tsukuriageru 作り上げる (concoct); keshō suru 化粧する (put on cosmetics); **make up for** ... no umeawase o suru ...の埋め合わせをする; **make up one's mind** kesshin suru 決心する.

make-believe, *adj.* misekake 見せかけ.

maker, *n.* 1. mēkā メーカー; seizōsha 製造者 (factory). 2. seisakusha 制作者 (maker of movies, etc.).

makeshift, *n.* maniawase 間に合わせ.

make-up, *n.* mēkyappu メーキャッ

プ; keshō 化粧 (cosmetics).

malady, *n.* 1. byōki 病気 (disease). 2. byōgai 病害 (social malady).

malaria, *n.* mararia マラリア.

male, *n., adj.* dansei (no) 男性 (の); otoko (no) 男 (の) (human); osu (no) 雄 (の) (animal).

malefactor, *n.* 1. hanzaisha 犯罪者 (criminal). 2. akunin 悪人 (person who does evil).

malevolent, *adj.* 1. akui ni michiteiru 悪意に満ちている (malicious). 2. kiken (na) 危険 (な) (injurious).

malice, *n.* akui 悪意 (desire to harm others).

malicious, *adj.* akui ni michiteiru 悪意に満ちている; ijiwaru (na) 意地悪 (な) (spiteful).

malign, *vb.* chūshō suru 中傷する.

malignant, *adj.* 1. akui ni michiteiru 悪意に満ちている (disposed to hurt others). 2. akusei (no) 悪性 (の) (tumor).

malinger, *vb.* kebyō o tsukau 仮病を使う.

mall, *n.* shoppingu-mōru ショッピングモール (shopping mall).

mallet, *n.* kizuchi 木槌.

malnutrition, *n.* eiyōfuryō 栄養不良.

malt, *n.* 1. bakuga 麦芽 (germinated barley). 2. moruto-bīru モルトビール (malt beer).

mama, *n.* mama ママ; okāsan お母さん.

mammal, *n.* honyūdōbutsu 哺乳動物.

mammoth, 1. *adj.* kyodai (na) 巨大 (な) (gigantic). 2. *n.* manmosu マンモス.

man, *n.* 1. hito 人 (person, human being); jinrui 人類 (human race). 2. otoko 男 (adult male).

manage, *vb.* 1. nantoka ... suru 何とか...する (succeed in accomplishing). 2. kontorōru suru コントロールする (control); atsukau 扱う (handle). 3. kantoku suru 監督する (supervise). 4. kanri suru 管理する (administer).

management, *n.* 1. keiei 経営; kanri 管理 (business administration). 2. kanrishoku 管理職 (executives).

manager, *n.* 1. manējā マネージャー; shihainin 支配人 (person who manages an enterprise). 2. kantoku 監督 (sports).

Mandarin, *n.* pekingo 北京語; chūgokugo 中国語 (language).

mandarin orange, *n.* mikan みかん.

mandate, *n.* kunrei 訓令; shirei 司令 (official order).

mandatory, *adj.* kyōsei-teki (na) 強制的 (な); gimu-teki (na) 義務的 (な).

mane, *n.* tategami たてがみ.

maneuver, 1. *n.* sakusen 作戦 (stratagem); **maneuvers** enshū 演習 (military). 2. *vb.* ugokasu 動かす (move); enshū o okonau 演習を行う (military).

manganese, *n.* mangan マンガン.

mangle, *vb.* 1. zuta-zuta ni suru ずたずたにする (disfigure). 2. sokonau 損う (spoil).

mango, *n.* mangō マンゴー.

mangy, *adj.* misuborashii みすぼらしい (shabby).

manhandle, *vb.* tearaku atsukau 手荒く扱う.

manhood, *n.* 1. seijin 成人 (state of being an adult). 2. otokorashisa 男らしさ (manly qualities). 3. dansei 男性 (men collectively).

mania, *n.* 1. nekkyō 熱狂 (excessive enthusiasm). 2. sōbyō 躁病 (psychological disorder).

-mania, -kyō 〜狂; -kichigai 〜気違い; **bibliomania** honkichigai 本気違い.

maniac, *n.* kichigai 気違い.

manicure, *n.* manikyua マニキュア.

manifest, 1. *adj.* meihaku (na) 明白 (な). 2. *vb.* meiji suru 明示する.

manifestation, *n.* meiji 明示 (act of showing clearly).

manifesto, *n.* seimeibun 声明文.

manifold, *adj.* iro-iro (na, no) 色々 (な、の) (various).

manipulate, *vb.* 1. sōsa suru 操作する (handle with skill). 2. ayatsuru 操る (influence by devious skill).

mankind, *n.* jinrui 人類.

manliness, *n.* otokorashisa 男らしさ (masculine qualities).

manly, *adj.* otokorashii 男らしい (having masculine qualities).

mannequin, *n.* manekin マネキン.

manner, *n.* 1. hōhō 方法 (way of doing). 2. taido 態度 (bearing).

mannerism, *n.* man'neri マンネリ (stereotypical quality).

manners, *n.* manā マナー; reigi(sahō) 礼儀(作法) (polite behavior); shūzoku 習俗 (prevailing customs).

manor, *n.* 1. shōen 荘園 (estate of medieval lord). 2. gōtei 豪邸 (mansion).

manpower, *n.* rōdōryoku 労働力.

mansion, *n.* gōtei 豪邸.

mantelpiece, *n.* danro no ue no tana 暖炉の上の棚.

manual, 1. *n.* manyuaru マニュア

ル; tebikisho 手引き書 (guidebook). 2. *adj.* shudō (no) 手動 (の) (operated by hand); teshigoto (no) 手仕事 (の) (involving work with the hands);

manual worker nikutai-rōdōsha 肉体労働者.

manufacture, 1. *n.* seizō 製造 (act of manufacturing); seihin 製品 (product). 2. *vb.* seizō suru 製造する (make with machinery); detchiageru でっち上げる (fabricate).

manufacturer, *n.* seizōsha 製造者 (producer).

manuscript, *n.* 1. genkō 原稿 (original text). 2. tegakibon 手書き本 (handwritten book).

many, *pron., adj.* takusan (no) たくさん (の); tasū (no) 多数 (の).

map, *n.* chizu 地図.

maple, *n.* momiji もみじ.

mar, *vb.* sokonau 損う (impair, spoil).

marathon, *n.* marason マラソン.

maraud, *vb.* ryakudatsu suru 略奪する.

marble, *n.* dairiseki 大理石 (stone); bīdama ビー玉 (glass sphere).

march, 1. *n.* māchi マーチ; kōshinkyoku 行進曲 (music); kōshin 行進 (act of marching). 2. *vb.* kōshin suru 行進する (walk with measured tread); susumu 進む (advance).

mare, *n.* meuma 雌馬 (female horse).

margarine, *n.* māgarin マーガリン.

margin, *n.* 1. yohaku 余白 (of a page). 2. hashi 端; fuchi 縁 (edge). 3. yoyū 余裕 (amount above what is necessary). 4. sa 差 (difference).

marginal, *adj.* toru ni tarinai 取る

に足りない (insignificant).

marijuana, *n.* mariwana マリワナ.

marina, *n.* marīna マリーナ.

marine, 1. *adj.* umi (no) 海 (の) (sea); senpaku (no) 船舶 (の) (ships); kaiheitai (no) 海兵隊 (の) (Marines). 2. *n.* kaiheitai'in 海兵隊員 (member of the Marine Corps).

mariner, *n.* suifu 水夫.

marionette, *n.* marionetto マリオネット; ayatsuriningyō 操り人形.

marital, *adj.* kon'in (no) 婚姻 (の); **marital status** kikonmikon no betsu 既婚未婚の別.

maritime, *adj.* 1. senpaku (no) 船舶 (の) (ships). 2. umi (no) 海 (の) (sea).

mark, 1. *n.* shimi 染み (stain); kizu 傷 (blemish); māku マーク; shirushi 印 (sign, symbol); ten 点 (score); mato 的 (target); maruku マルク (German money); **hit/miss the mark** mato ni ataru/o hazusu 的に当たる／を外す. 2. *vb.* shirushi o tsukeru 印を付ける (put a mark on); ... no shirushi de aru ...の印である (indicate); chūmoku suru 注目する (give heed to); ten o tsukeru 点を付ける (rate); **mark down/up** nesage/neage suru 値下げ／値上げする (price).

market, *n.* 1. māketto マーケット; ichiba 市場 (physical location). 2. shijō 市場 (potential buyers); **stock market** kabushiki shijō 株式市場.

marketing, *n.* māketingu マーケティング.

marksman, -woman, *n.* shashu 射手.

marmalade, *n.* māmarēdo マーマレード.

maroon, *n.* kuri'iro 栗色 (color).

marquis, *n.* kōshaku 侯爵.

marriage, *n.* 1. kekkon 結婚 (state of being married). 2. kekkonshiki 結婚式 (ceremony).

married, *adj.* 1. kikon (no) 既婚 (の) (marriage). 2. kekkon shiteiru 結婚している (united in marriage); **get married** kekkon suru 結婚する; **be married** kekkon shiteiru 結婚している.

marrow, *n.* 1. kotsuzui 骨髄 (in bones). 2. seizui 精髄 (essential part).

marry, *vb.* 1. kekkon suru 結婚する (take in marriage); kekkon saseru 結婚させる (cause to take in marriage). 2. **marry off** kekkon saseru 結婚させる.

Mars, *n.* kasei 火星.

marsh, *n.* shitchi 湿地.

marshal, 1. *n.* gensui 元帥 (military). 2. *vb.* seiton suru 整頓する (arrange).

marshmallow, *n.* mashumaro マシュマロ.

martial, *adj.* 1. kōsen-teki (na) 好戦的 (な) (inclined to war). 2. sensō (no) 戦争 (の) (war). 3. **martial arts** bugei 武芸; **martial law** kaigenrei 戒厳令.

martyr, *n.* junkyōsha 殉教者.

martyrdom, *n.* junkyō 殉教.

marvel, 1. *n.* kyōi 驚異 (wonder); kyōi no mato 驚異の的 (thing/person that arouses wonder). 2. *vb.* odoroku 驚く (wonder at).

marvelous, *adj.* kyōi-teki (na) 驚異的 (な); subarashii 素晴らしい (fabulous).

Marxism, *n.* marukusu-shugi マルクス主義.

mascara, *n.* masukara マスカラ.

mascot, *n.* masukotto マスコット.

masculine, *adj.* 1. otokorashii 男らしい (having qualities characteristic of men). 2. dansei (no) 男性 (の) (men).

masculinity, *n.* otokorashisa 男らしさ (quality characteristic of men).

mash, *vb.* suritsubusu 磨りつぶす.

mashed potatoes, *n.* masshupoteto マッシュポテト.

mask, 1. *n.* masuku マスク; (ka)men (仮)面. 2. *vb.* kamen o kaburu 仮面を被る (wear a mask); ōu 覆う (cover).

masochism, *n.* mazohizumu マゾヒズム.

mason, *n.* ishidaiku 石大工 (stone mason).

masquerade, 1. *n.* kamenbutōkai 仮面舞踏会 (masked ball); hensō 変装 (false outward show). 2. *vb.* hensō suru 変装する (go about under false pretenses).

mass, *n.* 1. tasū 多数 (great number of); tairyō 大量 (large amount of); **mass production** tairyōseisan; ryōsan 量産. 2. misa ミサ (religion). 3. **masses** taishū 大衆.

massacre, 1. *n.* tairyō-gyakusatsu 大量虐殺. 2. *vb.* minagoroshi ni suru 皆殺しにする.

massage, 1. *n.* massāji マッサージ. 2. *vb.* massāji o suru マッサージをする (give a massage).

massive, *adj.* 1. bōdai (na) 膨大 (な) (large in scale, amount, or degree). 2. kasabaru かさばる (bulky).

mast, *n.* masuto マスト.

master, *n.* 1. meijin 名人 (skilled person); goshujin 御主人 (employer of servants or workers); kachō 家長 (master of household); shūshi 修士 (degree holder); **master of ceremonies** shikai 司会. 2. *vb.* shihai suru 支配する (conquer).

mastermind, *vb.* shidō suru 指導する.

masterpiece, *n.* kessaku 傑作.

master's degree, *n.* shūshigō 修士号.

mastery, *n.* shihai 支配 (control).

masturbate, *vb.* jii ni fukeru 自慰に耽る.

mat, 1. *n.* matto マット (floor covering, border for picture, etc.); tatami 畳 (Japanese straw mat). 2. *vb.* matto o shiku マットを敷く (cover floor, etc., with a mat).

match, 1. *n.* matchi マッチ (short stick to make fire, game, competition); shiai 試合 (game, competition); gokaku no aite 互角の相手 (equal opponent); kekkon'aite 結婚相手 (partner in marriage). 2. *vb.* dōtō de aru 同等である (be equal to); ... ni hitteki suru ...に匹敵する (be the counterpart of, correspond to); ... to au ...と合う (fit together); kekkon saseru 結婚させる (unite in marriage).

matchmaker, *n.* nakōdo 仲人.

mate, 1. *n.* haigūsha 配偶者 (spouse); katahō 片方 (one of a pair); nakama 仲間 (companion). 2. *vb.* majiwaru 交わる (join as mates, copulate).

material, 1. *n.* zairyō 材料 (substance); nuno 布 (fabric); shiryō 資料 (material for research); **raw material** genryō 原料. 2. *adj.* busshitsu-teki (na) 物質的 (な) (corporeal).

materialism, *n.* busshitsushugi 物

質主義.

materialize, *vb.* jitsugen suru 実現する (realize).

maternal, *adj.* 1. haha (no) 母 (の) (mother). 2. hahakata (no) 母方 (の) (related through a mother).

maternity, *n.* 1. haha de aru koto 母であること (state of being a mother). 2. bosei 母性 (motherly quality).

mathematical, *adj.* sūgaku-teki (na) 数学的 (な).

mathematics, *n.* sūgaku 数学.

matinee, *n.* hiru no bu 昼の部 (afternoon performance).

matriarchy, *n.* bokenshakai 母権社会 (matriarchal social system).

matrimony, *n.* kekkon 結婚.

matrix, *n.* botai 母体 (something that gives origin to another).

matron, *n.* 1. fujin 婦人 (married woman). 2. joseikanrinin 女性管理人 (female supervisor).

matter, 1. *n.* busshitsu 物質 (material); kotogara 事柄 (affair); mondai 問題 (trouble); kakimono 書き物 (printed matter); **as a matter of course** tōzen 当然; **as a matter of fact** jissai 実際; **What's the matter?** Dō shita no. どうしたの. **no matter (how, what, etc.)** tatoe ... demo/temo たとえ...でも／ても. 2. *vb.* jūyō de aru 重要である (be important); **it doesn't matter** jūyō ja nai 重要じゃない.

mattress, *n.* mattoresu マットレス.

mature, 1. *adj.* seijuku shita 成熟した (fully developed); ōkiku natta 大きくなった (fully grown); ureta 熟れた (ripe). 2. *vb.* seijuku suru 成熟する (bring to full development); seiiku suru 成育する (grow); jukusuru 熟する

(become ripe).

maturity, *n.* seijuku 成熟 (state of being mature).

maudlin, *adj.* 1. senchimentaru (na) センチメンタル (な) (sentimental). 2. namidamoroi 涙脆い (tearful).

maul, *vb.* 1. tearaku atsukau 手荒く扱う (manhandle). 2. kega o saseru 怪我をさせる (bruise).

mausoleum, *n.* reibyō 霊廟.

maxim, *n.* kakugen 格言.

maximize, *vb.* 1. saidaigen made fuyasu 最大限まで増やす (increase to a maximum). 2. ōi ni katsuyō suru 大いに活用する (make fullest use of).

maximum, *n., adj.* 1. saidai (no) 最大 (の) (highest amount). 2. saidaigen (no) 最大限 (の) (upper limit).

may, *aux. vb.* 1. ...kamoshirenai ...かもしれない (to express contingency or possibility). 2. ...temo ii ...ても良い (permission). 3. ... yō ni ...ように (wish); **May you live long!** Nagaiki suru yō ni. 長生きするように. 4. **may as well do** ... shita hō ga ii ...した方が良い.

May, *n.* gogatsu 五月.

maybe, *adv.* osoraku おそらく.

mayonnaise, *n.* mayonēzu マヨネーズ.

mayor, *n.* shichō 市長 (city); chōchō 町長 (town); sonchō 村長 (village).

maze, *n.* meiro 迷路.

me, *pron.* watashi (o/ni) 私 (を／に); **with me** watashi to 私と.

meadow, *n.* kusahara 草原.

meager, *adj.* 1. yaseteiru やせている (thin). 2. sukunai 少ない (scanty). 3. mazushii 貧しい

(poor).

meal, *n.* gohan 御飯; shokuji 食事.

mean, 1. *n.* chūkan 中間 (midway between extremes); heikin 平均 (average). 2. *adj.* ijiwaru (na) 意地悪 (な) (malicious); iyashii 卑しい (ignoble); kechi (na) けち (な) (stingy); ototteiru 劣っている (inferior). 2. *vb.* (... suru) tsumori de aru (...する) つもりである (intend); imi suru 意味する (signify).

meaning, *n.* imi 意味 (purport, significance).

meaningful, *adj.* igibukai 意義深い.

means, *n.* 1. hōhō 方法; shudan 手段 (method, agency). 2. (o)kane (お)金 (money); tomi 富 (wealth). 3. **by all means** zehi 是非; **by means of** ... ni yotte ...によって; **by no means** kesshite ... nai 決して...ない.

meantime, *adv.* aida 間; **in the meantime** sono aida ni その間に.

meanwhile, *adv.* 1. sono aida ni その間に (meantime). 2. dōji ni 同時に (at the same time).

measles, *n.* hashika はしか.

measly, *adj.* hon no wazuka (no) ほんのわずか (の).

measure, 1. *n.* mejā メジャー (tape measure); monosashi 物差し (yardstick); hakari 秤 (scale); sunpō 寸法; ōkisa 大きさ (dimensions); omosa 重さ (weight); nagasa 長さ (length); shochi 処置 (action); hyōshi 拍子 (rhythm). 2. *vb.* hakaru はかる (ascertain size or extent).

measurement, *n.* 1. sunpō 寸法; ōkisa 大きさ (dimensions). 2. sokutei 測定 (process of measuring).

meat, *n.* niku 肉.

meatball, *n.* mītobōru ミートボール.

mechanic, *n.* 1. jukurenkō 熟練工 (skilled worker with tools, etc.). 2. seibishi 整備士 (repairer).

mechanical, *adj.* 1. kikai (no) 機械 (の) (pertaining to machinery). 2. kikai-teki (na) 機械的 (な) (going through the motions).

mechanics, *n.* 1. mekanikkusu メカニックス (technical aspect). 2. rikigaku 力学 (science).

mechanism, *n.* mekanizumu メカニズム; shikumi 仕組み; naritachi 成り立ち.

mechanize, *vb.* kikaika suru 機械化する (adapt to machinery).

medal, *n.* medaru メダル.

medallion, *n.* ōgata-medaru 大型メダル.

meddle, *vb.* kanshō suru 干渉する.

meddlesome, *adj.* osekkai (na) お節介 (な).

media, *n.* masukomi マスコミ (mass media).

mediate, *vb.* chōtei suru 調停する (settle dispute).

mediation, *n.* chōtei 調停.

mediator, *n.* chōteinin 調停人.

medical, *adj.* igaku (no) 医学 (の) (of the science of medicine).

medication, *n.* 1. kusurifukuyō 薬服用 (use of medicine). 2. kusuri 薬 (medical substance).

medicine, *n.* 1. kusuri 薬 (medical substance). 2. igaku 医学 (science of restoring health).

medieval, *adj.* chūsei (no) 中世 (の).

mediocre, *adj.* nami (no) 並 (の).

meditate, *vb.* meisō suru 瞑想する.

meditation, *n.* meisō 瞑想.

Mediterranean, *n., adj.* chichūkai

(no) 地中海 (の).

medium, 1. *n.* chūkan 中間 (mean, something intermediate); baitai 媒体 (intervening substance); hōhō 方法 (means of doing); kankyō 環境 (environment); reibai 霊媒 (spiritualist). 2. *adj.* chūkan (no) 中間 (の) (intermediate).

medley, *n.* 1. medorē メドレー (music). 2. gotamaze ごたまぜ (jumble).

meek, *adj.* jūjun (na) 従順 (な).

meet, 1. *n.* kyōgikai 競技会; taikai 大会 (athletic meet). 2. *vb.* (... ni) deau (...に) 出会う (encounter); au 会う (join at an agreed time or place); shiriau 知り合う (be introduced to); mukaeru 迎える (be present at the arrival of); atsumaru 集まる (assemble for action); mitasu 満たす (satisfy).

meeting, *n.* 1. kaigi 会議 (conference, business meeting). 2. deai 出会い (encounter). 3. shūkai 集会; tsudoi 集い (gathering for a purpose).

megahertz, *n.* megaherutsu メガヘルツ.

megaphone, *n.* megahon メガホン; kakuseiki 拡声器.

melancholy, *n., adj.* merankorī (na) メランコリー (な); yūutsu (na) 憂うつ (な).

mellow, *adj.* 1. jukushiteiru 熟している (ripe). 2. yutaka (na) 豊か (な) (rich). 3. yawarakai 柔らかい (soft).

melodrama, *n.* merodorama メロドラマ.

melody, *n.* merodī メロディー; senritsu 旋律.

melon, *n.* meron メロン.

melt, *vb.* tokeru 溶ける (become liquified, dissolve); tokasu 溶かす (reduce to a liquid state).

member, *n.* 1. menbā メンバー; kai'in 会員 (person belonging to an organization). 2. karada no ichibu 体の一部 (part of body).

membership, *n.* 1. menbāshippu メンバーシップ; kai'inshikaku 会員資格 (state of being a member). 2. kai'insū 会員数 (total number of members).

membrane, *n.* usumaku 薄膜.

memento, *n.* katami 形見; kinenhin 記念品.

memoir, *n.* kaisōki 回想記 (personal recollection).

memorable, *adj.* omoidebukai 思い出深い (worth remembering).

memorandum, *n.* memo メモ (reminder).

memorial, 1. *n.* kinenhi 記念碑 (monument honoring memory). 2. *adj.* kinen (no) 記念 (の) (serving to preserve the memory).

memorize, *vb.* anki suru 暗記する.

memory, *n.* 1. kioku 記憶 (faculty of remembering). 2. omoide 思い出 (recollection). 3. kinen 記念 (commemoration); **in memory of** ... o kinen shite ...を記念して. 4. memorī メモリー (computer).

menace, 1. *n.* kyōi 脅威 (something that threatens). 2. *vb.* obiyakasu 脅かす (threaten).

mend, *vb.* shūri suru 修理する (repair a machine); tsukurou 繕う (repair something by sewing).

menial, *adj.* tsumaranai つまらない (humble).

menopause, *n.* kōnenki 更年期.

menstruation, *n.* gekkei 月経; mensu メンス; seiri 生理.

mental, *adj.* 1. kokoro (no) 心 (の); seishin (no) 精神 (の) (of the

mind). 2. seishinbyō (no) 精神病
(の) (of mental disorder). 3.
atama no naka (no) 頭の中 (の)
(performed in the mind). 4.
chiteki (na) 知的 (な)
(intellectual).

mentality, *n.* 1. chinō 知能
(mental capacity). 2. kangaekata
考え方 (outlook).

mention, 1. *n.* genkyū 言及
(reference). 2. *vb.* noberu 述べる
(speak of); genkyū suru 言及する
(refer to, cite); **not to mention**
sono ue ni その上に.

mentor, *n.* onshi 恩師.

menu, *n.* menyū メニュー (list of
dishes).

meow, 1. *n.* neko no nakigoe 猫の
鳴き声; nyā-nyā にゃーにゃー. 2.
vb. nyā-nyā to naku にゃーにゃー
と鳴く.

mercenary, *n., adj.* kanemeate
(no) 金目当て (の) (wanting
money).

merchandise, *n.* shōhin 商品
(goods).

merchant, *n.* shōnin 商人.

merciful, *adj.* jihibukai 慈悲深い.

merciless, *adj.* mujihi (na) 無慈悲
(な); zankoku (na) 残酷 (な).

mercury, *n.* 1. suigin 水銀. 2.
Mercury suisei 水星.

mercy, *n.* jihi 慈悲 (benevolence);
dōjō 同情 (compassion); awaremi
哀れみ (pity); **at the mercy of** ...
no nasu ga mama de ...のなすがま
まで.

mercy killing, *n.* anrakushi 安楽
死.

mere, *adj.* tatta no たったの; hon
no ほんの.

merely, *adv.* tada ただ; ... dake ...
だけ.

merge, *vb.* 1. hitotsu ni naru/suru
一つになる／する (become
united/cause to unite or blend).
2. gappei suru 合併する
(business).

merger, *n.* gappei 合併 (business).

meridian, *n.* shigosen 子午線
(circle on earth's surface).

meringue, *n.* merenge メレンゲ.

merit, 1. *n.* meritto メリット;
kachi 価値 (worth); riten 利点
(something that deserves praise);
merits kōseki 功績 (state of
deserving). 2. *vb.* atai suru 値する
(deserve).

meritorious, *adj.* shōsan ni atai
suru 賞賛に値する.

mermaid, *n.* ningyo 人魚.

merry, *adj.* yukai (na) 愉快 (な);
tanoshii 楽しい.

merry-go-round, *n.* kaiten-
mokuba 回転木馬.

mesh, 1. *n.* messhu メッシュ; ami
網 (net). 2. *vb.* ami de toru 網で捕
る (catch in mesh).

mesmerize, *vb.* 1. saiminjutsu ni
kakeru 催眠術にかける
(hypnotize). 2. miwaku suru 魅惑
する (fascinate).

mess, 1. *n.* yogore 汚れ (dirty
jumble or condition); konzatsu 混
雑 (confusion); yakkai 厄介
(difficult situation); **in a mess**
chirakkate 散らかって (in
disorder); **make a mess of** ... o
dainashi ni suru ...を台無しにする
(ruin). 2. *vb.* chirakasu 散らかす
(disorder); yogosu 汚す (make
dirty); **mess up** mecha-mecha ni
suru めちゃめちゃにする
(disorder, ruin).

message, *n.* messēji メッセージ;
dengon 伝言.

messenger, *n.* messenjā メッセン
ジャー; tsukai 使い.

messy, *adj.* chirakatteiru 散らかっ
ている (disorderly); yogoreteiru
汚れている (dirty).

metabolism, *n.* shinchintaisha 新
陳代謝.

metal, *n.* metaru メタル; kinzoku
金属.

metamorphosis, *n.* henshin 変身
(of a person); henka 変化; hensei
変性 (of a thing or animal).

metaphor, *n.* in'yu 隠喩.

metaphysics, *n.* keijijōgaku 形而上
学 (philosophy).

meteor, *n.* nagareboshi 流れ星.

meter, *n.* 1. mētā メーター
(measuring instrument). 2.
mētoru メートル (unit of length).

method, *n.* hōhō 方法 (manner).

methodical, *adj.* 1. chitsujo
tadashii 秩序正しい (systematic).
2. shinchō (na) 慎重 (な)
(deliberate).

methodology, *n.* hōhōron 方法論.

meticulous, *adj.* saishin (na, no)
細心 (な、の).

metric, *adj.* mētoru (no) メートル
(の) (pertaining to the meter);
metric system mētoru-hō メート
ル法.

metropolis, *n.* daitokai 大都会.

metropolitan, *adj.* metoroporitan
(no) メトロポリタン (の); daitokai
(no) 大都会 (の).

Mexico, *n.* mekishiko メキシコ.

mezzanine, *n.* nikai-shōmenseki
二階正面席 (theater); chūnikai 中
二階 (architecture).

mica, *n.* unmo 雲母.

microbe, *n.* 1. biseibutsu 微生物
(microorganism). 2. baikin ばい
菌; saikin 細菌 (disease-causing
bacteria).

microcosm, *n.* shōuchū 小宇宙.

microfilm, *n.* maikuro-firumu マ
イクロフィルム.

microphone, *n.* maiku マイク.

microscope, *n.* kenbikyō 顕微鏡.

microscopic, *adj.* kyokushō (no)
極小 (の).

microwave oven, *n.* denshi-renji
電子レンジ.

mid, *adj.* man'naka (no) 真中 (の);
nakaba (no) 半ば (の) (being at
the middle point); **mid-autumn**
akinakaba 秋半ば.

middle, 1. *n.* chūkan 中間
(intermediate); man'naka 真中
(central point); chūō 中央
(center); **in the middle of** ... no
saichū ni ... の最中に (engaged
in). 2. *adj.* chūkan (no) 中間 (の);
man'naka (no) 真中 (の)
(intermediate); chūō (no) 中央
(の) (central).

middle-aged, *adj.* chūnen (no) 中
年 (の).

Middle Ages, *n.* chūsei 中世.

middle-class, *adj.* chūryūkaikyū
(no) 中流階級 (の).

Middle East, *n.* chūtō 中東.

middleman, *n.* nakagainin 仲買人.

middle school, *n.* chūgakkō 中学
校.

midget, *n.* kobito 小人.

midnight, *n.* mayonaka 真夜中.

midst, *n.* 1. man'naka 真中
(middle). 2. **in the midst of** ...
no tadanaka de/ni ...の只中で／に
(surrounded by); ... no saichū ni
... の最中に (engaged in).

midwife, *n.* josanpu 助産婦.

mien, *n.* mi no konashi 身のこなし
(bearing); fūsai 風采 (appearance);
yōsu 様子 (air).

might, *n.* chikara 力 (strength).

mighty, *adj.* 1. kyōryoku (na) 強力
(な) (powerful). 2. kyodai (na) 巨
大 (な) (huge).

migraine, *n.* hentōtsū 偏頭痛.

migrate, *vb.* idō suru 移動する.

migration, *n.* ijū 移住.

mikado, *n.* mikado 帝; ten'nō 天皇.

mild, *adj.* 1. odayaka (na) 穏やか (な) (gentle). 2. karui 軽い (light, not severe). 3. atatakai 暖かい (not cold); kaiteki (na) 快適 (な) (comfortable); **mild winter** ondan na fuyu 温暖な冬. 4. mairudo (na) マイルド (な) (not bitter or pungent). 5. yowai 弱い (moderate in force).

mildew, *n.* kabi かび.

mile, *n.* mairu マイル.

milestone, *n.* kakki-teki na koto 画期的なこと (epoch-making thing or event).

milieu, *n.* kankyō 環境.

militant, *adj.* sentō-teki (na) 戦闘的 (な).

military, *n., adj.* gun (no) 軍 (の); guntai (no) 軍隊 (の); **military man** gunjin 軍人.

militia, *n.* shimingun 市民軍.

milk, 1. *n.* miruku ミルク; gyūnyū 牛乳. 2. *vb.* chichi o shiboru 乳を搾る (draw milk); shiboritoru 搾り取る (exploit).

milkshake, *n.* mirukusēki ミルクセーキ.

milky, *adj.* miruku no yō (na) ミルクのよう (な) (like milk).

Milky Way, *n.* amanogawa 天の川.

mill, 1. *n.* kōjō 工場 (factory); konahikiki 粉碾き機 (machine for grinding beans or grain); kōhī-hiki コーヒー碾き (coffee mill). 2. *vb.* hiku 碾く (grind).

miller, *n.* konaya 粉屋.

milligram, *n.* miriguramu ミリグラム.

millimeter, *n.* miri ミリ.

million, *n., adj.* hyakuman (no) 百万 (の); **two million** nihyakuman (no) 二百万 (の).

millionaire, *n.* ōganemochi 大金持ち; chōja 長者.

mime, 1. *n.* pantomaimu パントマイム (pantomime). 2. *vb.* mane suru 真似する (mimic).

mimic, 1. *n.* monomaneshi 物真似師 (performer). 2. *vb.* mane suru 真似する (imitate).

mimicry, *n.* monomane 物真似 (act of imitating).

mince, *vb.* hiku 挽く (chop meat); komagire ni suru 細切れにする (chop foods).

mincemeat, *n.* hikiniku 挽き肉 (ground meat).

mind, 1. *n.* kokoro 心 (center of thoughts and emotions); chisei 知性 (intellect); ikō 意向 (intention); shōki 正気 (sound mental condition); kangae 考え (opinion); **bear/keep in mind** oboeteoku 覚えておく **be on one's mind** ki ni kakaru 気にかかる; **be out of one's mind** ki ga kuruu 気が狂う; **call to mind** omoidasu 思い出す; **make up one's mind** kesshin suru 決心する. 2. *vb.* ki ni suru 気にする (heed); chūi suru 注意する (pay attention to, be careful); sen'nen suru 専念する (apply oneself to); shinpai suru 心配する (care about).

mine, 1. *n.* kōzan 鉱山 (excavation). 2. *pron.* watashi no mono 私のもの. 3. *vb.* horidasu 掘り出す (dig).

miner, *n.* kōfu 坑夫.

mineral, *n.* 1. mineraru ミネラル (inorganic substance); **mineral water** mineraru-wotā ミネラルウォーター. 2. kōbutsu 鉱物

(ore).

mingle, *vb.* majiwaru 交わる; mazaru 混ざる (become mixed or blended); mazeru 混ぜる (mix, blend).

miniature, *n., adj.* minichua (no) ミニチュア (の).

minimal, *adj.* saishō(gendo no) 最小(限度の).

minimum, *n.* 1. saishōgendo 最小限度 (least amount possible). 2. saitei 最低 (lowest amount, value, etc.); **minimum wage** saiteichingin 最低賃金.

mining, *n.* kōgyō 鉱業 (mining industry).

minister, 1. *n.* daijin 大臣 (government); bokushi 牧師 (religion). 2. *vb.* tsukaeru 仕える.

ministry, *n.* 1. -shō -省 (government department); **Ministry of Education** monbushō 文部省. 2. seishoku 聖職 (religious calling); bokushi 牧師 (clergy).

mink, *n.* minku ミンク.

minor, 1. *n.* miseinen 未成年 (youth). 2. *adj.* (yori) chiisai (より) 小さい (lesser in seriousness, importance, etc.); (yori) sukunai (より) 少ない (lesser in amount); miseinen (no) 未成年 (の) (youth); tanchō (no) 短調 (の) (music).

minority, *n.* 1. shōsūha 少数派 (smaller group). 2. miseinen 未成年 (legal age).

minstrel, *n.* gin'yūshijin 吟遊詩人 (itinerant poet); kyūteishijin 宮廷詩人 (court poet).

mint, 1. *n.* minto ミント; hakka 薄荷 (herb); zōheikyoku 造幣局 (place where money is coined). 2. *vb.* chūzō suru 鋳造する (make by

stamping metal); tsukuridasu 作り出す (invent).

minus, *prep.* mainasu マイナス; hiku 引く (less by subtraction of).

minute, 1 *n.* fun 分 (sixty seconds); chotto ちょっと (short space of time); **Wait a minute!** Chotto matte kudasai. ちょっと待って下さい; **up to the minute** saishin (no) 最新 (の) (up-to-date). 2. *adj.* komakai 細かい (extremely small).

minutes, *n.* kaigiroku 会議録 (record of meeting).

miracle, *n.* kiseki 奇蹟.

miraculous, *adj.* kiseki-teki (na) 奇蹟的 (な).

mirage, *n.* shinkirō 蜃気楼.

mire, 1. *n.* doronuma 泥沼 (bog). 2. *vb.* doronuma ni hamarikomu 泥沼にはまり込む (be stuck in bog or difficulty).

mirror, *n.* mirā ミラー; kagami 鏡.

mirth, *n.* yorokobi 喜び.

misanthrope, *n.* ningengirai 人間嫌い.

misbehave, *vb.* gyōgi waruku suru 行儀悪くする.

misbehavior, *n.* busahō 無作法.

miscarriage, *n.* 1. ryūzan 流産 (miscarriage of a baby). 2. shippai 失敗 (failure).

miscellaneous, *adj.* samazama (na, no) 様々 (な、の).

mischief, *n.* 1. kigai 危害 (harm, evil); yakkai 厄介 (trouble). 2. itazura いたずら (petty annoyance). 3. chame 茶目 (harmless teasing).

mischievous, *adj.* 1. ijiwaru (na) 意地悪 (な) (malicious). 2. itazura (na) いたずら (な) (playfully annoying).

misconduct, *n.* busahō 無作法.

misdemeanor, *n.* keihanzai 軽犯罪.

miser, *n.* kechi けち.

miserable, *adj.* 1. aware (na) 哀れ (な); mijime (na) 惨め (な) (pitiable, wretched). 2. hidoi ひどい (despicable). 3. fukō (na) 不幸 (な) (unfortunate).

miserly, *adj.* kechi (na) けち (な).

misery, *n.* awaresa 哀れさ; mijimesa 惨めさ (wretchedness).

misfit, *n.* futekiōsha 不適応者.

misfortune, *n.* fu'un 不運 (bad luck).

misgiving, *n.* 1. kenen 懸念 (apprehension). 2. utagai 疑い (doubt).

mishap, *n.* sainan 災難.

mishmash, *n.* gotamaze ごたまぜ.

misinformation, *n.* gohō 誤報.

misinterpret, *vb.* gokai suru 誤解する.

mislead, *vb.* 1. machigawaseru 間違わせる (lead in the wrong direction). 2. damasu だます (deceive).

misnomer, *n.* ayamatta yobina 誤った呼び名.

misogyny, *n.* joseibesshi 女性蔑視; joseigirai 女性嫌い.

misplace, *vb.* 1. oki-machigaeru 置き間違える (put in wrong place). 2. oki-wasureru 置き忘れる (mislay, lose).

misrepresent, *vb.* tadashiku tsutaenai 正しく伝えない (inform incorrectly).

miss, 1. *n.* atesokonai 当て損ない (failure to hit); dokushinjosei 独身女性 (unmarried woman); **Miss** -san - さん; -様 (title); **Miss Oda** odasan 小田さん. 2. *vb.* atesokonau 当て損なう (fail to hit); nogasu 逃す (fail to catch,

take advantage of, etc.); nakusu 無くす (lose); nogareru 逃れる (escape); samishigaru 淋しがる (regret the absence of); yasumu 休む (be absent from); **be missing** ... ga nai ... が無い.

missile, *n.* misairu ミサイル.

missing, *adj.* yukuefumei (no) 行方不明 (の) (person, dog, etc.).

mission, *n.* 1. misshon ミッション; shimei 使命 (duty). 3. dendō 伝道; senkyō 宣教 (religious).

missionary, *n.* dendōshi 伝道師; senkyōshi 宣教師.

mist, *n.* kiri 霧; moya もや.

mistake, 1. *n.* ayamari 誤り; machigai 間違い; **by mistake** ayamatte 誤って; **make a mistake** machigaeru 間違える. 2. *vb.* machigaeru 間違える.

Mister, see **Mr.**

mistreat, *vb.* kokushi suru 酷使する (treat abusively); gyakutai suru 虐待する (treat cruelly).

mistress, *n.* 1. aijin 愛人; mekake 妾 (extramarital partner). 2. on'nashujin 女主人 (female head, female owner).

mistrust, *vb.* utagau 疑う.

misty, *adj.* 1. kiri ga kakatteiru 霧がかかっている (covered by mist). 2. hakkiri shinai はっきりしない (unclear).

misunderstand, *vb.* gokai suru 誤解する.

misunderstanding, *n.* gokai 誤解.

misuse, *vb.* 1. goyō suru 誤用する (use improperly). 2. kokushi suru 酷使する (use abusively).

mite, *n.* dani だに (insect).

mitigate, *vb.* yawarageru 和らげる.

mitten, *n.* miton ミトン; tebukuro 手袋.

mix, 1. *n.* mikkusu ミックス; kongō 混合 (mixture). 2. *vb.* mazeru 混ぜる (combine into one inseparable mass); hitotsu ni suru 一つにする (unite); ireru 入れる (add as an ingredient); **mix up** kondō suru 混同する (confuse).

mixture, *n.* mikkusu ミックス; kongō 混合.

mix-up, *n.* konran 混乱 (state of confusion).

moan, 1. *n.* umeki 呻き. 2. *vb.* umeku 呻く.

moat, *n.* hori 堀.

mob, *n.* 1. bōto 暴徒 (riotous crowd of people). 2. gunshū 群衆 (any large group of people).

mobile, 1. *n.* mōbiru モービル (sculpture). 2. *adj.* idōshiki (no) 移動式 (の) (movable).

mobility, *n.* idōsei 移動性 (quality of being mobile).

mobilize, *vb.* dōin suru 導引する (assemble armed forces); senjitaisei o shiku 戦時体制をしく (organize for service in time of war).

mock, *vb.* 1. azawarau 嘲笑う; karakau からかう (deride). 2. mohō suru 模倣する (imitate).

mockery, *n.* 1. karakai からかい (derision). 2. mohō 模倣 (imitation).

mode, *n.* 1. yōshiki 様式 (manner). 2. hōhō 方法 (method). 3. sutairu スタイル (style).

model, 1. *n.* moderu モデル (fashion model, ideal example, plastic model, etc.); mihon 見本 (standard for imitation); kata 型 (typical form). 2. *vb.* tsukuru 作る (shape, form).

moderate, 1. *adj.* datō (na) 妥当 (な) (kept within proper limits);

chū-gurai (no) 中位 (の) (of medium quantity, extent, etc.); odayaka (na) 穏やか (な) (calm weather, personality, etc.). 2. *vb.* yawarageru 和らげる (mitigate); shikai o suru 司会をする (preside over meeting, etc.).

moderation, *n.* setsudo 節度; tekido 適度 (temperance); **in moderation** tekido ni 適度に.

moderator, *n.* shikaisha 司会者 (at meeting).

modern, *adj.* modan (na) モダン (な); gendai-teki (na) 現代的 (な).

modernize, *vb.* gendaika suru 現代化する.

modest, *adj.* 1. kenkyo (na) 謙虚 (な) (humble in estimating oneself). 2. shisso (na) 質素 (な) (free from ostentation). 3. jōhin (na) 上品 (な) (decent).

modesty, *n.* 1. kenkyo 謙虚 (humbleness). 2. shisso 質素 (simplicity). 3. jōhinsa 上品さ (decency).

modify, *vb.* 1. shūsei suru 修正する (alter partially). 2. kagen suru 加減する (reduce in degree).

moist, *adj.* shimetteiru 湿っている (damp).

moisten, *vb.* shimeraseru 湿らせる.

moisture, *n.* shikke 湿気; suibun 水分.

molar, *n.* kyūshi 臼歯 (tooth).

mold, 1. *n.* kabi かび (fungus growth); kata 型 (cast). 2. *vb.* kata ni ireru 型に入れる (put into a mold); katachizukuru 形作る (shape).

moldy, *adj.* kabiteiru かびている.

mole, *n.* 1. hokuro ほくろ (spot on skin). 2. mogura もぐら (animal).

molecule, *n.* bunshi 分子.

molest, *vb.* 1. komaraseru 困らせ
る (annoy). 2. bōkō suru 暴行す
る (assault sexually).

moment, *n.* 1. shunkan 瞬間
(instant). 2. ima 今 (present
time). 3. toki 時 (definite period,
as in a course of events; occasion).
4. jūyōsa 重要さ (importance). 5.
at the last moment giri-giri no
toki ni ぎりぎりの時に; **at the
moment** tadaima 只今; **in a
moment** sugu ni すぐに.

momentary, *adj.* tsukanoma (no)
束の間 (の).

momentous, *adj.* jūyō (na) 重要
(な).

momentum, *n.* suishinryoku 推進
力; hazumi 弾み.

monarch, *n.* kunshu 君主.

monarchy, *n.* ōkoku 王国 (country
governed by monarch).

monastery, *n.* shūdōin 修道院.

Monday, *n.* getsuyōbi 月曜日.

monetary, *adj.* (o)kane (no) (お)金
(の).

money, *n.* (o)kane (お)金 (coin
and paper money).

money order, *n.* kawase 為替.

mongrel, *n., adj.* zasshu (no) 雑種
(の).

monitor, 1. *n.* kyūchō 級長
(student); monitā モニター (TV).
2. *vb.* miharu 見張る.

monk, *n.* sō 僧.

monkey, *n.* saru 猿.

monogram, *n.* monoguramu モノ
グラム.

monograph, *n.* ronbun 論文.

monologue, *n.* hitorigoto 独り言;
dokuhaku 独白.

monopolize, *vb.* dokusen suru 独
占する (obtain exclusive
possession of).

monopoly, *n.* dokusen 独占

(exclusive possession or control);
senbai 専売 (business).

monorail, *n.* monorēru モノレー
ル.

monotone, *n.* tanchō 単調.

monotonous, *adj.* 1. tanchō (na)
単調 (な) (sounded in one
unvarying tone). 2. taikutsu (na)
退屈 (な) (boring).

monsoon, *n.* monsūn モンスーン.

monster, *n.* kaibutsu 怪物
(creature of abnormal form,
wicked creature).

monstrosity, *n.* 1. kaibutsusei 怪
物性 (character of being
monstrous). 2. kaibutsu 怪物
(monster).

monstrous, *adj.* 1. shūaku (na) 醜
悪 (な) (extremely ugly). 2. hidoi
ひどい (shocking, outrageous). 3.
kyodai (na) 巨大 (な) (huge).

month, *n.* tsuki 月 (calendar
month).

monthly, 1. *n.* gekkanzasshi 月刊
雑誌 (monthly magazine). 2. *adj.*
hitotsuki (no) ひと月 (の);
ikkagetsu (no) 一か月 (の)
(month, computed by the month);
tsuki'ikkai (no) 月一回 (の) (once
a month); maitsuki (no) 毎月 (の)
(every month).

monument, *n.* monyumento モ
ニュメント (memorial structure);
kinenhi 記念碑 (memorial pillar).

monumental, *adj.* 1. kinen (no)
記念 (の) (of a monument). 2.
kakki-teki (na) 画期的 (な)
(historically significant).

moo, *n.* mō もー.

mood, *n.* 1. mūdo ムード; fun'iki
雰囲気 (prevailing emotional tone,
general attitude). 2. kibun 気分
(person's emotional state). 3.
johō 叙法 (grammar).

moody, *adj.* fukigen (na) 不機嫌 (な) (sullen); inki (na) 陰気 (な) (gloomy).

moon, *n.* tsuki 月.

moonlight, *n.* gekkō 月光.

moor, 1. *n.* areno 荒野 (peaty wasteland). 2. *vb.* teihaku suru 停泊する (secure a ship).

moose, *n.* mūsu ムース.

mop, 1. *n.* moppu モップ (for cleaning). 2. *vb.* moppu o kakeru モップをかける (clean with mop).

mope, *vb.* fukureru 膨れる (pout).

moral, 1. *n.* kyōkun 教訓 (moral teaching); *(pl.)* moraru モラル; dōtoku 道徳 (principles of right conduct). 2. *adj.* moraru (no) モラル (の); dōtoku-teki (na) 道徳的 (な) (right conduct); **moral support** seishin-teki na sasae 精神的な支え.

morale, *n.* shiki 士気.

morality, *n.* 1. dōtoku-teki okonai 道徳的行い (moral conduct). 2. dōtokusei 道徳性 (moral quality).

moralize, *vb.* sekkyō suru 説教する.

moratorium, *n.* moratoriamu モラトリアム; yūyo 猶予 (temporary cessation).

morbid, *adj.* 1. inki (na) 陰気 (な) (gloomy). 2. kimi ga warui 気味が悪い (gruesome). 3. byō-teki (na) 病的 (な) (sick).

more, *adj., adv.* 1. yori ōi より多い; motto もっと; sara ni 更に. 2. **all the more** naosara 尚更; **what is more** sono ue ni その上に; **more and more** masu-masu ますます; **more or less** hobo ほぼ; **more than ever** yori issō より一層; **no more** mohaya ... nai もはや...ない (no longer); **no more than** seizei せいぜい; **once more** mō ichido

もう一度; **the more the better** ōkereba ōi hodo ii 多ければ多い程良い.

moreover, *adv.* sono ue ni その上に.

morgue, *n.* shitaihokansho 死体保管所.

moribund, *adj.* shinikakete-iru 死にかけている.

morning, *n., adj.* 1. asa (no) 朝 (の); gozen (no) 午前 (の). 2. **in the morning** gozenchū ni 午前中に; **morning call** mōningu-kōru モーニングコール; **Good morning!** Ohayō gozaimasu. おはようございます.

moron, *n.* baka 馬鹿.

morose, *adj.* fukigen (na) 不機嫌 (な).

morphine, *n.* moruhine モルヒネ.

morsel, *n.* 1. kakera かけら (small piece). 2. hitokuchi 一口 (small piece of food).

mortal, 1. *n.* ningen 人間 (human being). 2. *adj.* ningen (no) 人間 (の) (of human beings); shinu sadame (no) 死ぬ定め (の) (subject to death); chimei-teki (na) 致命的 (な) (causing death); **mortal wound** chimeishō 致命傷.

mortality, *n.* 1. shibōritsu 死亡率 (death rate). 2. shinu sadame 死ぬ定め (mortal nature).

mortar, *n.* morutaru モルタル; shikkui 漆喰 (mixture of lime and cement).

mortgage, 1. *n.* teitō 抵当. 2. *vb.* teitō ni ireru 抵当に入れる.

mortify, *vb.* kuyashigara-seru 悔しがらせる (humiliate, anger).

mortuary, *n.* shitai-karianchisho 死体仮安置所.

mosaic, *n., adj.* mozaiku (no) モザ

イク (の).

Moslem, *n., adj.* isuramu-kyō (no) イスラム教 (の); kaikyō (no) 回教 (の).

mosque, *n.* mosuku モスク; kaikyō-jiin 回教寺院.

mosquito, *n.* ka 蚊.

moss, *n.* koke 苔.

most, 1. *adj.* ichiban ōi 一番多い (greatest in amount); daibubun (no) 大部分 (の) (the majority of). 2. *adv.* ichiban 一番; mottomo 最も (to the greatest extent). 3. **at most** seizei せいぜい; **for the most part** daibubun wa 大部分は; **make the most of** ... o katsuyō suru ...を活用する.

motel, *n.* mōteru モーテル.

moth, *n.* ga 蛾.

mothball, *n.* bōchūzai 防虫剤.

mother, *n.* haha 母; okāsan お母さん.

mother-in-law, *n.* gibo 義母; shūtome 姑.

mother-of-pearl, *n.* shinjugai 真珠貝.

motif, *n.* mochīfu モチーフ (subject); moyō 模様 (pattern).

motion, 1. *n.* ugoki 動き (action, movement); aizu 合図 (signal); teian 提案 (suggestion). 2. *vb.* aizu suru 合図する (signal).

motion picture, *n.* eiga 映画.

motivate, *vb.* suruki ni saseru する気にさせる.

motive, *n.* dōki 動機.

motor, *n.* mōtā モーター.

motorboat, *n.* mōtābōto モーターボート.

motorcycle, *n.* ōtobai オートバイ.

motorist, *n.* untensha 運転者.

mottled, *adj.* madara (no) まだら (の).

motto, *n.* mottō モットー.

mound, *n.* 1. maundo マウンド (baseball). 2. koyama 小山 (small hill).

mount, 1. *n.* yama 山 (mountain). 2. *vb.* noru 乗る (get on); noboru 登る (climb); agaru 上がる (rise); fueru 増える (increase); suetsukeru 据え付ける (install); hiraku 開く (launch).

mountain, *n.* yama 山.

mountaineer, *n.* tozanka 登山家.

mountainous, *adj.* 1. yama ga ōi 山が多い (full of mountains). 2. yama no yō (na) 山のよう (な) (resembling a mountain).

mountaintop, *n.* sanchō 山頂.

mourn, *n.* 1. itamu 悼む (mourn for someone's death). 2. kanashimu 悲しむ (lament).

mourning, *n.* mo 喪.

mouse, *n.* 1. nezumi ねずみ (animal). 2. mausu マウス (computer).

mousetrap, *n.* nezumitori ねずみ取り.

mouth, *n.* 1. kuchi 口 (of an animal, anything resembling a mouth); **mouth of a bottle** bin no kuchi 瓶の口. 2. kakō 河口 (of a river). 3. ana 穴 (opening). 4. iriguchi 入口 (entrance). 5. **by word of mouth** kuchi-komi de 口コミで.

mouthful, *n.* 1. kuchi ippai no ryō 口一杯の量 (as much as a mouth can hold). 2. shōryō 少量 (small portion).

movable, *adj.* ugokaseru 動かせる.

move, 1. *n.* ugoki 動き (movement, purposeful action); iten 移転 (act of going to a new apartment, office, etc.); te 手 (in chess); **get a move on** isogu 急ぐ; **on the move** kappatsu (na) 活発

(な) (active); hattenchū (no) 発展中 (の) (progressing). 2. *vb.* ugoku 動く (change place or position, go, run); ugokasu 動かす (cause to change); hikkosu 引越す (change one's abode); shinten suru 進展する (advance); kandō saseru 感動させる (affect emotionally); teian suru 提案する (propose); **move along** susumu 進む (move further); saru 去る (go away); **move around** ugokimawaru 動き回る; **move in** nyūkyo suru 入居する; **move on** utsuru 移る (change).

movement, *n.* 1. ugoki 動き (action, motion; course or trend of affairs). 2. undō 運動 (organized group of people). 3. idō 移動 (transference).

movie, *n.* eiga 映画; **movie theater** eigakan 映画館.

moving, *adj.* 1. kandō-teki (na) 感動的 (な) (touching). 2. ugoku 動く (that can move).

mow, *vb.* karu 刈る (grass).

Mr., -san -さん; -様 **Mr. Abe** abe-san 阿部さん.

Mrs., -san -さん; -様 **Mrs. Taki** taki-san 滝さん.

much, 1. *adj.* takusan (no) たくさん (の) (in great quantity). 2. *adv.* taihen 大変 (greatly); hobo ほぼ (nearly). 3. **as much as** ... to onaji hodo ...と同じ程; **How much?** Ikura. いくら; **make much of** omonjiru 重んじる; **much more** motto takusan もっとたくさん; **too much for (a person)** (... no) te ni oenai (...の) 手に負えない.

mud, *n.* doro 泥.

muddle, *vb.* 1. konran saseru 混乱させる (make confused). 2.

mecha-mecha ni suru めちゃめちゃにする (mix up).

muddy, 1. *adj.* doro darake (no) 泥だらけ (の) (full of mud). 2. *vb.* doro darake ni suru 泥だらけにする.

muffin, *n.* mafin マフィン.

muffle, *vb.* osaeru 抑える (suppress).

muffler, *n.* mafurā マフラー (scarf, car muffler).

mug, 1. *n.* magu マグ; ōgata-koppu 大型コップ (cup). 2. *vb.* gōtō o hataraku 強盗を働く (rob).

muggy, *adj.* mushiatsui 蒸し暑い.

mugging, *n.* gōtō 強盗.

mulberry, *n.* kuwa no mi 桑の実.

mule, *n.* raba 騾馬.

mull, *vb.* **mull over** kangaeru 考える.

multicolored, *adj.* tashoku (no) 多色 (の).

multinational, *n., adj.* takokuseki (no) 多国籍 (の).

multiple, *adj.* tayō (na) 多様 (な); samazama (no) 様々 (の) (consisting of many).

multiplication, *n.* kakezan 掛け算 (math).

multiplicity, *n.* tayōsei 多様性.

multiply, *vb.* 1. kakeru 掛ける (math). 2. fuyasu 増やす (increase).

multitude, *n.* tasū 多数.

mumble, *vb.* mogu-mogu iu もぐもぐ言う.

mummy, *n.* mīra ミイラ.

mumps, *n.* otafukukaze おたふく風邪.

munch, *vb.* kamu 噛む.

mundane, *adj.* arifureteiru ありふれている (commonplace).

municipal, *adj.* machi (no) 町 (の) (town); shi (no) 市 (の) (city).

municipality, *n.* jichitai 自治体.

munitions, *n.* ōgataheiki 大型兵器.

mural painting, *n.* hekiga 壁画.

murder, 1. *n.* satsujin 殺人. 2. *vb.* korosu 殺す.

murderer, *n.* satsujinsha 殺人者.

murky, *adj.* 1. inki (na) 陰気 (な) (gloomily dark). 2. bon'yari shiteiru ぼんやりしている (obscured with haze).

murmur, 1. *n.* sasayaki ささやき (soft speech); fuhei 不平 (complaint). 2. *vb.* sasayaku ささやく (speak softly); fuhei o iu 不平 を言う (complain).

muscle, *n.* kin'niku 筋肉.

muse, 1. *n.* **Muse** bungei-gakujutsu no megami 文芸学術の 女神. 2. *vb.* kangaekomu 考え込 む; hansū suru 反すうする (meditate).

museum, *n.* hakubutsukan 博物館 (any museum); bijutsukan 美術館 (art museum).

mushroom, *n.* kinoko きのこ.

music, *n.* ongaku 音楽 (art, score).

musical, 1. *n.* myūjikaru ミュージ カル. 2. *adj.* ongaku (no) 音楽 (の) (pertaining to music); ongaku-teki (na) 音楽的 (な) (melodious).

musical instrument, *n.* gakki 楽 器.

musician, *n.* ongakuka 音楽家.

musk, *n.* jakō じゃ香 (fragrance).

musket, *n.* shōjū 小銃.

must, 1. *n.* hitsujuhin 必需品 (anything necessary). 2. *aux. vb.* ... nakereba-naranai ...なければな らない (be obliged to); ... ni chigainai ...に違いない (be reasonably expected to); **must not do** ... subeki dewa nai ...すべ きではない.

mustache, *n.* kuchihige 口髭.

mustard, *n.* masutādo マスタード; karashi 辛子、芥子.

musty, *adj.* kabi kusai かび臭い.

mutant, *n.* henshu 変種 (new type of organism).

mutation, *n.* 1. totsuzenhen'i 突然 変異 (sudden change in offspring). 2. henka 変化 (change).

mute, 1. *n.* rōasha ろうあ者 (deaf person without speech). 2. *adj.* mugon (no) 無言 (の) (without speech).

mutilate, *vb.* sonshō suru 損傷する.

mutiny, 1. *n.* hanran 反乱. 2. *vb.* hanran o okosu 反乱を起こす.

mutt, *n.* zasshu 雑種 (mixed breed).

mutter, *vb.* 1. tsubuyaku 呟く (utter in low tone). 2. fuhei o iu 不平を言う (grumble).

mutton, *n.* maton マトン.

mutual, *adj.* 1. tagai (no) 互い (の) (reciprocal). 2. kyōtsū (no) 共通 (の) (common).

muzzle, *n.* 1. hanazura 鼻面 (snout). 2. kuchiwa 口輪 (to control animal). 3. jūkō 銃口 (rifle).

my, *adj.* watashi no 私の.

myopia, *n.* kinshi 近視; kingan 近 眼.

myriad, *n.* musū 無数.

myself, *pron.* watashijishin 私自身.

mysterious, *adj.* 1. nazo (no) 謎 (の); fushigi (na) 不思議 (な) (enigmatic). 2. shinpi-teki (na) 神 秘的 (な) (supernatural).

mystery, *n.* 1. misuterī ミステリ ー; nazo 謎 (enigma). 2. shinpi 神 秘 (supernatural event). 3.

mystery novel misuterī-shōsetsu ミステリー小説; suiri-shōsetsu 推 理小説.

mystic, *n.* shinpishugisha 神秘主義者.

mystify, *vb.* tōwaku saseru 当惑させる.

myth, *n.* 1. shinwa 神話 (legendary story). 2. meishin 迷信 (false popular belief).

mythology, *n.* 1. shinwa 神話 (body of myths). 2. shinwagaku 神話学 (study of myth).

N

nab, *vb.* tsukamaeru 捕まえる; toraeru 捕える.

nag, *vb.* gami-gami iu がみがみ言う (pester); shitsukoku kogoto o iu しつこく小言を言う (scold constantly).

nail, 1. *n.* kugi 釘 (metal); tsume 爪 (fingernail). 2. *vb.* kugi o utsu 釘を打つ (fasten); **nail down** kotei suru 固定する (fasten down); kakujitsu ni suru 確実にする (make definite).

nail polish, *n.* manikyua マニキュア.

naïve, *adj.* ubu (na) うぶ (な); soboku (na) 素朴 (な); naïbu (na) ナイーブ (な).

naked, *adj.* hadaka (no) 裸 (の).

nakedness, *n.* hadaka 裸.

name, 1. *n.* namae 名前; meishō 名称 (designating object or person); meisei 名声 (reputation). 2. *vb.* nazukeru 名付ける (give name to); na o ageru 名をあげる (identify); shimei/ninmei suru 指名／任命する (appoint); shitei suru 指定する (specify).

namely, *adv.* sunawachi 即ち; tsumari つまり.

nap, 1. *n.* hirune 昼寝 (daytime sleep); inemuri 居眠り (doze). 2. *vb.* hirune o suru 昼寝をする; inemuri o suru 居眠りをする.

nape, *n.* erikubi 襟首.

napkin, *n.* napukin ナプキン.

narcissus, *n.* suisen 水仙.

narcotic, *n.* 1. kakuseizai 覚醒剤; mayaku 麻薬 (drug). 2. masuizai 麻酔剤 (anesthetic).

narrate, *vb.* kataru 語る; hanasu 話す.

narration, *n.* katari 語り; hanashi 話.

narrative, 1. *n.* hanashi 話; monogatari 物語. 2. *adj.* monogatari (no) 物語 (の) (of a narrative); suji ga aru 筋がある (having a story).

narrator, *n.* katarite 語り手; narētā ナレーター.

narrow, 1. *adj.* semai 狭い (of little breadth or width); kagirareta 限られた (limited); yatto (no) やっと (の) (barely adequate or successful). 2. *vb.* sebameru 狭める (make narrow); kagiru 限る (limit).

narrowly, *adv.* nantoka 何とか; karōjite 辛うじて (barely).

narrow-minded, *adj.* kokoro no semai 心の狭い.

nasal, *adj.* 1. hana (no) 鼻 (の) (of nose). 2. bion (no) 鼻音 (の) (sound).

nasty, *adj.* 1. kitanai 汚い (unclean). 2. iya (na) 嫌 (な); fukai (na) 不快 (な) (unpleasant). 3. ijiwaru (na) 意地悪 (な); hiretsu (na) 卑劣 (な) (vicious, mean-spirited).

nation, *n.* 1. kokka 国家; kuni 国 (country). 2. kokumin 国民 (people).

national, *adj.* 1. kokka (no) 国家 (の); kuni (no) 国 (の). 2. kokumin (no) 国民 (の). 3. zenkoku (no) 全国 (の) (nationwide).

national debt, *n.* kokkazaisei-akaji 国家財政赤字.

nationalism, *n.* aikoku/kokka shugi 愛国／国家主義.

nationality, *n.* kokuseki 国籍.

nationalize, *vb.* kokueika suru 国営化する.

native, 1. *adj.* bokoku/jikoku (no) 母国／自国 (の) (of one's nation); umaretsuki (no) 生まれつき (の) (by birth); jimoto (no) 地元 (の) (of local area); genjūmin (no) 現住民 (の) (of original inhabitants); **native language** bokokugo/jikokugo. 2. *n.* jimoto no hito 地元の人 (local people); genjūmin 原住民 (original inhabitants); ... umare no hito ...生まれの人 (person born in a particular place).

natural, *adj.* 1. shizen (na, no) 自然 (な、の) (of nature, formed by nature; to be expected; unchanged). 2. umaretsuki (no) 生まれつき (の) (inborn). 3. ten'nen (no) 天然 (の) (existing in nature); **natural resources** ten'nenshigen 天然資源.

naturalize, *vb.* **be naturalized** 1. kika suru 帰化する (become a citizen). 2. dōka suru 同化する; tekiō suru 適応する (become adapted).

naturally, *adv.* 1. mochiron もちろ

ん; tōzen 当然 (as would be expected). 2. umaretsuki 生まれ つき; seirai 生来 (inherent in character). 3. shizen ni/to 自然 に／と (according to nature).

nature, *n.* 1. shizen 自然 (Nature). 2. seikaku 性格 (character of person); seishitsu/tokushitsu 性質／特質 (characteristic of animal or object). 3. shurui 種類 (sort).

naught, *n.* mu 無.

naughty, *adj.* 1. gyōgi ga warui 行儀が悪い (badly behaved). 2. futekitō (na) 不適当 (な) (improper).

nausea, *n.* 1. hakike 吐き気 (desire to vomit). 2. mukatsuki/iyake む かつき／嫌気 (disgust).

nautical, *adj.* sen'in (no) 船員 (の) (of sailors); fune (no) 船 (の) (of ships); kōkai (no) 航海 (の) (of navigation).

naval, *adj.* kaigun (no) 海軍 (の).

navel, *n.* (o)heso (お)へそ.

navigate, *vb.* 1. kōkō suru 航行す る (travel). 2. an'nai suru 案内す る (direct).

navigation, *n.* kōkō 航行.

navigator, *n.* kōkaishi 航海士 (ship); pairotto パイロット (aircraft).

navy, *n.* kaigun 海軍.

near, 1. *adj.* chikai 近い. 2. *adv.* chikaku de/ni 近くで／に. 3. *prep.* (... no) chikaku de/ni (...の) 近く で／に.

nearby, 1. *adj.* chikaku/soba (no) 近く／側 (の). 2. *adv.* chikaku/soba ni 近く／側に.

nearly, *adv.* hotondo ほとんど.

near-sighted, *adj.* kinshi/kingan (no) 近視／近眼 (の).

neat, *adj.* 1. kichin to shita きちん とした (tidy). 2. kireizuki (na) き

れい好き (な) (habitually orderly).
3. kirei (na) きれい (な) (good-looking); kimochi ga ii 気持がいい
(pleasant); ii 良い (good). 4. ki ga
kiita 気が利いた (cleverly
effective).

necessary, *adj.* hitsuyō (na) 必要
(な).

necessity, *n.* hitsuyō 必要.

neck, *n.* kubi 首.

necklace, *n.* kubikazari 首飾り;
nekkuresu ネックレス.

neckline, *n.* nekkurain ネックラ
イン.

necktie, *n.* nekutai ネクタイ.

need, 1. *n.* hitsuyō 必要
(necessity); hinkon 貧困
(poverty). 2. *vb.* hitsuyō to suru
必要とする; iru 要る (require).
　need to ... (shi)-nakerebanaranai
　...(し)なければならない (be
　obliged).

needle, *n.* hari 針.

needless, *adj.* fuyō (na) 不要 (な);
iranai 要らない; **needless to say**
mochiron もちろん.

needy, *adj.* mazushii 貧しい.

negate, *vb.* 1. uchikesu 打ち消す;
dame ni suru だめにする (nullify).
2. hitei suru 否定する (deny).

negative, 1. *adj.* hitei (no) 否定
(の); hitei-teki (na) 否定的 (な)
(expressing negation, denying);
shōkyoku-teki (na) 消極的 (な)
(lacking positive attitude); hantai
(no) 反対 (の) (contrary); mainasu
(no) マイナス (の) (negative
number, detracting quality). 2. *n.*
hitei 否定 (negation, denial);
hiteikei 否定形 (negative word);
nega ネガ; inga 陰画
(photographic image).

neglect, 1. *vb.* mushi suru 無視す
る (disregard); orosoka ni suru お

ろそかにする; okotaru 怠る (be
remiss). 2. *n.* mushi 無視
(disregard); hōchi 放置; taiman 怠
慢 (negligence).

negligée, *n.* negurije ネグリジェ.

negligent, *adj.* 1. taiman (na) 怠慢
(な) (guilty of neglect). 2. fuchūi
(na) 不注意 (な) (unheeding).

negligible, *adj.* toru ni tarinai 取る
に足りない; wazuka (na) わずか
(な).

negotiate, *vb.* kōshō suru 交渉す
る.

negotiation, *n.* kōshō 交渉.

neigh, 1. *n.* inanaki いななき. 2.
vb. inanaku いななく.

neighbor, *n.* kinjo no hito 近所の
人; rinjin 隣人.

neighborhood, *n.* kinjo 近所;
fukin 付近.

neighboring, *adj.* tonari (no) 隣り
(の); sessuru 接する.

neither, 1. *pron., adj.* dochira (no
...) mo ... nai どちら (の...) も...な
い; 2. *conj.* **neither ... nor** ... mo
... mo ... nai; ... mo (... nai).
　Neither can I. Watashi mo
　dekinai 私も出来ない.

neon, *n.* neon ネオン.

nephew, *n.* oi 甥.

nerve, *n.* 1. shinkei 神経 (physical).
2. yūki 勇気 (courage). 3.
atsukamashisa 厚かましさ
(impudence).

nervous, *adj.* 1. shinkeishitsu (na,
no) 神経質 (な、の) (easily upset,
fearful). 2. shinkei (no) 神経 (の)
(pertaining to nerves). 3. shinpai
(na) 心配 (な) (worried).

nest, *n.* su 巣.

net, 1. *adj.* shōmi (no) 正味 (の)
(amount). 2. *n.* ami 網; netto ネッ
ト (mesh). 3. *vb.* ami de kakomu
網で囲む (enclose); ami de toraeru

網で捕える (catch).

Netherlands, 1. *n.* oranda オラン
ダ. 2. *adj.* oranda (no) オランダ
(の) (of the Netherlands).

network, *n.* 1. nettowāku ネット
ワーク. 2. hōsōmō 放送網
(broadcasting).

neurology, *n.* shinkeigaku 神経学.

neurotic, 1. *adj.* shinkeishō (no) 神
経症 (の); noirōzē (no) ノイローゼ
ー (の). 2. *n.* shinkeishō no hito
神経症の人.

neuter, *adj.* chūsei (no) 中性 (の).

neutral, *adj.* chūritsu (no) 中立
(の) (impartial); chūsei (no) 中性
(の) (chemical).

neutrality, *n.* chūritsu 中立.

neutron, *n.* nyūtoron ニュート
ロン; chūseishi 中性子.

never, *adv.* kesshite/zettai ... nai 決
して／絶対...ない.

nevertheless, *adv.* sore nimo
kakawarazu それにもかかわらず;
sore demo それでも.

new, *adj.* atarashii 新しい.

new- 1. shin 新; **new theory**
shinsetsu 新説. 2. (... ta) bakari
(no) (...た) ばかり (の); **newborn**
umareta bakari (no) 生まれたばか
り (の).

newly, *adv.* atarashiku 新しく.

newlywed, *n.* shinkon(san) 新婚
(さん).

news, *n.* nyūsu ニュース.

newsboy, *n.* shinbunhaitatsu 新聞
配達 (deliverer); shinbun'uri 新聞
売り (seller).

newscast, *n.* nyūsu-bangumi
ニュース番組; nyūsu-hōsō ニュー
ス放送.

newsletter, *n.* kaihō 会報.

newspaper, *n.* shinbun 新聞.

newsstand, *n.* shinbunbaiten 新聞
売店.

New Year, *n.* shin'nen 新年.

New Year's Day, *n.* ganjitsu 元日;
gantan 元旦.

New Year's Eve, *n.* ōmisoka 大晦
日.

New York, *n.* nyū-yōku ニュー
ヨーク.

next, 1. *adj.* tsugi (no) 次 (の)
(immediately following); tonari
(no) 隣り (の) (adjacent). 2. *adv.*
tsugi ni 次に (nearest in space). 3.
next-door tonari no ie 隣りの家
(next-door neighbor); **next to** (...
no) tonari (...の) 隣り (adjacent);
hotondo ほとんど (almost); **next
day** yokujitsu 翌日; **next week**
raishū 来週; **next month** raigetsu
来月; **next year** rainen 来年.

nibble, *vb.* sukoshizutsu taberu 少
しずつ食べる; kajiru かじる.

nice, *adj.* 1. ii 良い (good, fine,
pleasant). 2. yasashii 優しい
(kind).

nickname, *n.* adana あだ名;
nikkunēmu ニックネーム.

niece, *n.* mei 姪.

night, *n.* yoru 夜; ban 晩; **good
night** oyasuminasai おやすみなさ
い; **last night** sakuban 昨晩; kinō
no ban/yoru 昨日の晩／夜.

night club, *n.* naito-kurabu ナイト
クラブ.

nightfall, *n.* yūgure 夕暮れ;
tasogare たそがれ.

nightgown, *n.* nemaki 寝巻.

nightingale, *n.* naichingēru ナイチ
ンゲール.

nightmare, *n.* akumu 悪夢.

nimble, *adj.* 1. keikai (na) 軽快
(な); kibin (na) 機敏 (な) (quick
and light in movement). 2.
monowakari ga hayai 物わかりが
早い (quick to understand).

nine, *n.* kyū 九; kokonotsu 九つ.

nine hundred, *n.* kyūhyaku 九百.

nineteen, *n.* jūkyū 十九.

ninety, *n.* kyūjū 九十.

ninth, *adj.* daikyū (no) 第九 (の); kyūbanme (no) 九番目 (の).

nip, *vb.* 1. hasamu 挟む (pinch). 2. kamu 噛む (bite).

nipple, *n.* chikubi 乳首.

nitrogen, *n.* chisso 窒素.

no, 1. *adj.* ... nai ...ない. 2. *adv.* iie いいえ.

nobility, *n.* 1. kizoku 貴族 (person). 2. kedakasa 気高さ (noble quality).

noble, *adj.* 1. kedakai 気高い; kōki (na) 高貴 (な) (moral excellence). 2. kizoku (no) 貴族 (の) (of high rank by birth).

nobleman, -woman, *n.* kizoku 貴族.

nobody, 1. *n.* mumei no hito 無名の人. 2. *pron.* daremo ... nai 誰も...ない.

nocturnal, *adj.* 1. ban/yoru (no) 晩／夜 (の); yakan (no) 夜間 (の) (of night). 2. yakōsei (no) 夜行性 (の) (animal).

nod, 1. *n.* unazuki 頷き (inclination of head). 2. *vb.* unazuku 頷く (incline head); inemuri suru 居眠りする (become sleepy).

noise, *n.* sōon 騒音; zatsuon 雑音.

noisy, *adj.* urusai うるさい.

nominal, *adj.* 1. namae dake (no) 名前だけ (の) (in name only). 2. wazuka (no) わずか (の) (small).

nominate, *vb.* 1. shimei suru 指名する; ageru あげる (name a candidate). 2. ninmei suru 任命する (appoint).

nomination, *n.* 1. shimei 指名 (select candidate). 2. ninmei 任命 (appointment).

nominee, *n.* kōhosha 候補者 (nominated person).

non- hi-, mu- 非、無-; **non-profit** hieiri (no) 非営利 (の).

nonchalant, *adj.* mutonchaku (na) 無着 (な).

noncommittal, *adj.* ayafuya (na) あやふや (な); aimai (na) あいまい (な).

nonconformist, *n.* kata ni hamaranai hito 型にはまらない人; hitsuizuisha 非追随者.

nondescript, *adj.* arifureta ありふれた (ordinary); tsumaranai つまらない (dull); hakkiri shinai はっきりしない (not easily described).

none, *pron.* nani/dore mo(... nai) 何／どれも(...ない) (not any); dare mo (... nai) 誰も(...ない) (nobody).

nonexistent, *adj.* (sonzai shi)nai (存在し)ない.

nonetheless, *adv.* sore nimo kakawarazu それにもかかわらず; soredemo それでも.

nonfiction, *n.* non-fikushon ノンフィクション.

nonsense, *n.* nansensu ナンセンス; tawagoto たわ言; kudaranai koto 下らない事.

nonsmoking, *adj.* kin'en (no) 禁煙 (の); **nonsmoking seat** kin'enseki 禁煙席.

nonstop, *adj.* chokkō (no) 直行 (の); non-sutoppu (no) ノンストップ (の).

noodle, *n.* men めん; udon うどん (wheat); soba そば (buckwheat).

nook, *n.* katasumi 片隅.

noon, *n.* shōgo 正午; gogo jūniji 午後十二時.

no one, *pron.* dare mo ... nai 誰も...ない.

nor, *conj.* (...) mo ... nai (...) も...な

い; **neither ... nor** ... mo ... mo ... nai ...も...も...ない.

norm, *n.* 1. kijun 基準 (standard). 2. noruma ノルマ (expected number).

normal, *adj.* futsū (no) 普通 (の); nōmaru (na) ノーマル (な).

north, *n., adj.* kita (no) 北 (の).

North America, *n.* kita-amerika 北アメリカ; hokubei 北米.

northeast, *n., adj.* hokutō (no) 北東 (の).

northern, *adj.* kita (no) 北 (の).

North Pole, *n.* hokkyoku 北極.

northwest, *n., adj.* hokusei (no) 北西 (の).

nose, *n.* hana 鼻.

nosebleed, *n.* hanaji 鼻血.

nosedive, *n.* kyūkōka 急降下.

nostalgia, *n.* kyōshū 郷愁; nosutarujia ノスタルジア.

nostalgic, *adj.* kyōshū-teki (na) 郷愁的 (な); natsukashii 懐かしい.

nostril, *n.* hana no ana 鼻の穴.

nosy, *adj.* sensakuzuki (na) 詮索好き (な).

not, *adv.* (de) nai (で) ない; **not at all** zen'zen/mattaku ... nai 全然／全く...ない.

notable, *adj.* chūmoku subeki 注目すべき.

notary, *n.* kōshōnin 公証人.

notch, *n.* kizamime 刻み目.

note, 1. *n.* 1. memo メモ (record); oboegaki 覚え書き (reminder); hashirigaki 走り書き (quick letter); jūyō 重要 (importance); chūmoku 注目 (notice); yakusoku-tegata 約束手形 (paper promising payment); onpu 音符 (music); **notes** shuki 手記; kiroku 記録 (written summary). 2. *vb.* memo o toru メモを取る (write); kiroku suru 記録する; chūmoku

suru 注目する (pay attention); kizuku 気付く (recognize); genkyū suru 言及する (mention).

notebook, *n.* nōto ノート; chōmen 帳面.

noted, *adj.* yūmei (na) 有名 (な).

noteworthy, *adj.* ichijirushii 著しい.

nothing, *n.* nani mo ... nai 何も...ない; **for nothing** tada de 只で (free of charge); muda ni 無駄に (in vain); **nothing but** ... nomi ... のみ; **have nothing to do with** ... towa kankei ga nai ...とは関係がない.

notice, 1. *n.* tsūchi 通知; shirase 知らせ (information); keikoku 警告 (warning); kaikotsūkoku 解雇通告 (termination of employment); chūi/chūmoku 注意／注目 (attention); **on short notice** kyū ni 急に; **take notice of** ... ni chūi/chūmoku suru. 2. *vb.* ... ni chūmoku suru ...に注目する (pay attention to); ... ni ki ga tsuku ...に気が付く (perceive); noberu 述べる (mention).

noticeable, *adj.* 1. akiraka (na) 明らか (な) (visible). 2. chūmoku ni atai suru 注目に値する (noteworthy).

notification, *n.* shirase 知らせ; tsūchi 通知.

notify, *vb.* (... ni) ... o shiraseru (...に) ... を知らせる; (... ni) ... o tsūchi suru (...に) ... を通知する.

notion, *n.* 1. gainen 概念 (general idea). 2. iken 意見; kangae 考え (opinion, view).

notoriety, *n.* akumyō 悪名.

notorious, *adj.* akumyō takai 悪名高い.

notwithstanding, *adv.* sore demo nao それでもなお; sore nimo

kakawarazu それにもかかわらず.

noun, *n.* meishi 名詞.

nourish, *vb.* yashinau 養う; eiyō o ataeru 栄養を与える.

nourishment, *n.* 1. eiyō 栄養 (nutrition). 2. ikusei 育成 (act of nourishing).

novel, 1. *adj.* atarashii 新しい (new). 2. *n.* shōsetsu 小説 (book).

novelist, *n.* shōsetsuka 小説家; sakka 作家.

novelty, *n.* 1. atarashisa 新しさ (being novel). 2. atarashii koto/mono 新しい事／物 (novel experience, thing).

November, *n.* jūichigatsu 十一月.

novice, *n.* shoshinsha 初心者 (beginner).

now, *adv.* ima 今; **now and then** tokidoki 時々; **by now** imagoro wa (mō) 今ごろは (もう); **from now on** korekara これから; **just now** tatta ima たった今 (a moment ago); mokka 目下 (at this moment); **right now** imasugu ni 今すぐに (right away).

nowadays, *adv.* kon'nichi 今日; chikagoro 近頃.

nowhere, *adv.* doko nimo ... nai ど こにも...ない.

nozzle, *n.* nozuru ノズル; kuchi 口.

nuance, *n.* nyuansu ニュアンス; bimyō na chigai 微妙な違い.

nuclear, *adj.* 1. kaku (no) 核 (の) (of nucleus). 2. genshiryoku (no) 原子力 (の) (of atomic energy); **nuclear power** genshiryoku 原子力.

nucleus, *n.* 1. chūshin 中心 (center). 2. kaku 核 (living cell). 3. genshikaku 原子核 (atom).

nude, *adj.* hadaka (no) 裸 (の); nūdo (no) ヌード (の).

nudge, *vb.* 1. hiji de tsuku 肘で突

く (push with one's elbow). 2. wakeiru 分け入る (push into).

nudist, *n.* nūdisuto ヌーディスト.

nudity, *n.* ratai 裸体; hadaka 裸.

nugget, *n.* 1. nagetto ナゲット (food). 2. katamari 塊 (lump).

nuisance, *n.* 1. meiwakumono 迷 惑者 (person). 2. meiwaku na koto 迷惑な事 (thing). 3. meiwaku 迷惑; yakkai 厄介 (annoyance, trouble).

null, *adj.* 1. mukō (na, no) 無効 (な、の) (of no effect). 2. zero (no) ゼロ (の); mu (no) 無 (の) (nil).

nullify, *vb.* mukō ni suru 無効にす る.

numb, *adj.* mukankaku (no) 無感 覚 (の); shibireta しびれた.

number, 1. *n.* kazu 数; sūji 数字 (figure, amount); bangō 番号 (assigned number); **telephone number** denwabangō; **a large number of** tasū (no) 多数 (の). 2. *vb.* kazoeru 数える (count); ... ni tassuru ...に達する (amount to); bangō o tsukeru 番号を付ける (give a number to).

numerical, *adj.* 1. kazu (no) 数 (の); bangō (no) 番号 (の); kazu ni kansuru 数に関する (pertaining to numbers).

numerous, *adj.* obitadashii 夥しい; takusan (no) たくさん (の).

nun, *n.* shūdōjo 修道女; shisutā シ スター.

nuptial, 1. *adj.* kekkon (no) 結婚 (の); kekkonshiki (no) 結婚式 (の). 2. *n.* **nuptials** kekkon (marriage); kekkonshiki (marriage ceremony).

nurse, 1. *n.* kangofu 看護婦 (person who cares for the sick); uba 乳母 (wet nurse); hobo 保母

(dry nurse). 2. *vb.* kango suru 看護する (tend in sickness); junyū suru 授乳する (suckle); sodateru 育てる (feed and tend).

nursemaid, *n.* komori 子守り.

nursery, *n.* 1. kodomobeya 子供部屋 (room). 2. hoikuen 保育園 (nursery school). 3. shubyōen 種苗園 (plants).

nursery rhyme, *n.* dōyō 童謡.

nursery school, *n.* hoikuen 保育園.

nursing home, *n.* 1. yōrōin 養老院; rōjin-hōmu 老人ホーム (for aged people). 2. ryōyōsho 療養所 (for the infirm).

nurture, *vb.* sodateru 育てる.

nut, *n.* ki/ko no mi 木の実; nattsu ナッツ (seed). 2. natto ナット (for bolt).

nutrient, *n.* yōbun 養分.

nutrition, *n.* eiyō 栄養.

nutritious, *adj.* eiyō ga aru 栄養がある; jiyō ni tomu 滋養に富む.

nylon, *n.* nairon ナイロン.

nymph, *n.* ninfu ニンフ; yōsei 妖精.

O

oaf, *n.* tonma 頓馬; usunoro 薄のろ (dunce).

oak, *n.* kashi (no ki) 樫 (の木); ōku オーク.

oar, *n.* kai 櫂; ōru オール.

oasis, *n.* oashisu オアシス.

oat, *n.* karasumugi 烏麦.

oath, *n.* 1. chikai 誓い (vow). 2. fukei na kotoba 不敬な言葉 (blasphemous words).

oatmeal, *n.* ōtomīru オートミール.

obedience, *n.* fukujū 服従.

obedient, *adj.* jūjun (na) 従順 (な); otonashii おとなしい.

obese, *adj.* futtoteiru 太っている; himan (no) 肥満 (の).

obey, *vb.* ... ni fukujū suru ...に服従する; ... ni shitagau ...に従う.

obituary, *n.* shibōkiji 死亡記事.

object, 1. *n.* buttai 物体; mono 物 (thing); taishō 対象 (focus of attention); mokuteki 目的 (end); mokutekigo 目的語 (grammatical). 2. *vb.* hantai suru 反対する.

objection, *n.* hantai 反対; igi 意義.

objective, 1. *adj.* kyakkan-teki (na) 客観的 (な). 2. *n.* mokuteki 目的 (end).

obligate, *vb.* gimuzukeru 義務づける.

obligation, *n.* 1. gimu 義務 (duty). 2. giri 義理 (moral indebtedness).

obligatory, *adj.* kyōsei-teki (na) 強制的 (な) (mandatory).

oblige, *vb.* 1. ... sezaru o enaku suru ...せざるを得なくする (require or constrain to do). 2. on ni kiseru 恩に着せる (place under debt of gratitude). 3. on o hodokosu 恩を施す (do favor for). 4. **be obliged** kansha suru 感謝する (feel grateful); **be obliged to do** ... shinakutewa-naranai ...しなくてはならない (must do).

oblique, *adj.* 1. naname (no) 斜め (の) (slanting). 2. kansetsu-teki (na) 間接的 (な) (indirect).

obliterate, *vb.* keshisaru 消し去る (erase).

oblivion, *n.* bōkyaku 忘却.

obnoxious, *adj.* hatameiwaku (na) はた迷惑 (な) (bothersome); fukai (na) 不快 (な) (unpleasant).

obscene, *adj.* hiwai (na) 卑猥 (な); midara (na) 淫ら (な).

obscenity, *n.* hiwai 卑猥; midara 淫ら.

obscure, 1. *adj.* aimai (na) あいまい (な); hakkirishinai はっきりしない (not clear); mumei (no) 無名 (の) (unknown); kurai 暗い (dark). 2. *vb.* kakusu 隠す (conceal, cover); kuraku suru 暗くする (make dark).

obsequious, *adj.* gokigentori (no) ご機嫌取り (の); kobiru 媚びる.

observance, *n.* 1. junshu 遵守; jikkō 実行 (obeying, following). 2. iwai 祝い (due celebration); shikiten 式典 (ceremony).

observant, *adj.* chūibukai 注意深い; surudoi 鋭い (alert).

observation, *n.* 1. kansatsu 観察 (act of watching closely). 2. kansatsuryoku 観察力 (ability to notice). 3. iken 意見 (remark).

observatory, *n.* tentai-kansokusho 天体観測所.

observe, *vb.* 1. kansatsu suru 観察する (watch closely). 2. chūi suru 注意する (pay attention). 3. mamoru 守る (obey). 4. iwau 祝う (celebrate). 5. noberu 述べる (comment).

observer, *n.* obuzābā オブザーバー; kansatsusha 観察者.

obsess, *vb.* toritsuku 取り憑く; **be obsessed with** ... ni toritsukarete iru ...に取り憑かれている.

obsession, *n.* toritsuki 取り憑き; kyōhakukan'nen 強迫観念.

obsolete, *adj.* 1. sutareta 廃れた (out of use). 2. haigo (no) 廃語 (の) (linguistic form).

obstacle, *n.* shōgai 障害.

obstetrics, *n.* sankagaku 産科学.

obstinate, *adj.* ganko (na) 頑固 (な).

obstruct, *vb.* jama suru 邪魔する; bōgai suru 妨害する.

obstruction, *n.* jama 邪魔; bōgai 妨害.

obtain, *vb.* te ni ireru 手に入れる; eru 得る (get, acquire).

obvious, *adj.* akiraka (na) 明らか (な); meihaku (na) 明白 (な).

occasion, 1. *n.* toki 時 (particular time); taisetsu na toki 大切な時 (important time); moyo'oshi 催し (event); kikai 機会 (opportunity); riyū 理由 (reason). 2. *vb.* hikiokosu 引き起こす.

occasional, *adj.* tokiori (no) 時折 (の); tokidoki (no) 時々 (の).

occasionally, *adv.* tokiori 時折; tokidoki 時々.

occult, *adj.* okaruto (no) オカルト (の); chōshizen-teki (na) 超自然的 (な).

occupant, *n.* 1. kyaku 客. 2. kyojūsha 居住者 (resident). 3. karite 借り手 (tenant).

occupation, *n.* 1. shokugyō 職業; shigoto 仕事 (work). 2. senryō 占領 (military takeover); **occupation army** senryōgun 占領軍.

occupy, *vb.* 1. (... o) shimeru (...を) 占める (fill, hold attention of). 2. (... ni) sumu (...に) 住む (inhabit); (... ni) iru (...に) いる (be in). 3. senryō suru 占領する (by military invasion).

occur, *vb.* 1. okoru 起こる (happen, present itself). 2. (kokoro ni) ukabu (心に) 浮かぶ (come to mind).

occurrence, *n.* dekigoto 出来事 (incident).

ocean, *n.* umi 海; -yō -洋; **Pacific**

Ocean taiheiyō 太平洋; **Atlantic Ocean** taiseiyō 大西洋.

o'clock, *adv.* -ji -時; **It is one o'clock.** Ichiji desu 一時です. **at two o'clock** niji ni 二時に.

October, *n.* jūgatsu 十月.

octopus, *n.* tako 蛸.

oculist, *n.* gankai 眼科医.

odd, *adj.* 1. kimyō (na) 奇妙 (な); kawatta 変わった (strange). 2. kisū (no) 奇数 (の) (number). 3. hanpa (no) 半ぱ (の) (not part of set).

oddity, *n.* henjin 変人 (person); hen na mono 変な物 (strange object).

odds, *n.* 1. kachime 勝ち目; kanōsei 可能性 (probability to win). 2. handikyappu ハンディキャップ (handicap). 3. **be at odds with** ... to (iken ga) awanai ...と (意見が) が合わない; **odds and ends** yoseatsume 寄せ集め; hanpamono 半ぱ物.

ode, *n.* jojōshi 叙情詩; shōka 唱歌.

odious, *adj.* hijō ni iya (na) 非常に嫌 (な).

odor, *n.* nioi 匂い.

of, *prep.* 1. ...no ...の (belonging to, by, possessed or ruled by). 2. ...kara ...から (from, so as to be rid of). 3. ...de ...で (owing to, made with). 4. ... no aru ...のある (having particular qualities). 5. ... ni tsuite no ...についての (concerning).

off, 1. *adj.* machigatteiru 間違っている (in error); torikesareta 取り消された (no longer in effect); hima (na) 暇 (な) (free from duty). 2. *adv.* hanarete 離れて (up, away); torete 取れて (coming off); mukō ni 向こうに (at a distance); tomatte 止まって (not

in operation); yasunde 休んで (in absence); **be off** ... o yasumu ...を休む (be absent); hanareru 離れる (leave); iku 行く (leave); **come off** toreru 取れる; **get off** oriru 降りる; **take off** nugu 脱ぐ (undress); **turn off** tomeru 止める; kesu 消す; **off and on** tokiori 時折 (with intervals between); **be well off** yutaka de aru 豊かである (be rich); **20 percent off** niwaribiki de 二割引で. 3. *prep.* ...kara ...から (away from); ... kara hanarete ...から離れて (apart from); ... yori shita de/ni ...より下で／に (below the standard); ... nashi de ...なしで (without).

offend, *vb.* okoraseru 怒らせる (anger); kizutsukeru 傷つける (hurt); **be offended** okoru 怒る.

offense, *n.* 1. hanzai 犯罪 (crime); ihan 違反 (violation). 2. kōgeki 攻撃 (attack). 3. rippuku 立腹 (anger); hankan 反感 (resentment); **take offense at** ni rippuku suru ...に立腹する.

offensive, *adj.* 1. fukai (na) 不快 (な) (irritating, unpleasant). 2. kōgeki (no) 攻撃 (の) (pertaining to attack).

offer, 1. *n.* mōshide 申し出 (something offered); mōshikomi 申し込み (proposal). 2. *vb.* teikyō suru 提供する (hold out); teian suru 提案する (propose); hikiukeru 引き受ける (volunteer).

offering, *n.* 1. (o)sonae(mono) (お)供え(物) (at altar). 2. kenkin 献金 (money given at church); saisen 賽銭 (money given at temple).

offhand, *adj.* sokuseki (no) 即席 (の) (unplanned); kudaketa 砕けた (informal).

office, *n.* 1. ofisu オフィス; jimusho 事務所; shigotoba 仕事場; kaisha 会社 (place of business). 2. shinsatsushitsu 診察室 (doctor's office); kurinikku クリニック (clinic). 3. yakusho 役所 (public office); **take office** shūnin suru 就任する.

office hours, *n.* 1. eigyōjikan 営業時間 (business). 2. shinsatsujikan 診察時間 (clinic). 3. mensetsu-jikan 面接時間 (school).

officer, *n.* 1. keikan 警官 (police). 2. shōkō 将校 (military). 3. kanryō 官僚 (government); yakuin 役員 (corporation).

official, 1. *adj.* kōshiki (no) 公式 (の) (formal); kōnin (no) 公認 (の) (authorized); ōyake (no) 公 (の) (public). 2. *n.* yakunin 役人; kōmuin 公務員 (public official).

offspring, *n.* shison 子孫.

often, *adv.* shiba-shiba しばしば; yoku よく.

off-the-record, *adj.* hikōkai (no) 非公開 (の).

ogle, *vb.* irome tappuri ni miru 色目たっぷりに見る.

oil, 1. *n.* abura 油 (liquid); sekiyu 石油 (petroleum); **oil painting** aburae; **oil well** yuden 油田. 2. *vb.* abura o sasu 油を注す.

oily, *adj.* 1. beto-beto shitaべとべとした (greasy). 2. abura ga ōi 油が多い (full of oil). 3. abura (no) 油 (の) (of oil). 4. nameraka (na) 滑らか (な) (smooth).

ointment, *n.* nankō 軟膏.

okay, O.K., *adj., adv., interj.* 1. ii 良い; ōkē オーケー; daijōbu 大丈夫 (good, right, adequate, feeling well; fine, all right). 2. wakarimashita 分かりました (in agreement).

okra, *n.* okura オクラ.

old, *adj.* 1. furui 古い (objects and concepts); toshi totta 年取った; toshiyori (no) 年寄り (の) (people, animals); **old man/woman** toshiyori 年寄り; rōjin 老人. 2. ... sai (no) ...歳 (の) (of one's age); ... **years old** ... sai desu ...歳です; **How old is ...?** ... wa nansai desu ka ...は何歳ですか. 3. mae (no) 前 (の) (former).

old age, *n.* rōnen 老年.

older, *adj.* toshiue (no) 年上 (の) (senior); **older than** ...yori toshiue (no) ...より年上 (の) (older than); **older brother** ani 兄; oniisan お兄さん.

old-fashioned, *adj.* jidaiokure (no) 時代遅れ (の); kyūshiki (na) 旧式 (な).

old maid, *n.* ōrudo-misu オールドミス.

olive, *n.* orību オリーブ.

olive oil, *n.* orību-oiru/-yu オリーブオイル／～油.

Olympics, *n.* orinpikku(-taikai) オリンピック(大会).

omelet, *n.* omuretsu オムレツ.

omen, *n.* maebure 前触れ; kizashi 兆し.

ominous, *adj.* fukitsu (na) 不吉 (な).

omission, *n.* shōryaku 省略.

omit, *vb.* 1. shōryaku suru 省略する (leave out on purpose); nukasu 抜かす (leave out by mistake). 2. wasureru 忘れる (forget).

omnipotent, *adj.* ban'nō (no) 万能 (の).

on, 1. *prep.* ... no ue de/ni ...の上で／に (on top of); ...ni ...に (at the time of); **on Sunday** nichiyōbi ni 日曜日に; ... ni tsuite ...について (concerning); ... no

soba de/ni ...の側で／に (near); ...
de ...で (by means of); ... no hō ni
...の方に (toward). 2. *adv.* ue
de/ni/e 上で／に／へ (above);
and so on ... nado など; sonota
その他.

once, 1. *adv.* katsute かつて;
mukashi 昔 (formerly);
ichido/ikkai 一度／一回 (one
time); **at once** dōji ni 同時に (at
the same time); sugu ni すぐに
(immediately); **once and for all**
kore o kagiri ni これを限りに;
once in a while tokidoki 時々;
once upon a time mukashi-
mukashi 昔々; **all at once**
totsuzen 突然; **once more** mō
ichido もう一度; **once a month**
hitotsuki ni ichido 一月に一度. 2.
conj. moshi ... shitara もし...したら
(if ever); ... shitara sugi ni ...した
らすぐに (as soon as).

one, 1. *n., pron.* ichi 一; hitotsu 一
つ (single item); hitori 一人 (single
person); **one after another** tsugi-
tsugi ni 次々に; **one another**
otagai (o, ni) お互い (を、に); **no
one** dare mo ... nai 誰も...ない;
that one are あれ; sore それ; **this
one** kore これ; **one by one** jun ni
順に. 2. *adj.* ichi (no) 一 (の);
hitotsu (no) 一つ (の); hitori (no)
一人 (の) (single); onaji (no) 同じ
(の) (the same); aru ある (some);
one day aru hi ある日.

oneself, *pron.* jibun 自分; **by
oneself** jibun de 自分で.

one-way, *adj.* 1. ippōtsūkō (no) 一
方通行 (の) (street). 2. katamichi
(no) 片道 (の) (ticket).

ongoing, *adj.* shinkōchū (no) 進行
中 (の).

onion, *n.* tamanegi 玉ねぎ.

only, 1. *adj.* yuiitsu (no) 唯一 (の)

(sole); tada hitotsu (no) 只一つ
(の) (item); tada hitori (no) 只一
人 (の) (person). 2. *adv.* tatta たっ
た (merely); ... dake ...だけ
(solely); **only you** anata dake.

onus, *n.* 1. futan 負担 (burden). 2.
gimu 義務 (responsibility).

onward, *adv.* saki ni/e/wa 先に／
へ／は.

ooze, *vb.* nijimu 滲む.

opal, *n.* opāru オパール.

opaque, *adj.* futōmei (na) 不透明
(な).

open, 1. *adj.* hiraita/hiraiteiru 開い
た／開いている; aita/aiteiru 開い
た／開いている (not shut,
enclosed, covered, filled); hirobiro
to shita 広々とした (wide space);
sotchoku (na) 率直 (な) (frank);
kaihō sareteiru 解放されている
(accessible); eigyōchū (no) 営業中
(の) (business); kaikanchū (no) 開
館中 (の) (museum, library);
open the market (... ni) shijō o
kaihō suru (...に) 市場を開放する.
2. *vb.* hiraku 開く; akeru 開ける
(make open); hajimaru 始まる
(begin); hajimeru 始める (cause to
begin); kaihō suru 解放する
(make accessible).

opening, *n.* aki 空き (vacancy);
ketsuin 欠員 (job).

opera, *n.* opera オペラ; kageki 歌
劇.

operate, *vb.* 1. sōsa suru 操作する;
ugokasu 動かす (operate
machine). 2. un'ei suru 運営する
(manage). 3. sayō suru 作用する
(have effect). 4. shujutsu o suru
手術をする (perform surgery).

operation, *n.* 1. shujutsu 手術
(surgery); **have an operation**
shujutsu o ukeru 手術を受ける.
2. sōsa 操作; unten 運転

(machine). 3. gunjikōdō 軍事行動 (military operation).

operator, *n.* denwakōkanshu 電話交換手 (telephone).

ophthalmologist, *n.* gankai 眼科医; meisha 眼医者.

opinion, *n.* iken 意見.

opinionated, *adj.* gōjō (na) 強情 (な); dokudan-teki (na) 独断的 (な).

opium, *n.* ahen 阿片.

opponent, *n.* 1. aite 相手; taikōsha 対抗者 (person on opposite side). 2. hantaisha 反対者 (person who opposes).

opportune, *adj.* 1. tekisetsu (na) 適切 (な) (suitable). 2. ii taimingu (no) 良いタイミング (の) (well-timed).

opportunist, *n.* hiyorimi-shugisha 日和見主義者.

opportunity, *n.* kōki 好機; kikai 機会.

oppose, *vb.* 1. (... ni) hantai suru (...に) 反対する (resist). 2. saegiru 遮る (obstruct).

opposite, 1. *adj.* hantai (no) 反対 (の) (reverse of); taisuru 対する (face to face). 2. *prep.* ... ni taishite ...に対して; ... no mukai ni ...の向かいに (across from).

opposition, *n.* 1. hantai 反対; teikō 抵抗 (act of opposing). 2. yatō 野党 (political party); hantaisha 反対者 (person, group).

oppress, *vb.* appaku suru 圧迫する.

oppression, *n.* appaku 圧迫.

oppressive, *adj.* yokuatsu-teki (na) 抑圧的 (な).

opt for, *vb.* ... o erabu ...を選ぶ.

optic, -al, *adj.* 1. me (no) 目 (の) (of the eyes). 2. kōgaku (no) 光学 (の) (of light and vision).

optician, *n.* meganeya 眼鏡屋.

optics, *n.* kōgaku 光学.

optimal, *adj.* saiteki (no) 最適 (の).

optimism, *n.* rakkan-/rakuten-shugi 楽観～／楽天主義.

optimistic, *adj.* rakkan-/rakuten-teki (na) 楽観／楽天的 (な).

optimum, *adj.* saiteki (no) 最適 (の).

option, *n.* sentaku no yochi 選択の余地; opushon オプション.

optional, *adj.* nin'i (no) 任意 (の); sentaku dekiru 選択できる.

optometrist, *n.* kenganshi 検眼師.

opulent, *adj.* yutaka (na) 豊か (な); hōfu (na) 豊富 (な).

opus, *n.* sakuhin 作品.

or, *conj.* 1. matawa 又は; soretomo それとも (used to represent alternatives). 2. tsumari つまり (that is). 3. samonaito さもないと (otherwise).

oracle, *n.* 1. shintaku 神託 (divination). 2. yogensha 預言者 (person).

oral, *adj.* kōtō (no) 口頭 (の) (uttered in words); hanashikotoba (no) 話し言葉 (の) (of spoken language); **oral exam** kōtōshiken 口頭試験.

orange, 1. *adj.* orenji (no) オレンジ (の). 2. *n.* orenji(-iro) オレンジ (色) (color); orenji オレンジ (fruit); mikan みかん (tangerine).

orator, *n.* 1. yūbenka 雄弁家 (eloquent speaker). 2. enzetsusha 演説者 (speaker).

oratory, *n.* 1. yūben 雄弁. 2. yūbenjutsu 雄弁術 (skill in oratory).

orbit, *n.* 1. kidō 軌道 (path).

orchard, *n.* kajuen 果樹園.

orchestra, *n.* ōkesutora オーケストラ; kangengakudan 管弦楽団; **symphony orchestra** kōkyōgakudan 交響楽団.

orchid, *n.* ran 蘭.

ordain, *vb.* 1. ninmei suru 任命する (religion). 2. meijiru 命じる (order).

ordeal, *n.* shiren 試練.

order, 1. *n.* meirei 命令 (command); junban 順番 (systematic arrangement); chitsujo 秩序 (neatness); chūmon 注文 (request); **in order that, in order to** ... suru tame ni ...するために; **out of order** koshōchū 故障中. 2. *vb.* meijiru 命じる (command); chūmon suru 注文する (place an order); seiri suru 整理する (put things in order).

orderly, *adj.* seiton sareta 整頓された; kichin to shita きちんとした (neatly arranged); kiritsu tadashii 規律正しい (calm, organized).

ordinal, *adj.* junban (no) 順番 (の); **ordinal number** josū 序数.

ordinance, *n.* hōrei 法令; jōrei 条例; hōritsu 法律 (law).

ordinary, *adj.* futsū (no) 普通 (の); arifureta ありふれた.

ore, *n.* kōseki 鉱石.

organ, *n.* 1. orugan オルガン (musical instrument). 2. kikan 器官 (body part). 3. kikan 機関 (organization).

organic, *adj.* 1. kikan (no) 器官 (の) (of bodily organs). 2. yūki (no) 有機 (の) (organic compound). 3. yūkisaibai (no) 有機栽培 (の) (grown without chemicals).

organization, *n.* soshiki 組織; dantai 団体.

organize, *vb.* 1. soshiki suru 組織する (form). 2. taikeidateru 体系だてる (systematize); totonoeru 整える (order).

orgasm, *n.* orugazumu オルガズム.

orgy, *n.* donchansawagi どんちゃん騒ぎ (drunken revelry); rankō-pātī 乱交パーティー (wild party with sex).

orient, 1. *n.* **the Orient** tōyō 東洋; oriento オリエント. 2. *vb.* tehodoki suru 手ほどきする (introduce).

Oriental, 1. *n.* tōyōjin 東洋人. 2. *adj.* tōyō (no) 東洋 (の).

orientation, *n.* 1. orientēshon オリエンテーション; tehodoki 手ほどき (introductory program). 2. hōkō 方向 (direction).

origin, *n.* 1. kigen 起源; hajimari 始まり (beginning, source). 2. umare 生まれ (birth, parentage).

original, 1. *n.* orijinaru オリジナル (original); genkei 原型 (primary type, form); gensho 原書 (book in the original language); gensakuhin 原作品 (original work as opposed to a copy). 2. *adj.* orijinaru (na, no) オリジナル (な、の) (original); dokusō-teki (na) 独創的 (な) (creative); hajime (no) 始め (の) (first); atarashii 新しい (new); moto (no) 元 (の) (not copied).

originate, *vb.* (... ni) motozuku (... に) 基づく; (... ni) hassuru (...に) 発する.

ornament, 1. *n.* kazari 飾り; sōshoku 装飾. 2. *vb.* kazaru 飾る.

ornamental, *adj.* kazari (no) 飾り (の) (of ornament); sōshoku-teki (na) 装飾的 (な) (decorative).

ornate, *adj.* 1. hade (na) 派手 (な) (pompous). 2. kazaritateta 飾りたてた (decorative).

ornithology, *n.* chōruigaku 鳥類学.

orphan, *n.* koji 孤児 (without parents); minashigo みなし児

(without protective affiliation).

orphanage, *n.* koji'in 孤児院.

orthodox, *adj.* ōsodokkusu (na) オーソドックス (な); seitō-teki (na) 正統的 (な) (generally accepted).

orthography, *n.* tsuzuri 綴り (spelling); tadashii tsuzuri 正しい 綴り (correct spelling).

orthopedic, *adj.* seikeigeka 整形外科.

oscillate, *vb.* 1. fureru 振れる (sway). 2. mayou 迷う (fluctuate).

ostensible, *adj.* misekake (no) 見せかけ (の); uwabedake (no) 上辺だけ (の).

ostentation, *n.* mie 見栄.

ostentatious, *adj.* koremiyogashi (no) これ見よがし (の); misebirakashi (no) 見せびらかし (の).

ostracism, *n.* murahachibu 村八分; nakama hazure 仲間外れ.

ostrich, *n.* dachō 駝鳥.

other, 1. *adj.* hoka (no) 他 (の); ta (no) 他 (の) (additional, different); mō hitotsu (no) もう一つ (の) (remaining one); **the other day** senjitsu 先日; **every other day** ichinichi oki ni 一日おきに; **on the other hand** sono ippō その一方; **in other words** tsumari つまり. 2. *pron.* **the others** hoka no hito 他の人 (other people); hoka no mono 他の物 (other things); **each other** otagai ni/o お互いに／を.

otherwise, *adv.* 1. sō de nakereba そうでなければ (if not). 2. sore o nozokeba それを除けば (apart from that). 3. chigatta fū niwa 違ったふうには (differently).

otter, *n.* rakko らっこ (sea otter); kawauso 川うそ (river otter).

ought, *aux. vb.* 1. ... beki ... べき (should); **ought to know** shiru beki 知るべき. 2. kitto (... ni) chigainai きっと (...に) 違いない (used to express probability).

ounce, *n.* onsu オンス.

our, *adj., pron.* watashitachi (no) 私達 (の); ware-ware (no) 我々 (の).

ours, *pron.* watashitachi no mono 私達のもの; ware-ware no mono 我々のもの.

ourselves, *pron.* watashitachi-jishin (wa, o) 私達自身 (は、を); ware-ware jishin (wa, o) 我々自身 (は、を).

oust, *vb.* tsuihō suru 追放する.

out, 1. *adv.* soto de/ni/e 外で／に／へ (outside); hanarete/hazurete 離れて／外れて (away from); sukkari すっかり (completely); nakunatte/kirete 無くなって／切れて (none left); **go out of a room** heya kara deru 部屋から出る; **out of pity** dōjō kara 同情から; **out of money** okane ga nakunatte お金が無くなって; **out of breath** iki ga kirete 息が切れて; **out of reach** te ga todokanai 手が届かない. 2. *prep.* ... kara ...から (out from).

outbreak, *n.* 1. hassei 発生; boppatsu 勃発 (sudden occurrence). 2. bōdō 暴動 (insurrection).

outburst, *n.* bakuhatsu 爆発 (outpouring, sudden spell of activity).

outcast, *n.* nokemono 除け者.

outcome, *n.* kekka 結果.

outcry, *n.* daihantai 大反対 (protest).

outdated, *adj.* jidaiokure (no) 時代遅れ (の) (old-fashioned).

outdo, *vb.* (... ni) masaru (...に) 勝る; (...o) shinogu (...を) 凌ぐ.

outdoor, 1. *adj.* kogai (no) 戸外 (の); soto (no) 外 (の). 2. *adv.* **outdoors** kogai de/ni 戸外で／に; soto de/ni 外で／に.

outer, *adj.* 1. soto (no) 外 (の) (exterior). 2. **outer space** uchū-kūkan 宇宙空間.

outfit, *n.* 1. sōbi 装備 (equipment). 2. fuku 服 (clothing).

outgoing, *adj.* 1. deteiku 出て行く (leaving). 2. gaikō-teki (na) 外交的 (な) (sociable).

outgrow, *vb.* 1. (... ga) hairanaku-naru (...が) 入らなくなる (grow too large for); **outgrow one's clothes** fuku ga hairanaku-naru 服が入らなくなる. 2. (... yori) ōkiku naru (...より) 大きくなる (grow more than).

outgrowth, *n.* 1. tōzen no kekka 当然の結果 (natural consequence). 2. nariyuki 成り行き (natural development).

outing, *n.* ensoku 遠足 (excursion); pikunikku ピクニック (picnic).

outlandish, *adj.* 1. iyō (na) 異様 (な) (odd). 2. ikokufū (na, no) 異国風 (な、の) (having a foreign appearance).

outlaw, 1. *n.* muhōmono 無法者; narazumono ならず者. 2. *vb.* kinshi suru 禁止する.

outlet, *n.* 1. deguchi 出口 (exit). 2. hakeguchi はけ口 (outlet for expression). 3. hanbaiten 販売店 (retailer); hanbairo 販売路 (market for goods). 4. konsento コンセント (electrical).

outline, 1. *n.* autorain アウトライン; rinkaku 輪郭 (line); gairyaku 概略 (general account). 2. *vb.* rinkaku o egaku 輪郭を描く (draw outline); gairyaku o noberu 概略を述べる (give an account).

outlook, *n.* 1. nagame 眺め (view). 2. mitōshi 見通し; yosō 予想 (speculation). 3. kangaekata 考え方 (mental view).

out-of-date, *adj.* 1. kigengire (no) 期限切れ (の) (no longer valid). 2. jidaiokure (no) 時代遅れ (の) (old-fashioned).

outpatient, *n.* gairaikanja 外来患者.

outpouring, *n.* hotobashiri ほとばしり.

output, *n.* 1. autoputto アウトプット; shutsuryoku 出力 (electrical or computer). 2. seisandaka 生産高 (quantity produced).

outrage, 1. *n.* bōryoku 暴力 (violence); gekido 激怒; ikari 怒り (fury); tondemonai koto とんでもないこと (unthinkable). 2. *vb.* gekido saseru 激怒させる (anger); okasu 犯す (violate).

outrageous, *adj.* hidoi ひどい; tondemonai とんでもない.

outright, *adj.* 1. mattaku no 全くの (complete). 2. akiraka (na) 明らか (な) (obvious).

outset, *n.* hajime/hajimari 始め／始まり; **from the outset** hajime kara 始めから.

outside, 1. *adj.* soto (no) 外 (の); gaibu (no) 外部 (の). 2. *n.* soto 外; sotogawa 外側. 3. *adv.* soto de/ni/e 外で／に／へ. 4. *prep.* ... no soto de/ni/e ...の外で／に／へ.

outsider, *n.* autosaidā アウトサイダー; bugaisha 部外者; yosomono よそ者.

outskirts, *n.* kōgai 郊外.

outsmart, *vb.* (... yori) uwate ni deru (...より) 上手に出る.

outspoken, *adj.* sotchoku (na) 率直 (な) (unreserved).

outstanding, *adj.* 1. namihazureta 並外れた; subarashii 素晴らしい (prominent). 2. mikaiketsu (no) 未解決 (の) (unsettled); miharai (no) 未払い (の) (unpaid).

outward, *adv.* sotogawa de/ni/e 外側で／に／へ (toward the outside).

oval, *n., adj.* daenkei (no) 楕円形 (の).

ovary, *n.* ransō 卵巣.

ovation, *n.* hakushu kassai 拍手喝采.

oven, *n.* ōbun オーブン; tenpi 天火.

over, 1. *adv.* ue de/ni 上で／に (above); ue no 上の (so as to cover); koete 超えて (across, beyond); mata また (again); sukkari すっかり (throughout); **over and over** kurikaeshite 繰り返して; **over here** koko de/ni ここで／に; **over there** mukō de/ni 向こうで／に; **all over** achikochi de/ni あちこちで／に (here and there); zentai ni 全体に (over entirety). 2. *prep.* ... no ue de/ni/e/o ...の上で／に／へ／を (above in place, authority, etc.); ... no mukō ni ...の向こうに (to the other side of); ... o koete ...を超えて (across); ... o tōtte ...を通って (through); ... ni wattate ...に渡って (throughout).

overall, 1. *adj.* zentai no 全体の. 2. *adv.* zentai(-teki) ni 全体(的)に.

overbearing, *adj.* ōhei (na) 横柄 (な).

overboard, *adv.* **go overboard** ikisugiru 行き過ぎる; kyokutan ni hashiru 極端に走る.

overcast, *adj.* 1. kumotta 曇った (cloudy). 2. inki (na) 陰気 (な) (gloomy).

overcoat, *n.* ōbā オーバー; gaitō 外套.

overcome, *vb.* 1. makasu 負かす (defeat). 2. (... ni) uchikatsu (...に) 打ち勝つ (prevail over). 3. kokufuku suru 克服する (conquer). 4. **be overcome by** ... ni uchinomesareru ...に打ちのめされる.

overdo, *vb.* 1. shisugiru し過ぎる (do to excess). 2. kochō suru 誇張する (exaggerate). 3. muri suru 無理する (exhaust). 4. yakisugiru 焼き過ぎる (overcook).

overdue, *adj.* 1. kigengire (no) 期限切れ (の) (past due). 2. minō (no) 未納 (の) (unpaid). 3. okureteiru 遅れている (delayed).

overflow, *vb.* afureru 溢れる.

overhaul, *vb.* 1. ōbāhōru o suru オーバーホールをする; zentai no kensa o suru 全体の検査をする (examine thoroughly). 2. sukkari shūri suru すっかり修理する (repair thoroughly).

overlap, *vb.* chōfuku suru 重複する; kasanaru 重なる.

overload, *vb.* 1. nimotsu o tsumisugiru 荷物を積み過ぎる (load to excess). 2. futan o kakesugiru 負担をかけ過ぎる (overburden).

overlook, *vb.* 1. misugosu 見過ごす (fail to notice). 2. minogasu 見逃す (disregard, excuse). 3. miorosu 見下ろす (look over from above).

overnight, *adv.* hitobanjū 一晩中 (all night); **stay overnight** ippaku suru 一泊する.

overpopulation, *n.* jinkōkajō 人口過剰.

overpower, *vb.* 1. attō suru 圧倒する (overwhelm). 2. (... ni) uchikatsu (...に) 打ち勝つ (overcome).

overrule, *vb.* kyakka suru 却下する.

overseas, 1. *adj.* kaigai (no) 海外 (の); gaikoku (no) 外国 (の). 2. *adv.* kaigai de/ni 海外で／に.

oversee, *vb.* kantoku suru 監督する (supervise).

oversight, *n.* miotoshi 見落とし.

overt, *adj.* akarasama (na) あからさま (な).

overtake, *vb.* (... ni) oitsuku (...に) 追い付く (catch up with).

overthrow, *vb.* 1. taosu 倒す (depose, put an end to). 2. hikkurikaesu ひっくり返す (topple).

overtime, *n.* 1. zangyō 残業; chōka-kinmu 超過勤務 (working overtime). 2. zangyōteate 残業手当て (payment).

overture, *n.* 1. jokyoku 序曲 (music). 2. teian 提案 (proposal); mōshide 申し出 (offer).

overturn, *vb.* 1. hikkurikaesu ひっくり返す (turn over). 2. taosu 倒す (depose).

overweight, *adj.* 1. jūryōchōka (no) 重量超過 (の) (load). 2. himan (no) 肥満 (の); futorisugi (no) 太り過ぎ (の) (person).

overwhelm, *vb.* attō suru 圧倒する.

overwork, 1. *n.* karō 過労. 2. *vb.* hataraki-sugiru 働き過ぎる.

owe, *vb.* 1. kari ga aru 借りがある (owe money); harawa-nakereba-naranai 払わなければならない (need to pay). 2. ... no okage de aru ...のおかげである; ... ni on ga aru ...に恩がある (indebted to); **owing to** ... no okage de ...のおかげで.

owl, *n.* fukurō ふくろう.

own, 1. *adj.* jishin no 自身の; hon'nin no 本人の. 2. *vb.* motsu 持つ; shoyū suru 所有する.

owner, *n.* mochinushi 持ち主; ōnā オーナー.

ox, *n.* oushi 雄牛.

oxygen, *n.* sanso 酸素.

oyster, *n.* kaki 牡蠣; oisutā オイスター.

ozone, *n.* ozon オゾン.

P

pace, *n.* 1. pēsu ペース; sokudo 速度 (rate of movement); shinpo no doai 進歩の度合い (rate of progress). 2. ippo 一歩 (single step).

Pacific Ocean, *n.* taiheiyō 太平洋.

pacifier, *n.* oshaburi おしゃぶり (baby).

pacifist, *n.* heiwashugisha 平和主義者.

pacify, *vb.* 1. nadameru なだめる (calm). 2. heiwa o motarasu 平和をもたらす (bring peace).

pack, 1. *n.* pakku パック; tsutsumi 包み (bundle); mure 群れ (dogs, crooks); hako 箱 (cigarettes); **a pack of cigarettes** tabako hito hako タバコ一箱. 2. *vb.* nimotsu o matomeru 荷物をまとめる (prepare for traveling, etc.); mitasu 満たす (fill with objects); tsumekomu 詰め込む (cram).

package, *n.* pakkēji パッケージ;

tsutsumi 包み.

pact, *n.* kyōtei 協定.

pad, 1. *n.* paddo パッド (cushion); hito toji 一綴じ (writing pad, etc.); **pad of paper** hito toji no kami 一綴じの紙. 2. *vb.* paddo o tsumeru パッドを詰める (cushion).

padding, *n.* paddo パッド; tsumemono 詰め物.

paddle, 1. *n.* raketto ラケット (table tennis); kai 櫂 (oar). 2. *vb.* kogu 漕ぐ (propel with a paddle).

padlock, *n.* nankinjō 南京錠.

pagan, 1. *n.* ikyōto 異教徒. 2. *adj.* ikyōto (no) 異教徒 (の).

page, *n.* pēji ページ (book, etc.).

pageant, *n.* pējento ページェント; supekutakuru スペクタクル.

pagoda, *n.* tō 塔.

paid-up, *adj.* shiharaizumi (no) 支払い済み (の).

pail, *n.* baketsu バケツ.

pain, *n.* 1. itami 痛み (bodily or mental suffering); kurushimi 苦しみ (pang, woe). 2. **pains** doryoku 努力 (effort). 3. **be in pain** kurushindeiru 苦しんでいる; **pain in the neck** yakkaimono 厄介もの (nuisance); **take pains** doryoku suru 努力する.

painful, *adj.* 1. itai 痛い (aching). 2. tsurai 辛い (excruciating).

painkiller, *n.* chintsūzai 鎮痛剤.

paint, 1. *n.* penki ペンキ (house paint); enogu 絵の具 (oil or watercolor paint); **Wet Paint.** Penki nuritate ペンキ塗り立て. 2. *vb.* penki o nuru ペンキを塗る (house, wall, etc.); e o kaku 絵を描く (picture).

paintbrush, *n.* fude 筆; burashi ブラシ.

painter, *n.* 1. penkinuri ペンキ塗り (worker). 2. gaka 画家; ekaki

絵かき (artist).

painting, *n.* e 絵; kaiga 絵画 (picture).

pair, *n.* pea ペア; futari 二人 (two people); ittsui 一対 (set of two).

pajamas, *n.* pajama パジャマ.

pal, *n.* shin'yū 親友.

palace, *n.* kyūden 宮殿.

palate, *n.* kōgai 口蓋 (mouth).

palatial, *adj.* kyūden no yō (na) 宮殿のよう (な).

pale, 1. *adj.* aojiroi 青白い (near-white); usui 薄い (dim). 2. *vb.* aozameru/-zamesaseru 青ざめる／～ざめさせる (become/make pale).

palette, *n.* paretto パレット (painting).

pall, 1. *n.* tobari 帳 (cover of darkness). 2. *vb.* otoroeru 衰える (fade); taikutsu ni naru 退屈になる (become uninterested).

pallid, *adj.* aojiroi 青白い.

palm, 1. *n.* tenohira 掌 (hand); yashi no ki 椰子の木 (tree). 2. *vb.* **palm off** damashite uritsukeru だまして売りつける.

palmistry, *n.* tesōhandan 手相判断.

palpable, *adj.* 1. kanjirareru 感じられる (tangible). 2. akiraka (na) 明らか (な) (obvious).

palpitate, *vb.* doki-doki suru どきどきする.

paltry, *adj.* kudaranai 下らない.

pamper, *vb.* amayakasu 甘やかす.

pamphlet, *n.* panfuretto パンフレット.

pan, *n.* nabe 鍋.

panacea, *n.* ban'nōyaku 万能薬.

pancake, *n.* pankēki パンケーキ.

panda, *n.* panda パンダ.

pander, 1. *n.* ponbiki ぽん引き (pimp). 2. *vb.* chūkai suru 仲介す

る (act as a go-between); **pander to** ... ni omoneru ... におもねる (cater to).

pane, *n.* mado-garasu 窓ガラス (windowpane).

panel, *n.* 1. hameita 羽目板 (of a door). 2. paneru パネル (on a wall, etc.). 3. i'inkai 委員会 (committee).

pang, *n.* kurushimi 苦しみ (pain).

panic, 1. *n.* panikku パニック. 2. *vb.* panikku o okosu パニックを起こす (feel panic); panikku ni otoshi'ireru パニックに陥れる (affect someone with panic).

panorama, *n.* panorama パノラマ.

pant, *vb.* aegu あえぐ.

panther, *n.* pansā パンサー; hyō ひょう.

panties, *n.* pantī パンティー.

pantomime, *n.* pantomaimu パントマイム.

pantry, *n.* shokuhin chozōshitsu 食品貯蔵室.

pants, *n.* 1. zubon ズボン (trousers). 2. pantī パンティー (panties).

pantyhose, *n.* pantī-sutokkingu パンティーストッキング.

paper, *n.* 1. kami 紙 (fibrous sheet). 2. shinbun 新聞 (newspaper). 3. kenkyū ronbun 研究論文 (research paper); ronbun 論文 (essay, thesis). 4. shorui 書類 (document).

paperback, *n.* pēpābakku ペーパーバック; bunkobon 文庫本.

paper clip, *n.* kurippu クリップ.

paper money, *n.* shihei 紙幣.

paperweight, *n.* bunchin 文鎮.

par, *n.* 1. dōtō 同等; onaji 同じ (parity); **on a par (with)** (... to) onaji (...と) 同じ. 2. pā パー (golf, etc.) 3. **below par** suijun ika 水準以下.

parade, 1. *n.* parēdo パレード (march). 2. *vb.* parēdo o suru パレードをする (march); misebirakasu 見せびらかす (show off).

paradise, *n.* paradaisu パラダイス (heavenly place); tengoku 天国 (Heaven).

paradox, *n.* gyakusetsu 逆説.

paradoxical, *adj.* gyakusetsu-teki (na) 逆説的 (な).

paragon, *n.* tenkei 典型 (model).

paragraph, *n.* paragurafu パラグラフ; danraku 段落.

parallel, 1. *n.* heikōsen 平行線 (parallel line); hitteki-butsu/-sha 匹敵物／～者 (a comparable thing/person). 2. *adj.* heikō (no) 平行 (の) (not converging or diverging); 3. *vb.* heikō suru 平行する (be parallel to); ... ni hitteki suru ...に匹敵する (be comparable to).

paralysis, *n.* mahi 麻痺.

paralyze, *vb.* mahi suru/saseru 麻痺する／させる (become/make paralyzed).

paramedic, *n.* ishi no joshu 医師の助手 (assistant to a doctor).

parameter, *n.* paramētā パラメーター; kettei-teki yōso 決定的の要素 (determining factor).

paranoid, *adj.* higai mōsō (no) 被害妄想 (の).

paraphernalia, *n.* 1. kodōgu 小道具 (equipment). 2. shojihin 所持品 (belongings).

paraphrase, 1. *n.* iikae 言い換え. 2. *vb.* iikaeru 言い換える.

paraplegic, *n., adj.* kahanshin mahi (no) 下半身麻痺 (の).

parasite, *n.* kiseichū 寄生虫 (animal, useless person).

parcel, *n.* kozutsumi 小包み (package); **parcel post** kozutsumi-yūbin 小包み郵便.

parch, *vb.* hiagaraseru 干上がらせる (make dry); **be parched** nodo ga kawaita 喉が乾いた (be thirsty).

parchment, *n.* mozōyōhishi 模造羊皮紙 (paper parchment).

pardon, 1. *n.* yurushi 許し (forgiveness); onsha 恩謝 (legal); **I beg your pardon?** Sumimasen, mō ichido itte kudasai. すみません、もう一度言って下さい. (Please repeat what you said.). 2. *vb.* yurusu 許す (excuse, forgive); onsha o ataeru 恩謝を与える (legal); **Pardon me.** Sumimasen すみません (Excuse me).

parent, *n.* kataoya 片親 (mother or father); chichi 父 (father); haha 母 (mother); **parents** ryōshin 両親.

parentage, *n.* umare 生まれ (birth).

parenthesis, *n.* kakko 括弧.

parity, *n.* 1. dōtō 同等 (equality). 2. paritī パリティー (equivalent value).

park, 1. *n.* kōen 公園 (public space). 2. *vb.* chūsha suru 駐車する (a vehicle).

parking, *n.* chūsha 駐車.

parking lot/place, *n.* chūshajō 駐車場.

parking meter, *n.* pākingu-mētā パーキングメーター.

parliament, *n.* gikai 議会; kokkai 国会.

parlor, *n.* 1. -pārā -パーラー; -ten -店; -ya -屋 (shop); **ice cream parlor** aisukurīmu-pārā アイスクリームパーラー. 2. ima 居間 (living room).

parody, 1. *n.* parodī パロディー.

2. *vb.* kokkeika suru 滑稽化する.

parole, *n.* karishakuhō 仮釈放.

paroxysm, *n.* bakuhatsu 爆発 (outburst).

parrot, *n.* ōmu おうむ.

parsley, *n.* paseri パセリ.

part, 1. *n.* bubun 部分 (portion or division of a whole); buntan 分担 (share of duty); buhin 部品 (mechanical); yaku 役 (theatrical); **for my part** watashi to shite wa 私としては; **for the most part** taitei 大抵; **in part** bubun-teki ni 部分的に; **on the part of** ... no hō de ...の方で; **take part in** ... ni sanka suru ...に参加する. 2. *vb.* wakeru 分ける (divide, separate); wakareru 分かれる (be divided, be separated); **part company with** ... to wakareru ...と別れる; **part with** ... o tebanasu ...を手放す (relinquish).

partial, *adj.* 1. bubun-teki (na) 部分的 (な) (incomplete). 2. ekohi'iki (no) えこひいき (の) (unfair, biased). 3. **partial to** ... ga toku ni suki ...が特に好き (especially fond of).

participant, *n.* sankasha 参加者.

participate, *vb.* sanka suru 参加する (take part in an event); **participate in** ... ni sanka suru ...に参加する.

participation, *n.* sanka 参加 (taking part in an event).

participle, *n.* bunshi 分詞.

particle, *n.* ryūshi 粒子 (extremely minute piece, elementary particle); kakera 欠けら (small portion, fragment).

particular, *adj.* 1. tokubetsu (na) 特別 (な) (noteworthy). 2. tokutei (no) 特定 (の) (pertaining to some one person, thing, etc.). 3. (... ni)

urusai (...に) うるさい
(fastidious). **4. in particular**
toku ni 特に.

parting, *n.* wakare 別れ
(departure, separation).

partition, 1. *n.* bunkatsu 分割
(division); shikiri 仕切り (interior
wall). 2. *vb.* wakeru 分ける
(divide, separate).

partly, *adv.* bubun-teki ni 部分的
に.

partner, *n.* 1. pātonā パートナー
(associate, sharer, etc.). 2.
haigūsha 配偶者 (wife or
husband). 3. kyōdō-keieisha 共同
経営者 (joint owner).

partnership, *n.* 1. kyōryoku 協力
(cooperation). 2. kyōdō-keiei 共
同経営 (joint ownership).

partridge, *n.* uzura うずら.

party, *n.* 1. pātī パーティー (social
gathering); **have a party** pātī o
suru パーティーをする. 2. dantai
団体 (group). 3. seitō 政党
(political). **4. third party**
daisansha 第三者.

pass, 1. *n.* kyoka 許可 (permit);
tōge 峠 (mountain pass); gōkaku
合格 (success in an exam). 2. *vb.*
tōru 通る (go forward); tsūka suru
通過する (go through); watasu 渡
す (hand over); sugosu 過ごす
(spend, as time); ... ni gōkaku
suru ...に合格する (succeed in an
examination); **pass away** shinu
死ぬ (die); **pass by** mushi suru 無
視する (ignore); **pass out** kubaru
配る (distribute).

passable, *adj.* 1. māmā (no) まあま
あ (の) (marginally adequate). 2.
tsūyō suru 通用する (valid,
acceptable). 3. tsūkō dekiru 通行
出来る (capable of being passed).

passage, *n.* 1. michi 道 (road,

way); rōka 廊下 (corridor). 2.
nagare 流れ (flow or lapse, as of
time). 3. issetsu 一節 (section of a
written work, etc.). 4. tsūka 通過
(act of passing). 5. funatabi 船旅
(journey by ship).

passenger, *n.* jōkyaku 乗客.

passer-by, *n.* tsūkōnin 通行人.

passion, *n.* passhon パッション;
jōnetsu 情熱.

passionate, *adj.* jōnetsu-teki (na)
情熱的 (な).

passive, *adj.* 1. shōkyoku-teki (na)
消極的 (な). 2. ukemikei (no) 受
身形 (の) (grammar).

passport, *n.* pasupōto パスポート.

password, *n.* aikotoba 合い言葉.

past, 1. *n.* kako 過去 (time gone
by); kakokei 過去形 (grammar).
2. *adj.* kako (no) 過去 (の) (gone
by, as in time); konomae no この
前の (of an earlier time, former);
owatta 終わった (over); kakokei
(no) 過去形 (の) (grammar); **in
the past few years** kono
sūnenkan この数年間. 3. *prep.* ...
sugi ...過ぎ (beyond, as in time or
age); ... no mukō ni ...の向こうに;
... o sugite ...を過ぎて (beyond);
ten past one ichiji juppun sugi 一
時十分過ぎ.

pasta, *n.* pasuta パスタ; menrui
めん類.

paste, *n.* 1. pēsuto ペースト (soft
sticky mixture). 2. nori 糊 (glue).

pastel, *n.* pasuteru パステル.

pasteurize, *vb.* teionsakkin suru 低
温殺菌する.

pastime, *n.* goraku 娯楽;
tanoshimi 楽しみ.

pastry, *n.* kēki ケーキ; yōgashi 洋
菓子 (pie, tart, etc.).

pasture, *n.* bokusōchi 牧草地.

pat, 1. *n.* hitonade 一撫で (light

touch). 2. *vb*. karuku tataku 軽く
たたく (strike gently).

patch, 1. *n*. tsugi 継ぎ (material
used to mend or protect); bubun
部分 (any small piece). 2. *vb*. tsugi
o ateru 継ぎを当てる (mend);
patch up tsukurou 繕う (mend,
fix); toriosameru 取り治める
(smooth over, as a quarrel, etc.).

patent, 1. *n*. tokkyo 特許
(copyright, etc.). 2. *adj*. akiraka
(na) 明らか (な) (obvious). 3. *vb*.
(... no) tokkyo o toru (... の) 特許
を取る (secure a patent on).

paternal, *adj*. 1. chichikata (no) 父
方 (の) (related through a father).
2. chichioya rashii 父親らしい
(fatherly).

paternity, *n*. (umi no) chichioya
(生みの) 父親 (descent from a
father); **paternity unknown**
chichioya-fumei 父親不明.

path, *n*. 1. komichi 小道 (narrow
way); tōrimichi 通り道 (passage).
2. kidō 軌道 (route).

pathetic, *adj*. 1. itamashii 痛ましい
(arousing pity). 2. aware (na) 哀
れ (な) (pitiful).

pathology, *n*. byōrigaku 病理学.

patience, *n*. nintai 忍耐; gaman 我
慢 (endurance).

patient, 1. *n*. kanja 患者. 2. *adj*. 我
慢強い gamanzuyoi.

patio, *n*. nakaniwa 中庭 (inner
open court).

patriarch, *n*. chōrō 長老
(venerable old man).

patriarchy, *n*. fukenshugi 父権主
義.

patriot, *n*. aikokusha 愛国者.

patriotic, *adj*. aikoku-teki (na) 愛
国的 (な).

patriotism, *n*. aikokushin 愛国心.

patrol, 1. *n*. patorōru パトロール.

2. *vb*. patorōru suru パトロールす
る.

patron, *n*. 1. shiensha 支援者
(supporter). 2. otokuikyaku お得
意客 (regular customer).

patronize, *vb*. 1. shien suru 支援す
る (support). 2. hi'iki ni suru ひ
いきにする (buy from regularly).
3. mottai buru 勿体ぶる (behave
haughtily).

pattern, *n*. 1. moyō 模様 (surface
design). 2. kata 型 (characteristic
mode). 3. mihon 見本 (excellent
example, sample). 4. katagami 型
紙 (sewing, stencil, etc.)

paunch, *n*. taikobara 太鼓腹.

pauper, *n*. binbōnin 貧乏人.

pause, 1. *n*. pōzu ポーズ; kyūshi 休
止 (temporary stop). 2. *vb*. kyūshi
suru 休止する (make a pause);
tamerau ためらう (hesitate).

pave, *vb*. hosō suru 舗装する
(cover with concrete, etc.); **pave
the way for** ... e no michi o
hiraku ...への道を開く.

pavement, *n*. hosōdōro 舗装道路
(paved road).

pavilion, *n*. pabirion パビリオン
(light open shelter).

paw, *n*. te 手 (foreleg); ashi 足
(hind leg).

pawn, *vb*. shichi ni ireru 質に入れ
る.

pawnbroker, *n*. shichiya 質屋.

pawnshop, *n*. shichiya 質屋.

pay, 1. *n*. kyūryō 給料 (wages,
salary). 2. *vb*. harau 払う (give
money to, give as compensation);
rieki o ageru 利益を上げる (yield
profit); **pay attention to** ... ni
chūi suru ...に注意する; **pay back**
haraikaesu 払い返す; **pay for** ...
no daikin o harau ...の代金を払う
(pay money for); ... no mukui o

ukeru ...の報いを受ける (be retaliated against); **pay off** zenbu harau 全部払う; **pay a visit** tazuneru 訪ねる.

payable, *adj.* shiharawareru-beki (no) 支払われるべき (の).

payday, *n.* kyūryōbi 給料日.

payment, *n.* 1. shiharai 支払い (act of paying). 2. shiharaikin 支払い金 (sum of money to be paid).

pay phone, *n.* kōshūdenwa 公衆電話.

payroll, *n.* 1. jūgyōinkyūryō-ichiranhyō 従業員給料一覧表 (list). 2. kyūryōsōgaku 給料総額 (sum total to be paid).

pea, *n.* endōmame えんどう豆.

peace, *n.* 1. heiwa 平和 (freedom from wars); anshin 安心 (freedom from troubles); heion 平穏 (calmness). 2. shizukesa 静けさ (quietness). 3. **make peace with** ... to nakayoku suru ...と仲良くする.

peaceable, *adj.* odayaka (na) 穏やか (な) (calm).

peaceful, *adj.* 1. heiwa-teki (na) 平和的 (な) (nonviolent). 2. shizuka (na) 静か (な) (tranquil).

peach, *n.* momo 桃.

peacock, *n.* kujaku 孔雀.

peak, *n.* 1. itadaki 頂 (mountain peak). 2. pīku ピーク; chōten 頂点 (highest point, culmination).

peal, 1. *n.* hibiki 響き (ringing of bells); todoroki とどろき (loud sound, as of thunder). 2. *vb.* hibiku 響く (ring out); todoroku とどろく (sound loudly).

peanut, *n.* pīnattsu ピーナッツ.

pear, *n.* nashi 梨.

pearl, *n.* shinju 真珠.

peasant, *n.* hyakushō 百姓; nōfu 農夫.

pebble, *n.* koishi 小石.

peck, *vb.* tsutsuku 突く (pick at, strike with beak).

peculiar, *adj.* 1. fūgawari (na) 風変わり (な) (strange). 2. **peculiar to** ... ni dokutoku (na, no) ...に独特 (な、の) (characteristic of).

pedal, 1. *n.* pedaru ペダル. 2. *vb.* pedaru o fumu ペダルを踏む.

pedagogy, *n.* kyōjuhō 教授法.

pedantic, *adj.* gengaku-teki (na) 衒学的 (な).

peddle, *vb.* gyōshō o suru 行商をする.

peddler, *n.* gyōshōnin 行商人.

pedestal, *n.* dai 台.

pedestrian, *n.* hokōsha 歩行者.

pediatrician, *n.* shōnikai 小児科医.

pedigree, *n.* 1. kettō 血統 (of a dog or cat); kettōsho 血統書 (certificate of ancestry). 2. kakei 家系 (lineage).

peek, 1. *n.* ichibetsu 一瞥; **have a peek** satto miru さっと見る. 2. *vb.* nozoku 覗く.

peel, 1. *n.* kawa 皮 (skin of fruit, etc.). 2. *vb.* kawa o muku 皮を剥く (remove the skin); kawa ga mukeru 皮が剥ける (lose the skin); hageru 剥げる (paint: come off).

peep, 1. *n.* ichibetsu 一瞥 (quick look). 2. *vb.* nozoku 覗く (look secretly).

peer, 1. *n.* dōhai 同輩 (equal); kizoku 貴族 (nobleman). 2. *vb.* yoku miru よく見る (look closely).

peeved, *adj.* okotteiru 怒っている.

peevish, *adj.* okorippoi 怒りっぽい (irritable); fukigen (na) 不機嫌 (な) (bad-tempered).

peg, *n.* kakekugi 掛け釘 (pin of

wood, metal, etc.)

pejorative, *adj.* keibetsu-teki (na) 軽蔑的 (な).

Peking, *n.* pekin 北京.

pelican, *n.* perikan ペリカン.

pellet, *n.* chiisai tama 小さい玉 (little ball).

pelt, 1. *n.* kegawa 毛皮 (skin of a beast). 2. *vb.* nagetsukeru 投げつける (throw); hageshiku furu 激しく降る (rain).

pelvis, *n.* kotsuban 骨盤.

pen, *n.* 1. pen ペン (instrument for writing). 2. kakoichi 囲い地 (enclosure).

penal, *adj.* keibatsu (no) 刑罰 (の) (of punishment); keihō (no) 刑法 (の) (of penal laws).

penalty, *n.* 1. keibatsu 刑罰 (punishment). 2. bakkin 罰金 (money).

penance, *n.* tsumihoroboshi 罪滅ぼし.

pencil, *n.* enpitsu 鉛筆.

pendant, *n.* pendanto ペンダント.

pending, *adj.* mikettei (no) 未決定 (の).

penetrate, *vb.* 1. tsuranuku 貫く (pierce); hairikomu 入り込む (enter). 2. minuku 見抜く (understand).

penguin, *n.* pengin ペンギン.

penicillin, *n.* penishirin ペニシリン.

peninsula, *n.* hantō 半島.

penis, *n.* penisu ペニス; inkei 陰茎.

penknife, *n.* poketto naifu ポケットナイフ.

pen name, *n.* pen-nēmu ペンネーム.

penniless, *adj.* ichimon nashi (no) 一文なし (の).

penny, *n.* sento セント; penī ペニー.

pension, *n.* nenkin 年金 (money).

pensive, *adj.* mono'omoi ni fuketteiru 物思いに耽っている.

penthouse, *n.* pentohausu ペントハウス.

pent-up, *adj.* tojikome-rarete-iru 閉じ込められている (shut up).

people, *n.* 1. hitobito 人々 (persons). 2. kokumin 国民 (nation); minzoku 民族 (race). 3. ichizoku 一族 (relatives).

pep, *n.* katsuryoku 活力.

pepper, *n.* 1. koshō 胡椒 (condiment). 2. pīman ピーマン (vegetable).

peppermint, *n.* hakka 薄荷 (herb).

per, *prep.* ... ni tsuki ... につき (for each ...).

perceive, *vb.* 1. satchi suru 察知する (discern, sense). 2. wakaru 分かる (understand). 3. mitomeru 認める (recognize).

percent, *n.* pāsento パーセント.

percentage, *n.* wari(ai) 割(合).

perception, *n.* 1. rikairyoku 理解力 (ability to understand). 2. ninshiki 認識 (recognition).

perceptive, *adj.* rikairyoku ni tomu 理解力に富む (keen).

perch, *vb.* 1. tomaru 止まる (of a bird). 2. suwaru 座る (of a person).

percolate, *vb.* kosu 漉す.

percussion, *n.* 1. shōdō 衝動 (violent impact). 2. dagakki 打楽器 (instrument).

perennial, *adj.* 1. taemanai 絶え間ない (constant). 2. eien (no) 永遠 (の) (lasting indefinitely). 3. tanensei (no) 多年性 (の) (plant).

perfect, *adj.* 1. kanpeki (na) 完璧 (な) (faultless). 2. kanzen (na) 完全 (な) (complete). 3. mattaku (no) 全く (の) (utter).

perfect tense, *n.* kanryōkei 完了形.

perfection, *n.* 1. kanpeki 完璧 (flawlessness). 2. kansei 完成 (completion).

perforate, *vb.* ana o akeru 穴を開ける (make a hole or holes).

perform, *vb.* 1. okonau 行う (execute). 2. ensō suru 演奏する (play an instrument). 3. enjiru 演じる (act). 4. ugoku 動く (move, function).

performance, *n.* 1. suikō 遂行 (execution). 2. seiseki 成績 (achievement, result). 3. ensō 演奏 (music). 4. engi 演技 (acting). 5. seinō 性能 (efficiency, as of a car, etc.).

performer, *n.* 1. ensōka 演奏家 (music). 2. engisha 演技者 (actor).

perfume, *n.* kōsui 香水.

perfunctory, *adj.* iikagen (na) 好い加減 (な).

perhaps, *adv.* tabun 多分.

peril, *n.* kiken 危険; **at one's peril** kiken o okashite 危険を冒して.

perilous, *adj.* kiken (na) 危険 (な).

perimeter, *n.* shūhen 周辺.

period, *n.* 1. kikan 期間 (portion of time). 2. jidai 時代 (epoch). 3. shūshifu 終止符 (punctuation).

periodic, *adj.* shūki-teki (na) 周期的 (な) (recurring regularly).

periodical, *n.* teiki-kankōbutsu 定期刊行物 (journal).

peripheral, *adj.* 1. mattan (no) 末端 (の) (of the periphery). 2. taishita koto nai 大したことない (of little importance).

periphery, *n.* shūhen 周辺.

perish, *vb.* 1. shinu 死ぬ (die). 2. horobiru 滅びる (be ruined or destroyed).

perishable, *adj.* kusareyasui 腐れ易い (of food).

perjury, *n.* gishō 偽証.

permanence, *n.* eien 永遠.

permanent, *adj.* 1. eien (no) 永遠 (の) (lasting). 2. eijū (no) 永住 (の) (of an address). 3. teishoku (no) 定職 (の) (of a job).

permeate, *adj.* 1. shintō suru 浸透する (penetrate). 2. ikiwataru 行き渡る (pervade).

permissible, *adj.* yurusareru 許される (that may be permitted).

permission, *n.* kyoka 許可.

permissive, *adj.* kan'yō (na) 寛容 (な) (tolerant).

permit, 1. *n.* kyokashō 許可書 (written statement, license). 2. *vb.* kyoka suru 許可する (allow, license); yurusu 許す (afford opportunity, allow).

pernicious, *adj.* yūgai (na) 有害 (な).

perpendicular, *adj.* suichoku (na, no) 垂直 (な、の) (vertical, meeting at right angle).

perpetrate, *vb.* okasu 犯す.

perpetual, *adj.* 1. eien (no) 永遠 (の) (lasting forever). 2. taemanai 絶え間ない (constant).

perpetuate, *vb.* eienka suru 永遠化する.

perplex, *vb.* tomadowaseru 戸惑わせる.

perplexed, *adj.* **be perplexed** tomadou 戸惑う.

persecute, *vb.* hakugai suru 迫害する.

persecution, *n.* hakugai 迫害.

perseverance, *n.* nintai 忍耐.

persevere, *vb.* nintaizuyoku tsuzukeru 忍耐強く続ける.

persimmon, *n.* kaki 柿.

persist, *vb.* 1. shitsukoku

tsuzukeru しつこく続ける
(continue stubbornly). 2. tsuzuku
続く (continue).

persistent, *adj.* shitsukoi しつこい
(stubborn).

person, *n.* hito 人; **in person**
hon'ninmizukara 本人自ら.

personal, *adj.* 1. kojin (no) 個人
(の); kojin-teki (na) 個人的 (な)
(of, by, or relating to a particular
person). 2. shiteki (na) 私的 (な)
(private).

personality, *n.* 1. kosei 個性
(personal character). 2. chomeijin
著名人 (famous person).

personify, *vb.* 1. gijinka suru 擬人
化する (attribute human character
to a thing). 2. gugen suru 具現す
る (embody). 3. ... no gonge de
aru ...の権化である (be a good
example of ...).

personnel, *n.* jin'in 人員.

perspective, *n.* 1. enkinhō 遠近法
(spatial relationship). 2. kenchi 見
地 (viewpoint). 3. tenbō 展望
(vista, view).

perspiration, *n.* ase 汗.

perspire, *vb.* ase o kaku 汗をかく.

persuade, *vb.* 1. settoku suru 説得
する (prevail on). 2. nattoku
saseru 納得させる (convince).

persuasion, *n.* 1. settoku 説得 (act
of persuading). 2. settokuryoku
説得力 (power of persuading). 3.
shin'nen 信念 (conviction).

pertain, *vb.* 1. ... ni zokusuru ...に
属する (belong to ...). 2. ... ni
kansuru ...に関する (have
reference to ...).

pertinent, *adj.* 1. kankei ga aru 関
係がある (related). 2. fusawashii
ふさわしい (appropriate).

perturb, *vb.* fuangaraseru 不安がら
せる.

perverse, *adj.* 1. tsumujimagari
(no) つむじ曲がり (の)
(stubbornly contrary). 2. ijō (na)
異常 (na) (abnormal).

perversion, *n.* 1. ijō 異常
(abnormality). 2. hentai-seiyoku
変態性欲 (sexual perversion).

pervert, 1. *n.* hentaisha 変態者
(perverted person). 2. *vb.* akuyō
suru 悪用する (turn something to
a wrong use); daraku saseru 堕落
させる (turn someone away from
the moral course).

pessimism, *n.* hikanshugi 悲観主
義.

pessimistic, *adj.* hikan-teki (na) 悲
観的 (な).

pest, *n.* 1. gaichū 害虫 (insect). 2.
iya na yatsu 嫌な奴 (person).

pester, *vb.* 1. komaraseru 困らせる
(bother). 2. segamu せがむ (ask
persistently).

pesticide, *n.* satchūzai 殺虫剤.

pet, 1. *n.* petto ペット (animal);
okini'iri お気に入り (favorite). 2.
vb. amayakasu 甘やかす (indulge);
aibu suru 愛撫する (fondle).

petal, *n.* hanabira 花びら.

petition, 1. *n.* chinjōsho 陳情書
(appeal signed by many people);
onegai お願い (request). 2. *vb.*
chinjō suru 陳情する (appeal in a
group); kongan suru 懇願する
(request earnestly).

petrify, *vb.* 1. kasekika suru 化石化
する (fossilize). 2. **be petrified**
kyōfu de tachisukumu 恐怖で立ち
すくむ (be paralyzed with fear).

petroleum, *n.* sekiyu 石油.

petty, *adj.* 1. chippoke (na) ちっぽ
け (な); sasai (na) 些細 (な)
(trivial). 2. henkyō (na) 偏狭 (な)
(small-minded).

petulant, *adj.* okorippoi 怒りっぽ

い.

pewter, *n.* suzu to namari no gōkin 錫と鉛の合金.

phallic, *adj.* dankon (no) 男根 (の).

phantom, *n.* obake お化け.

pharmacist, *n.* yakuzaishi 薬剤師.

pharmacy, *n.* yakkyoku 薬局.

phase, *n.* 1. kyokumen 局面; dankai 段階 (stage of change). 2. men 面 (aspect).

pheasant, *n.* kiji 雉子.

phenomenal, *adj.* kyōi-teki (na) 驚異的 (な) (marvelous).

phenomenon, *n.* 1. genshō 現象 (something observable). 2. kyōi 驚異 (marvel).

philanthropist, *n.* jizenka 慈善家 (person who helps the needy).

philanthropy, *n.* 1. jinruiai 人類愛 (concern for human beings). 2. jizen 慈善 (benevolent act).

philharmonic, *n.* kōkyōgakudan 交響楽団 (symphony orchestra).

Philippines, *n.* firipin フィリピン.

philosopher, *n.* tetsugakusha 哲学者.

philosophical, *adj.* tetsugaku-teki (na) 哲学的 (な) (of philosophy).

philosophy, *n.* tetsugaku 哲学.

phlegm, *n.* tan 痰 (mucus secretion).

phobia, *n.* kyōfu 恐怖.

phoenix, *n.* fushichō 不死鳥.

phone, 1. *n.* denwa 電話. 2. *vb.* denwa suru 電話する.

phonetic, *adj.* 1. onsei (no) 音声 (の) (of the sounds of human speech). 2. hatsuonkigō (no) 発音記号 (の) (of phonetic symbols).

phonetics, *n.* onseigaku 音声学.

phony, *adj.* nisemono (no) 偽物 (の) (fake).

phosphorus, *n.* rin 燐.

photo, *n.* shashin 写真.

photocopy, 1. *n.* kopī コピー. 2. *vb.* ... no kopī o suru ...のコピーをする.

photogenic, *adj.* shashin'utsuri ga ii 写真映りがいい.

photograph, *n.* shashin 写真; **take a photograph** shashin o toru 写真を撮る.

photographer, *n.* kameraman カメラマン.

photography, *n.* shashinjutsu 写真術.

phrase, 1. *n.* furēzu フレーズ; ku 句 (unit of words). 2. *vb.* hyōgen suru 表現する.

physical, *adj.* 1. nikutai (no) 肉体 (の) (of the body). 2. busshitsu-teki (na) 物質的 (な) (of matter). 3. butsurigaku (no) 物理学 (の) (of physics).

physician, *n.* naikai 内科医.

physicist, *n.* butsurigakusha 物理学者.

physics, *n.* butsurigaku 物理学.

physiology, *n.* seirigaku 生理学.

physique, *n.* taikaku 体格.

pianist, *n.* pianisuto ピアニスト.

piano, *n.* piano ピアノ.

piccolo, *n.* pikkoro ピッコロ.

pick, 1. *n.* sentaku 選択 (choice); pikku ピック (plectrum, pointed tool); **take one's pick** erabu 選ぶ. 2. *vb.* tsumiatsumeru 摘み集める (gather, as fruit, etc); tsumamiageru 摘まみ上げる (take up with fingers); erabu 選ぶ (choose); tsuku 突く (dig, break into); hiku 弾く (guitar); hojikuru ほじくる (teeth, nose); suru 掏る (pocket); **pick up;** tori ni iku 取りに行く (go and get a thing); mukae ni iku 迎えに行く (go and get a person); atsumeru 集める

(collect); yoku naru 良くなる (improve); oboeru 覚える (learn); kiku 聞く (hear).

pickle, *n.* tsukemono 漬物 (pickled vegetable).

pickpocket, *n.* suri すり.

picnic, *n.* pikunikku ピクニック.

picture, 1. *n.* e 絵 (drawing, painting); shashin 写真 (photograph); eiga 映画 (motion picture). 2. *vb.* egaku 描く (draw, paint); omoiegaku 思い描く (imagine).

picturesque, *adj.* 1. e no yō (na) 絵のよう (な) (looking as if in a picture). 2. kirei (na) きれい (な) (beautiful). 3. byōsha-teki (na) 描写的 (な) (descriptive).

pie, *n.* pai パイ.

piece, *n.* 1. bubun 部分 (part). 2. danpen 断片 (broken piece). 3. sakuhin 作品 (artistic work). 4. **a piece of** hitotsu (no) 一つ (の); **a piece of paper** kami ichimai 紙一枚.

pier, *n.* sanbashi 桟橋.

pierce, *vb.* tsuranuku 貫く.

piety, *n.* keikensa 敬虔さ.

pig, *n.* buta 豚 (animal, person).

pigeon, *n.* hato 鳩.

pigeon-toed, *adj.* uchimata (no) 内股 (の).

pigment, *n.* shikiso 色素.

pigpen, *n.* butagoya 豚小屋.

pile, 1. *n.* yama 山 (heap); takusan 沢山 (large quantity). 2. *vb.* tsumikasaneru 積み重ねる (make a pile); tamaru 溜まる (accumulate).

pilfer, *vb.* nusumu 盗む.

pilgrim, *n.* junreisha 巡礼者.

pilgrimage, *n.* junrei 巡礼.

pill, *n.* 1. jōzai 錠剤 (medicine). 2. hinin'yaku 避妊薬 (for birth control).

pillage, *vb.* gōdatsu suru 強奪する.

pillar, *n.* hashira 柱.

pillow, *n.* makura 枕 (for sleeping); **pillow case** makura-kabā 枕カバー.

pilot, 1. *n.* pairotto パイロット (ship or airplane). 2. *vb.* sōjū suru 操縦する (airplane); michibiku 導く (guide, lead).

pimento, *n.* pīman ピーマン.

pimp, *n.* ponbiki ぽん引き.

pimple, *n.* nikibi にきび.

pin, 1. *n.* pin ピン (for fastening). 2. *vb.* pin de tomeru ピンで留める.

pincers, *n.* yattoko やっとこ (tool); hasami 鋏 (crab).

pinch, 1. *n.* hitotsumami 一摘み (tiny amount); **in a pinch** hitsuyō naraba 必要ならば (if necessary). 2. *vb.* tsumamu 摘む (squeeze); tsuneru つねる (squeeze painfully); nusumu 盗む (steal); **be pinched** komatteiru 困っている (be in trouble).

pine, 1. *n.* matsu 松 (tree); **pine cone** matsukasa 松かさ. 2. *vb.* omoi kogareru 思い焦がれる (long painfully).

pineapple, *n.* painappuru パイナップル.

Ping-Pong, *n.* pinpon ピンポン.

pink, *n., adj.* pinku (no) ピンク (の); momoiro (no) 桃色 (の).

pinnacle, *n.* 1. itadaki 頂 (mountaintop). 2. chōten 頂点 (culmination).

pint, *n.* painto パイント.

pioneer, *n.* 1. senkusha 先駆者 (art, thought, etc.). 2. kaitakusha 開拓者 (first settler, explorer).

pious, *adj.* shinjinbukai 信心深い.

pipe, *n.* 1. kuda 管 (tube). 2. paipu

パイプ (smoking). 3. kangakki 管
楽器 (musical instrument).

piracy, *n.* chosakukenshingai 著作
権侵害 (violation of copyright).

pirate, *n.* kaizoku 海賊 (robber at
sea).

pistol, *n.* pisutoru ピストル.

piston, *n.* pisuton ピストン.

pit, *n.* ana 穴 (hole); kubomi 凹み
(hollow); naraku 奈落 (stage).

pitch, 1. *n.* pitchi ピッチ (musical
tone, baseball); kōbaido 勾配度
(slope); teido 程度 (degree). 2. *vb.*
nageru 投げる (throw); setchi
suru 設置する (set up); taoreru 倒
れる (fall); yureru 揺れる (drop
and rise).

pitcher, *n.* 1. mizusashi 水差し
(water container). 2. pitchā ピッ
チャー (baseball).

pitch-dark, *adj.* makkura (na, no)
真暗 (な、の).

pitfall, *n.* otoshiana 落とし穴
(trap).

pith, *n.* 1. zui 髄 (spongy tissue).
2. seizui 精髄 (essence).

pitiful, *adj.* 1. aware (na) 哀れ (な)
(lamentable). 2. nasakenai 情けな
い (contemptible).

pittance, *n.* namidakin 涙金.

pity, 1. *n.* awaremi 哀れみ
(sympathetic sorrow); zan'nen 残
念 (regret); **it is a pity that** ... to
wa zan'nen da ... とは残念だ;
What a pity! Zan'nen. 残念. 2.
vb. awaremu 哀れむ (feel pity for);
dōjō suru 同情する (sympathize
with).

pivot, *n.* kaitenjiku 回転軸 (shaft
on which something turns).

placard, *n.* purakādo プラカード;
keiji 掲示 (public notice).

placate, *vb.* nadameru なだめる.

place, 1. *n.* basho 場所; tokoro 所

(particular portion of space); chii
地位 (social standing); -i -位 (at a
competition); **first place** ichii 一
位; **in place** tekisetsu (na) 適切
(な) (proper); **out of place**
bachigai (na) 場違い (な)
(awkward); futekisetsu (na) 不適
切 (な) (improper); **take the
place of** ... ni totte kawaru ... に
取って代わる; **take place** okoru
起こる. 2. *vb.* oku 置く (put in
place); omoidasu 思い出す
(remember); **place an order**
chūmon o suru 注文をする.

placement office, *n.* shokugyō-
shōkaisho 職業紹介所.

placid, *adj.* odayaka (na) 穏やか
(な).

plagiarism, *n.* hyōsetsu 剽窃.

plagiarize, *vb.* hyōsetsu suru 剽窃
する.

plague, 1. *n.* pesuto ペスト
(bubonic plague); ekibyō 疫病
(contagious disease). 2. *vb.*
komaraseru 困らせる (annoy).

plain, 1. *n.* heichi 平地 (level area).
2. *adj.* meikai (na) 明快 (な)
(clear); shisso (na) 質素 (な)
(simple); muji (no) 無地 (の)
(without pattern); bukiryō (na) 不
器量 (な) (unattractive); sotchoku
(na) 率直 (な) (candid).

plaintiff, *n.* genkoku 原告.

plaintive, *adj.* kanashii 悲しい.

plan, 1. *n.* keikaku 計画 (project);
sekkeizu 設計図 (drawing). 2. *vb.*
keikaku suru 計画する (make a
plan); sekkei suru 設計する
(design).

plane, *n.* 1. heimen 平面 (flat
surface). 2. reberu レベル (level).
3. kan'na 鉋 (tool). 4. hikōki 飛行
機 (airplane).

planet, *n.* wakusei 惑星.

planetarium, *n.* puranetariumu プラネタリウム.

plank, *n.* ita 板 (lumber).

planner, *n.* keikakusha 計画者.

plant, 1. *n.* shokubutsu 植物 (organism); kōjō 工場 (factory); setsubi 設備 (apparatus). 2. *vb.* ueru 植える (set in ground for growth).

plantation, *n.* 1. purantēshon プランテーション (large estate for growing crops) 2. shokurin 植林 (trees).

plaque, *n.* 1. shikō 歯こう (on teeth). 2. meiban 銘板 (monumental tablet).

plasma, *n.* kesshō 血しょう (blood).

plaster, *n.* 1. shikkui 漆喰 (for construction). 2. bansōkō ばんそうこう (adhesive plaster).

plastic, *n.* purasuchikku プラスチック.

plastic bag, *n.* binīru-bukuro ビニール袋.

plastic surgery, *n.* biyōseikei 美容整形; seikeishujutsu 整形手術.

plate, *n.* 1. sara 皿 (dish). 2. ginshokki 銀食器 (silver plate). 3. kinzokuban 金属板 (metal sheet). 4. ireba 入れ歯 (denture).

plateau, *n.* kōgen 高原 (geology).

platform, *n.* 1. purattohōmu プラットホーム (at a railroad station). 2. dai 台 (raised flooring).

platinum, *n.* purachina プラチナ.

platitude, *n.* kimarimonku 決まり文句.

platter, *n.* moritsukezara 盛りつけ皿.

plausible, *adj.* shin'yō dekiru 信用出来る (believable).

play, 1. *n.* asobi 遊び (recreation, fun); purē プレー (sports); geki 劇 (theater). 2. *vb.* asobu 遊ぶ (amuse oneself); suru する (engage in, as a game); ensō suru 演奏する (perform on a musical instrument); enzuru 演ずる (play a part).

player, *n.* purēyā プレーヤー (audio or video player, sports participant); ongakuka 音楽家 (musician); engisha 演技者 (theater).

playboy, *n.* pureibōi プレイボーイ; on'natarashi 女たらし.

playful, *adj.* 1. tanoshii 楽しい (full of fun). 2. jōdan (no) 冗談 (の) (not serious).

playground, *n.* gakkō no asobiba 学校の遊び場 (at a school).

playmate, *n.* asobinakama 遊び仲間.

playwright, *n.* gekisakka 劇作家.

plaza, *n.* puraza プラザ.

plea, *n.* 1. kongan 懇願 (entreaty); kōjitsu 口実 (excuse); **on the plea that** ... to iu kōjitsu de ... という口実で. 2. tōben 答弁 (defendant's answer).

plead, *vb.* 1. kongan suru 懇願する (entreat). 2. mōshitateru 申し立てる (make a legal plea).

pleasant, *adj.* 1. kokoroyoi 快い (pleasing). 2. aisō ga ii 愛想がいい (friendly).

please, 1. *vb.* yorokobaseru 喜ばせる (give pleasure); **if you please** yokereba 良ければ (if you like); **Please yourself!** Sukikatte ni shiro. 好き勝手にしろ. 2. *adv.* onegai shimasu お願いします (used when making a request).

pleased, *adj.* ureshii 嬉しい (happy).

pleasure, *n.* 1. yorokobi 喜び (joy).

2. manzoku 満足 (satisfaction).

pleat, *n.* hida ひだ.

pledge, 1. *n.* shirushi 印 (sign); seiyaku 誓約 (solemn promise). 2. *vb.* seiyaku suru 誓約する (promise).

plentiful, *adj.* jūbun (na) 十分 (な).

plenty, *n.* jūbun 十分 (abundant quantity); **plenty of** jūbun na 十分な; **in plenty** jūbun ni 十分に.

pliable, *adj.* 1. shinayaka (na) しなやか (な) (supple). 2. sayū sareyasui 左右され易い (easily influenced).

pliers, *n.* puraiyā プライヤー (for holding); penchi ペンチ (for cutting wires).

plight, *n.* kyūchi 窮地; gyakkyō 逆境.

plod, *vb.* 1. tobo-tobo aruku とぼとぼ歩く (manner of walking). 2. kotsu-kotsu hataraku こつこつ働く (manner of working).

plot, 1. *n.* kukaku 区画 (piece of ground); inbō 陰謀 (secret scheme); arasuji 荒筋 (main story). 2. *vb.* zushi suru 図示する (mark on a map, etc.); takuramu 企む (conspire).

plow, 1. *n.* suki 鋤 (farming tool). 2. *vb.* suki de tagayasu 鋤で耕す (cultivate with a plow); oshisusumu 押し進む (move forcefully through).

pluck, 1. *n.* yūki 勇気 (courage). 2. *vb.* nuku 抜く (pull out); hane o mushiru 羽をむしる (pluck feathers); tsumabiku 爪弾く (strings); **pluck up courage** yūki o furuiokosu 勇気を奮い起こす.

plug, 1. *n.* sen 栓 (for stopping a hole); puragu プラグ (electrical). 2. *vb.* sen o suru 栓をする (stop

with a plug); **plug in** ... no puragu o soketto ni ireru ... のプラグをソケットに入れる (electrical).

plum, *n.* puramu プラム.

plumage, *n.* hane 羽.

plumb, 1. *n.* omori おもり (piece of lead). 2. *vb.* hakaru 測る、計る (measure depth of); saguru 探る (try to get to the root of).

plumber, *n.* haikankō 配管工.

plumbing, *n.* 1. haikan setsubi 配管設備 (system of water pipes). 2. haikan 配管 (work of a plumber).

plume, *n.* hane 羽.

plummet, *vb.* kyūgeki ni ochiru 急激に落ちる.

plump, *adj.* maru-maru to shiteiru 丸々としている.

plunder, 1. *n.* ryakudatsuhin 略奪品 (loot). 2. *vb.* ryakudatsu suru 略奪する (rob).

plunge, 1. *n.* tobikomi 飛び込み (dive). 2. *vb.* tsukkomu 突っ込む (put into); tobikomu 飛び込む (dive into); tosshin suru 突進する (move forward quickly); kyū ni sagaru 急に下がる (become low suddenly).

plural, *n., adj.* fukusūkei (no) 複数形 (の).

plus, *prep.* purasu プラス.

plush, *adj.* gōka (na) 豪華 (な) (luxurious).

plutonium, *n.* purutoniumu プルトニウム.

ply, 1. *n.* sō 層 (layer). 2. *vb.* ōfuku suru 往復する (travel regularly); **ply a trade** shōbai ni hagemu 商売に励む.

plywood, *n.* beniyaita ベニヤ板.

p.m., gogo 午後; **5:00 p.m.** gogo goji 午後五時.

pneumonia, *n.* haien 肺炎.

poach, *vb.* 1. yuderu ゆでる (boil);
otoshitamago ni suru 落し卵にす
る (poach an egg). 2. mitsuryō
suru 密猟する (catch animals
illegally).

pocket, 1. *n.* poketto ポケット (in
garment); koritsu shita tokoro 孤
立した所 (isolated area). 2. *vb.*
poketto ni ireru ポケットに入れる
(put into one's pocket);
chakufuku suru 着服する
(embezzle).

pocketbook, *n.* handobaggu ハン
ドバッグ.

pocketknife, *n.* pokettonaifu ポ
ケットナイフ.

pod, *n.* saya さや.

podium, *n.* dai 台.

poem, *n.* shi 詩.

poet, *n.* shijin 詩人.

poetess, *n.* joseishijin 女性詩人.

poetic, *adj.* 1. shi (no) 詩 (の) (of
poetry). 2. shi-teki (na) 詩的 (な)
(like poetry).

poetry, *n.* shi 詩.

poignant, *adj.* kokoroitamu 心痛
む.

point, 1. *n.* ten 点 (dot, score in
game, decimal point, detail in
conversation or writing); saki 先
(projecting part, tip); chiten 地点
(definite place); jiten 時点
(definite time); yōten 要点 (issue,
central topic); **at the point of** ...
no magiwa ni ...の間際に; **be
beside the point** yōten o
hazureteiru 要点を外れている;
make a point of doing kanarazu
...suru 必ず...する (do without
fail); **miss the point** mato o
hazusu 的を外す; **on the point
of doing** ... shiyō to suru tokoro
...しようとするところ; **point of
view** kenkai 見解; **to the point**

of hotondo ほとんど (almost). 2.
vb. sasu 指す (indicate); yubisasu
指差す (indicate with a finger);
mukeru 向ける (direct); **point
out** shiteki suru 指摘する.

point-blank, *adv.* kippari きっぱり
(bluntly and frankly).

pointed, *adj.* togatteiru 尖っている
(sharp).

point of view, *n.* kenkai 見解;
kanten 観点.

pointless, *adj.* muimi (na) 無意味
(な).

poise, *n.* 1. ochitsuki 落ち着き
(composure). 2. mi no tsuriai 身
の釣り合い (balance).

poison, 1. *n.* doku 毒. 2. *adj.*
yūdoku (na) 有毒 (な). 3. *vb.* ... ni
doku o moru ... に毒を盛る.

poisonous, *adj.* yūdoku (na) 有毒
(な).

poke, *vb.* tsutsuku 突く.

poker, *n.* 1. pōkā ポーカー (game).
2. hikakibō 火掻き棒 (tool for
tending fire).

polar, *adj.* kyokuchi (no) 極地 (の).

pole, *n.* bō 棒 (long slender piece of
wood, etc.). 2. kyoku 極
(geographical).

polemic, *n.* tōron 討論.

police, *n.* keisatsu 警察.

police officer, *n.* kei(satsu)kan 警
(察)官.

policy, *n.* 1. porishī ポリシー;
hōshin 方針 (course of action). 2.
hoken shōsho 保険証書
(insurance contract).

polio, *n.* porio ポリオ; shōnimahi
小児麻痺.

polish, 1. *n.* kenmazai 研磨剤
(polishing substance); kōtaku 光沢
(luster); senren 洗練 (refinement);
shoe polish kutsuzumi 靴墨. 2.
vb. migaku 磨く (make glossy,

refine).

polite, *adj.* 1. reigi tadashii 礼儀正しい (showing good manners). 2. jōhin (na) 上品 (な) (refined).

politeness, *n.* 1. reigitadashisa 礼儀正しさ (good manners). 2. jōhinsa 上品さ (refinement).

political, *adj.* seiji (no) 政治 (の); seiji-teki (na) 政治的 (な); **political prisoner** seijihan 政治犯.

politician, *n.* seijika 政治家.

politics, *n.* 1. seiji 政治 (administration of government). 2. seijigaku 政治学 (political science).

poll, *n.* 1. senkyo 選挙 (voting, votes). 2. senkyonin meibo 選挙人名簿 (list of voters). 3. seron-chōsa 世論調査 (analysis of public opinion).

pollen, *n.* kafun 花粉.

pollute, *vb.* osen suru 汚染する.

pollution, *n.* osen 汚染; **environmental pollution** kankyō osen 環境汚染.

pomegranate, *n.* zakuro ざくろ.

pomp, *n.* sōreisa 壮麗さ.

pompous, *adj.* sōrei (na) 壮麗 (な).

pond, *n.* ike 池.

ponder, *vb.* kangaeru 考える.

pony, *n.* kouma 子馬.

pool, *n.* 1. mizutamari 水溜まり (of water); **swimming pool** pūru プール. 2. tamatsuki 玉突き (game).

poor, *adj.* 1. mazushii 貧しい (destitute). 2. hinjaku (na) 貧弱 (な) (inferior). 3. kawaisō (na) 可哀そう (な) (unfortunate).

pop, 1. *n.* pon to iu oto ぽんと言う音 (short, quick sound); poppusu ポップス (music); tansan inryō 炭酸飲料 (soft drink). 2. *vb.* pon to

hajikeru ぽんとはじける (burst with a short, quick sound); tobideru 飛び出る (spring).

popcorn, *n.* poppukōn ポップコーン.

poppy, *n.* keshi けし.

populace, *n.* minshū 民衆.

popular, *adj.* 1. ninki ga aru 人気がある (liked). 2. taishū (no) 大衆 (の) (of the general public); taishūmuke (no) 大衆向け (の) (aimed at the general public). 3. hayari (no) はやり (の) (prevalent, current).

popularity, *n.* ninki 人気.

populated, *adj.* hito ga sundeiru 人が住んでいる.

population, *n.* jinkō 人口.

porcelain, *n.* jiki 磁器.

porch, *n.* pōchi ポーチ.

porcupine, *n.* yama'arashi 山荒し.

pore, *n.* keana 毛穴 (in the skin).

pork, *n.* pōku ポーク; butaniku 豚肉; **pork chop** pōku-choppu ポークチョップ.

pornography, *n.* poruno ポルノ.

porpoise, *n.* iruka いるか.

port, *n.* 1. minato 港 (harbor). 2. pōto-wain ポートワイン (type of wine).

portable, *adj.* keitaiyō (no) 携帯用 (の).

porter, *n.* pōtā ポーター.

portfolio, *n.* 1. kamibasami 紙挟み (case). 2. pōtoforio ポートフォリオ (securities held by an investor).

portion, *n.* 1. bubun 部分 (part). 2. wakemae 分け前 (share).

portly, *adj.* futotteiru 太っている.

portrait, *n.* pōtorēto ポートレート; shōzōga 肖像画.

portray, *vb.* egaku 描く (depict).

portrayal, *n.* byōsha 描写 (depiction).

pose, 1. *n.* pōzu ポーズ (bodily posture); kidori 気取り (affectation). 2. *vb.* pōzu o toru ポーズをとる (sit for a portrait, etc.); motarasu もたらす (give rise to); **pose as** ... no furi o suru ...のふりをする (feign).

position, *n.* 1. ichi 位置; basho 場所 (location). 2. chi'i 地位 (social standing). 3. tachiba 立場 (condition, state). 4. shoku 職 (job).

positive, *adj.* 1. tashika (na) 確か (な) (certain). 2. kōtei-teki (na) 肯定的 (な) (affirmative). 3. zettai (no) 絶対 (の) (definite). 4. kensetsu-teki (na) 建設的 (な) (constructive). 5. yōsei (no) 陽性 (の) (medical test).

possess, *vb.* 1. shoyū suru 所有する (own). 3. toritsuku 取り憑く (obsess).

possession, *n.* 1. shoyū 所有 (ownership). 2. shoyūhin 所有品 (something owned). 3. **be in possession of** ... o shoyū shiteiru ...を所有している; **take possession of** ... o te ni ireru ...を手に入れる.

possessive, *adj.* 1. dokusen'yoku ga tsuyoi 独占欲が強い (obsessed with dominating another). 2. shoyūkaku (no) 所有格 (の) (grammar).

possibility, *n.* kanōsei 可能性 (likelihood).

possible, *adj.* kanō (na) 可能 (な); **if possible** dekireba 出来れば; **as much as possible** dekirudake takusan 出来るだけ沢山.

post, 1. *n.* hashira 柱 (pole); shoku 職 (job); mochiba 持ち場 (place of duty); yūbin 郵便 (mail). 2. *vb.* keiji suru 掲示する (display, as a

notice); haichi suru 配置する (station); tōkan suru 投函する (mail).

postage, *n.* yūbinryōkin 郵便料金 (charge); **postage stamp** kitte 切手.

postal, *adj.* yūbin (no) 郵便 (の).

postbox, *n.* posuto ポスト (mailbox).

postcard, *n.* hagaki 葉書.

poster, *n.* posutā ポスター.

posterity, *n.* kōsei no hito 後世の人.

posthumous, *adj.* shigo (no) 死後 (の).

postman, *n.* yūbinhaitatsu 郵便配達.

postmark, *n.* keshi'in 消印.

post office, *n.* yūbinkyoku 郵便局.

post office box, *n.* shishobako 私書箱.

postpone, *vb.* enki suru 延期する.

postscript, *n.* tsuishin 追伸.

posture, *n.* shisei 姿勢 (position of the body).

pot, *n.* potto ポット (cooking, planting).

potable, *adj.* nomeru 飲める.

potato, *n.* poteto ポテト; jagaimo じゃが芋; **potato chip** poteto-chippu ポテトチップ.

potbelly, *n.* taikobara 太鼓腹.

potent, *adj.* 1. kyōryoku (na) 強力 (な) (powerful). 2. seishokukanō (na) 生殖可能 (な) (having sexual power).

potential, 1. *n.* senzainōryoku 潜在能力. 2. *adj.* senzainōryoku ga aru 潜在能力がある.

potion, *n.* mizugusuri 水薬 (liquid medicine).

potter, *n.* tōkō 陶工.

pottery, *n.* tōki 陶器.

pouch, *n.* fukuro 袋.

poultry, *n.* 1. kakin 家禽 (domestic fowl). 2. toriniku 鳥肉 (meat).

pounce on, *vb.* ... ni tobikakaru ... に飛びかかる.

pound, 1. *n.* pondo ポンド (unit of weight, currency). 2. *vb.* kudaku 砕く (crush by pounding); utsu 打つ (strike).

pour, *vb.* 1. sosogu 注ぐ (send a liquid flowing out); nagareru 流れる (flow out or along). 2. tsugu 注ぐ (tea).

pouring rain, *n.* doshaburi 土砂降り.

pout, *vb.* kuchi o togarasu 口を尖らす (thrust out the lips).

poverty, *n.* binbō 貧乏.

powder, *n.* kona 粉.

power, *n.* 1. chikara 力 (strength). 2. nōryoku 能力 (ability, faculty). 3. denryoku 電力 (electricity). 4. kenryoku 権力 (authority, control, domination).

powerful, *adj.* kyōryoku (na) 強力 (な).

power plant, *n.* hatsudensho 発電所.

practical, *adj.* 1. genjitsu-teki (na) 現実的 (な) (pragmatic, realistic). 2. jissai (no) 実際 (の) (real, actual). 3. yaku ni tatsu 役に立つ (useful).

practice, 1. *n.* renshū 練習 (repeated performance); jikkō 実行 (actual performance); genjitsu 現実 (actuality); shūkan 習慣 (customary action); kaigyō 開業 (pursuit, as of a profession); **in practice** genjitsu niwa 現実には; **put into practice** jikkō suru 実行する. 2. *vb.* renshū suru 練習する (perform repeatedly); kaigyō suru 開業する (pursue as profession); okonau 行う (do habitually).

practitioner, *n.* isha 医者 (medical).

pragmatic, *adj.* genjitsu-teki (na) 現実的 (な).

prairie, *n.* sōgen 草原.

praise, 1. *n.* shōsan 賞讃、称讃. 2. *vb.* shōsan suru 賞讃／称讃する.

prance, *vb.* tobihaneru 飛び跳ねる.

prank, *n.* itazura いたずら.

prawn, *n.* kuruma ebi 車えび.

pray, *vb.* inoru 祈る (make a devout petition).

prayer, *n.* inori 祈り (devout petition).

preach, *vb.* sekkyō suru 説教する (deliver a sermon, moralize).

preacher, *n.* bokushi 牧師.

preamble, *n.* maeoki 前置き.

precarious, *adj.* 1. abunakkashii 危なっかしい (dangerous). 2. fuantei (na) 不安定 (な) (unsteady).

precaution, *n.* yōjin 用心; **take precautions** yōjin suru 用心する.

precede, *vb.* mae ni kuru/okoru 前に来る／起こる (come/happen before).

precedence, *n.* yūsenken 優先権; **take precedence over** ... yori yūsenken ga aru ...より優先権がある.

precedent, *n.* 1. senrei 先例 (former example). 2. hanketsurei 判決例 (legal).

preceding, *adj.* sono mae no その前の.

precept, *n.* kisoku 規則 (rule).

precinct, *n.* 1. fukin 付近 (neighborhood). 2. kōnai 構内 (premises).

precious, *adj.* 1. kichō (na) 貴重 (な) (beloved, important). 2. kōka (na) 高価 (な) (valuable).

precipice, *n.* zeppeki 絶壁.

precipitate, *vb.* hayameru 早める (hasten occurrence of).

precipitous, *adj.* kewashii 険しい (extremely steep).

precise, *adj.* seikaku (na) 正確 (な).

precision, *n.* seikakusa 正確さ.

preclude, *vb.* fusegu 防ぐ.

precocious, *adj.* sōjuku (na) 早熟 (な).

precursor, *n.* senkusha 先駆者.

predatory, *adj.* tanin o ejiki ni suru 他人をえじきにする (plundering).

predecessor, *n.* zen'ninsha 前任者.

predicament, *n.* kyūchi 窮地.

predict, *vb.* yogen suru 予言する.

prediction, *n.* yogen 予言.

predisposition, *n.* keikōsei 傾向性 (tendency).

predominant, *adj.* kencho (na) 顕著 (な) (most conspicuous); shuyō (na) 主要 (な) (chief).

predominate, *vb.* uwamawaru 上回る (be greater in number, strength, etc.).

preeminent, *adj.* sugureteiru 優れている.

preface, *n.* jo 序.

prefer, *vb.* ... no hō o konomu ...の方を好む.

preferable, *adj.* ... hō ga ii ...方がいい.

preference, *n.* 1. konomi 好み; **have a preference for** ... o konomu ...を好む. 2. **give preference to** ... ni yūsenken o ataeru ...に優先権を与える.

prefix, *n.* settōji 接頭辞.

pregnancy, *n.* ninshin 妊娠.

pregnant, *adj.* ninshin shiteiru 妊娠している.

prejudice, 1. *n.* henken 偏見 (bigotry); sen'nyūkan 先入観 (preconception). 2. *vb.* **be**

prejudiced against ... ni taishite henken ga aru ...に対して偏見がある.

preliminary, *adj.* yobi (no) 予備 (の).

prelude, *n.* 1. maebure 前触れ (preliminary to a major event). 2. pureryūdo プレリュード; zensōkyoku 前奏曲 (music).

premature, *adj.* 1. jiki shōsō (no) 時期尚早 (の) (too early). 2. sōzan (no) 早産 (の) (of child).

premeditated, *adj.* keikaku-teki (na) 計画的 (な).

premier, *n.* shushō 首相.

premiere, *n.* shoen 初演.

premise, *n.* zentei 前提.

premium, *n.* 1. kakekin 掛け金 (periodic insurance payment). 2. puremiamu プレミアム (addition to ordinary charges).

premonition, *n.* mushi no shirase 虫の知らせ.

preoccupation, *n.* kanshinji 関心事 (chief concern).

preoccupied, *vb.* **preoccupied by/with** ... de atama ga ippai ...で頭が一杯.

preparation, *n.* junbi 準備 (act of preparing, things to be done beforehand).

preparatory, *adj.* yobi (no) 予備 (の).

prepare, *vb.* 1. junbi suru 準備する (get ready). 2. ryōri suru 料理する (cook). 3. kokorogamae o saseru 心構えをさせる (make someone ready to accept something new).

preponderance, *n.* yūsei 優勢.

preposition, *n.* zenchishi 前置詞.

preposterous, *adj.* bakagete iru 馬鹿げている.

prerogative, *n.* tokken 特権.

prescribe, *vb.* 1. meijiru 命じる (order). 2. shohō suru 処方する (medical).

prescription, *n.* shohōsen 処方箋 (written order for medicine); kusuri 薬 (prescribed medicine).

presence, *n.* 1. shusseki 出席 (attendance). 2. sonzai 存在 (existence, fact of being present); **presence of mind** ochitsuki 落ち着き (composure); **in my presence** watashi no me no mae de 私の目の前で. 3. sonzaikan 存在感 (perceived personal quality).

present, 1. *n.* purezento プレゼント; okurimono 贈り物 (gift); ima 今 (present time); **at present** ima 今; **for the present** ima no tokoro 今のところ. 2. *adj.* ima (no) 今 (の) (being or occurring now); kiteiru 来ている (being at particular place). 3. *vb.* purezento suru プレゼントする (give a gift); ataeru 与える (offer); motarasu もたらす (bring, pose); teishutsu suru 提出する (offer for consideration); miseru 見せる (exhibit); shōkai suru 紹介する (introduce).

presentation, *n.* 1. happyō 発表 (exhibition). 2. zōtei 贈呈 (bestowal). 3. teishutsu 提出 (submission).

present-day, *adj.* kon'nichi (no) 今日 (の).

presently, *adv.* 1. sugu すぐ (soon). 2. ima 今 (now).

preservation, *n.* hozon 保存 (act of keeping from decay); iji 維持 (act of keeping safe).

preservative, *n.* bōfuzai 防腐剤 (in food).

preserve, 1. *n.* jamu ジャム (jam). 2. *vb.* hozon suru 保存する (keep

from decay); hogo suru 保護する (keep safe); iji suru 維持する (maintain).

preside, *vb.* **preside over** ... no gijichō o tsutomeru ...の議事長を務める (committee, etc.).

presidency, *n.* daitōryō no chi'i 大統領の地位 (office of president of a republic).

president, *n.* daitōryō 大統領 (chief of state of a republic); shachō 社長 (company); gakuchō 学長 (college or university).

press, 1. puresu プレス (device for pressing); insatsuki 印刷機 (device for printing); hōdōkikan 報道機関 (newspapers, magazines, etc.); insatsu 印刷 (printing); shinbun 新聞 (newspapers); shuppansha 出版社 (publisher). 2. *vb.* osu 押す (push); atsuryoku o kakeru 圧力をかける (apply pressure to); ... ni airon o kakeru ...にアイロンをかける (iron); sekasu 急かす (urge to hurry); iiharu 言い張る (insist upon).

press conference, *n.* kishakaiken 記者会見.

pressing, *adj.* kinkyū (no) 緊急 (の) (urgent).

pressure, *n.* 1. puresshā プレッシャー (mental constraint). 2. atsuryoku 圧力 (exertion of force); **pressure cooker** atsuryokugama 圧力釜; **put pressure on** ... ni atsuryoku o kakeru ...に圧力をかける. 3. **water/air pressure** suiatsu/kiatsu 水圧／気圧.

prestige, *n.* meisei 名声.

prestigious, *adj.* nadakai 名高い.

presume, *vb.* katei suru 仮定する (suppose).

presumption, *n.* katei 仮定 (act of

supposing, something proposed).

presumptuous, *adj.* atsukamashii 厚構しい.

presupposition, *n.* zentei 前提.

pretend, *vb.* furi o suru 振りをする.

pretense, *n.* misekake 見せかけ (false appearance); kōjitsu 口実 (pretext); **make a pretense of** ... furi o suru ...振りをする.

pretension, *n.* kidori 気取り.

pretentious, *adj.* mottaibutte-iru 勿体ぶっている (ostentatious); kidotteiru 気取っている (affected).

pretext, *n.* kōjitsu 口実.

pretty, 1. *adj.* kirei (na) きれい (な) (beautiful); kawaii 可愛い (cute). 2. *adv.* kanari かなり.

prevail, *vb.* 1. katsu 勝つ (gain victory). 2. ikiwatatte-iru 行き渡っている (be widespread).

prevalent, *adj.* 1. ippan-teki (na) 一般的 (な) (most common). 2. ikiwatatte-iru 行き渡っている (widespread).

prevaricate, *vb.* gomakasu ごまかす.

prevent, *vb.* fusegu 防ぐ.

prevention, *n.* bōshi 防止.

preventive, preventative, *adj.* yobō (no) 予防 (の).

preview, *n.* shisha 試写 (advance showing of film); shien 試演 (advance performance of play).

previous, *adj.* mae (no) 前 (の); **previous to** ... no mae (no) ...の前 (の).

prey, 1. *n.* ejiki えじき (animal, victim). 2. *vb.* **prey on** ... o ejiki ni suru ...をえじきにする.

price, 1. *n.* nedan 値段 (sum of money); **at any price** dōshitemo どうしても (by all means); **at the**

price of ... o gisei ni shite ...を犠牲にして. 2. *vb.* nedan o tsukeru 値段を付ける (set the price of).

priceless, *adj.* 1. totemo kōka (na) とても高価 (な) (very expensive). 2. kakegae ga nai 掛け替えがない (very important).

prick, 1. *n.* tsukikizu 突き傷 (puncture wound); chottoshita itami ちょっとした痛み (pain). 2. *vb.* tsutsuku 突く (pierce); chiku-chiku sasu ちくちく刺す (stick, as with a needle).

pride, *n.* 1. hokori 誇り (high opinion of oneself, something that causes one to be proud); **take pride in** ... o hokori ni suru ...を誇りにする. 2. jisonshin 自尊心 (self-respect).

priest, *n.* shisai 司祭 (Christian); sō 僧 (Buddhist).

priestess, *n.* miko 巫女 (Shinto).

prim, *adj.* katakurushii 堅苦しい.

primary, *adj.* omo (na) 主 (な) (chief).

primary school, *n.* shōgakkō 小学校.

prime, 1. *n.* saiseiki 最盛期 (best stage of one's life). 2. *adj.* ichiban (no) 一番 (の) (first, best).

prime minister, *n.* sōridaijin 総理大臣.

primitive, *adj.* genshi-teki na 原始的な (early, unrefined).

prince, *n.* ōji(sama) 王子(様); **crown prince** kōtaishi 皇太子.

princess, *n.* ohimesama お姫様; ōjo(sama) 王女(様).

principal, 1. *n.* kōchō 校長 (elementary or secondary school); gankin 元金 (capital sum); shuyaku 主役 (leading performer). 2. *adj.* shuyō (na) 主要 (な) (main).

principle, *n.* 1. gensoku 原則 (general rule); **in principle** gensoku to shite 原則として. 2. shin'nen 信念 (faith, belief); **on principle** shin'nen kara 信念から.

print, 1. *n.* insatsu 印刷 (printed lettering); ato 跡 (mark, indentation); hanga 版画 (woodblock, etc.); shashin 写真 (photographic); **out of print** zeppan (no) 絶版 (の). 2. *vb.* insatsu suru 印刷する (reproduce from inked type); katsujitai de kaku 活字体で書く (write with printed-style letters); yakitsukeru 焼き付ける (photo).

printed matter, *n.* insatsubutsu 印刷物.

printer, *n.* 1. purintā プリンター (machine). 2. insatsuya 印刷屋 (a printing business or its owner).

printing, *n.* insatsu 印刷; **printing press** insatsuki 印刷機.

print shop, *n.* 1. hangaten 版画店 (gallery of Japanese prints). 2. insatsuya 印刷屋 (printer).

prior, *adj.* mae (no) 前 (の) (earlier); mae kara (no) 前から (の) (planned before); **prior to** ... no mae ni ...の前に.

priority, *n.* 1. yūsenken 優先権 (right). 2. yūsenjikō 優先事項 (urgent matter).

prism, *n.* purizumu プリズム.

prison, *n.* keimusho 刑務所.

prisoner, *n.* 1. shūjin 囚人 (in a prison). 2. horyo 捕虜 (captive in a war).

privacy, *n.* puraibashī プライバシー.

private, 1. *adj.* puraibēto (na) プライベート (な); shi-teki (na) 私的 (な) (personal, secret); kojin-teki (na) 個人的 (な) (individual);

hikōshiki (na, no) 非公式 (な、の) (unofficial); minkan (no) 民間 (の) (of the general population); shiritsu (no) 私立 (の) (of a private institution). 2. *n.* hohei 歩兵 (military); **in private** naimitsu ni 内密に (secretly).

privilege, *n.* tokken 特権.

privileged, *adj.* tokken o motsu 特権を持つ (enjoying privilege).

privy, *adj.* nainai kan'yo shiteiru 内々関与している (in on, as a secret).

prize, 1. *n.* shō 賞. 2. *vb.* taisetsu ni suru 大切にする.

probability, *n.* arisō na koto ありそうな事 (probable event, etc.); mikomi 見込み (likelihood).

probable, *adj.* arisō (na) ありそう (な) (likely).

probably, *adv.* tabun 多分.

probation, *n.* 1. minarai 見習い (test of ability). 2. shikkōyūyo 執行猶予 (legal).

probe, *vb.* saguru 探る (search).

problem, *n.* mondai 問題 (trouble, question).

problematic, *adj.* mondai ga aru 問題がある.

procedure, *n.* tejun 手順; shinkō 進行.

proceed, *vb.* 1. tsuzukeru 続ける (continue). 2. susumu 進む (advance).

proceedings, *n.* **bring legal proceedings against** ... o uttaeru ...を訴える.

proceeds, *n.* shūekikin 収益金.

process, 1. *n.* purosesu プロセス (procedure); katei 過程 (course); **in the process of** ... no katei de ...の過程で. 2. *vb.* kakō suru 加工する (food).

procession, *n.* gyōretsu 行列.

proclaim, *vb.* sengen suru 宣言する.

proclamation, *n.* sengen 宣言.

procrastinate, *vb.* guzu-guzu suru 愚図愚図する.

procreate, *vb.* ko o umu 子を産む.

procure, *vb.* 1. nyūshu suru 入手する (obtain). 2. ponbiki o suru ぽん引きをする (hire a prostitute).

prod, *vb.* tsutsuku 突く.

prodigal, *adj.* rōhiteki (na) 浪費的 (な).

prodigy, *n.* tensai 天才.

produce, 1. *n.* seihin 製品 (product); nōsanbutsu 農産物 (agricultural products). 2. *vb.* umu 産む (bear young); ... no mi ga naru ...の実がなる (bear fruit); sanshutsu suru 産出する (grow and supply); tsukuru 作る (make, create); shimesu 示す (show).

producer, *n.* 1. purodyūsā プロデューサー; seisakusha 製作者 (film, play). 2. seisansha 生産者 (crop, machine).

product, *n.* seihin 製品 (manufactured article).

production, *n.* 1. seisan 生産 (manufacturing, farming). 2. seisanryō 生産量 (amount produced). 3. sakuhin 作品 (film, play, etc.)

productive, *adj.* 1. minori ga ōi 実りが多い (fruitful). 2. tasan (na) 多産 (な) (prolific).

productivity, *n.* seisanryoku 生産力 (power of being productive).

profane, 1. *adj.* bōtoku-teki (na) 冒瀆的 (な). 2. *vb.* bōtoku suru 冒瀆する.

profanity, *n.* bōtoku 冒瀆.

profess, *vb.* genmei suru 言明する.

profession, *n.* 1. shokugyō 職業 (vocation). 2. genmei 言明 (declaration).

professional, 1. *n.* puro プロ (professional person). 2. *adj.* puro (no) プロ (の) (working for money); purofesshonaru (na) プロフェッショナル (な) (efficient and ethical).

professor, *n.* kyōju 教授.

proficient, *adj.* jukuren shiteiru 熟練している.

profile, *n.* 1. yokogao 横顔 (side view). 2. purofīru プロフィール (one's background or portrayal).

profit, 1. *n.* rieki 利益 (gain). 2. *vb.* rieki o ageru 利益を上げる (make profit); **profit from** ... kara manabu ...から学ぶ (learn from).

profitable, *adj.* 1. mōkeru 儲ける (moneymaking). 2. yūyō (na) 有用 (な) (useful).

profound, *adj.* fukai 深い (deep, thinking deeply).

progeny, *n.* kodomotachi 子供達.

prognosis, *n.* yosoku-teki shindan 予測的診断.

program, 1. *n.* keikaku 計画 (plan); puroguramu プログラム (computer); dashimono 出し物 (schedule of entertainments); bangumi 番組 (TV or radio program). 2. *vb.* setchi suru 設置する (arrange); puroguramu ni uchikomu プログラムに打ち込む (computer).

progress, 1. *n.* shinkō 進行 (act of moving forward); kaizen 改善 (improvement); hatten 発展 (growth); **in progress** shinkōchū 進行中; **make progress** hakadoru 捗る (get better, develop). 2. *vb.* shinkō suru 進行する (move forward); yoku naru 良くなる (improve); hatten suru 発展する (develop).

progressive, *adj.* shinpo-teki (na) 進歩的 (な) (loving new ideas).

prohibit, *vb.* kinjiru 禁じる.

prohibition, *n.* kinshi 禁止.

project, 1. *n.* purojekuto プロジェクト (enterprise, aim); keikaku 計画 (plan). 2. *vb.* keikaku suru 計画する (plan); tsukideru 突き出る (protrude); hassha suru 発射する (hurl); tōsha suru 投射する (display upon surface, attribute unconsciously).

projectile, *n.* dangan 弾丸 (gun).

projector, *n.* eishaki 映写機 (apparatus).

proliferate, *vb.* zōshoku suru 増殖する (spread rapidly).

prolific, *adj.* tasan (na) 多産 (な).

prologue, *n.* purorōgu プロローグ.

prolong, *vb.* nobasu 延ばす.

promenade, 1. *n.* sansaku 散策 (leisurely walk); puromunādo プロムナード (way). 2. *vb.* sansaku suru 散策する.

prominent, *adj.* 1. tsukideta 突き出た (projecting). 2. medatsu 目立つ (conspicuous). 3. chomei (na) 著名 (な) (well-known).

promiscuous, *adj.* sei-teki ni hōshō (na) 性的に放縦 (な) (sexually).

promise, 1. *n.* yakusoku 約束 (assurance); yūbōsei 有望性 (potentiality); **make/keep/break a promise** yakusoku o suru/mamoru/yaburu 約束をする／守る／破る. 2. *vb.* yakusoku suru 約束する (assure by promise); kitai saseru 期待させる (afford ground for expecting).

promote, *vb.* 1. shōshin saseru 昇進させる (cause to advance in position). 2. sokushin suru 促進する (further the progress of). 3.

senden suru 宣伝する (advertise). 4. kikaku suru 企画する (organize).

promotion, *n.* 1. shōshin 昇進 (advancement in position). 2. puromōshon プロモーション (advertising). 3. sokushin 促進 (act of fostering).

prompt, 1. *adj.* jinsoku (na) 迅速 (な) (swift); jikandōri (no) 時間通り (の) (punctual). 2. *vb.* hikiokosu 引き起こす (cause).

prone, *adj.* 1. utsubuse (no) うつぶせ (の) (lying flat). 2. **prone to** ... e no keikō ga aru ...への傾向があある (have a tendency toward).

prong, *n.* saki 先.

pronoun, *n.* daimeishi 代名詞.

pronounce, *vb.* 1. hatsuon suru 発音する (enunciate or articulate). 2. genmei suru 言明する (declare as one's opinion). 3. senkoku suru 宣告する (announce).

pronouncement, *n.* sengen 宣言.

pronunciation, *n.* hatsuon 発音.

proof, *n.* 1. shōko 証拠 (evidence). 2. do 度 (alcohol).

proofread, *vb.* kōsei suru 校正する.

prop, 1. *n.* sasae 支え (support). 2. *vb.* sasaeru 支える.

propaganda, *n.* senden 宣伝.

propagate, *vb.* 1. hanshoku suru 繁殖する (reproduce). 2. fukyū suru 普及する (transmit doctrine, etc.).

propel, *vb.* susumeru 進める (drive forward).

propeller, *n.* puropera プロペラ.

propensity, *n.* keikōsei 傾向性 (inclination); seiheki 性癖 (natural tendency).

proper, *adj.* 1. fusawashii ふさわしい (suitable). 2. tadashii 正しい

(right).

property, *n.* 1. bukken 物件 (assets, holdings, real estate). 2. tochi 土地 (land). 3. tokushitsu 特質 (attribute).

prophecy, *n.* yogen 予言.

prophesy, *vb.* yogen suru 予言する.

prophet, *n.* yogensha 予言者.

propitious, *adj.* 1. kōtsugō (na) 好都合 (な) (favorable). 2. saisaki ga ii 幸先が良い (auspicious).

proponent, *n.* shijisha 支持者.

proportion, *n.* 1. puropōshon プロポーション; tsuriai 釣り合い (balance); **be in proportion** tsuriai ga toreteiru 釣り合いが取れている. 2. wariai 割合 (percentage); hirei 比例 (comparative relation); **in proportion to** ... ni hirei shite ... に比例して.

proportional, proportionate, *adj.* **proportional to** ... ni hirei shite ...に比例して.

proposal, *n.* 1. teian 提案 (proposition). 2. kekkon-mōshikomi 結婚申し込み (offer of marriage).

propose, *vb.* 1. teian suru 提案する (suggest). 2. kekkon o mōshikomu 結婚を申し込む (offer marriage).

proposition, *n.* 1. teian 提案 (proposal). 2. chinjutsu 陳述 (statement).

proprietor, *n.* keieisha 経営者.

propriety, *n.* 1. datōsei 妥当性 (appropriateness). 2. reigi-tadashisa 礼儀正しさ (moral correctness).

prosaic, *adj.* arifureteiru ありふれている.

proscribe, *vb.* kinjiru 禁じる.

prose, *n.* sanbun 散文.

prosecute, *vb.* kiso suru 起訴する.

prosecution, *n.* kiso 起訴.

prospect, *n.* 1. kanōsei 可能性 (likelihood of success). 2. miharashi 見晴らし (view). 3. mitōshi 見通し (outlook).

prosper, *vb.* sakaeru 栄える.

prosperity, *n.* han'ei 繁栄.

prosperous, *adj.* 1. sakaeteiru 栄えている (successful). 2. yutaka (na) 豊か (な) (rich).

prostitute, 1. *n.* baishunfu 売春婦. 2. *vb.* baishun o suru 売春をする (sell one's body); uriwatasu 売り渡す (sell, degrade).

prostitution, *n.* baishun 売春.

prostrate, 1. *adj.* hirefushiteiru ひれ伏している. 2. *vb.* heifuku suru 平伏する.

protagonist, *n.* shujinkō 主人公.

protect, *vb.* mamoru 守る (defend).

protection, *n.* hogo 保護 (act of defending, thing that defends).

protégé, *n.* hihogosha 被保護者.

protein, *n.* tanpakushitsu 蛋白質.

protest, 1. *n.* kōgi 抗議. 2. *vb.* kōgi suru 抗議する.

Protestant, *n., adj.* purotesutanto (no) プロテスタント (の); shinkyō (no) 新教 (の).

protocol, *n.* gaikōgirei 外交儀礼 (diplomatic etiquette).

protract, *vb.* nagabikaseru 長引かせる.

protrude, *vb.* tsuki-deru/-dasu 突き出る／〜出す (project/cause to project).

protuberance, *n.* tosshutsu 突出.

proud, *adj.* 1. hokoritakai 誇り高い (having pride). 2. kōman (na) 高慢 (な) (arrogant).

prove, *vb.* 1. shōmei suru 証明する (establish as fact). 2. ... to hanmei suru ...と判明する (be or become ultimately).

proverb, *n.* kotowaza 諺.

provide, *vb.* 1. ataeru 与える (supply). 2. sadameru 定める (stipulate). 3. **provide for** yashinau 養う (raise, feed).

provided, providing, *conj.* ... to iu jōken de ...と言う条件で.

providence, *n.* setsuri 摂理 (God's care); kami no tasuke 神の助け (God's help).

province, *n.* shū 州.

provincial, *adj.* 1. shū (no) 州 (の) (of a province). 2. chihō-teki (na) 地方的 (な) (unsophisticated; characteristic of the provinces).

provision, *n.* 1. yōi 用意 (preparation). 2. kitei 規定 (condition). 3. kyōkyū 供給 (supply). 4. **provisions** shokuryō 食料 (food).

provisional, *adj.* zantei-teki (na) 暫定的 (な).

provocative, *adj.* chōhatsu-teki (na) 挑発的 (な).

provoke, *vb.* chōhatsu suru 挑発する.

prowess, *n.* sainō 才能.

prowl, *vb.* urotsuku うろつく.

proximity, *n.* **in the proximity of** ... no chikaku ni ...の近くに.

proxy, *n.* dairi 代理 (agent).

prudence, *n.* 1. funbetsu 分別 (discreetness). 2. shinchōsa 慎重さ (cautiousness).

prudent, *adj.* 1. funbetsu ga aru 分別がある (discreet). 2. shinchō (na) 慎重 (な) (cautious).

prune, 1. *n.* hoshi sumomo 干し李 (food). 2. *vb.* sentei suru 剪定する (tree).

pry, *vb.* sensaku suru 詮索する (investigate).

pseudonym, *n.* pen-nēmu ペンネーム.

psyche, *n.* seishin 精神.

psychiatrist, *n.* seishinkai 精神科医.

psychiatry, *n.* seishin igaku 精神医学.

psychoanalysis, *n.* seishin bunseki 精神分析.

psychological, *adj.* 1. shinri-teki (na) 心理的 (な) (of the mind). 2. shinrigaku (no) 心理学 (の) (of psychology).

psychology, *n.* 1. shinri 心理 (mind). 2. shinrigaku 心理学 (science).

psychotic, *n.* seishinbyō kanja 精神病患者.

puberty, *n.* shishunki 思春期.

pubic, *adj.* inbu (no) 陰部 (の).

public, 1. *n.* hitobito 人々 (people in general); **in public** ōyake no ba de 公の場で. 2. *adj.* kōkyō (no) 公共 (の) (for use of the public); ōyake (no) 公 (の) (open to view or knowledge of all); hitobito (no) 人々 (の) (of people).

publication, *n.* 1. shuppan 出版 (in print). 2. happyō 発表 (announcement).

publicity, *n.* 1. chūmoku 注目 (attention). 2. senden 宣伝 (promotion).

publicize, *vb.* senden suru 宣伝する.

public school, *n.* kōritsu gakkō 公立学校.

publish, *vb.* 1. shuppan suru 出版する (in printed form). 2. happyō suru 発表する (bring to public notice).

publisher, *n.* shuppansha 出版社

(company).

pudding, *n.* pudingu プディング.

puddle, *n.* mizutamari 水溜まり.

puff, 1. *n.* ippuku 一服 (cigarette). 2. *vb.* fukasu ふかす (cigarette); aegu あえぐ (breathe hard and fast); fukuramaseru 膨らませる (inflate); **puff up** fukureru 膨れる (swell).

pull, *vb.* 1. hiku 引く (draw); hipparu 引張る (draw with force). 2. saku 裂く (tear). 3. **pull apart** bara-bara ni suru ばらばらにする; **pull out** saru 去る (leave); nuku 抜く (extract); **pull through** kirinukeru 切り抜ける (manage); **pull up** tomaru 止まる (come to a stop).

pulley, *n.* kassha 滑車.

pulp, *n.* 1. parupu パルプ (for paper). 2. kaniku 果肉 (fruit).

pulpit, *n.* sekkyōdan 説教壇.

pulsate, *vb.* myaku utsu 脈打つ.

pulse, 1. *n.* kodō 鼓動; myaku 脈 (beat of arteries). 2. *vb.* myaku utsu 脈打つ (throb).

pump, *n.* ponpu ポンプ.

pumpkin, *n.* kabocha かぼちゃ.

pun, *n.* share しゃれ.

punch, 1. *n.* genko げんこ (blow); panchi パンチ (tool, drink). 2. *vb.* ana o akeru 穴を開ける (make a hole); naguru 殴る (strike).

punctual, *adj.* jikandōri (no) 時間通り (の).

punctuate, *vb.* kutōten o tsukeru 句読点を付ける (mark).

punctuation, *n.* kutōten 句読点 (mark).

puncture, 1. *n.* ana 穴 (hole); panku パンク (hole in a tire). 2. *vb.* ... ni ana o akeru ...に穴を開ける (make a hole in); panku suru

パンクする (get a flat tire); kujiku 挫く (discourage).

pungent, *adj.* tsukisasu yō (na) 突き刺すよう(な) (piercing); karai 辛い (hot).

punish, *vb.* bassuru 罰する.

punishment, *n.* 1. batsu 罰 (act of punishing). 2. keibatsu 刑罰 (judicial punishment).

punitive, *adj.* 1. batsu (no) 罰 (の) (of punishment). 2. kibishii 厳しい (severe).

puny, *adj.* hinjaku (na) 貧弱 (な).

pupil, *n.* 1. seito 生徒 (student). 2. hitomi 瞳 (eye).

puppet, *n.* ayatsuriningyō 操り人形 (stringed, etc.); yubiningyō 指人形 (hand).

puppeteer, *n.* ningyōtsukai 人形使い.

puppy, *n.* koinu 小犬.

purchase, 1. *n.* kōbai 購買 (act of buying); kōbaihin 購買品 (thing bought). 2. *vb.* kau 買う (buy).

pure, *adj.* 1. junsui (na, no) 純粋 (な、の) (unmixed, innocent). 2. junketsu (na) 純潔 (な) (chaste). 3. junshin (na) 純心 (な) (innocent). 4. mattaku (no) 全く (の) (utter).

purée, *n.* pyūre ピューレ.

purge, 1. *n.* kiyome 清め (act of purifying); tsuihō 追放 (act of getting rid of). 2. *vb.* kiyomeru 清める (purify, cleanse); tsuihō suru 追放する (get rid of).

purify, *vb.* 1. junka suru 純化する (make pure, as sugar, etc.). 2. kiyomeru 清める (purge, cleanse).

puritan, *n.* 1. katabutsu 堅物. 2. **Puritan** seikyōto 清教徒; shinkyōto 新教徒.

puritanical, *adj.* 1. kin'yoku-teki

(na) 禁欲的 (な) (ascetic). 2. genkaku (na) 厳格 (な) (strict in moral or religious matters).

purity, *n.* 1. kiyorakasa 清らかさ (clearness, chastity). 2. junsuisa 純粋さ (innocence).

purple, *adj.* murasaki (no) 紫 (の).

purpose, *n.* mokuteki 目的 (aim); **for the purpose of** ... no mokuteki de ...の目的で; **on purpose** wazato わざと.

purr, *vb.* nodo o narasu 喉を鳴らす (cat).

purse, *n.* 1. saifu 財布 (wallet). 2. handobaggu ハンドバッグ (handbag).

pursue, *vb.* 1. oikakeru 追いかける (chase). 2. tsuzukeru 続ける (carry on). 3. tsuikyū suru 追求する (search for, commit oneself to).

pursuit, *n.* 1. tsuikyū 追求 (chase, quest, commitment); **in pursuit of** ... o oikakete ...を追いかけて. 2. shumi 趣味 (hobby); shigoto 仕事 (occupation).

pus, *n.* umi 膿.

push, 1. *n.* oshi 押し. 2. *vb.* osu 押す (put pressure on, thrust, elbow, shoulder, urge); oshiwakeru 押し分ける (make one's way by pushing); ... ni chikara o ireru ...に力を入れる (promote).

put, *vb.* 1. oku 置く (lay, place). 2. ireru 入れる (put into). 3. hyōgen suru 表現する (express). 4. **put aside/by** takuwaeru 貯える (store up); totteoku 取って置く (save); **put away** shimau 仕舞う; **put down** kaku 書く (write); osaetsukeru 抑え付ける (suppress); **put an end to** ... o oeru ...を終える; **put in** kakeru かける (spend time); teishutsu suru 提出する (submit); **put in for** mōshikomu 申し込む (request, apply for); **put off** enki suru 延期する; sakeru 避ける (get rid of by evasion); **put on** kiru 着る (dress); haku 履く (footwear); kaburu 被る (hat); ... no furi o suru ...の振りをする (adopt, as an affectation); tsukeru 点ける (turn on); **put out** kesu 消す (light, fire); komaraseru 困らせる (annoy); **put up** tateru 建てる (construct, erect); **put up with** ... o gaman suru ... を我慢する.

puzzle, 1. *n.* pazuru パズル (game, toy); nazo 謎 (enigma). 2. *vb.* tomadowaseru 戸惑わせる (perplex); komaraseru 困らせる (trouble).

pyramid, *n.* piramiddo ピラミッド.

Q

quack, 1. *n.* yabuisha やぶ医者 (pretender to medical skill); gā-gā がーがー (duck). 2. *vb.* gā-gā to naku がーがーと鳴く.

quadruple, *vb.* yonbai suru 四倍する.

quail, *n.* uzura うずら.

quaint, *adj.* fūgawari (na) 風変わり (な).

quake, 1. *n.* jishin 地震 (earthquake); furue 震え (trembling). 2. *vb.* furueru 震える.

qualification, *n.* 1. shikaku 資格 (skill). 2. gentei 限定; seigen 制限

(restriction).

qualified, *adj.* 1. tekinin (no) 適任 (の); shikaku ga aru 資格がある (competent). 2. jōkentsuki (no) 条件付き (の) (limited).

qualify, *vb.* 1. shikaku o ataeru 資格を与える; atehamaraseru 当てはまらせる (make fit); shikaku ga aru 資格がある; atehamaru 当てはまる (fit). 2. shikaku o toru 資格を取る (get a license). 3. gentei/seigen suru 限定／制限する (limit).

quality, *n.* 1. shitsu 質 (grade of excellence). 2. ryōshitsu 良質 (excellence). 3. tokushoku 特色; seishitsu 性質 (characteristic).

qualm, *n.* 1. ryōshin no kashaku 良心の呵責 (pang of conscience). 2. fuan 不安 (apprehension).

quandary, *n.* jirenma ジレンマ; kon'waku 困惑.

quantity, *n.* ryō 量; **a large quantity** takusan (no) 沢山 (の).

quarantine, *n.* kakuri 隔離.

quarrel, 1. *n.* kenka 喧嘩 (fight); kōron 口論 (dispute). 2. *vb.* kenka suru 喧嘩する; kōron suru 口論する.

quarry, *n.* saisekijō 採石場.

quarter, *n.* 1. yonbun no ichi 四分の一 (one-fourth). 2. nijūgo sento 二十五セント (25 cents). 3. jūgofun 十五分 (15 minutes). 4. chiku 地区 (part of a town).

quarterly, *adj.* 1. nen ni yonkai (no) 年に四回 (の). 2. kikan no 季刊の (periodical).

quartet, *n.* shijūsō 四重奏; kuwarutetto クワルテット.

quartz, *n.* suishō 水晶.

quay, *n.* hatoba 波止場; futō 埠頭.

queasy, *adj.* 1. i ga mukatsuku 胃がむかつく (nauseated). 2. ki ga mukanai 気が向かない

(uncomfortable).

queen, *n.* jo'ō(sama) 女王(様).

queer, *adj.* hen (na) 変 (な); kimyō (na) 奇妙 (な).

quell, *vb.* osaeru 抑える; shizumeru 静める.

quench, *vb.* 1. kesu 消す (extinguish). 2. iyasu 癒す (satisfy).

quest, *n.* tankyū 探求.

question, 1. *n.* shitsumon 質問 (query); mondai 問題 (problem); gimon 疑問 (doubt); **question mark** kuesuchon-māku クエスチョンマーク; gimonfu 疑問符. 2. *vb.* shitsumon suru 質問する; kiku 聞く (ask question); gimonshi suru 疑問視する (doubt).

questionnaire, *n.* an'kēto アンケート; shitsumon(hyo) 質問(表).

queue, 1. *n.* (gyō)retsu (行)列 (line). 2. *vb.* narabu 並ぶ.

quibble, *vb.* iinogare o suru 言い逃れをする; gomakasu ごまかす (fudge).

quick, *adj.* 1. hayai 速い (prompt, swift). 2. rikō (na) 利口 (な) (alert).

quicken, *vb.* hayameru 速める (hasten); hayaku naru 速くなる (become quick).

quiet, 1. *n.* shizukesa 静けさ (noiselessness); heion 平穏 (calmness). 2. *adj.* shizuka (na) 静か (な) (free from noise); heion (na) 平穏 (な) (calm). 3. *vb.* shizumeru 静める.

quilt, *n.* kiruto キルト; sashiko 刺し子.

quintessence, *n.* shinzui 真髄; honshitsu 本質.

quintet, *n.* gojūsō 五重奏; kuintetto クインテット.

quip, *n.* keiku 警句.

quirk, *n.* kibatsu 奇抜 (peculiarity).

quit, *vb.* 1. yameru やめる (stop, resign). 2. deru 出る (depart from).

quite, *adv.* 1. mattaku 全く; sukkari すっかり (completely). 2. hontō ni 本当に (really).

quiver, 1. *n.* furue 震え (trembling). 2. *vb.* furueru 震える (tremble); yusuru 揺する (shake).

quiz, 1. *n.* shiken 試験; tesuto テスト. 2. *vb.* shiken/tesuto o suru 試験／テストをする.

quota, *n.* wariate 割当て.

quotation, *n.* 1. in'yō 引用; **quotation marks** in'yōfu 引用符. 2. kakaku 価格 (quoted price).

quote, *vb.* in'yō suru 引用する; hiku 引く (cite); nedan o tsukeru 値段を付ける (give price).

R

rabbit, *n.* usagi 兎; **rabbit hutch** usagigoya 兎小屋.

rabble, *n.* yajiuma 野次馬 (disorderly crowd).

rabies, *n.* kyōkenbyō 狂犬病.

race, 1. *n.* jinshu 人種; minzoku 民族 (group of persons of common origin); -rui 〜類; -shu 〜種 (class); rēsu レース (competition). 2. *vb.* kyōgikai ni deru 競技会に出る (participate in a race); kisou 競う (compete); isogu 急ぐ (move swiftly).

race track, *n.* rēsu-torakku レーストラック (course for racing); keibajō 競馬場 (course for horse racing).

racial, *adj.* jinshu (no) 人種 (の); minzoku (no) 民族 (の).

racism, *n.* jinshusabetsu 人種差別.

racist, *n.* jinshusabetsu-shugisha 人種差別主義者.

rack, 1. *n.* rakku ラック; amidana 網棚 (luggage rack); tana 棚 (storage unit). 2. *vb.* kurushimeru 苦しめる (afflict).

racket, *n.* 1. sōon 騒音 (noise). 2. raketto ラケット (tennis). 3. fusei 不正; inchiki いんちき (deception).

radar, *n.* rēdā レーダー.

radiance, *n.* hikari 光; kagayaki 輝き (light).

radiant, *adj.* hikatteiru 光っている; kagayaiteiru 輝いている (emitting light).

radiate, *vb.* 1. hikaru 光る; kagayaku 輝く (emit light). 2. hōsha suru 放射する (emit heat or radioactive energy).

radiation, *n.* hōsha 放射 (radiating of light, heat, etc.)

radical, 1. *n.* kagekiha 過激派 (extremist). 2. *adj.* kageki (na) 過激 (な) (militant); bappon-teki (na) 抜本的 (な) (complete, thorough).

radio, *n.* 1. musen 無線 (communication system). 2. rajio ラジオ (apparatus); **on the radio** rajio de ラジオで.

radioactive, *adj.* hōshasei (no) 放射性 (の).

radio station, *n.* hōsōkyoku 放送局.

radish, *n.* radisshu ラディッシュ (small); daikon 大根 (long Japanese radish).

radium, *n.* rajiumu ラジウム.

radius, *n.* hankei 半径.

raffle, *n.* takarakuji 宝くじ (lottery).

raft, *n.* ikada 筏 (floating platform).

rafter, *n.* hari 梁.

rag, *n.* borogire ぼろぎれ (old cloth); boro ぼろ (worn-out clothes).

rage, 1. *n.* gekido 激怒 (fury); ryūkō 流行 (fad). 2. *vb.* ikari kuru'u 怒り狂う (be in a fury).

ragged, *adj.* 1. boro-boro (no) ぼろ ぼろ (の) (worn-out). 2. zatsu na 雑な (uneven).

raid, 1. *n.* shūgeki 襲撃 (attack); teire 手入れ (police); **air raid** kūshū 空襲. 2. *vb.* shūgeki suru 襲撃する; teire suru 手入れする.

rail, 1. *n.* rēru レール; tesuri 手すり (handrail); senro 線路 (railroad); **by rail** densha de 電車で. 2. *vb.* urusaku monku o iu うるさく文句 を言う (complain).

railroad, *n.* senro 線路; tetsudō 鉄 道.

rain, 1. *n.* ame 雨. 2. *vb.* ame ga furu 雨が降る.

rainbow, *n.* niji 虹.

raincoat, *n.* reinkōto レインコー ト.

rainfall, *n.* uryō 雨量 (amount of rain).

rainy, *adj.* ame ga ōi 雨が多い (having a lot of rain); amefuri (no) 雨降り(の) (raining).

raise, 1. *n.* shōkyū 昇給 (increase in pay). 2. *vb.* ageru 上げる (lift up, increase); atsumeru 集める (collect); sodateru 育てる (bring up); hikiokosu 引き起こす (cause).

raisin, *n.* rēzun レーズン.

rake, *n.* kumade 熊手 (tool).

rally, 1. *n.* shūkai 集会 (meeting); rarī ラリー (car race, recovery in tennis). 2. *vb.* atsumaru 集まる (come together); atsumeru 集める (call together); kaifuku suru 回復 する (recover).

ram, 1. *n.* ohitsuji 雄羊 (sheep). 2. *vb.* gekitotsu suru 撃突する (collide violently).

ramble, *vb.* sansaku suru 散策する (stroll idly).

ramification, *n.* eikyō 影響 (consequence); kekka 結果 (result).

ramp, *n.* 1. surōpu スロープ (slope). 2. haiuē-iriguchi/ -deguchi ハイウエー入口／～出口 (highway entrance/exit).

rampage, *n.* abaremawaru 暴れ回 る.

rampant, *adj.* man'en shite iru 蔓 延している (widespread).

rampart, *n.* jōheki 城壁.

ramshackle, *adj.* onboro (no) おん ぼろ (の).

ranch, *n.* bokujō 牧場 (large farm for raising stock).

rancher, *n.* 1. bokujōnushi 牧場主 (ranch owner). 2. bokujōrōdōsha 牧場労働者 (worker).

rancid, *adj.* furui 古い (old); kusai 臭い (odorous).

rancor, *n.* urami 恨み.

random, *adj.* teatarishidai (no) 手 当り次第 (の); **at random** teatari-shidai ni 手当り次第に.

range, *n.* sanmyaku 山脈 (mountain range); retsu 列 (row); shatekijō 射的場 (place for target shooting); shatei 射程 (distance between gun and target); bokujō 牧場 (pasture); han'i 範囲 (extent); genkai 限界 (limit); renji レンジ (cooking range). 2. *vb.*

arukimawaru 歩き回る (wander); naraberu 並べる (arrange); mōra suru 網羅する (vary within specified limits); **range over** oyobu 及ぶ; wataru 渡る.

rank, 1. *n*. chi'i 地位 (official position); mibun 身分; kaikyū 階級 (social standing or class); kurai 位 (class in any scale of comparison); retsu 列 (row); **rank and file** ippanjin 一般人 (ordinary people). 2. *adj*. habikotteiru はびこっている (growing excessively); kusai 臭い (smelly). 3. *vb*. kurai suru 位する (be in a particular rank); kurai ni ireru 位に入れる (put in a particular rank).

ransack, *vb*. 1. ryakudatsu suru 略奪する (loot). 2. sagashimawaru 捜し回る (search).

ransom, *n*. minoshirokin 身代金.

rant, *vb*. wamekitateru 喚きたてる.

rap, *vb*. tataku 叩く (strike).

rape, 1. *n*. bōkō 暴行; gōkan 強姦. 2. *vb*. gōkan suru 強姦する.

rapid, *adj*. subayai 素早い; jinsoku (na) 迅速 (な).

rapport, *n*. kyōkan 共感.

rapture, *n*. kyōki 狂喜; uchōten 有頂天.

rare, *adj*. mare (na) 稀れ (な); mezurashii 珍しい (unusual). 2. namayake (no) 生焼け (の) (meat).

rarity, *n*. mezurashii mono 珍しい物 (uncommon thing).

rascal, *n*. narazumono ならず者.

rash, 1. *n*. hasshin 発疹. 2. *adj*. seikyū (na) 性急 (な) (thoughtlessly hasty); keisotsu (na) 軽率 (な) (imprudent).

raspberry, *n*. kiichigo 木苺; razuberī ラズベリー.

rat, *n*. ōnezumi 大ねずみ.

rate, 1. *n*. ritsu 率; wariai 割合 (percentage); sokudo 速度 (degree of speed); ryōkin 料金 (charge); tōkyū 等級 (rating); **at any rate** tonikaku とにかく; **at the rate of** ... no wariai de ...の割合で; **exchange rate** kawase-rēto 為替レート. 2. *vb*. hyōka suru 評価する (estimate).

rather, *adv*. 1. ikubun ka 幾分か (somewhat). 2. kanari かなり (quite). 3. mushiro むしろ (in preference); **rather than** ... yori mushiro ...よりむしろ; **I would rather** mushiro ... no hō ga ii むしろ...の方がいい. 4. gyaku ni 逆に (on the contrary).

ratify, *vb*. hijun suru 批准する.

rating, *n*. hyōka 評価 (assessment).

ratio, *n*. ritsu 率; wariai 割合.

ration, 1. *n*. haikyūryō 配給量; wariate 割当て (fixed allowance). 2. *vb*. haikyū suru 配給する (put on ration).

rational, *adj*. 1. risei-teki (na) 理性的 (な) (able to reason). 2. suji ga tōtteiru 筋が通っている (sensible).

rationale, *n*. konkyo 根拠.

rationalize, *vb*. gōrika suru 合理化する (find reasons).

rattle, 1. *n*. gara-gara がらがら (toy). 2. *vb*. gara-gara naru がらがら鳴る; gara-gara narasu がらがら鳴らす (make something rattle).

rattlesnake, *n*. gara-gara hebi がらがら蛇.

raucous, *adj*. kishiru 軋る.

ravage, *vb*. 1. hakai suru 破壊する (destroy). 2. ryakudatsu suru 略奪する (loot).

rave, *vb*. 1. wameku 喚く (talk wildly). 2. homechigiru 褒めちぎる (praise).

raven, *n.* karasu 烏.

ravine, *n.* kyōkoku 峡谷.

ravish, *vb.* 1. yorokobaseru 喜ばせる (fill with joy). 2. gōkan suru 強姦する (rape).

raw, *adj.* 1. nama (no) 生 (の) (uncooked). 2. mikakō (no) 未加工 (の) (unprocessed); gen- 原〜 (basic); **raw material** genzairyō 原材料. 3. mikeiken (no) 未経験 (の) (inexperienced). 4. kawa ga muketa 皮が剥けた (peeled skin).

ray, *n.* 1. kōsen 光線 (beam). 2. **a ray of** ichimatsu no 一抹の; hitosuji no 一筋の (a trace of). 3. ei えい (fish).

rayon, *n.* rēyon レーヨン.

raze, *vb.* 1. nagitaosu なぎ倒す (flatten). 2. kaimetsu suru 壊滅する (demolish).

razor, *n.* kamisori 剃刀 (for shaving); **razor blade** kamisori no ha 剃刀の刃.

re-, *pref.* sai- 再- (repetition); **rearmament** saigunbi 再軍備.

reach, 1. *n.* todoku han'i 届く範囲 (distance that one can touch or attain); ikeru han'i 行ける範囲 (distance that one can go); **within/beyond one's reach** (te no) todoku/todokanai han'i ni (手の) 届く／届かない範囲に. 2. *vb.* tsuku 着く (arrive at); todoku 届く (be able to touch); nobasu 伸ばす (extend); renraku o toru 連絡を取る (contact).

react, *vb.* 1. han'nō suru 反応する (respond). 2. **react against** hanpatsu suru 反発する.

reaction, *n.* han'nō 反応 (response).

reactionary, *n.* handōshugisha 反動主義者.

reactor, *n.* genshiro 原子炉

(nuclear).

read, *vb.* yomu 読む.

reader, *n.* dokusha 読者.

readily, *adv.* 1. yorokonde 喜んで (willingly). 2. kantan ni 簡単に (easily).

reading, *n.* dokusho 読書 (act of reading).

ready, 1. *adj.* (yōi ga) dekiteiru (用意が) 出来ている (fully prepared); jinsoku (na) 迅速 (な) (prompt); **be ready to do** yorokonde suru 喜んでする (willing to do). 2. *vb.* junbi suru 準備する.

real, *adj.* 1. jissai (no) 実際 (の); genjitsu (no) 現実 (の) (actual). 2. hontō (no) 本当 (の) (true). 3. honmono (no) 本物 (の) (genuine).

real estate, *n.* fudōsan 不動産.

realism, *n.* 1. genjitsusei 現実性 (actuality). 2. riarizumu リアリズム; shajitsushugi 写実主義 (in art).

realistic, *adj.* 1. genjitsu-teki (na) 現実的 (な) (practical). 2. shajitsu-teki (na) 写実的 (な) (lifelike).

reality, *n.* 1. genjitsu 現実; jijitsu 事実; jissai 実際 (real fact or thing); **in reality** jissai wa 実際は. 2. jitsuzai 実在 (real existence).

realize, *vb.* 1. satoru 悟る; wakaru 分かる (understand clearly). 2. jitsugen suru 実現する (happen). 3. rieki o eru 利益を得る (acquire profit).

really, *adv.* hontō ni 本当に (truly, thoroughly, indeed).

realm, *n.* 1. ōkoku 王国 (kingdom). 2. bun'ya 分野 (area of activity).

Realtor, *n.* fudōsangyōsha 不動産業者.

reap, *vb.* shūkaku suru 収穫する

(harvest).

rear, 1. *n.* ushiro 後ろ (back); (o)shiri (お)尻 (buttocks). 2. *vb.* sodateru 育てる (care for to maturity); ageru 上げる (lift up); tateru 立てる (raise, erect).

rear-view mirror, *n.* bakku-mirā バックミラー.

reason, 1. *n.* riyū 理由 (cause); risei 理性 (mental powers); shōki 正気 (sanity). 2. *vb.* handan suru 判断する (judge); suitei suru 推定 する (infer); **reason with** settoku suru 説得する (persuade).

reasonable, *adj.* 1. mottomo (na) もっとも (な); funbetsu ni kanau 分別に適う (sensible). 2. datō (na) 妥当 (な) (fair).

reassure, *vb.* anshin saseru 安心さ せる.

rebate, *n.* ribēto リベート; ichibu-haraimodoshi 一部払い戻し.

rebel, 1. *n.* hankōsha 反抗者. 2. *vb.* hankō suru 反抗する (fight).

rebellion, *n.* hangyaku 反逆 (against government); hankō 反抗 (against authority).

rebellious, *adj.* hankō-teki (na) 反 抗的 (な).

rebirth, *n.* fukkatsu 復活; saisei 再 生.

rebound, 1. *n.* hanekaeri 跳ね返り (act of rebounding); handō 反動 (reaction). 2. *vb.* hanekaeru 跳ね 返る.

rebuff, 1. *n.* kyozetsu 拒絶 (rejection). 2. *vb.* kyozetsu suru 拒絶する (reject).

rebuke, *vb.* tashinameru たしなめ る.

rebut, *vb.* hanron suru 反論する.

recalcitrant, *adj.* hankō-teki (na) 反抗的 (な).

recall, *vb.* omoidasu 思い出す

(remember). 2. yobimodosu 呼び 戻す (call back). 3. kaishū suru 回 収する (take off market). 4. torikesu 取り消す (withdraw).

recapitulate, *vb.* yōyaku suru 要約 する.

recede, *vb.* 1. shirizoku 退く (move back). 2. hageagaru 禿げ上がる (hair).

receipt, *n.* 1. reshīto レシート; ryōshūsho 領収書 (written statement). 2. uketori 受け取り (act of receiving).

receive, *vb.* 1. ukeru 受ける; uketoru 受け取る (get). 2. mukaeru 迎える (welcome). 3. ukeireru 受け入れる (accept).

receiver, *n.* 1. juwaki 受話器 (of a telephone). 2. jushinki 受信機 (of a radio or TV).

recent, *adj.* saikin (no) 最近 (の).

receptacle, *n.* yōki 容器.

reception, *n.* 1. resepushon レセプ ション (party). 2. uketsuke 受け 付け; furonto フロント (at hotel). 3. kangei 歓迎 (welcome). 4. jushin 受信 (of a radio or TV).

receptionist, *n.* uketsuke(-gakari) 受け付け(係).

recess, *n.* 1. yasumi 休み (pause). 2. kubomi 凹み (alcove). 3. **recesses** oku 奥.

recession, *n.* fukeiki 不景気; keiki-kōtai 景気後退 (economic).

recipe, *n.* ryōrihō 料理法; tsukurikata 作り方 (cooking).

recipient, *n.* uketorinin 受け取り 人.

reciprocal, *adj.* sōgo (no) 相互 (の) (mutual).

recital, *n.* risaitaru リサイタル; ensōkai 演奏会.

recite, *vb.* 1. anshō suru 暗誦する (repeat from memory). 2. kataru

語る (narrate).

reckless, *adj.* 1. mubō (na) 無謀
(な) (heedless). 2. seikyū (na) 性
急 (な) (hasty).

reckon, *vb.* 1. (... to) minasu (...と)
見なす (consider). 2. (... to) omou
(... と) 思う (suppose). 3. keisan
suru 計算する (calculate). 4.
reckon with atsukau 扱う (deal
with); kōryo ni ireru 考慮に入れ
る (include in consideration).

reclaim, *vb.* 1. henkan o
motomeru 返還を求める (ask the
return of). 2. umetateru 埋め立て
る (reclaim land). 3. saisei suru 再
生する (recycle).

recline, *vb.* motareru もたれる;
yorikakaru 寄り掛かる (lean).

recluse, *n.* inja 隠者.

recognition, *n.* 1. ninshiki 認識
(act of recognizing). 2. shōnin 証
認 (acknowledgment, approval).
3. **beyond recognition** mukashi
no omokage mo nai kurai ni 昔の
面影もない位に.

recognize, *vb.* 1. wakaru 分かる
(identify, see clearly, understand).
2. mitomeru 認める (admit,
acknowledge). 3. shōnin suru 証
認する (approve). 4. aisatsu suru
挨拶する (greet).

recoil, *vb.* mi o hiku 身を引く
(draw back).

recollect, *vb.* omoidasu 思い出す.

recollection, *n.* omoide 思い出.

recommend, *vb.* 1. suisen suru 推
薦する (commend as worthy). 2.
susumeru 勧める (advise).

recommendation, *n.* 1. susume
勧め (advice). 2. suisenjō 推薦状
(letter of recommendation).

recompense, 1. *n.* baishō 賠償
(payment for damage); hōshū 報
酬 (reward); **in recompense of** ...

no baishō/hōshū ni ...の賠償／報
酬に. 2. *vb.* baishō suru 賠償する
(compensate for damage);
mukuiru 報いる (reward).

reconcile, *vb.* wakai suru 和解す
る.

reconnaissance, *n.* teisatsu 偵察
(military).

reconnoiter, *vb.* teisatsu suru 偵察
する.

record, 1. *n.* kiroku 記録 (account,
documentation); keireki 経歴
(one's past history); shinkiroku 新
記録 (sports); rekōdo レコード
(phonograph); **keep a record**
kiroku suru 記録する; **off the
record** hikōshiki ni 非公式に; **on
the record** kōshiki ni 公式に
(officially). 2. *vb.* kiroku suru 記
録する (register, write down);
rokuon suru 録音する (tape);
shimesu 示す (indicate).

record player, *n.* purēyā プレー
ヤー.

recount, *vb.* 1. kataru 語る
(narrate). 2. kazoenaosu 数えなお
す (count again).

recoup, *vb.* torimodosu 取り戻す.

recourse, *n.* **have recourse to** ...
ni tayoru ...に頼る.

recover, *vb.* kaifuku suru 回復する;
torimodosu 取り戻す (regain,
restore).

recovery, *n.* kaifuku 回復;
torimodoshi 取り戻し
(restoration).

re-create, *vb.* saigen suru 再現する
(create anew).

recreation, *n.* rekuriēshon レクリ
エーション; goraku 娯楽.

recruit, 1. *n.* shin-menbā 新メン
バー (new member);
shin'nyūshain 新入社員 (new
company worker). 2. *vb.* boshū

suru 募集する (enlist).

rectangle, *n.* chōhōkei 長方形.

rectify, *vb.* tadasu 正す.

rectum, *n.* chokuchō 直腸.

recuperate, *vb.* genki ni naru 元気になる; kaifuku suru 回復する.

recur, *vb.* saihatsu suru 再発する (occur again); hinpatsu suru 頻発する (occur repeatedly).

recycle, *vb.* risaikuru suru リサイクルする.

red, 1. *adj.* akai 赤い (color); **turn red** akaku naru 赤くなる. 2. *n.* aka(iro) 赤(色) (color); **be in the red** akaji de aru 赤字である.

Red Cross, *n.* sekijūji 赤十字.

redeem, *vb.* 1. kaimodosu 買い戻す (buy back). 2. kaifuku suru 回復する (recover). 3. hatasu 果たす (fulfill). 4. sukuu 救う (deliver from sin).

red-handed, *adj.* genkōhan (no) 現行犯 (の).

red pepper, *n.* tōgarashi 唐辛子.

redress, 1. *n.* baishō 賠償 (recompense). 2. *vb.* tadasu 正す (set right); tsugunau 償う (recompense).

red tape, *n.* keishikishugi 形式主義.

reduce, *vb.* 1. herasu 減らす (make less in amount, weight, etc.). 2. sageru 下げる (lower in degree, rank, intensity, etc.); nesage suru 値下げする (lower price). 3. taijū ga heru 体重が減る (lose weight). 4. **reduce something/someone to** o ... ni shite shimau を... にしてしまう (change something/someone to); **be reduced to** ... ni natte shimau ...になってしまう (be changed into).

reduction, *n.* 1. genshō 減少; teika 低下 (making smaller); shukushō

縮小 (by use of copier). 2. nesage 値下げ (price reduction).

redundant, *adj.* 1. fuhitsuyō (na) 不必要 (な) (needless). 2. kudoi くどい (wordy).

reed, *n.* ashi 葦 (plant).

reef, *n.* anshō 暗礁.

reek, *vb.* akushū ga suru 悪臭がする (smell strongly).

reel, 1. *n.* rīru リール (film, fishing); itomaki 糸巻き (sewing). 2. *vb.* furatsuku ふらつく (stagger); maku 巻く (wind on reel).

refer (to), *vb.* 1. ... ni tsuite noberu ...について述べる; ... ni genkyū suru ...に言及する (mention). 2. ... o sankō ni suru ...を参考にする (draw information from). 3. makaseru 任せる (hand over for decision).

referee, *n.* shinpan 審判 (judge).

reference, *n.* 1. genkyū 言及 (mentioning). 2. sankō 参考 (direction to information source); **reference book** sankōsho 参考書. 3. suisenjō 推薦状 (letter of recommendation); suisen'nin 推薦人 (person who recommends). 4. **in reference to** ... ni kanshite ...に関して; **make reference to** ... ni genkyū suru ...に言及する.

referendum, *n.* jūmintōhyō 住民投票.

refill, 1. *n.* okawari お代わり (food); tsumekaehin 詰め替え品 (object). 2. *vb.* okawari o suru お代わりをする (food); futatabi mitasu 再び満たす (object, liquid, etc.).

refine, *vb.* seiren suru 精練する (object); senren suru 洗練する (person).

refinement, *n.* seiren 精練; senren

洗練.

refinery, *n.* seirensho 精練所.

reflect, *vb.* hansha suru 反射する (cast image/light back). 2. han'ei suru 反映する (mirror, express). 3. yoku kangaeru よく考える (meditate); **reflect on** ... ni tsuite yoku kangaeru ...についてよく考える (think carefully).

reflection, *n.* 1. hansha 反射 (reflected light); sugata 姿 (image in the mirror). 2. han'ei 反映 (indication). 3. jukkō 熟考 (contemplation).

reflector, *n.* hanshabutsu 反射物.

reflex, *n.* jidōhansha 自動反射.

reform, 1. *n.* kaisei 改正 (object); kaishin 改心 (person). 2. *vb.* kaisei suru 改正する (condition or object); kaishin suru 改心する (person).

reformation, *n.* 1. kaikaku 改革. 2. **Reformation** shūkyōkaikaku 宗教改革.

reformatory, *n.* shōnen'in 少年院.

reformer, reformist, *n.* kaikakusha 改革者.

refrain, 1. *n.* kurikaeshi 繰り返し (music). 2. *vb.* **refrain from** ... o hikaeru ... を控える (abstain).

refresh, *vb.* 1. genkizukeru 元気付ける (reinvigorate). 2. arata ni suru 新たにする (renew).

refreshments, *n.* inshokubutsu 飲食物 (food and drink).

refrigerate, *vb.* hiyasu 冷やす.

refrigerator, *n.* reizōko 冷蔵庫.

refuge, *n.* hinan(sho) 避難(所); **take refuge** hinan suru 避難する.

refugee, *n.* nanmin 難民.

refund, 1. *n.* haraimodoshi 払い戻し. 2. *vb.* haraimodosu 払い戻す.

refusal, *n.* kyohi 拒否.

refuse, 1. *n.* gomi ごみ (garbage);

haikibutsu 廃棄物 (any waste material). 2. *vb.* kyohi suru 拒否する; kotowaru 断る (decline).

refute, *vb.* hanron suru 反論する.

regain, *vb.* torimodosu 取り戻す.

regal, *adj.* igen ga aru 威厳がある.

regard, 1. *n.* sonkei 尊敬 (respect); kanshin 関心 (concern); **with regard to** ... ni kanshite ...に関して. 2. *vb.* miru 見る (look); sonkei suru 尊敬する (respect); **regard as** ... to minasu ...と見なす (consider to be); **regard highly** takaku hyōka suru 高く評価する (consider highly).

regarding, *prep.* ... ni kanshite/tsuite ...に関して／ついて.

regardless, *adv.* 1. tonikaku とにかく (despite everything, anyway). 2. **regardless of** ... ni kakawarazu ...にかかわらず (in spite of); ... o mushi shite ...を無視して (ignoring).

regime, *n.* seijikeitai 政治形態; seido 制度 (system of rule).

regiment, 1. *n.* rentai 連隊. 2. *vb.* shihai suru 支配する; tōsei suru 統制する (control).

region, *n.* chi'iki 地域 (area); chiku 地区 (district).

regional, *adj.* 1. chihō (no) 地方(の) (local). 2. chi'iki-teki (na) 地域的 (な) (of an area).

register, 1. *n.* tōrokubo 登録簿 (written list); sei'iki 声域 (voice); reji レジ (cash register). 2. *vb.* tōroku suru 登録する (enter in a register); namae o kaku 名前を書く (sign up); inshō ga nokoru 印象が残る (make some impression); shimesu 示す (show); kakitome de dasu 書留で出す (mail).

registered, *adj.* kakitome (no) 書

留 (の) (mail).

registration, *n.* 1. tōroku 登録 (act of entering in register). 2. kimei 記名 (act of signing up).

registrar, *n.* gakuseki-gakari 学籍係 (at a university or college).

registry, *n.* tōkisho 登記所 (place); tōrokubo 登録簿 (registration list).

regret, 1. *n.* kanashimi 悲しみ (grief); kōkai 後悔 (repentance). 2. *vb.* kuyamu 悔む (feel sorry about); kōkai suru 後悔する (repent).

regular, 1. *n.* jōren 常連 (regular visitor); otokuisama お得意様 (regular customer). 2. *adj.* regyurā (no) レギュラー (の); itsumo no いつもの; heijō (no) 平常 (の) (usual); futsū (no) 普通 (の) (ordinary); teiki-teki (na) 定期的 (な) (recurring at fixed intervals); kisoku-teki (na) 規則的 (な) (orderly); ittei (no) 一定 (の) (constant).

regulate, *vb.* 1. kisei suru 規制する (control by rules, method, etc.). 2. chōsei suru 調整する (adjust).

regulation, *n.* 1. kisoku 規則 (rule). 2. kisei 規制 (control).

rehabilitate, *vb.* 1. kaifuku suru 回復する (health, honor, etc.). 2. shakaifukki suru 社会復帰する (return to society).

rehabilitation, *n.* rihabiri リハビリ (restoration).

rehearsal, *n.* rihāsaru リハーサル; keiko 稽古.

rehearse, *vb.* keiko suru 稽古する.

reign, 1. *n.* chisei 治世 (royal rule). 2. *vb.* osameru 治める (have sovereign power); shihai suru 支配する (dominate).

reimburse, *vb.* haraimodosu 払い戻す.

rein, *n.* tazuna 手綱 (guiding straps).

reincarnation, *n.* 1. rin'ne 輪廻 (belief). 2. saisei 再生 (rebirth). 3. umarekawari 生まれ変わり (new embodiment).

reinforce, *vb.* hokyō suru 補強する; tsuyomeru 強める (strengthen with support).

reiterate, *vb.* kurikaeshi noberu 繰り返し述べる.

reject, *vb.* 1. kyohi suru 拒否する (decline). 2. suteru 捨てる (throw away).

rejoice, *vb.* yorokobu 喜ぶ.

rejuvenate, *vb.* wakagaeru 若返る (become young again); wakaku suru 若くする (make young again).

relapse, *vb.* 1. atomodori suru 後戻りする (revert). 2. saihatsu suru 再発する (fall back into illness).

relate, *vb.* 1. hanasu 話す (tell). 2. kankeizukeru 関係づける (connect in thought or meaning). 3. kankei ga aru 関係がある (have relation). 4. shitashimu 親しむ (establish a friendly or meaningful relationship).

relation, *n.* 1. kankei 関係 (connection); **in/with relation to** ... ni kanshite ...に関して. 2. shinseki 親戚 (relative).

relationship, *n.* 1. kankei 関係 (connection). 2. kankei 関係 (personal connection); shinseki kankei 親戚関係 (family connection).

relative, 1. *n.* shinseki 親戚 (family). 2. *adj.* sōtai-teki (na) 相対的 (な); hikaku-teki (na) 比較的 (な) (comparative).

relatively, *adj.* sōtai-teki ni 相対的に; hikaku-teki ni 比較的に.

relax, *vb.* 1. rirakkusu suru リラックスする; kutsurogu くつろぐ (rest). 2. yurumu 緩む (become slack); yurumeru 緩める (loosen).

relaxation, *n.* 1. ikinuki 息抜き (diversion). 2. kanwa 緩和 (relief from tension or restriction).

relay, 1. *n.* kōtai 交代 (new shift); rirē リレー (race); chūkeihōsō 中継放送 (TV). 2. *vb.* toritsugu 取り次ぐ (send message); kōtai saseru 交代させる (replace with fresh relays); chūkeihōsō suru 中継放送する (TV).

release, 1. *n.* fūkiri 封切り (movie); shakuhō 釈放 (prisoner); hōmen 放免 (setting free from an obligation). 2. *vb.* fūkiru 封切る (movie); shakuhō suru 釈放する (prisoner); hōmen suru 放免する (set free from an obligation).

relegate, *vb.* kakusage suru 格下げする (lower position).

relent, *vb.* yawaragu 和らぐ (become more mild or forgiving).

relevant, *adj.* 1. tekisetsu (na) 適切 (な) (appropriate). 2. kankei ga aru 関係がある (pertinent).

reliability, *n.* 1. shinraisei 信頼性 (dependability). 2. shinpyōsei 信憑性 (credibility).

reliable, *adj.* ate ni dekiru 当てに出来る; tayori ni naru 頼りになる (dependable, trustworthy). 2. shinjirareru 信じられる (credible).

relic, *n.* 1. sei'i 聖遺 (religious object). 2. ibutsu 遺物 (object surviving from the past).

relief, *n.* 1. anshin 安心 (from anxiety); keigen 軽減 (from pain). 2. kyūenbusshi 救援物資 (help, such as money, food, etc.). 3. kōtai 交代 (new shift). 4. rerīfu レリーフ (architecture). ·

relieve, *vb.* 1. anshin saseru 安心させる (anxiety); keigen suru 軽減する (pain); sukuu 救う (trouble). 2. kōtai suru 交代する (shift). 3. **relieve (someone) of (something)** ... o motte ageru ...を持ってあげる (carry).

religion, *n.* shūkyō 宗教.

religious, *adj.* 1. shūkyō (no) 宗教 (の) (of a religion). 2. shinkō-bukai 信仰深い (devout).

relinquish, *vb.* hōki suru 放棄する (surrender).

relish, 1. *n.* yorokobi 喜び (enjoyment); tsukemono 漬物 (pickles). 2. *vb.* mankitsu suru 満喫する; yorokobu 喜ぶ.

reluctant, *adj.* ki ga susumanai 気が進まない (hesitant).

rely on, *vb.* ... o ate ni suru ...を当てにする; shin'yō suru 信用する (put trust in).

remain, 1. *n.* **remains** nokori 残り (that which remains); itai 遺体 (corpse). 2. *vb.* nokoru 残る (stay); ... no mama de iru ...のままでいる (continue to be).

remainder, *n.* nokori 残り (rest).

remark, 1. *n.* iken 意見 (comment); chūmoku 注目 (attention); **make remarks** iken o noberu 意見を述べる. 2. *vb.* noberu 述べる (say); kizuku 気付く (notice).

remarkable, *adj.* subarashii 素晴らしい (wonderful).

remedy, 1. *n.* chiryō 治療. 2. *vb.* tadasu 正す (correct); naosu 治す (cure).

remember, *vb.* 1. omoidasu 思い出す (recall). 2. oboeteoku 覚えておく (keep in mind). 3. okurimono o suru 贈り物をする (give a present).

remind, *vb.* omoidasaseru 思い出させる.

reminder, *n.* 1. memo メモ (memorandum); tokusokujō 督促状 (letter). 2. chūkoku 忠告 (notification).

reminisce, *vb.* kaisō suru 回想する (recollect); omoide-banashi ni fukeru 思い出話しに耽る (talk about the past).

remiss, *adj.* fuchūi (na) 不注意 (な) (negligent).

remit, *vb.* 1. sōkin suru 送金する (send money). 2. menjo suru 免除する (pardon).

remittance, *n.* sōkin 送金.

remnant, *n.* 1. nokori 残り (remaining part). 2. nokorimono 残り物 (leftover).

remorse, *n.* kōkai 後悔.

remote, *adj.* 1. tōi 遠い (distant). 2. kasuka (na) 微か (な) (faint).

remote control, *n.* rimokon リモコン.

remove, *vb.* 1. torinozoku 取り除く (get rid of). 2. nugu 脱ぐ (take off). 3. korosu 殺す (murder). 4. utsusu 移す (move to another place). 5. kaiko suru 解雇する (dismiss).

remunerate, *vb.* mukuiru 報いる.

Renaissance, *n.* runessansu ルネッサンス.

rend, *vb.* hikisaku 引き裂く (tear).

render, *vb.* 1. ataeru 与える (provide). 2. (... ni) suru (...に) する (cause to be). 3. enjiru 演じる (perform). 4. **render aid** enjo suru 援助する.

rendezvous, *n.* 1. machiawase 待ち合わせ (appointment to meet). 2. machiawase-basho 待ち合わせ場所 (meeting place).

rendition, *n.* 1. engi 演技 (play);

ensō 演奏 (music). 2. kaishaku 解釈 (interpretation).

renegade, *n.* uragirimono 裏切り者.

renew, *vb.* 1. saikai suru 再開する (begin again). 2. arata ni suru 新たにする (make new). 3. kōshin suru 更新する (extend contract, etc.).

renewal, *n.* kōshin 更新 (extending contract, etc.).

renounce, *vb.* hōki suru 放棄する (give up).

renovate, *vb.* kaizō/shūri suru 改造／修理する (remodel/repair).

renown, *n.* meisei 名声.

renowned (for), *adj.* (... de) yūmei (na) (...で) 有名 (な).

rent, 1. *n.* karichin 借り賃 (payment); yachin 家賃 (house rent); yabure 破れ (tear); **house for rent** kashiya 貸家. 2. *vb.* kariru 借りる (pay for lease); kasu 貸す (grant a lease).

rental, *n.* rentaru-ryō レンタル料 (amount).

renunciation, *n.* hōki 放棄.

repair, 1. *n.* shūri 修理. 2. *vb.* shūri suru 修理する.

reparation, *n.* benshō 弁償 (compensation).

repay, *n.* hensai suru 返済する (pay back money).

repeal, *vb.* haishi suru 廃止する.

repeat, 1. *n.* ripīto リピート (repetition); saihōsō 再放送 (TV). 2. *vb.* kurikaesu 繰り返す (do or say again); saihōsō suru 再放送する (TV).

repel, *vb.* 1. gekitai suru 撃退する (drive back). 2. hanpatsu saseru 反発させる (excite disgust).

repellent, *n.* mushiyoke 虫除け (insect repellent).

repent, *vb.* kōkai suru 後悔する.

repentance, *n.* kōkai 後悔.

repercussion, *n.* eikyō 影響 (effect).

repertoire, *n.* 1. repātorī レパートリー.

repetition, *n.* kurikaeshi 繰り返し.

replace, *vb.* 1. modosu 戻す (return). 2. kawaru 代わる (take place of). 3. **replace (with)** (...to) torikaeru (...と) 取り替える (change one thing for another).

replacement, *n.* 1. torikae 取り替え (changing one thing for another). 2. kawari 代わり (substitute).

replenish, *vb.* futatabi mitasu 再び満たす.

replete, *adj.* 1. ippai (no) 一杯 (の) (filled). 2. manpuku (no) 満腹 (の) (full stomach).

replica, *n.* fukusei 複製.

reply, 1. *n.* henji 返事 (response); **in reply to** ... no henji ni ...の返事に. 2. *vb.* kotaeru 答える (answer).

report, 1. *n.* repōto レポート; hōkoku 報告 (account); uwasa 噂 (rumor); jūsei 銃声 (gunfire). 2. *vb.* hōkoku suru 報告する (give an account of); shiraseru 知らせる (make known).

report card, *n.* tsūchihyō 通知表.

reporter, *n.* repōtā レポーター; shinbunkisha 新聞記者 (newspaper reporter); terebi-kisha テレビ記者 (TV reporter).

repose, 1. *n.* yasumi 休み (rest); nemuri 眠り (sleep). 2. *vb.* yasumu 休む (rest); nemuru 眠る (sleep).

repository, *n.* sōko 倉庫 (storage).

represent, *vb.* 1. arawasu 現わす (signify). 2. daihyō suru 代表する

(act for). 3. egaku 描く (portray).

representation, *n.* 1. daihyō 代表 (being a representative). 2. hyōgen 表現; byōsha 描写 (depiction).

representative, 1. *n.* daihyōsha 代表者 (person who represents another); giin 議員 (member of a legislative body). 2. *adj.* daihyō-teki (na) 代表的 (な) (representing); tenkei-teki (na) 典型的 (な) (typical).

repress, *vb.* 1. osaeru 抑える (control). 2. yokuatsu suru 抑圧する (suppress by force).

repression, *n.* 1. yokusei 抑制 (control). 2. yokuatsu 抑圧 (suppression by force).

reprieve, *n.* 1. enki 延期 (delay). 2. shikkōenki 執行延期 (delay punishment).

reprimand, 1. *n.* chōkai 懲戒. 2. *vb.* chōkai suru 懲戒する.

reprisal, *n.* hōfuku 報復.

reproach, 1. *n.* hinan 非難. 2. *vb.* hinan suru 非難する.

reproduce, *vb.* 1. ko o umu 子を産む (procreate). 2. fukusei o tsukuru 複製を作る (copy). 3. saisei suru 再生する (produce anew or again).

reproduction, *n.* 1. hanshoku 繁殖 (procreation). 2. fukusei 複製 (copy). 3. saisei 再生 (act of producing anew or again).

reproof, *n.* shisseki 叱責.

reptile, *n.* hachūrui は虫類.

republic, *n.* kyōwakoku 共和国.

republican, *adj.* kyōwashugi (no) 共和主義 (の).

repudiate, *vb.* hitei suru 否定する (deny).

repugnance, *n.* ken'o 嫌悪 (aversion).

repugnant, *adj.* ozomashii おぞましい (disgusting).

repulse, *vb.* gekitai suru 撃退する (drive back with force).

repulsion, *n.* zōo 憎悪 (hatred).

reputable, *adj.* hyōban ga ii 評判が良い (well spoken of).

reputation, *n.* hyōban 評判.

repute, *n.* hyōban 評判.

request, 1. *n.* rikuesuto リクエスト; (o)negai (お)願い; yōbō 要望; **at the request of** ... no yōbō ni ōjite ...の要望に応じて; **on request** yōbō ga ari shidai 要望があり次第. 2. *vb.* tanomu 頼む (ask for).

require, *vb.* 1. hitsuyō to suru 必要とする (need); **be required to do** ... suru hitsuyō ga aru ...する必要がある. 2. yōkyū suru 要求する (demand).

requirement, *n.* 1. hitsuyōhin 必要品 (something necessary). 2. yōkyū 要求 (demand). 3. jōken 条件 (condition).

requisite, 1. *adj.* hitsuyō (na) 必要 (な). 2. *n.* hitsujuhin 必需品.

requisition, *n.* seikyū 請求 (demand).

rescind, *vb.* haishi suru 廃止する (repeal).

rescue, 1. *n.* kyūjo 救助. 2. *vb.* kyūjo suru 救助する.

research, 1. *n.* chōsa 調査 (investigation); kenkyū 研究 (advanced study). 2. *vb.* chōsa suru 調査する (investigate); kenkyū suru 研究する (study).

researcher, *n.* 1. chōsakan 調査官 (investigator). 2. kenkyūsha 研究者 (one who studies).

resemblance, *n.* sōji 相似.

resemble, *vb.* niteiru 似ている.

resent, *vb.* okoru 怒る (feel angry).

resentful, *adj.* okotteiru 怒っている.

resentment, *n.* fungai 憤慨.

reservation, *n.* 1. utagai 疑い (doubt). 2. yoyaku 予約 (booking).

reserve, 1. *n.* takuwae 貯え、蓄え (store); hogoku 保護区 (land); mukuchi 無口 (reticence); jisei 自制 (self-restraint); yobihei 予備兵 (military). 2. *vb.* yoyaku suru 予約する (book); totteoku 取っておく (keep, set apart).

reserved, *adj.* 1. yoyaku 予約 (booked). 2. mukuchi (na) 無口 (な) (reticent).

reservoir, *n.* chosuichi 貯水地; suigenchi 水源地.

reside, *vb.* sumu 住む.

residence, *n.* 1. jūkyo 住居 (dwelling place). 2. kyojū 居住 (act or fact of residing).

resident, *n.* jūnin 住人 (inhabitant).

residential, *adj.* jūtakuchi (no) 住宅地 (の).

residue, *n.* zanryūbutsu 残留物.

resign, *vb.* 1. yameru 辞める; jinin suru 辞任する (give up job, office, etc.). 2. **resign oneself to** akiramete ... o suru 諦めて...をする.

resignation, *n.* 1. jinin 辞任 (retirement). 2. jinintodoke 辞任届け (letter of resignation). 3. akirame 諦め (renunciation).

resilient, *adj.* 1. danryokusei ga aru 弾力性がある (springing back). 2. kaifuku ga hayai 回復が早い (recovering readily from adversity).

resin, *n.* jushi 樹脂.

resist, *vb.* 1. teikō suru 抵抗する (offer opposition to, remain

unaffected). 2. gaman suru 我慢
する (withstand).

resistance, *n.* 1. hantai 反対; teikō
抵抗 (opposition). 2. teikōryoku
抵抗力 (immunity).

resistant, *adj.* teikōryoku ga tsuyoi
抵抗力が強い.

resolute, *adj.* dankotaru 断固たる.

resolution, *n.* 1. katai ketsui 固い
決意 (firmness). 2. kaiketsu 解決
(solution). 3. kettei 決定
(decision).

resolve, *vb.* 1. kaiketsu suru 解決す
る (solve). 2. kimeru 決める
(decide).

resonant, *adj.* hibiki ga yoi 響きが
良い.

resort, 1. *n.* rizōto リゾート
(recreation place); shudan 手段
(recourse); **as a last resort** saigo
no shudan ni 最後の手段に. 2. *vb.*
resort to ... ni tayoru ...に頼る
(rely on).

resound, *vb.* hibiku 響く (echo).

resources, *n.* 1. shigen 資源;
natural resources ten'nenshigen
天然資源. 2. shiryoku 資力
(money).

respect, 1. *n.* sonkei 尊敬 (esteem);
ten 点 (point); kanshin 関心
(attention); **in all respects** subete
no ten de 全ての点で; **with
respect to** ... ni kanshite ...に関し
て. 2. *vb.* sonkei suru 尊敬する.

respectable, *adj.* 1. rippa (na) 立派
(な) (worthy of respect). 2. kanari
(no) かなり (の) (considerable).

respectful, *adj.* reigi tadashii 礼儀
正しい.

respective, *adj.* sorezore (no) それ
ぞれ (の).

respiration, *n.* kokyū 呼吸.

respite, *n.* kyūshi 休止 (temporary
pause).

respond, *vb.* 1. henji suru 返事す
る (answer). 2. ōjiru 応じる
(react).

response, *n.* 1. henji 返事
(answer). 2. han'nō 反応
(reaction).

responsibility, *n.* sekinin 責任.

responsible, *adj.* 1. sekinin ga aru
責任がある (accountable). 2.
sekininkan ga aru 責任感がある
(reliable).

responsive, *adj.* han'nō ga tsuyoi
反応が強い.

rest, 1. *n.* yasumi 休み (refreshing
quiet; cessation from motion,
work, etc.); sasae 支え (support);
nokori 残り (remainder, others);
at rest yasunde 休んで; **come to
rest** tomaru 止まる. 2. *vb.*
yasumu 休む (be quiet or at ease);
yameru 止める (stop); tomaru 止
まる (cease motion); yokotawaru
横たわる (lie); yokotaeru 横たえ
る (lay); **rest against** ... ni
motasekakeru ...にもたせかける;
rest on ... ni motozuku ...に基づ
く (be based on).

restaurant, *n.* resutoran レスト
ラン.

restitution, *n.* 1. henkan 返還
(return). 2. baishō 賠償
(reparation).

restless, *adj.* ochitsukanai 落ち着か
ない.

restoration, *n.* 1. kaifuku 回復
(recovery). 2. shūfuku 修復
(repair).

restore, *vb.* 1. kaifuku suru 回復す
る (bring back). 2. shūfuku suru
修復する (repair).

restrain, *vb.* 1. yokusei suru 抑制す
る (control). 2. fusegu 防ぐ
(prevent).

restraint, *n.* 1. yokuseiryoku 抑制

力 (restraining influence). 2. yokuatsu 抑圧 (constraint).

restrict, *vb.* seigen suru 制限する (limit).

restriction, *n.* seigen 制限.

restroom, *n.* (o)tearai (お)手洗; toire トイレ.

result, 1. *n.* kekka 結果 (outcome, consequence); **as a result** ... no kekka ... の結果. 2. *vb.* **result in** ... ni owaru ... に終わる.

resume, *vb.* 1. saikai suru 再開する (begin again).

résumé, *n.* rirekisho 履歴書 (curriculum vitae).

resurgence, *n.* fukkō 復興.

resuscitate, *vb.* sosei saseru 蘇生させる.

retail, *n., adv.* kouri (de) 小売り (で).

retailer, *n.* kourishō 小売商.

retain, *vb.* tamotsu 保つ.

retaliate, *vb.* hōfuku suru 報復する.

retard, *vb.* okuraseru 遅らせる (delay).

retarded, *adj.* chieokure (no) 知恵遅れ (の) (person).

reticence, *n.* mukuchi 無口; mugon 無言.

retina, *n.* mōmaku 網膜.

retire, *vb.* 1. taishoku suru 退職する (from profession). 2. sagaru 下がる (go).

retirement, *n.* intai 引退; taishoku 退職.

retort, *vb.* 1. iikaesu 言い返す (answer in anger). 2. ōsen suru 応戦する (answer smartly).

retract, *vb.* tekkai suru 撤回する (withdraw).

retreat, 1. *n.* taikyaku 退却 (military); kakurega 隠れ家 (private place). 2. *vb.* taikyaku

suru 退却する (military).

retribution, *n.* batsu 罰 (punishment).

retrieve, *vb.* 1. torimodosu 取り戻す (regain, restore, recover). 2. tsugunau 償う (make amends for).

retroactive, *adj.* sakanobotte yūkō (na) 遡って有効 (な).

retrospect, *n.* kaisō 回想; **in retrospect** kaisō suru to 回想すると.

return, 1. *n.* kaeri 帰り (act of coming or going back); kitaku 帰宅 (act of returning to one's home); henkyaku 返却 (act of giving back something); shinkoku 申告 (report); *(pl.)* rieki 利益 (profit); **by return mail** orikaeshi-yūbin de 折り返し郵便で; **in return (for)** (... no) okaeshi ni (...の) お返しに. 2. *vb.* kaeru 帰る (go or come back); kaesu 返す; modosu 戻す (give, put, or bring back); kotaeru 答える (reply).

reunite, *vb.* futatabi issho ni naru 再び一緒になる (join together after a separation).

reveal, *vb.* arawasu 現わす; shimesu 示す (disclose).

revel, 1. *n.* ukaresawagi 浮かれ騒ぎ. 2. *vb.* ukaresawagu 浮かれ騒ぐ.

revelation, *n.* 1. keiji 啓示 (religious). 2. bakuro 暴露 (act of revealing). 3. omoigakenai nyūsu 思いがけないニュース (surprising information).

revelry, *n.* ukaresawagi 浮かれ騒ぎ.

revenge, *n.* 1. fukushū 復讐 (vengeance). 2. hōfuku 報復 (retaliation); **in revenge for** ... no hōfuku ni ...の報復に.

revenue, *n.* shūnyū 収入 (income); sainyū 歳入 (income of government).

reverberate, *vb.* hankyō suru 反響する (echo).

revere, *vb.* keiai suru 敬愛する (respect).

reverent, *adj.* sonkei ni michita 尊敬に満ちた.

reverie, *n.* musō 夢想.

reverse, 1. *n.* hantai 反対; gyaku 逆 (reverse part, position, etc.); ura 裏 (back); fu'un 不運 (misfortune). **2.** *adj.* hantai (no) 反対 (の); gyaku (no) 逆 (の) (opposite); ura (no) 裏 (の) (back); ribāsu (no) リバース (の) (in car). **3.** *vb.* gyaku ni suru 逆にする (invert); uragaeshi ni suru 裏返しにする (turn inside out); bakku suru/saseru バックする／させる (go/cause to go backward in car).

revert, *vb.* modoru 戻る (go back).

review, 1. *n.* bunseki 分析 (analysis); kentō 検討 (consideration); fukushū 復習 (repeated study of something); hihyō 批評 (critical article); hyōronzasshi 評論雑誌 (magazine); **under review** kentōchū 検討中. **2.** *vb.* bunseki suru 分析する (analyze); kentō suru 検討する (examine, consider); hihyō suru 批評する (give criticism); fukushū suru 復習する (study again).

revise, *vb.* **1.** kaeru 変える (change). **2.** kaitei suru 改訂する (amend).

revision, *n.* **1.** kaitei 改訂 (act of amending). **2.** kaiteiban 改訂版 (revised edition).

revival, *n.* **1.** saisei 再生; fukkō 復興 (rebirth). **2.** ribaibaru リバイバル (film, play).

revive, *vb.* yomigaeru/yomigaeraseru 蘇る／蘇らせる (return/restore to life); fukkō suru/saseru 復興する／させる (come/bring back into use); kaifuku suru/saseru 回復する／させる (return/restore to consciousness, vigor, etc.).

revoke, *vb.* torikesu 取り消す (cancel).

revolt, 1. *n.* hankō 反抗; hangyaku 反逆 (rebellion). **2.** *vb.* hankō suru 反抗する; hangyaku suru 反逆する (rebel); ken'o suru/saseru 嫌悪する／させる (feel/cause to feel disgust).

revolution, *n.* **1.** kakumei 革命 (overthrow of an old political system; fundamental change). **2.** kaiten 回転 (rotation).

revolutionary, 1. *n.* kakumeika 革命家. **2.** *adj.* kakumei (no) 革命 (の) (of a revolution); kakumei-teki (na) 革命的 (な) (innovative).

revolutionize, *vb.* (... ni) kakumei o okosu (...に) 革命を起こす (cause a fundamental change in).

revolve, *vb.* **1.** mawaru 回る; kaiten suru 回転する. **2. revolve around** ... o chūshin ni mawaru ...を中心に回る.

revolver, *n.* riborubā リボルバー; renpatsujū 連発銃 (gun).

revolving, *adj.* kaiten(shiki no) 回転(式の); **revolving door** kaiten-doa 回転ドア.

reward, 1. *n.* hōshū 報酬; hōbi 褒美; **in reward** hōbi ni 褒美に. **2.** *vb.* hōshū o ataeru 報酬を与える; mukuiru 報いる.

rhapsody, *n.* **1.** rapusodī ラプソディー (music). **2.** netsuben 熱弁

(enthusiastic expression).

rhetoric, *n.* retorikku レトリック; shūjigaku 修辞学 (art of speech).

rheumatism, *n.* ryūmachi リューマチ.

rhinoceros, *n.* sai さい.

rhyme, 1. *n.* inbun 韻文 (verse); in 韻 (similar terminal sounds). 2. *vb.* in o fumu 韻を踏む.

rhythm, *n.* rizumu リズム.

rib, *n.* rokkotsu 肋骨 (bone).

ribbon, *n.* ribon リボン.

rice, *n.* raisu ライス; gohan 御飯 (cooked); kome 米 (uncooked).

rich, *adj.* 1. kanemochi (no) 金持ち (の) (of a wealthy person); **get rich** kanemochi ni naru 金持ちになる. 2. kotteri shiteiru こってりしている (containing butter, cream, etc.). 3. yutaka (na) 豊か (な) (affluent, abundant, fertile, sumptuous).

riches, *n.* tomi 富.

ricochet, *vb.* hanekaeru 跳ね返る.

rid, *vb.* 1. **rid oneself of, get rid of** ... o torinozoku ...を取り除く (free oneself from, eliminate); ... o oiharau ...を追い払う (drive away). 2. **be rid of** ... ga nai ...がない (be without a thing); ... ga inai ...がいない (be without a person).

riddle, *n.* nazo 謎.

ride, 1. *n.* jōsha 乗車 (in a vehicle); jōba 乗馬 (on a horse); **go for a ride** doraibu suru ドライブする (in a car); **take for a ride** damasu だます (deceive). 2. *vb.* (... ni) noru (...に) 乗る (ride a bicycle, horse, etc.; rest on something); notteiku 乗って行く (be carried in a vehicle); susumu 進む (move along).

rider, *n.* norite 乗り手 (person who rides).

ridge, *n.* one 尾根 (of a mountain); mune 棟 (of a roof); une 畝 (in plowed land).

ridicule, 1. *n.* karakai からかい. 2. *vb.* karakau からかう; baka ni suru 馬鹿にする.

ridiculous, *adj.* bakarashii 馬鹿らしい.

rife, *adj.* 1. michiteiru 満ちている (full of); **rife with** ... ni michiteiru ... に満ちている. 2. man'en shiteiru 蔓延している (widespread).

rifle, 1. *n.* raifuru ライフル. 2. *vb.* arasagashi o shite nusumu 荒捜しをして盗む (search through to rob).

rift, *n.* kiretsu 亀裂 (split).

right, 1. *adj.* migi (no) 右 (の) (side or direction); tadashii 正しい (correct, just, morally good); ii 良い (good); hontō (no) 本当 (の) (true); massugu (na) 真っ直ぐ (な) (straight). 2. *n.* migi 右 (side or direction); hoshuha 保守派 (conservative political group); tadashii koto 正しいこと (what is morally good); kenri 権利 (something justly due to a person); **turn to the right** migi ni magaru 右に曲がる. 3. *adv.* migi ni 右に (on/to the right); tadashiku 正しく (correctly); chōdo 丁度 (exactly); sugu すぐ (directly); sō そう (yes); **right away** sugu すぐ; **right now** tada ima 只今.

righteous, *adj.* 1. yūtoku (no) 有徳 (の) (virtuous); seigi (no) 正義 (の) (just). 2. mottomo (na) もっとも (な) (reasonable).

righthanded, *adj.* migikiki (no) 右利き (の).

rightist, *n., adj.* uyoku (no) 右翼
(の).

rigid, *adj.* 1. katai 硬い; 固い (stiff,
inflexible). 2. genkaku (na) 厳格
(な) (rigorous).

rigor, *n.* kibishisa 厳しさ
(strictness, hardship).

rigorous, *adj.* 1. kibishii 厳しい
(strict). 2. tsurai 辛い (painful).

rile, *vb.* okoraseru 怒らせる (vex).

rim, *n.* fuchi 縁; heri へり.

rind, *n.* kawa 皮.

ring, 1. *n.* wa 輪 (circular band,
line, etc.); yubiwa 指輪 (for
finger); ringu リング (boxing
ring); ichimi 一味 (group);
beru/denwa no oto ベル／電話の
音 (sound of a bell/telephone);
give someone a ring denwa o
suru 電話をする (telephone). 2.
vb. kakomu 囲む (encircle,
surround); narasu 鳴らす (cause
to sound); naru 鳴る (sound);
beru o narasu ベルを鳴らす
(signal by a bell); **ring true**
hontōrashiku kikoeru 本当らしく
聞こえる.

rink, *n.* sukēto-rinku スケートリン
ク (skating rink).

rinse, 1. *n.* rinsu リンス (for hair).
2. *vb.* yusugu ゆすぐ.

riot, *n.* 1. bōdō 暴動 (violent
disturbance by mob); sōdō 騒動
(tumult). 2. yukai na koto 愉快な
こと (fun).

rip, *vb.* 1. yaburu 破る (tear);
yabureru 破れる (be torn). 2. **rip
off** ne o fukikakeru 値を吹き掛け
る (charge too much); nusumu 盗
む (steal); **rip up** yaburu 破る.

ripe, *adj.* 1. ureteiru 熟れている (of
a fruit). 2. ki ga jukushiteiru 期が
熟している (ready).

ripen, *vb.* jukusu/jukusaseru 熟

す／熟させる (become/make
ripe).

ripple, 1. *n.* sazanami 小波 (wave);
seseragi せせらぎ (sound of small
waves). 2. *vb.* sazanami o tateru
小波を立てる (make ripples).

rise, 1. *n.* jōshō 上昇 (increase,
upward motion); neage 値上げ
(increase in price); kōryū 興隆
(ascendance to prosperity);
noborizaka 上り坂 (slope); **give
rise to** ... o hikiokosu ...を引き起
こす. 2. *vb.* okiru 起きる (get up);
noboru 昇る (sun); agaru 上がる
(move upward); hanran o okosu
反乱を起こす (revolt); arawareru
現われる (appear); **rise from** ...
yori shōjiru ...より生じる
(originate from).

risk, 1. *n.* risuku リスク; kiken 危
険 (danger); **at risk** kiken ni
sarasarete 危険に晒されて; **run a
risk** kiken o okasu 危険を冒す. 2.
vb. kakeru 賭ける (take the risk
of); kiken ni sarasu 危険に晒す
(expose to a risk).

risky, *adj.* kiken (na) 危険 (な).

rite, *n.* gishiki 儀式.

ritual, *n.* gishiki 儀式. 2. *adj.*
gishiki-teki (na) 儀式的 (な).

rival, 1. *n.* raibaru ライバル;
kyōsōaite 競争相手. 2. *vb.* (... to)
kisou (...と) 競う (compete with);
hitteki suru 匹敵する (match).

rivalry, *n.* 1. kyōsō 競争
(competition).

river, *n.* kawa 川.

rivet, 1. *n.* ribetto リベット (pin).
2. *vb.* ribetto de tomeru リベット
で留める (fix); hikitsukeru 引き付
ける (attract).

roach, *n.* gokiburi ごきぶり.

road, *n.* michi 道; dōro 道路; **on
the road** ryokōchū 旅行中

(traveling); jungyōchū 巡業中 (touring with a show).

roam, *vb.* samayou さまよう (wander).

roar, 1. *n.* hoegoe 吠え声 (animal); bakushō 爆笑 (laughter); unari 唸り (machine). 2. *vb.* hoeru 吠える (animal); bakushō suru 爆笑する (laugh); unaru 唸る (machine).

roast, *vb.* yaku 焼く; aburu あぶる.

roast beef, *n.* rōsuto-bīfu ロースト ビーフ.

rob, *vb.* nusumu 盗む; **rob someone of something** ... kara ... o nusumu ...から...を盗む.

robber, *n.* dorobō 泥棒.

robbery, *n.* settō 窃盗; nusumi 盗み.

robe, *n.* 1. rōbu ローブ (long loose garment). 2. shikifuku 式服 (for a ceremony).

robot, *n.* robotto ロボット.

robust, *adj.* kenkō (na) 健康 (な).

rock, 1. *n.* iwa 岩 (stone); rokku ロック (music); **on the rocks** on za rokku オン ザ ロック (drink); kiki ni hinshite 危機に瀕して (in difficulty). 2. *vb.* yusuru 揺する (child); yureru 揺れる (move back and forth); yusaburu 揺さぶる (shock).

rock and roll, *n.* rokkun-rōru ロックンロール.

rocker, *n.* rokkā ロッカー.

rocket, *n.* roketto ロケット.

rocking chair, *n.* yuri'isu 揺り椅子.

rocky, *adj.* iwa ga ōi 岩が多い.

rod, *n.* 1. tsue 杖 (for walking). 2. sao 竿 (for fishing).

rogue, *n.* narazumono ならず者 (criminally dishonest person).

role, *n.* 1. yaku(wari) 役(割) (part). 2. **play the role of** ... no yakuwari o suru ...の役割をする; ... no yaku o enjiru ...の役を演じる (theater).

roll, 1. *n.* maki 巻 (anything rolled); rōru-pan ロールパン (bread); todoroki とどろき (sound); meibo 名簿 (register); **call the roll** shusseki o toru 出席 をとる. 2. *vb.* mawaru 回る (revolve); susumu 進む (move forward); maku 巻く (form into a roll); marumeru 丸める (form into a ball); yusaburu 揺さぶる (rock); todoroku とどろく (have a deep, loud sound); **roll back** nedan o modosu 値段を戻す (reduce price); **roll in** takusan haittekuru 沢山入って来る (come in abundantly); **roll up** makiageru 巻き上げる (tuck up).

roll call, *n.* shukketsu 出欠; tenko 点呼.

roller, *n.* rōrā ローラー.

roller coaster, *n.* rōrā-kōsutā ローラーコースター.

romance, *n.* 1. romansu ロマンス; ren'ai 恋愛 (love). 2. monogatari 物語 (story). 3. yume 夢 (fantasy).

romantic, *adj.* romanchikku (na) ロマンチック (な).

romanticism, *n.* roman-shugi ロマン主義.

Rome, *n.* rōma ローマ.

romp, *vb.* asobisawagu 遊び騒ぐ.

roof, *n.* yane 屋根; **hit the roof** kan-kan ni okoru かんかんに怒る (be angry).

room, *n.* 1. heya 部屋 (compartment). 2. basho 場所 (space); **make room for** ... no tame ni basho o akeru ... のために 場所を空ける. 3. yochi 余地 (opportunity or scope for something); **room for improvement** kaizen no yochi 改善の余地.

roommate, *n.* rūmumēto ルームメート.

room service, *n.* rūmu-sābisu ルームサービス.

roomy, *adj.* hiroi 広い.

rooster, *n.* ondori 雄鶏.

root, 1. *n.* ne 根 (of a plant, tooth, etc.); konpon 根本 (origin); rūto ルート (math); **take root** ne o haru 根を張る (begin to grow). 2. *vb.* nezuku 根付く (grow roots); **root for** ... o ōen suru ...を応援する (lend support to); **root out** nekosogi ni suru 根こそぎにする.

rope, *n.* rōpu ロープ; tsuna 綱; nawa 縄.

rosary, *n.* juzu 数珠 (string of beads).

rose, *n.* bara ばら (flower).

roster, *n.* tōbanmeibo 当番名簿.

rostrum, *n.* dai 台 (platform).

rosy, *adj.* barairo (no) ばら色 (の) (rosy color, promising).

rot, 1. *n.* fuhai 腐敗 (decay). 2. *vb.* kusaru/kusaraseru 腐る／腐らせる (become/cause to spoil).

rotary, *adj.* kaitenshiki (no) 回転式 (の) (movement).

rotate, *vb.* 1. mawaru 回る (turn around); mawasu 回す (cause to turn around). 2. kōtai suru/saseru 交代する／させる (take or cause to take turns).

rotation, *n.* 1. kaiten 回転 (revolution). 2. kōtai 交代 (taking of turns).

rotten, *adj.* kusatteiru 腐っている (decayed, dishonest).

rotund, *adj.* futotteiru 太っている.

rouge, *n.* hōbeni 頬紅 (for cheeks).

rough, *adj.* 1. arai 粗い (not smooth). 2. arai 荒い (violent, tempestuous). 3. soya (na) 粗野 (な) (crude). 4. ōmaka (na) 大まか (な) (preliminary). 5. kurushii 苦しい (painful). 6. shagaregoe (no) しゃがれ声 (の) (voice).

roughneck, *n.* sobō na ningen 粗暴な人間 (rough, coarse person).

roulette, *n.* rūretto ルーレット.

round, 1. *n.* raundo ラウンド (sports); kai 回 (number of events); renzoku 連続 (complete series); junkai 巡回 (regular visit); marui mono 丸い物 (something round-shaped). 2. *adj.* marui 丸い (circular, globular); maru-maru shita 丸々した (fat); **round trip** ōfukuryokō 往復旅行. 3. *adv.* mawari ni 周りに (in circumference); mawatte 回って (moving in a circle) **all year round** ichinenjū 一年中. 4. *vb.* mawaru 回る (go around); marumeru 丸める (make round); **round up** atsumeru 集める.

roundabout, *adj.* 1. tōmawari (no) 遠回り (の) (of a road). 2. kansetsu-teki (na) 間接的 (な) (of a rumor, admonition, etc.).

roundup, *n.* 1. matome まとめ (summary). 2. yobiatsume 呼び集め (bringing together).

rouse, *vb.* 1. okosu 起こす (waken). 2. yobiokosu 呼び起こす (stir up).

rout, *vb.* haisō saseru 敗走させる (force to flee in disorder).

route, *n.* rūto ルート; michi 道.

routine, 1. *n.* itsumo no koto いつものこと (customary course of procedure); okimari no koto お決まりのこと (unimaginative procedure); **daily routine** nikka 日課. 2. *adj.* itsumo (no) いつも

(の) (regular); kimarikitta 決まり
きった (regular and dull).

rove, *vb.* samayou さまよう.

row, 1. *n.* narabi 並び; retsu 列
(line); sawagi 騒ぎ (noise); kenka
喧嘩 (quarrel). 2. *vb.* kogu 漕ぐ
(propel by oars); sawagu 騒ぐ
(make noise); kenka suru 喧嘩す
る (quarrel).

rowboat, *n.* bōto ボート.

rowdy, *adj.* ranbō (na) 乱暴 (な)
(rough and noisy).

royal, *adj.* kokuō/joō (no) 国王／
女王 (の) (of a king/queen).

royalty, *n.* 1. kōzoku 皇族 (royal
persons). 2. ōken 王権 (royal
power). 3. inzei 印税 (share).

rub, *vb.* kosuru 擦る (apply friction
or pressure).

rubber, *n.* gomu ゴム (substance);
rubber band wa-gomu 輪ゴム;
rubber plant gomu no ki ゴムの
木.

rubbish, *n.* 1. gomi ごみ (waste).
2. tawagoto たわ言 (nonsense).

rubble, *n.* gareki がれき.

ruby, *n.* rubī ルビー.

rude, *adj.* burei (na) 無礼 (な)
(impolite).

rudimentary, *adj.* 1. shoho-teki
(na) 初歩的 (な) (introductory).
2. kihon-teki (na) 基本的 (な)
(basic).

rue, *vb.* kōkai suru 後悔する
(regret).

ruffle, 1. *n.* hida ひだ (band of
cloth); midare 乱れ (break in
evenness). 2. *vb.* midasu 乱す
(destroy the smoothness of);
okoraseru 怒らせる (anger); shiwa
ni naru しわになる (become
wrinkled).

rug, *n.* kāpetto カーペット; jūtan
じゅうたん (floor covering).

rugged, *adj.* gotsu-gotsu shita ごつ
ごつした.

ruin, 1. *n.* hametsu 破滅
(destruction); shittsui 失墜
(downfall); haikyo 廃墟; iseki 遺跡
(remains). 2. *vb.* hakai suru 破壊
する (demolish); dainashi ni suru
台無しにする (spoil); hasan suru
破産する (bankrupt).

rule, 1. *n.* kisoku 規則 (regulation);
shihai 支配 (reign); jōgi 定規 (for
measurement); **as a rule** ippan ni
一般に (generally). 2. *vb.* shihai
suru 支配する (reign); kettei suru
決定する (decide); jōgi de sen o
hiku 定規で線を引く (mark with a
ruler); **rule out** jogai suru 除外す
る.

ruler, *n.* 1. jōgi 定規 (for
measurement). 2. shihaisha 支配
者 (one who rules).

ruling, 1. *n.* kettei 決定 (decision).
2. *adj.* omo na 主な
(predominant); shihai (no) 支配
(の) (governing).

rum, *n.* ramu-shu ラム酒.

rumble, *vb.* goro-goro naru ごろご
ろ鳴る (make rumbling sound).

ruminate, *vb.* yoku kangaeru よく
考える (think).

rummage, *vb.* kakimawasu 掻き回
す.

rumor, *n.* uwasa 噂 (gossip,
hearsay).

rump, *n.* (o)shiri (お)尻 (hind
part).

rumple, *vb.* midasu 乱す.

rumpus, *n.* kōron 口論 (quarrel);
sawagi 騒ぎ (noisy disturbance).

run, *vb.* 1. hashiru 走る (move
quickly); hashiraseru 走らせる
(cause to move quickly). 2. keiei
suru 経営する (run a business). 3.
rikkōho suru 立候補する (be a

candidate). 4. nagareru 流れる (flow). 5. tokeru 溶ける (melt). 6. nobiru 伸びる (extend). 7. ugoku 動く (be in operation). 8. jōen suru 上演する (be performed). 9. **run across** dekuwasu 出くわす; **run after** oikakeru 追いかける; **run away** nigeru 逃げる; **run into** butsukeru ぶつける (cause to hit); **run out of** ... ga kireru ...が切れる; **run over** hiku ひく (knock down with a car).

runner, *n.* ran'nā ランナー; sōsha 走者.

runway, *n.* kassōro 滑走路 (airplane).

rupture, 1. *n.* haretsu 破裂 (break). 2. *vb.* yaburu 破る (break).

rural, *adj.* inaka (no) 田舎 (の).

ruse, *n.* keiryaku 計略 (trick).

rush, 1. *n.* ōisogi 大急ぎ (hurried activity or state); sattō 殺倒 (eager rushing of people to one place); tosshin 突進 (sudden and hasty movement). 2. *vb.* isogu 急ぐ (hurry); isogaseru 急がせる (cause

to hurry); tobikakaru 飛びかかる (attack).

rush hour, *n.* rasshu-awā ラッシュアワー.

Russian, 1. *n.* roshiajin ロシア人 (person); roshiago ロシア語 (language). 2. *adj.* roshia (no) ロシア (の) (of Russia); roshiajin (no) ロシア人 (の) (of the Russians); roshiago (no) ロシア語 (の) (language).

rust, 1. *n.* sabi 錆. 2. *vb.* sabiru 錆びる.

rustic, *adj.* 1. inaka (no) 田舎 (の) (rural). 2. soboku (na) 素朴 (な) (simple).

rustle, *vb.* 1. kosuru oto o tateru 擦る音を立てる (make a rustling sound). 2. nusumu 盗む (steal).

rusty, *adj.* sabiteiru 錆びている (covered with rust, unused).

rut, *n.* 1. wadachi 轍; mizo 溝 (furrow). 2. **get into a rut** kata ni hamaru 型にはまる.

ruthless, *adj.* zan'nin (na) 残忍 (な) (cruel).

rye, *n.* rai-mugi ライ麦.

S

sabotage, *n.* sabotāju サボタージュ; bōgai kōsaku 妨害工作 (obstructive activities).

sack, *n.* 1. fukuro 袋 (bag). 2. ryakudatsu 略奪 (pillage).

sacred, *adj.* 1. shinsei (na) 神聖 (な) (holy). 2. shūkyō (no) 宗教 (の) (religious).

sacrifice, 1. *n.* ikenie 生け贄 (offering); gisei 犠牲 (victimization). 2. *vb.* ikenie ni suru 生け贄にする (offer as a

sacrifice); gisei ni suru 犠牲にする (give up).

sacrificial, *adj.* 1. ikenie (no) 生け贄 (の) (of an offering). 2. gisei (no) 犠牲 (の) (of victimization).

sacrilege, *n.* bōtoku 冒瀆.

sacrosanct, *adj.* shinsei fukashin (no) 神聖不可侵 (の).

sad, *adj.* 1. kanashii 悲しい (sorrowful). 2. nagekawashii 嘆かわしい (deplorable).

sadden, *vb.* kanashimaseru 悲しま

せる (make sad); kanashiku naru
悲しくなる (become sad).

saddle, 1. *n.* sadoru サドル (seat).
2. *vb.* **saddle with** ... de futan o
ataeru ... で負担を与える
(burden).

saddlebag, *n.* sadorubaggu サドル
バッグ.

sadistic, *adj.* sadisuchikku (na) サ
ディスティック.

sadness, *n.* kanashimi 悲しみ.

safe, 1. *n.* kinko 金庫. 2. *adj.* anzen
(na) 安全 (な) (secure, free from
danger); kakujitsu (na) 確実 (な)
(dependable).

safeguard, *n.* bōgyo 防御.

safety, *n.* anzen 安全 (freedom
from danger).

safety belt, *n.* anzen-beruto 安全
ベルト.

safety pin, *n.* anzen-pin 安全ピン.

saffron, *n.* safuran サフラン.

sag, *vb.* 1. tawamu たわむ (bend).
2. tareru 垂れる (hang loose).

saga, *n.* buyūdan 武勇談 (heroic
tale).

sagacity, *n.* meibinsa 明敏さ
(perspicacity); chisei 知性
(intelligence).

sage, *n.* 1. kenjin 賢人 (person). 2.
sēji セージ (plant).

sail, 1. *n.* ho 帆 (sheet); kōkō 航行
(trip on sailing vessel). 2. *vb.*
kōkai suru 航海する (travel over
the sea); funatabi o suru 船旅をす
る (voyage).

sailboat, *n.* kogata hosen 小型帆船
(small boat).

sailing, *n.* 1. sōjū 操縦 (skill of
navigation). 2. seiringu セイリン
グ (navigation).

sailor, *n.* sērā セーラー.

saint, *n.* seija 聖者.

saintly, *adj.* seija no yō (na) 聖者の

よう (な).

sake, *n.* 1. **for the sake of** ... no
tame ni ... の為に (for the good
of). 2. **for the sake of doing** ...
suru tame ni ... する為に (for the
purpose of doing).

salad, *n.* sarada サラダ; **salad
bowl** sarada-bōru サラダボール.

salad dressing, *n.* sarada-
doresshingu サラダドレッシング.

salamander, *n.* sanshōuo 山椒魚.

salami, *n.* sarami サラミ.

salaried man, *n.* sararī-man サラ
リーマン.

salaried woman, *n.* josei-sararī-
man 女性サラリーマン.

salary, *n.* kyūryō 給料; sararī サラ
リー.

sale, *n.* 1. hanbai 販売 (act of
selling). 2. sēru セール (bargain
sale). 3. **for sale** urimono 売り物;
on sale waribiki (de) 割り引き
(で) (able to be bought at reduced
prices).

salesclerk, -man, -lady, *n.* ten'in
店員.

sales tax, *n.* shōhizei 消費税.

saliva, *n.* daeki 唾液.

salmon, *n.* sake 鮭.

salon, *n.* saron サロン.

saloon, *n.* bā バー (bar).

salt, 1. *n.* shio 塩 (sodium
chloride). 2. *vb.* shioaji o tsukeru
塩味を付ける (season with salt);
shiozuke ni suru 塩漬けにする
(preserve).

salt shaker, *n.* shioire 塩入れ.

salty, *adj.* shiokarai 塩辛い.

salutation, *n.* aisatsu 挨拶
(greeting).

salute, *vb.* 1. ... ni aisatsu suru ...
に挨拶する (greet). 2. ... keirei
suru 敬礼する (make a gesture of
respect to a superior).

salvation, *n.* kyūsai 救済.

salve, *n.* nankō 軟膏 (ointment).

same, *adj.* onaji 同じ; **same as** ... to onaji ... と同じ; **all the same** sore demo それでも (even so); **Same to you!** Anata mo. あなたも.

sample, 1. *n.* sanpuru サンプル; mihon 見本. 2. *vb.* tamesu 試す (experiment, test).

sanatorium, *n.* sanatoriumu サナトリウム; ryōyōsho 療養所.

sanctify, *vb.* shinseika suru 神聖化する.

sanctimonious, *adj.* ikanimo shinjinbukasō (na) いかにも信心深そう (な).

sanction, 1. *n.* ninka 認可 (permission); seisai 制裁 (international law). 2. *vb.* mitomeru 認める (approve).

sanctity, *n.* shinseisa 神聖さ (holiness).

sanctuary, *n.* 1. sei'iki 聖域 (holy place). 2. hinansho 避難所 (safe place).

sand, 1. *n.* suna 砂. 2. *vb.* kamiyasuri o kakeru 紙やすりをかける (smooth with sandpaper).

sandal, *n.* sandaru サンダル.

sandpaper, *n.* kamiyasuri 紙やすり.

sandwich, *n.* sandoitchi サンドイッチ.

sandy, *adj.* 1. suna darake (no) 砂だらけ (の) (full of sand). 2. suna ga majitteiru 砂が混じっている (containing sand).

sane, *adj.* 1. shōki (no) 正気 (の) (not deranged). 2. funbetsu ga aru 分別がある (showing good sense).

sanguine, *adj.* 1. hogaraka (na) 朗らか (な) (cheerful). 2. kesshoku ga ii 血色が良い (ruddy).

sanitarium, *n.* see **sanatorium**.

sanitary, *adj.* 1. eisei (no) 衛生 (の) (hygienic). 2. seiketsu (na) 清潔 (な) (free from dirt, germs, etc.).

sanitary napkin, *n.* seiriyō-napukin 生理用ナプキン.

sanitation, *n.* gesuidō-shisetsu 下水道施設 (sewage system).

sanity, *n.* 1. shōki 正気 (soundness of mind). 2. funbetsu 分別 (soundness of judgment).

Santa Claus, *n.* santakurōsu サンタクロース.

sap, *vb.* yowaraseru 弱らせる (weaken).

sapphire, *n.* safaia サファイア.

sarcasm, *n.* iyami 嫌味.

sarcastic, *adj.* iyami tappuri (na, no) 嫌味たっぷり (な、の).

sardine, *n.* iwashi いわし.

sash, *n.* 1. obi 帯 (article of clothing). 2. sasshi サッシ; madowaku 窓枠 (framework for window).

Satan, *n.* 1. satan サタン (chief evil spirit). 2. akuma 悪魔 (devil).

satanic, *adj.* 1. akuma-teki (na) 悪魔的 (な) (fiendish). 2. reikoku (na) 冷酷 (な) (cruel).

satellite, *n.* sateraito サテライト; jinkōeisei 人工衛星.

satin, *n.* saten サテン.

satire, *n.* fūshi 諷刺.

satirical, *adj.* fūshi-teki (na) 諷刺的 (な).

satisfaction, *n.* 1. manzoku 満足 (contentment). 2. manzoku saseru koto 満足させること (act of satisfying).

satisfactory, *adj.* manzoku dekiru 満足出来る (good enough).

satisfied, *adj.* **be satisfied** manzoku shiteiru 満足している.

satisfy, *vb.* 1. manzoku saseru 満足させる (make contented). 2. mitasu 満たす (fulfill).

saturate, *vb.* 1. zubunure ni suru ずぶ濡れにする (soak completely). 2. michiafureru 満ちあふれる (permeate, overflow).

Saturday, *n.* doyōbi 土曜日.

sauce, *n.* sōsu ソース.

saucepan, *n.* sōsupan ソースパン.

saucer, *n.* ukezara 受け皿.

saucy, *adj.* burei (na) 無礼 (な) (insolent).

sausage, *n.* sōsēji ソーセージ.

sauté, 1. *n.* itamemono 炒め物. 2. *vb.* itameru 炒める.

savage, 1. *n.* yabanjin 野蛮人. 2. *adj.* yaban (na) 野蛮 (な) (uncivilized); dōmō (na) どうもう (な) (fierce).

save, 1. *n.* sēbu セーブ (sports). 2. *vb.* tasukeru 助ける (rescue); setsuyaku suru 節約する (economize); takuwaeru 貯える、蓄える (store up). 3. *prep.* ... o nozoite ...を除いて (except).

savings, *n.* chokin 貯金 (money).

savior, *n.* kyūseisha 救世者.

savor, *vb.* tanoshimu 楽しむ (enjoy); ajiwau 味わう (taste).

savory, *adj.* 1. oishii おいしい (tasty). 2. tanoshimeru 楽しめる (pleasing).

saw, 1. *n.* nokogiri 鋸 (tool). 2. *vb.* nokogiri de kiru 鋸で切る (cut).

sawdust, *n.* ogakuzu おが屑.

sawmill, *n.* seizaisho 製材所.

saxophone, *n.* sakusuhon サクスホン.

say, 1. *vb.* iu 言う (speak, state, utter); **that is to say** sunawachi 即ち; **it goes without saying** mochiron もちろん; **You don't say!** Masaka. まさか. 2. *adv.*

daitai 大体い (approximately); tatoeba 例えば (for example).

saying, *n.* kotowaza ことわざ (proverb).

scab, *n.* kasabuta かさぶた (crust).

scaffold, *n.* 1. ashiba 足場 (framework). 2. kōshudai 絞首台 (for execution).

scald, *vb.* yakedo saseru 火傷させる (burn).

scale, 1. *n.* uroko うろこ (fish); hakari 秤 (tool for weighing); tenbin 天秤 (balance); shakudo 尺度 (standard, relative measure); sukēru スケール; kibo 規模 (size, magnitude); onkai 音階 (music). 2. *vb.* noboru 登る (climb up); jōge suru 上下する (increase or decrease); **scale down** kibo o chiisaku suru 規模を小さくする.

scallion, *n.* wakegi わけぎ.

scallop, *n.* hotategai 帆立て貝.

scalp, *n.* tōhi 頭皮 (skin).

scalpel, *n.* mesu メス.

scaly, *adj.* uroko ga ōi うろこが多い (of fish).

scamper, *vb.* satto hashiru さっと走る.

scan, *vb.* 1. shiraberu 調べる (examine). 2. zatto me o tōsu ざっと目を通す (skim).

scandal, *n.* 1. sukyandaru スキャンダル; shūbun 醜聞 (disgrace). 2. uwasa 噂 (gossip).

scandalous, *adj.* hazubeki 恥ずべき.

scanner, *n.* sukyanā スキャナー (medical).

scant, *adj.* saishōgen (no) 最小限 (の) (barely adequate).

scanty, *adj.* fujūbun (na) 不十分 (な); sukunai 少ない (insufficient).

scapegoat, *n.* migawari 身代わり.

scar, *n.* kizuato 傷跡.

scarce, *adj.* sukunai 少ない (insufficient, sparse).

scarcely, *adv.* hotondo ... nai ほとんど ... ない.

scarcity, *n.* fusoku 不足.

scare, 1. *n.* kyōfu 恐怖 (fear). 2. *vb.* kowagaraseru 恐がらせる (frighten).

scarecrow, *n.* kakashi かかし.

scared, *adj.* **be scared** kowai 恐い.

scarf, *n.* erimaki 襟巻 (wool); sukāfu スカーフ (silk).

scarlet, *adj.* shinku (no) 真紅 (の).

scarlet fever, *n.* shōkōnetsu 猩紅熱.

scary, *adj.* osoroshii 恐ろしい.

scathing, *adj.* yōshanai 容赦無い.

scatter, *vb.* 1. makichirasu 撒き散らす (strew loosely about). 2. chirabaraseru 散らばらせる (cause to disperse); chirabaru 散らばる (disperse).

scatterbrain, *n.* awatemono あわて者.

scenario, *n.* shinario シナリオ; kyakuhon 脚本.

scene, *n.* 1. shīn シーン; bamen 場面 (film, play). 2. ba 場 (location of action). 3. kōkei 光景 (view). 4. **behind the scenes** kossori (to) こっそり (と) (secretly).

scenery, *n.* 1. fūkei 風景; keshiki 景色 (landscape). 2. butaihaikei 舞台背景 (theater).

scenic, *adj.* keshiki ga ii 景色が良い.

scent, 1. *n.* nioi 匂い (smell); kaori 香り (fragrance). 2. *vb.* kagu 嗅ぐ (smell).

scepter, *n.* ōshaku 王しゃく.

schedule, 1. *n.* sukejūru スケジュール; keikakuhyō 計画表 (list of plans, events, etc.); jikokuhyō 時刻表 (timetable of buses, planes, etc.); **ahead of/behind schedule** yotei yori hayaku/yori okurete 予定より早く／より遅れて; **on schedule** yoteidōri ni 予定通りに. 2. *vb.* yotei suru 予定する (plan).

scheme, 1. *n.* keikaku 計画 (plan); takurami 企み (plot). 2. *vb.* takuramu 企む (plot).

schism, *n.* bunretsu 分裂 (division into groups).

schizophrenia, *n.* seishin-bunretsushō 精神分裂症.

scholar, *n.* 1. gakusha 学者 (learned person). 2. gakusei 学生 (pupil).

scholarship, *n.* 1. shōgakukin 奨学金 (financial aid). 2. gakumon 学問 (learning).

scholastic, *adj.* gakumon (no) 学問 (の) (of learning).

school, *n.* 1. gakkō 学校 (place for instruction); gakubu 学部 (university department); **elementary school** shōgakkō 小学校; **middle school** chūgakkō 中学校; **high school** kōtōgakkō 高等学校. 2. ha 派 (group). 3. mure 群れ (fish).

schoolchild, *n.* seito 生徒.

schooling, *n.* kyōiku 教育.

schoolmaster, -mistress, *n.* sensei 先生.

schoolmate, *n.* gakuyū 学友.

schoolroom, *n.* kyōshitsu 教室.

school year, *n.* gakunen 学年.

science, *n.* kagaku 科学; **science fiction** esu-efu SF; kūsōkagaku shōsetsu 空想科学小説.

scientific, *adj.* kagaku-teki (na) 科学的 (な).

scientist, *n.* kagakusha 科学者.

scissors, *n.* hasami 鋏.

scoff, *vb.* **scoff at** ... o azawarau ...

を嘲笑う.

scold, *vb.* shikaru 叱る.

scoop, 1. *n.* sukūpu スクープ
(news report); sukoppu スコップ
(small shovel); sukui 掬い
(quantity taken up). **2.** *vb.* **scoop
up** sukuiageru 掬い上げる (take
up); **scoop out** sukuitoru 掬い取
る.

scooter, *n.* sukūtā スクーター.

scope, *n.* **1.** han'i 範囲 (extent). **2.**
genkai 限界 (limit). **3.** kikai 機会
(opportunity).

scorch, *vb.* kogasu 焦がす.

scorching, *adj.* kogetsuku yō (na)
焦げつくよう (な).

score, 1. *n.* tokuten 得点 (points
made in a game, examination,
etc.); riyū 理由 (reason); gakufu
楽譜 (written music); ongaku 音楽
(music used in a film, etc.); nijū 二
十 (twenty); **on that score** sono
ten dewa その点では; **settle a
score** fukushū suru 復習する
(retaliate). **2.** *vb.* tokuten o ageru
得点を上げる (game,
examination); ten o tsukeru 点を
付ける (keep a record); kizamime
o tsukeru 刻み目を付ける (notch);
kachieru 勝ち得る (gain, win).

scoreboard, *n.* tokutenhyō 得点表.

scorn, 1. *n.* keibetsu 軽蔑. **2.** *vb.*
keibetsu suru 軽蔑する.

scorpion, *n.* sasori さそり.

scotch, 1. *n.* **Scotch**
sukotchi(uisukī) スコッチ(ウイス
キー) (whiskey). **2.** *vb.* owaraseru
終わらせる (put an end to).

Scotch tape, *n.* serotēpu セロテー
プ.

scoundrel, *n.* akunin 悪人.

scour, *vb.* **1.** kosuriotosu 擦り落と
す (clean by rubbing). **2.**
sagashimawaru 捜し回る (range

in searching).

scourge, *n.* **1.** muchi 鞭 (whip). **2.**
genkyō 元凶; kunō no moto 苦悩
の元 (cause of affliction).

scout, 1. *n.* teisatsu 偵察 (person
sent ahead); bōi-sukauto ボーイス
カウト (Boy Scout). **2.** *vb.*
shirabemawaru 調べ回る
(explore); sagashimawaru 捜し回
る (seek).

scowl, 1. *n.* shikamettsura しかめ
っ面. **2.** *vb.* okotte kao o
shikameru 怒って顔をしかめる
(frown with anger).

scram, *vb.* deteiku 出て行く (get
out).

scramble, 1. *n.* yojinoboru koto よ
じ登ること (act of climbing);
arasoi 争い (struggle). **2.** *vb.*
yojinoboru よじ登る (climb);
aiarasou 相争う (struggle).

scrambled egg, *n.* iritamago 炒り
卵.

scrap, 1. *n.* kakera 欠けら
(fragment); kozeriai 小競り合い
(fight); **scraps** sukurappu スクラ
ップ (reusable discarded material);
tabenokoshi 食べ残し (leftover
food). **2.** *vb.* suteru 捨てる
(discard); kenka suru 喧嘩する
(fight).

scrapbook, *n.* sukurappubukku ス
クラップブック.

scrape, 1. *n.* kosuru koto 擦ること
(act of rubbing); kukyō 苦境
(predicament); surikizu 擦り傷
(wound). **2.** *vb.* kosuru 擦る (rub
harshly); kosuriotosu 擦り落とす
(remove by scraping).

scratch, 1. *n.* kakikizu 掻き傷
(mark from scratching); hikkaku
oto 引っ掻く音 (sound); **from
scratch** mattaku no hajime kara
全くの初めから. **2.** *vb.* hikkaku

引っ掻く (mark, tear, rub); kaku 掻く (rub slightly with the fingernails); **scratch off/out** kakikesu 掻き消す.

scrawl, 1. *n.* hashirigaki 走り書き (something written hastily); nagurigaki なぐり書き (something written carelessly). 2. *vb.* hashirigaki suru 走り書きする (write hastily); kakinaguru 書きなぐる (write carelessly).

scrawny, *adj.* yasekokete-iru やせこけている (skinny).

scream, 1. *n.* sakebigoe 叫び声. 2. *vb.* sakebu 叫ぶ.

screech, 1. *n.* kanakirigoe 金切り声 (shrill cry). 2. *vb.* kanakirigoe o ageru 金切り声を上げる.

screen, 1. *n.* tsuitate つい立て (partition); amido 網戸 (window screen); gamen 画面 (TV or movie screen). 2. *vb.* kakusu 隠す (hide); furui ni kakeru ふるいにかける (sift through a screen); shiraberu 調べる (examine); hōei suru 放映する (movie).

screw, 1. *n.* neji ねじ (fastener); sukuryū スクリュー (propeller). 2. *vb.* neji de tomeru ねじで留める (fasten).

screwdriver, *n.* nejimawashi ねじ回し (tool).

scribble, 1. *n.* hashirigaki 走り書き (something written hastily). 2. *vb.* hashirigaki suru 走り書きする (write hastily).

script, *n.* 1. kyakuhon 脚本 (play, film, etc.). 2. tegaki 手書き (handwriting).

scroll, *n.* 1. makimono 巻き物 (roll of inscribed paper). 2. kakejiku 掛け軸 (hanging scroll).

scrub, *vb.* 1. goshi-goshi arau ごしごし洗う (wash roughly). 2.

toriyameru 取り止める (cancel).

scruple, *n.* 1. dōgishin 道義心 (ethical consideration). 2. ryōshin 良心 (conscience).

scrupulous, *adj.* 1. ryōshin-teki (na) 良心的 (な) (conscientious). 2. nen'iri (na) 念入り (な) (painstaking).

scrutinize, *vb.* menmitsu ni shiraberu 綿密に調べる (examine).

scrutiny, *n.* menmitsu na chōsa 綿密な調査 (examination).

scuffle, *n.* rantō 乱闘 (fight).

sculptor, *n.* chōkokuka 彫刻家.

sculpture, *n.* chōkoku 彫刻.

scum, *n.* 1. kasu かす (film). 2. kuzu 屑 (person).

scythe, *n.* ōgama 大鎌.

sea, *n.* umi 海 (body of salty water, ocean); -kai -海; **Japan Sea** Nihonkai 日本海; **by sea** fune de 船で (by ship); **at sea** tohō ni kurete 途方に暮れて (at a loss).

seacoast, seaboard, *n.* kaigan 海岸.

seafarer, *n.* funanori 船乗り (sailor).

seafood, *n.* shīfūdo シーフード; gyokairui 魚貝類.

sea gull, *n.* kamome かもめ.

sea horse, *n.* tatsu no otoshigo 竜の落とし子.

seal, 1. *n.* in 印; han 判 (mark); fūin 封印 (means of closing); azarashi あざらし (mammal). 2. *vb.* ... ni in o osu ... に印を押す (affix seal to); fūin o suru 封印をする (close with a seal); fūjiru 封じる (close); **seal in** tojikomeru 閉じ込める.

sea level, *n.* kaibatsu 海抜.

sea lion, *n.* ashika あしか.

seam, *n.* nuime 縫い目 (line

formed in sewing).

seamstress, *n.* josei-shitatenin 女性仕立人.

séance, *n.* kōreikai 降霊会.

seaport, *n.* minatomachi 港町.

search, 1. *n.* sōsaku 捜索 (act of searching for someone or something missing); chōsa 調査 (investigation); **in search of** ... o motomete ... を求めて. 2. *vb.* sagasu 捜す (look for); chōsa suru 調査する (investigate); **search for** ... o sagasu ... を捜す.

searchlight, *n.* sāchiraito サーチライト.

seashore, *n.* kaigan 海岸.

seasickness, *n.* funayoi 船酔い.

season, 1. *n.* shīzun シーズン; kisetsu 季節 (any of the four periods of the year; best or usual time); **in season** shun (no) 旬 (の); **out of season** jikihazure (no) 時季外れ (の). 2. *vb.* ... ni aji o tsukeru ... に味を付ける (flavor).

seasonable, *adj.* jiki ni kanatteiru 時季に適っている.

seasonal, *adj.* kisetsu-teki (na) 季節的 (な).

seasoned, *adj.* keiken'yutaka (na) 経験豊か (な) (experienced).

seasoning, *n.* chōmiryō 調味料.

seat, 1. *n.* seki 席 (place for sitting); giseki 議席 (right to sit, as in Congress); tokoro 所 (site); **take a seat** suwaru 座る. 2. *vb.* suwaraseru 座らせる (place someone on a seat); **seat oneself** suwaru 座る; **be seated** suwaru 座る.

seat belt, *n.* shīto-beruto シートベルト.

sea urchin, *n.* uni うに.

seaweed, *n.* kaisō 海草.

secede, *vb.* dattai suru 脱退する.

secluded, *adj.* 1. koritsu shiteiru 孤立している (isolated). 2. hitozato hanareteiru 人里離れている (located in isolation).

seclusion, *n.* 1. inton 陰遁 (hermitage, retirement). 2. kakuri 隔離 (act of placing away from others).

second, 1. *n.* byō 秒 (sixtieth part of a minute); **seconds** nikyūhin 二級品 (imperfect goods); okawari お代わり (second helping). 2. *adj.* nibanme (no) 二番目 (の); daini (no) 第二 (の) (next after the first); **second to none** saijō (no) 最上 (の) (best). 3. *vb.* shiji suru 支持する (support).

secondary, *adj.* 1. chūtō (no) 中等 (の) (of the second stage, as education). 2. niji-teki (na) 二次的 (な) (deriving from the original, of lesser importance).

second-class, *adj.* ototteiru 劣っている; niryū (no) 二流 (の) (inferior).

second-hand, *adj.* 1. chūko (no) 中古 (の) (used). 2. matagiki (no) 又聞き (の) (indirect).

second-rate, *adj.* niryū (no) 二流 (の).

secrecy, *n.* himitsu 秘密 (state of being secret).

secret, 1. *n.* himitsu 秘密. 2. *adj.* himitsu (no) 秘密 (の).

secretary, *n.* 1. hisho 秘書 (clerical worker). 2. chōkan 長官 (head of department of government). 3. shoki 書記 (official in an organization).

secrete, *vb.* bunpitsu suru 分泌する.

secretion, *n.* bunpitsu 分泌 (liquid).

secretive, *adj.* himitsuzuki (na, no) 秘密好き (な、の) (disposed to keep things secret).

sect, *n.* ha 派 (group); shūha 宗派 (religious group); tōha 党派 (political group).

section, *n.* 1. bubun 部分 (separate part). 2. bu 部; ka 課 (part of an organization or company). 3. chi'iki 地域 (part of a town).

sector, *n.* 1. hōmen 方面 (area). 2. bumon 部門 (part of a business activity).

secular, *adj.* sezoku (no) 世俗 (の).

secure, 1. *adj.* anzen (na) 安全 (な) (safe); kakujitsu (na) 確実 (な) (assured); shikkari shiteiru しっかりしている (firm, reliable). 2. *vb.* kakuho suru 確保する (get); kakujitsu ni suru 確実にする (make certain); tomeru 留める (fasten).

security, *n.* 1. anzen 安全 (safety). 2. bōei 防衛 (protection). 3. tanpo 担保 (security for a loan).

sedan, *n.* sedan セダン.

sedate, *adj.* ochitsuite-iru 落ち着いている (composed).

sedative, *n.* chinseizai 鎮静剤 (medicine).

sedentary, *adj.* suwarigachi (no) 座りがち (の) (characterized by much sitting).

sediment, *n.* chindenbutsu 沈殿物.

sedition, *n.* sendō 扇動 (agitation, instigation).

seduce, *vb.* yūwaku suru 誘惑する.

seducer, *n.* yūwakusha 誘惑者.

seduction, *n.* yūwaku 誘惑.

see, *vb.* miru 見る; **see off** ... o miokuru ... を見送る; **see to** ... o kakujitsu ni suru ... を確実にする.

seed, 1. *n.* tane 種 (plant, cause of anything). 2. *vb.* tane o maku 種

を蒔く (plant seeds); tane o toru 種を取る (remove seeds).

seedy, *adj.* 1. tane ga ōi 種が多い (full of seeds). 2. misuborashii みすぼらしい (run-down).

seek, *vb.* 1. sagasu 捜す (search). 2. motomeru 求める (request). 3. **seek to do** ... shiyō to suru ... しようとする (try to do). 4. **be sought after** juyō ga ōi 需要が多い.

seem, *vb.* ... yō ni mieru ... ように見える (appear).

seeming, *adj.* mikakejō (no) 見掛け上 (の).

seemingly, *adv.* ikkenshita tokoro 一見したところ.

seemly, *adj.* fusawashii ふさわしい.

seep, *vb.* shintō suru 浸透する; **seep into** ... ni shimikomu ... に染み込む.

seer, *n.* yogensha 予言者.

seesaw, *n.* shīsō シーソー.

seethe, *vb.* wakitatsu 沸き立つ (surge or foam as if boiling).

segment, *n.* bubun 部分 (part).

segregate, *vb.* hikihanasu 引き離す (separate).

segregation, *n.* bunri 分離 (separation).

seismic, *adj.* jishin (no) 地震 (の).

seize, *vb.* 1. tsukamu 摑む (grab). 2. bosshū suru 没収する (confiscate). 3. **be seized with** ... ni toritsukareru ... に取り憑かれる.

seizure, *n.* 1. bosshū 没収 (confiscation). 2. hossa 発作 (attack).

seldom, *adv.* mettani ... nai めったに ... ない; **seldom come** mettani konai めったに来ない.

select, 1. *adj.* yorinuki (no) 選り抜

き (の) (carefully chosen). 2. *vb.*
erabu 選ぶ (choose).

selection, *n.* sentaku 選択 (act of
choosing).

selective, *adj.* 1. sentaku (no) 選択
(の) (characterized by selection).

self, *n.* 1. jibun 自分; jiko 自己
(person's own nature); **by
oneself** jibun de 自分で; hitori de
一人で. 2. rikoshin 利己心
(personal interest).

self-, 1. jidō- 自動- (automatic);
self-winding jidōmakishiki (no)
自動巻き式 (の). 2. jiko- 自己-
(oneself); **self-hatred** jikoken'o
自己嫌悪.

self-analysis, *n.* jikobunseki 自己
分析.

self-assertion, *n.* jikoshuchō 自己
主張.

self-assurance, *n.* jishin 自信.

self-centered, *adj.* jikochūshin-
teki (na) 自己中心的 (な).

self-confident, *adj.* jishin ga aru
自信がある.

self-conscious, *adj.* ji'ishiki ga
tsuyoi 自意識が強い.

self-control, *n.* jisei 自制.

self-defense, *n.* jikobōei 自己防衛.

Self-Defence Forces, *n.* jieitai 自
衛隊 (Japanese armed services).

self-denial, *n.* jikohitei 自己否定.

self-discipline, *n.* jikotanren 自己
鍛練.

self-employed, *adj.* jiei (no) 自営
(の).

self-esteem, *n.* jikosonchō 自己尊
重.

self-evident, *adj.* jimei (no) 自明
(の).

self-imposed, *adj.* jikokisei (no) 自
己規制 (の).

self-indulgent, *adj.* wagamama
(na) 我がまま (な).

self-introduction, *n.* jikoshōkai 自
己紹介.

selfish, *adj.* riko-teki (na) 利己的
(な).

self-made, *adj.* dokuryoku (no) 独
力 (の).

self-pity, *n.* jikorenbin 自己憐憫.

self-portrait, *n.* jigazō 自画像.

self-preservation, *n.* jikohozon 自
己保存.

self-respect, *n.* jisonshin 自尊心.

self-righteous, *adj.* hitoriyogari
(no) 一人よがり (の).

self-sacrifice, *n.* jikogisei 自己犠牲.

self-satisfaction, *n.* jikomanzoku
自己満足.

self-service, *n.* serufu-sābisu セル
フサービス.

self-taught, *adj.* dokugaku (no) 独
学 (の).

sell, *vb.* 1. uru 売る (part with in
exchange for money). 2. ureru 売
れる (find a buyer). 3. **sell out**
uritsukusu 売り尽くす; **be sold
out** urikire 売り切れ.

seller, *n.* urite 売り手.

semantics, *n.* imiron 意味論.

semblance, *n.* mikake 見掛け.

semen, *n.* seieki 精液.

semester, *n.* gakki 学期.

semi-, han- 半- (half); **semicircle**
han'en 半円.

semicolon, *n.* semikoron セミコロ
ン.

semimonthly, *adj.* hantsukigoto
(no) 半月毎 (の).

seminar, *n.* seminā セミナー.

seminary, *n.* shingakkō 神学校.

senate, *n.* jōin 上院.

senator, *n.* jōin giin 上院議員.

send, *vb.* 1. okuru 送る (cause to
go or be conveyed). 2. **send out**
hanatsu 放つ (emit); **send back**
okurikaesu 送り返す; **send for** ...

o yobu ... を呼ぶ (summon).

sender, *n.* okurinushi 送り主.

send-off, *n.* sōbetsu 送別 (a farewell).

senile, *adj.* mōroku shiteiru もうろくしている.

senior, 1. *n.* nenchōsha 年長者 (older person); jōshi 上司 (company worker of higher rank); senpai 先輩 (older colleague); yonensei 四年生 (fourth year college student). 2. *adj.* nenchō (no) 年長 (の) (older); jōkyū (no) 上級 (の) (higher in rank); yonensei (no) 四年生 (の) (of a fourth year student).

senior citizen, *n.* rōjin 老人; (o)toshiyori (お)年寄り.

seniority, *n.* nenchō 年長 (condition of being senior); sen'nin 先任 (precedence by length of service).

sensation, *n.* 1. kankaku 感覚 (ability to feel or sense). 2. kimochi 気持ち (impression, perception). 3. sensēshon センセーション; kōfun 興奮 (excitement).

sensational, *adj.* 1. sensēshonaru (na) センセーショナル (な) (startling). 2. subarashii 素晴らしい (outstanding).

sense, 1. *n.* imi 意味 (meaning); kankaku 感覚 (faculty for perceiving physical things); kanji 感じ (feeling so produced); funbetsu 分別 (rationality); **senses** gokan 五感 (five senses); ishiki 意識 (consciousness); **in a sense** aru imi de wa ある意味では; **make sense** suji ga tōru 筋が通る. 2. *vb.* kanjiru 感じる (perceive).

sense of humor, *n.* yūmoa no

sensu ユーモアのセンス.

sensible, *adj.* 1. funbetsu ga aru 分別がある (wise or practical). 2. ishiki shiteiru 意識している (aware).

sensitive, *adj.* 1. binkan (na) 敏感 (な) (easily affected). 2. omoiyari ga aru 思い遣りがある (compassionate). 3. okoriyasui 怒り易い (easily offended). 4. shinchō o yōsuru 慎重を要する (requiring prudence).

sensitivity, *n.* binkansa 敏感さ (susceptibility to stimulation).

sensual, *adj.* 1. kan'nō-teki (na) 官能的 (な) (gratifying to the senses). 2. nikuwaku-teki (na) 肉感的 (な) (carnal).

sensuous, *adj.* 1. kan'nō-teki (na) 官能的 (な) (gratifying to the senses). 2. kankaku-teki (na) 感覚的 (な) (of the senses).

sentence, 1. *n.* bun 文 (group of words); hanketsu 判決 (assignment of punishment). 2. *vb.* hanketsu o iiwatasu 判決を言い渡す.

sentiment, *n.* 1. kanjō 感情 (emotion). 2. iken 意見 (opinion).

sentimental, *adj.* senchimentaru (na) センチメンタル (な); kanshō-teki (na) 感傷的 (な).

sentry, *n.* hoshō 歩哨.

separate, 1. *adj.* betsu (no) 別 (の) (not connected); sorezore (no) それぞれ (の) (individual). 2. *vb.* wakareru 分かれる (come apart); wakareru 別れる (part company); wakeru 分ける (keep or put apart).

separation, *n.* 1. bunri 分離 (state of being separated). 2. betsuri 別離 (separation from family, etc.).

3. bekkyo 別居 (married couple).
4. aida 間 (gap).

September, *n.* kugatsu 九月.

septic, *adj.* kansen shiteiru 感染し
ている.

sequel, *n.* 1. tsuzuki 続き (film,
story). 2. kekka 結果
(consequence).

sequence, *n.* renzoku 連続 (series).

serenade, *n.* serenādo セレナード.

serene, *adj.* odayaka (na) 穏やか
(な) (calm).

sergeant, *n.* gunsō 軍曹 (military);
keibu 警部 (police).

serial, 1. *n.* tsuzukimono 続き物.
2. *adj.* renzoku (no) 連続 (の).

series, *n.* 1. shirīzu シリーズ (TV
program). 2. renzoku 連続 (things
in succession); **a series of** ichiren
no 一連の.

serious, *adj.* 1. shinken (na) 真剣
(な) (of deep thought, earnest). 2.
jūdai (na) 重大 (な) (significant).
3. shinkoku (na) 深刻 (な) (giving
cause for apprehension).

sermon, *n.* sekkyō 説教 (religious
discourse, lecture).

serpent, *n.* hebi 蛇 (snake).

serum, *n.* kessei 血清.

servant, *n.* meshitsukai 召し使い
(domestic servant).

serve, 1. *n.* sābu サーブ (sports). 2.
vb. tsukaeru 仕える (work for
someone); kyūji suru 給仕する
(wait on table); sashiageru 差し上
げる (provide, as with food or
drink); hōshi suru 奉仕する
(render assistance free); yō o nasu
用をなす (have definite use); yaku
ni tatsu 役に立つ (be useful);
tsutomeru 務める (perform the
duties of; serve as a juror, senator,
etc.); kei ni fukusuru 刑に服する
(submit to a criminal sentence);

sābu o suru サーブをする (sports).

service, *n.* 1. sābisu サービス; taiō
対応 (treatment in a hotel,
restaurant, etc.). 2. **services**
joryoku 助力 (assistance). 3.
heieki 兵役 (military service). 4.
shokumu 職務 (duty or work). 5.
shiki 式 (ritual). 6. shisetsu 施設
(supplier of gas, water, etc.). 7.
kōtsū no ben 交通の便
(transportation system). 8. seibi
整備 (maintenance and repair).

service station, *n.* gasorin-sutando
ガソリンスタンド.

servile, *adj.* hikutsu (na) 卑屈 (な).

sesame, *n.* goma 胡麻.

session, *n.* 1. kai 会 (assembly,
sitting); **in session** kaiteichū (no)
開廷中 (の) (court); kaikaichū
(no) 開会中 (の) (legislature). 2.
kōza 講座 (class).

set, 1. *n.* setto セット; soroi 揃い
(group); butai sōchi 舞台装置
(theater); terebi テレビ (TV set); **a
set of** hitosoroi no 一揃いの. 2.
adj. kimatteiru 決まっている
(fixed); junbibantan (no) 準備万端
(の) (ready); **set phrase**
kimarimonku 決まり文句. 3. *vb.*
oku 置く (place); setto suru セッ
トする (arrange, as hair, clock,
etc.); kimeru 決める (determine);
uchitateru 打ち立てる (establish);
shizumu 沈む (pass below
horizon); **set a record** kiroku o
uchitateru 記録を打ち立てる; **set
the table** shokutaku no junbi o
suru 食卓の準備をする; **set free**
jiyū ni suru 自由にする; **set aside**
betsu ni totte oku 別に取って置く
(reserve); **set back** okuraseru 遅
らせる (make late); **set forth**
noberu 述べる (state); **set off/out**
hajimeru 始める (start); tabidatsu

旅立つ (begin a journey); **set up** sōsetsu suru 創設する (establish).

setback, *n.* 1. tsumazuki つまずき (check to progress). 2. atomodori 後戻り (reverse).

settle, *vb.* 1. kimeru 決める (decide). 2. kaiketsu suru 解決する (resolve). 3. wakai suru 和解する (reconcile in a dispute). 4. sumitsuku 住みつく (take up residence). 5. shizumeru 静める (quiet). 6. shiharau 支払う (pay).

settlement, *n.* 1. kaiketsu 解決 (resolution). 2. kettei 決定 (decision). 3. wakai 和解 (reconciliation). 4. teijū 定住 (act of taking up residence). 5. shiharai 支払い (payment).

settler, *n.* nyūshokusha 入植者 (colonist).

setup, *n.* shikumi 仕組み (arrangement).

seven, *n.* nana/nanatsu/shichi 七／七つ／七.

seventeen, *n.* jūnana 十七.

seventeenth, *adj.* jūnanabanme (no) 十七番目 (な); daijūnana (no) 第十七 (の).

seventy, *n.* nanajū/shichijū 七十.

sever, *vb.* 1. hanareru 離れる; kireru 切れる (become separated). 2. kirihanasu 切り離す (separate by cutting). 3. tachikiru 断ち切る (break off, as relations).

several, *adj.* 1. ikutsuka (no) 幾つか (の) (things); sūnin (no) 数人 (の) (people). 2. sū- 数-; **several thousand** sūsen (no) 数千 (の).

severe, *adj.* 1. genkaku (na) 厳格 (な) (strict). 2. hageshii 激しい (violent, hard). 3. kibishii 厳しい (harsh, as weather). 4. kanso (na) 簡素 (な) (plain).

sew, *vb.* nu'u 縫う.

sewage, *n.* osui 汚水.

sewer, *n.* gesui 下水.

sewing, *n.* saihō 裁縫 (act of sewing); **sewing machine** mishin ミシン.

sex, *n.* 1. sekkusu セックス (intercourse); **have sex** sekkusu o suru セックスをする; neru 寝る. 2. sei 性 (gender); **opposite sex** isei 異性; **sex organ** seiki 性器.

sexism, *n.* seisabetsu 性差別.

sexist, *n.* seisabetsu-shugisha 性差別主義者.

sexual, *adj.* sei-teki (na) 性的 (な) (of sex); **sexual harassment** sekuhara セクハラ; **sexual intercourse** sekkusu セックス.

sexy, *adj.* sekushī (na) セクシー (な).

shabby, *adj.* 1. boro-boro (no) ぼろぼろ (の) (worn-out); misuborashii みすぼらしい (meager). 2. kudaranai 下らない (contemptible, inferior).

shack, *n.* hottategoya 堀立て小屋.

shackle, *n.* 1. tekase 手かせ (wrist); ashikase 足かせ (ankle). 2. shikkoku 桎梏 (hindrance).

shade, 1. *n.* kage 陰 (dimness); hikage 日陰 (shady place under the sun); yūrei 幽霊 (ghost); iroai 色合い (degree of color); hiyoke 日除け (window shade); kasa 傘 (of a lamp); sukoshi 少し (slight amount). 2. *vb.* saegiru 遮る (protect from light).

shadow, *n.* 1. kage 影 (dark image). 2. atokata 跡形 (trace).

shady, *adj.* 1. hikage (no) 日陰 (の) (in shade). 2. usankusai うさん臭い (suspicious).

shaft, *n.* 1. e 柄 (long slender rod); yagara 矢柄 (arrow shaft). 2. shinbō 心棒 (revolving bar in engine). 3. kōsen 光線 (beam of light).

shaggy, *adj.* 1. kemukujara (no) 毛むくじゃら (の) (covered with hair). 2. darashinai だらしない (untidy).

shake, *vb.* 1. furu 振る (agitate, as container, bottle, etc.). 2. yureru 揺れる (move with short movements); yusuburu 揺すぶる (cause to move with short movements). 3. furueru 震える (tremble); furuwaseru 震わせる (cause to tremble). 4. furiharau 振り払う (remove by shaking). 5. **shake hands** akushu suru 握手する; **shake one's head** kubi o yoko ni furu 首を横に振る.

shaky, *adj.* 1. fuantei (na) 不安定 (な) (insecure). 2. furueru 震える (tending to tremble).

shall, *aux. vb.* **Shall I (we)...?** ... mashō ka. ... ましょうか.

shallow, *adj.* asai 浅い (not deep).

sham, *n.* 1. inchiki いんちき (pretense). 2. mozōhin 模造品 (imitation).

shambles, *n.* konton 混沌 (chaos).

shame, 1. *n.* haji 恥 (painful feeling); fumeiyo 不名誉 (disgrace); **What a shame!** Nasakenai. 情けない (It is deplorable); **Shame on you!** Haji o shire. 恥を知れ. 2. *vb.* haji o kakaseru 恥をかかせる (cause to feel shame, disgrace).

shameful, *adj.* hazubeki (no) 恥ずべき (の).

shameless, *adj.* hajishirazu (na, no) 恥知らず (な、の) (brazen, unashamed).

shampoo, *n.* shanpū シャンプー.

shanty, *n.* hottategoya 堀立て小屋 (shack).

shape, 1. *n.* katachi 形 (form); jōtai 状態 (condition); **take shape** katachi o toru 形をとる. 2. *vb.* katachizukuru 形作る (form).

shapely, *adj.* katachi ga ii 形が良い.

share, 1. *n.* wakemae 分け前 (portion); buntan 分担 (allotment, assignment); kabu 株 (corporate stock). 2. *vb.* wakeru 分ける; buntan suru 分担する.

shareholder, *n.* kabunushi 株主.

shark, *n.* same 鮫.

sharp, 1. *adj.* surudoi 鋭い (acute, insightful); eibin (na) 鋭敏 (な) (keen, sensitive); kyū (na) 急 (な) (abrupt); meikaku (na) 明確 (な) (distinct); piritto suru ぴりっとする (in taste). 2. *n.* shāpu シャープ (music). 3. *adv.* chōdo 丁度 (of time).

sharpen, *vb.* togu 研ぐ (whet).

sharpener, *n.* enpitsukezuri 鉛筆削り (pencil).

shatter, *vb.* kudakeru 砕ける (break); kudaku 砕く (cause to be broken).

shave, *vb.* 1. soru 剃る (hair); **shave one's beard** hige o soru 髭を剃る. 2. kezuru 削る (cut or scrape in thin slices).

shaver, *n.* shēbā シェーバー.

shaving cream, *n.* shēbingu-kurīmu シェービングクリーム.

shawl, *n.* shōru ショール.

she, *pron.* kanojo 彼女.

sheaf, *n.* taba 束.

shear, *vb.* karitoru 刈り取る.

shears, *n.* ōbasami 大鋏.

sheath, *n.* saya さや.

shed, 1. *n.* koya 小屋 (hut). 2. *vb.* nagasu 流す (pour forth); otosu 落とす (throw off); dappi suru 脱皮する (of a snake or insect); **shed**

light on ... o akiraka ni suru ... を明らかにする.

sheen, *n.* kōtaku 光沢.

sheep, *n.* hitsuji 羊.

sheepish, *adj.* hanikami (no) はにかみ (の).

sheer, *adj.* mattaku (no) 全く (の) (utter, absolute).

sheet, *n.* 1. shītsu シーツ (bedding). 2. shīto シート (thin piece); -mai -枚 (paper); **sheet of paper** kami ichimai 紙一枚.

shelf, *n.* tana 棚 (furniture).

shell, 1. *n.* kara 殻 (hard outer covering); kaigara 貝殻 (sea shell); dan'yaku 弾薬 (shotgun cartridge). 2. *vb.* ... no kara o toru ... の殻を取る (remove the shell of); bakugeki suru 爆撃する (bombard); **shell out** harau 払う (pay).

shellfish, *n.* kōkakurui 甲殻類 (crustacean: lobster, crab, etc.); kai 貝 (mollusk: clam, oyster, etc.).

shelter, 1. *n.* hinansho 避難所 (place for protection); bōkūgō 防空壕 (from air-raid); ichiji-shukuhakusho 一時宿泊所 (temporary residence). 2. *vb.* hogo suru 保護する (protect); hinan suru 避難する (take shelter).

shepherd, -ess, *n.* hitsujikai 羊飼い.

sherbet, *n.* shābetto シャーベット.

sheriff, *n.* hoankan 保安官.

sherry, *n.* sherī-shu シェリー酒.

shield, 1. *n.* tate 盾 (armor); hogo sōchi 保護装置 (device for protection). 2. *vb.* mamoru 守る (protect).

shift, 1. *n.* henka 変化 (change); kōtai 交代 (work). 2. *vb.* utsusu 移す (transfer something); utsuru 移る (be transferred); kawaru 変わる (change); kaeru 変える (cause to change).

shiftless, *adj.* 1. dame (na) だめ (な) (inefficient). 2. namakemono (no) 怠け者 (の) (lazy).

shifty, *adj.* 1. shin'yō dekinai 信用出来ない (untrustworthy). 2. usankusai うさん臭い (appearing suspicious).

shilling, *n.* shiringu シリング.

shimmer, *vb.* matataku 瞬く.

shin, *n.* mukōzune 向こうずね.

shine, 1. *n.* kagayaki 輝き (radiance); kōtaku 光沢 (sheen); migaki 磨き (act of polishing); **rain or shine** nani ga attemo 何があっても (whatever happens). 2. *vb.* hikaru 光る; kagayaku 輝く (give forth light); migaku 磨く (polish).

shiny, *adj.* hikaru 光る.

ship, 1. *n.* fune 船 (boat). 2. *vb.* okuru 送る (send).

shipbuilding, *n.* zōsen 造船.

shipment, *n.* 1. yusō 輸送 (act of sending). 2. yusōhin 輸送品 (thing shipped).

shipwreck, 1. *n.* nanpa 難波. 2. *vb.* **be shipwrecked** nanpa suru 難波する.

shipyard, *n.* zōsensho 造船所; dokku ドック.

shirk, *vb.* okotaru 怠る.

shirt, *n.* shatsu シャツ.

shiver, *vb.* miburui suru 身震いする.

shock, 1. *n.* shokku ショック; shōgeki 衝撃 (emotional disturbance, blow, impact); seishin-teki dageki 精神的打撃 (emotional disturbance); dengeki 電撃 (electric). 2. *vb.* ... ni shokku o ataeru ... にショックを与える (strike with force, horror, etc.); **be shocked (by)** ... ni gakuzen to suru ... に愕然とする (become emotionally devastated).

shock absorber, *n.* kanshōki 緩衝器.

shocking, *adj.* shokkingu (na) ショッキング (な).

shoddy, *adj.* hinjaku (na) 貧弱 (な).

shoe, *n.* kutsu 靴.

shoehorn, *n.* kutsubera 靴べら.

shoelace, *n.* kutsuhimo 靴紐.

shoemaker, *n.* kutsushokunin 靴職人.

shoe polish, *n.* kutsuzumi 靴墨.

shoeshine man, *n.* kutsumigaki 靴磨き.

shoe store, *n.* kutsuya 靴屋.

shoestring, *n.* wazuka no okane わずかのお金 (small amount of money).

shogun, *n.* shōgun 将軍.

shoot, 1. *n.* me 芽 (new growth). 2. *vb.* utsu 撃つ (hit with bullet, discharge firearm); iru 射る (discharge, as bow).

shooting star, *n.* nagareboshi 流れ星.

shop, 1. *n.* mise 店 (store); kōjō 工場 (factory); shigotoba 仕事場 (workshop). 2. *vb.* kau 買う (purchase); **shop around** kurabemawaru 比べ回る (compare); **shop for** ... o sagasu ... を捜す (hunt for).

shopkeeper, *n.* tenshu 店主.

shoplifting, *n.* manbiki 万引き.

shopper, *n.* kaimonokyaku 買い物客.

shopping, *n.* shoppingu ショッピング; kaimono 買い物.

shore, 1. *n.* kishibe 岸辺 (land beside water); riku 陸 (land). 2. *vb.* **shore up** sasaeru 支える (support).

short, 1. *adj.* mijikai 短い (not long); hikui 低い (not tall); tarinai 足りない (not enough); bukkirabō (na) ぶっきらぼう (な) (rudely brief). 2. *adv.* kyū ni 急に (abruptly). 3. **fall short of** ... ni tasshinai ... に達しない (fail to reach); **for short** chijimete 縮めて (as a shorter form); **in short** yōsuru ni 要するに; **run short of** ... ga fusoku suru ... が不足する.

shortage, *n.* fusoku 不足.

shortcake, *n.* shōtokēki ショートケーキ.

short circuit, *n.* shōto ショート.

shortcoming, *n.* ketten 欠点.

shortcut, *n.* chikamichi 近道 (way or method).

shorten, *vb.* mijikaku suru 短くする.

shortening, *n.* shōtoningu ショートニング (food).

shorthand, *n.* sokki 速記.

shorthanded, *adj.* hitodebusoku (no) 人手不足 (の).

shortly, *adv.* 1. sugu ni すぐに (soon). 2. bukkirabō ni ぶっきらぼうに (impatiently).

shortness, *n.* mijikasa 短かさ.

shorts, *n.* 1. han-zubon 半ズボン (pants). 2. pantsu パンツ (underwear).

shortsighted, *adj.* 1. kingan (no) 近眼 (の) (nearsighted). 2. chōki-tenbō ni kakeru 長期展望に欠ける (lacking foresight).

short story, *n.* tanpenshōsetsu 短編小説.

short-tempered, *adj.* tanki (na) 短気 (な).

shortwave, *n.* tanpa 短波.

shot, *n.* 1. happō 発砲 (discharge of firearm); shashu 射手 (marksman); dangan 弾丸 (lead pellet). 2. shotto ショット (photography, film). 3. chūsha 注射 (injection). 4. shūto シュート (sports). 5. **big shot** ōmono 大物; **long shot** mikominashi 見込み無し; **have a shot** yattemiru やってみる.

shotgun, *n.* shottogan ショットガン.

should, *aux. vb.* ... beki ... べき.

shoulder, 1. *n.* kata 肩 (body). 2. *vb.* ninau 担う (carry); kata de osu 肩で押す (push).

shoulder blade, *n.* kenkōkotsu 肩甲骨.

shout, 1. *n.* sakebi 叫び (cry); kansei 歓声 (hurrah). 2. *vb.* sakebu 叫ぶ (yell).

shove, 1. *n.* hitooshi 一押し. 2. *vb.* tsuyoku osu 強く押す.

shovel, *n.* shaberu シャベル.

show, 1. *n.* shō ショー (entertainment, exhibition); tenjikai 展示会 (exhibition); misekake 見せ掛け (appearance); **on show** tenjichū 展示中 (on display). 2. *vb.* tenji suru 展示する (display at a show); miseru 見せる (allow to be seen); shimesu 示す (demonstrate); mieru 見える (be visible); jōen suru 上演する (theater); an'nai suru 案内する (guide); **show off** misebirakasu 見せびらかす; **show up** kuru 来る (arrive).

showcase, *n.* chinretsudana 陳列棚.

showdown, *n.* taiketsu 対決.

shower, 1. *n.* shawā シャワー (for bathing); niwaka'ame にわか雨 (rain); **take a shower** shawā o abiru シャワーを浴びる. 2. *vb.* niwaka'ame ga furu にわか雨が降る (rain briefly); fundan ni ataeru ふんだんに与える (give liberally).

show-off, *n.* misebirakashi-ya 見せびらかし屋.

showroom, *n.* shōrūmu ショールーム.

showy, *adj.* hade (na) 派手 (な) (loud).

shred, 1. *n.* kirehashi 切れ端 (narrow strip). 2. *vb.* kizamu 刻む (cut into shreds).

shrew, *n.* gami-gami on'na がみがみ女 (woman).

shrewd, *adj.* josainai 如才ない.

shriek, 1. *n.* kanakirigoe 金切り声 (loud shrill cry). 2. *vb.* kanakirigoe o ageru 金切り声を上げる (cry).

shrill, *adj.* mimi o tsunzaku yō (na) 耳をつんざくような (piercing).

shrimp, *n.* koebi 小海老.

shrine, *n.* seidō 聖堂 (sacred building); jinja 神社 (Shinto shrine).

shrink, *vb.* 1. chijimu 縮む (contract in size). 2. hikisagaru 引き下がる (draw back). 3. heru 減る (reduce).

shrivel, *vb.* shioreru しおれる (wrinkle and fade).

shroud, *n.* 1. kyōkatabira 経帷子 (burial). 2. ōi 覆い (cover).

shrub, *n.* yabu やぶ.

shrug, *vb.* kata o sukumeru 肩をすくめる; **shrug off** karuku inasu 軽くいなす (dismiss).

shudder, 1. *n.* senritsu 戦慄 (act of shuddering). 2. *vb.* furueru 震える (tremble); zotto suru ぞっとする (feel horrified).

shuffle, *vb.* ashi o hikizuru 足を引きずる (drag feet); kiru 切る

(cards).

shun, *vb.* sakeru 避ける (avoid).

shut, *vb.* 1. tojiru 閉じる (make closed). 2. tojikomeru 閉じ込める (confine). 3. shimeru 閉める (cause to cease operations). 4. shimaru 閉まる (become shut). 5. **shut down** kyūgyō suru 休業する (close temporarily); **Shut up!** Shizuka ni. 静かに (Be quiet!); Damare. だまれ (Don't say anything!).

shutter, *n.* shattā シャッター (door, camera).

shuttle, *n.* **shuttle bus** kinkyori-ōfuku-basu 近距離往復バス; **free shuttle service** sōgeisha 送迎車.

shy, 1. *adj.* uchiki (na) 内気 (な) (bashful); okubyō (na) 臆病 (な) (timid). 2. *vb.* **shy away** sakeru 避ける (avoid).

sibling, *n.* kyōdai 兄弟 (male); shimai 姉妹 (female).

sick, *adj.* 1. byōki (no) 病気 (の) (ill, of sickness). 2. hakike ga suru 吐き気がする (nauseated). 3. byō-teki (na) 病的 (な) (morbid). 4. **be sick of** ... ni unzari shiteiru ... にうんざりしている (be fed up with).

sicken, *vb.* mukatsukaseru むかつかせる (nauseate, disgust).

sickly, *adj.* 1. byōkigachi (no) 病気がち (の) (habitually ailing). 2. mukatsuku yō (na) むかつくよう (な) (nauseating). 3. byōki no yō (na) 病気のよう (な) (appearing ill).

sickness, *n.* 1. byōki 病気 (illness). 2. hakike 吐き気 (nausea).

side, 1. *n.* bubun 部分 (part); gawa 側 (part or group); yoko(gawa) 横 (側) (part other than front, back, top or bottom); men 面 (surface or aspect); fuchi 縁 (edge); soba 側 (nearby area); chi'iki 地域 (region); **side by side** narande 並んで; **take sides** mikata suru 味方する (be partial). 2. *vb.* **side with** ... o shien suru ... を支援する; ... no mikata o suru ... の味方をする (support).

sideburns, *n.* momiage 揉み上げ.

side effect, *n.* fukusayō 服作用.

sidestep, *vb.* sakeru 避ける.

sidewalk, *n.* hodō 歩道.

siege, *n.* hōi 包囲.

sieve, *n.* furui ふるい.

sift, *vb.* 1. furui ni kakeru ふるいに掛ける (separate with a sieve). 2. yoku shiraberu よく調べる (scrutinize).

sigh, 1. *n.* tameiki 溜め息. 2. *vb.* tameiki o tsuku 溜め息を吐く.

sight, 1. *n.* kōkei 光景 (vista); shiryoku 視力 (eyesight); shikai 視界 (range of vision); meisho 名所 (interesting place); **at first sight** hitome de 一目で; **on sight** sugu ni すぐに (immediately); **catch/ lose sight of** ... o mikakeru/ miushinau ... を見掛ける／見失う; **in sight** chikaku ni 近くに (nearby). 2. *vb.* miru 見る (see); mokugeki suru 目撃する (witness).

sightseeing, *n.* kankō 観光; kenbutsu 見物.

sign, 1. *n.* shirushi 印 (symbol); kigō 記号 (conventional mark, figure, etc.); kanban 看板 (advertising board); chōkō 兆候 (portent); aizu 合図 (signal through gesture); keiseki 形跡 (trace). 2. *vb.* shomei suru 署名する (put signature to); aizu suru 合図する (signal); **sign up** ōbo suru 応募する (enlist).

signal, 1. *n.* aizu 合図 (symbolic communication); shingō 信号 (traffic light). 2. *vb.* aizu suru 合図 する (communicate).

signatory, *n.* shomeisha 署名者 (person); chōinkoku 調印国 (country).

signature, *n.* shomei 署名.

signboard, *n.* kanban 看板.

signer, *n.* shomeisha 署名者.

significance, *n.* 1. imi 意味 (meaning). 2. jūdaisa 重大さ (importance).

significant, *adj.* 1. jūdai (na) 重大 (な) (important). 2. ichijirushii 著 しい (noticeable). 3. igibukai 意義 深い (meaningful).

signify, *vb.* 1. imi suru 意味する (mean). 2. shimesu 示す (indicate).

silence, 1. *n.* chinmoku 沈黙 (absence of sound); mugon 無言 (muteness). 2. *vb.* damaraseru 黙 らせる (make speechless).

silent, *adj.* 1. shizuka (na) 静か (な) (quiet). 2. mugon (no) 無言 (の) (speechless).

silhouette, *n.* shiruetto シルエッ ト.

silicon, *n.* shirikon シリコン.

silk, *n.* shiruku シルク; kinu 絹.

silky, *adj.* kinu no yō (na) 絹のよ う (な).

sill, *n.* shikii 敷居 (of a door or window).

silliness, *n.* bakasakagen 馬鹿さ加 減.

silly, *adj.* baka (na) 馬鹿 (な).

silver, 1. *n.* gin 銀 (metal); ginshokki 銀食器 (silverware). 2. *adj.* gin (no) 銀 (の) (of silver); ginsei (no) 銀製 (の) (made of silver).

silverware, *n.* ginshokki 銀食器.

similar, *adj.* dōyō (na, no) 同様 (な、の) (same); niteiru 似ている (resembling).

similarity, *n.* ruijiten 類似点.

simile, *n.* chokuyu 直喩.

simmer, *vb.* gutsu-gutsu nieru ぐ つぐつ煮える.

simple, *adj.* 1. kantan (na) 簡単 (な) (easy); tanjun (na) 単純 (な) (uncomplicated). 2. soboku (na) 素朴 (な) (unpretentious). 3. shisso (na) 質素 (な) (plain, undecorated). 4. tonma (na, no) 頓馬 (な、の) (foolish).

simpleton, *n.* tonma 頓馬.

simplicity, *n.* tanjunsa 単純さ; sobokusa 素朴さ (naiveté, plainness); kansosa 簡素さ (plainness).

simplify, *vb.* tanjunka suru 単純化 する.

simulate, *vb.* mohō suru 模倣する.

simultaneous, *adj.* dōji ni okoru 同時に起こる.

sin, 1. *n.* tsumi 罪. 2. *vb.* tsumi o okasu 罪を犯す.

since, 1. *adv.* sore kara それから. 2. *prep.* ... kara ... から. 3. *conj.* kara から.

sincere, *adj.* seijitsu (na) 誠実 (な).

sincerely, *adv.* **Sincerely yours** keigu 敬具.

sincerity, *n.* seijitsusa 誠実さ.

sinecure, *n.* kanshoku 閑職.

sinew, *n.* ken 腱 (tendon).

sinful, *adj.* tsumibukai 罪深い.

sing, *vb.* utau 歌う.

singe, *vb.* kogasu 焦がす.

singer, *n.* kashu 歌手.

singing, *n.* uta 歌 (act of singing); seigaku 声楽 (art of singing).

single, 1. *n.* dokushinsha 独身者 (unmarried person); shinguru シ ングル (record). 2. *adj.* hitotsu (no) 一つ (の) (one); yui'itsu (no) 唯一 (の) (only); dokushin (no) 独身 (の) (unmarried); koko (no) 個々 (の) (individual); hitoe (no) 一重 (の) (not multiple). 3. *vb.*

single out erabidasu 選び出す.

single file, *n.* ichiretsu 一列.

single-handed, *adj.* tandoku (no) 単独 (の).

singular, *adj.* 1. tansū (no) 単数 (の) (grammar). 2. namihazurete-iru 並外れている (extraordinary). 3. hen (na) 変 (な) (strange).

sinister, *adj.* bukimi (na) 無気味 (な).

sink, 1. *n.* nagashi 流し (kitchen). 2. *vb.* shizumu 沈む (submerge); shizumaseru 沈ませる (cause to submerge); heru 減る (decrease); taoreru 倒れる (fall); yowaru 弱る (deteriorate).

sinner, *n.* tsumibito 罪人.

sinuous, *adj.* magarikunette-iru 曲がりくねっている.

sinus, *n.* bikō 鼻腔.

sinusitis, *n.* bien 鼻炎 (temporary); chikunōshō 蓄膿症 (chronic).

sip, 1. *n.* hitosusuri 一すすり. 2. *vb.* susuru すする.

siphon, *n.* saihon サイホン.

sir, *n.* **Sir** -kyō -卿; **Sir Lawrence Olivier** Rōrensu Oribie-kyō ローレンスオリビエ卿.

siren, *n.* 1. sairen サイレン (device). 2. on'na-yūwakusha 女誘惑者 (seductress).

sirloin, *n.* sāroin サーロイン.

sissy, *n.* 1. josei-teki na otoko 女性的な男 (feminine man). 2. yowamushi 弱虫 (coward).

sister, *n.* 1. shimai 姉妹 (female family member); ane 姉; onēsan お姉さん (older sister); imōto 妹 (younger sister); **sister city**

shimaitoshi 姉妹都市. 2. shūdōjo 修道女 (Catholic).

sister-in-law, *n.* giri no shimai 義理の姉妹.

sit, *vb.* 1. suwaru 座る (take a seat); suwaraseru 座らせる (cause to take seat). 2. **sit back** kutsurogu 寛ぐ (rest); **sit down** suwaru 座る; **sit up** mi o okosu 身を起こす (rise); osoku made okiteiru 遅くまで起きている (stay up late).

site, *n.* basho 場所 (place).

sitting, *n.* 1. kai 会 (session). 2. suwatteiru jikan 座っている時間 (period of being seated).

situated, *adj.* **be situated in** … ni aru … にある.

situation, *n.* 1. jōkyō 状況 (state of affairs). 2. ichi 位置 (position). 3. shoku 職 (employment).

six, *n.* roku/muttsu 六／六つ.

six hundred, *n.* roppyaku 六百.

sixteen, *n.* jūroku 十六.

sixty, *n.* rokujū 六十.

sizable, *adj.* kanari (no) かなり (の).

size, *n.* 1. saizu サイズ (shoes, clothes, etc.). 2. ōkisa 大きさ (dimensions or extent). 3. kibo 規模 (scale).

sizzle, *vb.* jū-jū yakeru じゅーじゅー焼ける (cooking).

skate, 1. *n.* sukēto スケート. 2. *vb.* sukēto o suru スケートをする.

skater, *n.* sukētā スケーター.

skating, *n.* sukēto スケート.

skeleton, *n.* 1. gaikotsu 骸骨 (bones). 2. kokkaku 骨格 (framework).

skeptic, *n.* kaigisha 懐疑者.

skeptical, *adj.* kaigi-teki (na) 懐疑的 (な).

skepticism, *n.* kaigishugi 懐疑主義.

sketch, 1. *n.* suketchi スケッチ

(drawing). 2. *vb.* suketchi o suru スケッチをする (draw).

sketchy, *adj.* 1. fukanzen (na) 不完全 (な) (incomplete). 2. ayafuya (na) あやふや (な) (vague).

skewer, 1. *n.* kushi 串. 2. *vb.* kushi ni sasu 串に刺す.

ski, 1. *n.* sukī スキー. 2. *vb.* sukī o suru スキーをする.

skid, *vb.* yoko ni suberu 横に滑る.

skier, *n.* sukīyā スキーヤー.

skiing, *n.* sukī スキー.

skill, *n.* gijutsu 技術; udemae 腕前 (dexterity).

skilled, *adj.* jukuren shiteiru 熟練している.

skillful, *adj.* takumi (na) 巧み (な).

skim, *vb.* 1. sukuitoru 掬い取る (remove). 2. kasumeru 掠める (move lightly over).

skim milk, *n.* sukimu-miruku スキムミルク.

skimp, *n.* ken'yaku suru 倹約する.

skimpy, *adj.* fujūbun (na) 不十分 (な).

skin, 1. *n.* hada 肌 (animal, human being); kawa 皮 (plant, fruit); **get under one's skin** iradataseru 苛立たせる (irritate one). 2. *vb.* kawa o muku 皮を剝く (remove skin).

skin diving, *n.* sukin-daibingu スキンダイビング.

skinny, *adj.* (gari-gari ni) yaseteiru (がりがりに) やせている.

skip, 1. *n.* sukippu スキップ (jump). 2. *vb.* sukippu suru スキップする (spring); tobu 飛ぶ (jump, disregard order); **skip over** tobasu 飛ばす (leave out).

skipper, *n.* kyaputen キャプテン.

skirmish, *n.* kozeriai 小競り合い.

skirt, 1. *n.* sukāto スカート (garment). 2. *vb.* sakeru 避ける (avoid).

skull, *n.* zugaikotsu 頭蓋骨.

skunk, *n.* sukanku スカンク.

sky, *n.* sora 空.

skylark, *n.* hibari ひばり.

skylight, *n.* tenmado 天窓.

skyrocket, *vb.* kyūjōshō suru 急上昇する.

skyscraper, *n.* chōkōsō-biru 超高層ビル.

slab, *n.* atsuita 厚板 (flat piece); atsugiri 厚切り (food).

slack, 1. *adj.* yurui 緩い (loose, lenient); hima (na) 暇 (な) (not busy, slow); taiman (na) 怠慢 (な) (inattentive). 2. *vb.* **slack off** yurumeru 緩める; namakeru 怠ける (be lazy).

slacken, *vb.* yurumu 緩む (become loose); yurumeru 緩める (cause to become loose).

slacks, *n.* surakkusu スラックス.

slam, *vb.* 1. batan to shimeru ばたんと閉める (shut noisily). 2. hihan suru 批判する (criticize).

slander, 1. *n.* chūshō 中傷. 2. *vb.* chūshō suru 中傷する.

slang, *n.* surangu スラング; zokugo 俗語.

slant, 1. *n.* keisha 傾斜 (slope); kenkai 見解 (view). 2. *vb.* keisha suru 傾斜する (slope); henkō suru 偏向する (be biased).

slap, 1. *n.* hirateuchi 平手打ち. 2. *vb.* hirate de tataku 平手で叩く.

slapstick, *n.* dotabata-kigeki どたばた喜劇.

slash, 1. *n.* kirikizu 切り傷 (wound); surasshu スラッシュ; shasen 斜線 (symbol). 2. *vb.* kiritsukeru 切りつける (cut); nesage suru 値下げする (price).

slate, *n.* 1. yanefukiyō no sekiban 屋根葺き用の石板 (for roofing).

2. nenbangan 粘板岩 (rock). 3.
kōhoshameibo 候補者名簿 (list of
nominees).

slaughter, 1. *n.* gyakusatsu 虐殺
(massacre); tosatsu 屠殺 (killing of
animals). 2. *vb.* gyakusatsu suru
虐殺する (massacre); tosatsu suru
屠殺する (kill animals).

slaughterhouse, *n.* tosatsujō 屠殺
場.

slave, 1. *n.* dorei 奴隷. 2. *vb.*
akuseku hataraku あくせく働く.

slavery, *n.* 1. doreiseido 奴隷制度
(institution). 2. dorei no jōtai 奴
隷の状態 (condition of being a
slave).

slay, *vb.* korosu 殺す (kill);
gyakusatsu suru 虐殺する
(slaughter).

sleazy, *adj.* fuketsu (na) 不潔 (な)
(filthy, contemptibly
disreputable).

sleek, *adj.* 1. kakkoii かっこ良い
(stylish); iki (na) 粋 (な) (smooth
in manners). 2. nameraka (na) 滑
らか (な) (smooth, as hair).

sleep, 1. *n.* nemuri 眠り. 2. *vb.*
nemuru 眠る; neru 寝る **sleep off**
nemutte naosu 眠って治す (get
rid of by sleeping); **sleep with ...**
to sekkusu o suru ... とセックスを
する (have sex with).

sleeping bag, *n.* nebukuro 寝袋.

sleeping car, *n.* shindaisha 寝台車.

sleeping pill, *n.* nemurigusuri 眠
り薬.

sleepwalking, *n.* muyūbyō 夢遊
病.

sleepy, *adj.* 1. nemui 眠い
(drowsy). 2. kakki ga nai 活気が
無い (inactive).

sleet, *n.* mizore みぞれ.

sleeve, *n.* sode 袖 (garment); **keep
something up one's sleeve**

hisoka ni junbi suru 密かに準備す
る.

sleigh, *n.* sori そり.

slender, *adj.* hossori shiteiru ほつ
そりしている.

sleuth, *n.* tantei 探偵.

slice, 1. *n.* suraisu スライス (piece);
a slice of hitokire no 一切れの. 2.
vb. suraisu suru スライスする (cut
into slices); kiru 切る (cut through
with a knife).

slick, *adj.* 1. josai ga nai 如才がない
(shrewdly adroit). 2.
mottomorashii もっともらしい
(sleek but shallow).

slide, 1. *n.* suraido スライド (film
or microscope); suberidai 滑り台
(playground); suberi 滑り (act of
sliding); geraku 下落 (fall). 2. *vb.*
suberu 滑る (move); suberaseru
滑らせる (cause to move).

slight, 1. *n.* bujoku 侮辱 (insult).
2. *adj.* kasuka (na) 微か (な)
(small in amount or degree); sasai
(na) 些細 (な) (trivial); yaseteiru
やせている (slender). 3. *vb.* keishi
suru 軽視する (treat as
unimportant); bujoku suru 侮辱す
る (insult).

slim, *adj.* 1. hossori-shiteiru ほつそ
りしている (slender). 2. wazuka
(na, no) わずか (な、の) (slight).

slimy, *adj.* nuru-nuru suru ぬるぬ
るする.

sling, *n.* tsuribōtai 吊り包帯
(bandage).

slingshot, *n.* (gomu)pachinko (ゴ
ム)パチンコ.

slink, *vb.* koso-koso iku こそこそ行
く.

slip, 1. *n.* suberi 滑り (act of
slipping); machigai 間違い
(mistake); surippu スリップ
(garment); hitokire 一切れ (piece).

2. *vb.* suberu 滑る (glide); suberaseru 滑らせる (cause to glide); akka suru 悪化する (deteriorate); machigaeru 間違える (make a mistake); **slip into (a place)** ... ni kossori hairu ... にこっそり入る; **slip out of (a place)** ... o kossori deru ... をこっそり出る; **slip into/out of (a garment)** ... o sururi to kiru/nugu ... をするりと着る／脱ぐ.

slipper, *n.* surippa スリッパ.

slippery, *adj.* suberiyasui 滑り易い.

slit, 1. *n.* suritto スリット; kireme 切れ目 (narrow opening). 2. *vb.* kirihiraku 切り開く (cut open).

sliver, *n.* hahen 破片.

slob, *n.* darashinai ningen だらしない人間 (slovenly person); bukotsumono 武骨者 (boorish person).

slogan, *n.* surōgan スローガン.

slope, 1. *n.* surōpu スロープ; shamen 斜面 (surface, road); kōbai 勾配 (angle). 2. *vb.* keisha shiteiru/saseru 傾斜している／させる (incline/cause to incline).

sloppy, *adj.* 1. iikagen (na) 好い加減 (な) (careless). 2. darashi ga nai だらしがない (unkempt).

slot, *n.* ana 穴 (opening).

sloth, *n.* taida 怠惰 (laziness).

slot machine, *n.* surotto-mashin スロットマシーン.

slouch, 1. *n.* noroma のろま (lazy, inept person). 2. *vb.* darashinaku suwaru だらしなく座る (sit with a slovenly posture).

slovenly, *adj.* 1. darashinai だらしない (messy). 2. iikagen (na) 好い加減 (な) (careless).

slow, 1. *adj.* osoi 遅い (not fast); okureteiru 遅れている (delayed, as clock); taikutsu (na) 退屈 (な)

(boring); hima (na) 暇 (な) (not busy, slack); atama ga warui 頭が悪い (unintelligent). 2. *vb.* osoku naru/suru 遅くなる／する (become/make slower); **slow down** sokudo o otosu 速度を落とす (reduce speed); hima ni naru 暇になる (business).

slowly, *adv.* yukkuri ゆっくり.

slow motion, *n.* surō-mōshon スローモーション.

slug, *n.* namekuji なめくじ (mollusk).

sluggish, *adj.* 1. taida (na) 怠惰 (な) (lazy). 2. noroi のろい (slow).

slum, *n.* suramu スラム.

slumber, 1. *n.* madoromi まどろみ (nap). 2. *vb.* madoromu まどろむ (doze).

slump, 1. *n.* suranpu スランプ (of an athlete); fukeiki 不景気 (economic depression); gekigen 激減 (decline in number); bōraku 暴落 (decline in value). 2. *vb.* kuzureochiru 崩れ落ちる (drop heavily); kyūraku suru 急落する (drop suddenly).

slur, 1. *n.* wakarinikui hatsuon 分かりにくい発音 (indistinct speech); chūshō 中傷 (disparagement). 2. *vb.* mogo-mogo hanasu もごもご話す (pronounce indistinctly); chūshō suru 中傷する (disparage).

slush, *n.* handoke no yuki 半溶けの雪 (partly melted snow).

sly, *adj.* zurugashikoi ずる賢い (cunning).

smack, *vb.* 1. hirate de tataku 平手で叩く (slap). 2. ōkiku kisu o suru 大きくキスをする (kiss). 3. **smack of** ... kimi ga aru ... 気味がある (have taste or trace of).

small, *adj.* 1. chiisai 小さい (small in size, importance, degree, voice, etc.). 2. sukunai 少ない (small in amount).

small change, *n.* kozeni 小銭.

smallpox, *n.* ten'nentō 天然痘.

smart, 1. *adj.* atama ga ii 頭が良い (intelligent); ereganto (na) エレガント (な) (elegant); sumāto (na) (sophisticated); surudoi 鋭い (sharp). 2. *vb.* hiri-hiri suru ひりひりする (be a source of sharp pain); zuki-zuki itamu ずきずき痛む (feel a stinging pain); kutsujoku ni kurushimu 屈辱に苦しむ (suffer from shame).

smart aleck, *n.* hikerakashiya ひけらかし屋.

smash, 1. *n.* ichigeki 一撃 (blow); wareru oto 割れる音 (noise); sumasshu スマッシュ (tennis); ōatari 大当り (smash hit). 2. *vb.* konagona ni kudakeru/kudaku 粉々に砕ける／砕く (break/cause to break into pieces).

smattering, *n.* **a smattering of** sukoshi no 少しの.

smear, 1. *n.* yogore 汚れ (stain); chūshō 中傷 (defamation). 2. *vb.* nuru 塗る (spread); kegasu 汚す (stain); chūshō suru 中傷する (defame).

smell, 1. *n.* nioi 匂い (odor); kyūkaku 嗅覚 (sense). 2. *vb.* nioi ga suru 匂いがする (emit smell); kagu 嗅ぐ (perceive with nose); akushū ga suru 悪臭がする (stink); **smell of** ... no nioi ga suru ... の匂いがする.

smile, 1. *n.* hohoemi 微笑み. 2. *vb.* hohoemu 微笑む.

smirk, *vb.* nita-nita suru にたにたする.

smite, *vb.* uchinomesu 打ちのめす

(strike); **be smitten by** ... ni karareru ... に駆られる (be carried away by).

smith, *n.* kajiya 鍛冶屋 (blacksmith); kinzaikushi 金細工師 (goldsmith).

smock, *n.* sumokku スモック.

smoke, 1. *n.* kemuri 煙 (visible vapor); kitsuen 喫煙 (act of smoking). 2. *vb.* tabako o su'u 煙草を吸う (smoke a cigarette); kemuri o dasu 煙を出す (emit smoke); kunsei ni suru 薫製にする (food). 3. **No Smoking** Kin'en 禁煙; **smoking section** kitsuenseki 喫煙席; **nonsmoking section** kin'eneseki 禁煙席.

smoker, *n.* kitsuensha 喫煙者.

smoky, *adj.* kemutteiru 煙っている.

smolder, *vb.* 1. ibusu いぶす (burn without flame). 2. kusuburu くすぶる (have suppressed emotions).

smooth, 1. *adj.* nameraka (na) 滑らか (な) (even in surface or movement); junchō (na) 順調 (な) (free from difficulties); maroyaka (na) 円やか (な) (tasting smooth); odayaka (na) 穏やか (な) (tranquil). 2. *vb.* nameraka ni suru 滑らかにする (make smooth of surface); enkatsu ni suru 円滑にする (free from difficulties); **smooth away** torinozoku 取り除く (remove, as obstacles); **smooth out** nobasu 伸ばす (stretch or remove, as wrinkles); **smooth over** yawarageru 和らげる (mitigate).

smother, *vb.* chissoku saseru 窒息させる (suffocate); chissokushi saseru 窒息死させる (suffocate one to death).

smudge, *n.* yogosu 汚す.

smug, *adj.* dokuzen-teki (na) 独善的 (な).

smuggle, *vb.* mitsuyu suru 密輸する.

smuggler, *n.* mitsuyusha 密輸者.

smuggling, *n.* mitsuyu 密輸.

snack, *n.* sunakku スナック; keishoku 軽食.

snag, *n.* 1. tosshutsubutsu 突出物 (sharp projection). 2. omoigakenai mondai 思いがけない問題 (obstacle).

snail, *n.* katatsumuri かたつむり.

snake, *n.* hebi 蛇.

snap, 1. *n.* pokiri to iu oto ぽきりという音 (sound of breaking); pachiri to iu oto ぱちりという音 (sound of snapping fingers); sunappu スナップ (fastener). 2. *vb.* oreru 折れる (break); oru 折る (cause to break); kamu 噛む (bite); shashin o toru 写真を撮る (photograph); **snap up** hittakuru ひったくる (grab).

snapshot, *n.* sunappushotto スナップショット.

snare, 1. *n.* wana 罠 (trap). 2. *vb.* wana ni kakeru 罠に掛ける.

snarl, 1. *n.* unarigoe 唸り声 (growling, as of a dog). 2. *vb.* unaru 唸る (growl); donaru 怒鳴る (speak angrily).

snatch, *vb.* hittakuru ひったくる (grab); **snatch at** ... o tsukamō to suru ... を掴もうとする (try to get).

sneak, *vb.* 1. kossori iku/suru こっそり行く／する (go/act furtively). 2. **sneak into** ... ni shinobikomu ... に忍び込む (enter); **sneak something into** ... o kossori mochikomu ... をこっそり持ち込む (bring something into).

sneakers, *n.* sunīkā スニーカー.

sneer, 1. *n.* azawarai 嘲笑い. 2. *vb.* azawarau 嘲笑う.

sneeze, 1. *n.* kushami くしゃみ. 2. *vb.* kushami o suru くしゃみをする.

snicker, *n.* kusu-kusu warai くすくす笑い.

sniff, *vb.* 1. su'u 吸う (inhale). 2. kagu 嗅ぐ (smell).

snip, *vb.* hasami de kiru 鋏で切る (cut with scissors).

snipe, *vb.* 1. kakurete utsu 隠れて撃つ (shoot from concealment). 2. tokumei de kōgeki suru 匿名で攻撃する (attack anonymously).

snob, *n.* tomi ya katagaki ni yowai ningen 富や肩書きに弱い人間.

snobbish, *adj.* tomi ya katagaki ni yowai 富や肩書きに弱い.

snoop, *vb.* nozokimawaru 覗き回る.

snoopy, *adj.* sensakuzuki (no) 詮索好き (の).

snooze, *vb.* utatane suru うたた寝する.

snore, 1. *n.* ibiki いびき. 2. *vb.* ibiki o kaku いびきをかく.

snort, *vb.* hana o narasu 鼻を鳴らす.

snout, *n.* hanazura 鼻面 (muzzle).

snow, 1. *n.* yuki 雪. 2. *vb.* yuki ga furu 雪が降る.

snowball, *n.* yuki no bōru 雪のボール.

snowfall, *n.* kōsetsu 降雪.

snowflake, *n.* seppen 雪片.

snowstorm, *n.* fubuki 吹雪.

snowy, *adj.* yuki ga ōi 雪が多い (full of snow).

snub, *vb.* mushi suru 無視する (ignore).

snuff, *n.* kagi-tabako 嗅ぎタバコ (tobacco).

snug, *adj.* kaiteki (na) 快適 (な)

(comfortable).

so, 1. *adv.* sō そう (in the manner indicated); kono/sono yō ni この／そのように (in this/that way); totemo とても (very); sore hodo それほど (to such a degree); ... mo mata ... もまた (also); sorede それで (therefore); **... or so** ... hodo ... ほど (approximately); **so as to** ... tame ni ... ために (for the purpose of); **so far** kore made wa これまでは; **so far as I am concerned** ... watashi ni kansuru kagiri wa 私に関する限りは; **so much** son'na ni takusan そんなにたくさん; **so that** ... yō ni ... ように (with the effect that); **and so on** ... nado ... など。 **2.** *conj.* ... yō ni ... ように (in order that).

soak, *vb.* 1. tsukaru 浸かる (lie in liquid); tsukeru 浸ける (place something in liquid). 2. zubunure ni naru/suru ずぶ濡れになる／する (become/cause to become thoroughly wet). 3. shimikomu 染み込む (pass through something). 4. **soak up** ... o kyūshū suru ... を吸収する (absorb).

so-and-so, *n.* nanigashi 某 (unnamed person).

soap, *n.* sekken 石けん (bar).

soap opera, *n.* renzoku-merodorama 連続メロドラマ.

soar, *vb.* maiagaru 舞い上がる.

sob, *vb.* susurinaku すすり泣く.

sober, *adj.* 1. shirafu (no) 素面 (の) (not drunk). 2. omo-omoshii 重々しい (grave). 3. jimi (na) 地味 (な) (subdued).

so-called, *adj.* iwayuru いわゆる.

soccer, *n.* sakkā サッカー.

sociable, *adj.* shakō-teki (na) 社交的 (な).

social, *adj.* 1. shakai (no) 社会 (の); shakai-teki (na) 社会的 (な) (of human society). 2. shakō (no) 社交 (の) (relating to companionship).

socialism, *n.* shakaishugi 社会主義.

socialist, *n.* shakaishugisha 社会主義者.

socialize, *vb.* **socialize with** ... to tsukiau ... と付き合う.

social science, *n.* shakaikagaku 社会科学.

social security, *n.* shakaihoshō 社会保障.

social work, *n.* shakaifukushi-jigyō 社会福祉事業.

society, *n.* 1. shakai 社会 (human beings generally). 2. kyōkai 協会 (association). 3. jōryūshakai 上流社会 (fashionable people).

sociology, *n.* shakaigaku 社会学.

sock, *n.* kutsushita 靴下.

socket, *n.* 1. soketto ソケット (electrical). 2. ganka 眼窩 (eye socket).

sod, *n.* shibatsuchi 芝土 (turf).

soda, *n.* 1. sōda ソーダ. 2. tansan'inryō 炭酸飲料 (drink made with soda water).

sodium, *n.* natoriumu ナトリウム.

sofa, *n.* sofā ソファー.

soft, *adj.* 1. yawarakai 柔らかい (not strong; fluffy, pleasant, supple). 2. amai 甘い (too kind). 3. hi-arukōru (no) 非アルコール (の) (without alcohol). 4. **soft water** nansui 軟水.

soften, *vb.* yawarakaku suru 柔らかくする (make soft); yawarakaku naru 柔らかくなる (become soft).

softness, *n.* yawarakasa 柔らかさ.

soggy, *adj.* becha-becha (no) べちゃべちゃ (の) (soaked).

soil, 1. *n.* tsuchi 土. **2.** *vb.* yogosu

汚す.

soirée, *n.* yakai 夜会.

sojourn, *n.* ichiji taizai 一時滞在.

solace, 1. *n.* nagusame 慰め. 2. *vb.* nagusameru 慰める.

solar, *adj.* taiyō (no) 太陽 (の) (of the sun); **solar system** taiyōkei 太陽系.

solder, 1. *n.* handa はんだ (for joining metal). 2. *vb.* handa de setsugō suru はんだで接合する (join with solder).

soldier, *n.* heishi 兵士.

sole, 1. *n.* ashi no ura 足の裏 (foot); kutsuzoko 靴底 (shoe); karei かれい (fish). 2. *adj.* yui'itsu (no) 唯一 (の) (only).

solely, *adv.* dake だけ; **I am solely responsible** watashi dake ga sekinin ga aru 私だけが責任があ る.

solemn, *adj.* 1. shinken (na) 真剣 (な) (earnest or serious). 2. ogosoka (na) 厳か (な) (characterized by dignity, awe, or formality).

solemnity, *n.* 1. genshukusa 厳粛 さ (awesome dignity). 2. **solemnities** gishiki 儀式 (formal events).

solicit, *vb.* kou 乞う、請う (ask, request).

solicitous, *adj.* 1. shinpai shiteiru 心配している (worried). 2. negatteiru 願っている (eager).

solid, *adj.* 1. rittai (no) 立体 (の) (three-dimensional). 2. kotai (no) 固体 (の) (having definite shape and size). 3. naka ga tsumatteiru 中が詰まっている (not hollow). 4. ganjō (na) 頑丈 (な) (sturdy). 5. junsui (na, no) 純粋 (な、の) (unmixed).

solidarity, *n.* danketsu 団結

soliloquy, *n.* dokuhaku 独白.

solitary, *adj.* 1. kodoku (na) 孤独 (な) (lonely). 2. hitori dake (no) 一人だけ (の) (done alone).

solitude, *n.* kodoku 孤独 (loneliness).

solo, *n.* soro ソロ.

soloist, *n.* dokusōsha 独奏者 (of a musical instrument); dokushōsha 独唱者 (singer).

soluble, *adj.* **be soluble** tokeru 溶 ける.

solution, *n.* 1. kaiketsu 解決 (settlement or answer). 2. yōkaieki 溶解液 (liquid).

solve, *vb.* kaiketsu suru 解決する.

solvent, *adj.* shiharai-nōryoku ga aru 支払い能力がある (able to pay).

somber, *adj.* 1. inki (na) 陰気 (な) (gloomy). 2. usugurai 薄暗い (dark).

some, 1. *pron.* aru hitobito/mono ある人々／物 (unspecified people/things); sūnin 数人 (several people); ikutsuka 幾つか (unspecified number of things); ikuraka 幾らか (unspecified amount). 2. *adj.* sūnin (no) 数人 (の) (referring to people); ikutsuka (no) 幾つか (の) (referring to things); sū- 数- (unspecified in number, several); ikuraka (no) 幾らか (の) (unspecified in amount); aru ある (unspecified); nanika (no) 何か (の) (unknown); **to some extent** aru teido ある程度; **some weeks** sūshūkan 数週間. 3. *adv.* yaku 約 (approximately).

somebody, someone, *pron.* dareka 誰か; **someone else** dareka hoka no hito 誰か他の人.

someday, *adv.* itsuka いつか.

somehow, *adv.* 1. nantokashite 何とかして (in some way or other). 2. dōshiteka どうしてか (for an unknown reason).

somersault, *n.* chūgaeri 宙返り.

something, *pron.* nanika 何か.

sometime, *adv.* itsuka いつか.

sometimes, *adv.* tokidoki 時々.

somewhat, *adv.* ikubunka 幾分か.

somewhere, *adv.* dokoka どこか.

son, *n.* musuko 息子.

song, *n.* uta 歌.

sonic, *adj.* onpa (no) 音波 (の) (of sound waves).

son-in-law, *n.* giri no musuko 義理の息子.

sonnet, *n.* sonetto ソネット.

soon, *adv.* sugu すぐ (in a short time); **soon after (...)** (... no) sugu ato de (... の) すぐ後で; **sooner or later** osokare-hayakare 遅かれ早かれ; **as soon as ...** (suru) to sugu ni ... (する) とすぐに; **as soon as possible** dekirudake hayaku 出来るだけ早く.

soot, *n.* susu 煤.

soothe, *vb.* 1. shizumeru 静める (calm). 2. iyasu 癒す (make less painful).

soothing, *adj.* 1. kokoronagomu 心和む (for the mind). 2. yawarageru 和らげる (for pain).

soothsayer, *n.* yogensha 予言者.

sophisticated, *adj.* 1. senren sareteiru 洗練されている (refined). 2. fukuzatsu (na) 複雑 (な) (complicated). 3. yonareteiru 世慣れている (worldly).

sophomore, *n.* ninensei 二年生.

soprano, *n.* sopurano ソプラノ.

sorcerer, -ess, *n.* mahōtsukai 魔法使い.

sorcery, *n.* mahō 魔法.

sordid, *adj.* 1. asamashii 浅ましい (ignoble). 2. kitanai 汚ない (dirty).

sore, *adj.* itai 痛い (painful); **be sore** itamu 痛む.

sorrow, *n.* kanashimi 悲しみ.

sorry, *adj.* 1. zan'nen (na) 残念 (な) (feeling sad). 2. sumanaku omou すまなく思う (feeling regret); **I am sorry.** Sumimasen. すみません. 3. kinodoku (na) 気の毒 (な) (feeling pity); **feel sorry for ...** o kinodoku ni omou ... を気の毒に思う.

sort, 1. *n.* shurui 種類 (type); ningen 人間 (person); **sort of** ikubun ka 幾分か. 2. *vb.* bunrui suru 分類する (classify); **sort out** yoriwakeru 選り分ける.

so-so, 1. *adj.* māmā (no) まあまあ (の). 2. *adv.* māmā まあまあ.

soufflé, *n.* sufure スフレ.

soul, *n.* 1. tamashii 魂 (spirit, essence, heart). 2. hito 人 (person).

sound, 1. *n.* oto 音 (tone or noise); kaikyō 海峡 (strait). 2. *adj.* sukoyaka (na) 健やか (な) (untroubled); kenkō (na) 健康 (な) (healthy); kenjitsu (na) 堅実 (な) (firm or reliable); ii jōtai (no) 良い状態 (の) (being in a good condition). 3. *vb.* ... yō ni kikoeru ... ように聞こえる (seem); naru 鳴る (make sound); narasu 鳴らす (cause to make sound); hakaru 測る (measure); **sound out** dashin suru 打診する.

sound effects, *n.* onkyōkōka 音響効果.

soundtrack, *n.* saundotorakku サウンドトラック.

soup, *n.* sūpu スープ (Western-style); shiru 汁 (Japanese-style).

sour, *adj.* 1. suppai 酸っぱい (taste). 2. fukigen (na) 不機嫌 (な) (cross).

source, *n.* 1. minamoto 源 (origin or beginning). 2. kongen 根源 (basis or root). 3. dedokoro 出所 (source of information).

south, *n.* minami 南.

South Africa, *n.* minami-afurika 南アフリカ.

South America, *n.* minami-amerika 南アメリカ.

southeast, *n.* nantō 南東.

Southeast Asia, *n.* tōnan-ajia 東南アジア.

southeastern, *adj.* nantō (no) 南東 (の).

southern, *adj.* minami (no) 南 (の).

South Pole, *n.* nankyoku 南極.

southwest, *n.* nansei 南西.

southwestern, *adj.* nansei (no) 南西 (の).

souvenir, *n.* (o)miyage (お)土産.

sovereign, 1. *n.* kunshu 君主 (monarch). 2. *adj.* shuken (no) 主権 (の) (reigning).

sovereignty, *n.* shuken 主権.

soviet, *n.* hyōgikai 評議会.

Soviet Union, *n.* sobieto(-renpō) ソビエト(-連邦); soren ソ連.

sow, 1. *n.* mesubuta 雌豚 (female swine). 2. *vb.* tane o maku 種を蒔く (seed).

soy, *n.* daizu 大豆 (soybean).

soy sauce, *n.* shōyu しょう油.

spa, *n.* onsenchi 温泉地 (hot spring resort).

space, 1. *n.* kūkan 空間 (expanse); basho 場所 (place); aida 間 (interval or distance); kikan 期間 (time); yochi 余地 (room); uchū 宇宙 (outer space). 2. *vb.* aida o oku 間を置く (set some distance apart).

spaceship, *n.* uchūsen 宇宙船.

space shuttle, *n.* supēsu-shatoru スペースシャトル.

spacious, *adj.* hiroi 広い.

spade, *n.* 1. suki 鋤 (for digging). 2. supēdo スペード (cards).

spaghetti, *n.* supagettī スパゲッティー.

Spain, *n.* supein スペイン.

span, 1. *n.* kikan 期間 (length of time); kyori 距離 (distance). 2. *vb.* ... ni oyobu ... に及ぶ (extend over ...); ... no ue ni kakaru ... の上にかかる (make bridge over ...).

Spanish, 1. *n.* supeinjin スペイン人 (people); supeingo スペイン語 (language). 2. *adj.* supein (no) スペイン (の) (of Spain); supeinjin (no) スペイン人 (の) (of the Spanish people); supeingo (no) スペイン語 (の) (of the Spanish language).

spank, *vb.* ... no shiri o tataku ... の尻を叩く.

spanking, *n.* shiritataki 尻叩き.

spare, 1. *adj.* yobi (no) 予備 (の) (kept in reserve); yobun (no) 余分 (の) (extra); hima (na) 暇 (な) (free). 2. *vb.* yōsha suru 容赦する (refrain from hurting or destroying; deal leniently with); kureru くれる (give); habuku 省く (omit); oshimu 惜しむ (use grudgingly).

spare time, *n.* yoka 余暇.

spare tire, *n.* supeataiya スペアタイヤ.

spark, *n.* supāku スパーク (electrical); hibana 火花 (fire).

sparkle, *vb.* 1. kirameku きらめく (shine). 2. awadatsu 泡立つ (effervesce).

spark plug, *n.* tenka-puragu 天火

プラグ.

sparrow, *n.* suzume 雀.

sparse, *adj.* mabara (na) 疎ら (な).

spasm, *n.* 1. keiren けいれん (muscle). 2. hossa 発作 (fit).

spat, *n.* karui kenka 軽い喧嘩 (quarrel).

spate, *n.* **a spate of** ... no hotobashiri ... のほとばしり.

spatial, *adj.* kūkan (no) 空間 (の) (of space).

spatter, *vb.* hanetobasu 跳ね飛ばす (splash).

spatula, *n.* hera へら.

spawn, *n.* tamago 卵 (eggs).

speak, *vb.* hanasu 話す (talk, say); **so to speak** iwaba いわば; **speak about** ... ni tsuite hanasu ... について話す; **speak for** ... no daiben o suru ... の代弁をする (represent).

speaker, *n.* 1. hanashite 話し手 (person). 2. supīkā スピーカー (appliance).

spear, *n.* yari 槍.

spearmint, *n.* hakka 薄荷; supeaminto スペアミント.

special, *adj.* tokubetsu (na, no) 特別 (な、の) (particular, extraordinary).

special delivery, *n.* sokutatsu 速達.

specialist, *n.* senmonka 専門家.

specialize, *vb.* senmon ni suru 専門にする.

specialty, *n.* 1. senmon 専門 (field of special interest). 2. senmonhin 専門品 (specialty product); jimanryōri 自慢料理 (at a restaurant).

species, *n.* shu 種 (class).

specific, *adj.* 1. tokutei (no) 特定 (の) (definite or particular). 2. komakai 細かい (detailed). 3.

seikaku (na) 正確 (な) (precise).

specifically, *adv.* tokubetsu ni 特別に (especially).

specification, *n.* 1. shitei 指定 (act of specifying). 2. **specifications** shōsai 詳細 (details); shiyōgaki 使用書き (for a product, etc.).

specify, *vb.* shitei suru 指定する.

specimen, *n.* mihon 見本; sanpuru サンプル (sample).

specious, *adj.* mottomorashii もっともらしい (plausible but deceptive).

speck, *n.* 1. hanten 斑点 (dot). 2. shimi 染み (stain).

speckled, *adj.* hantenmoyō (no) 斑点模様 (の).

spectacle, *n.* 1. supekutakuru スペクタクル (large-scale public display). 2. sōkan 壮観 (impressive sight). 3. kōkei 光景 (view).

spectacular, *adj.* 1. daikibo (no) 大規模 (の) (grand in scale). 2. migoto (na) 見事 (な) (impressive). 2. waku-waku suru わくわくする (thrilling).

spectator, *n.* kanshū 観衆 (member of audience).

specter, *n.* yūrei 幽霊.

spectrum, *n.* supekutoru スペクトル (band of colors).

speculate, *vb.* 1. shisaku suru 思索する (meditate). 2. yosō suru 予想する (conjecture). 3. tōki suru 投機する (invest).

speech, *n.* 1. hanashikotoba 話し言葉 (spoken language). 2. gengo-nōryoku 言語能力 (faculty of speaking). 3. supīchi スピーチ; enzetsu 演説 (talk before an audience); **make a speech** supīchi o suru スピーチをする.

speed, 1. *n.* supīdo スピード;

hayasa 速さ (rapidity); sokudo 速度 (rate of motion); **at full speed** zensokuryoku de 全速力で. 2. *vb.* isogu 急ぐ (hurry); shissō suru 疾走する (run with speed); **speed up** hayameru 速める.

speeding, *n.* supīdo-ihan スピード違反 (traffic violation).

speed limit, *n.* seigensokudo 制限速度.

speedometer, *n.* sokudokei 速度計.

speedy, *adj.* hayai 速い (quick).

spell, 1. *n.* jumon 呪文 (incantation); **under a spell** mahō ni kakatte 魔法にかかって. 2. *vb.* tsuzuru 綴る (words); **spell out** wakariyasuku iu 分かり易く言う (explain plainly).

spellbound, *adj.* miwaku sareteiru 魅惑されている.

spelling, *n.* superu スペル; tsuzuri 綴り.

spend, *vb.* 1. tsukau 使う (pay out). 2. sugosu 過ごす (pass time).

spendthrift, *n.* rōhika 浪費家.

sperm, *n.* seishi 精子.

spew, *vb.* haku 吐く (vomit).

sphere, *n.* 1. kyū 球 (round ball). 2. tentai 天体 (heavenly body). 3. bun'ya 分野 (field). 4. han'i 範囲 (range).

spice, 1. *n.* supaisu スパイス (food). 2. *vb.* ... ni supaisu o kuwaeru ... にスパイスを加える (season).

spick-and-span, *adj.* pika-pika (no) ぴかぴか (の).

spicy, *adj.* piri-piri suru ぴりぴりする (hot or piquant).

spider, *n.* kumo 蜘蛛; **spider web** kumo no su 蜘蛛の巣.

spigot, *n.* sen 栓.

spike, *n.* 1. ōkugi 大釘 (large nail). 2. ho 穂 (ear of grain).

spill, *vb.* koboreru こぼれる (run over); kobosu こぼす (let run over).

spin, 1. *n.* kaiten 回転 (spinning motion). 2. *vb.* tsumugu 紡ぐ (make yarn); mawasu 回す (cause to rotate); mawaru 回る (revolve).

spinach, *n.* hōrensō ほうれん草.

spinal cord, *n.* sekizui 脊髄.

spine, *n.* 1. sekitsui 脊椎 (spinal column). 2. toge とげ (thorn).

spinster, *n.* ōrudo-misu オールドミス.

spiny, *adj.* 1. toge ga ōi とげが多い (thorny). 2. muzukashii 難しい (difficult).

spiral, 1. *n.* rasen らせん (curve). 2. *adj.* rasenjō (no) らせん状 (の).

spire, *n.* sentō 尖塔.

spirit, *n.* 1. kokoro 心; tamashii 魂 (soul). 2. seishin 精神 (mind, soul). 3. rei 霊 (supernatural being); bōrei 亡霊 (ghost). 4. **spirits** sake 酒 (liquor). 5. **spirits** kibun 気分 (feelings). 6. genki 元気 (vigor).

spiritual, *adj.* 1. seishin-teki (na) 精神的 (な) (pertaining to the mind or soul). 2. rei-teki (na) 霊的 (な) (supernatural). 3. shūkyō-teki (na) 宗教的 (な) (religious).

spiritualism, *n.* kōrei 降霊 (communication with the dead).

spit, 1. *n.* tsuba 唾. 2. *vb.* tsuba o haku 唾を吐く.

spite, *n.* 1. akui 悪意 (malice). 2. urami 恨み (grudge). 3. **in spite of** ... nimo kakawarazu ... にもかかわらず.

spiteful, *adj.* iji ga warui 意地が悪い.

splash, 1. *n.* haneru oto 跳ねる音

(noise); shibuki しぶき (spray). 2. *vb.* hanetobasu 跳ね飛ばす (spatter).

spleen, *n.* 1. hizō 脾臓. 2. fukigen 不機嫌 (ill humor).

splendid, *adj.* subarashii 素晴らしい (magnificent).

splendor, *n.* 1. subarashisa 素晴らしさ (magnificence). 2. kagayaki 輝き (brightness).

splinter, *n.* hahen 破片 (fragment).

split, 1. *n.* sakeme 裂け目 (rent); bunretsu 分裂 (separation). 2. *vb.* waru 割る (break); wareru 割れる (become broken); wakeru 分ける (divide, separate, share); wakareru 別れる (be separated, end marriage or friendship).

splurge, *vb.* 1. zeitaku o suru 贅沢をする (be extravagant). 2. misebirakasu 見せびらかす (show off).

spoil, 1. *n.* ryakudatsuhin 略奪品 (loot). 2. *vb.* dame ni suru だめにする (damage or ruin, cause to lose good quality); dame ni naru だめになる (be damaged or ruined, lose good quality); amayakasu 甘やかす (spoil someone by indulgence).

spoilsport, *n.* kyōzame na ningen 興醒めな人間.

spoke, *n.* supōku スポーク (bar or rod).

spokesman, -woman, -person, *n.* daibensha 代弁者; daihyōsha 代表者.

sponge, *n.* suponji スポンジ (for cleaning).

sponsor, 1. *n.* suponsā スポンサー (advertiser); hoshōnin 保証人 (endorser). 2. *vb.* suponsā de aru スポンサーである (be an advertiser); hoshō suru 保証する

(endorse).

spontaneous, *adj.* jihatsu-teki (na) 自発的 (な) (unpremeditated).

spoof, *n.* parodī パロディー.

spook, *n.* yūrei 幽霊.

spoon, *n.* supūn スプーン; saji さじ.

spoonful, *n.* hitosajibun 一さじ分; **a spoonful of sugar** hitosaji no satō 一さじの砂糖.

sporadic, *adj.* sanpatsu-teki (na) 散発的 (な).

spore, *n.* hōshi 胞子.

sport, *n.* supōtsu スポーツ; undō 運動 (athletic activity).

sportsman, -woman, *n.* supōtsu-ka スポーツ家.

sportsmanship, *n.* supōtsuman-shippu スポーツマンシップ.

spot, 1. *n.* ten 点 (dot); shimi 染み (stain); basho 場所 (place); bubun 部分 (part); **on the spot** sono ba de その場で (at the very place). 2. *vb.* ten o tsukeru 点を付ける (dot); mitsukeru 見つける (notice, find).

spotless, *adj.* shimihitotsunai 染み一つない (clean or pure).

spotlight, *n.* 1. supottoraito スポットライト. 2. **be in the spotlight** kyakkō o abiteiru 脚光を浴びている.

spouse, *n.* haigūsha 配偶者.

spout, 1. *n.* sosogiguchi 注ぎ口 (on a container). 2. *vb.* fukidasu 吹き出す (discharge).

sprain, 1. *n.* nenza 捻挫. 2. *vb.* nenza suru 捻挫する.

sprawl, *vb.* 1. buzama ni hirogaru 無様に広がる (be spread out ungracefully). 2. teashi o nagedasu 手足を投げ出す (lie or sit with limbs spread out).

spray, 1. *n.* kiri 霧 (mist); supurē

スプレー (appliance). 2. *vb.* ... ni supurē de fukikakeru ... にスプレーで吹きかける (apply spray to).

spread, 1. *n.* hirogari 広がり (expanse or stretch); rufu 流布 (act of spreading); supureddo スプレッド (food). 2. *vb.* hirogaru 広がる (extend over); hirogeru 広げる (cause to stretch out); hiromaru 広まる (become known); nuru 塗る (apply a thin layer).

spree, *n.* ukaresawagi 浮かれ騒ぎ (bout).

sprig, *n.* kukisaki 茎先 (end of a stem).

spring, 1. *n.* bane ばね (metal); haru 春 (season); izumi 泉 (water). 2. *vb.* tobiagaru 飛び上がる (jump); **spring over** ... o tobikosu ... を飛び越す; **spring up** shōjiru 生じる (arise).

sprinkle, *vb.* furikakeru 振り掛ける.

sprinkler, *n.* supurinkurā スプリンクラー.

sprint, *n.* tankyorikyōsō 短距離競走 (short race).

sprite, *n.* yōsei 妖精.

sprout, 1. *n.* me 芽 (shoot). 2. *vb.* mebaeru 芽生える (bud).

spruce, 1. *adj.* kogirei (na) 小ぎれい (な) (tidy and clean). 2. *vb.* **spruce up** mekasu めかす (dress up).

spry, *adj.* kakushakutaru かくしゃくたる.

spur, 1. *n.* shigeki 刺激 (incentive). 2. *vb.* hakusha o kakeru 拍車をかける (drive, urge).

spurn, *vb.* hanetsukeru はねつける.

spurt, 1. *n.* funshutsu 噴出 (forceful gush); funpatsu 奮発 (brief increase of effort). 2. *vb.* funshutsu suru 噴出する (gush or eject).

sputter, *vb.* kōkaku awa o tobasu 口角泡を飛ばす (speak excitedly); hayakuchi de shaberu 早口でしゃべる (utter hastily).

spy, 1. *n.* supai スパイ. 2. *vb.* nusumimiru 盗み見る (watch secretly); hisoka ni shiraberu 密かに調べる (search for); supai o suru スパイをする (act as a spy).

squabble, *n.* kozeriai 小競り合い.

squad, *n.* shō-gurūpu 小グループ (small group).

squadron, *n.* daibutai 大部隊.

squalid, *adj.* 1. kitanai 汚ない (filthy). 2. misuborashii みすぼらしい (wretched).

squall, *n.* sukōru スコール.

squander, *vb.* mudazukai suru 無駄使いする.

square, 1. *n.* seihōkei 正方形 (geometry); hiroba 広場 (public space); heihō 平方 (math). 2. *adj.* seihōkei (no) 正方形 (の) (being a square); shikakubatte-iru 四角張っている (formed with a right angle); suihei (na) 水平 (な) (level); heihō (no) 平方 (の) (math).

square root, *n.* heihōkon 平方根.

squash, 1. *n.* kabocha かぼちゃ (plant). 2. *vb.* oshitsubusu 押し潰す (crush).

squat, 1. *adj.* zunguri (no) ずんぐり (の). 2. *vb.* shagamu しゃがむ.

squawk, *vb.* 1. ganaritateru がなりたてる (cry). 2. fuhei o narasu 不平を鳴らす (complain loudly).

squeak, *vb.* kishiru 軋る (make a shrill sound, as a door).

squeal, 1. *n.* himei 悲鳴 (shrill cry,

as of pain). 2. *vb.* himei o ageru 悲鳴を上げる (utter a squeal).

squeamish, *adj.* 1. ōyōsa ni kakeru 鷹揚さに欠ける (easily shocked or disgusted). 2. shinkeishitsu (na) 神経質 (な) (overfastidious).

squeeze, *vb.* 1. shiboru 絞る (press together). 2. **squeeze (into)** (... ni) oshikomu (... に) 押し込む (cram); **squeeze out of** ... kara oshidasu ... から押し出す (push out).

squelch, *vb.* oshitsubusu 押し潰す (crush).

squid, *n.* ika いか.

squint, *vb.* me o hosomete miru 目を細めて見る.

squire, *n.* daijinushi 大地主 (landowner).

squirm, *vb.* mi o yojiru 身をよじる.

squirrel, *n.* risu りす.

squirt, *vb.* fukideru 吹き出る (gush out); fukidasu 吹き出す (cause to gush out).

stab, 1. *n.* sashikizu 刺し傷 (wound). 2. *vb.* tsukisasu 突き刺す.

stability, *n.* anteisei 安定性.

stabilize, *vb.* antei suru 安定する (become stable); antei saseru 安定させる (make stable).

stable, 1. *n.* umaya 馬屋 (for horses). 2. *adj.* antei shiteiru 安定している (firm, balanced).

stack, 1. *n.* yama 山 (heap); **stacks** shoka 書架 (books). 2. *vb.* tsumikasaneru 積み重ねる (pile in a stack); saiku suru 細工する (arrange unfairly).

stadium, *n.* sutajiamu スタジアム.

staff, *n.* shokuin 職員 (group of workers); kanbu 幹部 (administrators).

stag, *n.* ojika 雄鹿.

stage, 1. *n.* sutēji ステージ; butai 舞台 (in a theater); haiyūgyō 俳優業 (theatrical profession); dankai 段階 (single period or phase). 2. *vb.* jōen suru 上演する (present, as a play); kōdō ni utsusu 行動に移す (plan and carry out).

stagecoach, *n.* ekibasha 駅馬車.

stage fright, *n.* hitomae de agaru koto 人前で上がること.

stagger, *vb.* yoromeku よろめく.

stagnant, *adj.* 1. yodondeiru 淀んでいる (not flowing). 2. teitai shiteiru 停滞している (inactive).

stagnate, *vb.* 1. yodomu 淀む (cease to flow). 2. teitai suru 停滞する (become inactive).

staid, *adj.* kimajime (na) 生真面目 (な).

stain, 1. *n.* shimi 染み (blotch, blemish); chakushokuzai 着色剤 (coloring agent). 2. *vb.* shimi o tsukeru 染みを付ける (mark with stains); chakushoku suru 着色する (color).

stained glass, *n.* sutendo-gurasu ステンドグラス.

stainless, *adj.* sutenresu-sei (no) ステンレス製 (の) (of stainless material).

stairs, staircase, *n.* kaidan 階段.

stake, 1. *n.* kui 杭 (pointed post); kakekin 掛け金 (money wagered); **stakes** shōkin 賞金 (prize money); **at stake** kiki ni hinshite 危機に瀕して (in danger). 2. *vb.* kakeru 賭ける (risk or bet); **stake off** kui de kugiru 杭で区切る.

stale, *adj.* 1. furui 古い (not fresh). 2. chinpu (na) 陳腐 (な) (trite).

stalemate, *n.* ikizumari 行き詰まり (deadlock).

stalk, 1. *n.* kuki 茎 (plant stem). 2.

vb. kossori ou こっそり追う (pursue stealthily); noshiaruku のし歩く (march haughtily).

stall, 1. *n.* shikiri 仕切り (compartment); yatai 屋台 (sales booth). 2. *vb.* tomaru 止まる (stop functioning); iinogare o suru 言い逃れをする (delay by evasion); hikinobasu 引き延ばす (delay, put off).

stallion, *n.* taneuma 種馬.

stalwart, *adj.* 1. ganjō (na) 頑丈 (な) (sturdy and robust). 2. yūkan (na) 勇敢 (な) (brave). 3. yuruginai 揺るぎない (firm and steadfast).

stamina, *n.* seiryoku 精力.

stammer, *vb.* domoru 吃る.

stamp, 1. *n.* kitte 切手 (postage); sutanpu スタンプ (rubber stamp); shirushi 印 (mark). 2. *vb.* kitte o haru 切手を貼る (put a paper stamp on); sutanpu o osu スタンプを押す (mark with a rubber stamp); ashi o fuminarasu 足を踏みならす (trample).

stamp collecting, *n.* kitteshūshū 切手収集.

stampede, 1. *n.* panikku パニック (panic flight). 2. *vb.* awate-futameku あわてふためく (flee in a stampede); sattō suru 殺到する (rush).

stance, *n.* shisei 姿勢 (position, attitude).

stand, 1. *n.* kiritsu 起立 (act of standing); tachiba 立場 (position taken); sutando スタンド (furniture); baiten 売店 (stall); noriba 乗り場 (taxi); dai 台 (platform). 2. *vb.* tatsu 立つ (be upright); tateru 立てる (make upright); aru ある (be located); (... de) aru (... で) ある (be in a

certain condition); taeru 耐える (endure or bear); **stand by** tasukeru 助ける (help); taiki suru 待機する (be ready); **stand for** arawasu 表わす (represent); **stand out** medatsu 目立つ (be conspicuous); tsukideru 突き出る (protrude); **stand up** tachiagaru 立ち上がる (rise to one's feet); nagamochi suru 長持ちする (be durable).

standard, 1. *n.* mohan 模範 (approved model); kijun 基準 (basis for comparison); suijun 水準 (norm); hata 旗 (banner); **standard of living** seikatsu-suijun 生活水準. 2. *adj.* hyōjun (no) 標準 (の) (customary); hyōjun-teki (na) 標準的 (な) (being a model).

standardize, *vb.* kikakuka suru 企画化する.

standardized, *adj.* kikaku (no) 企画 (の).

stand-in, *n.* daiyōin 代用員.

standing, 1. *n.* chi'i 地位 (rank); kikan 期間 (length of continuance); **of long standing** nagai aida no 長い間の. 2. *adj.* keizoku-teki (na) 継続的 (な) (lasting).

stand-off, *n.* tai タイ (tie in a game).

stand-offish, *adj.* buaisō (na) 無愛想 (な).

standpoint, *n.* kenchi 見地.

standstill, *n.* teishi 停止 (stop).

stanza, *n.* sutanza スタンザ.

staple, 1. *n.* shuyōsanbutsu 主要産物 (principal product); shushoku 主食 (basic food); hotchikisu no hari ホッチキスの針 (for a stapler). 2. *vb.* hotchikisu de tomeru ホッチキスで留める.

stapler, *n.* hotchikisu ホッチキス.

star, *n.* 1. hoshi 星 (heavenly body, asterisk). 2. sutā スター (performer).

starch, 1. *n.* denpun でんぷん (food); nori 糊 (stiffening agent). 2. *vb.* nori o tsukeru 糊を付ける (stiffen).

stardom, *n.* sutā no za スターの座.

stare, 1. *n.* gyōshi 凝視. 2. *vb.* **stare (at)** (... o) mitsumeru (... を)見つめる.

starfish, *n.* hitode ひとで.

stark, 1. *adj.* mattaku (no) 全く (の) (utter); ikameshii いかめしい (severe). 2. *adv.* **stark naked** maruhadaka (no) 丸裸 (の).

start, 1. *n.* hajime 初め (beginning); kaishiten 開始点 (place or time of beginning); **from the start** hajime kara 初めから. 2. *vb.* hajimaru 始まる (begin on a course of action); hajimeru 始める (set something moving); shuppatsu suru 出発する (leave); **start doing/to do** ... shidasu ... しだす; **start all over again** hajime kara yarinaosu 初めからやり直す; **to start with** somo-somo そもそも.

starter, *n.* shidōsōchi 始動装置 (on an engine).

startle, *vb.* bikkuri saseru びっくりさせる; **be startled** bikkuri suru びっくりする.

starvation, *n.* ue 飢え.

starve, *vb.* ueru 飢える (suffer from hunger); uejini suru 飢え死にする (die from hunger).

starving, *adj.* 1. ueteiru 飢えている (suffering from hunger or desire). 2. onaka ga suiteiru お腹が空いている (hungry).

state, 1. *n.* jōtai 状態 (condition); kuni 国 (nation); shū 州 (commonwealth of a federal union). 2. *vb.* noberu 述べる; shitei suru 指定する (express).

stately, *adj.* dōdō to shiteiru 堂々としている (majestic).

statement, *n.* 1. seimei 声明 (declaration). 2. chinjutsu 陳述 (what is said). 3. shutsunyū-meisaisho 出入明細書 (bank).

statesman, -woman, *n.* beteran-seijika ベテラン政治家 (experienced politician).

static, *adj.* ittei (no) 一定 (の) (fixed).

static electricity, *n.* seidenki 静電気.

station, 1. *n.* hōsōkyoku 放送局 (radio or TV); kyoku 局 (headquarters for public services, police, fire); eki 駅 (bus, train, etc.); chūtonchi 駐屯地 (military); **police station** keisatsusho 警察署. 2. *vb.* haichi suru 配置する (assign place to).

stationary, *adj.* seishi shiteiru 静止している.

stationery, *n.* binsen 便せん (writing paper); bunbōgu 文房具 (writing materials); **stationery store** bunbōguten 文房具店.

station wagon, *n.* wagon-sha ワゴン車.

statistics, *n.* tōkei 統計.

statue, *n.* zō 像.

stature, *n.* 1. shinchō 身長 (person's height). 2. gyōseki 業績 (level of achievement).

status, *n.* 1. mibun 身分 (social standing); chii 地位 (professional standing). 2. jōkyō 状況 (present condition).

status quo, *n.* genjō 現状.

status symbol, *n.* sutētasushinboru ステータスシンボル.

statute, *n.* hōki 法規.

staunch, *adj.* yuruginai 揺るぎない (firm).

stave, *vb.* **stave off** kuitomeru 食い止める.

stay, 1. *n.* taizai 滞在 (temporary residence). 2. *vb.* taizai suru 滞在する (reside temporarily); tomaru 泊まる (be an overnight guest); nokoru 残る (remain at a place); ... mama de iru ... ままでいる (remain through time); tsuzukeru 続ける (continue); **stay away** chikayoranai 近寄らない (keep a distance); **stay up** osoku made okiteiru 遅くまで起きている.

steadfast, *adj.* yuruginai 揺るぎない.

steady, *adj.* 1. kakkotaru 確固たる (firm). 2. chakujitsu (na) 着実 (な) (regular or habitual). 3. antei shiteiru 安定している (stable).

steak, *n.* sutēki ステーキ.

steal, 1. *n.* okaidoku お買得 (bargain). 2. *vb.* nusumu 盗む (commit theft); kossori ugoku こっそり動く (move secretly); **steal away** kossori deru こっそり出る.

stealth, *n.* **by stealth** kossori (to) こっそり (と).

stealthy, *adj.* hisoka (na) 密か (な).

steam, 1. *n.* suchīmu スチーム; yuge 湯気 (vapor). 2. *vb.* musu 蒸す (cook).

steamboat, steamship, steamer, *n.* jōkisen 蒸気船.

steed, *n.* jōyōba 乗用馬.

steel, *n.* suchīru スチール; tekkō 鉄鋼 (metal); **steel mill** tekkōsho 鉄工所.

steep, *adj.* 1. kyū (na) 急 (な) (sloping or rising sharply). 2. hōgai (na) 法外 (な)

(unreasonably high).

steeple, *n.* sentō 尖塔.

steer, *vb.* 1. michibiku 導く (lead). 2. mukeru 向ける (direct).

steering wheel, *n.* handoru ハンドル.

stem, 1. *n.* kuki 茎 (of a plant); gokan 語幹 (of a word). 2. *vb.* tomeru 止める (stop); **stem from** ... ni yurai suru ... に由来する (originate from).

stench, *n.* akushū 悪臭.

stencil, *n.* kirinuki-katagami 切り抜き型紙.

stenographer, *n.* sokkisha 速記者.

step, 1. *n.* ayumi 歩み (movement of the foot); ippo 一歩 (distance of such movement); ashioto 足音 (sound); dankai 段階 (stage in a process); **steps** kaidan 階段 (stairs); suteppu ステップ (dancing); **take steps** kōdō o okosu 行動を起こす; **step by step** jojo ni 徐々に; **Watch your step!** Ashimoto ni chūi. 足元に注意. 2. *vb.* **step aside** yoko ni noku 横に退く; **step back** hikisagaru 引き下がる; **step in** ... ni hairu ... に入る (enter); naka ni hairu 中に入る (intervene); **step on** ... o fumu ... を踏む; **step out** hamidasu はみ出す.

stepbrother, *n.* ibokyōdai/ifukyōdai 異母兄弟／異父兄弟 (by a different mother/father).

stepfather, *n.* mamachichi 継父.

stepladder, *n.* kyatatsu 脚立.

stepmother, *n.* mamahaha 継母.

stepsister, *n.* iboshimai/ifushimai 異母姉妹／異父姉妹 (by a different mother/father).

stepson, -daughter, *n.* mamako 継子.

stereo, *n.* sutereo ステレオ.

stereotype, *n.* tenkei 典型.

sterile, *adj.* 1. fumō (no) 不毛 (の) (barren or fruitless). 2. funin (no) 不妊 (の) (incapable of producing offspring). 3. sakkin sareteiru 殺菌されている (free of germs).

sterilize, *vb.* 1. funin ni suru 不妊にする (make infertile). 2. sakkin suru 殺菌する (make free from germs).

sterling silver, *n.* jungin 純銀.

stern, 1. *adj.* kibishii 厳しい (rigid or severe). 2. *n.* senbi 船尾 (boat).

stethoscope, *n.* chōshinki 聴診器.

stew, 1. *n.* shichū シチュー (dish). 2. *vb.* torobi de niru とろ火で煮る (cook).

steward, *n.* suchuwādo スチュワード (airplane).

stewardess, *n.* suchuwādesu スチュワーデス (airplane).

stick, 1. *n.* eda 枝 (twig); sutekki ステッキ (cane or rod); bō 棒 (drumstick or club). 2. *vb.* tsukisasu 突き刺す (pierce or thrust); tsukisasaru 突き刺さる (have the point embedded); haru はる (glue); tsukeru 付ける (cause to adhere); kuttsuku くっつく (adhere); **stick by** ... ni chūjitsu o tsukusu ... に忠実を尽くす (be faithful to); **stick out** tsukideru 突き出る (protrude); **stick to** ... ni shigamitsuku ... にしがみつく (cling to); **stick up for** mamoru 守る (defend).

sticker, *n.* sutekkā ステッカー.

stickler, *n.* kodawariya こだわり屋.

sticky, *adj.* **be sticky** neba-neba suru ねばねばする.

stiff, *n.* 1. katai 固い (difficult to bend). 2. katakurushii 堅苦しい (formal).

stiffen, *vb.* kataku naru/suru 固くなる／する (become/make stiff).

stiffness, *n.* katasa 固さ.

stifle, *vb.* 1. osaeru 押える (repress). 2. ikizumaraseru 息詰まらせる (smother).

stigma, *n.* 1. oten 汚点 (blemish). 2. kutsujoku 屈辱 (feeling of shame).

still, 1. *n.* seijaku 静寂 (calmness or silence). 2. *adj.* shizuka (na) 静か (な) (quiet); ugokanai 動かない (motionless). 3. *vb.* shizumeru 静める (make calm). 4. *adv.* mada 未だ (as previously); sore demo それでも (in spite of that); sara ni 更に (further).

stillborn, *adj.* shizan 死産.

still life, *n.* seibutsuga 静物画 (painting).

stilted, *adj.* katakurushii 堅苦しい.

stilts, *n.* takeuma 竹馬.

stimulant, *n.* shigekizai 刺激剤 (drink, food, drug).

stimulate, *vb.* shigeki suru 刺激する (incite).

stimulus, *n.* shigeki 刺激 (incitement).

sting, 1. *n.* hari 針 (insect); sashikizu 刺し傷 (wound). 2. *vb.* sasu 刺す (wound, as a bee); chiku-chiku suru/saseru ちくちくする／させる (feel/cause to feel pain).

stingy, *adj.* kechi (na) けち (な).

stink, 1. *n.* akushū 悪臭. 2. *vb.* akushū ga suru 悪臭がする.

stinking, *adj.* 1. kusai 臭い (foul-smelling). 2. gesu (na) 下司 (な) (despicable).

stipend, *n.* 1. shōgakukin 奨学金 (scholarship allowance). 2. kyūkin 給金 (regular pay).

stipulate, *vb.* jōken o tsukeru 条件

をつける.

stir, 1. *n.* kakuhan かくはん (act of mixing); kōfun 興奮 (excitement). 2. *vb.* kakimazeru 掻き混ぜる (mix); ugoku 動く (move); ugokasu 動かす (cause to move).

stitch, 1. *n.* hitohari 一針 (complete movement of a needle); nuime 縫い目 (loop of thread); yokobara no gekitsū 横腹の激痛 (sharp pain in the side). 2. *vb.* nuu 縫う (sew).

stock, *n.* 1. zaiko 在庫 (goods on hand); **in stock** zaikoari 在庫あり; **out of stock** zaikogire 在庫切れ. 2. takuwae 貯え; 蓄え (supply). 3. kabu 株 (capital or share of a company, stem or trunk). 4. kachiku 家畜 (livestock). 5. iegara 家柄 (line of descent).

stockbroker, *n.* kabushiki-nakagainin 株式仲買人.

stock exchange, *n.* kabushiki-torihikisho 株式取引所.

stockholder, *n.* kabunushi 株主.

stocking, *n.* sutokkingu ストッキング.

stockpile, *vb.* bichiku suru 備蓄する.

stocky, *adj.* zunguri shiteiru ずんぐりしている.

stoic, *adj.* jiseishin ga tsuyoi 自制心が強い.

stoke, *vb.* kuberu くべる (tend a fire).

stole, *n.* sutōru ストール.

stolid, *adj.* kanjō ga toboshii 感情が乏しい.

stomach, *n.* i 胃.

stomachache, *n.* itsū 胃痛.

stone, 1. *n.* ishi 石 (small rock); tane 種 (of fruit). 2. *vb.* ... ni ishi o nageru ... に石を投げる (throw

stones at).

stooge, *n.* hosa 補佐 (subordinate).

stool, *n.* koshikake 腰掛け (seat).

stoop, *vb.* kagamu 屈む.

stop, 1. *n.* teishi 停止 (act of stopping); owari 終わり (end); tachiyori 立ち寄り (act of stopping by); teiryūsho 停留所 (bus stop); **put a stop to** ... o yamesaseru ... を止めさせる. 2. *vb.* owaru 終わる (come to an end); owaraseru 終わらせる (cause to end); tomaru 止まる (cease moving); tomeru 止める (prevent, cause to halt); saegiru 遮る (block); yamu 止む (of rain); **stop by** (tachi)yoru (立ち)寄る; **stop doing** ... suru no o yameru ... するのを止める; **stop over** tachiyoru 立ち寄る.

stopgap, *n.* anaume 穴埋め.

stop light, *n.* akashingō 赤信号 (red light).

stopover, *n.* sutoppuōbā ストップオーバー; tachiyori 立ち寄り.

stoppage, *n.* tsumari 詰まり (block in a pipe, etc.); shōgai 障害 (block in general).

stopper, *n.* sen 栓.

stop sign, *n.* teishishingō 停止信号.

stop watch, *n.* sutoppuwotchi ストップウォッチ.

storage, *n.* sōko 倉庫 (place).

store, 1. *n.* mise 店 (shop); takuwae 貯え; 蓄え (supply); **in store for** ... o machiukete ... を待ち受けて. 2. *vb.* takuwaeru 貯える; 蓄える (accumulate).

storekeeper, *n.* tenshu 店主 (owner).

storeroom, *n.* chozōshitsu 貯蔵室.

stork, *n.* kōnotori こうのとり.

storm, *n.* arashi 嵐.

stormy, *adj.* arekuru'u 荒れ狂う.

story, *n.* 1. hanashi 話; monogatari

物語 (tale); uso 嘘 (lie). 2. kiji 記事 (newspaper report). 3. kai 階 (floor).

storyteller, *n.* 1. hanashite 話し手 (speaker). 2. sakka 作家 (writer).

stout, *adj.* 1. ganjō (na) 頑丈 (な) (strong). 2. futotteiru 太っている (weighty).

stove, *n.* 1. sutōbu ストーブ (for heat). 2. renji レンジ (for cooking).

stow, *vb.* shimau 仕舞う (put away).

stowaway, *n.* mikkōsha 密航者.

strafe, *vb.* bakugeki suru 爆撃する (bombard).

straggle, *vb.* hagureru はぐれる (stray from course).

straight, 1. *adj.* massugu (na) 真っ直ぐ (な) (without a bend); tate (no) 縦 (の) (vertical); tadashii 正しい (correct); shōjiki (na) 正直 (な) (honest); sutorēto (na, no) ストレート (な、の) (without water added). 2. *adv.* massugu ni 真っ直ぐに (in a straight line, directly); **straight off** tadachi ni 直ちに (immediately).

straighten, *vb.* 1. massugu ni naru/suru 真っ直ぐになる／する (become/make straight). 2. kichin to suru きちんとする (tidy). 3. **straighten out** ... o tadasu ... を正す (correct); ... o kichin to suru ... をきちんとする (set right).

straightforward, *adj.* shōjiki (na) 正直 (な) (honest).

strain, 1. *n.* futan 負担 (severe pressure); kinchō 緊張 (tension); nenza 捻挫 (sprain). 2. *vb.* hipparu 引っ張る (pull); sei ippai tsutomeru 精一杯努める (exert to utmost); kujiku 挫く (sprain); kosu 漉す (filter).

strainer, *n.* koshiki 漉し器; zaru ざる.

straits, *n.* 1. kaikyō 海峡 (water). 2. kukyō 苦境 (a plight).

strand, 1. *n.* ito 糸 (thread). 2. *vb.* **be stranded** tachiōjō suru 立ち往生する.

strange, *adj.* 1. hen (na) 変 (な) (odd). 2. shiranai 知らない (unfamiliar).

stranger, *n.* shiranai hito 知らない人 (unfamiliar person); **be a stranger** hajimete de aru 初めてである (be a first-timer).

strangle, *vb.* shimekorosu 絞め殺す (kill).

strap, *n.* bando バンド (band).

stratagem, *n.* keiryaku 計略.

strategy, *n.* senryaku 戦略.

stratify, *vb.* sō o keisei suru 層を形成する (form in layers).

stratosphere, *n.* seisōken 成層圏.

stratum, *n.* sō 層.

straw, *n.* 1. wara わら (dried stalks). 2. sutorō ストロー (for drinking).

strawberry, *n.* ichigo 苺.

stray, 1. *adj.* maigo (no) 迷子 (の) (lost). 2. *vb.* samayou さまよう (wander); soreru 逸れる (digress).

stray bullet, *n.* nagaredama 流れ弾.

streak, 1. *n.* suji 筋 (line); **a streak of** ichijō no 一条の. 2. *vb.* suji o tsukeru 筋をつける (mark with streaks); mōshin suru 猛進する (run headlong).

stream, *n.* kawa 川 (river); nagare 流れ (current, flow, river).

streamer, *n.* fukinagashi 吹き流し.

streamline, *vb.* gōrika suru 合理化する (make efficient).

street, *n.* tōri 通り.

streetcar, *n.* romendensha 路面電

車.

strength, *n*. 1. tsuyosa 強さ; chikara 力 (power). 2. tsuyomi 強み (strong point).

strengthen, *vb*. tsuyomeru 強める (make strong); tsuyomaru 強まる (become strong).

strenuous, *adj*. 1. taihen (na) 大変 (な) (requiring great effort or energy). 2. seiryoku-teki (na) 精力的 (な) (energetic).

stress, 1. *n*. sutoresu ストレス (anxiety); atsuryoku 圧力 (physical pressure); kyōchō 強調 (emphasis). 2. *vb*. kyōchō suru 強調する (emphasize).

stretch, 1. *n*. hirogari 広がり (unbroken space); kikan 期間 (period of time). 2. *vb*. nobiru 伸びる (expand or extend); nobasu 伸ばす (cause to expand or extend); hirogaru 広がる (spread); hirogeru 広げる (cause to spread); ganbaru 頑張る (exert oneself to the limit).

stretcher, *n*. tanka 担架.

strew, *vb*. maku 撒く.

strict, *adj*. 1. kibishii 厳しい (stern). 2. genmitsu (na) 厳密 (な) (exact).

stride, 1. *n*. ōmata 大股 (long step). 2. *vb*. ōmata de aruku 大股で歩く (walk).

strident, *adj*. kandakai 甲高い.

strife, *n*. arasoi 争い.

strike, 1. *n*. utsu koto 打つこと (act of hitting); sutoraiku ストライク (sports); sutoraiki ストライキ (walkout); **be on strike** suto-kekkōchū de aru スト決行中である. 2. *vb*. tataku 叩く (deal a blow); utsu 打つ (hit); suru 擦る (of a match); kōgeki suru 攻撃する (attack); inshō-zukeru 印象付

ける (impress); mitsukeru 見つける (discover); **strike a bargain** gōi ni tassuru 合意に達する; **strike down** uchinomesu 打ちのめす (knock down; beat up); **strike up** hajimeru 始める.

strikebreaker, *n*. suto-yaburi スト破り.

striker, *n*. sutoraikā ストライカー (person on strike).

striking, *adj*. 1. subarashii 素晴らしい (outstanding). 2. kirei (na) きれい (な) (attractive).

string, *n*. 1. himo 紐 (cord). 2. gengakki 弦楽器 (musical instrument); gen 弦 (cord for an instrument).

stringent, *adj*. kibishii 厳しい.

strip, *vb*. 1. hagitoru 剥ぎ取る (remove). 2. nugu 脱ぐ (undress).

stripe, *n*. shimamoyō 縞模様 (pattern).

strive, *vb*. doryoku suru 努力する.

stroke, *n*. tokei no utsu oto 時計の打つ音 (sound of a striking clock); sutorōku ストローク (swimming); ichigeki 一撃 (blow); nōsotchū 脳卒中 (cerebral); kaku 画 (single movement of a pen). 2. *vb*. naderu 撫でる (pet).

stroll, *vb*. sansaku 散策.

stroller, *n*. bebī-kā ベビーカー; ubaguruma 乳母車 (baby stroller).

strong, *adj*. 1. tsuyoi 強い (powerful, sturdy). 2. koi 濃い (tea, coffee, etc.)

strongbox, *n*. kinko 金庫.

stronghold, *n*. toride 砦.

structure, *n*. 1. kōzō 構造 (formation). 2. kenchikubutsu 建築物 (building).

struggle, 1. *n*. tatakai 戦い (combat, strong effort). 2. *vb*.

tatakau 戦う (combat, strive).

strut, *vb.* noshiaruku のし歩く.

stub, 1. *n.* suisashi 吸いさし (cigarette); hanken 半券 (ticket). 2. *vb.* butsukeru ぶつける (toe).

stubborn, *adj.* ganko (na) 頑固 (な).

stubby, *adj.* zunguri shiteiru ずんぐりしている.

stuck-up, *adj.* kidotteiru 気取っている.

stud, *n.* taneuma 種馬 (horse).

student, *n.* gakusei 学生 (college student); seito 生徒 (elementary or secondary school student).

studio, *n.* 1. sutajio スタジオ (broadcasting). 2. atorie アトリエ (artist's workroom). 3. wanrūmu-manshon ワンルームマンション (apartment).

studious, *adj.* 1. benkyōka (no) 勉強家 (の) (devoted to study). 2. chūibukai 注意深い (careful).

study, 1. *n.* kenkyū 研究; benkyō 勉強; shosai 書斎 (room). 2. *vb.* kenkyū suru 研究する; benkyō suru 勉強する.

stuff, 1. *n.* mono 物 (material, things); bakageta koto 馬鹿げたこと (nonsense); soshitsu 素質 (character, qualities). 2. *vb.* ... ni tsumeru ... に詰める (fill); ... ni tsumemono o suru ... に詰め物をする (cooking).

stuffing, *n.* tsumemono 詰め物.

stuffy, *adj.* kūki ga yodondeiru 空気が淀んでいる (lacking fresh air).

stumble, *vb.* 1. tsumazuku つまずく (trip while walking). 2. shikujiru しくじる (blunder). 3. **stumble across** ... ni dekuwasu ... に出くわす.

stump, *n.* 1. kirikabu 切り株 (tree). 2. nokorihashi 残り端 (part remaining).

stun, *vb.* akke ni toraseru あっけにとらせる (surprise); **be stunned** akke ni torareru あっけにとられる.

stunning, *adj.* migoto (na) 見事 (な) (attractive).

stunt, 1. *n.* sakuryaku 策略 (trick). 2. *vb.* samatageru 妨げる (prevent growth of).

stupefy, *vb.* bōzen jishitsu saseru 茫然自失させる.

stupendous, *adj.* 1. namihazureteiru 並外れている (extraordinary). 2. kyodai (na) 巨大 (な) (immense).

stupid, *adj.* baka (na) 馬鹿 (な).

stupidity, *n.* baka na koto 馬鹿なこと.

stupor, *n.* 1. bōzen jishitsu 茫然自失 (condition caused by shock). 2. mahi 麻痺 (suspension of sensibility); **drunken stupor** doroyoijōtai 泥酔い状態.

sturdy, *adj.* ganjō (na) 頑丈 (な) (strong).

stutter, 1. *n.* domori 吃り. 2. *vb.* domoru 吃る.

sty, *n.* 1. butagoya 豚小屋 (pig pen). 2. monomorai 物貰い (eyelid).

style, *n.* 1. sutairu スタイル (mode of fashion or particular fashion). 2. yōshiki 様式 (particular manner).

stylish, *adj.* sutairisshu (na) スタイリッシュ (な); iki (na) 粋 (な).

stylist, *n.* sutairisuto スタイリスト.

subconscious, *n.* senzai'ishiki 潜在意識.

subdue, *vb.* 1. seifuku suru 征服する (conquer). 2. osaeru 抑える (control).

subdued, *adj.* osaeta 抑えた (made

calmer).

subject, 1. *n.* wadai 話題
(conversational topic); shudai 主
題 (theme); kamoku 科目 (field of
study); shugo 主語 (grammar);
shinmin 臣民 (person). 2. *adj.* **be
subject to** ... no kanōsei ga aru ...
の可能性がある (have the
possibility of); ... no shihai o
ukeru ... の支配を受ける (be
under the domination of); ... no
taishō ni nariyasui ... の対象にな
り易い (be vulnerable to); ...
shidai de aru ... 次第である (be
dependent on).

subjective, *adj.* shukan-teki (na)
主観的 (な).

subjugate, *vb.* fukujū saseru 服従
させる.

subjunctive, *n.* kateihō 仮定法.

sublet, *vb.* matagashi suru 又貸し
する.

sublime, *adj.* sūkō (na) 崇高 (な).

subliminal, *adj.* ishikika (no) 意識
下 (の).

submarine, 1. *n.* sensuikan 潜水艦
(boat). 2. *adj.* kaichū (no) 海中
(の) (being under the sea).

submerge, *vb.* moguru 潜る (go
under water).

submissive, *adj.* jūjun (na) 従順
(な).

submit, *vb.* 1. teishutsu suru 提出
する (present). 2. shitagau 従う
(obey).

subordinate, *n.* buka 部下.

subpoena, *n.* shōkanjō 召喚状.

subscribe, *vb.* **subscribe to** 1. ... o
teiki-kōdoku suru ... を定期購読す
る (periodical). 2. ... ni kifukin o
ataeru ... に寄付金を与える
(donate money to). 3. ... ni
shomei suru ... に署名する (sign).

subscriber, *n.* 1. teiki-kōdokusha

定期購読者 (periodical). 2.
shomeisha 署名者 (signer). 3.
kanyūsha 加入者 (participant).

subscription, *n.* 1. teiki-
kōdokuyō-daikin 定期購読用代金
(money for receiving a periodical);
kifukin 寄付金 (contribution). 2.
teiki-kōdoku 定期購読 (right to
receive a periodical).

subsequent, *adj.* sono go (no) その
後 (の).

subservient, *adj.* hikutsu (na) 卑屈
(な).

subside, *vb.* 1. shizumaru 静まる
(abate). 2. shizumu 沈む (sink).

subsidiary, 1. *adj.* hojo (no) 補助
(の) (auxiliary); jūzoku-teki (na)
従属的 (な) (subordinate). 2. *n.*
kogaisha 子会社 (company).

subsidize, *vb.* hojokin o dasu 補助
金を出す.

subsidy, *n.* hojokin 補助金.

subsist, *vb.* 1. ikiteiku 生きて行く
(exist). 2. tabeteiku 食べて行く
(live, as on food).

substance, *n.* 1. busshitsu 物質
(matter or material). 2. jisshitsu
実質 (substantial quality, content);
igi 意義 (significance).

substantial, *adj.* 1. kanari no かな
りの (fairly large). 2. ganjō (na)
頑丈 (な) (strong). 3. jisshitsu-teki
(na) 実質的 (な) (actual).

substantiate, *vb.* shōmei suru 証明
する (prove).

substitute, 1. *n.* kawari 代わり. 2.
vb. dairi o suru 代理をする
(person); daiyō suru 代用する
(thing).

subterfuge, *n.* kōjitsu 口実
(excuse).

subtitle, *n.* 1. fukudai 副題
(secondary title). 2. jimaku 字幕
(movie).

subtle, *adj.* 1. bimyō (na) 微妙 (な) (delicate). 2. kōmyō (na) 巧妙 (な) (crafty).

subtlety, *n.* bimyōsa 微妙さ (delicacy or refinement).

subtract, *vb.* hiku 引く.

suburb, *n.* kōgai 郊外.

suburban, *adj.* kōgai (no) 郊外 (の).

subversion, *n.* hakai 破壊 (destruction).

subversive, *adj.* hanseifu-teki (na) 反政府的 (な) (anti-government); hantaisei-teki (na) 反体制的 (な) (anti-Establishment).

subvert, *vb.* kutsugaesu 覆えす (overthrow); hakai suru 破壊する (destroy).

subway, *n.* chikatetsu 地下鉄.

succeed, *vb.* 1. **succeed (in)** (... ni) seikō suru (... に) 成功する (accomplish). 2. ... ni tsuzuku ... に続く (follow). 3. **succeed (to)** (... o) keishō suru (... を) 継承する (inherit).

succeeding, *adj.* tsuzuku 続く.

success, *n.* seikō 成功.

successful, *adj.* seikō shita 成功した; **be successful** seikō suru 成功する.

succession, *n.* 1. renzoku 連続 (series); **in succession** tsuzukete 続けて. 2. keishō 継承 (act of inheriting).

successive, *adj.* renzoku (no) 連続 (の).

successor, *n.* kōkeisha 後継者.

succinct, *adj.* kanketsu (na) 簡潔 (な).

succor, *n.* kyūjo 救助.

succulent, *adj.* shiruke tappuri (no) 汁気たっぷり (の) (food).

succumb, *vb.* **succumb to** ... ni kuppuku suru ... に屈服する (yield to).

such, 1. *pron.* sono yō na mono/hito そのような物／人 (such a thing/person). 2. *adj.* sono yō na そのような (of the kind indicated). 3. *adv.* sore hodo ni mo それほどにも (to so large an extent); taihen 大変 (very). 4. **as such** sono yō na koto de そのようなことで; **such as** ... no yō (na) ... のよう (な); tatoeba 例えば (for example).

suck, *vb.* 1. su'u 吸う (draw in). 2. shaburu しゃぶる (put in the mouth and draw upon).

suckle, *vb.* junyū suru 授乳する.

suction, *n.* kyūin 吸引.

sudden, *adj.* totsuzen (no) 突然 (の); **all of a sudden** totsuzen (ni) 突然 (に).

suddenly, *adv.* totsuzen (ni) 突然 (に).

suds, *n.* awa 泡 (foam).

sue, *vb.* kokuso suru 告訴する.

suede, *n.* suēdo スエード.

suffer, *n.* 1. kurushimu 苦しむ (undergo pain). 2. kōmuru 被る (experience an unpleasant condition). 3. teika suru 低下する (deteriorate).

sufferer, *n.* 1. byōnin 病人 (from illness). 2. higaisha 被害者 (victim).

suffering, *n.* kurushimi 苦しみ (pain).

suffice, *vb.* jūbun de aru 十分である.

sufficient, *adj.* jūbun (na) 十分 (な).

suffix, *n.* setsubiji 接尾辞.

suffocate, *vb.* chissoku suru/saseru 窒息する／させる (die/cause to die).

sugar, *n.* satō 砂糖.

sugar cane, *n.* satōkibi 砂糖きび.

sugary, *adj.* amai 甘い (sweet tasting).

suggest, *vb.* 1. teian suru 提案する (offer for consideration). 2. anji suru 暗示する (imply).

suggestion, *n.* 1. teian 提案 (proposal). 2. anji 暗示 (implication).

suicide, *n.* jisatsu 自殺; **commit suicide** jisatsu suru 自殺する.

suit, 1. *n.* sūtsu スーツ (clothing); soshō 訴訟 (lawsuit); **follow suit** ta ni narau 他に倣う. 2. *vb.* (... ni) au (... に) 合う; (... ni) teki suru (... に) 適する (be fitting or appropriate); (... ni totte) tsugō ga ii (... にとって) 都合が良い (be convenient); (... ni) niau (... に) 似合う (be becoming to).

suitable, *adj.* fusawashii ふさわしい.

suitcase, *n.* sūtsukēsu スーツケース.

suite, *n.* 1. suīto スイート (hotel). 2. kumikyoku 組曲 (music).

suitor, *n.* kyūkonsha 求婚者.

sulfur, *n.* iō 硫黄.

sulk, *vb.* fukureru ふくれる.

sullen, *adj.* 1. fukigen (na) 不機嫌 (na) (bad-tempered). 2. inki (na) 陰気 (na) (gloomy).

sully, *vb.* kegasu 汚す.

sultry, *adj.* atsukurushii 暑苦しい (hot and close).

sum, 1. *n.* gōkei 合計 (total); gōkeikin 合計金 (money); keisan 計算 (calculation); **in sum** yō suru ni 要するに (namely). 2. *vb.* **sum up** gōkei suru 合計する (total); yōyaku suru 要約する (summarize).

summarize, *vb.* yōyaku suru 要約する.

summary, *n.* yōyaku 要約.

summer, *n.* natsu 夏.

summit, *n.* chōjō 頂上.

summit meeting, *n.* samitto サミット.

summon, *vb.* 1. shōkan suru 召喚する (call or order). 2. **summon up** furuiokosu 奮い起こす.

summons, *n.* shōkan 召喚.

sumptuous, *adj.* gōka (na) 豪華 (な).

sun, *n.* 1. taiyō 太陽 (the star). 2. nikkō 日光 (sunshine).

sunburn, *n.* hiyake 日焼け.

sundae, *n.* sandē サンデー.

Sunday, *n.* nichiyōbi 日曜日.

sundial, *n.* hidokei 日時計.

sundry, *adj.* iro-iro (na, no) 色々 (な、の).

sunflower, *n.* himawari ひまわり.

sunglasses, *n.* sangurasu サングラス.

sunlight, *n.* nikkō 日光.

sunny, *adj.* 1. hare (no) 晴れ (の) (weather). 2. hiatari ga ii 日当たりが良い (bright with sunlight). 3. hogaraka (na) 朗らか (な) (cheerful).

sunny-side up, *adj.* medamayaki (no) 目玉焼き (の) (eggs).

sunrise, *n.* hinode 日の出.

sunset, *n.* nichibotsu 日没.

sunshine, *n.* nikkō 日光.

sunstroke, *n.* nisshabyō 日射病.

suntan, *n.* hiyake 日焼け.

super-, chō- 超-; **superhuman** chōningen-teki (na) 超人間的 (な).

superb, *adj.* subarashii 素晴らしい (wonderful).

superficial, *adj.* hyōmen-teki (na) 表面的 (な).

superfluous, *adj.* yobun (na, no) 余分 (な、の).

superintendent, *n.* 1. kantokusha 監督者 (manager). 2. kanrinin 管理人 (building superintendent).

superior, 1. *n.* jōshi 上司 (person of higher rank in a job). 2. *adj.* ue (no) 上 (の) (upper); jōshitsu (no) 上質 (の) (of high quality); **superior to** ... yori yoi ... より良い (better than).

superiority, *n.* yūshūsa 優秀さ (excellence).

superiority complex, *n.* yūetsukan 優越感.

superlative, *adj.* 1. saijō (no) 最上 (の) (best). 2. saijōkyūkei (no) 最上級型 (の) (grammar).

supermarket, *n.* sūpā(māketto) スーパー(マーケット).

supernatural, *adj.* chōshizen (no) 超自然 (の).

superpower, *n.* chōtaikoku 超大国 (nation).

supersede, *vb.* ... ni totte kawaru ... に取って代わる.

supersonic, *adj.* chō'onsoku (no) 超音速 (の).

superstition, *n.* meishin 迷信.

superstitious, *adj.* meishinbukai 迷信深い.

supervise, *vb.* kantoku suru 監督する.

supervisor, *n.* kantoku 監督.

supper, *n.* yūshoku 夕食; bangohan 晩御飯 (evening meal).

supplant, *vb.* 1. oshinokeru 押し退ける (take place of improperly). 2. totte kawaru 取って代わる (supersede).

supple, *adj.* shinayaka (na) しなやか (な).

supplement, 1. *n.* hosoku 補足. 2. *vb.* hosoku suru 補足する.

supplier, *n.* kyōkyūsha 供給者 (person or firm); gyōsha 業者 (firm).

supply, 1. *n.* kyōkyū 供給 (act of supplying); kyōkyūhin 供給品 (things supplied); **supplies** zaiko 在庫 (stores); **supplies** hitsujuhin 必需品 (necessities); **supply and demand** jukyū 需給. 2. *vb.* kyōkyū suru 供給する (provide); ataeru 与える (give).

support, 1. *n.* sasae 支え (prop); shiji 支持 (help, patronage); seikatsuhi 生活費 (money to live). 2. *vb.* sasaeru 支える (hold up, bear); shiji suru 支持する (advocate, encourage); fuyō suru 扶養する (provide with money to live).

supporter, *n.* shijisha 支持者 (person).

suppose, *vb.* 1. ... to omou ... と思う (think). 2. ... to katei suru ... と仮定する (assume). 3. **be supposed to** ... to kimerareteiru ... と決められている (be required to); ... to omowareteiru ... と思われている (be considered to).

supposition, *n.* 1. katei 仮定 (conjecture). 2. kangae 考え (guess).

suppress, *vb.* 1. dan'atsu suru 弾圧する (put down by force). 2. yokusei suru 抑制する (restrain). 3. sashitomeru 差し止める (prevent from appearing).

supremacy, *n.* 1. saikō 最高 (state of being the greatest). 2. shijōken 至上権 (supreme authority).

supreme, *adj.* ichiban (no) 一番 (の); saikō (no) 最高 (の) (greatest).

sure, *adj.* 1. tashika (na) 確か (な) (certain or reliable). 2. **be sure to do** kitto ... suru きっと... する; **make sure** tashikameru 確かめる

(confirm).

surf, *n.* kudakeru nami 砕ける波.

surfboard, *n.* sāfubōdo サーフボード.

surface, 1. *n.* omote 表; hyōmen 表面 (outside); **on the surface** hyōmenjō wa 表面上は. 2. *vb.* fujō suru 浮上する (come to the surface).

surfer, *n.* sāfā サーファー.

surfing, *n.* sāfin サーフィン.

surge, 1. *n.* dotō 怒とう (strong wave); sāji サージ (electricity). 2. *vb.* dotō no yō ni oshiyoseru 怒とうのように押し寄せる (move in a surge); wakitatsu 沸き立つ (rise up).

surgeon, *n.* gekai 外科医.

surgery, *n.* gekashujutsu 外科手術.

surgical, *adj.* gekashujutsu (no) 外科手術 (の).

surly, *adj.* 1. burei (na) 無礼 (な) (rude). 2. buaisō (na) 無愛想 (な) (unfriendly).

surmise, *vb.* suisoku suru 推測する.

surmount, *vb.* kokufuku suru 克服する (overcome).

surname, *n.* myōji 名字; sei 姓.

surpass, *vb.* uwamawaru 上回る; shinogu 凌ぐ (exceed or excel).

surplus, *n.* yojō 余剰; yobun 余分.

surprise, 1. *n.* odoroki 驚き. 2. *vb.* odorokaseru 驚かせる.

surprised, *adj.* odoroita 驚いた; **be surprised** odoroku 驚く.

surprising, *adj.* odorokubeki 驚くべき.

surrealism, *n.* chōgenjitsushugi 超現実主義.

surrender, 1. *n.* kōfuku 降伏 (act of yielding). 2. *vb.* kōfuku suru 降伏する (yield); hōki suru 放棄する (give up).

surreptitious, *adj.* himitsu (no) 秘密 (の).

surrogate, *n.* dairinin 代理人 (substitute, judge).

surround, *vb.* kakomu 囲む.

surrounding, *adj.* mawari (no) 周り (の).

surroundings, *n.* kankyō 環境.

surveillance, *n.* kanshi 監視; **under surveillance** kanshika (no) 監視下 (の).

survey, 1. *n.* gaikan 概観 (general view); chōsa 調査 (investigation); sokuryō 測量 (measurement). 2. *vb.* nagameru 眺める (view); shiraberu 調べる (investigate); sokuryō suru 測量する (measure).

surveyor, *n.* sokuryō gishi 測量技師.

survival, *n.* 1. seizon 生存 (living). 2. sonzokubutsu 存続物 (continuation).

survive, *vb.* 1. ikinokoru 生き残る (live after a disaster); ... yori nagaiki suru ... より長生きする (outlive). 2. sonzoku suru 存続する (continue to exist).

survivor, *n.* seizonsha 生存者 (after a disaster).

susceptible, *adj.* **susceptible to** 1. ... ni yowai ... に弱い (apt to be afflicted by). 2. ... no eikyō o ukeyasui ... の影響を受け易い (easily influenced by).

suspect, 1. *n.* yōgisha 容疑者. 2. *vb.* kengi o kakeru 嫌疑をかける (imagine to be guilty); ... to omou ... と思う (imagine); utagau 疑う (distrust).

suspend, *vb.* 1. tsurusu 吊す (hang). 2. horyū suru 保留する (keep temporarily inactive).

suspenders, *n.* zubon-tsuri ズボン吊り.

suspense, *n.* 1. kinchō 緊張 (tension). 2. fuan 不安 (anxiety).

suspicion, *n.* 1. utagai 疑い (distrust). 2. kengi 嫌疑 (act of suspecting guilt); **under suspicion** kengichū (no) 嫌疑中 (の).

suspicious, *adj.* 1. utagaibukai 疑い深い (distrustful). 2. ayashii 怪しい (causing suspicion).

sustain, *vb.* 1. sasaeru 支える (support). 2. jizoku suru 持続する (maintain).

svelte, *adj.* surari to shiteiru すらりとしている.

swab, *n.* menbō 綿棒.

swagger, *vb.* kata de kaze o kitte aruku 肩で風を切って歩く.

swallow, 1. *n.* tsubame つばめ (bird). 2. *vb.* nomikomu 飲み込む (gulp).

swamp, *n.* numa 沼.

swan, *n.* hakuchō 白鳥.

swanky, *adj.* shareteiru しゃれている.

swap, 1. *n.* kōkan 交換. 2. *vb.* kōkan suru 交換する.

swarm, 1. *n.* mure 群れ. 2. *vb.* muragaru 群がる (throng).

swat, *vb.* tataku 叩く.

sway, 1. *n.* yure 揺れ (act of swinging); shihai 支配 (rule). 2. *vb.* yureugoku 揺れ動く (swing); yuriugokasu 揺り動かす (cause to swing); sayū suru 左右する (influence).

swear, *vb.* chikau 誓う (vow).

sweat, 1. *n.* ase 汗. 2. *vb.* ase o kaku 汗をかく.

sweater, *n.* sētā セーター.

sweep, 1. *n.* sōji 掃除 (cleaning of a room); hitofuri 一振り (sweeping movement of the arm). 2. *vb.* haku 掃く (clean with a broom);

kasumeru 掠める (pass over a surface); oshiyoseru 押し寄せる (rush).

sweet, 1. *n.* (o)kashi (お)菓子 (food). 2. *adj.* amai 甘い (having the taste of sugar, honey, etc.); kokochiyoi 心地良い (pleasing); yasashii 優しい (gentle).

sweeten, *vb.* 1. satō o ireru 砂糖を入れる (add sugar). 2. amaku naru 甘くなる (become sweet).

sweetener, *n.* kanmiryō 甘味料.

sweetheart, *n.* koibito 恋人.

sweetness, *n.* 1. amasa 甘さ (taste of sugar, honey, etc.). 2. kokochiyosa 心地良さ (pleasantness). 2. yasashisa 優しさ (pleasing disposition).

sweet potato, *n.* satsuma imo さつま芋.

swell, *vb.* 1. hareru 腫れる (swell from injury). 2. fukureru 膨れる (puff up). 3. fueru 増える (increase).

swelling, *n.* hare 腫れ (from injury).

swelter, *vb.* asedaku ni naru 汗だくになる.

swerve, *vb.* kyū ni muki o kaeru 急に向きを変える.

swift, *adj.* hayai 速い (quick).

swim, *vb.* oyogu 泳ぐ.

swimmer, *n.* suimā スイマー.

swimming, *n.* oyogi 泳ぎ; suiei 水泳; suimingu スイミング.

swimming pool, *n.* pūru プール.

swimming trunks, *n.* kaisui-pantsu 海水パンツ.

swimsuit, *n.* mizugi 水着.

swindle, 1. *n.* sagi 詐欺. 2. *vb.* damashitoru 騙し取る.

swindler, *n.* sagishi 詐欺師.

swine, *n.* buta 豚 (pig).

swing, 1. *n.* buranko ブランコ

(suspended seat). 2. *vb.* yureru 揺
れる (move to and fro);
yuriugokasu 揺り動かす (cause to
move to and fro); furimawasu 振
り回す (cause to move in a
circular movement).

swipe, *vb.* 1. butsu 打つ (hit). 2.
nusumu 盗む (steal).

swirl, 1. *n.* uzumaki 渦巻き. 2. *vb.*
uzumaku 渦巻く.

swish, *vb.* utsu 打つ (cut through
the air).

switch, 1. *n.* henka 変化 (change);
suitchi スイッチ (electrical). 2. *vb.*
kawaru 変わる (change); kaeru 変
える (cause to change); **switch
off** kesu 消す; **switch on** tsukeru
点ける.

swivel, *vb.* mawaru 回る (turn);
mawasu 回す (cause to turn).

swiveling chair, *n.* kaiten isu 回転
椅子.

swoon, *vb.* kizetsu suru 気絶する.

swoop, *vb.* kyūkōka suru 急降下す
る.

sword, *n.* katana 刀; ken 剣.

swordsman, *n.* kenjutsushi 剣術
師.

sycophant, *n.* tsuishōsha 追従者.

syllable, *n.* onsetsu 音節.

syllabus, *n.* kōginaiyō-ichiranhyō
講義内容一覧表.

symbol, *n.* 1. shōchō 象徴
(representation). 2. kigō 記号
(sign).

symbolic, *adj.* shōchō-teki (na) 象
徴的 (な).

symbolism, *n.* shōchōshugi 象徴主
義.

symbolize, *vb.* shōchō suru 象徴す
る; arawasu 現す.

symmetrical, *adj.* taishō-teki (na)

対称的 (な).

sympathetic, *adj.* 1. dōjō-teki (na)
同情的 (な) (compassionate); **be
sympathetic towards** ... ni dōjō
suru ... に同情する. 2. dōchō-teki
(na) 同調的 (な) (supportive).

sympathize, *vb.* 1. dōjō suru 同情
する (feel compassionate). 2. dōi
suru 同意する (agree).

sympathy, *n.* 1. dōjō 同情
(compassion). 2. dōi 同意
(agreement).

symphony, *n.* 1. shinfonī シンフォ
ニー; kōkyōkyoku 交響曲 (music).
2. kōkyōgakudan 交響楽団
(orchestra).

symposium, *n.* shinpojiumu シン
ポジウム; tōronkai 討論会.

symptom, *n.* chōkō 徴候 (sign);
shōkō 症候 (indication of a
disease).

synagogue, *n.* yudaya-kyōkai ユダ
ヤ教会.

synchronize, *vb.* dōji ni okoru 同
時に起こる (occur at the same
time); awaseru 合わせる (clocks,
etc.).

syndrome, *n.* shōkōgun 症候群.

synonym, *n.* dōgigo 同義語.

synopsis, *n.* yōshi 要旨.

syntax, *n.* shintakkusu シンタック
ス; tōjiron 統辞論.

synthesis, *n.* gōsei 合成.

synthesize, *vb.* gōsei suru 合成する.

synthetic, *adj.* gōsei (no) 合成 (の).

syphilis, *n.* baidoku 梅毒.

syringe, *n.* chūshaki 注射器 (for
injection).

syrup, *n.* shiroppu シロップ.

system, *n.* 1. shisutemu システム;
seido 制度 (structure). 2. hōhō 方
法 (method).

T

tab, *n.* himo 紐 (flap, strip); sakuin'hyō 索引表 (file tab).

table, *n.* 1. tēburu テーブル (furniture); **at table** shokujichū ni 食事中に (during a meal); **under the table** kossori こっそり (covertly). 2. tabemono 食べ物 (food). 3. hyō 表 (columns of data); **table of contents** mokuji 目次.

tablecloth, *n.* tēburukurosu テーブルクロス; tēburu-kake テーブル掛け.

tablespoon, *n.* ōsaji 大さじ; tēburusupūn テーブルスプーン.

tablet, *n.* 1. jōzai 錠剤 (pill). 2. nōto-paddo ノートパッド (note pad). 3. ita 板 (slab, plaque).

tabloid, *n.* taburoido タブロイド (newspaper).

taboo, *n.* tabū タブー.

tacit, *adj.* anmoku (no) 暗黙 (の) (unspoken).

taciturn, *adj.* mukuchi (na, no) 無口 (な、の) (inclined to silence).

tack, *n.* byō 鋲 (nail). 2. *vb.* byō de tomeru (fasten with a nail) 鋲で留める.

tackle, *vb.* 1. torikumu 取り組む (undertake). 2. takkuru suru タックルする (sports).

tact, *n.* josainasa 如才なさ (social skill).

tactic(s), *n.* 1. sakusen 作戦 (maneuvering). 2. shudan 手段 (methods).

tadpole, *n.* otamajakushi おたまじゃくし.

tag, *n.* fuda 札 (label).

tail, *n.* 1. shippo 尻尾 (of an animal). 2. kōbu 後部 (back part).

tailor, *n.* tērā テーラー.

taint, 1. *n.* oten 汚点 (unfavorable trace). 2. *vb.* kegasu 汚す (tarnish, corrupt morally); sokonau 損なう (spoil, contaminate).

take, *vb.* 1. toru 取る (get into one's possession, react in a specified manner, get, win, steal, occupy or fill time or space, study, swallow medicine, write down); **take a math course** sūgaku o toru 数学を取る. 2. tsukamu 摑む (grasp); nigiru 握る (grip). 3. toraeru 捕える (catch a thief, etc.). 4. erabu 選ぶ (select). 5. uketoru 受け取る (receive and accept willingly, be the recipient of); **take someone's advice** adobaisu o ukeru アドバイスを受ける. 6. eru 得る (obtain). 7. mukaeru 迎える (receive into some relation); **take a wife** tsuma o mukaeru 妻を迎える. 8. kōdoku suru 購読する (subscribe). 9. hiku 引く (subtract). 10. motteiku 持って行く (carry with one). 11. atsukau 扱う (deal with, handle). 12. kakaru かかる (require a certain time). 13. ... ni noru ...に乗る (travel by). 14. shimeru 占める (occupy). 15. kau 買う (buy). 16. nomu 飲む (swallow); taberu 食べる (eat). 17. **take after** ... ni niru ...に似る (resemble); **take apart** bunkai suru 分解する (disassemble); **take away** torisaru 取り去る (remove); **take back** torimodosu 取り戻す (regain possession of); **take care of** ... no

mendō o miru ...の面倒を見る
(look after); **take for** ... to minasu
...と見なす (regard as); **take long**
jikan ga kakaru 時間がかかる
(take time); **take off** ririku suru
離陸する (plane); nugu 脱ぐ
(clothing); **take out** toridasu 取り
出す (remove); **take over**
hikitsugu 引き継ぐ (assume
responsibility for); **take part in** ...
ni kuwawaru ...に加わる; **take
up** toriageru 取り上げる (pick up,
choose as a topic); shimeru 占める
(occupy space or time); tsuzukeru
続ける (continue); **take a walk**
sanpo o suru 散歩をする.

takeoff, *n.* 1. ririku 離陸 (plane).
2. monomane 物真似 (mimicry).

takeout, *n.* mochikaeri 持ち帰り
(food).

talc, *n.* tarukamu-paudā タルカム
パウダー.

tale, *n.* hanashi 話; monogatari 物
語.

talent, *n.* tarento タレント; sainō
才能 (ability).

talented, *adj.* sainō ga aru 才能が
ある.

talisman, *n.* omamori お守り.

talk, 1. *n.* hanashi 話 (speech);
kaiwa 会話 (conversation); kaidan
会談 (negotiation session); uwasa
噂 (rumor). 2. *vb.* hanasu 話す
(speak, deliver a speech, discuss);
sōdan suru 相談する (consult);
uwasa suru 噂する (spread a
rumor); shaberu しゃべる
(chatter); kaiwa suru 会話する
(converse). 3. **talk about** ... ni
tsuite hanasu ... について話す;
talk big hora o fuku ほらを吹く;
talk back kuchigotae o suru 口答
えをする; **talk over** hanashiau 話
し合う (discuss); **talk to** ... ni

hanashikakeru ...に話し掛ける;
talk with ... to hanasu ...と話す.

talkative, *adj.* oshaberi (no) おし
ゃべり (の).

tall, *adj.* (se ga) takai (背が) 高い.

talon, *n.* tsume 爪.

tame, 1. *adj.* otonashii 大人しい
(gentle); tsumaranai つまらない
(uninteresting). 2. *vb.* narasu 慣ら
す (domesticate).

tamper, *vb.* **tamper with** ... o
ijiru ...をいじる (meddle with);
kaizan suru 改ざんする (alter,
falsify).

tampon, *n.* tanpon タンポン.

tan, 1. *adj.* shakudōshoku (no) 赤
銅色 (の) (of bronze color). 2. *vb.*
kawa o namesu 皮をなめす
(convert into leather); hi ni
yakeru 日に焼ける (be tanned by
the sun).

tang, *n.* tokuyū no nioi/aji 特有の
匂い／味 (special smell/taste).

tangent, *n.* sessen 接線
(geometry).

tangerine, *n.* mikan みかん.

tangible, *adj.* 1. yūkei (no) 有形
(の) (material); te ni kanjirareru
手に感じられる (discernible by
touch). 3. jissai (no) 実際 (の)
(real).

tangle, 1. *n.* motsure もつれ
(tangled mass). 2. *vb.* motsureru
もつれる; kongarakaru こんがら
かる (become confused);
motsuresaseru (snarl) もつれさせ
る.

tank, *n.* 1. tanku タンク
(receptacle). 2. sensha 戦車
(military).

tanker, *n.* tankā タンカー (oil
tanker).

tantalize, *vb.* jirasu 焦らす (tease).

tantamount, *adj.* (... ni) hitoshii

(...に) 等しい.

tap, 1. *n.* karuku utsu koto 軽く打つこと (light blow); jaguchi 蛇口 (faucet); sen 栓 (plug, stopper). 2. *vb.* karuku utsu 軽く打つ (strike lightly); sen o hineru 栓を捻る (open a plug); jaguchi o hineru 蛇口を捻る (open a faucet).

tape, 1. *n.* tēpu テープ (paper, cloth, adhesive, magnetic, etc.); kasetto-tēpu カセットテープ (cassette tape); rokuga-tēpu 録画テープ (videotape); makijaku 巻尺 (tape measure); himo 紐 (binding tape). 2. *vb.* rokuon suru 録音する (record sound); rokuga suru 録画する (videotape); shibaru 縛る (bind).

tape deck, *n.* tēpu dekki テープデッキ.

taper, *vb.* hosoku/chiisaku naru 細く／小さくなる (become thinner/smaller).

tape recorder, *n.* tēpu-rekōdā テープレコーダー.

tapestry, *n.* tapesutorī タペストリー.

tar, 1. *n.* tāru タール (viscid product). 2. *vb.* tāru o nuru タールを塗る (cover with tar).

tardy, *adj.* 1. osoi 遅い (late). 2. noroi のろい (slow).

target, *n.* 1. tāgetto ターゲット; mato 的 (aim, mark). 2. mokuhyō 目標 (purpose).

tariff, *n.* kanzei 関税 (duty).

tarnish, *vb.* 1. kumoru 曇る (lose luster); kumoraseru (cause to lose luster) 曇らせる. 2. kegasu 汚す (disgrace).

tart, 1. *n.* taruto タルト (pastry). 2. *adj.* suppai 酸っぱい (sour); shinratsu (na) 辛辣 (な) (sarcastic).

task, *n.* shigoto 仕事 (work).

tassel, *n.* fusa 房.

taste, 1. *n.* mikaku 味覚 (sense); aji 味 (flavor); hitokuchi 一口 (small portion of food); shumi 趣味 (sensitivity to beauty, etc.); **be in good/bad taste** shumi ga ii/warui 趣味が良い／悪い. 2. *vb.* ajiwau 味わう (enjoy eating/drinking; experience); hitokuchi taberu 一口食べる (eat a little bit); shishoku suru 試食する (sample food); **taste like** ... no yō na aji ga suru ...のような味がする.

tasty, *adj.* oishii おいしい.

tatters, *n.* boro ぼろ (ragged clothing).

tattered, *adj.* boro-boro (no) ぼろぼろ (の) (ragged).

tattle, *vb.* 1. hito no himitsu o morasu 人の秘密を漏らす (reveal another's secrets). 2. uwasa o suru 噂をする (gossip).

tattoo, *n.* irezumi 入れ墨 (design on the skin).

taunt, 1. *n.* karakai からかい. 2. *vb.* karakau からかう; baka ni suru 馬鹿にする.

taut, *adj.* 1. (of a rope) pin to hatta ぴんと張った (tightly drawn). 2. kinchō shiteiru 緊張している (emotionally tense).

tavern, *n.* sakaba 酒場 (bar).

tawdry, *adj.* keba-kebashii けばけばしい (showy and cheap).

tax, 1. *n.* zeikin 税金 (money levied). 2. *vb.* zeikin o kakeru 税金をかける (impose tax).

tax-free, *adj.* muzei (no) 無税 (の).

taxi, *n.* takushī タクシー.

taxpayer, *n.* nōzeisha 納税者.

tax rate, *n.* zeiritsu 税率.

tea, *n.* (o)cha (お)茶 (any tea);

kōcha 紅茶 (black tea); ryokucha 緑茶 (green tea).

tea bag, *n.* tī-baggu ティーバッグ.

teach, *vb.* 1. oshieru 教える (impart knowledge). 2. sensei o shiteiru 先生をしている (be employed as a teacher).

teacher, *n.* sensei 先生; kyōshi 教師.

teaching, *n.* 1. kyōshoku 教職 (profession of teaching); kyōiku 教育 (act of teaching). 2. **teachings** oshie 教え (doctrine).

teacup, *n.* tīkappu ティーカップ (Western style); yunomi 湯飲み (for green tea); chawan 茶碗 (for tea ceremony).

teahouse, *n.* kissaten 喫茶店 (cafe).

teakettle, *n.* yakan やかん; chagama 茶釜.

team, *n.* 1. chīmu チーム (team of people). 2. hitokumi 一組 (team of harnessed animals).

teapot, *n.* tīpotto ティーポット; kyūsu 急須.

tear, 1. *n.* yabure 破れ (rip, hole); namida 涙 (teardrop); **in tears** naiteiru 泣いている; **burst into tears** nakidasu 泣き出す; **tear gas** sairui-gasu 催涙ガス. 2. *vb.* saku 裂く; yaburu 破る (pull apart); yabureru 破れる (become torn); **tear down** torikowasu 取り壊す (pull down).

tease, *vb.* 1. karakau からかう (make fun of). 2. komaraseru 困らせる (annoy).

teaspoon, *n.* tīsupūn ティースプーン; chasaji 茶さじ.

teat, *n.* chikubi 乳首.

technical, *adj.* 1. gijutsujō (no) 技術上 (の); gijutsu-teki (na) 技術的 (な) (pertaining to skilled activity).

2. senmon (no) 専門の (pertaining to a particular art, science, etc.). 3. genmitsu (na) 厳密 (な) (considered in the strict sense).

technician, *n.* tekunishan テクニシャン; gijutsuka 技術家.

technique, *n.* tekunikku テクニック; gijutsu 技術.

technology, *n.* tekunorojī テクノロジー.

tedious, *adj.* taikutsu (na) 退屈 (な).

tedium, *n.* taikutsu 退屈.

teenage, *adj.* jūdai (no) 十代 (の).

teenager, *n.* tīn'ējā ティーンエージャー.

teeter, *vb.* 1. jōge ni yureru 上下に揺れる (seesaw). 2. fura-fura aruku ふらふら歩く (walk unsteadily).

telecast, *n.* terebi-hōsō テレビ放送.

telegram, *n.* denpō 電報 (message).

telegraph, *n.* 1. denshinki 電信機 (apparatus to send a message); denshin 電信 (process). 2. denpō 電報 (telegram).

telepathy, *n.* terepashī テレパシー.

telephone, 1. *n.* denwa 電話. 2. *adj.* denwa (no) 電話 (の). 3. *vb.* (... ni) denwa o suru/kakeru (... に) 電話をする／かける.

telephone booth, *n.* denwa-bokkusu 電話ボックス.

telephone call, *n.* denwa 電話.

telephone directory, *n.* denwachō 電話帳.

telephone number, *n.* denwa-bangō 電話番号.

telephone operator, *n.* kōkanshu 交換手.

telescope, *n.* bōenkyō 望遠鏡.

televise, *vb.* hōei suru 放映する.

television, *n.* terebi テレビ.

tell, *vb.* 1. iu 言う (say positively, communicate); hanasu 話す (relate). 2. kubetsu suru 区別する (distinguish). 3. oshieru 教える (inform). 4. meijiru 命じる (order). 5. **tell off** hinan suru 非難する (rebuke); **tell on** himitsu o barasu 秘密をばらす (tattle on).

teller, *n.* suitōgakari 出納係 (bank).

telltale, *n.* oshaberi おしゃべり (tattler).

temerity, *n.* atsukamashisa 厚かましさ.

temper, 1. *n.* kigen 機嫌 (particular state of mind); kishitsu 気質 (disposition); kanshaku 癇癪 (outburst of anger); **keep one's temper** gaman suru 我慢する; **lose one's temper** okoridasu 怒り出す; **out of temper** okotte (-iru) 怒って(いる). 2. *vb.* yawarageru 和らげる (moderate, soften).

temperament, *n.* seishitsu 性質 (mental disposition).

temperamental, *adj.* muraki (na, no) むら気 (な、の) (moody, unpredictable).

temperance, *n.* 1. jisei 自制 (self-control). 2. sessei 節制 (habitual moderation in any indulgence).

temperate, *adj.* 1. odayaka (na) 穏やか (な) (not extreme in opinion, statement, etc.). 2. ondan (na) 温暖 (な) (moderate in respect to temperature). 3. hikaeme (na, no) 控え目 (な、の) (moderate in any indulgence).

temperature, *n.* 1. ondo 温度 (degree of warmth or coldness). 2. taion 体温 (body temperature).

tempest, *n.* arashi 嵐.

tempestuous, *adj.* arashi no yō na 嵐のような (tumultuous, resembling a tempest).

template, *n.* kata 型 (mold, pattern).

temple, *n.* 1. shinden 神殿 (house of worship); (o)tera (お)寺 (Buddhism). 2. komekami こめかみ (side of head).

tempo, *n.* tenpo テンポ.

temporary, *adj.* ichiji-teki (na) 一時的 (な).

tempt, *vb.* 1. yūwaku suru 誘惑する (entice). 2. hikitsukeru 引きつける (appeal).

temptation, *n.* yūwaku 誘惑 (enticement).

tempura, *n.* tenpura 天ぷら (Japanese dish).

ten, *n.* jū 十; tō 十.

tenacious, *adj.* 1. tsuyoi 強い (firm). 2. shitsu(k)koi しつ(っ)こい (persistent). 3. **having a tenacious memory** kiokuryoku ga ii 記憶力が良い.

tenacity, *n.* ganbari 頑張り; konki 根気 (perseverance).

tenant, *n.* karite 借手; karinushi 借主 (person or group that rents).

tend, *vb.* 1. sewa o suru 世話をする (take care of); miharu 見張る (watch over). 2. keikō ga aru 傾向がある (be disposed in action or operation); mukau 向かう (lead in a particular direction).

tendency, *n.* keikō 傾向 (inclination, disposition).

tender, 1. *adj.* yawarakai 柔らかい (soft); yowai 弱い (weak); derikēto (na) デリケート (な) (delicate); osanai 幼い (young or immature); yasashii 優しい (gentle). 2. *vb.* teishutsu suru 提出する (present); teikyō suru 提供

する (offer).

tenderness, *n.* 1. yawarakasa 柔らかさ (softness). 2. yowasa 弱さ (weakness). 3. yasashisa 優しさ (gentleness).

tendon, *n.* ken 腱; **Achilles tendon** akiresu-ken アキレス腱.

tenement, *n.* rōkyū-apāto 老朽アパート (run-down apartment house).

tenet, *n.* shinjō 信条.

tennis, *n.* tenisu テニス.

tenor, *n.* 1. shushi 主旨 (purport). 2. tenōru テノール (music).

tense, 1. *n.* jisei 時制 (grammar). 2. *adj.* kataku hatta 固く張つた (stretched tight); katai 硬い、固い (stiff); kinchō shiteiru 緊張している (emotionally strained).

tension, *n.* 1. chōryoku 張力 (degree of tightness, as of a rope). 2. kinchō 緊張 (emotional strain, strained relationship between parties).

tent, *n.* tento テント.

tentacle, *n.* ashi 足.

tentative, *adj.* 1. ichiō (no) 一応 (の) (experimental). 2. futashika (na) 不確か (な) (uncertain).

tenth, *adj.* jūbanme (no) 十番目 (の).

tenuous, *adj.* 1. konkyo ga hakujaku (na) 根拠が薄弱 (な) (lacking a sound basis). 2. hosoi 細い (thin).

tenure, *n.* 1. zaishoku 在職 (holding of an office). 2. eikyū-koyō 永久雇用 (assurance of permanent work).

tepid, *adj.* namanurui 生ぬるい (lukewarm, dispassionate).

term, 1. *n.* kikan 期間 (period); gakki 学期 (division of a school year); na(mae) 名(前) (name);

yōgo 用語 (word, group of words); terms jōken 条件 (stipulations); **in terms of** ... ni kanshite ...に関して; **on good terms with** ... to naka ga ii ...と仲が良い; **come to terms** dōi suru 同意する. 2. *vb.* nazukeru 名付ける (name); yobu 呼ぶ (call).

terminal, 1. *n.* hashi 端 (extremity); tāminaru ターミナル (terminating point for trains, busses, etc.; computer terminal); tanshi 端子 (electrical). 2. *adj.* (... no) hashi ni aru (... の) 端にある (situated at the end); owari (no) 終わり (の) (closing); shi ni itaru 死に至る (leading to death).

terminate, *vb.* owaraseru 終わらせる (bring to an end); owaru 終わる (end).

termination, *n.* owari 終わり (act of terminating).

terminology, *n.* senmon'yōgo 専門用語 (nomenclature).

termite, *n.* shiroari 白蟻.

terrace, *n.* 1. terasu テラス (balcony); beranda ベランダ (veranda). 2. niwa 庭 (garden); nakaniwa 中庭 (patio). 3. daichi 大地 (plateau).

terrain, *n.* chi'iki 地域 (stretch of land); chikei 地形 topography.

terrible, *adj.* 1. kowai 恐い (scary). 2. hidoi ひどい (very bad, distressing).

terrific, *adj.* subarashii 素晴らしい (wonderful).

terrify, *vb.* kowagaraseru 恐がらせる (fill with fear).

territory, *n.* 1. ryōdo 領土 (land belonging to a state, etc.). 2. ryōiki 領域 (field of action or thought). 3. nawabari 縄張り (domain, sphere of influence).

terror, *n.* kyōfu 恐怖.

terrorism, *n.* tero(rizumu) テロ(リズム) (use of violence).

terrorist, *n.* terorisuto テロリスト.

terrorize, *vb.* kowagaraseru 恐がらせる (intimidate, scare).

terse, *adj.* kanketsu (na) 簡潔 (な) (pithy, as language).

test, 1. *n.* tesuto テスト; shiken 試験. 2. *vb.* shiken o ukeru 試験を受ける (undergo a test); shiken o suru 試験をする (conduct a test, subject to a test).

testament, *n.* isho 遺書; yuigon 遺言 (will).

testicle, *n.* kōgan 睾丸.

testify, *vb.* 1. shōgen suru 証言する (in court). 2. shōmei suru 証明する (give evidence).

testimony, *n.* 1. shōgen 証言 (in court). 2. shōko 証拠 (proof).

test tube, *n.* shikenkan 試験管.

tether, 1. *n.* tsuna 綱 (rope); kusari 鎖 (chain). 2. *vb.* tsunagu 繋ぐ (fasten); **be at the end of one's tether** genkai ni tassuru 限界に達する.

text, *n.* 1. honbun 本文 (main body of matter in a book). 2. genbun 原文 (original text).

textbook, *n.* tekisuto テキスト; kyōkasho 教科書.

textile, *n.* 1. orimono 織り物 (cloth). 2. sen'i 繊維 (fiber).

texture, *n.* 1. kime きめ (degree of smoothness); tezawari 手触り (tactile quality of a surface). 2. ori 織り (structure of the fibers that make up a textile fabric).

Thailand, *n.* tai タイ.

than, *conj.* ... yori ... より; **more than** ... ijō ... 以上.

thank, *vb.* kansha suru 感謝する; **Thank you.** Arigatō. 有難う; **No,**

thank you. Kekkō desu. 結構です.

thanks, 1. *n.* kansha no kotoba 感謝の言葉 (words expressing thankfulness); **thanks to** ... no okage de ... のおかげで. 2. *interj.* Arigatō. 有難う.

thankful, *adj.* kansha shiteiru 感謝している.

Thanksgiving Day, *n.* kanshasai 感謝祭.

that, 1. *pron.* are あれ; sore それ; **that is to say** tsumari つまり. 2. *adj.* ano あの; sono その. 3. *adv.* son'na ni そんなに; an'na ni あんなに; **that many, that much** son'na ni takusan そんなに沢山; an'na ni takusan あんなに沢山.

thaw, 1. *n.* yukidoke 雪解け (of snow). 2. *vb.* tokeru 溶ける (melt); tokasu 溶かす (cause to thaw); yawaragu 和らぐ (become less hostile).

the, *art.* ano あの; sono その (often not translated into Japanese.)

theater, *n.* 1. gekijō 劇場 (building). 2. butai 舞台 (place of performance). 3. **the theater** engeki 演劇 (drama).

theatrical, *adj.* 1. engeki (no) 演劇 (の) (pertaining to the theater). 2. geki-teki (na) 劇的 (な) (spectacular).

theft, *n.* nusumi 盗み; dorobō 泥棒.

their, *adj.* karera no 彼らの.

theirs, *pron.* karera no mono 彼らの物.

them, *pron.* karera o/ni 彼らを／に.

theme, *n.* tēma テーマ; shudai 主題.

themselves, *pron.* karera jishin 彼ら自身; **by themselves** karera jishin de 彼ら自身で; **they themselves** karera jishin 彼ら自身.

then, *adv.* 1. sono toki その時 (at that time). 2. soshite sugu ni そして すぐに (immediately after). 3. soshite そして; sore kara それから (next in order). 4. sore ni それに (in addition).

thence, *adv.* 1. soko kara そこから (from that place). 2. sore kara それから (from that time).

theology, *n.* shingaku 神学.

theoretical, *adj.* 1. rironjō (no) 理論上 (の) (existing only in theory). 2. riron (no) 理論 (の); riron-teki (na) 理論的 (な) (pertaining to theory).

theory, *n.* 1. riron 理論; gensoku 原則 (principle). 2. gakusetsu 学説 (proposed explanation). 3. iken 意見 (view, guess).

therapeutic, *adj.* chiryō (no) 治療 (の) (curative).

therapy, *n.* serapī セラピー; chiryō 治療.

there, *adv.* (a)soko de/ni (あ)そこで／に.

thereafter, *adv.* sore igo それ以後.

thereby, *adv.* sore ni yotte それによって (by that).

therefore, *adv., conj.* dakara だから; sorede それで.

thermometer, *n.* 1. ondokei 温度計. 2. **clinical thermometer** taionkei 体温計.

thermos, *n.* mahōbin 魔法瓶.

thermostat, *n.* sāmosutatto サーモスタット.

thesaurus, *n.* ruigigo-han'igo-jiten 類義語反意語辞典 (dictionary of synonyms and antonyms).

these, 1. *pron.* korera これら. 2. *adj.* korera (no) これら (の).

thesis, *n.* ronbun 論文 (research paper).

they, *pron.* karera 彼ら.

thick, *adj.* 1. futoi 太い (fat, as a cylindrical object or line); atsui 厚い (thick in depth, as a layer). 2. koi 濃い (dense, not watery). 3. tsumatta 詰まった (compact). 4. **thick fog** fukai kiri 深い霧.

thicken, *vb.* 1. futoku naru 太くなる (become fat); futoku suru 太くする (make fat). 2. atsuku naru 厚くなる (become thick, as a layer); atsuku suru 厚くする (make thick, as a layer). 3. koku naru 濃くなる (become dense); koku suru 濃くする (make dense).

thicket, *n.* shigemi 繁み.

thickness, *n.* 1. futosa 太さ (fatness). 2. atsusa 厚さ (width). 3. kosa 濃さ (denseness).

thief, *n.* dorobō 泥棒.

thigh, *n.* futomomo 太股.

thin, 1. *adj.* hosoi 細い (slender); usui 薄い (small in extent between two surfaces, as a layer; of relatively slight consistency; lacking volume); yaseta やせた (skinny); mabara (na) 疎ら (な) (sparse). 2. *vb.* hosoku suru 細くする (make slender); usumeru 薄める (make less thick or dense); mabara ni suru 疎らにする (make sparse).

thing, *n.* 1. mono 物 (material object, substance). 2. koto こと、事 (intangible object, object of thought). 3. jitai 事態; jōkyō 状況 (things, general state of affairs). 4. jijitsu 事実 (fact). 5. okonai 行い (deed); dekigoto 出来事 (event). 6. **things** yōgu 用具 (utensils). 7. **things** shoyūhin 所有品 (personal possessions).

think, *vb.* 1. omou 思う (believe, regard). 2. kangaeru 考える (reason, meditate). 3. **think about** ... ni tsuite kangaeru ... について考える; **think of** (people, things) ... no koto o omou ...のことを思う; **think of doing** ... shiyō to omou ...しようと思う; **think over** ... ni tsuite yoku kangaeru ... についてよく考える.

third, 1. *n.* sanbun no ichi 三分の一 (one-third). 2. *adj.* sanbanme (no) 三番目 (の).

third party, *n.* daisansha 第三者.

third person, *n.* san'ninshō 三人称 (grammar).

thirst, 1. *n.* kawaki 渇き (need for water, desire for anything). 2. *vb.* **thirst for** ... o katsubō suru ...を渇望する.

thirsty, *adj.* 1. **be thirsty** nodo ga kawaiteiru 喉が渇いている (need to drink). 2. ueteiru 餓えている (eager to obtain something).

thirteen, *n.* jūsan 十三.

thirty, *n.* sanjū 三十.

this, 1. *pron.* kore これ (thing); kochira こちら (person). 2. *adj.* kono この; ko(n)- こ(ん)-; **this country** kono kuni この国; **this week** konshū 今週; **this year** kotoshi 今年.

thistle, *n.* azami あざみ.

thorn, *n.* toge とげ.

thorny, *adj.* 1. toge ga ōi とげが多い (prickly). 2. mendō (na) 面倒 (な) (difficult).

thorough, *adj.* 1. tettei-teki (na) 徹底的 (な); kanzen (na) 完全 (な) (complete). 2. kichōmen (na) 几帳面 (な) (meticulous).

thoroughbred, *n., adj.* 1. sarabureddo (no) サラブレッド

(の) (horse). 2. junketsushu (no) 純血種 (の) (pure breed).

thoroughfare, *n.* 1. ōdōri 大通り (main street). 2. **No thoroughfare** Tsūkōkinshi 通行禁止.

those, *pron., adj.* sorera (no) それら (の); arera (no) あれら (の).

though, 1. *adv.* dakedo だけど; sore demo それでも (however). 2. *conj.* dakedo だけど; sore nimo kakawarazu それにもかかわらず (notwithstanding that); **as though** ... marude ... ka no yō ni まるで...かのように.

thought, *n.* 1. kangae 考え (product of mental activity, idea, opinion). 2. shikō 思考 (mental activity). 3. shikōryoku 思考力 (capacity of reasoning). 4. omoi 思い (meditation). 5. ito 意図 (intention). 6. kōryo 考慮 (consideration). 7. shisō 思想 (ideas characteristic of a place or time); **Greek thought** girisha-shisō ギリシャ思想.

thoughtful, *adj.* 1. omoiyari ga aru 思い遣りがある (considerate). 2. chūi bukai 注意深い (characterized by careful thought). 3. shikō-teki (na) 思考的 (な) (meditative).

thousand, *n.* 1. sen 千. 2. **thousands (of)** sūsen (no) 数千 (の) (thousands of); takusan (no) 沢山 (の) (great number or amount). 3. **two thousand** nisen 二千; **three thousand** sanzen 三千; **ten thousand** ichiman 一万; **one hundred thousand** jūman 十万.

thrash, *vb.* 1. tataku 叩く (beat). 2. uchimakasu 打ち負かす (defeat).

thread, *n.* 1. ito 糸 (for sewing). 2. sujimichi 筋道 (line of reasoning).

threadbare, *adj.* surikireta 擦り切れた (of cloth).

threat, *n.* 1. odoshi 脅し (declaration to hurt). 2. kiken 危険 (danger).

threaten, *vb.* odosu 脅す (declare to hurt).

three, *n.* san 三; mittsu 三つ.

three dimensional, *adj.* rittai-teki (na) 立体的 (な).

three hundred, *n.* sanbyaku 三百.

threshold, *n.* 1. shiki'i 敷居 (sill of a doorway). 2. hajimari 始まり (beginning).

thrift, *n.* ken'yaku 倹約 (economical management).

thrifty, *adj.* ken'yakuka (no) 倹約家 (の) (frugal).

thrill, 1. *n.* suriru スリル. 2. *vb.* waku-waku saseru わくわくさせる (cause to feel excited); waku-waku suru わくわくする (feel excited).

thrilling, *adj.* 1. suriru ga aru スリルがある (producing fear). 2. waku-waku suru わくわくする (exciting).

thrive, *vb.* 1. sakaeru 栄える (prosper). 2. yoku sodatsu よく育つ (grow well).

throat, *n.* nodo 喉.

throb, 1. *n.* dōki 動悸 (pulsation of the heart); shindō'on 振動音 (vibration, as a sound). 2. *vb.* dōki ga suru 動悸がする (of the heart); utsu 打つ (of a machine, etc.).

throe, *n.* 1. keiren けいれん (spasm). 2. **throes** kutsū 苦痛 (pain).

throne, *n.* 1. ōza 王座 (chair). 2. ōi 王位 (office of a sovereign).

throng, *n.* mure 群れ (a great number of people or things).

through, *prep.* 1. ... o tōtte ...を通って (in at one end and out at the other, by way of, across). 2. ... no aida zutto ...の間ずっと (throughout). 3. ... no kekka ...の結果 (as a result of). 4. ... ni yotte ... によって (by means of). 5. ... made ...まで (to and including). 6. **be through** owaru 終わる (be over with).

throughout, 1. *prep.* ... no itaru tokoro ni ... の至る所に (in all parts of); ... no aida zutto ...の間ずっと (from beginning to end). 2. *adv.* itaru tokoro de/ni 至る所で／に (in every part).

throw, 1. *n.* nageru koto 投げること (act of throwing). 2. *vb.* nageru 投げる (cast, hurl, send forth); nagetaosu 投げ倒す (cause to fall on the ground). 3. **throw away** rōhi suru 浪費する (waste); nogasu 逃す (miss); suteru 捨てる (discard); **throw in** omake suru おまけする (add as a bonus); **throw over** misuteru 見捨てる (forsake); **throw up** haku 吐く (vomit).

thrust, 1. *n.* oshi 押し; tsuki 突き (push). 2. *vb.* osu 押す; tsuku 突く (push); tsukisasu 突き刺す (stab).

thug, *n.* kyōakuhan 凶悪犯 (vicious criminal).

thumb, *n.* oyayubi 親指 (of the hand).

thumbtack, *n.* gabyō 画鋲.

thunder, 1. *n.* raimei 雷鳴 (noise accompanying lightning). 2. *vb.* kaminari ga naru 雷が鳴る (give forth thunder).

Thursday, *n.* mokuyōbi 木曜日.

thus, *adv.* 1. kono yō ni (shite) こ

626

のように (して) (in this way). 2.
sore de それで (consequently). 3.
thus far kore made no tokoro こ
れまでのところ (to this extent).

thwart, *vb.* 1. kujiku 挫く
(frustrate). 2. samatageru 妨げる
(prevent).

tic, *n.* hikitsuri 引きつり.

tick, 1. *n.* chikutaku チクタク
(sound of a clock); dani だに
(insect). 2. *vb.* chikutaku naru ち
くたく鳴る (make a sound).

ticket, *n.* 1. chiketto チケット;
kippu 切符; ken 券. 2. jōshaken
乗車券 (for vehicular travel);
nyūjōken 入場券 (admission);
chūshaihanken 駐車違反券 (for
parking violation); **ticket office**
kippu'uriba 切符売り場; **ticket
window** kippuhanbai-madoguchi
切符販売窓口.

tickle, *vb.* 1. kusuguru くすぐる
(touch with the fingers). 2.
manzoku saseru 満足させる
(gratify).

ticklish, *adj.* kusuguttai くすぐっ
たい.

tidal wave, *n.* tsunami 津波.

tide, *n.* 1. shio no michihi 潮の満ち
干 (periodic rise and fall of the
waters). 2. chōryū 潮流 (current
of water). 3. nagare 流れ (trend).
4. ugoki 動き (movement).

tidy, 1. *adj.* kichin to shita きちん
とした (neat, orderly). 2. *vb.*
kichin to suru きちんとする;
katazukeru 片付ける (make tidy).

tie, 1. *n.* himo 紐 (string); nekutai
ネクタイ (necktie); tai タイ
(sports). 2. *vb.* musubu 結ぶ
(bind); tai ni naru タイになる
(sports); **tie down** shibaritsukeru
縛りつける (confine); **tie up**
tomeru 留める (secure by tying);

be tied up isogashii 忙しい (be
busy).

tier, *n.* kai 階; sō 層; **second tier**
nikai 二階.

tiger, *n.* taigā タイガー; tora 虎.

tight, *adj.* 1. kitsui きつい (firmly
fixed in place, fitting closely,
scarce, as money). 2. katai 固い
(firmly knotted). 3. kataku hatta
固く張った (taut, as a rope). 4.
bōsui (no) 防水 (の) (waterproof);
kimitsusei (no) 気密性 (の) (air-
tight). 5. tsumatta 詰まった (fully
packed). 6. muzukashii 難しい
(difficult). 7. kibishii 厳しい
(rigid).

tighten, *vb.* kitsuku suru きつくす
る; shimeru 締める (make firmly
fixed).

tile, *n.* tairu タイル (any tile);
kawara 瓦 (roof tile).

till, 1. *n.* okaneire お金入れ
(money box). 2. *vb.* tagayasu 耕す
(cultivate). 3. *prep.* ... made ...ま
で. 4. *conj.* ... made ... まで.

tilt, 1. *n.* katamuki 傾き; naname
斜め (slope). 2. *vb.* katamukeru
傾ける (cause to incline);
katamuku (incline) 傾く.

timber, *n.* zaimoku 材木 (wood for
building); zaimoku no tame no ki
材木のための木 (standing timber).

time, *n.* 1. jikan 時間 (duration,
definite point in time, hour,
particular period in a day,
appointed time). 2. kikan 期間
(period). 3. jidai 時代 (era,
period). 4. -do/-kai -度／-回
(each occasion of a recurring
action or event); **do something
five times** ... o go-do/-kai suru ...
を五度／～回する. 5. **times** -bai
-倍 (multiplication); **five times
faster** gobai hayai 五倍早い. 6.

ahead of time hayaku 早く;
ahead of one's time jisei ni
sakinjite 時勢に先んじて; **all the
time** zutto ずっと; **a long time**
nagai aida 長い間; **a long time
ago** mukashi 昔; **at the same
time** dōji ni 同時に
(simultaneously); **at times**
tokidoki 時々; **behind the times**
jidaiokure (no) 時代遅れ (の); **for
a time** shibaraku 暫く (for a
while); **for the time being** ichiji-
teki (ni) 一時的 (に)
(temporarily); sashiatatte 差し当
たって (for the present); **from
time to time** tokidoki 時々; **to
have a good time** tanoshimu 楽
しむ; **in time** jikan'nai ni 時間内
に (early enough); chikai uchi ni
近いうちに (in the future); **it's
time to do** ... suru jikan da/desu
...する時間だ／です; **kill time**
jikan o tsubusu 時間を潰す; **on
time** teikoku ni 定刻に
(punctually); **once upon a time**
mukashi-mukashi 昔々; **What
time is it?** Ima nanji desu ka. 今
何時ですか.

time, *vb.* jikan o hakaru 時間を計
る (measure the duration of).

time-consuming, *adj.* jikan ga
kakaru 時間がかかる.

timely, *adj.* taimingu ga ii タイミン
グが良い; jigi ni kanatta 時宜に
適った.

timer, *n.* taimā タイマー (device).

times, *prep.* kakeru 掛ける
(multiplied by); **five times six** go
kakeru roku 五掛ける六.

timetable, *n.* jikokuhyō 時刻表
(bus, train, etc.).

time zone, *n.* jikantai 時間帯.

timid, *adj.* okubyō (na) 臆病 (な).

tin, *n.* 1. buriki ブリキ (tinplate).

2. suzu 錫 (element). 3. **tin can**
kan 缶; **tinfoil** gingami 銀紙.

tinge, 1. *n.* kasuka na iro 微かな色
(color); kasukasa 微かさ (slight
admixture). 2. *vb.* kasuka ni iro o
tsukeru 微かに色をつける (tint);
kasuka ni mazeru 微かに混ぜる
(impart some taste or smell).

tingle, *vb.* hiri-hiri suru ひりひりす
る.

tinker, *vb.* **tinker with** ijikuru い
じくる (try to repair clumsily).

tinkle, *vb.* rin-rin to naru りんりん
と鳴る (make sounds, as a small
bell).

tint, 1. *n.* iro(ai) 色(合い) (hue). 2.
vb. iro o tsukeru 色をつける (give
a tint to).

tiny, *adj.* chiisai 小さい.

tip, 1. *n.* hashi 端; saki 先 (end);
chippu チップ (gratuity). 2. *vb.*
chippu o ageru チップを上げる
(give money to); katamukeru 傾け
る (cause to tilt); taosu 倒す
(cause to overturn).

tipsy, *adj.* chotto yotteiru ちょっと
酔っている.

tiptoe, *n.* **on tiptoe**
tsumasakidatte 爪先立って.

tirade, *n.* ikari no chōkōzetsu 怒り
の長広舌.

tire, 1. *n.* taiya タイヤ (of a car). 2.
vb. tsukareru 疲れる (become
weary); tsukare saseru 疲れさせる
(make weary).

tired, *adj.* 1. tsukareteiru/
tsukareta 疲れている／疲れた
(exhausted). 2. akiteiru 飽きてい
る (bored). 3. chinpu (na) 陳腐
(な) (hackneyed).

tireless, *n.* tsukare shirazu (no) 疲
れ知らず (の) (untiring).

tiresome, *adj.* 1. tsukaresaseru 疲
れさせる (causing fatigue). 2.

unzari saseru うんざりさせる
(causing boredom).

tissue, *n.* 1. soshiki 組織 (body). 2.
tisshū ティッシュー (tissue paper;
facial tissue).

title, *n.* taitoru タイトル; dai(mei)
題(名) (name of a book, film, etc.);
katagaki 肩書き (appellation of
rank or office).

to, *prep.* 1. ... e/ni ...へ／に (so as to
reach, toward, on). 2. ... made ...
まで (until). 3. **in order to do** ...
suru tame ni ...するために; **to
and fro** achikochi ni あちこちに.

toad, *n.* kaeru 蛙; hikigaeru ひき
蛙.

toast, 1. *n.* tōsuto トースト
(bread); kanpai 乾杯 (ceremonial
drink). 2. *vb.* yaku 焼く (brown
bread, cheese, etc.); kanpai suru
乾杯する (drink to).

toaster, *n.* tōsutā トースター.

tobacco, *n.* tabako タバコ.

today, *n., adv.* 1. kyō 今日 (this
present day). 2. kon'nichi 今日
(the present age, nowadays).

to-do, *n.* sawagi 騒ぎ.

toe, *n.* 1. ashi no yubi 足の指 (of
the foot). 2. tsumasaki 爪先
(forepart of a shoe).

together, *adv.* 1. issho ni 一緒に;
tomo ni 共に (in a single mass, in
cooperation); **together with** ... to
issho ni ...と一緒に. 2. dōji ni 同
時に (at the same time).

toil, 1. *n.* kurō 苦労; nangi 難儀
(laborious task). 2. *vb.* nangi suru
難儀する (move with great effort);
akuseku suru あくせくする (labor
arduously).

toilet, *n.* 1. benki 便器 (toilet
fixture). 2. toire トイレ; (o)tearai
(お)手洗い (bathroom);
keshōshitsu 化粧室 (powder

room). 3. mizukuroi 身繕い
(dressing oneself). 4. **toilet paper**
toiretto-pēpā トイレットペーパー.

token, *n.* 1. shirushi 印; shōchō 象
徴 (representation). 2. shōko 証拠
(evidence). 3. kinenhin 記念品
(memento). 4. jōshayō-koin 乗車
用コイン (metal disk for riding a
bus, etc.). 5. **by the same token**
dōyō ni 同様に (in the same
manner); **in token of** ... no
shirushi ni ...の印に (as a sign of).

Tokyo, *n.* tōkyō 東京.

tolerance, *n.* 1. kan'yō 寛容
(permissive attitude toward
difference). 2. gaman 我慢; nintai
忍耐 (endurance).

tolerant, *adj.* kan'yō (na) 寛容 (な)
(lenient).

tolerate, *vb.* yurusu 許す (permit).
2. gaman suru 我慢する; taeru 耐
える (put up with, endure).

toll, *n.* 1. tsūkōryōkin 通行料金
(fee for passage). 2. tsūwaryōkin
通話料金 (fee for telephone call);
toll call chōkyoridenwa 長距離電
話 (long distance call).

tomato, *n.* tomato トマト.

tomb, *n.* haka 墓.

tombstone, *n.* hakaishi 墓石.

tomorrow, *n., adv.* ashita 明日;
tomorrow morning/night
ashita no asa/ban 明日の朝／晩;
the day after tomorrow asatte
あさって.

tone, *n.* 1. oto 音 (sound). 2.
onshitsu 音質 (quality of sound);
seishitsu 声質 (quality of voice);
gochō 語調 (expressive quality of
voice). 3. shikichō 色調 (hue). 4.
yōsu 様子 (appearance, manner).

tongs, *n.* kanabasami 金鋏; yattoko
やっとこ.

tongue, *n.* 1. shita 舌 (organ). 2.

kotoba 言葉 (language); kokugo
国語 (national language); **mother
tongue** bokokugo 母国語.

tonic, *n.* 1. kyōsōzai 強壮剤
(medicine). 2. **tonic water**
tonikku-wōtā トニックウォー
ター.

tonight, *n., adv.* kon'ya 今夜;
konban 今晩.

tonsil, *n.* hentōsen 扁桃腺.

too, *adv.* 1. ... mo (mata) ... も (又);
sono ue ni その上に (also, in
addition). 2. amari ni 余りに;
... sugiru ... 過ぎる (excessively);
Too bad! Zan'nen da. 残念だ; **too
many** ōsugiru 多過ぎる.

tool, *n.* dōgu 道具.

toot, 1. *n.* pū-pū iu oto ぷーぷーい
う音 (sound of horn or whistle).
2. *vb.* pū-pū narasu ぷーぷー鳴ら
す (sound a horn or whistle).

tooth, *n.* ha 歯.

toothache, *n.* haita 歯痛.

toothbrush, *n.* ha-burashi 歯ブラ
シ.

toothless, *adj.* hanashi (no) 歯なし
(の).

toothpaste, *n.* nerihamigaki 練り
歯磨き.

toothpick, *n.* tsumayōji 爪楊枝.

top, 1. *n.* toppu トップ (highest
part); chōten 頂点 (highest point);
ichiban 一番 (highest rank or
quality); futa 蓋 (lid); koma こま
(toy). 2. *adj.* ichiban ue (no) 一番
上 (の) (situated at the highest
point, highest in degree). 2. *vb.*
kabuseru 被せる (put something
on top of); shinogu 凌ぐ (surpass).

topic, *n.* 1. topikku トピック; tēma
テーマ (theme of a discourse). 2.
wadai 話題 (subject of
conversation).

topknot, *n.* chonmage ちょんまげ

(of a samurai or sumo wrestler).

topping, *n.* 1. sōsu ソース (sauce).
2. kazari 飾り; soemono 添え物
(garnish).

topple, *vb.* taoreru 倒れる (fall
forward); taosu 倒す (overthrow).

topsy-turvy, *adv.* sakasama ni 逆
さまに (upside down).

torch, *n.* taimatsu 松明 (flaming
stick).

torment, 1. *n.* kurushimi 苦しみ
(agony). 2. *vb.* kurushimeru 苦し
める (inflict agony on).

tornado, *n.* tatsumaki 竜巻.

torrent, *n.* 1. gekiryū 激流 (violent
stream). 2. doshaburi 土砂降り
(violent rain).

torrid, *adj.* yaketsuku yō (na) 焼け
つくよう (な) (burning).

torso, *n.* dōtai 胴体 (trunk of
human body).

tortoise, *n.* kame 亀.

tortoiseshell, *n.* bekkō べっ甲.

tortuous, *adj.* 1. magarikunette-iru
曲がりくねっている (twisted). 2.
mawarikudoi 回りくどい
(indirect).

torture, 1. *n.* kutsū 苦痛 (anguish);
gōmon 拷問 (act of inflicting
severe pain). 2. *vb.* kurushimeru
苦しめる (inflict with anguish);
gōmon ni kakeru 拷問にかける
(subject to torture).

toss, *vb.* 1. nageru 投げる (throw).
2. korogemawaru 転げ回る
(writhe about); yureru 揺れる
(rock). 3. karuku mazeru 軽く混
ぜる (mix lightly).

tot, *n.* yōji 幼児 (small child).

total, 1. *n.* gōkei 合計; zenbu 全部
(sum, full amount); **in total**
zenbu de 全部で. 2. *adj.* zenbu
(no) 全部 (の); gōkei (no) 合計
(の) (comprising the whole);

mattaku (no) 全く (の) (complete). 3. *vb*. gōkei suru 合計する (bring to a total).

totalitarianism, *n*. zentaishugi 全体主義.

totality, *n*. zentaisei 全体性 (state of being total).

tote, *vb*. motteiku 持って行く; hakobu 運ぶ (carry).

totem, *n*. tōtemu トーテム.

touch, 1. *n*. fureru koto 触れること (act of touching); shokkaku 触覚 (sense); tezawari 手触り (feel); sesshoku 接触 (coming or being in contact with); renraku 連絡 (communication); udemae 腕前 (skill); kimi 気味 (slight addition or change, trace); **a touch of** sukoshi no 少しの; **keep in touch with** ... to renraku shiau ... と連絡し合う; **be out of touch** tōzakatteiru 遠ざかっている. 2. *vb*. (... ni) fureru (... に) 触れる (put the hand on, be adjacent to, strike lightly, deal with as a topic); ...to narabu ... と並ぶ (be equal with); ... ni kankei suru ... に関係する (concern); kandō saseru 感動させる (cause to feel sympathy); **touch on** ... ni fureru ...に触れる (refer to).

touching, *adj*. kandō-teki (na) 感動的 (な).

touchy, *adj*. 1. okoriyasui 怒り易い (easily offended). 2. bimyō (na) 微妙 (な) (sensitive).

tough, *adj*. 1. katai 固い (not easily broken, hard to chew). 2. ganjō (na) 頑丈 (な) (sturdy). 3. muzukashii 難しい (difficult). 4. ganko (na) 頑固 (な) (stubborn).

toughen, *vb*. kataku suru 固くする (make hard or unbreakable).

toupee, *n*. katsura かつら (wig).

tour, 1. *n*. ryokō 旅行 (trip); tsuā ツアー (pleasure trip; group tour; concert tour); kengaku 見学 (trip through a place to view or inspect it). 2. *vb*. ryokō suru 旅行する (make a tour); kengaku suru 見学する (travel through a place for viewing or inspection).

tourism, *n*. kankō 観光.

tourist, *n*. tsūrisuto ツーリスト; kankōkyaku 観光客.

tournament, *n*. tōnamento トーナメント.

tout, *vb*. shitsukoku tanomu しつこく頼む (solicit importunately); sakan ni senden suru 盛んに宣伝する (praise extravagantly.

tow, *vb*. ken'in suru けん引する (pull by a rope).

toward, *prep*. 1. ... no hō e/ni ...の方へ／に (in the direction of). 2. ... no tame ni ...のために (for, as a contribution to). 3. ... ni taishite ...に対して (turned to). 4. ... goro/koro ...頃 (shortly before in time).

towel, *n*. taoru タオル.

tower, *n*. tawā タワー; tō 塔.

town, *n*. 1. machi 町 (populated area smaller than city); **town hall** yakuba 役場; yakusho 役所. 2. machi no chūshin 町の中心 (center of a city).

toxic, *adj*. yūdoku (na, no) 有毒 (な、の) (poisonous).

toxin, *n*. dokuso 毒素.

toy, *n*. omocha おもちゃ; gangu 玩具.

trace, 1. *n*. ato 跡; keiseki 形跡 (mark left behind); shōryō 少量 (small amount). 2. *vb*. tsuiseki suru 追跡する (follow); tadoru 辿る (follow the course, history, etc., of); utsusu 写す (copy).

track, 1. *n.* atokata 跡形 (mark); michi 道 (path); torakku トラック (sports); senro 線路 (train). 2. *vb.* ato o ou 後を追う (follow the track of); **track down** tsukitomeru 突き止める.

tract, *n.* chitai 地帯 (expanse of land).

tractor, *n.* torakutā トラクター (vehicle).

trade, 1. *n.* shōgyō 商業; torihiki 取り引き (commerce); bōeki 貿易 (foreign trade); kōkan 交換 (exchange of things); shokugyō 職業 (occupation). 2. *vb.* kōkan suru 交換する (exchange); **trade in** akinau 商う; torihiki o suru 取り引きをする (buy and sell).

trademark, *n.* torēdomāku トレードマーク; shōhyō 商標.

trade union, *n.* rōdōkumiai 労働組合.

trade wind, *n.* bōekifū 貿易風.

tradition, *n.* dentō 伝統.

traditional, *adj.* dentō-teki (na) 伝統的 (な).

traffic, 1. *n.* kōtsū 交通 (traveling persons and things); **traffic jam** kōtsūjūtai 交通渋滞; **traffic light, signal** kōtsūshingō 交通信号; baibai 売買 (buying and selling). 2. *vb.* baibai suru 売買する (buy and sell).

tragedy, *n.* higeki 悲劇 (drama, sad event).

tragic, *adj.* 1. higeki (no) 悲劇 (の) (of a drama). 2. higeki-teki (na) 悲劇的 (な) (sad).

trail, 1. *n.* ato 跡 (tracks, traces); torēru トレール; michi 道 (path). 2. *vb.* hikizuru 引きずる (drag along the ground); ato ni hiku 後に引く (draw behind); ou 追う (follow).

trailer, *n.* torērā トレーラー.

train, 1. *n.* ressha 列車 (railway train); gyōretsu 行列 (moving line of people, vehicles, etc.). 2. *vb.* kyōiku suru 教育する (instruct); kyōiku o ukeru 教育を受ける (undergo instruction); kunren suru 訓練する (make fit or proficient by exercise or practice).

training, *n.* torēningu トレーニング; kunren 訓練 (exercise, practice).

trait, *n.* tokuchō 特徴 (characteristic).

traitor, *n.* uragirimono 裏切り者.

tram, *n.* romendensha 路面電車 (streetcar).

tramp, 1. *n.* ashioto 足音 (walking sound); furōsha 浮浪者 (vagabond). 2. *vb.* aruku 歩く (travel on foot); dota-dota aruku どたどた歩く (walk with heavy, noisy steps); fumu 踏む (step on).

trample, *vb.* fumitsukeru 踏みつける.

trance, *n.* konsuijōtai 昏睡状態 (half-conscious state); saiminjōtai 催眠状態 (hypnotic state); kōkotsujōtai 恍惚状態 (ecstatic state).

tranquil, *adj.* shizuka (na) 静か (な) (quiet); heiwa (na) 平和 (な) (peaceful).

tranquilize, *vb.* shizuka ni saseru 静かにさせる (make quiet); shizuka ni naru 静かになる (become quiet).

tranquilizer, *n.* chinseizai 鎮静剤.

tranquillity, *n.* shizukesa 静けさ (quietness).

transact, *vb.* torihiki suru 取り引きする.

transaction, *n.* torihiki 取り引き.

transcend, *vb.* 1. chōetsu suru 超

越する (rise above ordinary limits). 2. masaru 勝る (excel).

transcendental, *adj.* chōetsu-teki (na) 超越的 (な) (superior, supernatural).

transcribe, *vb.* 1. utsusu 写す (copy). 2. kiroku suru 記録する (make record of).

transcript, *n.* 1. kopī コピー; utsushi 写し (copy). 2. seisekihyō 成績表 (copy of one's academic record).

transfer, 1. *n.* idō 移動 (moving from one place to another); norikaeken 乗り換え券 (ticket for passenger). 2. *vb.* utsuru/utsusu 移る／移す; idō suru/saseru 移動する／させる (move/cause to move from one place to another); jōto suru 譲渡する (make over the legal title of).

transform, *vb.* kaeru 変える (change).

transformation, *n.* henka 変化.

transformer, *n.* hen'atsuki 変圧器 (electrical).

transfuse, *vb.* yuketsu suru 輸血する (perform a blood transfusion).

transgress, *vb.* 1. do o kosu 度を越す (go beyond). 2. ihan suru 違反する (violate a law).

transgression, *n.* ihō 違法 (violation of a law).

transient, *adj.* 1. tsukanoma (no) 束の間 (の) (passing). 2. ichiji-teki (na) 一時的 (な) (existing temporarily).

transistor, *n.* toranjisutā トランジスター.

transit, *n.* 1. tsūkō 通行 (act of passing). 2. yusō 輸送 (conveyance).

transition, *n.* henka 変化; ikō 移行 (passage from one condition, etc.,

to another).

transitive verb, *n.* tadōshi 他動詞.

transitory, *adj.* mijikai 短い; tsukanoma (no) 束の間 (の) (brief).

translate, *vb.* hon'yaku suru 翻訳する (change from one language to another).

translation, *n.* hon'yaku 翻訳.

translator, *n.* hon'yakusha/hon'yakuka 翻訳者／翻訳家.

transmission, *n.* 1. dentatsu 伝達 (act of sending out, communication). 2. hōsō 放送 (broadcasting).

transmit, *vb.* 1. utsusu 移す (pass from one person, place, or thing to another). 2. okuru 送る (send out). 3. hōsō suru 放送する (broadcast). 4. tsutaeru 伝える (cause to pass through, communicate).

transparent, *adj.* tōmei (na) 透明 (な).

transpire, *vb.* 1. hanmei suru 判明する (become known). 2. okoru 起こる (take place).

transplant, *vb.* 1. utsusu 移す (remove from one place to another). 2. ishoku suru 移植する (plant, body organ).

transport, 1. *n.* yusō 輸送 (conveyance). 2. *vb.* hakobu 運ぶ (convey).

transportation, *n.* 1. yusō 輸送 (conveyance of goods). 2. kōtsū-shudan 交通手段 (means of carrying passengers).

transpose, *vb.* irekaeru 入れ替える (interchange).

transvestite, *n.* josōshumisha 女装趣味者.

trap, 1. *n.* wana 罠 (snare). 2. *vb.* wana ni kakeru 罠に掛ける

(ensnare); tojikomeru 閉じ込める (confine).

trash, *n.* 1. garakuta がらくた; kuzu 屑 (worthless thing, garbage). 2. tawagoto 戯言 (nonsense).

trauma, *n.* 1. kizu 傷 (wound). 2. seishin-teki dageki 精神的打撃; shokku ショック (psychological trauma).

travel, 1. *n.* tabi 旅; ryokō 旅行 (journey); ugoki 動き (movement); **travel agency** ryokō-dairiten/-gaisha 旅行代理店／〜会社. 2. *vb.* ryokō suru 旅行する (journey); susumu 進む (move).

traveler, *n.* tabibito 旅人; ryokōsha 旅行者; **traveler's check** ryokō-kogitte 旅行小切手.

traverse, *vb.* yokogiru 横切る (pass across).

travesty, *n.* parodī パロディー (parody).

tray, *n.* bon 盆 (flat, shallow container).

treachery, *n.* uragiri 裏切り (betrayal).

tread, 1. *n.* arukiburi 歩き振り (manner of walking); ashioto 足音 (walking sound). 2. *vb.* aruku 歩く (walk); fumu 踏む (trample).

treason, *n.* 1. uragiri 裏切り (treachery). 2. hangyaku 反逆 (disloyalty to one's country).

treasure, 1. *n.* zaisan 財産 (accumulated wealth); takara 宝 (valuable thing, jewel). 2. *vb.* taisetsu ni suru 大切にする (retain carefully, cherish); shimau 仕舞う (put away for future use).

treasurer, *n.* kaikei 会計 (person in charge of monetary matters).

treasury, *n.* 1. kokko 国庫 (place

for keeping government funds). 2. hōko 宝庫 (collection of treasures).

treat, 1. *n.* ogori 奢り (food, etc., paid for by another). 2. *vb.* atsukau 扱う (deal with); motenasu もてなす (entertain); ogoru 奢る (provide food at one's own expense); chiryō suru 治療する (give medical care to).

treatise, *n.* ronbun 論文.

treatment, *n.* 1. atsukai 扱い (act, manner, or process of dealing with). 2. chiryō 治療 (medical).

treaty, *n.* jōyaku 条約 (formal agreement between states).

tree, *n.* ki 木.

trek, *n.* tsurai tabi 辛い旅 (journey involving hardship).

trellis, *n.* kōshi 格子 (latticework).

tremble, *vb.* furueru 震える (shake, as from cold, etc.); yureru 揺れる (quake).

tremendous, *adj.* 1. bakudai/kyodai (na) 莫大/巨大 (な) (extraordinarily great in amount/size). 2. saikō (no) 最高 (の) (excellent).

tremor, *n.* 1. yure 揺れ (vibration). 2. miburui 身震い (involuntary shaking of the limbs).

trench, *n.* mizo 溝 (ditch).

trenchant, *adj.* 1. surudoi 鋭い (keen). 2. kōka-teki (na) 効果的 (な) (effective). 3. shinratsu (na) 辛辣 (な) (caustic).

trend, *n.* 1. ryūkō 流行 (vogue). 2. nagare 流れ (general course); keikō 傾向 (tendency).

trespass, *vb.* 1. shin'nyū suru 侵入する (enter illicitly). 2. shingai suru 侵害する (encroach).

tresses, *n.* nagai kami 長い髪.

trial, *n.* 1. saiban 裁判 (judicial). 2.

shiken 試験 (test). 3. kokoromi 試
み (attempt). 4. shiren 試練 (act
of being tested, hardship). 5. kurō
no tane 苦労の種 (source of
distress). 6. **on trial** tameshi ni 試
しに (in order to test); **stand trial**
saiban ni kakerareru 裁判にかけら
れる (be tried in a court); **trial
and error** shikō sakugo 試行錯誤.

triangle, *n.* sankakkei 三角形.

tribe, *n.* buzoku 部族; shuzoku 種
族 (people united by common
descent).

tribulation, *n.* kunan 苦難
(grievous trouble).

tribunal, *n.* hōtei 法廷 (court of
justice).

tributary, *n.* shiryū 支流 (stream).

tribute, *n.* 1. kansha no
okurimono 感謝の贈り物 (gift
given as an expression of
gratitude). 2. sanji 賛辞 (praise);
pay tribute to ... ni sanji o okuru
...に賛辞を送る.

trick, 1. *n.* keiryaku 計略
(stratagem); warufuzake 悪ふざけ
(prank); kotsu こつ (knack); tejina
手品 (feat of magic). 2. *vb.*
damasu だます (deceive).

trickery, *n.* damashi だまし;
keiryaku 計略 (stratagem).

trickle, *vb.* shitataru 滴る (flow or
fall by drops).

trickster, *n.* petenshi ぺてん師
(deceiver).

tricky, *adj.* 1. zurugashikoi ずる賢
い (sly). 2. mendō (na) 面倒 (な)
(difficult).

trifle, 1. *n.* kudaranai mono/koto
下らない物／事 (useless or trivial
thing or matter); **a trifle** chotto ち
ょっと (a little bit, somewhat). 2.
vb. **trifle away** rōhi suru 浪費す
る; **trifle with** moteasobu 弄ぶ

(play with); zonzai ni atsukau ぞ
んざいに扱う (deal with without
respect).

trigger, 1. *n.* hikigane 引き金 (of a
gun). 2. *vb.* hikiokosu 引き起こす
(provoke).

trill, *n.* toriru トリル (music).

trilogy, *n.* sanbusaku 三部作.

trim, 1. *adj.* kichin to shita きちん
とした (neat). 2. *vb.* kichin to
suru きちんとする (make tidy);
kichin to karu きちんと刈る
(make neat by cutting); kazaru 飾
る (ornament).

trio, *n.* torio トリオ; sanjūsō 三重
奏 (music).

trip, 1. *n.* ryokō 旅行 (journey);
tsumazuki つまずき (stumble). 2.
vb. tsumazuku つまずく
(stumble); tsumazukaseru つまず
かせる (cause to stumble);
shikujiru しくじる (make a
mistake).

tripe, *n.* garakuta がらくた
(worthless thing).

triple, *adj.* sanbai (no) 三倍 (の)
(three times as great); sanjū (no)
三重 (の) (threefold).

triplets, *n.* mitsugo 三つ子 (three
offspring born at one birth).

tripod, *n.* sankyaku 三脚.

trite, *adj.* chinpu (na) 陳腐 (な);
arifureta ありふれた (banal).

triumph, 1. *n.* shōri 勝利 (victory
or success). 2. *vb.* shōri suru 勝利
する; uchikatsu 打ち勝つ (be
victorious).

triumphant, *adj.* shōri (no) 勝利
(の) (victorious).

trivia, *n.* kudaranai mono/koto 下
らない物／事 (inconsequential
things or matters).

trivial, *adj.* 1. toru ni tarinai 取るに
足りない (insignificant). 2.

arifureta ありふれた (ordinary).

trolley, *n*. shigaidensha 市街電車 (streetcar).

troop, *n*. 1. gurūpu グループ; ichidan 一団 (group). 2. **troops** guntai 軍隊.

trophy, *n*. torofī トロフィー.

tropical, *adj*. nettai (no) 熱帯 (の) (of the tropics).

tropic, *n*. kaikisen 回帰線 (parallel of latitude).

tropics, *n*. nettai 熱帯.

trot, *vb*. sassa to aruku さっさと歩く (walk briskly).

trouble, 1. *n*. kon'nan 困難 (difficulty); kurō 苦労 (distress); mondai 問題 (annoyance, problem); mendō 面倒 (inconvenience); shinpai 心配 (worry); kiken 危険 (danger); **be in trouble** komatteiru 困っている. 2. *vb*. shinpai saseru 心配させる (cause to be worried); mendō o kakeru 面倒をかける (cause inconvenience to); kurushimeru 苦しめる (cause pain to).

troublemaker, *n*. toraburumēkā トラブルメーカー.

troublesome, *adj*. yakkai (na) 厄介 (な); muzukashii 難しい.

trough, *n*. esabako 餌箱 (food container); mizuire 水入れ (water container).

trounce, *vb*. uchinomesu 打ちのめす (beat severely).

trousers, *n*. zubon ズボン; surakkusu スラックス.

trousseau, *n*. yomeiridōgu 嫁入り道具.

trout, *n*. masu ます.

trowel, *n*. kote こて.

truant, *adj*. mudankessekisha 無断欠席者 (of a student).

truce, *n*. kyūsen 休戦.

truck, *n*. torakku トラック (vehicle); **truck driver** torakku-untenshu トラック運転手.

trudge, *vb*. tobo-tobo aruku とぼとぼ歩く (walk wearily).

true, *adj*. 1. hontō (no) 本当 (の) (actual, sincere, genuine). 2. jissai (no) 実際 (の) (actual). 3. honmono (no) 本物 (の) (real, genuine). 4. seijitsu (na) 誠実 (な) (sincere). 5. seikaku (na) 正確 (な) (exact). 6. **come true** jitsugen suru 実現する; **be true to** ... ni chūjitsu de aru ...に忠実である.

true-life, *adj*. jijitsu ni motozuku 事実に基づく.

truly, *adv*. hontō ni 本当に (sincerely, really); **yours truly** keigu 敬具 (in complimentary close of letter).

trumpet, *n*. toranpetto トランペット.

trunk, *n*. toranku トランク (for traveling, of a car); miki 幹 (of a tree); dō(tai) 胴(体) (of a human body); hana 鼻 (of an elephant).

trust, 1. *n*. shinrai 信頼; shin'yō 信用 (belief); sekinin 責任 (responsibility); sewa 世話 (care). 2. *vb*. shinrai suru 信頼する; shin'yō suru 信用する (believe, have faith in); ate ni suru 当てにする (rely on); makaseru 任せる (entrust); tayoru 頼る.

trustworthy, *adj*. shin'yō dekiru 信用出来る.

truth, *n*. 1. shinjitsu 真実 (true fact). 2. shinjitsusei 真実性 (quality of being true). 3. seijitsusa 誠実さ (sincerity). 4. shinri 真理 (principle, concept). 5. **in truth** hontō ni 本当に; **to tell the truth** jitsu wa 実は.

truthful, *adj.* 1. shinjitsu (no) 真実 (の) (conforming to truth). 2. shōjiki (na) 正直 (な) (telling the truth).

try, 1. *n.* kokoromi 試み (attempt); doryoku 努力 (effort). 2. *vb.* tamesu 試す (test); kokoromiru 試みる (attempt); doryoku suru 努力する (make an effort); saiban ni kakeru 裁判にかける (examine judically); **try on** ... o kite miru ...を着てみる (try on a garment); **try to do** ... shiyō to suru ... しようとする.

trying, *adj.* taihen (na) 大変 (な) (difficult).

tryout, *n.* shien 試演 (theater).

tryst, *n.* aibiki 逢い引き (meeting of lovers).

T-shirt, *n.* tī-shatsu ティーシャツ.

tub, *n.* 1. oke 桶 (wide, round container). 2. furo'oke 風呂桶 (bathtub).

tube, *n.* 1. chūbu チューブ (container for toothpaste, oil paint, etc.). 2. kuda 管 (very narrow pipe: test tube, etc.); tsutsu 筒; paipu パイプ (comparatively wider pipe, drainage pipe).

tuberculosis, *n.* kekkaku 結核.

tuck, 1. *n.* takku タック (fold). 2. *vb.* oshikomu 押し込む (thrust); tsumekomu 詰め込む (cram).

Tuesday, *n.* kayōbi 火曜日.

tuft, *n.* fusa 房 (bunch).

tug, *vb.* 1. hipparu 引っ張る (pull hard). 2. hikizuru 引きずる (move by pulling).

tugboat, *n.* taggubōto タッグボート.

tuition, *n.* jugyōryō 授業料 (fee).

tulip, *n.* chūrippu チューリップ.

tumble, *vb.* 1. korogaru 転がる (roll). 2. ochiru 落ちる (fall). 3. tsumazuku つまずく (stumble).

tummy, *n.* hara 腹; onaka お腹.

tumor, *n.* shuyō 腫瘍.

tumult, *n.* sōdō 騒動 (commotion); konran 混乱 (confusion).

tuna, *n.* maguro 鮪.

tune, 1. *n.* merodī メロディー; kyoku 曲 (melody); tadashii chōshi 正しい調子 (proper condition); **in/out of tune** oto ga atte/hazurete 音が合って／外れて (music); **in/out of tune with** ... ni au/awanai に合う／合わない (compatible/incompatible with). 2. *vb.* chōritsu suru 調律する (adjust musical instrument); chōsetsu suru 調節する (adjust a motor, etc.); **tune in** chan'neru o awaseru チャンネルを合わせる (TV).

tunnel, *n.* ton'neru トンネル.

turbulent, *adj.* hageshii 激しい (violent); arekuru'u 荒れ狂う (stormy).

turf, *n.* shibafu 芝生 (grassy earth).

turkey, *n.* shichimenchō 七面鳥.

turmoil, *n.* sōdō 騒動 (tumult); konran 混乱 (confusion).

turn, 1. *n.* kaiten 回転 (revolution, rotation, twirl); henka 変化 (change); ban 番 (shift); keikō 傾向 (inclination); **at every turn** itsumo いつも (at every moment); **in turn** junban ni 順番に (in due order); **take turns** kōtai de suru 交代でする. 2. *vb.* mawaru 回る (move around); mawasu 回す (cause to move around, as a faucet); magaru 曲がる (at corner); kawaru 変わる (change). 3. **turn around** furimuku 振り向く; **turn back** kaeru/kaesu 返る／返す (return/cause to return);

turn down kotowaru 断る (reject); **turn in** teishutsu suru 提出する (submit); **turn into** ... ni naru ...になる (become); **turn off** kesu 消す (gas, light, etc.); shimeru 閉める (faucet); **turn on** tsukeru 点ける (gas, light, etc.); **turn out to be ...** kekkyoku ... to naru 結局...となる (become ultimately); **turn to the right** migi ni magaru 右に曲がる; **turn up** tsuku 着く (arrive).

turncoat, *n.* uragirimono 裏切り者.

turning point, *n.* tenki 転機.

turnip, *n.* kabu かぶ.

turnover, *n.* 1. kaiten 回転 (act of turning over). 2. uriagedaka 売り上げ高 (total amount of business done in a given time). 3. rōdōsha-idōritsu 労働者移動率 (rate of replacement of employees); shōhin-kaitenritsu 商品回転率 (rate of replacement of goods).

turntable, *n.* kaitenban 回転板; tāntēburu ターンテーブル (of record player).

turpitude, *n.* harenchi はれんち.

turquoise, *n.* toruko-ishi トルコ石 (gemstone).

turret, *n.* hōtō 砲塔 (on tank, warship).

turtle, *n.* kame 亀.

turtledove, *n.* kijibato 雉子鳩.

tusk, *n.* kiba 牙.

tussle, *n.* tsukamiai 摑み合い.

tutelage, *n.* 1. kōken 後見 (guardianship). 2. hogo 保護 (protection).

tutor, 1. *n.* kateikyōshi 家庭教師 (private tutor). 2. *vb.* oshieru 教える.

tuxedo, *n.* takishīdo タキシード.

twang, *n.* 1. gen no oto 弦の音 (sound of a string instrument). 2. hanagoe 鼻声 (nasal sound).

tweezers, *n.* kenuki 毛抜き.

twelve, *n.* jūni 十二.

twenty, *n.* nijū 二十.

twice, *adv.* 1. nido 二度; nikai 二回 (two times). 2. nibai ni 二倍に (in twofold quantity).

twig, *n.* koeda 小枝.

twilight, *n.* yūgure 夕暮れ (dim light of the early evening).

twin, *n.* futago 双子 (one of two offspring born at the same time).

twin bed, *n.* tsuin(-beddo) ツイン(ベッド).

twine, 1. *n.* himo 紐 (cord). 2. *vb.* makitsuku 巻き付く (wind around); yoru よる (twist together).

twinge, *n.* 1. itami 痛み (pain). 2. ryōshin no kashaku 良心の呵責 (qualm).

twinkle, 1. *n.* kirameki きらめき; matataki 瞬き (brightness). 2. *vb.* kirameku きらめく; matataku 瞬く (shine).

twirl, 1. *n.* kyūkaiten 急回転 (sudden spin). 2. *vb.* kyūkaiten suru 急回転する (spin); maku 巻く (curl).

twist, 1. *n.* magari 曲がり (curve); kaiten 回転 (spin); waikyoku 歪曲 (distortion, as of meaning); igai na tenkai 以外な展開 (unexpected development). 2. *vb.* yoriawaseru より合わせる (combine by winding); yugameru 歪める (distort); makitsukeru 巻き付ける (wind around something); magaru 曲がる (bend, wind about); mageru 曲げる (cause to bend); mawasu 回す (turn).

twitch, 1. *n.* hikitsuri 引きつり (tic); keiren けいれん (spasm); kyū na hiki 急な引き (sudden pull). 2. *vb.* hikitsuru 引きつる; keiren suru けいれんする (contract); piku-piku ugokasu ぴくぴく動かす (pull with a jerking movement); kyū ni hiku 急に引く (pull suddenly).

two, *n.* ni 二; futatsu 二つ.

twofold, *adj.* 1. nijū (no) 二重 (の) (having two parts). 2. nibai (no) 二倍 (の) (twice as much).

two hundred, *n.* nihyaku 二百.

twosome, *n.* futari-hitokumi 二人一組.

tycoon, *n.* ōdatemono 大立て者.

type, *n.* 1. katsuji 活字; taipu タイプ (printing). 2. shurui 種類 (kind, class). 3. mihon 見本; tenkei 典型 (representative specimen).

typewrite, *vb.* taipu(raitā) o utsu タイプ(ライター)を打つ.

typewriter, *n.* taipuraitā タイプライター.

typhoon, *n.* taifū 台風.

typical, *adj.* tenkei-teki (na) 典型的 (な).

typing, *n.* taipingu タイピング.

typist, *n.* taipisuto タイピスト.

tyranny, *n.* 1. bōgyaku 暴虐 (despotic abuse). 2. assei 圧政 (despotism).

tyrant, *n.* bōkun 暴君.

U

ubiquitous, *adj.* achikochi ni aru あちこちにある.

udder, *n.* chichi 乳; chibusa 乳房.

ugliness, *n.* minikusa 醜さ.

ugly, *adj.* minikui 醜い (ugly to the sight).

ulcer, *n.* kaiyō 潰瘍.

ulterior, *adj.* 1. kakusareta 隠された (concealed). 2. ato no 後の (later).

ultimate, *adj.* 1. saigo (no) 最後 (の) (final). 2. kyūkyoku (no) 究極 (の) (highest). 3. konpon-teki (na) 根本的 (な) (basic).

ultimatum, *n.* saishūtsūkoku 最終通告 (final demand).

ultra-, chō- 超-, sai- 最-; **ultraleft** saisayoku 最左翼.

ultraviolet rays, *n.* shigaisen 紫外線.

umbrella, *n.* kasa 傘.

umpire, *n.* anpaia アンパイア; shinpan 審判.

unabashed, *adj.* heizentaru 平然たる.

unable, *adj.* (... koto ga) dekinai (... ことが) 出来ない.

unabridged, *adj.* kanzen (na) 完全 (な).

unaccustomed, *adj.* 1. funare (na) 不慣れ (な) (unfamiliar). 2. ijō (na) 異常 (な) (unusual).

unanimous, *adj.* manjōitchi (no) 満場一致 (の); kanzengōi (no) 完全合意 (の).

unapproachable, *adj.* chikayori-gatai 近寄りがたい (unfriendly).

unarmed, *adj.* bukinashi (no) 武器無し (の).

unavoidable, *adj.* sakerarenai 避けられない; yamu o enai やむを得ない.

unaware, *adj.* kizukanai 気付かない.

unawares, *adv.* kizukazu ni 気付かずに; shiranai de 知らないで.

unbalanced, *adj.* fukinkō (na) 不均衡 (な); fuantei (na) 不安定 (な); katayotta 片寄った.

unbearable, *adj.* gaman dekinai 我慢出来ない; taerarenai 耐えられない.

unbelievable, *adj.* shinjirarenai 信じられない.

uncertain, *adj.* 1. futashika (na) 不確か (な); hakkiri shinai はっきりしない (unclear, changeable). 2. ate ni dekinai 当てに出来ない (unreliable).

unchanged, *adj.* fuhen (no) 不変 (の); kawaranai 変わらない.

uncivilized, *adj.* yaban (na) 野蛮 (な).

uncle, *n.* oji(san) 伯父(さん).

uncomfortable, *adj.* fukai (na) 不快 (な); iya (na) 嫌 (な).

uncommitted, *adj.* gimu/sekinin ga nai 義務／責任がない.

uncommon, *adj.* 1. mezurashii 珍しい (unusual). 2. hibon (na) 非凡 (な) (outstanding).

unconditional, *adj.* 1. mujōken (no) 無条件 (の) (without conditions). 2. museigen (no) 無制限 (の) (without reservations).

unconscious, 1. *n.* muishiki 無意識 (the unconscious). 2. *adj.* muishiki (no) 無意識 (の).

unconsciousness, *n.* muishiki 無意識.

unconstitutional, *adj.* kenpōihan (no) 憲法違反 (の).

uncontrollable, *adj.* te ni oenai 手に負えない.

uncooked, *adj.* nama (no) 生 (の).

uncouth, *adj.* 1. soya (na) 粗野 (な) (clumsy). 2. burei (na) 無礼 (な) (rude).

uncover, *vb.* 1. futa o toru 蓋を取る (remove lid). 2. arawasu 現わす (reveal).

undamaged, *adj.* mukizu (no) 無傷 (の); buji (na) 無事 (な).

undecided, *adj.* mitei/miketsu (no) 未定／未決 (の).

undefeatable, *adj.* muteki (no) 無敵 (の).

undeniable, *adj.* tashika/meihaku (na) 確か／明白 (な).

under, *prep.* ... no shita de/ni ...の下で／に (beneath, below); ... yori ika/shita (no) ...より以下／下 (の) (less than, lower than); ... no moto de/ni ...のもとで／に (subject to condition, influence, etc., of; protected or watched by; during the rule of); ... chū de ...中で (in the process of).

undercover, *adj.* 1. himitsu (no) 秘密 (の) (clandestine). 2. supai (no) スパイ (の) (acting as a spy).

undercut, *vb.* 1. ... yori yasuku uru ...より安く売る (sell cheaper than...); ... yori yasuku hataraku ...より安く働く (work cheaper than...). 2. sokonau 損なう (injure).

underdeveloped country, *n.* hattentojōkoku 発展途上国.

underdog, *n.* 1. makeinu 負け犬 (loser). 2. giseisha 犠牲者 (victim).

underestimate, *vb.* kashōhyōka suru 過小評価する.

undergo, *vb.* 1. taeru 耐える (endure). 2. keiken suru 経験する (experience).

undergraduate, *n.* daigakusei 大学生; gakubusei 学部生.

underground, 1. *n.* chika 地下 (place); chikasoshiki 地下組織 (resistance group); chikatetsu 地下鉄 (subway system). 2. *adj.* chika (no) 地下 (の) (under the ground, hidden); himitsu (no) 秘密 (の) (secret); zen'ei (no) 前衛 (の) (avant-garde).

underhand, *adj.* koso-koso shita こそこそした; naimitsu (no) 内密 (の) (stealthy).

underlie, *vb.* 1. ... no shita ni aru ...の下にある (lie beneath). 2. ... no moto ni naru ...の元になる (be basis of).

underline, *vb.* 1. kasen o hiku 下線を引く; andārain o hiku アンダーラインを引く (mark). 2. kyōchō suru 強調する (stress).

underling, *n.* shitappa 下っ端.

underlying, *adj.* 1. shita ni yokotawatte-iru 下に横たわっている (lying beneath). 2. kihon-teki (na) 基本的 (な) (basic).

undermine, *vb.* sokonau 損なう; kizutsukeru 傷つける (injure).

underneath, 1. *adv.* shita ni 下に. 2. *prep.* ... no shita ni/de ...の下に／で.

undernourished, *adj.* eiyōbusoku (no) 栄養不足 (の).

underpants, *n.* pantsu パンツ.

underpay, *vb.* yasuku hatarakaseru 安く働かせる.

underprivileged, *adj.* shakai-teki ni furi (na) 社会的に不利 (な) (socially disadvantaged); mazushii 貧しい (poor); kasōkaikyū (no) 下層階級 (の) (of the lower classes).

underrate, *vb.* kashōhyōka suru 過小評価する.

undersea, *adj.* kaitei (no) 海底 (の); kaichū (no) 海中 (の).

undershirt, *n.* andāshatsu アンダーシャツ; hadagi 肌着.

understaffed, *adj.* hitodebusoku (no) 人手不足 (の).

understand, *vb.* 1. wakaru 分かる; rikai suru 理解する (know

meaning, sympathize). 2. shōchi suru 承知する (accept).

understandable, *adj.* nattoku/rikai dekiru 納得／理解出来る.

understate, *vb.* waribiki shite iu 割り引きして言う.

undertake, *vb.* 1. kokoromiru 試みる (attempt). 2. hikiukeru 引き受ける (take upon oneself, take in charge). 3. ukeau 請け合う (warrant). 4. yakusoku suru 約束する (promise).

undertaker, *n.* sōgiya 葬儀屋 (funeral director).

undertaking, *n.* 1. jigyō 事業 (enterprise). 2. shigoto 仕事 (task). 3. yakusoku 約束 (promise).

undervalue, *vb.* kashōhyōka suru 過小評価する.

underwear, *n.* shitagi 下着; hadagi 肌着.

underworld, *n.* ankokugai 暗黒街; hanzaisoshiki 犯罪組織 (criminal element).

underwrite, *vb.* hoshō suru 保証する (guarantee).

undesirable, *adj.* nozomashikunai 望ましくない.

undeveloped, *adj.* mikaihatsu (no) 未開発 (の); mikaitaku (no) 未開拓 (の).

undo, *vb.* 1. moto ni modosu 元に戻す (return to original state). 2. hodoku 解く; hazusu 外す (unfasten, untie); akeru 開ける (open). 3. hametsu saseru 破滅させる (bring to ruin).

undone, *adj.* mikansei (no) 未完成 (の) (not completed).

undoubtedly, *adv.* machigainaku 間違いなく.

undress, *vb.* kimono o nugu 着物を脱ぐ (remove one's clothing);

kimono o nugaseru 着物を脱がせる (remove clothing of).

unearned, *adj.* furōshotoku (no) 不労所得 (の) (not earned by work).

unearth, *vb.* 1. horidasu 掘り出す (dig out). 2. mitsukeru 見つける (discover).

uneasy, *adj.* fuan (na) 不安 (な); ochitsukanai 落ち着かない.

unemployed, *adj.* mushoku (no) 無職 (の); shitsugyō (no) 失業 (の).

unemployment, *n.* mushoku 無職; shitsugyō 失業.

unemployment benefit, *n.* shitsugyōteate 失業手当て.

unemployment insurance, *n.* shitsugyōhoken 失業保険.

unequal, *adj.* 1. fuzoroi (no) 不揃い (の); futsuriai (no) 不釣り合い (の) (uneven, disproportionate). 2. tarinai 足りない (inadequate).

unessential, *adj.* dōdemo ii どうでも良い; honshitsu-teki ja nai 本質的じゃない.

uneven, *adj.* 1. dekoboko (no) でこぼこ (の) (not flat). 2. fuzoroi (no) 不揃い (の) (irregular). 3. kisū (no) 奇数 (の) (number).

unexpected, *adj.* omoigakenai 思いがけない; yosōgai (no) 予想外 (の) (unforeseen).

unfair, *adj.* fukōhei (na) 不公平 (な) (not just).

unfaithful, *adj.* 1. fuchūjitsu (na) 不忠実 (な) (not loyal). 2. fujitsu (na) 不実 (な) (adulterous). 3. fuseikaku (na) 不正確 (な) (not accurate).

unfamiliar, *adj.* 1. shiranai 知らない (unacquainted). 2. funare (na, no) 不慣れ (な、の) (unused to). 3. mezurashii 珍しい (unusual).

unfavorable, *adj.* 1. furi (na) 不利 (な) (disadvantageous). 2. konomashikunai 好ましくない (undesirable).

unfinished, *adj.* mikan(sei) (no) 未完(成) (の).

unfit, *adj.* awanai 合わない; futekitō (na) 不適当 (な).

unfold, *vb.* akeru 開ける; hiraku 開く.

unforeseen, *adj.* yosōgai (no) 予想外 (の); furyo (no) 不慮 (の).

unforgettable, *adj.* wasure-rarenai 忘れられない.

unforgivable, *adj.* yurushigatai 許し難い.

unfortunate, *adj.* fu'un (na) 不運 (な); zan'nen (na) 残念 (な).

unfortunately, *adv.* ainiku あいにく; unwaruku 運悪く.

unfriendly, *adj.* aisō ga warui 愛想が悪い; tsumetai 冷たい.

unfurnished, *adj.* kagunashi (no) 家具なし (の).

ungrammatical, *adj.* bunpō ni awanai 文法に合わない.

ungrateful, *adj.* onshirazu (no) 恩知らず (の).

unhappy, *adj.* fushiawase (na) 不幸せ (な); fukō (na) 不幸 (な).

unharmed, *adj.* buji (na) 無事 (な).

unhealthy, *adj.* 1. fukenkō (na) 不健康 (な) (physically unhealthy). 2. fukenzen (na) 不健全 (な) (morally corrupt).

uniform, 1. *n.* seifuku 制服; yunifōmu ユニフォーム. 2. *adj.* kin'itsu (no) 均一 (の); kakuitsu-teki (na) 画一的 (な).

uniformity, *n.* kin'itsusei 均一性.

unify, *vb.* hitotsu ni suru 一つにする (make a single unit); hitotsu ni naru 一つになる (become a single unit).

unilateral, *adj.* katagawa dake (no) 片側だけ (の); ippō dake (no) 一方だけ (の).

unimaginable, *adj.* sōzō dekinai 想像出来ない; kangaerarenai 考えられない.

unimportant, *adj.* dōdemo ii どうでも良い; jūyō de nai 重要でない.

unintelligible, *adj.* wakaranai 分からない; rikai dekinai 理解出来ない.

unintentional, *adj.* muishiki (no) 無意識 (の).

uninteresting, *adj.* omoshirokunai 面白くない; tsumaranai つまらない.

union, *n.* 1. yunion ユニオン; rōdō-kumiai 労働組合 (labor). 2. ketsugō 結合 (uniting).

unique, *adj.* yunīku (na) ユニーク (な); dokutoku (na/no) 独特 (な／の).

unisex, *adj.* unisekkusu (no) ユニセックス (の); danjoryōyō (no) 男女両用 (の).

unison, *n.* 1. yunizon ユニゾン; seishō 斉唱 (chorus). 2. chōwa 調和 (harmony).

unit, *n.* yunitto ユニット; tan'i 単位.

unite, *vb.* hitotsu ni suru 一つにする (make into one); hitotsu ni naru 一つになる (become one).

United Nations, *n.* koku(sai)ren(gō) 国(際)連(合).

United States, *n.* amerika-gasshūkoku アメリカ合衆国; beikoku 米国.

unity, *n.* 1. tan'itsusei 単一性 (oneness). 2. matomari まとまり; chōwa 調和; tōitsu 統一 (harmonious combination).

universal, *adj.* 1. zenbu (no) 全部 (の) (of all). 2. ippan (no) 一般 (の) (general). 3. fuhen-teki (na) 普遍的 (な) (existing everywhere). 4. uchū (no) 宇宙 (の) (of the universe); sekai (no) 世界 (の) (of the world).

universe, *n.* 1. uchū 宇宙 (cosmos). 2. zensekai 全世界 (whole world).

university, *n.* daigaku 大学.

unjust, *adj.* 1. fusei (na) 不正 (な); futō (na) 不当 (な) (not right). 2. fukōhei (na) 不公平 (な) (unfair).

unjustifiable, *adj.* benkai dekinai 弁解出来ない (inexcusable).

unkempt, *adj.* 1. moja-moja (no) もじゃもじゃ (の) (disheveled). 2. midareta 乱れた (messy).

unkind, *adj.* tsumetai 冷たい; fushinsetsu (na) 不親切 (な).

unknowable, *adj.* shiru koto ga dekinai 知ることが出来ない.

unknown, *adj.* 1. michi (no) 未知 (の) (not known, not explored). 2. mumei (no) 無名 (の) (obscure).

unlawful, *adj.* ihō/fuhō (no) 違法／不法 (の).

unleash, *vb.* 1. toku 解く (let loose). 2. kaihō suru 解放する (release).

unless, *conj.* ... de nakereba ... でなければ; ... (shi)nakereba ... (し)なければ.

unlike, 1. *adj.* chigau 違う; kotonaru 異なる (different). 2. *prep.* ... to chigau/kotonaru ...と違う／異なる (different from); ... rashikunai ...らしくない (not typical of).

unlikely, *adj.* arisō ni nai ありそうにない; muri (na) 無理 (な).

unlimited, *adj.* museigen (no) 無制限 (の).

unload, *vb.* ni o orosu 荷を下ろす (remove cargo).

unlock, *vb.* 1. kagi o akeru 鍵を開ける (undo lock). 2. akeru 開ける; hiraku 開く (open).

unlucky, *adj.* un ga warui 運が悪い; fu'un (na) 不運 (な).

unmanageable, *adj.* te ni oenai 手に負えない.

unmarried, *adj.* dokushin (no) 独身 (の); mikon (no) 未婚 (の).

unmask, *vb.* 1. kamen o toru 仮面を取る (strip mask). 2. arawasu 現わす (disclose).

unmistakable, *adj.* akiraka (na) 明らか (な); machigai (ga) nai 間違い (が) 無い.

unnatural, *adj.* fushizen (na) 不自然 (な).

unnecessary, *adj.* iranai 要らない; fuhitsuyō (na) 不必要 (な).

unnoticed, *adj.* kizuka(re)nai 気付か(れ)ない.

unofficial, *adj.* hikōshiki (no) 非公式 (の).

unpack, *vb.* ni o toku 荷を解く; nakami o toridasu 中身を取り出す.

unpaid, *adj.* miharai (no) 未払い (の).

unparalleled, *adj.* zendaimimon (no) 前代未聞 (の).

unpleasant, *adj.* fukai (na) 不快 (な).

unpopular, *adj.* funinki (no) 不人気 (の).

unprecedented, *adj.* zendai-mimon (no) 前代未聞 (の).

unpredictable, *adj.* yochi dekinai 予知出来ない.

unprejudiced, *adj.* henken ga nai 偏見がない.

unpretentious, *adj.* shizen (na) 自然 (な); sunao (na) 素直 (な).

unproductive, *adj.* hiseisan-teki (na) 非生産的 (な).

unprofessional, *adj.* puro-rashikunai プロらしくない (improper).

unprofitable, *adj.* rieki ni naranai 利益にならない; mueki (na, no) 無益 (な、の).

unpublished, *adj.* 1. happyō sarete-inai 発表されていない (not printed). 2. shirasarete-inai 知らされていない (not made known).

unqualified, *adj.* shikaku ga nai 資格がない.

unquestionable, *adj.* utagainai 疑いない.

unravel, *vb.* toku 解く (disentangle, solve).

unreal, *adj.* 1. sonzai shinai 存在しない (not existing). 2. kakū/sōzō (no) 架空／想像 (の) (imaginary). 3. nise (no) 偽 (の) (false).

unrealistic, *adj.* higenjitsu-teki (na) 非現実的 (な).

unreasonable, *adj.* 1. fugōri (na) 不合理 (な) (irrational). 2. hōgai (na) 法外 (な) (exorbitant).

unreliable, *adj.* ate ni naranai 当てにならない; shinrai dekinai 信頼出来ない.

unrequited love, *n.* kataomoi 片思い.

unrest, *n.* fuan 不安.

unruly, *adj.* te ni oenai 手に負えない.

unsafe, *adj.* abunai 危ない; kiken (na) 危険 (な).

unscientific, *adj.* hikagaku-teki (na) 非科学的 (な).

unscrupulous, *adj.* sessō no nai 節操のない; iikagen (na) 好い加減 (な).

unselfish, *adj.* mushimuyoku (no) 無私無欲 (の); hito ga ii 人が良い.

unsettled, *adj.* 1. fukakutei (na) 不
確定 (な) (not fixed). 2.
ochitsukanai 落ち着かない;
kawariyasui 変わり易い
(constantly changing).

unskilled, *adj.* mijukuren (no) 未
熟練 (の).

unstable, *adj.* fuantei (na) 不安定
(な).

unsuccessful, *adj.* shippai (no) 失
敗 (の).

unsuitable, *adj.* tekisanai 適さな
い; futekitō (na) 不適当 (な).

untie, *vb.* toku 解く; hodoku 解く.

until, 1. *prep.* ... made ... まで. 2.
conj. ... suru made ... するまで.

untrue, *adj.* uso (no) 嘘 (の).

unusual, *adj.* kawatta 変わった;
mezurashii 珍しい (uncommon).

unvoiced, *adj.* mugon (no) 無言
(の).

unwelcome, *adj.* kangei sarenai 歓
迎されない; meiwaku (na) 迷惑
(な).

unwell, *adj.* 1. kibun ga warui 気分
が悪い (not well). 2. byōki (no)
病気 (の) (ill).

unwilling, *adj.* ki ga susumanai 気
が進まない; iya-iyanagara (no)
嫌々ながら (の); **unwilling to do**
... suru no/koto ga iya ...するの／
ことが嫌.

unwitting, *adj.* kizukanai 気付かな
い; shiranai 知らない.

unworthy, *adj.* fusawashikunai ふ
さわしくない; atai shinai 値しな
い.

up, 1. *adv.* ue de/e/ni 上で／へ／に
(to or in a higher place); agatte 上
がって (high); okite 起きて (out of
bed); nobotte 昇って (above the
horizon); **come up** nobottekuru
昇って来る; **Get up.** Okite
kudasai. 起きて下さい. **Stand up.**

Tachiagatte kudasai. 立ち上がって
下さい. 2. *prep.* ... no ue de/e/ni
...の上で／へ／に (up onto or
into); ue no hō ni 上の方に
(upward). 3. **be up** okiteiru 起き
ている (out of bed); **be up to
(someone)** ... shidai de aru ...次
第である; **What's up?**
Dōshitano. どうしたの.

upbringing, *n.* sodachi 育ち.

update, *vb.* saishin no mono ni
suru 最新の物にする (update
something).

upgrade, *vb.* kōjō saseru 向上させ
る (improve).

upheaval, *n.* hendō 変動.

uphold, *vb.* 1. mamoru 守る
(defend). 2. shiji suru 支持する;
sasaeru 支える (support).

upholsterer, *n.* isu no kiji harikae-
shokunin 椅子の生地張り替え職
人.

upon, *prep.* ... no ue de/e/ni ...の上
で／へ／に.

upper, *adj.* (... yori) ue no (...より)
上の; motto takai もっと高い.

upper-class, *adj.* jōryūkaikyū (no)
上流階級 (の).

upper hand, *n.* yūri 有利; yūsei 優
勢.

upright, *adj.* 1. tate (no) 縦 (の);
suichoku (no) 垂直 (の) (erect). 2.
shōjiki (na) 正直 (な) (righteous).

uprising, *n.* bōdō 暴動.

uproar, *n.* ōsawagi 大騒ぎ.

uproot, *vb.* nekosogi ni suru 根こ
そぎにする.

upset, 1. *n.* tentō 転倒
(overturning); igai na haiboku 意
外な敗北 (defeat). 2. *adj.* kōfun
shiteiru 興奮している (disturbed);
chōshi ga warui 調子が悪い
(slightly ill); **have an upset
stomach** i no chōshi ga warui 胃

の調子が悪い. 3. vb. kutsugaesu
覆す; hikkurikaesu ひっくり返す
(overturn); kōfun saseru 興奮させ
る (disturb someone); makasu 負
かす (defeat).

upside down, adv. sakasama ni 逆
さまに.

upstairs, adv. nikai (de/e/ni) 二階
(で／へ／に) (on or to the second
floor); ue no kai (de/e/ni) 上の階
(で／へ／に) (on or to an upper
floor).

up-to-date, adj. saishin (no) 最新
(の).

upward, adv. ue ni 上に; ue ni
mukatte 上に向かって.

uranium, n. uraniumu ウラニウ
ム.

urban, adj. tokai (no) 都会 (の);
machi (no) 町 (の).

urchin, n. 1. wanpaku 腕白; gaki
餓鬼 (child). 2. uni うに
(seafood).

urge, 1. n. shōdō 衝動 (impulse).
2. vb. segamu せがむ (persuade);
sekitateru 急き立てる (force);
iiharu 言い張る (insist).

urgency, n. kinkyū 緊急.

urgent, adj. kinkyū (no) 緊急 (の).

urinal, n. 1. danseiyō'otearai 男性
用お手洗 (men's room). 2.
shōbenki 小便器 (urinal).

urinate, vb. nyō/oshikko/shōben o
suru 尿／おしっこ／小便をする.

urine, n. nyō 尿; shōben 小便;
oshikko おしっこ.

urn, n. tsubo 壺; kame 瓶.

us, pron. watashitachi (o/ni) 私達
(を／に); ware-ware (o/ni) 我々
(を／に); **with us** watashitachi to
issho ni 私達と一緒に.

usage, n. 1. shūkan 習慣 (custom).
2. atsukai 扱い; yōhō 用法
(treatment). 3. kan'yōgohō 慣用

語法 (customary usage of words).

use, 1. n. shiyō 使用 (act of using);
shiyōhō 使用法 (way of using);
shiyōmokuteki 使用目的 (purpose
for which something is used);
riyō-kachi 利用価値 (usefulness);
it's no use muda (desu/da) 無駄
(です／だ); **in use** tsukawarete-
iru 使われている; **out of use**
tsukawarete-inai 使われていない;
sutareta 廃れた. 2. vb. tsukau 使
う; riyō suru 利用する (utilize);
use up tsukaihatasu 使い果たす;
used to do ... mukashi yoku ...
shita mono datta/deshita 昔よく...
したものだった／でした.

used, adj. 1. chūko (no) 中古 (の)
(secondhand); **used car** chūkosha
中古車. 2. nareta 慣れた
(accustomed); **be used to** ... ni
narete iru ... に慣れている; **get
used to** ... ni nareru ... に慣れる.

useful, adj. yaku ni tatsu 役に立つ;
benri (na) 便利 (な).

usefulness, n. benrisa 便利さ;
jitsuyōsei 実用性.

useless, adj. yaku ni tatanai 役に立
たない.

user, n. shiyōsha 使用者.

usher, 1. n. an'naigakari 案内係. 2.
vb. **usher in** michibiku 導く.

usual, adj. 1. itsumo (no) いつも
(の) (customary); **as usual** itsumo
no yō ni いつものように. 2. futsū
(no) 普通 (の) (ordinary).

usurer, n. kōrigashi 高利貸し.

usurp, vb. 1. ubaitoru 奪い取る
(seize by force). 2. nusumitoru 盗
み取る (take unlawfully).

utensil, n. dōgu 道具; yōgu 用具.

uterus, n. shikyū 子宮.

utility, n. 1. benrisa 便利さ;
jitsuyōsei 実用性 (usefulness). 2.
kōkyōjigyō 公共事業 (public

service enterprise).

utilize, *vb.* tsukau 使う; riyō suru 利用する.

utmost, *adj.* ichiban (no) 一番 (の);
saidai (no) 最大 (の).

utter, 1. *adj.* mattaku (no) 全く (の). 2. *vb.* iu 言う.

utterance, *n.* hatsugen 発言.

V

vacancy, *n.* 1. akibeya 空き部屋 (vacant room); akichi 空き地 (vacant place). 2. ketsuin 欠員 (vacant position). 3. kūkyo 空虚 (emptiness).

vacant, *adj.* 1. aiteiru 空いている (not occupied or filled). 2. kara (no) 空 (の) (empty). 3. nai 無い (devoid). 4. bon'yari shita ぼんやりした (lacking in thought).

vacate, *vb.* 1. akeru 空ける (make vacant). 2. saru 去る (leave).

vacation, *n.* yasumi 休み; kyūka 休暇.

vaccinate, *vb.* yobōsesshu o suru 予防接種をする; wakuchin o suru ワクチンをする.

vaccine, *n.* yobōsesshu 予防接種; wakuchin ワクチン.

vacillate, *vb.* yureugoku 揺れ動く; guratsuku ぐらつく.

vacuum, *n.* shinkū 真空; kūhaku 空白.

vacuum cleaner, *n.* denkisōjiki 電気掃除機.

vagabond, *n.* 1. furōsha 浮浪者 (homeless person). 2. nagaremono 流れ者 (wanderer).

vagina, *n.* chitsu 膣.

vagrant, *n.* furōsha 浮浪者 (homeless person).

vague, *adj.* aimai (na) あいまい (な); bon'yari shita ぼんやりした; hakkiri shinai はっきりしない.

vain, *adj.* 1. unubore ga tsuyoi うぬぼれが強い (conceited). 2. muda (na) 無駄 (な); munashii 空しい (futile); **in vain** munashiku 空しく; muda ni 無駄に.

valet, *n.* bōi ボーイ (hotel).

valiant, *adj.* yūkan (na) 勇敢 (な).

valid, *adj.* 1. seitō (na) 正当 (な) (logical, sound). 2. yūkō (na) 有効 (な); tsūyō suru 通用する (effective).

validity, *n.* 1. seitōsei 正当性. 2. yūkō 有効; tsūyō 通用.

valley, *n.* tani 谷.

valor, *n.* yūki 勇気.

valuable, *adj.* kichō (na) 貴重 (な); kachi ga aru 価値がある.

value, 1. *n.* kachi 価値 (worth, importance); kakaku 価格 (price); hyōka 評価 (estimation). 2. *vb.* hyōka suru 評価する; ne o tsukeru 値を付ける (estimate); sonchō suru 尊重する (respect).

valve, *n.* barubu バルブ; ben 弁.

vampire, *n.* kyūketsuki 吸血鬼.

van, *n.* unsōsha 運送車 (moving van); ban バン (vehicle).

vandalize, *vb.* hakai suru 破壊する.

vanguard, *n.* 1. zen'ei 前衛 (army). 2. shidōsha/senkusha 指導者／先駆者 (movement leader).

vanish, *vb.* kieru 消える.

vanity, *n.* kyoei 虚栄; mie 見栄 (excessive pride).

vanquish, *vb.* datō suru 打倒する;

uchikatsu 打ち勝つ.

vapor, *n.* moya もや (haze); yuge 湯気; jōki 蒸気 (steam); kiri 霧 (mist).

variable, *adj.* kawariyasui 変わり易い.

variant, *n.* betsu no katachi 別の形; henkei 変形.

variation, *n.* 1. henka 変化 (change). 2. henkaryō 変化量 (amount of change). 3. henkei 変形 (variant).

variety, *n.* 1. tayōsei 多様性; henka 変化 (diversity). 2. iro-iro na koto 色々な事 (number of different things). 3. shurui 種類 (kind).

various, *adj.* 1. iro-iro (na, no) 色々 (な, の) (many, of different sorts). 2. ikutsuka (no) 幾つか (の) (several).

varnish, 1. *n.* (wa)nisu (ワ)ニス. 2. *vb.* nisu o nuru ニスを塗る.

vary, *vb.* 1. kawaru 変わる; henka suru 変化する (change). 2. kaeru 変える (cause to change). 3. chigau 違う (differ).

vase, *n.* 1. kabin 花瓶 (for flowers).

vast, *adj.* 1. kōdai (na) 広大 (な) (large and wide). 2. bōdai (na) 膨大 (な) (immense).

vat, *n.* taru 樽.

vault, *n.* 1. dōmu ドーム (dome). 2. maru tenjō 丸天井 (ceiling); maru yane 丸屋根 (roof). 3. chika-sōko 地下倉庫 (basement storage).

veal, *n.* koushi (no) niku 子牛 (の) 肉.

veer, *vb.* muki o kaeru 向きを変える.

vegetable, *n.* yasai 野菜 (food); shokubutsu 植物 (plant).

vegetarian, 1. *n.* saishoku-shugisha 菜食主義者. 2. *adj.*

saishoku (no) 菜食 (の).

vegetation, *n.* shokubutsu 植物.

vehement, *adj.* hageshii 激しい.

vehicle, *n.* 1. norimono 乗り物 (for transport). 2. shudan 手段 (means).

veil, 1. *n.* bēru ベール; ōi 覆い (covering). 2. *vb.* bēru o kakeru ベールをかける; ōu 覆う.

vein, *n.* 1. jōmyaku 静脈 (blood vessel). 2. mokume 木目 (wood grain).

velvet, *n.* berubetto ベルベット; birōdo ビロード.

velocity, *n.* sokudo 速度.

vendor, *n.* 1. urite 売り手. 2. rotenshō 露店商 (street vendor).

venerable, *adj.* tōtoi 尊い.

venerate, *vb.* tōtobu 尊ぶ; uyamau 敬う.

venereal, *adj.* seibyō (no) 性病 (の).

vengeance, *n.* fukushū 復讐.

venom, *n.* 1. dokueki 毒液 (liquid). 2. akui 悪意 (malice).

vent, 1. *n.* tsūkikō 通気孔; kanki-mado 換気窓 (opening for air, etc.); hakeguchi はけ口 (outlet for anger, etc.). 2. *vb.* hakidasu 吐き出す (express); dasu 出す (release).

ventilate, *vb.* kūki o tōsu/kaeru 空気を通す／換える.

ventilation, *n.* kanki 換気; tsūki 通気.

venture, 1. *n.* bōken 冒険 (undertaking); tōki 投機 (business venture). 2. *vb.* kakeru 賭ける (risk).

veracity, *n.* shinjitsusei 真実性.

veranda, *n.* beranda ベランダ.

verb, *n.* dōshi 動詞.

verbal, *adj.* 1. kotoba (no) 言葉 (の) (of words). 2. kōtō (no) 口頭

(の) (oral). 3. dōshi (no) 動詞 (の) (of verbs).

verbose, *adj.* kudoi くどい.

verdict, *n.* hanketsu 判決.

verge, 1. *n.* fuchi 縁; hashi 端; **on the verge of** ... sunzen (no) ... 寸前 (の); ... setogiwa (no) ... 瀬戸際 (の). 2. *vb.* (...ni/to) sessuru (... に／と) 接する; (...ni) chikazuku (...に) 近づく.

verify, *vb.* 1. shōmei suru 証明する (prove). 2. tashikameru 確める (ascertain).

versatile, *adj.* 1. tasai (na) 多才 (な) (multi-talented). 2. tamokuteki (no) 多目的 (の) (of many uses).

verse, *n.* shi 詩; inbun 韻文.

version, *n.* 1. hon'yaku 翻訳 (translation). 2. hanashi 話; kaishaku 解釈 (account, interpretation). 3. -ban -版 (different form, copy).

versus, *prep.* tai 対.

vertical, *adj.* suichoku (na, no) 垂直 (な、の); tate (no) 縦 (の).

very, 1. *adj.* onaji (no) 同じ (の) (same); hon (no) ほん (の) (mere); mattaku (no) 全く (の) (utter); shin (no) 真 (の) (true); jissai (no) 実際 (の) (actual). 2. *adv.* totemo とても; taihen 大変; hijō ni 非常に (in a high degree); chōdo 丁度; masani 正に (exactly).

vessel, *n.* 1. fune 船 (boat). 2. yōki 容器 (container). 3. kekkan 血管 (blood vessel).

vest, *n.* besuto ベスト; chokki チョッキ.

vestige, *n.* konseki 痕跡.

veteran, 1. *n.* taiekigunjin 退役軍人 (soldier); beteran ベテラン (experienced person). 2. *adj.*

jukuren shita 熟練した (experienced).

veterinarian, *n.* jūi 獣医.

veto, 1. *n.* kyohiken 拒否権 (official right); kinshi 禁止 (prohibition). 2. *vb.* kyohi suru 拒否する; kinshi suru 禁止する.

vex, *vb.* 1. okoraseru 怒らせる; ira-ira saseru いらいらさせる (irritate). 2. nayamaseru 悩ませる (trouble).

via, *prep.* 1. -keiyu de -経由で (by way of); **via Hawaii** hawai-keiyu de ハワイ経由で. 2. (...o) tōshite (...を) 通して; (...ni) yotte (...に) よって (by means of).

viable, *adj.* 1. sei'iku dekiru 成育出来る (capable of living). 2. jikkō dekiru 実行出来る (practicable).

viaduct, *n.* kōkakyō 高架橋.

vibrate, *vb.* yureru 揺れる; shindō suru 震動する.

vibration, *n.* shindō 震動.

vicarious, *adj.* 1. kansetsu-teki (na) 間接的 (な) (indirect). 2. dairi (no) 代理 (の) (substitute).

vice, *n.* 1. aku(toku) 悪(徳) (wickedness). 2. fuhinkō 不品行; fudōtoku 不道徳 (immoral conduct or habit). 3. ketten 欠点 (fault).

vice-, fuku- 副-; **vice-chairman** fuku-gichō 副議長; **vice president** fuku-daitōryō 副大統領.

vicinity, *n.* fukin 付近; kinjo 近所.

vicious, *adj.* 1. iji ga warui 意地が悪い; akui ni michita 悪意に満ちた (malicious). 2. daraku shita 堕落した (depraved). 3. dōmō (na) どうもう (な) (ferocious).

victim, *n.* giseisha 犠牲者; higaisha 被害者.

victimize, *vb.* gisei ni suru 犠牲に

する; kurushimeru 苦しめる.

victor, *n.* shōrisha 勝利者.

victorious, *adj.* shōri (no) 勝利 (の); kagayakashii 輝かしい.

victory, *n.* shōri 勝利.

video, *n.* bideo ビデオ.

videocassette, *n.* bideokasetto ビ デオカセット; **videocassette recorder** bideokasetto-rekōdā ビ デオカセットレコーダー.

videodisc, *n.* bideodisuku ビデオ ディスク.

video game, *n.* terebi-/bideo-gēmu テレビ〜/ビデオゲーム.

videotape, *n.* bideotēpu ビデオテ ープ.

Vietnam, *n.* betonamu ベトナム.

Vietnamese, 1. *n.* betonamujin ベ トナム人 (person); betonamugo ベトナム語 (language). 2. *adj.* betonamu (no) ベトナム (の) (of Vietnam); betonamujin (no) ベト ナム人 (の) (of the Vietnamese); betonamugo (no) ベトナム語 (の) (of the Vietnamese language).

view, 1. *n.* nagame 眺め (scene); keshiki 景色 (landscape); shikai 視 界 (range of vision); iken 意見 (opinion). 2. *vb.* miru 見る (see); shiraberu 調べる (survey); ...to minasu ...と見なす (consider to be).

viewer, *n.* 1. kenbutsunin 見物人 (bystander). 2. shichōsha 視聴者 (TV viewer).

viewpoint, *n.* mikata 見方; kenchi 見地.

vigil, *n.* nezu/tetsuya no ban 寝 ず/徹夜の番.

vigilant, *adj.* yōjinbukai 用心深い.

vigor, *n.* 1. kakki 活気 (energy). 2. chikara 力 (strength).

vigorous, *adj.* 1. kakki ga aru 活気 がある (energetic). 2. kyōryoku

(na) 強力 (な) (strong).

vile, *adj.* 1. iyashii 卑しい (degraded). 2. iya (na) 嫌 (な) (repulsive). 3. gehin (na) 下品 (な) (morally unpure).

villa, *n.* bessō 別荘.

village, *n.* mura 村.

villager, *n.* murabito 村人.

villain, *n.* warumono 悪者; akunin 悪人.

vindicate, *vb.* 1. mujitsu o shōmei suru 無実を証明する (clear from suspicion). 2. shōmei suru 証明す る (prove).

vindictive, *adj.* shūnenbukai 執念 深い.

vine, *n.* 1. tsurukusa つる草; tsuta 蔦 (ivy, etc.). 2. budō no ki 葡萄 の木 (grapevine).

vinegar, *n.* su 酢.

vineyard, *n.* budōen 葡萄園.

vinyl, *n.* binīru ビニール.

violate, *vb.* okasu 犯す／侵す; yaburu 破る.

violation, *n.* 1. ihan 違反 (infringement). 2. bōgai 妨害 (disturbance). 3. gōkan 強姦 (rape).

violence, *n.* 1. hageshisa 激しさ (great force). 2. bōryoku 暴力 (harm).

violent, *adj.* 1. hageshii 激しい (uncontrollable, intense). 2. bōryoku-teki (na) 暴力的 (な) (destructive).

violet, *n.* 1. sumire 菫 (plant). 2. murasaki(iro) 紫(色) (color).

violin, *n.* baiorin バイオリン.

viper, *n.* 1. dokuhebi 毒蛇 (snake). 2. hiretsukan 卑劣漢 (person).

virgin, *n.* 1. shojo 処女 (woman); dōtei 童貞 (chaste man); bājin バージン.

virginity, *n.* junketsu 純潔

(purity); shojo(sei) 処女(性) (woman); dōtei 童貞 (chastity).

virile, *adj.* 1. otokorashii 男らしい (manly). 2. chikarazuyoi 力強い (strong).

virtual, *adj.* jisshitsu-teki (na) 実質的 (な).

virtue, *n.* 1. (bi)toku (美)徳 (moral excellence). 2. biten 美点; chōsho 長所 (merit). 3. teisetsu 貞節 (chastity). 4. **by virtue of** (...no) okage de (...の) おかげで.

virtuous, *adj.* 1. kōketsu (na) 高潔 (な) (moral). 2. teisetsu (na) 貞節 (な) (chaste).

virus, *n.* uirusu ウイルス; saikin 細菌.

visa, *n.* biza ビザ; sashō 査証.

visible, *adj.* 1. mieru 見える (can be seen). 2. meihaku (na) 明白 (な) (clear).

vision, *n.* 1. shikaku 視覚 (sense of sight). 2. shiryoku 視力 (power of sight). 3. senken 先見 (foresight). 4. bijon ビジョン; sōzōryoku 想像力 (mental image). 5. maboroshi 幻 (supernatural appearance).

visionary, *n.* risōka 理想家; kūsōka 空想家.

visit, 1. *n.* hōmon 訪問. 2. *vb.* hōmon suru 訪問する; tazuneru 訪ねる.

visitor, *n.* hōmonsha 訪問者; (o)kyaku(san) (お)客(さん).

visual, *adj.* shikaku (no) 視覚 (の); mieru 見える.

vital, *adj.* 1. seimei (no) 生命 (の) (of life). 2. iki-iki shita 生き生きした (lively). 3. jūyō (na) 重要 (な) (important). 4. fukaketsu (na) 不可欠 (な) (essential).

vitamin, *n.* bitamin ビタミン.

vivacious, *adj.* yōki (na) 陽気 (な); kakki ga aru 活気がある.

vivid, *adj.* 1. senmei (na) 鮮明 (な); azayaka (na) 鮮やか (な) (bright, perceptible). 2. iki-iki shita 生き生きした (lively).

vocabulary, *n.* goi 語彙; bokyaburarī ボキャブラリー.

vocal, *adj.* 1. koe (no) 声 (の) (voice). 2. yakamashiku shuchō suru やかましく主張する (adamant on issue).

vocalist, *n.* seigakuka 声楽家; kashu 歌手.

vocation, *n.* shokugyō 職業; shigoto 仕事.

vogue, *n.* 1. ryūkō 流行 (fashion). 2. ninki 人気 (popularity).

voice, 1. *n.* koe 声 (sound); tai 態 (grammar). 2. *vb.* iu 言う.

void, 1. *n.* kūkan 空間 (empty space). 2. *adj.* mukō (no) 無効 (の) (without legal force); kara (no) 空 (の) (empty). 3. *vb.* mukō ni suru 無効にする (invalidate).

volatile, *adj.* 1. kawariyasui 変わり易い; utsurigi (na, no) 移り気 (な, の) (emotionally changeable). 2. kihatsusei (no) 揮発性 (の) (evaporating). 3. bakuhatsu shiyasui 爆発し易い (explosive).

volcano, *n.* kazan 火山; **active volcano** kakkazan 活火山.

volition, *n.* 1. ishi 意志 (will). 2. ketsudan 決断 (choice).

volleyball, *n.* barē(bōru) バレー (ボール).

volt, *n.* boruto ボルト.

volume, *n.* 1. boryūmu ボリューム; ryō 量 (quantity, amount). 2. hon 本 (book); -kan -巻 -satsu -冊 (counter for books). 3. yōseki 容積 (size in three dimensions).

voluntary, *adj.* jihatsu-teki (na) 自発的 (な); shigan (no) 志願 (の) (willing).

volunteer, 1. *n.* borantia ボランティア; shigansha 志願者; tokushika 篤志家. 2. *vb.* shigan suru 志願する; susunde hikiukeru 進んで引き受ける.

voluptuous, *adj.* kan'nō-teki (na) 官能的 (な).

vomit, 1. *n.* ōto 嘔吐. 2. *vb.* haku 吐く.

voracious, *adj.* 1. taishoku/ōgui (no) 大食／大食い (の) (eating much). 2. don'yoku (na) 貪欲 (な) (avid).

vortex, *n.* uzu(maki) 渦(巻).

vote, 1. *n.* tōhyō 投票 (expression of choice); tōhyōken 投票権 (right). 2. *vb.* tōhyō suru 投票する.

voter, *n.* tōhyōsha 投票者.

voting, *n.* tōhyō 投票.

vouch for, *vb.* hoshō suru 保証する.

vow, 1. *n.* chikai 誓い. 2. *vb.* chikau 誓う.

vowel, *n.* boin 母音.

voyage, 1. *n.* nagatabi 長旅. 2. *vb.* tabi suru 旅する; ryokō suru 旅行する.

voyager, *n.* tabibito 旅人; ryokōsha 旅行者.

vulgar, *adj.* zokuaku (na) 俗悪 (な); gehin (na) 下品 (な); chinpu (na) 陳腐 (な).

vulgarity, *n.* zokuakusa 俗悪さ; gehinsa 下品さ; chinpusa 陳腐さ.

vulnerable, *adj.* kizutsuki-yasui 傷つき易い.

vulture, *n.* hagetaka 禿鷹.

W

wade, *vb.* 1. wataru 渡る. 2. kurōshite susumu 苦労して進む (proceed laboriously).

waffle, *n.* waffuru ワッフル.

wag, *vb.* furu 振る.

wage, *n.* chingin 賃金; kyūryō 給料; kyūyo 給与; sararī サラリー (salary).

wage earner, *n.* kyūyoshotokusha 給与所得者.

wager, 1. *n.* kake 賭け. 2. *vb.* kakeru 賭ける.

wagon, *n.* 1. wagon ワゴン. 2. nibasha 荷馬車 (horse drawn).

waif, *n.* 1. furōsha 浮浪者 (homeless person). 2. mayoi'inu 迷い犬 (lost dog).

wail, 1. *n.* nageki 嘆き (lament). 2. *vb.* nageki-kanashimu 嘆き悲しむ (cry).

waist, *n.* uesuto ウエスト; koshi 腰.

wait, *vb.* 1. matsu 待つ; **wait for** ... o matsu ... を待つ. 2. kyūji suru 給仕する (serve food); **wait on (a person)** (... ni) tsukaeru. (...に) 仕える

waiter, *n.* ueitā ウエイター; bōi ボーイ.

waiting list, *n.* junbanmachi no risuto 順番待ちのリスト.

waitress, *n.* ueitoresu ウエイトレス.

waive, *vb.* 1. sashihikaeru 差し控える (forgo). 2. hōki suru 放棄する (give up).

wake, 1. *n.* tsuya 通夜 (vigil beside corpse); ato 跡 (track). 2. *vb.* mezameru 目覚める (become awake); mezame-saseru 目覚めさ

せる; okosu 起こす (cause to wake).

walk, 1. *n.* aruki 歩き (act of walking); hodō 歩道 (sidewalk); **take a walk** sanpo suru 散歩する; **be a ten minute walk** aruite juppun kakaru 歩いて十分かかる. 2. *vb.* aruku 歩く.

wall, *n.* kabe 壁; hei 塀.

wallet, *n.* saifu 財布.

wallpaper, *n.* kabegami 壁紙.

walnut, *n.* kurumi 胡桃.

walrus, *n.* seiuchi せいうち.

waltz, *n.* warutsu ワルツ; enbukyoku 円舞曲.

wan, *adj.* aojiroi 青白い (pale).

wand, *n.* mahō no tsue 魔法の杖 (magic wand).

wander, *vb.* 1. arukimawaru 歩き回る (walk about). 2. mayou 迷う (go astray). 3. soreru 逸れる (deviate).

wanderer, *n.* hōrōsha 放浪者.

wane, *vb.* 1. kakeru 欠ける (of the moon). 2. suitai suru 衰退する (decline).

want, 1. *n.* hitsuyō 必要 (need); ketsubō 欠乏 (lack); mazushisa 貧しさ (poverty); **be in want of ...** ga iru ...が要る; **for want of ...** ga nai node ...が無いので. 2. *vb.* ... ga iru ...が要る (need); ... ga hoshii ...が欲しい (desire); ... ga kakete-iru ...が欠けている (lack); **want to do** ... shitai ...したい; **want to go** ikitai 行きたい.

wanton, *adj.* 1. hidoi ひどい (malicious and unjustifiable). 2. kimagure (na) 気紛れ (な) (capricious). 3. fushidara (na) ふしだら (な) (lewd).

war, *n.* sensō 戦争; tatakai 戦い; **be at war (with)** (... to) sensō shite-iru (... と) 戦争している; **wage**

war against ... to tatakau ... と戦う.

ward, 1. *n.* ku 区 (district); byōtō 病棟 (of hospital); hihogosha 被保護者 (person under legal guardianship); hogo 保護 (custody). 2. *vb.* **ward off ...** o kawasu/sakeru ...をかわす／避ける.

warden, *n.* keimushochō 刑務所長 (chief prison officer).

wardrobe, *n.* 1. fuku 服; ishō 衣装 (clothes). 2. yōfukudansu 洋服だんす (cabinet).

ware, *n.* 1. shōhin 商品 (merchandise). 2. seihin 製品 (manufactured article); **silverware** ginseihin 銀製品; **earthenware** tōki 陶器.

warehouse, *n.* sōko 倉庫.

warfare, *n.* sensō 戦争.

warm, 1. *adj.* atatakai 暖かい (having moderate heat); kokoro ga komotta 心がこもった (cordial); nesshin (na) 熱心 (な) (lively); shinsetsu (na) 親切 (な) (kind). 2. *vb.* atatameru 暖める (make warm); atatakaku naru 暖かくなる (become warm); **warm up** wōmingu-appu suru ウォーミングアップする.

warmth, *n.* atatakasa 暖かさ.

warn, *vb.* keikoku suru 警告する; chūkoku suru 忠告する.

warning, *n.* keikoku 警告; chūkoku 忠告.

warp, *vb.* soru 反る; magaru 曲がる (become bent).

warrant, 1. *n.* tadashii riyū 正しい理由 (justification); hoshō 保証 (guarantee); reijō 令状 (writ). 2. *vb.* riyū ni naru 理由になる (serve as justification); hoshō suru 保証する (guarantee).

warranty, *n.* hoshō 保証.

warrior, *n.* 1. senshi 戦士. 2. samurai 侍; bushi 武士 (Japanese warrior).

warship, *n.* gunkan 軍艦; senkan 戦艦.

wart, *n.* ibo いぼ.

wary, *adj.* yōjinbukai 用心深い.

wash, *vb.* arau 洗う (cleanse in water); sentaku suru 洗濯する (wash clothes).

washing, *n.* 1. sentaku 洗濯 (washing clothes). 2. sentakumono 洗濯物 (things washed or to be washed); **washing machine** denki-sentakuki 電気洗濯機.

wasp, *n.* suzumebachi 雀蜂.

waste, 1. *n.* rōhi 浪費 (useless expenditure); arechi 荒れ地 (uncultivated land); haikibutsu 廃棄物 (leftovers from manufacturing). 2. *vb.* rōhi suru 浪費する (spend uselessly); muda ni suru 無駄にする (fail to use); suijaku suru 衰弱する (decay in health); shōmō saseru 消耗させる (wear away).

wastebasket, *n.* gomibako ごみ箱; kuzuire 屑入れ.

wasteful, *adj.* fukeizai (na) 不経済 (な) (uneconomical).

watch, 1. *n.* udedokei 腕時計 (wristwatch); mihari 見張り; ban 番 (guard, watchman); yōjin 用心 (caution). 2. *vb.* miru 見る (look); (... ni) ki o tsukeru (...に) 気をつける; (... ni) yōjin suru (...に) 用心する (be watchful); miharu 見張る (keep under surveillance); **watch out** ki o tsukeru. 気をつける

watchdog, *n.* banken 番犬 (dog).

watchful, *adj.* yōjinbukai 用心深い.

watchmaker, *n.* tokeiya 時計屋.

watchman, *n.* yakei 夜警.

water, 1. *n.* mizu 水 (cold water); oyu お湯 (hot water). 2. *vb.* mizu o yaru 水をやる (give water).

watercolor, *n.* 1. suisaienogu 水彩絵の具 (paint). 2. suisaiga 水彩画 (painting).

waterfall, *n.* taki 滝.

watering can, *n.* jōro 如雨露.

water lily, *n.* suiren 水蓮.

watermelon, *n.* suika 西瓜.

waterproof, *adj.* bōsui (no) 防水 (の); **waterproof watch** bōsuidokei 防水時計.

water wheel, *n.* suisha 水車.

watt, *n.* watto ワット.

wave, 1. *n.* nami 波 (undulation, rush, mass movement); yure 揺れ (vibration); kābu カーブ (curve); **short wave** tanpa 短波. 2. *vb.* yureru 揺れる (move back and forth); furu 振る (flag, hand, etc.).

waver, *vb.* 1. yuragu 揺らぐ (sway). 2. tamerau ためらう (hesitate). 3. yureugoku 揺れ動く (fluctuate).

wavy, *adj.* namiutteiru 波打っている; namijō (no) 波状 (の).

wax, 1. *n.* wakkusu ワックス; rō ろう (beeswax); mimiaka 耳垢 (earwax); **wax paper** parafin-shi パラフィン紙. 2. *vb.* (... ni) wakkusu o nuru (...に) ワックスを塗る (apply wax); (tsuki ga) michiru (月が) 満ちる (moon).

way, *n.* 1. hōhō 方法; yarikata やり方 (manner, mode, method). 2. michi 道 (passage, road). 3. hōkō 方向 (direction). 4. michinori 道程 (distance). 5. **a long way** nagai michinori 長い道程; **by the way** tokoro de ところで; **by way of** ... keiyu de ... 経由で; **in a way**

654

aru teido ある程度 (to some extent); **on the way to** ... ni iku tochū de ...に行く途中で; **that way** achira あちら; **this way** kochira こちら; **which way** dochira どちら.

we, *pron.* watashitachi 私達; ware-ware 我々.

weak, *adj.* 1. yowai 弱い (feeble, fragile). 2. heta (na) 下手 (な) (deficient). 3. usui 薄い (tea, coffee, etc.).

weaken, *vb.* yowameru 弱める (make weak); yowamaru 弱まる (become weak).

weakness, *n.* 1. yowasa 弱さ (feebleness). 2. ketten 欠点 (fault). 3. **have a weakness for** ... ga daisuki ...が大好き.

wealth, *n.* tomi 富; yutakasa 豊かさ.

wealthy, *adj.* 1. yutaka (na) 豊か (な) (abundant, affluent). 2. kanemochi (no) 金持ち (の) (possessing riches).

wean, *vb.* chichibanare saseru 乳離れさせる.

weapon, *n.* buki 武器.

wear, 1. *n.* fuku 服 (clothing); shōmō 消耗 (deterioration, exhaustion). 2. *vb.* kiru 着る (waist up: shirt, jacket, etc.); haku はく (waist down: pants, shoes, socks); kaburu 被る (hat); kakeru かける (glasses); hameru はめる (gloves); mi ni tsukeru 身に着ける (accessories); suriherasu 擦り減らす (diminish, impair); tsukaifurusu 使い古す (damage, cause to deteriorate by use); kutabireru くたびれる (get exhausted); **wear out** shōmō suru 消耗する.

weary, *adj.* 1. hirō shiteiru 疲労し

ている (exhausted). 2. unzari saseru うんざりさせる (tedious).

weasel, *n.* itachi いたち.

weather, *n.* tenki 天気; kishō 気象; **weather forecast** tenkiyohō 天気予報.

weatherman, -woman, *n.* tenki-yohōin 天気予報員.

weather vane, *n.* kazamidori 風見鶏.

weave, *vb.* oru 織る (fabric); amu 編む (basket).

weaver, *n.* hataori(-shokunin) 機織り(職人).

web, *n.* 1. orimono 織り物 (fabric). 2. kumo no su 蜘蛛の巣 (cobweb).

wed, *vb.* 1. (... to) kekkon suru (... と) 結婚する (get married). 2. musubitsukeru 結び付ける (attach firmly).

wedding, *n.* kekkonshiki 結婚式; **wedding ring** kekkon'yubiwa 結婚指輪.

wedge, *n.* kusabi くさび.

wedlock, *n.* kon'in 婚姻; kekkon-seikatsu 結婚生活.

Wednesday, *n.* suiyōbi 水曜日.

wee, *adj.* chiisai 小さい.

weed, 1. *n.* zassō 雑草. 2. *vb.* zassō o toru 雑草を取る (weed grass); **weed out** nozoku 除く.

week, *n.* shū(kan) 週(間); **once a week** shū ni ichido 週に一度 **last week** senshū 先週; **this week** konshū 今週; **next week** raishū 来週.

weekday, *n.* uīkudē ウイークデー; heijitsu 平日.

weekend, *n.* uīkuendo ウイークエンド; shūmatsu 週末.

weekly, 1. *n.* shūkanshi 週刊誌 (weekly magazine). 2. *adj.* shū ni ichido (no) 週に一度 (の) (done once a week); isshūkan (no) 一週

間 (の) (computed by the week).

weep, *vb.* naku 泣く.

weigh, *vb.* 1. omosa o hakaru 重さ を計る／量る (measure heaviness). 2. ... no omosa ga aru ... の重さが ある (have the stated weight). 3. yoku kangaeru よく考える (consider).

weight, *n.* omosa 重さ (heaviness).

weird, *adj.* kikai (na) 奇怪 (な); kawatta 変わった; hen (na) 変 (な).

welcome, 1. *n.* kangei 歓迎. 2. *adj.* kangei subeki; 歓迎すべき yorokobashii 喜ばしい; **you're welcome** dō itashimashite どうい たしまして (response to "thank you"). 3. *vb.* kangei suru 歓迎す る. 4. *interj.* yōkoso ようこそ; irrasshai(mase) いらっしゃい (ませ).

weld, *vb.* yōsetsu suru 溶接する; tsukeru 付ける.

welfare, *n.* 1. seikatsuhogo 生活保 護 (public relief); fukushi 福祉 (social welfare). 2. kōfuku 幸福 (well-being).

well, 1. *n.* ido 井戸 (for water). 2. *adj.* genki (na) 元気 (な) (healthy). 3. *adv.* yoku よく (excellently, properly, thoroughly); **as well** ... mo (mata) ...も (又); **as well as** ... sono ue ni ... その上に...; sore kara それから (in addition); **be doing well** junchō de aru 順調で ある; **get well** genki ni naru 元気 になる; **Well done!** Yoku yatta. よくやった. 4. *interj.* sate さて; jā じゃあ.

well-balanced, *adj.* 1. tsuriai ga toreta 釣り合いが取れた. 2. jōshiki ga aru 常識がある (person).

well-being, *n.* 1. ii jinsei/seikatsu 良い人生／生活 (good condition

of life). 2. fukushi 福祉 (welfare).

well-bred, *adj.* 1. reigi tadashii 礼 儀正しい (polite). 2. sodachi ga ii 育ちが良い (of good birth).

well-chosen, *adj.* erabi-nukareta 選び抜かれた.

well-done, *adj.* 1. umaku dekite- iru うまく出来ている (skillful). 2. weru-dan ウェルダン; yoku yaketeiru よく焼けている (meat).

well-dressed, *adj.* minari ga ii 身 なりがいい.

well-educated, *adj.* kyōiku ga aru 教育がある.

well-founded, *adj.* tashika (na) 確 か (な).

well-informed, *adj.* yoku shitte- iru よく知っている.

well-known, *adj.* yoku shirarete- iru よく知られている; yūmei (na) 有名 (な).

well-made, *adj.* yoku dekiteiru よ く出来ている.

well-off, *adj.* 1. megumarete-iru 恵 まれている (in favorable circumstances). 2. kanemochi (no) 金持ち (の) (prosperous).

well-paid, *adj.* kyūryō ga ii 給料が 良い.

well-to-do, *adj.* kanemochi (no) 金持ち (の).

wend, *vb.* susumu 進む.

werewolf, *n.* ōkamiotoko 狼男.

west, 1. *n.* nishi 西; **the West** seiō 西欧 (Europe and America); seiyō 西洋 (western part of the world); seibu 西部 (western part of a country). 2. *adj.* see **western.**

western, 1. *adj.* nishi (no) 西 (の); seiō (no) 西欧 (の); seiyō (no) 西 洋 (の); seibu (no) 西部 (の). 2. *n.* seibugeki 西部劇 (cowboy movie).

wet, 1. *adj.* nureta 濡れた (soaked with water); shimetta 湿った

(moist, damp); **get wet** nureru 濡れる. 2. *vb.* nurasu 濡らす.

whale, *n.* kujira 鯨.

wharf, *n.* futō 埠頭.

what, 1. *adj.* nan no 何の; don'na どんな; **what time** nanji 何時. 2. *pron.* nani/nan 何; **What for?** Dōshite どうして. **what about** wa dō desuka ...はどうですか; **What do you think?** Dō omou. どう思う. **what I like** watashi no sukina mono 私の好きなもの. 3. *interj.* nan to ... 何と... (what a ...).

whatever, 1. *adj.* don'na ... demo どんな...でも (no matter what); **whatever reason** don'na riyū demo どんな理由でも. 2. *pron.* ... koto o nan demo ... ことを何でも... (... anything that...); **Do whatever you like.** Sukina koto o nan demo shinasai. 好きなことを何でもしなさい. nani ga/o ... temo 何が／を...ても (no matter what...); **whatever happens** nani ga okottemo 何が起こっても; **whatever I say** nani o ittemo 何を言つても.

wheat, *n.* komugi 小麦.

wheel, *n.* kuruma 車; sharin 車輪; **wheel chair** kurumaisu 車椅子; **steering wheel** handoru ハンドル.

wheeze, 1. *n.* aegi あえぎ. 2. *vb.* aegu あえぐ.

when, 1. *adv.* itsu いつ. 2. *conj.* ... toki ...時 (at or during the time that); **when I feel sad** kanashii toki 悲しい時; ... -nara/-kereba ...-なら／-ければ (if ...); ... kara ... から (as, since ...); ... hazu no toki ni ...はずの時に (whereas ...); sono toki その時 (upon which).

whenever, 1. *adv.* (when ever, emphatic form of **when**) ittai-

zentai itsu 一体全体いつ. 2. *conj.* ... toki wa itsumo ...時はいつも (every time ...); itsu demo いつでも (at any time).

where, 1. *adv.* doko de/ni どこで／に (in or at what place); **Where is he?** Kare wa doko ni imasu ka. 彼はどこにいますか. **Where do you live?** Doko ni sunde imasu ka. どこに住んでいますか. doko e/ni どこへ／に (to what place); doko kara/de どこから／で (from what source or place). 2. *conj.* tokoro 所; **Find where he is.** Kare no iru tokoro o sagase. 彼のいる所を探せ.

whereabouts, *n.* idokoro 居所; yukue 行方 (person); basho 場所 (thing).

wherever, 1. *adv.* ittaizentai doko de/ni 一体全体どこで／に (where ever, emphatic form of **where**). 2. *conj.* ... tokoro wa doko demo ... 所はどこでも (at whatever place ...).

wherewithal, *n.* 1. shudan 手段 (means). 2. (o)kane (お)金 (money).

whet, *vb.* togu 研ぐ (a blade).

whether, *conj.* ... ka dōka ...かどうか (if... or not); **do not know whether he has come or not** kita ka dōka wakaranai 来たかどうか分からない.

which, 1. *adj.* dono どの; dochira no どちらの. 2. *pron.* dore どれ; dochira どちら.

whichever, 1. *adj.* dono ... demo どの...でも. 2. *pron.* dore demo どれでも (any one that); dochira ga/o ... temo どちらが／を...ても (no matter which one is .../no matter which one you ...).

while, 1. *n.* aida 間 (interval);

after a while shibaraku shite kara 暫くしてから; **all the while** zutto ずっと; **a while ago** sukoshi mae ni 少し前に; **once in a while** tokidoki 時々; **for a while** shibaraku 暫く; **worth one's while** kai ga aru 甲斐がある. 2. *conj.* ... aida ni ...間に (during the time that ...); ... kagiri wa ...限りは (as long as ...); keredomo けれども (even though).

whim, *n.* kimagure 気紛れ.

whimper, 1. *n.* susurinaki すすり泣き. 2. *vb.* susurinaku すすり泣く.

whimsical, *adj.* kimagure (na) 気紛れ (な).

whine, 1. *n.* nakigoto 泣き言; guchi 愚痴 (complaint). 2. *vb.* nakigoto/guchi o iu 泣き言／愚痴を言う (complain).

whip, 1. *n.* muchi 鞭 (instrument). 2. *vb.* muchiutsu 鞭打つ (strike); awadateru 泡立てる (beat into a foam).

whipped cream, *n.* hoippu-kurīmu ホイップクリーム.

whirl, *vb.* mawaru 回る.

whirlpool, *n.* uzu(maki) 渦(巻き).

whirlwind, *n.* tsumujikaze 旋風.

whiskers, *n.* hoohige 頬髭 (man); hige 髭 (cat).

whiskey, *n.* uisukī ウイスキー.

whisper, 1. *n.* sasayaki 囁き. 2. *vb.* sasayaku 囁く.

whistle, *n.* 1. kuchibue 口笛 (from human mouth); fue no yō na oto 笛のような音 (any whistling sound). 2. **blow the whistle** abaku 暴く (expose).

white, 1. *adj.* shiroi 白い (lacking color); aojiroi 青白い (pale); hakujin (no) 白人 (の) (race). 2. *n.* shiro(iro) 白(色) (color);

hakujin 白人 (race or person).

white-collar, 1. *adj.* howaito-karā ホワイトカラー. 2. *n.* **white-collar worker** sararī-man サラリーマン.

White House, *n.* howaito-hausu ホワイトハウス.

whiten, *vb.* shiroku suru 白くする.

whittle, *vb.* herasu 減らす (reduce).

who, *pron.* dare ga 誰が; donata ga どなたが.

whoever, *pron.* 1. dare demo 誰でも (whatever person). 2. dare ga ... temo 誰が...ても (whoever does ...).

whole, 1. *adj.* zenbu no 全部の; subete no 全ての. 2. *n.* zenbu 全部; subete 全て; **as a whole** zentai-teki ni mite 全体的に見て; **on the whole** gaishite 概して.

wholesale, *adj.* oroshiuri (no) 卸し売り (の).

wholesaler, *n.* oroshiuriya 卸し売り屋.

wholesome, *adj.* 1. kenzen (na) 健全 (な) (morally good). 2. kenkō ni ii 健康に良い (good for the health).

whom, *pron.* dare o 誰を; donata o どなたを.

whore, *n.* baishunfu 売春婦.

whose, *pron.* dare no 誰の; donata no どなたの.

why, *adv., conj.* naze 何故; dōshite どうして.

wicked, *adj.* 1. ja'aku (na) 邪悪 (な); ijiwarui 意地悪い (evil). 2. tsumibukai 罪深い (sinful). 3. itazura (na) いたずら (な) (naughty).

wicker, *n.* tō(seihin) 籐(製品).

wide, 1. *adj.* waido (na) ワイド (な); hiroi 広い; ōkii 大きい. 2.

adv. hiroku 広く; ōkiku 大きく;
wide open ōkiku aketeiru 大きく
開けている.

widen, *vb.* 1. hiroku suru 広くす
る; ōkiku suru 大きくする (make
wide). 2. hirogaru 広がる
(become wide).

widespread, *adj.* hiromatteiru 広
まっている.

widow, *n.* mibōjin 未亡人.

widower, *n.* otoko yamome 男や
もめ.

widowhood, *n.* mibōjingurashi 未
亡人暮らし.

width, *n.* hirosa 広さ; haba 幅.

wield, *vb.* furu'u 振るう.

wife, *n.* tsuma 妻; kanai 家内
(one's own wife); okusan 奥さん
(someone's wife).

wig, *n.* katsura かつら.

wild, *adj.* 1. yasei (no) 野性 (の)
(living or growing in nature). 2.
yaban (na) 野蛮 (な) (uncivilized).
3. arekuru'u 荒れ狂う (violent).
4. te ni oenai 手に負えない
(unruly). 5. mugamuchū (no) 無
我夢中 (の) (unrestrained). 6.
mujin (no) 無人 (の)
(uninhabited).

wilderness, *n.* kōya 荒野.

wildlife, *n.* yasei no dōbutsu 野性
の動物.

wile, *n.* warudakumi 悪巧み;
keiryaku 計略.

will, 1. *n.* ishi 意志 (power of the
mind, intention); yuigon 遺言
(testament). 2. *vb.* nozomu 望む
(wish); yuigon ni nokosu 遺言に
残す (bequeath). 3. *aux. vb.* ...
deshō ...でしょう; ... darō ...だろ
う (probability); ... shitai ...したい
(willingness); ... suru tsumori ...す
るつもり (intention).

willful, *adj.* 1. gōjō (na) 強情 (な)

(obstinate). 2. waza to (no) わざ
と (の); koi (no) 故意 (の)
(intentional).

willing, *adj.* **be willing to ...**
yorokonde ... suru 喜んで...する.

willingly, *adv.* yorokonde 喜んで;
susunde 進んで.

willow, *n.* yanagi 柳.

willpower, *n.* ishiryoku 意志力.

wilt, *vb.* kareru 枯れる.

win, 1. *n.* shōri 勝利; kachi 勝ち
(victory). 2. *vb.* shōri suru 勝利す
る; katsu 勝つ (gain victory);
kachieru 勝ち得る (get by effort);
ateru 当てる (win lottery).

wince, *vb.* tajirogu たじろぐ.

wind, 1. *n.* kaze 風 (air in motion).
2. *vb.* kaze ni ateru 風に当てる
(expose to the air); maku 巻く
(coil, roll); magarikuneru 曲がり
くねる (move in a curving
course).

windfall, *n.* mōkemono 儲け物.

winding, *adj.* 1. magatteiru 曲がっ
ている (curving); magarikunette-
iru 曲がりくねっている (sinuous).
2. rasenjō (no) らせん状の
(spiral).

windmill, *n.* fūsha 風車.

window, *n.* 1. mado 窓. 2.
madoguchi 窓口 (ticket, teller's).
3. uindō ウインドー (display).

windowpane, *n.* mado-garasu 窓
ガラス.

window shade, *n.* buraindo ブラ
インド.

windshield, *n.* uindo-shīrudo ウイ
ンドシールド; **windshield wiper**
waipā ワイパー.

windy, *adj.* kaze ga tsuyoi 風が強
い.

wine, *n.* wain ワイン; budōshu 葡
萄酒.

wine cellar, *n.* wain-chozōsho ワ

イン貯蔵所.

wing, *n.* hane 羽; tsubasa 翼; uingu ウイング; **on the wing** tondeiru 飛んでいる; **take wing** tobitatsu 飛び立つ; **under one's wing** (... ni) mamorarete (...に) 守られて.

wink, 1. *n.* uinku ウインク; mabataki 瞬き. 2. *vb.* uinku/mabataki suru ウインク／瞬きする.

winner, *n.* shōrisha 勝利者.

winter, *n.* fuyu 冬.

wipe, *vb.* fuku 拭く; nugu'u 拭う; **wipe out** hakai suru 破壊する (destroy); korosu 殺す (kill).

wire, 1. *n.* waiyā ワイヤー; harigane 針金 (metal strand); densen 電線 (electric wire); denwasen 電話線 (telephone wire); denpō 電報 (telegram). 2. *vb.* waiyā de shibaru ワイヤーで縛る (tie with wire); denpō o utsu 電報を打つ (telegraph); haisen o suru 配線をする (install wiring).

wisdom, *n.* sōmeisa 聡明さ; chie 知恵 (knowledge and judgment).

wise, *adj.* sōmei (na) 聡明 (な); kashikoi 賢い.

wise guy, *n.* shittakaburi 知ったかぶり.

wish, 1. *n.* kibō 希望; negai 願い (desire, hope, something desired or hoped); **My best wishes to your father.** Otōsan ni yoroshiku. お父さんによろしく. 2. *vb.* kibō suru 希望する; negau 願う (desire, hope); **wish to do** ... shitai ...したい; **wish someone to do** ... ni ... shite moraitai ...に...してもらいたい; **wish him to come** kare ni kite moraitai 彼に来てもらいたい.

wishy-washy, *adj.* 1. tsumaranai つまらない (insipid). 2. niekiranai 煮え切らない (irresolute).

wit, *n.* chie 知恵 (intelligence); kichi 機知; uitto ウイット (cleverness).

witch, *n.* majo 魔女.

witchcraft, *n.* mahō 魔法; majutsu 魔術.

with, *prep.* 1. ... to issho ni ...と一緒に (accompanied by). 2. ... de ...で (by means of, because of); **cut with a knife** naifu de kiru ナイフで切る. 3. ... ga aru ...がある (having); **a woman with ambition** yashin ga aru josei 野心がある女性. 4. ... to tomo ni ...と共に (in proportion to). 5. ... to ...と (against, separate from); **fight with the enemy** teki to tatakau 敵と戦う.

withdraw, *vb.* 1. hikisagaru 引き下がる (draw oneself back); hikkomeru 引っ込める (draw something back); kaishū suru 回収する (take out of circulation). 2. hikidasu 引き出す (draw out). 3. torikesu 取り消す (retract); toriyameru 取り止める (cancel). 4. teppei suru 撤兵する (army retreat).

withdrawal, *n.* 1. taishutsu 退出 (withdrawing oneself); kaishū 回収 (withdrawing something from circulation). 2. hikidashi 引き出し (withdrawing money). 3. tekkai 撤回 (retraction); toriyame 取り止め (cancellation). 4. teppei 撤兵 (army).

wither, *vb.* shibomu しぼむ; kareru 枯れる.

withhold, *vb.* 1. kotowaru 断る (refuse). 2. gensenchōshū suru 源泉徴収する (taxes). 3. sashihikaeru 差し控える (hold back).

within, 1. *adv.* naka de/ni/e 中で／に／へ (inside). 2. *prep.* ... no naka de/ni ...の中で／に (in, inside of, in the scope of); ... inai ni ...以内に (within a certain distance or time); ... jū ni ...中に (within a certain time).

without, 1. *adv.* soto de/ni 外で／に (outside). 2. *prep.* ... nashi de ... 無しで (not having); **do without** ... nashi de sumasu ... 無しで済ます.

withstand, *vb.* 1. (... ni) uchikatsu (...に) 打ち勝つ (resist successfully). 2. taeru 耐える (tolerate).

witness, 1. *n.* mokugekisha 目撃者 (person who witnesses); shōnin 証人 (person who gives testimony, who attests by signature); shōgen 証言 (testimony); shōko 証拠 (evidence). 2. *vb.* mokugeki suru 目撃する (see); shōnin ni naru 証人になる (be present as a formal witness); shōgen suru 証言する (testify); hoshōnin no shomei o suru 保証人の署名をする (attest by signature).

witticism, *n.* kichi ni tonda kotoba 機知に富んだ言葉.

witty, *adj.* kichi ni tonda 機知に富んだ.

wizard, *n.* mahōtsukai 魔法使い.

wobble, *vb.* guratsuku ぐらつく (move); guratsukaseru ぐらつかせる (cause to move); furueru 震える (tremble).

woe, *n.* 1. hiai 悲哀; kanashimi 悲しみ (sorrow). 2. sainan 災難 (trouble).

wolf, *n.* ōkami 狼.

woman, *n.* josei 女性; on'na (no hito) 女 (の人).

womanhood, *n.* josei de aru koto 女性であること (being a woman).

womanizer, *n.* purēbōi プレーボーイ; on'natarashi 女たらし.

womanly, *adj.* on'narashii 女らしい.

womb, *n.* shikyū 子宮.

wonder, 1. *n.* odoroki 驚き (surprise); kyōi 驚異 (marvel); fushigi 不思議 (puzzlement); **no wonder** tōzen 当然. 2. *vb.* kangaeru 考える (speculate); (... ni) odoroku (...に) 驚く (be surprised, marvel); fushigi ni omou 不思議に思う (be puzzled); shiritai 知りたい (want to know); **wonder if/how/what/etc.** ... ka to omou ...かと思う.

wonderful, *adj.* subarashii 素晴らしい.

wont, 1. *n.* shūkan 習慣 (customary habit). 2. *adj.* (... ni) narete iru (... に) 慣れている (accustomed).

woo, *vb.* 1. kou 請う (seek). 2. kyūkon suru 求婚する (ask for in marriage).

wood, *n.* 1. ki 木. 2. zaimoku 材木 (lumber); maki 薪 (firewood). 3. mori 森 (grove).

woodblock print, *n.* 1. mokuhanga 木版画. 2. ukiyoe 浮世絵 (antique print).

woodcut, *n.* 1. hangi 版木 (woodblock). 2. mokuhanga 木版画 (woodblock print).

woodcutter, *n.* kikori 樵 (woodman).

wooden, *adj.* 1. mokusei (no) 木製 (の) (made of wood). 2. katakurushii 堅苦しい (stiff).

woodpecker, *n.* kitsutsuki きつつき.

woodwind, *n.* mokkangakki 木管楽器.

woodwork, *n*. mokuseihin 木製品 (wooden object); mokuzōbubun 木造部分 (in a house).

wool, *n*. ūru ウール; yōmō 羊毛.

word, *n*. 1. tango 単語; kotoba 言葉 (unit of language). 2. kotoba 言葉 (something said or written). 3. hitokoto 一言; hanashi 話 (short talk). 4. yakusoku 約束 (promise). 5. nyūsu ニュース (news). 6. **words** kashi 歌詞 (lyrics); kenka 喧嘩 (angry speech). 7. **in a word** tsumari つまり; **in other words** iikaeru to 言い換えると; **keep/break one's word** yakusoku o mamoru/yaburu 約束を守る／破る; **take one at one's word** kotobadōri ni toru 言葉通りにとる; **would like to have a word with you** chotto hanashi ga aru ちょっと話しがある.

wording, *n*. iimawashi 言い回し.

word processor, *n*. wāpuro ワープロ.

wordy, *adj*. kudoi くどい.

work, 1. *n*. shigoto 仕事 (employment, task); rōdō 労働 (labor); sakuhin 作品 (result of work, writing, painting, etc.); doryoku 努力 (exertion); **at work** shigotochū 仕事中 (at one's job); **in the works** junbichū 準備中; **out of work** shitsugyōchū 失業中. 2. *vb*. shigoto suru 仕事する; hataraku 働く (do work, be employed); isoshimu いそしむ (engage oneself in); benkyō suru 勉強する (work on an academic subject); ugoku 動く (operate, function); kiku 効く (function effectively); **The medicine won't work.** Kusuri wa kikanai darō. 薬は効かないだろう.

workaholic, *n*. shigoto-chūdokusha 仕事中毒者.

workbook, *n*. wāku-bukku ワークブック; renshūchō 練習帳.

workday, *n*. 1. shigoto-/kinmu-bi 仕事～／勤務日 (day on which one works).

worker, *n*. wākā ワーカー; rōdōsha 労働者.

working class, *n*. rōdōshakaikyū 労働者階級.

working hours, *n*. kinmu jikan 勤務時間.

workmanship, *n*. gijutsu 技術; ude 腕 (technique).

workout, *n*. renshū 練習 (practice).

workshop, *n*. 1. wākushoppu ワークショップ (seminar). 2. shigotoba 仕事場 (place where work is done); shūriya 修理屋 (repair shop).

world, *n*. 1. sekai 世界 (globe, universe, part of the earth, group of living things); **world war** sekai taisen 世界大戦. 2. jinrui 人類 (human race). 3. seken 世間; shakai 社会 (public). 4. nakama 仲間 (group of people). 5. bun'ya 分野 (area of interest).

worldly, *adj*. 1. konoyo (no) この世 (の) (of this world). 2. zoku (na) 俗 (な) (mundane).

worldwide, *adv*. sekaijū de 世界中で.

worm, *n*. mimizu みみず (earthworm).

worn, *adj*. surihetta 擦り減った; tsukaifurushita 使い古した.

worn-out, *adj*. 1. surikireta 擦り切れた (threadbare). 2. tsukarekitta 疲れ切った (exhausted).

worried, *adj*. shinpai (na) 心配 (な) (anxious); shinpaisō (na) 心

配そう (な) (worried seeming).

worry, 1. *n*. shinpai 心配. 2. *vb*. shinpai saseru 心配させる (make anxious); shinpai suru 心配する (feel anxious).

worse, *adj., adv.* (... yori) sara ni warui (...より) 更に悪い.

worsen, *vb*. akka suru 悪化する.

worship, 1. *n*. sūhai 崇拝 (admiration); reihai 礼拝 (religious service, religious worship). 2. *vb*. sūhai suru 崇拝する; reihai suru 礼拝する.

worshiper, *n*. 1. sūhaisha 崇拝者. 2. reihaisha 礼拝者.

worst, *adj., adv.* saiaku (no) 最悪 (の); ichiban warui 一番悪い; **at worst** ichiban warukute mo 一番悪くても; **if worst comes to worst** saiaku no bāi niwa 最悪の場合には.

worth, 1. *n*. kachi 価値 (value, importance). 2. *prep*. ... (no) kachi ga aru (...の) 価値がある (having value of ..., deserving of ...); **worth it** kai ga aru 甲斐がある.

worthless, *adj*. kachi ga nai 価値が無い; kudaranai 下らない.

worthwhile, *adj*. kachi ga aru 価値がある.

worthy, *adj*. 1. **be worthy (of)** (... ni) atai suru (...に) 値する. 2. rippa (na) 立派 (な) (having great merit).

would, *aux. vb*. 1. ... shita mono datta ...したものだった (used to do ...). 2. **Would you please ...?** ... kudasaimasen ka ...下さいませんか.

wound, 1. *n*. kizu 傷; kega 怪我. 2. *vb*. kizutsukeru 傷つける.

wrap, *vb*. tsutsumu 包む.

wrapping, *n*. tsutsumigami 包み紙

(wrapping paper).

wrath, *n*. ikari 怒り.

wrathful, *adj*. ikarikurutte-iru 怒り狂っている.

wreak, *vb*. 1. ataeru 与える (inflict); **wreak havoc** dageki o ataeru 打撃を与える. 2. harasu 晴らす (carry out); **wreak vengeance** urami o harasu 恨みを晴らす.

wreath, *n*. hanawa 花輪.

wreck, 1. *n*. zangai 残骸 (ruin); nanpasen 難破船 (ship); haijin 廃人 (person); hakai 破壊 (destruction). 2. *vb*. nanpa suru 難破する (shipwreck); hakai suru 破壊する (destroy).

wrench, 1. *n*. renchi レンチ; supanā スパナー (tool); hineri 捻り (twist); nenza 捻挫 (injury). 2. *vb*. mogitoru もぎ取る (pull away); hineru 捻る (twist); nenza suru 捻挫する (injure).

wrest, *vb*. mogitoru もぎ取る (pull away).

wrestle, *vb*. 1. resuringu o suru レスリングをする (engage in wrestling). 2. (... to) tatakau (... と) 戦う (struggle with).

wrestling, *n*. resuringu レスリング; sumō 相撲.

wretched, *adj*. 1. mijime (na) 惨め (な) (miserable); aware (na) 哀れ (な) (pitiable). 2. mukatsuku (yō na) むかつく (ような) (despicable).

wring, *vb*. 1. hineru 捻る; nejiru ねじる (twist). 2. shiboru しぼる (twist and compress to force out liquid).

wrinkle, 1. *n*. shiwa しわ. 2. *vb*. shiwa o yoseru しわを寄せる (form wrinkles in); shiwa ga yoru しわが寄る (become wrinkled).

wrist, *n.* tekubi 手首.

wristwatch, *n.* udedokei 腕時計.

write, *vb.* 1. kaku 書く. 2. **write down** kakitomeru 書き留める; **write off** torikesu 取り消す; kyanseru suru キャンセルする (cancel); **write in** kakikomu 書き込む.

writer, *n.* sakka 作家; chosha 著者.

writhe, *vb.* mogaku もがく; notautsu のたうつ.

writing, *n.* 1. shippitsu 執筆 (activity of writing); chosaku katsudō 著作活動 (activity of writing books). 2. hisseki 筆跡 (handwriting). 3. kakimono 書き物 (anything written); chosaku 著作; chosho 著書 (book); bunsho 文書 (legal document, written form). 4. sakkaseikatsu 作家生活 (profession of a writer).

writing desk, *n.* tsukue 机.

wrong, 1. *n.* fusei 不正 (injustice); aku 悪 (evil); gai 害 (damage); **do wrong to others** tanin ni gai o ataeru 他人に害を与える; **in the wrong** machigatteiru 間違っている. 2. *adj.* machigai (no) 間違い (の); ayamari (no) 誤り (の) (erroneous, deviating from the truth); warui 悪い (evil, erroneous, unjust, not suitable); fusei (na) 不正 (な) (unjust); **something wrong with** ... ga kowarete iru ... が壊れている (out of order). 3. *vb.* gai o ataeru 害を与える (harm).

wrongdoing, *n.* 1. warui okonai 悪い行い (wrong behavior). 2. akuji 悪事 (sin).

wrong number, *n.* machigai-denwa 間違い電話.

X

xenophobia, *adj.* haita-teki (na) 排他的 (な); heisashugi (no) 閉鎖主義 (の); gaikokujin-girai (no) 外国人嫌い (の).

xerox, *n.* zerokkusu ゼロックス.

x-ray, 1. *n.* rentogen レントゲン; ekkusu-sen エックス線. 2. *vb.* rentogen o toru レントゲンを撮る.

xylophone, *n.* mokkin 木琴.

Y

yacht, *n.* yotto ヨット.

yank, 1. *n.* tsuyoku hiku koto 強く引くこと. 2. *vb.* tsuyoku hiku 強く引く.

yard, *n.* 1. yādo ヤード (measure). 2. niwa 庭 (land).

yarn, *n.* ito 糸 (thread); keito 毛糸 (woolen yarn).

yawn, 1. *n.* akubi あくび. 2. *vb.* akubi o suru あくびをする.

year, *n.* toshi 年; nen 年 (12 months); **all year round** ichinenjū 一年中.

yearbook, *n.* nenpō 年報; nenkan 年鑑.

yearly, *adj.* maitoshi (no) 毎年 (の);

nen ni ichido (no) 年に一度 (の).

yearn, *vb.* netsubō suru 熱望する; akogareru 憧れる.

yearning, *n.* netsubō 熱望; akogare 憧れ.

yeast, *n.* īsuto イースト; kōbo 酵母.

yell, 1. *n.* sakebigoe 叫び声 (scream). 2. *vb.* sakebu 叫ぶ (scream); donaru どなる (shout).

yellow, 1. *adj.* kiiroi 黄色い. 2. *n.* ki(iro) 黄(色) (color).

yen, *n.* 1. en 円 (currency). 2. yokkyū 欲求; akogare 憧れ (desire).

yes, *adv.* hai はい; ee ええ; sō desu そうです; sono tōri desu その通りです.

yesterday, *adv.* kinō 昨日; sakujitsu 昨日.

yet, 1. *adv.* mada まだ (still); mō もう; sude ni すでに (already); **not yet** mada (...nai) まだ (...ない). 2. *conj.* soredemo それでも.

yield, 1. *n.* shūkaku 収穫 (crop); rieki 利益 (profit); seisandaka 生産高 (quantity produced). 2. *vb.* umu 産む; motarasu もたらす (produce); kuppuku suru 屈服する (surrender).

yin and yang, *n.* in/on (to) yō 陰 (と) 陽.

yoga, *n.* yoga ヨガ.

yogurt, *n.* yōguruto ヨーグルト.

yolk, *n.* kimi 黄身.

you, *pron.* 1. anata あなた; (pl.)

anata-tachi あなた達, anatagata あなた方; **with you** anata to (issho ni) あなたと(一緒に). 2. kimi 君; (pl.) kimi-tachi 君達 (familiar form used by men).

young, 1. *adj.* wakai 若い (youthful); atarashii 新しい (new); mijuku (na) 未熟 (な) (inexperienced). 2. *n.* wakamono 若者 (young people); ko 子 (offspring).

youngster, *n.* 1. wakamono 若者 (young person). 2. kodomo 子供 (child).

your, *adj.* 1. anata no あなたの; (pl.) anata-tachi no あなた達の. 2. kimi no 君の; (pl.) kimi-tachi no 君達の (familiar form used by men).

yours, *pron.* 1. anata no mono あなたの物; (pl.) anata-tachi no mono あなた達の物. 2. kimi no mono 君の物; (pl.) kimi-tachi no mono 君達の物 (familiar form used by men).

yourself, -selves, *pron.* jibun 自分; anata jishin あなた自身; (pl.) anata-tachi jishin あなた達自身.

youth, *n.* 1. wakasa 若さ (age). 2. seishunjidai 青春時代 (early life). 3. wakamono 若者 (young person).

youthful, *adj.* 1. waka-wakashii 若々しい (vigorous). 2. wakai 若い (young).

Z

zany, *adj.* odoketa おどけた (comical).

zap, *vb.* nagitaosu なぎ倒す (destroy); yattsukeru やっつける

(conquer).

zeal, *n.* netsui 熱意.

zealot, *n.* kyōshinsha 狂信者.

zealous, *adj.* nesshin (na) 熱心 (な).

zebra, *n.* shimauma 縞馬.

Zen, *n.* zen 禅 (Buddhist sect).

zenith, *n.* 1. tenchō 天頂 (celestial point). 2. chōten 頂点 (peak).

zero, *n.* zero ゼロ; rei 零.

zest, *n.* 1. yakumi 薬味 (spice). 2. miryoku 魅力 (appeal). 3. nesshinsa 熱心さ (dedication).

zigzag, 1. *n.* jiguzagu ジグザグ. 2. *vb.* jiguzagu ni susumu ジグザグに進む.

zinc, *n.* aen 亜鉛; totan トタン.

zip, 1. *n.* genki 元気 (energy). 2. *vb.* ikioi yoku susumu 勢いよく進む (zoom forward); ugokimawaru 動き回る (move with energy).

zip code, *n.* yūbinbangō 郵便番号.

zipper, *n.* chakku チャック; jippā ジッパー.

zodiac, *n.* 1. kōdōtai 黄道帯 (belt of the heavens). 2. jūnikyū 十二宮 (twelve signs); eto 干支 (Chinese zodiac diagram).

zone, *n.* chiku 地区 (district); chitai 地帯 (area).

zoo, *n.* dōbutsuen 動物園.

zoology, *n.* dōbutsugaku 動物学.

zoom, *vb.* 1. subayaku iku 素早く行く (go quickly); hayaku ugoku 速く動く (move quickly). 2. kyūjōshō suru 急上昇する (rise rapidly).

zoom lens, *n.* zūmu-renzu ズームレンズ.